Comprehensive

BUSINESS STATISTICS

B. Com. II

B.I.M.

B.B.A.

SALIENT FEATURES OF THE PRESENT EDITION :

- ★ It has **simplified theory** supplemented with **neat diagrams** and **examples.**
- ★ It has **adequate number of unsolved problems** of all types in exercises.
- ★ It has **working rules for solving problems** before exercises.
- ★ It has **unsolved exercises** covering each type of questions.
- ★ It has **hints of tricky problems** after relevant exercises.
- ★ It has latest questions appeared in the university examinations conducted by **M.D.U.** and **K.U.**
- ★ To help the students to attempt theory question in examination, the necessary material is also given in simple **Hindi language.**

Other books by the same author :

1. **Comprehensive Mathematics XI**
2. **Comprehensive Mathematics XII**

Note. These books are approved by C.B.S.E. to be used as textbooks.

3. **Comprehensive IIT-JEE Screening Model Test Papers**
4. **Comprehensive Mathematics** *(For Indian Civil Services Exam.)*
5. **Comprehensive Objective Mathematics** *(For Engg. Entrance Tests)*
6. **Comprehensive Algebra and Trigonometry** *(For B.A./B.Sc.I)*
7. **Comprehensive Calculus** *(For B.A./B.Sc.I)*
8. **Comprehensive Differential Equations and Calculus of Variations** *(For B.A./B.Sc.II)*
9. **Comprehensive Differential Equations and Differential Geometry** *(For B.A./B.Sc.II)*
10. **Comprehensive Abstract Algebra** *(For B.A./B.Sc.III)*
11. **Comprehensive Discrete Mathematics** *(For B.A./B.Sc.III)*
12. **Comprehensive Business Mathematics** *(For B.Com. I and B.T.M)*

Comprehensive

BUSINESS STATISTICS

व्यावसायिक सांख्यिकी

(English and Hindi Medium)

(B.Com. IInd Year)

(Strictly as per M.D.U., Rohtak ; K.U., Kurukshetra and other Indian Universities Syllabus and also for B.I.M. and B.B.A. Courses)

By

PARMANAND GUPTA

M.Sc. M.Phil (Maths)

M.A.(Economics)

Head, Deptt. of Mathematics

Indira Gandhi National College, Ladwa

KURUKSHETRA UNIVERSITY

LAXMI PUBLICATIONS (P) LTD

An ISO 9001:2015 Company

BENGALURU • CHENNAI • GUWAHATI • HYDERABAD

KOCHI • KOLKATA • LUCKNOW • RANCHI

NEW DELHI

Printed and bound in India
Third Edition : *2008, New Edition* : 2025
ISBN *:* 978-81-3180-262-5

Branches

✆	Bengaluru	080-26 75 69 30
✆	Chennai	044-24 34 47 26
✆	Guwahati	0361-254 36 69
✆	Hyderabad	040-27 55 53 83
✆	Kochi	0484-405 13 03
✆	Kolkata	033-40 04 77 79
✆	Lucknow	0522-430 36 13
✆	Ranchi	0651-224 24 64

Published in India by

LAXMI PUBLICATIONS (P) LTD
An ISO 9001:2015 Company
113, GOLDEN HOUSE, GURUDWARA ROAD, DARYAGANJ,
NEW DELHI - 110002, INDIA
Corporate Office : B-33, Sector-5, Noida,
Gautambuddha Nagar (U.P.) - 201 301, INDIA
Telephone : +91-120-44 46 900
www.laxmipublications.com
info@laxmipublications.com

Dedicated to my teachers whose teaching have made me able to grasp some of the fundamentals of Mathematics and Statistics

CONTENTS

PREFACE TO THE THIRD EDITION

It is a matter of great pleasure for me to write the preface for the third edition of this book.

The present book is to serve as a textbook for **Business Statistics** course for B. Com. II students of M.D.U., Rohtak and K.U., Kurukshetra Universities. This edition is in strict conformity with the latest syllabus for the session 2007–2008 and onwards. The present book also covers the complete syllabus of B.I.M. and B.B.A. courses.

Questions appeared in the universities examinations up to April 2007 have also been included in the book.

The author feels that generally the students do understand the contents of theory in English but sometime face difficulty in reproducing the same in the examination. To meet this end, the author has not created a hotch-potch mixing of English and Hindi material in the book. Rather, the whole book has been divided into two parts :

Part I. This part contains theory and practicals portion. Very simple English has been used so that students may enjoy studying the book.

Part II. This part contains important theory questions which are answered in Hindi. This part is titled :

"महत्त्वपूर्ण सैद्धान्तिक प्रश्नों के हिन्दी में उत्तर"

The author maintains that there is always scope for improvement. Suggestions and comments from worthy readers would be gratefully received and acknowledged.

—Author

SYLLABUS

BUSINESS STATISTICS

Class B.Com. II

(Latest Syllabus for M.D.U., Rohtak and K.U., Kurukshetra)

Time : 3 Hours *Max. Marks : 100*

UNIT I *(Chapters 1, 2, 4, 5, 6, 7, 8, 9, 10, 11)*

Introduction : Statistics as a subject, Statistical Data ; Meaning and types ; Collection and Rounding of data ; Classification and Presentation of data.

Analysis of Univariate Data : Construction of a frequency distribution ; Concepts of Central tendency and dispersion and their measures ; Skewness and measures ; Kurtosis and measures.

Analysis of Bivariate Data : Linear regression and correlation.

UNIT II *(Chapters 12, 13)*

Index Numbers : Meaning, types and uses ; Methods of constructing price and quantity indices (simple and aggregate) ; Tests of adequacy ; Chain-base index numbers ; Base shifting, splicing and deflating ; Problems in constructing index numbers ; Consumer price index.

Analysis of Time Series : Causes of variations in time series data ; Components of a time series ; Decomposition—Additive and multiplicative models ; Determination of trend—Moving averages method and method of least squares (including linear, second degree, parabolic, and exponential trend) ; Computation of seasonal indices by simple averages, ratio-to-trend, ratio-to-moving average and link relative methods.

UNIT III *(Chapters 15, 16, 17)*

Theory of Probability : Probability as a concept ; Approaches to defining probability ; Addition and multiplication laws of probability ; Conditional probability ; Bayes' Theorem.

Probability Distributions : Probability distribution as a concept ; Binomial, Poisson, and Normal distributions—their properties and parameters.

Note for M.D.U. Students : Ten questions shall be set in the question paper covering the whole syllabus. The candidates will be required to attempt any five questions.

Note for K.U. Students : Ten questions shall be set in the question paper with at least three questions from each unit. The candidates will be required to attempt five questions in all, selecting at least one question but not more than two from each unit.

SYLLABUS

K.U., KURUKSHETRA

Class B.I.M.

BIM–104 : Quantitative Techniques
(BUSINESS STATISTICS)

Time : 3 Hours

Max. Marks : 100
External : 90
Internal : 10

Note. Ten questions shall be set in the question-paper. The candidates shall be required to attempt five questions in all, selecting at least one question from each of the five units.

UNIT I (*Chapters 1, 2, 4, 5, 6, 7, 8*)

Introduction, importance and uses of statistics. Quantitative techniques in business decisions. Methods of presenting statistical information and collection of data. Frequency distribution, Measures of central tendency, mean, mode, median. Measures of dispersion; range, quartile deviation, mean deviation, standard deviation, coefficient of variation and skewness.

UNIT II (*Chapters 15, 16, 17*)

Probability Theory : Definition of probability, event, counting rules and computation of probabilities. Addition and multiplication rules, Conditional probability. Rule of Bayes, permutation and combination. Probability Distributions : introduction, binomial model, Poisson model and normal distribution.

UNIT III (*Chapters 14, 18, 19*)

Sampling and sampling techniques. Forecasting : meaning, nature and techniques (Qualitative and Quantitative Techniques. Curve fitting and method of least squares.

UNIT IV (*Chapters 10, 11, 13*)

Correlation and regression analysis : nature and significance of correlation, types of correlation, methods of correlation, graphic methods, non-graphic methods, Karl Pearson's, rank and concurrent deviation methods. Regression : Nature and use of regression analysis, regression equations (two variables only). Time series : nature, components, models of time series, measure of trends, graphic methods, method of moving average, method of least square; secular trends, cyclical, seasonal and irregular fluctuations.

UNIT V (*Chapter 12*)

Index numbers : nature, use, problems in index number construction. Unweighted index numbers, weighted index numbers. Application of operational research techniques.

SYLLABUS

M.D.U., ROHTAK

Class B.B.A. (IIIrd Semester) (Paper III)

BUSINESS STATISTICS

Time : 3 Hours | *Theory Marks : 75*
Internal Assessment : 25

Note. Eight questions shall be set in the question paper. The candidates are required to attempt five questions. Select at least one question for each unit.

UNIT I (*Chapters 1, 4*)

Classification, Tabulation and Presentation of Data. Meaning, objectives and types of classification, formation of frequency distributions, role of tabulation; types of tables, significance of diagram and graphs, rules for construction and types of diagram and graphs.

UNIT II (*Chapters 5, 6, 7, 8*)

Measures of Central Tendency and Dispersion. Meaning and objectives of measures of central tendency, different measures viz. arithmetic mean, median, mode, geometric mean and harmonic mean, characteristics, applications and limitations of these measures. Measures of variation viz. range, quartile deviation, mean deviation, standard deviation, coefficient of variation and skewness.

UNIT III (*Chapters 10, 11*)

Correlation and Regression. Meaning of correlation, types of correlation : positive or negative correlation, simple, partial and multiple correlation; method of studying correlation; scatter diagram, graphic and direct method. Properties of correlation coefficient, rank correlation, coefficient of determination, Lines of regression, coefficient of regression, standard error of estimate.

UNIT IV (*Chapters 12, 13, 14*)

Index numbers and Time series. Index number and their uses in business, construction of simple and weighted price, quantity and value index numbers. Test for an ideal index number. Components of Time series viz.-secular trend, cyclical, seasonal and irregular variations, methods of estimating secular trend. Seasonal and cyclical indices, its use in business. Forecasting and limitations.

3. DEFINITION OF STATISTICS IN PLURAL SENSE (AS DATA)

Horace Secrist defined statistics as aggregate of facts, affected to a marked extent by multiplicity of causes, numerically expressed, enumerated or estimated according to reasonable standard of accuracy, collected in a systematic manner for a predetermined purpose and placed in relation to each other.

Aggregate of facts. Statistics refers to set of numerical data. It does not recognise individual items. Suppose, the height of Mr. X is 70 inches. This statement does not constitute statistical data. If we are given the profit figures of a particular firm for the last twenty years, that would constitute statistical data.

Multiplicity of causes. This is an important characteristic of statistics. Economic and business phenomenon are very complex. These are influenced by a large number of forces. For example, the statistics of production of a crop is in general affected by a number of factors like soil conditions, quantity of fertilizers used, quantity of rainfall, method of cultivation, quality of land, quality of seed, state agriculture policy etc. Whatsoever may be the nature of statistical variable, its value is likely to be affected by causes like human psychology, state policies, market conditions, social relations etc.

Numerically expressed. According to professor *Horace Secrist*, "the statistical approach to a subject is numerical. Things, attributes and conditions are counted, totalled, divided and sub-divided and analysed". Data regarding qualitative variables like beauty, intelligence, honesty, poverty cannot be expressed directly.

Reasonable standard of accuracy. In statistical data, we do not require hundred per cent accuracy in measurement, which is neither possible nor indispensable. Suppose, we are considering the height of students of a class. It will be quite sufficient to measure upto 1/10 of a centimetre. Most of the times the data is expressed in round figures. A statistician would be contented to take 0.3 as the value of 1/3, but on the other hand, its exact value is 0.33333......

Systematic manner. It means that the data collected should be in a systematic manner. Suppose, we have data regarding the income and age of population of a certain city. It would be advisable to arrange the data in accordance with increasing values of the variables under consideration.

Pre-determined purpose. The data must be collected with a pre-determined purpose in view. An enumerator cannot collect data about any business and economic variable unless he is told about the purpose. Suppose the data is collected for preparing index number, then it must be very much clear to the enumerator, whether whole sale price-index or consumer price-index is to be calculated.

Placed in relation to each other. It means that all data, which is collected, should be comparable. The data may be comparable w.r.t. time, place etc. The data regarding the total strength of a particular college from 1975-86 is a statistical data. On the other hand, we may also collect the data regarding the strength of different colleges in Haryana in the year 1986.

From this definition, we see that all numerical data are not statistical data. On the other hand, all statistical data are numerical data.

4. DEFINITION OF STATISTICS IN THE SINGULAR SENSE (AS A SUBJECT)

In the singular sense, the word 'statistics' is defined as a subject. This subject mainly deals with the analysis of classified data. The tools of mathematics are used extensively in this subject. *Croxton* and *Cowden* defined the subject statistics as the collection, presentation, analysis and interpretation of numerical data. In statistics, we learn the methods of classifying data, graphical presentation of data, averages of data, dispersion of data. We also study skewness and kurtosis of distribution. We also study correlation, regression, index numbers, analysis of time series, probability, theoretical distributions, tests of significance. In brief, we can say that the subject statistics is concerned with the scientific methods of collecting, summarizing, presenting and analysing data, as well as drawing valid conclusions and making reasonable decisions on the basis of such analysis. In nutshell, we can remark that statistics studies statistics. The subject matter of the subject statistics is divided in two parts namely, *descriptive statistics* and *inferential statistics*.

5. DESCRIPTIVE STATISTICS

The part of the subject statistics which deals with the analysis of a given group without drawing conclusions about a larger group is called **descriptive statistics.** Descriptive statistics includes, collection of data, presentation of data, measures of averages, dispersion, skewness, kurtosis, correlation, regression, index numbers, components of time series. In our present course, we shall be mainly dealing with descriptive statistics. Descriptive statistics is also known as **deductive statistics.**

6. INFERENTIAL STATISTICS

The part of the subject statistics which deals with the analysis of a given group and drawing conclusions about a larger group is called **inferential statistics.** For studying data regarding a group of individuals or objects, such as heights, weights, income, expenditure of persons in a locality or number of defective and non-defective articles produced in a factory, it is generally impracticable to collect and study data regarding the entire group. Instead of examining the entire group, we concentrate on a small part of the group called a **sample.** If this sample happen to be a true representative of the entire group, called **population,** important conclusions can be drawn from the analysis of the sample. The conditions under which the conclusions for samples can be considered valid for the corresponding populations are studied in inferential statistics. Since such conclusions cannot be absolutely certain, the language of probability is often used in stating conclusions. Theoretical distributions are also needed in inferential statistics. In the present course, we shall be studying probability and theoretical distributions. Binomial, Poisson and Normal. Inferential statistics is also known as **inductive statistics.**

7. SCOPE

The importance of statistics cannot be underestimated. It is considered to be both a science and an art. According to *Tippett*, "Statistics is both a science and an art. It is a science in that its methods are basically systematic and have general application and an art in that their successful application depends to a considerable degree on the skill and special experience of the statistician and on his knowledge of the field of application *e.g.*, economics". Statistical methods help simplifying complexities. Statistical tools like diagrams and graphs presents data in simple and attractive form. That is why, diagrams and graphs are used for presenting data in exhibitions etc. On the extreme end, statistical methods are used to prepare control charts and for analysis of variance etc. Statistical methods are helping in enlarging human experience and is becoming indispensable. Statistics is related to almost every other discipline of knowledge like planning, mathematics, economics, physical science, psychology etc.

(*i*) **Statistics and Planning**. Statistical methods are powerful tools in the hands of the Government. The modern era is the era of Planning. In almost every country of the world, governments prepare their future plans well before time. This is very essential for the economic development of the country. The success of a plan depends upon the proper use of suitable statistical methods.

(*ii*) **Statistics and Mathematics.** Statistics is very closely related with mathematics. Statistical formulae are developed on the sound knowledge of mathematics. Contributors to statistics were primarily talented mathematicians. *Connor* defined statistics as the branch of applied Mathematics which specialises in data. Advancement in this field is impossible without the use of mathematics. Role of mathematics in the development of statistics is ever increasing.

(*iii*) **Statistics and Economics.** Methods of statistics are very much important in the formulation of economic policies. Data regarding the consumption pattern of people helps in knowing the standard of their living and their taxable capacity. Government adjust the dearness allowance of its employees on the basis of cost of living index, which is prepared by using the statistics regarding the consumption pattern of the people concerned. Statistical methods are used very widely in solving economic problems relating to wages, prices, consumption function, analysis of time series, etc. The ever increasing use of statistics in the field of economics has led to the development of a new subject 'Econometrics'.

(*iv*) **Statistics and Business.** Statistics is quite indispensible in business. In big business concerns, it is very much difficult for the owner to act as salesmen, accountant, store-manager etc. It is quite difficult for him to maintain direct contact with his customers. The success of business depends upon accuracy of his statistical forecasting. Business houses avails the services of trained and skilled statisticians. Without making use of statistical tools, it is impossible to take decisions about the effect of different forces acting on the 'profit' variable.

(*v*) **Statistics and Physical Sciences.** The methods of statistics are very much used in Physical sciences like Physics, Biology, Astronomy, Medical Sciences, Geology etc. *Professor Karl Pearson* studied that the 'theory of heredity' is based on Statistics. In Astronomy, the 'normal laws of errors' were developed by using the 'Principle of least squares'. In medical science, χ^2-test and other tests of significance are used widely to see whether a particular medicine is useful in curing a certain disease or not.

8. LIMITATIONS

Statistics is considered to be a science as well as an art, which is used as an instrument of research in almost every sphere of our activities. There are limitations of statistics also. Care must be taken of these limitations while using statistical methods. *Newsholme* has well said, "It must be regarded as an instrument of research of great value but having several limitations which are not possible to overcome and as such they need our careful attention". Some of the limitations of statistics are as follows :

1. **Statistics suits to the study of quantitative data only.** Statistics deals with the study of quantitative data only. By using the methods of statistics, the problems regarding production, income, price, wage, height, weight etc. can be studied. Such characteristics are quantitative in nature. The characteristics like honesty, goodwill, duty, character, beauty, intelligence, efficiency, integrity etc. are not capable of quantitative measurement and hence cannot be directly dealt with statistical methods. These characteristics are qualitative in nature. In such type of characteristics, only comparison is possible. The statistical methods may be tried in studying qualitative characteristics only if they are expressed quantitatively. For example, the efficiency of workers in a hand made paper factory, may be studied by considering the number of paper sheets prepared daily by each worker. The use of statistical methods is

limited to quantitative characteristics and those qualitative characteristics which are capable of being expressed numerically.

2. **Statistical results are not exact.** The task of statistical analysis is performed under certain conditions. It is not always possible, rather not advisable, to consider the entire population during statistical investigations. The use of samples is called for in statistical investigations. And the results obtained by using samples may not be universally true for the entire population. Data collected for a statistical enquiry may not be hundred percent true. Statistical results are true on an average. If we comment that the students of a particular class are intelligent, it does not necessarily imply that each and every student of the class is intelligent. The probability of getting a head in a single trial of an unbiased coin is 1/2, but we may not get exactly one head in two trials of the coin. That is why, statistics is not considered an exact science like Physics, Mathematics etc.

3. **Statistics deals with aggregates only.** Statistics does not recognise individual items. Consider the statement, "The weight of Mr. X in the college is 70 kg". This statement does not constitute statistical data. Statistical methods are not going to investigate anything about this statement. Whereas, if the weights of all the students of the college are given, the statistical methods may be applied to analyse that data. According to *Tippett*, "Statistics is essentially totalitarian because it is not concerned with individual values, but only with classes". Statistics is used to study group characteristics of aggregates. If we are given the profit figure of a firm manufacturing a particular item, it does not help in commenting on the performance of the company. On the other hand, if we are given the profit figures of the firm for the ten or fifteen consecutive years, we can make use of statistical methods to comment on the performance of the firm.

4. **Statistics is useful for experts only.** Statistics is both a science and an art. It is systematic and find applications in studying problems in Economics, Business, Astronomy, Physics, Medicines etc. Statistical methods are sophisticated in nature. Everyone is not expected to possess the intelligence required to understand and to apply these methods to practical problems. This is the job of an expert, who is well-versed with statistical methods. *W.I. King* says, "Statistics is a most useful servant but only of great value to those who understand its proper use".

A skilled statistician can never advise the public to walk in the middle of the road just on the plea that the number of padestrians who died in road accidents during 1975-86, on a particular road, was less for those who walked in the middle than those who walked on the road side. Such statements can only be given by those who cannot be considered as experts in using statistical methods. If such a type of decision is to be taken, then we must also consider the number of persons, who walk on the middle and on the sides of the road. In fact, if some body, accepts the advice of such an expert and start walking in the middle of the road, he is not hoped to survive much longer. *Yule* and *Kendall* has rightly said that "statistical methods are most dangerous tools in the hands of inexperts".

The methods of statistics must be tried by experts only. The results derived by using statistical methods would very much depends upon the skill of the user. According to *King*, "Statistics are like clay of which one can make a god or devil as one pleases".

5. **Statistics does not provide solutions to the problems.** The statistical methods are used to explore the essentials of problems. It does not find use in inventing solutions to problems. For example, the methods of statistics may reveal the fact that the average result of a particular class in a college is deteriorating for the last ten years, *i.e.*, the trend of the result is downward, but statistics cannot provide solution to this problem. It cannot help in

Merits

(*a*) This method is economical in respect of money, labour and time.

(*b*) This method can be very easily used if the area to be covered is widely spread.

Demerits

(*a*) This method is not useful in case the informants are illiterate or semi-literate.

(*b*) The collected data is not expected to be very accurate due to lack of seriousness in the informants.

(*c*) The response of the informants is expected to be poor because people generally avoid giving reply in written statement form.

(*d*) The reliability of the data collected cannot be judged by the investigator.

(*e*) The data may be unduly affected by the expected bias of the informants.

8. THROUGH SCHEDULES FILLED IN BY ENUMERATORS

In this method of collecting data, the informants are not directly contacted by the investigator, but instead, the enumerators are deputed to contact the informants and to fill in the schedules on the spot, after collecting data as per the need of the schedule. The basic difference between this method and the previous method is that, in this method the schedules are filled in by the enumerators after getting information from the informants, whereas in the previous method, the questionnaires were to be filled in by the informants themselves. The suitability of this method depends upon the enumerators. The enumerators are expected to be skilled honest, hard working, well-behaved and free from bias. This method of collecting data is suitable in case the informants are illiterate or semi-literate. In our country, census data about all the citizens is collected after every ten years by using this method.

Merits

(*a*) In this method of collecting data, the degree of accuracy is expected to be very high.

(*b*) The data collected is very reliable.

(*c*) Because of the direct contact between the enumerators and the informants, data can also be gathered about sensitive questions by twisting the questions accordingly.

(*d*) The data collected is least affected by the bias of the enumerators and the informants.

(*e*) This method can also be used in case the informants are illiterate or semi-literate.

Demerits

(*a*) This method of collecting data is very expensive.

(*b*) Much time is taken in collecting data.

(*c*) The enumerator have to be trained before they are deputed to start collecting data.

9. REQUISITES OF A GOOD 'QUESTIONNAIRE' AND 'SCHEDULE'

In the last two methods of collecting primary data, we discussed the method of questionnaires to be filled in by the informants and the method of filling schedules by the enumerators. In fact, there is no fundamental difference between a questionnaire and a schedule. Both questionnaire and schedule contain some questions. The only difference between the two is that the former is filled in by the informants themselves, whereas in the case of later, the data concerning the informants is filled in by the enumerators. The success of collecting data by using either questionnaire or schedule depends upon the quality of itself. Preparation of questionnaire and schedule is an art. Now we shall discuss in detail the requisites of a good questionnaire and schedule.

(*i*) **Forwarding Letter.** The investigator must include a forwarding letter in case of sending questionnaires to the informants. The investigator must request the informants to fill in the same and to return it back after filling it. The object of the investigation should also be mentioned in the latter. The informants should also be ensured that the filled questionnaires would be kept secretly, if desired. To encourage the response of informants, special concessions and free gifts may be offered to the informants.

(*ii*) **Questions should be Minimum in Number.** The number of questions in a questionnaire or a schedule should be as small as possible. Unnecessary questions should never be included. Inclusion of more than 20 or 25 questions would be undesirable.

(*iii*) **Questions should be Simple to Understand.** The questions included in a questionnaire or a schedule should be simple to understand. The questions should not be confusing in nature. The language used should also be simple and the use of highly technical terms should also be avoided.

(*iv*) **Questions should be Logically Arranged.** The questions in a questionnaire or a schedule also be logically arranged. The questions should be arranged so that there is natural and spontaneous reaction of the informants to the questions. It is not fair to ask the informant whether he is employed or unemployed after asking his monthly income. Such sequence of questions create bad impression on the mind of the informants.

(*v*) **Only well-defined terms should be used in questions.** In drafting questions for a questionnaire or a schedule, only well defined terms should be used. For example, the term 'income' should be clearly defined in the sense whether it is to include allowances etc. along with the basic income or not. Similarly, in case of businessman, whether the informants are to inform about their gross profits or net profits etc.

(*vi*) **Prohibited questions should not be included.** No such question should be included in the questionnaire or schedule which may immediately agitate the mind of the informants. Question like, "Have you given up the habit of telling a lie" or "How many times in a month, do you quarrel with your wife", would immediately mar the spirit of the informants.

(*vii*) **Irrelevant questions should be avoided.** In questionnaire or schedule, only those questions should be included which bears direct link with the object of the investigation. If the object is to study the problem of unemployment, then it would be useless to collect data regarding the heights and weights of the informants.

(*viii*) **Pilot Survey.** Before the questionnaire is sent to all the informants for collecting data, it should be checked before hand for its workability. This is done by sending the questionnaire to a selected sample and the replies received are studied thoroughly. If the investigator finds that most of the informants in the sample have left some questions unanswered then those questions should be modified or deleted altogether, provided the object of the investigation permits to do so. This is called *Pilot Survey*. Pilot Survey must be carried out before the questionnaire is finally accepted.

II. SECONDARY DATA

10. DEFINITION

Data is called **secondary** if it is not originally collected in the process of investigation, but instead, the data collected by some other agency is used for the purpose. If the investigation is not of very special nature, then the use of secondary data may be made provided that can serve the purpose. Suppose we want to investigate the extent of poverty in our country, then this investigation can be carried out by using the national census data which is obtained regularly after every 10 years. The use of secondary data economise the money spent. It also reduces the time period of investigation to a great extent. If in an investigation some secondary data could be made use of, then we must use the same. The secondary data are ought to be used very carefully. In this context, *Connor* has remarked, "Statistics, especially other peoples' statistics are full of pitfalls for the user."

11. METHODS OF COLLECTING SECONDARY DATA

(*i*) Collection from Published Data

(*ii*) Collection from Un-published Data.

12. COLLECTION FROM PUBLISHED DATA

There are agencies which collect statistical data regularly and publish it. The published data is very important and is used frequently by investigators. The main sources of published data are as follows :

(*a*) *International Publications*. International Organisations and Govt. of foreign countries collect and publish statistical data relating to various characteristics. The data is collected regularly as well as on ad-hoc basis. Some of the publications are :

(*i*) U.N.O. Statistical Year Book

(*ii*) Annual Reports of I.L.O.

(*iii*) Annual Reports of the Economic and Social Commission for Asia and Pacific (ESCAP)

(*iv*) Demography Year Book

(*v*) Bulletins of World Bank.

(*b*) *Govt. Publications*. In India, the Central Govt. and State Govt. collects data regarding various aspects. This data is published and is found very useful for investigation purpose. Some of the publications are :

(*i*) Census Report of India (*ii*) Five-Year Plans

(*iii*) Reserve Bank of India Bulletin

(*iv*) Annual Survey of Industries (*v*) Statistical Abstracts of India.

(*c*) *Report of Commissions and Committees*. The Central Govt. and State Govt. appoints Commissions and Committees to study certain issues. The reports of such investigations are very useful. Some of these are :

(*i*) Reports of National Labour Commission

(*ii*) Reports of Finance Commission

(*iii*) Report of Hazari Committee etc.

(*d*) *Publications of Research Institutes*. There are number of research institutes in India which regularly collect data and analyse it. Some of the agencies are :

(*i*) Central Statistical Organisation (C.S.O.)

(*ii*) Institute of Economic Growth

(*iii*) Indian Statistical Institute

(*iv*) National Council of Applied Economic Research etc.

(*e*) *Newspapers and Magazines.* There are many newspapers and magazines which publish data relating to various aspects. Some of these are :

(*i*) Economic Times (*ii*) Financial Express

(*iii*) Commerce (*iv*) Transport

(*v*) Capital etc.

(*f*) *Reports of Trade Associations.* The trade associations also collect data and publish it. Some of the agencies are :

(*i*) Stock Exchanges (*ii*) Trade Unions

(*iii*) Federation of Indian Chamber of Commerce and Industry.

13. COLLECTION FROM UN-PUBLISHED DATA

The Central Government, State Government and Research Institutes also collect data which is not published due to some reasons. This type of data is called un-published data. Unpublished data can also be made use of in Investigations. The data collected by research scholars of Universities is also generally not published.

14. PRECAUTIONS IN THE USE OF SECONDARY DATA

The secondary data must be used very carefully. The applicability of the secondary data should be judged keeping in view the object and scope of the Investigation. *Prof. Bowley* has remarked, "Secondary data should not be accepted at their face value." Following are the basis on which the applicability of secondary data is to be judged.

(*i*) **Reliability of Data.** Reliability of data is assessed by reliability of the agency which collected that data. The agency should not be biased in any way. The enumerators who collected the data should have been unbiased and well trained. Degree of accuracy achieved should also be judged.

(*ii*) **Suitability of Data.** The suitability of the data should be assessed keeping in view the object and scope of Investigation. If the data is not suitable for the investigation, then it is not to be used just for the sake of economy of time and money. The use of unsuitable data can lead to only misleading results.

(*iii*) **Adequacy of Data.** The adequacy of data should also be judged keeping in view the object and scope of the investigation. If the data is found to be inadequate, it should not be used. For example, if the object of investigation is to study the problem of unemployment in India, then the data regarding unemployment in one state say U.P. would not serve the purpose.

III. ROUNDING OF DATA

15. ROUNDING OF DATA

Suppose we are considering the data regarding population of various districts in India. The magnitude of the entries would be in thousand and lacs. Suppose the population of a district is 2,84,639. For the sake of simplicity, we say that the population is about 3 lacs because 2,84,639 is closer to 3 lacs than to 2 lacs.

In general, the data collected consists of long figures, running into several digits. Such long figures are very inconvenient to read, write and speak. Moreover, the computation work with such long figures is very cumbersome. For the sake of easiness in calculation work, the given data is rounded to desired level. In rounding 3850 to the nearest hundred, we are faced with a dilemma since 3850 is just as far from 3800 as from 3900. It has become the practice in such cases to round to the *even integer* preceding the 5. Thus 3850 is rounded to 3800.

Example 1. *Round each of the following numbers to the indicated accuracy :*

(*i*) *569784 to the nearest hundred.*

(*ii*) *569784 to the nearest thousand.*

(*iii*) *4379.3 to the nearest hundred.*

(*iv*) *23.695 to the nearest unit.*

(*v*) *24.72 to the nearest tenth.*

(*vi*) *823.5693 to the nearest hundredth.*

(*vii*) *84500 to the nearest thousand.*

(*viii*) *7750 to the nearest hundred.*

Sol. (*i*) 569784 rounded to the nearest hundred is **569800.**

(*ii*) 569784 rounded to the nearest thousand is **570000.**

(*iii*) 4379.3 rounded to the nearest hundred is **4400.**

(*iv*) 23.695 rounded to the nearest unit is **24.**

(*v*) 24.72 rounded to the nearest tenth is **24.7.**

(*vi*) 823.5693 rounded to the nearest hundredth is **823.57.**

(*vii*) 84500 rounded to the nearest thousand is **84000.**

(*viii*) 7750 rounded to the nearest hundred is **7800.**

EXERCISE 1

1. Distinguish between Primary and secondary data (*MDU 2005*)
2. Explain the various methods that are used in the collection of Primary Data, pointing out their merits and demerits. (*MDU 1998*)
3. Distinguish between primary source and secondary source of statistical data. What precautions would you take before using data from a secondary source ? (*KU 1995 C*)
4. What are the various methods of collection of primary data ? Briefly explain two such methods, pointing out their merits and demerits.
5. Discuss the sources, advantages and limitations of secondary data. What precautions should be taken while using secondary data ? (*MDU 2007*)
6. Describe the points that you would consider in drafting a questionnaire ? (*KU 1995 C*)
7. Why is it necessary that secondary data must be scrutinised and edited before use ? What precautions would you take before making use of such statistical data ?
8. Distinguish clearly between primary and secondary data. Explain the various methods of collecting primary data and point out their respective merits and demerits. (*MDU 1997 ; KU 2005, 2006*)
9. What are the various methods of collecting statistical data ? Which of these are not reliable and why ? (*KU 1997 C*)
10. What are the various methods of collecting primary data ? Why we prefer primary data than secondary data ? Explain. (*MDU 1999*)

3

Summation Operation

1. INTRODUCTION

Most of the methods of statistics involve summation of values of various variables. To simplify the statistical treatment, the sum of values of a variable is written in a compact form.

2. SUMMATION OPERATION

The summation operation is denoted by 'Σ', the Greek capital letter *Sigma*.

If $x_1, x_2, \ldots\ldots, x_n$ be n values of a variable x, then their sum $x_1 + x_2 + \ldots\ldots + x_n$ is denoted by $\sum_{i=1}^{n} x_i$.

Thus, $$\sum_{i=1}^{n} x_i = x_1 + x_2 + \ldots\ldots + x_n.$$

In $\sum_{i=1}^{n}$, 1 and n are called the **lower limit** of Σ and **upper limit** of Σ respectively.

For example :

(*i*) $\sum_{i=1}^{7} x_i = x_1 + x_2 + x_3 + x_4 + x_5 + x_6 + x_7$

(*ii*) $\sum_{j=4}^{8} y_j = y_4 + y_5 + y_6 + y_7 + y_8$

(*iii*) $\sum_{k=2}^{100} x_k = x_2 + x_3 + x_4 + \ldots\ldots + x_{99} + x_{100}.$

Example 1. *Express the following in the summation notation :*

(*i*) $x_1 + x_2 + x_3 + \ldots\ldots + x_{10}$

(*ii*) $X_4^2 + X_5^2 + X_6^2 + \ldots\ldots + x_{17}^2$

(*iii*) $f_1 x_1 + f_2 x_2 + f_3 x_3 + \ldots\ldots + f_{20} x_{20}$

(*iv*) $f_1 (x_1 - k)^2 + f_2 (x_2 - k)^2 + \ldots\ldots + f_n (x_n - k)^2.$

Sol. (*i*) $x_1 + x_2 + x_3 + \ldots\ldots + x_{10}$ is the sum of values x_i, where i ranges from 1 to 10.

∴ Given sum = $\sum_{i=1}^{10} x_i$.

3. If $x_1 = 1, x_2 = 5, x_3 = 7, x_4 = 9, x_5 = 3$, find the value of :

(i) $\sum_{i=1}^{4} x_i$ (ii) $\sum_{j=1}^{5} x_j$ (iii) $\sum_{j=4}^{4} x_j$ (iv) $\sum_{k=2}^{5} x_k$.

4. If $X_i = \frac{i(i+3)}{2}$ for $i = 1, 2, 3, \ldots, 10$, find the value of :

(i) $\sum_{i=1}^{3} X_i$ (ii) $\sum_{j=5}^{10} X_j$ (iii) $\sum_{k=1}^{9} X_k$ (iv) $\sum_{j=10}^{10} X_j$.

5. If $x_1 = 2, x_2 = -2, x_3 = 5, x_4 = 3, x_5 = -1$, find the value of :

(i) $\sum_{i=1}^{5}(x_i + 6)$ (ii) $\sum_{j=1}^{4}(x_j - 11)$ (iii) $\sum_{i=1}^{5}(9x_i)$ (iv) $\sum_{i=1}^{4}\left(\frac{x_i}{7}\right)$.

6. If $x_1 = 18, x_2 = 20, x_3 = 27, x_4 = -29$, find the value of :

(i) $\sum_{i=1}^{4}(2x_i + 3)$ (ii) $\sum_{i=1}^{4}(1 - 7x_i)$ (iii) $\sum_{j=1}^{3}(5x_j + 7)$ (iv) $\sum_{i=1}^{4}(9x_i - 3)$.

7. If $x_1 = 5, x_2 = 3, x_3 = 9, x_4 = 8, x_5 = 3, x_6 = 1$, find the value of :

(i) $\sum_{i=1}^{6} x_i^2$ (ii) $\sum_{i=1}^{5}(2x_i^2 - x_i)$ (iii) $\sum_{i=1}^{6} x_i^3$ (iv) $\sum_{i=1}^{6}(4x_i^3 - 6)$.

8. If $\sum_{i=1}^{10} x_i = -3$, $\sum_{i=1}^{10} x_i^2 = 100$, find the value of :

(i) $\sum_{i=1}^{10}(2x_i + 5)$ (ii) $\sum_{i=1}^{10}(10 - 3x_i)$ (iii) $\sum_{i=1}^{10} x_i(x_i + 5)$ (iv) $\sum_{i=1}^{10} 2x_i(1 - x_i)$.

9. If $\sum_{i=1}^{50} x_i = -36$, $\sum_{i=1}^{50} x_i^2 = 104$, find the value of :

(i) $\sum_{i=1}^{50}(2x_i + 3)^2$ (ii) $\sum_{i=1}^{50}(3x_i - 5)^2$

(iii) $\sum_{i=1}^{50}(x_i + 1)(3x_i + 8)$ (iv) $\sum_{i=1}^{50}(3x_i - 1)(2x_i + 3)$.

Answers

1. (i) $\sum_{i=1}^{57} x_i$ (ii) $\sum_{i=3}^{18} y_i$ (iii) $\sum_{i=1}^{11} x_i^2$ (iv) $\sum_{i=4}^{20} x^3$

2. (i) $\sum_{i=1}^{14} f_i x_i$ (ii) $\sum_{i=1}^{n} f_i y_i^2$ (iii) $\sum_{i=1}^{15} f_i x_i y_i$ (iv) $\sum_{i=1}^{45} f_i(x_i - 6)^2$.

3.	(*i*) 22	(*ii*) 25	(*iii*) 9	(*iv*) 24
4.	(*i*) 16	(*ii*) 245	(*iii*) 210	(*iv*) 65
5.	(*i*) 37	(*ii*) –36	(*iii*) 63	(*iv*) 8/7
6.	(*i*) 84	(*ii*) – 248	(*iii*) 346	(*iv*) 312
7.	(*i*) 189	(*ii*) 348	(*iii*) 1421	(*iv*) 5648
8.	(*i*) 44	(*ii*) 109	(*iii*) 85	(*iv*) – 206
9.	(*i*) 434	(*ii*) 3266	(*iii*) 316	(*iv*) 222.

The sum (Σf) of all the items is denoted by N. The data is also classified according to different classes of values of variable. This would also help in condensing the data to a great extent. In the above example, we can have classes of the values of the variable as 40 and under 45, 45 and under 50 and so on. In the class 40 and under 45, we shall count all the items with values 40 or more but less than 45. Using these classes, the above frequency distribution takes the form :

Weight (in kg)	*No. of students (f)*
40 and under 45	2
45 and under 50	18
50 and under 55	4
55 and under 60	7
60 and under 65	5
65 and under 70	2
70 and under 75	2
	N = 40

12. METHODS OF FORMING CLASSES

There are two methods of forming classes :

(*a*) Exclusive Method

(*b*) Inclusive Method

Let us discuss these methods in detail :

(*a*) **Exclusive Method.** In this method of writing classes, the lower limit of a class is equal to the upper limit of the previous class. For example, we may form the classes like 0 and under 10, 10 and under 20, 20 and under 30 and so on.

An item with value 10 would be counted in the class 10 and under 20 and not in 0 and under 10. For all practical purposes, the above classes are written as 0—10, 10—20, 20—30 and so on.

(*b*) **Inclusive Method.** In this method of writing classes, the lower limit of a class is not equal to the upper limit of the previous class. For example, we may have classes like 10—19, 20—29, 30—39 and so on. In the class 10—19, all items with value greater or equal to 9.5 but less than 19.5 are to be taken. Similarly, in the class 20—29, all items with value greater or equal to 19.5 but less than 29.5 are to be taken. Thus, we see that the actual class limits of the classes 10—19, 20—29, 30—39 ... are 9.5—19.5, 19.5—29.5, 29.5—39.5 and so on. For all practical purposes, the actual class limits are taken as the class limits.

The following points must be taken care of while preparing classes of the values of the variable :

1. The width (Upper limit-Lower limit) of classes should be preferably kept equal.

2. The lower limit and upper limit of classes should be preferably multiples of 5 or 10. This will facilitate application of statistical methods.

3. The number of classes may be found out by using formula given by *Prof. H.A. Sturges*. The formula is :

$$n = 1 + 3.222 \log N$$

where N = total number of items

n = number of classes.

For example, let N = 45

$$\therefore \quad n = 1 + 3.222 \log 45 = 1 + 3.222\,(1.6532)$$
$$= 1 + 5.327 \text{ or } 6 \text{ (Approx.)}$$

The width of classes would depend upon the values of the variable. If L and S are the largest and smallest values of the variable, then the *width* (h) of the classes is obtained by

$$h = \frac{L - S}{n}$$

The value of h as obtained by this formula is preferably approximated to the nearest multiple of 5 or 10.

13. CUMULATIVE FREQUENCY

The **cumulative frequency** of a value (or class of values) of variable is obtained by adding all the frequencies of all values (or classes of values) less than or equal to that under consideration. The cumulative frequency is generally denoted by 'c.f.'. The concept of cumulative frequency would be specifically used in estimating partition values of distributions.

Let us consider the following frequency distribution :

No. of children (X)	0	1	2	3	4	5	6
No. of families (f)	40	55	44	22	6	2	1

In this frequency distribution, we are given the data regarding the number of children in 170 families.

The cumulative frequencies for different values of the variable would be 40,

$40 + 55 = 95$, $40 + 55 + 44 = 139$,

$40 + 55 + 44 + 22 = 161$, $40 + 55 + 44 + 22 + 6 = 167$,

$40 + 55 + 44 + 22 + 6 + 2 = 169$ and $40 + 55 + 44 + 22 + 6 + 2 + 1 = 170$.

The cumulative frequency 95 means that there are 95 families having either no child or 1 child. The c.f. 139 means that there are 139 families having either no child or 1 child or 2 children and so on. If the families are arranged in ascending order of no. of children in family, then the c.f. can also be interpreted as follows. The c.f. 40 means that the first 40 families are having no child. The c.f. 95 means that 41st family to 95th family are having 1 child. The c.f. 139 means that 96th family to 139th family are having 2 children and so on. The simple frequencies and cumulative frequency can also be arranged in a table as follows :

No. of children (X)	*No. of families (f)*	*Cumulative frequencies (c.f.)*
0	40	40
1	55	95
2	44	139
3	22	161
4	6	167
5	2	169
6	1	170 = N
	N = 170	

From this table, we find that there are four children in the 165th family, because 6 families from 162th to 167th are having 4 children. Similarly c.f. can also be used to find the number of children in any family. Thus, we see that c.f. is very useful in finding the size of any item provided the items are arranged in order of magnitude.

Example 1. *Following is the data regarding the number of children in 50 families in a locality. Prepare a frequency distribution :*

3	2	0	4	4	6	5	0	2	1
4	3	1	5	4	4	6	5	2	4
2	0	2	3	0	3	6	2	2	2
0	5	2	2	1	2	0	2	1	1
5	4	1	3	5	2	2	1	2	5.

Sol. Let 'X' denotes the variable 'number of children'.

X	*Tally bars*	*No. of families (f)*
3	⅂⅃ (5)	5
4	𝍸 II	7
2	𝍸 𝍸 𝍸	15
0	𝍸 I	6
5	𝍸 II	7
1	𝍸 II	7
6	III	3
		N = 50

We write this distribution once again, arranging the values of the variable in ascending order :

No. of children (X)	0	1	2	3	4	5	6
No. of families (f)	6	7	15	5	7	7	3

Example 2. *Following are the marks (out of 100) obtained by 50 students in Statistics paper :*

70	46	39	25	45	41	45	18	52	63
40	33	53	53	75	64	53	65	65	42
48	56	50	42	49	20	26	63	36	54
45	56	61	65	39	15	60	58	45	35
51	64	55	59	30	35	42	82	45	52

Make a frequency distribution taking class interval of 10 marks.

Sol. In the given data, the smallest item = 15

Largest item = 82

The class interval is given to be 10.

We take the classes as 10—20, 20—30, ..., 80—90.

Classes	*Tally bars*	*No. of students (f)*
10—20	||	2
20—30	|||	3
30—40	~~||||~~ ||	7
40—50	~~||||~~ ~~||||~~ |||	13
50—60	~~||||~~ ~~||||~~ |||	13
60—70	~~||||~~ ||||	9
70—80	||	2
80—90	|	1
		N = 50

We can write the frequency distribution as :

Marks	10—20	20—30	30—40	40—50	50—60	60—70	70—80	80—90
No. of Students (f)	2	3	7	13	13	9	2	1

Example 3. *Convert the following into a frequency distribution :*

12 students get less than 10 marks

18 students get less than 20 marks

30 students get less than 30 marks

40 students get less than 40 marks

56 students get less than 50 marks.

Sol. The given data can be written as :

Marks	*No. of students*
Less than 10	12
Less than 20	18
Less than 30	30
Less than 40	40
Less than 50	56

There are 12 students getting less than 10 marks. Therefore, the frequency of the class 0—10 is 12. There are 18 students getting less than 20 marks whereas there are 12 students who are getting less than 10 marks, therefore 18 – 12 = 6 students must be getting marks between 10—20. Therefore, the frequency of the class 10— 20 is 6. Similarly, the frequency of the class 20—30 can be obtained by subtracting the number of students getting less than 20 marks from the number of students getting less than 30 marks. Therefore, the frequency of the class 20—30 is 30 – 18 = 12. Similarly, we can obtain the frequencies of the classes 30—40, 40—50. We can show the computation of frequencies as follows :

Classes	*No. of students (f)*
0—10	12
10—20	18 – 12 = 6
20—30	30 – 18 = 12
30—40	40 – 30 = 10
40—50	56 – 40 = 16
	N = 56

EXERCISE 1

1. Following is the data regarding the number of children in 40 families. Represent it in the form of a frequency distribution.

3	4	4	0	1	4	6	0
4	6	3	0	5	4	2	2
2	2	2	1	6	3	3	4
1	2	1	2	2	2	1	3
5	1	0	2	1	2	5	2

2. Monthly wages of 30 labourers are as follows :
Represent the data in the form of a frequency distribution with class interval equal to Rs. 10/.

510	590	535	530	535	536
512	585	540	535	536	578
508	504	555	545	533	532
540	506	590	590	540	568
560	520	590	598	545	569

3. Read the following passage and form a frequency distribution taking number of letters in a word as the variable :

"Success in the examination confers no absolute right to appointment, unless Govt. is satisfied, after such enquiry as may be considered necessary that the candidate is suitable in all respect for the appointment".

4. Arrange the following passage into a frequency distribution according to the number of letters in each word :

"Statistics are aggregate of facts affected to a marked extent by multiplicity of causes numerically expressed, enumerated or estimated according to reasonable standard of accuracy, collected in a systematic manner and placed in relation to each other".

5. Represent the following data in the form of a frequency distribution :

Less than	0	10	15	25	40	55	70
No. of items	0	10	15	25	40	55	70

6. Convert the following frequency distribution into an individual series :

X	2	3	4	5
f	1	2	3	1

7. Following are the marks obtained by the students of a class. Arrange the data in the form of frequency distribution with classes.

12	38	11	40	45
18	40	12	42	46
30	20	6	46	49
45	22	7	17	23
4	17	3	31	26
7	6	3	23	29
19	5	2	32	30
20	19	15	32	16

Answers

1.

No. of children (X)	0	1	2	3	4	5	6
No. of families (f)	4	7	12	5	6	3	3

2.

Monthly wages (in Rs.)	*No. of Labourers*	*Monthly wages (in Rs.)*	*No. of Labourers*
500—510	3	550—560	1
510—520	2	560—570	3
520—530	1	570—580	1
530—540	8	580—590	1
540—550	5	590—600	5

3.

No. of letters (X)	2	3	4	5	6	7	8	9	10	11
No. of words (f)	8	6	3	2	1	4	2	3	1	3

4.

No. of letters (X)	1	2	3	4	5	6	8	9	10	11	12
No. of words (f)	2	10	2	1	2	5	4	5	4	1	1

5.

Classes	0—10	10—15	15—25	25—40	40—55	55—70
Frequency	10	5	10	15	15	15

6. X : 2, 3, 3, 4, 4, 4, 5

7.

Marks	0—10	10—20	20—30	30—40	40—50
No. of students	9	10	7	6	8

14. GRAPHS OF FREQUENCY DISTRIBUTIONS

We know that a frequency distribution is obtained by classifying the data according to the values of some quantitative variable. The number of times a different value of the variable is repeated, is called its frequency. Now we shall consider the graphical representation of frequency distributions.

15. TYPES OF GRAPHS OF FREQUENCY DISTRIBUTIONS

(*i*) Histogram (*ii*) Frequency Polygon

(*iii*) Frequency Curve (*iv*) Ogives.

We discuss each type of the above mentioned graphs of frequency distribution, in detail.

16. HISTOGRAM

A **histogram** is a set of rectangles with class intervals as basis and corresponding frequencies as heights, provided the classes in the distribution are of equal widths and are in ascending order of magnitude. In case, the classes are not of equal width, then before constructing histogram, the width of classes are made equal. If the width of a particular class is double then those of other classes, then it is divided into two classes with frequencies also equally divided. We know that the frequency of a class is always a whole number. If the frequency of the class which is to be broken into two classes is odd, say 15, then the frequencies of the classes are to be as 8, 7 or 7, 8. If the classes are given in inclusive form, then the actual class limits are taken into account while drawing the histogram. The frequencies are to be measured along Y-axis. On the Y-axis, scale must begin from '0'. On the 'X' axis, the classes are marked and it not necessary to start the scale from '0'.

Example 1. *Construct a histogram from the following data :*

Marks	*10—19*	*20—29*	*30—39*	*40—49*	*50—59*
No. of Students	*15*	*20*	*35*	*10*	*4*

Sol. The actual class limits of the given classes are 9.5–19.5, 19.5–29.5,.........

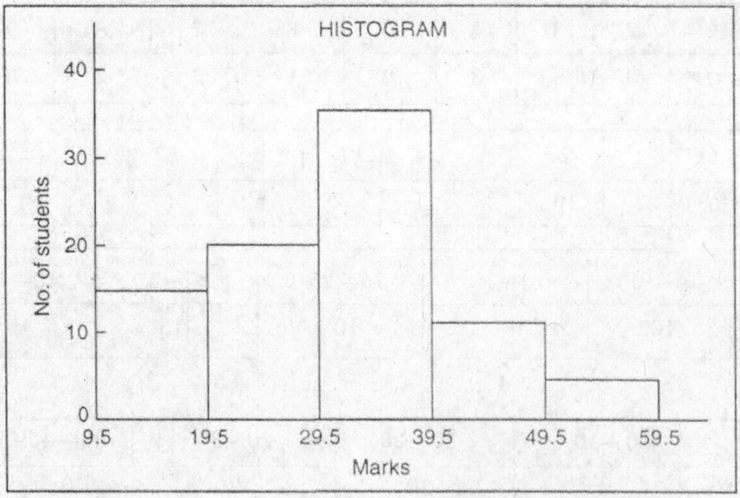

Example 2. *Represent the following data by means of a histogram :*

Weekly Wages (in Rs.)	*10—15*	*15—20*	*20—25*	*25—30*	*30—40*	*40—50*	*60—80*
No. of Workers	*7*	*19*	*27*	*15*	*12*	*12*	*8*

(MDU 2005)

Sol. In this distribution, the classes are not of equal width. The smallest width is 5. We shall modify the classes, whose width is greater than 5. The frequency of the class 30—40 is 12. This class would be broken into classes 30—35 and 35—40, each with frequency '6'. Similarly, the class 40—50 would be broken in 2 classes 40—45 and 45—50 with frequencies 6 each. The class 60—80 would be broken in to four classes, 60—65, 65—70, 70—75, 75—80, each with frequency 2. We rewrite the classes as :

Classes	*No. of workers*	*Classes*	*No. of workers*
10—15	7	45—50	6
15—20	19	50—55	0
20—25	27	55—60	0
25—30	15	60—65	2
30—35	6	65—70	2
35—40	6	70—75	2
40—45	6	75—80	2

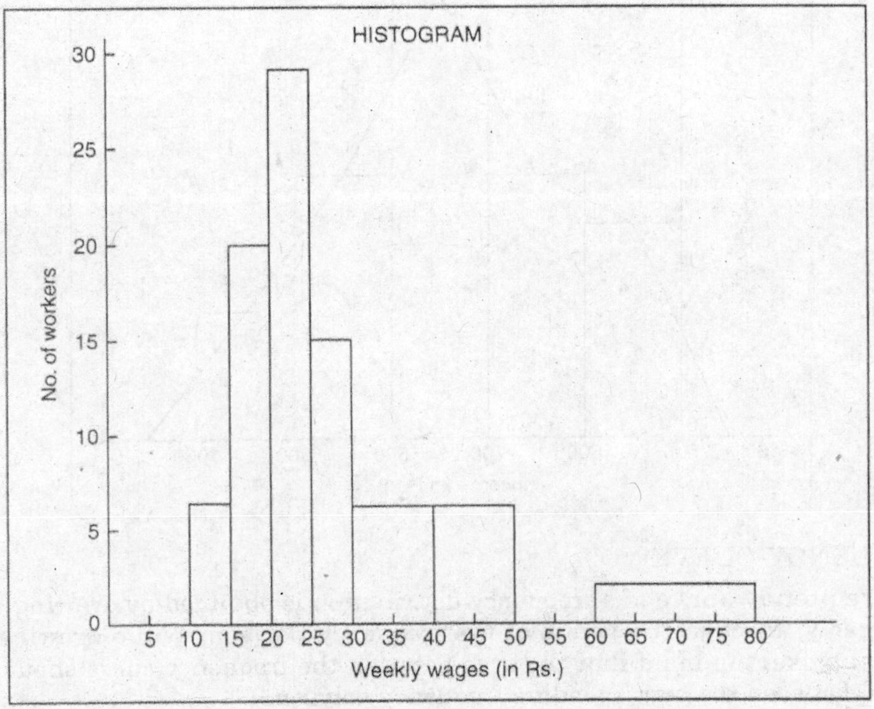

The vertical lines through the class limits which were not given in the original data, are not drawn.

17. FREQUENCY POLYGON

The **frequency polygon** of a frequency distribution is obtained by joining the mid-points of upper sides of rectangles with that for the adjacent rectangles. The polygon is closed by taking two classes on either sides with '0' frequency each. The frequency polygon can also be drawn without the help of histogram. The classes and frequencies are to be measured along

X-axis and Y-axis as we did in the case of histogram. The points are taken with abscissas as mid-points of classes and ordinates as their respective frequencies. Two additional points are also taken on the X-axis corresponding to two classes on each end with '0' frequencies. It may be noted that the area between the histogram and the frequency polygon would always be exactly equal.

Example 3. *Draw a frequency polygon for the data given below :*

Income less than (in Rs.)	*500*	*600*	*700*	*800*	*900*	*1000*
No. of employees	*0*	*25*	*55*	*105*	*135*	*150*

Sol. We first convert the data in the form of a frequency distribution.

Income (in Rs.)	500—600	600—700	700—800	800—900	900—1000
No. of employees	25	30	50	30	15

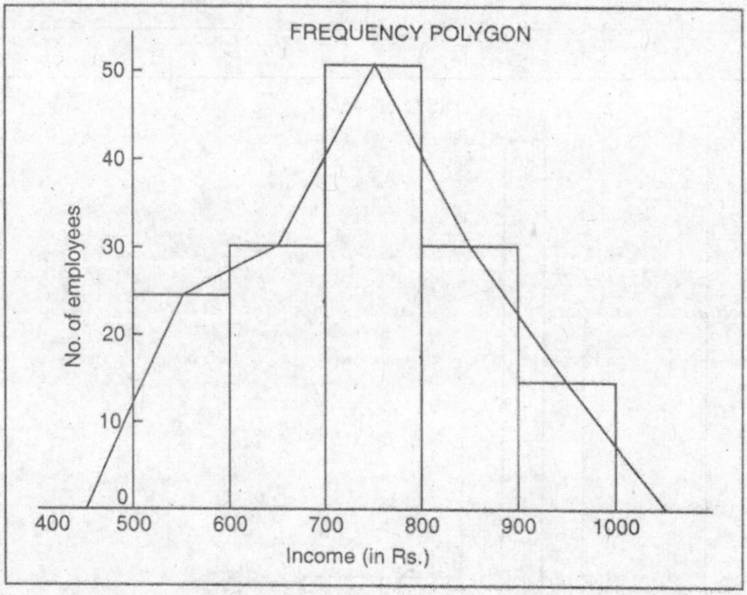

18. FREQUENCY CURVE

The **frequency curve** of a frequency distribution is obtained by drawing a free hand curve, preferably, through the points of the frequency polygon. While drawing frequency curves it is to be kept in mind that the area between the frequency curve should be almost equal to that between the corresponding frequency polygon.

Example 4. *Draw a 'Histogram', 'Frequency polygon' and 'Frequency curve' to the data given below :*

Marks	*10—20*	*20—30*	*30—40*	*40—50*	*50—60*
No. of Students	*15*	*25*	*17*	*49*	*60*
Marks	*60—70*	*70—80*	*80—90*	*90—100*	
No. of Students	*45*	*45*	*50*	*14*	

Sol.

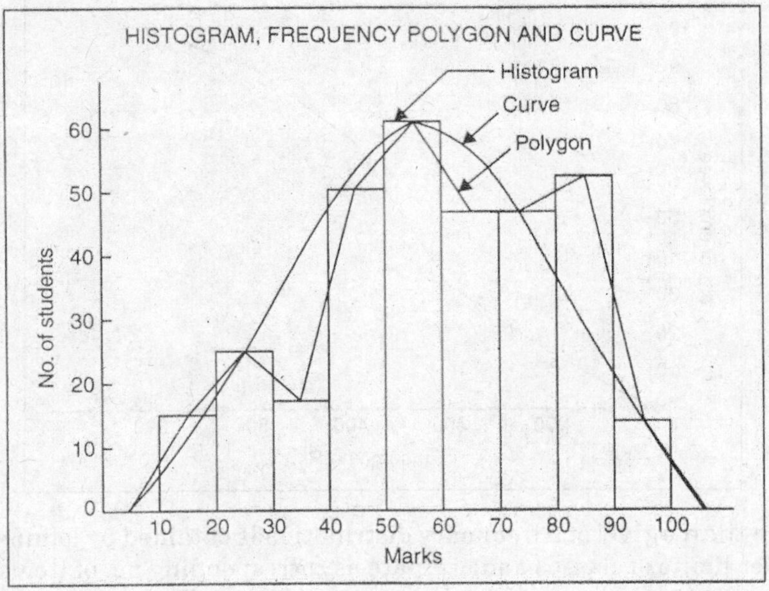

19. OGIVES

Ogives are also called cumulative frequency curves. Ogives are of two types : (*i*) 'Less than ogive' (*ii*) 'More than Ogive'. The **'less than ogive'** of a frequency distribution is obtained by joining the points with abscissas as upper limit of classes and ordinate as corresponding number of items less than that upper limit. The point (lower limit of first class, 0) is also taken. Let us take an example.

Income (in Rs.)	100—200	200—300	300—400	400—500	500—600
No. of employees	15	20	40	20	5

We rewrite this data as follows :

Income less than	100	200	300	400	500	600
No. of employees	0	15	35	75	95	100

The *'less than ogive'* would be obtained by joining the points (100, 0), (200, 15), (300, 35), (400, 75), (500, 95), (600, 100) on the graph paper.

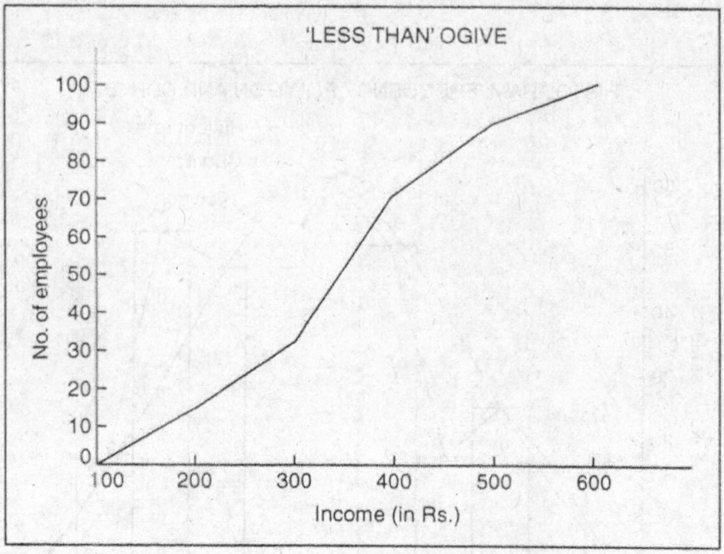

The '**more than ogive**' of a frequency distribution is obtained by joining the points with abscissas as lower limits of classes and ordinate as corresponding no. of items more than that lower limit. The point (upper limit of last class, 0) is also taken. The above-mentioned frequency distribution can also be expressed as :

Income more than	100	200	300	400	500	600
No. of employees	100	85	65	25	5	0

The *more than* ogive would be obtained by joining the points (100, 100), (200, 85), (300, 65) etc. on the graph paper.

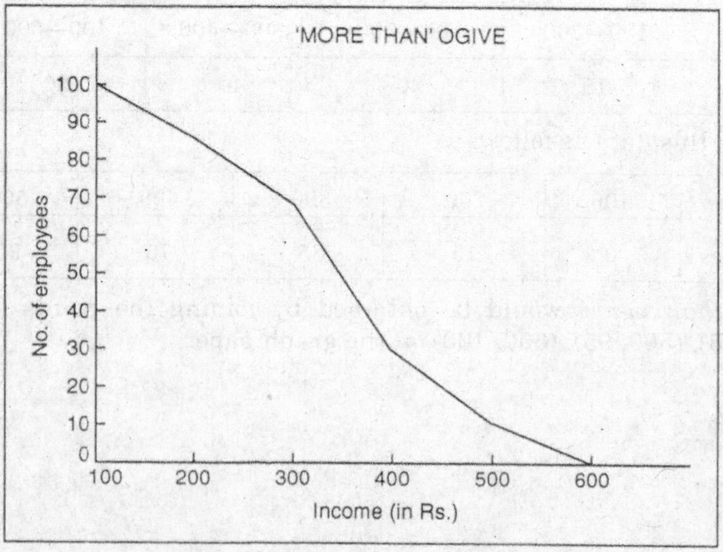

Both '*less than*' and '*more than*' ogives can also be drawn on the same graph paper.

WORKING RULES FOR DRAWING OGIVES

Step I. *Arrange the classes in ascending order of magnitude. The classes must be in 'exclusive form'. The widths of classes may not be equal.*

Step II. *On the vertical axis, cumulative frequencies would be marked.*

Step III. *(i) For the 'less than' ogive, take the points (x, y) where :*

x = upper limit of a class

y = number of items less than x

The point (lower limit of first-class, 0) is also taken.

(ii) For the 'more than' ogive, take the points (x, y) where :

x = lower limit of a class

y = number of items more than x.

The point (upper limit of last class, 0) is also taken.

Step IV. *The points obtained in **step III** are joined by straight lines. The 'less than' ogive is left to right rising while the 'more than' ogive is left to right falling.*

EXERCISE 2

1. The following table gives the wages and number of workers receiving the wages in a company. Draw a histogram to this data :

Daily wages (in Rs.)	10—15	15—20	20—25	25—30	30—35
No. of workers	40	70	60	80	60

2. Draw a histogram to the following data regarding the percentage of marks obtained by 800 students in a college :

Marks	11—20	21—30	31—40	41—50	51—60
No. of students	151	330	161	108	50

3. Draw a frequency polygon and frequency curve to the data given below :

Height (in inches)	60—62	63—65	66—68	69—71	72—74
No. of students	15	21	35	19	10

4. Draw a histogram, frequency polygon and frequency curve to the data given below :

Profit (,000 Rs.)	500—550	550—600	600—650	650—750	750—900
No. of companies	20	25	20	20	15

5. Draw both ogives to the following data :

Weight (in kg)	30—34	35—39	40—44	45—49	50—54	55—59	60—64
Frequencies	3	5	12	18	14	6	2

(MDU 2006)

6. Draw 'less than' as well as 'more than' ogives to the following data :

Classes	15—19	20—24	25—29	30—34	35—39	40—44	45—49
Frequencies	150	169	300	78	49	42	12

7. From the following data, construct : (1) Frequency Histogram, (2) Frequency Polygon and (3) Frequency curve.

Wage groups (in Rs.)	0—10	10—20	20—30	30—40	40—50
No. of workers	2	4	11	15	25
Wage groups (in Rs.)	50—60	60—70	70—80	80—90	
No. of workers	18	15	4	2	

8. Draw a frequency polygon for the following data :

Marks	0—10	10—20	20—30	30—40	40—50	50—60	60—70
No. of students	4	8	11	15	12	6	3

(MDU 1997)

9. Draw a histogram, frequency polygon and frequency curve of the following data :

Marks	10—20	20—30	30—40	40—50	50—60
No. of students	15	30	15	10	20

(MDU 1998)

II. PRESENTATION OF DATA

20. DEFINITION

Tabulation is a statistical method in which data is *presented* systematically using rows and columns. It is a fact that unarranged data cannot be analysed effectively. Tabulation helps to bring items with common characteristics to come together. *Tuttle* defined a statistical table exhaustively in the following words, "A statistical table is the logical listing of related quantitative data in vertical columns and horizontal rows of numbers, with sufficient explanatory and qualifying words, phrases and statements in the form of titles, headings and notes to make clear the full meaning of the data and their origin".

21. OBJECTS OF TABULATION

The process of tabulation is carried to achieve the following objectives :

(*i*) Data is tabulated to condense it by using rows and columns.

(*ii*) Data is tabulated to bring out the points of similarities and dissimilarities in the data.

(*iii*) Data is tabulated to facilitate comparison.

(*iv*) Data is tabulated so that statistical methods may be used effectively.

(*v*) Data is tabulated so that classified data may be arranged systematically in rows and columns.

(*vi*) Data is tabulated to economise space and time.

22. GENERAL RULES FOR TABULATION

The following points must be kept in mind while presenting the data in tables :

(*i*) It should be presented in an attractive form.

(*ii*) The data may be approximated to a reasonable standard.

(*iii*) The totals of different columns and rows should also be shown.

(*iv*) Title must be provided with every table.

(*v*) Source of data should also be mentioned in the table.

(*vi*) It should not be made unduly complex by introducing too many rows and columns.

23. MAIN PARTS OF A TABLE

A good table is expected to have the following parts :

(*i*) **Title.** Every table must possess a suitable title. Title should be self-explanatory in nature. It should also be brief.

(*ii*) **Table Number.** Every table should be provided with a table number. It helps in locating it.

(*iii*) **Captions.** The headings of columns are called **captions**. A table may have more than one caption. The captions should be brief and self-explanatory. Captions should also be numbered.

(*iv*) **Stubs.** The headings of rows are called **stubs**. A table may have more than one stub. The stubs should also be brief and self-explanatory. The stubs should also be numbered.

(*v*) **Body.** The part of the table which contains the numerical figures is called the **body** of the table. If the entries in a particular row or column are in the same units, then instead of mentioning units with every entry, the units are mentioned in the corresponding stub or column.

(*vi*) **Ruling and spacing.** For the table to look attractive and clear, it very necessary to make use of ruling between different stubs and columns. The different stubs and columns should also be preferably at equal distances.

(*vii*) **Footnotes.** Any other necessary information regarding the contents of the table which are not covered in the stubs, columns, title etc. may be given in the footnotes.

(*viii*) **Source of data.** The source of data in the table should also be mentioned therein.

24. SPECIMEN OF TABLE

The following is a specimen of table showing the places for its different parts :

TITLE

Table No.

	Caption	*Caption*	⟶	*Caption*	*Total*
Stub					
Stub					
↓			Body		
Stub					
Total					

Footnotes ......

Source ......

25. TYPES OF TABLES

Tables are classified as :

(*i*) Simple Table (*ii*) Complex Table

(*i*) **Simple Table.** When the data in a table is tabulated on the basis of only one characteristic, it is called a **simple table**. Simple table is also called **one-way table**. For example, the table showing the number of students in different faculties in a University is a simple table.

No. of students in the University in the year 1986-87

Faculties	*No. of students*
Arts	...
Commerce	...
Law	...
Non-Medical	...
Medical	...
Total	...

(*ii*) **Complex Table.** When the data in a table is tabulated on the basis of more than one characteristic, it is called a **complex table**. A complex table is also called a **manifold table**. When two characteristics are used in the table, then it is called a **double table** or **two-way table**. In the above example, if we also tabulate the number of boys and girls in different faculties, it would be a two-way table :

When three characteristics are used in a table, then it is also called a **trable table** or **three-way table**. In the above example, if we also show the number of hostlers and day scholars separately, it would become a trable table.

No. of students in the University in the year 1986-87

Faculties	*No. of students*		*Total*
	Boys	*Girls*	
Arts	...	...	...
Commerce	...	...	...
Law	...	...	...
Non-Medical	...	...	...
Medical	...	...	...
Total	...	...	...

No. of Students in the University in the Year 1986-87

Faculties	*No. of students*				*Total*		*TOTAL*
	Boys		*Girls*				
	Hostlers	*Day Scholars*	*Hostlers*	*Day Scholars*	*Hostlers*	*Day Scholars*	
Arts	...	...	...	...	...	...	...
Commerce	...	...	...	...	...	...	...
Law	...	...	...	...	...	...	...
Non-Medical	...	...	...	...	...	...	...
Medical	...	...	...	...	...	...	...
Total	...	...	...	...	...	...	...

The above table can also be extended to show the fourth characteristic "Age Groups". When four characteristics are used in a table then it may also be called a **four-way table**.

No. of Students in the University in the Year 1986-87

Faculties	*Age Group (in years)*	*No. of students*						*Total*		
		Boys			*Girls*					
		Hostlers	*Day Scholars*	*Total*	*Hostlers*	*Day Scholars*	*Total*	*Hostlers*	*Day Scholars*	*Total*
Arts	Less than 20	—	—	—	—	—	—	—	—	—
	20—25	—	—	—	—	—	—	—	—	—
	25 and above	—	—	—	—	—	—	—	—	—
Commerce	Less than 20	—	—	—	—	—	—	—	—	—
	20—25	—	—	—	—	—	—	—	—	—
	25 and above	—	—	—	—	—	—	—	—	—
Law	Less than 20	—	—	—	—	—	—	—	—	—
	20—25	—	—	—	—	—	—	—	—	—
	25 and above	—	—	—	—	—	—	—	—	—
Nonmedical	Less than 20	—	—	—	—	—	—	—	—	—
	20—25	—	—	—	—	—	—	—	—	—
	25 and above	—	—	—	—	—	—	—	—	—
Medical	Less than 20	—	—	—	—	—	—	—	—	—
	20—25	—	—	—	—	—	—	—	—	—
	25 and above	—	—	—	—	—	—	—	—	—
Total		—	—	—	—	—	—	—	—	—

Example 1. *Prepare a blank table to show the following characteristics regarding the employees of establishment 'X'.*

(i) Employees in the years 1985, 1986.

(ii) Male and Female.

(iii) Grade II, III, IV employees.

Sol. Table showing employees of establishment 'X' (1985-86)

Year	*No. of Employees*											
	Male				*Female*				*Total*			
	Grade II	*Grade III*	*Grade IV*	*Total*	*Grade II*	*Grade III*	*Grade IV*	*Total*	*Grade II*	*Grade III*	*Grade IV*	*Total*
1985												
1986												
Total												

Example 2. *A college organised a trip of 65 persons, out of which 60 were students of different classes. One servant and one lady lecturer also joined with other male lecturers accompanying the trip. 15 girls students also participated. Present the above data in the form of a table.*

Sol. Total number of participants $= 65$

Number of students $= 60$

Therefore, others $= 65 - 60 = 5$

Number of servants $= 1$

Number of lady lecturers $= 1$

Therefore, number of male lecturers $= 5 - 1 - 1 = 3$

Girls students $= 15$

Therefore, boys students $= 60 - 15 = 45$

Participants	*Sex*		*Total*
	Males	*Females*	
Students	45	15	60
Lectures	3	1	4
Servants	0	1	1
Total	48	17	65

EXERCISE 3

1. Prepare a blank table to show the following characteristics regarding the students of the B.Com. I class :

(*i*) Male, Female

(*ii*) Age groups, less than 20, 20 and above.

2. Prepare a blank table to show the following characteristics regarding the population in city 'X' :

(*i*) Male, Female

(*ii*) Age groups, less than 30, 30—45, 45 and above

(*iii*) Employed and unemployed.

3. Draft a blank table, showing the distribution of students of a college according to classes and sex.

4. Draft a blank table, showing the distribution of students of a college according to classes, sex and age.

5. There are 1000 employees in a factory, out of which 200 are females. There are only 50 class-II female employees and all other female employees are class-III. The number of class-II male employees is 200 and the rest are class-III employees. Represent the above data in the tabular form.

6. Submit a proforma of table which could explain the distribution of students of a college on the following basis : Faculty wise, Rural or Urban, Male or Female, hostlers or day scholar.

7. Define 'classification'. Explain the purpose and methods of classification of data giving suitable examples.

8. What is a statistical table ? Mention the rules of the construction of a table. (*KU 2000*)

9. "The statistical table is a systematic arrangement and numerical data presented in columns and rows for purpose of comparison." Elucidate the above statement and mention the rules for the construction of a statistical table.

10. Distinguish between classification and tabulation. Discuss the purpose, methods and importance of classification. (*MDU 2006*)

11. What are the different components of a table ? Explain the main precautions, you would take in tabulating your data.

12. Define classification and tabulation and show their importance in statistical studies.

13. What are the different problems and considerations in determining the classification of data ?

14. Discuss the considerations that would guide you in determining :

(*i*) the number of classes

(*ii*) the magnitude of each class and

(*iii*) the class limits.

15. Differentiate between classification and tabulation. Explain the purpose and methods of classification of data by giving suitable examples. (*KU 2006 S*)

16. Define classification. Discuss the basic objective of classification. (*KU 2005*)

17. Discuss the role of diagrams in presenting statistical data. (*KU 2005 S*)

5

Measures of Central Tendency

1. INTRODUCTION

In the previous chapters, we studied the different methods of presenting statistical data. The story does not end here. We have to go a long way with these well-presented statistical data. Suppose we have the data regarding the marks obtained by all the students of a class and we are to give an impression about the performance of students, to someone. It would not be desirable rather impracticable to tell him the marks obtained by all the students of the class. Perhaps, it may not be possible for him to gather any impression about the standard of students of that class. Similarly suppose we intend to compare the wage distribution of workers in two sugar factories and to decide as to which factory is paying more to individual workers, than the other. In this case also, if we proceed with comparing the wages of workers of one factory with that of the other on individual basis, we may not be able get any "thing". Even this type of comparison may not be possible if the number of workers in two factories are different.

2. MEANING

In fact, such type of problems can be easily dealt with, if we could find a single value of the variable which may be considered as a representative of the entire data. This type of representative which help in describing the characteristics of the entire data is called an *average* of the data. The individual values of the variable usually cluster around it. An average is also called a *measure of central tendency*, because it tends to lie centrally with the values of the variable arranged according to magnitude. Thus, we see that an *average* or a *measure of central tendency* of a statistical data is that single value of the variable which represent the entire data.

3. REQUISITES OF A GOOD AVERAGE

1. It should be easy to understand.

2. It should be simple to compute.

3. It should be well-defined in the sense that it is defined algebraically and should not depend upon personal bias.

4. It should be based on all the items.

5. It should not be unduly affected by extreme items in the series.

6. It should be capable of further algebraic treatment. For example, if we are given the averages of some groups, then we should be able to find the average of all the items taken together.

7. It should have sampling stability. By this we mean that the averages of different samples, drawn from the same population, should not vary significantly. Though it cannot be claimed that all the samples would have exactly the same average, but we expect that the values of the averages, should not vary significantly.

4. TYPES OF MEASURES OF CENTRAL TENDENCY (Averages)

I. Arithmetic Mean (A.M.) II. Geometric Mean (G.M.)
III. Harmonic Mean (H.M.) IV. Median
V. Mode.

I. ARITHMETIC MEAN (A.M.)

5. DEFINITION

This is the most popular and widely used measure of central tendency. The popularity of this average can be judged from the fact that it is generally referred to as 'mean'. The **arithmetic mean** of a statistical data is defined as the quotient of the sum of all the values of the variable by the total number of items and is generally denoted by $\bar{x}$.

∴ (*a*) **For an individual series**, the A.M. is given by

$$\text{A.M.} = \frac{x_1 + x_2 + ... + x_n}{n} = \frac{\sum_{i=1}^{n} x_i}{n} \text{ or more briefly as } \frac{\Sigma x}{n}$$

i.e., $$\bar{\mathbf{x}} = \frac{\Sigma \mathbf{x}}{\mathbf{n}}$$

where $x_1, x_2, ..., x_n$ are the values of the variable, under consideration.

(*b*) **For a frequency distribution,**

$$\text{A.M.} = \frac{f_1x_1 + f_2x_2 + ... + f_nx_n}{f_1 + f_2 + ... + f_n} = \frac{\sum_{i=1}^{n} f_i x_i}{\sum_{i=1}^{n} f_i} = \frac{\Sigma fx}{\Sigma f} = \frac{\Sigma fx}{\text{N}},$$

i.e., $$\bar{\mathbf{x}} = \frac{\Sigma \mathbf{fx}}{\mathbf{N}}$$

where f_i is the frequency of x_i $(1 \le i \le n)$. For simplicity, Σf, *i.e.*, the total number of items is denoted by N.

When the values of the variable are given in the form of classes, then their respective mid-points are taken as the values of the variable (x).

WORKING RULES TO FIND A.M.

Rule I. *In case of an individual series, first find the sum of all the items. In the second step, divide this sum by n, total number of items. This gives the value of* $\bar{x}$.

Rule II. *In case of a frequency distribution, find the products (fx) of frequencies and value of items. In the second step, find the sum (Σfx) of these products. Divide this sum by the sum (N) of all frequencies. This gives the value of* $\bar{x}$.

Rule III. *If the values of the variable are given in the form of classes, then their respective mid-points are taken as the values of the variable.*

Example 1. *Find the A.M. of the following data :*

Roll No.	*1*	*2*	*3*	*4*	*5*	*6*	*7*	*8*
Marks in Maths	*12*	*8*	*6*	*9*	*7*	*8*	*7*	*14*

Sol. Let the variable 'marks in maths' be denoted by x.

$$\therefore \quad \bar{x} = \frac{\text{Sum of values of } x}{\text{Number of items}} = \frac{12+8+6+9+7+8+7+14}{8} = \frac{71}{8} = \textbf{8.875 marks.}$$

Example 2. *The average weight of a group of 24 boys was calculated to be 78.4 kg. It was later discovered that one weight was misread as 69 kg instead of 96 kg. Calculate the correct average (Average used is A.M.).*

Sol. No. of items = 25

Incorrect average = 78.4 kg

Incorrect item = 69 kg

Correct item = 96 kg

Let the variable 'weight' be denoted by 'x'.

Now $\bar{x} = \frac{\Sigma x}{n}$

$$\therefore \quad \text{Incorrect } \bar{x} = \frac{\text{incorrect } \Sigma x}{25}$$

$$\therefore \quad 78.4 = \frac{\text{incorrect } \Sigma x}{25}$$

$$\therefore \quad \text{Incorrect } \Sigma x = 78.4 \times 25 = 1960 \text{ kg}$$

The correct $\bar{x}$ is obtained by using correct Σx in the formula.

$$\text{Correct } \Sigma x = \text{incorrect } \Sigma x - \text{incorrect item} + \text{correct item}$$

$$= 1960 - 69 + 96 = 1987 \text{ kg}$$

$$\therefore \quad \text{Correct } \bar{x} = \frac{\text{correct } \Sigma x}{25} = \frac{1987}{25} = \textbf{79.48 kg.}$$

Example 3. *The A.M. of 9 items is 15. If one more item is added to this series, the A.M. becomes 16. Find the value of the 10th item.*

Sol. Let the values of 9 items be $x_1, x_2, ..., x_9$.

$$\therefore \quad 15 = \frac{x_1 + x_2 + ... + x_9}{9}$$

$$\therefore \quad x_1 + x_2 + ... + x_9 = 15 \times 9 = 135$$

Let x_{10} be the 10th item.

$\therefore$ A.M. of $x_1, x_2, ..., x_9, x_{10}$ is 16

$$\therefore \quad 16 = \frac{x_1 + x_2 + ... + x_9 + x_{10}}{10}$$

$$\therefore \quad x_1 + x_2 + ... + x_9 + x_{10} = 160$$

$$\therefore \quad 135 + x_{10} = 160$$

$$\therefore \quad x_{10} = 160 - 135 = \textbf{25.}$$

Example 4. *If the A.M. of $x_1, x_2, ..., x_n$ be $\bar{x}$, then show that :*

(i) the A.M. of $x_1 + a, x_2 + a, ..., x_n + a$ is $\bar{x} + a$

(ii) the A.M. of $3x_1, 3x_2, ..., 3x$ is $3\bar{x}$

(iii) the A.M. of $ax_1, ax_2, ..., ax_n$ is $a\bar{x}$.

Sol. A.M. of $x_1, x_2, ..., x_n$ is $\bar{x}$.

$$\therefore \quad \bar{x} = \frac{x_1 + x_2 + ... + x_n}{n}$$

(*i*) A.M. of $x_1 + a, x_2 + a, ..., x_n + a$

$$= \frac{(x_1 + a) + (x_2 + a) + ... + (x_n + a)}{n}$$

$$= \frac{(x_1 + x_2 + ... + x_n) + na}{n} = \frac{x_1 + x_2 + ... + x_n}{n} + \frac{na}{n} = \mathbf{\bar{x} + a.}$$

$$(ii) \text{ A.M. of } 3x_1, 3x_2, ..., 3x_n = \frac{3x_1 + 3x_2 + ... + 3x_n}{n} = 3\left(\frac{x_1 + x_2 + ... + x_n}{n}\right) = \mathbf{3\bar{x}}.$$

$$(iii) \text{ A.M. of } ax_1, ax_2, ..., ax_n = \frac{ax_1 + ax_2 + ... + ax_n}{n} = a\left(\frac{x_1 + x_2 + ... + x_n}{n}\right) = \mathbf{a\bar{x}}.$$

Example 5. *(a) The marks obtained by 20 students in a test were :*

13, 17, 11, 5, 18, 16, 11, 14, 13, 12, 18, 11, 9, 6, 8, 17, 21, 22, 7, 6.

Find the mean marks per student.

(b) If extra 5 marks are given to each student, show that the mean marks are also increased by 5 marks.

Sol. (*a*) Mean marks $= \dfrac{\text{Sum of marks obtained by 20 students}}{20}$

$$= \frac{\begin{array}{c}13 + 17 + 11 + 5 + 18 + 16 + 11 + 14 + 13 \\ + 12 + 18 + 11 + 9 + 6 + 8 + 17 + 21 + 22 + 7 + 6\end{array}}{20} = \frac{255}{20} = \mathbf{12.75.}$$

(*b*) New marks are :

13 + 5 = 18,	17 + 5 = 22,	11 + 5 = 16,	5 + 5 = 10,
18 + 5 = 23,	16 + 5 = 21,	11 + 5 = 16,	14 + 5 = 19,
13 + 5 = 18,	12 + 5 = 17,	18 + 5 = 23,	11 + 5 = 16,
9 + 5 = 14,	6 + 5 = 11,	8 + 5 = 13,	17 + 5 = 22,
21 + 5 = 26,	22 + 5 = 27,	7 + 5 = 12,	6 + 5 = 11.

$\therefore$ New mean marks

$$= \frac{\begin{array}{c}18 + 22 + 16 + 10 + 23 + 21 + 16 + 19 + 18 + 17 \\ + 23 + 16 + 14 + 11 + 13 + 22 + 26 + 27 + 12 + 11\end{array}}{20}$$

$$= \frac{355}{20} = 17.75 = 12.75 + 5 = \textbf{old mean marks + 5.}$$

Example 6. *Calculate A.M. for the following data :*

Income (in Rs.)	*500*	*520*	*550*	*600*	*800*	*1000*
No. of employees	*4*	*10*	*6*	*5*	*3*	*2*

Sol. **Calculation of A.M.**

S. No.	*Income (in Rs.)* x	*No. of employees* f	fx
1	500	4	2000
2	520	10	5200
3	550	6	3300
4	600	5	3000
5	800	3	2400
6	1000	2	2000
		N = 30	Σfx = 17900

Now $\bar{x} = \dfrac{\Sigma fx}{N} = \dfrac{17900}{30}$ = **Rs. 596.67.**

Example 7. *Calculate the A.M. for the following data :*

Marks	*0—10*	*10—30*	*30—40*	*40—50*	*50—80*	*80—100*
No. of students	*5*	*7*	*15*	*8*	*3*	*2*

Sol. **Calculation of A.M.**

Marks	*No. of students* f	*Mid-points of classes* x	fx
0—10	5	5	25
10—30	7	20	140
30—40	15	35	525
40—50	8	45	360
50—80	3	65	195
80—100	2	90	180
	N = 40		Σfx = 1425

∴ $\bar{x} = \dfrac{\Sigma fx}{N} = \dfrac{1425}{40}$ = **35.625 marks.**

6. STEP DEVIATION METHOD

When the values of the variable (x) and their frequencies (f) are large, the calculation of A.M. may become quite tedious. The calculation work can be reduced considerably by taking *step deviations* of the values of the variable.

Let A be any number, called **assumed mean**, then $d = x - A$ are called the **deviations** of the values of x, from A.

If the values of x are $x_1, x_2, \ldots\ldots, x_n$, then the values of deviations are $d_1 = x_1 - A$, $d_2 = x_2 - A, \ldots\ldots, d_n = x_n - A$. We define $u = \dfrac{x - A}{h}$, where h is some suitable common factor in the deviations of values of x from A. The definition of 'u' is meaningful, because at least $h = 1$ is a common factor for all the values of the deviations. The different values of $u = \dfrac{x - A}{h}$ are called the **step deviations** of the corresponding values of x. In this case, the values of the step deviations are $u_1 = \frac{x_1 - A}{h}, u_2 = \frac{x_2 - A}{h}, \ldots\ldots, u_n = \frac{x_n - A}{h}$.

$\therefore$ For $1 \le i \le n, \quad u_i = \frac{x_i - A}{h} \quad$ *i.e.,* $x_i = A + u_i h$

$$\therefore \quad \bar{x} = \frac{1}{N}\Sigma f_i x_i = \frac{1}{N}\Sigma f_i (A + u_i h) = \frac{1}{N}\Sigma f_i A + \frac{1}{N}\Sigma f_i u_i h$$

$$= A \cdot \frac{\Sigma f_i}{N} + \frac{1}{N}(\Sigma f_i u_i)h = A + \frac{\Sigma f_i u_i}{N} h \qquad (\because \Sigma f_i = N)$$

$$\therefore \quad \bar{\mathbf{x}} = \mathbf{A} + \left(\frac{\Sigma \mathbf{f_i u_i}}{\mathbf{N}}\right)\mathbf{h}.$$

In brief, the above formula is written as $\bar{\mathbf{x}} = \mathbf{A} + \left(\frac{\Sigma \mathbf{fu}}{\mathbf{N}}\right)\mathbf{h}$.

In case of individual series, this formula takes the form $\bar{\mathbf{x}} = \mathbf{A} + \left(\frac{\Sigma \mathbf{u}}{\mathbf{n}}\right)\mathbf{h}$.

In dealing with practical problems, it is advisable to first take deviations (d) of the values of the variable (x) from some suitable number (A). Then we see, if there is any common factor, greater than one in the values of the deviations. If there is a common factor $h(> 1)$, then we calculate $u = \frac{d}{h} = \frac{x - A}{h}$ in the next column. In case, there is no common factor other than one, then we take $h = 1$ and u becomes $\frac{d}{1} = d = x - A$. In this case, the formulae reduces as given below :

$$\bar{\mathbf{x}} = \mathbf{A} + \frac{\Sigma \mathbf{d}}{\mathbf{n}} \qquad \textbf{(For Individual Series)}$$

$$\bar{\mathbf{x}} = \mathbf{A} + \frac{\Sigma \mathbf{fd}}{\mathbf{N}} \qquad \textbf{(For Frequency Distribution)}$$

where d = x – A and A is any constant ; to be chosen suitably.

WORKING RULES TO FIND A.M.

Rule I. *In case of an individual series, choose a number A. Find deviations $d(= x - A)$ of items from A. Find the sum 'Σd' of the deviations. Divide this sum by n, the total number of items. This quotient is added to A to get the value of $\bar{x}$.*
If some common factor h (> 1) is available in the values of d, then we calculate 'u' by dividing the values of d by h and find $\bar{x}$ by using the formula :

$$\bar{x} = A + \left(\frac{\Sigma x}{n}\right)h.$$

Rule II. *In case of a frequency distribution, choose a number A. Find deviations $d(= x - A)$ of items from A. Find the products fd of f and d. Find the sum 'Σfd' of these products. Divide this sum by N, the total number of items. This quotient is added to A to get the value of $\bar{x}$.*

If some common factor h(> 1) is available in the values of d, then we calculate 'u' dividing d by h and find $\bar{x}$ by using the formula :

$$\bar{x} = A + \left(\frac{\Sigma fu}{N}\right) h.$$

Rule III. *If the values of the variable are given in the form of classes, then their respective mid-points are taken as the values of the variable.*

Example 8. *Find the A.M. for the following individual series :*

12.36, 14.36, 16.36, 18.36, 20.36, 24.36.

Sol. **Calculation of A.M.**

Variable x	$d = x - A$ $A = 16.36$	$u = d/h$ $h = 2$
12.36	– 4	– 2
14.36	– 2	– 1
16.36	0	0
18.36	2	1
20.36	4	2
24.36	8	4
		$\Sigma u = 4$

Now $\bar{x} = A + \left(\frac{\Sigma u}{n}\right) h = 16.36 + \left(\frac{4}{6}\right) 2 = 16.36 + 1.33 = \mathbf{17.69}.$

Example 9. *Calculate A.M. for the following data :*

Temp. (in°C)	*– 40 to – 30*	*– 30 to – 20*	*– 20 to – 10*	*– 10 to 0*
No. of days	*10*	*28*	*30*	*42*
Temp. (in°C)	*0 – 10*	*10 – 20*	*20 – 30*	
No. of days	*65*	*180*	*10*	

Sol. **Calculation of A.M.**

Temp. (in°C)	*No. of days* f	*Mid-points of classes* x	$d = x - A$ $A = -5$	$u = d/h$ $h = 10$	fu
– 40 to – 30	10	– 35	– 30	– 3	– 30
– 30 to – 20	28	– 25	– 20	– 2	– 56
– 20 to – 10	30	– 15	– 10	– 1	– 30
– 10 to 0	42	– 5	0	0	0
0—10	65	5	10	1	65
10—20	180	15	20	2	360
20—30	10	25	30	3	30
	N = 365				$\Sigma fu = 339$

Now $\bar{x} = A + \left(\frac{\Sigma fu}{N}\right)h = -5 + \left(\frac{339}{365}\right)10 = -5 + 9.2877 = \mathbf{4.2877°C.}$

Example 10. *Find the A.M. for the following distribution :*

Marks	*No. of students*	*Marks*	*No. of students*
Above 0	*80*	*Above 60*	*28*
Above 10	*77*	*Above 70*	*16*
Above 20	*72*	*Above 80*	*10*
Above 30	*65*	*Above 90*	*8*
Above 40	*55*	*Above 100*	*0*
Above 50	*43*		

Sol. **Calculation of A.M.**

Marks	*Mid-points* x	*No. of students* f	$d = x - A$ $A = 55$	$u = d/h$ $h = 10$	fu
0—10	5	3	– 50	– 5	– 15
10—20	15	5	– 40	– 4	– 20
20—30	25	7	– 30	– 3	– 21
30—40	35	10	– 20	– 2	– 20
40—50	45	12	– 10	– 1	– 12
50—60	55	15	0	0	0
60—70	65	12	10	1	12
70—80	75	6	20	2	12
80—90	85	2	30	3	6
90—100	95	8	40	4	32
		N = 80			$\Sigma fu = -26$

Now $\bar{x} = A + \left(\frac{\Sigma fu}{N}\right)h = 55 + \left(\frac{-26}{80}\right)10 = 55 - 3.25 = \mathbf{51.75\ marks.}$

7. A.M. OF COMBINED GROUP

Theorem. If $\bar{x}_1$ and $\bar{x}_2$ are the A.M. of two groups having n_1 and n_2 items, then the A.M. ($\bar{x}$) of the combined group is given by

$$\bar{x} = \frac{n_1\bar{x}_1 + n_2\bar{x}_2}{n_1 + n_2}$$

Proof. Let $x_1, x_2, ..., x_{n_1}$ and $y_1, y_2, ..., y_{n_2}$ be the items in the two groups respectively.

$$\therefore \quad \bar{x}_1 = \frac{x_1 + x_2 + ... + x_{n_1}}{n_1}$$

$$\bar{x}_2 = \frac{y_1 + y_2 + ... + y_{n_2}}{n_2}$$

$\therefore \quad x_1 + x_2 + ... + x_{n_1} = n_1\bar{x}_1$

$y_1 + y_2 + ... + y_{n_2} = n_2\bar{x}_2$

Now $$\bar{x} = \frac{\text{sum of items in both groups}}{n_1 + n_2}$$

$$= \frac{x_1 + x_2 + ... + x_{n_1} + y_1 + y_2 + ... + y_{n_2}}{n_1 + n_2} = \frac{n_1\bar{x}_1 + n_2\bar{x}_2}{n_1 + n_2}$$

$$\therefore \quad \mathbf{\bar{x} = \frac{n_1\bar{x}_1 + n_2\bar{x}_2}{n_1 + n_2}}.$$

This formula can also be extended to more than two groups.

Example 11. *The mean wage of 1000 workers in a factory running two shifts of 700 and 300 workers is Rs. 500. The mean wage of 700 workers, working in the day shift, is Rs. 450. Find the mean wage of workers, working in the night shift.*

Sol. No. of workers in the day shift (n_1) = 700

No. of workers in the night shift (n_2) = 300

Mean wage of workers in the day shift ($\bar{x}_1$) = Rs. 450

Mean wage of all workers ($\bar{x}$) = Rs. 500

Let mean wage of workers in the night shift $= \bar{x}_2$

Now $$\bar{x} = \frac{n_1\bar{x}_1 + n_2\bar{x}_2}{n_1 + n_2}$$

$$\therefore \quad 500 = \frac{700\,(450) + 300\,(\bar{x}_2)}{700 + 300} \quad \text{or} \quad 500000 = 315000 + 300\bar{x}_2$$

$$\therefore \quad 300\bar{x}_2 = 185000$$

$$\therefore \quad \bar{x}_2 = \frac{185000}{300} = \textbf{Rs. 616.67.}$$

8. WEIGHTED A.M.

If all the values of the variable are not of equal importance, or in other words, these are of varying significance, then we calculate **weighted A.M.**

$$\text{Weighted A.M.} = \bar{x}_w = \frac{\Sigma wx}{\Sigma w}$$

where $w_1, w_2, ..., w_n$ are the weights of the values $x_1, x_2, ..., x_n$ of the variable, under consideration.

Example 12. *An examination was held to decide the award of a scholarship. The weights given to different subjects were different. The marks were as follows :*

Subjects	*Weight*	*Marks of A*	*Marks of B*	*Marks of C*
Statistics	4	63	60	65
Accountancy	3	65	64	70
Economics	2	58	56	63
Mercantile Law	1	70	80	52

The candidate getting the highest marks is to be awarded the scholarship. Who should get it ?

Sol. **Calculation of weighted A.M.**

Subject	*Weight* w	*Marks of* A x_1	wx_1	*Marks of* B x_2	wx_2	*Marks of* C x_3	wx_3
Statistics	4	63	252	60	240	65	260
Accountancy	3	65	195	64	192	70	210
Economics	2	58	116	56	112	63	126
Mercantile Law	1	70	70	80	80	52	52
	$\Sigma w = 10$		$\Sigma wx_1 = 633$		$\Sigma wx_2 = 624$		$\Sigma wx_3 = 648$

Weighted A.M. of $A = \frac{\Sigma wx_1}{\Sigma w} = \frac{633}{10} = \mathbf{63.3}$

Weighted A.M. of $B = \frac{\Sigma wx_2}{\Sigma w} = \frac{624}{10} = \mathbf{62.4}$

Weighted A.M. of $C = \frac{\Sigma wx_3}{\Sigma w} = \frac{648}{10} = \mathbf{64.8}$

$\therefore$ **The student 'C' is to get the scholarship.**

9. MATHEMATICAL PROPERTIES OF A.M.

1. In a statistical data, the sum of the deviations of items from A.M. is always zero

i.e., $\sum_{i=1}^{n} f_i (x_i - \bar{x}) = 0,$

where f_i is the frequency of x_i $(1 \le i \le n)$.

2. In a statistical data, the sum of squares of the deviations of items from A.M. is always least *i.e.*, $\sum_{i=1}^{n} f_i (x_i - \bar{x})^2$ is least, where f_i is the frequency of x_i $(1 \le i \le n)$.

10. MERITS OF A.M.

1. It is the simplest average to understand.
2. It is easy to compute.
3. It is well-defined.
4. It is based on all the items.
5. It is capable of further algebraic treatment.
6. It has sampling stability.
7. It is specially used in finding the average speed, when time taken at different speeds are varying, or are equal.

11. DEMERITS OF A.M.

1. It may not be present in the given series itself. For example, the A.M. of 4, 5, 6, 6 is $\frac{4+5+6+6}{4}$ = 5.25, which is not present in the series. So, sometimes it becomes theoretical.

2. It cannot be calculated for qualitative data.

3. It may be badly affected by the extreme item.

EXERCISE 1

1. Find the A.M. of the series 4, 6, 8, 10, 12.
2. The mean marks of 100 students was found to be 40. Later on, it was discovered that a score of 53 was misread as 83. Find the correct mean.
3. The A.M. of 25 items is found to be 78.4. If at the time of calculation, two items were wrongly taken as 96 and 43 instead of 69 and 34, find the value of the correct mean. (*KU 1995*)
4. The marks obtained by 5 students are 11, 17, 9, 16, 22. Later on, 3 grace marks were awarded to each student. Find the mean marks of the increased marks of the students.
5. Find the arithmetic mean for the following data :

x	6	7	8	9	10
f	7	10	12	6	5

6. Find the A.M. for the following frequency distribution :

x	10	11	12	13	14	15
f	2	6	8	6	2	6

7. Find the A.M. for the following data :

Marks	18	19	20	21	22	23	24
No. of students	169	320	530	698	230	140	105

8. The postal expenses on the letters despatched from an office on a given day resulted in the following frequency distribution :

Postage (in paise)	15	30	35	60	70
No. of letters	47	33	56	41	25

Find the mean postage per letter. Convert the postal charges in rupees and then calculate the mean postage per letter.

9. Two hundred people were interviewed by a public opinion polling agency. The following frequency distribution gives the ages of people interviewed. Calculate A.M.

Age Groups (Years)	80—89	70—79	60—69	50—59
No. of Persons	2	2	6	20
Age Groups (Years)	40—49	30—39	20—29	10—19
No. of Persons	56	40	40	42

10. Find the A.M. for the following frequency distribution :

Marks obtained	0—7	7—14	14—21	21—28
No. of Students	19	25	36	72
Marks obtained	28—35	35—42	42—49	
No. of Students	51	43	28	

(*KU 2000*)

11. Find the A.M. for the following data :

Class intervals	– 2 to 2	3—7	8—12	13—17	18—22	23—27
Frequency	3277	4096	2048	512	64	3

12. Find the A.M. for the following data :

Income	20—30	Below 40	Below 50	Below 60	Below 70	Below 80	80—90
No. of Persons	16	36	61	76	87	95	5

13. Calculate the arithmetic mean for the following data :

Wages (in Rs.)	*No. of persons*	*Wages (in Rs.)*	*No. of workers*
Less than 10	30	40 and above	332
Less than 20	70	50 and above	308
20—30	50	60—70	132
20—40	98	70 and above	14

14. From the following information, find out :

(*i*) Which of the factor pays larger amount as daily wages.

(*ii*) What is the average daily wage of the workers of two factories taken together.

	Factory A	*Factory B*
No. of wage earners	250	200
Average daily wages	Rs. 20	Rs. 25

15. The mean wage of 100 workers in a factory running two shifts of 60 and 40 workers is Rs. 38. The mean wage of 60 workers working in the day shift is Rs 40. Find the mean wage of workers, working in the night shift. (*KU 2002 C*)

16. The mean weight of 15 students is 110 lbs. The mean weight of 5 of them is 100 lbs and of another 5 is 125 lbs. What is the mean weight of the remaining students ?

17. Fifty students took up a test. The result of those who passed the test is given below :

Marks	4	5	6	7	8	9
No. of students	8	10	9	6	4	3

If the average of all the 50 students was 5.16 marks, find the average of those who failed.

18. The average weight of 150 students in a class is 80 kg. The average weight of boys in the class is 85 kg and that of girls is 70 kg. Tell the number of boys and girls in the class separately.

19. If a student gets the following marks : English 80, Hindi 70, Mathematics 85, Physics 75 and Chemistry 67, find the weighted mean marks if the weights of the subjects are 1, 2, 1, 3, 1 respectively.

20. The following table gives the number of students in different classes in a Government Senior Secondary School and their tuition fees. Find the average tuition fees per student.

Class	*No. of students*	*Tuition fee (Rs.)*
V	65	0.50
VI	80	0.75
VII	95	1.00
VIII	90	1.50
IX	70	2.00

21. From the following results of two colleges A and B, find out which of the two is better.

Examination	*College A*		*College B*	
	Appeared	*Passed*	*Appeared*	*Passed*
B.Sc.	100	90	240	200
M. Com.	60	45	200	160
B. Com.	120	75	160	60
B.A.	200	150	200	140
Total	480	360	800	560

Answers

1. 8 **2.** 39.7 marks **3.** 76.96 **4.** 18 marks
5. 7.8 **6.** 12.6 **7.** 20.61 marks
8. Paise 38.94, Rs. 0.39 **9.** 34.9 years **10.** 26.4927 marks **11.** 4.9995
12. Rs. 47.90 **13.** Rs. 46.60
14. (*i*) Both factories are paying equal amount (*ii*) Rs. 22.22 **15.** Rs. 35
16. 105 lbs **17.** 2.1 marks **18.** Boys = 100, Girls = 50
19. 74.625 marks **20.** Rs. 1.16 **21.** College A is better.

II. GEOMETRIC MEAN (G.M.)

12. DEFINITION

The **geometric mean** of a statistical data is defined as the *n*th root of the product of all the *n* values of the variable.

For an individual series, the G.M. is given by

$$\text{G.M.} = (x_1 x_2 \ldots\ldots x_n)^{1/n}$$

where $x_1, x_2, \ldots\ldots, x_n$ are the values of the variable, under consideration. From the definition of G.M. we see that it involves the *n*th root of a product, which is not possible to evaluate by using simple arithmetical tools. To solve this problem, we take the help of logarithms.

Now $G = \text{Antilog}\left(\frac{\Sigma f \log x}{N}\right) = \text{Antilog}\left(\frac{81.9092}{68}\right)$

$= \text{Antilog}\,(1.2045) = \mathbf{16.02\ quintals.}$

13. G.M. OF COMBINED GROUP

Theorem. If G_1 and G_2 are the GMs of two groups having n_1 and n_2 items, then the G.M. (G) of the combined group is given by

$$G = \text{Antilog}\left(\frac{n_1 \log G_1 + n_2 \log G_2}{n_1 + n_2}\right).$$

Proof. Let $x_1, x_2, \ldots\ldots, x_{n_1}$ and $y_1, y_2, \ldots\ldots, y_{n_2}$ be the items in the two groups respectively.

$\therefore \quad G_1 = \text{Antilog}\left(\frac{\Sigma \log x}{n_1}\right)$

$\therefore \quad \log G_1 = \frac{\Sigma \log x}{n_1}$

$\therefore \quad n_1 \log G_1 = \Sigma \log x$

Similarly, $n_2 \log G_2 = \Sigma \log y$

Now $G = \text{Antilog}\left(\frac{\text{sum of logarithms of all items}}{\text{no. of items in both groups}}\right)$

$= \text{Antilog}\left(\frac{\Sigma \log x + \Sigma \log y}{n_1 + n_2}\right)$

$\therefore \quad G = \text{Antilog}\left(\frac{n_1 \log G_1 + n_2 \log G_2}{n_1 + n_2}\right)$

This formula can also be extended to more than two groups.

Example 4. *The G.M. of wages of 200 workers working in a factory is Rs. 700. The G.M. of wages of 300 workers, working in another factory is Rs. 1000. Find the G.M. of wages of all the workers taken together.*

Sol. No. of workers in I factory (n_1) = 200

No. of workers in II factory (n_2) = 300

G.M. of wages of workers of I factory (G_1) = Rs. 700

G.M. of wages of workers of II factory (G_2) = Rs. 1000

Let G be the G.M. of wages of all the workers taken together.

$\therefore \quad G = \text{Antilog}\left(\frac{n_1 \log G_1 + n_2 \log G_2}{n_1 + n_2}\right) = \text{Antilog}\left(\frac{200 \log 700 + 300 \log 1000}{200 + 300}\right)$

$= \text{Antilog}\left(\frac{200\,(2.8451) + 300\,(3.0000)}{500}\right) = \text{Antilog}\left(\frac{569.0200 + 900}{500}\right)$

$= \text{Antilog}\,(2.9380) = \mathbf{Rs.\ 867.}$

14. AVERAGING OF PERCENTAGES

Geometric mean is specially used to find the average rate of increase or decrease in sale, production, population etc.

If V_0 and V_n are the values of a variable at the beginning of the first and at the end of the nth period, then

$$\mathbf{V_n = V_0 (1 + r)^n}, \text{ where } \mathbf{r} \text{ is the average rate of growth per unit.}$$

Example 5. *A gave Rs. 10,000 to B on the terms that after expiry of 5 years, B will return him Rs. 12,294. What is the rate of interest ?* (KU 1995 C)

Sol. Here $V_0 = 10{,}000$ and $V_5 = 12{,}294$.

Let r be the average rate of interest per rupee.

$$\therefore \quad V_5 = V_0 (1 + r)^5$$

$$\text{or} \quad 12{,}294 = 10{,}000 (1 + r)^5$$

$$\text{or} \quad (1 + r)^5 = \frac{12{,}294}{10{,}000} = 1.2294$$

$$\therefore \quad 5 \log (1 + r) = \log 1.2294 = 0.1120$$

$$\therefore \quad \log (1 + r) = 0.0224$$

$$\therefore \quad 1 + r = \text{Antilog } 0.0224 = 1.053$$

$$\therefore \quad r = 1.053 - 1 = 0.053$$

$\therefore$ Average percentage rate of interest = 0.053 × 100 = **5.3%.**

Example 6. *At what rate of interest would Rs. 100 double in 10 years.*

Sol. Here $V_0 = 100$ and $V_{10} = 200$.

Let r be the average rate of interest per rupee

$$\therefore \quad V_{10} = V_0 (1 + r)^{10}$$

$$\text{or} \quad 200 = 100(1 + r)^{10} \quad \text{or} \quad (1 + r)^{10} = 2$$

$$\therefore \quad 10 \log (1 + r) = \log 2 = 0.3010$$

$$\therefore \quad \log (1 + r) = 0.03010$$

$$\therefore \quad 1 + r = \text{Antilog } 0.0301 = 1.074$$

$$\therefore \quad r = 1.074 - 1 = 0.074$$

$\therefore$ Average percentage rate of interest = 0.074 × 100 = **7.4%.**

Example 7. *The machinery of an industrial house is depreciated by 50% in the first year, 30% in the second year and by 10% in the following three years. Find out the average rate of depreciation for the entire period.*

Sol.

Year	*Rate of depreciation*	*Depreciated value of the machine at the end of the year taking 100 in the beginning (x)*	*log x*
I	50%	50	1.6990
II	30%	70	1.8451
III	10%	90	1.9542
IV	10%	90	1.9542
V	10%	90	1.9542
			$\Sigma \log x = 9.4067$

$$\therefore \quad \text{G.M.} = \text{Antilog}\left(\frac{\Sigma \log x}{n}\right) = \text{Antilog}\left(\frac{9.4067}{5}\right)$$

$$= \text{Antilog}\,(1.88134) = 76.08$$

∴ Average rate of depreciation = 100 – 76.08 = **23.92%.**

Example 8. *The annual rate of growth of output of a factory in 5 years are 5.0, 7.5, 2.5, 5.0 and 10.0 percent respectively. What is compound rate of growth per annum for the period ?* (KU 1996)

Sol.

Year	*Rate of growth*	*Production at the end of the year, taking 100 in the beginning* x	*log x*
I	10%	105	2.0212
II	7.5%	107.5	2.0314
III	2.5%	102.5	2.0107
IV	5%	105	2.0212
V	10%	110	2.0414
			$\Sigma \log x = 10.1259$

$$\therefore \quad \text{G.M.} = \text{antilog}\left(\frac{\Sigma \log x}{n}\right) = \text{Antilog}\left(\frac{10.1259}{5}\right)$$

$$= \text{Antilog } 2.02518 = 105.9$$

∴ Average rate of growth = 105.9 – 100 = **5.9%.**

15. WEIGHTED G.M.

If all the values of the variable are not of equal importance, or in other words, these are of varying significance, then we calculate **weighted G.M.**

$$\text{Weighted G.M.} = \text{Antilog}\left(\frac{\Sigma w \log x}{\Sigma w}\right),$$

where $w_1, w_2, \ldots\ldots, w_n$ are the weights of the values $x_1, x_2, \ldots\ldots, x_n$ of the variable, under consideration.

Example 9. *The weighted G.M. of four numbers 8, 25, 17 and 30 is 15.3. If the weights of the first three numbers are 5, 3 and 4 respectively, find the weight of the fourth number.*

Sol. Let K be the weight of the fourth number.

x	w	*log x*	*w log x*
8	5	0.9031	4.5155
25	3	1.3979	4.1937
17	4	1.2304	4.9216
30	K	1.4771	1.4771 K
	$\Sigma w = 12 + \text{K}$		$\Sigma w \log x = 13.6308 + 1.4771\text{ K}$

Now weighted G.M. $= \text{Antilog}\left(\dfrac{\Sigma w \log x}{\Sigma w}\right)$

$$\therefore \quad 15.3 = \text{Antilog}\left(\frac{13.6308 + 1.4771\,K}{12 + K}\right).$$

$$\therefore \quad (12 + K) \log 15.3 = 13.6308 + 1.4771\,K$$

$$\therefore \quad (1.1847)(12 + K) = 13.6308 + 1.4771\,K$$

or $$14.2164 + 1.1847\,K = 13.6308 + 1.4771\,K$$

or $$14.2164 - 13.6308 = (1.4771 - 1.1847)\,K$$

or $$K = \frac{0.5856}{0.2924} = 2.0027 = \mathbf{2\ (Approx.)}.$$

Example 10. *The G.M. of 15 observations is found to be 12. Later on, it was discovered that the item 21 was misread as 14. Calculate the correct value of G.M.*

Sol. No. of items = 15

Incorrect G.M. = 12

Correct item = 21

Incorrect item = 14

Now $$G = \text{Antilog}\left(\frac{\Sigma \log x}{n}\right)$$

$$\therefore \quad 12 = \text{Antilog}\left(\frac{\text{incorrect } \Sigma \log x}{15}\right)$$

or $$\log 12 = \frac{\text{incorrect } \Sigma \log x}{15}$$

$$\therefore \quad \text{Incorrect } \Sigma \log x = 15 \log 12 = 15(1.0792) = 16.1880$$

Now $$\text{Correct } \Sigma \log x = 16.1880 - \log 14 + \log 21$$
$$= 16.1880 - 1.1461 + 1.3222 = 16.3641.$$

$$\therefore \quad \text{Correct G.M.} = \text{Antilog}\left(\frac{16.3641}{15}\right) = \text{Antilog}\,(1.0909) = \mathbf{12.33}.$$

16. MERITS OF G.M.

1. It is well defined.
2. It is based on all the items.
3. It is capable of further algebraic treatment.
4. It is used to find the average rate of increase or decrease in the variables like sale, production, population etc.
5. It is specially used in the construction of index numbers.
6. It is used when larger weights are to be given to smaller items and smaller weights to larger items.
7. It has sampling stability.

17. DEMERITS OF G.M.

1. It is not simple to understand.
2. It is not easy to compute.

3. It may become imaginary in the presence of negative items.

4. If any one item is zero, then its value would be zero, irrespective of magnitude of other items.

EXERCISE 2

1. (*i*) Find the G.M. of the following individual series :

15, 1.5, 1500, 0.0015.

(*ii*) Find the G.M. of the following series :

10, 110, 120, 50, 52, 80, 37, 60.

2. From the monthly incomes of ten families given below, calculate G.M.

S. No.	1	2	3	4	5	6	7	8	9	10
Income (in Rs.)	145	367	268	73	185	619	280	115	870	315

3. Find the G.M. for the following data relating to the profit of 30 firms :

Profit ('000 Rs.)	25	26	27	28	29	30
No. of firms	4	7	12	2	4	1

4. Find the G.M. for the following frequency distribution :

x	8	10	12	14	16	18
f	6	10	20	8	5	1

5. Find the G.M. for the following frequency distribution :

Marks	0—10	10—20	20—30	30—40	40—50
No. of students	4	8	10	6	7

6. Calculate G.M. for the following data :

Income (in Rs.)	100—300	100—500	100—700	100—1000	100—1500
No. of employees	12	18	30	50	100

7. Find G.M. from the following :

Marks obtained (below)	10	20	30	40	50
No. of candidates	12	27	72	92	100

8. A firm declared bonus according to respective salary groups as given below :

Salary Group (in Rs.)	60—75	75—90	90—105
Rate of Bonus	60	70	80
No. of employees	3	4	5
Salary Group (in Rs.)	105—120	120—135	135—150
Rate of Bonus	90	100	110
No. of employees	5	7	6

Calculate A.M. of salaries and G.M. of the bonus payable to the employees.

9. The G.M. of salaries paid to all employees of a company is Rs. 1700. The G.M. of salaries of male and female employees are Rs. 1800 and Rs. 1600 respectively. Determine the percentage of males and females employed in the company. *(KU 1994, 97 C)*
10. The population of a country is increased from 40 crore to 70 crore in 30 years. Find out the annual average rate of growth.
11. If the price of a commodity is doubled in five years, find out the annual average rate of increase. *(KU 1993)*
12. A Principal increased the number of students in his college in the year 1983 by 15%. Then increased again in 1984 by 5% but in 1985, it decreased by 20% due to introduction of 10 + 2 system. Hence the number of students becomes the same as it was before 1983. Do you agree, if not give reasons.
13. The population of a town increased from 10000 to 20000 in 20 years. Find the annual average rate of growth.
14. A machine is assumed to depreciate 40% in value in the I year, 25% in the II year and 10% for the next 3 years, each percentage being calculated on the diminishing value. Find the average rate of depreciation for the five years. *(KU 2005 S)*
15. Find the weighted G.M. of the items 15, 17, 19, 23, 29 with weights 1, 2, 1, 3, 1 respectively.
16. The G.M. of 20 items was found to be 10. Later on, it was found that one item 18 was misread as 8. Find the correct value of the G.M.

Answers

1. *(i)* 2.668 *(ii)* 52.84 2. Rs. 252.40 3. Rs. 26.9 thousand
4. 11.82 5. 22.06 marks 6. Rs. 794.10 7. 21.4 marks
8. Average salary = Rs. 111 ; Average bonus = Rs. 87.44
9. Males = 51.37%, Females = 48.63% 10. 1.9% 11. 14.9%
12. No, G.M. is to be used, 1.14% decrease 13. 3.5% 14. 19.98%
15. 20.32 16. 10.41.

III. HARMONIC MEAN (H.M.)

18. DEFINITION

The **harmonic mean** of a statistical data is defined as the quotient of the number of items by the sum of the reciprocals of all the values of the variable.

(*a*) **For an individual series**, the H.M. is given by

$$\text{H.M.} = \frac{n}{\frac{1}{x_1} + \frac{1}{x_2} + \ldots\ldots + \frac{1}{x_n}} = \frac{\text{n}}{\sum \frac{1}{\text{x}}},$$

where $x_1, x_2, \ldots\ldots, x_n$ are the values of the variable, under consideration.

(*b*) **For a frequency distribution**,

$$\text{H.M.} = \frac{f_1 + f_2 + \ldots\ldots + f_n}{f_1\left(\frac{1}{x_1}\right) + f_2\left(\frac{1}{x_2}\right) + \ldots\ldots + f_n\left(\frac{1}{x_n}\right)} = \frac{\Sigma f}{\sum f\left(\frac{1}{x}\right)} = \frac{\text{N}}{\sum\left(\frac{\text{f}}{\text{x}}\right)},$$

where f_i is the frequency of x_i $(1 \le i \le n)$.

When the values of the variable are given in the form of classes, then the mid-points of classes are taken as the values of the variable (x).

WORKING RULES TO FIND H.M.

Rule I. *In case of an individual series, first find the sum of the reciprocals of all the items. In the second step, divide n, the total number of items by this sum of reciprocals. This gives the value of the H.M.*

Rule II. *In case of a frequency distribution, find the quotients (f/x) of frequencies by the value of items. In the second step, find the sum (Σ(f/x)) of these quotients. Divide N, the total of all frequencies by this sum of quotients. This gives the value of the H.M.*

Rule III. *If the values of the variable are given in the form of classes, then their respective mid-points are taken as the values of the variable.*

Example 1. *Calculate the H.M. for the following individual series :*

x	*4*	*7*	*10*	*12*	*19*

Sol. **Calculation of H.M.**

S. No.	*x*	*1/x*
1	4	0.2500
2	7	0.1429
3	10	0.1000
4	12	0.0833
5	19	0.0526
$n = 5$		$\sum\left(\frac{1}{x}\right) = 0.6288$

Now $$\text{H.M.} = \frac{n}{\sum\left(\frac{1}{x}\right)} = \frac{5}{0.6288} = \mathbf{7.9516.}$$

Example 2. *Find the H.M.for the following frequency distribution :*

Profit ('000 Rs.)	*12*	*13*	*14*	*15*	*16*	*17*
No. of firms	*4*	*8*	*6*	*5*	*9*	*2*

Sol. **Calculation of H.M.**

Profit ('000 Rs.) x	*No. of firms* f	$\frac{f}{x}$
12	4	0.3333
13	8	0.6154
14	6	0.4286
15	5	0.3333
16	9	0.5625
17	2	0.1176
	N = 34	$\sum\left(\frac{f}{x}\right) = 2.3907$

Now $\text{H.M.} = \dfrac{N}{\sum\left(\dfrac{f}{x}\right)} = \dfrac{34}{2.3907}$ = Rs. 14.22178 thousand = **Rs. 14221.78.**

Example 3. *Calculate the value of H.M. for the following data :*

Marks	*0—10*	*0—20*	*0—30*	*0—40*	*0—50*	*0—60*	*0—70*
No. of students	*4*	*8*	*15*	*23*	*51*	*60*	*70*

Sol. **Calculation of H.M.**

Class	*No. of students* f	*Mid-points* x	$\dfrac{f}{x}$
0—10	4	5	0.8000
10—20	4	15	0.2667
20—30	7	25	0.2800
30—40	8	35	0.2286
40—50	28	45	0.6222
50—60	9	55	0.1636
60—70	10	65	0.1538
	N = 70		$\sum\left(\dfrac{f}{x}\right) = 2.5149$

Now $\text{H.M.} = \dfrac{N}{\sum\left(\dfrac{f}{x}\right)} = \dfrac{70}{2.5149}$ = **27.83 marks.**

19. H.M. OF COMBINED GROUP

Theorem. If H_1 and H_2 are the H.M. of two groups having n_1 and n_2 items, then the H.M. of the combined group is given by

$$\mathbf{H} = \frac{\mathbf{n_1 + n_2}}{\dfrac{\mathbf{n_1}}{\mathbf{H_1}} + \dfrac{\mathbf{n_2}}{\mathbf{H_2}}}.$$

Proof. Let $x_1, x_2, \ldots\ldots, x_{n_1}$ and $y_1, y_2, \ldots\ldots, y_{n_2}$ be the items in the two groups respectively.

$$\therefore \qquad H_1 = \frac{n_1}{\sum \dfrac{1}{x}}, \qquad H_2 = \frac{n_2}{\sum \dfrac{1}{y}}$$

$$\therefore \qquad \sum \frac{1}{x} = \frac{n_1}{H_1}, \qquad \sum \frac{1}{y} = \frac{n_2}{H_2},$$

Now $$H = \frac{\text{no. of items in both groups}}{\text{sum of reciprocals of all the items in both groups}}$$

$$= \frac{n_1 + n_2}{\sum \frac{1}{x} + \sum \frac{1}{y}} \qquad \therefore \quad \mathbf{H} = \frac{\mathbf{n_1 + n_2}}{\frac{\mathbf{n_1}}{\mathbf{H_1}} + \frac{\mathbf{n_2}}{\mathbf{H_2}}}.$$

This formula can also be extended to more than two groups.

Example 4. *The H.M. of two groups containing 10 and 12 items are found to be 29 and 35. Find the H.M. of the combined group.*

Sol. Here $n_1 = 10, \quad n_2 = 12$

$H_1 = 29, \quad H_2 = 35$

Let H be the H.M. of the combined group

$$\therefore \quad H = \frac{n_1 + n_2}{\frac{n_1}{H_1} + \frac{n_2}{H_2}} = \frac{10 + 12}{\frac{10}{29} + \frac{12}{35}} = \frac{22}{0.3448 + 0.3429} = \frac{22}{0.6877} = \mathbf{31.9907.}$$

20. WEIGHTED H.M.

If all the values of the variable are not of equal importance or in other words, these are of varying importance, then we calculate **weighted H.M.**

$$\text{Weighted H.M.} = \frac{\sum w}{\sum \left(\frac{w}{x}\right)}$$

where $w_1, w_2, \ldots\ldots, w_n$ are the weights of the values $x_1, x_2, \ldots\ldots, x_n$ of the variable, under consideration.

Example 5. *Find the weighted H.M. of the items 4, 7, 12, 19, 25 with weights 1, 2, 1, 1, 1 respectively.*

Sol. **Calculation of weighted H.M.**

x	w	w/x
4	1	0.2500
7	2	0.2857
12	1	0.0833
19	1	0.0526
25	1	0.0400
	$\sum w = 6$	$\sum \left(\frac{w}{x}\right) = 0.7116$

$$\text{Now weighted H.M.} = \frac{\sum w}{\sum \left(\frac{w}{x}\right)} = \frac{6}{0.7116} = \mathbf{8.4317.}$$

21. AVERAGING OF SPEEDS

The H.M. is specially used in finding the average of speeds. We have already noted that in certain circumstances A.M. is also used in averaging speeds. The reader is advised to note the following results regarding the averaging of speeds :

1. If equal distances are covered at different speeds (x), then simple H.M. is to be **used.**

2. If unequal distances are covered at different speeds (x), then weighted H.M. **is to be** used with corresponding distances as the weights (w).

3. If for equal time periods, different speeds (x) are maintained, then simple **A.M. is** to be used.

4. If for unequal time periods, different speeds are maintained, the weighted A.M. is to be used with corresponding time periods as the weights (w).

Example 6. *A car covers first 30 km at an average speed of 80 km/hr, another 20* **km at** *30 km/hr and the last 20 km at 20 km/hr. Find the average speed for the entire journey.*

Sol. Since unequal distances are covered at different speeds, the average speed **is given** by the weighted H.M. of the speeds with corresponding distances as weights.

Calculation of average speed

Speed (in km/hr) x	*Distance covered (in km)* w	$\frac{w}{x}$
80	30	$\frac{30}{80} = 0.3750$
30	20	$\frac{20}{30} = 0.6667$
20	20	$\frac{20}{20} = 1.0000$
	$\Sigma w = 70$	$\Sigma\left(\frac{w}{x}\right) = 2.0417$

$$\therefore \quad \text{Average speed} = \frac{\Sigma w}{\Sigma\left(\frac{w}{x}\right)} = \frac{70}{2.0417} = \mathbf{34.2851\ km/hr.}$$

Example 7. *A motorist covers distances 20 km, 30 km, 10 km at the speeds* **50 kph,** *60 kph and 22 kph respectively. Calculate the average speed of the motorist.*

Sol. **Calculation of Average Speed**

Speed (in kph) x	*Distance covered (in km)* w	$\frac{w}{x}$
50	20	0.4000
60	30	0.5000
22	10	0.4545
	$\sum w = 60$	$\sum\left(\frac{w}{x}\right) = 1.3545$

$$\therefore \quad \text{Average Speed} = \frac{\sum w}{\sum\left(\frac{w}{x}\right)} = \frac{60}{1.3545} = \mathbf{44.2968\ kph.}$$

Example 8. *The H.M. of 100 observations is found to be 17. Later on, it was discovered that one item 20 was misread as 28. Find the correct value of the H.M.*

Sol. Here, no. of items = 100

Incorrect H.M. = 17

Correct item = 20

Incorrect item = 28

Now $$\text{H.M.} = \frac{n}{\sum\left(\frac{1}{x}\right)}$$

$$\therefore \quad 17 = \frac{100}{\text{Incorrect} \sum\left(\frac{1}{x}\right)}$$

$$\therefore \quad \text{Incorrect} \sum \frac{1}{x} = \frac{100}{17}$$

$$\therefore \quad \text{Correct} \sum \frac{1}{x} = \frac{100}{17} - \frac{1}{28} + \frac{1}{20} = 5.8966$$

$$\therefore \quad \text{Correct H.M.} = \frac{100}{5.8966} = \mathbf{16.9589.}$$

22. MERITS OF H.M.

1. It is well-defined.
2. It is based on all the items.
3. It is capable of further algebraic treatment.
4. It has sampling stability.
5. It is specially used in finding the average speed, when the distances covered at different speeds are equal or unequal.

23. DEMERITS OF H.M.

1. It is not simple to understand.
2. It is not easy to compute.
3. It gives higher weightage to smaller items, which may not be desirable in some problems.

EXERCISE 3

1. Find the H.M. for the following series :

2, 4, 7, 12, 19.

2. Find the H.M. for the following series :

3, 5, 6, 6, 7, 10, 12.

3. Find the H.M. for the following series :

15, 20, 21, 22, 26, 29.

4. Find the H.M. for the following series :

0.874, 0.989, 0.012, 0.008, 0.00009.

5. Calculate (*a*) the Arithmetic Mean, (*b*) the Geometric Mean and (*c*) the Harmonic Mean for the following incomes :
10, 17, 29, 95, 95, 100, 175, 250, 750.

6. The following table gives the marks obtained by students in a class. Calculate the H.M :

Marks	18	21	30	45
No. of students	6	12	9	2

(*MDU 1998*)

7. Find the H.M. for the following frequency distribution :

x	10	11	12	13	14	15
f	4	7	6	2	2	1

8. Calculate the H.M. for the following :

Income (in Rs.)	10	20	30	40	50
No. of persons	2	4	3	0	1

9. The following table gives the marks (out of 30) obtained by a group of students in a test. Calculate the harmonic mean of this series :

Marks	20	21	22	23	24	25
No. of students	4	2	7	1	3	1

10. The following table gives the marks (out of 50) obtained by 70 students in a class. Calculate the H.M.

Marks	18	21	24	26	30	38	45
No. of students	6	12	15	19	9	7	2

11. Find the H.M. for the following frequency distribution :

Class	2—4	4—6	6—8	8—10
Frequency	20	40	30	10

12. Calculate the H.M. for the following frequency distribution :

Marks	0—10	10—20	20—30	30—40	40—50
No. of students	4	7	28	12	9

13. Find the H.M. for the following data :

Class	0—7	7—14	14—21	21—28	28—35	35—42
f	2	5	8	8	5	2

14. The H.M. of a group containing 150 items is found to be 17. The H.M. of another group containing 250 items is 22. Find the H.M. of the combined group.

15. An aeroplane flies along the four sides of a square at speeds 100 kph, 200 kph, 300 kph and 400 kph respectively. What is the average speed of the plane in its flight around the square ?

16. A cyclist covers his first three km at an average speed of 8 km per hour, another two km at 3 km per hour and the last 2 km at 2 km per hour. Find the average speed for the entire journey. *(KU 1995)*

17. A train starts from rest and travels successive quarters of a kilometre at average speeds of 12, 16, 24 and 48 kph. The average speed over the whole mile is 19.2 kph and not 25 kph. Explain the statement as you would to a layman and verify the arithmetic.

18. A man buy mangoes from one shop at the rate of Rs. 20 per kg, from the second shop at the rate of Rs. 25 per kg, from the third shop at the rate of Rs. 30 per kg, from the fourth shop at the rate of Rs. 35 per kg. Find the average rate in rupees per kg. if he buys mangoes of Rs. 10 from each shop. *(MDU 2005)*

(**Hint.** Use weighted H.M. with rates as x and amounts as w.)

19. The H.M. of the 200 observations is found to be 18. Later on, it was discovered that one item 20 was misread as 18. Find the correct value of H.M.

20. The H.M. of 50 items was found to be 125. Later on, it was discovered that two items 100 and 200 were misread as 90 and 250 respectively. Calculate the correct value of the H.M. *(KU 1996 C)*

Answers

1. 4.86	2. 5.9	3. 21.2251	4. 0.0004416
5. (*a*) 169, (*b*) 80.74, (*c*) 38.2328		6. 23.2147 marks	7. 11.5803
8. Rs. 19.23	9. 21.9 marks	10. 25.09 marks	11. 4.98
12. 20.48 marks	13. 14.6917	14. 19.8146	15. 192 kph
16. 3.4286 kph	17. H.M. is to be used	18. Rs. 26.33 per kg	19. 18.009
20. 125.0347.			

IV. MEDIAN

24. DEFINITION

The **median** of a statistical series is defined as the size of the middle most item (or the A.M. of two middle most items), provided the items are in order of magnitude. For example, the median for the series 4, 6, 10, 12, 18 is 10 and for the series 4, 6, 10, 12, 18, 22, the value of median would be $\frac{10+12}{2} = 11$. It can be observed that 50% items in the series would have value less than or equal to median and 50% items would be with value greater or equal to the value of the median.

For an individual series, the median is given by,

$$\text{Median} = \text{size of } \frac{n+1}{2} \text{th item}$$

where $x_1, x_2, ..., x_n$ are the values of the variable under consideration. The values $x_1, x_2, ..., x_n$ are supposed to have been arranged in order of magnitude. If $\frac{n+1}{2}$ comes out to be in decimal, then we take median as the A.M. of size of $\frac{n}{2}$th and $\left(\frac{n}{2}+1\right)$th items.

WORKING RULES FOR FINDING MEDIAN FOR AN INDIVIDUAL SERIES

Step I. *Arrange the given items in order of magnitude.*

Step II. *Find the total number 'n' of items.*

Step III. *Write : median = size of* $\frac{n+1}{2}$*th item.*

Step IV. *(i) If* $\frac{n+1}{2}$ *is a whole number, then* $\frac{n+1}{2}$*th item gives the value of median.*

(ii) If $\frac{n+1}{2}$ *is in fraction, then the A.M. of* $\frac{n}{2}$*th and* $\left(\frac{n}{2}+1\right)$*th items gives the value of median.*

For a frequency distribution, in which frequencies (*f*) of different values (*x*) of the variable are given, we have

$$\textbf{Median} = \textbf{size of } \frac{N+1}{2} \textbf{ th item.}$$

Remark. The values of the variable are supposed to have been arranged in order of magnitude.

WORKING RULES FOR FINDING MEDIAN FOR A FREQUENCY DISTRIBUTION

Step I. *Arrange the values of the variable in order of magnitude and find the cumulative frequencies (c.f.).*

Step II. *Find the total 'N' of all frequencies and check that it is equal to the last c.f.*

Step III. *Write : median = size of* $\frac{N+1}{2}$*th item.*

Step IV. *(a) If* $\frac{N+1}{2}$ *is a whole number, then* $\frac{N+1}{2}$*th item gives the value of median. For this, look at the cumulative frequency column and find that total which is either equal to* $\frac{N+1}{2}$ *or the next higher than* $\frac{N+1}{2}$ *and determine the value of the variable corresponding to this. This gives the value of median.*

(b) If $\frac{N+1}{2}$ *is in friction, then the A.M. of* $\frac{N}{2}$*th and* $\left(\frac{N}{2}+1\right)$*th items gives the value of median.*

In case, the values of the variable are given in the form of classes, we shall assume that items in the classes are uniformly distributed in the corresponding classes. We define

$$\textbf{Median} = \textbf{size of } \frac{N}{2} \textbf{ th item.}$$

Here we shall get the class in which N/2th item is present. This is called the **median class**. To ascertain the value of median in the median class, the following formula is used.

$$\textbf{Median} = \mathbf{L} + \left(\frac{\mathbf{N/2 - c}}{\mathbf{f}}\right)\mathbf{h}$$

where L = lower limit of the median class

c = cumulative frequency of the class preceding the median class

f = simple frequency of the median class

h = width of the median class.

Remark. In problems on **Averages** or in other problems in the following chapters, where we need only the mid values of class intervals in the formula, we need not convert the classes written using *'inclusive method'*.

The following points must be taken care of, while calculating median :

1. The values of the variable must be in order of magnitude. In case of classes of values of the variable, the classes must be strictly *in ascending* order of magnitude.

2. If the classes are in inclusive form, then the actual limits of the median class are to be taken for finding L and h.

3. The classes may not be of equal width *i.e.*, h need not be the common width of all classes. It is the width of the *"median class"*.

4. In case of open end classes, it is advisable to find average by using median.

WORKING RULES FOR FINDING MEDIAN FOR A FREQUENCY DISTRIBUTION WITH CLASS INTERVALS

Step I. *Arrange the classes in the ascending order of magnitude. The classes must be in 'exclusive form'. The widths of classes may not be equal. Find the cumulative frequencies (c.f.).*

Step II. *Find the total 'N' of all frequencies and check that it is equal to the last c.f.*

Step III. *Write : median = size of* $\frac{N}{2}$ *th item.*

Step IV. *Look at the cumulative frequency column and find that total which is either equal to* $\frac{N}{2}$ *or the next higher than* $\frac{N}{2}$ *and determine the class corresponding to this. That gives the 'median class'.*

Step V. *Write : median* $= L + \left(\frac{N/2 - c}{f}\right)$ *h. Put the values of L, N/2, c, f, h and calculate the value of median.*

Example 1. *Find the median of the series :*

4, 6, 9, 4, 2, 8, 10.

Sol. The values of the variable arranged in ascending order are

x : 2, 4, 4, 6, 8, 9, 10

Here $n = 7$. $\therefore \frac{n+1}{2} = \frac{7+1}{2} = 4$

$\therefore$ Median = size of 4th item = **6.**

Example 2. *Find the median for the series :*

25, 20, 23, 32, 40, 27, 30, 25, 20, 10, 55, 41.

Sol. The values of the variable arranged in the ascending order are

x : 10, 20, 20, 23, 25, 25, 27, 30, 32, 40, 41, 55

Here $n = 12$

$$\therefore \quad \frac{n+1}{2} = \frac{12+1}{2} = 6.5$$

$\therefore$ Median = 'size of 6.5th' item

$$= \frac{\text{6th item + 7th item}}{2} = \frac{25+27}{2} = \mathbf{26.}$$

Example 3. *The following are the marks obtained by a batch of 10 students in a certain class test in Statistics and Accountancy :*

Roll No.	*1*	*2*	*3*	*4*	*5*	*6*	*7*	*8*	*9*	*10*
Marks in Statistics	*63*	*64*	*62*	*32*	*30*	*60*	*47*	*46*	*35*	*28*
Marks in Accountancy	*68*	*65*	*35*	*42*	*26*	*85*	*44*	*80*	*33*	*72*

In which subject is the level of knowledge of students higher ?

Sol. In this problem, median is the most suitable average.

The marks in Statistics arranged in ascending order are :

28, 30, 32, 35, 46, 47, 60, 62, 63, 64.

Here $n = 10$. $\frac{n+1}{2} = \frac{10+1}{2} = 5.5$

$\therefore$ Median = size of 5.5th item

$$= \frac{\text{size of 5th item + size of 6th item}}{2}$$

$$= \frac{46+47}{2} = \mathbf{46.5\ marks.}$$

The marks in Accountancy arranged in ascending order are :

26, 33, 35, 42, 44, 65, 68, 72, 80, 85.

Here $n = 10$. $\frac{n+1}{2} = \frac{10+1}{2} = 5.5$

$\therefore$ Median = size of 5.5th item

$$= \frac{\text{size of 5th item + size of 6th item}}{2}$$

$$= \frac{44+65}{2} = \mathbf{54.5\ marks.}$$

$\therefore$ Level of knowledge is higher in accountancy.

Example 4. *Find the median for the following frequency distribution :*

x	*0*	*1*	*2*	*3*	*4*	*5*	*6*
f	*5*	*9*	*10*	*12*	*6*	*4*	*2*

Sol. **Calculation of Median**

x	f	c.f.
0	5	5
1	9	14
2	10	24
3	12	36
4	6	42
5	4	46
6	2	48 = N
	N = 48	

Here, $\frac{N+1}{2} = \frac{48+1}{2} = 24.5$

$\therefore$ Median = size of 24.5th item

$$= \frac{\text{size of 24th item + size of 25th item}}{2} = \frac{2+3}{2} = \mathbf{2.5.}$$

Example 5. *The following table gives the weekly expenditure of 100 families. Find the median.*

Weekly expenditure (in Rs.)	*0—10*	*10—20*	*20—30*	*30—40*	*40—50*
No. of families	*14*	*23*	*27*	*21*	*15*

Sol. **Calculation of Median**

Weekly expenditure (in Rs.)	*No. of families* f	*c.f.*
0—10	14	14
10—20	13	37 = c
L = 20—30	27 = f	64
30—40	21	85
40—50	15	100 = N
	N = 100	

$$\frac{N}{2} = \frac{100}{2} = 50$$

$\therefore$ Median = size of 50th item

$\therefore$ Median class is 20—30.

Now, $$\textbf{median} = L + \left(\frac{\frac{N}{2} - c}{f}\right) h = 20 + \left(\frac{50-37}{27}\right) 10 = 20 + 4.81 = \textbf{Rs. 24.81.}$$

Example 6. *The following table gives the ages in years of 800 persons. Find out the median age.*

Age (in years)	*20—60*	*20—55*	*20—40*	*20—30*
No. of persons	*800*	*740*	*400*	*120*
Age (in years)	*20—50*	*20—45*	*20—25*	*20—35*
No. of persons	*670*	*550*	*50*	*220*

Sol. **Calculation of Median**

Age (in years)	*No. of persons (f)*	*c.f.*
20—25	50	50
25—30	120 – 50 = 70	50 + 70 = 120
30—35	220 – 120 = 100	120 + 100 = 220 = *c*
L = 35—40	400 – 220 = 180 = *f*	220 + 180 = 400
40—45	550 – 400 = 150	400 + 150 = 550
45—50	670 – 550 = 120	550 + 120 = 670
50—55	740 – 670 = 70	670 + 70 = 740
55—60	800 – 740 = 60	740 + 60 = 800
	N = 800	

$$\frac{N}{2} = \frac{800}{2} = 400$$

∴ Median = size of 400th item

∴ Median class is 35—40.

$$\therefore \quad \text{Median} = L + \left(\frac{\frac{N}{2} - c}{f}\right) h$$

$$= 35 + \left(\frac{400 - 220}{180}\right) 5$$

$$= 35 + 5 = \textbf{40 years.}$$

Example 7. *Find the median for the following wage distribution in a certain factory :*

Monthly wages (Rs.)	*50—80*	*80—100*	*100—110*	*110—120*
No. of workers	*30*	*127*	*140*	*240*
Monthly wages (Rs.)	*120—130*	*130—150*	*150—180*	*180—200*
No. of workers	*176*	*135*	*20*	*3*

Sol. **Calculation of Median**

Monthly wages (Rs.)	*No. of workers f*	*c. f.*
50—80	30	30
80—100	127	157
100—110	140	297 = c
L = 110—120	240 = f	537
120—130	176	713
130—150	135	848
150—180	20	868
180—200	3	871 = N
	N = 871	

$$\frac{N}{2} = \frac{871}{2} = 435.5$$

∴ Median = size of 435.5th item

∴ Median class is 110—120.

∴ $$\text{Median} = L + \left(\frac{N/2 - c}{f}\right)h = 110 + \left(\frac{435.5 - 297}{240}\right)10$$

$$= 110 + 5.77 = \textbf{Rs. 115.77.}$$

Example 8. *Calculate the median for the following data :*

Wages upto (in Rs.)	*15*	*30*	*45*	*60*	*75*	*90*	*105*	*120*
No. of workers	*12*	*30*	*65*	*107*	*157*	*202*	*222*	*230*

Sol. **Calculation of Median**

Wages (in Rs.)	*No. of workers f*	*c.f.*
0—15	12	12
15—30	30 – 12 = 18	30
30—45	65 – 30 = 35	65
45—60	107 – 65 = 42	107 = c
L = 60—75	157– 107= 50 = f	157
75—90	202– 157= 45	202
90—105	222– 202= 20	222
105—120	230– 222= 8	230 = N
	N = 230	

$$\frac{N}{2} = \frac{230}{2} = 115$$

∴ Median = size of 115th item

∴ Median class is 60—75.

∴ $$\text{Median} = L + \left(\frac{\frac{N}{2} - c}{f}\right)h = 60 + \left(\frac{115 - 107}{50}\right)15 = 60 + 2.4 = \textbf{Rs. 62.40.}$$

Example 9. *The following table gives the marks obtained by 50 students. Find the median :*

Marks	*10—14*	*15—19*	*20—24*	*25—29*
No. of students	*5*	*8*	*6*	*7*
Marks	*30—34*	*35—39*	*40—44*	*45—49*
No. of students	*6*	*3*	*9*	*6*

Sol. Here the classes are given in 'inclusive form'. These classes in 'exclusive form' are :

9.5—14.5, 14.5—19.5, ..., 44.5—49.5.

Calculation of Median

Marks	*No. of students (f)*	*c.f.*
9.5—14.5	5	5
14.5—19.5	8	13
19.5—24.5	6	19 = *c*
L = 24.5—29.5	7 = *f*	26
29.5—34.5	6	32
34.5—39.5	3	35
39.5—44.5	9	44
44.5—49.5	6	50 = N
	N = 50	

$$\frac{N}{2} = \frac{50}{2} = 25$$

$\therefore$ Median = size of 25th item

$\therefore$ Median class is 24.5—29.5

$$\therefore \quad \text{Median} = L + \left(\frac{\frac{N}{2} - c}{f}\right) h = 24.5 + \left(\frac{25 - 19}{7}\right) 5$$

$$= 24.5 + 4.286 = \mathbf{28.786 \text{ marks.}}$$

Example 10. *You are given the following incomplete frequency distribution. It is known that the total frequency is 1000 and that the median is 413.11. Estimate the missing frequencies.*

Value	*Frequency*	*Value*	*Frequency*
300—325	*5*	*400—425*	*326*
325—350	*17*	*425—450*	*?*
350—375	*80*	*450—475*	*88*
375—400	*?*	*475—500*	*9*

Sol. Let the missing frequencies of the classes 375—400 and 425— 450 be *a* and *b* respectively.

Value	*Frequency f*	*c.f.*
300—325	5	5
325—350	17	22
350—375	80	102
375—400	a	$102 + a = c$
L = 400—425	$326 = f$	$428 + a$
425—450	b	$428 + a + b$
450—475	88	$516 + a + b$
475—500	9	$525 + a + b = 1000$
	N = 1000	

Median is given to be 413.11.

∴ Median class is 400—425.

Now, $\text{Median} = L + \left(\frac{N/2 - c}{f}\right)h$

Here $L = 400, N/2 = 500, c = 102 + a, \; h = 25.$

$$\therefore \quad 413.11 = 400 + \left(\frac{500 - (102 + a)}{326}\right) 25$$

$$\therefore \quad (13.11)\, 326 = (500 - 102 - a)\, 25$$

or $4273.86 = (398 - a)\, 25$

or $398 - a = 170.9544$ or $a = 227.0456 = 227$

Also $525 + a + b = 1000$

$$\therefore \quad b = 1000 - 525 - 227 = 228$$

∴ The missing frequencies are **227** and **228.**

25. GRAPHICAL LOCATION OF MEDIAN

The value of median can also be estimated by making use of ogives. We know that there are 50% items with values less than or equal to the value of the median. We shall use this fact in estimating median by using 'less than ogive' of the data.

On the graph of 'less than' ogive, we mark the point N/2 on the y-axis. Then a line parallel to the x-axis is drawn to meet the 'less than' ogive. From this point of intersection, a perpendicular is drawn on the x-axis. The point where this perpendicular meet the x-axis would give the value of the median.

We also know that there are 50% items with values more than or equal to the value of the median. This fact can also be made use of in estimating median from 'more than' ogive of the data. For this, we mark the point N/2 on the y-axis and a line is drawn parallel to x-axis to meet the ogive. From this point of intersection a perpendicular is drawn on the x-axis. The point where this perpendicular meet the x-axis would give the value of the median.

In case, we have drawn both ogives for the data, then the values of the median is very easily found out by drawing a perpendicular, from the point of intersection of ogives, on the x-axis. The point where this perpendicular meets the x-axis would give the value of the median.

WORKING RULES FOR FINDING MEDIAN BY USING OGIVES

Method 1. Using 'less than' ogive

Step I. *Draw 'less than' ogive on the graph paper.*

Step II. *Mark N/2 on the vertical axis. Draw a horizontal line from this point and cutting the 'less than' ogive at A.*

Step III. *Draw a perpendicular from A to meet the horizontal axis at A′. The reading at A′ gives the value of the median.*

Method 2. Using both ogives

Step I. *Draw both ogives on the graph paper.*

Step II. *Let the ogives intersect at B.*

Step III. *Draw a perpendicular from B to meet the horizontal axis at B′. The reading at B′ gives the value of the median.*

Example 11. *Find the median income from the following data by using ogives :*

Income (in Rs.)	*500—600*	*600—700*	*700—800*
No. of employees	*45*	*60*	*30*
Income (in Rs.)	*800—900*	*900—1000*	*1000—1100*
No. of employees	*12*	*7*	*2*

Sol.

Income (in Rs.)	*No. of employees*	*For 'less than ogive'*		*For 'more than ogive'*	
		Income (in Rs.)	*No. of employees*	*Income (in Rs.)*	*No. of employees*
—	—	Less than 500	0	—	—
500—600	45	" " 600	45	More than 500	156
600—700	60	" " 700	105	" " 600	111
700—800	30	" " 800	135	" " 700	51
800—900	12	" " 900	147	" " 800	21
900—1000	7	" " 1000	154	" " 900	9
1000—1100	2	" " 1100	156	" " 1000	2
—	—	—	—	" " 1100	0

For 'less than' ogive, the points (500, 0), (600, 45), (700, 105), (800, 135), (900, 147), (1000, 154), (1100, 156) are marked on the graph paper. These points are joined by straight lines. This gives the 'less than' ogive. For 'more than' ogive, the points (500, 156), (600, 111), (700, 51), (800, 21), (900, 9), (1000, 2), (1100, 0) are marked on the graph paper. The points are joined by straight lines. This gives the 'more than' ogive.

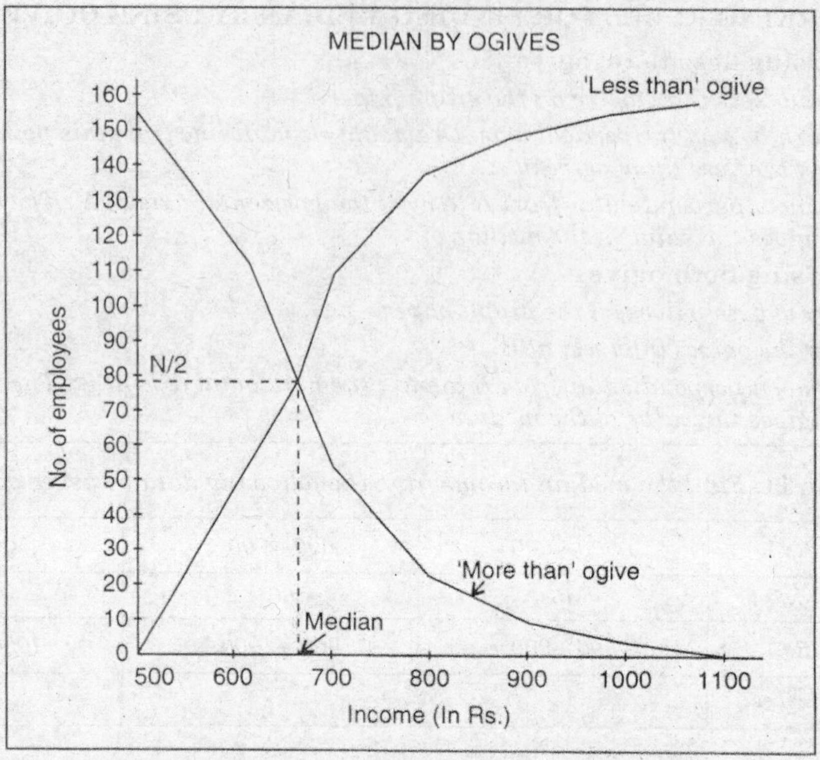

From the graphs, we see that median is **Rs. 655.**

26. MATHEMATICAL PROPERTY OF MEDIAN

In a statistical data, the sum of numerical values of deviations of items from median is always least, *i.e.*,

$$\sum_{i=1}^{n} f_i \,|\, x_i - \text{Median} \,|\ \text{is always least,}$$

where f_i is the frequency of x_i $(1 \le i \le n)$.

27. MERITS OF MEDIAN

1. It is simple to understand.
2. It is easy to compute.
3. It is well-defined.
4. It is not affected by the extreme items.
5. It is best suited for open end classes.
6. It can also be located graphically.

28. DEMERITS OF MEDIAN

1. It is not based on all the items.
2. It is not capable of further algebraic treatment.
3. It can only be calculated when the data is in order of magnitude.

EXERCISE 4

1. Find the value of the median for the series :
   8, 6, 6, 5, 11, 80, 12.
2. Find the value of the median for the following series :
   4, 6, 7, 8, 12, 10, 13, 14.
3. Find the value of median for the following data :

x	1	2	3	4	5	6	7	8	9
f	5	6	7	2	2	1	2	1	1

4. Find the median for the following frequency distribution :

x	5	10	15	20	25
f	2	4	6	8	10

5. Find the median for the following frequency distribution :

No. of students	6	4	16	7	8	2
Marks	20	9	25	50	40	80

6. Find the median for the following frequency distribution :

Marks	0—10	10—20	20—30	30—40	40—50	50—60
No. of students	15	17	19	27	19	12

(*KU 1998*)

7. Find the median marks for the following distribution :

Marks less than	10	20	30	40	50	60
No. of students	4	10	30	40	47	50

8. For the following frequency distribution, find out the value of median :

Marks	0—7	7—14	14—21	21—28
Frequency	3	4	7	11
Marks	28—35	35—42	42—49	
Frequency	0	16	9	

9. Find the value of median for the following series :

Class	1—10	11—20	21—30	31—40	41—50
No. of items	10	21	51	45	26

[**Hint.** The actual limits of classes are :
0.5—10.5, 10.5—20.5, 20.5—30.5, 30.5—40.5 and 40.5—50.5.]

10. Calculate median and arithmetic average for the following data :

Class Interval	10—20	10—30	10—40	10—50
Frequency	4	6	56	97
Class Interval	10—60	10—70	10—80	10—90
Frequency	124	137	146	150

11. Calculate median for the following data :

Mid-value	115	125	135	145	155	165	175	185	195
Frequency	6	25	48	72	116	60	38	22	3

12. Calculate the median for the following distribution :

Height (in inches)	60—63	63—66	66—69	69—72	72—75	75—78
No. of men	8	28	118	66	16	4

13. Find A.M. and Median for the following frequency distribution.

Marks	*No. of students*
0–7	19
7–14	25
14–21	36
21–28	72
28–35	51
35–42	43
42–49	28

(*KU 2000*)

14. In a frequency distribution of 100 families given below, the median is known to be 50. Find the missing frequencies.

Expenditure (in Rs.)	0–20	20–40	40–60	60–80	80–100
No. of families	14	?	27	?	15

(*KU 2000*)

15. An incomplete frequency distribution is given below :

Variable	10—20	20—30	30—40	40—50	50—60	60—70	70—80
Frequency	12	30	?	65	?	25	18

It is given that median value is 46 and the total number of items is 229. You are required to find the missing frequencies. (*KU 1998 C*)

16. Find the missing frequencies in the following distribution, if N = 100 and median of the distribution is 30 :

Marks	0—10	10—20	20—30	30—40	40—50	50—60
No. of students	10	?	25	30	?	10

17. Find the missing frequencies in the following distribution, if N = 74 and median of the distribution is 36 :

Marks	0—10	10—20	20—30	30—40
No. of students	2	8	?	20
Marks	40—50	50—60	60—70	70—80
No. of students	12	?	4	3

18. Find the median for the following data using ogives :

Wages (in Rs.)	20—40	40—60	60—80	80—100
No. of workers	4	6	10	16
Wages (in Rs.)	100—120	120—140	140—160	
No. of workers	12	7	3	

19. Find the median for the following data from ogives. Also verify the result algebraically :

Marks	0—5	5—10	10—15	15—20
No. of students	4	6	10	10
Marks	20—25	25—30	30—35	35—40
No. of students	25	22	18	5

20. From the following data, find the value of median by using 'less than' ogive and 'more than' ogive separately. Also verify your result by calculating the value of median algebraically.

Class	5—10	10—15	15—20	20—25	25—30	30—35	35—40
No. of items	81	72	63	45	32	16	8

(KU 1995, 98 C)

Answers

1. 8	**2.** 9	**3.** 3	**4.** 20
5. 25 marks	**6.** 31.2963 marks	**7.** 27.5 marks	**8.** 28 marks
9. 29.4216	**10.** 44.6341, 47	**11.** 153.7931	**12.** 68.1356 inches
13. 26.49, 30.82	**14.** 22, 22	**15.** 34, 45	**16.** 15, 10
17. 15, 10	**18.** Rs. 91.25	**19.** 24 marks	**20.** 15.42.

V. MODE

29. DEFINITION

The **mode** of a statistical series is defined as that value of the variable around which the values of the variable tend to be most heavily concentrated. It can also be defined as that value of the variable whose own frequency is dominating and at the same time, the frequencies of its neighbouring items are also dominating. Thus, we see that mode is that value of the variable around which the items of the series cluster densily. Let us consider the data regarding the sale of ready made shirts :

Size (in inches)	30	32	34	36	38	40	42
No. of shirts sold	5	22	24	38	16	8	2

Here we see that the frequency of 36 is highest and the frequencies of its neighbouring items (34, 38) are also dominating. Here the most fashionable, modal size is 36 inches. Technically, we shall say that the mode of the distribution is 36 inches.

In case of mode, we are to deal with the frequencies of values of the items, thus if we are to find the value of mode for an individual series, we will have to see the repetition of different items. *i.e.*, we would be in a way expressing it in the form of frequency distribution. Thus, we start our discussion for evaluating mode for frequency distributions. There are two methods of finding mode of a frequency distribution.

30. MODE BY INSPECTION

Sometimes the frequencies in a frequency distribution are so distributed that we would be able to find the value of mode just, by inspection. For example, let us consider the frequency distribution :

x	4	5	6	7	8	9	10	11	12
f	1	2	1	5	12	4	2	2	1

Here we can say, at once, that mode is 8.

31. MODE BY GROUPING

Let us consider the distribution :

x	4	5	6	7	8	9	10	11	12
f	4	5	7	14	8	15	2	2	1

Here the frequency of 9 is more than the frequency of 7, whereas the frequencies of neighbouring items of 7 are more than that for 9. In such a case, we would not be able to judge the value of mode just by inspecting the data. In case there is even slight doubt as to which is the value of mode, we go for this method. In this method, two tables are drawn. These tables are called 'Grouping Table' and 'Analysis Table'. In the grouping table, six columns are drawn. The column of frequencies is taken as the column I. In the column II, the sum of two frequencies are taken at a time. In the column III, we exclude the first frequency and take the sum of two frequencies at a time. In the column IV, we take the sum of three frequencies at a time. In the column V, we exclude the first frequency and take the sum of frequencies, taking three at a time. In the last column, we exclude the first two frequencies and take the sum of three frequencies at a time. The next step is to mark the maximum sums in each of the six columns.

In the analysis table, six rows are drawn corresponding to each column in the grouping table. In this table, columns are made for those values of the variable whose frequencies accounts for giving maximum totals in the columns of the grouping table. In this table, marks are given to the values of the variable as often as their frequencies are added to make the total maximum in the columns of the grouping table. The value of the variable which get the maximum marks is declared to be the mode of the distribution.

In case, the values of the variable are given in the form of classes, we shall assume that the items in the classes are uniformly distributed in the corresponding classes. Here we shall get a 'class' either by the method of inspection or the method of grouping. This class is called the **modal class**. To ascertain the value of mode in the modal class, the following formula is used.

$$\textbf{Mode} = L + \left(\frac{\Delta_1}{\Delta_1 + \Delta_2}\right) h$$

where L = lower limit of modal class

Δ_1 = difference of frequencies of modal class and pre-modal class

Δ_2 = difference of frequencies of modal class and post-modal class

h = width of the modal class.

The following points must be taken care of while calculating mode :

1. The values (or classes of values) of the variable must be in ascending order of magnitude.

2. If the classes are in inclusive form, then the actual limits of the modal class are to be taken for finding L and h.

3. The classes must be of equal width.

It may be noted that while analysing the analysis table, we may find two or more values (or classes of values) of the variable getting equal marks. In such a case, the grouping method fails. Such distribution is called a **multi-modal distribution**.

32. EMPIRICAL MODE

In case of a multi-modal distribution, we find the value of mode by using the relation

Mode = 3 Median – 2 A.M.

This mode is called **empirical mode** in the sense that this relation cannot be established algebraically. But it is generally observed that in distributions, the value of mode is approximately equal to 3 Median – 2 A.M. That is why, this mode is called *empirical mode.*

WORKING RULES FOR FINDING MODE

Step I. *If mode is not evident by the 'method of inspection', then the 'method of grouping' should be used.*

Step II. *In case, the values of variable are given in terms of classes of equal width, then* ***step I****, will give the 'modal class'.*

Step III. *To find value of the mode, use the formula :*

$$mode = L + \left(\frac{\Delta_1}{\Delta_1 + \Delta_2}\right) h.$$

Step IV. *In case, the distribution is multimodal, then find the value of mode by using the formula : 'mode = 3 median – 2 A.M'.*

Example 1. *Find the mode for the following individual series :*

5, 7, 3, 5, 2, 1, 5, 8, 5.

Sol. **Calculation of Mode**

x	*Tally bars*	*Frequency (f)*
1	|	1
2	|	1
3	|	1
5	||||	4
7	|	1
8	|	1

By inspection, we can say that mode is **5.**

Example 2. *Find the mode for the following distribution* :

Profit ('000 Rs.)	*28*	*29*	*30*	*31*	*32*	*33*
No. of firms	*4*	*7*	*10*	*6*	*2*	*1*

Sol. **Calculation of Mode**

Profit ('000 Rs.) x	*No. of firms* f
28	4
29	7
30	10
31	6
32	2
33	1

By inspection we can say that mode is **Rs. 30,000**. This is so because the frequency of 30,000 is very high as compared with the frequencies of other values of x. Moreover, the frequencies of the neighbouring items are also dominating.

Example 3. *Find the value of mode for the following distribution* :

x	*4*	*5*	*6*	*7*	*8*	*9*	*10*	*11*	*12*
f	*15*	*18*	*12*	*30*	*27*	*40*	*20*	*20*	*12*

Sol. For the given distribution, we cannot judge the value of mode, just by inspection. In this case, we shall apply the method of grouping. The values of the variable are already in order of magnitude.

Grouping Table

x	*I* f	*II*	*III*	*IV*	*V*	*VI*
4	15	33				
5	18		30	45		

6	12	42			60	
7	30		57			
8	27	**67**		**97**		**69**
9	**40**		60		**87**	
10	20	40				
11	20		32	52		**80**
12	12					

Analysis Table

Column	*9*	*8*	*10*	*7*	*11*
I	1				
II	1	1			
III	1		1		
IV	1	1		1	
V	1	1	1		
VI	1		1		1
Total	6	3	3	1	1

∴ Mode = **9**.

Example 4. *Find the mode for the following frequency distribution :*

x	*5*	*10*	*15*	*20*	*25*	*30*	*35*	*40*
f	*4*	*15*	*25*	*20*	*17*	*26*	*10*	*3*

Sol. We find the 'mode' by using the 'method of grouping'.

Grouping Table

x	*f* *I*	*II*	*III*	*IV*	*V*	*VI*
5	4	19				
10	15		40	44		
15	**25**	**45**			**60**	
20	20		37			
25	17	43		**63**		**62**
30	**26**		36			
35	10	13			53	39
40	3					

Analysis Table

Column	*30*	*15*	*20*	*10*	*25*
I	1				
II		1	1		
III		1		1	
IV	1		1	1	1
V		1	1	1	
VI		1	1		1
	2	4	4	2	2

Since the totals for 15 and 20 are equal, the given frequency distribution is bimodal. For this distribution, we find mode by using the formula :

mode = 3 median – 2 A.M.

Calculation of $\overline{X}$ and median

x	f	*c.f.*	$d = x - A$ $A = 20$	$u = d/h$ $h = 5$	fu
5	4	4	– 15	– 3	– 12
10	15	19	– 10	– 2	– 30
15	25	44	– 5	– 1	– 25
20	20	64	0	0	0
25	17	81	5	1	17
30	26	107	10	2	52
35	10	117	15	3	30
40	3	120	20	4	12
	N = 120				$\Sigma fu = 44$

Now, $\bar{x} = A + \left(\frac{\Sigma fu}{N}\right) h$

$\therefore$ $\bar{x} = 20 + \left(\frac{44}{120}\right) 5 = 20 + 1.833 = 21.833.$

$\frac{N+1}{2} = \frac{20+1}{2} = 60.5$

$\therefore$ Median = size of 60.5th item = $\frac{20+20}{2} = 20.$

$\therefore$ Mode = 3 median – 2$\bar{x}$ = 3(20) – 2(21.833) = **16.334.**

Example 5. *Find the mode for the following frequency distribution :*

Class	*10—20*	*20—30*	*30—40*	*40—50*	*50—60*	*60—70*
f	*10*	*15*	*30*	*12*	*8*	*6*

Sol. By 'inspection', modal class is 30—40.

Now, $$\text{mode} = L + \left(\frac{\Delta_1}{\Delta_1 + \Delta_2}\right) h$$

Here $L = 30$, $\Delta_1 = 30 - 15 = 15$,
$\Delta_2 = 30 - 12 = 18$, $h = 10$

$$\therefore \quad \text{Mode} = 30 + \left(\frac{15}{15+18}\right) 10 = 30 + 4.545 = \mathbf{34.545}.$$

Example 6. *Find the mode for the following frequency distribution :*

Class	*0—5*	*5—10*	*10—15*	*15—20*	*20—25*
f	*6*	*9*	*4*	*2*	*10*
Class	*25—30*	*30—35*	*35—40*	*40—45*	*45—50*
f	*8*	*7*	*5*	*1*	*3*

Sol. We find the 'modal class' by using the 'method of grouping'.

Grouping Table

Class	*f* *I*	*II*	*III*	*IV*	*V*	*VI*
0—5	6	15				
5—10	9		13	19		
10—15	4	6			15	
15—20	2		12			16
20—25	**10**	**18**		**20**		
25—30	8		**15**		**25**	
30—35	7	12				**20**
35—40	5		6	13		
40—45	1	4			9	
45—50	3					

Analysis Table

Column	*20—25*	*25—30*	*30—35*	*15—20*	*35—40*
I	1				
II	1	1			
III		1	1		
IV	1	1		1	
V	1	1	1		
VI		1	1		1
Total	4	5	3	1	1

Since the total is maximum for the class 25—30, the modal class is 25—30.

Now $\qquad \text{mode} = L + \left(\dfrac{\Delta_1}{\Delta_1 + \Delta_2}\right) h$

Here $\qquad L = 25, \Delta_1 = 10 - 8 = 2, \Delta_2 = 8 - 7 = 1, h = 5.$

$\therefore \qquad \text{Mode} = 25 + \left(\dfrac{2}{2+1}\right) 5 = 25 + 3.333 = \mathbf{28.333}.$

Example 7. *Calculate the value of mode for the following frequency distribution :*

Class	*Frequency*	*Class*	*Frequency*
1—4	*2*	*21—24*	*14*
5—8	*5*	*25—28*	*14*
9—12	*8*	*29—32*	*15*
13—16	*9*	*33—36*	*11*
17—20	*12*	*37—40*	*13*

Sol. In this problem, we shall make use of 'grouping method' to find the modal class.

Grouping Table

Class	*Frequency* *I*	*II*	*III*	*IV*	*V*	*VI*
1—4	2	7				
5—8	5		13	15		
9—12	8	17			22	
13—16	9		21			29
17—20	12	26		35		
21—24	14		**28**		**40**	
25—28	14	**29**				**43**
29—32	**15**		26	**40**		
33—36	11	24			39	
37—40	13					

Analysis Table

Column	*29—32*	*25—28*	*21—24*	*33—36*	*17—20*
I	1				
II	1	1			
III		1	1		
IV	1	1		1	
V		1	1		1
VI	1	1	1		
Total	4	5	3	2	1

∴ Modal class is 25—28.

Now $\text{mode} = L + \left(\dfrac{\Delta_1}{\Delta_1 + \Delta_2}\right) h$

Here $L = 24.5, \Delta_1 = 14 - 14 = 0, \Delta_2 = 15 - 14 = 1, h = 28.5 - 24.5 = 4$

∴ $\text{Mode} = 24.5 + \left(\dfrac{0}{0+1}\right) 4 = 24.5 + 0 = \mathbf{24.5.}$

Remark. The modal class 25—28 expressed in 'exclusive form' is 24.5—28.5.

Example 8. *If the mode and mean of a moderately asymmetrical series are 16 m and 15.6 m respectively, what would be its most probable median ?* (KU 1997)

Sol. We have mode = 16 m and mean = 15.6 m.

The formulae is mode = 3 median – 2 A.M.

∴ 16 = 3 median – 2(15.6)

⇒ 3 median = 16 + 31.2 = 47.2

∴ $\text{median} = \dfrac{47.2}{3} = \mathbf{15.73\ m.}$

Example 9. *What are the relationships between mathematical averages ?* (KU 1997)

Sol. The following are the relations between mathematical averages :

(I) A.M. ≥ G.M. ≥ H.M.

In particular, if all the items are identical, then

A.M. = G.M. = H.M.

(II) A.M., G.M. and H.M. are in geometric progression *i.e.*,

$(\text{G.M.})^2 = (\text{A.M.})(\text{H.M.})$

(III) Mode = 3 Median – 2 A.M. (Approximately).

Example 10. *If a, b are positive numbers, then show that*

(i) A.M. ≥ G.M. ≥ H.M.

(ii) $G.M. = \sqrt{A.M. \times H.M.}$ (KU 1997)

Sol. We have $\text{A.M.} = \dfrac{a+b}{2}, \quad \text{G.M.} = \sqrt{ab}, \quad \text{H.M.} = \dfrac{2}{\frac{1}{a}+\frac{1}{b}} = \dfrac{2ab}{a+b}.$

(i)
$$\text{A.M.} - \text{G.M.} = \frac{a+b}{2} - \sqrt{ab} = \frac{a+b-2\sqrt{ab}}{2}$$
$$= \frac{(\sqrt{a})^2 + (\sqrt{b})^2 - 2\sqrt{a}\sqrt{b}}{2} = \frac{(\sqrt{a}-\sqrt{b})^2}{2} \geq 0$$

∴ A.M. – G.M. ≥ 0 *i.e.*, A.M. ≥ G.M. ...(1)

$$\text{G.M.} - \text{H.M.} = \sqrt{ab} - \frac{2ab}{a+b} = \frac{\sqrt{ab}\,(a+b-2\sqrt{ab})}{a+b}$$
$$= \frac{\sqrt{ab}\,((\sqrt{a})^2 + (\sqrt{b})^2 - 2\sqrt{a}\sqrt{b})}{a+b} = \frac{\sqrt{ab}\,(\sqrt{a}-\sqrt{b})^2}{a+b} \geq 0.$$

∴ G.M. – H.M. ≥ 0 *i.e.*, G.M. ≥ H.M. ...(2)

Combining (1) and (2), we have

$$\textbf{A.M.} \geq \textbf{G.M.} \geq \textbf{H.M.}$$

In particular if $a = b$, then

$$\text{A.M.} = \frac{a+b}{2} = \frac{a+a}{2} = a, \ \text{G.M.} = \sqrt{ab} = \sqrt{aa} = a$$

and $$\text{H.M.} = \frac{2ab}{a+b} = \frac{2aa}{a+a} = \frac{2a^2}{2a} = a$$

i.e., $$\textbf{A.M.} = \textbf{G.M.} = \textbf{H.M.}$$

(*ii*) $$\sqrt{\text{A.M.} \times \text{H.M.}} = \sqrt{\frac{a+b}{2} \times \frac{2ab}{a+b}} = ab \quad \text{and} \quad \text{G.M.} = (\sqrt{ab})^2 = ab$$

$$\therefore \qquad \textbf{G.M.} = \sqrt{\textbf{A.M.} \times \textbf{H.M.}}$$

33. MODE IN CASE OF CLASSES OF UNEQUAL WIDTHS

When the values of the variable are given in the form of classes and the classes are not of equal width, then we would not be able to proceed directly to find the modal class either by the method of inspection or by the method of grouping. In fact, we are to compare the frequencies of different classes in order to observe the concentration of items about some item. If the classes happen to be of unequal width, then we would not be able to compare the frequencies in different classes. To make the comparison meaningful, we will first make classes of equal width by grouping two or more classes or by breaking classes, as per the need.

Example 11. *Calculate mode for the following distribution* :

Marks	*No. of students*	*Marks*	*No. of students*
0—2	*8*	*25—30*	*45*
2—4	*12*	*30—40*	*60*
4—10	*20*	*40—50*	*20*
10—15	*10*	*50—60*	*13*
15—20	*16*	*60—80*	*15*
20—25	*25*	*80—100*	*4*

Sol. In this frequency distribution, the classes are not of equal width. Before ascertaining the modal class, we shall make the widths of classes equal.

Marks	*No. of students*
0—20	8 + 12 + 20 + 10 + 16 = 66
20—40	25 + 45 + 60 = 130
40—60	20 + 13 = 33
60—80	15
80—100	4

By inspection, modal class is 20—40.

Now $\quad \text{mode} = L + \left(\frac{\Delta_1}{\Delta_1 + \Delta_2}\right) h$

Here $\quad L = 20, \Delta_1 = 130 - 66 = 64, \Delta_2 = 130 - 33 = 97, h = 20$

$\therefore \quad \text{Mode} = 20 + \left(\frac{64}{64 + 97}\right) 20 = 20 + 7.9503 = \mathbf{27.9503.}$

Example 12. *Calculate median and mode for the following data :*

Class	*2*	*3*	*4*	*5—7*	*7—10*	*10—15*	*15—20*	*20—25*
Frequency	*1*	*2*	*2*	*3*	*5*	*10*	*8*	*4*

(KU 1996)

Sol. We make classes as 0—5, 5—10, 10—15, 15—20 and 20—25.

Class	*Frequency* *f*	*c.f.*
0—5	1 + 2 + 2 = 5	5
5—10	3 + 5 = 8	13
10—15	10	23
15—20	8	31
20—25	4	35 = N
	N = 35	

Calculation of Median

$$\frac{N}{2} = \frac{35}{2} = 17.5$$

$\therefore \quad$ Median = size of 17.5th item

$\therefore \quad$ Median class is 10—15.

$\therefore \quad \text{Median} = L + \left(\frac{N/2 - c}{f}\right) h \quad = 10 + \left(\frac{17.5 - 13}{10}\right) 5 = 10 + 2.25 = \mathbf{12.25.}$

Calculation of Mode

By inspection, modal class is 10—15.

Now $\quad \text{Mode} = L + \left(\frac{\Delta_1}{\Delta_1 + \Delta_2}\right) h$

Here, $\quad L = 10, \Delta_1 = 10 - 8 = 2, \Delta_2 = 10 - 8 = 2, h = 5.$

$\therefore \quad \text{Mode} = 10 + \left(\frac{2}{2 + 2}\right) 5 = 10 + 2.5 = \mathbf{12.5.}$

34. GRAPHICAL LOCATION OF MODE

Generally, the value of mode can also be found out by making use of histogram. This method is applicable when the mode appears to be in the class which has maximum frequency. In this method, two lines are drawn diagonally from the upper corners of the modal class bar to the upper corners of the adjacent bars, touching the modal class bar.

Now from the point of intersection of these lines, a perpendicular is drawn on the x-axis. The point where this line meet the x-axis gives the value of the mode.

Example 13. *Draw histogram to the following frequency distribution and estimate the value of mode from the histogram. Verify its value from the value of mode as calculated by using the algebraical formula.*

Profit ('000 Rs.)	*0—15*	*15—30*	*30—45*	*45—60*	*60—75*
No. of companies	*3*	*7*	*18*	*25*	*20*
Profit ('000 Rs.)	*75—90*	*90—105*	*105—120*	*120—135*	*135—150*
No. of companies	*12*	*6*	*5*	*2*	*2*

(KU 1997 C)

Sol. Graphically. Graph given below :

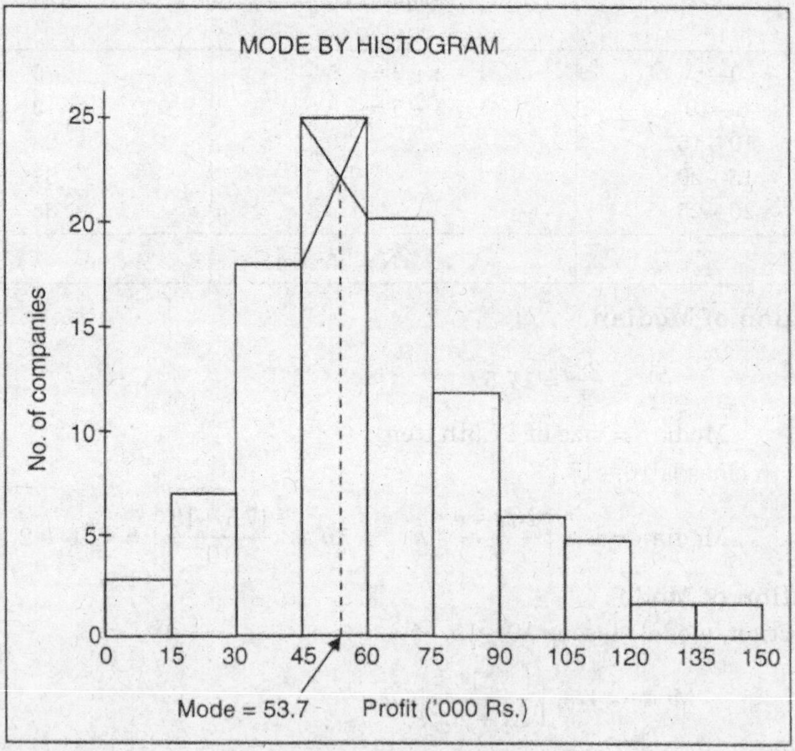

From the graph, mode = Rs. 53.7 thousand = **Rs. 53,700**

Algebraically. By inspection, modal class is 45—60.

Now $\quad \text{Mode} = L + \left(\dfrac{\Delta_1}{\Delta_1 + \Delta_2}\right) h$

Here $\quad L = 45, \Delta_1 = 25 - 18 = 7,$

$\Delta_2 = 25 - 20 = 5, h = 15$

$$\therefore \qquad \text{Mode} = 45 + \left(\frac{7}{7+5}\right) 15 = 45 + 8.75 = \text{Rs. } 53.75 \text{ thousand}$$

$$= \textbf{Rs. 53,750}$$

We see that both values are approximately equal.

35. MERITS OF MODE

1. It is easy to compute.
2. It is not affected by the extreme items.
3. It can be located graphically.

36. DEMERITS OF MODE

1. It is not simple to understand.
2. It is not well defined. There are number of formulae to calculate mode, not necessarily giving the same answer.
3. It is not capable of further algebraic treatment.

EXERCISE 5

1. Find the value of mode for the following series :

10, 12, 17, 12, 10, 12, 16, 11.

2. Find the mode for the following series :

3, 5, 6, 2, 5, 4, 5, 9, 5.

3. Find the value of mode for the following frequency distribution :

x	10	11	12	13	14	15	16	17	18
f	2	4	6	8	10	9	6	2	1

4. Calculate the mode for the following frequency distribution :

x	4	5	6	7	8	9	10	11	12	13
f	2	5	8	9	12	14	14	15	11	13

5. Find the mode for the following frequency distribution :

x	1	2	3	4	5	6	7	8	9	10	11	12
f	3	8	15	23	35	40	32	28	20	45	14	6

6. The number of fully formed apples on 100 plants were counted with the following results :

2	plants	had	0	apples
5	”	”	1	”
7	”	”	2	”
11	”	”	3	”
18	”	”	4	”
24	”	”	5	”
12	”	”	6	”

8	,,	,,	7	,,
6	,,	,,	8	,,
4	,,	,,	9	,,
3	,,	,,	10	,,

(*i*) How many apples are there ?

(*ii*) What is the average number of apples per plant ?

(*iii*) What is the modal number of apples ?

7. Find the mode for the following frequency distribution :

Class	0—4	4—8	8—12	12—16
f	4	8	5	6

8. Find the mode for the following frequency distribution :

Marks	0—5	5—10	10—15	15—20	20—25	25—30	30—35
No. of students	11	20	31	45	30	12	6

9. The following table gives the weight of 50 students of a class. Find the modal weight :

Weight (in kg)	37—41	42—46	47—51	52—56	57—61	62—66	67—71
No.of students	3	7	11	14	7	6	2

10. Calculate the modal value for the following frequency distribution :

Marks	*No. of candidates*	*Marks*	*No. of candidates*
0—9	6	50—59	263
10—19	29	60—69	133
20—29	87	70—79	43
30—39	181	80—89	9
40—49	247	90—99	2

11. Following table shows the marks obtained by 60 students. Calculate (*i*) median (*ii*) mode and (*iii*) arithmetic average.

Marks	*No. of students*
More than 70%	8
,, 60%	18
,, 50%	40
,, 40%	40
,, 30%	55
,, 20%	60

12. Obtain the mean, median and mode for the following series :

Marks	10—25	25—40	40—55	55—70	70—85	85—100
Frequency	6	20	44	26	3	1

13. Calculate median and arithmetic average for the following data. Also calculate mode with the help of median and A.M.

Variable	100—110	110—120	120—130	130—140
Frequency	4	6	20	32
Variable	150—160	160—170	170—180	
Frequency	33	8	2	

14. Find the mean, median and mode for the following distribution :

Wages (in Rs.)	5—15	15—25	25—35	35—45	45—55	55—65
No. of employees	4	6	10	5	3	2

15. The following table shows the distribution of 100 families according to their expenditure per week. Number of families corresponding to the groups Rs. 1000—2000 and Rs. 3000—4000 are missing. The mode is given to be Rs. 2,400. Calculate the missing frequencies :

Expenditure (Rs.)	0—1000	1000—2000	2000— 3000	3000—4000	4000—5000
No. of families	14	?	27	?	15

[**Hint.** Let the frequencies of the classes 1000—2000 and 3000—4000 be a and b respectively.

$$\therefore \quad 2400 = 2000 + \left(\frac{27 - a}{(27 - a) + (27 - b)}\right) 1000 \text{ i.e., } 400 = \frac{(27 - a)\,100}{54 - a - b}.$$

Also $\quad a + b = 44.$]

16. Calculate mode for the following distribution :

Class	0—4	4—6	6—8	8—12	12—18	18—20
Frequency	4	6	8	12	7	2

17. Find the mode for the following data :

Size of items	*Frequency*	*Size of items*	*Frequency*
0—4	5	20—24	14
4—8	7	24—28	6
8—12	9	28—32	3
12—16	17	32—36	1
16—20	15	36—40	0

18. Calculate the median and mode for the following distribution :

Class	*Frequency*	*Class*	*Frequency*
10—20	4	10—60	124
10—30	16	10—70	137
10—40	56	10—80	146
10—50	97	10—90	150

(*KU 1995 C, 99*)

19. Calculate median and mode from the following table :

Income	100—200	100—300	100—400	100—500	100—600
No. of persons	15	33	63	83	100

(MDU 2004)

20. Find out missing frequencies in the following incomplete distribution :

Class	0—10	10—20	20—30	30—40	40—50
Frequency	3	?	20	12	?

The values of Median and Mode are 27 and 26 respectively. *(KU 2004)*

[**Hint.** Let missing frequencies be a and b.

$\therefore$ we have $27 = 20 + \dfrac{(35 + a + b)/2 - (3 + a)}{20} . 10$ and $26 = 20 + \dfrac{20 - a}{(20 - a) + (20 - 12)} . 10$.]

21. Draw a histogram to the following frequency distribution and estimate the value of mode from the histogram. Verify its value from the value of mode as calculated by using algebraical formula :

Income (Rs.)	0—15	15—30	30—45	45—60	60—75	75—90
No. of families	3	7	18	25	20	10

(KU 1997 C)

22. Find the mode and the median from the following table by the use of graphs and check the results by calculations :

Marks	*Students*
0—10	2
10—20	18
20—30	30
30—40	45
40—50	35
50—60	20
60—70	6
70—80	3

(MDU 2000)

Answers

1. 12 **2.** 5 **3.** 14 **4.** 10
5. 6 **6.** (*i*) 486 (*ii*) 4.86 (*iii*) 5
7. 6.286 **8.** 17.414 **9.** 53 **10.** 47.5488
11. (*i*) 54.54% marks (*ii*) 56.47% marks (*iii*) 51.67% marks
12. 47.95 marks, 48.18 marks, 48.57 marks
13. 137.03, 140.14, 130.81 **14.** Rs. 31, Rs. 30, Rs. 29.44
15. 23, 21 **16.** 7 **17.** 18.67 **18.** 44.63, 40.67
19. 356.67, 354.55 **20.** 8, 7 **21.** Rs. 53.75 **22.** 36, 36.56.

PARTITION VALUES

37. DEFINITIONS

We have already seen than the median divide the items in a series into two equal parts. On the same lines, we can think of those values of the variable which may partition the series into four equal parts or ten equal parts or hundred equal parts. The values of the variable which partition a series into equal parts, are called **partition values**.

The values of the variable which partition the series into four equal parts are called **quartiles** (Q_1, Q_2, Q_3). In the distribution, 25% items would have value less than or equal to Q_1 and 75% items would be having value greater than or equal to Q_1. Similarly, we can interpret Q_2 and Q_3. It may be noted that Q_2 would be same as the median.

The values of the variable which partition the series into ten equal parts, are called **deciles** (D_1, D_2, ..., D_9). In the distribution, 10 K% items would be $\leq D_K$ and (100—10 K)% items would be having value $\geq D_K$, $(1 \leq K \leq 9)$.

The values of the variable which partition the series into 100 equal parts, are called **percentiles** (P_1, P_2, ..., P_{99}). In the distribution, K% items would be $\leq P_K$ and (100—K)% items would be having value $\geq P_K$, $(1 \leq K \leq 99)$.

It may be noted very carefully that these quartiles, deciles and percentiles are not averages, but even then these measures are finding place in this chapter on account of their similarity with median. These measures would be very much useful in our further discussion.

For an individual series, the partition values are given by

$$Q_K = \text{size of} \quad K\left(\frac{n+1}{4}\right)\text{th item,} \quad K = 1, 2, 3.$$

where $x_1, x_2, ..., x_n$ are the values of the variable under consideration. The values $x_1, x_2, ..., x_n$ are supposed to have been arranged strictly in *ascending* order of magnitude. If $K\left(\frac{n+1}{4}\right)$ comes out to be in decimal, then we find Q_K by the 'method of interpolation'.

Similarly,

$$D_K = \text{size of} \quad K\left(\frac{n+1}{10}\right)\text{th item,} \quad K = 1, 2, ..., 9.$$

$$P_K = \text{size of} \quad K\left(\frac{n+1}{100}\right)\text{th item,} \quad K = 1, 2, ..., 99.$$

WORKING RULES FOR FINDING POSITIONAL MEASURES OF AN INDIVIDUAL SERIES

Step I. *Arrange the given items in the ascending order of magnitude.*

Step II. *Find the total number 'n' of items.*

Step III. *Write :* (i) $Q_K = \text{size of } K\left(\frac{n+1}{4}\right)\text{th item,} \quad K = 1, 2, 3.$

(ii) $D_K = \text{size of } K\left(\frac{n+1}{10}\right)\text{th item,} \quad K = 1, 2, ..., 9.$

(iii) P_K = *size of* $K\left(\dfrac{n+1}{100}\right)$ *th item,* $K = 1, 2, ..., 99.$

Step IV. *If* $K\left(\dfrac{n+1}{4}\right)$ *or* $K\left(\dfrac{n+1}{10}\right)$ *or* $K\left(\dfrac{n+1}{100}\right)$ *is in fraction, then the corresponding positional measure is found by the 'method of interpolation'.*

For a frequency distribution, we define

$$Q_K = \text{size of } K\left(\frac{N+1}{4}\right)\text{th item,} \quad K = 1, 2, 3.$$

$$D_K = \text{size of } K\left(\frac{N+1}{10}\right)\text{th item,} \quad K = 1, 2, ..., 9.$$

$$P_K = \text{size of } K\left(\frac{N+1}{100}\right)\text{th item,} \quad K = 1, 2, ..., 99.$$

Here also the values of the variable are supposed to have been arranged in the ascending order of magnitude.

WORKING RULES FOR FINDING POSITIONAL MEASURES OF A FREQUENCY DISTRIBUTION

Step I. *Arrange the values of the variable in the ascending order of magnitude and find the cumulative frequencies (c.f.).*

Step II. *Find the total 'N' of all frequencies and check that it is equal to the last c.f.*

Step III. *Write : (i)* Q_K = *size of* $K\left(\dfrac{N+1}{4}\right)$ *th item,* $K = 1, 2, 3.$

(ii) D_K = *size of* $K\left(\dfrac{N+1}{10}\right)$ *th item,* $K = 1, 2, ..., 9.$

(iii) P_K = *size of* $K\left(\dfrac{N+1}{100}\right)$ *th item,* $K = 1, 2, ..., 99.$

Step IV. *We have* Q_1 = *size of* $\dfrac{N+1}{4}$ *th item.*

(a) If $\dfrac{N+1}{4}$ *is a whole number, then* $\dfrac{N+1}{4}$ *th item gives the value of* Q_1. *For this, look at the cumulative frequency column and find that total which is either equal to* $\dfrac{N+1}{4}$ *or the next higher than* $\dfrac{N+1}{4}$ *and determine the value of the variable corresponding to this. That gives the value of* Q_1.

(b) If $\dfrac{N+1}{4}$ *is in fraction, then* Q_1 *is found by the method of interpolation.*

Same procedure is followed for finding other positional measures.

In case the values of the variable are given in the form of classes, then we shall assume that the items in the classes are uniformly distributed in the corresponding classes. Here we define

$$Q_K = \text{size of} \quad K\left(\frac{N}{4}\right)\text{th item,} \quad K = 1, 2, 3.$$

$$D_K = \text{size of} \quad K\left(\frac{N}{10}\right)\text{th item,} \quad K = 1, 2, \ldots\ldots, 9.$$

$$P_K = \text{size of} \quad K\left(\frac{N}{100}\right)\text{th item,} \quad K = 1, 2, \ldots\ldots, 99.$$

By using these formulae, we shall get the class in which the corresponding partition value would lie. This class is called the corresponding *partition value class*. To ascertain the partition value, we shall use the required formula from the list given below :

$$Q_K = L + \left(\frac{K\left(\frac{N}{4}\right) - c}{f}\right) h, \quad K = 1, 2, 3.$$

$$D_K = L + \left(\frac{K\left(\frac{N}{10}\right) - c}{f}\right) h, \quad K = 1, 2, \ldots\ldots, 9.$$

$$P_K = L + \left(\frac{K\left(\frac{N}{100}\right) - c}{f}\right) h, \quad K = 1, 2, \ldots\ldots, 99.$$

where L = lower limit of the corresponding partition value class

c = cummulative frequency of the class preceding the corresponding partition value class

f = simple frequency of the corresponding partition value class

h = width of the corresponding partition value class.

The following points must be taken care of while calculating partition values :

1. The values (classes of values) of the variable must be strictly in the *ascending* order of magnitude.

2. If the classes are in inclusive form, then actual limits of the partition value class are to be taken for finding L and h.

3. The classes may not be of equal width.

WORKING RULES FOR FINDING POSITIONAL MEASURES OF A FREQUENCY DISTRIBUTION WITH CLASS INTERVALS

Step I. *Arrange the classes in the ascending order of magnitude. The classes must be in exclusive form. The width of the classes may not be equal. Find the cumulative frequencies (c.f.).*

Step II. *Find the total 'N' of all frequencies and check that it is equal to the last c.f.*

Step III. *Write : (i)* Q_K = *size of* $K\left(\frac{N}{4}\right)$*th item,* $K = 1, 2, 3.$

(ii) D_K = *size of* $K\left(\frac{N}{10}\right)$*th item,* $K = 1, 2, ..., 9.$

(iii) P_K = *size of* $K\left(\frac{N}{100}\right)$*th item,* $K = 1, 2, ..., 99.$

Step IV. *We have* Q_1 = *size of* $\frac{N}{4}$ *th item. Look at the cumulative frequency column and find that total which is either equal to* $\frac{N}{4}$ *or the next higher than* $\frac{N}{4}$ *and determine the class corresponding to this. That gives the 'Q_1-class'.*

Step V. *Write :* $Q_1 = L + \left(\frac{N/4 - c}{f}\right) h$*. Put the values of L, N/4, c, f, h and calculate the value of* Q_1*. Same procedure is followed for finding other positional measures.*

Example 1. *Calculate the partition values* $Q_1, Q_3, D_2, D_7, P_{22}, P_{38}, P_{80}$ *for the following data :*

4, 7, 3, 9, 4, 12, 7, 12, 6, 18, 19, 20, 4, 7, 6, 5, 17, 16, 19.

Sol. The values of the variable arranged in ascending order of magnitude are

3, 4, 4, 4, 5, 6, 6, 7, 7, 7, 9, 12, 12, 16, 17, 18, 19, 19, 20.

Here $n = 19$

$\mathbf{Q_1}$: $\frac{n+1}{4} = \frac{19+1}{4} = 5$ $\therefore$ Q_1 = size of 5th item = **5.**

$\mathbf{Q_3}$: $3\left(\frac{n+1}{4}\right) = 3\left(\frac{19+1}{4}\right) = 15$ $\therefore$ Q_3 = size of 15th item = **17.**

$\mathbf{D_2}$: $2\left(\frac{n+1}{10}\right) = 2\left(\frac{19+1}{10}\right) = 4$ $\therefore$ D_2 = size of 4th item = 4.

$\mathbf{D_7}$: $7\left(\frac{n+1}{7}\right) = 7\left(\frac{19+1}{10}\right) = 14$ $\therefore$ D_7 = size of 14th item = **16.**

$\mathbf{P_{22}}$: $22\left(\frac{n+1}{100}\right) = 22\left(\frac{19+1}{100}\right) = 4.4$

$\therefore$ P_{22} = size of 4.4th item

= size of 4th item + 0.4 (size of 5th item – size of 4th item)

= 4 + 0.4(5 – 4) = **4.4.**

$\mathbf{P_{38}}$: $38\left(\frac{n+1}{100}\right) = 38\left(\frac{19+1}{100}\right) = 7.6$

$\therefore$ P_{38} = size of 7.6th item

$= \text{size of 7th item} + 0.6\ (\text{size of 8th item} - \text{size of 7th item})$

$= 6 + 0.6(7 - 6) = \mathbf{6.6}.$

$\mathbf{P_{80}}:\ 80\left(\frac{n+1}{100}\right) = 80\left(\frac{19+1}{100}\right) = 16 \quad \therefore \quad P_{80} = \text{size of 16th item} = \mathbf{18.}$

Example 2. *Calculate the median and quartiles for the following data :*

Marks	*0—10*	*10—20*	*20—30*	*30—40*
No. of students	5	7	8	12
Marks	*40—50*	*50—60*	*60—70*	*70—80*
No. of students	28	22	10	8

(KU 2001 C)

Sol. **Calculation of median, Q_1 and Q_3**

Marks	*No. of students f*	*c.f.*
0—10	5	5
10—20	7	12
20—30	8	20
30—40	12	32
40—50	28	60
50—60	22	82
60—70	10	92
70—80	8	100 = N
	N = 100	

Median

$$\frac{N}{2} = \frac{100}{2} = 50$$

$\therefore$ Median = size of 50th item

$\therefore$ Median class is 40—50.

$$\therefore \quad \text{Median} = L + \left(\frac{N/2 - c}{f}\right)h$$

$$= 40 + \left(\frac{50 - 32}{28}\right)10 = 40 + 6.429 = \mathbf{46.429\ marks.}$$

First Quartile (Q_1)

$$\frac{N}{4} = \frac{100}{4} = 25$$

$\therefore$ Q_1 = size of 25th item

$\therefore$ Q_1 class is 30—40.

$$\therefore \quad Q_1 = L + \left(\frac{N/4 - c}{f}\right)h$$

$$= 30 + \left(\frac{25 - 20}{12}\right) 10 = 30 + 4.167 = \mathbf{34.167\ marks.}$$

Third Quartile (Q_3)

$$3\left(\frac{N}{4}\right) = 3\left(\frac{100}{4}\right) = 75$$

∴ Q_3 = size of 75th item

∴ Q_3 class is 50—60.

$$\therefore \quad Q_3 = L + \left(\frac{3(N/4) - c}{f}\right)h = 50 + \left(\frac{75 - 60}{22}\right)10$$

$$= 50 + 6.818 = \mathbf{56.818\ marks.}$$

Example 3. *The following table gives the mark obtained by 70 students in Mathematics paper. Calculate Q_1, D_3 and P_{95} for this distribution.*

Marks more than	*80*	*70*	*60*	*50*	*40*	*30*	*20*
No. of students	*0*	*7*	*18*	*40*	*40*	*63*	*70*

Sol. We shall first express the data in the form of frequency distribution, with classes of values as 20—30, 30—40, ..., 70—80.

Calculation of Partition Values

Marks	*No. of students*	*c.f.*
20—30	7	7
30—40	23	30
40—50	0	30
50—60	22	52
60—70	11	63
70—80	7	70 = N
	N = 70	

Q_1 : $\frac{N}{4} = \frac{70}{4} = 17.5$ ∴ Q_1 = size of 17.5th item

∴ Q_1 class is 30—40

$$\therefore \quad Q_1 = L + \left(\frac{N/4 - c}{f}\right)h = 30 + \left(\frac{17.5 - 7}{23}\right)10 = 30 + 4.565 = \mathbf{34.565\ marks.}$$

D_3 : $3\left(\frac{N}{10}\right) = 3\left(\frac{70}{10}\right) = 21$ ∴ D_3 = size of 21st item

∴ D_3 class is 30—40

$$\therefore \quad D_3 = L + \left(\frac{3N/10 - c}{f}\right)h = 30 + \left(\frac{21 - 7}{23}\right)10 = 30 + 6.087 = \mathbf{36.087\ marks.}$$

P_{95} : $95\left(\frac{N}{100}\right) = 95\left(\frac{70}{100}\right) = 66.5$ $\therefore$ P_{95} = size of 66.5th item

$\therefore$ P_{95} class is 70—80

$$\therefore \quad P_{95} = L + \left(\frac{95N/100 - c}{f}\right)h = 70 + \left(\frac{66.5 - 63}{7}\right)10$$

$$= 70 + 5 = \mathbf{75\ marks.}$$

38. GRAPHICAL LOCATION OF PARTITION VALUES

The partition values of a distribution can also be found out graphically by making use of 'less than' ogive of the data. To find Q_1 (or Q_3), we mark the point $\frac{N}{4}$ $\left(\text{or } \frac{3N}{4}\right)$ on the y-axis. Then a line is drawn parallel to x-axis so that it may cut the ogive. From this point of intersection, a perpendicular is drawn on the x-axis. The point where this perpendicular meet the x-axis would give the value of Q_1 (or Q_3).

Similarly, we can find deciles and percentile by using 'less than' ogive.

WORKING RULES FOR FINDING POSITIONAL MEASURES BY USING 'LESS THAN' OGIVE

Step I. *Draw 'less than' ogive on the graph paper.*

Step II. *For quartiles, mark N/4 and 3N/4 on the vertical axis. Draw horizontal lines from these points and cutting the less than ogive at A and B respectively.*

Step III. *Draw perpendiculars from A and B to meet the horizontal axis at A′ and B′ respectively. The readings at A′ and B′ gives the values of Q_1 and Q_3 respectively. Same procedure is followed for finding other positional measures.*

Example 4. *Draw 'less than' ogive for the following frequency distribution and find the values of quartiles graphically :*

Class	*4—5*	*5—6*	*6—7*	*7—8*	*8—9*	*9—10*	*10—11*	*11—12*
Frequency	*5*	*9*	*18*	*35*	*42*	*32*	*15*	*18*

Sol.

Class	*Frequency*	*For 'less than' ogive*	
		Value	*No. of items*
—	—	Less than 4	0
4—5	5	Less than 5	5
5—6	9	Less than 6	14
6—7	18	Less than 7	32
7—8	35	Less than 8	67
8—9	42	Less than 9	109
9—10	32	Less than 10	141
10—11	15	Less than 11	156
11—12	18	Less than 12	174 = N

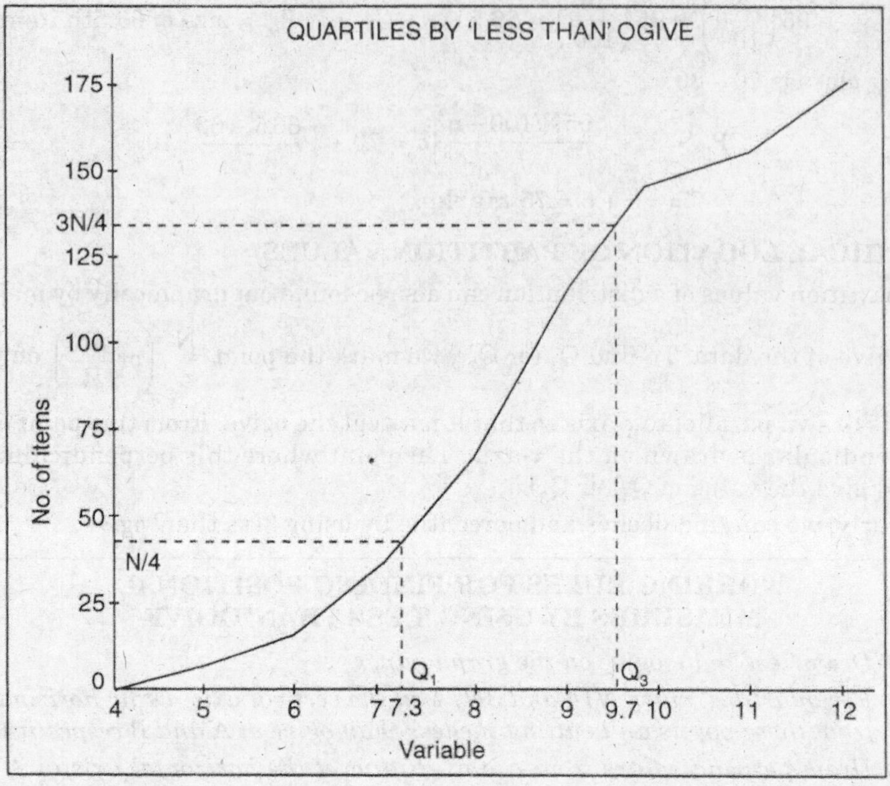

Q_1 = size of $\frac{174}{4}$ th item = size of 43.5th item = **7.3 (Graphically)**

Q_3 = size of $3\left(\frac{174}{4}\right)$ th item = size of 130.5th item = **9.7 (Graphically).**

Example 5. *Draw an 'ogive' for the following distribution. Read the median from the graph and verify the result by calculation. How many workers earn monthly wages between Rs. 60 and Rs. 72 ?*

Monthly wages (in Rs.)	*No.of workers*
50—55	*6*
55—60	*10*
60—65	*22*
65—70	*30*
70—75	*16*
75—80	*12*
80—100	*15*

(MDU 1999)

Sol. We draw *'less than'* ogive.

Monthly wages (in Rs.)	*No. of workers*	*For 'less than' ogive*	
		Monthly wages (in Rs.)	*No. of workers*
—	—	Less than 50	0
50—55	6	Less than 55	6
55—60	10	Less than 60	16
60—65	22	Less than 65	38
65—70	30	Less than 70	68
70—75	16	Less than 75	84
75—80	12	Less than 80	96
80—100	15	Less than 100	111

For 'less than' ogive, the points (50, 0), (55, 6), (60, 16), (65, 38), (70, 68), (75, 84), (80, 96), (100, 111) are marked on the graph paper. These points are joined by straight lines. This gives the 'less than' ogive.

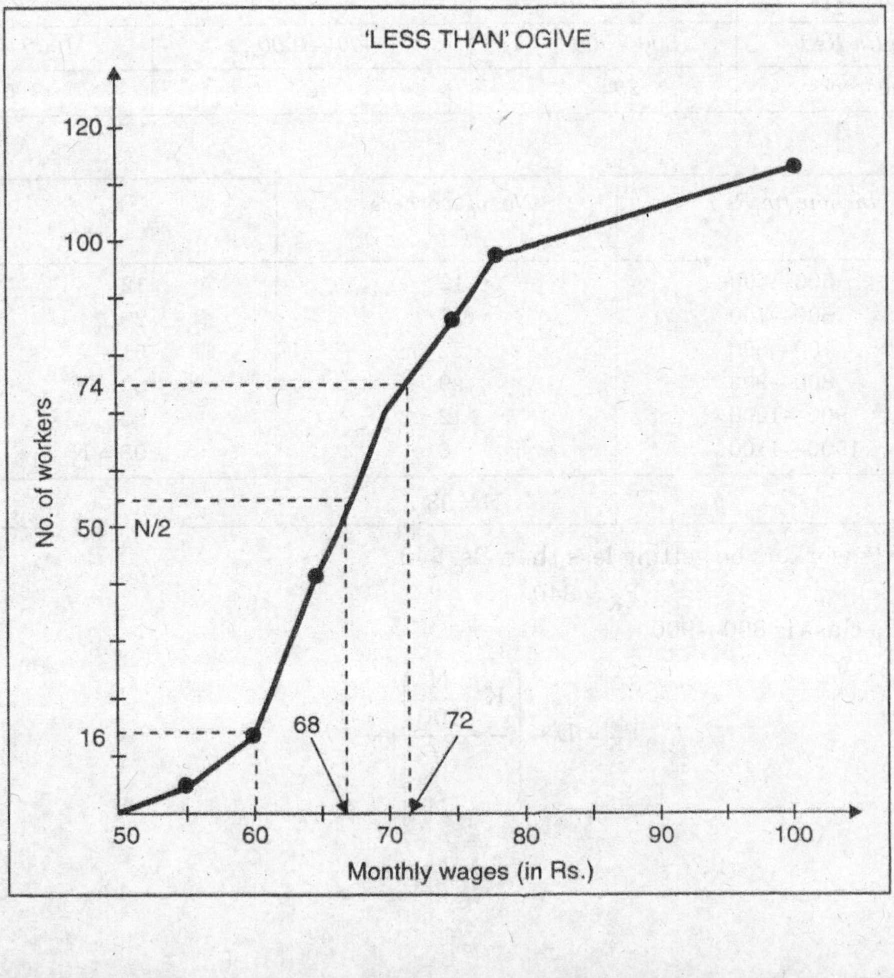

$$\frac{N}{2} = \frac{111}{2} = 55.5$$

∴ Median = size of 55.5th item = **Rs. 68 (Graphically).**

Algebraically

Median class = 65—70

∴ $$\text{Median} = L + \left(\frac{\frac{N}{2} - c}{f}\right) h = 65 + \left(\frac{55.5 - 38}{30}\right) 5 = 65 + 2.92 = \textbf{Rs. 67.92.}$$

Workers getting between Rs. 60 and Rs. 72

From the graph :

No. of workers getting less than Rs. 72 = 74

No. of workers getting less than Rs. 60 = 16

∴ No. of workers getting between Rs. 60 and Rs. 72 = 74 – 16 = **58.**

Example 6. *Find the percentage of workers who earned more than Rs. 840.*

Income (in (Rs.)	*500—600*	*600—700*	*700—800*
No. of workers	*12*	*17*	*22*
Income (in Rs.)	*800—900*	*900—1000*	*1000—1100*
No. of workers	*29*	*12*	*6*

Sol.

Income (in Rs.)	*No. of workers* f	*c.f.*
500—600	12	12
600—700	17	29
700—800	22	51
800—900	29	80
900—1000	12	92
1000—1100	6	98 = N
	N = 98	

Let K% workers be getting less than Rs. 840.

∴ $P_K = 840$

∴ P_K class is 800—900

Now $$P_K = L + \left(\frac{K\left(\frac{N}{100}\right) - c}{f}\right) h$$

$$\therefore \quad 840 = 800 + \left(\frac{K\left(\frac{98}{100}\right) - 51}{29}\right) 100$$

$$\therefore \quad 40 = \left(\frac{0.98K - 51}{29}\right) 100$$

$$\therefore \quad 1160 = 98K - 5100$$

$$\therefore \quad 98K = 6260$$

$$\therefore \quad K = \frac{6260}{98} = 63.88.$$

∴ **% of workers getting less than Rs. 840 = 63.88**

∴ **% of workers getting more than Rs. 840 = 100 – 63.88 = 36.12**

∴ **36.12% workers are getting more than Rs. 840.**

EXERCISE 6

1. Find the value of Q_1 and Q_3 for the series :
   7, 6, 9, 4, 8, 7, 5.
2. Find quartiles for the following series :

Size	*Frequency*	*Size*	*Frequency*
4	40	12	50
5	48	13	52
6	52	14	41
7	56	15	57
8	60	16	63
9	63	17	52
10	57	18	48
11	55	19	40

3. From the figures given below, find the quartiles :

Age (in years)	20—25	25—30	30—35	35—40
No. of Persons	50	70	100	180
Age (in years)	40—45	45—50	50—55	55—60
No. of Persons	150	120	70	59

4. For the following data, find out the values of Q_1, Q_3 and D_1.

Size of item	0—10	10—20	20—30	30—40
Frequency	2	18	30	45
Size of item	40—50	50—60	60—70	70—80
Frequency	35	20	6	3

5. The following series relates to the marks obtained by students, in a class test :

Marks	0—10	10—20	20—30	30—40	40—50
No. of students	11	18	25	28	30
Marks	50—60	60—70	70—80	80—90	90—100
No. of students	33	22	15	12	10

Find the median, the quartiles and the first and the ninth deciles.

6. Calculate the quartiles and the fourth decile for the following data :

Marks	5—10	10—15	15—20	20—25
No. of students	5	6	15	10
Marks	25—30	30—35	35—40	40—45
No. of students	5	4	2	2

7. Find the median, mode and quartiles for the following data :

Wage (in Rs.)	0—10	10—20	20—30	30—40	40—50
No. of workers	22	35	46	35	20

8. Calculate Q_1, Q_3, D_2, P_5, P_{90} for the following data :

Marks	0—10	10—20	20—40	40—60	60—80	80—100
No. of students	8	10	22	25	10	5

9. Determine the first quartile and the median for the following data :

Income (in Rs.)	Below 30	30—40	40—50	50—60
No. of persons	69	167	207	65
Income (in Rs.)	60—70	70—80	80 and above	
No. of persons	58	27	10	

10. Find the median, lower and upper quartiles for the following table :

Marks below	10	20	30	40	50	60	70	80
No. of students	15	35	60	84	94	127	198	249

(KU 1996 C)

11. Draw a 'less than' ogive for the following data and then find the values of quartiles graphically :

Wages (in Rs.)	50—55	55—60	60—65	65—70
No. of workers	6	10	22	30
Wages (in Rs.)	70—75	75—80	80—85	
No. of workers	16	12	15	

Answers

1. $Q_1 = 5, Q_3 = 8$ 2. $Q_1 = 8, Q_3 = 15$
3. $Q_1 = 33.99$ years, $Q_3 = 47.05$ years
4. $Q_1 = 26.58, Q_3 = 46.93, D_1 = 17.72$
5. Median = 46.67 marks, $Q_1 = 28.80$ marks, $Q_3 = 63.64$ marks, $D_1 = 15.22$ marks, $D_9 = 81.33$ marks
6. $Q_1 = 15.41$ marks, $Q_3 = 25.75$ marks, $D_4 = 17.86$ marks
7. Median = Rs. 24.45, mode = Rs. 24.21, Q_1 = Rs. 14.80, Q_3 = Rs. 34.21
8. $Q_1 = 21.8$ marks, $Q_3 = 56$ marks, $D_2 = 18$ marks, $P_5 = 5$ marks, $P_{90} = 74$ marks
9. Q_1 = Rs. 34.89, median = Rs. 43.16
10. Median = 59.24 marks, $Q_1 = 30.94$ marks, $Q_3 = 68.41$ marks
11. Q_1 = Rs. 64.8, Q_3 = Rs. 74.8.

EXERCISE 7

1. What is meant by 'Central Tendency' ? Describe the various methods of measuring it and point out the usefulness of each method. *(MDU 1997)*
2. What are the properties of median ?
3. Describe the merits and demerits of arithmetic mean, median and mode.
4. What are the requisites of a good average ?
5. What is the relationship among mode, median and arithmetic average in a symmetrical series ?
6. What do you mean by 'Central Tendency' ? What are the desirable properties for an average to possess ?
7. What purpose is served by an average ? Discuss the relative merits and shortcomings of various types of statistical averages.
8. Give different measures of central tendency with their formulae. Also state the situations where these measures are used. *(KU 1998)*
9. Define geometric mean, for individual series and frequency distribution and give their computational formulae. *(KU 1999 C)*
10. What are the desirable properties of an average ? Which of the averages you know possesses most of them ? *(KU 2004)*

6

Measures of Dispersion

1. INTRODUCTION

We have already seen that an average of a statistical series is a representative of the series. It tells us about the concentration of the items about an average value of the distribution. Let us consider the following series :

I	10	10	10	10	10
II	10	9	11	12	8
III	1	45	1	2	1

In all the three series, there are five items in each and A.M. of each series is 50/5 = 10. But there is a lot of difference in their formation. In the first series, all the items are coinciding with 10, *i.e.*, the A.M. and there are no deviations of items from A.M. In the second series, the deviations are very small in magnitude. In the third series, we find that the deviations are very large and it is not justified to keep 10 as the average of the series. Thus, we see that the number of items and A.M. of all the series are the same, but even then there is lot of difference in their formation.

2. MEANING

Suppose there are two classes of students with average percentage of marks 56% each, it would not be justified to take for guaranteed that the students of both classes are approximately of same level of intelligence. It may be just possible that the students of first class are getting marks between 50% and 59% and the students of the second class getting between 8% and 90%. Thus, we see that even if the average value of two series are same, the items may be of quite different in nature, in two series. The measures of central tendency are inadequate to give the complete idea about the items in the series, we would be very much helped, if we are also given some idea about the *scatter* of items about the average value. The measure of scatteredness of items about some average is also called measure of dispersion. We may define **measure of dispersion** for a statistical data as the measurement of the spread of the items about an average value.

3. REQUISITES OF A GOOD MEASURE OF DISPERSION

The requisites of a good measure of a dispersion are the same as those for a good measure of central tendency. For the sake of completeness, we list the requisites as under :

1. It should be simple to understand.
2. It should be easy to compute.
3. It should be well-defined.

4. It should be based on all the items.
5. It should not be unduly affected by the extreme items.
6. It should be capable of further algebraic treatment.
7. It should have sampling stability.

4. METHODS OF MEASURING DISPERSION

I. Range
II. Quartile Deviation (Q.D.)
III. Mean Deviation (M.D.)
IV. Standard Deviation (S.D.)
V. Lorenz Curve.

I. RANGE

5. DEFINITION

The **range** of a statistical data is defined as the difference between the largest and the smallest values of the variable.

$\therefore$ **Range = L – S,**

where L = largest value of the variable
S = smallest value of the variable.

In case, the values of the variable are given in the form of classes, then L is taken as the upper limit of the largest value class and S as the lower limit of the smallest value class.

Example 1. *Find the range of the series :*

4, 2, 6, 8, 10.

Sol. Here L = 10, S = 2.

$\therefore$ Range = L – S = 10 – 2 = **8.**

Example 2. *Find the range of the following distribution* :

Age (in years)	*16—18*	*18—20*	*20—22*	*22—24*	*24—26*	*26—28*
No. of students	*0*	*4*	*6*	*8*	*2*	*2*

Sol. Here L = 28, S = 18

$\therefore$ Range = L – S = 28 – 18 = **10 years.**

It may be noted that S ≠ 16, though it is the lower limit of the smallest value class, but there is no item in this class and so this class is meaningless so far as the calculation of range is concerned.

Let us consider the market value of shares of companies A and B, during a particular week.

Day	*Monday*	*Tuesday*	*Wednesday*	*Thursday*	*Friday*	*Saturday*
M.V. of shares of company A (in Rs.)	12	11	10	13	16	20
M.V. of shares of company B (in Rs.)	60	50	55	62	70	75

From the data, we see that Range (A) = 20 – 10 = Rs. 10 and Range (B) = 75 – 50 = Rs. 25. From these results, one is likely to infer that there is more variability in the II series. But this is not so, because the M.V. of shares of A has increased by 100% in the week, whereas there is only 50% rise in the M.V. of shares of B, during that week. Thus, variability is more in the first series. Thus, we see that range may give misleading results if used for comparing two or more series for variability (scatteredness, dispersion). For comparison purpose, we use its corresponding relative measure, called '*coefficient of range*'. This is defined as

$$\textbf{Coeff. of Range} = \frac{\mathbf{L-S}}{\mathbf{L+S}}.$$

Now $\quad \text{Coeff. of Range for A} = \frac{20-10}{20+10} = \frac{10}{30} = \mathbf{0.3333.}$

$$\text{Coeff. of Range for B} = \frac{75-50}{75+50} = \frac{25}{125} = \mathbf{0.2000.}$$

∴ Coeff. of Range (A) > Coeff. of Range (B)

∴ Variability is more in the M.V. of shares of company A.

6. MERITS OF RANGE

1. It is simple to understand.
2. It is easy to compute.
3. It is well-defined.
4. It helps in giving an idea about the variation, just by giving the lowest value and the greatest value of variable.

7. DEMERITS OF RANGE

1. It is not based on all the items.
2. It is highly affected by the extreme items. In fact, if extreme items are present, then range would be calculated by taking only extreme items.
3. It does not take into account the frequencies of items in the middle of the series.
4. It is not capable of further algebraic treatment.
5. It does not have sampling stability.

EXERCISE 1

1. Calculate the range for the following series :

   17, 10, 12, 8, 12, 16, 19.

2. Find the value of range for the following frequency distribution :

Age (in years)	14	15	16	17	18	19	20
No. of students	1	2	2	2	6	4	0

3. Find the range for the following data :

Profit ('000 Rs.)	0—10	10—20	20—30	30—40	40—50
No. of firms	0	6	0	7	15

4. Find the coefficient of range for the following data :

Marks less than	10	20	30	40	50	60	70
No. of students	0	4	7	10	14	18	20

5. Compare the following series for variability :

Days	M	T	W	T	F	S
M.V. of shares of company X (in Rs.)	48	47	46	49	43	45
M.V. of shares of company Y (in Rs.)	10	9	12	12	14	12

Answers

1. 11 **2.** 5 years **3.** Rs. 40,000 **4.** 0.75

5. $\left.\begin{array}{l}\text{Coeff. of Range (X)} = 0.0652\\ \text{Coeff. of Range (Y)} = 0.2174\end{array}\right\}$ Variability is more in the second series.

II. QUARTILE DEVIATION (Q.D.)

8. INADEQUACY OF RANGE

Consider the series

I : 4, 4, 4, 5, 5, 6, 4, 5, 5, 1000.

II : 4, 4, 4, 5, 5, 6, 4, 5, 5.

$$\text{For series I, Coeff. of Range} = \frac{1000-4}{1000+4} = \frac{996}{1004} = 0.992$$

$$\text{For series II, Coeff. of Range} = \frac{6-4}{6+4} = \frac{2}{10} = 0.200.$$

On comparing the values of coeff. of range for these series, one is likely to conclude that these is marked difference in variability in the series. In fact, the series II is obtained from the series I, just by ignoring the extreme item 1000. Thus, we see that extreme items can distort the value of range and even the coefficient of range. If we have a glance at the definitions of these measures, we would find that only extreme items are required in their calculation, if at all extreme items are present. Even if extreme items are present in a series, the middle 50% values of the variable would be expected to vary quite smoothly, keeping this in view, we define another measure of dispersion, called 'Quartile Deviation'.

9. DEFINITION

The **quartile deviation** of a statistical data is defined as

$$\frac{Q_3 - Q_1}{2} \text{ and is denoted as Q.D.}$$

This is also called *semi-inter quartile* range. We have already studied the method of calculating quartiles. The value of Q.D. is obtained by subtracting Q_1 from Q_3 and then dividing it by 2.

For comparing two or more series for variability, the absolute measure Q.D. would not work. For this purpose, the corresponding relative measure, called coeff. of Q.D. is calculated. This is defined as :

$$\text{Coeff. of Q.D.} = \frac{Q_3 - Q_1}{Q_3 + Q_1}.$$

Example 1. *Find Q.D. and its coefficient for the following series :*

x (in Rs.) : 4, 7, 6, 5, 9, 12, 19.

Sol. The values of the variable arranged in ascending order are

x (in Rs.) : 4, 5, 6, 7, 9, 12, 19.

Here $n = 7$.

Q_1 : $\frac{n+1}{4} = \frac{7+1}{4} = 2$ $\therefore$ Q_1 = size of 2nd item = Rs. 5

Q_3 . $3\left(\frac{n+1}{4}\right) = 3\left(\frac{7+1}{4}\right) 6$ $\therefore$ Q_3 = size of 6th item = Rs. 12

$$\therefore \quad \text{Q.D.} = \frac{Q_3 - Q_1}{2} = \frac{12-5}{2} = \textbf{Rs. 3.5.}$$

$$\text{Coeff. of Q.D.} = \frac{Q_3 - Q_1}{Q_3 + Q_1} = \frac{12-5}{12+5} = \frac{7}{17} = \textbf{0.4118.}$$

Example 2. *Find the quartile deviation for the following distribution :*

Marks	*2*	*3*	*4*	*5*	*6*	*7*	*8*	*9*
No. of students	*10*	*11*	*12*	*13*	*5*	*12*	*7*	*5*

Sol. **Calculation of Quartiles**

Marks	*No. of students* *f*	*c.f.*
2	10	10
3	11	21
4	12	33
5	13	46
6	5	51
7	12	63
8	7	70
9	5	75 = N
	N = 75	

Q_1 : $\frac{N+1}{4} = \frac{75+1}{4} = 19$ $\therefore$ Q_1 = size of 19th item = 3 marks

Q_3 : $3\left(\frac{N+1}{4}\right) = 3\left(\frac{75+1}{4}\right) = 57$ $\therefore$ Q_3 = size of 57th item = 7 marks

$\therefore$ $$\text{Q.D.} = \frac{Q_3 - Q_1}{2} = \frac{7-3}{2} = \textbf{2 marks.}$$

Example 3. *Find the coeff. of Q.D. for the following distribution :*

Marks	*0—4*	*4—8*	*8—12*	*12—14*
No. of students	*10*	*12*	*18*	*7*
Marks	*14—18*	*18—20*	*20—25*	*25 and above*
No. of students	*5*	*8*	*4*	*6*

Sol. **Calculation of Quartiles**

Marks	*No. of students* *f*	*c.f.*
0—4	10	10
4—8	12	22
8—12	18	40
12—14	7	47
14—18	5	52
18—20	8	60
20—25	4	64
25 and above	6	70 = N
	N = 70	

Q_1 : $\frac{N}{4} = \frac{70}{4} = 17.5$ $\therefore$ Q_1 = size of 17.5th item

$\therefore$ Q_1 class is 4—8.

$\therefore$ $$Q_1 = L + \left(\frac{N/4 - c}{f}\right)h = 4 + \left(\frac{17.5 - 10}{12}\right)4 = 4 + 2.5 = 6.5 \text{ marks.}$$

Q_3 : $3\left(\frac{N}{4}\right) = 3\left(\frac{70}{4}\right) = 52.5$ $\therefore$ Q_3 = size of 52.5th item

$\therefore$ Q_3 class is 18—20.

$\therefore$ $$Q_3 = L + \left(\frac{3N/4 - c}{f}\right)h = 18 + \left(\frac{52.5 - 52}{8}\right)2 = 18 + 0.125 = 18.125 \text{ marks.}$$

$$\text{Coeff. of Q.D.} = \frac{Q_3 - Q_1}{Q_3 + Q_1} = \frac{18.125 - 6.5}{18.125 + 6.5} = \frac{11.625}{24.625} = \textbf{0.4721.}$$

Example 4. *For the following data, calculate :*

(i) the coefficient of range

(ii) interquartile range, and

(iii) percentile range

Marks	*5—9*	*10—14*	*15—19*	*20—24*
No. of students	*1*	*3*	*8*	*5*
Marks	*25—29*	*30—34*	*35—39*	
No. of students	*4*	*2*	*2*	

(KU 1995 C)

Sol. The first and the last classes in the exclusive form are 4.5—9.5 and 34.5—39.5 respectively.

$$\therefore \quad \text{Coeff. of range} = \frac{L-S}{L+S} = \frac{39.5-4.5}{39.5+4.5} = \frac{35}{44} = \mathbf{0.7955.}$$

Calculation of Q_1, Q_3, P_{10}, P_{90}

Marks	*No. of students* f	*c.f.*
4.5—9.5	1	1
9.5—14.5	3	4
14.5—19.5	8	12
19.5—24.5	5	17
24.5—29.5	4	21
29.5—34.5	2	23
34.5—39.5	2	25 = N
	N = 25	

Q_1 : $\frac{N}{4} = \frac{25}{4} = 6.25.$ $\quad \therefore \quad Q_1$ = size of 6.25th item

$\therefore \quad Q_1$ class is 14.5—19.5

$$\therefore \quad Q_1 = L + \left(\frac{N/4 - c}{f}\right)h = 14.5 + \left(\frac{6.25-4}{8}\right)5$$

$$= 14.5 + 1.4063 = 15.9063 \text{ marks}$$

Q_3 : $3\left(\frac{N}{4}\right) = 3\left(\frac{25}{4}\right) = 18.75$ $\quad \therefore \quad Q_3$ = size of 18.75th item

$\therefore \quad Q_3$ class is 24.5--29.5

$$\therefore \quad Q_3 = L + \left(\frac{3(N/4) - c}{f}\right)h = 24.5 + \left(\frac{18.75-17}{4}\right)5$$

$$= 24.5 + 2.1875 = 26.6875 \text{ marks}$$

$\therefore$ Interquartite range

$$= Q_3 - Q_1 = 26.6875 - 15.9063 = \mathbf{10.7812 \text{ marks}}$$

Percentile range is defined as $P_{90} - P_{10}$.

P_{10}: $10\left(\frac{N}{100}\right) = 10\left(\frac{25}{100}\right) = 2.5$ $\therefore$ P_{10} = size of 2.5th item

$\therefore$ P_{10} class is 9.5—14.5.

$$\therefore \quad P_{10} = L + \left(\frac{10\,(N/100) - c}{f}\right)h = 9.5 + \left(\frac{2.5 - 1}{3}\right)5 = 9.5 + 2.5 = 12 \text{ marks.}$$

P_{90}: $90\left(\frac{N}{100}\right) = 90\left(\frac{25}{100}\right) = 22.5$ $\therefore$ P_{90} = size of 22.5th item

$\therefore$ P_{90} class is 29.5—34.5.

$$\therefore \quad P_{90} = L + \left(\frac{90\,(N/100) - c}{f}\right)h$$

$$= 29.5 + \left(\frac{22.5 - 21}{2}\right)5 = 29.5 + 3.75 = 33.25 \text{ marks}$$

$\therefore$ Percentile range = $P_{90} - P_{10}$ = 33.25 – 12 = **21.25 marks.**

10. MERITS OF Q.D.

1. It is simple to understand.
2. It is easy to calculate.
3. It is well-defined.
4. It helps in studying the middle 50% items in the series.
5. It is not affected by the extreme items.
6. It is useful in the case of open end classes.

11. DEMERITS OF Q.D.

1. It is not based on all the items.
2. It is not capable of further algebraic treatment.
3. It does not have sampling stability.

EXERCISE 2

1. Find the Q.D. and its coefficient for the given data regarding the age of 7 students.

   Age (in years) : 17, 19, 22, 26, 19, 28, 17.

2. Compare the following two series of figures in respect of their dispersion by quartile measures :

Height (in inches)	58	56	62	61	63	64	65	59	62	65	55
Weight (in pounds)	117	112	127	123	125	130	106	119	121	132	108

3. Find the coefficient of Q.D. for the following frequency distribution :

Age (in years)	15	16	17	18	19	20
No. of students	241	500	600	550	700	750

4. Calculate the coefficient of Q.D. of the marks of 39 students in statistics given below :

Marks	0—5	5—10	10—15	15—20	20—25	25—30
No. of students	4	6	8	12	7	2

5. For the following data, calculate Q.D. and its coefficient :

Class	10—20	20—30	30—40	40—50	50—60	60—70
Frequency	3	5	15	10	4	2

(*MDU 1996*)

6. Calculate the values of Q.D. and its coefficient for the following data :

Size	4—8	8—12	12—16	16—20	20—24
Frequency	6	10	18	30	15
Size	24—28	28—32	32—36	36—40	
Frequency	12	10	6	2	

7. Calculate Quartile Deviation and its coefficient for the data given below :

Daily wages (in Rs.)	1—5	6—10	11—15	16—20
No. of workers	3	8	14	11
Daily wages (in Rs.)	21—25	26—30	31—35	36—40
No. of workers	7	6	5	2

8. Find Quartile deviation for the following data :

Mid-point	2	3	4	5	6	7	8	9	10	11
Frequency	2	3	5	6	8	12	16	7	5	4

(*KU 2002 C*)

Answers

1. Q.D. = 4.5 years, Coeff. of Q.D. = 0.2093
2. Coeff. of Q.D. (Height) = 0.0492,
   Coeff. of Q.D. (Weight) = 0.0628
   Variability is more in the II series.
3. 0.0555
4. 0.3356
5. Q.D. = 7.5416, Coeff. of Q.D. = 0.1948
6. Q.D. = 5.2083, Coeff. of Q.D. = 0.2643
7. Q.D. = 6.6072, Coeff. of Q.D. = 0.3635
8. Q.D. = 1.406.

III. MEAN DEVIATION (M.D.)

12. DEFINITION

Mean deviation is also called **average deviation**. The **mean deviation** of a statistical data is defined as the arithmetic mean of the numerical values of the deviations of items from some average. Generally, A.M. and median are used in calculating mean deviation. Let '*a*' stand for the average used for calculating M.D.

For an **individual series**, the M.D. is given by

$$\textbf{M.D.} = \frac{\sum_{i=1}^{n} |x_i - a|}{n} = \frac{\Sigma|x - a|}{n}$$

where $x_1, x_2, \ldots\ldots, x_n$ are the values of the variable, under consideration.

For a **frequency distribution,**

$$\textbf{M.D.} = \frac{\sum_{i=1}^{n} f_i |x_i - a|}{N} = \frac{\Sigma f|x - a|}{N}$$

where f_i is the frequency of x_i $(1 \le i \le n)$.

When the values of the variable are given in the form of classes, then their respective mid-points are taken as the values of the variable.

Median is used in calculating M.D., because of its property that the sum of numerical values of deviations of items from median is always least. So, if median is used in the calculation of M.D., its value would come out to be least. M.D. is also calculated by using A.M. because of its simplicity and popularity. In problems, it is generally given as to which average is to be used in the calculation of M.D. If it is not given, then either of the two can be made use of.

13. COEFFICIENT OF M.D.

For comparing two or more series for variability, the corresponding relative measure, 'Coefficient of M.D.', is used. This is defined as :

$$\textbf{Coeff. of M.D.} = \frac{\textbf{M.D.}}{\textbf{Average}}.$$

If M.D. is calculated about A.M., then M.D. is written as M.D.$(\bar{x})$. Similarly, M.D.(Median) would mean that median has been used in calculating M.D.

∴ We can write

$$\textbf{Coeff. of M.D.}(\bar{x}) = \frac{\textbf{M.D.}(\bar{x})}{\bar{x}}$$

$$\textbf{Coeff. of M.D.(Median)} = \frac{\textbf{M.D.(Median)}}{\textbf{Median}}$$

WORKING RULES TO FIND M.D. ($\bar{x}$)

Rule I. *In case of an individual series, first find $\bar{x}$ by using the formula $\bar{x} = \frac{\Sigma x}{n}$. In the second step, find the values of $x - \bar{x}$. In the next step, find the numerical values $|x - \bar{x}|$ of $x - \bar{x}$. Find the sum $\Sigma|x - \bar{x}|$ of these numerical values $|x - \bar{x}|$. Divide this sum by n to get the value of M.D.($\bar{x}$).*

Rule II. *In case of a frequency distribution, first find $\bar{x}$ by using the formula $\bar{x} = \frac{\Sigma fx}{N}$. In the second step, find the values of $x - \bar{x}$. In the next step, find the numerical values $|x - \bar{x}|$ of $x - \bar{x}$. Find the products of the values of $|x - \bar{x}|$ and their corresponding frequencies. Find the sum $\Sigma f|x - \bar{x}|$ of these products. Divide this sum by N to get the value of M.D.($\bar{x}$).*

Rule III. *If the values of the variable are given in the form of classes, then their respective mid-points are taken as the values of the variable.*

Rule IV. *To find the coefficient of M.D.($\bar{x}$), divide M.D.($\bar{x}$) by $\bar{x}$.*

Remark. Similar working rules are followed to find the values of M.D.(median) and coefficient of M.D. (median).

Example 1. *Find M.D.($\bar{x}$) and M.D.(median) for the following statistical series :*

7, 10, 12, 13, 15, 20, 21, 27, 30, 35.

Sol. **Calculation of M.D. ($\bar{x}$)**

S. No.	*x*	$x - \bar{x}$ $\bar{x} = 19$	$\lvert x - \bar{x} \rvert$
1	7	− 12	12
2	10	− 9	9
3	12	− 7	7
4	13	− 6	6
5	15	− 4	4
6	20	1	1
7	21	2	2
8	27	8	8
9	30	11	11
10	35	16	16
$n = 10$	$\Sigma x = 190$		$\Sigma\lvert x - \bar{x}\rvert = 76$

$$\bar{x} = \frac{\Sigma x}{n} = \frac{190}{10} = 19.$$

$$\therefore \quad \text{M.D.}(\bar{x}) = \frac{\Sigma|x - \bar{x}|}{n} = \frac{76}{10} = \mathbf{7.6}.$$

Calculation of M.D.(median)

S. No.	x	x – median median = 17.5	| x – median |
1	7	– 10.5	10.5
2	10	– 7.5	7.5
3	12	– 5.5	5.5
4	13	– 4.5	4.5
5	15	– 2.5	2.5
6	20	2.5	2.5
7	21	3.5	3.5
8	27	9.5	9.5
9	30	12.5	12.5
10	35	17.5	17.5
n = 10			Σ| x – median | = 76

$$\frac{n+1}{2} = \frac{10+1}{2} = \mathbf{5.5}$$

$$\therefore \quad \text{Median} = \frac{\text{Size of 5th item} + \text{size of 6th item}}{2} = \frac{15+20}{2} = 17.5$$

$$\therefore \quad \text{M.D.(median)} = \frac{\Sigma|x - \text{median}|}{n} = \frac{76}{10} = \mathbf{7.6.}$$

Example 2. *Find the M.D. from A.M. for the following data :*

x	*3*	*5*	*7*	*9*	*11*	*13*
f	*2*	*7*	*10*	*9*	*5*	*2*

Sol. **Calculation of M.D. ($\overline{x}$)**

x	f	fx	$x - \overline{x}$	$\|x - \overline{x}\|$	$f\|x - \overline{x}\|$
3	2	6	– 4.8	4.8	9.6
5	7	35	– 2.8	2.8	19.6
7	10	70	– 0.8	0.8	8.0
9	9	81	1.2	1.2	10.8
11	5	55	3.2	3.2	16.0
13	2	26	5.2	5.2	10.4
	N = 35	Σfx = 273			$\Sigma f\|x - \overline{x}\|$ = 74.4

$$\overline{x} = \frac{\Sigma fx}{N} = \frac{273}{35} = 7.8$$

Now $$\text{M.D.}(\overline{x}) = \frac{\Sigma f|x - \overline{x}|}{N} = \frac{74.4}{35} = \mathbf{2.1257.}$$

Example 3. *Find the coeff. of M.D.(Median) for the following frequency distribution :*

Marks	*0—10*	*10—20*	*20—30*	*30—40*	*40—50*
No. of students	*5*	*8*	*15*	*16*	*6*

Sol. **Calculation of M.D.(Median)**

Marks	*No. of students* (*f*)	*c.f.*	*Mid-points of classes* *x*	*x–median* (*med.* = 28)	$\lvert x - med. \rvert$	$f\lvert x - med. \rvert$
0—10	5	5	5	– 23	23	115
10—20	8	13	15	– 13	13	104
20—30	15	28	25	– 3	3	45
30—40	16	44	35	7	7	112
40—50	6	50 = N	45	17	17	102
	N = 50					$\Sigma f\lvert x - med. \rvert$ = 478

Median = size of 50/2th item = size of 25th item.

∴ Median class is 20—30

$$\text{Median} = L + \left(\frac{N/2 - c}{f}\right)h = 20 + \left(\frac{25 - 13}{15}\right) 10 = 28$$

Now
$$\text{M.D.(Median)} = \frac{\Sigma f\,|x - \text{median}|}{N} = \frac{478}{50} = 9.56 \text{ marks.}$$

$$\therefore \text{ Coeff. of M.D.(Median)} = \frac{\text{M.D.(Median)}}{\text{Median}} = \frac{9.56}{28} = \mathbf{0.3414.}$$

14. SHORT-CUT METHOD FOR M.D.

We know that the calculation of M.D. involve taking of deviations of items from some average. If the value of the average under consideration is a whole number, we can easily take the deviations and proceed without any difficulty. But in case, the value of the average comes out to be in decimal like 18.6747, the calculation of M.D. would become quite tedious. In such a case, we would have to approximate the value of the average up to one or two places of decimal for otherwise we would have to bear the heavy calculation work involved. If the value of the average is in decimal, the following short-cut method is preferred.

$$\mathbf{M.D.} = \frac{(\Sigma fx)_A - (\Sigma fx)_B - ((\Sigma f)_A - (\Sigma f)_B)\,a}{N}$$

where '*a*' is the average about which M.D. is to be calculated. In this formula, suffixes A and B denote the sums corresponding to the values of $x \geq a$ and $x < a$ respectively.

This formula can also be used for an individual series, by taking '*f*' equal to 1 for each *x*, in the series. In this case, the formula reduces to

$$\mathbf{M.D.} = \frac{(\Sigma x)_A - (\Sigma x)_B - ((n)_A - (n)_B)\,a}{n}$$

where $(n)_A$ and $(n)_B$ are the number of items whose values are greater than or equal to *a* and less than *a* respectively.

If short-cut method is to be used to find M.D.($\bar{x}$), then it is advisable to use *direct method* to find $\bar{x}$, because we would be needing $(\Sigma fx)_A$ and $(\Sigma fx)_B$ in the calculation of M.D.($\bar{x}$).

Example 4. *Calculate M.D.(Median) for the following data :*

x : 4, 6, 10, 12, 18, 19.

Sol. **Calculation of M.D. (Median)**

S. No.	x		x – median	| x – median |
1	4		–7	7
2	6	$(\Sigma x)_B$	–5	5
3	10	= 20	–1	1
4	12		1	1
5	18	$(\Sigma x)_A$	7	7
6	19	= 49	8	8
n = 6				Σ| x – median | = 29

$$\text{Median} = \text{size of } \frac{6+1}{2} \text{th item} = \text{size of 3.5th item} = \frac{10+12}{2} = 11.$$

Direct Method

$$\text{M.D. (Median)} = \frac{\Sigma|x - \text{median}|}{n} = \frac{29}{6} = \mathbf{4.8333.}$$

Short-cut Method

$$\text{M.D. (Median)} = \frac{(\Sigma x)_A - (\Sigma x)_B - ((n)_A - (n)_B)\text{ median}}{n}$$

$$= \frac{49 - 20 - (3-3).11}{6} = \frac{29}{6} = \mathbf{4.8333.}$$

Example 5. *Calculate the mean deviation from the median for the following distribution :*

x	20	40	60	80	100	120	140	160	180	200	220	240
f	3	13	43	102	175	220	204	139	69	25	6	1

(KU 1999 C)

Sol. **Calculation of M.D. (median)**

S. No.	x	f		c.f.	fx	
1	20	3		3	60	
2	40	13		16	520	
3	60	43	$(\Sigma f)_B$	59	2580	$(\Sigma fx)_B$
4	80	102	= 556	161	8160	= 55220
5	100	175		336	17500	
6	120	220		556	26400	
7	140	204		760	28560	
8	160	139		899	22240	
9	180	69	$(\Sigma f)_A$	968	12420	$(\Sigma fx)_A$
10	200	25	= 444	993	5000	= 69780
11	220	6		999	1320	
12	240	1		1000	240	
		N = 1000			Σfx = 125000	

$$\frac{N+1}{2} = \frac{1000+1}{2} = 500.5$$

$$\therefore \quad \text{Median} = \text{size of 500.5th item} = \frac{120+120}{2} = 120.$$

$$\text{Now, M.D. (median)} = \frac{(\Sigma fx)_A - (\Sigma fx)_B - [(\Sigma f)_A - (\Sigma f)_B] \text{ median}}{N}$$

$$= \frac{69780 - 55220 - (444 - 556)\,120}{1000} = \frac{28000}{1000} = \mathbf{28.}$$

Example 6. *Calculate M.D.($\bar{x}$) and its coefficient for the following data :*

Profit (in Rs.)	*No. of firms*	*Profit (in Rs.)*	*No. of firms*
5000—6000	*10*	*0—1000*	*4*
4000—5000	*15*	*– 1000 to 0*	*6*
3000—4000	*30*	*– 2000 to – 1000*	*8*
2000—3000	*10*	*– 3000 to – 2000*	*10*
1000—2000	*5*		

Sol. **Calculation of M.D.($\bar{x}$)**

Profit (in Rs.)	*No. of firms (f)*	*x*	*fx*
– 3000 to – 2000	10	– 2500	– 25000
– 2000 to – 1000	8	– 1500	– 12000
– 1000 to 0	6 $(\Sigma f)_B = 33$	– 500	– 3000 $(\Sigma fx)_B = -30500$
0—1000	4	500	2000
1000—2000	5	1500	7500
2000—3000	10	2500	25000
3000—4000	30 $(\Sigma f)_A = 65$	3500	105000 $(\Sigma fx)_A = 252500$
4000—5000	15	4500	67500
5000—6000	10	5500	55000
	N = 98		Σfx = 222000

$$\bar{x} = \frac{\Sigma fx}{N} = \frac{222000}{98} = \text{Rs. } 2265.3061$$

$$\text{Now} \quad \text{M.D.}(\bar{x}) = \frac{(\Sigma fx)_A - (\Sigma fx)_B - [(\Sigma f)_A - (\Sigma f)_B]\,\bar{x}}{N}$$

$$= \frac{252500 - (-30500) - (65 - 33)\,2265.3061}{98}$$

$$= \frac{210510.21}{98} = \textbf{Rs. 2148.0633}$$

$$\text{Coeff. of M.D.}(\bar{x}) = \frac{\text{M.D.}(\bar{x})}{\bar{x}} = \frac{2148.0633}{2265.3061} = \mathbf{0.9482.}$$

15. MERITS OF M.D.

1. It is simple to understand.
2. It is easy to compute.
3. It is well-defined.
4. It is based on all the items.
5. It is not unduly affected by the extreme items.
6. It can be calculated by using any average.

16. DEMERITS OF M.D.

1. It is not capable of further algebraic treatment.
2. It does not take into account the signs of the deviations of items from the average value.

EXERCISE 3

1. Calculate M.D.($\bar{x}$) and its coefficient for the following individual series :
21, 23, 25, 28, 30, 32, 38, 39, 46, 48.

2. Compute M.D.($\bar{x}$) for the following data :

Marks	10	15	20	25	30
No. of students	2	4	6	8	5

3. Find the mean deviation about A.M. for the following data :

x	2	3	5	9	10
f	3	6	10	7	4

4. Find the mean deviation about median for the following data :

x	6	12	18	24	30	36	42
f	4	7	9	18	15	10	5

5. The following table gives the monthly distribution of wages of 1000 employees in a certain factory :

Wages (in Rs.)	20	40	60	80	100	120
No. of employees	3	13	43	102	175	220
Wages (in Rs.)	140	160	180	200	220	240
No. of employees	204	139	69	25	6	1

Calculate coefficients of M.D. about mean and median.

6. Find the mean deviation about the mean for the following frequency distribution :

Class	0—4	4—8	8—12	12—16	16—20
f	4	6	8	5	2

7. Calculate the mean deviation about median and its coefficient for the following frequency distribution :

Marks	0—10	10—20	20—30	30—40	40—50
No. of students	6	7	15	16	6

8. Calculate M.D. about A.M. and also about median for the following data :

Income per week (in Rs.)	20—30	30—40	40—50	50—60	60—70
No. of families	120	201	150	75	25

9. Calculate the M.D.$(\bar{x})$ for the following data regarding the difference in age between husbands and wives :

Difference in age (in years)	0—5	5—10	10—15	15—20
No. of couples	449	705	507	281
Difference in age (in years)	20—25	25—30	30—35	35—40
No. of couples	109	52	16	4

10. Calculate coefficient of mean deviation and coefficient of median deviation for the following :

Marks	140—150	150—160	160—170
No. of students	4	6	10
Marks	170—180	180—190	190—200
No. of students	18	9	3

11. Find M.D.$(\bar{x})$ for the following distribution :

Class	15—24	25—34	35—44	45—54	55—64
Frequency	4000	16000	28000	33000	28000

12. Find M.D. and coefficient of M.D. about median for the following data :

Size	5	6	7	8	9	10
Frequency	8	12	18	8	3	1

13. Calculate median and M.D.(Median) for the following frequency distribution :

Age (in years)	*No. of persons*	*Age (in years)*	*No. of persons*
1—5	7	26—30	18
6—10	10	31—35	10
11—15	16	36—40	5
16—20	32	41—45	1
21—25	24		

Answers

1. M.D.($\bar{x}$) = 7.8, coeff. of M.D.($\bar{x}$) = 0.2364.
2. M.D.($\bar{x}$) = 5.12 marks.
3. 2.54
4. 7.5
5. Coeff. of M.D.($\bar{x}$) = 0.2285, Coeff. of M.D.(median) = 0.2333
6. 3.84
7. 9.76 marks, 0.3485.
8. M.D.($\bar{x}$) = Rs. 9.22, M.D.(median) = Rs. 9.07.
9. M.D.($\bar{x}$) = 5.34 years.
10. Coeff. of M.D.($\bar{x}$) = 0.062, Coeff. of M.D.(median) = 0.059.
11. M.D.($\bar{x}$) = 9.656.
12. M.D.(median) = 0.9, Coeff. of M.D.(median) = 0.1286.
13. Median = 19.95 years, M.D.(median) = 7.1 years.

IV. STANDARD DEVIATION (S.D.)

17. DEFINITION

It is the most important measure of dispersion. It finds indispensable place in advanced statistical methods. The **standard deviation** of a statistical data is defined as the positive square root of the A.M. of the squared deviations of items from the A.M. of the series under consideration. The S.D. is often denoted by the greek letter 'σ'.

For an **individual series**, the S.D. is given by

$$\text{S.D.} = \sqrt{\frac{\sum_{i=1}^{n} (x_i - \bar{x})^2}{n}} = \sqrt{\frac{\Sigma (x - \bar{x})^2}{n}}$$

where $x_1, x_2, \ldots\ldots, x_n$ are the value of the variable, under consideration.

For a **frequency distribution**,

$$\text{S.D.} = \sqrt{\frac{\sum_{i=1}^{n} f_i (x_i - \bar{x})^2}{N}} = \sqrt{\frac{\Sigma f(x - \bar{x})^2}{N}}$$

where f_i is the frequency of x_i $(1 \le i \le n)$.

When the values of the variable are given in the form of classes, then their respective mid-points are taken as the values of the variable.

18. COEFFICIENT OF S.D., C.V., VARIANCE

For comparing two or more series for variability, the corresponding relative measure, called coefficient of S.D. is calculated. This measure is defined as :

$$\textbf{Coefficient of S.D.} = \frac{\text{S.D.}}{\bar{x}}.$$

The product of coefficient of S.D. and 100 is called as the *coefficient of variation*.

$$\therefore \quad \textbf{Coefficient of variation} = \left(\frac{\text{S.D.}}{\bar{x}}\right) 100.$$

This measure is denoted as C.V.

$$\therefore \quad \text{C.V.} = \left(\frac{\text{S.D.}}{\bar{x}}\right) 100.$$

In practical problems, we prefer comparing C.V. instead of comparing coefficient of S.D. The coefficient of variation is also represented as percentage. The square of S.D. is called the **variance** of the distribution.

WORKING RULES TO FIND S.D.

Rule I. *In case of an individual series, first find* $\bar{x}$ *by using the formula* $\bar{x} = \frac{\Sigma x}{n}$. *In the second step, find the values of* $x - \bar{x}$. *In the next step, find the squares* $(x - \bar{x})^2$ *of the values of* $x - \bar{x}$. *Find the sum* $\Sigma (x - \bar{x})^2$ *of the values of* $(x - \bar{x})^2$. *Divide this sum by n. Take the positive square root of this to get the value of S.D.*

Rule II. *In case of a frequency distribution, first find* $\bar{x}$ *by using the formula* $\bar{x} = \frac{\Sigma fx}{N}$. *In the second step, find the values of* $x - \bar{x}$. *In the next step, find the squares* $(x - \bar{x})^2$ *of the values of* $x - \bar{x}$. *Find the products of the values of* $(x - \bar{x})^2$ *and their corresponding frequencies. Find the sum* $\Sigma f(x - \bar{x})^2$ *of these products. Divide this sum by N. Take the positive square root of this to get the value of S.D.*

Rule III. *If the values of the variable are given in the form of classes, then their respective mid-points are taken as the values of the variable.*

Rule IV. (i) *Coeff. of S.D.* $= \frac{S.D.}{A.M.}$

(ii) *Coeff. of variation (C.V.)* $= \frac{S.D.}{A.M.} \times 100$

(iii) *Variance* $= (S.D.)^2$.

Example 1. *Find the S.D. and C.V. for the following data :*

4, 6, 10, 12, 18.

Sol. **Calculation of S.D. and C.V.**

S. No.	x	$x - \bar{x}$ $\bar{x} = 10$	$(x - \bar{x})^2$
1	4	−6	36
2	6	−4	16
3	10	0	0
4	12	2	4
5	18	8	64
$n = 5$	$\Sigma x = 50$		$\Sigma(x - \bar{x})^2 = 120$

$$\bar{x} = \frac{\Sigma x}{n} = \frac{50}{5} = 10.$$

Now $$\text{S.D.} = \sqrt{\frac{\Sigma (x - \bar{x})^2}{n}} = \sqrt{\frac{120}{5}} = \sqrt{24} = \mathbf{4.8989.}$$

$$\text{C.V.} = \left(\frac{\text{S.D.}}{\bar{x}}\right) 100 = \left(\frac{4.8989}{10}\right) 100 = \mathbf{48.989\%.}$$

Example 2. *Calculate S.D. and C.V. for the following data :*

x	*5*	*15*	*25*	*35*	*45*	*55*
f	*12*	*18*	*27*	*20*	*17*	*6*

Sol. **Calculation of S.D. and C.V.**

x	f	fx	$x - \bar{x}$	$(x - \bar{x})^2$	$f(x - \bar{x})^2$
5	12	60	– 23	529	6348
15	18	270	– 13	169	3042
25	27	675	– 3	9	243
35	20	700	7	49	980
45	17	765	17	289	4913
55	6	330	27	729	4374
	N = 100	$\Sigma fx = 2000$			$\Sigma f(x - \bar{x})^2 = 19900$

$$\bar{x} = \frac{\Sigma fx}{\text{N}} = \frac{2800}{100} = 28.$$

Now $$\text{S.D.} = \sqrt{\frac{\Sigma f(x - \bar{x})^2}{\text{N}}} = \sqrt{\frac{19900}{100}} = \sqrt{199} = \mathbf{14.1067.}$$

$$\text{C.V.} = \left(\frac{\text{S.D.}}{\bar{x}}\right) 100 = \left(\frac{14.1067}{28}\right) 100 = \mathbf{50.3811\%.}$$

Example 3. *Calculate S.D. and C.V. for the following frequency distribution :*

Class	*Frequency*	*Class*	*Frequency*
4—8	*11*	*24—28*	*9*
8—12	*13*	*28—32*	*17*
12—16	*16*	*32—36*	*6*
16—20	*14*	*36—40*	*4*
20—24	*14*		

Sol. **Calculation of S.D. and C.V.**

Class	x	f	fx	$x-\bar{x}$	$(x-\bar{x})^2$	$f(x-\bar{x})^2$
4—8	6	11	66	– 14	196	2156
8—12	10	13	130	– 10	100	1300
12—16	14	16	224	– 6	36	576
16—20	18	14	252	– 2	4	56
20—24	22	14	308	2	4	56
24—28	26	9	234	6	36	324
28—32	30	17	510	10	100	1700
32—36	34	6	204	14	196	1176
36—40	38	4	152	18	324	1296
		N = 104	Σfx = 2080			$\Sigma f(x-\bar{x})^2$ = 8640

$$\bar{x} = \frac{\Sigma fx}{N} = \frac{2080}{104} = 20.$$

Now $$\text{S.D.} = \sqrt{\frac{\Sigma f(x-\bar{x})^2}{N}} = \sqrt{\frac{8640}{104}} = \mathbf{9.1146.}$$

$$\text{C.V.} = \left(\frac{\text{S.D.}}{\bar{x}}\right)100 = \left(\frac{9.1146}{20}\right)100 = \mathbf{45.573\%.}$$

Example 4. *The mean of 5 observations is 4 and variance is 5.2. If three of the five observations are 1, 2 and 6, find the other two.* (KU 2001 C)

Sol. Given observations are 1, 2, 6. Let the other two observations be a and b.

$$\text{A.M.} = 4 \Rightarrow \frac{\Sigma x}{n} = 4$$

$$\Rightarrow \frac{1+2+6+a+b}{5} = 4 \Rightarrow a+b = 20-9 = 11$$

$$\therefore \quad a+b = 11 \quad \text{...(1)}$$

Also $$\text{Variance} = \frac{\Sigma(x-\bar{x})^2}{n}$$

$$\Sigma(x-\bar{x})^2 = \Sigma(x^2+\bar{x}^2-2n\bar{x}) = \Sigma x^2 + n\bar{x}^2 - 2\bar{x}\,\Sigma x$$

$$= \Sigma x^2 + n\bar{x}^2 - 2\bar{x}\left(\frac{\Sigma x}{n}\right)n = \Sigma x^2 + n\bar{x}^2 - 2n\bar{x}^2 = \Sigma x^2 - n\bar{x}^2.$$

$$\therefore \quad \text{Variance} = \frac{\Sigma x^2 - n\bar{x}^2}{n} = \frac{\Sigma x^2}{n} - \bar{x}^2.$$

$$\therefore \quad 5.2 = \frac{1^2+2^2+6^2+a^2+b^2}{5} - (4)^2 \Rightarrow 5.2 = \frac{41+a^2+b^2}{5} - 16$$

$$\Rightarrow a^2+b^2+41 = (21.2)\times 5 = 106 \Rightarrow a^2+b^2 = 65 \quad \text{...(2)}$$

Solving (1) and (2), we get a = **4**, b = **7.**

19. SHORT-CUT METHOD FOR S.D.

We have seen in the above examples that the calculations of S.D. involves a lot of computation work. Even if the value of A.M. is a whole number, the calculations are not so simple. In case, A.M. is in decimal, then the calculation work would become more tedious. In problems, where A.M. is expected to be in decimal, we shall use this method, which is based on deviations (or step deviations) of items in the series.

For an individual series $x_1, x_2, ..., x_n$, we have

$$\text{S.D.} = \sqrt{\frac{\sum_{i=1}^{n} u_i^2}{n} - \left(\frac{\sum_{i=1}^{n} u_i}{n}\right)^2} \cdot h = \sqrt{\frac{\Sigma u^2}{n} - \left(\frac{\Sigma u}{n}\right)^2} \cdot h$$

where $u_i = \frac{x_i - A}{h}$, $1 \le i \le n$.

For a frequency distribution, this formula takes the form

$$\text{S.D.} = \sqrt{\frac{\sum_{i=1}^{n} f_i u_i^2}{N} - \left(\frac{\sum_{i=1}^{n} f_i u_i}{N}\right)^2} \cdot h = \sqrt{\frac{\Sigma fu^2}{N} - \left(\frac{\Sigma fu}{N}\right)^2} \cdot h$$

where f_i is the frequency of x_i $(1 \le i \le n)$ and $u_i = \frac{x_i - A}{h}$, $1 \le i \le n$.

A and h are constants to be chosen suitably. This method is also known as *step deviation method*.

In practical problems, it is advisable to first take deviations 'd' of the values of the variable (x) from some suitable number 'A'. Then we see if there is any common factor greater than one, in the values of the deviations. If there is a common factor h (> 1), then we calculate $u = \frac{d}{h} = \frac{x - A}{h}$ in the next column. In case, there is no common factor greater one, then we take $h = 1$ and u becomes $u = \frac{d}{1} = x - A$.

In this case, the formula reduces as given below :

$$\text{S.D.} = \sqrt{\frac{\Sigma d^2}{n} - \left(\frac{\Sigma d}{n}\right)^2} \qquad \textbf{(Individual Series)}$$

$$\text{S.D.} = \sqrt{\frac{\Sigma fd^2}{N} - \left(\frac{\Sigma fd}{N}\right)^2} \qquad \textbf{(Frequency Distribution)}$$

where d = x – A and A is any constant, to be chosen suitably.

WORKING RULES TO FIND S.D.

Rule I. *In case of an individual series, choose a number A. Find deviations $d(= x - A)$ of items from A. Find the squares 'd^2' of the values of d. Find S.D. by using the formula*

$$\sqrt{\frac{\Sigma d^2}{n} - \left(\frac{\Sigma d}{n}\right)^2}.$$

If some common factor h (> 1) is available in the values of d, then we calculate 'u' by dividing the values of d by h. Find the squares 'u^2' of the values of u. Find S.D. by using the formula : $\sqrt{\frac{\Sigma u^2}{n} - \left(\frac{\Sigma u}{n}\right)^2} \times h.$

Rule II. *In case of a frequency distribution, choose a number A. Find deviations $d(= x - A)$ of items from A. Find the products fd of f and d. Next, find the products of fd and d. Find the sums Σfd and Σfd^2. Find S.D. by using the formula :*

$$\sqrt{\frac{\Sigma fd^2}{N} - \left(\frac{\Sigma fd}{N}\right)^2}.$$

If some common factor h(> 1) is available in the values of d, then we calculate 'u' by dividing the values of d by h. Find the product fu of f and u. Next find the products of fu and u. Find the sums Σfu and Σfu^2. Find S.D. by using the formula :

$$\sqrt{\frac{\Sigma fu^2}{N} - \left(\frac{\Sigma fu}{N}\right)^2} \times h.$$

Rule III. *If the values of the variable are given in the form of classes, then their respective mid-points are taken as the values of the variable.*

Example 5. *Find the C.V. of the following individual series :*

2.76398, 4.76398, 6.76398, 8.76398, 12.76398, 10.76398.

Sol. **Calculation of S.D. and $\bar{x}$**

S.No.	*x*	*d = x – A* *A = 8.76398*	*u = d/h* *h = 2*	u^2
1	2.76398	– 6	– 3	9
2	4.76398	– 4	– 2	4
3	6.76398	– 2	– 1	1
4	8.76398	0	0	0
5	12.76398	4	2	4
6	10.76398	2	1	1
n = 6			$\Sigma u = -3$	$\Sigma u^2 = 19$

Now $\bar{x} = A + \left(\frac{\Sigma u}{n}\right)h = 8.76398 + \left(\frac{-3}{6}\right).2 = 7.76398$

$$\text{S.D.} = \sqrt{\frac{\Sigma u^2}{n} - \left(\frac{\Sigma u}{n}\right)^2} \,.\, h = \sqrt{\frac{19}{6} - \left(\frac{-3}{6}\right)^2} \times 2 = \sqrt{2.9167} \times 2 = 3.4157.$$

$$\therefore \quad \text{C.V.} = \left(\frac{\text{S.D.}}{\bar{x}}\right) 100 = \left(\frac{3.4157}{7.76398}\right) 100 = \mathbf{43.9942\%}.$$

Example 6. *Find the value of coefficient of variation for the following frequency distribution :*

Class	*0—5*	*5—10*	*10—15*	*15—20*	*20—25*
No. of items	*20*	*24*	*32*	*28*	*20*
Class	*25—30*	*30—35*	*35—40*	*40—45*	
No. of items	*16*	*34*	*10*	*16*	

Sol. **Calculation of S.D. and $\bar{x}$**

Class	*f*	*x*	$d = x - A$ $A = 22.5$	$u = d/h$ $h = 5$	*fu*	fu^2
0—5	20	2.5	– 20	– 4	– 80	320
5—10	24	7.5	– 15	– 3	– 72	216
10—15	32	12.5	– 10	– 2	– 64	128
15—20	28	17.5	– 5	– 1	– 28	28
20—25	20	22.5	0	0	0	0
25—30	16	27.5	5	1	16	16
30—35	34	32.5	10	2	68	136
35—40	10	37.5	15	3	30	90
40—45	16	42.5	20	4	64	256
	N = 200				Σfu = – 66	Σfu^2 = 1190

Now $$\bar{x} = \text{A} + \left(\frac{\Sigma fu}{\text{N}}\right) h = 22.5 + \left(\frac{-66}{200}\right) 5 = 20.85$$

$$\text{S.D.} = \sqrt{\frac{\Sigma fu^2}{\text{N}} - \left(\frac{\Sigma fu}{\text{N}}\right)^2} \,.\, h = \sqrt{\frac{1190}{200} - \left(\frac{-66}{200}\right)^2} \times 5 = \sqrt{5.8411} \times 5 = 12.0842.$$

$$\therefore \quad \text{C.V.} = \left(\frac{\text{S.D.}}{\bar{x}}\right) 100 = \left(\frac{12.0842}{20.85}\right) 100 = \mathbf{57.9578\%}.$$

Example 7. *The scores of two batsmen A and B for 20 innings are tabulated below. Which of the two may be regarded as the more consistent batsman ?*

Score		*50*	*51*	*52*	*53*	*54*	*55*	*56*	*57*
No. of	*A*	*1*	*0*	*0*	*4*	*3*	*6*	*3*	*3*
innings	*B*	*1*	*2*	*2*	*6*	*3*	*4*	*2*	*0*

(KU 1996 C)

Sol. **Calculation of C.V. for Batsman A**

Score x	*No. of innings* f	$d = x - A$ $A = 53$	$u = d$	fu	fu^2
50	1	– 3	– 3	– 3	9
51	0	– 2	– 2	0	0
52	0	– 1	– 1	0	0
53	4	0	0	0	0
54	3	1	1	3	3
55	6	2	2	12	24
56	3	3	3	9	27
57	3	4	4	12	48
	N = 20			$\Sigma fu = 33$	$\Sigma fu^2 = 111$

$$\bar{x} = A + \frac{\Sigma fu}{N} = 53 + \frac{33}{20} = 54.65$$

$$\text{S.D.} = \sqrt{\frac{\Sigma fu^2}{N} - \left(\frac{\Sigma fu}{N}\right)^2} = \sqrt{\frac{111}{20} - \left(\frac{33}{20}\right)^2} = 1.6815$$

$$\therefore \quad \text{C.V. for A} = \left(\frac{\text{S.D.}}{\bar{x}}\right) 100 = \left(\frac{1.6815}{54.65}\right) 100 = \mathbf{3.0768\%.}$$

Calculation of C.V. for Batsman B

Score x	*No. of innings* f	$u = d = x - A$ $A = 53$	fu	fu^2
50	1	– 3	– 3	9
51	2	– 2	– 4	8
52	2	– 1	– 2	2
53	6	0	0	0
54	3	1	3	3
55	4	2	8	16
56	2	3	6	18
57	0	4	0	0
	N = 20		$\Sigma fu = 8$	$\Sigma fu^2 = 56$

$$\bar{x} = A + \frac{\Sigma fu}{N} = 53 + \frac{8}{20} = 53.4$$

$$\text{S.D} = \sqrt{\frac{\Sigma fu^2}{N} - \left(\frac{\Sigma fu}{N}\right)^2} = \sqrt{\frac{56}{20} - \left(\frac{8}{20}\right)^2} = 1.6248$$

$$\therefore \quad \text{C.V. for B} = \left(\frac{\text{S.D.}}{\bar{x}}\right) 100 = \left(\frac{16248}{53.4}\right) 100 = \mathbf{3.0427\%.}$$

∴ C.V. for A > C.V. for B

∴ Batsman B is more consistent.

Example 8. *For the data given below, state which team (A or B) is more consistent.*

No. of goals scored in a match	*No. of matches*	
	A	*B*
0	*27*	*1*
1	*9*	*5*
2	*8*	*8*
3	*5*	*9*
4	*1*	*27*

Sol. **Calculation of C.V. for Team A**

x	f	$u = d = x - A$ $A = 2$	fu	fu^2
0	27	− 2	− 54	108
1	9	− 1	− 9	9
2	8	0	0	0
3	5	1	5	5
4	1	2	2	4
	N = 50		$\Sigma fu = -56$	$\Sigma fu^2 = 126$

$$\bar{x} = A + \frac{\Sigma fu}{N} = 2 + \left(\frac{-56}{50}\right) = 0.88$$

$$\text{S.D.} = \sqrt{\frac{\Sigma fu^2}{N} - \left(\frac{\Sigma fu}{N}\right)^2} = \sqrt{\frac{126}{50} - \left(\frac{-56}{50}\right)^2} = 1.1249$$

$$\therefore \quad \text{C.V. for team A} = \left(\frac{\text{S.D.}}{\bar{x}}\right) 100 = \frac{1.1249}{0.88} \times 100 = \mathbf{127.8295\%.}$$

Calculation of C.V. for Team B

x	f	$u = d = x - A$ $A = 2$	fu	fu^2
0	1	− 2	− 2	4
1	5	− 1	− 5	5
2	8	0	0	0
3	9	1	9	9
4	27	2	54	108
	N = 50		$\Sigma fu = 56$	$\Sigma fu^2 = 126$

$$\bar{x} = A + \frac{\Sigma fu}{N} = 2 + \frac{56}{50} = 3.12$$

$$\text{S.D.} = \sqrt{\frac{\Sigma fu^2}{N} - \left(\frac{\Sigma fu}{N}\right)^2} = \sqrt{\frac{126}{50} - \left(\frac{56}{50}\right)^2} = 1.1249$$

$\therefore$ C.V. for team B = $\left(\frac{\text{S.D.}}{\bar{x}}\right) 100 = \left(\frac{1.1249}{3.12}\right) 100 = \mathbf{36.0545\%}.$

$\therefore$ C.V. for team A > C.V. for team B.

$\therefore$ Team B is more consistent.

Example 9. *For the following data, find out which group is more uniform :*

Age group (years)	*No. of persons*	
	Group A	*Group B*
0—10	*5*	*7*
10—20	*15*	*12*
20—30	*20*	*22*
30—40	*25*	*30*
40—50	*18*	*20*
50—60	*10*	*5*
60—70	*7*	*4*

Sol. **Calculation of C.V. for group A**

Age group (years)	*No. of persons f*	*x*	*d = x – A* *A = 35*	*u = d/h* *h = 10*	*fu*	*fu*^{2}
0—10	5	5	– 30	– 3	– 15	45
10—20	15	15	– 20	– 2	– 30	60
20—30	20	25	– 10	– 1	– 20	20
30—40	25	35	0	0	0	0
40—50	18	45	10	1	18	18
50—60	10	55	20	2	20	40
60—70	7	65	30	3	21	63
	N = 100				$\Sigma fu = -6$	$\Sigma fu^2 = 246$

$$\bar{x} = A + \left(\frac{\Sigma fu}{N}\right) h = 35 + \left(\frac{-6}{100}\right) 10 = 34.4$$

$$\text{S.D.} = \sqrt{\frac{\Sigma fu^2}{N} - \left(\frac{\Sigma fu}{N}\right)^2} \,.\, h = \sqrt{\frac{246}{100} - \left(\frac{-6}{100}\right)^2} \,.\, 10 = 15.6729$$

$$\therefore \quad \text{C.V. for group A} = \frac{\text{S.D.}}{\bar{x}} \times 100$$

$$= \frac{15.6729}{34.4} \times 100 = \mathbf{45.5608\%}.$$

Calculation of C.V. for Group B

Age group (years)	*No. of person (f)*	*x*	*d = x − A* *A = 35*	*u = d/h* *h = 10*	*fu*	*fu²*
0—10	7	5	− 30	− 3	− 21	63
10—20	12	15	− 20	− 2	− 24	48
20—30	22	25	− 10	− 1	− 22	22
30—40	30	35	0	0	0	0
40—50	20	45	10	1	20	20
50—60	5	55	20	2	10	20
60—70	4	65	30	3	12	36
	N = 100				$\Sigma fu = -25$	$\Sigma fu^2 = 209$

$$\bar{x} = A + \left(\frac{\Sigma fu}{N}\right) h = 35 + \left(\frac{-25}{100}\right) 10 = 32.5$$

$$\text{S.D.} = \sqrt{\frac{\Sigma fu^2}{N} - \left(\frac{\Sigma fu}{N}\right)^2} \,.\, h = \sqrt{\frac{209}{100} - \left(\frac{-25}{100}\right)^2} \,.\, 10 = 14.2390$$

$\therefore$ C.V. for group B = $\frac{\text{S.D.}}{\bar{x}} \times 100 = \frac{14.2390}{32.5} \times 100 =$ **43.8123%**

$\therefore$ C.V. for Group A > C.V. for Group B.

$\therefore$ Group B is more uniform.

Example 10. *The A.M. of the runs scored by three batsmen A, B and C in the same series of 10 innings are 58, 48 and 12 respectively. The S.D. of their runs are respectively 15, 12 and 2. Who is the most consistent of the three ? If one of these is to be selected, who will be selected ?*

Sol. We have

$\bar{x}$ (A) = 58 σ (A) = 15

$\bar{x}$ (B) = 48 σ (B) = 12

$\bar{x}$ (C) = 12 σ (C) = 2

$\therefore$ C.V. (A) = $\left(\frac{15}{58}\right) 100 = 25.86\%$

C.V. (B) = $\left(\frac{12}{48}\right) 100 = 25.00\%$

C.V. (C) = $\left(\frac{2}{12}\right) 100 = 16.67\%$.

From this, we conclude that player C is most consistent, whereas the average score is highest for A. If the selection committee is to select the player on the basis of consistency of performance, then C would be selected. If on the other hand, scoring of highest runs is the basis, then A would be selected.

Example 11. *A student obtained the A.M. and S.D. of 100 observations as 40 and 5.1 respectively. Later on, it was discovered that he had wrongly copied down an observation as 50 instead of 40. Calculate the correct value of S.D.* (KU 2001)

Sol. We have

No. of items $= 100$

Incorrect $\bar{x}$ $= 40$

Incorrect S.D. $= 5.1$

Correct item $= 40$

Incorrect item $= 50$

Now $$\bar{x} = \frac{\Sigma x}{n}$$

$$\therefore \quad 40 = \frac{\text{Incorrect } \Sigma x}{100} \quad \text{or} \quad \text{Incorrect } \Sigma x = 4000$$

$$\therefore \quad \text{Correct } \Sigma x = 4000 - 50 + 40 = 3990$$

$$\therefore \quad \text{Correct } \bar{x} = \frac{3990}{100} = 39.9.$$

Now $$\text{S.D.} = \sqrt{\frac{\Sigma (x - \bar{x})^2}{n}} = \sqrt{\frac{\Sigma x^2}{n} - (\bar{x})^2}.$$

Note. The reader is advised to note this form of S.D. carefully.

$$\therefore \quad 5.1 = \sqrt{\frac{\text{Incorrect } \Sigma x^2}{100} - (40)^2}$$

or $$26.01 = \frac{\text{Incorrect } \Sigma x^2}{100} - 1600$$

$$\therefore \quad \text{Incorrect } \Sigma x^2 = (1626.01)\, 100 = 162601$$

$$\therefore \quad \text{Correct } \Sigma x^2 = 162601 - (50)^2 + (40)^2 = 161701$$

$$\text{Now Correct S.D.} = \sqrt{\frac{161701}{100} - (39.9)^2} = \sqrt{1617.01 - 1592.01} = \mathbf{5.}$$

20. S.D. OF COMBINED GROUP

Let σ_1 and σ_2 be the S.D. of two groups containing n_1 and n_2 items respectively. Let $\bar{x}_1$ and $\bar{x}_2$ be their respective A.M. Let $\bar{x}$ and σ be the A.M. and S.D. of the **combined group** respectively.

$$\therefore \quad \bar{x} = \frac{n_1\bar{x}_1 + n_2\,\bar{x}_2}{n_1 + n_2}$$

We define $$d_1 = \bar{x}_1 - \bar{x}$$
$$d_2 = \bar{x}_2 - \bar{x}$$

The S.D. of the combined group is given by the formula,

$$\sigma = \sqrt{\frac{\mathbf{n_1\,\sigma_1^{\,2} + n_2\,\sigma_2^{\,2} + n_1 d_1^{\,2} + n_2 d_2^{\,2}}}{\mathbf{n_1 + n_2}}}.$$

This result can be extended to even more than two groups.

Example 12. *The following data give the A.M. and S.D. of three sub-groups. Calculate the A.M. and S.D. of the combined group.*

Sub-group	*No. of men*	*Average wage (in Rs.)*	*S.D. (in Rs.)*
A	*50*	*61*	*8*
B	*100*	*70*	*9*
C	*120*	*80.5*	*10*

(KU 1997 C)

Sol. Let suffixes 1, 2, 3 be referred to information regarding groups A, B, C respectively.

$\therefore \quad n_1 = 50 \quad \bar{x}_1 = 61 \quad \sigma_1 = 8$

$n_2 = 100 \quad \bar{x}_2 = 70 \quad \sigma_2 = 9$

$n_3 = 120 \quad \bar{x}_3 = 80.5 \quad \sigma_3 = 10$

Let $\bar{x}$ and σ be the A.M.and S.D. of the combined group respectively.

Now
$$\bar{x}_1 = \frac{n_1 \bar{x}_1 + n_2\bar{x}_2 + n_3\bar{x}_3}{n_1 + n_2 + n_3}$$
$$= \frac{50\,(61) + 100\,(70) + 120\,(80.5)}{50 + 100 + 120} = \frac{19710}{270} = \text{Rs. } 73.$$

$\therefore$
$$d_1 = \bar{x}_1 - \bar{x} = 61 - 73 = -12$$
$$d_2 = \bar{x}_2 - \bar{x} = 70 - 73 = -3$$
$$d_3 = \bar{x}_3 - \bar{x} = 80.5 - 73 = 7.5.$$

Now
$$\sigma = \sqrt{\frac{n_1 \sigma_1^2 + n_2\sigma_2^2 + n_3\sigma_3^2 + n_1 d_1^2 + n_2 d_2^2 + n_3 d_3^2}{n_1 + n_2 + n_3}}$$
$$= \sqrt{\frac{50(8)^2 + 100(9)^2 + 120(10)^2 + 50(-12)^2 + 100(-3)^2 + 120(7.5)^2}{50 + 100 + 120}}$$
$$= \sqrt{\frac{3200 + 8100 + 12000 + 7200 + 900 + 6750}{270}}$$
$$= \sqrt{\frac{38150}{270}} = \sqrt{141.2963} = \mathbf{11.8868.}$$

Example 13. *Find the missing information from the following :*

	Group A	*Group B*	*Group C*	*Combined Group*
No. of items	*50*	*?*	*90*	*200*
A.M.	*113*	*?*	*115*	*116*
S.D.	*6*	*7*	*?*	*7.746*

Sol. Let suffixes 1, 2, 3 be referred to information regarding groups A, B, C respectively.

$\therefore \quad n_1 = 50 \qquad \bar{x}_1 = 113 \qquad \sigma_1 = 6$

$n_2 = ? \qquad \bar{x}_2 = ? \qquad \sigma_2 = 7$

$n_3 = 90 \qquad \bar{x}_3 = 115 \qquad \sigma_3 = ?$

The number of items in the combined group is 200.

$$\therefore \quad n_1 + n_2 + n_3 = 200$$

$$50 + n_2 + 90 = 200$$

$$n_2 = 200 - 140 = \mathbf{60.}$$

The A.M. $(\bar{x})$ of the combined group is 116.

$$\therefore \quad 116 = \frac{n_1\bar{x}_1 + n_2\bar{x}_2 + n_3\bar{x}_3}{n_1 + n_2 + n_3} = \frac{50(113) + 60\bar{x}_2 + 90(115)}{200}$$

$$\therefore \quad 23200 = 5650 + 60\bar{x}_2 + 10350$$

$$\bar{x}_2 = \frac{23200 - 16000}{60} = \frac{7200}{60} = \mathbf{120.}$$

Now

$$d_1 = \bar{x}_1 - \bar{x} = 113 - 116 = -3$$

$$d_2 = \bar{x}_2 - \bar{x} = 120 - 116 = 4$$

$$d_3 = \bar{x}_3 - \bar{x} = 115 - 116 = -1$$

The S.D. (σ) of the combined group is 7.746.

$$\therefore \quad 7.746 = \sqrt{\frac{n_1\sigma_1^2 + n_2\sigma_2^2 + n_3\sigma_3^2 + n_1d_1^2 + n_2d_2^2 + n_3d_3^2}{n_1 + n_2 + n_3}}$$

$$= \sqrt{\frac{50(6)^2 + 60(7)^2 + 90\sigma_3^2 + 50(-3)^2 + 60(4)^2 + 90(-1)^2}{200}}$$

$$\therefore \quad 60 = \frac{1800 + 2940 + 90\sigma_3^2 + 450 + 960 + 90}{200}$$

or

$$12000 = 90\sigma_3^2 + 6240$$

or

$$\sigma_3^2 = \frac{12000 - 6240}{90} = \frac{5760}{90} = 64$$

$$\therefore \quad \sigma_3 = \mathbf{8.}$$

Example 14. *An original frequency distribution with A.M. = 11 and variance 9.9 was lost but the following table derived from it was found. Construct the original table :*

Step Deviations	*– 2*	*– 1*	*0*	*1*	*2*
Frequency	*1*	*6*	*7*	*4*	*2*

Sol. Let u denotes the step deviations.

u	f	fu	fu^2
-2	1	-2	4
-1	6	-6	6
0	7	0	0
1	4	4	4
2	2	4	8
	N = 20	$\Sigma fu = 0$	$\Sigma fu^2 = 22$

Let $$u = \frac{x - A}{h}$$

Now $$\text{S.D.} = \sqrt{\frac{\Sigma fu^2}{N} - \left(\frac{\Sigma fu}{N}\right)^2}\; h$$

$\therefore$ $$\text{Variance} = (\text{S.D.})^2 = \left(\frac{\Sigma fu^2}{N} - \left(\frac{\Sigma fu}{N}\right)^2\right) h^2$$

or $$9.9 = \left(\frac{22}{20} - \left(\frac{0}{20}\right)^2\right) h^2 \quad \text{or} \quad \frac{99}{10} = \frac{22}{20} h^2$$

or $$h^2 = \left(\frac{99}{10}\right)\left(\frac{20}{22}\right) = 9$$

$\therefore$ $$h = 3.$$

Also $$\bar{x} = A + \left(\frac{\Sigma fu}{N}\right) h$$

$\therefore$ $$11 = A + \left(\frac{0}{20}\right) 3 = A + 0$$

$\therefore$ $$A = 11.$$

Now $$u = \frac{x - A}{h}$$

$\therefore$ $$x = A + uh$$

$\therefore$ Values of x are

$11 + (-2)3$, $11 + (-1)3$, $11 + (0)3$, $11 + (1)3$, $11 + (2)3$

or 5, 8, 11, 14, 17

$\therefore$ **The classes of values of the variable are**

3.5 – 6.5, 6.5– 9.5, 9.5– 12.5, 12.5 – 15.5, 15.5 – 18.5

$\therefore$ The original table is

Class	3.5—6.5	6.5—9.5	9.5—12.5	12.5—15.5	15.5—18.5
Frequency	1	6	7	4	2

21. RELATION BETWEEN MEASURES OF DISPERSION

It has been observed that in frequency distribution, the following relations hold.

1. Q.D. is approximately equal to $\frac{2}{3}$ S.D.

2. M.D. is approximately equal to $\frac{4}{5}$ S.D.

22. MERITS OF S.D.

1. It is simple to understand.
2. It is well-defined.
3. In the calculation of S.D., the signs of deviations of items are also taken into account.
4. It is based on all the items.
5. It is capable of further algebraic treatment.
6. It has sampling stability.
7. It is very useful in the study of "Tests of Significance".

23. DEMERITS OF S.D.

1. It is not easy to calculate.

2. It is unduly affected by the extreme items, because the squares of deviations of extreme items would be either extremely low or extremely high.

EXERCISE 4

1. (*a*) Find S.D. and C.V. for the following individual series :

4, 4, 4, 4, 4, 4, 4.

(*b*) The A.M. of the runs scored by three batsmen A, B, C in the same innings are 58, 48, 12 respectively. The S.D. of their runs are 15, 12 and 2 respectively. Find who is most consistent of the three.

2. Calculate mean, standard deviation and its coefficient for the following data :

Wages up to (in Rs.)	10	20	30	40	50	60	70	80
No. of persons	12	30	65	107	157	202	220	230

(*KU 1995*)

3.

Class interval	60—70	50—60	40—50	30—40	20—30	10—20
Frequency	3	6	10	12	15	6

Find coefficient of variation for the above data. (*KU 1999 C*)

4. Find the standard deviation for the following data :

Wages (Rs.)	50—60	60—70	70—80	80—90	90—100	100—110
No. of workers	8	10	16	14	10	5

(*KU 1997 ; MDU 1998*)

5. Find which of the following batsman is more consistent in scoring :

Batsman A	5	7	16	27	53	80
Batsman B	0	4	16	21	43	83

(*MDU 1998*)

6. Find which of the following batsman is more consistent in scoring :

Batsman A	5	7	16	27	39	53	56	61	80	101	105
Batsman B	0	4	16	21	41	43	57	78	83	90	95

7. A group of 100 selected students is with average height 168.8 cm and coefficient of variation 3.2%. What is the S.D. of their height ? (*MDU 2000*)

8. (*a*) The mean of 5 observations is 4.4 and the variance is 8.24. If three of the five observations are 1, 2 and 6, find the other two. (*KU 1997*)

(*b*) Mean of 48 items is 9 and their standard deviation is 1.6. Find the sum of the squares of all items. (*MDU 2001*)

9. Goals scored by two teams in a football season were as follows :

No. of goals scored in a match	*No. of matches*	
	Team A	*Team B*
0	15	20
1	10	10
2	07	05
3	05	04
4	03	02
5	02	01
Total	42	42

Calculate coefficient of variation and state which team is more consistent.

10. The following are scores made by two Batsmen Gavaskar and Kapil in a series of innings :

Gavaskar	12	115	6	73	7	19	119	36	84	29
Kapil	47	12	76	42	4	51	37	48	13	0

(*i*) Who is the better run getter ?

(*ii*) Who is more consistent ?

11. From the data given below, state which series is more variable :

Variable	10—20	20—30	30—40	40—50	50—60	60—70
Group A	10	18	32	22	40	18
Group B	18	22	40	18	32	10

12. If the S.D. of a series is 7.5, find the most likely value of the mean deviation. (*MDU 1999*)

13. The following is the data relating to two models of televisions :

Life (No. of years)	*No. of televisions*	
Model :	*Crown*	*Dyanora*
0—2	5	2
2—4	16	7
4—6	13	12
6—8	7	19
8—10	5	9
10—12	4	1

(*i*) What is the average life of each model of these televisions ?

(*ii*) Which model has more uniformity ?

14. From the prices of shares of x and y given below, state which share is more stable in value :

x	41	44	43	48	45	46	49	50	42	40
y	91	93	96	92	90	97	99	94	98	95

(*MDU 2004*)

15. The following table gives the distribution of wages in the two branches of an industrial concern. Find out which branch has greater variability in wages relating to the average wage :

Monthly wages (in Rs.)	*No. of workers*	
	Branch A	*Branch B*
50—100	20	8
100—150	35	17
150—200	42	43
200—250	45	20
250—300	58	12
Total	200	100

16. In a cricket season, batsman A gets an average score of 64 runs per inning with a S.D. of 18 runs, while batsman B gets an average score of 43 runs with a S.D. of 9 runs in about an equal number of innings. Discuss the efficiency and consistency of both the batsmen.

17. Mean and standard deviation of 200 items are found to be 60 and 20. If at the time of calculations two items are wrongly taken as 3 and 67 instead of 13 and 17, find the correct mean and the standard deviation. (*KU 1996*)

18. The mean and S.D. of 20 items is found to be 10 and 2 respectively. At the time of checking, it was found that one item 8 was incorrect. Calculate the correct mean and S.D., if :

(*i*) the wrong item is omitted. (*ii*) it is replaced by 12.

19. The analysis of the results of a budget survey of 150 families gave an average monthly expenditure of Rs. 120 on food items with a S.D. of Rs. 15. After the analysis was completed it was noticed that the figure recorded for one household was wrongly taken as Rs. 15 instead of Rs. 105. Determine the correct value of the average expenditure and its S.D.

20. For a group of 50 male workers, the mean and standard deviation of their weekly wages are Rs. 63 and Rs. 9 respectively. For a group of 40 female workers, these measures are respectively Rs. 54 and Rs. 6. Find the mean and the S.D. for the combined group of 90 workers.

21. Following is the data related to two factories :

	Factory A	*Factory B*
Numbers of Workers	200	250
Average wage per hour	Rs. 15.00	Rs. 12.00
Variance (σ^2)	Rs. 16	Rs. 9

Find the following :

(*i*) Which factory pays larger amount as total wages per hour ?

(*ii*) Which factory is more variable ?

(*iii*) Find combined S.D. (*KU 2004*)

22. Following table gives height of boys and girls studying in a college :

	Boys	*Girls*
Number	72	38
Average height	68 inches	61 inches
Variance	9 inches	4 inches

Find the (*i*) S.D. of the height of boys and girls taken together and (*ii*) whose heights are more variable.

23. In the following data, two class frequencies are missing :

Class	*Frequency*	*Class*	*Frequency*
100—110	4	150—160	—
110—120	7	160—170	16
120—130	15	170—180	10
130—140	—	180—190	6
140—150	40	190—200	3

However, it was possible to ascertain that the total number of items was 150 and that the median has been correctly found out to be 146.25. You are required to find with the help of the given information :

(*i*) two missing frequencies. (*ii*) value of A.M. (*iii*) value of C.V.

24. A.M. and S.D. of the following frequency distribution are 31 and 15.937 respectively. The distribution after taking step deviations is as follows :

u	– 3	– 2	– 1	0	1	2	3
f	10	15	25	25	10	10	5

Determine the class intervals.

25. The values of the arithmetic mean and standard deviation of the following distribution of a continuous variable calculated from step-deviation method are 135.3 kg and 9.6 kg respectively :

Step deviations	– 4	– 3	– 2	– 1	0	+ 1	+ 2	+ 3
Frequency	2	5	8	18	22	13	8	4

Determine the actual class intervals. (*KU 1997*)

26. Calculate C.V. for the following data :

x	50	51	52	53	54	55	56	57
f	1	2	2	6	3	4	2	0

(KU 1998 ; MDU 2002)

27. A collar manufacture is considering the production of new style of collar to attract young man. The following statistics of neck circumference are available based upon measurement of a typical group of college students :

Mid-values (in Inches)	12.5	13.0	13.5	14.0	14.5	15.0	15.5	16.0	16.5
No. of students	4	19	30	63	66	29	18	1	1

Compute standard deviation and use criterion ($\bar{x} \pm 3\sigma$) to determine the largest and smallest size of collar he should make in order to meet the needs of practically all the consumer bearing in mind that collar are worn, on an average 3/4 inch longer than the neck size. *(KU 2006)*

28. The following data give the A.M. and S.D. of the three subgroups. Find the A.M. and S.D. of the combined group :

Subgroup	*No. of men*	*Average wage (in Rs.)*	*S.D. (in Rs.)*
A	150	20	2
B	150	10	3
C	200	12.5	4

Answers

1. (*a*) S.D. = 0, C.V. = 0
   (*b*) C.V. (A) = 25.86%, C.V. (B) = 25.00%,
   C.V. (C) = 16.67% ∴ C is most consistent.
2. $\bar{x}$ = Rs. 40.52, S.D. = Rs. 17.41, Coeff. of S.D. = 0.4296
3. C.V. = 38.708 4. Rs. 14.5079
5. C.V. for A = 81.0306%, C.V. for B = 101.6502%, A is consistent.
6. C.V. for A = 67.0738%, C.V. for B = 69.5120% } A is consistent. 7. S.D. = 5.4016 cm
8. (*a*) 4, 9 (*b*) 4010.9
9. C.V. for A = 102.1259, C.V. for B = 124.5434 } A is consistent.
10. (*i*) A.M. for Gavaskar = 50 Runs, A.M. for Kapil = 33
    ∴ Gavaskar is better run getter.
    (*ii*) C.V. for Gavaskar = 83.6612%, C.V. for Kapil = 70.8209%
    ∴ Kapil is more consistent.
11. C.V. for A = 33.8496%, C.V. for B = 38.2442%
    Group B is more variable. 12. M.D. = 6
13. (*i*) A.M. for Crown = 5.12 yrs, A.M. for Dyanora = 6.16 yrs
    (*ii*) C.V. for Crown = 54.9158%, C.V. for Dyanora = 36.2068%
    ∴ Dyanora model has more uniformity.

14. S.D. for X = 3.2496, S.D. for Y = 2.8723
C.V. for X = 7.2536%, C.V. for Y = 3.0395%
Stability is more in series Y.

15. C.V. for A = 33.9015%. C.V. for B = 29.8077%
Variability is more in branch A.

16. C.V. for A = 28.125%, C.V. for B = 20.9302%
If average is the criterion, then A is efficient.
If consistency is the criterion, then B is efficient.

17. 59.8, 20.0938

18. (*i*) Correct $\bar{x}$ = 10.1053, Correct S.D. = 1.997
(*ii*) Correct $\bar{x}$ = 10.2, Correct S.D. = 1.9899

19. Correct A.M. = Rs. 120.60, Correct S.D. = Rs. 12.35

20. $\bar{x}$ = Rs. 59, S.D. = Rs. 9

21. (*i*) Same amount Rs. 3,000
(*ii*) A (*iii*) Rs. 3.786

22. (*i*) S.D. = 4.2839 inches
(*ii*) C.V. for boys = 4.4118%, C.V. for girls = 3.2887%
Heights of boys are more variable.

23. (*i*) 24, 25 (*ii*) A.M. = 147.3333 (*iii*) C.V. = 13.0302

24. 0—10, 10—20, 20—30, 30—40, 40—50, 50—60, 60—70

25. 109.5—115.5, 115.5—121.5, ..., 151.5—157.5 **26.** 3.0427%

27. S.D. = 0.75 inches, smallest size = (14.23 – 3(0.75)) + 0.75 = 12.73 inches,
largest size = (14.23 + 3(0.75)) + 0.75 = 17.23 inches

28. 14, 5.1769.

V. LORENZ CURVE

24. MEANING

This is a graphic method of studying dispersion in a given distribution. This method was devised by famous economic statistician Dr. Max. O. Lorenz. **Lorenz Curve** is used to study the distribution of wealth, land, profit, income etc. For drawing a Lorenz curve, the values of the variable and the frequencies are separately cumulated. These are then expressed as percentage of their respective aggregates. The two sets of percentage of cumulative totals are then plotted against each other on a graph paper. This graph is called the Lorenz curve. A line is drawn through the points (0, 0) and (100, 100) on the graph paper. This line is called the line of equal distribution. The distance of the Lorenz curve is observed from this line of equal distribution. This distance is the measure of variability in the distribution. Greater the distance from the line of equal distribution would mean greater variability.

Example. *The following table gives the weekly wages of workers in two factories A and B. Represent the data graphically by using Lorenz curve.*

Weekly wages (in Rs.)	*0—20*	*20—40*	*40—60*	*60—80*	*80—100*
No. of workers (Factory A)	5	7	8	6	4
No. of workers (Factory B)	3	6	10	2	1

Sol.

Weekly wages (in Rs.)				*Factory A*			*Factory B*		
Wages (in Rs.)	*Mid-points*	*Cumu. wages*	*% of Cumu. wages*	*No. of workers*	*Cumu. no. of workers*	*% of Cumu. no. of workers*	*No. of workers*	*Cumu. no. of workers*	*% of Cumu. no. of workers*
0—20	10	10	4	5	5	16.67	3	3	13.64
20—40	30	40	16	7	12	40.00	6	9	40.91
40—60	50	90	36	8	20	66.67	10	19	86.36
60—80	70	160	64	6	26	86.67	2	21	95.45
80—100	90	250	100	4	30	100.00	1	22	100.00

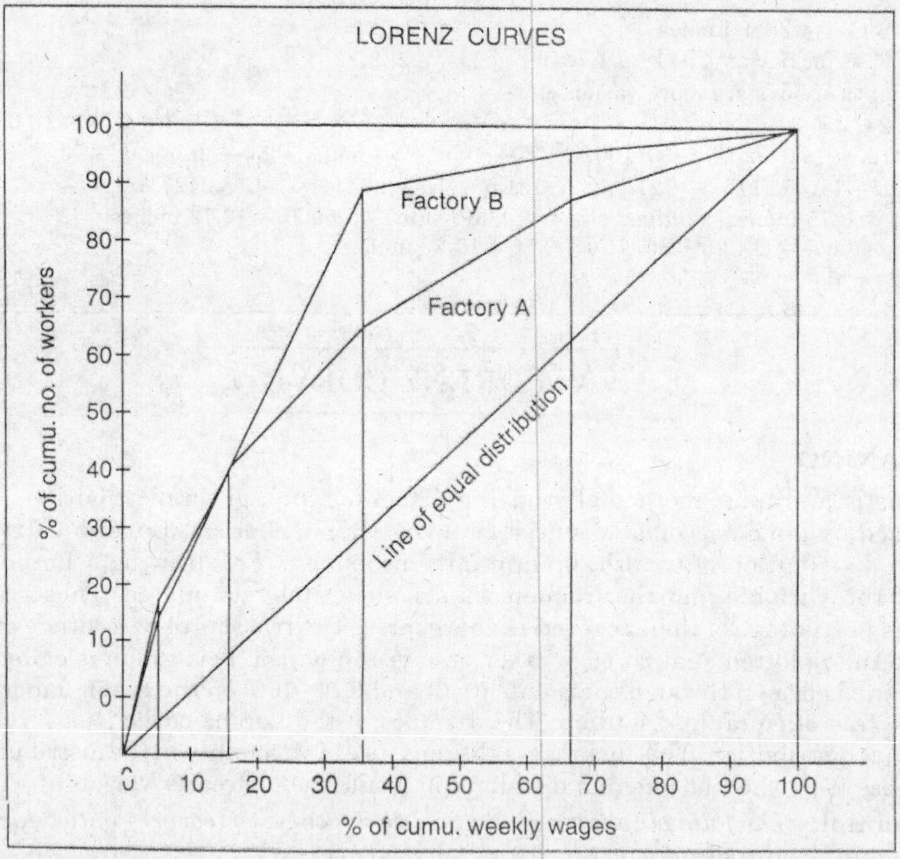

From the graph of Lorenz curves, we see that variability is greater in the wage distribution in factory B.

25. MERITS OF LORENZ CURVE METHOD

1. It is a graphical method. It gives an idea about the variability in the distribution, very easily.

2. It is also understandable to those who do not have knowledge of statistics.

26. DEMERITS OF LORENZ CURVE METHOD

1. It involves much calculation work.
2. It does not give quantitative measure of variability.

EXERCISE 5

1. Draw a Lorenz curve for the following data :

Income (in Rs.)	500	600	700	800	900	1000
No. of employees	4	8	15	6	2	1

2. You are given data relating to the marks obtained by 50 students. Draw a Lorenz curve to this data :

Marks	0—10	10—20	20—30	30—40	40—50
No. of students	5	7	20	12	6

3. The following table gives the profit earned by companies of two localities A and B. Show the data by Lorenz curves and interpret the curves.

Profit (000 Rs.)	10	11	12	13	14	15
No. of companies (Locality A)	4	6	8	7	4	1
No. of companies (Locality B)	5	5	10	12	18	5

4. The frequency distribution of income of two groups are as follows :

Annual income (in Rs.)	*No. of persons*	
	A	*B*
12000	400	200
13000	500	400
14000	550	800
15000	500	1000
16000	600	950
17000	700	950
18000	550	600

Show the data by Lorenz curves and interpret the curves.

EXERCISE 6

1. Define dispersion and discuss its various measures.
2. Explain the merits of quartile deviation method of measuring dispersion over the range method.
3. What are the requisites of a good measure of dispersion ?
4. What is meant by dispersion ? What are the requirements of a good measure of dispersion ? In the light of those, comment on some of the well-known measures of dispersion.
5. Write a short note on 'Lorenz Curve' method of measuring dispersion.

7

Moments

1. INTRODUCTION

Moments are statistical tools, used in statistical investigations. In our present course, we shall be using the moments in studying 'Skewness' and 'Kurtosis' of statistical distributions. The *moments* of a distribution are the arithmetic means of the various powers of the deviations of items from some number.

2. MOMENTS ABOUT MEAN

For an individual series, the **rth moment about mean**, written as μ_r, is defined as

$$\mu_r = \frac{\sum_{i=1}^{n}(x_i - \bar{x})^r}{n} = \frac{\Sigma(x-\bar{x})^r}{n}, \quad r = 0, 1, 2, \ldots\ldots$$

where $x_1, x_2, \ldots\ldots, x_n$ are the values of the variable under consideration.

For a frequency distribution,

$$\mu_r = \frac{\sum_{i=1}^{n} f_i(x_i - \bar{x})^r}{N} = \frac{\Sigma f(x-\bar{x})^r}{N}, \quad r = 0, 1, 2, \ldots\ldots$$

where f_i is the frequency of x_i $(1 \le i \le n)$.

When the values of the variable are given in the form of classes, then their respective mid-points are taken as values of the variable (x).

Putting $r = 0$, $\quad \mu_0 = \frac{\Sigma f(x-\bar{x})^0}{N} = \frac{\Sigma f}{N} = 1.$

$\therefore$ **For any distribution, $\mu_0 = 1$.**

Putting $r = 1$, $\quad \mu_1 = \frac{\Sigma f(x-\bar{x})^1}{N} = \frac{0}{N} = 0$

because we know that the sum of deviations of items from $\bar{x}$ is always zero.

$\therefore$ **For any distribution, $\mu_1 = 0$.**

Also, $\quad \mu_2 = \frac{\Sigma f(x-\bar{x})^2}{N} = (\text{S.D.})^2 = \text{Variance}.$

$\therefore$ **For any distribution, μ_2 coincides with the variance of the distribution.**

Remark 1. The results :

(*i*) $\mu_0 = 1$ (*ii*) $\mu_1 = 0$ (*iii*) μ_2 = variance are also true for data given in the form of an *individual series*.

Remark 2. The moments about mean are also called **central moments.**

Remark 3. $\mu_1, \mu_2, \mu_3, \mu_4$ are generally referred to as the *"first four central moments"*.

WORKING RULES FOR FINDING CENTRAL MOMENTS

Rule I. *In case of an individual series, first find $\bar{x}$ by using the formulae $\bar{x} = \frac{\Sigma x}{n}$. In the second step, find $x - \bar{x}$, $(x - \bar{x})^2$, $(x - \bar{x})^3$, $(x - \bar{x})^4$ and their respective sum. In the third step, find*

$$\mu_1 = \frac{\Sigma(x-\bar{x})}{n}, \quad \mu_2 = \frac{\Sigma(x-\bar{x})^2}{n}, \quad \mu_3 = \frac{\Sigma(x-\bar{x})^3}{n} \quad \text{and} \quad \mu_4 = \frac{\Sigma(x-\bar{x})^4}{n}.$$

Rule II. *In case of a frequency distribution, first find $\bar{x}$ by using the formula $\bar{x} = \frac{\Sigma fx}{N}$.*

In the second step, find $f(x-\bar{x})$, $f(x-\bar{x})^2$, $f(x-\bar{x})^3$, $f(x-\bar{x})^4$ and their respective sum. In the third step, find

$$\mu_1 = \frac{\Sigma f(x-\bar{x})}{N}, \quad \mu_2 = \frac{\Sigma f(x-\bar{x})^2}{N}, \quad \mu_3 = \frac{\Sigma f(x-\bar{x})^3}{N} \quad \text{and} \quad \mu_4 = \frac{\Sigma f(x-\bar{x})^4}{N}.$$

Rule III. *If the values of the variable are given in the form of classes, then their respective mid-points are taken as the values of the variable.*

Rule IV. *μ_1 is always 0.*

Example 1. *Find the first four moments for the following individual series :*

x	3	6	8	10	18

Sol. **Calculation of Moments**

S. No.	*x*	$x - \bar{x}$ $\bar{x} = 9$	$(x - \bar{x})^2$	$(x - \bar{x})^3$	$(x - \bar{x})^4$
1	3	– 6	36	– 216	1296
2	6	– 3	9	– 27	81
3	8	– 1	1	– 1	1
4	10	1	1	1	1
5	18	9	81	729	6561
$n = 5$	$\Sigma x = 45$	$\Sigma(x - \bar{x}) = 0$	$\Sigma(x - \bar{x})^2$ = 128	$\Sigma(x - \bar{x})^3$ = 486	$\Sigma(x - \bar{x})^4$ = 7940

Now $\bar{x} = \frac{\Sigma x}{n} = \frac{45}{5} = 9$

$\therefore$ $\mu_1 = \frac{\Sigma(x-\bar{x})}{n} = \frac{0}{5} = \mathbf{0}$

$$\mu_2 = \frac{\Sigma(x-\bar{x})^2}{n} = \frac{128}{5} = \mathbf{25.6}$$

$$\mu_3 = \frac{\Sigma(x-\bar{x})^3}{n} = \frac{486}{5} = \mathbf{97.2}$$

$$\mu_4 = \frac{\Sigma(x-\bar{x})^4}{n} = \frac{7940}{5} = \mathbf{1588.}$$

Example 2. *Calculate μ_1, μ_2, μ_3, μ_4 for the following frequency distribution :*

Marks	*5—15*	*15—25*	*25—35*	*35—45*	*45—55*	*55—65*
No. of students	*10*	*20*	*25*	*20*	*15*	*10*

Sol. **Calculation of Moments**

Marks	*No. of Students (f)*	*Mid-points x*	*fx*	*$x-\bar{x}$ $\bar{x}=34$*	*$f(x-\bar{x})$*	*$f(x-\bar{x})^2$*	*$f(x-\bar{x})^3$*	*$f(x-\bar{x})^4$*
5—15	10	10	100	– 24	– 240	5760	– 138240	3317760
15—25	20	20	400	– 14	– 280	3920	– 54880	768320
25—35	25	30	750	– 4	– 100	400	– 1600	6400
35—45	20	40	800	6	120	720	4320	25920
45—55	15	50	750	16	240	3840	61440	983040
55—65	10	60	600	26	260	6760	175760	4569760
	N = 100		Σfx = 3400		$\Sigma f(x-\bar{x})$ = 0	$\Sigma f(x-\bar{x})^2$ = 21400	$\Sigma f(x-\bar{x})^3$ = 46800	$\Sigma f(x-\bar{x})^4$ = 9671200

Now $$\bar{x} = \frac{\Sigma fx}{N} = \frac{3400}{100} = \mathbf{34}$$

$\therefore$ $$\mu_1 = \frac{\Sigma f(x-\bar{x})}{N} = \frac{0}{100} = \mathbf{0}$$

$$\mu_2 = \frac{\Sigma f(x-\bar{x})^2}{N} = \frac{21400}{100} = \mathbf{214}$$

$$\mu_3 = \frac{\Sigma f(x-\bar{x})^3}{N} = \frac{46800}{100} = \mathbf{468}$$

$$\mu_4 = \frac{\Sigma f(x-\bar{x})^4}{N} = \frac{9671200}{100} = \mathbf{96712.}$$

3. SHEPPARD'S CORRECTION FOR MOMENTS

Let the values of the variable in a frequency distribution be given in the form of classes. In this case, we would suppose that the items in a class are concentrated at the mid-points of the respective classes. In other words, we suppose that the values of all items lying in a class are equal to the mid-point of the respective classes.

This assumption leads to some error, in the values of the moments. This error is called **grouping error.** This error is corrected by using the following formulae given by **W.F. Sheppard :**

$$\mu_2 \text{ (corrected)} = \mu_2 - \frac{h^2}{12}$$

and
$$\mu_4 \text{ (corrected)} = \mu_4 - \frac{1}{2} h^2 \mu_2 + \frac{7}{240} h^4$$

where h is the width of the intervals. μ_1 **and** μ_3 **require no correction.**

Example 3. *Find the corrected values of the following moments using Sheppard's correction. The width of classes in the distribution is 10.*

$$\mu_2 = 214, \quad \mu_3 = 468, \quad \mu_4 = 96712.$$

Sol. We have $\mu_2 = 214$, $\mu_3 = 468$

$\mu_4 = 96712$, $h = 10$.

Now $$\mu_2 \text{ (corrected)} = \mu_2 - \frac{h^2}{12} = 214 - \frac{(10)^2}{12} = 214 - 8.333 = \mathbf{205.667}.$$

$$\mu_3 \text{ (corrected)} = \mu_3 = \mathbf{468}$$

$$\mu_4 \text{ (corrected)} = \mu_4 - \frac{h^2}{2} \mu_2 + \frac{7}{240} h^4$$

$$= 96712 - \frac{(10)^2}{2} (214) + \frac{7}{240} (10)^4$$

$$= 96712 - 10700 - 291.667 = \mathbf{86303.667}.$$

4. ALTERNATIVE METHOD FOR FINDING MOMENTS

We have seen in the above examples that the calculation of '*moments about mean*' involves a lot of calculation work. Even if the value of A.M. is a whole number, the calculation work is not so simple. Now, let us imagine a frequency distribution with $\bar{x} = 6.88642$. In such a case, one can easily imagine the difficulties which would arise during the computation of moments. This problem is solved by first finding the *moments of distribution about any convenient point.* The **rth moment about a number 'A'** is denoted by μ_r' and is defined by

$$\mu_r' = \frac{\sum_{i=1}^{n} (x_i - A)^r}{n} = \frac{\Sigma(x - A)^r}{n}, \quad r = 0, 1, 2, ...$$

where $x_1, x_2, ..., x_n$ are the values of the variable under consideration.

For a frequency distribution,

$$\mu_r' = \frac{\sum_{i=1}^{n} f_i (x_i - A)^r}{N} = \frac{\Sigma f(x - A)^r}{N}, \quad r = 0, 1, 2, ...$$

where f_i is the frequency of x_i $(1 \le i \le n)$.

In the calculation work, if we find that there is some common factor h (> 1) in the values of $x - A$, then we can further ease our calculation work by defining :

$$u = \frac{x - A}{h}.$$

In this case, we have

$$\mu_r' = \left(\frac{\sum_{i=1}^{n} u_i^r}{n}\right) h^r = \left(\frac{\Sigma u^r}{n}\right) h^r, \quad r = 0, 1, 2, \ldots\ldots \qquad \text{(For individual series)}$$

and

$$\mu_r' = \left(\frac{\sum_{i=1}^{n} f_i u_i^r}{N}\right) h^r = \left(\frac{\Sigma f u^r}{N}\right) h^r, \quad r = 0, 1, 2, \ldots\ldots \text{ (For frequency distribution)}$$

The moments about any arbitrary number are also called **raw moments.**

Remark 1. Putting $r = 0$, we get $\mu_0' = \frac{\Sigma f(x-A)^0}{N} = \frac{\Sigma f}{N} = 1.$

$\therefore$ μ_0' is always 1.

Remark 2. Putting $r = 1$, we get

$$\mu_1' = \frac{\Sigma f(x-A)}{N} = \left(A + \frac{\Sigma f(x-A)}{N}\right) - A = \bar{x} - A.$$

$$\therefore \quad \bar{\mathbf{x}} = \mathbf{A} + \mu_1'.$$

After calculating moments about arbitrary number 'A', the moments about mean are calculated by using the formulae :

$$\mu_1 = 0 \qquad \text{(always)}$$

$$\mu_2 = \mu_2' - \mu_1'^2$$

$$\mu_3 = \mu_3' - 3\mu_2'\mu_1' + 2\mu_1'^3$$

and

$$\mu_4 = \mu_4' - 4\mu_3'\mu_1' + 6\mu_2'\mu_1'^2 - 3\mu_1'^4.$$

This method of finding central moments (μ_r) seems to be lengthy but it is not so in practice. In this method, the choice of 'A' is at our discretion. In this method, the value of A.M. is not required for the computation of central moments.

WORKING RULES FOR FINDING CENTRAL MOMENTS

Step I. *This method is used when the A.M. of the given distribution is not expected to be a whole number.*

Step II. *Choose a suitable number 'A' and find $f(x-A)$, $f(x-A)^2$, $f(x-A)^3$, $f(x-A)^4$ and their respective sums.*

Step III. *Find raw moments :*

$$\mu_1' = \frac{\Sigma f(x-A)}{N}, \ \mu_2' = \frac{\Sigma f(x-A)^2}{N}, \ \mu_3' = \frac{\Sigma f(x-A)^3}{N} \ \text{and} \ \mu_4 = \frac{\Sigma f(x-A)^4}{N}.$$

Step IV. *Find central moments by using the formulae :*

$$\mu_1 = 0,\ \mu_2 = \mu_2' - \mu_1'^2,\ \mu_3 = \mu_3' - 3\mu_2'\mu_1' + 2\mu_1'^3$$

and $\mu_4 = \mu_4' - 4\mu_3'\mu_1' + 6\mu_2'\mu_1'^2 - 3\mu_1'^4.$

Example 4. *The first three moments of a distribution, about the value '3' of the variable are 2, 10 and 30. Find the values of* μ_1, μ_2, μ_3. (KU 2000 C)

Sol. We have $\mu_1' = 2, \mu_2' = 10$ and $\mu_3' = 30$.

Now $\mu_1 = \mathbf{0}$ (always)

$$\mu_2 = \mu_2' - \mu_1'^2 = 10 - (2)^2 = \mathbf{6}.$$

$$\mu_3 = \mu_3' - 3\mu_2'\mu_1' + 2(\mu_1')^3$$

$$= 30 - 3(10)(2) + 2(2)^3 = 30 - 60 + 16 = \mathbf{-14}.$$

Example 5. *The first three moments of a distribution, about the value '2' of the variable are 1, 16 and – 40. Show that the mean is 3, variance is 15 and* $\mu_3 = -86$.

Sol. We have $A = 2, \mu_1' = 1, \mu_2' = 16$ and $\mu_3' = -40$.

$$\therefore \quad \mu_1' = \frac{\Sigma f(x - A)}{N} = 1$$

Now

$$\bar{x} = A + \frac{\Sigma f(x - A)}{N} = 2 + 1 = \mathbf{3}$$

$$\text{Variance} = \mu_2 = \mu_2' - \mu_1'^2 = 16 - (1)^2 = \mathbf{15}$$

$$\mu_3 = \mu_3' - 3\mu_2'\mu_1' + 2(\mu_1')^3$$

$$= -40 - 3(16)(1) + 2(1)^3 = -40 - 48 + 2 = \mathbf{-86}.$$

Example 6. *The first four moments of a distribution, about the value of '35' are – 1.8, 240, – 1020 and 144000. Find the values of* μ_1, μ_2, μ_3, μ_4.

Sol. $\mu_1 = \mathbf{0}$

$$\mu_2 = \mu_2' - \mu_1'^2 = 240 - (-1.8)^2 = \mathbf{236.76}$$

$$\mu_3 = \mu_3' - 3\mu_2'\mu_1' + 2\mu_1'^3 = -1020 - 3(240)(-1.8) + 2(-1.8)^3 = \mathbf{264.36}$$

$$\mu_4 = \mu_4' - 4\mu_3'\mu_1' + 6\mu_2'\mu_1'^2 - 3\mu_1'^4$$

$$= 144000 - 4(-1020)(-1.8) + 6(240)(-1.8)^2 - 3(-1.8)^4$$

$$= \mathbf{141290.11}.$$

Example 7. *From the following data, calculate the first four moments about the mean :*

Class	*0—10*	*10—20*	*20—30*	*30—40*	*40—50*	*50—60*	*60—70*
Frequency	*4*	*8*	*11*	*15*	*11*	*7*	*4*

(KU 1996)

Sol. **Calculation of Moments**

Class	*f*	*x*	$d = x - A$ $A = 35$	$u = d/h$ $h = 10$	*fu*	fu^2	fu^3	fu^4
0—10	4	5	– 30	– 3	– 12	36	– 108	324
10—20	8	15	– 20	– 2	– 16	32	– 64	128
20—30	11	25	– 10	– 1	– 11	11	– 11	11
30—40	15	35	0	0	0	0	0	0
40—50	11	45	10	1	11	11	11	11
50—60	7	55	20	2	14	28	56	112
60—70	4	65	30	3	12	36	108	324
	N = 60				$\Sigma fu = -2$	$\Sigma fu^2 = 154$	$\Sigma fu^3 = -8$	$\Sigma fu^4 = 910$

Now, $\mu_1' = \left(\frac{\Sigma fu}{N}\right) h = \left(\frac{-2}{60}\right) 10 = -0.33$

$$\mu_2' = \left(\frac{\Sigma fu^2}{N}\right) h^2 = \left(\frac{154}{60}\right) (10)^2 = 256.67$$

$$\mu_3' = \left(\frac{\Sigma fu^3}{N}\right) h^3 = \left(\frac{-8}{60}\right) (10)^3 = -133.33$$

$$\mu_4' = \left(\frac{\Sigma fu^4}{N}\right) h^4 = \left(\frac{910}{60}\right) (10)^4 = 151666.67.$$

Moments about mean

$$\mu_1 = \mathbf{0}$$

$$\mu_2 = \mu_2' - \mu_1'^2 = 256.67 - (-0.33)^2 = \mathbf{256.56}.$$

$$\mu_3 = \mu_3' - 3\mu_2'\mu_1' + 2\mu_1'^3$$

$$= -133.33 - 2(256.67)(-0.33) + 2(-0.33)^3 = \mathbf{120.70}.$$

$$\mu_4 = \mu_4' - 4\mu_3'\mu_1' + 6\mu_2'\mu_1'^2 - 3\mu_1'^4$$

$$= 151666.67 - 4(-133.33)(-0.33) + 6(256.67)(-0.33)^2 - 3(-0.33)^4$$

$$= \mathbf{151658.35}.$$

Example 8. *Calculate the first four moments of the following data. Also make Sheppard's correction.*

Values	*10—20*	*20—30*	*30—40*	*40—50*	*50—60*	*60—70*	*70—80*
Frequency	*1*	*20*	*69*	*108*	*78*	*22*	*2*

Sol. **Calculation of Moments**

Values	*f*	*x*	$d = x - A$ $A = 45$	$u = \frac{x - A}{h}$ $h = 10$	*fu*	fu^2	fu^3	fu^4
10—20	1	15	– 30	– 3	– 3	9	– 27	81
20—30	20	25	– 20	– 2	– 40	80	– 160	320
30—40	69	35	– 10	– 1	– 69	69	– 69	69
40—50	108	45	0	0	0	0	0	0
50—60	78	55	10	1	78	78	78	78
60—70	22	65	20	2	44	88	176	352
70—80	2	75	30	3	6	18	54	162
	N = 300				Σfu = 16	Σfu^2 = 342	Σfu^3 = 52	Σfu^4 = 1062

Now $\mu_1' = \left(\frac{\Sigma fu}{N}\right) h = \left(\frac{16}{300}\right) 10 = 0.533$

$$\mu_2' = \left(\frac{\Sigma fu^2}{N}\right) h^2 = \left(\frac{342}{300}\right) (10)^2 = 114$$

$$\mu_3' = \left(\frac{\Sigma fu^3}{N}\right) h^3 = \left(\frac{52}{300}\right)(10)^3 = 173.33$$

$$\mu_4' = \left(\frac{\Sigma fu^4}{N}\right) h^4 = \left(\frac{1062}{300}\right)(10)^4 = 35400.$$

Moment about mean

$\mu_1 = 0$ (always)

$\mu_2 = \mu_2' - \mu_1'^2 = 114 - (0.53)^2 = \mathbf{113.72}$

$\mu_3 = \mu_3' - 3\mu_2'\mu_1' + 2\mu_1'^3 = 173.33 - 3(114)(0.53) + 2(0.53)^3 = \mathbf{-7.63}$

$\therefore$ $\mu_4 = \mu_4' - 4\mu_3'\mu_1' + 6\mu_2'\mu_1'^2 - 3\mu_1'^4$

$= 35400 - 4(173.33)(0.53) + 6(114)(0.53)^2 - 3(0.53)^4 = \mathbf{35224.44.}$

Sheppard's correction

μ_1 (Corrected) $= \mu_1 = 0$

$$\mu_2 \text{ (Corrected)} = \mu_2 - \frac{h^2}{12} = 113.72 - \frac{(10)^2}{12} = \mathbf{105.39.}$$

μ_3 (Corrected) $= \mu_3 = \mathbf{-7.63}$

$$\mu_4 \text{ (Corrected)} = \mu_4 - \frac{1}{2}h^2\mu_2 + \frac{7}{240}h^4$$

$$= 35224.44 - \frac{1}{2}(10)^2(113.72) + \frac{7}{240}(10)^4 = \mathbf{29830.11.}$$

Example 9. *Compute the classes and the first four moments about the mean for the following data :*

Mid values of the variate	*5*	*10*	*15*	*20*	*25*	*30*	*35*
Frequency	*8*	*15*	*20*	*32*	*23*	*17*	*5*

Sol. The mid values 5, 10, ..., 35 are at equal intervals. The difference between consecutive mid values is 5.

$\therefore$ The lower and upper limits of the first class are respectively

$$5 - \frac{1}{2}(5) = 2.5 \text{ and } 5 + \frac{1}{2}(5) = 7.5.$$

$\therefore$ The first class is **2.5—7.5.**

Similarly other classes are **7.5—12.5, 12.5—17.5, 17.5—22.5, ..., 32.5—37.5.**

Calculation of Moments

Class	*f*	*x*	*d = x – A* *A = 20*	*u = d/h* *h = 5*	*fu*	*fu²*	*fu³*	*fu⁴*
2.5—7.5	8	5	– 15	– 3	– 24	72	– 216	648
7.5—12.5	15	10	– 10	– 2	– 30	60	– 120	240
12.5—17.5	20	15	– 5	– 1	– 20	20	– 20	20
17.5—22.5	32	20	0	0	0	0	0	0
22.5— 27.5	23	25	5	1	23	23	23	23
27.5—32.5	17	30	10	2	34	68	136	272
32.5—37.5	5	35	15	3	15	45	135	405
	N = 120				Σfu = – 2	Σfu^2 = 288	Σfu^3 = – 62	Σfu^4 = 1608

Now $$\mu_1' = \left(\frac{\Sigma fu}{N}\right)h = \left(\frac{-2}{120}\right)5 = -0.083$$

$$\mu_2' = \left(\frac{\Sigma fu^2}{N}\right)h^2 = \left(\frac{288}{120}\right)(5)^2 = 60$$

$$\mu_3' = \left(\frac{\Sigma fu^3}{N}\right)h^3 = \left(\frac{-62}{120}\right)(5)^3 = -64.583$$

$$\mu_4' = \left(\frac{\Sigma fu^4}{N}\right)h^4 = \left(\frac{1608}{120}\right)(5)^4 = 8375.$$

Moments about mean

$\mu_1 = 0$ (always)

$\mu_2 = \mu_2' - \mu_1'^2 = 60 - (-0.083)^2 = 60 - 0.007 = \mathbf{59.99}$

$\mu_3 = \mu_3' - 3\mu_2'\mu_1' + 2\mu_1'^3 = -64.583 - 3(60)(-0.083) + 2(-0.083)^3$

$= -64.583 + 14.94 - 0.001 = \mathbf{-49.64}$

$\mu_4 = \mu_4' - 4\mu_3'\mu_1' + 6\mu_2'\mu_1'^2 - 3\mu_1'^4$

$= 8375 - 4(-64.583)(-0.083) + 6(60)(-0.83)^2 - 3(-0.083)^4$

$= 8375 - 21.442 + 2.48 - 0 = \mathbf{8356.038.}$

5. MOMENTS ABOUT ORIGIN

Let $x_1, x_2, ..., x_n$ be the values of a variable x with corresponding frequencies $f_1, f_2, ..., f_n$. The **rth moment about origin,** written as ν_r, is defined as

$$\nu_r = \frac{\Sigma f_i x_i^{\,n}}{N}, \quad r = 0, 1, 2, ...$$

If $\bar{x}$, μ_2, μ_3 and μ_4 are given, then ν_1, ν_2, ν_3, ν_4 are calculated by using the following formulae :

$\nu_1 = \bar{x}$

$\nu_2 = \mu_2 + \bar{x}^2$

$\nu_3 = \mu_3 + 3\mu_2\,\bar{x} + \bar{x}^3$

and $\nu_4 = \mu_4 + 4\mu_3\bar{x} + 6\mu_2\bar{x}^2 + \bar{x}^4$.

Example 10. *The first three moments of a distribution about the value 2 of the variable are 1, 16 and – 40 respectively.*

(i) Show that the mean, variance and the value of μ_3 are respectively 3, 15 and – 86.

(ii) Find the values of the first three moments about the origin.

Sol. We have $A = 2$, $\mu_1' = 1$, $\mu_2' = 16$ and $\mu_3' = -40$.

(i) $$\mu_1' = 1 \Rightarrow \frac{\Sigma f_i (x_i - 2)}{N} = 1 \qquad (\because A = 2)$$

$$\Rightarrow \frac{(\Sigma f_i x_i - 2\Sigma f_i)}{N} = 1 \Rightarrow \frac{\Sigma f_i x_i}{N} - \frac{(2N)}{N} = 1$$

$\Rightarrow \quad \bar{x} - 2 = 1$ or $\bar{x} = 3$.

$$\text{Variance} = \mu_2 = \mu_2' - \mu_1'^2 = 16 - (1)^2 = \mathbf{15}.$$

$$\mu_3 = \mu_3' - 3\mu_2'\mu_1' + 2\mu_1'^3 = -40 - 3(16)(1) + 2(1)^3 = \mathbf{-86}.$$

(ii) $\nu_1 = \bar{x} = \mathbf{3}$

$$\nu_2 = \mu_2 + \bar{x}^2 = 15 + (3)^2 = \mathbf{24}$$

$$\nu_3 = \mu_3 + 3\mu_2\bar{x} + \bar{x}^3 = -86 + 3(15)(3) + (3)^3 = \mathbf{76}.$$

Example 11. *The first four moments of a distribution about x = 2 are 1, 2.5, 5.5 and 16. Calculate the four moments about the mean and about zero.* (KU 1996 C)

Sol. We have $A = 2, \mu_1' = 1, \mu_2' = 2.5, \mu_3' = 5.5$ and $\mu_4' = 16$.

Moments about mean

$$\mu_1 = \mathbf{0}$$

$$\mu_2 = \mu_2' - \mu_1'^2 = 2.5 - (1)^2 = \mathbf{1.5}$$

$$\mu_3 = \mu_3' - 3\mu_2'\mu_1' + 2\mu_1'^3 = 5.5 - 3(2.5)(1) + 2(1)^3 = \mathbf{0}$$

$$\mu_4 = \mu_4' - 4\mu_3'\mu_1' + 6\mu_2'\mu_1'^2 - 3\mu_1'^4$$

$$= 16 - 4(5.5)(1) + 6(2.5)(1)^2 - 3(1)^4 = \mathbf{6}.$$

Moments about zero

Let ν_r be the *r*th moment about zero. We have the following formulae :

$$\nu_1 = \bar{x} = A + \mu_1', \quad \nu_2 = \mu_2 + \bar{x}^2$$

$$\nu_3 = \mu_3 + 3\mu_2\bar{x} + \bar{x}^3, \quad \nu_4 = \mu_4 + 4\mu_3\bar{x} + 6\mu_2\bar{x}^2 + \bar{x}^4.$$

$\therefore \quad \nu_1 = \bar{x} = 2 + 1 = \mathbf{3}, \quad \nu_2 = 1.5 + (3)^2 = \mathbf{10.5}$

$$\nu_3 = 0 + 3(1.5)(3) + (3)^3 = \mathbf{40.5}$$

$$\nu_4 = 6 + 4(0)(3) + 6(1.5)(3)^2 + (3)^4 = \mathbf{168}.$$

Example 12. *For the following data, calculate first four moments about (i) assumed mean 25 (ii) actual mean (iii) zero :*

Variable	*0—10*	*10—20*	*20—30*	*30—40*
Frequency	*1*	*3*	*4*	*2*

Sol. **Calculation of moments**

Variable	*f*	*x*	*d = x − 25*	*u = d/h* *h = 10*	*fu*	*fu*²	*fu*³	*fu*⁴
0—10	1	5	− 20	− 2	− 2	4	− 8	16
10—20	3	15	− 10	− 1	− 3	3	− 3	3
20—30	4	25	0	0	0	0	0	0
30—40	2	35	10	1	2	2	2	2
	N = 10				Σ*fu* = − 3	Σ*fu*² = 9	Σ*fu*³ = − 9	Σ*fu*⁴ = 21

(i) **Moments about 25**

$$\mu_1' = \left(\frac{\Sigma fu}{N}\right) h = \left(-\frac{3}{10}\right) 10 = -3$$

$$\mu_2' = \left(\frac{\Sigma fu^2}{N}\right)h^2 = \left(\frac{9}{10}\right)(10)^2 = \mathbf{90}$$

$$\mu_3' = \left(\frac{\Sigma fu^3}{N}\right)h^3 = \left(\frac{-9}{10}\right)(10)^3 = -\mathbf{900}$$

$$\mu_4' = \left(\frac{\Sigma fu^4}{N}\right)h^4 = \left(\frac{21}{10}\right)(10)^4 = \mathbf{21000.}$$

(*ii*) **Moments about actual mean**

$\mu_1 = \mathbf{0}$ (always)

$\mu_2 = \mu_2' - \mu_1'^2 = 90 - (-3)^2 = \mathbf{81}$

$\mu_3 = \mu_3' - 3\mu_2'\mu_1' + 2\mu_1'^3 = -900 - 3(90)(-3) + 2(-3)^3$

$= -900 + 810 - 54 = -\mathbf{144}$

$\mu_4 = \mu_4' - 4\mu_3'\mu_1' + 6\mu_2'\mu_1'^2 - 3\mu_1'^4$

$= 21000 - 4(-900)(-3) + 6(90)(-3)^2 - 3(-3)^4$

$= 21000 - 10800 + 4860 - 243 = \mathbf{14817.}$

(*iii*) **Moments about zero**

We have $\mu_1' = -3.$

$$\Rightarrow \left(\frac{\Sigma fu}{N}\right)h = 3 \Rightarrow \frac{\Sigma f(uh)}{N} = -3 \Rightarrow \frac{\Sigma f(x-25)}{N} = -3$$

$$\Rightarrow \frac{\Sigma fx}{N} - 25\left(\frac{\Sigma f}{N}\right) = -3 \Rightarrow \bar{x} - 25(1) = -3 \Rightarrow \bar{x} = 25 - 3 = 22.$$

Now $\nu_1 = \frac{\Sigma fx}{N} = \bar{x} = \mathbf{22}$

$\nu_2 = \mu_2 + \bar{x}^2 = 81 + (22)^2 = \mathbf{565}$

$\nu_3 = \mu_3 + 3\mu_2\bar{x} + \bar{x}^3 = -144 + 3(81)(22) + (22)^3 = \mathbf{15850}$

$\nu_4 = \mu_4 + 4\mu_3\bar{x} + 6\mu_2\bar{x}^2 + \bar{x}^4$

$= 14817 + 4(-144)(22) + 6(81)(22)^2 + (22)^4 = \mathbf{471625.}$

Alternative method

Calculation of moments about zero

Variable	*f*	*x*	*fx*	fx^2	fx^3	fx^4
0—10	1	5	5	25	125	625
10—20	3	15	45	675	10125	51875
20—30	4	25	100	2500	62500	1562500
30—40	2	35	70	2450	85750	3001250
	N = 10		Σfx = 220	Σfx^2 = 5650	Σfx^3 = 158500	Σfx^4 = 4716250

$$\therefore \quad v_1 = \frac{\Sigma fx}{N} = \frac{220}{10} = 22, \qquad v_2 = \frac{\Sigma fx^2}{N} = \frac{5650}{10} = 565$$

$$v_3 = \frac{\Sigma fx^3}{N} = \frac{158500}{10} = 15850, \qquad v_4 = \frac{\Sigma fx^4}{N} = \frac{4716250}{10} = 471625.$$

EXERCISE 1

1. Calculate first four moments about mean, for the following individual series :
   5, 5, 5, 5, 5, 5.
2. Find the corrected values of the following moments using Sheppard's correction. The width of classes in the distribution is 10 :
   $\mu_2 = 113.72$, $\mu_3 = -8.11$, $\mu_4 = 35225$. *(KU 2001 C)*
3. Find the first four moments about the mean for the following series :
   1, 3, 7, 9, 10.
4. Calculate $\mu_1, \mu_2, \mu_3, \mu_4$ for the series : 4, 7, 10, 13, 16, 19, 22.
5. The first three moments of a distribution about the value 4 of the variable are 1.5, 17 and – 30. Find the moments about mean.
6. The first four moments of a distribution about $x = 4$ are 1, 4, 10 and 45. Show that the mean is 5, the variance is 3, μ_3 is 0 and μ_4 is 26.
7. The first four moments of a distribution about $x = 2$ are 1, 2.5, 5.5 and 16 respectively. Calculate the values of first four central moments.
8. If the first four moments of a distribution about the value 5 are equal to – 4, 22, – 117 and 560. Determine the corresponding moments :
   (*i*) about the mean, and (*ii*) about zero. *(MDU 2005)*
9. Find the first four moments for the following frequency distribution :

x	1	2	3	4	5	6	7	8	9
f	1	2	3	4	5	4	3	2	1

10. Find the first four moments about mean for the following frequency distribution :

Marks	0—10	10—20	20—30	30—40	40—50
No. of students	5	10	40	20	25

11. Calculate the first four moments about mean for the following data :

Wages (in Rs.)	0—10	10—20	20—30	30—40	40—50	50—60	60—70	70—80
No. of persons	15	23	35	49	32	28	12	6

12. Calculate the first four moments about mean for the following frequency distribution :

Classes	5—15	15—25	25—35	35—45	45—55
f	14	22	36	18	10

13. Calculate the first four moments about mean for the following frequency distribution :

Class interval	0—10	10—20	20—30	30—40	40—50
Frequency	5	8	15	16	6

14. Calculate the first four moments about $x = 15$ and hence find the moments about the mean for the following distribution :

x	10	11	12	13	14	15	16	17	18	19	20	21
f	9	36	75	105	116	107	88	66	45	30	18	5

15. For the following data, calculate the first four moments about the mean :

Class	0—10	10—20	20—30	30—40	40—50	50—60	60—70
Frequency	4	8	11	15	11	7	4

16. Calculate the first four moments about $x = 40.45$ of the following distribution and hence find μ_2, μ_3 and μ_4.

Class	30.0—32.9	33.0—35.9	36.0—38.9
Frequency	2	4	26
Class	39.0—41.9	42.0—44.9	45.0—47.9
Frequency	47	15	6

Answers

1. $\mu_1 = 0, \mu_2 = 0, \mu_3 = 0, \mu_4 = 0$
2. $\mu_2 = 105.39, \mu_3 = -8.11, \mu_4 = 29830.67$
3. $\mu_1 = 0, \mu_2 = 12, \mu_3 = -12, \mu_4 = 208.8$
4. $\mu_1 = 0, \mu_2 = 36, \mu_3 = 0, \mu_4 = 2268$
5. $\mu_1 = 0, \mu_2 = 14.75, \mu_3 = -99.75$
7. $\mu_1 = 0, \mu_2 = 1.5, \mu_3 = 0, \mu_4 = 6$
8. (*i*) 0, 6, 19, 32 (*ii*) 1, 7, 38, 145
9. $\mu_1 = 0, \mu_2 = 4, \mu_3 = 0, \mu_4 = 37.6$
10. $\mu_1 = 0, \mu_2 = 125, \mu_3 = -300, \mu_4 = 37625$
11. $\mu_1 = 0, \mu_2 = 303.79, \mu_3 = 696.2, \mu_4 = 225029.91$
12. $\mu_1 = 0, \mu_2 = 134.56, \mu_3 = 126.14, \mu_4 = 41840.82$
13. $\mu_1 = 0, \mu_2 = 132, \mu_3 = -480, \mu_4 = 40656$
14. $\mu_1 = 0, \mu_2 = 5.5, \mu_3 = 4.4, \mu_4 = 77.8$
15. $\mu_1 = 0, \mu_2 = 256.56, \mu_3 = 120.70, \mu_4 = 151658.35$
16. $\mu_2 = 8.758, \mu_3 = -2.924, \mu_4 = 281.453.$

8

Skewness

1. INTRODUCTION

We have already seen that a single statistical measure is not capable of telling everything about a statistical distribution. A single measure cannot explore all the characteristics of a distribution. As we have already seen that an average of a distribution gives us an idea about the concentration of items about some value. Distributions with same average may differ widely in nature. We have already studied the scatter of items around some average value, in our discussion of measure of dispersion. Now we shall consider the aspect of 'symmetry' in curves of frequency distributions. The shape of the frequency curve depends upon the frequencies of different values of the variable under consideration. If the frequencies of items increases with the equally spaced increasing values of the variable and after a particular stage, the frequencies start decreasing exactly in the same way these were increased, then the frequency curve of the distribution would be *symmetrical, bell-shaped*.

2. MEANING

In symmetrical distribution, the values of mean, mode and median, would coincide. If the curve of the distribution is not symmetrical, it may admit of tail on either side of the distribution. Such a distribution lack in symmetry. **Skewness** is the word used for lack of symmetry. A distribution which is not symmetrical is called **asymmetrical** or **skewed**. We can define '**skewness**' of a distribution as the tendency of a distribution to depart from symmetry.

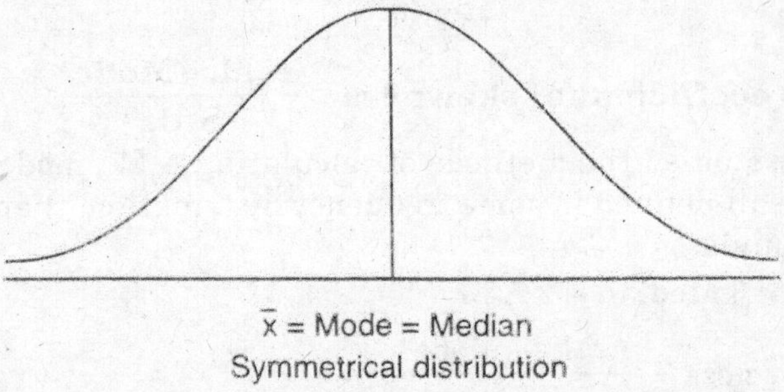

$\bar{x}$ = Mode = Median

Symmetrical distribution

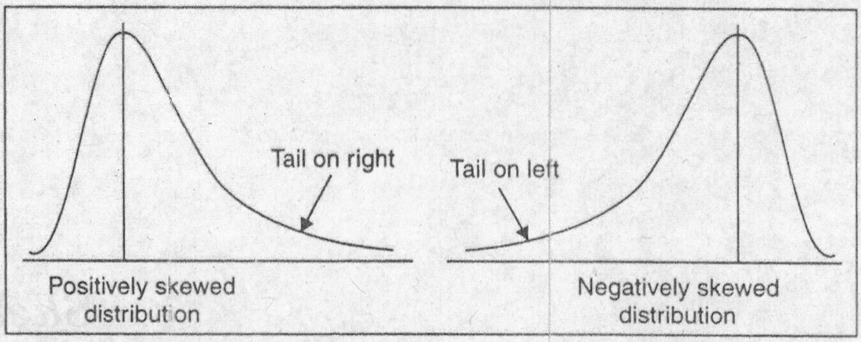

If the tail of an asymmetrical distribution is on the right side, then the distribution is called a **positively skewed distribution**. If the tail is on left side, then the distribution is defined to be **negatively skewed distribution**. Now we shall account for the situations when skewness can be expected in a distribution.

3. TESTS OF SKEWNESS

1. If A.M. = mode = median, then there is no skewness in the distribution. In other words, the curve of the frequency distribution would be symmetrical, bell-shaped.

2. If A.M. is less than (greater than), the value of mode, the tail would on left (right) side, *i.e.*, the distribution is negatively (positively) skewed.

3. If sum of frequencies of values less than mode is equal to the sum of frequencies of values greater than mode, then there would be no skewness.

4. If quartiles are equidistant from median, then there would be no skewness.

4. METHODS OF MEASURING SKEWNESS

1. Karl Pearson's Method
2. Bowley's Method
3. Kelly's Method
4. Method of Moments

5. KARL PEARSON'S METHOD

This method is based on the fact that in a symmetrical distribution, the value of A.M. is equal to that of mode. As we have already noted that the distribution is positively skewed if A.M. > Mode and negatively skewed if A.M. < Mode. The Karl Pearson's coefficient of skewness is given by

$$\textbf{Karl Pearson's coefficient of skewness} = \frac{\textbf{A.M.} - \textbf{Mode}}{\textbf{S.D.}}.$$

We have already studied the methods of calculating A.M., mode and S.D. of frequency distributions. If mode is ill-defined in some frequency distribution, then the value of empirical mode is used in the formula.

Empirical mode = 3 Median – 2 A.M.

$$\therefore \quad \text{Coeff. of skewness} = \frac{\text{A.M.} - \text{Mode}}{\text{S.D.}}$$

$$= \frac{\text{A.M.} - (3\text{ Median} - 2\text{ A.M.})}{\text{S.D.}} = \frac{3\text{ A.M.} - 3\text{ Median}}{\text{S.D.}}$$

$\therefore$ **Karl Pearson's coefficient of skewness** $= \dfrac{\textbf{3 (A.M. – Median)}}{\textbf{S.D.}}$

The coefficient of skewness as calculated by using this method would give magnitude as well as direction of skewness, present in the distribution. Practically, its value lies between – 1 and 1. For a symmetrical distribution, its value comes out to be zero.

The Karl Pearson's coefficient of skewness is generally denoted by 'SK_P'.

WORKING RULES FOR SOLVING PROBLEMS

Rule I. *If the values of $\bar{x}$, σ and mode are given, then find SK_P by using the formula :*

$$SK_P = \frac{\bar{x} - mode}{\sigma}.$$

Rule II. *If the values of $\bar{x}$, σ and median are given, then find SK_P by using the formula :*

$$SK_P = \frac{3(\bar{x} - median)}{\sigma}.$$

Rule III. *If the values of $\bar{x}$, σ and mode are not given, then calculate these. If mode is ill-defined, then find median.*

Rule IV. *Find SK_P by using formulae given in above rules.*

Example 1. *Karl Pearson's coefficient of skewness of a distribution is 0.32, its standard deviation is 6.5 and mean is 29.6. Find the mode of the distribution.*

Sol. We have $SK_P = 0.32$, S.D. = 6.5, $\bar{x} = 29.6$.

Now $SK_P = \dfrac{\bar{x} - \text{Mode}}{\text{S.D.}}$

$\therefore \quad 0.32 = \dfrac{29.6 - \text{Mode}}{6.5}$

$\Rightarrow \quad 29.6 - \text{Mode} = 0.32 \times 6.5 = 2.08$

$\Rightarrow \quad \text{Mode} = 29.6 - 2.08 = \mathbf{27.52.}$

Example 2. *For a moderately skewed data, the arithmetic mean is 100, the variance is 35 and Karl Pearson's coefficient of skewness is 0.2. Find its mode and median.*

Sol. We have $\bar{x} = 100$, variance = 35, $SK_P = 0.2$.

Now $SK_P = \dfrac{\bar{x} - \text{Mode}}{\sigma}.$

$\therefore \quad 0.2 = \dfrac{100 - \text{Mode}}{\sqrt{35}}$ $\quad (\because \text{ S.D.} = \sqrt{\text{variance}})$

$\Rightarrow \quad 100 - \text{Mode} = 0.2 \times 5.92 = 1.184$

$\Rightarrow \quad \text{Mode} = 100 - 1.184 = \mathbf{98.816.}$

Also $\quad \text{Mode} = 3 \text{ Median} - 2\bar{x}$ implies

$98.816 = 3 \text{ Median} - 2(100).$

$\therefore \quad 3 \text{ Median} = 98.816 + 200 = 298.816$

$\therefore \quad \text{Median} = \dfrac{298.816}{3} = \mathbf{99.61.}$

Example 3. *In a certain distribution, the following results were obtained :*

A.M. = 45, Median = 48, Coefficient of Skewness = – 0.4. The person who gave you this data, failed to give the value of S.D. You are required to estimate it with the help of available data.

Sol. We have

coeff. of skewness = – 0.4, A.M. = 45, median = 48.

$$\text{Now, coeff. of skewness} = \frac{3(\bar{x} - \text{Median})}{\text{S.D.}}$$

$$\Rightarrow \quad -\frac{4}{10} = \frac{3(45-48)}{\text{S.D.}} = \frac{-9}{\text{S.D.}} \quad \Rightarrow \quad 4\text{ S.D.} = 90$$

$$\Rightarrow \quad \text{S.D.} = \frac{90}{4} = \mathbf{22.5.}$$

Example 4. *The sum of 20 observations is 300 and sum of their squares is 5000. The median is 15. Find the Karl Pearson's coefficient of skewness and coefficient of variation.*

Sol. Let 'x' be the variable under consideration.

We have $n = 20$, $\Sigma x = 300$, $\Sigma x^2 = 5000$, median = 15.

$$\text{Now,} \quad \bar{x} = \frac{\Sigma x}{n} = \frac{300}{20} = 15$$

$$\text{S.D.} = \sqrt{\frac{\Sigma x^2}{n} - \bar{x}^2} = \sqrt{\frac{5000}{20} - (15)^2} = \sqrt{250 - 225} = \sqrt{25} = 5.$$

Now, Karl Pearson's coeff. of skewness

$$= \frac{3(\bar{x} - \text{Median})}{\text{S.D.}} = \frac{3(15-15)}{5} = \frac{0}{5} = \mathbf{0}$$

$$\text{C.V.} = \frac{\text{S.D.}}{x}(100) = \frac{5}{15} \times 100 = \mathbf{33.33\%}.$$

Example 5. *Find the coefficient of skewness by Karl Pearson's method for the following data :*

Value	*6*	*12*	*18*	*24*	*30*	*36*	*42*
Frequency	*4*	*7*	*9*	*18*	*15*	*10*	*3*

Sol. **Calculation of $\bar{x}$, S.D.**

Value x	f	$d = x - A$ $A = 24$	$u = d/h$ $h = 6$	fu	fu^2
6	4	– 18	– 3	– 12	36
12	7	– 12	– 2	– 14	28
18	9	– 6	– 1	– 9	9
24	18	0	0	0	0
30	15	6	1	15	15
36	10	12	2	20	40
42	3	18	3	9	27
	N = 66			$\Sigma fu = 9$	$\Sigma fu^2 = 155$

A.M. $\bar{x} = A + \left(\frac{\Sigma fu}{N}\right)h = 24 + \left(\frac{9}{66}\right)6 = 24.82$

S.D. $SD = \sqrt{\frac{\Sigma fu^2}{N} - \left(\frac{(\Sigma fu)}{N}\right)^2} \times h = \sqrt{\frac{155}{66} - \left(\frac{9}{66}\right)^2} \times 6$

$= \sqrt{2.35 - 0.12} \times 6 = 1.49 \times 6 = 8.94.$

Mode.

Grouping Table

x	*I* *f*	*II*	*III*	*IV*	*V*	*VI*
6	4	11				
12	7		16	20		
18	9	**27**			**34**	
24	**18**		**33**			**42**
30	15	25		**43**		
36	10		13		28	
42	3					

Analysis Table

Column	*24*	*18*	*30*	*36*	*12*
I	1				
II	1	1			
III	1		1		
IV	1		1	1	
V	1	1			1
VI	1	1	1		
Total	6	3	3	1	1

∴ Mode = 24

∴ $SK_P = \frac{\bar{x} - \text{Mode}}{\text{S.D}} = \frac{24.82 - 24}{8.94} = \frac{0.82}{8.94} = \mathbf{0.092.}$

Example 6. *Calculate Karl Pearson's coefficient of skewness for the following data :*

Income (in Rs.)	*500—600*	*600—700*	*700—800*
No. of employees	*8*	*12*	*4*
Income (in Rs.)	*800—900*	*900—1000*	*1000—1100*
No. of employees	*2*	*1*	*1*

Sol. **Calculation of $\bar{x}$, Mode, S.D.**

Income (in Rs.)	*No. of employees f*	*Mid-points of classes x*	$d = x - A$, $A = 750$	$u = d/h$, $h = 100$	*fu*	fu^2
500—600	8	550	– 200	– 2	– 16	32
600—700	12	650	– 100	– 1	– 12	12
700—800	4	750	0	0	0	0
800—900	2	850	100	1	2	2
900—1000	1	950	200	2	2	4
1000—1100	1	1050	300	3	3	9
	N = 28				$\Sigma fu = -21$	$\Sigma fu^2 = 59$

A.M., $$\bar{x} = A + \left(\frac{\Sigma fu}{N}\right)h = 750 + \left(-\frac{21}{28}\right)(100) = 750 - 75 = \text{Rs. } 675$$

Mode. By inspection, modal class is 600—700.

$$\therefore \quad \text{Mode} = L + \left(\frac{\Delta_1}{\Delta_1 + \Delta_2}\right)h$$

Here $L = 600, \Delta_1 = 12 - 8 = 4, \Delta_2 = 12 - 4 = 8, h = 100$

$$\therefore \quad \text{Mode} = 600 + \left(\frac{4}{4+8}\right)(100) = 600 + 33.33 = \text{Rs. } 633.33$$

S.D., $$\text{S.D.} = \sqrt{\frac{\Sigma fu^2}{N} - \left(\frac{\Sigma fu}{N}\right)^2} \times h = \sqrt{\frac{59}{28} - \left(-\frac{21}{28}\right)^2} \times 100$$

$$= \sqrt{2.1071 - 0.5625} \times 100 = \sqrt{1.5446} \times 100$$

$$= 1.2428 \times 100 = \text{Rs. } 124.28$$

Now, Karl Pearson's coeff. of skewness

$$= \frac{\bar{x} - \text{Mode}}{\text{S.D.}} = \frac{675 - 633.33}{124.28} = \mathbf{0.34.}$$

Example 7. *Following is data regarding the position of wages in a factory before and after the settlement of an industrial dispute. Comment on the gains and losses from the point of view of the workers and management.*

	Before settlement	*After settlement*
No. of workers	*2400*	*2350*
A.M. of wages	*Rs. 455*	*Rs. 475*
Median of wages	*Rs. 480*	*Rs. 450*
S.D. of wages	*Rs. 120*	*Rs. 100*

Sol. Let x denote the variable 'wage'.

(*i*) No. of workers before settlement = 2400

No. of workers after settlement = 2350.

$\therefore$ After settlement, 50 workers were thrown out of their job. This is a certain loss to the workers, who lost their job.

(*ii*) A.M. of wages before settlement = Rs. 455

A.M. of wages after settlement = Rs. 475.

$\therefore$ After settlement, the wages of workers have increased. This is a gain to the workers.

(*iii*) Median wages before settlement = Rs. 480

$\therefore$ 50% workers were getting less than or equal to Rs. 480.

Median wage after settlement = Rs. 450

After settlement, 50% workers were getting less than or equal to Rs. 450.

(*iv*) $\bar{x} = \dfrac{\Sigma x}{n}$ $\quad\therefore\quad \Sigma x = n.\ \bar{x}$

$\therefore$ Wage bill before settlement = Rs. 2400(455) = Rs. 10,92,000

Wage bill after settlement = Rs. 2350(475) = Rs. 11,16,250

$\therefore$ Increase in wage bill = Rs. 11,16,250 − 10,92,000 = Rs. 24,250

This is a loss to the management.

(*v*) C.V. before settlement $= \dfrac{120}{455} \times 100 = 26.374\%$

C.V. after settlement $= \dfrac{100}{475} \times 100 = 21.053\%$.

We see that C.V. has decreased after settlement.

$\therefore$ Disparity in wages has decreased after settlement.

(*vi*) Coeff. of skewness (before settlement)

$$= \frac{3\,(\bar{x} - \text{Median})}{\text{S.D.}} = \frac{3\,(455 - 480)}{120} = -\,0.625$$

$\therefore$ Tail of frequency curve is on left side.

Coeff. of skewness (after settlement)

$$= \frac{3\,(475 - 450)}{100} = 0.750$$

$\therefore$ Tail of frequency curve is on right side.

$\therefore$ After settlement, the management reduced the number of workers getting high wages.

EXERCISE 1

1. (*i*) A frequency distribution gives the following results :
coeff. of variation = 5, Karl Pearson's coeff. of skewness = 0.5,
S.D. = 2.
Find A.M. and Mode of the distribution.
(*ii*) In a certain distribution, the following results were obtained :
coefficient of variation (C.V.) = 40%, $\overline{X}$ = 25, and mode = 20.
Find the coefficient of skewness. (*MDU 2006*)

2. Find the coeff. of variation of a frequency distribution with the help of following information :

A.M. = 50 Mode = 56

Karl Pearson's coeff. of skewness = – 0.4.

3. For the following data, find Karl Pearson's coefficient of skewness :

Height (in inches)	58	59	60	61	62	63
No. of persons	10	18	30	42	35	28

(MDU 1998)

4. Find Pearson's coeff. of skewness for the following frequency distribution :

Wage (in Rs.)	50.00—59.99	60—69.99	70—79.99	80—89.99
No. of employees	8	10	16	14
Wage (in Rs.)	90—99.99	100—109.99	110—119.99	
No. of employees	10	5	2	

5. Find Pearson's coeff. of skewness for the following frequency distribution :

Height (in inches)	60—62	63—65	66—68	69—71	72—74
Frequency	5	18	42	27	8

(KU 2000)

6. For the following data, calculate the coefficient of skewness based on mean, median and S.D.

Variable	100—110	110—120	120—130	130—140
Frequency	4	16	36	52
Variable	140—150	150—160	160—170	170—180
Frequency	64	40	32	11

7. Calculate skewness and its coefficient from the following data. (Use Karl Pearson's formula) :

Wage (in Rs.)	10	11	12	13	14	15	16
No. of Workers	4	7	9	15	8	5	2

(MDU 2004)

8. Calculate Karl Pearson's coefficient of skewness for the following frequency distribution :

Marks more than	0	10	20	30	40	50	60	70
No. of students	100	90	75	50	25	15	5	0

9. For the following frequency distribution, calculate the value of Karl Pearson's coeff. of skewness :

Temp. (°C)	– 40 to – 30	– 30 to – 20	– 20 to – 10	– 10 to 0
No. of days	10	28	30	42
Temp. (°C)	0—10	10—20	20—30	
No. of days	65	180	10	

10. For the following data, calculate Karl Pearson's coefficient of skewness :

Marks (above)	0	10	20	30	40	50	60	70	80
No. of students	150	140	100	80	80	70	30	14	0

(*KU 2006 S, 2007*)

11. Find the mean wage and coefficient of skewness for the following data :

35 men gets at the rate of Rs. 4.5 per man	125 men gets at the rate of Rs. 8.5 per man
40 men gets at the rate of Rs. 5.5 per man	87 men gets at the rate of Rs. 9.5 per man
48 men gets at the rate of Rs. 6.5 per man	43 men gets at the rate of Rs. 10.5 per man
100 men gets at the rate of Rs. 7.5 per man	22 men gets at the rate of Rs. 11.5 per man

12. Calculate Karl Fearson's coefficient of skewness for the following data :

Wage (in Rs.)	70—80	80—90	90—100	100—110
No. of workers	12	18	35	42
Wage (in Rs.)	110—120	120—130	130—140	140—150
No. of workers	50	45	20	8

13. Find Pearson's coeff. of skewness from the following frequency distribution :

Scores	10—15	15—20	20—25	25—30	30—35	35—40	40—45	45—50	50—55	55—60
f	2	8	6	12	7	6	4	3	1	1

(*KU 2005*)

Answers

1. (*i*) $\bar{x}$ = 40, mode = 39 (*ii*) 0.5   2. C.V. = 30%   3. – 0.0208
4. 0.1454   5. 0.0356   6. – 0.0087   7. 1.52, – 0.14
8. – 0.0627   9. – 0.6617   10. – 0.7539
11. Mean wage = Rs. 8.07, Coeff. of skewness = – 0.2445   12. – 0.3314
13. 0.23.

6. BOWLEY'S METHOD

This method is based on the fact that in a symmetrical distribution, the quartiles are equidistant from the median. In a skewed distribution, this would not happen. The Bowley's coefficient of skewness is given by

$$\textbf{Bowley's coefficient of skewness} = \frac{Q_3 + Q_1 - 2\,\text{Median}}{Q_3 - Q_1}.$$

For a symmetrical distribution, its values would come out to be zero. The value of Bowley's coefficient of skewness lies between – 1 and + 1. The coefficient of skewness as calculated by using this, would give magnitude as well as direction of skewness present in the distribution. In problems, it is generally given as to which method is to be used. But in case, the method to be used is not specifically mentioned, then it is advisable to use Bowley's method. The calculation of Bowley's coefficient of skewness would involve the calculation of Q_1, Q_3 and median. The calculation of these measures would definitely take lesser time than for the calculation of $\bar{x}$, mode and S.D. It may also be noted that the values of coefficient of skewness as calculated by using different formulae may not be same. This method is also useful in case of open end classes in the distribution.

The Bowley's coefficient of skewness is generally denoted by 'SK_B'.

WORKING RULES FOR SOLVING PROBLEMS

Rule I. *If the values of medium, Q_1 and Q_3 are given, then find SK_B by using the formula :*

$$SK_B = \frac{Q_3 + Q_1 - 2Median}{Q_3 - Q_1}.$$

Rule II. *If the values of median, Q_1 and Q_3 are not given, then find these by using cumulative frequencies of the distribution.*

Rule III. *If the name of the method is not mentioned, then the coefficient should be calculated by Bowley's method. This method will take less time.*

Example 1. *For a distribution, the Bowley's coefficient of skewness = – 0.36, Q_1 = 8.6 and median 12.3. What is the value of the coefficient of Q.D. ?*

Sol. We have, median = 12.3, $Q_1 = 8.6$
and Bowley's coeff. of skewness = – 0.36.

$$\text{Bowley's coeff. of skewness} = \frac{Q_3 + Q_1 - 2\text{ Median}}{Q_3 - Q_1}$$

$$\therefore \quad -0.36 = \frac{Q_3 + 8.6 - 2(12.3)}{Q_3 - 8.6}$$

$$\therefore \quad -0.36\, Q_3 + 3.096 = Q_3 - 16$$

$$\therefore \quad 1.36\, Q_3 = 19.096$$

$$\therefore \quad Q_3 = \frac{19.096}{1.36} = 14.0412$$

Now $$\text{coeff. of Q.D.} = \frac{Q_3 - Q_1}{Q_3 + Q_1} = \frac{14.0412 - 8.6}{14.0412 + 8.6} = \frac{5.4412}{22.6412} = \mathbf{0.2403.}$$

Example 2. *In a frequency distribution, the following measures were calculated :*

Bowley's coeff. of skewness = 0.35
Median = 75
Q.D. = 6

Find the value of the coefficient of Q.D.

Sol. We have coeff. of skewness = 0.35, median = 75 and Q.D. = 6.

Now $$\text{Q.D.} = \frac{Q_3 - Q_1}{2}$$

$$\Rightarrow \quad \frac{Q_3 - Q_1}{2} = 6 \quad \Rightarrow \quad Q_3 - Q_1 = 12.$$

Also $$\text{coeff. of skewness} = \frac{Q_3 + Q_1 - 2\text{ Median}}{Q_3 - Q_1}$$

$$\Rightarrow \quad 0.35 = \frac{Q_3 + Q_1 - 2(75)}{12}$$

$$\Rightarrow \quad 4.2 = Q_3 + Q_1 - 150 \quad \Rightarrow \quad Q_3 + Q_1 = 154.2$$

Now coeff. of Q.D. $= \frac{Q_3 - Q_1}{Q_3 + Q_1} = \frac{12}{154.2} = \mathbf{0.0778.}$

Example 3. *For the following data, compute quartiles and the coefficient of skewness :*

Income (Rs.)	*Below 200*	*200—400*	*400—600*	*600—800*	*800—1000*	*above 1000*
No. of persons	*25*	*40*	*80*	*75*	*20*	*16*

Sol. **Calculation of Q_1, Q_3 and median**

Classes	*No. of persons (f)*	*c.f.*
Below 200	25	25
200—400	40	65
400—600	80	145
600—800	75	220
800—1000	20	240
above 1000	16	256 = N
	N = 256	

Q_1 : $\frac{N}{4} = \frac{256}{4} = 64$

$\therefore$ Q_1 = size of 64th item

$\therefore$ Q_1 class is 200—400

$\therefore$ $$Q_1 = L + \left(\frac{N/4 - c}{f}\right)h = 200 + \left(\frac{64 - 25}{40}\right) 200 = 200 + 195 = 395.$$

Q_3 : $3\left(\frac{N}{4}\right) = 3\left(\frac{256}{4}\right) = 192$

$\therefore$ Q_3 = size of 192th item

$\therefore$ Q_3 class is 600—800.

$\therefore$ $$Q_3 = L + \left(\frac{3(N/4) - c}{f}\right)h = 600 + \left(\frac{192 - 145}{75}\right) 200$$

$$= 600 + 125.33 = 725.33.$$

Median : $\frac{N}{2} = \frac{256}{2} = 128$

$\therefore$ Median = size of 128th item

$\therefore$ Median class is 400—600.

$\therefore$ $$\text{Median} = L + \left(\frac{N/2 - c}{f}\right)h = 400 + \left(\frac{128 - 65}{80}\right) 200$$

$$= 400 + 157.5 = 557.5.$$

∴ Bowley's coefficient of skewness

$$= \frac{Q_3 + Q_1 - 2\,\text{Median}}{Q_3 - Q_1}$$

$$= \frac{725.33 + 395 - 2\,(557.5)}{725.33 - 395} = \frac{5.33}{330.33} = \mathbf{0.016.}$$

Example 4. *Calculate the Bowley's coefficient of skewness for the following frequency distribution :*

Classes	*1—5*	*6—10*	*11—15*	*16—20*	*21—25*	*26—30*	*31—35*
Frequency	*3*	*4*	*68*	*30*	*10*	*6*	*2*

Sol. **Calculation of Q_1, Q_3 and median**

Classes	*f*	*c.f.*
1—5	3	3
6—10	4	7
11—15	68	75
16—20	30	105
21—25	10	115
26—30	6	121
31—35	2	123 = N
	N = 123	

Q_1 : $\frac{N}{4} = \frac{123}{4} = 30.75$

∴ Q_1 = size of 30.75th item

∴ Q_1 class is 10.5—15.5 (actual class limits)

∴ $Q_1 = L + \left(\frac{N/4 - c}{f}\right) h = 10.5 + \left(\frac{30.75 - 7}{68}\right) 5 = 10.5 + 1.746 = 12.246.$

Q_3 : $3\left(\frac{N}{4}\right) = 3\left(\frac{123}{4}\right) = 92.25$

∴ Q_3 = size of 92.25th item

∴ Q_3 class is 15.5—20.5 (actual class limits)

∴ $Q_3 = L + \left(\frac{3\,(N/4) - c}{f}\right) h = 15.5 + \left(\frac{92.25 - 75}{30}\right) 5$

$= 15.5 + 2.875 = 18.375.$

Median : $\frac{N}{2} = \frac{123}{2} = 61.5$

∴ Median = size of 61.5th item

$\therefore$ Median class is 10.5—15.5 (actual class limits)

$$\therefore \quad \text{Median} = L + \left(\frac{N/2 - c}{f}\right) h = 10.5 + \left(\frac{61.5 - 7}{68}\right) 5 = 10.5 + 4.007 = 14.507.$$

Now, Bowley's coefficient of skewness

$$= \frac{Q_3 + Q_1 - 2\,\text{Median}}{Q_3 - Q_1}$$

$$= \frac{18.375 + 12.246 - 2\,(14.507)}{18.375 - 12.246} = \frac{1.607}{6.129} = \mathbf{0.262.}$$

Example 5. *From the information given below, calculate Karl Pearson's coefficient of skewness and also Bowley's coefficient of skewness :*

Measure	*Place A*	*Place B*
Mean	*150*	*140*
Median	*142*	*155*
S.D.	*30*	*55*
Third Quartile	*195*	*260*
First Quartile	*62*	*80*

Sol. Place A

We have $\bar{x} = 150$, median = 142, S.D. = 30, $Q_3 = 195$, $Q_1 = 62$.

$$\therefore \quad SK_P(A) = \frac{3\,(\bar{x} - \text{Median})}{\text{S.D.}} = \frac{3\,(150 - 142)}{30} = \frac{24}{30} = \mathbf{0.8.}$$

$$SK_B(A) = \frac{Q_3 + Q_1 - 2\,\text{Median}}{Q_3 - Q_1} = \frac{195 + 62 - 2\,(142)}{195 - 62} = \frac{-27}{133} = \mathbf{-0.203.}$$

Place B

We have $\bar{x} = 140$, median = 155, S.D. = 55, $Q_3 = 260$, $Q_1 = 80$.

$$\therefore \quad SK_P(B) = \frac{3\,(\bar{x} - \text{Median})}{\text{S.D.}} = \frac{3\,(140 - 155)}{55} = \frac{-45}{55} = \mathbf{-0.818.}$$

$$SK_B(B) = \frac{Q_3 + Q_1 - 2\,\text{Median}}{Q_3 - Q_1} = \frac{260 + 80 - 2\,(155)}{260 - 80} = \frac{30}{180} = \mathbf{0.167.}$$

EXERCISE 2

1. In a frequency distribution, the difference of quartiles is 25 and their sum is 45. The median is found to be 15. Find Bowley's coefficient of skewness.
2. In a frequency distribution, it is found that $Q_1 = 14.6$ cm, median = 18.8 cm and $Q_3 = 25.2$ cm. Find the coefficient of Q.D. and the Bowley's coefficient of skewness. *(KU 1997)*
3. In a frequency distribution, the Bowley's coefficient of skewness is 0.80. The sum of upper and lower quartiles is 130. The median is 60. Calculate the values of the quartiles.
4. Calculate Bowley's coefficient of skewness for the following data :

Wage (in Rs.)	85	90	95	100	105	110	115	120	125
No. of persons	15	18	25	19	15	7	28	12	11

5. Calculate the Bowley's coefficient of skewness for the following frequency distribution :

More than	*No. of items*	*More than*	*No. of items*
0	5474	60	2718
10	5426	70	1406
20	5259	80	764
30	5023	90	370
40	4475	100	160
50	3712	110	39

6. Calculate the quartile coefficient of skewness for the following frequency distribution :

Weight (in kg)	*No. of persons*	*Weight (in kg)*	*No. of persons*
Under 100	1	150—159	65
100—109	14	160—169	31
110—119	66	170—179	12
120—129	122	180—189	5
130—139	145	190—199	2
140—149	121	200 and above	2

7. Calculate coefficient of skewness based upon quartiles for the data given below :

Marks (Less than)	10	20	30	40	50	60
No. of students	5	12	20	35	40	50

(KU 1997 C)

8. Find Bowley's coefficient of skewness for the following data and show which section of carpenters is more skewed ?

Daily wage (in Rs.)	55—58	58—61	61—64	64—67	67—70
No. of carpenters (Locality A)	12	17	23	18	11
No. of carpenters (Locality B)	20	22	25	13	7

9. For the following table, state in which section the coefficient of skewness is higher :

Marks Obtained	*No. of Students*	
	Section A	*Section B*
0—10	1	0
10—20	4	5
20—30	10	10
30—40	22	13
40—50	30.	42
50—60	35	30
60—70	10	10
70—80	7	8
80—90	1	2

Answers

1. 0.6
2. Coeff. of Q.D. = 0.2663, Coeff. of skewness = 0.2075
3. $Q_1 = 58.75$, $Q_3 = 71.25$
4. 0.5
5. – 0.1628
6. 0.0233
7. – 0.0425
8. Coeff. of skewness (for A) = – 0.01429
   Coeff. of skewness (for B) = – 0.0597
   ∴ Skewness is greater for section B
9. Coeff. of skewness (for A) = – 0.0984
   Coeff. of skewness (for B) = 0.1177
   ∴ Skewness is greater for section B.

---

7. KELLY'S METHOD

This method is based on the fact that in a symmetrical distribution **the 10th percentile** and 90th percentile are equidistant from the median. **In a skewed distribution, this equality** would not hold. The Kelly's coefficient of skewness is given by

$$\textbf{Kelly's coefficient of skewness} = \frac{P_{90} + P_{10} - 2\text{ Median}}{P_{90} - P_{10}}.$$

For a symmetrical distribution, its value would come out to be zero. This coefficient of skewness would lie between – 1 and + 1. The coefficient of skewness as calculated by this method would give magnitude as well as direction of skewness present in the distribution.

WORKING RULES FOR SOLVING PROBLEMS

Rule I. *If the values of median, P_{10} and P_{90} are given, then find Kelly's coefficient of skewness by using the formula :*

$$SK = \frac{P_{90} + P_{10} - 2\text{ Median}}{P_{90} - P_{10}}.$$

Rule II. *Kelly's coefficient of skewness is also equal to* $\dfrac{D_9 + D_1 - 2\text{ Median}}{D_9 - D_1}$.

Rule III. *If the values of median, P_{10} and P_{90} are not given, then find these by using the cumulative frequencies of the distribution.*

Example 1. *In a frequency distribution,*

$$P_{10} = 5,\ \text{Median} = 12 \text{ and } P_{90} = 22.$$

Find Kelly's coefficient of skewness.

Sol. We have $P_{10} = 5$, median = 12 and $P_{90} = 22$.

Kelly's coeff. of skewness

$$= \frac{P_{90} + P_{10} - 2\text{ Median}}{P_{90} - P_{10}} = \frac{22 + 5 - 2(12)}{22 - 5} = \frac{3}{17} = \mathbf{0.1765}.$$

Example 2. *Calculate Kelly's coefficient of skewness for the following frequency distribution :*

Daily wage (in Rs.)	*20—25*	*25—30*	*30—35*	*35—40*	*40—45*	*45—50*
No. of Workers	*12*	*16*	*5*	*4*	*2*	*1*

Sol. **Calculation of Kelly's Coefficient of Skewness**

Daily wages (in Rs.)	*No. of workers (f)*	*c.f.*
20—25	12	12
25—30	16	28
30—35	5	33
35—40	4	37
40—45	2	39
45—50	1	40 = N
	N = 40	

$\mathbf{P_{10}}$: $10\left(\frac{N}{100}\right) = 10\left(\frac{40}{100}\right) = 4$

$\therefore$ P_{10} = size of 4th item

$\therefore$ P_{10} class is 20—25

$$\therefore \quad P_{10} = L + \left(\frac{10\,(N/100) - c}{f}\right) h$$

$$= 20 + \left(\frac{4 - 0}{12}\right) 5 = 20 + 1.67 = \text{Rs. } 21.67.$$

$\mathbf{P_{90}}$: $90\left(\frac{N}{100}\right) = 90\left(\frac{40}{100}\right) = 36$

$\therefore$ P_{90} = size of 36th item

$\therefore$ P_{90} class is 35—40.

$$\therefore \quad P_{90} = L + \left(\frac{90\,(N/100) - c}{f}\right) h = 35 + \left(\frac{36 - 33}{4}\right) 5$$

$$= 35 + 3.75 = \text{Rs. } 38.75.$$

Median : $\frac{N}{2} = \frac{40}{2} = 20$

$\therefore$ Median = size of 20th item

$\therefore$ Median class is 25—30

$$\therefore \quad \text{Median} = L + \left(\frac{N/2 - c}{f}\right) h = 25 + \left(\frac{20 - 12}{16}\right) 5 = 25 + 2.5 = \text{Rs. } 27.50$$

Now, Kelly's coefficient of skewness

$$= \frac{Q_3 + Q_1 - 2\text{ Median}}{Q_3 - Q_1}$$

$$= \frac{38.75 + 21.67 - 2\,(27.50)}{38.75 - 21.67} = \frac{5.42}{17.08} = \mathbf{0.3173.}$$

EXERCISE 3

1. In a frequency distribution, $P_{10} = 10$, median = 22 and $P_{90} = 25$. Calculate Kelly's coefficient of skewness.
2. In a frequency distribution, $P_{10} = 17$, $P_{90} = 53$ and median = 38. Find Kelly's coefficient of skewness.
3. Find Kelly's coefficient of skewness for the following distribution :

x	8	9	10	11	12	13	14
f	6	10	12	18	17	9	1

4. Calculate the coefficient of skewness, using P_{10} and P_{90}, for the following data :

x	10	11	12	13	14	15	16	17
f	3	11	18	15	12	9	6	3

5. Calculate Kelly's coefficient of skewness for the following frequency distribution :

Marks less than	10	20	30	40	50	60	70
No. of students	0	5	7	10	12	18	30

Answers

1. – 0.6 2. – 0.17 3. 0 4. 0.2 5. – 0.51.

8. METHOD OF MOMENTS

In this method, second and third central moments of the distribution are used. This measure of skewness is called the **Moment coefficient of skewness** and is given by

$$\textbf{Moment coefficient of skewness} = \frac{\mu_3}{\sqrt{{\mu_2}^3}}.$$

For a symmetrical distribution, its value would come out to be zero. The coefficient of skewness as calculated by this method gives the magnitude as well as direction of skewness present in the distribution.

In statistics, we define $\beta_1 = \dfrac{{\mu_3}^2}{{\mu_2}^3}$.

∴ Moment coefficient of skewness can also be written as

$$= \frac{\mu_3}{\sqrt{{\mu_2}^3}} = \pm\sqrt{\left(\frac{\mu_3}{\sqrt{{\mu_2}^3}}\right)^2} = \pm\sqrt{\frac{{\mu_3}^2}{{\mu_2}^3}} = \pm\sqrt{\beta_1}.$$

The sign with $\sqrt{\beta_1}$ is to be taken as that of μ_3. The moment coefficient of skewness is also denoted by γ_1.

The moment coefficient of skewness is generally denoted by 'SK_M'.

WORKING RULES FOR SOLVING PROBLEMS

Rule I. *If the values of μ_2 and μ_3 are given, then find SK_M by using the formula :*

$$SK_M = \frac{\mu_3}{\sqrt{\mu_2^{\,3}}}.$$

Rule II. *If raw moments μ_1', μ_2' and μ_3' are given, then calculate : $\mu_2 = \mu_2' - \mu_1'^2$ and $\mu_3 = \mu_3' - 3\mu_2'\mu_1' + 2\mu_1'^3$.*

Now, find $SK_M = \dfrac{\mu_3}{\sqrt{\mu_2^{\,3}}}$.

Rule III. *If moments are not given, then first find μ_2 and μ_3 by using the given data and then use the formula :* $SK_M = \dfrac{\mu_3}{\sqrt{\mu_2^{\,3}}}$.

Rule IV. $\beta_1 = \dfrac{\mu_3^{\,2}}{\mu_2^{\,3}}$ *and* $\gamma_1 = \dfrac{\mu_3}{\sqrt{\mu_2^{\,3}}}$.

Example 1. *The first three central moments of a distribution are 0, 15, – 31. Find the moment coefficient of skewness.*

Sol. We have $\mu_1 = 0$, $\mu_2 = 15$ and $\mu_3 = -31$.

Moment coefficient of skewness

$$= \frac{\mu_3}{\sqrt{\mu_2^{\,3}}} = \frac{-31}{\sqrt{(15)^3}} = -\frac{31}{\sqrt{3375}} = -\frac{31}{58.09} = \mathbf{-0.53}.$$

Example 2. *The first four moments of a distribution about the value 5 of the variable are 2, 20, 40 and 50. Calculate the moment coefficient of skewness.*

Sol. We have $A = 5, \mu_1' = 2, \mu_2' = 20$

$\mu_3' = 40$ and $\mu_4' = 50$.

Now $\mu_2 = \mu_2' - (\mu_1')^2 = 20 - (2)^2 = 16$

$\mu_3 = \mu_3' - 3\mu_1'\mu_2' + 2\mu_1'^3$

$= 40 - 3(2)(20) + 2(2)^3 = 40 - 120 + 16 = -64$

Moment coefficient of skewness $= \dfrac{\mu_3}{\sqrt{\mu_2^{\,3}}} = \dfrac{-64}{\sqrt{(16)^3}} = \dfrac{-64}{\sqrt{64}} = \mathbf{-1.}$

Example 3. *Calculate the moment coefficient of skewness for the following distribution*

Class	*2.5—7.5*	*7.5—12.5*	*12.5—17.5*	*17.5—22.5*
Frequency	*8*	*15*	*20*	*32*
Class	*22.5—27.5*	*27.5—32.5*	*32.5—37.5*	
Frequency	*23*	*17*	*5*	

Sol. **Calculation of 'SK$_M$'**

Classes	*Frequency* *f*	*Mid-pts.* *x*	*d = x − A* *A = 20*	*u = d/h* *h = 5*	*fu*	*fu*^{2}	*fu*^{3}
2.5—7.5	8	5	− 15	− 3	− 24	72	− 216
7.5—12.5	15	10	− 10	− 2	− 30	60	− 120
12.5—17.5	20	15	− 5	− 1	− 20	20	− 20
17.5—22.5	32	20	0	0	0	0	0
22.5—27.5	23	25	5	1	23	23	23
27.5—32.5	17	30	10	2	34	68	136
32.5—37.5	5	35	15	3	15	45	135
	N = 120				Σ*fu* = − 2	Σ*fu*^{2} = 288	Σ*fu*^{3} = − 62

Now $\mu_1' = \left(\frac{\Sigma fu}{N}\right) h = \left(\frac{-2}{120}\right) 5 = -0.083$

$$\mu_2' = \left(\frac{\Sigma fu^2}{N}\right) h^2 = \left(\frac{288}{120}\right) (5)^2 = 60$$

$$\mu_3' = \left(\frac{\Sigma fu^3}{N}\right) h^3 = \left(\frac{-62}{162}\right) (5)^3 = -64.583.$$

Now $\mu_2 = \mu_2' - \mu_1'^2 = 60 - (-0.083)^2 = 59.993$

$$\mu_3 = \mu_3' - 3\mu_1' \mu_2' + 2\mu_1'^3$$

$$= -64.583 - 3(-0.083)(60) + 2(-0.083)^3 = -49.644.$$

Moment coefficient of skewness $= \frac{\mu_3}{\sqrt{\mu_2^3}} = \frac{-49.644}{\sqrt{(59.993)^3}} = \frac{-49.644}{464.676} = \mathbf{-0.1068.}$

Example 4. *Find the second and third central moments for the frequency distribution given below. Hence find the coefficient of skewness :*

Class	*110.0—114.9*	*115.0—119.9*	*120.0—124.9*	*125.0—129.9*
Frequency	*5*	*15*	*20*	*35*
Class	*130.0—134.9*	*135.0—139.9*	*140.0—144.9*	
Frequency	*10*	*10*	*5*	

Sol. **Computation of moments**

Class	*f*	*x*	*d = x − A* *A = 127.45*	*u = d/h* *h = 5*	*fu*	*fu*^{2}	*fu*^{3}
110.0—114.9	5	112.45	−15	− 3	− 15	45	− 135
115.0—119.9	15	117.45	− 10	− 2	− 30	60	− 120
120.0—124.9	20	122.45	− 5	− 1	− 20	20	− 20
125.0—129.9	35	127.45	0	0	0	0	0
130.0—139.9	10	132.45	5	1	10	10	10
140.0—144.9	10	137.45	10	2	20	40	80
	5	142.45	15	3	15	45	135
	N = 100				Σ*fu* = − 20	Σ*fu*^{2} = 220	Σ*fu*^{3} = − 50

Now $\mu_1' = \left(\frac{\Sigma fu}{N}\right) h = \left(\frac{-20}{100}\right) 5 = -1$

$$\mu_2' = \left(\frac{\Sigma fu^2}{N}\right) h^2 = \left(\frac{220}{100}\right) (5)^2 = 55$$

$$\mu_3' = \left(\frac{\Sigma fu^3}{N}\right) h^3 = \left(\frac{-50}{100}\right) (5)^3 = -62.5.$$

Central moments

$$\mu_2 = \mu_2' - \mu_1'^2 = 55 - (-1)^2 = \mathbf{54}$$

$$\mu_3 = \mu_3' - 3\mu_2'\mu_1' + 2\mu_1'^3 = -62.5 - 3(55)(-1) + 2(-1)^3$$

$$= -62.5 + 165 - 2 = \mathbf{100.5.}$$

∴ **Moment coefficient of skewness**

$$= \frac{\mu_3}{\sqrt{\mu_2^3}} = \frac{100.5}{\sqrt{(54)^3}} = \frac{100.5}{54 \times 7.35} = \mathbf{0.253.}$$

EXERCISE 4

1. **The first three central moments of a distribution are 0, 2.5, 0.7. Find the values of S.D. and the moment coefficient of skewness.**
2. **In a certain distribution, the first four moments about the point 4 are – 1.5, 17, – 30 and 308. Calculate the moment coefficient of skewness.** *(KU 2001)*
3. **The first three moments of a frequency distribution about origin '5' are – 0.55, 4.46 and – 0.43. Find the moment coefficient of skewness.**
4. **Find the moment coefficient of skewness for the following series :**

x	3	6	8	10	18

5. **For the following frequency distribution, find the first four moments about the mean. Also find the value of β_1. Is it a symmetrical distribution ?**

x	2	3	4	5	6
f	1	3	7	3	1

6. **Calculate the A.M., coefficient of variation and the moment coefficient of skewness for the following data :**

x	0	1	2	3	4	5	6	7	8
f	1	8	28	56	70	56	28	8	1

(KU 1998 C)

7. **Calculate the C.V. and the moment coefficient of skewness for the following data :**

Marks	0—10	10—20	20—30	30—40	40—50	50—60	60—70
No. of students	8	12	20	30	15	10	5

(KU 1997)

Answers

1. 1.5811, 0.1771 2. 0.7017 3. 0.7781 4. 0.7504
5. 0, 0.933, 0, 2.533, 0, yes
6. A.M. = 4, C.V. = 35.3553%, coefficient of skewness = 0
7. C.V. = 46.3464%, coefficient of skewness = 0.0726.

EXERCISE 5

1. "Averages, Measures of Disperson and Skewness are complementary to one another in understanding a frequency distribution". Elucidate.
2. Define skewness. Explain the difference between positive skewness and negative skewness.
3. Explain what do you undertand by "Skewness". What are the various methods of measuring skewness ? *(MDU 2002)*
4. Explain the use of moments in studying skewness in frequency distributions.
5. How does 'Skewness' differ from 'Dispersion' ? Explain the different methods of studying skewness.
6. Explain the use of quartiles in studying skewness in frequency distributions.
7. Explain with formulae different measures of skewness. *(KU 1999 C)*
8. What is skewness ? How does it differ from dispersion ? *(MDU 2005)*
9. Explain skewness. *(KU 2007)*

9

Kurtosis

1. INTRODUCTION

We have already discussed some of the characteristics of statistical distributions. The measures of central tendency tells us about the concentration of the observations about an average value of the distribution whereas the measure of dispersion gives the idea of scatter of the observations about some average. The measure of skewness helps us in judging the extent of symmetry in the curves of frequency distributions. Now we shall consider the peakedness and flatness of frequency distributions. The measure of peakedness or flatness or the curve of a frequency distribution, relative to the curve of normal distribution, is called the measure of 'Kurtosis'. Kurtosis refers to the bulginess of the curve of a frequency distribution.

2. DEFINITIONS

The curve of a frequency distribution is called '**Mesokurtic**', if it is neither flat nor sharply peaked. The curve of normal distribution is mesokurtic. The curve of a frequency distribution is called '**Leptokurtic**', if it is more peaked than normal curve. The curve of a frequency distribution is called '**Platykurtic**', if it is more flat-topped than the normal curve.

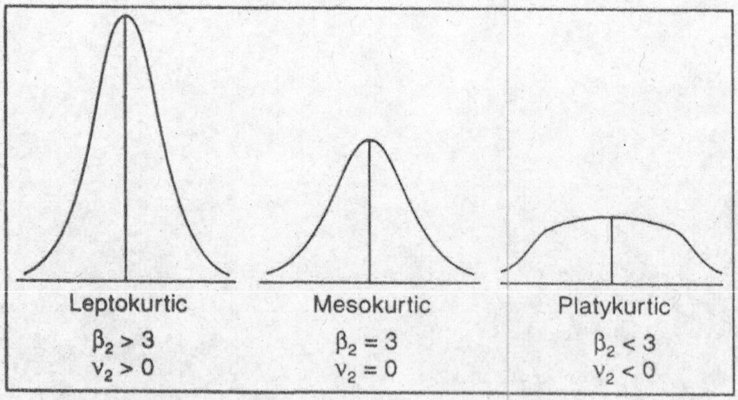

3. MEASURE OF KURTOSIS

The measure of kurtosis is denoted by β_2 and is defined as

$$\beta_2 = \frac{\mu_4}{\mu_2^{\,2}}$$

where μ_2 and μ_4 are respectively the second and fourth moments, about mean of the distribution. If $\beta_2 > 3$, the distribution is Leptokurtic. If $\beta_2 = 3$, the distribution is Mesokurtic. If $\beta_2 < 3$, the distribution is Platykurtic. The kurtosis of a distribution is also measured by using Greek letter 'ν_2', which is defined as $\nu_2 = \beta_2 - 3$.

$\therefore$ $\nu_2 > 0 \Rightarrow \beta_2 - 3 > 0 \Rightarrow \beta_2 > 3 \Rightarrow$ the distribution is Leptokurtic.

Similarly, if $\nu_2 = 0$, then $\beta_2 = 3$

$\therefore$ The distribution is mesokurtic.

$\nu_2 < 0 \Rightarrow \beta_2 < 3 \Rightarrow$ the distribution is Platykurtic.

WORKING RULES FOR SOLVING PROBLEMS

Rule I. *If the values of* μ_2 *and* μ_4 *are given, then find* β_2 *by using the formula :* $\beta_2 = \dfrac{\mu_4}{\mu_2^{\,2}}$.

Rule II. *If raw moments* μ_1', μ_2', μ_3' *and* μ_4' *are given, then calculate :*

$\mu_2 = \mu_2' - \mu_1'^2$ *and* $\mu_4 = \mu_4' - 4\mu_3'\mu_1' + 6\mu_2'\mu_1'^2 - 3\mu_1'^4$

Now, find $\beta_2 = \dfrac{\mu_4}{\mu_2^{\,2}}$.

Rule III. *If moments are not given, then first find* μ_2 *and* μ_4 *by using the given data and then use the formula :* $\beta_2 = \dfrac{\mu_4}{\mu_2^{\,2}}$.

Rule IV. *The given distribution is leptokurtic, mesokurtic and platykurtic according as* $\beta_2 > 3$, $\beta_2 = 3$ *and* $\beta_2 < 3$ *respectively.*

Rule V. $\gamma_2 = \beta_2 - 3$. *The given distribution is leptokurtic, mesokurtic and platykurtic according as* $\gamma_2 > 0$, $\gamma_2 = 0$ *and* $\gamma_2 < 0$ *respectively.*

Example 1. *The first four moments about mean of a frequency distribution are 0, 100, – 7 and 35000. Discuss the kurtosis of the distribution.*

Sol. We have $\mu_1 = 0, \mu_2 = 100, \mu_3 = -7$ and $\mu_4 = 35000$.

Now $$\beta_2 = \frac{\mu_4}{\mu_2^{\,2}} = \frac{35000}{(100)^2} = 3.5 > 3.$$

$\therefore$ The distribution is **leptokurtic.**

Example 2. *The first four moments of a distribution about the value '4' of the variable are – 1.5, 17, – 30 and 108. Discuss the kurtosis of the distribution.* (KU 1999 C, 2000)

Sol. We have $\mu_1' = 1.5, \mu_2' = 17, \mu_3' = -30$ and $\mu_4' = 108$.

$\therefore$ $\mu_2 = \mu_2' - (\mu_1')^2 = 17 - (-1.5)^2 = 14.75$

$$\mu_4 = \mu_4' - 4\mu_1'\mu_3' + 6\mu_2'.(\mu_1')^2 - 3(\mu_1')^4$$
$$= 108 - 4(-1.5)(-30) + 6(17)(-1.5)^2 - 3(-1.5)^4 = 142.3125.$$

Now, $$\beta_2 = \frac{\mu_4}{(\mu_2)^2} = \frac{142.3125}{(14.75)^2} = \frac{142.3125}{217.5625} = 0.654 < 3.$$

$\therefore$ The distribution is **platykurtic.**

Example 3. *The first four moments of a distribution about* $x = 4$ *are 1, 4, 10 and 45. Find the mean and* β_2 *of the distribution.*

Sol. We have $\mu_1' = 1, \mu_2' = 4, \mu_3' = 10$ and $\mu_4' = 45$.

Now $$\bar{x} = 4 + \frac{\Sigma f(x-4)}{N} = 4 + \mu_1' = 4 + 1 = 5$$

$$\mu_2 = \mu_2' - (\mu_1')^2 = 4 - (1)^2 = 3$$

$$\mu_4 = \mu_4' - 4\mu_3'\mu_1' + 6\mu_2'(\mu_1')^2 - 3(\mu_1')^4$$
$$= 45 - 4(10)(1) + 6(4)(1)^2 - 3(1)^4 = 45 - 40 + 24 - 3 = 26.$$

$$\therefore \quad \beta_2 = \frac{\mu_4}{\mu_2^2} = \frac{26}{3^2} = \mathbf{2.8889.}$$

Example 4. *Compute the coefficient of skewness and kurtosis based on moments for the following distribution :*

x	*4.5*	*14.5*	*24.5*	*34.5*	*44.5*	*54.5*	*64.5*	*74.5*	*84.5*	*94.5*
f	*1*	*5*	*12*	*22*	*17*	*9*	*4*	*3*	*1*	*1*

Sol. **Calculation of moments**

x	*f*	*d = x – A* A = 44.5	*u = d/h* h = 10	*fu*	*fu*²	*fu*³	*fu*⁴
4.5	1	– 40	– 4	– 4	16	– 64	256
14.5	5	– 30	– 3	– 15	45	– 135	405
24.5	12	– 20	– 2	– 24	48	– 96	192
34.5	22	– 10	– 1	– 22	22	– 22	22
44.5	17	0	0	0	0	0	0
54.5	9	10	1	9	9	9	9
64.5	4	20	2	8	16	32	64
74.5	3	30	3	9	27	81	243
84.5	1	40	4	4	16	64	256
94.5	1	50	5	5	25	125	625
	N = 75			Σ*fu* = – 30	Σ*fu*² = 224	Σ*fu*³ = – 6	Σ*fu*⁴ = 2072

Moments about 44.5

$$\mu_1' = \left(\frac{\Sigma fu}{N}\right) h = \left(-\frac{30}{75}\right) 10 = -4$$

$$\mu_2' = \left(\frac{\Sigma fu^2}{N}\right) h^2 = \left(\frac{224}{75}\right) (10)^2 = 298.667$$

$$\mu_3' = \left(\frac{\Sigma fu^3}{N}\right) h^3 = \left(\frac{-6}{75}\right) (10)^3 = -80$$

$$\mu_4' = \left(\frac{\Sigma fu^4}{N}\right) h^4 = \left(\frac{2072}{75}\right) (10)^4 = 276266.667.$$

Central moments μ_2, μ_3, μ_4

$$\mu_2 = \mu_2' - \mu_1'^2 = 298.667 - (-4)^2 = 282.667$$

$$\mu_3 = \mu_3' - 3\mu_2'\mu_1' + 2\mu_1'^3 = -80 - 3(298.667)(-4) + 2(-4)^3 = 3376.004$$

$$\mu_4 = \mu_4' - 4\mu_3'\mu_1' + 6\mu_2'\mu_1'^2 - 3\mu_1'^4$$

$$= 276266.667 - 4(-80)(-4) + 6(298.667)(-4)^2 - 3(-4)^4 = 302890.7.$$

Skewness

Moment coefficient of skewness,

$$\gamma_1 = \frac{\mu_3}{\sqrt{\mu_2^3}} = \frac{3376.004}{\sqrt{(282.667)^3}} = \frac{3376.004}{282.667\sqrt{282.667}} = \mathbf{0.71}.$$

$\therefore$ The distribution is **positively skewed.**

Kurtosis

$$\gamma_2 = \frac{\mu_4}{\sqrt{\mu_2^2}} - 3 = \frac{302890.7}{(282.667)^2} - 3 = 3.79 - 3 = 0.79 > 0.$$

$\therefore$ The distribution is **leptokurtic.**

Example 5. *Discuss the kurtosis for the following distribution :*

Marks	*0—10*	*10—20*	*20—30*	*30—40*	*40—50*	*50—60*	*60—70*
No. of students	*8*	*12*	*20*	*30*	*15*	*10*	*5*

(KU 2001 C)

Sol. In order to calculate β_2, the measure of kurtosis, we will have to find the values of μ_2 and μ_4.

Marks	*No. of students* f	*Mid pts* x	$d = x - A$, $A = 35$	$u = d/h$, $h = 10$	fu	fu^2	fu^3	fu^4
0—10	8	5	– 30	– 3	– 24	72	– 216	648
10—20	12	15	– 20	– 2	– 24	48	– 96	192
20—30	20	25	– 10	– 1	– 20	20	– 20	20
30—40	30	35	0	0	0	0	0	0
40—50	15	45	10	1	15	15	15	15
50—60	10	55	20	2	20	40	80	160
60—70	5	65	30	3	15	45	135	405
	N = 100				$\Sigma fu =$ – 18	$\Sigma fu^2 =$ 240	$\Sigma fu^3 =$ – 102	$\Sigma fu^4 =$ 1440

Now,

$$\mu_1' = \left(\frac{\Sigma fu}{N}\right) h = \left(\frac{-18}{100}\right) 10 = -1.8$$

$$\mu_2' = \left(\frac{\Sigma fu^2}{N}\right) h^2 = \left(\frac{240}{100}\right) (10)^2 = 240$$

$$\mu_3' = \left(\frac{\Sigma fu^3}{N}\right) h^3 = \left(\frac{-102}{100}\right) (10)^3 = -1020$$

$$\mu_4' = \left(\frac{\Sigma fu^4}{N}\right) h^4 = \left(\frac{1440}{100}\right)(10)^4 = 144000.$$

Now, $\mu_2 = \mu_2' - (\mu_1')^2 = 240 - (-1.8)^2 = 236.76$

$\mu_4 = \mu_4' - 4\mu_1'\mu_3' + 6(\mu_1')^2\mu_2' - 3(\mu_1')^4$

$= 144000 - 4(-1.8)(-1020) + 6(-1.8)^2(240) - 3(-1.8)^4$

$= 144000 - 7344 + 4665.6 - 31.4928 = 141290.11.$

$$\therefore \quad \beta_2 = \frac{\mu_4}{(\mu_2)^2} = \frac{141290.11}{(236.76)^2} = \frac{141290.11}{56055.297} = 2.5205 < 3.$$

$\therefore$ The distribution is **platykurtic.**

Example 6. *Find the measure of kurtosis for the following distribution :*

Class	*45—52*	*52—59*	*59—66*	*66—73*	*73—80*	*80—87*	*87—94*
Frequency	*4*	*9*	*12*	*4*	*3*	*2*	*1*

(KU 1995 C)

Sol. In order to calculate β_2, the measure of kurtosis, we will have to find the values of μ_2 and μ_4.

Class	*Frequency*	*Mid-points x*	*d = x − A A = 69.5*	*u = d/h h = 7*	*fu*	*fu²*	*fu³*	*fu⁴*
45—52	4	48.5	− 21	− 3	− 12	36	− 108	324
52—59	9	55.5	− 14	− 2	− 18	36	− 72	144
59—66	12	62.5	− 7	− 1	− 12	12	− 12	12
66—73	4	69.5	0	0	0	0	0	0
73—80	3	76.5	7	1	3	3	3	3
80—87	2	83.5	14	2	4	8	16	32
87—94	1	90.5	21	3	3	9	27	81
	N = 35				Σfu = − 32	Σfu² = 104	Σfu³ = − 146	Σfu⁴ = 596

Now, $\mu_1' = \left(\frac{\Sigma fu}{N}\right) h = \left(\frac{-32}{35}\right) 7 = -6.4$

$$\mu_2' = \left(\frac{\Sigma fu^2}{N}\right) h^2 = \left(\frac{104}{35}\right)(7)^2 = 145.6$$

$$\mu_3' = \left(\frac{\Sigma fu^3}{N}\right) h^3 = \left(\frac{-146}{35}\right)(7)^3 = -1430.8$$

$$\mu_4' = \left(\frac{\Sigma fu^4}{N}\right) h^4 = \left(\frac{596}{35}\right)(7)^4 = 40885.6$$

$\therefore \quad \mu_2 = \mu_2' - (\mu_1')^2 = 145.6 - (-6.4)^2 = 104.64$

$\mu_4 = \mu_4' - 4\mu_1'\mu_3' + 6(\mu_1')^2 \mu_2' - 3(\mu_1')^4$

$= 40885.6 - 4(-6.4)(-1430.8) + 6(-6.4)^2(145.6) - 3(-6.4)^4$

$= 40885.6 - 36628.48 + 35782.656 - 5033.1648 = 35006.612.$

$$\therefore \quad \beta_2 = \frac{\mu_4}{(\mu_2)^2} = \frac{35006.612}{(104.64)^2} = 3.1971 > 3.$$

$\therefore$ The distribution is **leptokurtic.**

Example 7. *Obtain coefficients of skewness and kurtosis for the following data :*

Income in Rs. (below)	*90*	*110*	*130*	*150*	*170*
No. of workers	*8*	*11*	*18*	*19*	*24*

(MDU 1999)

Sol. To obtain the coefficients of skewness and kurtosis, we find first four central moments.

Income (in Rs.)	*No. of workers (f)*	*Mid-points x*	*d = x − A A = 120*	*u = d/h h = 20*	*fu*	*fu²*	*fu³*	*fu⁴*
70—90	8	80	− 40	− 2	− 16	32	64	128
90—110	11 − 8 = 3	100	− 20	− 1	− 3	3	− 3	3
110—130	18 − 11 = 7	120	0	0	0	0	0	0
130—150	19 − 18 = 1	140	20	1	1	1	1	1
150—170	24 − 19 = 5	160	40	2	10	20	40	80
	N = 24				Σfu = − 8	Σfu^2 = 56	Σfu^3 = − 26	Σfu^4 = 212

Now $\quad \mu_1' = \left(\frac{\Sigma fu}{N}\right) h = \left(\frac{-8}{24}\right) 20 = -6.67$

$$\mu_2' = \left(\frac{\Sigma fu^2}{N}\right) h^2 = \left(\frac{56}{24}\right) (20)^2 = 933.33$$

$$\mu_3' = \left(\frac{\Sigma fu^3}{N}\right) h^3 = \left(\frac{-26}{24}\right) (20)^3 = 8666.67$$

$$\mu_4' = \left(\frac{\Sigma fu^4}{N}\right) h^4 = \left(\frac{212}{24}\right) (20)^4 = 1413333.33.$$

$\therefore \quad \mu_2 = \mu_2' - (\mu_1')^2 = 933.33 - (-6.67)^2 = 888.44$

$\mu_3 = \mu_3' - 3\mu_2'\mu_1' + 2(\mu_1')^3$

$= 8666.67 - 3(933.33)(-6.67) + 2(-6.67)^3 = 26749.12$

$\mu_4 = \mu_4' - 4\mu_3'\mu_1' + 6\mu_2'(\mu_1')^2 - 3(\mu_1')^4$

$= 1413333.33 - 4(8666.67)(-6.67) + 6(933.33)(-6.67)^2 - 3(-6.67)^4$

$= 1714365.8$

Moment coefficient of skewness

$$= \frac{\mu_3}{\sqrt{\mu_2^3}} = \frac{26749.12}{\sqrt{(888.44)^3}} = \frac{26749.12}{26481.47} = \mathbf{1.01.}$$

$$\text{Coefficient of kurtosis } (\beta_2) = \frac{\mu_4}{\mu_2^2} = \frac{1714365.8}{(888.44)^2} = \frac{1714365.8}{789325.63} = \mathbf{2.17.}$$

Example 8. *For a distribution, the mean is 10, variance is 16. If $\gamma_1 = 1$, $\beta_2 = 4$, find the first four moments about the mean and about the origin.* (KU 1998)

Sol. We have $\bar{x} = 10$, variance = 16, $\gamma_1 = 1$, $\beta_2 = 4$.

We know $\mu_1 = \mathbf{0}$ (always), μ_2 = variance = **16**

$$\gamma_1 = \frac{\mu_3}{\sqrt{\mu_2^3}} \Rightarrow 1 = \frac{\mu_3}{\sqrt{(16)^3}} \Rightarrow \mu_3 = 16 \times 4 = \mathbf{64}$$

$$\beta_2 = \frac{\mu_4}{\mu_2^2} \Rightarrow 4 = \frac{\mu_4}{(16)^2} \Rightarrow \mu_4 = 4 \times 256 = \mathbf{1024.}$$

Moments about origin

$$\gamma_1 = \bar{x} = \mathbf{10}$$

$$\gamma_2 = \mu_2 + \bar{x}^2 = 16 + (10)^2 = \mathbf{116}$$

$$\gamma_3 = \mu_3 + 3\mu_2 \bar{x} + \bar{x}^3 = 64 + 3(16)(10) + (10)^3 = \mathbf{1544}$$

$$\gamma_4 = \mu_4 + 4\mu_3 \bar{x} + 6\mu_2 \bar{x}^2 + \bar{x}^4$$

$$= 1024 + 4(64)(10) + 6(16)(10)^2 + (10)^4 = \mathbf{23184.}$$

EXERCISE 1

1. Define kurtosis. How is it measured ? *(MDU 2007)*
2. How does kurtosis differ from skewness ?
3. Explain the method of studying kurtosis.
4. What are Skewness and Kurtosis ? Give formula for measuring them. *(KU 1998 C)*
5. How would you analyse a frequency distribution through the method of moments ? *(KU 2006 S)*
6. Define Kurtosis. Give Fisher's measure of Kurtosis. Draw rough sketches for different cases. *(KU 1999)*
7. The first four moments about mean of a frequency distribution are 0, 60, – 50 and 8020 respectively. Discuss the kurtosis of the distribution.
8. The μ_2 and μ_4 for a distribution are found to be 2 and 12 respectively. Discuss the kurtosis of the distribution.
9. The first four central moments of a distribution are 0, 2.5, 0.7 and 18.75. Test the kurtosis of the distribution. *(KU 1997)*
10. The standard deviation of a symmetric distribution is 3. What must be the value of μ_4, so that the distribution may be mesokurtic ? *(KU 2002)*

11. Calculate the value of β_2 for the following distribution :

Class	Frequency	Class	Frequency
2.5—7.5	8	22.5—27.5	23
7.5—12.5	15	27.5—32.5	17
12.5—17.5	20	32.5—37.5	5
17.5—22.5	32		

12. If the first four moments about the value '5' of the variable are – 4, 22, – 117 and 560, find the value of β_2 and discuss the kurtosis.

13. Compute the value of β_2 for the following distribution. Is the distribution platykurtic ?

Class	10—20	20—30	30—40	40—50	50—60	60—70	70—80
Frequency	1	20	69	108	78	22	2

(*KU 1997 C*)

14. From the following data of the wages of 50 workers of a factory, compute the first four moments about mean and also the value of β_2.

Monthly Wage (Rs.)	*No. of Workers*
100—120	1
120—140	3
140—160	7
160—180	20
180—200	12
200—220	4
220—240	3

(*KU 1995*)

15. Calculate β_1 and β_2 for the following distribution :

Age (in years)	25—30	30—35	35—40	40—45
Number of workers	2	8	18	27
Age (in years)	45—50	50—55	55—60	60—65
Number of workers	25	16	7	2

(*KU 1999*)

Answers

7. $\beta_2 = 2.2278$, Platykurtic **8.** $\beta_2 = 3$, Mesokurtic **9.** $\beta_2 = 3$, Mesokurtic
10. $\mu_4 = 243$ **11.** $\beta_2 = 2.3216$, Platykurtic **12.** $\beta_2 = 0.8889$, Platykurtic
13. $\beta_2 = 2.7240$, Yes **14.** $\mu_1 = 0$, $\mu_2 = 636.96$, $\mu_3 = 642.816$, $\mu_4 = 1338557.8$, $\beta_2 = 3.2992$
15. $\beta_1 = 0.033, \beta_2 = 2.7$.

10

Measures of Correlation

1. INTRODUCTION

In practical life, we come across certain situations, where movements in one variable are accompanied by movements in other variables. For example, the expenditure of a family is very much related to the income of the concerned family. An increase in income is expected to be accompanied by an increase in the expenditure. If the data relating to a number of families is collected, then it would be found that the variables 'income' and 'expenditure' are moving in sympathy in the same direction. An increase in the day temperature may be accompanied by an increase in the sale of cold drinks. The marks in Accountancy and Mathematics papers of students in a class move in the same direction, on an average, because a student who is brilliant in one subject is expected to be so in the other subjects also.

2. DEFINITION

If the changes in the values of one variable are accompanied by changes in the values of the other variable, then the variables are said to be **correlated.** The correlated variables move in sympathy, on an average, either in the same direction or in the opposite directions. According to *L.R. Connor*, "If two or more quantities vary in sympathy so that movements in one tend to be accompanied by corresponding movements in the other(s), then they are said to be correlated". In other words, variables are said to be correlated if the variations in one variable are followed by variations in the others.

3. CORRELATION AND CAUSATION

Two variables may be related in the sense that the changes in the values of one variable are accompanied by changes in the values of the other variable. But this cannot be interpreted in the sense that the changes in one variable has necessarily caused changes in the other variable. Their movement in sympathy may be due to mere chance. A high degree correlation between two variables may not necessarily imply the existence of a cause-effect relationship between the variables. On the other hand, if there is a cause-effect relationship between the variables, then the correlation is sure to exist between the variables under consideration. A high degree correlation between 'income' and 'expenditure' is due to the fact that expenditure is affected by the income.

Now we shall outline the reasons which may be held responsible for the existence of correlation between variables.

The correlation between variables may be due to the effect of some common cause. For example, positive correlation between the number of girls seeking admission in colleges A and B of a city may be due to the effect of increasing interest of girls towards higher education.

The correlation between variables may be due to mere chance. Consider the data regarding six students selected at random from a college.

Students	*A*	*B*	*C*	*D*	*E*	*F*
% of marks obtained in the previous exam.	42%	47%	60%	80%	55%	40%
Height (in inches)	60	62	65	70	64	59

Here the variables are moving in the same direction and a high degree of correlation is expected between the variables. We cannot expect this degree of correlation to hold good for any other sample drawn from the concerned population. In this case, the correlation has occurred just due to chance.

The correlation between variables may be due to the presence of some cause-effect relationship between the variables. For example, a high degree correlation between 'temperature' and 'sale of coffee' is due to the fact that people like taking coffee in the winter season.

The correlation between variables may also be due to the presence of interdependent relationship between the variables. For example, the presence of correlation between amount spent on entertainment of family and the total expenditure of family is due to the fact that both variables effects each other. Similarly, the variables, 'total sale' and 'advertisement expenses' are interdependent.

TYPES OF CORRELATION

Correlation is classified in the following ways :

(*i*) Positive and Negative Correlation.

(*ii*) Linear and Non-linear Correlation.

(*iii*) Simple, Multiple and Partial Correlation.

4. POSITIVE AND NEGATIVE CORRELATION

The correlation between two variables is said to be **positive** if the variables, on an average, move in the same direction. That is, an increase (or decrease) in the value of one variable is accompanied, on an average, by an increase (or decrease) in the value of the other variable. We do not stress that the variables should move strictly in the same direction. For example, consider the data :

x	2	3	6	8	11
y	14	15	13	18	22

Here the values of y has increased corresponding to every increasing value of x, except for $x = 6$. The correlation between the variables x and y is positive.

The correlation between two variables is said to be **negative** if the variables, on an average, move in the opposite directions. That is, an increase (or decrease) in the value of one variable is accompanied, on an average, by a decrease (or increase) in the value of the other variable.

Here also, we do not stress that the variables should move strictly in the opposite directions. For example, consider the data :

x	110	107	105	95	80
y	8	15	14	27	36

Here, a decrease in the value of x is accompanied by an increase in the value of y, except for $x = 105$. The correlation between x and y is negative.

Thus, we see that the correlation between two variables is positive or negative according as the movements in the variables are in same direction or in the opposite directions, on an average.

5. LINEAR AND NON-LINEAR CORRELATION

The correlation between two variables is said to be **linear** if the ratio of change in one variable to the change in the other variable is almost constant. The correlation between the 'number of students' admitted and the 'monthly fee collected' is linear in nature. Let x and y be two variables such that the ratio of change in x to the change in y is almost constant and if a scatter diagram is prepared corresponding to the variables x and y, the points in the diagrams would be almost along a line.

The extent of linear correlation is found by using Karl Pearson's method, Spearman's rank correlation method and concurrent deviation method.

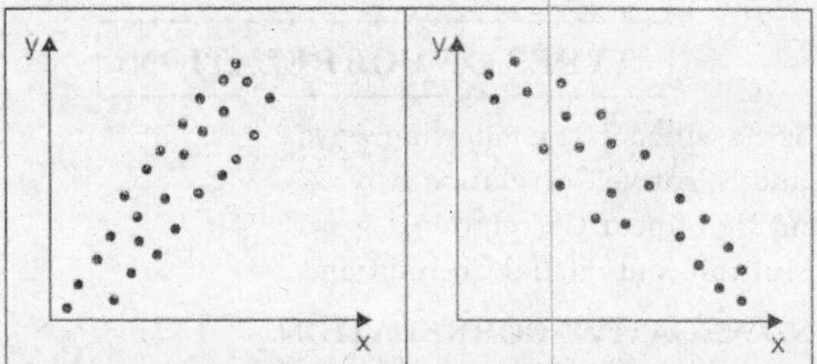

Positive linear correlation　　Negative linear correlation

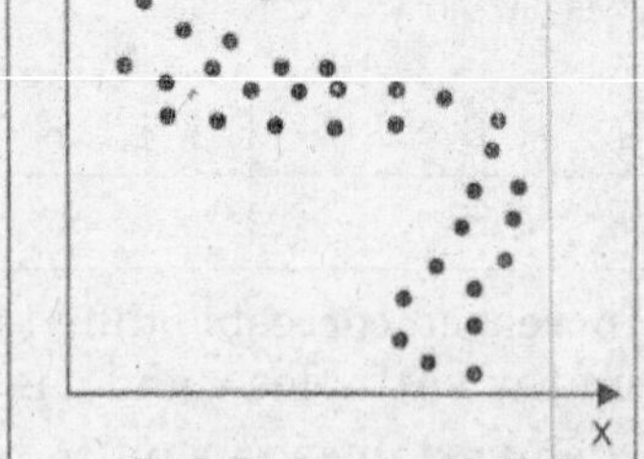

Non-linear correlation

The correlation between two variables is said to be **non-linear** if the ratio of change in one variable to the change in the other variable is not constant. The correlation between 'profit' and 'advertisement expenditure' of a company is non-linear, because if the expenditure on advertisement is doubled, the profit may not be doubled. Let x and y be two variables in which the ratio of change in x to the change in y is not constant and if a scatter diagram is drawn corresponding to the data, the points in the diagram would not be having linear tendency.

6. SIMPLE, MULTIPLE AND PARTIAL CORRELATION

The correlation is said to be **simple** if there are only two variables under consideration. The correlation between sale and profit figures of a departmental store is simple. If there are more than two variables under consideration, then the correlation is either multiple or partial. Multiple and partial coefficients of correlation are called into play when the values of one variable are influenced by more than one variable. For example, the expenditure of salaried class of people may be influenced by their monthly incomes, secondary sources of income, legacy (money etc. handed down from ancestors) etc. If we intend to find the effect of all these variables on the expenditure of families, this will be a problem of multiple correlation. In **multiple correlation,** the combined effect of a number of variables on a variable is considered. Let x_1, x_2, x_3 be three variables, then $R_{1.23}$ denotes the multiple correlation coefficient of x_1 on x_2 and x_3. Similarly $R_{2.31}$ denotes the multiple correlation coefficient of x_2 on x_3 and x_1. In **partial correlation,** we study the relationship between any two variables, from a group of more than two variables, after eliminating the effect of other variables mathematically on the variables under consideration. Let x_1, x_2, x_3 be three variables, then $r_{12.3}$ denotes the partial correlation coefficient between x_1 and x_2. Similarly, $r_{13.2}$ denotes the partial correlation coefficient between x_1 and x_3. The methods of computing multiple and partial correlation coefficients are beyond the scope of this book. Thus, we shall be discussing the methods of computing only simple correlation coefficient.

7. METHODS OF MEASURING CORRELATION

The followings are the methods of measuring correlation between two variables :

I. Scatter Diagram Method

II. Correlation Graph Method

III. Karl Pearson's Method

IV. Spearman's Rank Correlation Method

V. Concurrent Deviations Method.

I. SCATTER DIAGRAM METHOD

8. MEANING

Let $(x_1, y_1), (x_2, y_2), ..., (x_n, y_n)$ be n pairs of values of two variables x and y with respect to some characteristic (time, place etc.). On the graph paper, x variable is measured horizontally whereas the y-variable is measured vertically. The scales on the axes may not be started from zero. The points $\{(x_i, y_i), i = 1, 2, ..., n\}$ are plotted on the graph paper. The diagram so formed is called the '**scatter diagram**', corresponding to the given data. There will be n points on the scatter diagram. If a pair is having exactly same values of variables as that of some other pair, then such point is to be shown separately touching the corresponding point. In order to see, if there is any linear correlation between the variables, the scatter diagram is analysed in the following manner :

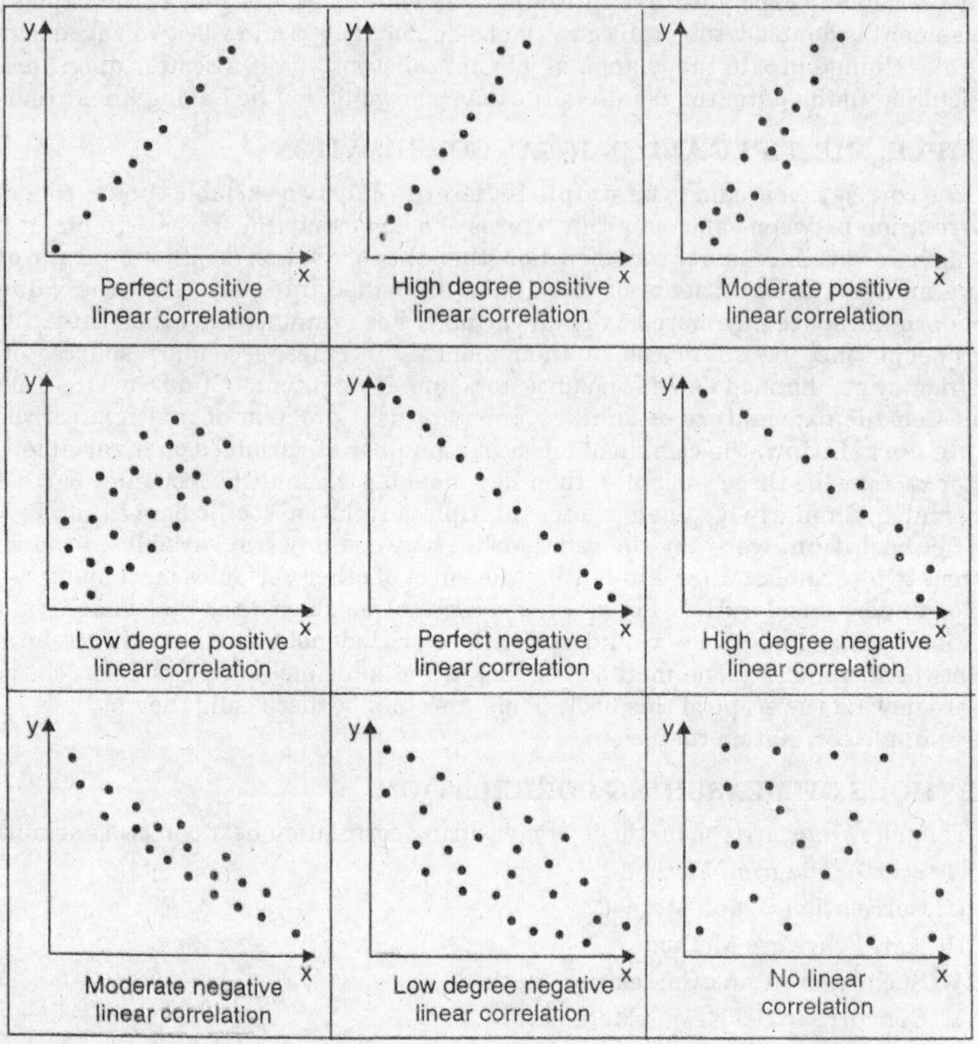

(*i*) If all the plotted points lies on a straight line rising from lower left to upper right, then there is *perfect positive linear correlation* between the variables.

(*ii*) If all the plotted points do not lie on a straight line, but their tendency is to rise from lower left to upper right, then there is *positive linear correlation* between the variables.

(*iii*) If all the plotted points lie on a straight line falling from upper left to lower right, then there is *perfect negative linear correlation* between the variables.

(*iv*) If all the plotted points do not lie on a straight line, but their tendency is to fall from upper left to lower right, then there is *negative linear correlation* between the variables.

(*v*) If it cannot be ascertained as to whether the trend of the plotted points is rising or falling then there is *no linear correlation* between the variables.

Remark. If all the plotted points cluster around some curve, then the correlation between the variables is *non-linear*.

Example 1. *From the following data, ascertain with the help of scatter diagram, whether the income and expenditure of the workers of a factory are correlated or not.*

Years	*1979*	*1980*	*1981*	*1982*	*1983*	*1984*	*1985*	*1986*
Average income (in Rs.)	*210*	*215*	*215*	*222*	*230*	*236*	*245*	*255*
Average expenditure (in Rs.)	*205*	*208*	*212*	*218*	*225*	*230*	*237*	*250*

Sol. From the scatter diagram, we see that there is high degree positive linear correlation between the variables.

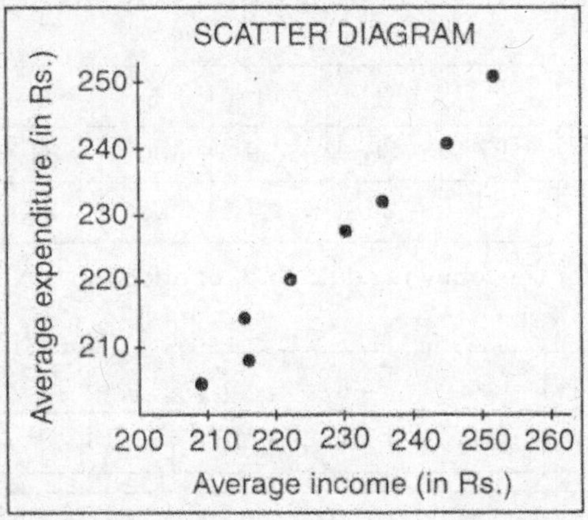

9. MERITS

1. This is simplest of all the methods of measuring correlation.
2. This method is most suitable if just an idea is to be formed whether the variables are correlated or not.
3. This method is least affected by the extreme items.
4. Scatter diagrams are attractive and can be used in exhibition for displaying the correlation between variables.

10. DEMERITS

1. This method is subjective in nature.
2. The degree of correlation assessed cannot be numerically expressed.

EXERCISE 1

1. Draw a scatter diagram for the following data :

x	4	6	8	10	12	14	16	18
y	20	30	40	50	60	70	80	90

2. Draw a scatter diagram for the following data and ascertain if there is any correlation between the variables :

x	80	65	25	40	33	17	38	42	50	52
y	75	54	29	35	41	37	25	40	33	62

3. Draw a scatter diagram for the following data and comment on the presence of correlation between the variables :

x	1	2	3	4	5	6	7	8	9	10
y	4	6	6	7	8	9	10	11	12	12

4. By using scatter diagram, find out if there is any correlation between the ages of husbands and wives given below :

No. of pair	1	2	3	4	5	6	7	8	9	10
Husband's Age	23	27	28	29	30	31	33	35	36	39
Wife's Age	18	22	23	24	25	26	26	28	29	30

5. Draw a scatter diagram for the following data and comment on the presence of correlation between the variables :

Marks in Statistics	18	20	6	15	11	17	16	12
Marks in Accountancy	15	10	18	14	10	18	18	10

II. CORRELATION GRAPH METHOD

11. MEANING

Let (x_1, y_1), (x_2, y_2), ..., (x_n, y_n) be n pairs of values of two variables x and y with respect to some characteristic (time, place etc.). Graphs of both variables are drawn on the same graph paper. The common characteristic is measured along x-axis, whereas the variables x and y are measured along y-axis. The false base line may be used, if need be. If the variables are measured in different units or if their magnitudes vary widely, then the use of double scale on the vertical axis is made. Points are taken corresponding to variables x and y. These points are joined to get graphs of both variables. This is called the **correlation graphs** of variables x and y. This graph is interpreted as follows :

(*i*) If the graphs move in the same direction for almost all values of the common characteristic, then the correlation is linear and positive.

(*ii*) If the graphs move in the opposite direction for almost all values of the common characteristic, then the correlation is linear and negative.

(*iii*) If the graphs move neither in the same direction nor in the opposite direction for almost all values of the common characteristic, then there is no linear correlation between the variables.

12. MERITS

1. This method is suitable if just an idea is to be formed whether the variables are correlated or not.
2. Correlation graphs are attractive and can be used in exhibitions.

13. DEMERITS

1. Correlation graph is effected by the presence of extreme items.
2. The degree of correlation assessed cannot be numerically expressed.
3. This method is subjective in nature.

Example 1. *From the following data, ascertain with the help of correlation graph, whether the income and expenditure of the workers of a factory are correlated or not :*

Years	*1979*	*1980*	*1981*	*1982*	*1983*	*1984*	*1985*	*1986*
Average Income (in Rs.)	*210*	*215*	*215*	*222*	*230*	*236*	*245*	*255*
Average expenditure (in Rs.)	*205*	*208*	*212*	*218*	*225*	*230*	*237*	*250*

Sol. From the correlation graph, we see that there is high degree positive linear correlation between the variables.

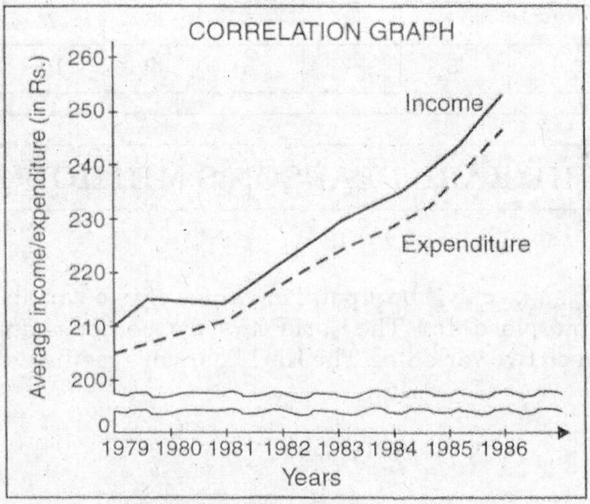

EXERCISE 2

1. Draw correlation graph, showing correlation between demand and price of a certain commodity.

Price (in Rs.)	2	3	5	6	8	9	12	15
Demand (no. of units)	40	35	33	25	22	14	10	5

2. Draw correlation graph for the following data and comment on the presence of correlation between the variables :

x	15	16	19	22	27	27	29	30
y	20	16	10	10	6	6	5	4

3. Draw correlation graph for the data regarding the income and expenditure of 10 families in a locality. Also comment on the presence of correlation between the variables :

Family	1	2	3	4	5	6	7	8	9	10
Income (in Rs.)	500	700	1000	600	900	950	800	500	900	650
Expenditure (in Rs.)	450	700	900	650	800	800	775	550	800	600

4. Depict the following data by using correlation graph and interpret it :

x	200	250	200	200	150	75	50	40	25
y	250	240	200	190	130	60	45	30	15

5. Draw correlation graph for the following data and comment on the presence of correlation between the variables :

x	1	2	3	4	5	6	7	8	9	10
y	4	6	6	7	8	9	10	11	12	12

III. KARL PEARSON'S METHOD

14. DEFINITION

Let $(x_1, y_1), (x_2, y_2), ..., (x_n, y_n)$ be n pairs of values of two variables x and y with respect to some characteristic (time, place etc.). The Karl Pearson's method is used to study the presence of *linear correlation* between two variables. The Karl Pearson's coefficient of correlation, denoted by $r(x, y)$ is defined as :

$$r(x, y) = \frac{\sum_{i=1}^{n} (x_i - \bar{x})(y_i - \bar{y})}{\sqrt{\sum_{i=1}^{n} (x_i - \bar{x})^2} \sqrt{\sum_{i=1}^{n} (y_i - \bar{y})^2}}$$

or simply,

$$\mathbf{r} = \frac{\Sigma(\mathbf{x} - \bar{\mathbf{x}})(\mathbf{y} - \bar{\mathbf{y}})}{\sqrt{\Sigma(\mathbf{x} - \bar{\mathbf{x}})^2} \sqrt{\Sigma(\mathbf{y} - \bar{\mathbf{y}})^2}}$$

where $\bar{x}$ and $\bar{y}$ are the A.M.'s of x-series and y-series respectively.

This is called the *direct method* of computing Karl Pearson's coefficient of correlation.

If there is no chance of confusion, we write $r(x, y)$, just as r.

It can be proved mathematically that $-1 \le r \le 1$.

If the correlation between the variables is *linear*, then the value of Karl Pearson's coefficient of correlation is interpreted as follows :

Value of 'r'	*Degree of linear correlation between the variables*
$r = +1$	Perfect positive correlation
$0.75 \le r < 1$	High degree positive correlation
$0.50 \le r < 0.75$	Moderate degree positive correlation
$0 < r < 0.50$	Low degree positive correlation
$r = 0$	No correlation
$-0.50 < r < 0$	Low degree negative correlation
$-0.75 < r \le -0.50$	Moderate degree negative correlation
$-1 < r \le -0.75$	High degree negative correlation
$r = -1$	Perfect negative correlation

Remark 1. The Karl Pearson's coefficient of correlation is also referred to as **product moment correlation coefficient** or as **Karl Pearson's product moment correlation coefficient.**

Remark 2. The Karl Pearson's coefficient of correlation, r, is also denoted by $\rho(x, y)$ or simply by ρ. The letter ρ is the Greek letter 'rho'.

Remark 3. The square of Karl Pearson's coefficient of correlation is called the **coefficient of determination.**

For example, if $r = 0.753$, then the coefficient of determination is $(0.753)^2 = 0.567$.

The *coefficient of determination* always lies between 0 and 1, both inclusive.

Remark 4. $$r = \frac{\Sigma(x-\bar{x})(y-\bar{y})}{\sqrt{\Sigma(x-\bar{x})^2}\sqrt{\Sigma(y-\bar{y})^2}}$$ implies

$$r = \frac{\Sigma(x-\bar{x})(y-\bar{y})}{n\sqrt{\dfrac{\Sigma(x-\bar{x})^2}{n}}\sqrt{\dfrac{\Sigma(y-\bar{y})^2}{n}}}$$

$$\therefore \qquad \mathbf{r} = \frac{\Sigma(\mathbf{x}-\bar{\mathbf{x}})(\mathbf{y}-\bar{\mathbf{y}})}{\mathbf{n}\sigma_{\mathbf{x}}\,\sigma_{\mathbf{y}}}.$$

Example 1. *From the data given below calculate coefficient of correlation and interpret it :*

	x	y
Number of items	8	8
Mean	68	69
Sum of squares of deviations from mean	36	44

Sum of products of deviations of x and y from their respective means = 24.

Sol. We are given

$$n = 8,\ \bar{x} = 68,\ \bar{y} = 69,\ \Sigma(x-\bar{x})^2 = 36,\ \Sigma(y-\bar{y})^2 = 44,\ \Sigma(x-\bar{x})(y-\bar{y}) = 24.$$

Coefficient of correlation,

$$r = \frac{\Sigma(x-\bar{x})(y-\bar{y})}{\sqrt{\Sigma(x-\bar{x})^2}\sqrt{\Sigma(y-\bar{y})^2}} = \frac{24}{\sqrt{36}\sqrt{44}} = \frac{24}{39.7995} = +\mathbf{0.603}.$$

∴ There is moderate degree positive linear correlation between the variables x and y.

Example 2. *The coefficient of correlation between two variables X and Y is 0.48. The covariance is 36. The variance of X is 16. Find the standard deviation of Y.*

Sol. We have $r = 0.48$, Covariance = 36, $\sigma_X^2 = 16$.

$$r = \frac{\Sigma(X-\overline{X})(Y-\overline{Y})}{\sqrt{\Sigma(X-\overline{X})^2}\sqrt{\Sigma(Y-\overline{Y})^2}} \text{ implies}$$

$$r = \frac{\frac{\Sigma(X-\overline{X})(Y-\overline{Y})}{n}}{\sqrt{\frac{\Sigma(X-\overline{X})^2}{n}}\sqrt{\frac{\Sigma(Y-\overline{Y})^2}{n}}} = \frac{\text{Covariance}^*}{\sigma_X\,\sigma_Y}.$$

$$\therefore \quad 0.48 = \frac{36}{\sqrt{16}.\sigma_Y} \quad \text{or} \quad \frac{48}{100} = \frac{9}{\sigma_Y} \quad \text{or} \quad \sigma_Y = \mathbf{18.75.}$$

Example 3. *Calculate the Karl Pearson's coefficient of correlation from the data given below :*

x	4	6	8	10	12
y	2	3	4	6	10

Sol. **Calculation of 'r'**

S. No.	x	y	$x-\bar{x}$ $\bar{x}=8$	$y-\bar{y}$ $\bar{y}=5$	$(x-\bar{x})(y-\bar{y})$	$(x-\bar{x})^2$	$(y-\bar{y})^2$
1	4	2	−4	−3	12	16	9
2	6	3	−2	−2	4	4	4
3	8	4	0	−1	0	0	1
4	10	6	2	1	2	4	1
5	12	10	4	5	20	16	25
$n=5$	$\Sigma x = 40$	$\Sigma y = 25$			$\Sigma(x-\bar{x})(y-\bar{y}) = 38$	$\Sigma(x-\bar{x})^2 = 40$	$\Sigma(y-\bar{y})^2 = 40$

$$\bar{x} = \frac{\Sigma x}{n} = \frac{40}{5} = 8, \quad \bar{y} = \frac{\Sigma y}{n} = \frac{25}{5} = 5$$

Now $$r = \frac{\Sigma(x-\bar{x})(y-\bar{y})}{\sqrt{\Sigma(x-\bar{x})^2}\sqrt{\Sigma(y-\bar{y})^2}} = \frac{38}{\sqrt{40}.\sqrt{40}} = \frac{38}{40} = \mathbf{0.95.}$$

It shows that there is high degree positive linear correlation between the variables.

Example 4. *Two variable x and y when expressed as deviations from their respective means are as given below :*

---

* **Covariance** between variables X and Y is defined as $\frac{\Sigma(X-\overline{X})(Y-\overline{Y})}{n}$.

X	– 3	– 2	– 1	0	+ 1	+ 2	+ 3
Y	– 3	– 1	0	+ 2	+3	+ 1	+ 2

Find the coefficient of correlation between x and y.

Sol. We have $X = x - \bar{x}$ and $Y = y - \bar{y}$.

Also $r(x, y) = \dfrac{\Sigma(x - \bar{x})(y - \bar{y})}{\sqrt{\Sigma(x - \bar{x})^2}\sqrt{\Sigma(y - \bar{y})^2}}$ $\therefore$ $r(x, y) = \dfrac{\Sigma XY}{\sqrt{\Sigma X^2}\sqrt{\Sigma Y^2}}$ ...(1)

Calculation of r(x, y)

S. No.	X	Y	XY	X^2	Y^2
1	– 3	– 3	9	9	9
2	– 2	– 1	2	4	1
3	– 1	0	0	1	0
4	0	+ 2	0	0	4
5	+ 1	+ 3	3	1	9
6	+ 2	+ 1	2	4	1
7	+ 3	+ 2	6	9	4
$n = 7$	$\Sigma X = 0$	$\Sigma Y = 4$	$\Sigma XY = 22$	$\Sigma X^2 = 28$	$\Sigma Y^2 = 28$

$\therefore$ (1) implies $r(x, y) = \dfrac{22}{\sqrt{28}\sqrt{28}} = \dfrac{22}{28} = \mathbf{0.7857.}$

Example 5. *Calculate the Karl Pearson's coefficient of correlation from the data given below :*

x	4	6	8	10	11
y	2	3	4	6	12

Sol. **Calculation of 'r'**

S. No.	x	y	$x - \bar{x}$ $\bar{x} = 7.8$	$y - \bar{y}$ $\bar{y} = 5.4$	$(x - \bar{x})(y - \bar{y})$	$(x - \bar{x})^2$	$(y - \bar{y})^2$
1	4	2	– 3.8	– 3.4	12.92	14.44	11.16
2	6	3	– 1.8	– 2.4	4.32	3.24	2.76
3	8	4	0.2	– 1.4	– 0.28	0.04	1.96
4	10	6	2.2	0.6	1.32	4.84	0.36
5	11	12	3.2	6.6	21.12	10.24	43.56
$n = 5$	$\Sigma x = 39$	$\Sigma y = 27$			$\Sigma(x - \bar{x})(y - \bar{y}) = 39.4$	$\Sigma(x - \bar{x})^2 = 32.8$	$\Sigma(y - \bar{y})^2 = 63.2$

$$\bar{x} = \frac{\Sigma x}{n} = \frac{39}{5} = 7.8, \qquad \bar{y} = \frac{\Sigma y}{n} = \frac{27}{5} = 5.4$$

Now $$r = \frac{\Sigma(x-\bar{x})(y-\bar{y})}{\sqrt{\Sigma(x-\bar{x})^2}\sqrt{\Sigma(y-\bar{y})^2}} = \frac{39.4}{\sqrt{32.8}\sqrt{63.2}} = \frac{39.4}{(5.7271)(7.9498)}$$

$$= \frac{39.4}{45.5293} = \mathbf{0.8654.}$$

It shows that there is high degree positive linear correlation between the variables.

Example 6. *From the data given below, find the correlation coefficient between variables X and Y ; n = 10, Σxy = 120, Σx² = 90, S.D. of Y series = 8, where x and y denote the deviations of items of X and Y from their respective A.M.*

Sol. We have $n = 10$, $\Sigma xy = 120$, $\Sigma x^2 = 90$, $\sigma_Y = 8$.

Also $x = X - \bar{X}$ and $y = Y - \bar{Y}$.

$\therefore$ $\Sigma(X-\bar{X})(Y-\bar{Y}) = \Sigma xy = 120$, $\Sigma(X-\bar{X})^2 = \Sigma x^2 = 90$

$\sigma_Y = 8$ implies $\sqrt{\frac{\Sigma(Y-\bar{Y})^2}{n}} = 8$ or $\Sigma(Y-\bar{Y})^2 = (8)^2 \times 10 = 640.$

$$\therefore \quad r(X, Y) = \frac{\Sigma(X-\bar{X})(Y-\bar{Y})}{\sqrt{\Sigma(X-\bar{X})^2}\sqrt{\Sigma(Y-\bar{Y})^2}} = \frac{120}{\sqrt{90}\times\sqrt{640}} = \frac{120}{3\sqrt{10}\times 8\sqrt{10}}$$

$$= \frac{120}{240} = \frac{1}{2} = \mathbf{0.5.}$$

15. ALTERNATIVE FORM OF 'r'

In the above examples, the calculations involved in **Example 5** is much more than in other examples. This is due to the fractional values of $\bar{x}$ and $\bar{y}$ in the data. Suppose for some data, we get $\bar{x} = 27.374$ and $\bar{y} = 14.873$, then it can be well imagined that lot of time and energy would be consumed in computing the Karl Pearson's coefficient of correlation. There are very few chances to get $\bar{x}$ and $\bar{y}$ as whole numbers. In order to avoid the chance of facing difficulty in computing deviations of the values of variables from their respective arithmetic means, an alternative form is used which is discussed below :

We have $$r = \frac{\Sigma(x_i-\bar{x})(y_i-\bar{y})}{\sqrt{\Sigma(x_i-\bar{x})^2}\sqrt{\Sigma(y_i-\bar{y})^2}}.$$

Now, $$\Sigma(x_i-\bar{x})(y_i-\bar{y}) = \Sigma(x_i y_i - x_i\bar{y} - \bar{x}y_i + \bar{x}\bar{y})$$

$$= \Sigma x_i y_i - (\Sigma x_i)\,\bar{y} - \bar{x}\,(\Sigma y_i) + n\bar{x}\,\bar{y}$$

$$= \Sigma x_i y_i - \Sigma x_i \left(\frac{\Sigma y_i}{n}\right) - \left(\frac{\Sigma x_i}{n}\right)\Sigma y_i + n\left(\frac{\Sigma x_i}{n}\right)\left(\frac{\Sigma y_i}{n}\right)$$

$$= \Sigma x_i y_i - \frac{(\Sigma x_i)(\Sigma y_i)}{n} = \frac{n\Sigma x_i y_i - (\Sigma x_i)(\Sigma y_i)}{n}.$$

Also $\Sigma(x_i - \bar{x})^2 = \Sigma(x_i^2 + \bar{x}^2 - 2x_i\bar{x}) = \Sigma x_i^2 + n\bar{x}^2 - 2(\Sigma x_i)\,\bar{x}$.

$$= \Sigma x_i^2 + n\left(\frac{\Sigma x_i}{n}\right)^2 - 2(\Sigma x_i)\left(\frac{\Sigma x_i}{n}\right)$$

$$= \Sigma x_i^2 - \frac{(\Sigma x_i)^2}{n} = \frac{n\Sigma x_i^2 - (\Sigma x_i)^2}{n}.$$

Similarly, $\Sigma(y_i - \bar{y})^2 = \dfrac{n\Sigma y_i^2 - (\Sigma y_i)^2}{n}$

$$\therefore \qquad r = \frac{\Sigma(x_i - \bar{x})(y_i - \bar{y})}{\sqrt{\Sigma(x_i - \bar{x})^2}\sqrt{\Sigma(y_i - \bar{y})^2}} \text{ implies}$$

$$r = \frac{\dfrac{n\Sigma x_i y_i - (\Sigma x_i)(\Sigma y_i)}{n}}{\sqrt{\dfrac{n\Sigma x_i^2 - (\Sigma x_i)^2}{n}}\sqrt{\dfrac{n\Sigma y_i^2 - (\Sigma y_i)^2}{n}}}.$$

$$\therefore \qquad \mathbf{r} = \frac{\mathbf{n\Sigma x_i y_i - (\Sigma x_i)(\Sigma y_i)}}{\sqrt{\mathbf{n\Sigma x_i^2 - (\Sigma x_i)^2}}\sqrt{\mathbf{n\Sigma y_i^2 - (\Sigma y_i)^2}}}.$$

For simplicity, we write

$$\mathbf{r} = \frac{\mathbf{n\Sigma xy - (\Sigma x)(\Sigma y)}}{\sqrt{\mathbf{n\Sigma x^2 - (\Sigma x)^2}}\sqrt{\mathbf{n\Sigma y^2 - (\Sigma y)^2}}}.$$

Example 7. *Find the coefficient of correlation for the following data :*

$n = 10, \Sigma x = 50, \Sigma y = -30, \Sigma x^2 = 290, \Sigma y^2 = 300, \Sigma xy = -115.$

Sol.
$$r = \frac{n\Sigma xy - (\Sigma x)(\Sigma y)}{\sqrt{n\Sigma x^2 - (\Sigma x)^2}\sqrt{n\Sigma y^2 - (\Sigma y)^2}}$$

$$= \frac{10(-115) - (50)(-30)}{\sqrt{10(290) - (50)^2}\sqrt{10(300) - (-30)^2}}$$

$$= \frac{350}{\sqrt{400}\sqrt{2100}} = \frac{35}{\sqrt{8400}} = \text{AL}\left[\log\left(\frac{350}{\sqrt{8400}}\right)\right]$$

$$= \text{AL}\left[\log 35 - \frac{1}{2}\log 8400\right] = \text{AL}\left[1.5441 - \frac{1}{2}(3.9243)\right]$$

$$= \text{AL}(-0.4181) = \text{AL}(\bar{1}.5819) = \mathbf{0.3819}.$$

Example 8. *Calculate the Karl Pearson's coefficient of correlation for the data given below :*

x	*4*	*6*	*8*	*10*	*11*
y	*2*	*3*	*4*	*6*	*12*

Sol. **Calculation of 'r'**

S. No.	x	y	xy	x^2	y^2
1	4	2	8	16	4
2	6	3	18	36	9
3	8	4	32	64	16
4	10	6	60	100	36
5	11	12	132	121	144
$n = 5$	$\Sigma x = 39$	$\Sigma y = 27$	$\Sigma xy = 250$	$\Sigma x^2 = 337$	$\Sigma y^2 = 209$

$$r = \frac{n\Sigma xy - (\Sigma x)(\Sigma y)}{\sqrt{n\Sigma x^2 - (\Sigma x)^2}\sqrt{n\Sigma y^2 - (\Sigma y)^2}} = \frac{5(250) - (39)(27)}{\sqrt{5(337) - (39)^2}\sqrt{5(209) - (27)^2}}$$

$$= \frac{197}{\sqrt{164}\sqrt{316}} = \frac{197}{227.6488} = \mathbf{0.8654.}$$

Remark. We have already found 'r' for the above data in **example 5.** The reader must have felt comfortable in using the alternative form of $r(x, y)$.

Example 9. *Calculate the Karl Pearson's coefficient for the data given below :*

x	2	3	5	7	3
y	15	17	4	5	4

Sol. **Calculation of 'r'**

S. No.	x	y	xy	x^2	y^2
1	2	15	30	4	225
2	3	17	51	9	289
3	5	4	20	25	16
4	7	5	35	49	25
5	3	4	12	9	16
$n = 5$	$\Sigma x = 20$	$\Sigma y = 45$	$\Sigma xy = 148$	$\Sigma x^2 = 96$	$\Sigma y^2 = 571$

$$r = \frac{n\Sigma xy - (\Sigma x)(\Sigma y)}{\sqrt{n\Sigma x^2 - (\Sigma x)^2}\sqrt{n\Sigma y^2 - (\Sigma y)^2}} = \frac{5(148) - (20)(45)}{\sqrt{5(96) - (20)^2}\sqrt{5(571) - (45)^2}}$$

$$= \frac{-160}{\sqrt{80}\sqrt{830}} = \frac{-16}{\sqrt{664}} = -\text{AL}\left[\log\left(\frac{16}{\sqrt{664}}\right)\right]$$

$$= -\text{AL}\left[\log 16 - \frac{1}{2}\log 664\right] = -\text{AL}\left[1.2041 - \frac{1}{2}(2.8222)\right]$$

$$= -\text{AL}(-0.207) = -\text{AL}(-1 + 1 - 0.207)$$

$$= -\text{AL}(\bar{1}.793) = \mathbf{-0.6209.}$$

Example 10. *Calculate the Karl Pearson's coefficient of correlation for the data given below :*

(4, 2), (6, 3), (8, 4), (10, 6), (11, 12).

Sol. Let x and y respectively denote the first and the second variables.

Calculation of 'r'

S. No.	x	y	xy	x^2	y^2
1	4	2	8	16	4
2	6	3	18	36	9
3	8	4	32	64	16
4	10	6	60	100	36
5	11	12	132	121	144
$n = 5$	$\Sigma x = 39$	$\Sigma y = 27$	$\Sigma xy = 250$	$\Sigma x^2 = 337$	$\Sigma y^2 = 209$

$$r = \frac{n\Sigma xy - (\Sigma x)(\Sigma y)}{\sqrt{n\Sigma x^2 - (\Sigma x)^2}\ \sqrt{n\Sigma y^2 - (\Sigma y)^2}} = \frac{5(250) - (39)(27)}{\sqrt{5(337) - (39)^2}\ \sqrt{5(209) - (27)^2}}$$

$$= \frac{197}{\sqrt{164}\ \sqrt{316}} = \text{AL}\left[\log \frac{197}{\sqrt{164}.\sqrt{316}}\right]$$

$$= \text{AL}\left[\log 197 - \frac{1}{2}(\log 164 + \log 316)\right]$$

$$= \text{AL}\left[2.2945 - \frac{1}{2}(2.2148 + 2.4997)\right]$$

$$= \text{AL}\,(2.2945 - 2.3573) = \text{AL}\,(-0.0628)$$

$$= \text{AL}\,(-1 + 1 - 0.0628) = \text{AL}\,(\bar{1}.9372) = \mathbf{0.8654}.$$

Example 11. *Calculate 'r' for the following data :*

x	*– 3*	*– 2*	*– 1*	*0*	*1*	*2*	*3*
y	*9*	*4*	*1*	*0*	*1*	*4*	*9*

Sol.

Calculation of 'r'

S. No.	x	y	xy	x^2	y^2
1	– 3	9	– 27	9	81
2	– 2	4	– 8	4	16
3	– 1	1	– 1	1	1
4	0	0	0	0	0
5	1	1	1	1	1
6	2	4	8	4	16
7	3	9	27	9	81
$n = 7$	$\Sigma x = 0$	$\Sigma y = 28$	$\Sigma xy = 0$	$\Sigma x^2 = 28$	$\Sigma y^2 = 196$

$$r = \frac{n\Sigma xy - (\Sigma x)(\Sigma y)}{\sqrt{n\Sigma x^2 - (\Sigma x)^2}\sqrt{n\Sigma y^2 - (\Sigma y)^2}} = \frac{7(0) - (0)(28)}{\sqrt{7(28) - (0)^2}\sqrt{7(196) - (28)^2}} = \mathbf{0.}$$

Remark. In the above example, $r = 0$ indicates that there is no linear correlation between the variables. In fact, the variables x and y are very well correlated and there also exists algebraic relation $y = x^2$ between the variables. The correlation between x and y is curvilinear and Karl Pearson's coefficient of correlation does not help in estimating curvilinear correlation.

Example 12. *Calculate the coefficient of correlation between x and y :*

x	*22*	*24*	*25*	*27*	*21*	*22*	*23*
y	*41*	*44*	*45*	*48*	*40*	*42*	*44*

Sol. **Calculation of 'r'**

S. No.	*x*	*y*	*xy*	x^2	y^2
1	22	41	902	484	1681
2	24	44	1056	576	1936
3	25	45	1125	625	2025
4	27	48	1296	729	2304
5	21	40	840	441	1600
6	22	42	924	484	1764
7	23	44	1012	529	1936
$n = 7$	$\Sigma x = 164$	$\Sigma y = 304$	$\Sigma xy = 7155$	$\Sigma x^2 = 3868$	$\Sigma y^2 = 13246$

$$r = \frac{n\Sigma xy - (\Sigma x)(\Sigma y)}{\sqrt{n\Sigma x^2 - (\Sigma x)^2}\sqrt{n\Sigma y^2 - (\Sigma y)^2}}$$

$$= \frac{7(7155) - (164)(304)}{\sqrt{7(3868) - (164)^2}\sqrt{7(13246) - (304)^2}}$$

$$= \frac{229}{\sqrt{180}\sqrt{306}} = \frac{229}{234.6913} = \mathbf{0.9757.}$$

Example 13. *Calculate coefficient of correlation between Density of population and Death rate for the following data :*

Region	*Area (in sq. km.)*	*Population*	*Deaths*
A	*200*	*40,000*	*480*
B	*150*	*75,000*	*1,200*
C	*120*	*72,000*	*1,080*
D	*80*	*20,000*	*270*

(KU 2001)

Sol. Let the variables x and y denote 'density of population' and 'death rate' respectively.

We have

$$\text{Density of population}^* = \frac{\text{Population}}{\text{Area}} \quad \text{and} \quad \text{Death rate}^* = \frac{\text{No. of deaths}}{\text{Population}} \times 100.$$

$\therefore$ For region A, $x = \frac{40000}{200} = 200,\quad y = \frac{480}{40000} \times 100 = 1.2.$

For region B, $x = \frac{75000}{150} = 500,\quad y = \frac{1200}{75000} \times 100 = 1.6.$

For region C, $x = \frac{72000}{120} = 600,\quad y = \frac{1080}{72000} \times 100 = 1.5.$

For region D, $x = \frac{20000}{80} = 250,\quad y = \frac{270}{20000} \times 100 = 1.35.$

Correlation between x and y

S.No.	x	y	xy	x^2	y^2
1	200	1.2	240	40000	1.44
2	500	1.6	800	250000	2.56
3	600	1.5	900	360000	2.25
4	250	1.35	337.5	62500	1.8225
$n = 4$	$\Sigma x = 1550$	$\Sigma y = 5.65$	$\Sigma xy = 2277.5$	$\Sigma x^2 = 712500$	$\Sigma y^2 = 8.0725$

$$r = \frac{n\Sigma xy - (\Sigma x)(\Sigma y)}{\sqrt{n\Sigma x^2 - (\Sigma x)^2}\sqrt{n\Sigma y^2 - (\Sigma y)^2}}$$

$$= \frac{4(2277.5) - (1550)(5.65)}{\sqrt{4(712500) - (1550)^2}\sqrt{4(8.0725) - (5.65)^2}}$$

$$= \frac{352.5}{\sqrt{447500}\sqrt{0.3675}} = \frac{352.5}{405.532} = \mathbf{0.8692}.$$

Example 14. *Calculate the coefficient of correlation between X and Y from the following data and interpret the result :*

$\Sigma XY = 8425,\ \bar{X} = 28.5,\ \bar{Y} = 28.0,\ \sigma_X = 10.5,\ \sigma_Y = 5.6$, *and* $n = 10$. (KU 2002)

Sol. We have

$$\Sigma XY = 8425,\ \bar{X} = 28.5,\ \bar{Y} = 28,\ \sigma_X = 10.5,\ \sigma_Y = 5.6, \quad \text{and} \quad n = 10.$$

Now $\bar{X} = \frac{\Sigma X}{n} \Rightarrow 28.5 = \frac{\Sigma X}{10} \Rightarrow \Sigma X = 285$

and $\bar{Y} = \frac{\Sigma Y}{n} \Rightarrow 28 = \frac{\Sigma Y}{10} \Rightarrow \Sigma Y = 280.$

*There are standard formulae and should be remembered.

Also $\sigma_X = \sqrt{\dfrac{\Sigma X^2}{n} - \left(\dfrac{\Sigma X}{n}\right)^2} \Rightarrow \sqrt{n\Sigma X^2 - (\Sigma X)^2} = n\,\sigma_X = 10 \times 10.5 = 105$

and $\sigma_Y = \sqrt{\dfrac{\Sigma Y^2}{n} - \left(\dfrac{\Sigma Y}{n}\right)^2} \Rightarrow \sqrt{n\Sigma Y^2 - (\Sigma Y)^2} = n\,\sigma_Y = 10 \times 5.6 = 56.$

Now $r = \dfrac{n\Sigma XY - (\Sigma X)(\Sigma Y)}{\sqrt{n\Sigma X^2 - (\Sigma X)^2}\,\sqrt{n\Sigma Y^2 - (\Sigma Y)^2}}$

$\therefore$ $r = \dfrac{10(8425) - (285)(280)}{105 \times 56} = \dfrac{4450}{105 \times 56} = \mathbf{0.7568}.$

The value of r shows that there is high degree positive linear correlation between the variables X and Y.

Example 15. *A computer while calculating the correlation coefficient between the variables X and Y obtained the following results :*

$$N = 30,\ \Sigma X = 120,\ \Sigma X^2 = 600,\ \Sigma Y = 90,\ \Sigma Y^2 = 250,\ \Sigma XY = 356.$$

It was however later discovered at the time of checking that it had copied down two pairs of observations as

X	*Y*
8	*10*
12	*7*

while the correct values were

X	*Y*
8	*12*
10	*8*

. Obtain the correct value of the coefficient of correlation between X and Y.

Sol. We have N = 30, $\Sigma X = 120$, $\Sigma X^2 = 600$, $\Sigma Y = 90$, $\Sigma Y^2 = 250$, $\Sigma XY = 356$.

Incorrect pairs are

X	Y
8	10
12	7

and correct pairs are

X	Y
8	12
10	8

Corrected sums

$$\Sigma X = 120 - (8 + 12) + (8 + 10) = 118$$

$$\Sigma Y = 90 - (10 + 7) + (12 + 8) = 93$$

$$\Sigma X^2 = 600 - (8^2 + 12^2) + (8^2 + 10^2) = 556$$

$$\Sigma Y^2 = 250 - (10^2 + 7^2) + (12^2 + 8^2) = 309$$

$$\Sigma XY = 356 - (8 \times 10 + 12 \times 7) + (8 \times 12 + 10 \times 8) = 368.$$

Now, correct $r = \dfrac{N\Sigma XY - (\Sigma X)(\Sigma Y)}{\sqrt{N\Sigma X^2 - (\Sigma X)^2}\,\sqrt{N\Sigma Y^2 - (\Sigma Y)^2}}$

$\therefore$ $r = \dfrac{30(368) - (118)(93)}{\sqrt{30(556) - (118)^2}\,\sqrt{30(309) - (93)^2}}$

$= \dfrac{66}{\sqrt{2756}\,\sqrt{621}} = \dfrac{66}{1308.23} = \mathbf{0.05}.$

Example 16. *In two sets of variables of X and Y with 50 observations of each, the following data were observed :*

$$\overline{X} = 10, \text{ S.D. of } X = 3, \overline{Y} = 6, \text{ S.D. of } Y = 2, r_{XY} = +0.3.$$

However, on subsequent verification it was found that one pair with value of X (= 10) and value of Y (= 6) was inaccurate and hence weeded out. With the remaining 49 pairs of values, how is the original value of correlation coefficient affected ? (KU 2001)

Sol. We have $n = 50, \overline{X} = 10, \sigma_X = 3, \overline{Y} = 6, \sigma_Y = 2, r_{XY} = 0.3.$

$$\overline{X} = \frac{\Sigma X}{n} \Rightarrow 10 = \frac{\Sigma X}{50} \Rightarrow \Sigma X = 500$$

$$\overline{Y} = \frac{\Sigma Y}{n} \Rightarrow 6 = \frac{\Sigma Y}{50} \Rightarrow \Sigma Y = 300$$

$$\sigma_X = 3 \Rightarrow \sqrt{\frac{\Sigma X^2}{n} - \overline{X}^2} = 3 \Rightarrow \frac{\Sigma X^2}{50} - (10)^2 = 9$$

$$\Rightarrow \quad \Sigma X^2 = 109 \times 50 = 5450$$

$$\sigma_Y = 2 \Rightarrow \sqrt{\frac{\Sigma Y^2}{n} - \overline{Y}^2} = 2 \Rightarrow \frac{\Sigma Y^2}{50} - (6)^2 = 4$$

$$\Rightarrow \quad \Sigma Y^2 = 40 \times 50 = 2000.$$

Also
$$r_{XY} = \frac{n\Sigma XY - (\Sigma X)(\Sigma Y)}{\sqrt{n\Sigma X^2 - (\Sigma X)^2}\sqrt{n\Sigma Y^2 - (\Sigma Y)^2}}$$

$$\therefore \quad 0.3 = \frac{50\Sigma XY - (500)(300)}{\sqrt{50 \times 5450 - (500)^2}\sqrt{50 \times 2000 - (300)^2}} = \frac{50\,\Sigma XY - 150000}{150 \times 100}$$

$$\Rightarrow \quad 0.3 \times 15000 = 50\,\Sigma XY - 150000.$$

$$\Rightarrow \quad 50\,\Sigma XY = 4500 + 150000 \Rightarrow \Sigma XY = 3090.$$

After dropping the incorrect pair (X = 10, Y = 6), we have 49 pairs of values. Now we find correct values of ΣX, ΣY, ΣX^2, ΣY^2 and ΣXY.

Corrected sums

$$\Sigma X = 500 - 10 = 490, \quad \Sigma Y = 300 - 6 = 294,$$

$$\Sigma X^2 = 5450 - (10)^2 = 5350, \quad \Sigma Y^2 = 2000 - (6)^2 = 1964,$$

$$\Sigma XY = 3090 - (10 \times 6) = 3030.$$

$$\therefore \quad \text{Correct } r_{XY} = \frac{n\Sigma XY - (\Sigma X)(\Sigma Y)}{\sqrt{n\Sigma X^2 - (\Sigma X)^2}\sqrt{\Sigma Y^2 - (\Sigma Y)^2}}$$

$$= \frac{49(3030) - (490)(294)}{\sqrt{49(5350) - (490)^2}\sqrt{49(1964) - (294)^2}}$$

$$= \frac{4410}{\sqrt{22050}\sqrt{9800}} = \frac{4410}{14700} = \mathbf{0.3.}$$

Example 17. *Show that correlation coefficient is independent of the change of origin and scale.* (MDU 1999)

Sol. Let x and y be any two variables. If A and B be any constants, then $x - A, y - B$ are called variables obtained by changing the origin. If h and k are positive constants, then $\frac{x}{h}$ and $\frac{y}{k}$ are called variables obtained by changing the scale.

Let $$u = \frac{x - A}{h} \quad \text{and} \quad v = \frac{y - B}{k}.$$

$\therefore$ u and v are variables obtained by changing origin and scale of given variables x and y respectively.

$$\therefore \quad x = A + hu \quad \text{and} \quad y = B + kv$$

Summing both sides and dividing by the number of values, we get

$$\bar{x} = A + h\bar{u} \quad \text{and} \quad \bar{y} = B + k\bar{v}.$$

$$\therefore \quad x - \bar{x} = (A + hu) - (A + h\bar{u}) = h(u - \bar{u})$$

and $$y - \bar{y} = (B + kv) - (B + k\bar{v}) = k(v - \bar{v})$$

Now, $$r(x, y) = \frac{\Sigma(x - \bar{x})(y - \bar{y})}{\sqrt{\Sigma(x - \bar{x})^2}\sqrt{\Sigma(y - \bar{y})^2}} = \frac{\Sigma[h(u - \bar{u}) \times k(v - \bar{v})]}{\sqrt{\Sigma[h(u - \bar{u})]^2}\sqrt{\Sigma[k(v - \bar{v})]^2}}$$

$$= \frac{hk\,\Sigma(u - \bar{u})(v - \bar{v})}{\sqrt{h^2}\,.\sqrt{k^2}\sqrt{\Sigma(u - \bar{u})^2}\sqrt{\Sigma(v - \bar{v})^2}}$$

$$= \frac{hk}{hk}\cdot\frac{\Sigma(u - \bar{u})(v - \bar{v})}{\sqrt{\Sigma(u - \bar{u})^2}\sqrt{\Sigma(v - \bar{v})^2}} \qquad \begin{pmatrix} h > 0 \Rightarrow \sqrt{h^2} = h, \\ k > 0 \Rightarrow \sqrt{k^2} = k \end{pmatrix}$$

$$= \frac{\Sigma(u - \bar{u})(v - \bar{v})}{\sqrt{\Sigma(u - \bar{u})^2}\sqrt{\Sigma(v - \bar{v})^2}} = r(u, v).$$

$\therefore$ Correlation coefficient between the variables x and y is same as that between the variables u and v.

$\therefore$ Correlation coefficient is independent of the change of origin and scale.

EXERCISE 3

1. From the data given below, calculate the coefficient of correlation :

	x	y
Number of items	15	15
A.M.	25	18
Sum of squares of deviations from mean	136	138

Sum of products of deviations of x and y from their respective means = 122. *(MDU 1996)*

2. Find the coefficient of correlation for the following data :

x	5	4	3	2	1
y	5	2	10	8	4

3. Find the coefficient of correlation for the following data :

x	1	2	3	4	5
y	7	6	5	4	3

4. Find the coefficient of correlation for the following data :

x	2	10	8	6	8
y	4	6	7	10	6

5. Find the coefficient of correlation for the following data :

x	2	3	4	5	6
y	4	3	2	8	10

6. Find the Karl Pearson's coefficient of correlation for the following data :

x	1	2	8.	4	5
y	10	9	8	8	7

7. Find Karl Pearson's coefficient of correlation between x and y for the following data :

x	1	2	3	4	5
y	2	5	7	8	10

8. Calculate the coefficient of correlation between x and y for the following data :

x	2	4	5	6	3	6	8	10
y	5	6	6	8	4	8	12	15

9. Find Karl Pearson's coefficient of correlation between x and y for the following data :

x	3	4	8	9	6	2	1
y	5	3	7	7	6	9	2

10. Find the coefficient of correlation for the following data :

x	1	3	5	7	8	10
y	8	12	15	17	18	20

11. Find the coefficient of correlation for the following data :

x	1	2	3	4	5	6	7	8	9	10
y	10	9	8	8	6	12	4	3	18	1

12. Calculate the coefficient of correlation between X and Y for the following data :

X	1	2	3	4	5	6	7	8	9
Y	9	8	10	12	11	13	14	16	15

13. Calculate the coefficient of correlation for the following data :

x	10	7	12	12	9	16	12	18	8	12	14	16
y	6	4	7	8	10	7	10	15	5	6	11	13

14. Calculate the coefficient of correlation between the values of X and Y given below :

X	– 15	+ 18	– 12	– 10	+ 15	– 20	– 25	+ 15	+ 16	– 14
Y	+ 8	– 10	+ 5	+ 12	– 6	+ 4	+ 11	– 9	– 7	+ 13

15. Calculate the Karl Pearson's coefficient of correlation for the following data :

x	28	32	38	42	46	52	54	57	58	63
y	0	1	3	4	2	5	4	6	7	8

16. With the following data in 6 cities, calculate the coefficient of correlation by Pearson's method between the density of population and the death rate.

City	*Area in square kilometres*	*Population (in thousands)*	*No. of deaths*
A	150	30	300
B	180	90	1440
C	100	40	560
D	60	42	840
E	120	72	1224
F	80	24	312

17. A computer while calculating correlation coefficient between two variables X and Y from 25 pairs of observations obtained the following results :

$$\Sigma X = 125, \Sigma Y = 100, \Sigma X^2 = 650, \Sigma Y^2 = 460, \Sigma XY = 508.$$

It was however discovered at the time of checking that two pairs of observations were not correctly copied. They were taken as (6, 14) and (8, 6) while the correct values were (8, 12) and (6, 8). Show that the correct value of the correlation coefficient should be 2/3.

18. Coefficient of correlation between variables x and y for 20 pairs is 0.3 ; means of x and y are respectively 15 and 20, standard deviations are 4 and 5 respectively. After calculations, it was found that one pair with values (27, 35) was taken as (17, 30). Find the correct coefficient of correlation between x and y.

Answers

1. 0.8906	**2.** $r = -0.1980$	**3.** $r = -1$	**4.** $r = 0.2859$
5. $r = 0.7825$	**6.** $r = 0.7206$	**7.** $r = 0.9851$	**8.** $r = 0.9623$
9. $r = 0.4078$	**10.** $r = 0.9879$	**11.** $r = -0.1840$	**12.** $r = 0.95$
13. $r = 0.748$	**14.** – 0.912	**15.** 0.9293	**16.** $r = 0.9876$
18. $r = 0.521$.			

16. STEP DEVIATION METHOD

When the values of x and y are numerically high, as in **Example 12** of Article **10.15,** the step deviation method is used.

Deviations of values of variables x and y are calculated from some chosen arbitrary numbers, called A and B. Let h be a *positive* common factor of all the deviations $(x - A)$ of items in the x-series. The definition of h is valid, since at least one common factor "1" exist for all the deviations. Similarly let k be a *positive* factor of all the deviations $(y - B)$ of items in the y-series.

Let $$u = \frac{x - A}{h} \quad \text{and} \quad v = \frac{y - B}{k}.$$

∴ The variables u and v are obtained by changing origin and scale of the variables x and y respectively.

Since correlation coefficient is independent of change of origin and scale, we have

$$r(x, y) = r(u, v).$$

$$\therefore \quad r(x, y) = \frac{\Sigma(u - \bar{u})(v - \bar{v})}{\sqrt{\Sigma(u - \bar{u})^2}\sqrt{\Sigma(v - \bar{v})^2}}$$

On simplification, we get

$$\mathbf{r(x, y)} = \frac{\mathbf{n\Sigma uv - (\Sigma u)(\Sigma v)}}{\sqrt{\mathbf{n\Sigma u^2 - (\Sigma u)^2}}\sqrt{\mathbf{n\Sigma v^2 - (\Sigma v)^2}}}.$$

The values of u and v are called the **step deviations** of the values of x and y respectively. In the above form :

Σu is the sum of step deviations of the items of x-series.

Σv is the sum of step deviations of the items of y-series.

Σuv is the sum of the products of the step deviations of items of x-series with the corresponding step deviations of items of y-series.

Σu^2 is the sum of the squares of the step deviations of items of x-series.

Σv^2 is the sum of the squares of the step deviations of items of y-series.

In practical problems, the choice of common factors h and k would not create any problem. Even if we do not care to compute step deviations, by dividing the deviations of values of x and y by some common factor, the formula would still work. Suppose we have taken deviations (u) of the items of x-series from A,

i.e., $$u = x - A = \frac{x - A}{1}.$$

We can consider the values of u as the step deviations of the items of x-series, taking '1' as the common factor. Similar argument would also work for y-series.

Therefore, in solving problems, we first calculate deviations of items of x-series and y-series from some convenient and suitable assumed means A and B respectively. These deviations of x-series and y-series are then divided by positive common factors, if at all desired. If we do not bother to divide these deviations by common factors, then these deviations would be thought of as *step deviations* of items of given series with '1' as the common factor for both series.

Thus if u = x – A and v = y – B, then, we have

$$\mathbf{r(x, y)} = \frac{\mathbf{n\Sigma uv - (\Sigma u)(\Sigma v)}}{\sqrt{\mathbf{n\Sigma u^2 - (\Sigma u)^2}}\sqrt{\mathbf{n\Sigma v^2 - (\Sigma v)^2}}}.$$

Example 1. *From the given data, calculate the Karl Pearson's coefficient of correlation :*

Months	*Price of Commodity*	
	A	*B*
Jan.	*35*	*65*
Feb.	*36*	*72*
March	*40*	*78*
April	*38*	*77*
May	*37*	*76*
June	*39*	*77*
July	*41*	*80*
August	*40*	*79*
Sept.	*36*	*76*
Oct.	*38*	*75*

Use 38 as assumed mean for commodity A and 75 for commodity B.

Sol. Let the variables 'price of A' and 'price of B' be denoted by x and y respectively.

Calculation of 'r'

Months	x	y	$u = x - A$ $A = 38$	$v = y - B$ $B = 75$	uv	u^2	v^2
Jan.	35	65	− 3	− 10	30	9	100
Feb.	36	72	− 2	− 3	6	4	9
March	40	78	2	3	6	4	9
April	38	77	0	2	0	0	4
May	37	76	− 1	1	− 1	1	1
June	39	77	1	2	2	1	4
July	41	80	3	5	15	9	25
August	40	79	2	4	8	4	16
Sept.	36	76	− 2	1	− 2	4	1
Oct	38	75	0	0	0	0	0
$n = 10$			$\Sigma u = 0$	$\Sigma v = 5$	$\Sigma uv = 64$	$\Sigma u^2 = 36$	$\Sigma v^2 = 169$

$$\therefore \quad r = \frac{n\Sigma uv - (\Sigma u)(\Sigma v)}{\sqrt{n\Sigma u^2 - (\Sigma u)^2}\sqrt{n\Sigma v^2 - (\Sigma v)^2}}$$

$$= \frac{10(64) - (0)(5)}{\sqrt{10(36) - (0)^2}\sqrt{10(169) - (5)^2}} = \frac{640}{\sqrt{360}\sqrt{1665}} = \text{AL}\left[\log \frac{640}{\sqrt{360 \times 1665}}\right]$$

$$= \text{AL}\left[\log 640 - \frac{1}{2}(\log 360 + \log 1665)\right]$$

$$= \text{AL}\left[\log 2.8064 - \frac{1}{2}(2.5563 + 3.2214)\right]$$

$$= \text{AL}(-0.08245) = \text{AL}(-1 + 1 - 0.08245) = \text{AL}(\bar{1}.91755) = \mathbf{0.8271.}$$

$\therefore$ There is high degree positive linear correlation between the prices of commodities A and B.

Example 2. *Find the correlation coefficient between 'height of father' and 'height of son', for the following data :*

Height of father (in inches)	65	66	67	67	68	69	70	72
Height of son (in inches)	67	68	65	68	72	72	69	71

Sol. Let x and y denote the variables 'height of father' and 'height of son' respectively.

Calculation of 'r'

S. No.	x	y	$u = x - A$ $A = 68$	$v = y - B$ $B = 69$	uv	u^2	v^2
1	65	67	– 3	– 2	6	9	4
2	66	68	– 2	– 1	2	4	1
3	67	65	– 1	– 4	4	1	16
4	67	68	– 1	– 1	1	1	1
5	68	72	0	3	0	0	9
6	69	72	1	3	3	1	9
7	70	69	2	0	0	4	0
8	72	71	4	2	8	6	4
$n = 8$			$\Sigma u = 0$	$\Sigma v = 0$	$\Sigma uv = 24$	$\Sigma u^2 = 36$	$\Sigma v^2 = 44$

Now
$$r = \frac{n\Sigma uv - (\Sigma u)(\Sigma v)}{\sqrt{n\Sigma u^2 - (\Sigma u)^2}\sqrt{n\Sigma v^2 - (\Sigma v)^2}}$$

$$= \frac{8(24) - 0 \times 0}{\sqrt{8(36) - 0^2}\sqrt{8(44) - 0^2}} = \frac{8(24)}{\sqrt{8}\sqrt{36}\sqrt{8}\sqrt{44}}$$

$$= \frac{24}{6 \times \sqrt{44}} = \frac{4}{\sqrt{4} \times \sqrt{11}} = \frac{2}{\sqrt{11}}$$

$$= \text{AL}\left\{\log 2 - \frac{1}{2}\log 11\right\} = \text{AL}\left\{0.3010 - \frac{1}{2}(1.0414)\right\}$$

$$= \text{AL}\{0.3010 - 0.5207\} = \text{AL}\{-0.2197\}$$

$$= \text{AL}\{-1 + 1 - 0.2197\} = \text{AL}\{\bar{1}.7803\} = 0.6030.$$

$\therefore$ $\mathbf{r = 0.6030.}$

It shows that there is moderate degree positive linear correlation between the variables.

Example 3. *Psychology test of intelligence and of arithmetical ability were applied to 10 children. Here is a record of ungrouped data showing intelligence and arithmetic ratios. Calculate Karl Pearson's coefficient of correlation :*

Child	*A*	*B*	*C*	*D*	*E*	*F*	*G*	*H*	*I*	*J*
I.R.	*105*	*104*	*102*	*101*	*100*	*99*	*98*	*96*	*93*	*92*
A.R.	*101*	*103*	*100*	*98*	*95*	*96*	*104*	*92*	*97*	*94*

Sol. Let x and y denote the variables I.R. and A.R. respectively.

Child	x	y	$u = x - A$, $A = 100$	$v = y - B$, $B = 96$	uv	u^2	v^2
A	105	101	5	5	25	25	25
B	104	103	4	7	28	16	49
C	102	100	2	4	8	4	16
D	101	98	1	2	2	1	4
E	100	95	0	− 1	0	0	1
F	99	96	− 1	0	0	1	0
G	98	104	− 2	8	− 16	4	64
H	96	92	− 4	− 4	16	16	16
I	93	97	− 7	1	− 7	49	1
J	92	94	− 8	− 2	16	64	4
$n = 10$			$\Sigma u = 10$	$\Sigma v = -20$	$\Sigma uv = 72$	$\Sigma u^2 = 180$	$\Sigma v^2 = 180$

Now
$$r = \frac{n\Sigma uv - \Sigma u \Sigma v}{\sqrt{n\Sigma u^2 - (\Sigma u)^2}\sqrt{n\Sigma v^2 - (\Sigma v)^2}}$$

$$= \frac{10(72) - (-10)(20)}{\sqrt{10(180) - (-10)^2}\sqrt{10(180) - (20)^2}}$$

$$= \frac{720 + 200}{\sqrt{1800 - 100}\sqrt{1800 - 400}} = \frac{920}{\sqrt{1700}\sqrt{1400}}$$

$$= \text{AL}\left\{\log 920 - \frac{1}{2}(\log 1700 + \log 1400)\right\}$$

$$= \text{AL}\left\{2.9638 - \frac{1}{2}(3.2304 + \log 3.1461)\right\}$$

$$= \text{AL}\{-0.2244\} = \text{AL}\{\bar{1}.7756\} = 0.5965.$$

$\therefore$ **r = 0.5965.**

It shows that there is moderate degree positive linear correlation between the variables.

Example 4. *Calculate the coefficient of correlation for the data given below :*

Age of husband (in years)	*23*	*27*	*28*	*28*	*29*	*30*	*31*	*33*	*35*	*36*
Age of wife (in years)	*18*	*20*	*22*	*27*	*21*	*29*	*27*	*29*	*28*	*29*

Sol. Let x and y denote the variables 'Age of Husband' and 'Age of Wife' respectively.

Calculation of 'r'

S. No.	x	y	$u = x - A$ $A = 30$	$v = y - B$ $B = 24$	uv	u^2	v^2
1	23	18	−7	−6	42	49	36
2	27	20	−3	−4	12	9	16
3	28	22	−2	−2	4	4	4
4	28	27	−2	3	−6	4	9
5	29	21	−1	−3	3	1	9
6	30	29	0	5	0	0	25
7	31	27	1	3	3	1	9
8	33	29	3	5	15	9	25
9	35	28	5	4	20	25	16
10	36	29	6	5	30	36	25
$n = 10$			$\Sigma u = 0$	$\Sigma v = 10$	$\Sigma uv = 123$	$\Sigma u^2 = 138$	$\Sigma v^2 = 174$

Now $$r = \frac{n\Sigma uv - (\Sigma u)(\Sigma v)}{\sqrt{n\Sigma u^2 - (\Sigma u)^2}\sqrt{n\Sigma v^2 - (\Sigma v)^2}} = \frac{10(123) - (0)(10)}{\sqrt{10(138) - (0)^2}\sqrt{10(174) - (-10)^2}}$$

$$= \frac{1230}{\sqrt{1380}\sqrt{1740 - 100}} = \frac{1230}{\sqrt{1380}\sqrt{1640}}$$

$$= \text{AL}\left\{\log 1230 - \frac{1}{2}(\log 1380 + \log 1640)\right\}$$

$$= \text{AL}\left\{3.0899 - \frac{1}{2}(3.1399 + 3.2148)\right\} = \text{AL}\left\{3.0899 - \frac{1}{2}(6.3547)\right\}$$

$$= \text{AL}\{3.0899 - 3.1773\} = \text{AL}\{-0.0874\} = \text{AL}\{\bar{1}.9126\} = 0.8177$$

$\therefore$ **r = 0.8177.**

It shows that there is high degree positive linear correlation between the variables.

Example 5. *Given :*

No. of pairs of observations	*= 10*
Sum of deviations of x	*= – 170*
Sum of deviations of y	*= – 20*
Sum of squares of deviations of x	*= 8288*
Sum of squares of deviations of y	*= 2264*
Sum of product of deviations of x and y	*= 3044*

Find out coefficient of correlation when the arbitrary means of x and y are 82 and 68 respectively.

Sol. Let $u = x - 82$, $v = y - 68$.

$\therefore$ We are given

$\Sigma u = -170$ $\qquad \Sigma v = -20,$ $\qquad \Sigma u^2 = 8288,$

$\Sigma v^2 = 2264,$ $\qquad \Sigma uv = 3044.$

Let 'r' be the coefficient of correlation between the variables x and y.

$$\therefore \quad r = \frac{n\Sigma uv - (\Sigma u)(\Sigma v)}{\sqrt{n\Sigma u^2 - (\Sigma u)^2}\sqrt{n\Sigma v^2 - (\Sigma v)^2}}$$

$$= \frac{10(3044) - (-170)(-20)}{\sqrt{10(8288) - (-170)^2}\sqrt{10(2264) - (-20)^2}}$$

$$= \frac{30440 - 3400}{\sqrt{82880 - 28900}\sqrt{22640 - 400}} = \frac{27040}{\sqrt{53980}\sqrt{22240}}$$

$$= \text{AL}\left\{\log 27040 - \frac{1}{2}(\log 53980 + \log 22240)\right\}$$

$$= \text{AL}\left\{4.4320 - \frac{1}{2}(4.7322 + 4.3472)\right\} = \text{AL}\left\{4.4320 - \frac{1}{2}(9.0794)\right\}$$

$$= \text{AL}\{4.4320 - 4.5397\} = \text{AL}\{-0.1077\} = \text{AL}\{\bar{1}.8923\} = 0.7803.$$

$\therefore$ **r = 0.7803.**

Example 6. *Complete the coefficient of correlation between the variables x and y from the given data :*

No. of pairs of x and y series	*= 8*
x-series A.M.	*= 74.5*
x-series S.D.	*= 13.07*
x-series assumed mean	*= 69*
y-series A.M.	*= 125.5*
y-series S.D.	*= 15.85*
y-series assumed mean	*= 112*

Sum of products of corresponding deviations of x and y series = 2176.

Sol. Let A = 69, B = 112

and $u = x - 69$, $v = y - 112$.

Let 'r' be the coefficient of correlation between x and y variables.

$$\therefore \quad r = \frac{n\Sigma uv - (\Sigma u)(\Sigma v)}{\sqrt{n\Sigma u^2 - (\Sigma u)^2}\sqrt{n\Sigma v^2 - (\Sigma v)^2}}. \qquad \text{...(1)}$$

We are given

$$\Sigma uv = 2176,\ \bar{x} = 74.5,\ \bar{y} = 125.5$$

$$\sigma_x = 13.07,\ \sigma_y = 15.85,\ n = 8,\ \text{A} = 69,\ \text{B} = 112.$$

We know that $\bar{x} = \text{A} + \dfrac{\Sigma u}{n}$.

$$\therefore \quad 74.5 = 69 + \frac{\Sigma u}{8} \quad i.e.,\ \Sigma u = 8(74.5 - 69) = 44$$

Also $\bar{y} = \text{B} + \dfrac{\Sigma v}{n}$

$$\therefore \quad 125.5 = 112 + \frac{\Sigma v}{8} \quad i.e.,\quad \Sigma v = 8(125.5 - 112) = 108$$

Again $\sigma_x = \sqrt{\frac{\Sigma u^2}{n} - \left(\frac{\Sigma u}{n}\right)^2} = \sqrt{\frac{n\Sigma u^2 - (\Sigma u)^2}{n^2}}$

$\therefore \quad \sqrt{n\Sigma u^2 - (\Sigma u)^2} = n\sigma_x = 8(13.07) = 104.56$

Also $\sigma_y = \sqrt{\frac{\Sigma v^2}{n} - \left(\frac{\Sigma v}{n}\right)^2} = \sqrt{\frac{n\Sigma v^2 - (\Sigma v)^2}{n^2}}$

$\therefore \quad \sqrt{n\Sigma v^2 - (\Sigma v)^2} = n\sigma_y = 8(15.85) = 126.8$

$\therefore \quad (1) \Rightarrow \quad r = \frac{8(2176) - (44)(108)}{(104.56)(126.8)} = \frac{12656}{13258.208} = \mathbf{0.9546.}$

Example 7. *From the following table giving the distribution of students and also regular players among them according to age group, find out correlation coefficient between 'age' and 'playing habit' :*

Age	*15-16*	*16-17*	*17-18*	*18-19*	*19-20*	*20-21*
No. of students	*200*	*270*	*340*	*360*	*400*	*300*
No. of regular players	*150*	*162*	*170*	*180*	*180*	*120*

(KU 1995 C)

Sol. We are to find the degree of correlation between the variables 'age' and 'playing habit.' The numbers of students in each age group is not same. So, first of all we shall express the number of regular players in each age group as the percentage of students in the corresponding age group. Let x and y denote the variables 'age' and 'percentage of regular players' respectively.

Calculation of 'r'

Age	*Mid-pts. of age groups* x	*No. of students*	*No. of regular players*	*% of regular players* y	$u = x - A$ $A = 17.5$	$v = y - B$ $B = 50$	uv	u^2	v^2
15—16	15.5	200	150	75	– 2	25	– 50	4	625
16—17	16.5	270	162	60	– 1	10	– 10	1	100
17—18	17.5	340	170	50	0	0	0	0	0
18—19	18.5	360	180	50	1	0	0	1	0
19—20	19.5	400	180	45	2	– 5	– 10	4	25
20—21	20.5	300	120	40	3	– 10	– 30	9	100
$n = 6$					$\Sigma u = 3$	$\Sigma v = 20$	$\Sigma uv = -100$	$\Sigma u^2 = 19$	$\Sigma v^2 = 850$

Now
$$r = \frac{n\Sigma uv - (\Sigma u)(\Sigma v)}{\sqrt{n\Sigma u^2 - (\Sigma u)^2}\sqrt{n\Sigma v^2 - (\Sigma v)^2}}$$
$$= \frac{6(-100) - (3)(20)}{\sqrt{6(19) - (3)^2}\sqrt{6(850) - (20)^2}}$$
$$= \frac{-660}{\sqrt{105}\sqrt{4700}} = \frac{-660}{702.4956} = \mathbf{-0.9395.}$$

It shows that there is high degree negative linear correlation between the variables.

EXERCISE 4

1. Calculate the coefficient of correlation for the following ages of husbands and wives :

Age of husband	23	27	28	28	29	30	31	33	35	36
Age of wife	18	20	20	27	21	29	27	29	28	29

2. Find the coefficient of correlation for the following data. Also explain, what does it express.

x	300	350	400	450	500	550	600	650	700
y	800	900	1000	1100	1200	1300	1400	1500	1600

3. The following table gives the value of iron ore exported and value of steel imported in India during 1970–71 to 1976–77. Find the value of correlation coefficient between exports and imports.

Year	1970–71	1971–72	1972–73	1973–74	1974–75	1975–76	1976–77
Export of iron ore ('000 Rs.)	42	44	58	55	89	98	66
Import of steel ('000 Rs.)	56	49	53	58	65	76	58

4. Calculate the coefficient correlation between the values of x and y given below :

x	78	89	96	69	59	79	68	61
y	125	137	156	112	107	136	123	108

(You may use 69 as working mean for x and 112 that for y).

5. Compute the coefficient of correlation between sales tax collected and sales of product '*M*' in ten countries selected at random from those served by the company.

Country	A	B	C	D	E	F	G	H	I	J
Sales tax collected (x) (in pounds)	16	24	32	15	20	12	18	14	10	29
Units of 'M' sold (y)	40	50	68	36	45	27	42	36	29	67

6. Find the coefficient of correlation between income and expenditure of a wage-earner and comment on the result.

Month	Jan.	Feb.	Mar.	Apr.	May	June	July
Income (Rs.)	46	54	56	56	58	60	62
Expenditure (Rs.)	36	40	44	54	42	58	54

7. Calculate K.P's coefficient of correlation for the given series :

Husband's age	24	27	28	28	29	30	32	33	35	35	40
Wife's age	18	20	22	25	22	28	28	30	27	30	22

8. The following table gives the distribution of the total population and those who are wholly or partially blind among them. Find out if there is any relation between 'age' and 'blindness'.

Age	0–10	10–20	20–30	30–40	40–50	50–60	60–70	70–80
No. of persons ('000)	100	60	40	36	24	11	6	3
No. of blinds	55	40	40	40	36	22	18	15

9. Find the correlation coefficient between age and playing habit of the following students :

Age (in years)	*No. of students*	*Regular players*
15	250	200
16	200	150
17	150	90
18	120	48
19	100	30
20	80	12

(KU 1997 C ; MDU 2000)

10. Find the coefficient of correlation between the variables 'income' and 'expenditure'.

Family	A	B	C	D	E	F	G	H	I	J
Income (Rs.)	95	90	110	100	85	105	95	100	105	95
Expenditure (Rs.)	90	95	115	95	85	110	90	95	95	95

11. Calculate the coefficient of correlation between the marks obtained by 12 students in Statistics and Accountancy paper :

Marks in Statistics	52	74	93	55	41	23	92	64	40	71	33	71
Marks in Accountancy	45	80	63	60	35	40	70	58	43	64	51	75

12. Calculate the coefficient of correlation and its probable error between the heights of fathers and sons for the following data :

Height of Father (in inches)	65	66	67	68	69	70	71
Height of Son (in inches)	67	68	66	69	72	72	69

13. Calculate the coefficient of correlation for the following data :

x	100	200	300	400	500	600	700
y	30	50	60	80	100	110	130

14. From the following data, calculate the coefficient of correlation between 'age' and 'playing habit'.

Age group	*No. of employees*	*No. of regular players*
20–30	25	10
30–40	60	30
40–50	40	12
50–60	20	2
60–70	20	1

15. From the following table, given the distribution of students and also regular players among them according to age group, find the correlation between 'age' and 'playing habit'.

Age	15–16	16–17	17–18	18–19	19–20	20–21
No. of students	200	270	340	360	400	300
Regular players	180	162	170	180	180	60

16. Calculate Karl Pearson's coefficient of correlation for the following paired data :

x	28	41	40	38	35	33	40	32	36	33
y	23	34	33	34	30	26	28	31	36	38

17. Calculate Karl Pearson's coefficient of correlation for the following data :

(*i*) sum of deviations of $x = 5$ (*ii*) sum of deviations of $y = 4$

(*iii*) sum of squares of deviations of $x = 40$ (*iv*) sum of squares of deviations of $y = 50$

(*v*) sum of products of deviations of x and $y = 32$ (*vi*) no. of pairs of observations = 10

18. Calculate correlation coefficient for the following data :

$$n = 10,\ \Sigma x = 140,\ \Sigma y = 150,\ \Sigma(x-10)^2 = 180,\ \Sigma(y-15)^2 = 215,\ \Sigma(x-10)(y-15) = 60.$$

(**Hint.** Let $u = x - 10$, $v = y - 15$. $\therefore$ $\Sigma u^2 = 180$, $\Sigma v^2 = 215$, $\Sigma uv = 60$.

Now $\Sigma u = \Sigma(x-10) = \Sigma x - n(10) = 140 - 10 \times 10 = 40$ etc.)

19. Calculate 'r' from the following data :

$\Sigma X = 225$, $\Sigma Y = 189$, $n = 10$, $\Sigma(X-22)^2 = 85$,

$\Sigma(Y-19)^2 = 25$ and $\Sigma(X-22)(Y-19) = 43$. (MDU 2006)

Answers

1. $r = 0.8067$	2. $r = 1$	3. $r = 0.9042$	4. $r = 0.9544$
5. $r = 0.9854$	6. $r = 0.769$	7. $r = 0.504$	8. $r = 0.8982$
9. $r = -0.9276$	10. $r = 0.8152$	11. $r = 0.7886$	
12. $r = 0.668$, P.E. = 0.1412	13. $r = 0.9972$	14. $r = -0.904$	15. $r = -0.936$
16. $r = 0.4403$	17. $r = 0.7042$	18. 0.915	19. 0.9597.

17. CORRELATION IN GROUPED SERIES

When the frequencies are distributed corresponding to different values of two variables, then the distribution is called **Bivariate frequency distribution.** Consider the following bivariate frequency distribution :

		x					
		18	*19*	*20*	*21*	*22*	*Total*
y	0–5	0	0	0	3	1	4
	5–10	0	0	0	3	2	5
	10–15	0	0	7	10	0	17
	15–20	0	5	4	0	0	9
	20–25	3	2	0	0	0	5
	Total	3	7	11	16	3	40

Here the frequency '7' means that 7 pairs in the data are with values of $x = 20$ and value of y lying in the class 10–15. Similarly, there is no pair with $x = 21$ and y in the class 20–25. These frequencies are called **cell frequencies.** The sum of cell frequencies of I column, II column, ... correspond to the values 18, 19, ... of x-variable respectively.

Similarly, the sums of cell frequencies of I row, II row, ... corresponds to the values of the y-variable in the classes 0–5, 5–10, ... respectively.

Our objective is to find the Karl Pearson's coefficient of correlation for bivariate frequency distributions. If either x or y or both variables represent classes, then their respective mid-points are taken as their representatives.

In case of a bivariate frequency distribution, the formula used is :

$$\mathbf{r} = \frac{\mathbf{N\Sigma fuv - (\Sigma fu)(\Sigma fv)}}{\sqrt{\mathbf{N\Sigma fu^2 - (\Sigma fu)^2}}\sqrt{\mathbf{N\Sigma fv^2 - (\Sigma fv)^2}}}$$

where N is the total number of pairs.

u and v are the step deviations of x and y variables respectively.

Σfu is the sum of the products of the class frequencies of x-series with their respective step deviations.

Σfv is the sum of the products of the class frequencies of y-series with their respective step deviations.

Σfuv is the sum of the products of the cell frequencies with the steps deviations of the corresponding values of x and y variables.

Σfu^2 is the sum of the products of the class frequencies of x-series with the squares of their corresponding step deviations.

Σfv^2 is the sum of the products of the class frequencies of y-series with the squares of their corresponding step deviations.

The values of fuv, corresponding to the cell frequency f is written in the same cell. If either of f or u or v is zero, then the product fuv would be zero.

The common factors to be used for calculating step deviations of x-series and y-series should both be *positive*. For calculating different quantities needed in the calculation of 'r' the following type of correlation table is drafted.

Draft of Correlation Table

y \ x		x_1	x_2	....	x_m	f	fv	fv^2	fuv
	u \ v	u_1	u_2	....	u_m				
y_1	v_1								
y_2	v_2								
.	.								
.	.								
.	.								
y_n	v_n								
f						N	Σfv	Σfv^2	Σfuv
fu						Σfu			
fu^2						Σfu^2			
fuv						Σfuv			

Example 1. *Calculate Karl Pearson's coefficient of correlation for the following table :*

		x					
		18	*19*	*20*	*21*	*22*	*Total*
	0–5	*0*	*0*	*0*	*3*	*1*	*4*
	5–10	*0*	*0*	*0*	*3*	*2*	*5*
y	*10–15*	*0*	*0*	*7*	*10*	*0*	*17*
	15–20	*0*	*5*	*4*	*0*	*0*	*9*
	20–25	*3*	*2*	*0*	*0*	*0*	*5*
	Total	*3*	*7*	*11*	*16*	*3*	*40*

(KU 2001 C, 2006 C)

Sol.

Values of x	:	18	19	20	21	22
Deviations (u) from 20	:	– 2	– 1	0	1	2
Classes of y	:	0–5	5–10	10–15	15–20	20–25
Mid-points	:	2.5	7.5	12.5	17.5	22.5
Deviation from 12.5	:	– 10	– 5	0	5	10
Step deviation by 5	:	– 2	– 1	0	1	2

$$\left(v = \frac{y - 12.5}{5}\right)$$

Correlation Table

y ↓ x →	v ↓ u →	18	19	20	21	22	f	fv	fv^2	fuv
		−2	−1	0	1	2				
0–5	−2	(0) 0	(0) 0	(0) 0	(−6) 3	(−4) 1	4	−8	16	−10
5–10	−1	(0) 0	(0) 0	(0) 0	(−3) 3	(−4) 2	5	−5	5	−7
10–15	0	(0) 0	(0) 0	(0) 7	(0) 10	(0) 0	17	0	0	0
15–20	1	(0) 0	(−5) 5	(0) 4	(0) 0	(0) 0	9	9	9	−5
20–25	2	(−12) 3	(−4) 2	(0) 0	(0) 0	(0) 0	5	10	20	−16
f		3	7	11	16	3	$N = 40$	$\Sigma fv = 6$	$\Sigma fv^2 = 50$	$\Sigma fuv = -38$
fu		−6	−7	0	16	6	$\Sigma fu = 9$			
fu^2		12	7	0	16	12	$\Sigma fu^2 = 47$			
fuv		−12	−9	0	−9	−8	$\Sigma fuv = -38$			

Now
$$r = \frac{N\Sigma fuv - (\Sigma fu)(\Sigma fv)}{\sqrt{N\Sigma fu^2 - (\Sigma fu)^2}\ \sqrt{N\Sigma fv^2 - (\Sigma fv)^2}}$$

$$= \frac{40(-38) - (6)(9)}{\sqrt{40(47) - (9)^2}\ \sqrt{40(50) - (6)^2}} = \frac{-1574}{\sqrt{1799}\ \sqrt{1964}}$$

$$= -\text{AL}\left\{\log 1574 - \frac{1}{2}(\log 1799 + \log 1964)\right\}$$

$$= -\text{AL}\left\{3.1942 - \frac{1}{2}(3.2551 + 3.2931)\right\}$$

$$= -\text{AL}\{3.1942 - 3.2741\}$$

$$= -\text{AL}\{-0.0799\} = -\text{AL}\{\bar{1}.9201\}$$

$$\mathbf{r = -0.8320.}$$

It shows that there is high degree negative linear correlation between the variables x and y.

Example 2. *The following table shows the ages of daughters and mothers. Calculate the coefficient of correlations between the variables 'age of daughter' and 'age of mother'.*

Age of mother	*Age of daughter*				
	5–10	*10–15*	*15–20*	*20–25*	*25–30*
15–25	*6*	*3*	*0*	*0*	*0*
25–35	*3*	*16*	*10*	*0*	*0*
35–45	*0*	*10*	*15*	*7*	*0*
45–55	*0*	*0*	*7*	*10*	*4*
55–65	*0*	*0*	*0*	*4*	*5*

Sol. Let x and y denote the variables 'age of daughter' and 'age of mother' respectively.

Classes of x	:	5–10	10–15	15–20	20–25	25–30
Mid-points	:	7.5	12.5	17.5	22.5	27.5
Deviations from 17.5	:	– 10	– 5	0	5	10
Step deviations by 5 $\left(u = \frac{x - 17.5}{5}\right)$	:	– 2	– 1	0	1	2
Classes of y	:	15–25	25–35	35–45	45–55	55–65
Mid-points	:	20	30	40	50	60
Deviations from 40	:	– 20	– 10	0	10	20
Step deviations by 10 $\left(v = \frac{y - 40}{10}\right)$	:	– 2	– 1	0	1	2

Correlation Table

(Each cell shows the frequency, with the product fuv in the box in brackets.)

y ↓ / x →		5–10	10–15	15–20	20–25	25–30	f	fv	fv^2	fuv
	v ↓ / u →	– 2	– 1	0	1	2				
15–25	– 2	6 [24]	3 [6]				9	– 18	36	30
25–35	– 1	3 [6]	16 [16]	10 [0]			29	– 29	29	22
35–45	0		10 [0]	15 [0]	7 [0]		32	0	0	0
45–55	1			7 [0]	10 [0]	4 [8]	21	21	21	18
55–65	2				4 [8]	5 [20]	9	18	36	28
f		9	29	32	21	9	N = 100	$\Sigma fv = -8$	$\Sigma fv^2 = 122$	$\Sigma fuv = 98$
fu		– 18	– 29	0	21	18	$\Sigma fu = -8$			
fu^2		36	29	0	21	36	$\Sigma fu^2 = 122$			
fuv		30	22	0	18	28	$\Sigma fuv = 98$			

Now
$$r = \frac{N\Sigma fuv - (\Sigma fu)(\Sigma fv)}{\sqrt{N\Sigma fu^2 - (\Sigma fu^2)}\,\sqrt{N\Sigma fv^2 - (\Sigma fv)^2}} = \frac{100(98) - (-8)(-8)}{\sqrt{100(122) - (-8)^2}\,\sqrt{100(122) - (-8)^2}}$$

$$= \frac{9736}{\sqrt{12136}\,\sqrt{12136}} = \frac{9736}{12136} = \mathbf{0.8022.}$$

It shows that there is high degree positive linear correlation between the variables.

Example 3. *Calculate Karl Pearson's coefficient of correlation for the following table relating to the marks obtained by 25 students in Economics and Statistics.*

Marks in Economics	*Marks in Statistics*			
	30—40	*40—50*	*50—60*	*60—70*
30–40	*3*	*1*	*1*	*0*
40–50	*2*	*6*	*1*	*2*
50–60	*1*	*2*	*2*	*1*
60–70	*0*	*1*	*1*	*1*

Sol. Let x and y denote the variables 'marks in Statistics' and 'marks in Economics' respectively.

Classes of x	:	30–40	40–50	50–60	60–70
Mid-points	:	35	45	55	65
Deviations from 45	:	– 10	0	10	20
Step deviation by 10 $\left(u = \dfrac{x-45}{10}\right)$	:	– 1	0	1	2
Classes of y	:	30–40	40–50	50–60	60–70
Mid-points	:	35	45	55	65
Deviations from 45	:	– 10	0	10	20
Step deviations by 10 $\left(v = \dfrac{y-45}{10}\right)$	:	– 1	0	1	2

Correlation Table

y \ x	v \ u	30–40 – 1	40–50 – 0	50–60 1	60–70 2	f	fv	fv^2	fuv
30–40	– 1	[3] 3	[0] 1	[–1] 1	0	5	– 5	5	2
40–50	0	[0] 2	[0] 6	[0] 1	[0] 2	11	0	0	0
50–60	1	[– 1] 1	[0] 2	[2] 2	[2] 1	6	6	6	3
60–70	2		[0] 1	[2] 1	[4] 1	3	6	12	6
f		6	10	5	4	N = 25	$\Sigma fv = 7$	$\Sigma fv^2 = 23$	$\Sigma fuv = 11$
fu		– 6	0	5	8	$\Sigma fu = 7$			
fu^2		6	0	5	16	$\Sigma fu^2 = 27$			
fuv		2	0	3	6	$\Sigma fuv = 11$			

Now $$r = \frac{N\Sigma fuv - (\Sigma fu)(\Sigma fv)}{\sqrt{N\Sigma fu^2 - (\Sigma fu^2)}\sqrt{N\Sigma fv^2 - (\Sigma fv)^2}}$$

$$= \frac{25(11) - (7)(7)}{\sqrt{25(27) - (7)^2}\sqrt{25(23) - (7)^2}} = \frac{226}{\sqrt{626}\sqrt{526}}$$

$$= \text{AL}\left\{\log 226 - \frac{1}{2}(\log 626 + \log 526)\right\} = \text{AL}\left\{2.3541 - \frac{1}{2}(2.7966 + 2.7210)\right\}$$

$$= \text{AL}\{2.3541 - 2.7588\} = \text{AL}\{-0.4047\} = \text{AL}\{\bar{1}.5953\} = \mathbf{0.3939}.$$

It shows that there is high degree positive linear correlation between the variables.

18. PROBABLE ERROR (P.E.) OF CORRELATION COEFFICIENT

The *probable error* (P.E.) of correlation coefficient is used to test the significance of an observed correlation coefficient. It indicates whether the coefficient of correlation obtained for a sample would also hold good for other samples drawn from the same population or not. According to *Horace Secrist*, "The probable error of '*r*' is an amount if added to and subtracted from the average correlation coefficient produces amounts within which the chances are even that a coefficient of correlation from a series selected at random will fall". The probable error is also used to fix the limits within which the correlation coefficient is expected to vary for different samples drawn from the same population. The formula to compute probable error is given by :

$$\textbf{P.E.} = \mathbf{0.6745}\ \frac{\mathbf{1 - r^2}}{\sqrt{\mathbf{n}}}$$

where r = Correlation coefficient for the sample

n = number of pairs in the sample.

The value of P.E. is used as follows :

(*i*) If $r <$ P.E. then r is not considered to be significant.

(*ii*) IF $r > 6$ P.E. then r is significant.

The lower and upper limits within which the correlation coefficient for any other sample, drawn from the same population, is expected to lie are r – P.E. and r + P.E.

Example 4. *Find the value of P.E. for the following data :*

$r = 0.9$; $n = 25$ (no. of pairs of values).

Sol. We have $r = 0.9$, $n = 25$.

$$\text{P.E.} = 0.6745\left(\frac{1 - r^2}{\sqrt{n}}\right) = 0.6745\left(\frac{1 - (0.9)^2}{\sqrt{25}}\right)$$

$$= \frac{6745}{10000} \times \frac{19}{100} \times \frac{1}{5} = 0.0256.$$

$\therefore$ P.E. = **0.0256.**

Example 5. *Test the significance of 'r' for the following data :*

$r = 0.9$; $n = 16$.

Sol. We have $r = 0.9,\ n = 16.$

$$\text{P.E.} = 0.6745\left(\frac{1-r^2}{\sqrt{n}}\right) = 0.645\left(\frac{1-(0.9)^2}{\sqrt{16}}\right) = \frac{0.6745\,(0.19)}{4} = 0.03204.$$

$$6\ \text{P.E.} = 6(0.03204) = 0.19224 < r$$

$\therefore$ $r = 0.9$ is significant.

19. MERITS

1. The coefficient of correlation indicates magnitude as well as direction of linear correlation between the variables.
2. This is a mathematical method and there is no chance of personal bias in its computation.
3. This method is considered as the best method among all the method of computing simple linear correlation.

20. DEMERITS

1. This is difficult to compute.
2. This is applicable only when the correlation between the variables is linear.
3. This is affected by the extreme items.

EXERCISE 5

1. Find the coefficient of correlation between 'age' and 'days lost' for the following data :

	Age (in years)					
Days lost	*20–30*	*30–40*	*40–50*	*50–60*	*60–70*	*Total*
1–2	4	0	4	0	0	8
3–4	8	8	4	4	0	24
5–6	4	12	16	0	0	32
7–8	0	4	8	4	0	16
9–10	0	0	12	0	0	12
11–12	0	0	0	7	1	8
Total	16	24	44	15	1	100

2. Calculate the coefficient of correlation between the ages of 100 husbands and wives for the following data :

Age of Husband (in years)	*Age of Wife (in years)*					*Total*
	10–20	*20–30*	*30–40*	*40–50*	*50–60*	
15—25	6	3	0	0	0	9
25—35	3	16	10	0	0	29
35—45	0	10	15	7	0	32
45—55	0	0	7	10	4	21
55—65	0	0	0	4	5	9
Total	9	29	32	21	9	100

(MDU 2005)

3. The following table gives the marks obtained by 100 students in Statistics and Accountancy. Calculate the coefficient of correlation.

Marks in Accountancy	*Marks in Statistics*						*Total*
	40–49	*50–59*	*60–69*	*70–79*	*80–89*	*90–99*	
90–99	0	0	0	2	4	4	10
80–89	0	0	1	4	6	5	16
70–79	0	0	5	10	8	1	24
60–69	1	4	9	5	2	0	21
50–59	3	6	6	2	0	0	17
40–49	3	5	4	0	0	0	12
Total	7	15	25	23	20	10	100

(*KU 2004*)

4. The following table gives the frequencies according to age groups and marks obtained by 67 students in an intelligence test. Measure the degree of relationship between 'age' and 'marks'.

Marks	*Age (in years)*				*Total*
	18	*19*	*20*	*21*	
200–250	4	4	2	1	11
250–300	3	5	4	2	14
300–350	2	6	8	5	21
350–400	1	4	6	10	21
Total	10	19	20	18	67

5. Calculate the coefficient of correlation for the following data :

y	*x*					*Total*
	15–18	*18–21*	*21–24*	*24–27*	*27–30*	
10–11	0	0	0	3	1	4
11–12	0	0	0	3	2	5
12–13	0	0	7	10	0	17
13–14	0	5	4	0	0	9
14–15	3	2	0	0	0	5
Total	3	7	11	16	3	40

6. Calculate the coefficient of correlation for the following table :

y	*x*			
	16–18	*18–20*	*20–22*	*22–24*
10–20	2	1	1	0
20–30	3	2	3	2
30–40	3	4	5	6
40–50	2	2	3	4
50–60	0	1	2	2
60–70	0	1	2	1

7. From the following table calculate coefficient of correlation between the age of husbands and wives :

Age of Wives (in years)	*Age of Husbands (in years)*					*Total*
	20–30	*30–40*	*40–50*	*50–60*	*60–70*	
15–25	5	9	3			17
25–35		10	25	2		37
35–45		1	12	2		15
45–55			4	16	5	25
55–65				4	2	6
Total	5	20	44	24	7	100

(KU 1996)

8. Find the coefficient of correlation for the following data :

Marks in English	*Marks in Economics*			
	5–15	*15–25*	*25–35*	*35–45*
0–10	1	1	—	—
10–20	3	6	5	1
20–30	1	8	9	2
30–40	—	3	9	3
40–50	—	—	4	4

9. Find the coefficient of correlation for the following data :

$x \rightarrow$ / $y \downarrow$	*0–500*	*500–1000*	*1000–1500*	*1500–2000*	*2000–2500*
0–200	12	6	—	—	—
200–400	2	18	4	2	1
400–600	—	4	7	3	—
600–800	—	1	—	2	1
800–1000	—	—	—	1	2

(KU 1999)

10. If $r = 0.64$ and $n = 9$, test the significance of 'r'.

11. Find the value of the coefficient of correlation 'r' from the following data :
P.E. = 0.009, $n = 9$.

12. If $r = 0.6$ for a pair of 64 observations, find the probable error of r and determine the limits for the measure for the population.

13. A student calculated the value of r as 0.7 when the number of items (n) in the sample is 25. Find the limits within which r lies for another sample from the same universe.

Answers

1. $r = 0.5534$	2. $r = 0.802$	3. $r = 0.7686$	4. $r = 0.4151$
5. $r = -0.84$	6. $r = 0.28$	7. $r = 0.7952$	8. $r = 0.533$
9. $r = 0.7466$	10. P.E. = 0.1327	11. $r = 0.9798$.	
12. 0.054, 0.546 and 0.654	13. 0.6312 and 0.7688.		

IV. SPEARMAN'S RANK CORRELATION METHOD

21. MEANING

In practical life, we come across problems of estimating correlation between variables, which are not quantitative in nature. Suppose, we are interested in deciding if there is any correlation between the variables 'honesty' and 'smartness' among a group of students. Here the variables 'honesty' and 'smartness' are not capable of quantitative measurement. These variables are qualitative in nature. Ranking is possible in case of qualitative variables.

Spearman's rank correlation method is used for studying linear correlation between variables which are not necessarily quantitative in nature. This method works for both quantitative as well as qualitative variables.

Let n pairs of values of variables x and y be given. The first step is to express the values of the variables in ranks. In case of qualitative variables, the data would be given in the desired form. For quantitative variables, the ranks are allotted according to the magnitude of the values of the variables. Generally the I rank is allotted to the item with highest value. If the highest value of the first variable is allotted I rank, then the same method is to be adopted for finding the ranks of the values of the other variable. In allotting ranks, difficulty arises when the values of two or more items in a series are equal. We shall consider this case separately.

22. CASE I. NON-REPEATED RANKS

Let R_1 and R_2 represent the ranks of the items corresponding to the variables x and y respectively.

The coefficient of rank correlation (r_k) is given by the formula :

$$r_k = 1 - \frac{6\Sigma D^2}{n(n^2 - 1)},$$

where n is the number of pairs and D denotes the difference between ranks *i.e.*, $(R_1 - R_2)$ of the corresponding values of the variables.

Example 1. *Ten students of a class are ranked in intelligence tests given by two teachers. Find the coefficient of rank corretation.*

Student	*1*	*2*	*3*	*4*	*5*	*6*	*7*	*8*	*9*	*10*
Ranks by Teacher A	*6*	*7*	*3*	*2*	*10*	*1*	*9*	*8*	*4*	*5*
Ranks by Teacher B	*7*	*10*	*4*	*1*	*9*	*3*	*8*	*6*	*2*	*5*

Sol. Let R_1 and R_2 denote the ranks allotted by teachers A and B respectively.

Calculation of 'r_k'

S. No.	R_1	R_2	$D = R_1 - R_2$	D^2
1	6	7	− 1	1
2	7	10	− 3	9
3	3	4	− 1	1
4	2	1	1	1
5	10	9	1	1
6	1	3	− 2	4
7	9	8	1	1
8	8	6	2	4
9	4	2	2	4
10	5	5	0	0
$n = 10$				$\Sigma D^2 = 26$

Coefficient of rank correlation,

$$r_k = 1 - \frac{6\Sigma D^2}{n(n^2-1)} = 1 - \frac{6(26)}{10(10^2-1)} = 1 - 0.1567 = \mathbf{0.8424.}$$

It shows that there is high degree positive linear correlation between the variables.

Example 2. *Two judges in a beauty competition rank the 12 entries as follows :*

x	*1*	*2*	*3*	*4*	*5*	*6*	*7*	*8*	*9*	*10*	*11*	*12*
y	*12*	*9*	*6*	*10*	*3*	*5*	*4*	*7*	*8*	*2*	*11*	*1*

What degree of agreement is there between the judges ?

Sol. Here the ranks are denoted by x and y, therefore, $D = x - y$.

Calculation of 'r_k'

S. No.	x	y	$D = x - y$	D^2
1	1	12	− 11	121
2	2	9	− 7	49
3	3	6	−3	9
4	4	10	− 6	36
5	5	3	2	4
6	6	5	1	1
7	7	4	3	9
8	8	7	1	1
9	9	8	1	1
10	10	2	8	64
11	11	11	0	0
12	12	1	11	121
$n = 12$				$\Sigma D^2 = 416$

Coefficient of rank correlation,

$$r_k = 1 - \frac{6\Sigma D^2}{n(n^2-1)} = 1 - \frac{6(416)}{12(12^2-1)} = 1 - 1.4545 = \mathbf{-0.4545.}$$

It shows that there is low degree negative linear correlation between the variables. This means that the judges are not agreeing, though the degree of disagreement is low.

Example 3. *Ten competitors in a beauty contest are ranked by three judges in the following order :*

Ist judge	*1*	*5*	*4*	*8*	*9*	*6*	*10*	*7*	*3*	*2*
IInd judge	*4*	*8*	*7*	*6*	*5*	*9*	*10*	*3*	*2*	*1*
IIIrd judge	*6*	*7*	*8*	*1*	*5*	*10*	*9*	*2*	*3*	*4*

Use the rank correlation coefficient to discuss which pair of judges has the nearest approach to common taste in beauty.

Sol. Let R_1, R_2 and R_3 denote the variables 'ranks by Ist judge', ranks by IInd judge' and 'ranks by IIIrd judge' respectively. Let r_{12}, r_{23} and r_{13} stand for the coefficients of rank correlation between the variables R_1 and R_2, R_2 and R_3, R_1 and R_3 respectively.

Calculation of r_{12}, r_{23} and r_{13}

S. No.	R_1	R_2	R_3	$D_{12} = R_1 - R_2$	$D_{23} = R_2 - R_3$	$D_{13} = R_1 - R_3$	D_{12}^2	D_{23}^2	D_{13}^2
1	1	4	6	−3	−2	−5	9	4	25
2	5	8	7	−3	1	−2	9	1	4
3	4	7	8	−3	−1	−4	9	1	16
4	8	6	1	2	5	7	4	25	49
5	9	5	5	4	0	4	16	0	16
6	6	9	10	−3	−1	−4	9	1	16
7	10	10	9	0	1	1	0	1	1
8	7	3	2	4	1	5	16	1	25
9	3	2	3	1	−1	0	1	1	0
10	2	1	4	1	−3	−2	1	9	4
$n = 10$							$\Sigma D_{12}^2 = 74$	$\Sigma D_{23}^2 = 44$	$\Sigma D_{13}^2 = 156$

We have $$r_{12} = 1 - \frac{6\Sigma D_{12}^2}{n(n^2-1)} = 1 - \frac{6(74)}{10(10^2-1)} = \mathbf{0.5515.}$$

$$r_{23} = 1 - \frac{6\Sigma D_{23}^2}{n(n^2-1)} = 1 - \frac{6(44)}{10(10^2-1)} = \mathbf{0.7333.}$$

$$r_{13} = 1 - \frac{6\Sigma D_{13}^2}{n(n^2-1)} = 1 - \frac{6(156)}{10(10^2-1)} = \mathbf{0.0545.}$$

By comparing the rank correlation coefficients, we find that r_{23} is the greatest (and positive) and so we conclude that the IInd judge and IIIrd judge have the nearest approach to common taste in beauty.

Example 4. *Calculate the coefficient of correlation for the following data by the method of rank differences :*

x	75	88	95	70	60	80	81	50
y	120	130	150	115	110	140	142	100

Sol. Let R_1 and R_2 denote the ranks of the variables x and y respectively. The first rank is allotted to the greatest item in each series.

Calculation of 'r_k'

S. No.	x	y	R_1	R_2	$D = R_1 - R_2$	D^2
1	75	120	5	5	0	0
2	88	130	2	4	− 2	4
3	95	150	1	1	0	0
4	70	115	6	6	0	0
5	60	110	7	7	0	0
6	80	140	4	3	1	1
7	81	142	3	2	1	1
8	50	100	8	8	0	0
$n = 8$						$\Sigma D^2 = 6$

Coefficient of rank correlation,

$$r_k = 1 - \frac{6\Sigma D^2}{n(n^2 - 1)} = 1 - \frac{6(6)}{8(8^2 - 1)} = \mathbf{0.9286.}$$

It shows that there is high degree positive linear correlation between the variables.

Example 5. *The ranks of 16 students in tests in 'Mathematics' and 'Statistics' were as follows. The two numbers within the brackets denoting the ranks of the same student in Mathematics and Statistics respectively.*

(1, 1), (2, 10), (3, 3), (4, 4), (5, 5), (6, 7), (7, 2), (8, 6), (9, 8),

(10, 11), (11, 15), (12, 9), (13, 14), (14, 12), (15, 16), (16, 13).

(i) Calculate the rank correlation coefficient for proficiencies of this group in Mathematics and Statistics.

(ii) What does the value of the coefficient obtained indicates ?

(iii) If you had found out Karl Pearson's coefficient of correlation between the ranks of these 16 students, would your result be the same as obtained in (i) or different ?

(KU 2000)

Sol. Let R_1 and R_2 denote the ranks in 'Mathematics' and Statistics respectively.

Calculation of 'r_k'

S. No.	R_1	R_2	$D = R_1 - R_2$	D^2
1	1	1	0	0
2	2	10	− 8	64
3	3	3	0	0
4	4	4	0	0
5	5	5	0	0
6	6	7	− 1	1
7	7	2	5	25

S. No.	R_1	R_2	$D = R_1 - R_2$	D^2
8	8	6	2	4
9	9	8	1	1
10	10	11	– 1	1
11	11	15	– 4	16
12	12	9	3	9
13	13	14	– 1	1
14	14	12	2	4
15	15	16	– 1	1
16	16	13	3	9
$n = 16$				$\Sigma D^2 = 136$

Coefficient of rank correlation,

$$r_k = 1 - \frac{6\Sigma D^2}{n(n^2 - 1)} = 1 - \frac{6(136)}{16((16)^2 - 1)} = 1 - 0.2 = \mathbf{0.8.}$$

(*ii*) The value of $r_k = 0.8$ shows that there is high degree positive linear correlation between the variables ranks in Mathematics and Statistics.

(*iii*) Let x and y denote the ranks in 'Mathematics' and 'Statistics' respectively *i.e.*, $x = R_1$ and $y = R_2$

Calculation of r

S. No.	x	y	xy	x^2	y^2
1	1	1	1	1	1
2	2	10	20	4	100
3	3	3	9	9	9
4	4	4	16	16	16
5	5	5	25	25	25
6	6	7	42	36	49
7	7	2	14	49	4
8	8	6	48	64	36
9	9	8	72	81	64
10	10	11	110	100	121
11	11	15	165	121	225
12	12	9	108	144	81
13	13	14	182	169	196
14	14	12	168	196	144
15	15	16	240	225	256
16	16	13	208	256	169
$n = 16$	$\Sigma x = 136$	$\Sigma y = 136$	$\Sigma xy = 1428$	$\Sigma x^2 = 1496$	$\Sigma y^2 = 1496$

∴ Karl Pearson's coefficient of correlation,

$$r = \frac{n\Sigma xy - (\Sigma x)(\Sigma y)}{\sqrt{n\Sigma x^2 - (\Sigma x)^2}\sqrt{n\Sigma y^2 - (\Sigma y)^2}}$$

$$= \frac{16(1428) - (136)(136)}{\sqrt{16(1496) - (136)^2}\sqrt{16(1496) - (136)^2}}$$

$$= \frac{4352}{\sqrt{5440}\sqrt{5440}} = \frac{4352}{5440} = \mathbf{0.8.}$$

This coefficient is same as the rank correlation coefficient.

Remark. If the non-repeated ranks are given in the data, then the Karl Pearson's coefficient of correlation and Spearman's coefficient are always equal.

Example 6. *What is Rank Correlation ? Find the formula for the rank correlation coefficient.* **(KU 1999 C)**

Sol. Let $(x_1, y_1), (x_2, y_2), ..., (x_n, y_n)$ be n pairs of ranks of two variables x and y.

We have
$$r = \frac{\Sigma(x-\bar{x})(y-\bar{y})}{\sqrt{\Sigma(x-\bar{x})^2}\sqrt{\Sigma(y-\bar{y})^2}} \quad ...(1)$$

Since the values of x represent ranks, the values $x_1, x_2, ..., x_n$ of x are distinct and take values from 1 to n.

$$\therefore \quad \Sigma x = 1 + 2 + 3 + ... + n = \frac{n(n+1)}{2}$$

and
$$\Sigma x^2 = 1^2 + 2^2 + 3^2 + ... + n^2 = \frac{n(n+1)(2n+1)}{6}$$

$$\therefore \quad \bar{x} = \frac{\Sigma x}{n} = \frac{1}{n} \cdot \frac{n(n+1)}{2} = \frac{n+1}{2}$$

Now
$$\Sigma(x-\bar{x})^2 = \Sigma(x^2 + \bar{x}^2 - 2x\bar{x}) = \Sigma x^2 + n\bar{x}^2 - 2\bar{x}\Sigma x$$

$$= \Sigma x^2 + n\bar{x}^2 - 2\bar{x} \,.\, n\bar{x} = \Sigma x^2 - n\bar{x}^2$$

$$= \frac{n(n+1)(2n+1)}{6} - n.\left(\frac{n+1}{2}\right)^2$$

$$= \frac{n(n+1)}{2}\left[\frac{2n+1}{3} - \frac{n+1}{2}\right] = \frac{n(n+1)}{2} \times \frac{n-1}{6} = \frac{n(n^2-1)}{12}.$$

Similarly,
$$\bar{y} = \frac{n+1}{2} \quad \text{and} \quad \Sigma(y-\bar{y})^2 = \frac{n(n^2-1)}{12}.$$

Let
$$D = x - y.$$

$$\therefore \quad D = (x-\bar{x}) - (y-\bar{y}) \qquad (\because \bar{x} = \bar{y})$$

$$\Rightarrow \quad D^2 = (x-\bar{x})^2 + (y-\bar{y})^2 - 2(x-\bar{x})(y-\bar{y})$$

$$\Rightarrow \quad 2(x-\bar{x})(y-\bar{y}) = (x-\bar{x})^2 + (y-\bar{y})^2 - D^2$$

$$\Rightarrow \quad 2\Sigma\,(x-\bar{x})(y-\bar{y}) = \Sigma(x-\bar{x})^2 + \Sigma(y-\bar{y})^2 - \Sigma D^2$$

$$= \frac{n(n^2-1)}{12} + \frac{n(n^2-1)}{12} - \Sigma D^2 = \frac{n(n^2-1)}{6} - \Sigma D^2$$

$$\therefore \quad \Sigma(x-\bar{x})(y-\bar{y}) = \frac{n(n^2-1)}{12} - \frac{\Sigma D^2}{2}.$$

Now,
$$r = \frac{\Sigma(x-\bar{x})(y-\bar{y})}{\sqrt{\Sigma(x-\bar{x})^2}\sqrt{\Sigma(y-\bar{y})^2}} = \frac{\dfrac{n(n^2-1)}{12} - \dfrac{\Sigma D^2}{2}}{\sqrt{\dfrac{n(n^2-1)}{12}}\sqrt{\dfrac{n(n^2-1)}{12}}}$$

$$= \frac{\dfrac{n(n^2-1)}{12} - \dfrac{\Sigma D^2}{2}}{\dfrac{n(n^2-1)}{12}} = 1 - \frac{6\Sigma D^2}{n(n^2-1)}$$

$$\therefore \quad \mathbf{r = 1 - \frac{6\Sigma D^2}{n(n^2-1)}}.$$

23. CASE II. REPEATED RANKS

Here we shall consider the case, when the values of two or more items in a series are equal. In such cases, we allot equal ranks to all the items with equal values. Suppose that the values of three items in a series are equal at the fourth place, then each item with equal value would be allotted rank $\frac{4+5+6}{3} = 5$. Similarly, if there happen to be two items in a series with equal values at the seventh place, then each item with equal value would be allotted rank $\frac{7+8}{2} = 7.5$.

In case of repeated ranks, the coefficient of rank correlation is given by the formula,

$$\mathbf{r_k = 1 - \frac{6\left\{\Sigma D^2 + \frac{1}{12}(m^3 - m) + \ldots\right\}}{n(n^2-1)}}$$

where n is the number of pairs and D denote the difference between ranks $(R_1 - R_2)$ of the corresponding values of the variables. In $\frac{1}{12}(m^3 - m)$, m is number of items whose ranks are equal. The term $\frac{1}{12}(m^3 - m)$ is to be added for each group of items with equal ranks. Now, we shall illustrate this method by taking some examples.

Example 7. *Calculate the rank coefficient of correlation for the following data :*

x	80	78	75	75	68	67	60	59
y	12	13	14	14	14	16	15	17

(KU 1997)

Sol. Let R_1 and R_2 denote the ranks of the variables x and y respectively. The first rank is allotted to the greatest item in each series.

Calculation of 'r_k'

S. No.	x	y	R_1	R_2	$D = R_1 - R_2$	D^2
1	80	12	1	8	– 7	49
2	78	13	2	7	– 5	25
3	75	14	3.5	5	– 1.5	2.25
4	75	14	3.5	5	– 1.5	2.25
5	68	14	5	5	0	0
6	67	16	6	2	4	16
7	60	15	7	3	4	16
8	59	17	8	1	7	49
n = 8						$\Sigma D^2 = 159.5$

Now $$r_k = 1 - \frac{6\left\{\Sigma D^2 + \frac{1}{12}(m^3 - m) + ...\right\}}{n(n^2 - 1)} = 1 - \frac{6\left\{159.5 + \frac{1}{12}(2^3 - 2) + \frac{1}{12}(3^3 - 3)\right\}}{8(8^2 - 1)}$$

$$= 1 - \frac{6\,\{159.5 + 0.5 + 2\}}{8 \times 63} = 1 - \frac{6 \times 162}{8 \times 63} = 1 - \frac{27}{14} = -\frac{13}{14} = \mathbf{-0.9286.}$$

It shows that there is a high degree negative linear correlation between the variables.

Example 8. *Following are the marks obtained by ten students in Hindi and English. Calculate coefficient of correlation by method of rank differences.*

Roll No.	*1*	*2*	*3*	*4*	*5*	*6*	*7*	*8*	*9*	*10*
Marks in Hindi	*45*	*56*	*39*	*54*	*45*	*40*	*56*	*60*	*30*	*36*
Marks in English	*40*	*36*	*30*	*44*	*36*	*32*	*45*	*42*	*20*	*36*

Sol. Let R_1 and R_2 denote the ranks of the variables 'marks in Hindi' and 'marks in English' respectively. The first rank is allotted to the greatest item in each series.

Calculation of 'r_k'

Roll No.	Marks in Hindi	Marks in English	R_1	R_2	$D = R_1 - R_2$	D^2
1	45	40	5.5	4	1.5	2.25
2	56	36	2.5	6	– 3.5	12.25
3	39	30	8	9	– 1	1
4	54	44	4	2	2	4
5	45	36	5.5	6	– 0.5	0.25
6	40	32	7	8	– 1	1
7	56	45	2.5	1	1.5	2.25
8	60	42	1	3	– 2	4
9	30	20	10	10	0	0
10	36	36	9	6	3	9
n = 10						$\Sigma D^2 = 36$

Now $$r_k = 1 - \frac{6\left\{\Sigma D^2 + \frac{1}{12}(m^3 - m) + ...\right\}}{n(n^2 - 1)}$$

$$= 1 - \frac{6\left\{36 + \frac{1}{12}(2^3 - 2) + \frac{1}{12}(2^3 - 2) + \frac{1}{12}(3^3 - 3)\right\}}{10(10^2 - 1)}$$

$$= 1 - \frac{6\left\{36 + \frac{1}{2} + \frac{1}{2} + 2\right\}}{990} = 1 - \frac{39}{165} = \mathbf{0.7636.}$$

It shows that there is a high degree positive linear correlation between the variables.

Example 9. *Calculate the rank coefficient of correlation for the following data :*

X-series	*112*	*106*	*109*	*84*	*95*	*95*	*117*	*97*	*95*	*115*
Y-series	*70*	*68*	*80*	*65*	*71*	*60*	*77*	*68*	*63*	*75*

Sol. **Let R_1 and R_2 denote the ranks of the variables X and Y respectively. The first rank is allotted to the greatest item in each series.**

Calculation of 'r_k'

S. No.	*X*	*Y*	*R_1*	*R_2*	*$D = R_1 - R_2$*	*D^2*
1	112	70	3	5	– 2	4
2	106	68	5	6.5	– 1.5	2.25
3	109	80	4	1	3	9
4	84	65	10	8	2	4
5	95	71	8	4	4	16
6	95	60	8	10	– 2	4
7	117	77	1	2	– 1	1
8	97	68	6	6.5	– 0.5	0.25
9	95	63	8	9	– 1	1
10	115	75	2	3	– 1	1
n = 10						$\Sigma D^2 = 42.5$

Now, $$r_k = 1 - \frac{6\left\{\Sigma D^2 + \frac{1}{12}(m^3 - m) + ...\right\}}{n(n^2 - 1)}$$

$$= 1 - \frac{6\left\{42.5 + \frac{1}{12}(3^3 - 3) + \frac{1}{12}(2^3 - 2)\right\}}{10(10^2 - 1)}$$

$$= 1 - \frac{6\left\{42.5 + 2 + \frac{1}{2}\right\}}{990} = 1 - \frac{45}{165} = \mathbf{0.7273.}$$

It shows that there is a moderate degree positive linear correlation between the variables.

Example 10. *Find the coefficient of correlation between x and y by method of rank differences.*

x	*48*	*33*	*40*	*9*	*16*	*16*	*65*	*24*	*16*	*57*
y	*13*	*13*	*24*	*6*	*15*	*4*	*20*	*9*	*6*	*19*

Sol. Let R_1 and R_2 denote the ranks of the variables x and y respectively. The first rank is allotted to the greatest item in each series.

Calculation of 'r_k'

S. No.	*x*	*y*	R_1	R_2	$D = R_1 - R_2$	D^2
1	48	13	3	5.5	− 2.5	6.25
2	33	13	5	5.5	− 0.5	0.25
3	40	24	4	1	3	9
4	9	6	10	8.5	1.5	2.25
5	16	15	8	4	4	16
6	16	4	8	10	− 2	4
7	65	20	1	2	− 1	1
8	24	9	6	7	− 1	1
9	16	6	8	8.5	− 0.5	0.25
10	57	19	2	3	− 1	1
$n = 10$						$\Sigma D^2 = 41$

Now, the coefficient of rank correlation is

$$r_k = 1 - \frac{6\left\{\Sigma D^2 + \frac{1}{12}(m^3 - m) + \ldots\right\}}{n(n^2 - 1)}$$

Here the items 16, 13, 6 are repeated thrice, twice, twice respectively. Therefore, we shall add the correcting factor $\frac{1}{12}(m^3 - m)$ three times in the values of ΣD^2, with the values of m as 3, 2, 2.

$$\therefore \quad r_k = 1 - \frac{6\left\{41 + \frac{1}{12}(3^3 - 3) + \frac{1}{12}(2^3 - 2) + \frac{1}{12}(2^3 - 2)\right\}}{10(10^2 - 1)}$$

$$= 1 - \frac{6\left\{41 + 2 + \frac{1}{2} + \frac{1}{2}\right\}}{990} = 1 - \frac{44}{165} = \mathbf{0.7333.}$$

It shows that there is a moderate degree positive linear correlation between the variables.

Example 11. *The rank correlation coefficient between marks obtained by some students in 'Statistics' and 'Accountancy' is 0.8. If the total of squares of rank difference is 33, find the number of students.*

Sol. We have $r_k = 0.8, \Sigma D^2 = 33.$

Let number of students be n.

$$\therefore \quad r_k = 1 - \frac{6\Sigma D^2}{n(n^2-1)} \quad \text{or} \quad 0.8 = 1 - \frac{6 \times 33}{n(n^2-1)}$$

$$\Rightarrow \quad \frac{198}{n(n^2-1)} = 0.2 = \frac{1}{5} \quad \Rightarrow \quad n(n^2-1) = 990$$

$$\Rightarrow \quad n(n^2-1) = 2 \times 5 \times 3 \times 3 \times 11$$

$$\Rightarrow \quad (n+1)n\,(n-1) = 11 \times 10 \times 9$$

i.e., $$(n+1)n\,(n-1) = (10+1)\,10\,(10-1)$$

$$\therefore \quad n = \mathbf{10}.$$

Example 12. *The coefficient of rank correlation of the marks obtained by 10 students in Auditing and Accounting was found to be 0.5. It was later discovered that the difference in ranks in the two subjects obtained by one of the students was wrongly taken as 3 instead of 7. Find the correct coefficient of rank correlation.* (MDU 2001)

Sol. We have

Incorrect $r_k = 0.5$

$n = 10$

Incorrect difference of ranks (D) $= 3$

Correct difference of rank (D) $= 7$

We know that $$r_k = 1 - \frac{6\Sigma D^2}{n(n^2-1)}$$

$$\therefore \quad \text{Incorrect } r_k = 1 - \frac{6(\text{incorrect } \Sigma D^2)}{n(n^2-1)}$$

$$\therefore \quad 0.5 = 1 - \frac{6(\text{incorrect } \Sigma D^2)}{10(10^2-1)}$$

$$\therefore \quad \text{Incorrect } \Sigma D^2 = 82.5.$$

Now $$\text{Correct } \Sigma D^2 = \text{incorrect } \Sigma D^2 - (\text{incorrect } D^2) + (\text{correct } D^2)$$

$$= 82.5 - (3)^2 + (7)^2 = 82.5 - 9 + 49 = 122.5.$$

$$\text{Correct } r_k = 1 - \frac{6(\text{correct } \Sigma D^2)}{n(n^2-1)} = 1 - \frac{6(122.5)}{10(10^2-1)}$$

$$= 1 - 0.7424 = \mathbf{0.2575}.$$

24. MERITS

1. This method is applicable to both qualitative and quantitative variables.
2. Only this method in applicable when ranks are given.
3. This method involves less calculation work as compared to Karl Pearson's method.

25. DEMERITS

This method is applicable only when the correlation between the variables is linear.

EXERCISE 6

1. From the following data, calculate Spearman's Rank Correlation coefficient.

S. No.	1	2	3	4	5	6	7	8	9	10
Rank Difference	− 2	− 4	− 1	+ 3	+ 2	0	− 2	+ 3	+ 3	2

2. The following are the ranks obtained by a group of 7 students in intelligence tests conducted by two teachers separately. Calculate the rank correlation coefficient.

Student	1	2	3	4	5	6	7
Ranks by Teacher 'A'	6	5	7	4	3	2	1
Ranks by Teacher 'B'	3	5	7	1	2	4	6

3. Ten competitors in a beauty contest are ranked by three judges in the following order :

Ist judge	1	6	5	10	3	2	4	9	7	8
IInd judge	3	5	8	4	7	10	2	1	6	9
IIIrd judge	6	4	9	8	1	2	3	10	5	7

Use the rank correlation coefficient to discuss which pair of judges has the nearest approach to common taste in beauty. *(MDU 1995, 97 ; KU 2002 C)*

4. Ten students were examined in Economics and Statistics. The ranks obtained by the students are as follows :

Economics	1	2	3	4	5	6	7	8	9	10
Statistics	2	4	1	5	3	9	7	10	6	8

Calculate the coefficient of rank correlation.

5. Ten students got following percentage of marks in Mathematics and Accountancy papers.

Mathematics	81	36	98	25	75	82	92	62	65	39
Accountancy	84	51	91	60	68	62	86	58	35	49

Find the rank correlation coefficient.

6. The following data relates to the monthly income and expenditure of 10 families. Find the coefficient of rank correlation between the variables.

Family	A	B	C	D	E	F	G	H	I	J
Income (in Rs.)	1000	700	870	500	900	950	1100	400	1500	800
Expenditure (in Rs.)	900	600	800	490	810	860	910	450	1200	750

7. Compute the coefficient of rank correlation between x and y from the data given below :

x	8	10	7	15	3	20	21	5	10	14	8	16	22	19	6
y	3	12	8	13	20	9	14	11	4	16	15	10	18	23	25

8. Calculate the coefficient of rank correlation for the following data of marks of eight students in Statistics and Accountancy :

Marks in Statistics	52	63	45	36	72	65	45	25
Marks in Accountancy	62	53	51	25	79	43	60	30

9. Following are the ranks obtained by 10 students in two subjects Statistics and Economics. To what extent knowledge of students in two subjects is related ?

Statistics	1	2	3	4	5	6	7	8	9	10
Economics	2	4	1	5	3	9	7	10	6	8

10. Ten competitors in an intelligence test are ranked by three examiners in the following order :

Ist Examiner	9	3	7	5	1	6	2	4	10	8
IInd Examiner	9	1	10	4	3	8	5	2	7	6
IIIrd Examiner	6	3	8	7	2	4	1	5	9	10

Calculate the appropriate rank correlation to help you answer the following questions :

(*i*) Which pair of examiners agree the most ?

(*ii*) Which pair of examiners disagree the most ?

11. An office has 12 clerks. The long serving clerks feel that they should have a seniority increment based on length of service. An assessment of their efficiency by their departmental manager and the personnel department produces a ranking of efficiency. This is shown below together with a ranking of their length of service. Do the data support the claim of clerks for a seniority increment ?

Ranking according to length of service	1	2	3	4	5	6	7	8	9	10	11	12
Ranking according to efficiency	2	3	5	1	9	10	11	12	8	7	6	4

12. The coefficient of rank correlation of the marks obtained by 10 students in Mathematics and Accountancy was found to be + 0.91. It was later discovered that the difference in ranks in the two subjects obtained by one of the students was wrongly taken as 0 instead of 3. Find the correct coefficient of rank correlation.

13. Calculate rank coefficient of correlation for the following data :

A	115	109	112	87	98	98	120	100	98	118
B	75	73	85	70	76	65	82	73	68	80

(*KU 1995*)

14. Find the coefficient of correlation between x and y by the method of rank differences :

x	42	48	35	50	50	57	45	40	50	39
y	90	110	95	95	95	120	115	128	116	130

15. Calculate coefficient of rank correlation from the following data :

X	15	10	20	28	12	10	16	18
Y	16	14	10	12	11	15	18	12

(KU 2005 C, 2007)

Answers

1. $r_k = 0.6364$ 2. $r_k = 0.143$ 3. Ist and IIIrd 4. $r_k = 0.7575$
5. $r_k = 0.7575$ 6. $r_k = 1$ 7. $r_k = 0.0425$ 8. $r_k = 0.643$
9. $r_k = 0.7576$ 10. (*i*) Ist and IIIrd (*ii*) IInd and IIIrd 11. $r_k = 0.3776$, No
12. Correct $r_k = 0.855$. 13. $r_k = 0.7212$ 14. $r_k = -0.0556$ 15. $r = -0.369$.

V. CONCURRENT DEVIATIONS METHOD

26. METHOD

This method is best suited when only the direction of correlation is wanted. Let n pairs of values of variables x and y are given. In this method, the deviations of the values of x and y series are considered from their corresponding preceding values. Moreover, we record only the signs of these deviations. If the deviation of a value from its preceding value is zero, then we shall write '0' in the column of signs. This is done for both series. The next step is to multiply these signs in accordance with the following rules :

$$(+)(+) = + \qquad (-)(-) = +$$
$$(-)(+) = - \qquad (+)(-) = -$$
$$(0)(+) = 0 \qquad (0)(-) = 0.$$

The products of the signs are written in a separate column. The '+' signs are counted in this column. This sum represents the number of *concurrent* deviations. This same is denoted by 'c'.

The formula for computing the coefficient of correlation is

$$r_c = \pm\sqrt{\pm\left(\frac{2c - N}{N}\right)}$$

where c = number of concurrent deviations

N = one less than the number of pairs *i.e.*, $N = n - 1$.

We know that the square root of only a non-negative quantity can be a real number.

The number $\frac{2c - N}{N}$ may be either positive or zero or negative.

If $\frac{2c - N}{N}$ is positive or zero, we take $r_c = +\sqrt{+\left(\frac{2c - N}{N}\right)}$.

If $\frac{2c - N}{N}$ is negative, then we take $r_c = -\sqrt{-\left(\frac{2c - N}{N}\right)}$.

In other words, we borrow sign from ± according to the sign of $\frac{2c - N}{N}$, so that the quantity under the sign of square root may become non-negative.

Example 1. *Find the coefficient of concurrent deviations correlation for the following data :*

Year	*1990*	*1991*	*1992*	*1993*	*1994*	*1995*	*1996*
Supply	*150*	*154*	*160*	*172*	*160*	*165*	*180*
Price	*200*	*180*	*170*	*160*	*190*	*180*	*172*

Sol. Let x and y denote the variables 'Supply' and 'Price' respectively. Let dx and dy represent the signs of the deviations of the values of x and y variables from their respective preceding values.

Calculation of 'r_c'

S. No.	x	y	dx	dy	$dx \cdot dy$
1	150	200			
2	154	180	+	–	–
3	160	170	+	–	–
4	172	160	+	–	–
5	160	190	–	+	–
6	165	180	+	–	–
7	180	172	+	–	–
$n = 7$					$c = 0$

Now $$r_c = \pm \sqrt{\pm\left(\frac{2c - N}{N}\right)}$$

Here $c = 0$, $N = n - 1 = 7 - 1 = 6$

$\therefore$ $$r_c = \pm \sqrt{\pm\left(\frac{2(0) - 6}{6}\right)} = \pm \sqrt{\pm(-1)}$$

$$= -\sqrt{-(-1)} = -\sqrt{1} = -1.$$

Example 2. *Calculate the coefficient of concurrent deviation for the following :*

Year	*1991*	*1992*	*1993*	*1994*	*1995*	*1996*	*1997*	*1998*
Supply (units)	*180*	*184*	*192*	*202*	*186*	*190*	*198*	*212*
Price (units)	*232*	*290*	*270*	*234*	*276*	*264*	*240*	*200*

(KU 1999)

Sol. Let x and y denote the variables 'Supply' and 'Price' respectively.

Let dx and dy represent the signs of deviations of values of x and y variables from their corresponding preceding values.

Calculation of 'r_c'

S. No.	x	y	dx	dy	$dxdy$
1	180	232			
2	184	290	+	+	+
3	192	270	+	−	−
4	202	234	+	−	−
5	186	276	−	+	−
6	190	264	+	−	−
7	198	240	+	−	−
8	212	200	+	−	−
$n = 8$					$c = 1$

Now $$r_c = \pm\sqrt{\pm\left(\frac{2c - N}{N}\right)}$$

Here $c = 1, N = n - 1 = 8 - 1 = 7$

$$\therefore \quad r_c = \pm\sqrt{\pm\left(\frac{2(1) - 7}{7}\right)} = \pm\sqrt{\pm\left(\frac{-5}{7}\right)}$$

$$= -\sqrt{-\left(\frac{-5}{7}\right)} = -\sqrt{\frac{5}{7}} = -\sqrt{0.7143} = \mathbf{-0.8452.}$$

Example 3. *Calculate the coefficient of concurrent deviation for the following data :*

Year	*1973*	*1974*	*1975*	*1976*	*1977*	*1978*	*1979*	*1980*
Supply	*160*	*164*	*172*	*182*	*166*	*170*	*178*	*192*
Price	*222*	*280*	*260*	*224*	*266*	*254*	*230*	*190*

(KU 1998)

Sol. Let x and y denote the variables 'Supply' and 'Price' respectively. Let dx and dy represent the signs of deviations of values of x and y variables from their corresponding preceding values.

Calculation of 'r_c'

S. No.	x	y	dx	dy	$dxdy$
1	160	222			
2	164	280	+	+	+
3	172	260	+	−	−
4	182	224	+	−	−
5	166	266	−	+	−
6	170	254	+	−	−
7	178	230	+	−	−
8	192	190	+	−	−
$n = 8$					$c = 1$

Now $$r_c = \pm\sqrt{\pm\left(\frac{2c-N}{N}\right)}.$$

Here $c = 1$, $N = n - 1 = 8 - 1 = 7$

$$\therefore \quad r_c = \pm\sqrt{\pm\left(\frac{2(1)-7}{7}\right)} = \pm\sqrt{\pm\left(\frac{-5}{7}\right)}$$

$$= -\sqrt{-\left(\frac{-5}{7}\right)} = -\sqrt{\frac{5}{7}} = -\sqrt{0.7143} = \mathbf{-0.8452.}$$

Example 4. *Calculate the coefficient of correlation by the method of concurrent deviations, for the following data :*

Year	*1991*	*1992*	*1993*	*1994*	*1995*	*1996*	*1997*	*1998*	*1999*
x	*80*	*82*	*86*	*91*	*83*	*85*	*89*	*96*	*93*
y	*146*	*140*	*130*	*117*	*133*	*127*	*115*	*95*	*100*

Sol. Let dx and dy denote the signs of the deviations of the values of x and y variables from their corresponding preceding values.

S. No.	*Year*	*x*	*y*	*dx*	*dy*	*dx . dy*
1	1991	80	146			
2	1992	82	140	+	–	–
3	1993	86	130	+	–	–
4	1994	91	117	+	–	–
5	1995	83	133	–	+	–
6	1996	85	127	+	–	–
7	1997	89	115	+	–	–
8	1998	96	95	+	–	–
9	1999	93	100	–	+	–
$n = 9$						$c = 0$

Now, $$r_c = \pm\sqrt{\pm\left(\frac{2c-N}{N}\right)}$$

Here $N = n - 1 = 9 - 1 = 8$ and $c = 0$

$$\therefore \quad r_c = \pm\sqrt{\pm\left(\frac{2(0)-8}{8}\right)} = \pm\sqrt{\pm(-1)} = -\sqrt{-(-1)} = -\sqrt{1} = \mathbf{-1.}$$

Example 5. *Calculate the coefficient of correlation by the method of concurrent derivations for the following data :*

Years	*1977*	*1978*	*1979*	*1980*	*1981*	*1982*	*1983*	*1984*	*1985*	*1986*
Annual income (in Rs.)	*12000*	*13000*	*13000*	*16000*	*16500*	*18000*	*15000*	*19000*	*20000*	*20000*
Annual Expenditure (in Rs.)	*10000*	*10500*	*12000*	*14000*	*14000*	*15000*	*14000*	*15000*	*16000*	*17000*

Sol. Let x and y denote the variables 'annual income' and 'annual expenditure' respectively. Let dx and dy represent the signs of deviations of values of x and y variables from their corresponding preceding values.

Calculation of 'r_c'

S. No.	*Year*	x	y	dx	dy	$dxdy$
1	1977	12000	10000			
2	1978	13000	10500	+	+	+
3	1979	13000	12000	0	+	0
4	1980	16000	14000	+	+	+
5	1981	16500	14000	+	0	0
6	1982	18000	15000	+	+	+
7	1983	15000	14000	–	–	+
8	1984	19000	15000	+	+	+
9	1985	20000	16000	+	+	+
10	1986	20000	17000	0	+	0
$n = 10$						$c = 6$

Now, $$r_c = \pm\sqrt{\pm\left(\frac{2c - N}{N}\right)}$$

Here $N = n - 1 = 10 - 1 = 9$ and $c = 6$

$$\therefore \quad r_c = \pm\sqrt{\pm\left(\frac{2(6) - 9}{N}\right)} = \pm\sqrt{\pm\left(\frac{1}{3}\right)} = +\sqrt{+\left(\frac{1}{3}\right)} = +\mathbf{0.5773.}$$

27. MERITS

1. This method is best suited when the purpose is only to know the direction of the correlation.
2. This method is simple to understand.
3. The coefficient of correlation is simple to compute.

28. DEMERITS

1. This method does not give the magnitude of the correlation correctly.
2. This is not an accurate method, because we take in to consideration only the direction of the deviations and do not bother for the magnitude of the deviations.

EXERCISE 7

1. Calculate the coefficient of correlation for the following data by using the method of concurrent deviations :

x	6	10	12	5	15	18
y	4	8	6	4	10	12

2. Compute the coefficient of correlation between *x* and *y* series by the method of concurrent deviations :

x-series	26	30	30	24	29	25	25	32	32	38
y-series	62	58	55	68	67	64	64	75	81	78

(*KU 2000 C*)

3. Calculate the coefficient of concurrent deviations for the following data :

x	28	41	40	38	35	33	40	32	36	33
y	23	34	33	34	30	26	28	31	36	38

4. The following statistics relate to income and expenditure of 11 workers of a factory. Find the correlation between the variables 'income' and 'expenditure' by the method of concurrent deviations :

Income (in Rs.)	65	40	35	75	63	80	35	20	80	60	50
Expenditure (in Rs.)	60	55	50	56	30	70	40	35	80	75	80

(*KU 2001 C*)

5. Calculate the coefficient of correlation using concurrent deviations for the following data :

x	1	4	3	8	9	5
y	15	14	18	15	12	14

6. Calculate the coefficient of correlation using concurrent deviations for the following data :

Student	A	B	C	D	E	F	G	H
Height (in inches)	60	65	59	70	72	60	62	64
Weight (in kgs.)	70	72	70	80	80	75	75	78

7. Following are the data relating to the income and expenditure of eight families. Find the coefficient of correlation using concurrent deviations.

Family	1	2	3	4	5	6	7	8
Income (in Rs.)	500	437	630	725	429	608	709	1050
Expenditure (in Rs.)	450	425	600	700	430	550	600	900

8. Calculate the coefficient of correlation using concurrent deviations for the following data :

Year	1989	1990	1991	1992	1993	1994	1995	1996
Expenses on Advertisements (in Rs.)	1000	1500	1400	2000	2000	2500	2200	2500
Profit (in Rs.)	20000	22000	22000	32000	34000	30000	37000	40000

9. Calculate the coefficient of correlation for the data given below by using the method of concurrent deviations :

Price	22	21	24	20	22	26	25	29	28	27
Imports	384	395	403	400	385	368	384	385	361	347

(KU 1998 C)

10. Find the coefficient of correlation for the following data, by using the method of concurrent deviations :

Year	1991	1992	1993	1994	1995	1996
Sale (in Rs.)	50000	60000	55000	70000	76000	74000
Profit (in Rs.)	10000	15000	15000	20000	22000	24000

11. What is correlation ? Calculate the coefficient of correlation from the following data by the method of concurrent deviations :

Year	*Export*	*Import*	*Year*	*Export*	*Import*
1990	70	22	1996	72	20
1991	68	18	1997	76	29
1992	85	25	1998	82	18
1993	80	16	1999	77	24
1994	75	15	2000	64	17
1995	69	12			

12. From the following data calculate the coefficient of correlation by concurrent deviations method :

Months	*x-series*	*y-series*
January	89	32
February	85	33
March	98	35
April	102	37
May	100	39
June	105	41
July	96	40
August	68	38
September	85	42
October	98	40
November	76	36
December	75	35

13. Calculate the coefficient of correlation by concurrent deviation method from the following data :

X	112	125	126	118	118	121	125	125	131	135
Y	106	102	102	104	98	96	97	97	95	90

(MDU 2006)

Answers

1. $r_c = 0.7747$ **2.** $r_c = -0.7454$ **3.** $r_c = -0.5774$ **4.** $r_c = 0.8945$
5. $r_c = -1$ **6.** $r_c = 0.6547$ **7.** $r_c = 1$ **8.** $r_c = -0.3779$
9. $r_c = 1/3$ **10.** $r_c = 0.4472$ **11.** $r_c = 0.7746$ **12.** $r_c = 0.6742$
13. $r_c = -0.881$.

EXERCISE 8

1. Explain the meaning of the term 'Correlation'. Does it always signify cause and effect relationship ? *(KU 2005)*
2. What is correlation ? Distinguish between positive and negative correlation.
3. If the '*r*' between the annual values of exports during the last ten years and the annual number of children born during the same period is + 0.8. What interference, if any, would you draw ?
4. How would you interpret the sign and magnitude of a calculated '*r*'. Consider in particular the values $r = 0$, $r = -1$ and $r = +1$.
5. What is a scatter diagram ?
6. Explain the meaning of the term 'correlation'. Name the different measures of correlation and discuss their uses.
7. Define correlation and discuss its significance in statistical analysis. *(KU 2002 ; MDU 2002)*
8. Explain different methods of computing correlation *(MDU 2003 ; KU 1995, 2006)*
9. What do you understand by correlation ? Explain its various types in detail. *(KU 2000 C)*
10. What is coefficient of concurrent deviation ? How it is determined ? *(KU 1997, 99 C)*
11. Elucidate the main features of Karl Pearson's coefficient of correlation. *(MDU 2000)*
12. What is correlation ? *(KU 2001)*
13. What are the degrees and types of correlation ? How is Karl Pearson's coefficient of correlation calculated ? *(MDU 2001)*
14. Define correlation and discuss its significance in statistical analysis. Does it signify cause and effect relationship between the two variables ? *(KU 2002)*
15. What is coefficient of concurrent deviation ? How it is determined ? *(KU 2005)*
16. Does correlation always show cause and effect relationship between two variables ? *(MDU 2007)*

11

Regression Analysis

1. INTRODUCTION

In the discussion of correlation, we estimated the degree of relationship between variables. The coefficient of correlation r, $(-1 \leq r \leq 1)$ measured the *degree* of relationship between variables. A numerically high value of 'r' resulted because of closeness of relation between the variables, under consideration. The coefficient of correlation is unable to depict the *nature* of relationship between the variable. For a given data regarding the corresponding values of two related variables, the coefficient of correlation cannot give the *estimated value* of a variable, corresponding to a certain value of the other related variable. For example, the coefficient of correlation between 'height' and 'weight' of a group of students of a university cannot help to give the estimated weight (resp. height) of a student with given height (resp. weight). This type of assignment is dealt with the tools of *regression analysis*.

2. MEANING

The literal meaning of the word 'regression' is 'stepping back towards the average'. British biometrician *Sir Francis Galton* (1822–1911) studies the heights of many persons and concluded that the offspring of abnormally tall or short parents tend to *regress* to the average population height. In statistics, *regression analysis* is concerned with the measure of average relationship between variables. Here we shall deal with the derivation of appropriate functional relationships between variables. Regression explains the nature of relationship between variables.

There are two types of variables. The variable whose value is influenced or is to be predicted is called *dependent variable (or regressed variable or predicted variable or explained variable)*. The variable which influences the value of dependent variable is called *independent variable (or regressor or predictor or explanator)*. Prediction is possible in regression analysis, because here we study the average relationship between related variables.

3. USES OF REGRESSION ANALYSIS

The tools of regression analysis are definitely more important and useful than those of correlation analysis. Some of the important uses of regression analysis are as follows :

(*i*) Regression analysis helps in establishing relationship between dependent variable and independent variables. The independent variables may be more than one. Such relationships are very useful in further studies of the variables, under consideration.

(*ii*) Regression analysis is very useful for prediction. Once a relation is established between dependent variable and independent variables, the value of dependent variable can be predicted for given values of the independent variables. This is very useful for predicting sale, profit, investment, income, population etc.

(*iii*) Regression analysis is specially used in Economics for estimating demand function, production function, consumption function, supply function etc. A very important branch of Economics, called *Econometrics,* is based on the techniques of regression analysis.

(*iv*) The coefficient of correlation between two variables can be found easily by using the regression lines between the variables.

4. TYPES OF REGRESSION

If there are only two variables under consideration, then the regression is called **simple regression.** For example, the study of regression between 'income' and 'expenditure' for a group of family would be termed as simple regression. If there are more than two variables under consideration then the regression is called **multiple regression.** In this text, we shall restrict ourselves to the study of only simple regression. The regression is called **partial regression** if there are more than two variables under consideration and relation between only two variables is established after excluding the effect of other variables. The simple regression is called **linear regression** if the point on the scatter diagram of variables lies almost along a line otherwise it is termed as **non-linear regression** or **curvilinear regression.**

5. COMPARISON BETWEEN CORRELATION AND REGRESSION

There is no denying the fact that there are some basic differences in studying correlation and regression between variables. These are as follows :

Correlation	*Regression*
1. It studies the *degree* of relationship between variables.	1. It studies the *nature* of relationship between variables.
2. It need not imply cause and effect relationship between variables.	2. It implies cause and effect relationship between variables.
3. There may be non-sense correlation between the variables.	3. In regression analysis, there is nothing like non-sense regression.
4. The correlation coefficient is independent of change of origin and scale.	4. The regression coefficients are independent of origin but not of scale.
5. The correlation coefficient cannot be used for prediction.	5. The regression lines can be used for prediction.

6. REGRESSION LINES

Let the variables under consideration be denoted by 'x' and 'y'. The line used to estimate the value of y for a given value of x is called the *regression line* of y *on* x. Similarly, the line used to estimate the value of x for a given value of y is called the *regression line of* x *on* y. In regression line of y on x (x on y), the variable y is considered as the dependent (independent) variable whereas x is considered as the independent (dependent) variable. The position of regression lines depends upon the given pairs of value of the variables. Regression lines are also known as *estimating lines.* We shall see that in case of perfect correlation between the variables, the regression lines will be coincident. The angle between the regression lines will increases for 0° to 90° as the correlation coefficient numerically decreases from 1 to 0. If for a particular pair of variables, $r = 0$, then the regression lines will be perpendicular to each other. The regression lines will be determined by using the *principle of least squares.*

7. REGRESSION EQUATIONS

We have already noted that for two variables x and y, there can be two regression lines. If the intention is to depict the change in y for a given change in x, then the regression line of y on x is to be used. Similar argument also works for regression line of x on y.

(*i*) **Regression equation of y on x.** The regression equation of y on x is estimated by using the 'principle of least squares'. This principle will ensure that the sum of the squares of the *vertical* deviations of actual values of y from estimated values for all possible values of x is minimum.

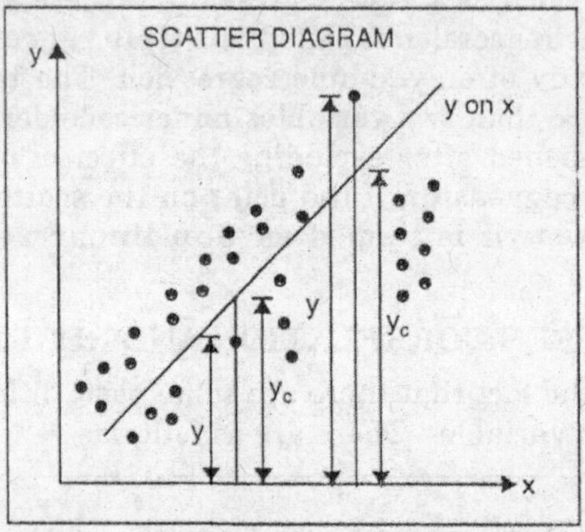

Mathematically, $\Sigma(y - y_c)^2$ is least, where y and y_c are the corresponding actual and computed values of y for a particular value of x.

Let n pairs of values $(x_1, y_1), (x_2, y_2), ..., (x_n, y_n)$ of two variables x and y be given.

Let the regression equation of y on x be $y = a + bx$. ...(1)

By using derivatives, it can be proved that the constants a and b are found by using the *normal equations :*

$$\Sigma y = an + b\Sigma x \quad ...(2)$$

and

$$\Sigma xy = a\Sigma x + b\Sigma x^2. \quad ...(3)$$

Dividing (2) by n, we get

$$\frac{\Sigma y}{n} = a + b\frac{\Sigma x}{n}.$$

$$\Rightarrow \quad \bar{y} = a + b\,\bar{x} \quad ...(4)$$

Subtracting (4) from (1), we get

$$y - \bar{y} = b(x - \bar{x}) \quad ...(5)$$

Multiplying (2) by Σx and (3) by n and subtracting, we get

$$(\Sigma x)(\Sigma y) - n\Sigma xy = b(\Sigma x)^2 - bn\Sigma x^2$$

$$\Rightarrow \quad n\Sigma xy - (\Sigma x)(\Sigma y) = b(n\Sigma x^2 - (\Sigma x)^2)$$

$$\therefore \quad b = \frac{n\Sigma xy - (\Sigma x)(\Sigma y)}{n\Sigma x^2 - (\Sigma x)^2}.$$

The constant b is denoted by b_{yx} and is called **regression coefficient** of y on x.

$\therefore$ (5) $\Rightarrow$ $y - \bar{y} = b_{yx}(x - \bar{x})$, where $b_{yx} = \dfrac{n\Sigma xy - (\Sigma x)(\Sigma y)}{n\Sigma x^2 - (\Sigma x)^2}$.

Remark. $b_{yx} = \dfrac{n\Sigma xy - (\Sigma x)(\Sigma y)}{n\Sigma x^2 - (\Sigma x)^2}$ implies

$$b_{yx} = \frac{n\Sigma xy - (\Sigma x)(\Sigma y)}{\sqrt{n\Sigma x^2 - (\Sigma x)^2}\sqrt{n\Sigma y^2 - (\Sigma y)^2}} \times \frac{\dfrac{\sqrt{n\Sigma y^2 - (\Sigma y)^2}}{n}}{\dfrac{\sqrt{n\Sigma x^2 - (\Sigma x)^2}}{n}} = r \times \frac{\sqrt{\dfrac{\Sigma y^2}{n} - \left(\dfrac{\Sigma y}{n}\right)^2}}{\sqrt{\dfrac{\Sigma x^2}{n} - \left(\dfrac{\Sigma x}{n}\right)^2}} = r\frac{\sigma_y}{\sigma_x}.$$

$$\therefore \qquad \mathbf{b_{yx} = r\,\frac{\sigma_y}{\sigma_x}}.$$

Thus we see that the regression equation of y on x is $\mathbf{y - \bar{y} = b_{yx}(x - \bar{x})}$, where $\mathbf{\bar{x} = \dfrac{\Sigma x}{n}}$, $\mathbf{\bar{y} = \dfrac{\Sigma y}{n}}$, $\mathbf{b_{yx} = \dfrac{n\Sigma xy - (\Sigma x)(\Sigma y)}{n\Sigma x^2 - (\Sigma x)^2}}$, which is also equal to $\mathbf{r\,\dfrac{\sigma_y}{\sigma_x}}$.

Example 1. *Find b_{yx} from the following data :*

$\{(x, y)\} = \{(5, 2), (7, 4), (8, 3), (4, 2), (6, 4)\}$.

Sol. **Calculation of b_{yx}**

S. No.	*x*	*y*	*xy*	x^2
1	5	2	10	25
2	7	4	28	49
3	8	3	24	64
4	4	2	8	16
5	6	4	24	36
$n = 5$	$\Sigma x = 30$	$\Sigma y = 15$	$\Sigma xy = 94$	$\Sigma x^2 = 190$

$$b_{yx} = \frac{n\Sigma xy - (\Sigma x)(\Sigma y)}{n\Sigma x^2 - (\Sigma x)^2} = \frac{5(94) - (30)(15)}{5(190) - (30)^2} = \frac{20}{50} = \mathbf{0.4}.$$

Example 2. *Find the regression equation of y on x when we know :*

$\bar{x} = 68.2,\ \bar{y} = 9.9,\ \dfrac{\sigma_y}{\sigma_x} = 0.44,\ r = 0.76.$ (MDU 2000)

Sol. We have $\bar{x} = 68.2$, $\bar{y} = 9.9$, $\dfrac{\sigma_y}{\sigma_x} = 0.44$, $r = 0.76$.

The regression equation of *y* on *x* is $y - \bar{y} = b_{yx}(x - \bar{x})$.

$\Rightarrow \quad y - \bar{y} = r\dfrac{\sigma_y}{\sigma_x}(x - \bar{x}) \quad \Rightarrow \quad y - 9.9 = (0.76)(0.44)(x - 68.2)$

$\Rightarrow \quad y - 9.9 = 0.3344\,(x - 68.2) \quad \Rightarrow \quad y = 0.3344x + 9.9 - (0.3344)(68.2)$

$\Rightarrow \quad \mathbf{y = 0.3344x - 12.9061.}$

Example 3. *Find the most likely price in Mumbai corresponding to price of Rs. 75 at Calcutta from the following data :*

	Calcutta	*Mumbai*
Average price	*Rs. 65*	*Rs. 68*
Standard deviation	*Rs. 2.5*	*Rs. 3.5*

Coefficient of correlation between two prices = 0.78. (KU 1996 C)

Sol. Let the 'price in Calcutta' and 'price in Mumbai' be denoted by x and y respectively.

We have $\bar{x}$ = Rs. 65, $\bar{y}$ = Rs. 68,

σ_x = Rs. 2.5, σ_y = Rs. 3.5, $r = 0.78$.

The regression line of y on x is $y - \bar{y} = b_{yx}(x - \bar{x})$.

$$\Rightarrow \quad y - \bar{y} = r\frac{\sigma_y}{\sigma_x}(x - \bar{x}) \quad \Rightarrow \quad y - 68 = 0.78 \times \frac{3.5}{2.5}(x - 65)$$

$$\Rightarrow \quad y - 68 = 1.092(x - 65) \quad \Rightarrow \quad y = 1.092x + 68 - (1.092 \times 65)$$

$$\Rightarrow \quad y = 1.092x - 2.98.$$

When x is Rs. 75, the expected value of

$$y = 1.092(75) - 2.98 = \text{Rs. } 78.92.$$

∴ Price at Mumbai = **Rs. 78.92.**

Example 4. *x and y are correlated variables. Ten observations of values of (x, y) have the following results :*

$$\Sigma x = 55,\ \Sigma y = 55,\ \Sigma xy = 350,\ \Sigma x^2 = 385.$$

Predict the value of y when the value of x is 6.

Sol. To predict the value of y for a given value of x, we shall require the equation of regression line of y on x.

The equation of regression line of y on x is

$$y - \bar{y} = b_{yx}(x - \bar{x}). \qquad ...(1)$$

We have $\Sigma x = 55,\ \Sigma y = 55,\ \Sigma xy = 350,\ \Sigma x^2 = 385,\ n = 10$

Now $$\bar{x} = \frac{\Sigma x}{n} = \frac{55}{10} = 5.5,\quad \bar{y} = \frac{\Sigma y}{n} = \frac{55}{10} = 5.5$$

$$b_{yx} = \frac{n\Sigma xy - (\Sigma x)(\Sigma y)}{n\Sigma x^2 - (\Sigma x)^2} = \frac{10(350) - (55)(55)}{10(385) - (55)^2} = \frac{475}{825} = 0.5758.$$

$$\therefore \quad (1) \Rightarrow \quad y - 5.5 = 0.5758(x - 5.5)$$

$$\Rightarrow \quad y = 0.5758x + 2.3331.$$

This is the equation of regression line of y on x.

When $x = 6$, the predicted value of y

$$= 0.5758(6) + 2.3331 = \mathbf{5.7879}.$$

Example 5. *For the following data, find the regression line of y on x :*

x	*1*	*2*	*3*	*4*	*5*	*8*	*10*
y	*9*	*8*	*10*	*12*	*14*	*16*	*15*

Sol. **Regression line of y on x**

S. No.	x	y	xy	x^2
1	1	9	9	1
2	2	8	16	4
3	3	10	30	9
4	4	12	48	16
5	5	14	70	25
6	8	16	128	64
7	10	15	150	100
$n = 7$	$\Sigma x = 33$	$\Sigma y = 84$	$\Sigma xy = 451$	$\Sigma x^2 = 219$

The regression line of y on x is $y - \bar{y} = b_{yx}(x - \bar{x})$

$$\bar{x} = \frac{\Sigma x}{n} = \frac{33}{7} = 4.714, \quad \bar{y} = \frac{\Sigma y}{n} = \frac{84}{7} = 12$$

$$b_{yx} = \frac{n\Sigma xy - (\Sigma x)(\Sigma y)}{n\Sigma x^2 - (\Sigma x)^2} = \frac{7(451) - (33)(84)}{7(219) - (33)^2} = \frac{385}{444} = 0.867.$$

$\therefore$ The equation of regression line of y on x is

$$y - 12 = 0.867\,(x - 4.714)$$

or $$y = 0.867x + 12 - (0.867)(4.714)$$

or $$\mathbf{y = 0.867x + 7.913.}$$

(*ii*) **Regression equation of x on y.** The regression equation of x on y is also estimated by using the 'principle of least squares'. This principle will ensure that the sum of the squares of the *horizontal* deviations of actual values of x from estimated values for all possible values of y is minimum. Mathematically, $\Sigma(x - \bar{x}_c)^2$ is least, where x and x_c are the corresponding actual and computed values of x for a particular value of y.

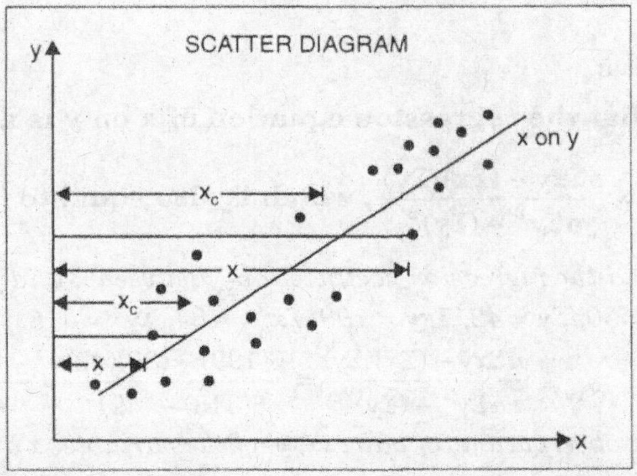

Let n pairs of values $(x_1, y_1), (x_2, y_2), \ldots, (x_n, y_n)$ of two variables x and y be given.

Let the regression equation of x on y be $x = a + by$ ...(1)

By using derivatives, it can be proved that the constants a and b are found by using the *normal equations* :

$$\Sigma x = ax + b\Sigma y \qquad ...(2)$$

and

$$\Sigma xy = a\Sigma y + b\Sigma y^2. \qquad ...(3)$$

Dividing (2) by n, we get

$$\frac{\Sigma x}{n} = a + b\frac{\Sigma y}{n}$$

$$\Rightarrow \quad \bar{x} = a + b\bar{y} \qquad ...(4)$$

Subtracting (4) from (1), we get

$$x - \bar{x} = b(y - \bar{y}) \qquad ...(5)$$

Multiplying (2) by Σy and (3) by n and subtracting, we get

$$(\Sigma x)(\Sigma y) - n\Sigma xy = b(\Sigma y)^2 - bn\Sigma y^2$$

$$\Rightarrow \quad n\Sigma xy - (\Sigma x)(\Sigma y) = b(n\Sigma y^2 - \Sigma y)^2$$

$$\therefore \quad b = \frac{n\Sigma xy - (\Sigma x)(\Sigma y)}{n\Sigma y^2 - (\Sigma y)^2}.$$

The constant b is denoted by b_{xy} and is called **regression coefficient** of x on y.

$$\therefore \quad (5) \Rightarrow \quad x - \bar{x} = b_{xy}(y - \bar{y}), \text{ where } \quad b_{xy} = \frac{n\Sigma xy - (\Sigma x)(\Sigma y)}{n\Sigma y^2 - (\Sigma y)^2}$$

Remark. $b_{xy} = \frac{n\Sigma xy - (\Sigma x)(\Sigma y)}{n\Sigma y^2 - (\Sigma y)^2}$ implies

$$b_{xy} = \frac{n\Sigma xy - (\Sigma x)(\Sigma y)}{\sqrt{n\Sigma x^2 - (\Sigma x)^2}\sqrt{n\Sigma y^2 - (\Sigma y)^2}} \times \frac{\dfrac{\sqrt{n\Sigma x^2 - (\Sigma x)^2}}{n}}{\dfrac{\sqrt{n\Sigma y^2 - (\Sigma y)^2}}{n}} = r \times \frac{\sqrt{\dfrac{\Sigma x^2}{n} - \left(\dfrac{\Sigma x}{n}\right)^2}}{\sqrt{\dfrac{\Sigma y^2}{n} - \left(\dfrac{\Sigma y}{n}\right)^2}} = r\frac{\sigma_x}{\sigma_y}.$$

$$\therefore \quad \mathbf{b_{xy} = r\frac{\sigma_y}{\sigma_x}}.$$

Thus we see that the regression equation of x on y is $\mathbf{x - \bar{x} = b_{xy}(y - \bar{y})}$, where

$$\mathbf{\bar{x} = \frac{\Sigma x}{n},\ \bar{y} = \frac{\Sigma y}{n},\ b_{xy} = \frac{n\Sigma xy - (\Sigma x)(\Sigma y)}{n\Sigma y^2 - (\Sigma y)^2}}, \textbf{ which is also equal to } \mathbf{r\frac{\sigma_x}{\sigma_y}}.$$

Example 6. *Find the regression coefficient b_{xy} between x and y for the following data :*

$$\Sigma x = 30,\ \Sigma y = 42,\ \Sigma xy = 199,\ \Sigma x^2 = 184,\ \Sigma y^2 = 318,\ n = 6.$$

Sol.

$$b_{xy} = \frac{n\Sigma xy - (\Sigma x)(\Sigma y)}{n\Sigma y^2 - (\Sigma y)^2} = \frac{6(199) - (30)(42)}{6(318) - (42)^2} = \frac{-66}{144} = \mathbf{-0.4583.}$$

Example 7. *For observations of pairs (x, y) of the variables x and y, the following results are obtained :*

$$\Sigma x = 110,\ \Sigma y = 70,\ \Sigma x^2 = 2500,\ \Sigma y^2 = 2000,\ \Sigma xy = 100,\ n = 20.$$

Find the equation of the regression line of x on y. Estimate the value of x when y = 4.

Sol. We have

$$\Sigma x = 110, \Sigma y = 70, \Sigma x^2 = 2500, \Sigma y^2 = 2000, \Sigma xy = 100, n = 20.$$

The equation of regression line of x on y is

$$x - \bar{x} = b_{xy}(y - \bar{y}). \qquad ...(1)$$

Now $\bar{x} = \frac{\Sigma x}{n} = \frac{110}{20} = 5.5, \quad \bar{y} = \frac{\Sigma y}{n} = \frac{70}{20} = 3.5$

$$b_{xy} = \frac{n\Sigma xy - (\Sigma x)(\Sigma y)}{n\Sigma y^2 - (\Sigma y)^2} = \frac{20(100) - (110)(70)}{20(2000) - (70)^2} = \frac{-5700}{35100} = -0.1624$$

$\therefore$ (1) $\Rightarrow$ $x - 5.5 = -0.1624\,(y - 3.5)$

$\Rightarrow$ $x = -0.1624y + (0.1624)(3.5) + 5.5$

$\Rightarrow$ $\mathbf{x = -0.1624y + 6.0684.}$

This is the regression equation of x on y.

When $y = 4$, the estimated value of y

$$= -0.1624(4) + 6.0684 = \mathbf{5.4188.}$$

Example 8. *Find the two regression equations from the following data and estimate the value of X, if Y is 6 :*

X	*1*	*2*	*3*	*4*	*5*
Y	*2*	*5*	*3*	*8*	*7*

(KU 2001 C)

Sol. **Regression Equations**

S. No.	*X*	*Y*	*XY*	*X²*	*Y²*
1	1	2	2	1	4
2	2	5	10	4	25
3	3	3	9	9	9
4	4	8	32	16	64
5	5	7	35	25	49
$n = 5$	$\Sigma X = 15$	$\Sigma Y = 25$	$\Sigma XY = 88$	$\Sigma X^2 = 55$	$\Sigma Y^2 = 151$

$$\bar{X} = \frac{\Sigma X}{n} = \frac{15}{5} = 3, \quad \bar{Y} = \frac{\Sigma Y}{n} = \frac{25}{5} = 5$$

The regression equation of Y on X is $Y - \bar{Y} = b_{YX}(X - \bar{X})$.

$$b_{YX} = \frac{n\Sigma XY - (\Sigma X)(\Sigma Y)}{n\Sigma X^2 - (\Sigma X)^2} = \frac{5(88) - (15)(25)}{5(55) - (15)^2} = \frac{65}{50} = 1.3$$

$\therefore$ The equation is

$$Y - 5 = 1.3\,(X - 3)$$

or $Y = 1.3X + 5 - 3.9$ or $\mathbf{Y = 1.3X + 1.1.}$

The regression equation of X on Y is $X - \bar{X} = b_{XY}(Y - \bar{Y})$.

$$b_{XY} = \frac{n\Sigma XY - (\Sigma X)(\Sigma Y)}{n\Sigma Y^2 - (\Sigma Y)^2} = \frac{5(88) - (15)(25)}{5(151) - (25)^2} = \frac{65}{130} = 0.5$$

∴ The equation is

$$X - 3 = 0.5\,(Y - 5)$$

or $X = 0.5\,Y + 3 - 2.5$ or $\mathbf{X = 0.5Y + 0.5.}$

For estimating the value of X, we shall use the regression equation of X on Y.

The regression equation of X on Y is $X = 0.5Y + 0.5$.

∴ When Y = 6, we have

$$X = 0.5 \times 6 + 0.5 = \mathbf{3.5.}$$

Example 9. *Find the equations of the line of regression of y on x and x on y for the data :*

x	*5*	*2*	*1*	*4*	*3*
y	*5*	*8*	*4*	*2*	*10*

Sol. **Regression Equations**

S. No.	x	y	xy	x^2	y^2
1	5	5	25	25	25
2	2	8	16	4	64
3	1	4	4	1	16
4	4	2	8	16	4
5	3	10	30	9	100
$n = 5$	$\Sigma x = 15$	$\Sigma y = 29$	$\Sigma xy = 83$	$\Sigma x^2 = 55$	$\Sigma y^2 = 209$

$$\bar{x} = \frac{\Sigma x}{n} = \frac{15}{5} = 3, \quad \bar{y} = \frac{\Sigma y}{n} = \frac{29}{5} = 5.8$$

The regression equation of y on x is $y - \bar{y} = b_{yx}\,(x - \bar{x})$.

$$b_{yx} = \frac{n\Sigma xy - (\Sigma x)(\Sigma y)}{n\Sigma x^2 - (\Sigma x)^2} = \frac{5(83) - (15)(29)}{5(55) - (15)^2} = \frac{-20}{50} = -0.4$$

∴ The equation is

$$y - 5.8 = -0.4\,(x - 3)$$

or $y = -0.4x + (0.4)3 + 5.8$

or $\mathbf{y = -0.4x + 7.}$

The regression equation of x on y is $x - \bar{x} = b_{xy}\,(y - \bar{y})$.

$$b_{xy} = \frac{n\Sigma xy - (\Sigma x)(\Sigma y)}{n\Sigma y^2 - (\Sigma y)^2} = \frac{5(83) - (15)(29)}{5(209) - (29)^2} = \frac{-20}{204} = -0.098$$

∴ The equation is

$$x - 3 = -0.098\,(y - 5.8)$$

or $x = 0.098y + (0.098)(5.8) + 3$

or $\mathbf{x = -0.098y + 3.5684.}$

Example 10. *You are given below the following information about advertisement and sales :*

	Advt. Expenditure (x) (in crore rupees)	Sales (y) (in crore rupees)
Mean	20	120
S.D.	5	25

Coefficient of correlation = 0.8.

(i) Calculate the regression equations.

(ii) Find the likely sales when advertisement expenditure is Rs. 25 crores.

(iii) What should be advertisement budget if the company wants to attain sales target of Rs. 150 crores ?

Sol. We have

$$\bar{x} = 20, \bar{y} = 120, \sigma_x = 5, \sigma_y = 25, r = 0.8$$

(*i*) The regression equation of y on x is $y - \bar{y} = b_{yx}(x - \bar{x})$.

$$\Rightarrow \quad y - \bar{y} = r\frac{\sigma_y}{\sigma_x}(x - \bar{x}) \quad \Rightarrow \quad y - 120 = (0.8)\frac{25}{5}(x - 20)$$

$$\Rightarrow \quad y - 120 = 4(x - 20) \quad \Rightarrow \quad \mathbf{y = 4x + 40.}$$

The regression equation of x on y is $x - \bar{x} = b_{xy}(y - \bar{y})$.

$$\Rightarrow \quad x - \bar{x} = r\frac{\sigma_x}{\sigma_y}(y - \bar{y}) \quad \Rightarrow \quad x - 20 = (0.8)\frac{5}{25}(y - 120)$$

$$\Rightarrow \quad x - 20 = 0.16(y - 120) \quad \Rightarrow \quad \mathbf{x = 0.16y + 0.8.}$$

(*ii*) We are to estimate the value of y for a given value of x.

∴ We use regression equation of y on x which is $y = 4x + 40$.

∴ When $x = 25$, the estimated value of $y = 4(25) + 40 = 140$

∴ Estimated sales = **Rs. 140 crores.**

(*iii*) We are to estimate the value of x for a given value of y.

∴ We use regression equation of x on y which is $x = 0.16y + 0.8$

∴ When $y = 150$, the estimated value of $x = (0.16)(150) + 0.8 = 24.8$

∴ Estimated advt. expenditure = **Rs. 24.8 crores.**

Example 11. *The coefficient of correlation between ages of husbands and wives in a community was found to be + 0.8, the average of husband's age is 25 years and that of wive's age was 22 years. Their standard deviations were 4 years and 5 years respectively. Find with the help of regression equations :*

(i) The expected age of husband when wife's age is 12 years.

(ii) The expected age of wife when husband's age is 20 years. (KU 2000)

Sol. Let x and y denote the variables 'age of husband' and 'age of wife' respectively.

∴ We have

$$r = 0.8, \quad \bar{x} = 25 \text{ years}, \bar{y} = 22 \text{ years}, \sigma_x = 4 \text{ years and } \sigma_y = 5 \text{ years.}$$

(*i*) We are to find the expected age of husband (x) for a given age of wife (y).

∴ We use regression equation of x on y which is given by

$$x - \bar{x} = b_{xy}(y - \bar{y}).$$

$\Rightarrow \quad x - \bar{x} = r \dfrac{\sigma_x}{\sigma_y}(y - \bar{y}) \quad \Rightarrow \quad x - 25 = (0.8)\dfrac{4}{5}(y - 22)$

$\Rightarrow \quad x - 25 = 0.64(y - 22) \quad \Rightarrow \quad x = 0.64y + 25 - (0.64)\,22$

$\Rightarrow \quad x = 0.64y + 10.92.$

When $y = 12$ years, the expected value of

$$x = 0.64\,(12) + 10.92 = \mathbf{18.6 \text{ years.}}$$

(*ii*) We are to find the expected age of wife (y) for a given age of husband (x).

$\therefore$ We use regression equation of y on x which is given by

$$y - \bar{y} = b_{yx}(x - \bar{x}).$$

$\Rightarrow \quad y - \bar{y} = r \dfrac{\sigma_y}{\sigma_x}(x - \bar{x}) \quad \Rightarrow \quad y - 22 = (0.8)\dfrac{5}{4}(x - 25)$

$\Rightarrow \quad y - 22 = x - 25 \quad \Rightarrow \quad y = x - 3.$

When $x = 20$ years, the expected value of $y = 20 - 3 =$ **17 years.**

Example 12. *Given :*

	x-series	*y-series*
Mean	5	4
S.D.	1.224	1.414

Sum of products of deviations from means of x and y series = 6

Number of items = 8.

(*i*) *Obtain the regression equations*

(*ii*) *Estimate the value of x when y = 5.* (KU 1997 C)

Sol. (*i*) We have $\bar{x} = 5$, $\bar{y} = 4$, $\sigma_x = 1.224$, $\sigma_y = 1.414$, $\Sigma(x - \bar{x})(y - \bar{y}) = 6$ and $n = 8$.

Now
$$r = \frac{\Sigma(x - \bar{x})(y - \bar{y})}{\sqrt{\Sigma(x - \bar{x})^2}\sqrt{\Sigma(y - \bar{y})^2}} = \frac{6}{n\sqrt{\dfrac{\Sigma(x - \bar{x})^2}{n}}\sqrt{\dfrac{\Sigma(y - \bar{y})^2}{n}}}$$

$$= \frac{6}{8\sigma_x\sigma_y} = \frac{3}{4(1.224)(1.414)} = 0.433.$$

Regression equation of y on x is

$$y - \bar{y} = b_{yx}(x - \bar{x}).$$

$\Rightarrow \quad y - \bar{y} = r \dfrac{\sigma_y}{\sigma_x}(x - \bar{x}) \quad \Rightarrow \quad y - 4 = 0.433 \times \dfrac{1.414}{1.224}(x - 5)$

$\Rightarrow \quad y - 4 = 0.5(x - 5) \quad \Rightarrow \quad y = 0.5x + 4 - 2.5$

$\Rightarrow \quad \mathbf{y = 0.5x + 1.5.}$

Regression equation of x on y is

$$x - \bar{x} = b_{xy}(y - \bar{y}).$$

$\Rightarrow \quad x - \bar{x} = r \dfrac{\sigma_x}{\sigma_y}(y - \bar{y}) \quad \Rightarrow \quad x - 5 = 0.433 \times \dfrac{1.224}{1.414}(y - 4)$

$\Rightarrow \quad x - 5 = 0.375\,(y - 4) \quad \Rightarrow \quad x = 0.375y + 5 - (0.375) \times 4$

$\Rightarrow \quad \mathbf{x = 0.375y + 3.5.}$

(*ii*) When $y = 5$, the estimated value of $x = (0.375)\,5 + 3.5 = \mathbf{5.375.}$

(By using regression equation of x on y)

Example 13. *You are given the following data :*

$\Sigma x = 300$, $\bar{x} = 50$, $\Sigma y = 240$, variance of $x = 2.56$, variance of $y = 1.96$, coefficient of correlation between x and y = + 0.6.

Find :

(i) Two regression coefficients

(ii) Two regression equations. (KU 2001 C)

Sol. We have

$$\Sigma x = 300, \quad \bar{x} = 50, \Sigma y = 240, \sigma_x^2 = 2.56 \quad \sigma_y^2 = 2.25, r = +0.6.$$

$$\bar{x} = \frac{\Sigma x}{n} \Rightarrow 50 = \frac{300}{n} \Rightarrow n = \frac{300}{50} = 6$$

$$\sigma_x^2 = 2.56 \quad \Rightarrow \quad \sigma_x = +\sqrt{2.56} = 1.6$$

$$\sigma_y^2 = 1.96 \quad \Rightarrow \quad \sigma_y = +\sqrt{1.16} = 1.4.$$

(*i*) $$b_{yx} = r\frac{\sigma_y}{\sigma_x} = 0.6 \times \frac{1.4}{1.6} = 0.525$$

and $$b_{xy} = r\frac{\sigma_x}{\sigma_y} = 0.6 \times \frac{1.6}{1.4} = 0.686.$$

(*ii*) Regression equation of y on x is $y - \bar{y} = b_{yx}(x - \bar{x})$.

$\Rightarrow \quad y - 40 = 0.525\,(x - 50) \qquad \left(\bar{y} = \dfrac{\Sigma y}{n} = \dfrac{240}{6} = 40\right)$

$\Rightarrow \quad y = 0.525x + 40 - (0.525)\,50$

$\Rightarrow \quad \mathbf{y = 0.525x + 13.75.}$

Regression equation of x on y is $x - \bar{x} = b_{xy}(y - \bar{y})$.

$\Rightarrow \quad x - 50 = 0.686\,(y - 40)$

$\Rightarrow \quad x = 0.686y + 50 - (0.686)(40)$

$\Rightarrow \quad \mathbf{x = 0.686y + 22.56.}$

Example 14. *From the following data, find the regression equations :*

x	*6*	*2*	*10*	*4*	*8*
y	*9*	*11*	*5*	*8*	*7*

Sol. **Estimation of Regression Equations**

S. No.	x	y	xy	x^2	y^2
1	6	9	54	36	81
2	2	11	22	4	121
3	10	5	50	100	25
4	4	8	32	16	64
5	8	7	56	64	49
$n = 5$	$\Sigma x = 15$	$\Sigma y = 40$	$\Sigma xy = 214$	$\Sigma x^2 = 220$	$\Sigma y^2 = 340$

$$\bar{x} = \frac{\Sigma x}{n} = \frac{30}{5} = 6, \qquad \bar{y} = \frac{\Sigma y}{n} = \frac{40}{5} = 8.$$

The regression equation of y on x is $y - \bar{y} = b_{yx}(x - \bar{x})$.

$$b_{yx} = \frac{n\Sigma xy - (\Sigma x)(\Sigma y)}{n\Sigma x^2 - (\Sigma x)^2} = \frac{5(214) - (30)(40)}{5(220) - (30)^2} = \frac{-130}{200} = -0.65.$$

∴ The equation is

$$y - 8 = -0.65(x - 6) \quad \text{or} \quad y = -0.65x + (0.65)6 + 8$$

or **y = 11.9 – 0.65x.**

The regression equation of x on y is $x - \bar{x} = b_{xy}(y - \bar{y})$.

$$b_{xy} = \frac{n\Sigma xy - (\Sigma x)(\Sigma y)}{n\Sigma y^2 - (\Sigma y)^2} = \frac{5(214) - (30)(40)}{5(340) - (40)^2} = \frac{-130}{100} = -1.3.$$

∴ The equation is

$$x - 6 = -1.3(y - 8) \quad \text{or} \quad x = -1.3y + (1.3)8 + 6$$

or **x = 16.4 – 1.3y.**

Example 15. *For the following data, find the regression line of x on y. Also show the regression line on a graph paper :*

x	*1*	*2*	*3*	*4*	*5*	*6*	*7*
y	*9*	*8*	*10*	*12*	*11*	*13*	*14*

Sol. **Regression line of x on y**

S. No.	x	y	xy	y^2
1	1	9	9	81
2	2	8	16	64
3	3	10	30	100
4	4	12	48	144
5	5	11	55	121
6	6	13	78	169
7	7	14	98	196
$n = 7$	$\Sigma x = 28$	$\Sigma y = 77$	$\Sigma xy = 83$	$\Sigma y^2 = 875$

The regression line of x on y is $x - \bar{x} = b_{xy}(y - \bar{y})$.

$$\bar{x} = \frac{\Sigma x}{n} = \frac{28}{7} = 4, \quad \bar{y} = \frac{\Sigma y}{n} = \frac{77}{7} = 11.$$

$$b_{xy} = \frac{n\Sigma xy - (\Sigma x)(\Sigma y)}{n\Sigma y^2 - (\Sigma y)^2} = \frac{7(334) - (28)(77)}{7(875) - (77)^2} = \frac{182}{196} = 0.929.$$

$\therefore$ The equation of regression line of x on y is

$$x - 4 = 0.929\,(y - 11) \quad \text{or} \quad x = 0.929y + 4 - 11\,(0.929)$$

or $$\mathbf{x = 0.929y - 6.219.}$$

To draw this line on the graph paper, we take two points on it.

$$y = 8 \quad \Rightarrow \quad x = 0.929(8) - 6.219 = 1.213$$

$$y = 12 \quad \Rightarrow \quad x = 0.929(12) - 6.219 = 4.929.$$

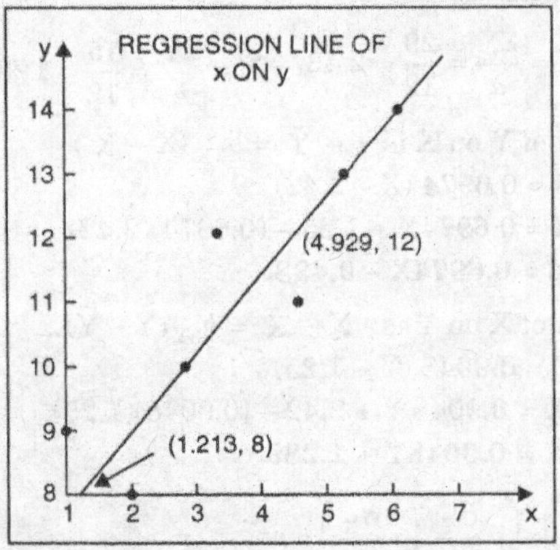

$\therefore$ The points (1.213, 8) and (4.929, 12) are on the regression line of x on y. The line joining these points is the required regression line of x on y.

Example 16. *In order to find the correlation coefficient between two variables X and Y from 12 pairs of observations, the following calculation were made :*

$$\Sigma X = 30,\ \Sigma X^2 = 670,\ \Sigma Y = 5,\ \Sigma Y^2 = 285,\ \Sigma XY = 344.$$

On subsequent verification, it was discovered that the pair (X = 11, Y = 4) was copied wrongly, the correct values being X = 10 and Y = 14. After making necessary correction, find the :

(i) regression coefficients

(ii) regression equations and

(iii) correlation coefficient. (MDU 2002)

Sol. We have $\Sigma X = 30,\ \Sigma X^2 = 670,\ \Sigma Y = 5,\ \Sigma Y^2 = 285,\ \Sigma XY = 344.$

Incorrect pair = (X = 11, Y = 4)

Correct pair = (X = 10, Y = 14)

Corrected sums

$$\Sigma X = 30 - 11 + 10 = 29$$
$$\Sigma Y = 5 - 4 + 14 = 15$$
$$\Sigma X^2 = 670 - (11)^2 + (10)^2 = 649$$
$$\Sigma Y^2 = 285 - (4)^2 + (14)^2 = 465$$
$$\Sigma XY = 344 - (11 \times 4) + (10 \times 14) = 440.$$

(*i*) **Regression coefficients**

$$b_{YX} = \frac{n\Sigma XY - (\Sigma X)(\Sigma Y)}{n\Sigma X^2 - (\Sigma X)^2} = \frac{12(440) - (29)(15)}{12(649) - (29)^2} = \frac{4845}{6947} = \mathbf{0.6974}$$

$$b_{XY} = \frac{n\Sigma XY - (\Sigma X)(\Sigma Y)}{n\Sigma Y^2 - (\Sigma Y)^2} = \frac{12(440) - (29)(15)}{12(465) - (15)^2} = \frac{4845}{5355} = \mathbf{0.9048.}$$

(*ii*) **Regression equations**

$$\overline{X} = \frac{\Sigma X}{n} = \frac{29}{12} = 2.42, \quad \overline{Y} = \frac{\Sigma Y}{n} = \frac{15}{12} = 1.25$$

Regression equation of Y on X is $Y - \overline{Y} = b_{YX}(X - \overline{X})$.

$\Rightarrow$ $Y - 1.25 = 0.6974 (X - 2.42)$

$\Rightarrow$ $Y = 0.6974X + 1.25 - (0.6974)(2.42)$

$\Rightarrow$ $\mathbf{Y = 0.6974X - 0.438.}$

Regression equation of X on Y is $X - \overline{X} = b_{XY}(Y - \overline{Y})$.

$\Rightarrow$ $X - 2.42 = 0.9048 (Y - 1.25)$

$\Rightarrow$ $X = 0.9048\,Y + 2.42 - (0.9048)(1.25)$

$\Rightarrow$ $\mathbf{X = 0.9048Y + 1.289.}$

(*iii*) $$b_{YX} \cdot b_{XY} = \left(r\frac{\sigma_Y}{\sigma_X}\right)\left(r\frac{\sigma_X}{\sigma_Y}\right) = r^2$$

$\therefore$ $$r = \pm\sqrt{b_{YX} \cdot b_{XY}}$$

$\therefore$ $$r = \pm\sqrt{0.6974 \times 0.9048} = \pm\, 0.7944$$

$$b_{YX} > 0 \Rightarrow r > 0. \qquad \left(\because \frac{\sigma_y}{\sigma_x} > 0\right)$$

$\therefore$ $\mathbf{r = +\,0.7944.}$

Example 17. *Show that regression coefficients are independent of the change of origin but not of scale.* (MDU 1999)

Sol. Let x and y be any two variables. Let A, B, h and k be any constant.

Let $$u = \frac{x - A}{h} \quad \text{and} \quad v = \frac{y - B}{k}.$$

$\therefore$ u and v are variables obtained by changing origin and scale of given variables x and y respectively.

$\therefore \qquad x = A + hu \quad \text{and} \quad y = B + kv$

Summing both sides and dividing by the number of values, we get

$$\bar{x} = A + h\bar{u} \quad \text{and} \quad \bar{y} = B + k\bar{v}.$$

$$\therefore \qquad x - \bar{x} = (A + hu) - (A + h\bar{u}) = h(u - \bar{u})$$

and $$y - \bar{y} = (B + kv) - (B + k\bar{v}) = k(v - \bar{v}).$$

Now $$b_{yx} = r\frac{\sigma_y}{\sigma_x} = \frac{\Sigma(x-\bar{x})(y-\bar{y})}{\sqrt{\Sigma(x-\bar{x})^2}\sqrt{\Sigma(y-\bar{y})^2}} \cdot \frac{\sqrt{\frac{\Sigma(y-\bar{y})^2}{n}}}{\sqrt{\frac{\Sigma(x-\bar{x})^2}{n}}}$$

$$= \frac{\Sigma(x-\bar{x})(y-\bar{y})}{\Sigma(x-\bar{x})^2} = \frac{\Sigma[h(u-\bar{u}) \times k(v-\bar{v})]}{\Sigma[h(u-\bar{u})]^2}$$

$$= \frac{hk}{h^2} \cdot \frac{\Sigma(u-\bar{u})(v-\bar{v})}{\Sigma(u-\bar{u})^2} = \frac{k}{h} \cdot b_{vu}.$$

Also $$b_{xy} = r\frac{\sigma_x}{\sigma_y} = \frac{\Sigma(x-\bar{x})(y-\bar{y})}{\sqrt{\Sigma(x-\bar{x})^2}\sqrt{\Sigma(y-\bar{y})^2}} \cdot \frac{\sqrt{\frac{\Sigma(x-\bar{x})^2}{n}}}{\sqrt{\frac{\Sigma(y-\bar{y})^2}{n}}}$$

$$= \frac{\Sigma(x-\bar{x})(y-\bar{y})}{\Sigma(y-\bar{y})^2} = \frac{\Sigma[h(u-\bar{u}) \times k(v-\bar{v})]}{\Sigma[k(v-\bar{v})]^2}$$

$$= \frac{hk}{k^2} \cdot \frac{\Sigma(u-\bar{u})(v-\bar{v})}{\Sigma(v-\bar{v})^2} = \frac{h}{k} \cdot b_{uv}.$$

$\therefore$ Regression coefficients are independent of change of origin but not of scale.

EXERCISE 1

1. Find b_{yx} from the following data :
   $\Sigma x = 30, \Sigma y = 42, \Sigma xy = 199, \Sigma x^2 = 184, \Sigma y^2 = 318, n = 6.$
2. Find b_{yx} from the following data :
   $\Sigma x = 24, \Sigma xy = 306, \Sigma x^2 = 164, \Sigma y = 44, \Sigma y^2 = 574, n = 4.$
3. Find the regression coefficient b_{xy} between x and y for the following data :
   $\Sigma x = 55, \Sigma y = 88, \Sigma x^2 = 385, \Sigma y^2 = 1114, \Sigma xy = 586, n = 10.$
4. Find the regression coefficient b_{xy} between x and y for the following data :
   $\Sigma x = 24, \Sigma y = 44, \Sigma xy = 306, \Sigma x^2 = 164, \Sigma y^2 = 574, n = 4.$
5. Find the regression line of y on x, where :
   $\Sigma x = 55, \Sigma y = 88, \Sigma x^2 = 385, \Sigma y^2 = 1114, \Sigma xy = 586, n = 10.$
6. x and y are correlated variables. Eight observations of (x, y) have the following results :
   $\Sigma x = 55, \Sigma y = 55, \Sigma xy = 350, \Sigma x^2 = 385.$

   Predict the value of y when the value of x is 8.

7. For observations of pairs (x, y) of variables x and y, the following results are obtained :

$$\Sigma x = 125, \Sigma y = 100, \Sigma x^2 = 1650, \Sigma y^2 = 1500, \Sigma xy = 50 \text{ and } n = 25.$$

Find the equation of the line of regression of x and y. Estimate the value of x if $y = 5$.

8. Find out the regression coefficients from the following data. Also calculate the value of coefficient of correlation.

$$\Sigma X = 50, \overline{X} = 5, \Sigma Y = 60, \overline{Y} = 6, \Sigma XY = 350, \text{Variance of X} = 4, \text{Variance of Y} = 9.$$

(**Hint.** Use : Var. $X = \frac{\Sigma X}{n} - (\overline{X})^2$ to find ΣX^2). *(MDU 2003)*

9. Find the value of X when Y = 60, and the value of Y when X = 50 from the following information :

	Variable X	*Variable Y*
Mean	24	140
S.D.	16	48

Also, $r = 0.6$. *(KU 2003)*

10. The following results were worked out from scores in Statistics and Mathematics in a certain examination :

	Scores in Statistics (x)	*Scores in Mathematics (y)*
A.M.	39.5	47.5
S.D.	10.8	17.8

Karl Pearson's coefficient of correlation is 0.42. Find both regression lines. Estimate the value of y when $x = 50$ and x when $y = 30$.

11. From the following data find the yield of wheat in kg per unit area when the rain fall is 9 inches :

	Mean	*S.D.*
Yield of wheat per unit area (in kg)	10	8
Annual rainfall (in inches)	8	2

Coefficient of correlation = 0.5. *(KU 1995 C)*

12. You are given below the following information about advertisement expenditure and sales :

	Advt. Expenditure (x) (in crore rupees)	*Sales (y) (in crore rupees)*
Mean	10	90
S.D.	3	12

Coefficient of correlation = + 0.8.

(*i*) Calculate two regression equations.

(*ii*) Find the likely sales when advertisement expenditure is Rs. 30 crores

(*iii*) What should be the advertisement budget if the company wants to attain sales target of Rs. 150 crores ?

13. Given the following data, find what will be : (*a*) the height of a policeman whose weight is 200 pounds, (*b*) the weight of a policeman who is 5 ft tall.
Average height = 68 inches, average weight = 150 pounds, coefficient of correlation between height and weight = 0.6, S.D. of height = 2.5 inches, S.D. of weight = 20 pounds. (*KU 1998 C*)

14. Find the equations of regression lines for the following data :

x	1	2	3	4	5
y	7	8	10	12	13

15. Find the equations of regression lines for the following pairs (x, y) for variables x and y :
(1, 2), (2, 5), (3, 3), (4, 8), (5, 7).

16. For the following data, determine the regression lines :

x	6	2	10	4	8
y	9	11	5	8	7

From these regression lines, estimate the value of :
(*i*) y when $x = 5$ and (*ii*) x when $y = 10$.

17. Find the regression lines for the following pairs (x, y) for variables x and y :
(1, 6), (5, 1), (3, 0), (2, 0), (1, 1), (1, 2), (7, 1), (3, 5).

18. By using the following data regarding pairs (x, y) for variables x and y, find the most likely value of y, when $x = 6.2$:
(1, 9), (2, 8), (3, 10), (4, 12), (5, 11), (6, 13), (7, 14), (8, 16), (9, 15).

19. Find the equations of two regression lines from the following data :

x	1	2	3	4	5
y	7	6	5	4	3

Hence find the estimated value of y for $x = 3.5$ from the appropriate line of regression.

20. The data of sales and promotion expenditure on a product for 10 years are given below :

Sales (Rs. lakh)	8	10	9	12	10	11	12	13	14	15
Promotion expenditure (Rs. thousand)	2	2	3	4	5	5	5	6	7	8

Use two-variable regression model to estimate the promotion expenditure for a given sale of Rs. 20 lakh. Forecast the sales when the company wants to spends Rs. 10 thousand on promotion.

21. A computer while calculating the correlation coefficient between two variables x and y obtained the following constants :

$$n = 25, \Sigma x = 127, \Sigma y = 100, \Sigma x^2 = 650, \Sigma y^2 = 450, \Sigma xy = 516.$$

It was however, later discovered at the time of checking that it copied down two pairs of observations as :

x	y
8	12
6	8

while the correct values were :

x	y
8	10
6	10

. After making the necessary corrections, find the :

(*i*) regression coefficients (*ii*) regression equations and
(*iii*) correlation coefficient.

22. A computer while calculating the correlation coefficient between two variables x and y obtained the following constants :

$$n = 25, \Sigma x = 125, \Sigma y = 100, \Sigma x^2 = 650, \Sigma y^2 = 460, \Sigma xy = 508$$

It was however, later discovered at the time of checking that it had copied down two pairs of observations as :

x	y
6	14
8	6

while the correct values were :

x	y
8	12
6	8

. After making the necessary corrections, find the :
(*i*) regression coefficients (*ii*) regression equations and
(*iii*) correlation coefficient.

Answers

1. – 0.3235 **2.** 2.1 **3.** 0.3004 **4.** 0.4667
5. $y = 1.2364x + 1.9998$ **6.** 2.2727 **7.** $x = -0.4091y + 6.6364$, 4.5909
8. $b_{yx} = 5/4$, $b_{xy} = 5/9$, $r = 5/6$ **9.** 8, 186.8
10. $y = 0.6922x + 20.1581$, $x = 0.2548y + 27.397$, 54.77, 35.04 **11.** 12 kg
12. (*i*) $x = 0.2y - 8$, $y = 3.2x + 58$, (*ii*) Rs. 154 crores (*iii*) Rs. 22 crores
13. (*a*) 71.75 inches (*b*) 111.6 pounds **14.** $y = 1.6x + 5.2$, $x = 0.615y - 3.15$
15. Regression line of y on x : $y = 1.1 + 1.3x$;
Regression line of x on y : $x = 0.5 + 0.5y$
16. $y = 11.9 - 0.65x$, $x = 16.4 - 1.3y$ (*i*) 8.65 (*ii*) 3.4
17. $y = 2.8745 - 0.3042x$, $x = 3.4306 - 0.2778y$ **18.** 13.14
19. Regression line of y on x : $y = -x + 8$;
Regression line of x on y : $x = -y + 8$; $y = 4.5$ when $x = 3.5$
20. $y = 0.815x - 4.591$, when $x = 20$, $y = 11.709$; $x = 1.003y + 6.686$, when $y = 10$, $x = 16.716$.
21. (*i*) $b_{yx} = 0.826$, $b_{xy} = 0.095$
(*ii*) Regression equation of y on x : $y = 0.826x - 1.96$
Regression equation of x on y : $x = 0.095y + 4.7$
(*iii*) $r = 0.28$
22. (*i*) $b_{yx} = 0.8$, $b_{xy} = 0.555$
(*ii*) Regression equations of y on x : $y = 0.8x$,
Regression equations of x on y : $x = 0.555y + 2.78$,
(*iii*) $r = 0.667$.

8. STEP DEVIATION METHOD

When the values of x and y are numerically high, the step deviation method is used.

Deviations of values of variables x and y are calculated from some chosen arbitrary numbers, called A and B. Let h be a positive common factor of all deviations $(x - A)$ of items in the x-series. Similarly let k be a positive factor of all deviations $(y - B)$ of items in the y-series. The step deviations are :

$$u = \frac{x - A}{h}, \quad v = \frac{x - B}{k}.$$

In practical problems, if we do not bother to divide the deviations by common factors, then these deviations would be thought of as step deviations of items of given series with '1' as the common factor for both series.

The equation of regression line of y on x in terms of step deviations is

$$y - \bar{y} = b_{yx}(x - \bar{x}),$$

where $$\bar{x} = A + \left(\frac{\Sigma u}{n}\right)h, \quad \bar{y} = B + \left(\frac{\Sigma v}{n}\right)k$$

and $$b_{yx} = b_{vu} \cdot \frac{k}{h} = \frac{n\Sigma uv - (\Sigma u)(\Sigma v)}{n\Sigma u^2 - (\Sigma u)^2} \cdot \frac{k}{h}.$$

The equation of regression line of x on y in terms of step deviations is

$$x - \bar{x} = b_{xy}(y - \bar{y}),$$

where $$\bar{x} = A + \left(\frac{\Sigma u}{n}\right)h, \quad \bar{y} = B + \left(\frac{\Sigma v}{n}\right)k$$

and $$b_{xy} = b_{uv} \cdot \frac{h}{k} = \frac{n\Sigma uv - (\Sigma u)(\Sigma v)}{n\Sigma v^2 - (\Sigma v)^2} \cdot \frac{h}{k}.$$

Remark. In particular if $u = x - A$ and $v = y - B$ *i.e.*, when $h = 1$, $k = 1$, we have

$$\bar{x} = A + \frac{\Sigma u}{n}, \quad \bar{y} = B + \frac{\Sigma v}{n},$$

$$b_{yx} = \frac{n\Sigma uv - (\Sigma u)(\Sigma v)}{n\Sigma u^2 - (\Sigma u)^2} \quad \text{and} \quad b_{xy} = \frac{n\Sigma uv - (\Sigma u)(\Sigma v)}{n\Sigma v^2 - (\Sigma v)^2}.$$

Example 1. *For a bivariate data, you are given the following information :*

$$\Sigma(x - 44) = -5, \ \Sigma(y - 26) = -6, \ \Sigma(x - 44)^2 = 255,$$
$$\Sigma(y - 26)^2 = 704, \ \Sigma(x - 44)(y - 26) = -306.$$

Number of pairs of observations = 12.

Find the regression equations.

Sol. Let $u = x - 44$ and $v = y - 26$.

$\therefore$ $\Sigma u = -5, \Sigma v = -6, \Sigma u^2 = 255, \Sigma v^2 = 704, \Sigma uv = -306, n = 12.$

$$\bar{x} = 44 + \frac{\Sigma u}{n} = 44 + \frac{(-5)}{12} = 43.58$$

$$\bar{y} = 26 + \frac{\Sigma v}{n} = 26 + \frac{(-6)}{12} = 25.5$$

$$b_{yx} = \frac{n\Sigma uv - (\Sigma u)(\Sigma v)}{n\Sigma u^2 - (\Sigma u)^2} = \frac{12(-306) - (-5)(-6)}{12(255) - (-5)^2} = \frac{-3702}{3035} = -1.22$$

$$b_{xy} = \frac{n\Sigma uv - (\Sigma u)(\Sigma v)}{n\Sigma v^2 - (\Sigma v)^2} = \frac{12(-306) - (-5)(-6)}{12(704) - (-6)^2} = \frac{-3702}{8412} = -0.44.$$

Regression equation of y on x is $y - \bar{y} = b_{yx}(x - \bar{x})$.

$\Rightarrow \quad y - 25.5 = -1.22(x - 43.58)$

$\Rightarrow \quad y = -1.22x + 25.5 + (1.22)(43.58)$

$\Rightarrow \quad \mathbf{y = -1.22x + 78.67.}$

Regression equation of x on y is $x - \bar{x} = b_{xy}(y - \bar{y})$.

$\Rightarrow \quad x - 43.58 = -0.44(y - 25.5)$

$\Rightarrow \quad x = -0.44y + 43.58 + (0.44)(25.5)$

$\Rightarrow \quad \mathbf{x = -0.44y + 54.8.}$

Example 2. *An investigation into the demand for television sets in 7 towns has resulted in the following data :*

Population x (in thousand)	*11*	*14*	*14*	*17*	*17*	*21*	*25*
No. of T.V. sets demanded, y	*15*	*27*	*27*	*30*	*34*	*38*	*46*

Calculate the regression equation of y on x and estimate the demand for T.V. sets for a town with a population of 30 thousands. (KU 2000 C)

Sol. Computation of Regression Equation of y on x

S. No.	*x*	*y*	$u = x - A$ $A = 17$	$v = y - B$ $B = 27$	*uv*	u^2
1	11	15	− 6	− 12	72	36
2	14	27	− 3	0	0	9
3	14	27	− 3	0	0	9
4	17	30	0	3	0	0
5	17	34	0	7	0	0
6	21	38	4	11	44	16
7	25	46	8	19	152	64
$n = 7$			$\Sigma u = 0$	$\Sigma v = 28$	$\Sigma uv = 268$	$\Sigma u^2 = 134$

Regression equation of y on x is $y - \bar{y} = b_{yx}(x - \bar{x})$.

We have $\bar{x} = A + \dfrac{\Sigma u}{n} = 17 + \dfrac{0}{7} = 17$

$$\bar{y} = B + \frac{\Sigma v}{n} = 27 + \frac{28}{7} = 31$$

$$b_{yx} = \frac{n\Sigma uv - (\Sigma u)(\Sigma v)}{n\Sigma u^2 - (\Sigma u)^2} = \frac{7(268) - (0)(28)}{7(134) - (0)^2} = \frac{268}{134} = 2$$

$\therefore$ **The required equation is**

$$y - 31 = 2(x - 17) \quad \text{or} \quad \mathbf{y = 2x - 3.}$$

When population is 30 thousand *i.e.*, $x = 30$, **the estimated value of**

$$y = 2(30) - 3 = 57.$$

$\therefore$ **The estimated demand for T.V. sets is 57.**

Example 3. *Obtain the regression equations of 'x on y' and 'y on x' taking origin as 2 and 200 for x and y respectively :*

x	*1*	*2*	*3*	*4*	*5*
y	*166*	*184*	*142*	*180*	*338*

Sol. **Computation of Regression Equations**

S. No.	x	y	$u = x - A$ $A = 2$	$v = y - B$ $B = 200$	uv	u^2	v^2
1	1	166	– 1	– 34	34	1	1156
2	2	184	0	– 16	0	0	256
3	3	142	1	– 58	– 58	1	3364
4	4	180	2	– 20	– 40	4	400
5	5	338	3	138	414	9	19044
$n = 5$			$\Sigma u = 5$	$\Sigma v = 10$	$\Sigma uv = 350$	$\Sigma u^2 = 15$	$\Sigma v^2 = 24220$

Regression equation of 'x on y'

The regression equation of x on y is $x - \bar{x} = b_{xy}(y - \bar{y})$.

We have $\bar{x} = A + \dfrac{\Sigma u}{n} = 2 + \dfrac{5}{5} = 3$

$$\bar{y} = B + \frac{\Sigma v}{n} = 200 + \frac{10}{5} = 202$$

$$b_{xy} = \frac{n\Sigma uv - (\Sigma u)(\Sigma v)}{n\Sigma v^2 - (\Sigma v)^2} = \frac{5(350) - (5)(10)}{5(24220) - (10)^2} = \frac{1700}{121000} = 0.014.$$

∴ The required equation is $x - 3 = 0.014\ (y - 202)$

or $x = 0.014y + 3 - (0.014)(202)$

or $\mathbf{x = 0.014y + 0.172.}$

Regression equation of 'y on x'

The regression equation of y on x is $y - \bar{y} = b_{yx}(x - \bar{x})$.

$$\bar{x} = 3,\ \bar{y} = 202$$

$$b_{yx} = \frac{n\Sigma uv - (\Sigma u)(\Sigma v)}{n\Sigma u^2 - (\Sigma u)^2} = \frac{5(350) - (5)(10)}{5(15) - (5)^2} = \frac{1700}{50} = 34.$$

∴ The regression equation is $y - 202 = 34(x - 3)$

or $y = 34x + 202 - 34(3)$

or $\mathbf{y = 34x + 100.}$

Example 4. *Obtain the two regression equations from the following data :*

x	*25*	*28*	*35*	*32*	*31*	*36*	*29*	*38*	*34*	*32*
y	*43*	*46*	*49*	*41*	*36*	*32*	*31*	*30*	*33*	*39*

Also find the value of y when x is equal to 30. (KU 1997, 2005 C)

Sol. **Computation of Regression Equations**

S. No.	x	y	$u = x - A$ $A = 32$	$v = y - B$ $B = 38$	uv	u^2	v^2
1	25	43	− 7	5	− 35	49	25
2	28	46	− 4	8	− 32	16	64
3	35	49	3	11	33	9	121
4	32	41	0	3	0	0	9
5	31	36	− 1	− 2	2	1	4
6	36	32	4	− 6	− 24	16	36
7	29	31	− 3	− 7	21	9	49
8	38	30	6	− 8	− 48	36	64
9	34	33	2	− 5	− 10	4	25
10	32	39	0	1	0	0	1
$n = 10$			$\Sigma u = 0$	$\Sigma v = 0$	$\Sigma uv = -93$	$\Sigma u^2 = 140$	$\Sigma v^2 = 398$

Regression equation of 'y on x'

The regression equation of y on x is $y - \bar{y} = b_{yx}(x - \bar{x})$.

$$\bar{x} = A + \frac{\Sigma u}{n} = 32 + \frac{0}{10} = 32$$

$$\bar{y} = B + \frac{\Sigma v}{n} = 38 + \frac{0}{10} = 38$$

$$b_{yx} = \frac{n\Sigma uv - (\Sigma u)(\Sigma v)}{n\Sigma u^2 - (\Sigma u)^2} = \frac{10(-93) - (0)(0)}{10(140) - (0)^2} = -\frac{93}{140} = -0.6643.$$

∴ The required equation is $y - 38 = -0.6643(x - 32)$.

⇒ $y = -0.6643x + 38 + (0.6643)(32)$

⇒ $\mathbf{y = -0.6643x + 59.2576.}$

When $x = 30$, the estimated value of $y = (-0.6643)(30) + 59.2576 = \mathbf{39.3286.}$

Regression equation of 'x on y'

The regression equation of x on y is $x - \bar{x} = b_{xy}(y - \bar{y})$.

$$\bar{x} = 32, \ \bar{y} = 38$$

$$b_{xy} = \frac{n\Sigma uv - (\Sigma u)(\Sigma v)}{n\Sigma v^2 - (\Sigma v)^2} = \frac{10(-93) - (0)(0)}{10(398) - (0)^2} = -\frac{93}{398} = -0.2337.$$

∴ The required equation is $x - 32 = -0.2337(y - 38)$.

⇒ $x = -0.2337y + 32 + (0.2337)(38)$

⇒ $\mathbf{x = -0.2337y + 40.8806.}$

Example 5. *Find (i) r and (ii) regression equations for the following data :*

x	75	89	97	69	59	79	68	61
y	125	137	156	112	107	136	123	108

Sol. Computation of 'r' and Regression Equations

S. No.	x	y	$u = x - A$ $A = 100$	$v = y - B$ $B = 100$	uv	u^2	v^2
1	75	125	– 25	25	– 625	625	625
2	89	137	– 11	37	– 407	121	1369
3	97	156	– 3	56	– 168	9	3136
4	69	112	– 31	12	– 372	961	144
5	59	107	– 41	7	– 287	1681	49
6	79	136	– 21	36	– 756	441	1296
7	68	123	– 32	23	– 736	1024	529
8	61	108	– 39	8	– 312	1521	64
$n = 8$			$\Sigma u = -203$	$\Sigma v = 204$	$\Sigma uv = -3663$	$\Sigma u^2 = 6383$	$\Sigma v^2 = 7212$

(*i*)
$$r = \frac{n\Sigma uv - (\Sigma u)(\Sigma v)}{\sqrt{n\Sigma u^2 - (\Sigma u)^2}\sqrt{n\Sigma v^2 - (\Sigma v)^2}}$$

$$= \frac{8(-3663) - (-203)(204)}{\sqrt{8(6383) - (-203)^2}\sqrt{8(7212) - (204)^2}} = \frac{12108}{\sqrt{9855}\sqrt{16080}} = \mathbf{0.9619.}$$

(*ii*) **Regression equation of 'y on x'**

The regression equation of y on x is $y - \bar{y} = b_{yx}(x - \bar{x})$.

$$\bar{x} = A + \frac{\Sigma u}{n} = 100 + \frac{(-203)}{8} = 74.625$$

$$\bar{y} = B + \frac{\Sigma v}{n} = 100 + \frac{204}{8} = 125.5$$

$$b_{yx} = \frac{n\Sigma uv - (\Sigma u)(\Sigma v)}{n\Sigma u^2 - (\Sigma u)^2} = \frac{8(-3663) - (-203)(204)}{8(6383) - (-203)^2} = \frac{12108}{9855} = 1.2286$$

∴ The required equation is $y - 125.5 = 1.2286\ (x - 74.625)$

or $y = 1.2286x + 125.5 - (1.2286)(74.625)$

or $\mathbf{y = 1.2286x + 33.8157.}$

Regression equation of x on y

The regression equation of x on y is $x - \bar{x} = b_{xy}(y - \bar{y})$.

$$\bar{x} = 74.625,\ \bar{y} = 125.5$$

$$b_{xy} = \frac{n\Sigma uv - (\Sigma u)(\Sigma v)}{n\Sigma v^2 - (\Sigma v)^2} = \frac{8(-3663) - (-203)(204)}{8(7212) - (-204)^2} = \frac{12108}{16080} = 0.753$$

∴ The required equation is $x - 74.625 = 0.753\ (y - 125.5)$

or $x = 0.753y + 74.625 - (0.753)(125.5)$

or $\mathbf{x = 0.753y - 19.8765.}$

Example 6. *Following are the heights of fathers and sons in inches :*

Height of father	*65*	*66*	*67*	*68*	*69*	*71*	*73*	*67*
Height of son	*67*	*68*	*64*	*72*	*70*	*69*	*70*	*68*

Find the two lines of regression and estimate the height of the son when the height of the father is 67.5 inches. (KU 1998, 2006)

Sol. Let the variables 'height of father' and 'height of son' be denoted by x and y respectively.

Computation of Regression Equations

S. No.	x	y	$u = x - A$ $A = 68$	$v = y - B$ $B = 68$	uv	u^2	v^2
1	65	67	– 3	– 1	3	9	1
2	66	68	– 2	0	0	4	0
3	67	64	– 1	– 4	4	1	16
4	68	72	0	4	0	0	16
5	69	70	1	2	2	1	4
6	71	69	3	1	3	9	1
7	73	70	5	2	10	25	4
8	67	68	– 1	0	0	1	0
$n = 8$			$\Sigma u = 2$	$\Sigma v = 4$	$\Sigma uv = 22$	$\Sigma u^2 = 50$	$\Sigma v^2 = 42$

Regression equation of 'y on x'

The regression equation of y on x is $y - \bar{y} = b_{yx}(x - \bar{x})$.

$$\bar{x} = A + \frac{\Sigma u}{n} = 68 + \frac{2}{8} = 68.25 \text{ inches}$$

$$\bar{y} = B + \frac{\Sigma v}{n} = 68 + \frac{4}{8} = 68.5 \text{ inches}$$

$$b_{yx} = \frac{n\Sigma uv - (\Sigma u)(\Sigma v)}{n\Sigma u^2 - (\Sigma u)^2} = \frac{8(22) - (2)(4)}{8(50) - (2)^2} = \frac{168}{396} = 0.4242$$

∴ The required equation is

$$y - 68.5 = 0.4242\,(x - 68.25).$$

$$\Rightarrow \quad y = 0.4242x + 68.5 - (0.4242)(68.25)$$

$$\Rightarrow \quad \mathbf{y = 0.4242x + 39.4835.}$$

Regression equation of 'x on y'

The regression equation of x on y is $x - \bar{x} = b_{xy}(y - \bar{y})$.

$$\bar{x} = 68.25 \text{ inches}, \quad \bar{y} = 68.5 \text{ inches}$$

$$b_{xy} = \frac{n\Sigma uv - (\Sigma u)(\Sigma v)}{n\Sigma v^2 - (\Sigma v)^2} = \frac{8(22) - (2)(4)}{8(42) - (4)^2} = \frac{168}{320} = 0.525$$

∴ The required equation is

$$x - 68.25 = 0.525\,(y - 68.5).$$

$\Rightarrow$ $x = 0.525y + 68.25 - (0.525)(68.5)$

$\Rightarrow$ $\mathbf{x = 0.525y + 32.2875.}$

To find the estimated value of height of son (y) for a given value of height of father (x), we require regression equation of y on x *i.e.*,

$$y = 0.4242x + 39.4835.$$

$\therefore$ When $x = 67.5$ inches, the estimated value of

$$y = (0.4242)(67.5) + 39.4835 = \mathbf{68.117\ inches.}$$

Example 7. *A panel of judges A and B graded seven debtors and independently awarded the following marks :*

Debtors	*1*	*2*	*3*	*4*	*5*	*6*	*7*
Marks by A	*40*	*34*	*28*	*30*	*44*	*38*	*31*
Marks by B	*32*	*39*	*26*	*30*	*38*	*34*	*28*

The eighth debtor was awarded 36 marks by judge A while judge B was not present. If judge B was also present, how many marks would you expect him to award to the eighth debtor assuming that the same degree of relationship exists in their judgement.

Sol. Let the variables 'marks by A' and 'marks by B' be denoted by 'x' and 'y' respectively. We shall estimate the marks given by judge B to the eighth debtor by using the fact that he has been awarded 36 marks by judge A. In other words, we shall estimate the value of y, when $x = 36$. For this, we shall need the regression equation of y on x.

Computation of Regression Line of y on x

Debtor	x	y	$u = x - A$, $A = 35$	$v = y - B$, $B = 35$	uv	u^2
1	40	32	5	−3	−15	25
2	34	39	−1	4	−4	1
3	28	26	−7	−9	63	49
4	30	30	−5	−5	25	25
5	44	38	9	3	27	81
6	38	34	4	−1	−3	9
7	31	28	−4	−7	28	16
$n = 7$			$\Sigma u = 0$	$\Sigma v = -18$	$\Sigma uv = 121$	$\Sigma u^2 = 206$

The regression line of y on x is $y - \bar{y} = b_{yx}(x - \bar{x})$.

We have
$$\bar{x} = A + \frac{\Sigma u}{n} = 35 + \frac{0}{7} = 35$$

$$\bar{y} = B + \frac{\Sigma v}{n} = 35 + \frac{(-18)}{7} = 32.429$$

$$b_{yx} = \frac{n\Sigma uv - (\Sigma u)(\Sigma v)}{n\Sigma u^2 - (\Sigma u)^2} = \frac{7(121) - 0(-18)}{7(206) - (0)^2} = \frac{121}{206} = 0.5874$$

$\therefore$ The required equation is $y - 32.429 = 0.5874(x - 35)$

or $y = 0.5874x + 32.429 - (0.5874)35$

or $\mathbf{y = 0.5874x + 11.87.}$

∴ When $x = 36$, the estimated value of

$$y = (0.5874)36 + 11.87 = 33.0164 \simeq 33.$$

∴ The judge B would have awarded **33 marks** to the eighth debtor.

Example 8. *Students of a class have obtained marks as given below in Paper I and Paper II of Statistics :*

Paper I	*45*	*55*	*56*	*58*	*60*	*65*	*68*	*70*	*75*	*80*	*85*
Paper II	*56*	*50*	*48*	*60*	*62*	*64*	*65*	*70*	*74*	*82*	*90*

Find the means, coefficient of correlation, regression coefficients and regression equations.

(KU 1999 C)

Sol. Let the variables 'marks in Paper I' and 'marks in Paper II' be denoted by x and y respectively.

Computation of $\bar{x}, \bar{y}, r$

S. No.	x	y	$u = x - A$ $A = 60$	$v = y - B$ $B = 70$	uv	u^2	v^2
1	45	56	– 15	– 14	210	225	196
2	55	50	– 5	– 20	100	25	400
3	56	48	– 4	– 22	88	16	484
4	58	60	– 2	– 10	20	4	100
5	60	62	0	– 8	0	0	64
6	65	64	5	– 6	– 30	25	36
7	68	65	8	– 5	– 40	64	25
8	70	70	10	0	0	100	0
9	75	74	15	4	60	225	16
10	80	82	20	12	240	400	144
11	85	90	25	20	500	625	400
$n = 11$			$\Sigma u = 57$	$\Sigma v = -49$	$\Sigma uv = 1148$	$\Sigma u^2 = 1709$	$\Sigma v^2 = 1865$

Means $\bar{x} = A + \dfrac{\Sigma u}{n} = 60 + \dfrac{57}{11} = \mathbf{65.1818.}$

$$\bar{y} = B + \frac{\Sigma v}{n} = 70 + \frac{(-49)}{11} = \mathbf{65.5455.}$$

Coefficient of correlation

$$r = \frac{n\Sigma uv - (\Sigma u)(\Sigma v)}{\sqrt{n\Sigma u^2 - (\Sigma u)^2}\sqrt{n\Sigma v^2 - (\Sigma v)^2}}$$

$$= \frac{11(1148) - (57)(-49)}{\sqrt{11(1709) - (57)^2}\sqrt{11(1865) - (-49)^2}}$$

$$= \frac{15421}{\sqrt{15550}\sqrt{18114}} = \frac{\mathbf{15421}}{\mathbf{124.70 \times 134.59}} = \mathbf{0.9188.}$$

Regression coefficients

$$b_{yx} = \frac{n\Sigma uv - (\Sigma u)(\Sigma v)}{n\Sigma u^2 - (\Sigma u)^2} = \frac{11(1148) - (57)(-49)}{11(1709) - (57)^2} = \frac{15421}{15550} = \mathbf{0.9917}$$

$$b_{xy} = \frac{n\Sigma uv - (\Sigma u)(\Sigma v)}{n\Sigma v^2 - (\Sigma v)^2} = \frac{11(1148) - (57)(-49)}{11(1865) - (-49)^2} = \frac{15421}{18114} = \mathbf{0.8513.}$$

Regression equations

Regression equation of y on x is $y - \bar{y} = b_{yx}(x - \bar{x})$.

$\Rightarrow \quad y - 65.5455 = 0.9917(x - 65.1818)$

$\Rightarrow \quad y = 0.9917x + 65.5455 - (0.9917)(65.1818)$

$\Rightarrow \quad \mathbf{y = 0.9917x + 0.9047.}$

Regression equation of x on y is $x - \bar{x} = b_{xy}(y - \bar{y})$.

$\Rightarrow \quad x - 65.1818 = 0.8513(y - 65.5455)$

$\Rightarrow \quad x = 0.8513y + 65.1818 - (0.8513)(65.5455)$

$\Rightarrow \quad \mathbf{x = 0.8513y + 9.3829.}$

EXERCISE 2

1. For a bivariate data, you are given the following information :

$$n = 10,\ \Sigma x = 320,\ \Sigma y = 380,\ \Sigma(x - 32)^2 = 140,$$
$$\Sigma(y - 38)^2 = 398,\ \Sigma(x - 32)(y - 38) = -93.$$

Find the :

(*i*) regression coefficients (*ii*) regression equations

(*iii*) correlation coefficient.

(**Hint.** Let $u = x - 32$ and $v = y - 38$.

$\therefore \quad \Sigma u^2 = 140, \quad \Sigma v^2 = 398, \quad \Sigma uv = -93$

$\Sigma u = \Sigma(x - 32) = \Sigma x - 32n = 320 - 32 \times 10 = 0$

$\Sigma v = \Sigma(y - 38) = \Sigma y - 38n = 380 - 38 \times 10 = 0$

$$\bar{x} = 32 + \frac{\Sigma u}{n} = 32 + \frac{0}{10} = 32$$

$$\bar{y} = 38 + \frac{\Sigma v}{n} = 38 + \frac{0}{10} = 38.$$

2. Find the regression equations for the following data :

Age of husband, x	36	23	27	28	28	29	30	31	33	35
Age of wife, y	29	18	20	22	27	21	29	27	29	28

3. The following data relates to 'advertising expenditure' (in lakhs of rupees) and 'sales' (in crores of rupees)

Advertising expenditure (in lakhs of rupees)	10	12	15	23	20
Sales (in crores of rupees)	14	17	23	25	21

Estimate (*i*) the sales corresponding to advertising expenditure of Rs. 30 lakhs and (*ii*) the advertising expenditure for a sales target of 35 crores.

4. From the following data, obtain the two regression equations :

Sales	91	97	108	121	67	124	51
Purchase	71	75	69	97	70	91	39

5. The following data gives the experience of machine operators and their performance rating as given by the number of good pieces turned out per 100 pieces :

Operator	1	2	3	4	5	6	7	8
Experience (in years)	16	12	18	4	3	10	5	12
Performance rating	87	88	89	68	78	80	75	83

Calculate the regression line of performance rating on experience and estimate the probable performance rating if an operator has seven years experience.

6. Find two lines of regression from the following data :

Age of husband	25	22	28	26	35	20	22	40	20	18
Age of wife	18	15	20	17	22	14	16	21	15	14

Hence estimate (*i*) the age of husband when the age of wife is 19 years and (*ii*) the age of wife when the age of husband is 30 years.

7. Find the regression equation of y on x for the following data :

x	78	89	97	69	59	79	68	61
y	125	137	156	112	107	136	124	108

8. The following table gives the aptitude test scores and productivity indices of 10 workers selected at random :

Aptitude score, x	60	62	65	70	72	48	53	73	65	82
Productivity index, y	68	60	62	80	85	40	52	62	60	81

Calculate the two regression equations and estimate the productivity index of a worker whose test score is 78 and the test score of a worker whose productivity index is 88. (*MDU 1999*)

9. Find the two regression equations for the following series. What is the most likely value of x when $y = 20$ and most likely value of y when $x = 22$?

x	35	25	29	31	27	24	33	36
y	23	27	26	21	24	20	29	30

10. Find the regression equations for the following data :

x	23	26	39	31	36	21	30	39
y	45	48	45	42	31	39	38	32

Also find :

(*i*) the value of y when $x = 30$

(*ii*) correlation coefficient between x and y. (*KU 2002 C*)

11. Obtain the lines of regression and show them on the graph paper for the following data :

x	65	66	67	67	68	69	71	71
y	67	68	64	68	70	70	69	68

(*KU 2001*)

Answers

1. (*i*) $b_{yx} = -0.6643$, $b_{xy} = -0.2337$
   (*ii*) Regression equation of y on x : $y = -0.6643x + 59.2576$
   Regression equation of x on y : $x = -0.2337y + 40.881$
   (*iii*) $r = -0.394$
2. Regression equation of y on x : $y = 0.8913x - 1.739$
   Regression equation of x on y : $x = 0.75y + 11.25$
3. (*i*) 29.9666 crore rupees (*ii*) 31.75 lakh rupees
4. If x and y represent the variables 'sales' and 'purchases' respectively, then
   Regression equation of y on x : $y = 0.607x + 15.998$
   Regression equation of x on y : $x = 1.286y + 0.081$
5. $y = 1.133x + 69.67$, $y = 78$ when $x = 7$
6. If x and y respectively represent 'age of husband' and 'age of wife' then the regression equations are $x = 2.23y - 12.76$ and $y = 0.385x + 7.34$
   (*i*) 30 years nearly (*ii*) 19 years nearly
7. $y = 1.212x + 34.725$
8. Regression equation of x on y : $x = 0.596y + 26.26$
   Regression equation of y on x : $y = 1.168x - 10.92$
   $y = 80.184$ when $x = 78$, $x = 78.708$ when $y = 88$
9. Regression equation of x on y : $x = 0.543y + 16.425$
   Regression equation of y on x : $y = 0.352x + 14.44$
   $x = 27.285$ when $y = 20$, $y = 22.184$ when $x = 22$
10. Regression equation of y on x : $y = 0.4x + 27.75$
    Regression equation of x on y : $x = 0.511y + 10.185$
    (*i*) 39.75 (*ii*) 0.452
11. Regression equation of y on x : $y = 0.2353x + 52$
    Regression equation of x on y : $x = 0.4615y + 36.618$.

9. REGRESSION LINES FOR GROUPED DATA

In case of grouped data if either x or y or both variables represent classes, then their respective mid-points are taken as their representatives.

In this case, if $u = \dfrac{x - A}{h}$, $v = \dfrac{y - B}{k}$,

then the regression line of y on x is $y - \bar{y} = b_{yx}(x - \bar{x})$,

where $\bar{x} = A + \left(\dfrac{\Sigma fu}{N}\right) h$,

$\bar{y} = B + \left(\dfrac{\Sigma fv}{N}\right) k$

and $b_{yx} = \dfrac{N\Sigma fuv - (\Sigma fu)(\Sigma fv)}{N\Sigma fu^2 - (\Sigma fu)^2} \cdot \dfrac{k}{h}$

The regression line of x on y is

$$x - \bar{x} = b_{xy}(y - \bar{y}),$$

where $\bar{x} = A + \left(\dfrac{\Sigma fu}{N}\right) h$,

$\bar{y} = B + \left(\dfrac{\Sigma fv}{N}\right) k$

and $b_{xy} = \dfrac{N\Sigma fuv - (\Sigma fu)(\Sigma fv)}{N\Sigma fv^2 - (\Sigma fv)^2} \cdot \dfrac{h}{k}$.

Example 1. *Calculate regression lines for the following data :*

		x					*Total*
		18	*19*	*20*	*21*	*22*	
	0—5	*0*	*0*	*0*	*3*	*1*	*4*
	5—10	*0*	*0*	*0*	*3*	*2*	*5*
y	*10—15*	*0*	*0*	*7*	*10*	*0*	*17*
	15—20	*0*	*5*	*4*	*0*	*0*	*9*
	20—25	*3*	*2*	*0*	*0*	*0*	*5*
	Total	*3*	*7*	*11*	*16*	*3*	*40*

Sol.

Values of x	:	18	19	20	21	22
Deviation (u) from A = 20	:	– 2	– 1	0	1	2
Class of y	:	0—5	5—10	10—15	15—20	20—25
Mid-point (y)	:	2.5	7.5	12.5	17.5	22.5
Deviation from B = 12.5	:	– 10	– 5	0	5	10
Step deviation by k = 5 $\left(v = \dfrac{y - 12.5}{5}\right)$	:	– 2	– 1	0	1	2

Regression Table

(In each cell of the correlation table, the boxed product value is shown first, followed by the frequency.)

y \ x		18	19	20	21	22	f	fv	fv^2	fuv
y	v \ u	− 2	− 1	0	1	2				
0–5	− 2	[0] 0	[0] 0	[0] 0	[− 6] 3	[− 4] 1	4	− 8	16	− 10
5–10	− 1	[0] 0	[0] 0	[0] 0	[− 3] 3	[− 4] 2	5	− 5	5	− 7
10–15	0	[0] 0	[0] 0	[0] 7	[0] 10	[0] 0	17	0	0	0
15–20	1	[0] 0	[− 5] 5	[0] 4	[0] 0	[0] 0	9	9	9	− 5
20–25	2	[−12] 3	[− 4] 2	[0] 0	[0] 0	[0] 0	5	10	20	− 16
f		3	7	11	16	3	$N = 40$	$\Sigma fv = 6$	$\Sigma fv^2 = 50$	$\Sigma fuv = -38$
fu		− 6	− 7	0	16	6	$\Sigma fu = 9$			
fu^2		12	7	0	16	12	$\Sigma fu^2 = 47$			
fuv		− 12	− 9	0	− 9	− 8	$\Sigma fuv = -38$			

Now
$$\bar{x} = A + \left(\frac{\Sigma fu}{N}\right) h = 20 + \left(\frac{9}{40}\right) 1 = 20.225$$

$$\bar{y} = B + \left(\frac{\Sigma fv}{N}\right) k = 12.5 + \left(\frac{6}{40}\right) 5 = 13.25$$

$$b_{yx} = \frac{N\Sigma fuv - (\Sigma fu)(\Sigma fv)}{N\Sigma fu^2 - (\Sigma fu)^2} \cdot \frac{k}{h} = \frac{40(-38) - (9)(6)}{40(47) - (9)^2} \cdot \frac{5}{1}$$

$$= \frac{-7870}{1799} = -4.375$$

$$b_{xy} = \frac{N\Sigma fuv - (\Sigma fu)(\Sigma fv)}{N\Sigma fv^2 - (\Sigma fv)^2} \cdot \frac{h}{k} = \frac{40(-38) - (9)(6)}{40(50) - (6)^2} \cdot \frac{1}{5}$$

$$= \frac{-1574}{9820} = -0.160.$$

The regression line of y on x is $y - \bar{y} = b_{yx}(x - \bar{x})$

or $y - 13.25 = -4.375(x - 20.225)$

or $y = -4.375x + 13.25 + (4.375)(20.225)$

or $\mathbf{y = -4.375x + 101.734.}$

The regression line of x on y is $x - \bar{x} = b_{xy}(y - \bar{y})$

or $x - 20.225 = -0.16(y - 13.25)$

or $x = -0.16y + 20.225 + (0.16)(13.25)$

or $\mathbf{x = -0.16y + 22.345.}$

Example 2. *Compute regression lines corresponding to the marks obtained by 25 students in Economics and Statistics :*

	Marks in Statistics			
Marks in Economics	*30–40*	*40–50*	*50–60*	*60–70*
30–40	*3*	*1*	*1*	*0*
40–50	*2*	*6*	*1*	*2*
50–60	*1*	*2*	*2*	*1*
60–70	*0*	*1*	*1*	*1*

Sol. Let x and y denote the variables 'marks in Statistics' and 'marks in Economics' respectively.

Class of x	:	30–40	40–50	50–60	60–70
Mid-point (x)	:	35	45	55	65
Deviation from A = 45	:	– 10	0	10	20
Step deviation by h = 10 $\left(u = \frac{x-45}{10}\right)$	:	– 1	0	1	2
Class of y	:	30–40	40–50	50–60	60–70
Mid-point (y)	:	35	45	55	65
Deviation from B = 45	:	– 10	0	10	20
Step deviation by k = 10 $\left(v = \frac{y-45}{10}\right)$	:	– 1	0	1	2

Regression Table

y \ x		30–40	40–50	50–60	60–70				
	v \ u	− 1	0	1	2	f	fv	fv^2	fuv
30–40	− 1	$\boxed{3}$ 3	$\boxed{0}$ 1	$\boxed{-1}$ 1	0	5	− 5	5	2
40–50	0	$\boxed{0}$ 2	$\boxed{0}$ 6	$\boxed{0}$ 1	$\boxed{0}$ 2	11	0	0	0
50–60	1	$\boxed{-1}$ 1	$\boxed{0}$ 2	$\boxed{2}$ 2	$\boxed{2}$ 1	6	6	6	3
60–70	2	0	$\boxed{0}$ 1	$\boxed{2}$ 1	$\boxed{4}$ 1	3	6	12	6
f		6	10	5	4	N = 25	$\Sigma fv = 7$	$\Sigma fv^2 = 23$	$\Sigma fuv = 11$
fu		− 6	0	5	8	$\Sigma fu = 7$			
fu^2		6	0	5	16	$\Sigma fu^2 = 27$			
fuv		2	0	3	6	$\Sigma fuv = 11$			

Now $$\bar{x} = A + \left(\frac{\Sigma fu}{N}\right) h = 45 + \left(\frac{7}{25}\right) 10 = 47.8$$

$$\bar{y} = B + \left(\frac{\Sigma fv}{N}\right) k = 45 + \left(\frac{7}{25}\right) 10 = 47.8$$

$$b_{yx} = \frac{N\Sigma fuv - (\Sigma fu)(\Sigma fv)}{N\Sigma fu^2 - (\Sigma fu)^2} \cdot \frac{k}{h} = \frac{25(11) - (7)(7)}{25(27) - (7)^2} \cdot \frac{10}{10} = \frac{2260}{6260} = 0.361$$

$$b_{xy} = \frac{N\Sigma fuv - (\Sigma fu)(\Sigma fv)}{N\Sigma fv^2 - (\Sigma fv)^2} \cdot \frac{h}{k} = \frac{25(11) - (7)(7)}{25(23) - (7)^2} \cdot \frac{10}{10} = \frac{2260}{5260} = 0.429$$

The regression line of y on x is $y - \bar{y} = b_{yx}(x - \bar{x})$

or $$y - 47.8 = 0.361(x - 47.8)$$

or $$y = 0.361x + 47.8 - (0.361)(47.8)$$

or $$\mathbf{y = 0.361x + 30.544.}$$

The regression line of x on y is $x - \bar{x} = b_{yx}(y - \bar{y})$

or $x - 47.8 = 0.429\,(y - 47.5)$

or $x = 0.429y + 47.8 - (0.429)(47.8)$

or $\mathbf{x = 0.429y + 27.294.}$

EXERCISE 3

1. The following table shows the ages of daughters and mothers. Calculate the coefficients of regression and the regression equations :

	Age of daughter (x)				
Age of mother (y)	*5—10*	*10—15*	*15—20*	*20—25*	*25—30*
15—25	6	3	0	0	0
25—35	3	16	10	0	0
35—45	0	10	15	7	0
45—55	0	0	7	10	4
55—65	0	0	0	4	5

2. The following table gives the frequency, according to groups of marks obtained by 67 students in an intelligence test. Compute the regression lines between the variables age (x) and marks (y) :

Test marks	*Age (in years)*			
	18	*19*	*20*	*21*
200—250	4	4	2	1
250—300	3	5	4	2
300—350	2	6	8	5
350—400	1	4	6	10

3. Following is the data relating 'Annual dividend (x)' and 'Security price (y)'. Compute the regression lines :

Security prices (in Rs.)	*Annual Dividend (in Rs.)*					
	6—8	*8—10*	*10—12*	*12—14*	*14—16*	*16—18*
130—140	0	0	1	3	4	2
120—130	0	1	3	3	3	1
110—120	0	1	2	3	2	0
100—110	0	2	3	2	0	0
90—100	2	2	1	1	0	0
80—90	3	1	1	0	0	0
70—80	2	1	0	0	0	0

4. Following is the distribution of students according to their height and weight :

Height (in inches)	*Weight (in lbs)*			
	90—100	*100—110*	*110—120*	*120—130*
50—55	4	7	5	2
55—60	6	10	7	4
60—65	6	12	10	7
65—70	3	8	6	3

Obtain (*i*) the coefficients of regression (*ii*) the regression equations (*iii*) coefficient of determination. (*KU 1995 ; MDU 2006*)

Answers

1. $b_{yx} = 1.6045$, $b_{xy} = 0.4011$, $y = 1.6045x + 11.763$, $x = 0.4011y + 1.3769$
2. $y = 21.5134x - 109.7157$, $x = 0.008y + 17.1727$
3. $y = 4.8042x + 55.8869$, $x = 0.1186y - 1.6032$
4. (*i*) $b_{yx} = 0.152$, $b_{xy} = 0.041$ (*ii*) $y = 0.152x + 99.93$, $x = 0.041y + 55.88$
(*iii*) $(0.152)(0.041) = 0.0062$.

---

10. PROPERTIES OF REGRESSION COEFFICIENTS AND REGRESSION LINES

(*i*) We have $b_{yx} = r \cdot \dfrac{\sigma_y}{\sigma_x}$ and $b_{xy} = r \cdot \dfrac{\sigma_x}{\sigma_y}$

σ_x and σ_y are always non-negative.

$\therefore$ The signs of b_{yx} and b_{xy} are same as that of r.

$\therefore$ The signs of regression coefficients and correlation coefficient are same.

Thus $\mathbf{b_{yx}}$, $\mathbf{b_{xy}}$ and r are all either positive or negative.

(*ii*) $b_{yx} \cdot b_{xy} = r \dfrac{\sigma_y}{\sigma_x} \cdot r \dfrac{\sigma_x}{\sigma_y} = r^2$.

Now $0 \le r^2 \le 1$ because $-1 \le r \le 1$.

$\therefore$ $0 \le b_{yx} b_{xy} \le 1$.

$\therefore$ **The product of regression coefficients is non-negative and cannot exceed one.**

(*iii*) $b_{yx} \cdot b_{xy} = r \dfrac{\sigma_y}{\sigma_x} \cdot r \dfrac{\sigma_x}{\sigma_y} = r^2$

$$\therefore \quad \mathbf{r = \pm \sqrt{b_{yx}\, b_{xy}}}\,. \qquad (MDU\ 1999)$$

The sign of r is taken as that of regression coefficients.

(*iv*) The regression line of y on x is $y - \bar{y} = b_{yx}(x - \bar{x})$.

$$\Rightarrow \quad y = b_{yx}\, x + (\bar{y} - b_{yx}\, \bar{x})$$

$\therefore$ **When y is kept on the left side, then the coefficient of x on the right side gives the regression coefficient of y on x.**

For example, let $4x + 7y - 9 = 0$ be the regression line of y on x.

We write this as $y = -\dfrac{4}{7}x + \dfrac{9}{7}$.

$\therefore$ Regression coefficient of y on x = coefficient of $x = -\dfrac{4}{7}$.

The regression line of x on y is $x - \bar{x} = b_{xy}(y - \bar{y})$.

$\Rightarrow \quad x = b_{xy}\, y + (\bar{x} - b_{xy}\, \bar{y})$

$\therefore$ **When x is kept on the left side, then the coefficient of y on the right side gives the regression coefficient of x on y.**

For example, let $5x + 9y - 8 = 0$ be the regression line of x on y.

We write this as $x = -\dfrac{9}{5}y + \dfrac{8}{5}$.

$\therefore$ Regression coefficient of x on y = coefficient of $y = -\dfrac{9}{5}$.

(*v*) The regression line of y on x is $y - \bar{y} = b_{yx}(x - \bar{x})$.

This equation is satisfied by the point $(\bar{x}, \bar{y})$. This point also lies on the regression line of x on y :

$$x - \bar{x} = b_{xy}(y - \bar{y})$$

$\therefore$ **The point $(\bar{x}, \bar{y})$ is common to both regression lines. In other words, if the correlation between the variables is not perfect, then the regression lines intersect at $(\bar{x}, \bar{y})$.**

(*vi*) **Angle between the lines of regression** (*KU 1998*)

The regression line of y on x is $y - \bar{y} = b_{yx}(x - \bar{x})$.

$\Rightarrow \quad y = b_{yx}\, x + (\bar{y} - b_{yx}\, \bar{x}) \quad \therefore$ Slope $= b_{yx} = m_1$ (say)

The regression line of x on y is $x - \bar{x} = b_{xy}(y - \bar{y})$.

$$\Rightarrow \quad y = \frac{1}{b_{xy}}x + \left(\bar{y} - \frac{1}{b_{xy}}\bar{x}\right) \quad \therefore \text{ Slope} = \frac{1}{b_{xy}} = m_2 \text{ (say)}$$

Let θ be the acute angle between the regression lines.

$$\therefore \quad \tan\theta = \left|\frac{m_1 - m_2}{1 + m_1 m_2}\right| = \left|\frac{b_{yx} - \dfrac{1}{b_{xy}}}{1 + b_{yx} \cdot \dfrac{1}{b_{xy}}}\right| = \left|\frac{b_{yx}b_{xy} - 1}{b_{xy} + b_{yx}}\right|$$

$$= \left|\frac{r\dfrac{\sigma_y}{\sigma_x} \cdot r\dfrac{\sigma_x}{\sigma_y} - 1}{r\dfrac{\sigma_x}{\sigma_y} + r\dfrac{\sigma_y}{\sigma_x}}\right| = \left|\frac{r^2 - 1}{r\left(\dfrac{\sigma_x^2 + \sigma_y^2}{\sigma_x\sigma_y}\right)}\right|$$

$$= \frac{|r^2 - 1||\sigma_x\sigma_y|}{|r||\sigma_x^2 + \sigma_y^2|} = \frac{(1 - r^2)\,\sigma_x\sigma_y}{|r|(\sigma_x^2 + \sigma_y^2)}$$

$$\therefore \quad \mathbf{\tan\theta = \frac{(1 - r^2)\,\sigma_x\sigma_y}{|r|(\sigma_x^2 + \sigma_y^2)}}.$$

Particular cases :

(*i*) **r = 0.** In this case, tan θ is not defined.

∴ θ = 90° *i.e.*, the regression lines are *perpendicular* to each other.

(*ii*) **r = 1 (or – 1).** In this case, tan θ = 0.

∴ The regression lines are *coincident*, because the point $(\bar{x}, \bar{y})$ is on both the regression lines.

Thus, we see that if the variables are not correlated, then the regression lines are perpendicular to each other and if the variables are perfectly correlated, then the regression lines are coincident. The closeness of regression lines measure the degree of linear correlation between the variables.

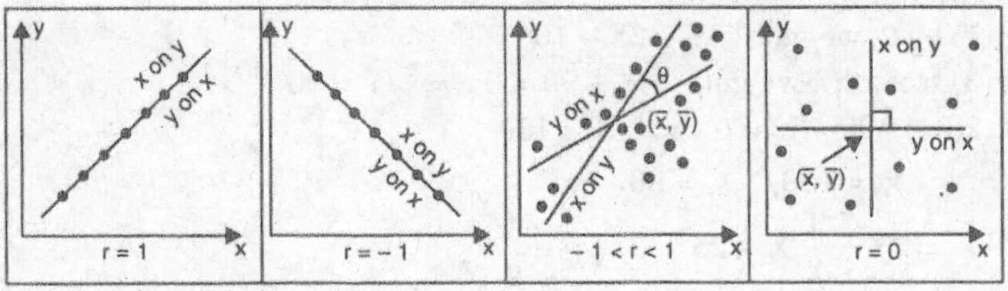

Example 1. *Are the following statements correct ? Give reasons :*

(*i*) *The regression coefficient of y on x is 3.2 and that of x on y is 0.8.*

(*ii*) *The two regression coefficients are 0.8 and – 0.2.*

(*iii*) *The two regression coefficients are given to be 0.8 and 0.2 and the coefficient of correlation is 0.4.*

(*iv*) *40x – 18y = 5 and 8x – 10y + 7 = 0 are respectively the regression equations of y on x and x on y.*

Sol. (*i*) We have $b_{yx} = 3.2,\ b_{xy} = 0.8.$

$$b_{yx} \cdot b_{xy} = 3.2 \times 0.8 = 2.56 > 1.$$

This is impossible, because $0 \le b_{yx} \cdot b_{xy} \le 1$.

∴ The given statement is **false.**

(*ii*) We have $b_{yx} = 0.8$ and $b_{xy} = -0.2$.

This is impossible, because the regression coefficients are either both +ve or both –ve.

∴ The statement is **false.**

(*iii*) We have $b_{yx} = 0.8$ and $b_{xy} = 0.2$.

$$\therefore \quad r = +\sqrt{b_{yx} \cdot b_{xy}} = +\sqrt{(0.8)(0.2)} = +0.4.$$

∴ The statement is **true.**

(*iv*) The regression line of *y* on *x* is 40*x* – 18*y* = 5.

$$\Rightarrow \quad 18y = 40x - 5 \quad \Rightarrow \quad y = \frac{40}{18}x - \frac{5}{18}$$

$$\therefore \quad b_{yx} = \frac{40}{18} = \frac{20}{9}$$

The regression line of *x* on *y* is 8*x* – 10*y* + 7 = 0.

$$\Rightarrow \quad 8x = 10y - 7 \quad \Rightarrow \quad x = \frac{10}{8}y - \frac{7}{8}.$$

$\therefore \quad b_{xy} = \frac{10}{8} = \frac{5}{4}.$

$\therefore \quad b_{yx} \cdot b_{xy} = \frac{20}{9} \times \frac{5}{4} = \frac{100}{36} > 1.$ This is impossible.

$\therefore$ The given statement is **false.**

Example 2. *Find the mean of the variable X and Y and correlation coefficient from the following informations :*

Regression equation of Y on X : $2Y - X - 50 = 0$.
Regression equation of X on Y : $3Y - 2X - 10 = 0$. (KU 2001)

Sol. Regression equation of Y on X is $2Y - X - 50 = 0$ ...(1)

Regression equation of X on Y is $3Y - 2X - 10 = 0$ ...(2)

Multiplying (1) by 2, we get $4Y - 2X - 100 = 0$ ...(3)

Subtracting (3) from (2), we get $-Y + 90 = 0 \Rightarrow Y = 90$

$\therefore$ (1) $\Rightarrow 2(90) - X - 50 = 0 \Rightarrow X = 130$

$\therefore \quad \overline{X} = \mathbf{130}, \quad \overline{Y} = \mathbf{90}.$

(1) $\Rightarrow \quad Y = \frac{1}{2}X + 25 \Rightarrow b_{yx} = \frac{1}{2}$

(2) $\Rightarrow \quad X = \frac{3}{2}Y - 5 \Rightarrow b_{xy} = \frac{3}{2}$

Now $r = +\sqrt{b_{yx} \cdot b_{xy}}$ (Regression coefficients are + ve)

$= \sqrt{\frac{1}{2} \times \frac{3}{2}} = \frac{\sqrt{3}}{2} = \mathbf{0.866}.$

Example 3. *Out of the following two regression lines, find the line of regression of y on x :*

$$4x - 5y + 33 = 0 \text{ and } 20x - 9y - 107 = 0.$$

Sol. The regression lines are

$4x - 5y + 33 = 0$ ...(1)

$20x - 9y - 107 = 0.$ ...(2)

Let (1) be the regression line of y on x.

$\therefore$ (2) is the regression line of x on y.

(1) $\Rightarrow \quad y = \frac{4}{5}x + \frac{33}{5} \quad \therefore \quad b_{yx} = \frac{4}{5}$

(2) $\Rightarrow \quad x = \frac{9}{20}y + \frac{107}{20} \quad \therefore \quad b_{xy} = \frac{9}{20}$

b_{yx} and b_{xy} are of same signs.

Also $\quad b_{yx}\, b_{xy} = \frac{4}{5} \times \frac{9}{20} = \frac{36}{100} \le 1.$

$\therefore$ Our choice of regression lines is correct.

$\therefore$ Regression line of y on x is $\mathbf{4x - 5y + 33 = 0.}$

Example 4. *Out of the following two regression lines, find the line of regression of x on y : $2x + 3y = 7$ and $5x + 4y = 9$.*

Sol. The regression lines are

$$2x + 3y = 7 \quad ...(1) \qquad \text{and} \qquad 5x + 4y = 9. \quad ...(2)$$

Let (1) be the regression line of x on y.

$\therefore$ (2) is the regression line of y on x.

$$(1) \Rightarrow \quad x = -\frac{3}{2}y + \frac{7}{2} \qquad \therefore \quad b_{xy} = -\frac{3}{2}$$

$$(2) \Rightarrow \quad y = -\frac{5}{4}x + \frac{9}{4} \qquad \therefore \quad b_{yx} = -\frac{5}{4}$$

b_{xy} and b_{yx} are of same sign.

Also $\quad b_{xy} \,.\, b_{yx} = \left(-\frac{3}{2}\right)\left(-\frac{5}{4}\right) = \frac{15}{8} > 1.$

This is impossible because $0 \le b_{xy} \,.\, b_{yx} \le 1$.

Our choice of regression line is incorrect.

(1) is not the regression line of x and y.

The regression line of x on y is $\mathbf{5x + 4y = 9}$.

Example 5. *Find the regression coefficients b_{yx} and b_{xy} when the lines of regression are $4x + 3y + 7 = 0$ and $3x + 4y + 8 = 0$.*

Sol. The regression lines are

$$4x + 3y + 7 = 0 \quad ...(1) \qquad \text{and} \qquad 3x + 4y + 8 = 0 \quad ...(2)$$

Let (1) be the regression line of y on x.

$\therefore$ (2) is the regression line of x on y.

$$(1) \Rightarrow \quad y = -\frac{4}{3}x - \frac{7}{3} \qquad \therefore \quad b_{yx} = -\frac{4}{3}$$

$$(2) \Rightarrow \quad x = -\frac{4}{3}y - \frac{8}{3} \qquad \therefore \quad b_{xy} = -\frac{4}{3}$$

$$b_{yx} \,.\, b_{xy} = \left(-\frac{4}{3}\right)\left(-\frac{4}{3}\right) = \frac{16}{9} > 1$$

This is impossible, because $0 \le b_{yx} \,.\, b_{xy} \le 1$.

$\therefore$ Our supposition is wrong.

(1) is the regression line of x on y and (2) is the regression line y on x.

$$(1) \Rightarrow \quad x = -\frac{3}{4}y - \frac{7}{4}$$

and $$(2) \Rightarrow \quad y = -\frac{3}{4}x - 2$$

$$\therefore \quad b_{xy} = -\frac{3}{4} \quad \text{and} \quad b_{yx} = -\frac{3}{4}.$$

Example 6. *The equations of two regression lines obtained in a correlation analysis are $3x + 12y = 19$ and $3y + 9x = 46$. Obtain :*

(i) the mean values of x and y,

(ii) the value of correlation coefficient.

Sol. The regression equations are

$$3x + 12y = 19 \quad ...(1) \qquad 9x + 3y = 46 \quad ...(2)$$

(*i*) We know that the regression lines passes through the point $(\bar{x}, \bar{y})$.

$\therefore$ The values of $\bar{x}$ and $\bar{y}$ can be obtained by solving the regression equations.

(1) × 3 $\Rightarrow$ $9x + 36y = 57$ ...(3)

(2) – (3) $\Rightarrow$ $0 - 33y = -11$

or $y = \frac{-11}{-33} = \frac{1}{3}$ $\Rightarrow$ $\bar{y} = \frac{1}{3}$

$\therefore$ (1) $\Rightarrow$ $3x + 12(1/3) = 19$ $\Rightarrow$ $\bar{x} = 5$.

$\therefore$ The means of x and y are 5 and 1/3 respectively.

(*ii*) We don't know exactly as to which of the above equations is regression equation of y on x. Let us suppose that (1) is regression equation of x on y and (2) is regression equation of y on x.

(1) $\Rightarrow$ $x = -4y + \frac{19}{3}$ $\therefore$ $b_{xy} = -4$

(2) $\Rightarrow$ $y = -3x + \frac{46}{3}$ $\therefore$ $b_{yx} = -3$

$\therefore$ $b_{xy} \cdot b_{yx} = (-4)(-3) = 12 > 1$. This is impossible.

$\therefore$ Our supposition is wrong.

$\therefore$ (1) is the regression equation of y on x and (2) is the regression equation of x on y

(1) $\Rightarrow$ $y = -\frac{1}{4}x + \frac{19}{12}$ $\therefore$ $b_{yx} = -\frac{1}{4}$

(2) $\Rightarrow$ $x = -\frac{1}{3}y + \frac{46}{9}$ $\therefore$ $b_{xy} = -\frac{1}{3}$

$\therefore$ $r = -\sqrt{b_{yx} \cdot b_{xy}} = -\sqrt{\left(-\frac{1}{4}\right)\left(-\frac{1}{3}\right)} = \mathbf{-0.2887}$.

Example 7. *The equations of regression lines are given by $4x - 5y + 35 = 0$ and $5x - 2y = 20$.*

Also, variance of x-series is 9. Find :

(*i*) *mean values of x and y variables*

(*ii*) *correlation coefficient between x and y variables*

(*iii*) *standard deviation of y series.* (MDU 1998)

Sol. The equations of regression lines are

$4x - 5y + 35 = 0$ ...(1)

$5x - 2y - 20 = 0$ ...(2)

(*i*) (1) × 2 $\Rightarrow$ $5x - 10y + 70 = 0$ ...(3)

(2) × 5 $\Rightarrow$ $25x - 10y - 100 = 0$ ...(4)

(3) – (4) $\Rightarrow$ $-17x + 170 = 0$ $\Rightarrow$ $x = 10$

$\therefore$ (1) $\Rightarrow$ $4(10) - 5y + 35 = 0$

$\Rightarrow$ $5y = 40 + 35 = 75$ $\Rightarrow$ $y = 15$

$\therefore$ (10, 15) is on both lines.

$\therefore$ $\mathbf{\bar{x} = 10, \bar{y} = 15.}$

(*ii*) Let (1) be the regression line of y on x.

$\therefore$ (2) is the regression line of x on y.

(1) $\Rightarrow$ $y = \frac{4}{5}x + 7$ $\therefore$ $b_{yx} = \frac{4}{5}$

(2) $\Rightarrow$ $x = \frac{2}{5}y + 4$ $\therefore$ $b_{xy} = \frac{2}{5}$

$\therefore$ b_{yx} and b_{xy} are of same sign.

Also $b_{yx} \cdot b_{xy} = \left(\frac{4}{5}\right)\left(\frac{2}{5}\right) = \frac{8}{25} \le 1$

$\therefore$ Our choice of regression lines is correct.

$$\therefore \quad b_{yx} = \frac{4}{5} \text{ and } b_{xy} = \frac{2}{5}$$

$$\therefore \quad r = +\sqrt{b_{yx} \cdot b_{xy}} = +\sqrt{\frac{4}{5} \times \frac{2}{5}} = \frac{2\sqrt{2}}{5} = \mathbf{0.5657.}$$

(iii) $b_{yx} = \frac{4}{5} \quad \Rightarrow \quad r\frac{\sigma_y}{\sigma_x} = \frac{4}{5}$

$$\Rightarrow \quad \frac{2\sqrt{2}}{5} \cdot \frac{\sigma_y}{3} = \frac{4}{5} \qquad (\because \text{ var. } x = 9 \Rightarrow \sigma_x = \sqrt{9} = 3)$$

$$\Rightarrow \quad \sigma_y = \frac{4 \times 3}{2\sqrt{2}} = 2\sqrt{2} = \mathbf{4.2426.}$$

Example 8. *For the following observations, find the regression coefficients b_{yx} and b_{xy} and hence find the correlation coefficient between x and y :*

{(x, y) : (4, 2), (2, 3), (3, 2), (4, 4), (2, 4)}.

Sol. **Calculation of b_{yx} and b_{xy}**

S. No.	x	y	xy	x^2	y^2
1	4	2	8	16	4
2	2	3	6	4	9
3	3	2	6	9	4
4	4	4	16	16	16
5	2	4	8	4	16
$n = 5$	$\Sigma x = 15$	$\Sigma y = 15$	$\Sigma xy = 44$	$\Sigma x^2 = 49$	$\Sigma y^2 = 49$

$$b_{yx} = \frac{n\Sigma xy - (\Sigma x)(\Sigma y)}{n\Sigma x^2 - (\Sigma x)^2} = \frac{5(44) - (15)(15)}{5(49) - (15)^2} = \frac{-5}{20} = -\frac{1}{4}$$

$$b_{xy} = \frac{n\Sigma xy - (\Sigma x)(\Sigma y)}{n\Sigma y^2 - (\Sigma y)^2} = \frac{5(44) - (15)(15)}{5(49) - (15)^2} = \frac{-5}{20} = -\frac{1}{4}.$$

The regression coefficients are –ve, so the correlation coefficient is also –ve.

$$r = -\sqrt{(b_{yx})(b_{xy})} = -\sqrt{\left(-\frac{1}{4}\right)\left(-\frac{1}{4}\right)} = -\frac{1}{4}.$$

Example 9. *Equations of two regression lines are :*

$4x + 3y + 7 = 0$ and $3x + 4y + 8 = 0$

Find :

(i) mean of x, mean of y ;

(ii) regression coefficients b_{yx} and b_{xy} and

(iii) correlation coefficient between x and y.

Sol. The equations of regression lines are :

$$4x + 3y + 7 = 0 \quad ...(1)$$

and

$$3x + 4y + 8 = 0 \quad ...(2)$$

(i) (1) × 4 $\Rightarrow$ $16x + 12y + 28 = 0$ ...(3)

(2) × 3 $\Rightarrow$ $9x + 12y + 24 = 0$ ...(4)

(3) – (4) $\Rightarrow$ $7x + 4 = 0 \Rightarrow x = -4/7.$

∴ (1) $\Rightarrow 4(-4/7) + 3y + 7 = 0$

$$\Rightarrow \quad y = \frac{-7 + (16/7)}{3} = -\frac{11}{7}$$

∴ (– 4/7, – 11/7) is on both lines.

Since regressions lines intersects at $(\bar{x}, \bar{y})$, we have

$$\bar{x} = -4/7, \ \bar{y} = -11/7.$$

(ii) Let (1) be the regression line of y on x.

∴ (2) is the regression line of x on y.

(1) $\Rightarrow$ $y = -\frac{4}{3}x - \frac{7}{3}$ ∴ $b_{yx} = -\frac{4}{3}$

(2) $\Rightarrow$ $x = -\frac{4}{3}y - \frac{8}{3}$ ∴ $b_{xy} = -\frac{4}{3}$

$$\therefore \quad b_{yx} \cdot b_{xy} = \left(-\frac{4}{3}\right)\left(-\frac{4}{3}\right) = \frac{16}{9} > 1$$

This is impossible, because $0 \le b_{yx} \cdot b_{xy} \le 1$.

∴ Our supposition is wrong.

∴ (1) is the regression line of x on y and (2) is the regression line of y on x.

(1) $\Rightarrow$ $x = -\frac{3}{4}y - \frac{7}{4}$. ∴ $b_{xy} = -\frac{3}{4}$

(2) $\Rightarrow$ $y = -\frac{3}{4}x - 2$ ∴ $b_{yx} = -\frac{3}{4}$.

(iii) $$r = -\sqrt{b_{yx}b_{xy}} = -\sqrt{\left(-\frac{3}{4}\right)\left(-\frac{3}{4}\right)} = -\frac{3}{4}.$$

Example 10. *The two regression lines obtained by a student were as given below :*

$$3X - 4Y = 5 \ ; \quad 8X + 16Y = 15$$

Do you agree with him ? Explain with reasons. (KU 2002)

Sol. The regression lines are

$3X - 4Y = 5$ ...(1) $8X + 16Y = 15$ ...(2)

Let (1) be the regression line of Y on X.

∴ (2) is the regression line of X on Y.

(1) $\Rightarrow$ $\qquad Y = \frac{3}{4}X - \frac{5}{4}$ $\qquad \therefore \quad b_{YX} = \frac{3}{4}$

(2) $\Rightarrow$ $\qquad X = -2Y + \frac{15}{8}$ $\qquad \therefore \quad b_{XY} = -2$

This is impossible because regression coefficients cannot be of different signs.

Let (1) be the regression line of X on Y.

$\therefore$ (2) is the regression line of Y on X.

(1) $\Rightarrow$ $\qquad X = \frac{4}{3}Y + \frac{5}{3}$ $\qquad \therefore \quad b_{XY} = \frac{4}{3}$

(2) $\Rightarrow$ $\qquad Y = -\frac{1}{2}X + \frac{15}{16}$ $\qquad \therefore \quad b_{YX} = -\frac{1}{2}$

This is also impossible.

$\therefore$ We do not agree with the student.

Example 11. *Show that the mean of the two regression coefficients is greater than the coefficient of correlation, if coefficient of correlation is positive.* (KU 1998 C)

Sol. A.M. of regression coefficients $= \dfrac{b_{yx} + b_{xy}}{2} = \dfrac{1}{2}\left[r\dfrac{\sigma_y}{\sigma_x} + r\dfrac{\sigma_x}{\sigma_y}\right]$

$$= \frac{r}{2}\left(\frac{\sigma_y^2 + \sigma_x^2}{\sigma_y\,\sigma_x}\right) = r\left(\frac{\sigma_x^2 + \sigma_y^2}{2\sigma_x\sigma_y}\right)$$

$$= r\left(\frac{\sigma_x^2 + \sigma_y^2}{2\sigma_x\sigma_y} - 1 + 1\right) = r\left(\frac{\sigma_x^2 + \sigma_y^2 - 2\sigma_x\sigma_y}{2\sigma_x\sigma_y}\right) + r$$

$$= r\,.\,\frac{(\sigma_x - \sigma_y)^2}{2\sigma_x\sigma_y} + r > r\,. \qquad (\because\; r > 0,\ (\sigma_x - \sigma_y)^2 > 0,\ 2\sigma_x\,\sigma_y > 0)$$

$\therefore$ A.M. of regression coefficients > coefficient of correlation.

EXERCISE 4

1. If two regression coefficients are 2 and 0.45, what will be the coefficient of correlation ?
2. In a problem of regression analysis, the two regression coefficients are found to be – 0.6 and – 1.4. What is the correlation coefficient ?
3. Out of the following two regression lines, find the regression line of y on x :
   (*i*) $3x + 12y = 8$, $3y + 9x = 46$
   (*ii*) $x + 2y - 5 = 0$, $2x + 3y = 8$.
4. Out of the following two regression lines, find the regression line of x on y :
   (*i*) $13x - 10y + 11 = 0$, $2x - y - 1 = 0$
   (*ii*) $x + 4y + 11 = 0$, $4x + y - 7 = 0$.
5. From the following data :

x	4	7	10	12	18
y	12	15	8	13	18

Verify that correlation coefficient is G.M. between the regression coefficients.

6. Find the correlation coefficient when the lines of regression are

$$2x - 9y + 6 = 0,\ x - 2y + 1 = 0.$$

7. The regression lines between two variables x and y are found to be

$$4x - 5y + 33 = 0 \text{ and } 20x - 9y = 107.$$

Find the coefficient of correlation.

8. The equations of two regression lines obtained in a correlation analysis are as follows :

$$3x + 13y = 19,\ x + 3y = 5.$$

Obtain (*i*) the means of x and y
(*ii*) regression coefficients b_{yx} and b_{xy}
(*iii*) correlation coefficient.

9. The equations of two regression lines obtained in a correlation analysis are as follows :

$$2x + 3y - 10 = 0,\ 4x + y - 5 = 0.$$

Obtain (*i*) means of x and y
(*ii*) regression coefficients b_{yx} and b_{xy}
(*iii*) correlation coefficient.

10. In a partially destroyed record, the following data are available :
Variance of $x = 25$.
Regression equation of x on y : $5x - y = 22$.
Regression equation of y on x : $64x - 45y = 24$.
Find : (*i*) mean values of x and y
(*ii*) coefficient of correlation between x and y
(*iii*) standard deviation of y.

11. A student obtained the two regression equations as :

$$2x - 5y - 7 = 0 \text{ and } 3x + 2y - 8 = 0.$$

Do you agree with him ?

12. The regression equations of a bivariate distribution are :
Regression equation of y on x : $4y = 9x + 15$
Regression equation of x on y : $25x = 6y + 7$.
Find : (*i*) coefficient of correlation
(*ii*) ratio of means of x and y
(*iii*) ratio of S.D. of x and y

13. Given the regression equations :

$$x + 2y - 5 = 0,\ 2x + 3y - 8 = 0 \text{ and } \sigma_x^2 = 12,$$

Find : (*i*) the mean values of x and y
(*ii*) regression coefficients (*iii*) correlation coefficient between x and y
(*iv*) standard deviation of y. (*MDU 2001, 2005*)

14. In a partially destroyed laboratory record of an analysis of correlation data, the following results are legible :
Variance of $x = 9$
Regression equations : $4x - 5y + 33 = 0$
$20x - 9y = 107$.
On the basis of above information, find :
(*i*) mean values of x and y
(*ii*) standard deviation of y-series
(*iii*) coefficient of correlation.

15. The equations of regression lines are given to be

$$3x + 2y = 26 \text{ and } 6x + y = 31.$$

A student obtained the mean values $\bar{x} = 7$, $\bar{y} = 4$ and coefficient of correlation $r = 0.5$. Do you agree with him ? If not, suggest your results.

16. The equations of regression lines are given to be $3x + 2y - 26 = 0$ and $6x + y - 31 = 0$. Find the values of $\bar{x}$, $\bar{y}$ and r. *(MDU 1997, 2004)*

17. Two regression equations are given below :

Find out :

(*i*) Mean values of X and Y :

(*ii*) Standard deviation of Y.

(*iii*) Coefficient of correlation between X and Y.

The regression equations are $8X - 10Y + 70 = 0$, $15X - 6Y = 60$, variance of X = 9. *(MDU 1998)*

Answers

1. 0.9487	2. -0.9165	3. (*i*) $3x + 12y = 8$	(*ii*) $x + 2y - 5 = 0$
4. (*i*) $2x - y - 1 = 0$	(*ii*) $4x + y - 7 = 0$	6. $r = 0.6667$	7. $r = 0.6$
8. (*i*) $\bar{x} = 2$, $\bar{y} = 1$	(*ii*) $b_{yx} = -\frac{3}{13}$, $b_{xy} = -3$		(*iii*) $r = -\frac{3}{\sqrt{13}}$
9. (*i*) $\bar{x} = \frac{1}{2}$, $\bar{y} = 3$	(*ii*) $b_{yx} = -\frac{2}{3}$, $b_{xy} = -\frac{1}{4}$		(*iii*) $r = -\frac{1}{\sqrt{6}}$
10. (*i*) $\bar{x} = 6$, $\bar{y} = 8$	(*ii*) $r = 8/15$	(*iii*) $\sigma_y = 40/3$	11. No
12. (*i*) $r = 0.7348$	(*ii*) $\bar{x}/\bar{y} = 59/219$	(*iii*) $\sigma_x/\sigma_y = \sqrt{8}/\sqrt{75}$	
13. (*i*) $\bar{x} = 1$, $\bar{y} = 2$	(*ii*) $b_{yx} = -0.5$, $b_{xy} = -1.5$	(*iii*) $r_{xy} = -0.866$	(*iv*) $\sigma_y = 2$
14. (*i*) $\bar{x} = 13$, $\bar{y} = 17$	(*ii*) $\sigma_y = 4$	(*iii*) $r = 0.6$	
15. No. $\bar{x} = 4$, $\bar{y} = 7$, $r = -0.5$		16. $\bar{x} = 4$, $\bar{y} = 7$, $r = -0.5$	
17. (*i*) $\bar{X} = 10$, $\bar{Y} = 15$	(*ii*) $\sigma_y = 3\sqrt{2}$	(*iii*) $r = 2\sqrt{2}/5$.	

11. STANDARD ERROR OF ESTIMATE

We know that standard deviation measures the scatter of items of a series around its arithmetic mean. Similarly, here we shall look for some measure of scatteredness of points on a scatter diagram about a regression line. In regression analysis, we have two regression lines *i.e.*, regression line of y on x and regression line of x on y. If y_c denote the estimated values of y for given x, then the deviations $y - y_c$ accounts for the scatter of points about the regression line of y on x. This measure of scatterness is technically called the **standard error of estimate of y on x** and is defined by $\sqrt{\frac{\Sigma(y - y_c)^2}{n}}$ and is denoted by S_{yx}.

$$\therefore \qquad S_{yx} = \sqrt{\frac{\Sigma(y - y_c)^2}{n}}.$$

Similarly, we define the **standard error of estimate of x on y** as

$$\sqrt{\frac{\Sigma(x - x_c)^2}{n}} \text{ and is denoted by } S_{xy}.$$

$$\therefore \qquad \mathbf{S_{xy}} = \sqrt{\frac{\Sigma(\mathbf{x}-\mathbf{x_c})^2}{\mathbf{n}}}.$$

Here x_c denotes the estimated values of x for given y, by using the regression line of x on y.

In general, $S_{yx} \neq S_{xy}$.

Let $y = a + bx$ be the regression line of y on x.

$$\therefore \qquad S_{yx}^{\ 2} = \frac{\Sigma(y-y_c)^2}{n} = \frac{\Sigma(y-a-bx)^2}{n} \qquad (\because \ y_c \text{ is given by } y = a + bx)$$

$$= \frac{\Sigma(y-a-bx)(y-a-bx)}{n}$$

$$= \frac{\Sigma[y(y-a-bx) - a(y-a-bx) - bx(y-a-bx)]}{n}$$

$$= \frac{\Sigma y(y-a-bx) - a\Sigma(y-a-bx) - b\Sigma(xy-ax-bx^2)}{n}$$

$$= \frac{\Sigma y(y-a-bx) - a[\Sigma y - an - b\Sigma x] - b[\Sigma xy - a\Sigma x - b\Sigma x^2]}{n}$$

$$= \frac{\Sigma(y^2 - ay - bxy) - a \times 0 - b \times 0}{n}$$

$$(\because \ \Sigma y = an - b\Sigma x \ \Rightarrow \ \Sigma y - an - b\Sigma x = 0 \text{ and } \Sigma xy = a\Sigma x - b\Sigma x^2 \ \Rightarrow \ \Sigma xy - a\Sigma x - b\Sigma x^2 = 0)$$

$$= \frac{\Sigma y^2 - a\Sigma y - b\Sigma xy}{n}$$

$$\therefore \qquad \mathbf{S_{yx}} = \sqrt{\frac{\mathbf{\Sigma y^2 - a\Sigma y - b\Sigma xy}}{\mathbf{n}}}.$$

Similarly if $x = a + by$ be the regression line of x on y then

$$\mathbf{S_{xy}} = \sqrt{\frac{\mathbf{\Sigma x^2 - a\Sigma x - b\Sigma xy}}{\mathbf{n}}}.$$

Example 1. *For the data given below :*

x	*1*	*2*	*3*	*4*	*5*
y	*2*	*5*	*3*	*8*	*7*

the regression line of y on x is y = 1.3x + 1.1. Find the standard error of estimate of y on x.

Sol. **Computation of S_{yx}**

S. No.	*x*	*y*	$y_c = 1.3x + 1.1$	$y - y_c$	$(y - y_c)^2$
1	1	2	(1.3)1 + 1.1 = 2.4	– 0.4	0.16
2	2	5	(1.3)2 + 1.1 = 3.7	1.3	1.69
3	3	3	(1.3)3 + 1.1 = 5.0	– 0.2	4.00
4	4	8	(1.3)4 + 1.1 = 6.3	1.7	2.89
5	5	7	(1.3)5 + 1.1 = 7.6	– 0.6	0.36
n = 5					$\Sigma(y - y_c)^2 = 9.10$

Now, $$S_{yx} = \sqrt{\frac{\Sigma(y - y_c)^2}{n}} = \sqrt{\frac{9.10}{5}} = \mathbf{1.349.}$$

Example 2. *For the data given below :*

x	*6*	*2*	*10*	*4*	*8*
y	*9*	*11*	*5*	*8*	*7*

find the value of standard error of estimate of x on y.

Sol. For computing S_{xy}, we shall be needing the regression line of x on y.

Computation of Regression Line of x on y

S. No.	x	y	x^2	y^2	xy	$x_c = 16.4 - 1.3y$	$x - x_c$	$(x - x_c)^2$
1	6	9	36	81	54	4.7	1.3	1.69
2	2	11	4	121	22	2.1	– 0.1	0.01
3	10	5	100	25	50	9.9	0.1	0.01
4	4	8	16	64	32	6.0	– 2.0	4.00
$n = 5$	8	7	64	49	56	7.3	0.7	0.49
Total	30	40	220	340	214			6.20

The regression line of x on y is $x - \bar{x} = b_{xy}(y - \bar{y})$. ...(1)

$$x = \frac{\Sigma x}{n} = \frac{30}{5} = 6, \quad y = \frac{\Sigma y}{n} = \frac{40}{5} = 8$$

$$b_{xy} = \frac{n\Sigma xy - (\Sigma x)(\Sigma y)}{n\Sigma y^2 - (\Sigma y)^2} = \frac{5(214) - (30)(40)}{5(340) - (40)^2} = \frac{-130}{100} = -1.3$$

$\therefore$ (1) $\Rightarrow$ $x - 6 = -1.3(y - 8)$

$\Rightarrow$ $x = -1.3y + 6 + 8(1.3)$

$\Rightarrow$ $x = 16.4 - 1.3y.$

Now, $$S_{xy} = \sqrt{\frac{\Sigma(x - x_c)^2}{n}} = \sqrt{\frac{6.20}{5}} = \mathbf{1.1135.}$$

Alternative method

$$S_{xy} = \sqrt{\frac{\Sigma x^2 - a\Sigma x - b\Sigma xy}{n}}$$

$$= \sqrt{\frac{220 - 16.4(30) - (-1.3)(2.14)}{5}} \qquad \begin{pmatrix} a = 16.4 \\ b = -1.3 \end{pmatrix}$$

$$= \sqrt{\frac{6.20}{5}} = \mathbf{1.1135.}$$

EXERCISE 5

1. For the data given below :

x	1	2	3	4	5	6	7	8	9
y	9	8	10	12	11	13	14	16	15

the regression line of y on x is $y = 0.95x + 7.25$. Find the standard error of estimate of y on x.

2. For the data given below :

x	1	2	3	4	5	6	7	8	9
y	9	8	10	12	11	13	14	16	15

the regression line of x on y is $x = 0.95y - 6.4$. Find the standard error of estimate of x on y.

3. For the data given below :

x	14	19	24	21	26	22	15	20	19
y	31	36	48	37	50	45	33	41	39

find the standard error of estimate of x on y.

4. From the following data, obtain the regression equations and also compute the standard errors of estimates.

x	3	5	6	7	9
y	2	3	4	6	5

Answers

1. 0.8062 2. 0.8062 3. 1.1712
4. $y = 0.6x + 0.4$, $x = 1.2y + 1.2$, 0.748, 1.058.

12. TOTAL, EXPLAINED AND UNEXPLAINED VARIATION

Let $\bar{y}$ be the A.M. of the values of the variable y. The sum of the squares of the deviations of the values of y from $\bar{y}$ *i.e.*, $\Sigma(y - \bar{y})^2$ is called the **total variation** of the variable y.

Let y_c denote the estimated value of y for given x, then the deviations $(y_c - \bar{y})$ have a definite pattern. The sum of the squares of the deviations of the values of y_c from $\bar{y}$ *i.e.*, $\Sigma(y_c - \bar{y})^2$ is called the **explained variation** of the variable y.

The deviations $(y - y_c)$ behave in a random manner. The sum of the squares of the deviation of the values of y from their corresponding value of y_c *i.e.*, $\Sigma(y - y_c)^2$ is called the **unexplained variation** of the variable y.

On the same pattern, the sum $\Sigma(x - \bar{x})^2$, $\Sigma(x_c - \bar{x})^2$ and $\Sigma(x - x_c)^2$ respectively called the **total variation, explained variation** and **unexplained variation** of the variable x.

∴ Let $y = a + bx$ be the regression line of y on x.

∴ y_c for a value of x is equal to the value of $a + bx$ for that corresponding value of x.

The normal equations used to find the values of a and b are :

$$\Sigma y = an + b\Sigma x \quad ...(1) \qquad \text{and} \qquad \Sigma xy = a\Sigma x + b\Sigma x^2. \quad ...(2)$$

Dividing (1) *by n*, we get

$$\bar{y} = a + b\bar{x}$$

$$\therefore \quad y_c - \bar{y} = (a + bx) - (a + b\bar{x}) = b(x - \bar{x})$$

$$\Rightarrow \quad (y_c - \bar{y})^2 = b^2(x - \bar{x})^2$$

$$\Rightarrow \quad \Sigma(y_c - \bar{y})^2 = b^2\Sigma(x - \bar{x})^2 = \left[\frac{\Sigma(x - \bar{x})(y - \bar{y})}{\Sigma(x - \bar{x})^2}\right]^2 . \Sigma(x - \bar{x})^2$$

(Note that b is the regression coefficient of y on x *i.e.*, b_{yx})

$$= \frac{(\Sigma(x - \bar{x})(y - \bar{y}))^2}{\Sigma(x - \bar{x})^2}$$

$$\therefore \quad \frac{\Sigma(y_c - \bar{y})^2}{\Sigma(y - \bar{y})^2} = \frac{(\Sigma(x - \bar{x})(y - \bar{y}))^2}{\Sigma(x - \bar{x})^2 \, . \, \Sigma(y - \bar{y})^2} = \left(\frac{\Sigma(x - \bar{x})(y - \bar{y})}{\sqrt{\Sigma(x - \bar{x})^2}\sqrt{\Sigma(y - \bar{y})^2}}\right)^2 = r^2 .$$

$$\therefore \quad \frac{\textbf{Explained variation of y}}{\textbf{Total variation of y}} = \mathbf{r^2}$$

The ratio on the left side is called the **coefficient of determination.**

$\therefore$ **Coefficient of determination = $\mathbf{r^2}$.**

Similarly, we can show that

$$\frac{\textbf{Explained variation of x}}{\textbf{Total variation of x}} = \mathbf{r^2}.$$

Theorem. Prove that (i) $\mathbf{S_{yx} = \sigma_y\sqrt{1 - r^2}}$ (ii) $\mathbf{S_{xy} = \sigma_x\sqrt{1 - r^2}}$.

Proof. We have

$$y - \bar{y} = (y - y_c) + (y_c - \bar{y}) .$$

$$\therefore \quad (y - \bar{y})^2 = (y - y_c)^2 + (y_c - \bar{y})^2 + 2(y - y_c)(y_c - \bar{y})$$

Summing, we get

$$\Sigma(y - \bar{y})^2 = \Sigma(y - y_c)^2 + \Sigma(y_c - \bar{y})^2 + 2\Sigma(y - y_c)(y_c - \bar{y}) \quad ...(1)$$

Let $y = a + bx$ be the regression line of y on x. The values of the constants a and b are given by the normal equations :

$$\Sigma y = an + b\Sigma x \quad ...(2)$$

$$\Sigma xy = a\Sigma x + b\Sigma x^2. \quad ...(3)$$

Now $\Sigma(y - y_c)(y_c - \bar{y}) = \Sigma(y - a - bx)(a + bx - \bar{y})$

($\because$ The values of y_c are given by $a + bx$)

$$= \Sigma a(y - a - bx) + b\Sigma x(y - a - bx) - \bar{y}\Sigma(y - a - bx)$$

$$= a(\Sigma y - an - b\Sigma x) + b(\Sigma xy - a\Sigma x - b\Sigma x^2) - \bar{y}(\Sigma y - an - b\Sigma x)$$

$$= a.0 + b.0 - \bar{y}.0 = 0. \quad \text{[Using (2) and (3)]}$$

$$\therefore \quad (1) \Rightarrow \Sigma(y - \bar{y})^2 = \Sigma(y - y_c)^2 + \Sigma(y_c - \bar{y})^2 + 2 \times 0$$

$$\Rightarrow \quad \Sigma(y - \bar{y})^2 = \Sigma(y_c - \bar{y})^2 + \Sigma(y - y_c)^2 \quad ...(4)$$

$\therefore$ **Total variation of y**

= Explained variation of y + unexplained variation of y

$$(4) \Rightarrow \quad \frac{\Sigma(y-\bar{y})^2}{\Sigma(y-\bar{y})^2} = \frac{\Sigma(y_c-\bar{y})^2}{\Sigma(y-\bar{y})^2} + \frac{\Sigma(y-y_c)^2}{\Sigma(y-\bar{y})^2}$$

$$\Rightarrow \quad 1 = r^2 + \frac{\frac{\Sigma(y-y_c)^2}{n}}{\frac{\Sigma(y-\bar{y})^2}{n}} \quad \Rightarrow 1 - r^2 = \frac{S^2_{yx}}{\sigma_y^{\ 2}}$$

$$\Rightarrow \quad S^2_{yx} = \sigma_y^{\ 2}(1-r^2)$$

$$\therefore \quad \mathbf{S_{yx} = \sigma_y \sqrt{1-r^2}}.$$

Similarly, we can prove that

$$\mathbf{S_{xy} = \sigma_x \sqrt{1-r^2}}.$$

Example 1. *For a bivariate data, we have*

$$r = -0.4382, \sigma_x = 109.545, \sigma_y = 5.$$

Find the values of S_{yx} and S_{xy}.

Sol. We have $\quad S_{yx} = \sigma_y \sqrt{1-r^2}$.

$$\therefore \quad S_{yx} = 5 \times \sqrt{1-(-0.4382)^2} = 5 \times \sqrt{1-0.192} = 5 \times \sqrt{0.808}$$

$$= 5 \times 0.8989 = \mathbf{4.4945}.$$

Also $\quad S_{xy} = \sigma_x \sqrt{1-r^2}$.

$$\therefore \quad S_{xy} = 109.545 \times \sqrt{1-(-0.4382)^2} = 109.545 \times 0.8989 = \mathbf{98.47}.$$

Example 2. *If unexplained variation of y = 19.22 and explained variation of y = 19.70, find (i) coefficient of determination (ii) coefficient of correlation.*

Sol. (*i*) We have $\quad r^2 = \dfrac{\text{Explained variation of } y}{\text{Total variation of } y}$

$$= \frac{\text{Explained variation of } y}{\text{Explained variation of } y + \text{unexplained variation of } y}$$

$$= \frac{19.70}{19.70 + 19.22} = \frac{19.70}{38.92} = 0.5062.$$

$\therefore$ Coefficient of determination = **0.5062.**

(*ii*) We have $\quad r^2 = 0.5062$

$\therefore$ Coefficient of correlation = $\pm \sqrt{0.5062} = \pm$ **0.7115.**

Remark. The given data is insufficient to fix the sign of 'r'.

Example 3. *From the following data :*

Age of husband (years)	*18*	*19*	*20*	*21*	*22*	*23*	*24*	*25*	*26*	*27*
Age of wife (years)	*17*	*17*	*18*	*18*	*18*	*19*	*19*	*20*	*21*	*21*

obtain the following :

(*i*) *The regression equation of age of husband on the age of wife.*

(*ii*) *Total variation in the age of husband.*

(iii) The magnitude of variation in age of the husband explained by the regression equation.

(iv) Standard error of the estimate of age of husband. (KU 2002)

Sol. Let the variables 'age of husband' and 'age of wife' be denoted by x and y respectively.

Computation of Regression Equation of x on y

S. No.	x	y	$u = x - A$ $A = 22$	$v = y - B$ $B = 19$	uv	u^2	v^2
1	18	17	– 4	– 2	8	16	4
2	19	17	– 3	– 2	6	9	4
3	20	18	– 2	– 1	2	4	1
4	21	18	– 1	– 1	1	1	1
5	22	18	0	– 1	0	0	1
6	23	19	1	0	0	1	0
7	24	19	2	0	0	4	0
8	25	20	3	1	3	9	1
9	26	21	4	2	8	16	4
10	27	21	5	2	10	25	4
$n = 10$			$\Sigma u = 5$	$\Sigma v = -2$	$\Sigma uv = 38$	$\Sigma u^2 = 85$	$\Sigma v^2 = 20$

(*i*) The regression equation of x on y is $x - \bar{x} = b_{xy}(y - \bar{y})$.

$$\bar{x} = A + \frac{\Sigma u}{n} = 22 + \frac{5}{10} = 22.5 \quad \text{and} \quad \bar{y} = B + \frac{\Sigma v}{n} = 19 + \frac{-2}{10} = 18.8$$

$$b_{xy} = \frac{n\Sigma uv - (\Sigma u)(\Sigma v)}{n\Sigma v^2 - (\Sigma v)^2} = \frac{10(38) - (5)(-2)}{10(20) - (-2)^2} = \frac{390}{196} = 1.99.$$

$\therefore$ The required equation is $x - 22.5 = 1.99(y - 18.8)$

or $x = 1.99y + 22.5 - (19.9)(18.8)$ or $\mathbf{x = 1.99y - 14.912.}$

(*ii*) Total variation in the age of husband $= \Sigma(x - \bar{x})^2$.

Total Variation in x

x	$(x - \bar{x})$ $\bar{x} = 22.5$	$(x - \bar{x})^2$
18	– 4.5	20.25
19	– 3.5	12.25
20	– 2.5	6.25
21	– 1.5	2.25
22	– 0.5	0.25
23	0.5	0.25
24	1.5	2.25
25	2.5	6.25
26	3.5	12.25
27	4.5	20.25
		$\Sigma(x - \bar{x})^2 = 82.5$

$\therefore$ Total variation in the age of husband $= \Sigma(x - \bar{x})^2 = \mathbf{82.5\ years.}$

(*iii*) Explained variation in the age of husband $= \Sigma(x_c - \bar{x})^2$

Explained variation in x

x	y	x_c (= 1.99y – 14.912)	$x_c - \bar{x}$ $\bar{x} = 22.5$	$(x_c - \bar{x})^2$
18	17	(1.99)17 – 14.912 = 18.918	– 3.582	12.8307
19	17	(1.99)17– 14.912 = 18.918	– 3.582	12.8307
20	18	(1.99)18 – 14.912 = 20.908	– 1.592	2.5345
21	18	(1.99)18 – 14.912 = 20.908	– 1.592	2.5345
22	18	(1.99)18 – 14.912 = 20.908	– 1.592	2.5345
23	19	(1.99)19 – 14.912 = 22.898	0.398	0.1584
24	19	(1.99)19 – 14.912 = 22.898	0.398	0.1584
25	20	(1.99)20 – 14.912 = 24.888	2.388	5.7025
26	21	(1.99)21 – 14.912 = 26.878	4.378	19.1669
27	21	(1.99)21 – 14.912 = 26.878	4.378	19.1669
				$\Sigma(x_c - \bar{x})^2 = 77.618$

∴ Explained variation in the age of husband = $\Sigma(x_c - \bar{x})^2$ = **77.618 years.**

(*iv*) Standard error of the estimate of age of husband = $S_{xy} = \sqrt{\dfrac{\Sigma(x - x_c)^2}{n}}$.

Computation of S_{xy}

x	x_c (= 1.99y – 14.912)	$x - x_c$	$(x - x_c)^2$
18	18.918	– 0.918	0.8427
19	18.918	0.082	0.0067
20	20.908	– 0.908	0.8245
21	20.908	0.092	0.0085
22	20.908	1.092	1.1925
23	22.898	0.102	0.0104
24	22.898	1.102	1.2144
25	24.888	0.112	0.0125
26	26.878	– 0.878	0.7709
27	26.878	0.122	0.0149
		$\Sigma(x - x_c) = 0$	$\Sigma(x - x_c)^2 = 4.898$

$$S_{xy} = \sqrt{\frac{\Sigma(x - x_c)^2}{n}} = \sqrt{\frac{4.898}{10}} = \mathbf{0.6999\ years.}$$

Remark. In the above example, we have :

(*i*) $\Sigma(x - x_c) = 0$ and

(*ii*) sum of explained and unexplained variation of x is approximately equal to the total variation of x.

EXERCISE 6

1. If the coefficient of correlation between x and y is 0.65 and S.D. of y-series is 4.2, then find the standard error of estimate of y on x.

2. If the standard error of estimate of x on y is 1.02 and the standard deviation of x-axis is 2, then find the coefficient of determination.
3. Find the standard errors of estimates :
$$\sigma_x = 4.4, \sigma_y = 2.2, r = 0.8.$$ *(KU 1996)*
4. If the explained variation of $y = 4.37$ and unexplained variation of $y = 9.85$, find (*i*) coefficient of determination (*ii*) coefficient of correlation.
5. (*i*) If the coefficient of correlation between variables x and y is 1, find the standard error of estimate of y on x.
   (*ii*) If the coefficient of correlation between variables x and y is – 1, find the standard error of estimate of x on y.
6. Find S_{yx} and S_{xy} if $\sigma_x = 5$, $\sigma_y = 12$ and r is equal to (*i*) 0 (*ii*) 0.5 (*iii*) – 1.
7. Find the means of X and Y variables and the coefficient of correlation between them from the following two regression equations :
$$2Y - X - 50, 3Y - 2X - 10 = 0.$$
Also calculate the standard error of estimate of Y on X, given that the standard deviation of X is 3. *(KU 2005 C)*

Answers

1. 3.1917	2. 0.7399	3. $S_{yx} = 1.32$, $S_{xy} = 2.64$	
4. (*i*) 0.3073	(*ii*) ± 0.5544	5. (*i*) 0	(*ii*) 0
6. (*i*) 12, 5	(*ii*) 10.39, 4.33	(*iii*) 0, 0	

7. $\overline{X} = 130$, $\overline{Y} = 90$, $r = \sqrt{3}/2$, $S_{YX} = \sqrt{3}/2$.

EXERCISE 7

1. Briefly explain the concept of 'regression' and write down the equations of regression lines. *(MDU 2005)*
2. Distinguish clearly between 'Correlation' and 'Regression'. Why should there be two lines of regression in a bivariate distribution ? *(MDU 1998, 2007)*
3. What are regression coefficients ? Show that $r^2 = b_{yx} \cdot b_{xy}$.
4. Point out the role of regression analysis in business with the help of few examples.
5. What is regression ? Why are there, in general two regression lines ? Under what conditions can there be only one regression line ? *(KU 2004)*
6. Write a short note on regression coefficients.
7. Define regression coefficients and describe their utility. How are they related with Karl Pearson's coefficient of correlation ? *(MDU 2007)*
8. What is regression analysis ? Explain its use in business problems with suitable examples.
9. Explain the concept of regression. Discuss its uses. What is difference between 'correlation' and 'regression' ? *(MDU 1995 ; KU 1996, 2002 C)*
10. Differentiate between standard error and probable error. *(KU 2002, 2006)*
11. What do you mean by regression coefficients ? What are the uses of regression analysis ? *(KU 1997)*
12. Differentiate between Correlation and Regression. Show that θ, the acute angle between two lines of regression is given by
$$\tan\theta = \frac{(1-r^2)\sigma_x\sigma_y}{|r|(\sigma_x^2 + \sigma_y^2)}$$. Interpret the case, when $r = 0, \pm 1$. *(KU 1998)*
13. Write a note on 'standard error of estimate'. *(KU 1997, 99, 99 C ; MDU 2000)*
14. Give difference between correlation and regression. *(KU 2001 C, 2003, 2005 C, 2006)*
15. Explain standard error of estimate and derive the formulae for their evaluation. *(KU 1998 C)*

12
Index Numbers

1. INTRODUCTION

We are generally interested in knowing as to whether the price level of a particular group of commodities is rising or falling. A teacher is interested in estimating the growth of intelligence in his students. Government may declare that the exports have increased during the current year. In all such statements, it is not possible to measure the changes in the concerned variables directly. If the exports for the current year have increased, it may not mean that exports of every item has increased. Exports of different items might have increased in different proportions, even the exports might have decreased for some of the items. We may compare the general price level of commodities in 1986 with that of price level in 1980. For this purpose, we will have to take into account the prices of all important items for both years. But, the percentage rise or fall in the prices of items is not expected to be same for each item. Had it been so, we would have immediately declared the rise or fall in the general price level of items in 1986. The change in price vary for different items. The percentage rise may be different for different commodities. It may even decrease for some items as well. Under such circumstances, we feel the necessity of some statistical device which may help us in facing such problems. The statistical devices used to measure such changes are called *Index Numbers*. Let us define 'index numbers' in a formal way.

2. DEFINITION AND CHARACTERISTICS OF INDEX NUMBERS

The **index numbers** are defined as specialized averages used to measure change in a variable or a group of related variables with respect to time or geographical location or some other characteristic.

In our course of discussion, we shall restrict ourselves to the study of changes in a group of related variables with respect to time only. Changes in related variables are expressed clearly by using index numbers, because these are generally expressed as percentages.

The index numbers are used to measure the change in production, prices, values etc., in related variables over time or geographical location. The barometers are used to study changes in whether conditions, similarly the index numbers are used to study the changes in economic and business activities. That is, why, the index numbers are also called **'Economic Barometers'.**

3. PURPOSE OF CONSTRUCTING INDEX NUMBERS

1. Index numbers are used for computing real incomes from money incomes. The wages, dearness allowances etc., are fixed on the basis of real income. The money income is divided by an appropriate consumer's price index number to get real income.

2. Index numbers are constructed to compare the changes in related variables over time. Index numbers of industrial production can be used to see the change in the production that has occurred in the current period.

3. Index numbers are used to study the changes occurred in the past. This knowledge help in forecasting.

4. Index numbers are used to study the changes in prices, industrial production, purchasing powers of money, agricultural production etc., of different countries. With the use of index numbers, the comparative study is also made possible for such variables.

4. PROBLEMS INVOLVED IN THE CONSTRUCTION OF INDEX NUMBERS

The following points are to be kept under consideration, in the construction of index numbers.

(1) **Definition of the purpose.** The first point in the construction of an index number is to define its purpose. We must decide as to what is to be measured. A single index number cannot be used for all purposes. Different index numbers are used in different situations. An index number is of great importance if it is computed strictly in accordance with its purpose. If we are interested in estimating the change in the cost of rice, then it is not advisable to collect figures of import of rice from other countries. In order to compute consumer price index number, it is not correct to take wholesale prices into consideration. In converting money income to real income, only consumer price index number is to be used.

(2) **Selection of items.** The items which should be included in the computation of index numbers, largely depend upon the purpose of constructing it. It is not possible to include each and every item in the construction of index number, because this would cause heavy calculations. The selection of items mainly depend upon the availability of funds, time and also on the degree of accuracy desired. If we are interested in computing general price index for certain period, then it is neither possible nor very important to include every item in the construction of index number. It is true that the accuracy of the index number will increase with an increase in the number of items, but at the same time, the number of items cannot go beyond certain limit. The items selected for the index number must be representative by nature. In computing consumer price index number, we must include the items which represents the habits, tastes etc. of the people for whom the index number is being computed. Only those items are to be included in the index which can be recognised even after certain years.

(3) **Collection of data regarding items.** After the decision about the items has been taken, the next step is to obtain data regarding these items for the periods under consideration. Data must be collected through specially trained agents. In order to avoid any possibility of personal bias, cross check must be imposed. Data may be collected from magazines, journals etc., if available. The periodicity of collecting data will depend upon the purpose of the index. In preparing consumer price index numbers, only retail prices must be used. Difficulty may have to be encountered in collecting prices from retailers. This happens because of great variability of prices in different shops. Price of commodities are expressed either in money prices or in quantity prices. In **money pricing system,** the price of commodity is expressed per unit of commodity. For example, Rs. 2 per kg, Rs. 3 per litre etc. In **quantity pricing system,** the quantity of commodity is expressed per rupee. For example, 3 kg per rupee, 4 m per rupee etc.

(4) **Choice of base period.** The period with which comparison is made is called the **base period,** we cannot think of computing index number without a base period. So far as the formulae for constructing index numbers are concerned, we can use any of the period as base

period. But in practice, base period is selected keeping in view the purpose of the index number. The following points must be kept in mind while deciding the base period.

(*a*) The base period should be such that the data relating to this period should neither be exceptionally low nor exceptionally high than those for other periods. If the data corresponding to items in the base period are exceptionally low, then the index number would seem to be elevated. And on the other hand, if the data corresponding to items are exceptionally high, the index number for the current period will be unnecessarily depressed. To avoid this, the base period is taken to be a normal one. Normal in the sense that it should be free from abnormalities like flood, famine, earthquake, boom, depression, war etc. If no single period is available which may be considered as normal, then average of data covering one complete cycle may be considered as base.

(*b*) The base period should be a period of recent past. The consumer price index number for 2003 will be of very little use, if it is computed with 1940 as the base year. If the purpose of the index number is to see, whether the wages of employees should be increased or not, then the consumer price, index number must be calculated by taking that year as the base year, after which the wages have not been increased.

(*c*) There are two types of base, namely fixed base and chain base. In computing **fixed base index numbers,** the comparison of all periods is made with a fixed period. Whereas in **chain base indices,** the comparison of periods is made with corresponding preceding periods. Either of the base can be used for computing index numbers. The index number for the base period is always taken to be 100.

(5) **Choice of average.** In constructing index numbers, we need averaging the changes in the items under consideration. Theoretically, any of the methods of averaging can be used for computing index numbers. The selection of the average much depend on the nature of data. Generally arithmetic mean and geometric mean are used in calculating index numbers.

The use of arithmetic mean in computing index numbers involve less calculation work. Moreover, this method of averaging is easy to understand. The use of A.M. is condemned on the ground that it is much affected by extreme items, present in the series. Moreover, it is not capable of measuring relative changes.

Inspite of heavy calculations involved in the calculation of G.M., its use is much advocated in computing index numbers. The availability of sophisticated computers has also eliminated the fear of facing difficulties in computing G.M. Geometric mean represents the changes occurred in the variables effectively, because it gives equal weights to equal ratios of changes in the variables. It gives more importance to smaller items and *vice versa*.

(6) **Choice of weights.** In practical life, we observe that all commodities which we use, are not of equal importance. Different commodities serve different purpose and hence cannot be considered to be of same significance. In computing consumer price index number, food and entertainment items cannot be kept at equal footing. An increase of 10% in the price of wheat cannot be balanced with a discount of 10% in the rate of cinema ticket. Similarly, the production index number would also give misleading results if proper weights are not attached with the items under consideration. If the production of cane-sugar increases by 20% and the production of opium decreases by 20% during a particular year, then it cannot be interpreted from the index numbers of cane-sugar and opium that there has occurred no change in the volume of production in that year.

Therefore, in computing index numbers, weights must be attached to the items under consideration. In computing price index numbers, the weights assigned to different items are of two types, namely **quantity weights** and **value weights.** These weights may correspond either to current period or to base period or to any other appropriate period. The choice of corresponding period much depend on the nature of data. Quantity weights are used in aggregative methods whereas value weights are used in price relative methods.

(7) **Choice of formula.** Choice of proper formula for computing index numbers is also a typical problem. It is neither possible nor advisable to treat the data by using any of the available formulae. The choice of formula would depend on the nature of the given data. The purpose of the index also affects the choice of the formula. There is no formula for computing index numbers, which may suit in all circumstances. For example, an index number used for deflating a time series is expected to satisfy the factor reversal test. The 'base shifting' in index numbers is possible only if the index number method satisfies the circular test.

5. TYPES OF INDEX NUMBERS

There are mainly three of index numbers :

I. Price Index Numbers.
II. Quantity Index Numbers.
III. Value Index Numbers.

In our course of discussion, we shall confine mainly to 'Price Index Numbers'. Price index numbers measure the changes is prices of commodities in the current period in comparison with the prices of commodities in the base period.

I. PRICE INDEX NUMBERS

6. METHODS

For constructing price index numbers, the following method are used :

(*i*) Simple Aggregative Method
(*ii*) Simple Average of Price Relatives Method
(*iii*) Laspeyre's Method
(*iv*) Paasche's Method
(*v*) Dorbish and Bowley's Method
(*vi*) Fisher's Method
(*vii*) Marshall Edgeworth's Method
(*viii*) Kelly's Method
(*ix*) Weighted Average of Price Relatives Method
(*x*) Chain Base Method.

First nine methods are fixed base methods of constructing price index number.

7. SIMPLE AGGREGATIVE METHOD

This is the simplest method of computing index number. In this method, we have

$$P_{01} = \frac{\Sigma p_1}{\Sigma p_0} \times 100$$

where 0 and 1 suffixes stand for base period and current period respectively.

P_{01} = price index number for the current period
Σp_1 = sum of prices of commodities per unit in the current period
Σp_0 = sum of prices of commodities per unit in the base period.

In other words, this price index number is the sum of prices of commodities in the current period expressed as percentage of the sum of prices in the base period. Consider the data :

Item	*Price in base period* p_0*(in Rs.)*	*Price in current period* P_1*(in Rs.)*
A	5	6
B	8	10
C	18	27
D	112	84
E	12	15
F	6	9
Total	$\Sigma p_0 = 161$	$\Sigma p_1 = 151$

Here $$P_{01} = \frac{\Sigma p_1}{\Sigma p_0} \times 100 = \frac{151}{161} \times 100 = \mathbf{93.79.}$$

This index number shows that there is fall in the prices of commodities to the extent of 6.21%. It may be noted that the prices of every item has increased in the current period except for the item *D*. On the other hand, the index number is declaring a decrease in prices on an average. This is not in consistency with the definition of index numbers. In fact, this unwanted result is due to the presence of an extreme item (*D*) in the series. So, in the presence of extreme items, this method is liable to give misleading results. This is a demerit of this method.

Let us find price index number for the data given below :

Item	*Unit*	*Price (in Rs.)*	
		1994 (p_0)	*1996* (p_1)
Sugar	kg	6	7
Milk	litre	3	4
Ghee	kg	45	50

Here $$\Sigma p_0 = 6 + 3 + 45 = 54$$

and $$\Sigma p_1 = 7 + 4 + 50 = 61$$

$$\therefore \quad P_{01} = \frac{\Sigma p_1}{\Sigma p_0} \times 100 = \frac{61}{54} \times 100 = \mathbf{112.96.}$$

Here we have considered the price of sugar per kg. Now we use the price of sugar per quintal, for calculating index number for the year 1996.

Item	*Unit*	*Price (in Rs.)*	
		1994 (p_0)	*1996* (p_1)
Sugar	quintal	600	700
Milk	litre	3	4
Ghee	kg	45	50

In this case, $\Sigma p_0 = 600 + 3 + 45 = 648$

and $\Sigma p_1 = 700 + 4 + 50 = 754$

$$\therefore \quad P_{01} = \frac{\Sigma p_1}{\Sigma p_0} \times 100 = \frac{754}{648} \times 120 = \mathbf{116.36.}$$

The index number has changed, whereas we have not affected any change in the data except for writing the price of sugar in a different unit. This type of variation in the value of index numbers is beyond one's expectation. This is another limitation with this method.

8. SIMPLE AVERAGE OF PRICE RELATIVES METHOD

Before introducing this method of finding index number, we shall first explain the concept of 'price relative'. The **price relative** of a commodity in the current period with respect to base period is defined as the price of the commodity in the current period expressed as a percentage of the price in the base period. Mathematically,

$$\textbf{Price Relative (P)} = \frac{\mathbf{p_1}}{\mathbf{p_0}} \times \mathbf{100.}$$

For example, if the prices of a commodity be Rs. 5 and Rs. 6 in the years 1995 and 1996 respectively, then the price relative of the commodity in 1996 w.r.t. 1995 is

$$\frac{6}{5} \times 100 = 120.$$

In the simple average of price relatives method of computing index numbers, simple average of price relatives of all the items is the required index number.

Mathematically,

$$P_{01} = \frac{\sum\left(\frac{p_1}{p_0} \times 100\right)}{n} \qquad \text{(if A.M. is used)}$$

i.e.,

$$\mathbf{P_{01}} = \frac{\mathbf{\Sigma P}}{\mathbf{n}}$$

where P_{01} is the required price index number,

$\frac{p_1}{p_0} \times 100$ = Price relative = P

n = no. of commodities under consideration.

In averaging price relatives, geometric mean is also used. In this case, the formula is

$$\mathbf{P_{01}} = \textbf{Antilog}\left(\frac{\mathbf{\Sigma \log P}}{\mathbf{n}}\right)$$

It has already been observed that the index number computed by using simple aggregative method is unduly affected by the extreme items, present in the series.

We shall just show that this method of computing index number is not at all affected by the extreme items. We compute the index number for the data considered in the previous method.

Index No. by simple A.M. of P.R. Method

Item	*Price in the base period (p_0) (in Rs.)*	*Price in the current period p_1 (in Rs.)*	*Price Relatives* $P = \frac{p_1}{p_0} \times 100$
A	6	6	120
B	8	10	125
C	18	27	150
D	112	84	75
E	12	15	125
F	6	9	150
			$\Sigma P = 745$

$$\therefore \quad P_{01} = \frac{\Sigma P}{n} = \frac{745}{6} = \mathbf{124.17.}$$

Here the index number is advocating the fact that the prices of commodities have raised on an average.

There is one more advantage of using this method. The index number, computed by averaging the price relatives is not affected by the change in measuring unit of any commodity. We illustrate this by using the data taken in the previous method :

Item	*Unit*	p_0	p_1	$P = \frac{p_1}{p_0} \times 100$
Sugar	kg	6	7	116.67
Milk	litre	3	4	133.33
Ghee	kg	45	50	111.11
				$\Sigma P = 361.11$

$$\therefore \quad P_{01} = \frac{\Sigma P}{n} = \frac{361.11}{3} = \mathbf{120.37.}$$

Now, we consider this data once again and change the measuring units for sugar :

Item	*Unit*	p_0	p_1	$P = \frac{p_1}{p_0} \times 100$
Sugar	quintal	600	700	116.67
Milk	litre	3	4	133.33
Ghee	kg	45	50	111.11
				$\Sigma P = 361.11$

$$\therefore \qquad P_{01} = \frac{\Sigma P}{n} = \frac{361.11}{3} = 120.37.$$

We see that this index number is same as that for the data when the rate of sugar was expressed in kg.

Thus, the index number as calculated by this method is not affected by changing measuring units.

In averaging the price relatives, we can also make use of median, harmonic mean etc. But, only A.M. and G.M. are generally used for this purpose.

Example 1. *Construct index number for each year from the following annual wholesale prices of cotton with 1984 as base.*

Year	*Wholesale price (in Rs.)*	*Year*	*Whole sale price (in Rs.)*
1984	*75*	*1989*	*70*
1985	*50*	*1990*	*69*
1986	*65*	*1991*	*75*
1987	*60*	*1992*	*84*
1988	*72*	*1993*	*80*

Sol. **Calculation of Index Nos. (1984 = 100)**

Year	*Whole sale price (in Rs.)*	*Index No. (1984 = 100)*
1984	75	**100**
1985	50	$\frac{50}{75} \times 100 = 66.67$
1986	65	$\frac{65}{75} \times 100 = 86.67$
1987	60	$\frac{60}{75} \times 100 = 80$
1988	72	$\frac{72}{75} \times 100 = 96$
1989	70	$\frac{70}{75} \times 100 = 93.33$
1990	69	$\frac{69}{75} \times 100 = 92$
1991	75	$\frac{75}{75} \times 100 = 100$
1992	84	$\frac{84}{75} \times 100 = 112$
1993	80	$\frac{80}{75} \times 100 = 106.67$

Example 2. *Calculate index number for 1994 on the basis of the prices of 1991 for the following data :*

Article	*A*	*B*	*C*	*D*	*E*
Prices in 1991	*12*	*25*	*10*	*5*	*6*
Prices in 1994	*15*	*20*	*12*	*10*	*15*

(KU 1995 C)

Sol. **Calculation of Inedx Nos (1991) = 100)**

Article	p_0	p_1	$P = \frac{p_1}{p_0} \times 100$
A	12	15	$\frac{15}{12} \times 100 = 125$
B	25	20	$\frac{20}{25} \times 100 = 80$
C	10	12	$\frac{12}{10} \times 100 = 120$
D	5	10	$\frac{10}{5} \times 100 = 200$
E	6	15	$\frac{15}{6} \times 100 = 250$
	$\Sigma p_0 = 58$	$\Sigma p_1 = 72$	$\Sigma P = 775$

By simple aggregative method

$$P_{01} = \frac{\Sigma p_1}{\Sigma p_0} \times 100 = \frac{72}{58} \times 100 = \mathbf{124.41.}$$

By A.M. of price relatives method

$$P_{01} = \frac{\Sigma P}{n} = \frac{775}{5} = \mathbf{155.}$$

Example 3. *Prepare index numbers of price for three years with average price as base.*

Year	*Rate per Rupee*		
	Wheat	*Cotton*	*Oil*
Ist year	*10 seers*	*4 seers*	*3 seers*
IInd year	*9 seers*	*3.5 seers*	*3 seers*
IIIrd year	*9 seers*	*3 seers*	*2.5 seers*

Sol. Here the prices of commodities are given in the form of 'quantity prices', we shall convert these quantity prices into money prices.

Price of wheat in the Ist year is 10 seers per rupee.

$\therefore$ Price of 1 maund wheat $= \frac{40}{10} =$ Rs. 4 ($\because$ 1 maund = 40 seers)

Similarly, we shall express the prices of other commodities per maund.

ty	Unit	Ist year		IInd year		IIIrd year		Average pr
		p_1	P	p_1	P	p_1	P	p_0
	Maund	$\frac{40}{10} = 4$	$\frac{4}{4.29} \times 100$ $= 93.24$	$\frac{40}{9} = 4.44$	$\frac{4.44}{4.29} \times 100$ $= 103.50$	$\frac{40}{9} = 4.44$	$\frac{4.44}{4.29} \times 100$ $= 103.50$	$\frac{4 + 4.44 +}{3}$ $= 4.29$
	Maund	$\frac{40}{4} = 10$	$\frac{10}{11.59} \times 100$ $= 86.28$	$\frac{40}{3.5} \times 11.43$	$\frac{11.43}{11.59} \times 100$ $= 98.62$	$\frac{40}{3} = 13.33$	$\frac{13.33}{11.59} \times 100$ $= 115.01$	$\frac{10 + 11.43 +}{3}$ $= 11.59$
	Maund	$\frac{40}{3} = 13.33$	$\frac{13.33}{14.22} \times 100$ $= 93.74$	$\frac{40}{3} = 13.33$	$\frac{13.33}{14.22} \times 100$ $= 93.74$	$\frac{40}{2.5} = 16$	$\frac{16}{14.22} \times 100$ $= 112.52$	$\frac{13.33 + 13.33}{3}$ $= 14.22$
		27.33	273.26	29.20	295.86	33.77	331.03	30.10

Index numbers by Simple Aggregative Method

Index no. for Ist year

$$= \frac{\Sigma p_1}{\Sigma p_0} \times 100 = \frac{27.33}{30.10} \times 100 = \mathbf{90.80}$$

Index no. for IInd year

$$= \frac{\Sigma p_1}{\Sigma p_0} \times 100 = \frac{29.20}{30.10} \times 100 = \mathbf{97.01}$$

Index no. for IIIrd year

$$= \frac{\Sigma p_1}{\Sigma p_0} \times 100 = \frac{33.77}{30.10} \times 100 = \mathbf{112.19}$$

Index numbers by Simple A.M. of Price Relatives Method

Index no. for Ist year

$$= \frac{\Sigma P}{n} = \frac{273.26}{3} = \mathbf{91.09}$$

Index no. for IInd year

$$= \frac{\Sigma P}{n} = \frac{295.86}{3} = \mathbf{98.62}$$

Index no. for IIIrd year

$$= \frac{\Sigma P}{n} = \frac{331.03}{3} = \mathbf{110.34.}$$

Example 4. *From the information given below, prepare index numbers of prices for three years with average price as base :*

Rate per rupee

Year	*Wheat*	*Rice*	*Sugar*
1st year	*1.38 kg*	*1 kg*	*0.40 kg*
2nd year	*1.6 kg*	*0.8 kg*	*0.40 kg*
3rd year	*1 kg*	*0.75 kg*	*0.25 kg*

Sol. Since the prices of commodities are given in the form of 'quantity prices', we shall convert these quantity prices into 'money prices'.

Price of wheat in the 1st year

$$= 2 \text{ kg per rupee}$$

∴ Price of wheat per quintal

$$= \frac{100}{2} = \text{Rs. } 50$$

Similarly, we shall express the prices of other commodities per quintal.

-ity	Unit	1st year		2nd year		3rd year		Average
		p_1	P	p_1	P	p_1	P	p
eat	Quintal	$\frac{100}{1.38} = 72.46$	$\frac{50}{78.33} \times 100$ $= 63.83$	$\frac{100}{1.6} = 62.5$	$\frac{62.5}{78.33} \times 100$ $= 79.79$	$\frac{100}{1} = 100$	$\frac{100}{78.33} \times 100$ $= 127.67$	$\frac{72.46 + 6}{3}$ $= 78$
	Quintal	$\frac{100}{1} = 100$	$\frac{100}{119.44} \times 100$ $= 83.72$	$\frac{100}{0.8} = 125$	$\frac{125}{119.44} \times 100$ $= 104.66$	$\frac{100}{0.75} \times 100$ $= 133.33$	$\frac{133.33}{119.44} \times 100$ $= 111.63$	$\frac{100 + 125}{3}$ $= 11$
ar	Quintal	$\frac{100}{0.4} = 250$	$\frac{250}{300} \times 100$ $= 83.33$	$\frac{100}{0.4} = 250$	$\frac{250}{300} \times 100$ $= 83.33$	$\frac{100}{0.25} = 400$	$\frac{400}{300} = 100$ $= 133.33$	$\frac{250 + 25}{3}$ $= 3$
l		400	230.88	437.5	267.78	633.33	372.63	497

Index numbers by Simple Aggregative Method

Index no. for 1st year $= \frac{\Sigma p_1}{\Sigma p_0} \times 100 = \frac{400}{497.77} \times 100 = \mathbf{83.36}$

Index no. for 2nd year $= \frac{\Sigma p_1}{\Sigma p_0} \times 100 = \frac{437.5}{497.77} \times 100 = \mathbf{87.89}$

Index no. for 3rd year $= \frac{\Sigma p_1}{\Sigma p_0} \times 100 = \frac{633.33}{497.77} \times 100 = \mathbf{127.23}$

Index numbers by Simple A.M. of Price Relatives Method

Index no. for 1st year $= \frac{\Sigma P}{n} = \frac{230.88}{3} = \mathbf{76.96}$

Index no. for 2nd year $= \frac{\Sigma P}{n} = \frac{267.78}{3} = \mathbf{89.26}$

Index no. for 3rd year $= \frac{\Sigma P}{n} = \frac{372.63}{3} = \mathbf{124.21.}$

EXERCISE 1

1. Construct price index number for the year 1995, by using the following series. Simple aggregative method is to be used.

Commodity	*A*	*B*	*C*	*D*	*E*
Price (1994) (in Rs.)	4	2	6	8	12
Price (1995) (in Rs.)	5	2	8	9	10

2. From the following data, construct an index number for 1996 by using the method of taking A.M. of price relatives :

Item	*A*	*B*	*C*	*D*	*E*	*F*
Price in 1995 (in Rs.)	10	12	6	5	5	9
Price in 1996 (in Rs.)	10	15	8	6	6	18

3. For the data given below, calculate the index numbers by taking :

(*i*) 1980 as the base year

(*ii*) 1982 as the base year.

Year	1978	1979	1980	1981	1982	1983	1984	1985
Price of 'x' (in Rs.)	4	7	10	10	12	11	15	16

4. From the following data, construct price index nos. for the year 1996 by the methods :
(i) simple A.M. of price relatives
(ii) simple G.M. of price relatives.

Commodity	*A*	*B*	*C*	*D*	*E*	*F*
Price in 1995 (in Rs.)	4	5	10	7	3	9
Price in 1996 (in Rs.)	6	8	12	14	6	12

5. Find the price index numbers for three years by simple aggregative method. The average price is to be used as base :

	Price per rupee		
Year	*A*	*B*	*C*
I	4 kg	2 kg	10 kg
II	5 kg	2.5 kg	12 kg
III	3 kg	2.5 kg	8 kg

6. From the following data, construct the price index number with average price as base :

	Rate per rupee		
Year	*Wheat*	*Rice*	*Oil*
I	10 kg	4 kg	2 kg
II	8 kg	2.5 kg	2 kg
III	5 kg	2 kg	1 kg

7. From the following data, construct the price index numbers with average price as base :

	Rate per rupee		
Year	*Wheat*	*Rice*	*Sugar*
2001	2 kg	1.25 kg	500 gm
2002	1.25 kg	1 kg	400 gm
2003	1 kg	800 gm	250 gm

(KU 2005 C)

Answers

1. 106.25 2. 133.05
3. (i) 40, 70, 100, 100, 120, 110, 150, 160
(ii) 33.33, 58.33, 83.33, 83.33, 100, 91.67, 125, 133.33
4. (i) 160.55 (ii) 157.7 5. 106.62, 85.71, 107.66
6. 70.26, 89.16, 140.53 by using simple A.M. of price relative method
7. 69.88, 94.96, 128.86 by using simple A.M. of price relative method.

9. LASPEYRE'S METHOD

This is a method for finding weighted index numbers. In this method, base period quantities (q_0) are used as weights. If P_{01} is the index number for the current period, then we have

$$P_{01} = \frac{\Sigma p_1 q_0}{\Sigma p_0 q_0} \times 100$$

where '0' and '1' suffixes stand for base period and current period respectively.

$\Sigma p_1 q_0$ = sum of products of prices of the commodities in the current period with their corresponding quantities used in the base period.

$\Sigma p_0 q_0$ = sum of product of prices of the commodities in the base period with their corresponding quantities used in the base period.

10. PAASCHE'S METHOD

This is a method for finding weighted index numbers. In this methods, current period quantities (q_1) are used as weights.

If P_{01} is the required index number for the current period, then

$$P_{01} = \frac{\Sigma p_1 q_1}{\Sigma p_0 q_1} \times 100$$

where p_0, p_1 represents prices per unit of commodities in the base period and current period respectively.

11. DORBISH AND BOWLEY'S METHOD

This is a method for computing weighted index numbers.

If P_{01} is the required index number for the current period, then

$$P_{01} = \frac{\left(\dfrac{\Sigma p_1 q_0}{\Sigma p_0 q_0} + \dfrac{\Sigma p_1 q_1}{\Sigma p_0 q_1}\right)}{2} \times 100$$

where p_0, p_1 represents prices per unit of commodities in the base period and current period respectively, q_0, q_1 represents number of units in the base period and current period respectively.

We have $$P_{01} = \frac{\left(\dfrac{\Sigma p_1 q_0}{\Sigma p_0 q_0} + \dfrac{\Sigma p_1 q_1}{\Sigma p_0 q_1}\right)}{2} \times 100 = \frac{\dfrac{\Sigma p_1 q_0}{\Sigma p_0 q_0} \times 100 + \dfrac{\Sigma p_1 q_1}{\Sigma p_0 q_1} \times 100}{2}$$

$$= \frac{\text{Laspeyre's index no + Paasche's index no.}}{2}$$

$\therefore$ Dorbish and Bowely's index number can also be obtained by taking A.M. of Laspeyre's and Paasche's index numbers.

12. FISHER'S METHOD

This is a method for computing weighted index numbers.

If P_{01} is the required index number for the current period, then

$$P_{01} = \sqrt{\frac{\Sigma p_1q_0}{\Sigma p_0q_0} \times \frac{\Sigma p_1q_1}{\Sigma p_0q_1}} \times 100$$

where symbols p_0, q_0, p_1, q_1 have their usual meaning.

We have $$P_{01} = \sqrt{\frac{\Sigma p_1q_0}{\Sigma p_0q_0} \times \frac{\Sigma p_1q_1}{\Sigma p_0q_1} \times 100} = \sqrt{\left(\frac{\Sigma p_1q_0}{\Sigma p_0q_0} \times 100\right)\left(\frac{\Sigma p_1q_1}{\Sigma p_0q_1} \times 100\right)}$$

$$= \sqrt{\begin{pmatrix}\text{Laspeyre's}\\ \text{Index no.}\end{pmatrix}\begin{pmatrix}\text{Paasche's}\\ \text{Index no.}\end{pmatrix}}$$

∴ Fisher's index numbers can also be obtained by taking G.M. of Laspeyre's and Paasche's index numbers. Fisher's method is considered to be the best method of computing index numbers because this method, satisfies unit test, time reversal test and factor reversal test. That is why, this method is also known as *Fisher's Ideal Method*.

13. MARSHALL EDGEWORTH'S METHOD

This is a method of computing weighted index numbers. In this method the sum of base period quantities and current period quantities are used as weights.

If P_{01} is the required index number for the current period, then

$$P_{01} = \frac{\Sigma p_1(q_0 + q_1)}{\Sigma p_0(q_0 + q_1)} \times 100$$

where p_0, q_0, p_1, q_1 have their usual meaning.

We can also write this index numbers as

$$P_{01} = \frac{\Sigma p_1q_0 + \Sigma p_1q_1}{\Sigma p_0q_0 + \Sigma p_0q_1} \times 100$$

This form is generally used for computing index numbers.

14. KELLY'S METHOD

This is a method of computing weighted index numbers. In this method, the quantities (q) corresponding to any period can be used as weights. We can also use the average of quantities for two or more periods as weights.

If P_{01} is the required index numbers for the current period, then

$$P_{01} = \frac{\Sigma p_1q}{\Sigma p_0q} \times 100$$

where q represents the quantities which are to be used as weights. p_0, p_1 have their usual meanings. This index number is also known as **Fixed Weights Aggregative Method.**

15. WEIGHTED AVERAGE OF PRICE RELATIVES METHOD (KU 2001 C)

This is a method of computing weighted index numbers. In weighted index numbers, we give weights to every commodity in the series so that each commodity may have due influence on the index number. Till now quantity weights were used for constructing price index numbers.

In the weighted average of price relatives method, value weights (W) are used. The values of commodities may correspond to either base period or current period or any other period.

If P_{01} is the required index number for the current period, then

$$P_{01} = \frac{\Sigma WP}{\Sigma W}, \quad \text{where } P = \frac{p_1}{p_0} \times 100.$$

p_0, p_1 have their usual meanings.

In this method, we have infact taken the weighted arithmetic mean of the price relatives. In constructing this index number, geometric mean is also used. In this case, the formula is

$$P_{01} = \text{Antilog}\left(\frac{\Sigma W \log P}{\Sigma W}\right).$$

Example 1. *Calculate Laspeyre's and Paasche's price index numbers for the year 1991 from the following data :*

Commodity	*1981*		*1991*	
	Quantity (in kg)	*Price (in Rs.)*	*Quantity (in kg)*	*Price (in Rs.)*
Wheat	*60*	*1.00*	*50*	*1.25*
Rice	*25*	*1.50*	*20*	*2.50*
Sugar	*10*	*2.00*	*10*	*3.00*
Ghee	*3*	*12.00*	*4*	*18.00*
Fuel	*40*	*0.10*	*60*	*0.15*

Sol. **Calculation of Index Nos. (1981 = 100)**

Commodity	p_0	q_0	p_1	q_1	p_0q_0	p_1q_1	p_0q_1	p_1q_0
Wheat	1.00	60	1.25	50	60.0	62.5	50.0	75.0
Rice	1.50	25	2.50	20	37.5	50.5	30.0	62.5
Sugar	2.00	10	3.00	10	20.0	30.0	20.0	30.0
Ghee	12.00	3	18.00	4	36.0	72.0	48.0	54.0
Fuel	0.10	40	0.15	60	4.0	9.0	6.0	6.0
Total					157.5	223.5	154.0	227.5

$$\text{Laspeyre's price index number} = \frac{\Sigma p_1q_0}{\Sigma p_0q_0} \times 100 = \frac{227.5}{157.5} \times 100 = \mathbf{144.44.}$$

$$\text{Paasche's price index number} = \frac{\Sigma p_1q_1}{\Sigma p_0q_1} \times 100 = \frac{223.5}{154.0} \times 100 = \mathbf{145.13.}$$

Example 2. *Calculate Fisher's Ideal Index No. from the following informations and also give three reversibility tests :*

Item	*Base Year*		*Current Year*	
	Price	*Quantity*	*Price*	*Quantity*
A	*2*	*4*	*6*	*5*
B	*4*	*5*	*8*	*4*
C	*6*	*2*	*9*	*3*
D	*8*	*1*	*6*	*2*
E	*10*	*1*	*5*	*2*

(KU 2001)

Sol. **Calculation of Index Number**

Item	p_0	q_0	p_1	q_1	p_0q_0	p_1q_1	p_0q_1	p_1q_0
A	2	4	6	5	8	30	10	24
B	4	5	8	4	20	32	16	40
C	6	2	9	3	12	27	18	18
D	8	1	6	2	8	12	16	6
E	10	1	5	2	10	10	20	5
Total					58	111	80	93

Fisher's price index number

$$= \sqrt{\frac{\Sigma p_1q_0}{\Sigma p_0q_0} \times \frac{\Sigma p_1q_1}{\Sigma p_0q_1}} \times 100 = \sqrt{\frac{93}{58} \times \frac{11}{80}} \times 100 = \mathbf{149.16.}$$

The reversibility tests : Time Reversal Test, Factor Reversal Test and Circular Tests are discussed in the section "Test of adequacy of index numbers".

Example 3. *Calculate Paasche's index number and Fisher's ideal index number for the year 1995 from the following data :*

Commodity	*1992*		*1995*	
	Price	*Quantity*	*Price*	*Quantiy*
A	*6*	*50*	*10*	*56*
B	*2*	*100*	*2*	*120*
C	*4*	*60*	*6*	*60*
D	*10*	*30*	*12*	*24*
E	*8*	*40*	*12*	*36*

Sol. **Calculation of Index Nos. (1992 = 100)**

Commodity	p_0	q_0	p_1	q_1	p_0q_0	p_1q_1	p_0q_1	p_1q_0
A	6	50	10	56	300	560	336	500
B	2	100	2	120	200	240	240	200
C	4	60	6	60	240	360	240	360
D	10	30	12	24	300	288	240	360
E	8	40	12	36	320	432	288	480
Total					1360	1880	1344	1900

Paasche's price index number $= \frac{\Sigma p_1q_1}{\Sigma p_0q_1} \times 100 = \frac{1880}{1344} \times 100 = \mathbf{139.88.}$

Fisher's price index number $= \sqrt{\frac{\Sigma p_1q_0}{\Sigma p_0q_0} \times \frac{\Sigma p_1q_1}{\Sigma p_0q_1}} \times 100$

$$= \sqrt{\frac{1900}{1360} \times \frac{1880}{1344}} \times 100 = \mathbf{139.79.}$$

Example 4. *Construct index numbers of price for the year 1994 from the following data by applying :*

1. Laspeyre's method *2. Paasche's method*
3. Bowley's method *4. Fisher's method*
5. Marshall Edgeworth's method

Commodity	*1993*		*1994*	
	Price	*Quantity*	*Price*	*Quantity*
A	*2*	*8*	*4*	*6*
B	*5*	*10*	*6*	*5*
C	*4*	*14*	*5*	*10*
D	*2*	*19*	*2*	*13*

Sol. **Calculation of Index Nos. (1993 = 100)**

Commodity	p_0	q_0	p_1	q_1	p_0q_0	p_1q_1	p_0q_1	p_1q_0
A	2	8	4	6	16	24	12	32
B	5	10	6	5	50	30	25	60
C	4	14	5	10	56	50	40	70
D	2	19	2	13	38	26	26	38
Total					160	130	103	200

Laspeyre's price index number $= \dfrac{\Sigma p_1q_0}{\Sigma p_0q_0} \times 100 = \dfrac{200}{160} \times 100 = \mathbf{125.}$

Paasche's price index number $= \dfrac{\Sigma p_1q_1}{\Sigma p_0q_1} \times 100 = \dfrac{130}{103} \times 100 = \mathbf{126.21}$

Bowley's price index number

$$= \frac{\left(\dfrac{\Sigma p_1q_0}{\Sigma p_0q_0} + \dfrac{\Sigma p_1q_1}{\Sigma p_0q_1}\right)}{2} \times 100 = \frac{\left(\dfrac{200}{160} + \dfrac{130}{103}\right)}{2} \times 100 = \mathbf{125.607.}$$

Fisher's price index number

$$= \sqrt{\frac{\Sigma p_1q_0}{\Sigma p_0q_0} \times \frac{\Sigma p_1q_1}{\Sigma p_0q_1}} \times 100 = \sqrt{\frac{200}{160} \times \frac{130}{103}} \times 100 = \mathbf{125.605.}$$

Marshall Edgeworth's price index number

$$= \frac{\Sigma p_1(q_0 + q_1)}{\Sigma p_0(q_0 + q_1)} \times 100 = \frac{\Sigma p_1q_0 + \Sigma p_1q_1}{\Sigma p_0q_0 + \Sigma p_0q_1} \times 100$$

$$= \frac{200 + 130}{160 + 103} \times 100 = \mathbf{125.47.}$$

Example 5. *Prepare the index number for 1982 on the basis of 1962 for the following data :*

Year	Commodity A		Commodity B		Commodity C	
	Price	Expenditure	Price	Expenditure	Price	Expenditure
1962	5	50	8	48	6	24
1982	4	48	7	49	5	15

Sol. We calculate price index number for the year 1982 by using **Fisher's method.**

Calculation of Index Number

Commodity	1962			1982			p_0q_1	p_1q_0
	p_0	p_0q_0	q_0	p_1	p_1q_1	q_1		
A	5	50	10	4	48	12	60	40
B	8	48	6	7	49	7	56	42
C	6	24	4	5	15	3	18	20
Total		122			112		134	102

Fisher's price index number

$$= \sqrt{\frac{\Sigma p_1q_0}{\Sigma p_0q_0} \times \frac{\Sigma p_1q_1}{\Sigma p_0q_1}} \times 100 = \sqrt{\frac{102}{122} \times \frac{112}{134}} \times 100 = \mathbf{83.59.}$$

Example 6. *Calculate the weighted price index number for 2000 for the following data :*

Material required	*Unit*	*Quantity required*	*Price during*	
			1999 Rs.	*2000* Rs.
A	*100 kg*	*500 kg*	5	8
B	*mt*	*2000 mt*	9.5	14.2
C	*kg*	*50 kg*	34	42.2
D	*litre*	*20 litres*	12	24

Sol. Here we shall use **Kelly's method** because quantities are fixed irrespective of base and current years.

Calculation of Index Number (1999 = 100)

Material	p_0	p_1	q	p_0q	p_1q
A	5	8	$\frac{500}{100} = 5$	25	40
B	9.5	14.2	2000	19000	28400
C	34	42.2	50	1700	2110
D	12	24	20	240	480
Total				20965	31030

Kelly's price index number $= \frac{\Sigma p_1 q}{\Sigma p_0 q} \times 100 = \frac{31030}{20965} \times 100 = \mathbf{148.}$

Example 7. *Construct an index number for the following data using weighted average (A.M. and G.M.) of price relatives method :*

Commodity	*Current year prices (in Rs.)*	*Base year prices (in Rs.)*	*Weights*
A	*4*	*5*	*1*
B	*6*	*5*	*2*
C	*10*	*8*	*3*
D	*12*	*10*	*1*

Sol. Calculation of Index Numbers

Commodity	p_0	p_1	*W*	$P = \frac{p_1}{p_0} \times 100$	*log P*	*WP*	*W log P*
A	5	4	1	80	1.9031	80	1.9031
B	5	6	2	120	2.0792	240	4.1584
C	8	10	3	125	2.0969	375	6.2907
D	10	12	1	120	2.0792	120	2.0792
Total			7			815	14.4314

Price index no. by weighted A.M.

$$= \frac{\Sigma WP}{\Sigma W} = \frac{815}{7} = \mathbf{116.43.}$$

Price index no. by weighted G.M.

$$= \text{AL}\left(\frac{\Sigma W \log P}{\Sigma W}\right) = \text{AL}\left(\frac{14.4314}{7}\right)$$

$$= \text{AL}\,(2.0616) = \mathbf{115.3.}$$

Example 8. *Prepare Index Number from the following information for the year 1980 taking the prices of 1975 as base :*

	Commodity			
	Wheat	*Rice*	*Gram*	*Pulse*
Price 1975	*10*	*5*	*2*	*2*
Price 1980	*12*	*7*	*3*	*4*

Give weights to above commodities as 4, 3, 2, 1 respectively.

Sol. **Calculation of Index Number**

Commodity	p_0	p_1	*W*	$P = \frac{p_1}{p_0} \times 100$	*WP*
Wheat	10	12	4	120	480
Rice	5	7	3	140	420
Gram	2	3	2	150	300
Pulse	2	4	1	200	200
Total			10		1400

$\therefore$ Price index no. by weighted A.M. $= \frac{\Sigma WP}{\Sigma W} = \frac{1400}{10} =$ **140.**

Example 9. *Show that Fisher's price index number lies between Laspeyre's and Paasche's price index numbers.*

Sol. Let L, P and F represent Laspeyre's Pasasche's and Fisher's price index numbers respectively.

$$\therefore \quad L = \frac{\Sigma p_1 q_0}{\Sigma p_0 q_0} \times 100, \; P = \frac{\Sigma p_1 q_1}{\Sigma p_0 q_1} \times 100 \quad \text{and} \quad F = \sqrt{\frac{\Sigma p_1 q_0}{\Sigma p_0 q_0} \times \frac{\Sigma p_1 q_1}{\Sigma p_0 q_1}} \times 100$$

$$\sqrt{LP} = \sqrt{\frac{\Sigma p_1 q_0}{\Sigma p_0 q_0} \times 100 \times \frac{\Sigma p_1 q_1}{\Sigma p_0 q_1} \times 100} = \sqrt{\frac{\Sigma p_1 q_0}{\Sigma p_0 q_0} \times \frac{\Sigma p_1 q_1}{\Sigma p_0 q_1}} \times 100 = F.$$

Also, L, P, F are positive numbers.

Let $\quad L < P.$

$\therefore \quad L < P \Rightarrow LL < LP \Rightarrow \sqrt{LL} < \sqrt{LP} \Rightarrow L < F$

Also, $\quad L < P \Rightarrow LP < PP \Rightarrow \sqrt{LP} < \sqrt{PP} \Rightarrow F < P$

$\therefore \quad$ **L < F < P.**

EXERCISE 2

1. From the following data calculate price index by using :
   (*i*) Laspeyre's method
   (*ii*) Paasche's method.

Commodity	*Base year*		*Current year*	
	Quantity	*Price*	*Quantity*	*Price*
A	20	4	30	6
B	40	5	60	7
C	60	3	70	4
D	30	2	50	3

2. Calculate price index numbers for the year 1990, by using the following methods :

(*i*) Laspeyre's method (*ii*) Paasche's method

(*iii*) Bowley's method (*iv*) Fisher's method

(*v*) Marshall's method.

Commodity	*1989*		*1990*	
	Price	*Quantity*	*Price*	*Quantity*
A	20	8	40	6
B	50	10	60	5
C	40	15	50	15
D	20	20	20	25

3. Apply Fisher's method and calculate the price index number for 1995 from the following data :

Commodity	*1994*		*1995*	
	p_0	q_0	p_1	q_1
A	10	4	12	3
B	15	6	20	5
C	2	5	5	6
D	4	4	4	4

4. Compute price index number by using Fisher's method.

Commodity	*Base year*		*Current year*	
	Price	*Quantity*	*Price*	*Quantity*
A	10	12	12	15
B	7	15	5	20
C	5	24	9	20
D	16	5	14	5

5. Compute Fisher's ideal price index number for 1994 for the following data :

Commodity	*1993*		*1994*	
	Price per unit	*Expenditure*	*Price per unit*	*Expenditure*
A	5	125	6	180
B	10	50	15	90
C	2	30	3	60
D	3	36	5	75

(*MDU 1995*)

6. From the following data construct a price index number of the group of four commodities by using an appropriate formula :

Commodity	Base year		Current year	
	Price per unit	*Expenditure (in Rs.)*	*Price per unit*	*Expenditure (in Rs.)*
A	2	40	5	75
B	4	16	8	40
C	1	10	2	24
D	5	25	10	60

7. Use the data given below and calculate Fisher's ideal price index number for the year 1993 with 1990 as base :

Commodity	Unit	Price (in Rs.)		Quantity	
		1990	*1993*	*1990*	*1993*
Wheat	Quintal	90	100	20	25
Potatoes	Kilogram	1	1.20	100	130
Tomatoes	Kilogram	1	1.30	50	40

8. Calculate weighted aggregative price index number taking 1992 as base, from the following data :

Commodity	*Quantity consumed in 1992*	*Units*	*Price in Base year 1992*	*Price in current year 1997*
Wheat	4 Qtls	per Qtl	80	100
Rice	1 Qtl	per Qtl	120	250
Gram	1 Qtl	per Qtl	100	150
Pulses	2Qtls	per Qtl	200	300

9. Construct Fisher's and Marshall's price index numbers by using the following data :

Commodity	*Base year price*	*Base year quantity*	*Current year price*	*Current year quantity*
A	12	100	20	120
B	4	200	4	240
C	8	120	12	120
D	20	60	24	48
E	16	80	24	52

10. The prices of four different commodities for 1995 and 1996 are given below. Calculate the price index number for 1996 with 1989 as base, by using weighted A.M. of price relatives :

Commodity	*Weight*	*Price in 1995 (in Rs.)*	*Price in 1996 (in Rs.)*
A	5	4.5	2.0
B	7	3.2	2.5
C	6	4.5	3.0
D	2	1.8	1.0

11. Calculate weighted average of price relative index number from the following data :

Item	*Unit*	*Base Year Quantity*	*Base Year Price (Rs.)*	*Current Year Price (Rs.)*
Wheat	Per qnt	4 qnt	200	250
Sugar	Per kg	50 kg	5	7
Milk	Per litre	50 litre	5	6
Cloth	Per metre	20 metre	10	15
House	Per house	1	50	80

12. From the following data, find price index number for the year 2002 : *(KU 2001 C)*

Item	*Price per unit*		*Value*
	2001	*2002*	*(2001)*
A	Rs. 13.75	Rs. 13.75	Rs. 8364
B	Rs. 9.70	Rs. 9.70	Rs. 2207
C	Rs. 6.03	Rs. 8.00	Rs. 876
D	Rs. 466.00	Rs. 433.00	Rs. 701
E	Rs. 1.25	Rs. 1.75	Rs. 534

13. It is stated that Marshal Edge worth index number is a good approximation to the Fisher's index number. Verify this by using the following data :

Item	*1999*		*2001*	
	Price	*Quantity*	*Price*	*Quantity*
A	2	74	3	82
B	5	125	4	140
C	7	40	6	33

14. Given the data :

Commodity

	A	*B*
p_0	1	1
q_0	10	5
p_1	2	x
q_1	5	2

where p and q respectively stand for price and quantity and subscripts stand for time periods. Find x if the ratio between Laspeyre's (L) and Paasche's (P) index numbers is L : P : : 28 : 27.

Answers

1. (*i*) 140.38	(*ii*) 141.14	2. 124.699, 121.769, 123.234, 123.225, 123.323	
3. 135.4	4. 115.75	5. 137.11	
6. Fisher's price index no. = 219.12		7. 111.98	8. 148.94
9. 139.729, 139.728	10. 64.01	11. 130.9	12. 103.53
14. 4			

16. CHAIN BASE METHOD

In this method of computing index numbers, link relatives are required. The prices of commodities in the current period are expressed as the percentages of their prices in the preceding period. These are called **link relatives.**

Mathematically,

$$\textbf{Link Relative (L.R.)} = \frac{\textbf{Price in current period}}{\textbf{Price in preceding period}} \times 100$$

If there are more than one commodity under consideration then averages of link relatives (A.L.R.) are calculated for each period. Generally A.M. is used for averaging link relatives. These averages of link relatives (A.L.R.) for different time periods are called **chain index numbers.** The chain index number of a particular period represent the index number of that period with preceding period as the base period. This would be so except for this first period.

These chain indices can further be used to get index numbers for various periods with a particular period as the base period. These index numbers are called **chain index numbers chained to a fixed base.**

For calculating these index numbers, the following formula is used :

$$\textbf{C.B.I. for current period (Base fixed)}$$
$$= \frac{\textbf{A. L. R. for current period} \times \textbf{C. B. I. for preceding period (Base fixed)}}{100}$$

There are certain advantages of using this method. By using chain base method, comparison is possible between any two successive periods. The average of link relatives represent the index number with preceding period as the base period. This characteristic of chain base index numbers benefit businessmen to a good extent. In calculating chain base index number, some items can be introduced or withdrawned during any period. In practice, the chain base index numbers are used only in those circumstances, where the list of items changes very frequently.

Example 1. *From the following data, find index numbers with 1998 as base by using (i) fixed base method (ii) chain base method :*

Year	*1998*	*1999*	*2000*	*2001*	*2002*
Price per unit (in Rs.)	*40*	*50*	*60*	*75*	*120*

Sol. **Calculation of index numbers (1998 = 100)**

Year	*p*	*F.B.I.*	*Link Relative*	*C.B.I.*
1998	40	100	100	100
1999	50	$\frac{50}{40} \times 100 = \mathbf{125}$	$\frac{50}{40} \times 100 = 125$	$\frac{125 \times 100}{100} = \mathbf{125}$
2000	60	$\frac{60}{40} \times 100 = \mathbf{150}$	$\frac{60}{50} \times 100 = 120$	$\frac{120 \times 125}{100} = \mathbf{150}$
2001	75	$\frac{75}{40} \times 100 = \mathbf{187.5}$	$\frac{75}{60} \times 100 = 125$	$\frac{125 \times 150}{100} = \mathbf{187.5}$
2002	120	$\frac{120}{40} \times 100 = \mathbf{300}$	$\frac{120}{75} \times 100 = 160$	$\frac{160 \times 187.5}{100} = \mathbf{300}$

∴ F.B.I. for 1999, 2000, 2001, 2002 with base 1998 are **125, 150, 187.5, 300** respectively.

C.B.I. for 1999, 2000, 2001, 2002 with base 1998 are **125, 150, 187.5, 300** respectively.

Remark. If there is only one series then F.B.I. and C.B.I. with fix base are always same.

Example 2. *Calculate the fixed base index numbers and chain base index numbers from the following data. Are the two results same ? If not, why ?*

Commodity	*Price (in rupees)*				
	1986	*1987*	*1988*	*1989*	*1990*
X	2	3	5	7	8
Y	8	10	12	4	18
Z	4	5	7	9	12

(KU 1997)

Sol. **Calculation of F.B.I. (1996 = 100)**

Commodity	*Price Relatives*				
	1986	*1987*	*1988*	*1989*	*1990*
X	100	$\frac{3}{2} \times 100 = 150$	$\frac{5}{2} \times 100 = 250$	$\frac{7}{2} \times 100 = 350$	$\frac{8}{2} \times 100 = 400$
Y	100	$\frac{10}{8} \times 100 = 125$	$\frac{12}{8} \times 100 = 150$	$\frac{4}{8} \times 100 = 50$	$\frac{18}{8} \times 100 = 225$
Z	100	$\frac{5}{4} \times 100 = 125$	$\frac{7}{4} \times 100 = 175$	$\frac{9}{4} \times 100 = 225$	$\frac{12}{4} \times 100 = 300$
Total	300	400	575	625	925
Average of P.R or F.B.I. (1986 = 100)	100	$\frac{400}{3} = \mathbf{133.33}$	$\frac{575}{3} = \mathbf{191.67}$	$\frac{625}{3} = \mathbf{208.33}$	$\frac{925}{3} = \mathbf{308.33}$

∴ F.B.I. for years 1987, 1988, 1989, 1990 with base 1986 are **133.33, 191.67, 208.33, 308.33** respectively.

Calculation of C.B.I. (1986 = 100)

Commodity	*Link Relatives*				
	1986	*1987*	*1988*	*1989*	*1990*
X	100	$\frac{3}{2} \times 100 = 150$	$\frac{5}{3} \times 100 = 166.67$	$\frac{7}{5} \times 100 = 140$	$\frac{8}{7} \times 100 = 114.29$
Y	100	$\frac{10}{8} \times 100 = 125$	$\frac{12}{10} \times 100 = 120$	$\frac{4}{12} \times 100 = 33.33$	$\frac{18}{4} \times 100 = 450$
Z	100	$\frac{5}{4} \times 100 = 125$	$\frac{7}{5} \times 100 = 140$	$\frac{9}{7} \times 100 = 128.57$	$\frac{12}{9} \times 100 = 133.33$
Total	300	400	426.67	301.9	697.62
Average of L.R. or C.B.I.	100	$\frac{400}{3} = 133.33$	$\frac{426.67}{3} = 142.22$	$\frac{301.9}{3} = 100.643$	$\frac{697.62}{3} = 232.54$
C.B.I. (1986 = 100)	100	$\frac{133.33 \times 100}{100}$ **= 133.33**	$\frac{142.22 \times 133.33}{100}$ **= 189.62**	$\frac{100.63 \times 189.62}{100}$ **= 190.81**	$\frac{232.54 \times 190.81}{100}$ **= 443.71**

$\therefore$ C.B.I. for years 1987, 1988, 1989, 1990 with base 1986 are **133.33, 189.62, 190.81, 443.71** respectively.

Example 3. *The average wholesale prices of three groups of commodities for the years 1988 to 1992 are given below. Compute chain base index numbers with 1988 as base :*

Group	*1988*	*1989*	*1990*	*1991*	*1992*
I	*6*	*9*	*15*	*21*	*24*
II	*24*	*30*	*36*	*42*	*54*
III	*12*	*15*	*21*	*27*	*36*

(KU 2000 C)

Sol. **Calculation of C.B.I. (1988 = 100)**

Group	*Link Relatives*				
	1988	*1989*	*1990*	*1991*	*1992*
I	100	$\frac{9}{6} \times 100 = 150$	$\frac{15}{9} \times 100 = 166.67$	$\frac{21}{15} \times 100 = 140$	$\frac{24}{21} \times 100 = 114.29$
II	100	$\frac{30}{24} \times 100 = 125$	$\frac{36}{30} \times 100 = 120$	$\frac{42}{36} \times 100 = 116.67$	$\frac{54}{42} \times 100 = 128.57$
III	100	$\frac{15}{12} \times 100 = 125$	$\frac{21}{15} \times 100 = 140$	$\frac{27}{21} \times 100 = 128.57$	$\frac{36}{27} \times 100 = 133.33$
Total	300	400	426.67	385.24	376.19
Average of L.R. or C.B.I.	100	$\frac{400}{3} = 133.33$	$\frac{426.67}{3} = 142.22$	$\frac{385.24}{3} = 128.41$	$\frac{376.19}{3} = 125.40$
C.B.I. (1988 = 100)	100	$\frac{133.33 \times 100}{100}$ **= 133.33**	$\frac{142.22 \times 133.33}{100}$ **= 189.62**	$\frac{128.41 \times 189.62}{100}$ **= 243.49**	$\frac{125.40 \times 243.49}{100}$ **= 305.34**

∴ C.B.I. for years 1989, 1990, 1991, 1992 with base 1988 are **133.33, 189.62, 243.49, 305.34** respectively.

Example 4. *The following table gives the average wholesale prices of three groups of commodities for the years 1991 to 1995. Compute chain base index numbers chained to 1991.*

Group	*Year*				
	1991	*1992*	*1993*	*1994*	*1995*
I	*4*	*6*	*8*	*10*	*12*
II	*16*	*20*	*24*	*30*	*36*
III	*8*	*10*	*16*	*20*	*24*

Sol. **Calculation of C.B.I. (1991 = 100)**

Group	*Link Relatives*				
	1991	*1992*	*1993*	*1994*	*1995*
I	100	$\frac{6}{4} \times 100 = 150$	$\frac{8}{6} \times 100 = 133.33$	$\frac{10}{8} \times 100 = 125$	$\frac{12}{10} \times 100 = 120$
II	100	$\frac{20}{16} \times 100 = 125$	$\frac{24}{20} \times 100 = 120$	$\frac{30}{24} \times 100 = 125$	$\frac{36}{30} \times 100 = 120$
III	100	$\frac{10}{8} \times 100 = 125$	$\frac{16}{10} \times 100 = 160$	$\frac{20}{16} \times 100 = 125$	$\frac{24}{20} \times 100 = 120$
Total	300	400	413.33	375	360
Average of L.R. of C.B.I.	100	$\frac{400}{3} = 133.33$	$\frac{413.33}{3} = 137.78$	$\frac{375}{3} = 125$	$\frac{360}{3} = 120$
C.B.I. (1991 = 100)	100	$\frac{133.33 \times 100}{100}$ = **133.33**	$\frac{137.78 \times 133.33}{100}$ = **183.70**	$\frac{125 \times 183.70}{100}$ = 229.62	$\frac{120 \times 229.62}{100}$ = **275.54**

∴ C.B.I. for years 1992, 1993, 1994, 1995 with base 1991 are **133.33, 183.70, 229.62, 275.54** respectively.

Example 5. *Construct, by chain base method, index number of prices in Kanpur on base 1990, for the following data :*

Commodity	*Year*			
	1990	*1991*	*1992*	*1993*
Rice	*7.5*	*8.0*	*6.0*	*5.5*
Wheat	*8.0*	*6.0*	*5.5*	*5.0*
Pulses	*7.0*	*8.0*	*6.5*	*5.5*
Gur	*6.5*	*7.5*	*6.0*	*5.0*
Cotton	*34.0*	*30.0*	*28.0*	*25.0*

Sol. **Calculation of C.B.I. (1990 = 100)**

Commodity	Link Relatives			
	1990	*1991*	*1992*	*1993*
Rice	100	$\frac{8}{7.5} \times 100 = 106.67$	$\frac{6}{8} \times 100 = 75$	$\frac{5.5}{6} \times 100 = 91.67$
Wheat	100	$\frac{6}{8} \times 100 = 75$	$\frac{5.5}{6} \times 100 = 91.67$	$\frac{5}{5.5} \times 100 = 90.91$
Pulses	100	$\frac{8}{7} \times 100 = 114.29$	$\frac{6.5}{8} \times 100 = 81.25$	$\frac{5.5}{6.5} \times 100 = 84.61$
Gur	100	$\frac{7.5}{6.5} \times 100 = 115.38$	$\frac{6}{7.5} \times 100 = 80$	$\frac{5}{6} \times 100 = 83.33$
Cotton	100	$\frac{30}{34} \times 100 = 88.23$	$\frac{28}{30} \times 100 = 93.33$	$\frac{25}{28} \times 100 = 89.29$
Total	500	499.57	421.25	439.81
A.L.R. or C.B.I.	100	$\frac{499.5}{3} = 99.91$	$\frac{421.25}{3} = 84.25$	$\frac{439.81}{3} = 87.96$
C.B.I. (1990 = 100)	100	$\frac{99.91 \times 100}{100} = \mathbf{99.91}$	$\frac{84.25 \times 99.91}{100} = \mathbf{84.17}$	$\frac{87.96 \times 84.17}{100} = \mathbf{74.04}$

∴ C.B.I. for years 1991, 1992, 1993 with base 1990 are **99.91, 84.17, 74.04** respectively.

EXERCISE 3

1. From the following data, find index numbers with 1996 as base by using (*i*) fixed base method (*ii*) chain base method. Verify that the index numbers are same :

Year	*1996*	*1997*	*1998*	*1999*	*2000*	*2001*	*2002*
Price per unit (in Rs.)	5	7	10	8	15	12	17

2. From the following average prices of the groups of commodities given in rupees per unit, find chain base index numbers with 1988 as the base year :

Group	*1988*	*1989*	*1990*	*1991*	*1992*
Ist	2	3	4	5	6
IInd	8	10	12	15	18
IIIrd	4	5	8	10	12

3. Compute the fixed base index numbers and chain base index numbers with 1982 as base, for the following data :

Commodity	*Price (in Rs.)*				
	1982	*1983*	*1984*	*1985*	*1986*
A	2	3	6	6	9
B	10	10	10	15	15
C	4	6	12	15	18

4. Calculate the chain base index numbers chained to 1997 from the average prices of following commodities :

Commodity	*1997*	*1998*	*1999*	*2000*	*2001*
Rice	16	20	24	30	36
Sugar	8	10	16	20	24
Wheat	4	6	8	10	12

(*KU 2006*)

5. The following table gives the average wholesale prices of three groups of commodities for the year 1993 to 1996. Compute chain base index number chained to 1993.

Group	*Year*			
	1993	*1994*	*1995*	*1996*
I	400	400	550	600
II	225	400	300	350
III	400	400	425	500

6. Compute chain base index number for 1996 with 1993 as base, by using the following data :

Commodity	*Year*			
	1993	*1994*	*1995*	*1996*
Sugar (Price per kg)	6.4	6.5	6	6.5
Gur (Price per kg)	4	3.7	4	4.5

Answers

1. 100, 140, 200, 160, 300, 240, 340
2. 100, 133.33, 183.70, 229.62, 275.54
3. 100, 133.33, 233.33, 275, 350 ; 100, 133.33, 222.22, 277.77, 342.57
4. 100, 133.33, 183.7, 229.63, 275.56
5. 100, 125.93, 133.80, 153.16
6. 107.03.

II. QUANTITY INDEX NUMBERS

17. METHODS

Quantity index numbers are used to show the average change in the quantities of related goods with respect to time. These index numbers are also used to measure the level of production. In computing quantiy index numbers, either prices or values are used as weights.

Let Q_{01} denotes the quantity index number for the current period. The formulae for calculating quantity index numbers are obtained by interchanging the role of 'p' and 'q' in the formulae for computing price index numbers. Various methods for computing quantity index numbers are as follows :

1. Simple Aggregative Method

$$Q_{01} = \frac{\Sigma q_1}{\Sigma q_0} \times 100.$$

2. Simple Average of Quantity Relative Method

$$Q_{01} = \frac{\Sigma Q}{n} \qquad \text{(Using A.M.)}$$

$$= \text{Antilog}\left(\frac{\Sigma \log Q}{n}\right) \qquad \text{(Using G.M.)}$$

where $\quad Q = \text{quantity relative} = \frac{q_1}{q_0} \times 100.$

3. Laspeyre's Method

$$Q_{01} = \frac{\Sigma q_1 p_0}{\Sigma q_0 p_0} \times 100.$$

4. Paasche's Method

$$Q_{01} = \frac{\Sigma q_1 p_1}{\Sigma q_0 p_1} \times 100.$$

5. Dorbish and Bowley's Method

$$Q_{01} = \frac{\left(\frac{\Sigma q_1 p_0}{\Sigma q_0 p_0} + \frac{\Sigma q_1 p_1}{\Sigma q_0 p_1}\right)}{2} \times 100.$$

6. Fisher's Ideal Method

$$Q_{01} = \sqrt{\frac{\Sigma q_1 p_0}{\Sigma q_0 p_0} \times \frac{\Sigma q_1 p_1}{\Sigma q_0 p_1}} \times 100.$$

7. Marshall Edgeworth's Method

$$Q_{01} = \frac{\Sigma q_1 (p_0 + p_1)}{\Sigma q_0 (p_0 + p_1)} \times 100.$$

8. Kelly's Method

$$Q_{01} = \frac{\Sigma q_1 p}{\Sigma q_0 p} \times 100.$$

9. Weighted Average of Quantity Relative Method

$$Q_{01} = \frac{\Sigma WQ}{\Sigma W} \qquad \text{(Using A.M.)}$$

$$= \text{Antilog}\left(\frac{\Sigma W \log Q}{\Sigma W}\right) \qquad \text{(Using G.M.)}$$

10. Chain Base Method

Here also, we define chain base quantity index numbers for a period as the average of link relatives (L.R.) for that particular period. These chain indices can be used to obtain quantity index numbers with a common base.

In all the above formulae, suffixes '0' and '1' stand for base period and current period respectively and

p_1 = current period price of an item

p_0 = base period price of an item

q_1 = current period quantity of an item

q_0 = base period quantity of an item

Q = quantity relative of an item = $\frac{q_1}{q_0} \times 100$

W = value weight for an item

p = price of an item in a fixed period

n = no. of item under consideration.

18. INDEX NUMBERS OF INDUSTRIAL PRODUCTION

The indices of industrial production are calculated by using the methods of quantity index numbers. In the formulae for quantity index numbers, we shall take *production* in place of quantities.

Example 1. *From the following data, construct the index of industrial production for the year 1996 and 1997 by the methods :*

(i) Simple aggregative method.

(ii) Simple A.M. of production relatives.

(iii) Simple G.M. of production relatives.

Commodity	*Annual Production*		
	1995	*1996*	*1997*
A	*20,000 units*	*25,000 units*	*26,000 units*
B	*4,000 units*	*5,000 units*	*4,000 units*
C	*7,000 units*	*7,000 units*	*12,000 units*

Sol. Let the suffixes 0, 1, 2 refer to the data relating to years 1995, 1996 and 1997 respectively.

Calculation of Index Numbers

Commodity	*Annual Production*			*Production Relatives*			
	q_0	q_1	q_1	$Q_1 = \frac{q_1}{q_0} \times 100$	$Q_2 = \frac{q_2}{q_0} \times 100$	*log* Q_1	*log* Q_2
A	20,000	25,000	26,000	125	130	2.0969	2.1139
B	4,000	5,000	4,000	125	100	2.0969	2.0000
C	7,000	7,000	12,000	100	171.43	2.0000	2.2340
Total	31,000	37,000	42,000	350	401.43	6.1938	6.3479

(*i*) Index of industrial production of 1996 with base 1995

$$= Q_{01} = \frac{\Sigma q_1}{\Sigma q_0} \times 100 = \frac{37000}{31000} \times 100 = \mathbf{119.35}$$

Index of industrial production of 1997 with base 1995

$$= Q_{02} = \frac{\Sigma q_2}{\Sigma q_0} \times 100 = \frac{42000}{31000} \times 100 = \mathbf{135.48.}$$

(*ii*) Index of industrial production of 1996 with base 1995

$$= Q_{01} = \frac{\Sigma Q_1}{n} = \frac{350}{3} = \mathbf{116.67}$$

Index of industrial production of 1997 with base 1995

$$= Q_{02} = \frac{\Sigma Q_2}{n} = \frac{401.43}{3} = \mathbf{133.81.}$$

(*iii*) Index of industrial production of 1996 with base 1995

$$= Q_{01} = \text{AL}\left(\frac{\Sigma \log Q_1}{n}\right) = \text{AL}\left(\frac{6.1938}{3}\right) = \text{AL}\ (2.0646) = \mathbf{116.10}$$

Index of industrial production of 1997 with base 1995

$$= Q_{02} = \text{AL}\left(\frac{\Sigma \log Q_2}{n}\right) = \text{AL}\left(\frac{6.3479}{3}\right) = \text{AL}\ (2.1160) = \mathbf{130.60.}$$

Example 2. *Calculate the quantity index number for 1986 by using Fisher's formula for the following data :*

Commodity	*1995*		*1996*	
	Price	*Quantity*	*Price*	*Quantity*
A	6	70	8	120
B	8	90	10	100
C	12	140	16	280

Sol. Calculation of Fisher's Quantity Index No. (1995 = 100)

Commodity	p_0	q_0	p_1	q_1	q_0p_0	q_1p_1	q_0p_1	q_1p_0
A	6	70	8	120	420	960	560	720
B	8	90	10	100	720	1000	900	800
C	12	140	16	280	1680	4480	2240	3360
Total					2820	6440	3700	4880

Fisher's quantity index number $= \sqrt{\dfrac{\Sigma q_1p_0}{\Sigma q_0p_0} \times \dfrac{\Sigma q_1p_1}{\Sigma q_0p_1}} \times 100$

$$= \sqrt{\frac{4880}{2820} \times \frac{6440}{3700}} \times 100 = \mathbf{173.55.}$$

Example 3. *From the following data, construct quantity index numbers for 1986, by using the following methods :*

(i) Simple aggregative method
(ii) Laspeyre's method
(iii) Paasche's method
(iv) Dorbish and Bowley's method
(v) Fisher's method
(vi) Marshall Edgeworth's method

Commodity	*1995*		*1996*	
	Price	*Value*	*Price*	*Value*
A	8	80	10	110
B	10	90	12	108
C	16	256	20	340

Sol. Calculation of Quantity Index Nos. (1995 = 100)

Commodity	p_0	*Value* q_0p_0	q_0	p_1	*Value* q_1p_1	q_1	q_1p_0	q_0p_1
A	8	80	10	10	110	11	88	100
B	10	90	9	12	108	9	90	108
C	16	256	16	20	340	17	272	320
Total		426	35		558	37	450	528

(i) Q_{01} by simple aggregative method

$$= \frac{\Sigma q_1}{\Sigma q_0} \times 100 = \frac{37}{35} \times 100 = \mathbf{105.71}$$

(ii) Laspeyre's quantity index no.

$$= \frac{\Sigma q_1 p_0}{\Sigma q_0 p_0} \times 100 = \frac{450}{426} \times 100 = \mathbf{105.63}$$

(iii) Paasche's quantity index no.

$$= \frac{\Sigma q_1 p_1}{\Sigma q_0 p_1} \times 100 = \frac{558}{528} \times 100 = \mathbf{105.68}$$

(iv) Dorbish and Bowley's quantity index no.

$$= \frac{\left(\frac{\Sigma q_1 p_0}{\Sigma q_0 p_0} + \frac{\Sigma q_1 p_1}{\Sigma q_0 p_1}\right)}{2} \times 100 = \frac{\left(\frac{450}{426} + \frac{558}{528}\right)}{2} \times 100 = \mathbf{105.66}$$

(v) Fisher's quantity index no.

$$= \sqrt{\frac{\Sigma q_1 p_0}{\Sigma q_0 p_0} \times \frac{\Sigma q_1 p_1}{\Sigma q_0 p_1}} \times 100 = \sqrt{\frac{450}{426} \times \frac{558}{528}} \times 100 = \mathbf{105.66}$$

(*vi*) Marshall Edgeworth's quantity index no.

$$= \frac{\Sigma q_1(p_0 + p_1)}{\Sigma q_0(p_0 + p_1)} \times 100 = \frac{\Sigma q_1 p_0 + \Sigma q_1 p_1}{\Sigma q_0 p_0 + \Sigma q_0 p_1} \times 100 = \frac{450 + 558}{426 + 528} \times 100 = \mathbf{105.66.}$$

III. VALUE INDEX NUMBERS

19. SIMPLE AGGREGATIVE METHOD

The simple aggregative method of computing value index number (V_{01}) is given by

$$\mathbf{V_{01}} = \frac{\Sigma \mathbf{p_1 q_1}}{\Sigma \mathbf{p_0 q_0}} \times \mathbf{100}$$

where $\Sigma p_1 q_1$ = sum of values of items in the current period

$\Sigma p_0 q_0$ = sum of values of items in the base period.

Example 4. *Calculate value index number for 2000 for the following data :*

Item	*1998*		*2000*	
	Price	*quantity*	*Price*	*Quantity*
A	*4*	*12*	*5*	*18*
B	*8*	*15*	*12*	*10*
C	*12*	*6*	*10*	*8*
D	*5*	*10*	*5*	*12*

Sol. Calculation of value index number (1998 = 100)

Item	p_0	q_0	p_1	q_1	p_0q_0	p_1q_1
A	4	12	5	18	48	120
B	8	15	12	10	120	120
C	12	6	10	8	72	80
D	5	10	5	12	50	60
Total					290	380

Value index number $= \frac{\Sigma p_1 q_1}{\Sigma p_0 q_0} \times 100 = \frac{380}{290} \times 100 = \mathbf{131.03.}$

EXERCISE 4

1. Compute by Fisher's index formula, the quantity index number for the data given below :

Commodity	*Base year*		*Current year*	
	Price	*Total value*	*Price*	*Total value*
A	10	100	8	96
B	16	96	14	98
C	12	36	10	40

2. Compute a suitable quantity index number by using the following data :

Commodity	*Price in the base period*	*Quantity*	
		Base period	*Current period*
A	4	7	10
B	5	8	9
C	4	10	9
D	3	12	8

3. By using the following methods, calculate quantity index numbers for the year 1995 for the following data :

(*i*) Simple A.M. of quantity relatives (*ii*) Laspeyre's method
(*iii*) Paasche's method (*iv*) Dorbish's method
(*v*) Fisher's method (*vi*) Marshall's method.

Commodity	*1993*		*1995*	
	Price	*Quantity*	*Price*	*Quantity*
A	4	10	5	12
B	6	8	7	10
C	10	5	12	4
D	3	12	4	15
E	5	7	5	8

4. Construct index numbers of quantity for the given data, by using the following methods :

(*i*) Simple aggregative method
(*ii*) Fisher's method
(*iii*) Weighted average (A.M.) of quantity relatives by using base period value as weights.

Commodity	*Base year*		*Current year*	
	Price	*Quantity*	*Price*	*Quantity*
A	2	8	4	6
B	5	10	6	5
C	4	14	5	10
D	2	19	2	13

5. Calculate quantity index numbers for the given data, by using the following methods :

(*i*) Dorbish's method (*ii*) Fisher's method
(*iii*) Marshall's method.

Item	*Base year*		*Current year*	
	Price per unit	*Quantity*	*Price per unit*	*Quantity*
A	5	7	7	4
B	3	2	4	3
C	1	5	1	5
D	4	4	3	6
E	2	8	2	10
F	1	2	2	6
G	4	5	6	4

6. Using Paasche's formula, compute the quantity index number and the price index number for 2000 with 1999 as base year :

Commodity	*Quantity Units*		*Value in (Rs.)*	
	1999	*2000*	*1999*	*2000*
A	100	150	500	900
B	80	100	320	500
C	60	72	150	360
D	30	33	360	297

For the above problem, also compute price index number by :
(*i*) Dorbish-Bowley Method (*ii*) Fisher's method
(*iii*) Marshall-Edworth method.

7. Calculate value index number for the following data :

Commodity	*Base year*		*Current year*	
	Price	*Quantity*	*Price*	*Quantity*
A	2	8	4	6
B	5	10	6	5
C	4	14	5	10
D	2	19	2	13

Answers

1. 120.654 2. 100.694
3. 112.857, 111.483, 111.647, 111.565, 111.565, 111.572
4. 66.667, 64.687, 64.375 5. 97.984, 97.963, 97.768
6. 131.02, 119.18 (*i*) 118.61 (*ii*) 118.61 (*iii*) 118.62 7. 81.25.

20. MEAN OF INDEX NUMBERS

If $I_1, I_2, \ldots\ldots, I_n$ are the index numbers of n groups of related items, then the index numbers of all the items of n groups taken together is calculated by taking the average of these index numbers. Generally, A.M. is used for averaging the index numbers. If weights are attached with different index numbers, then weighted A.M. is to be calculated.

Let I be the index number of all the items of n groups taken together, then

$$I = \frac{I_1 + I_2 + \ldots. + I_n}{n} \quad i.e., \quad \mathbf{I} = \frac{\Sigma \mathbf{I}}{\mathbf{n}}.$$

If $W_1, W_2, \ldots\ldots, W_n$ be the weights of index numbers $I_1, I_2, \ldots\ldots, I_n$ respectively, then

$$I = \frac{W_1 I_1 + W_2 I_2 + \ldots. + W_n I_n}{W_1 + W_2 + \ldots. + W_n} \quad \text{or} \quad \mathbf{I} = \frac{\Sigma \mathbf{WI}}{\Sigma \mathbf{W}}.$$

If G.M. is to be used for finding index number of combined group, then

$$I = AL\left(\frac{W_1 \log I_1 + W_2 \log I_2 + \ldots. + W_n \log I_n}{W_1 + W_2 + \ldots. + W_n}\right) \quad \text{or} \quad \mathbf{I} = \mathbf{AL}\left(\frac{\Sigma \mathbf{W} \log \mathbf{I}}{\mathbf{SW}}\right).$$

Example 1. *Construct the index number of business activity in India for the following data :*

Item	*Weightage*	*Index*
(i) Industrial Production	*36*	*250*
(ii) Mineral Production	*7*	*135*
(iii) Internal Trade	*24*	*200*
(iv) Financial Activity	*20*	*135*
(v) Exports and Imports	*7*	*325*
(vi) Shipping Activity	*6*	*300*

Sol. **Calculation of Index No. of Business Activity**

Item	*Weightage W*	*Index I*	*WI*
(*i*) Industrial Production	36	250	9000
(*ii*) Mineral Production	7	135	945
(*iii*) Internal Trade	24	200	4800
(*iv*) Financial Activity	20	135	2700
(*v*) Exports and Imports	7	325	2275
(*vi*) Shipping Activity	6	300	1800
Total	100		21520

$$\text{Index No. of combined group} = \frac{\Sigma WI}{\Sigma W} = \frac{21520}{100} = \mathbf{215.2.}$$

Example 2. *A textile worker in the city of Bombay earns Rs. 350 a month. The cost of living index for a particular month is given as 136. Using the following data, find out the amount he spends on clothings and house rent.*

Group	*Food*	*Clothing*	*House rent*	*Fuel*	*Misc.*
Expenditure	*140*	*?*	*?*	*56*	*63*
Group Index	*180*	*150*	*100*	*110*	*80*

Sol. Let '*a*' and '*b*' denote the expenditure on clothing and house rent respectively.

Group	*Expenditure W*	*Group Index I*	*WI*
Food	140	180	25200
Clothing	a	150	$150a$
House rent	b	100	$100b$
Fuel	56	110	6160
Misc.	63	80	5040
Total	$259 + a + b = 350$		$36400 + 150a + 100b$

Now $\quad 259 + a + b = 350$

$\therefore \quad a + b = 350 - 259 = 91$

$\therefore \quad b = 91 - a.$

Now, cost of living index $= \frac{\Sigma WI}{\Sigma W}$

$$\therefore \quad 136 = \frac{36400 + 150a + 100b}{350}$$

$$\therefore \quad 47600 = 36400 + 150a + 100(91 - a)$$

$$\therefore \quad 11200 = 150a + 9100 - 100a$$

$$\therefore \quad 2100 = 50a$$

$$\therefore \quad a = \mathbf{42}$$

$$\therefore \quad b = 91 - a = 91 - 42 = \mathbf{49}.$$

Example 3. *Calculate the index number of crime for 1994 with 1993 as base.*

Crime group	*1993*	*1994*	*Weight*
Robberies	*13*	*8*	*6*
Car thefts	*15*	*22*	*5*
Cycle thefts	*249*	*185*	*4*
Pocket picking	*328*	*259*	*1*
Thefts by servants	*497*	*448*	*2*

Sol. Calculation of Index No. of Crime

Crime group	C_0	C_1	*W*	$I = \frac{C_1}{C_0} \times 100$	*WI*
Robberies	13	8	6	61.54	369.24
Car thefts	15	22	5	146.67	733.35
Cycle thefts	249	185	4	74.30	297.20
Pocket picking	328	259	1	78.96	78.96
Thefts by servants	497	448	2	90.14	180.28
Total			18		1659.03

Index No. of combined group $= \frac{\Sigma WI}{\Sigma W} = \frac{1659.03}{18} = \mathbf{92.17}.$

EXERCISE 5

1. Construct index number of combined group for the following data :

Group	*A*	*B*	*C*	*D*	*E*
Index No.	110	95	160	170	200
Weight	4	2	1	1	2

2. The following are the group index numbers and group weights of an average working class family's budget. Construct the cost of living index.

Group	*Food*	*Fuel*	*Clothing*	*Rent*	*Misc.*
Index Nos.	352	220	230	160	190
Weight	48	10	8	12	15

3. Find the index number of combined group for the following data :

Group	*A*	*B*	*C*	*D*	*E*	*F*
Index No.	125	142	118.7	92	169	157
% of Weightage	25	15	10	12	13	25

4. From the following data relating to working class consumers of a city, calculate index numbers for 1993 and 1995.

Group	*Weight*	*Group Index*	
		1993	*1995*
Food	48	110	130
Clothing	8	120	125
Fuel	7	110	120
House rent	13	100	100
Miscellaneous	14	115	135

5. The combined index number for the following data is 138.858. You are required to find the group index for the group 'D'.

Group	A	B	C	D	E	F
Index No.	135	152	124	?	107	139
Weight	61	73	19	41	26	82

Answers

1. 136 2. 276.409 3. 136.68 4. 110.222, 125.222
5. 148

IV TESTS OF ADEQUACY OF INDEX NUMBER FORMULAE

21. MEANING

We have studied a large number of methods of constructing index numbers. Statisticians have developed certain mathematical criterion for deciding the superiority of one method over others. The following are the tests for judging the adequacy of a particular index number method :

(*i*) Unit Test.
(*ii*) Time Reversal Test.
(*iii*) Factor Reversal Test.
(*iv*) Circular Test.

22. UNIT TEST (U.T.)

An index number method is said to satisfy **unit test** if it is not changed by a change in the measuring units of some items, under consideration. All methods, except simple aggregative method, satisfies this test.

23. TIME REVERSAL TEST (T.R.T.)

An index numbers method is said to satisfy **time reversal test,** if

$$I_{01} \times I_{10} = 1$$

where I_{01} and I_{10} are the index numbers for two periods with base period and current period reversed. Here the index numbers I_{01} and I_{10} are not expressed as percentages.

The following methods of constructing index numbers satisfies this test :

(*i*) Simple Aggregative Method.

(*ii*) Simple G.M. of Price (or Quanity) Relatives Method.

(*iii*) Fisher's Method.

(*iv*) Marshall Edgeworth's Method.

(*v*) Kelly's Method.

Now, we shall illustrate this test by verifying its validity for Fisher's price index number method.

We have $$P_{01} = \sqrt{\frac{\Sigma p_1q_0}{\Sigma p_0q_0} \times \frac{\Sigma p_1q_1}{\Sigma p_0q_1}} \quad \text{and} \quad P_{10} = \sqrt{\frac{\Sigma p_0q_1}{\Sigma p_1q_1} \times \frac{\Sigma p_0q_0}{\Sigma p_1q_0}}$$

where P_{01} and P_{10} are the price index numbers for the periods t_1 and t_0 with base periods t_0 and t_1 respectively.

Now $$P_{01} \times P_{10} = \sqrt{\frac{\Sigma p_1q_0}{\Sigma p_0q_0} \times \frac{\Sigma p_1q_1}{\Sigma p_0q_1}} \times \sqrt{\frac{\Sigma p_0q_1}{\Sigma p_1q_1} \times \frac{\Sigma p_0q_0}{\Sigma p_1q_0}}$$

$$= \sqrt{\frac{\Sigma p_1q_0}{\Sigma p_0q_0} \times \frac{\Sigma p_1q_1}{\Sigma p_0q_1} \times \frac{\Sigma p_0q_1}{\Sigma p_1q_1} \times \frac{\Sigma p_0q_0}{\Sigma p_1q_0}} = \sqrt{1} = 1.$$

$\therefore$ $P_{01} \times P_{10} = 1.$

Example 1. *Calculate price index number for the year 1996 from the following data. Use geometric mean of price relatives. Also reverse the base (1996 as base) and show whether the two results are consistent or not.*

Commodity	*Average price 1990 (Rs.)*	*Average Price 1996 (Rs.)*
A	*16.1*	*14.2*
B	*9.2*	*8.7*
C	*15.1*	*12.5*
D	*5.6*	*4.8*
E	*11.7*	*13.4*
F	*100*	*117*

(MDU 2000)

Sol. **Index No. for 1996**

Commodity	p_0	p_1	$P = \frac{p_1}{p_0} \times 100$	$\log P$
A	16.1	14.2	$\frac{14.2}{16.1} \times 100 = 80.20$	1.9455
B	9.2	8.7	$\frac{8.7}{9.2} \times 100 = 94.57$	1.9757
C	15.1	12.5	$\frac{12.5}{15.1} \times 100 = 82.78$	1.9179
D	5.6	4.8	$\frac{4.8}{5.6} \times 100 = 85.71$	1.9331
E	11.7	13.4	$\frac{13.4}{11.7} \times 100 = 114.53$	2.0589
F	100	117	$\frac{117}{100} \times 100 = 117$	1.0682
$n = 6$				$\Sigma \log P = 11.8993$

$\therefore$ Price index no. for 1996 = $\text{AL}\left(\frac{\Sigma \log P}{n}\right) = \text{AL}\left(\frac{11.8993}{6}\right) = \text{AL } 1.9832 =$ **96.20.**

Index No. for 1990

Commodity	p_0	p_1	$P = \frac{p_1}{p_0} \times 100$	$\log P$
A	14.2	16.1	$\frac{16.1}{14.2} \times 100 = 113.38$	2.0547
B	8.7	9.2	$\frac{9.2}{8.7} \times 100 = 105.75$	2.0244
C	12.5	15.1	$\frac{15.1}{12.5} \times 100 = 120.80$	2.0820
D	4.8	5.6	$\frac{5.6}{4.8} \times 100 = 116.67$	2.0671
E	13.4	11.7	$\frac{11.7}{13.4} \times 100 = 87.31$	1.9410
F	117	100	$\frac{100}{117} \times 100 = 85.47$	1.9319
$n = 6$				$\Sigma \log P = 12.1011$

$\therefore$ Price index no. for 1990 = $\text{AL}\left(\frac{\Sigma \log P}{n}\right) = \text{AL}\left(\frac{12.1011}{6}\right) = \text{AL } 2.0169 = 104.$

Product of index numbers = 96.20 × 104 = 10004.8 = 10000 (nearly)

Since the index numbers are expressed as percentages, the T.R.T. is satisfied if their products is $(100)^2$, which is 10000.

$\therefore$ The index numbers are consistent.

24. FACTOR REVERSAL TEST (F.R.T.)

An index number method is said to satisfy **factor reversal test** if the product of price index number and quantity index number, as calculated by the same method, is equal to the value index number.

In other words, if P_{01} and Q_{01} are the price index number and quantity index number for the period t_1 corresponding to base period t_0, then we must have

$$P_{01} \times Q_{01} = V_{01} = \frac{\Sigma p_1 q_1}{\Sigma p_0 q_0}$$

Fisher's index number method is *the only method* which satisfies this test.

Let P_{01} and Q_{01} be the Fisher's price index number and quantity index numbers respectively, then

$$P_{01} = \sqrt{\frac{\Sigma p_1 q_0}{\Sigma p_0 q_0} \times \frac{\Sigma p_1 q_1}{\Sigma p_0 q_1}} \quad \text{and} \quad Q_{01} = \sqrt{\frac{\Sigma q_1 p_0}{\Sigma q_0 p_0} \times \frac{\Sigma q_1 p_1}{\Sigma q_0 p_1}}.$$

Now $$P_{01} \times Q_{10} = \sqrt{\frac{\Sigma p_1 q_0}{\Sigma p_0 q_0} \times \frac{\Sigma p_1 q_1}{\Sigma p_0 q_1}} \times \sqrt{\frac{\Sigma q_1 p_0}{\Sigma q_0 p_0} \times \frac{\Sigma q_1 p_1}{\Sigma q_0 p_1}}$$

$$= \sqrt{\frac{\Sigma p_1 q_0}{\Sigma p_0 q_0} \times \frac{\Sigma p_1 q_1}{\Sigma p_0 q_1} \times \frac{\Sigma q_1 p_0}{\Sigma q_0 p_0} \times \frac{\Sigma q_1 p_1}{\Sigma q_0 p_1}}$$

$$= \sqrt{\frac{\Sigma p_1 q_0}{\Sigma p_0 q_0} \times \frac{\Sigma p_1 q_1}{\Sigma p_0 q_1} \times \frac{\Sigma p_0 q_1}{\Sigma p_0 q_0} \times \frac{\Sigma p_1 q_1}{\Sigma p_1 q_0}} = \sqrt{\frac{\Sigma p_1 q_1 \times \Sigma p_1 q_1}{\Sigma p_0 q_0 \times \Sigma p_0 q_0}} = \frac{\Sigma p_1 q_1}{\Sigma p_0 q_0}$$

= Value index number.

$\therefore$ **Fisher's method satisfies this test.**

25. CIRCULAR TEST (C.T.) *(MDU 2000)*

An index number method is said to satisfy the **circular test** if $I_{01}, I_{12}, I_{23}, \ldots\ldots, I_{n-1n}$ and I_{n0} are the index numbers for the periods $t_1, t_2, t_3, \ldots\ldots, t_n, t_0$ corresponding to base periods $t_0, t_1, t_2, \ldots\ldots, t_{n-1}, t_n$ respectively, then

$$I_{01} \times I_{12} \times I_{23} \times \ldots\ldots \times I_{n-1n} \times I_{n0} = 1.$$

Here, also, the index numbers have not been expressed as percentages by multiplying by 100.

If n = I, we have $I_{01} \times I_{10} = 1$.

This is nothing but the condition of T.R.T. Thus, we see that the circular test is an extension of T.R.T.

If $n = 2$, we have

$$I_{01} \times I_{12} \times I_{20} = 1 \quad \text{or} \quad I_{01} \times I_{12} = I_{02}. \qquad (\because \; I_{02} \times I_{20} = 1)$$

The following methods satisfies circular test :

(*i*) Simple Aggregative Method.

(*ii*) Simple G.M. of Price (or Quantity) Relatives Method.

(*iii*) Kelly's Method.

Now, we shall illustrate this test by verifying its validity for simple aggregative method for price index numbers.

Here $P_{01} = \frac{\Sigma p_1}{\Sigma p_0}, P_{12} = \frac{\Sigma p_2}{\Sigma p_1}, P_{20} = \frac{\Sigma p_0}{\Sigma p_2}$.

$$\therefore \quad P_{01} \times P_{12} \times P_{20} = \frac{\Sigma p_1}{\Sigma p_0} \times \frac{\Sigma p_2}{\Sigma p_1} \times \frac{\Sigma p_0}{\Sigma p_2} = 1.$$

∴ Simple aggregative method satisfies this test.

Example 2. *With the help of following data show that Fisher's ideal index satisfies time and factor reversal tests.*

Commodity	*1993*		*1994*	
	Price	*Value*	*Price*	*Value*
A	*8*	*80*	*10*	*100*
B	*10*	*20*	*12*	*36*
C	*5*	*25*	*5*	*30*
D	*4*	*16*	*8*	*40*

(KU 1998)

Sol. Let suffixes '0' and '1' refers to data for periods 1993 and 1994 respectively.

Verification of T.R.T. and F.R.T. for Fisher's Method

Commodity	p_0	p_0q_0	p_1	p_1q_1	q_0	q_1	p_1q_0	p_0q_1
A	8	80	10	100	10	10	100	80
B	10	20	12	36	2	3	24	30
C	5	25	5	30	5	6	25	30
D	4	16	8	40	4	5	32	20
Total		141		206			181	160

Verification of T.R.T.

P_{01} = Fisher's price index number for 1994 with base 1993 (= 1)

$$= \sqrt{\frac{\Sigma p_1q_0}{\Sigma p_0q_0} \times \frac{\Sigma p_1q_1}{\Sigma p_0q_1}} = \sqrt{\frac{181}{141} \times \frac{206}{160}} = 1.28559$$

P_{10} = Fisher's price index number for 1993 with base 1994 (= 1)

$$= \sqrt{\frac{\Sigma p_0q_1}{\Sigma p_1q_1} \times \frac{\Sigma p_0q_0}{\Sigma p_1q_0}} = \sqrt{\frac{160}{206} \times \frac{141}{181}} = 0.77785.$$

Now $P_{01} \times P_{10} = 1.28559 \times 0.77785 = 0.9999961 = 1$ (nearly).

∴ T.R.T. is verified.

Verification. of F.R.T.

P_{01} = Fisher's price index number for 1994 with base 1993 (= 1)

$$= \sqrt{\frac{\Sigma p_1q_0}{\Sigma p_0q_0} \times \frac{\Sigma p_1q_1}{\Sigma p_0q_1}} = \sqrt{\frac{181}{141} \times \frac{206}{160}} = 1.28559$$

Q_{01} = Fisher's quantity index number for 1994 with base 1993 (= 1)

$$= \sqrt{\frac{\Sigma q_1 p_0}{\Sigma q_0 p_0} \times \frac{\Sigma q_1 p_1}{\Sigma q_0 p_1}} = \sqrt{\frac{\Sigma p_0 q_1}{\Sigma p_0 q_0} \times \frac{\Sigma p_1 q_1}{\Sigma p_1 q_0}} = \sqrt{\frac{160}{141} \times \frac{206}{181}} = 1.13643.$$

V_{01} = Value index number for 1994 with base 1993 (= 1)

$$= \frac{\Sigma V_1}{\Sigma V_0} = \frac{\Sigma p_1 q_1}{\Sigma p_0 q_0} = \frac{206}{141} = 1.46099.$$

Now, $P_{01} \times Q_{01} = 1.28559 \times 1.13643 = 1.46098 = V_{01}$ (nearly).

$\therefore$ F.R.T. is verified.

Example 3. *Construct Fisher's Ideal Index number from the following data and show that it satisfies the factor reversal test :*

Year	*Article A*		*Article B*		*Article C*	
	Price	*Quantity*	*Price*	*Quantity*	*Price*	*Quantity*
1975	*16*	*4*	*4*	*4*	*2*	*2*
1982	*30*	*3.5*	*14*	*1.5*	*6*	*2.5*

(KU 1998 C)

Sol. Let suffixes '0' and '1' refers to data for the periods 1975 and 1982 respectively.

Calculation of Fisher's Index Numbers

Article	p_0	q_0	p_1	q_1	p_0q_0	p_1q_1	p_1q_0	p_0q_1
A	16	4	30	3.5	64	105	120	56
B	4	4	14	1.5	16	21	56	6
C	2	2	6	2.5	4	15	12	5
Total					84	141	188	67

Now, Fisher's Ideal index number

$$= P_{01} = \sqrt{\frac{\Sigma p_1 q_0}{\Sigma p_0 q_0} \times \frac{\Sigma p_1 q_1}{\Sigma p_0 q_1}} \times 100 = \sqrt{\frac{188}{84} \times \frac{141}{67}} \times 100 = \mathbf{217.03}$$

Verification of F.R.T.

P_{01} = Fisher's price index no. for 1982 with base 1975 (= 1)

$$= \frac{217.03}{100} = 2.1703$$

Q_{01} = Fisher's quantity index number for 1982 with base 1975 (= 1)

$$= \sqrt{\frac{\Sigma q_1 p_0}{\Sigma q_0 p_0} \times \frac{\Sigma q_1 p_1}{\Sigma q_0 p_1}} = \sqrt{\frac{67}{84} \times \frac{141}{188}} = 0.7734 \qquad \text{(Not as \%)}$$

V_{01} = Value index number of 1982 with base 1975 (= 1)

$$= \frac{\Sigma V_1}{\Sigma V_0} = \frac{\Sigma p_1 q_1}{\Sigma p_0 q_0} = \frac{141}{84} = 1.6786 \qquad \text{(Not as \%)}$$

Now, $P_{01} \times Q_{01} = 2.1703 \times 0.7734 = 1.6785 = V_{01}$ (nearly)

$\therefore$ F.R.T. is verified.

EXERCISE 6

1. Compute Fisher's ideal index number for the following data and show that it satisfies time reversal test and factor reversal test.

Commodity	*1989*		*1990*	
	Price	*Quantity*	*Price*	*Quantity*
A	4	40	5	50
B	8	64	9	80
C	10	70	10	70
D	2	10	4	16

2. Find Fisher's price index from the following data and show how does it satisfy the time reversal tests :

Item	*2003 (Base Year)*		*2004 (Current Year)*	
	Price	*Expenditure*	*Price*	*Expenditure*
A	5	50	4	48
B	8	48	7	49
C	6	24	5	15

(*KU 2006*)

3. Prove using the following data that time reversal test and factor reversal test are satisfied by Fisher's Ideal Formula for Index Numbers :

Commodity	*2004*		*2003*	
	Price	*Value*	*Price*	*Value*
A	10	120	8	80
B	12	96	10	120
C	5	50	5	40
D	3	60	4	56
E	25	150	20	100

(*KU 2007*)

4. Show with the help of the following data that the time reversal test and factor reversal test are satisfied by Fisher's Ideal formula for index number construction :

Commodity	*Base year*		*Current year*	
	Price (Rs.)	*Quantity (kg.)*	*Price (Rs.)*	*Quantity (kg.)*
A	8	500	10	600
B	2	1000	4	800
C	6	600	8	500
D	10	300	12	400
E	4	800	2	1000

5. Verify the 'factor reversal test' by using the following data :

Item	1993		1994	
	Price per unit	*Expenditure*	*Price per unit*	*Expenditure*
A	5	125	6	180
B	10	50	15	90
C	2	30	3	60
D	3	36	5	75

(MDU 1995)

6. By using the given data show that Fisher's method of computing index numbers satisfies T.R.T. and F.R.T.

Item	1993		1995	
	Price	*Value*	*Price*	*Value*
A	4	12	7	21
B	60	120	65	195
C	11	44	9	36
D	27	108	30	90
E	12	72	20	100
F	25	100	20	100

7. With the help of data gaiven below, compute Fisher's Ideal Index and show that it satisfies the time reversal and factor reversal tests.

Commodity	1996 (Base year)		2002 (Current year)	
	Price (Rs.)	*Qty.*	*Price (Rs.)*	*Qty.*
A	40	30	60	20
B	50	40	60	40
C	70	20	90	20
D	20	30	10	50

(KU 2002)

V. CONSUMER PRICE INDEX NUMBERS (C.P.I.)

26. MEANING

There is no denying the fact that the rise or fall in the prices of commodities affect every family. But, this effect is not same for every family because different families consume different commodities and in different quantities. Car is not found is every house. Milk is used in almost every family but there are very few families who can afford to purchase even more than 5 litres of it, daily.

The index numbers which measures the effect of rise or fall in the prices of various goods and services, consumed by a particular group of people are called **consumer price**

index numbers for that particular group of people. The consumer price index numbers help in estimating the average change in the cost of maintaining particular standard of living by a particular class of people.

27. SIGNIFICANCE OF C.P.I.

(*i*) The consumer price index numbers are used in deflating money income to real income. Money income is divided by a proper consumer price index number to obtain real income.

(*ii*) The consumer price index numbers are used in wage fixation and automatic increase in wages. Generally, escalator clauses are provided for automatic increase in wages in accordance with increase in consumer price index number.

(*iii*) The consumer price index numbers are used by the planning commission for framing rent policy, taxation policy, price policy etc.

28. ASSUMPTIONS

The consumer price index numbers are computed under certain assumptions. These assumptions are as follows :

(*i*) It is assumed that the quantities of different goods and services consumed are same for base period and current period.

(*ii*) It is assumed that the prices of commodities are approximately same in the region covered by the consumer price index number.

(*iii*) It is assumed that the commodities used in preparing C.P.I. are used in equal quantities in every family in the region covered by the index number.

(*iv*) It is assumed that the families in the region covered by the C.P.I. are of same economic standard. Their demands are common.

These are very strong assumptions and cannot be fully met in practical life. That is why, the C.P.I. for a region will not be exactly true for every family covered by the index number.

29. PROCEDURE

The first step in computing consumer price index number is to decide the category of people for whom the index is to be computed. While fixing the domain of the index, the income and occupation of families must be taken in to consideration. Different families consume different commodities and that too in different quantities. For a particular category of people, it can be expected that their expenditure on different commodities will be almost same.

For computing index, enquiry is made about the expenditure of families on various commodities. The commodities are generally classified in the following heads :

(*a*) Food

(*b*) Clothing

(*c*) Fuel and lighting

(*d*) House rent

(*e*) Miscellaneous.

After the decision about commodities is taken, the next step is to collect prices of these commodities. The price quotations must be obtained from that market, from where the concerned class of people purchase commodities. The price quotations must be absolutely free from the personal bias of the agent obtaining price quotations. The price quotations must preferably be cross checked in order to eliminate any possibility of personal bias.

All the commodities which are used by a particular class of people cannot be expected to have equal importance. For example, entertainment and house rent can not be given equal weightage. Weights are taken in accordance with the consumption in the base period. Either base period quantities or base period expenditure on different items are generally used as weights for constructing C.P.I. The base period selected for this purpose must also be normal.

30. METHODS

There are two methods of computing consumer price index numbers.

(*i*) Aggregate expenditure method.

(*ii*) Family budget method.

31. AGGREGATE EXPENDITURE METHOD

In this method, generally base period quantities are used as weights.

$$\textbf{Consumer Price Index No.} = \frac{\Sigma p_1 q_0}{\Sigma p_0 q_0} \times 100$$

where '0' and '1' suffixes stand for base period and current period respectively.

$\Sigma p_1 q_0$ = sum of the products of the prices of commodities in the current period with their corresponding quantities used in the base period.

$\Sigma p_0 q_0$ = sum of the products of the prices of commodities in the base period with their corresponding quantities used in the base period.

Sometimes, current period quantities are also used for finding consumer price index numbers.

Example 1. *Calculate weighted average of price relative index number from the following data :*

Item	*Unit*	*Base year quantity*	*Base year Price (Rs.)*	*Current year Price (Rs.)*
Wheat	*Per Qtl*	*4 Qtl*	200	250
Sugar	*Per kg*	*50 kg*	5	7
Milk	*Per litre*	*50 litres*	5	6
Cloth	*Per meter*	*20 metres.*	10	15
House	*Per house*	*1*	50	80

(KU 2001 C)

Sol. **Calculation of Cost of Living Index Number**

Item	q_0	p_0	p_1	p_0q_0	p_1q_0
Wheat	4	200	250	800	1000
Sugar	50	5	7	250	350
Milk	50	5	6	250	300
Cloth	20	10	15	200	300
House	1	50	80	50	80
Total				1550	2030

$$\text{Cost of living index number} = \frac{\Sigma p_1 q_0}{\Sigma p_0 q_0} \times 100 = \frac{2030}{1550} \times 100 = \mathbf{130.97.}$$

Example 2. *Calculate the cost of living index from the following data by using aggregate expenditure method.*

Item	*Quantity consumed in the given year*	*Price in base year*	*Price in given year*
Rice	$2\frac{1}{2}$ *Qtl. × 12*	*12*	*25*
Pulses	*3 kg × 12*	*0.4*	*0.6*
Oil	*2 kg × 12*	*1.5*	*2.2*
Clothing	*6 mt. × 12*	*0.75*	*1*
Housing		*20 P.M.*	*30 P.M.*
Miscellaneous		*10 P.M.*	*15 P.M.*

Sol. Calculation of Cost of Living Index Number

Item	q_1	p_0	p_1	p_1q_1	p_0q_1
Rice	30	12	25	750	360
Pulses	36	0.4	0.6	21.6	14.4
Oil	24	1.5	2.2	52.8	36
Clothing	72	0.75	1.0	72	54
Housing	12	20	30	360	240
Miscellaneous	12	10	15	180	120
Total				1436.4	824.4

$$\text{Cost of living index no.} = \frac{\Sigma p_1 q_1}{\Sigma p_0 q_1} \times 100 = \frac{1436.4}{824.4} \times 100 = \mathbf{174.24.}$$

32. FAMILY BUDGET METHOD

In this method, the expenditure on different commodities in the base period, are used as weights.

$$\textbf{Consumer Price Index No.} = \frac{\Sigma PW}{\Sigma W}$$

where $P = \text{Price relative} = \frac{p_1}{p_0} \times 100.$

p_0, p_1 refers to prices of commodities in the base period and current period respectively.

$W = p_0 q_0.$

$$\text{We have C.P.I.} = \frac{\Sigma PW}{\Sigma W} = \frac{\Sigma\left(\frac{p_1}{p_0} \times 100\right) p_0 q_0}{p_0 q_0} = \frac{\Sigma(p_1 \times 100) q_0}{\Sigma p_0 q_0} = \frac{\Sigma p_1 q_0}{\Sigma p_0 q_0} \times 100.$$

Therefore, the C.P.I. calculated by using both methods would be same. Family budget method is particularly used when the expenditures on various items used in the base period are given on percentage basis.

Example 3. *An enquiry into the budgets of middle class families in a certain city gave the following information :*

Item	*% of total Expenditure*	*Price in 2000 (in Rs.)*	*Price in 2002 (in Rs.)*
Food	*35%*	*150*	*145*
Fuel	*10%*	*25*	*23*
Clothing	*20%*	*75*	*65*
Rent	*15%*	*30*	*30*
Miscellaneous	*20%*	*40*	*45*

What is the cost of living index number of 2002 as compared with 2000 ? (KU 2004)

Sol. Calculation of C.P.I. by Family Budget Method

Item	p_0	p_1	$P = \frac{p_1}{p_0} \times 100$	*W*	*PW*
Food	150	145	96.67	35	3383.45
Fuel	25	23	92	10	920
Clothing	75	65	86.67	20	1733.4
Rent	30	30	100	15	1500
Miscellaneous	40	45	112.5	20	2250
Total				100	9786.85

$$\text{Consumer Price Index No.} = \frac{\Sigma PW}{\Sigma W} = \frac{9786.85}{100} = \mathbf{97.865.}$$

Example 4. *The cost of living index for the working class families in 1988 was 168.12. The retail price indices with base 1984 = 100 and the percentages of family expenditure in 1984 are given below. Find the retail price for the rent, fuel and light group :*

Group	*% of Family Expenditure in 1984*	*Retail Price I in 1988 (1984 = 100)*
Food	*40*	*132*
Rent, Fuel and Light	*18*	*?*
Clothing	*9*	*210*
Miscellaneous	*33*	*200*

Sol. Let 'x' be the retail price index for rent, fuel and light group :

Group	*% of Family Expenditure W*	*Retail Price Index I*	*IW*
Food	40	132	5280
Rent, Fuel and Light	18	x	$18x$
Clothing	9	210	1890
Miscellaneous	33	200	6600
Total	100		$13770 + 18x$

$$\text{Cost of living index for 1938} = \frac{\Sigma IW}{\Sigma W}$$

$$\therefore \quad 168.12 = \frac{13770 + 18x}{100}$$

$$\therefore \quad 16812 = 13770 + 18x$$

$$\therefore \quad x = \frac{16812 - 13770}{18} = \mathbf{169.}$$

Example 5. *The group indices and corresponding weights for the working class cost of living index numbers in an industrial city for the years 1989 and 1990 are given below :*

Group	*Weight*	*Group Index for 1989*	*Group Index for 1990*
Food	*71*	*370*	*380*
Clothing	*3*	*423*	*504*
Fuel	*9*	*469*	*336*
House rent	*7*	*110*	*116*
Miscellaneous	*10*	*279*	*283*

Compute the cost of living index numbers for the years 1989 and 1990. If a worker was getting Rs. 3,000 per month in 1989, do you think that he should be given some extra allowance so that he can maintain his 1989 standard of living ? If so, what should be the minimum amount of this extra allowance ?

Sol. Calculation of Cost of Living Indices for 1989 and 1990

Group	*Weight* W	*1989* I	IW	*1990* I	IW
Food	71	370	26270	380	26980
Clothing	3	423	1296	504	1512
Fuel	9	469	4221	336	3024
House rent	7	110	770	116	812
Miscellaneous	10	279	2790	283	2830
Total	100		35320		35158

$$\text{Cost of living index for 1989} = \frac{\Sigma IW}{\Sigma W} = \frac{35320}{100} = \mathbf{353.20}$$

$$\text{Cost of living index for 1990} = \frac{\Sigma IW}{\Sigma W} = \frac{35158}{100} = \mathbf{351.58.}$$

The worker should not be given any extra allowance, because the cost of living index has not increased in 1990.

Example 6. *From the following data relating to working class consumer price index of a city, calculate index numbers for 1999 and 2001.*

Group	*Food*	*Clothing*	*Fuel*	*House rent*	*Misc.*
Weight	*48*	*18*	*7*	*13*	*14*
Index number 1999	*110*	*120*	*110*	*100*	*110*
Index number 2001	*130*	*125*	*120*	*100*	*135*

The wages were increased by 8% in 2001. Is this increase sufficient ?

Sol. **Calculation of C.P.I. for 1999 and 2001**

Group	*Weight (W)*	*I. No. 1999 (I_1)*	*I. No. 2001 (I_2)*	*WI_1*	*WI_2*
Food	48	110	130	5280	6240
Clothing	18	120	125	2160	2250
Fuel	7	110	120	770	840
House rent	13	100	100	1300	1300
Misc.	14	110	135	1540	1890
Total	100			11050	12520

$$\text{C.P.I. for 1999} = \frac{\Sigma WI_1}{\Sigma W} = \frac{11050}{100} = \mathbf{110.5}$$

$$\text{C.P.I. for 2001} = \frac{\Sigma WI_2}{\Sigma W} = \frac{12520}{100} = \mathbf{125.2}$$

$$\%\text{ increase in C.P.I. in 2001} = \frac{125.2 - 110.5}{110.5} \times 100 = \frac{14.7}{110.5} \times 100 = 13.3\%$$

$\therefore$ **An increase of 8% in wages is insufficient to maintain the standard of living as in** 1999.

Example 7. *From the information given below, calculate the cost of living index number for 1975, with 1974 as base year by the Family Budget method :*

Item	*Quantity consumed*	*Unit*	*Price*	
			1974	*1975*
Wheat	*2 Quintals*	*Quintal*	*75*	*125*
Rice	*25 kilograms*	*kg*	*12*	*16*
Sugar	*10 kilograms*	*kg*	*12*	*16*
Ghee	*5 kilograms*	*kg*	*10*	*15*
Clothing	*25 metres*	*metre*	*4.5*	*5*
Fuel	*40 litres*	*litre*	*10*	*12*
Rent	*one house*	*one*	*25*	*40*

Sol. **Calculation of C.P.I. by Family Budget Method**

Item	*q*	p_0	p_1	$P = \frac{p_1}{p_0} \times 100$	$W = p_0q$	*WP*
Wheat	2	75	125	166.67	150	25000.50
Rice	25	12	16	133.33	300	39999.00
Sugar	10	12	16	133.33	120	15999.60
Ghee	5	10	15	150.00	50	7500.00
Clothing	25	4.5	5	111.11	112.5	12499.87
Fuel	40	10	12	120.00	400	48000.00
Rent	1	25	40	160.00	25	4000.00
Total					1157.5	152998.97

Now, consumer price index number = $\frac{\Sigma WP}{\Sigma W} = \frac{152998.97}{1157.5}$ = **132.18.**

EXERCISE 7

1. Construct the cost of living index number from the following data :

Group	*Index for 1992*	*% of Expenditure*
Food	550	46
Clothing	215	10
Fuel and Lighting	220	7
House rent	160	12
Miscellaneous	275	25

2. In the construction of a certain cost of living index number, the following group index numbers were found. Calculate the cost of living index by using weighted A.M.

Group	*Index No.*	*Weight*
Food	350	5
Fuel and Lighting	200	1
Clothing	240	1
House rent	160	1
Miscellaneous	250	2

3. Calculate the cost of living index for the following data :

Group	*Price in Base year*	*Price in Current year*	*Weight*
Food	39	47	4
Fuel	8	12	1
Clothing	14	18	3
House rent	12	15	2
Miscellaneous	25	30	1

4. The following are the group index numbers and group weights of an average working class family budget. Construct the cost of living index number by assigning the given weights :

Group	*Index No.*	*Weight*
Food	352	48
Fuel and Lighting	220	10
Clothing	230	8
House rent	160	12
Miscellaneous	190	15

5. Construct a cost of living index number from the following price relatives for the year 1985 and 1986 with 1982 as base giving weightage to the following groups in the proportion of 30, 8, 6, 4 and 2 respectively.

Group	*1982*	*1985*	*1986*
Food	100	114	116
Rent	100	115	125
Clothing	100	108	110
Fuel	100	105	104
Misc.	100	102	104

6. Construct with the help of data given below the cost of living index numbers for the years 1960 and 1961, taking 1959 as the base year :

Group	*Unit*	*Price in 1959*	*Price in 1960*	*Price in 1961*
Foodgrains	per md.	16.00	18.00	20.00
Clothing	per mt	2.00	1.80	2.20
Fuel	per md.	4.00	5.00	5.50
Electricity	per unit	0.20	0.25	0.25
House rent	per room	10.00	12.00	15.00
Miscellaneous	per unit	0.50	0.60	0.75

Give weightage to the above groups in the proportion of 6, 4, 2, 2, 4 and 2 respectively.

7. From the following data, find the cost of living index number of 1980 on the basis of 1970 by the Family budget method :

Item	*Quantity consumed*	*Unit*	*Prices*	
			1970	*1980*
Wheat	2 quintals	Qtl.	50	75
Rice	25 kilograms	Qtl.	100	120
Sugar	10 kilograms	Qtl.	80	120
Ghee (Desi)	5 kilograms	kg.	10	10
Ghee (Dalda)	5 kilograms	kg.	3	5
Oil	25 kilograms	Qtl.	200	200
Clothing	25 metres	metre	4	5
Fuel	4 quintals	Qtl.	8	10
Rent	One House	House	20	25

(KU 1996, 2005)

8. From the following figures, prepare the cost of living index number by using "Aggregate Expenditure Method".

Article	*Quantity Consumed in Base year*	*Units*	*Price in Base year 1971*	*Price in Current year 1981*
Wheat	4 Qtls.	Qtl.	100	240
Rice	1 Qtl.	Qtl.	120	300
Gram	1 Qtl.	Qtl.	80	200
Pulses.	2Qtls.	Qtl.	160	400
Ghee	50 kg.	kg.	20	40
Sugar	50 kg.	kg.	2	6
Fire-wood	5 Qtls.	Qtl.	16	40
House rent	1 House	House	50	100

9. Taking 1996 as base, construct a consumer index for the year 1998 from the following data :

Item	*Unit*	*Price (1996)*	*Price (1998)*	*Weight*
A	Kg.	0.50	0.75	10%
B	Litre	0.60	0.75	25%
C	Dozen	2.00	2.40	20%
D	Kg.	0.80	1.00	40%
E	One pair	8.00	10.00	5%

(KU 1999)

10. Construct cost of living index for 1996 based on 1990 from the following data :

Group	*Food*	*Housing*	*Clothing*	*Fuel*	*Misc.*
Index No. for 1996 (Base 1990)	122	140	112	116	106
Weight	32	10	10	6	42

(MDU 2001)

11. An enquiry into the budgets of the middle class families of a certain city revealed that on an average the percentage expenses on the different groups were :

Food 45, Rent 15, Clothing 12, Fuel 8, Miscellaneous 20.

The group index numbers for the current year as compared with a fixed base year were respectively 410, 150, 343, 248 and 285. Calculate the cost of living index number for the current year.

Mr. X was getting Rs. 7200 p.m. in the base year and Rs. 12900 p.m in the current year. State how much he ought to have received as extra allowance to maintain his former standard of living.

Answers

1. 377.85 **2.** 285 **3.** 126.16 **4.** 276.41
5. 112.24, 115.28 **6.** 112.75, 130.75 **7.** 126.75 **8.** 226.05
9. 126.50 **10.** 115.72 **11.** Rs. 10500.

VI. CHANGE OF BASE PERIOD OF INDEX NUMBERS

33. MEANING

In this section, we shall discuss different situations when the base of an index number is desired to be changed. In our discussion, we shall denote chain base index numbers by C.B.I. and fixed base index numbers by F.B.I. For C.B.I. of a certain period, the base is the preceding period. We shall discuss the following processes :

(*i*) Conversion of F.B.I. to C.B.I.

(*ii*) Conversion of C.B.I. to F.B.I.

(*iii*) Base shifting.

(*iv*) Splicing.

34. CONVERSION OF F.B.I. TO C.B.I.

In this case, a series of fixed base index numbers will be given. All these index numbers will be having a common base period. In evaluating chain base index numbers, from these fixed base index numbers, the following formula is used :

$$\textbf{C.B.I. for current period} = \frac{\textbf{F.B.I. for current period}}{\textbf{F.B.I. for preceding period}} \times \textbf{100.}$$

Example 1. *From the following fixed base index numbers, prepare chain base index numbers :*

Year	*1981*	*1982*	*1983*	*1984*	*1985*	*1986*
Index No. (1980 = 100)	*110*	*150*	*180*	*250*	*300*	*440*

Sol. **Calculation of C.B.I.**

Year	*F.B.I. (1980 = 100)*	*C.B.I.*
1981	110	110
1982	150	136.364
1983	180	120
1984	250	138.889
1985	300	120
1986	440	146.667

C.B.I. for 1981 = F.B.I. for 1981, because for 1981, preceding year and fixed base are both 1980.

$$\text{C.B.I. for 1982} = \frac{150}{110} \times 100 = \mathbf{136.364}$$

$$\text{C.B.I. for 1983} = \frac{180}{150} \times 100 = \mathbf{120}$$

$$\text{C.B.I. for 1984} = \frac{250}{180} \times 100 = \mathbf{138.889}$$

$$\text{C.B.I. for 1985} = \frac{300}{250} \times 100 = \mathbf{120}$$

$$\text{C.B.I. for 1986} = \frac{440}{300} \times 100 = \mathbf{146.667.}$$

Example 2. *Calculate chain base index numbers for the following series of fixed base index numbers :*

Year	*1981*	*1982*	*1983*	*1984*	*1985*	*1986*
Index No. (1975 = 100)	*210*	*220*	*250*	*400*	*300*	*400*

Sol. **Calculation of C.B.I.**

Year	*F.B.I. (1975 = 100)*	*C.B.I.*
1981	210	—
1982	220	104.762
1983	250	113.636
1984	400	160
1985	300	75
1986	400	133.333

C.B.I. for 1981 is the index number for 1981 with 1980 as the base year. From the given data, we cannot estimate this index number.

$$\text{C.B.I. for 1982} = \frac{220}{210} \times 100 = \mathbf{104.762}$$

$$\text{C.B.I. for 1983} = \frac{250}{220} \times 100 = \mathbf{113.636}$$

$$\text{C.B.I. for 1984} = \frac{440}{250} \times 100 = \mathbf{160}$$

$$\text{C.B.I. for 1985} = \frac{300}{400} \times 100 = \mathbf{75}$$

$$\text{C.B.I. for 1986} = \frac{400}{300} \times 100 = \mathbf{133.333.}$$

35. CONVERSION OF C.B.I. TO F.B.I.

In this case, a series of chain index numbers will be given. We know that the base period for a C.B.I. is the preceding period. We want to find the index numbers for the periods under consideration, with some common base. In evaluating F.B.I. from a given series of C.B.I., the F.B.I. for the first period is taken equal to the C.B.I. for the first period, it the period preceding the first period is to be taken as the common base for F.B.I. But, if the common base is the first period in the series, then the F.B.I. for the first period would be 100. We illustrate this point by considering the data :

Year	1982	1983	1984	1985	1986
C.B.I.	105	115	140	150	155

If the F.B.I. are to be calculated with 1982 as base, then F.B.I. for 1982 would be taken as 100. If F.B.I. for 1982 is taken as 105, then the common base for all F.B.I. would be 1981. So, the F.B.I. for the first period is taken in accordance with the fixed base. The F.B.I. for other periods are calculated by using the following formula :

F.B.I. for current period

$$= \frac{\textbf{F.B.I. of preceding period} \times \textbf{C.B.I. for current period}}{\textbf{100}}$$

Example 3. *From the following series of chain base index number, compute fixed base index numbers with 1980 as the fixed base :*

Year	*1981*	*1982*	*1983*	*1984*	*1985*	*1986*
C.B.I.	*110*	*136.364*	*120*	*138.889*	*120*	*146.667*

Sol. Calculation of F.B.I. (1980 = 100)

Year	*C.B.I.*	*F.B.I. (1980 = 100)*
1981	110	110
1982	136.364	150
1983	120	180
1984	138.889	250
1985	120	300
1986	146.667	440

F.B.I. for 1981 = C.B.I. for 1981, because for 1981, fixed base and preceding year are both 1980.

F.B.I. for 1982 $= \frac{110 \times 136.364}{100} = \mathbf{150}$

F.B.I. for 1983 $= \frac{150 \times 120}{100} = \mathbf{180}$

F.B.I. for 1984 $= \frac{180 \times 138.889}{100} = \mathbf{250}$

F.B.I. for 1985 $= \frac{250 \times 120}{100} = \mathbf{300}$

F.B.I. for 1986 $= \frac{300 \times 146.667}{100} = \mathbf{440.}$

Example 4. *From the following series of chain base index numbers, compute fixed base index numbers with 1981 as the fixed base :*

Year	*1981*	*1982*	*1983*	*1984*	*1985*	*1986*
C.B.I.	*110*	*136.364*	*120*	*138.889*	*120*	*146.667*

Sol. **Calculation of F.B.I. (1981 = 100)**

Year	*C.B.I.*	*F.B.I. (1981 = 100)*
1981	110	100
1982	136.364	136.364
1983	120	163.637
1984	138.889	227.274
1985	120	272.729
1986	146.667	400

F.B.I. for 1981 = **100** because fixed base is 1981.

$$\text{F.B.I. for 1982} = \frac{100 \times 136.364}{100} = \mathbf{136.364}$$

$$\text{F.B.I. for 1983} = \frac{136.364 \times 120}{100} = \mathbf{163.637}$$

$$\text{F.B.I. for 1984} = \frac{163.637 \times 138.889}{100} = \mathbf{227.274}$$

$$\text{F.B.I. for 1985} = \frac{227.274 \times 120}{100} = \mathbf{272.729}$$

$$\text{F.B.I. for 1986} = \frac{272.729 \times 146.667}{100} = \mathbf{400.}$$

36. BASE SHIFTING

Base shifting of index numbers means the change of base period to some other period. It is always desired that the base period is not far distant in the past. In order to keep the base period not going too distant in the past, we would have to shift the base period accordingly. We may also need this technique for comparing index numbers series with different base periods. By shifting the base of one series, we can make the base periods of both series same.

One way of shifting the base is to prepare index numbers afresh with new base period. But this is a very time consuming method. The index numbers corresponding to new base period can also be computed by using the following formula :

Index number for current period (with new base)

$$= \frac{\textbf{Index number of current period (with old base)}}{\textbf{Index number of new base period (with old base)}} \times \mathbf{100.}$$

Example 5. *Construct a new series of index numbers by shifting the base from 1980 to 1981 :*

Year	*1980*	*1981*	*1982*	*1983*	*1984*	*1985*	*1986*
Index No. (1980 = 100)	*100*	*110*	*150*	*180*	*250*	*300*	*440*

Sol. **Shifting of Base from 1980 to 1981**

Year	*Index No. (1980 = 100)*	*Index No. (1981 = 100)*
1980	100	90.909
1981	110	100
1982	150	136.364
1983	180	163.636
1984	250	227.273
1985	300	272.727
1986	440	400

Index No. for 1980 = $\frac{100}{110} \times 100 = \mathbf{90.909}$.

Index No. for 1981 = **100**.

Index No. for 1982 = $\frac{150}{110} \times 100 = \mathbf{136.364}$.

Index No. for 1983 = $\frac{180}{110} \times 100 = \mathbf{163.636}$.

Index No. for 1984 = $\frac{250}{110} \times 100 = \mathbf{227.273}$.

Index No. for 1985 = $\frac{300}{110} \times 100 = \mathbf{272.727}$.

Index No. for 1986 = $\frac{440}{110} \times 100 = \mathbf{400}$.

37. SPLICING

The process of converting two index numbers series to get one continuous series of index numbers is called **splicing.** The index numbers of the second series are spliced to first series. In other words, we can say that the spliced index numbers are nothing but the index numbers of the second series corresponding to the base period of the first series. The spliced index numbers are obtained by using the following formula :

Spliced Index No. for current period

$$= \frac{\textbf{Index No. of current period with new base} \times \textbf{Index No. of new base period with old base}}{\textbf{100}}$$

Example 6. *Construct a single series of index numbers (1975 = 100) based on two separate series given below :*

Year	*1975*	*1976*	*1977*	*1978*	*1979*	*1980*	*1981*	*1982*	*1983*	*1984*	*1985*	*1986*
Index No. (1975 = 100)	*100*	*110*	*150*	*200*	*200*	*250*	*300*	*350*	—	—	—	—
Index No. (1982 = 100)	—	—	—	—	—	—	—	*100*	*120*	*150*	*180*	*200*

Sol. **Calculation of Spliced Index Numbers**

Year	*Index No. (1975 = 100)*	*Index No. (1982 = 100)*	*Single series of Index Nos.(1975 = 100)*
1975	100	—	100
1976	110	—	110
1977	150	—	150
1978	200	—	200
1979	200	—	200
1980	250	—	250
1981	300	—	300
1982	350	100	350
1983	—	120	420
1984	—	150	525
1985	—	180	630
1986	—	200	700

$$\text{Spliced Index No. for 1983} = \frac{120 \times 350}{100} = \mathbf{420}$$

$$\text{Spliced Index No. for 1984} = \frac{150 \times 350}{100} = \mathbf{525}$$

$$\text{Spliced Index No. for 1985} = \frac{180 \times 350}{100} = \mathbf{630}$$

$$\text{Spliced Index No. for 1986} = \frac{200 \times 350}{100} = \mathbf{700.}$$

Example 7. *Given below are two sets of indices, one with 1949 as base and the other with 1957 as base :*

(a) Year	*1949*	*1950*	*1951*	*1952*	*1953*	*1954*	*1955*	*1956*	*1957*
Index Nos.	*100*	*120*	*130*	*200*	*300*	*350*	*370*	*380*	*400*
(b) Year	*1957*	*1958*	*1959*	*1960*	*1961*	*1962*	*1963*	*1964*	
Index Nos.	*100*	*110*	*90*	*98*	*101*	*110*	*98*	*96*	

It is desired to splice the second index numbers series with 1957 base to the first index number series, for the sake of continuity.

You are to prepare a combined series with 1949 as base.

Sol. Calculation of Spliced Index Numbers

Year	*Index No. (1949 = 100)*	*Index No. (1957 = 100)*	*Continuous series of index numbers (1949 = 100)*
1949	100	—	100
1950	120	—	120
1951	130	—	130
1952	200	—	200
1953	300	—	300
1954	350	—	350
1955	370	—	370
1956	380	—	380
1957	400	100	400
1958	—	110	440
1959	—	90	360
1960	—	98	392
1961	—	101	404
1962	—	110	440
1963	—	98	392
1964	—	96	384

Spliced Index No. for 1958 $= \frac{110 \times 400}{100} = \mathbf{440}$

Spliced Index No. for 1959 $= \frac{90 \times 400}{100} = \mathbf{360}$

Spliced Index No. for 1960 $= \frac{98 \times 400}{100} = \mathbf{392}$

Spliced Index No. for 1961 $= \frac{101 \times 400}{100} = \mathbf{404}$

Spliced Index No. for 1962 $= \frac{110 \times 400}{100} = \mathbf{440}$

Spliced Index No. for 1963 $= \frac{98 \times 400}{100} = \mathbf{392}$

Spliced Index No. for 1964 $= \frac{96 \times 400}{100} = \mathbf{384.}$

EXERCISE 8

1. From the fixed base index numbers given below, prepare chain base index numbers :

Year	1982	1983	1984	1985	1986
F.B.I. (1975 = 100)	267	275	280	290	320

2. From the fixed base index numbers given below, prepare chain base index numbers :

Year	1981	1982	1983	1984	1985	1986
F.B.I. (1980 = 100)	110	120	130	141	200	180

3. From the chain base index numbers given below, prepare fixed base index numbers with 1978 as base year :

Year	1979	1980	1981	1982	1983	1984
C.B.I.	94	104	104	93	103	102

4. From the chain base index numbers given below, prepare fixed base index numbers with 1979 as base year :

Year	1979	1980	1981	1982	1983	1984
C.B.I.	94	104	104	93	103	102

5. From the fixed base index numbers given below, find chain base index numbers :

Year	1976	1977	1978	1979	1980	1981
Index No.	200	220	240	250	280	300

6. Shift the base of following index numbers to 1980 :

Year	1978	1979	1980	1981	1982	1983	1984
Index No. (1978 = 100)	100	110	120	150	140	200	180

7. From the following data, find out the index numbers with 1982 as the base year :

Year	1980	1981	1982	1983	1984	1985
Index No.	100	105	100	190	200	205

8. Reconstruct the following indices using 1986 as base :

Year	1984	1985	1986	1987	1988	1989	1990
Index No.	110	130	150	175	180	200	220

9. Construct a single series of index numbers, based on two separate series with base 1956 :

Year	1956	1957	1958	1959	1960	1961	1962	1963	1964	1965
Index No. (Ist Series)	100	120	125	140	127	—	—	—	—	—
Index No. (IInd Series)	—	—	—	—	100	150	172	207	215	263

10. Construct a single series of index numbers, based on two separate series with base 1980 :

Year	1980	1981	1982	1983	1984	1985	1986
Index No. (Ist series)	100	107	119	139	—	—	—
Index No. (IInd series)	—	—	—	100	105	110	111

Answers

1. Year : 1983 1984 1985 1986
C.B.I. : 102.99 101.82 103.57 110.34

2. Year : 1981 1982 1983 1984 1985 1986
C.B.I. : 110 109.09 108.33 108.46 141.84 90

3. Year : 1979 1980 1981 1982 1983 1984
C.B.I. : 94 97.76 101.67 94.55 97.39 99.34
(1978 = 100)

4. Year : 1979 1980 1981 1982 1983 1984
F.B.I. : 100 104 108.16 100.59 103.61 105.68
(1979 = 100)

5. Year : 1976 1977 1978 1979 1980 1981
C.B.I. : — 110 109.09 104.17 112 107.14

6. Year : 1978 1979 1980 1981 1982 1983 1984
Index No.
(1980 = 100) : 83.33 91.67 100 125 116.67 166.67 150

7. Year : 1980 1981 1982 1983 1984 1985
Index No.
(1982 = 100) : 100 105 100 190 200 205

8. 73.33, 86.67, 100, 116.67, 120, 133.33, 146.67

9. 100, 120, 125, 140, 127, 190.5, 218.44, 262.89, 273.05, 334.01

10. 100, 107, 119, 139, 145.95, 152.9, 154.29.

VII. DEFLATING

38. MEANING

Index numbers are used to compute real income from money income. It is not always necessary that the condition of wage earners may improve with an increase in their money income. The condition of wage earners would deteriorate if the prices of goods and services rise more rapidly than their money income. The condition of a wage earner can be better only if his real income increases. Increase in real income means increase in his purchasing power. That is why, wage earners are always interested in getting their real incomes increased. **Real income** is calculated by using the following formula :

$$\textbf{Real income} = \frac{\textbf{Money income}}{\textbf{Consumor Price Index No.}} \times 100$$

Index numbers of real incomes are calculated by using the formula :

Real income index no. for current period

$$= \frac{\textbf{Real income of current period}}{\textbf{Real income of base period}} \times 100.$$

Example 1. *The following table gives the per-capita income and the cost of living index of a particular community. Calculate the index numbers of real income taking into account the rise in the cost of living :*

Year	*1979*	*1980*	*1981*	*1982*	*1983*	*1984*	*1985*	*1986*
Cost of living Index (1979 = 100)	*100*	*104*	*115*	*160*	*210*	*260*	*300*	*320*
Per capita income (in Rs.)	*360*	*400*	*480*	*520*	*550*	*590*	*610*	*650*

Sol. Construction of Real Income Index Numbers

Year	*Per capita income (in Rs.)*	*Cost of living index*	*Real income (in Rs.)*	*Real income index nos. (1979 = 100)*
1979	360	100	360.00	**100**
1980	400	104	384.61	**106.84**
1981	480	115	417.39	**115.94**
1982	520	160	325.00	**90.28**
1983	550	210	261.90	**72.75**
1984	590	260	226.92	**63.03**
1985	610	300	203.33	**56.48**
1986	650	320	203.12	**56.42**

Example 2. *The annual wages (in Rs.) of a worker are given along with price indices. Find the real wage indices :*

Year	*1970*	*1971*	*1972*	*1973*	*1974*	*1975*	*1976*
Wage (Rs.)	*180*	*220*	*340*	*360*	*365*	*370*	*375*
Price index	*100*	*170*	*300*	*320*	*330*	*340*	*350*

Sol. Construction of Real Wage Index Numbers

Year	*Wage(in Rs.)*	*Price Index*	*Real wage* $= \frac{Wage}{C.P.I} \times 100$	*Real wage index no. (1970 = 100)*
1970	180	100	180	**100**
1971	220	170	129.41	**71.89**
1972	340	300	113.33	**62.96**
1973	360	320	112.50	**62.50**
1974	365	330	110.61	**61.45**
1975	370	340	108.82	**60.45**
1976	375	350	107.14	**59.52**

EXERCISE 9

1. The following data gives the per-capita income and the cost of living index number for a particular class of people. Deflate the per-capita income by taking into account the changes in the cost of living :

Year	1979	1980	1981	1982	1983	1984	1985	1986
Per-capita income (in Rs.)	300	320	340	350	375	405	425	480
Cost of living index	120	125	150	160	175	220	240	250

2. Find the real incomes from the data given below :

Year	1980	1981	1982	1983	1984	1985	1986
Average monthly income	400	410	450	500	600	750	800
Cost of living index (1975 = 100)	120	140	141	150	160	180	205

3. From the figures given below, calculate index numbers of real wages taking 1980 as base :

Year	1980	1981	1982	1983	1984	1985	1986
Average monthly wage (in Rs.)	1000	1100	1150	1200	1250	1300	1350
Consumer price index no. (1976 = 100)	142	180	200	205	220	220	240

4. From the following data, calculate real incomes :

Year	1980	1981	1982	1983	1984	1985
Money Income (,000 Rs.)	20	22	24	30	40	42
C.P.I. (1980 = 100)	100	110	130	150	160	180

5. Calculate the index numbers of real wages from the following information using 1981 as base year :

Year	1981	1982	1983	1984	1985	1986
Average monthly wage (in Rs.)	1200	1320	1430	1500	1710	2000
C.P.I.	100	120	130	150	190	200

6. The following table gives annual wages and cost of living index numbers. Calculate :
   (*i*) Real wages
   (*ii*) Index numbers of real wages with 1979 as base.

Year	*Wage*	*Cost of living index number*
1979	180	100
1980	200	150
1981	240	200
1982	300	225
1983	350	250

Answers

1. 250, 256, 226.67, 218.75, 214.29, 184.09, 177.08,192
2. 333.33, 292.86, 319.15,333.33, 375, 416.67, 390.24
3. 100, 86.78, 81.65, 83.12, 80.68, 83.91, 79.87
4. 20000, 20000, 18461.54, 20000, 25000, 23333.33
5. 100, 91.67, 91.67, 83.33, 75, 83.33
6. (*i*) 180, 133.33, 120, 133.33, 140, (*ii*) 100, 74.07, 66.67, 74.07, 77.78.

39. LIMITATIONS

Inspite of great significance, index numbers suffer from limitations also. Index numbers are valid on an average basis. An index number cannot be exactly true for every item, on individual basis. An index number may indicate that the industrial production has increased by 10% as compared with the previous year. This index number not necessarily imply that the production in every industrial unit has increased to the extent of 10%.

Index numbers much depend on the method used in their preparation. The selection of base period, number of items, average, weights of items etc., affect the index number considerably. Moreover, index numbers are constructed on sample basis. Accuracy of index number much depend upon the size of the sample. But, the sample size cannot be increased beyond certain limit. Increase of sample size causes difficulties in constructing index numbers. This may also increase the cost of preparing it.

Different index numbers meet different purposes. For example, the wholesale price index number of a market cannot work as a substitute for consumer price index number for the people residing in that area. Even the consumer price index number constructed for a particular group of people will not suit to every type of family.

EXERCISE 10

1. "Index Numbers are economic barometers". Discuss this statement. What precautions will you take while construction an index number ? (*KU 1995 C, 99, 2000 ; MDU 2006*)
2. "An index number is a special type of average." Discuss.
3. Distinguish between fixed base and chain base index numbers. (*KU 1997, 99 C*)
4. Write a short note on "Factor Reversal Test".
5. State the different uses of index numbers.
6. What is Fisher's ideal method of computing index numbers ? Why is it called ideal ? (*KU 2002 C, 2003*)

7. Explain the use of Index Numbers. What are the difficulties in the construction of Index Numbers ? *(MDU 1996, 2003 ; KU 2002 C, 2005)*
8. What main points should be taken into consideration while constructing simple index nos ? Explain the procedure of construction of simple index numbers taking example of five commodities.
9. Explain different types of index numbers. Examine the various problems involved in the construction of an index number. Discuss in brief the use of an index number. *(KU 1995, 2003)*
10. Why Fisher's Ideal formula called 'Ideal' ? Explain by giving an example that it satisfies time and factor reversal tests. *(KU 2004)*
11. State and explain the Fisher's, ideal formula for price index number. Show how it satisfies the time reversal and factor reversal test. Why is it used little in practice ? *(MDU 1998)*
12. What is Index Number ? What problems are involved in the construction of index numbers ? Give different formulae of index numbers and state which of these is best and why ? *(KU 1999 ; MDU 2005)*
13. Discuss the problems involved in the construction of an index number. *(KU 1997, 2003)*
14. What are consumer price index number ? What is their significance ? Discuss the steps involved in constructing a consumer price index number. *(MDU 1999, 2002 ; KU 2003 C)*
15. Explain the 'Factor-Reversal Test' of Adequacy of Index Number. *(MDU 2001)*
16. What is meant by an ideal index nymber ? Describe Fisher's index number. Why is it called an ideal index number ? *(KU 2002 C)*
17. Explain "The Circular Test' of adequancy of an Index Number. *(MDU 2000)*
18. Discuss the limitations of Index Numbers *(KU 2005 C)*
19. Explain any *three* of the following :
    (*i*) Base Shifting (*ii*) Chain Index
    (*iii*) Splicing (*iv*) Deflating of Index Number. *(MDU 2004)*
20. Explain the following :
    (*i*) Consumer Price Index (*ii*) Deflating of Index Numbers. *(KU 2007)*
21. (*a*) Why are index numbers called economic barometers ? *(MDU 2007)*
    (*b*) Using illustration, explain how are chain base index numbers computed ? *(MDU 2007)*

13

Analysis of Time Series

1. INTRODUCTION

We know that a **time series** is a collection of values of a variable taken at different time periods. If $y_1, y_2, \ldots\ldots, y_n$ be the values of a variable y taken at time periods $t_1, t_2, \ldots\ldots t_n$, then we write this time series as $\{(t_i, y_i)\ ;\ i = 1, 2, \ldots\ldots, n\}$. The given time series data is arranged chronologically. If we consider the sale figures of a company for over 20 years, the data will constitute a time series. Population of a town, taken annually for 15 years, would form a time series. There are plenty of variables whose value depends on time.

2. MEANING

In a time series, the values of the concerned variable is not expected to be same for every time period. For example, if we consider the price of 1 kg tea of a particular brand, for over twenty years, we will note that the price is not the same for every year. What has caused the price to vary ? In fact, there is nothing special with tea, this can happen for any variable, we consider.

There are number of economic, psychological, sociological and other forces which may cause the value of the variable to change with time. In this chapter, we shall locate, measure and interpret the changes in the values of the variable, in a time series. We shall investigate the factors, which may be held responsible for causing changes in the values of the variable with respect to time.

3. UTILITY OF TIME SERIES ANALYSIS

We have already noted that the variables whose values depend on time are not few in number. People from all walks of life have to deal with time series. A student may be interested in analysing the time series of the percentage of marks obtained in each lower class, he has passed. A doctor would be analysing the time series of temperature of a patient, recorded after every 15 minutes. Some of the reasons for which the analysis of time series is considered significant are as follows :

(*i*) **Study of fluctuations.** The fluctuations in any time series is a universal phenomenon. The time series of variables like sale, profit, temperature, population, production, import, export, national income etc. are all expected to depict fluctuations. The analysis of the time series would help in understanding the probable causes of fluctuations in the values.

(*ii*) **Assessment of present achievements.** The value of the variable for current period can be compared with that of expected value of the variable for the current period, on the basis of analysis of time series of previous periods. If the sale for current period is Rs. 50 thousand against the expected sale of Rs. 40 thousand then it can be concluded that the affecting forces have acted favourably. Similarly, if the actual value is less than the expected value then one may investigate the causes responsible for it.

(*iii*) **Forecasting.** The analysis of time series is used very frequently for forecasting, *i.e.*, to estimate the likely value of the variable for some future period. This is generally done by projecting the trend of the time series for the required future period. The forecasting is based on the assumption that the trend will continue. With the knowledge of seasonal variations present in the time series, a businessman can adjust his stock holding during the year. By studying cyclical variations present in the time series, a businessman can benefit himself by the knowledge of expected ups and downs to take place in business. Governments also plan their future programmes on the basis of forecasting of concerned time series.

(*iv*) **Comparison.** Different time series are compared and useful conclusions are drawn. For example, per capita income, literacy ratio, population, production, export, import, etc., can be compared between any two countries by studying the concerned time series.

4. COMPONENTS OF TIME SERIES

We have already noted that the value of variable in a time series are very rarely constant. The graph of its time series will be a zig-zag line. The variation in the values of time series are due to psychological, sociological, economic etc. forces. The variations in a time series are classified in to four types and are called **components** of the time series. The components are as follows :

(*i*) Secular trend or long-term variations
(*ii*) Seasonal variations
(*iii*) Cyclical variations
(*iv*) Irregular variations.

5. SECULAR TREND OR LONG TERM VARIATIONS

The general tendency of the values of the variable in a time series to grow or to decline over a long period of time is called **secular trend** of the times series. It indicates the general direction in which the graph of the time series appears to be going over a long period of time. The graph of the secular trend is either a straight line or a curve. This graph depends upon the nature of data and the method used to determine secular trend.

The secular trend of a time series depends much on factors which changes very slowly, *e.g.*, population, habits, technical development, scientific research etc.

If the secular trend for a particular time series is upward (downward), it does not necessarily imply that the values of the variable must be strictly increasing (decreasing). For example, consider the data :

Year	1978	1979	1980	1981	1982	1983	1984	1985	1986	1987
Profit ('000 Rs.)	18	17	20	21	25	22	26	27	28	35

We observe that the profit figures for the years 1979 and 1983 are less than those of their corresponding previous years, but for all other years the profit figures are greater than their corresponding previous years. In this time series, the general tendency of the profit figures is to grow.

If from the definition of secular trend, we drop the condition of having time series data for a long period of time, the definition will become meaningless. For example, if we consider the data :

Year	2002	2003
Price of sugar (1 kg)	Rs. 14	Rs. 14.50

From this time series, we cannot have the idea of the general tendency of the time series. In this connection, it is not justified to assert that the values of the variable must be taken for time periods covering 6 months or 10 years or 15 years. Rather we must see that the values of the variable are sufficient in number. Thus, in estimating trend, it is not the total time period that matters, but it is the number of time periods for which the values of the variable are known.

6. SEASONAL VARIATIONS

The **seasonal variations** in a time series counts for those variations in the series which occur annually. In a time series, seasonal variations occurs quite regularly. These variations play a very important role in business activities. There are number of factors which causes such variations. We know that the demand for raincoats rises automatically during rainy season. Producers of tea and coffee feels that the demand of their products is more in winter season rather than in summer season. Similarly, there is greater demand for cold drinks during summer season. Retailers on Hill stations are also affected by the seasonal variations. Their profits are heavily increased during summer season.

Even Banks have not escaped from seasonal variations. Banks observe heavy withdrawals in the first week of every month. Agricultural yield is also seasonal and so the farmers income is unevenly divided over the year. This has direct effect on business activities.

Customs and habits also plays an important role in causing seasonal variations in time series. On the eve of festivals, we are accustumed of purchasing sweets and new clothes. Generally, people get their houses white washed before Deepawali. Sale figures of retailers dealing with fireworks immediately boost up on the eve of Deepawali and in the season of marriages.

The study of seasonal variations in a time series is also very useful. By studying the seasonal variations, the businessman can adjust his stock holding during the year. He will not feel the danger of shortfall of stock during any particular period, in the year.

7. CYCLICAL VARIATIONS

The **cyclical variations** in a time series counts for the swings of graph of time series about its trend line (curve). Cyclical variations are seldom periodic and they may or may not follow same pattern after equal interval of time.

In particular, business and economic time series are said to have cyclical variations if these variations recur after time interval of more than one year. In business and economic time series, *business cycles* are example of cyclical variations. There are four phases of a business cycle. These are :

(*a*) Depression (*b*) Recovery

(*c*) Boom (*d*) Decline.

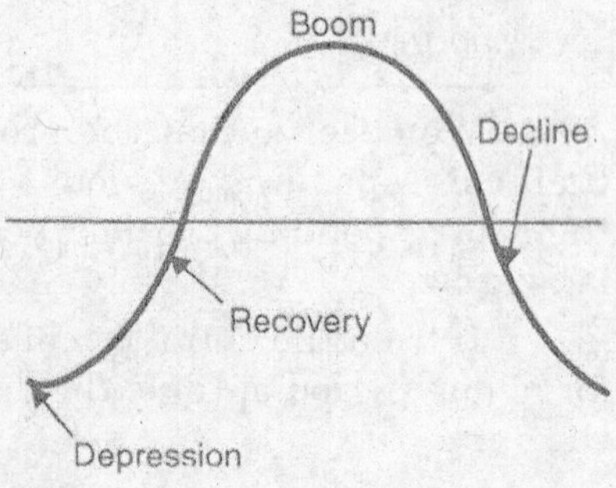

These four phases of business cycle follows each other in this order.

(*a*) **Depression.** We start with the situation of depression in business cycle. In this phase, the employment is very limited. Employees get very low wages. The purchasing power of money is high. This is the period of pessimism in business. New equilibrium is achieved in business at low level of cost, profit and prices.

(*b*) **Recovery.** The new equilibrium in the depression phase of a cycle ; last for few years. This phase is not going to continue for ever. In the phase of depression, even efficient workers are available at very low wages. In the depression period, prices are low and the costs also too low. These factors replaces pessimism by optimism. Businessman, with good financial support is optimistic in such circumstances. He invests money in repairing plants. New plants are purchased. This also boost the business of allied industries. People get employment and spend money on consumers good. So, the situation changes altogether. This is called the phase of recovery in business cycle.

(*c*) **Boom.** There is also limit to recovery. Investment is revived in recovery phase. Investment in one industry affects investment in other industries. People get employment. Extension in demand is felt. Prices go high. Profits are made very easily. All these leads to over development of business. This phase of business cycle is described as *boom*.

(*d*) **Decline.** In the phase of boom, the business is over developed. This is because of heavy profits. Wages are increased and on the contrary their efficiency decreases. Money is demanded everywhere. This results in the increase in rate of interest. In other words, the demand for production factors increases very much and this results in increase in their prices. This results in the increases in the cost of production. Profits are decreased. Banks insists for repayment of loans under these circumstances. Businessmen give concession in prices so that cash may be secured. Consumers start expecting more reduction in prices. Condition become more worse. Products accumulates with businessmen and repayment of loan does not take place. Many business houses fails. All these leads to depression phase and the business cycle continues itself.

The length of a business cycle is in general between 3 to 10 years. Moreover, the lengths of business cycles are not equal.

8. IRREGULAR VARIATIONS

The **irregular variations** in a time series counts for those variations which cannot be predicted before hand. This component is different from the other three components in the sense that irregular variations in a time series are very irregular. Nothing can be predicted about the occurrence of irregular variations. It is very true that floods, famines, wars, earthquakes, strikes etc. do affect the economic and business activities. The component *irregular variations* refers to the variations in time series which are caused due to the occurrence of events like flood, famine, war, earthquake, strike, etc.

9. ADDITIVE AND MULTIPLICATIVE MODELS OF DECOMPOSITION OF TIME SERIES

Let T, S, C and I represent the trend component, seasonal component, cyclical component and irregular component of a time series, respectively. Let the variable of the time series be denoted by Y. There are mainly two models of decomposition of time series.

(*i*) **Additive model.** In this model, we have

$$Y = T + S + C + I.$$

In this case, the components T, S, C and I represent absolute values. Here S, C and I may admit of negative values. In this model, we assume that all the four components are independent of each other.

(*ii*) **Multiplicative model.** In this model, we have

$$Y = T \times S \times C \times I.$$

In this case, the components T is in abosolute value where as the components S, C and I represent relative indices with base value unity. In this model, the four components are not necessarily independent of each other.

10. DETERMINATION OF TREND

Before we go in the detail of methods of measuring secular trend, we must be clear about the purpose of measuring trend. We know that the secular trend is the tendency of time series to grow or to decline over a long period of time. By studying the trend line (or curve) of the profits of a company for a number of years, it can be well-decided as to whether the company is progressing or not. Similarly, by studying the trend of *consumer price index numbers*, we can have an idea about the rate of growth (or decline) in the prices of commodities.

We can also make use of trend characteristics in comparing the behaviour of two different industries in India. It can equally be used for comparing the growth of industries in India with those functioning in some other country.

The secular trend is also used for forecasting. This is achieved by projecting the trend line (curve) for the required future value.

The secular trend is also measured in order to eliminate itself from the given time series. After this, only three components are left and these are studied separately. The following are the methods of measuring the secular trend of a time series :

(*i*) Free Hand Graphic Method

(*ii*) Semi-Average Method

(*iii*) Moving Average Method

(*iv*) Least Squares Method.

11. FREE HAND GRAPHIC METHOD

This is a graphic method. Let $\{(t_i, y_i) : i = 1, 2, ..., n\}$ be the given time series. On the graph paper, time is measured horizontally, whereas the values of the variable y are measured vertically. Points (t_1, y_1) (t_2, y_2), ..., (t_n, y_n) are plotted on the graph paper. These plotted points are joined by straight lines to get the graph of actual time series data.

In this method, trend line (or curve) is fitted by inspection. This is a subjective method. The trend line (or curve) is drawn through the graph of actual data so that the following are satisfied as far as possible :

(*i*) The algebraic sum of the deviations of actual values from the trend values is zero.

(*ii*) The sum of the squares of the deviations of actual values from the trend values is least.

(*iii*) The area above the trend is equal to area below it.

(*iv*) The trend line (or curve) is smooth.

Example 1. *Fit a straight line trend to the following data, by using free hand graphic method :*

Year	*1980*	*1981*	*1982*	*1983*	*1984*	*1985*	*1986*
Profit of Firm X ('000 Rs.)	*20*	*30*	*25*	*40*	*42*	*30*	*50*

Sol.

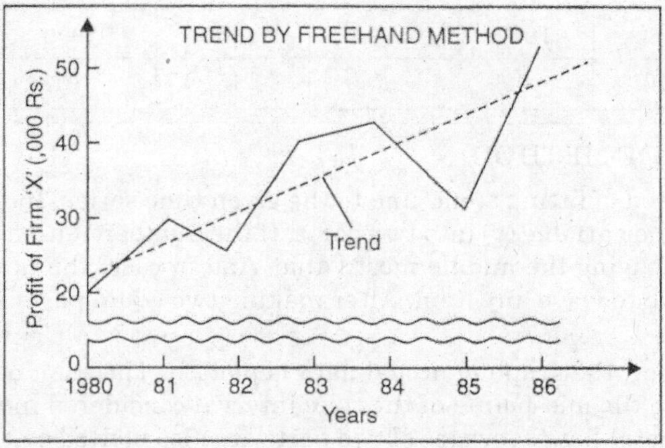

12. MERITS AND DEMERITS

Merits 1. This is the simplest of all the methods of measuring trend.

2. This is a non-mathematical method and it can be used by any one who does not have mathematical background.

3. This method proves very useful for one who is well acquainted with the economic history of the concern, under consideration.

4. For rough estimates, this method is best suited.

Demerits 1. This method is not rigidly defined.

2. This method is not suited when accurate results are desired.

3. This is a subjective method and can be affected by the personal bias of the person, drawing it.

EXERCISE 1

1. Fit a straight line trend to the following data by using free hand graphic method :

Year	1992	1993	1994	1995	1996
Import (in crores of Rs.)	45	47	30	32	27

2. Fit a straight line trend to the following data by using free hand graphic method :

Year	1992	1993	1994	1995	1996	1997
Profit (in Rs.)	27000	28000	30000	35000	42000	40000

3. Fit a straight line trend to the following data by using free hand graphic method :

Year	1931	1941	1951	1961	1971	1981
Population of city X (in lakhs)	45	47	50	55	60	70

4. Fit a straight line trend to the following data by using free hand graphic method :

Year	1992	1993	1994	1995	1996	1997	1998
X	10	8	7	15	16	25	30

13. SEMI AVERAGE METHOD

This is a method of fitting trend line to the given time series. In this method, we divide the given values of the variable (y) into two parts. If the number of items is odd, then we make two equal parts by leaving the middle most value. And in case, the number of items is even, then we will not have to leave any item. After making two equal parts, the A.M. of both parts are calculated.

On graph paper, the graph of actual data is plotted. The A.M. of two parts are considered to correspond to the mid-points of the time interval considered in making the parts. The points corresponding to these averages of two parts are also plotted on the graph paper. These points are then joined by a straight line. This line represents the trend by semi average method. From the trend line, we can easily get the trend values. This trend line can also be used for predicting the value of the variable for any future period.

Example 1. *Fit a straight line trend to the following data by using semi average method :*

Year	*1981*	*1982*	*1983*	*1984*	*1985*	*1986*
Cost of Living Index No.	*100*	*110*	*120*	*118*	*130*	*159*

Sol. **Trend line by Semi-Average Method**

Year	*Cost of Living Index*		*Year*	*Cost of Living Index*	
1981	100		1984	118	
1982	110	$\frac{330}{3} = 100$	1985	130	$\frac{407}{3} = 135.67$
1983	120		1986	159	

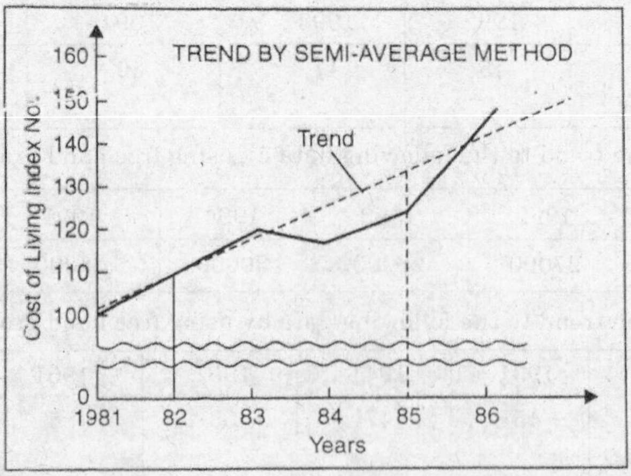

Example 2. *Fit a straight line trend by using the following data :*

Year	*1981*	*1982*	*1983*	*1984*	*1985*	*1986*	*1987*
Profit ('000 Rs.)	*20*	*22*	*27*	*26*	*30*	*29*	*40*

Semi Average Method is to be used. Also estimate the profit for the year 1988.

Sol. **Trend Line by Semi-Average Method**

Year	*Profit (,000 Rs.)*		*Year*	*Profit (,000 Rs.)*	
1981	20		1985	30	
1982	22	$\frac{69}{3} = 23$	1986	29	$\frac{99}{3} = 33.$
1983	27		1987	40	
1984	26				

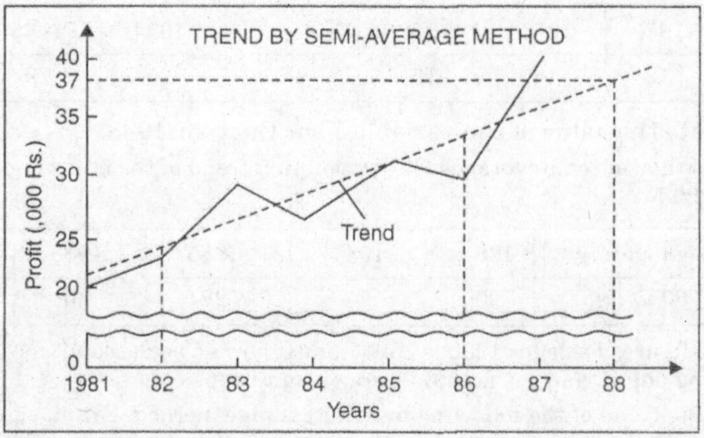

The estimated profit for the year 1988 is **Rs. 37000.**

14. MERITS AND DEMERITS

Merits 1. This method is rigidly defined.

2. This method is simple to understand.

Demerits 1. This method assumes a straight line trend, which is not always true.

2. Since this method is based on A.M., all the demerits of A.M. becomes the demerits of this method also.

EXERCISE 2

1. Fit a straight line trend by the method of semi-average from the following data :

Year	1993	1994	1995	1996	1997	1998
Sales ('000 Units)	20	24	22	30	28	32

2. Fit a straight line trend for the following data, by using semi-average method :

Year	1990	1991	1992	1993	1994	1995
Profit ('000 Rs.)	80	82	85	70	89	95

3. Fit a straight line trend for the following data, by using semi-average method :

Year	1980	1981	1982	1983	1984	1985	1986
Profit ('000 Rs.)	80	82	85	70	89	95	105

4. Estimate the production for the year 1987, by using semi-average method :

Year	1980	1981	1982	1983	1984	1985	1986
Production	50	40	45	55	75	70	72

5. Fit a straight line trend for the following data, by using semi-average method :

Year	1980	1981	1982	1983	1984	1985	1986	1987
Y	12	14	16	20	25	29	31	28

Also estimate the value of the variable Y for the year 1988.

6. Apply the method of semi-averages for determining trend of the following data and estimate the value for 1990 :

Year (March-ending)	1983	1984	1985	1986	1987	1988
Sale (in '000 units)	20	24	22	30	28	32

If the actual figure of sale for 1990 is 35000 units, how do you account for the difference between the figure you obtain and the actual figure given to you.

7. Determine the trend of the following by semi-average method. Graph should be neat.

Year	*Sales (,000 Rs.)*	*Year*	*Sales (,000 Rs.)*
1965	18	1971	30
1966	25	1972	20
1967	21	1973	35
1968	15	1974	32
1969	26	1975	23
1970	31		

15. MOVING AVERAGE METHOD

Let $\{(t_i, y_i) : i = 1, 2, ..., n\}$ be the given time series. Here $y_1, y_2, ..., y_n$ are the values of the variable (y) corresponding to time periods $t_1, t_2, ..., t_n$ respectively.

We define **moving totals of order m** as $y_1 + y_2 + ... + y_m$, $y_2 + y_3 + ... + y_{m+1}$, $y_3 + y_4 + ... + y_{m+2}$, ...

The **moving averages of order m** are defined as

$$\frac{y_1 + y_2 + \dots + y_m}{m}, \quad \frac{y_2 + y_3 + \dots + y_{m+1}}{m}, \quad \frac{y_3 + y_4 + \dots + y_{m+2}}{m}, \dots .$$

These moving averages will be called **m yearly moving averages** if the values, $y_1, y_2, \dots y_n$ of y are given annually. Similarly, if the data are given monthly, then the moving averages will be called **m monthly moving averages.**

In using moving averages in estimating the trend, we shall have to decide as to what should be the order of the moving averages. The order of the moving averages should be equal to the length of the cycles in the time series. In case, the order of the moving averages is given in the problem itself, then we shall use that order for computing the moving averages. The order of the moving averages may either be odd or even.

Let the order of moving averages be 3. The moving averages will be

$$\frac{y_1 + y_2 + y_3}{3}, \quad \frac{y_2 + y_3 + y_4}{3}, \quad \frac{y_3 + y_4 + y_5}{3}, \dots, \frac{y_{n-2} + y_{n-1} + y_n}{3}.$$

These moving averages will be considered to correspond to 2nd, 3rd, 4th, ... $(n - 1)$th years respectively.

Similarly, the 5 yearly moving averages will be

$$\frac{y_1 + y_3 + y_3 + y_4 + y_5}{5}, \quad \frac{y_2 + \dots + y_6}{5}, \dots\dots, \frac{y_{n-4} + \dots + y_n}{5}.$$

These 5 yearly moving averages will be considered to correspond to 3rd, 4th, ..., ... $(n - 2)$th years respectively. These moving averages are called the trend values.

Calculation of trend values, by using moving averages of *even* order is slightly complicated. Suppose we are to find trend values by using 4 yearly moving averages. The 4 yearly moving averages are :

$$\frac{y_1 + y_2 + y_3 + y_4}{4}, \quad \frac{y_2 + y_3 + y_4 + y_5}{4}, \dots\dots, \frac{y_{n-3} + y_{n-2} + y_{n-1} + y_n}{4}.$$

These moving averages will not correspond to time periods, under consideration. The first moving average will correspond to the mid of t_2 and t_3. Similarly, others.

In order that these moving averages may correspond to original periods, we will have to resort to a process, called *centering of moving averages.* There are two methods of finding centered moving averages. Suppose we are to find 4 yearly centered moving averages for the times series :

$$\{(t_i, y_i)\} : i = 1, 2, \dots\dots, n\}.$$

16. METHOD I

In this method, we first calculate 4 yearly moving totals from the given data. Of these 4 year moving totals, 2 yearly moving totals are computed. These 2 yearly moving totals are then divided by 8 to get 4 yearly *centered moving averages*. These centered moving averages will correspond to 3rd, 4th, ... $(n - 2)$th years, in the table.

17. METHOD II

In this method, we first calculate 4 yearly moving averages. The first 4 yearly moving average will correspond to the mid of 2nd and 3rd years. Similarly, others. We now calculate 2 yearly moving averages of these 4 yearly moving averages. These averages will be 4 yearly *centered moving averages*. These averages will correspond to 3rd, 4th, ..., $(n-2)$th years, in the table.

It may be carefully noted that the centered moving averages as calculated by using these methods will be exactly same.

In the moving average method of finding trend, the moving averages will be the trend values. These trend values may be plotted on the graph. The graph of the trend values will not be a straight line, in general.

Example 1. *Find the trend values by taking three yearly moving averages for the following data :*

Year	*1980*	*1981*	*1982*	*1983*	*1984*	*1985*	*1986*	*1987*
Profit ('000 Rs.)	*8*	*21*	*20*	*25*	*29*	*27*	*35*	*42*

Also find short term fluctuations assuming additive model.

Sol. **Trend by 3 year Moving Averages**

Year	*Profit ('000 Rs.)*	*3 yearly moving total*	*Trend value 3 yearly moving average*
1980	18	—	—
1981	21	18 + 21 + 20 = 59	**19.667**
1982	20	21 + 20 + 25 = 66	**22**
1983	25	20 + 25 + 29 = 74	**24.667**
1984	29	25 + 29 + 27 = 81	**27**
1985	27	29 + 27 + 35 = 91	**30.333**
1986	35	27 + 35 + 42 = 104	**34.667**
1987	42	—	—

Short term fluctuations

Year	*Actual value* y	*Trend value* y_c	*Short term fluctuations* $y - y_c$
1980	18	—	—
1981	21	19.667	**1.333**
1982	20	22	**– 2**
1983	25	24.667	**0.333**
1984	29	27	**2**
1985	27	30.333	**– 3.333**
1986	35	34.667	**0.333**
1987	42	—	—

Example 2. *From the following data, find trend, using five yearly moving averages and plot the results on a graph paper :*

Year	*Annual production*	*Year*	*Annual production*	*Year*	*Annual production*
1	*156*	*11*	*135*	*21*	*122*
2	*143*	*12*	*127*	*22*	*114*
3	*148*	*13*	*130*	*23*	*110*
4	*150*	*14*	*135*	*24*	*115*
5	*155*	*15*	*140*	*25*	*120*
6	*145*	*16*	*130*	*26*	*109*
7	*135*	*17*	*118*	*27*	*105*
8	*138*	*18*	*122*	*28*	*98*
9	*142*	*19*	*127*	*29*	*104*
10	*146*	*20*	*130*	*30*	*110*

Sol. **Trend by 5 yearly Moving Averages**

Year	*Annual Production*	*5 yearly moving total*	*5 yearly moving average i.e. trend value*
1	156	—	—
2	143	—	—
3	148	752	**150.4**
4	150	741	**148.2**
5	155	733	**146.6**
6	145	723	**144.6**
7	135	715	**143**
8	138	706	**141.2**
9	142	696	**139.2**
10	146	688	**137.6**
11	135	680	**136**
12	127	673	**134.6**
13	130	667	**133.4**
14	135	662	**132.4**
15	140	653	**130.6**
16	130	645	**129**
17	118	637	**127.4**
18	122	627	**125.4**
19	127	619	**123.8**
20	130	615	**123**
21	122	603	**120.6**
22	114	591	**118.2**
23	110	581	**116.2**
24	115	568	**113.6**
25	120	559	**111.8**
26	109	547	**109.4**
27	105	536	**107.2**
28	98	526	**105.2**
29	104	—	—
30	110	—	—

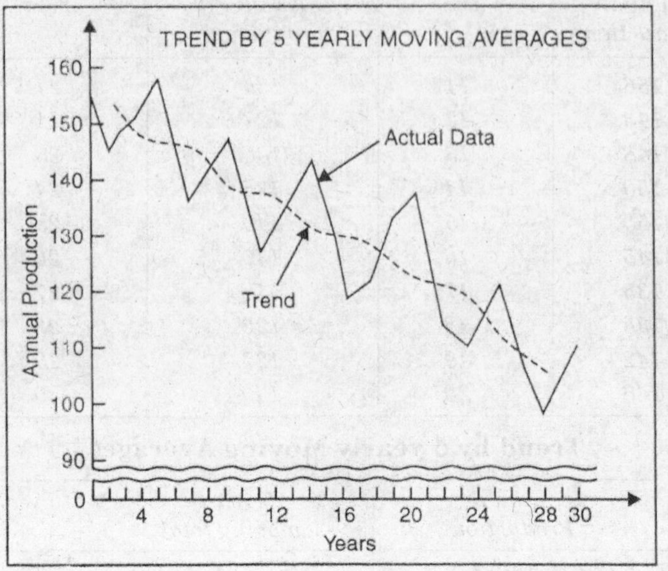

Example 3. *Compute 5 yearly, 7 yearly and 9 yearly moving averages for the following time series :*

Year	*Value of the Variable*	*Year*	*Value of the Variable*
1955	*8*	*1965*	*9*
1956	*10*	*1966*	*11*
1957	*11*	*1967*	*13*
1958	*10*	*1968*	*9*
1959	*10*	*1969*	*10*
1960	*9*	*1970*	*8*
1961	*9*	*1971*	*11*
1962	*11*	*1972*	*9*
1963	*7*	*1973*	*12*
1964	*9*	*1974*	*11*

Sol. **Trend by Moving Average Method**

Year	*Value of the Variable*	*5 Yearly m.t.*	*5 Yearly m.a.*	*7 Yearly m.t.*	*7 Yearly m.a.*	*9 Yearly m.t.*	*9 Yearly m.a.*
1955	8	—	—	—	—	—	—
1956	10	—	—	—	—	—	—
1957	11	49	**9.8**	—	—	—	—
1958	10	50	**10**	67	**9.57**	—	—
1959	10	49	**9.8**	70	**10**	85	**9.44**
1960	9	49	**9.8**	67	**9.57**	86	**9.55**
1961	9	46	**9.2**	65	**9.29**	85	**9.44**
1962	11	45	**9**	64	**9.14**	85	**9.44**

1963	7	45	**9**	65	**9.29**	88	**9.78**
1964	9	47	**9.4**	69	**9.86**	87	**9.67**
1965	9	49	**9.8**	69	**9.86**	88	**9.78**
1966	11	51	**10.2**	68	**9.71**	87	**9.67**
1967	13	52	**10.4**	69	**9.86**	87	**9.67**
1968	9	51	**10.2**	71	**10.14**	89	**9.89**
1969	10	51	**10.2**	71	**10.14**	92	**10.22**
1970	8	47	**9.4**	72	**10.29**	94	**10.44**
1971	11	50	**10**	70	**10**	—	—
1972	9	51	**10.2**	—	—	—	—
1973	12	—	—	—	—	—	—
1974	11	—	—	—	—	—	—

Example 4. *Following figures relate to output of cloth in a factory (output in lakhs of metres) :*

Year	*1967*	*1968*	*1969*	*1970*	*1971*	*1972*	*1973*	*1974*	*1975*	*1976*
Output	*72*	*68*	*64*	*60*	*68*	*72*	*72*	*76*	*72*	*68*

Calculate 4 yearly moving averages.

Sol. **Trend by Moving Average Method**

Year	*Output*	*4 yearly moving total*	*2 yearly moving total of column 3*	*4 yearly centered moving average*
1967	72		—	—
1968	68		—	—
		264		
1969	64		524	**65.5**
		260		
1970	60		524	**65.5**
		264		
1971	68		536	**67**
		272		
1972	72		560	**70**
		288		
1973	72		580	**72.5**
		292		
1974	76		580	**72.5**
		288		
1975	72		—	—
1976	68		—	—

Example 5. *Estimate the trend values using the data given below by taking a four yearly moving average. Also plot the actual and trend values on the graph paper :*

Year	*Value*	*Year*	*Value*
1969	*4*	*1975*	*24*
1970	*7*	*1976*	*36*
1971	*20*	*1977*	*25*
1972	*15*	*1978*	*40*
1973	*30*	*1979*	*42*
1974	*28*	*1980*	*45*

Sol. **Trend by Moving Average Method**

Year	*Value*	*4 yearly moving total*	*4 yearly moving average*	*4 yearly centered moving average*
1969	4			—
1970	7			—
		46	11.5	
1971	20			**14.75**
		72	18	
1972	15			**20.625**
		93	23.25	
1973	30			**23.75**
		97	24.25	
1974	28			**26.875**
		118	29.5	
1975	24			**28.875**
		113	28.25	
1976	36			**29.75**
		125	31.25	
1977	25			**33.5**
		143	35.75	
1978	40			**36.875**
		152	38	
1979	42			—
1980	45			—

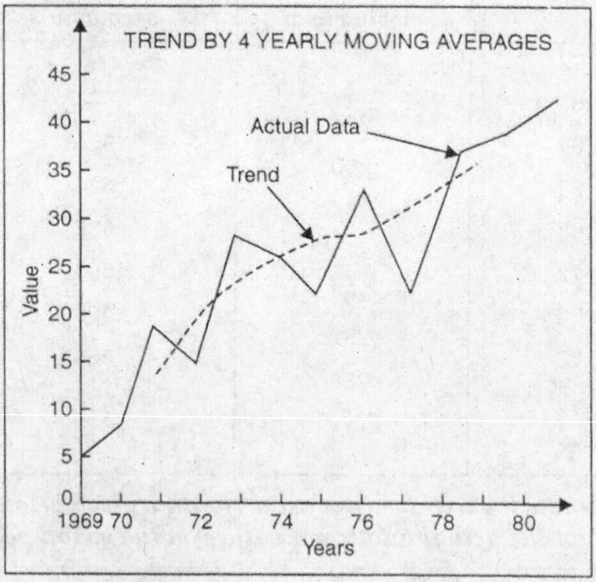

Remark. In the above two examples, centering of moving averages has been done by adopting **method 1** and **method 2** respectively.

Example 6. *Calculate 4 yearly moving averages from the following :*

Year	*1972*	*1973*	*1974*	*1975*	*1976*	*1977*	*1978*	*1979*	*1980*	*1981*
Sale	*30*	*40*	*80*	*60*	*70*	*110*	*90*	*100*	*140*	*120*

Sol. **Trend by Moving Average Method**

Year	*Sale*	*4 yearly moving total*	*2 yearly moving totals of column 3*	*4 yearly centered moving average*
1972	30		—	—
1973	40		—	—
		210		
1974	80		460	**57.5**
		250		
1975	60		570	**71.25**
		320		
1976	70		650	**81.95**
		330		
1977	110		700	**87.5**
		370		
1978	90		810	**101.25**
		440		
1979	100		890	**111.25**
		450		
1980	140		—	—
1981	120		—	—

18. MERITS AND DEMERITS

Merits. 1. This method is rigidily defined, so it cannot be affected by the personal prejudice of the person computing it.

2. If the order of the moving averages is exactly equal to the length of the cycle in the time series, the cyclical variations are eliminated.

3. If some more values of the variable are added at the end of the time series, the entire calculations are not changed.

4. This method is best suited for the time series whose trend is not linear. For such series, the general movement of the variable will be best shown by moving averages.

Demerits. 1. Moving averages are strongly affected by the presence of extreme items, in the series.

2. It is difficult to decide the order of the moving averages, because the cycles in time series are seldom regular in duration.

3. In this method, we lose trend values at each end of the series. For example, if the order of the moving averages is five, we lose trend values for two years at each end of the series.

4. Forecasting is not possible in this method, because we cannot objectively project the graph of the trend values, for a future period.

EXERCISE 3

1. Calculate three yearly moving averages for the following data :

Year	1982	1983	1984	1985	1986
Production (in tonnes)	15	17	20	28	30

2. Find trend values for the following data, by using 3 yearly moving averages :

Year	*Production (Lakh tonnes)*	*Year*	*Production (Lakh tonnes)*
1973	17.2	1981	25.3
1974	17.3	1982	24.9
1975	17.7	1983	23.2
1976	18.9	1984	24.3
1977	19.2	1985	25.2
1978	19.3	1986	26.3
1979	18.1	1987	27.3
1980	20.2		

3. Find trend values for the following data, by using 5 yearly moving averages. Also plot the actual data and trend values on a graph :

Year	*Profit ('000 Rs.)*	*Year*	*Profit ('000 Rs.)*
1970	80	1977	90
1971	82	1978	92
1972	84	1979	97
1973	88	1980	95
1974	70	1981	99
1975	72	1982	80
1976	90	1983	99

4. Calculate a 7 yearly moving average for the following data on the number of commercial and industrial failures in a country during 1929–44 :

Year	*No. of failures*	*Year*	*No. of failures*
1929	23	1937	9
1930	26	1938	13
1931	28	1939	11
1932	32	1940	14
1933	20	1941	12
1934	12	1942	9
1935	12	1943	3
1936	10	1944	1

5. Compute 3 yearly and 5 yearly moving averages of the following data. Also plot them on a graph paper along with original data :

Year	*Value*	*Year*	*Value*
1	1	11	3
2	2	12	4
3	3	13	5
4	2	14	4
5	1	15	3
6	2	16	4
7	3	17	5
8	4	18	6
9	3	19	5
10	2	20	4

6. Work out the centered 4 yearly moving averages for the following data :

Year	*Tonnage of cargo cleared*	*Year*	*Tonnage of cargo cleared*
1957	1102	1963	1452
1958	1250	1964	1549
1959	1180	1965	1586
1960	1440	1966	1476
1961	1212	1967	1625
1962	1317	1968	1586

7. The following table gives the number of workers employed in a small industry during 1980–87. Calculate the trend values by using 3 yearly moving averages :

Year	1980	1981	1982	1983	1984	1985	1986	1987
No. of workers	20	24	25	18	27	26	28	30

8. Obtain the trend of bank clearances by the method of moving averages (assume a five yearly cycle) :

Year	1951	1952	1953	1954	1955	1956	1957	1958	1959	1960	1961	1962
Bank Clearance (in crores of rupees)	53	79	76	66	69	94	105	87	79	104	97	92

9. Compute 4 yearly and 5 yearly moving averages from the following data :

Year	*Value (in Rs.)*	*Year*	*Value (in Rs.)*
1960	365	1971	255
1961	360	1972	250
1962	355	1973	245
1963	330	1974	225
1964	300	1975	210
1965	330	1976	200
1966	340	1977	230
1967	290	1978	225
1968	280	1979	200
1969	250	1980	195
1970	235		

10. Find the trend values for the following data, by using 4 yearly moving averages :

Year	1995	1996	1997	1998	1999	2000	2001	2002
Sale (in thousands of rupees)	108	112	110	120	140	120	100	135

(MDU 2003)

11. From the given data, compute trend by moving average method assuming 'a four-yearly cycle' Also find short term variations assuming additive model.

Year	*Sales*	*Year*	*Sales*
1984	75	1990	70
1985	60	1991	75
1986	55	1992	85
1987	60	1993	100
1988	65	1994	70
1989	70		

(*KU 1995*)

12. Calculate trend from the following data by using four yearly moving averages :

Year	*Production*	*Year*	*Production*
1	52.7	8	87.2
2	79.4	9	79.3
3	76.3	10	103.6
4	66.0	11	97.3
5	68.6	12	92.4
6	93.8	13	100.7
7	104.7		

13. Assuming a four year cycle calcualate the trend by the method of moving averages from the following data :

Year	*Value*	*Year*	*Value*
1991	464	1996	540
1992	515	1997	557
1993	518	1998	571
1994	467	1999	586
1995	502	2000	612

(*MDU 2002*)

Answers

1. 17.333, 21.667, 26

2. 17.4, 17.967, 18.6, 19.133, 18.867, 19.2, 21.2, 23.467, 24.467, 24.133, 24.233, 25.267, 26.267

3. 80.8, 79.2, 80.8, 82, 82.8, 88.2, 92.8, 94.6, 92.6, 94

4. 21.857, 20, 17.571, 15.429, 12.429, 11.571, 11.571, 11.143, 10.143,9

5. 3 yearly moving averages : 2, 2.33, 2, 1.67, 2, 3, 3.33, 3, 2.67, 3, 4, 4.33, 4, 3.67, 4, 5, 5.33, 5
5 yearly moving averages : 1.8, 2, 2.2, 2.4, 2.6, 2.8, 3, 3.2, 3.4, 3.6, 3.8, 4, 4.2, 4.4, 4.6, 4.8

6. 1256.75, 1278.875, 1321.25, 1368.875, 1429.25, 1495.875, 1537.375, 1563.625

7. 23, 22.333, 23.333, 23.667, 27, 28

8. 68.6, 76.8, 82, 84.2, 86.8, 93.8, 94.4, 91.8

9. 4 yearly moving averages : 344.375, 332.5, 326.875, 320, 312.5, 300, 276.875, 259.375, 251.25, 246.875, 245, 238.125, 226.25, 218.125, 216.25, 215, 213.125

5 yearly moving averages : 342, 335, 331, 318, 308, 298, 279, 262. 254, 247, 242, 237, 226, 222, 218, 213, 210

10. 116.5, 121.5, 121.25, 121.87

11. 61.25, 61.25, 64.38, 68.13, 72.50, 78.75, 82.5 ; – 6.25, – 1.25, 0.62, 1.87, 2.50, – 3.75, 2.50

12. 70.59, 74.38, 79.73, 85.93, 89.91, 92.48, 92.78, 92.50, 95.82

13. 495.75, 503.625, 511.625, 529.5, 553, 572.5.

19. LEAST SQUARES METHOD

This is a mathemetical method. Let $\{(t_i, y_i) : i = 1, 2, \ldots\ldots, n\}$ be the given time series. By using this method, we can find linear trend as well as non-linear trend of the corresponding data.

In this method, trend values (y_e) of the variable (y) are computed so as to satisfy the following two conditions :

(*i*) The sum of the deviations of values of y ($= y_1, y_2, \ldots\ldots, y_n$) from their corresponding trend values, is zero, *i.e.*, $\Sigma(y - y_e) = 0$.

(*ii*) The sum of the squares of the deviations of the values of y from their corresponding trend values is least *i.e.*, $\Sigma(y - y_e)^2$ is least.

On the graph paper, we shall measure the actual values and the estimated values (trend values) of the variable y, along the vertical axis. Let x denote the deviations of the time periods $(t_1, t_2, \ldots\ldots, t_n)$ from some fixed time period. The fixed time period is called the *origin*.

20. LINEAR TREND

From the knowledge of coordinate geometry, we know that the equation of the required trend line can be expressed as

$$y_e = a + bx,$$

where a and b are constants. We have already mentioned that our trend line will satisfy the conditions :

(*i*) $\Sigma(y - y_e) = 0$ and (*ii*) $\Sigma(y - y_e)^2$ is least.

In order to meet these requirements, we will have to use those values of a and b in the trend line equation which satisfies the following *normal equations :*

$$\Sigma y = an + b\Sigma x \qquad \ldots(1)$$

$$\Sigma xy = a\Sigma x + b\Sigma x^2 \qquad \ldots(2)$$

In the equation $y_e = a + bx$, of the trend, a represents the trend value of the variable when $x = 0$ and b represents the *slope* of the trend line. If b is positive, the trend will be upward and if b is negative, the trend of the time series will be downward.

It is very important to mention the origin and the x unit with the trend line equation. If either of the two is not given with the equation of the trend, we will not be able to get the trend values of the variable, under consideration.

Example 1. *Below are given the figures of production (in thousand maunds) of a sugar factory :*

Year	*1981*	*1982*	*1983*	*1984*	*1985*	*1986*	*1987*
Production	*80*	*90*	*92*	*83*	*94*	*99*	*92*

(i) Find the slope of a straight line trend of these figures. Also find trend values.

(ii) Plot these figures on a graph and show the trend line.

(iii) Do these figures show a rising or a falling trend ? *(KU 2001)*

Sol. We shall fit a straight line trend by the method of least squares. Let y denote the variable production (in thousand maunds).

Linear Trend by Least Squares Method

S. No.	*Year*	*y*	*x = Year – 1981*	x^2	*xy*
1	1981	80	0	0	0
2	1982	90	1	1	90
3	1983	92	2	4	184
4	1984	83	3	9	249
5	1985	94	4	16	376
6	1986	99	5	25	495
$n = 7$	1987	92	6	36	552
Total		630	21	91	1946

Let the equation of the trend line by $y = a + bx$.

$\therefore$ The normal equations are :

$$\Sigma y = an + b\Sigma x \quad \text{...(1)}$$

and $$\Sigma xy = a\Sigma x + b\Sigma x^2. \quad \text{...(2)}$$

(1) $\Rightarrow$ $630 = 7a + 21b$ ...(3)

(2) $\Rightarrow$ $1946 = 21a + 91b$ ...(4)

(3) × 3 $\Rightarrow$ $1890 = 21a + 63b$ ...(5)

(4) – (5) $\Rightarrow$ $56 = 28b$ $\Rightarrow$ $b = 2$.

$\therefore$ (3) $\Rightarrow$ $630 = 7a + 21(2)$ $\Rightarrow$ $a = 588/7 = 84$.

$\therefore$ The equation of trend is $y_e = 84 + 2x$, with origin 1981 and x unit = 1 year.

(*i*) The slope of straight line trend = **2.**

For 1981, $x = 1981 - 1981 = 0$, $\therefore$ $y_e\,(1981) = 84 + 2(0) =$ **84**

For 1982, $x = 1982 - 1981 = 1$. $\therefore$ $y_e\,(1982) = 84 + 2(1) =$ **86**

For 1983, $x = 1983 - 1981 = 2$. $\therefore$ $y_e\,(1983) = 84 + 2(2) =$ **88**

For 1984, $x = 1984 - 1981 = 3$. $\therefore$ $y_e\,(1984) = 84 + 2(3) =$ **90**

For 1985, $x = 1985 - 1981 = 4$. $\therefore$ $y_e\,(1985) = 84 + 2(4) =$ **92**

For 1986, $x = 1986 - 1981 = 5$. $\therefore$ $y_e\,(1986) = 84 + 2(5) =$ **94**

For 1987, $x = 1987 - 1981 = 6$. $\therefore$ $y_e\,(1987) = 84 + 2(6) =$ **96.**

(*ii*)

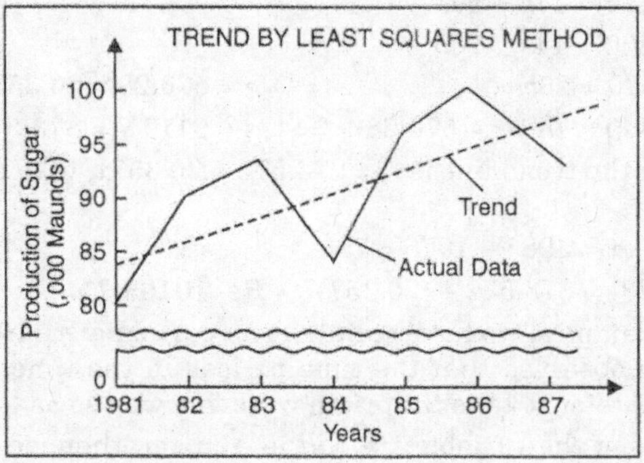

(*iii*) The figures shows a *rising* trend.

Example 2. *Calculate trend values by the method of least squares and estimate sales for 1983 :*

Year	*1975*	*1976*	*1977*	*1978*	*1979*	*1980*	*1981*
Sale (Rs.)	*800*	*900*	*920*	*930*	*940*	*980*	*930*

(KU 1997)

Sol. **Trend Line by Least Squares Method**

S. No.	*Year*	*Sales y*	*x = year – 1976*	x^2	*xy*	$y_e = a + bx$
1	1975	800	– 1	1	– 800	873.572 + 20.357 (– 1) = **853.215**
2	1976	900	0	0	0	873.572 + 20.357(0) = **873.572**
3	1977	920	1	1	920	873.572 + 20.357(1) = **893.929**
4	1978	930	2	4	1860	873.572 + 20.357(2) = **914.286**
5	1979	940	3	9	2820	873.572 + 20.357(3) = **934.643**
6	1980	980	4	16	3920	873.572 + 20.357(4) = **955.000**
n = 7	1981	930	5	25	4650	873.572 + 20.357(5) = **975.357**
Total		6400	14	56	13370	

Let the equation of the trend line by $y_e = a + bx$.

The normal equations are :

$$\Sigma y = an + b\Sigma x \qquad ...(1)$$

and

$$\Sigma xy = a\Sigma x + b\Sigma x^2. \qquad ...(2)$$

(1) $\Rightarrow$ $6400 = 7a + 14b$ ...(3)

(2) $\Rightarrow$ $13370 = 14a + 56b$ ...(4)

(3) × 2 $\Rightarrow$ $12800 = 14a + 28b$ ...(5)

(4) – (5) $\Rightarrow$ $570 = 28b$ $\Rightarrow$ $b = 570/28 = 20.357.$

$\therefore$ (3) $\Rightarrow$ $6400 = 7a + 14(570/28)$ $\Rightarrow$ $a = 6115/7 = 873.572.$

$\therefore$ The equation of the trend line is $y_e = 873.572 + 20.357x$, with origin 1976 and x unit = 1 year.

For 1983, $x = 1983 - 1976 = 7.$

$\therefore$ $y_e(1983) = 873.572 + (20.357)7 =$ **Rs. 1016.071.**

In the above two examples, we have seen that no particular rule is applied in choosing the origin. It is generally observed that the time periods in the time series are of uniform duration. If this is so, we prefer to take the origin in such a way so as to make $\Sigma x = 0$.

If the known values of the variable are *odd* in number, then we take the middle most time period as the origin. This choice would make $\Sigma x = 0$.

If the known values of the variable are *even* in number, then we take the A.M. of the two middle most time periods as the origin. Here also, this choice of origin would make $\Sigma x = 0$.

If for a time series, the origin is chosen so that $\Sigma x = 0$, then the normal equations reduces to

$$\Sigma y = an + b.0 \quad \text{and} \quad \Sigma xy = a.0 + b\Sigma x^2.$$

$$\therefore \quad \mathbf{a} = \frac{\Sigma \mathbf{y}}{\mathbf{n}} \quad \text{and} \quad \mathbf{b} = \frac{\Sigma \mathbf{xy}}{\Sigma \mathbf{x}^2}.$$

In practical problems, we prefer to choose origin in such a way that $\Sigma x = 0$. This will facilitate the computation of constants a and b.

Example 3. *Below are given figures of production (in ,000 tonnes) of a sugar factory :*

Year	*1981*	*1982*	*1983*	*1984*	*1985*	*1986*	*1987*
Production	*80*	*90*	*92*	*83*	*94*	*99*	*92*

Find the slope of a straight line trend to these figures by the method of least squares. (Plot the trend values on the graph).

Sol. Here the number of periods is equal to seven. Therefore, we shall take 1984 (the middle most period) as the origin.

Linear Trend by Least Square Method

S. No.	*Year*	*Production y (in '000 tonnes)*	*x = year – 1984*	x^2	*xy*
1	1981	80	– 3	9	– 240
2	1982	90	– 2	4	– 180
3	1983	92	– 1	1	– 92
4	1984	83	0	0	0
5	1985	94	1	1	94
6	1986	99	2	4	198
$n = 7$	1987	92	3	9	276
Total		630	0	28	56

Let the equation of trend line be $y_e = a + bx$.

The normal equations are :

$$\Sigma y = an + b\Sigma x \quad ...(1)$$

and

$$\Sigma xy = a\Sigma x + b\Sigma x^2. \quad ...(2)$$

(1) $\Rightarrow$ $630 = 7a + b.0 \Rightarrow a = 90$

(2) $\Rightarrow$ $56 = a.0 + 28b \Rightarrow b = 2$

$\therefore$ The equation of trend is $y_e = 90 + 2x$, with origin 1984 and x unit = 1 year.

The slope of the straight line trend is 2. This represent the average rate of increase of y w.r.t. time. The graph of the trend values is same as that in example 1.

Example 4. *Below are given figures of production (in thousand tonnes) of a sugar factory :*

Year	*1976*	*1977*	*1978*	*1979*	*1980*	*1981*	*1982*
Production	*77*	*88*	*94*	*85*	*91*	*98*	*90*

(i) *Fit a straight line trend by the method of least squares and calculate the trend values.* **(KU 1999, 2005 C)**

(ii) *What is the monthly increase in production.*

(iii) *Eliminate the trend by assuming* **(KU 2005 C)**

(a) *additive model* (b) *multiplicative model.*

Sol. Here the number of periods, 7 is odd.

We take the middle most period 1979 as the origin.

$\therefore$ $x = \text{year} - 1979$

Let y denotes the variable 'production (in thousand tonnes)'

Trend Line by Least Squares Method

S. No.	*Year*	*y*	*x = year – 1979*	x^2	*xy*
1	1976	77	– 3	9	– 231
2	1977	88	– 2	4	– 176
3	1978	94	– 1	1	– 94
4	1979	85	0	0	0
5	1980	91	1	1	91
6	1981	98	2	4	196
$n = 7$	1982	90	3	9	270
Total		623	0	28	56

Let the equation of trend line be $y_e = a + bx$.

The normal equations are :

$$\Sigma y = an + b\Sigma x \quad ...(1)$$

and

$$\Sigma xy = a\Sigma x + b\Sigma x^2. \quad ...(2)$$

(1) $\Rightarrow$ $623 = a(7) + b(0) \Rightarrow a = \dfrac{623}{7} = 89$

(2) $\Rightarrow$ $56 = a(0) + b(28) \Rightarrow b = \dfrac{56}{28} = 2.$

∴ **The equation of the trend line is $y_e = 89 + 2x$, with origin 1979 and x unit = 1 year.**

Trend values

For 1976, $x = -3$ ∴ $y_e(1976) = 89 + 2(-3) = 83$

For 1977, $x = -2.$ ∴ $y_e(1977) = 89 + 2(-2) = 85$

For 1978, $x = -1.$ ∴ $y_e(1978) = 89 + 2(-1) = 87$

For 1979, $x = 0$ ∴ $y_e(1979) = 89 + 2(0) = \mathbf{89}$

For 1980, $x = 1.$ ∴ $y_e(1980) = 89 + 2(1) = \mathbf{91}$

For 1981, $x = 2.$ ∴ $y_e(1981) = 89 + 2(2) = \mathbf{93}$

For 1982, $x = 3.$ ∴ $y_e(1982) = 89 + 2(3) = \mathbf{95}.$

(*ii*) Value of '*b*' = 2

∴ Annual increase of production = 2 × 1000 tonnes = 2000 tonnes

because the unit of *y* is thousand tonnes

∴ Monthly increase in production $= \frac{2000}{12}$ tonnes = **166.67 tonnes.**

(*iii*) (*a*) Time series model is **additive.**

∴ The trend eliminated values are given by $y - y_e$.

Year	*y*	y_e	*Trend eliminated value* $y - y_e$
1976	77	83	77—83 = **– 6**
1977	88	85	88—85 = **3**
1978	94	87	94—87 = **7**
1979	85	89	85—89 = **– 4**
1980	91	91	91—91 = **0**
1981	98	93	98—93 = **5**
1982	90	95	90—95 = **– 5**

(*b*) Trend series model is *multiplicative.*

∴ The trend eliminated values are given by y/y_e.

Year	*y*	y_e	*Trend eleminated value* y/y_e
1976	77	83	77 ÷ 83 = **0.928**
1977	88	85	88 ÷ 85 = **1.035**
1978	94	87	94 ÷ 87 = **1.080**
1979	85	89	85 ÷ 89 = **0.955**
1980	91	91	91 ÷ 91 = **1.000**
1981	98	93	98 ÷ 93 = **1.054**
1982	90	95	90 ÷ 95 = **0.947**

Example 5. *Find the trend values for the following series by the method of least squares :*

Year	*1976*	*1977*	*1978*	*1979*	*1980*	*1981*
Production (in crores kg)	*7*	*10*	*12*	*14*	*17*	*24*

(MDU 1996 ; KU 2006)

Sol. Here the number of periods is equal to six. Therefore, we take $\frac{1978+1979}{2} = 1978.5$ as the origin. Let y denote the variable 'production (in crores kg)'.

Trend Line by Least Squares Method

S. No.	*Year*	*y*	*x = year – 1978.5*	x^2	*xy*
1	1976	7	– 2.5	6.25	– 17.5
2	1977	10	– 1.5	2.25	– 15
3	1978	12	– 0.5	0.25	– 6
4	1979	14	0.5	0.25	7
5	1980	17	1.5	2.25	25.5
$n = 6$	1981	24	2.5	6.25	60
Total		84	0	17.50	54

Let the equation of trend line be $y_e = a + bx$.

The normal equations are :

$$\Sigma y = an + b\Sigma x \quad ...(1)$$

and
$$\Sigma xy = a\Sigma x + b\Sigma x^2. \quad ...(2)$$

(1) $\Rightarrow$ $84 = 6a + b(0)$ $\Rightarrow$ $a = \frac{84}{6} = 14$

(2) $\Rightarrow$ $54 = a(0) + b(17.5)$ $\Rightarrow$ $b = \frac{54}{17.5} = 3.0857.$

$\therefore$ The equation of trend line is $y_e = 14 + 3.0857x$, with origin 1978.5 and x unit = 1 year.

Trend Values

For 1976, $x = -2.5$ $\therefore$ $y_e\,(1976) = 14 + (3.0857)(-2.5) = \mathbf{6.2857}$

For 1977, $x = -1.5$ $\therefore$ $y_e\,(1977) = 14 + (3.0857)(-1.5) = \mathbf{9.3714}$

For 1978, $x = -0.5$ $\therefore$ $y_e\,(1978) = 14 + (3.0857)(-0.5) = \mathbf{12.4571}$

For 1979, $x = 0.5$ $\therefore$ $y_e\,(1979) = 14 + (3.0857)(0.5) = \mathbf{15.5428}$

For 1980, $x = 1.5$ $\therefore$ $y_e\,(1980) = 14 + (3.0857)(1.5) = \mathbf{18.6285}$

For 1981, $x = 2.5$ $\therefore$ $y_e\,(1981) = 14 + (3.085)(2.5) = \mathbf{21.7142.}$

Example 6. *The number of units of a product exported during 1980 – 1987 are given below. Fit a straight line trend to the data. Plot the data showing also the trend line. Find an estimate for 1988.*

Year	*1980*	*1981*	*1982*	*1983*	*1984*	*1985*	*1986*	*1987*
No. of units (in thousands)	*12*	*13*	*13*	*16*	*19*	*23*	*21*	*23*

(KU 1998)

Sol. Here the number of periods is eight. We take $\frac{1983+1984}{2} = 1983.5$ as the origin. In order to avoid decimals in the deviations, we define

$x = (\text{year} - 1983.5)2.$

Let y denote the variable 'no. of units in thousands'

Trend Line by Least Squares Method

S. No.	*Year*	*y*	*x*	x^2	*xy*
1	1980	12	– 7	49	– 84
2	1981	13	– 5	25	– 65
3	1982	13	– 3	9	– 39
4	1983	16	– 1	1	– 16
5	1984	19	1	1	19
6	1985	23	3	9	69
7	1986	21	5	25	105
$n = 8$	1987	23	7	49	161
Total		140	0	168	150

Let the equation of the trend line be $y_e = a + bx$.

The normal equations are :

$$\Sigma y = an + b\Sigma x \quad ...(1)$$

and $$\Sigma xy = a\Sigma x + b\Sigma x^2. \quad ...(2)$$

(1) $\Rightarrow$ $140 = 8a + b.0 \Rightarrow a = 140/8 = 17.5$

(2) $\Rightarrow$ $150 = a.0 + 168b \Rightarrow b = 150/168 = 0.89.$

$\therefore$ **The equation of trend line is y_e = 17.5 + 0.89x with origin = 1983.5 and x unit = 1/2 year.**

For 1988, $x = (1988 - 1983.5)2 = 4.5 \times 2 = 9.$

$\therefore$ The estimate value of $y(1988) = 17.5 + (0.89)9 =$ **25.51 thousand units.**

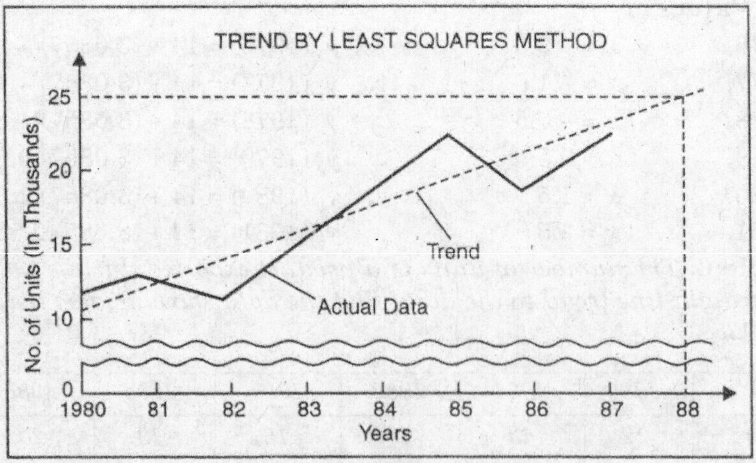

Example 7. *Find trend values by least squares method :*

Year	*1985*	*1986*	*1987*	*1988*	*1989*	*1990*	*1991*	*1992*
Production	*102.3*	*101.9*	*105.8*	*112.0*	*114.8*	*118.7*	*124.5*	*102.9*

(KU 1993)

Sol. Here the number of periods is even, we take $\frac{1988+1989}{2} = 1988.5$ as the origin. In order to avoid decimals in the deviations, we take $x = 2(\text{year} - 1988.5)$.

Let y denote the variable 'production'.

Trend Line by Least Squares Method

S. No.	Year	y	x	x^2	xy
1	1985	102.3	– 7	49	– 716.1
2	1986	101.9	– 5	25	– 509.5
3	1987	105.8	– 3	9	– 317.4
4	1988	112.0	– 1	1	– 112.0
5	1989	114.8	1	1	114.8
6	1990	118.7	3	9	356.1
7	1991	124.5	5	25	622.5
$n = 8$	1992	102.9	7	49	720.3
Total		882.9	0	170	158.7

Let the equation of the trend line by $y_e = a + bx$.

∴ The normal equations are :

$$\Sigma y = an + b\Sigma x \quad \text{...(1)}$$

and

$$\Sigma xy = a\Sigma x + b\Sigma x^2 \quad \text{...(2)}$$

$$(1) \Rightarrow \quad 882.9 = a(8) + b(0) \quad \Rightarrow a = \frac{882.9}{8} = 110.363$$

$$(2) \Rightarrow \quad 158.7 = a(0) + b(170) \quad \Rightarrow b = \frac{158.7}{170} = 0.934$$

∴ The equation of the trend line is $y_e = 110.363 + 0.934x$ with origin = 1988.5 and x unit = 1/2 year.

Trend values

For 1985, $x = -7$. ∴ $y_e(1985) = 110.363 + (0.934)(-7) = \mathbf{103.825}$

For 1986, $x = -5$. ∴ $y_e(1986) = 110.363 + (0.934)(-5) = \mathbf{105.693}$

For 1987, $x = -3$. ∴ $y_e(1987) = 110.363 + (0.934)(-3) = \mathbf{107.561}$

For 1988, $x = -1$. ∴ $y_e(1988) = 110.363 + (0.934)(-1) = \mathbf{109.429}$

For 1989, $x = 1$. ∴ $y_e(1989) = 110.363 + (0.934)(1) = \mathbf{111.297}$

For 1990, $x = 3$. ∴ $y_e(1990) = 110.363 + (0.934)(3) = \mathbf{113.165}$

For 1991, $x = 5$. ∴ $y_e(1991) = 110.363 + (0.934)(5) = \mathbf{115.033}$

For 1992, $x = 7$. ∴ $y_e(1992) = 110.363 + (0.934)(7) = \mathbf{116.901}$.

Example 8. *Below are given figures of production (in thousand tonnes) of a sugar factory :*

Year	*1976*	*1978*	*1979*	*1980*	*1981*	*1982*	*1985*
Production	*77*	*88*	*94*	*85*	*91*	*98*	*90*

Fit a straight line by the least squares method and calculate the trend values.

Sol. We define x = year – 1980 and y = production.

Trend Line by Least Squares Method

S. No.	Year	y	x = year – 1980	x^2	xy
1	1976	77	– 4	16	– 308
2	1978	88	– 2	4	– 176
3	1979	94	– 1	1	– 94
4	1980	85	0	0	0
5	1981	91	1	1	91
6	1982	98	2	4	196
$n = 7$	1985	90	5	25	450
		623	1	51	159

Let the equation of the trend line be $y_e = a + bx$.

The normal equations are :

$$\Sigma y = an + b\Sigma x \quad ...(1)$$

and $$\Sigma xy = a\Sigma x + b\Sigma x^2. \quad ...(2)$$

(1) $\Rightarrow$ $623 = 7a + b$ ...(3)

(2) $\Rightarrow$ $159 = a + 51b$ ...(4)

(4) × 7 $\Rightarrow$ $1113 = 7a + 357b$ ...(5)

(5) – (3) $\Rightarrow$ $490 = 356b \Rightarrow b = \dfrac{490}{356} = 1.376$

$\therefore$ (4) $\Rightarrow$ $a = 159 - 51b = 159 - 51(1.376) = 88.824$

$\therefore$ The equation of the trend line is **y_e = 88.824 + 1.376x with origin = 1980 and x unit = 1 year.**

Trend values

For 1976, $x = -4$. $\therefore$ $y_e(1976) = 88.824 + 1.376(-4) = \mathbf{83.32}$

For 1978, $x = -2$. $\therefore$ $y_e(1978) = 88.824 + 1.376(-2) = \mathbf{86.072}$

For 1979, $x = -1$. $\therefore$ $y_e(1979) = 88.824 + 1.376(-1) = \mathbf{87.448}$

For 1980, $x = 0$. $\therefore$ $y_e(1980) = 88.824 + 1.376(0) = \mathbf{88.824}$

For 1981, $x = 1$. $\therefore$ $y_e(1981) = 88.824 + 1.376(1) = \mathbf{90.2}$

For 1982, $x = 2$. $\therefore$ $y_e(1982) = 88.824 + 1.376(2) = \mathbf{91.576}$

For 1985, $x = 5$. $\therefore$ $y_e(1985) = 88.824 + 1.376(5) = \mathbf{95.704.}$

EXERCISE 4

1. Fit a straight line trend and find trend values for the following data by the method of least squares :

Year	1990	1991	1992	1993	1994
Profit (in thousand Rupees)	4	7	3	6	8

(KU 2000 C)

2. Fit a straight line trend by the method of Least Squares for the following series :

Year	1981	1982	1983	1984	1985	1986
Production	7	17	12	19	22	27

3. The production figures of a sugar factory are given below. Fit a straight line trend by the method of least squares and draw it on a graph paper along with the actual production figures :

Year	1951	1952	1953	1954	1955	1956	1957
Production (in thousand quintals)	80	90	92	83	94	99	92

4. Below are given the production (thousand quintals) figures of a sugar factory. Fit a straight line by Least Squares method and tabulate the trend values :

Year	1972	1973	1974	1975	1976	1977	1978
Production	12	10	14	11	13	15	16

5. Compute the straight line trend for the following data by using the method of least squares and show it graphically :

Year	1973	1974	1975	1976	1977	1978	1979	1980
Production (million tonnes)	38	40	65	72	69	60	87	95

6. Find out trend values by the method of Least Squares for the following series :

Year	1980	1981	1982	1983	1984	1985
Production (in lakh units)	7	10	12	14	17	24

7. Fit a straight line trend by the method of least squares for the following data :

Year	*Milk consumption (million gallons)*	*Year*	*Milk consumption (million gallons)*
1960	102.3	1965	118.7
1961	101.9	1966	124.5
1962	105.8	1967	129.9
1963	112.0	1968	134.8
1964	114.8		

8. Fit a straight line trend for the following series by the method of least squares. Also, estimate the value for the year 1993 :

Year	1984	1985	1986	1987	1988	1989	1990
Output	125	128	133	135	140	141	143

9. From the following data, determine the long-term trend, using the method of least squares :

Year	1963	1964	1965	1966	1967	1968	1969	1970
Income (in Lakh Rs.)	38	40	65	72	69	87	95	106

10. Compute secular trend by least square method from the following data :

Year	1970	1971	1972	1973	1974	1975	1976
Supply	23	25	26	24	25	29	30

11. Compute the trend values by the method of least squares from the data given below :

Year	*Output*	*Year*	*Output*
1972	5600	1976	4200
1973	5500	1977	3800
1974	5100	1978	3500
1975	4700	1979	3200

12. Your are given the annual profits (in ,000) for a certain firm for the years 1982-1988. Make an estimate of profit for the year 1989. You may assume linear trend in profits :

Year	1982	1983	1984	1985	1986	1987	1988
Profit (in ,000 Rs.)	60	72	75	65	80	85	95

13. Calculate trend values by the method of least squares and estimate production for the year 1995 :

Year	1984	1985	1986	1987	1988	1989	1990
Production of steel (in 10 lakh tonnes)	60	72	75	65	80	85	95

(MDU 1997)

14. Explain clearly what is meant by time series anlysis.
The following are the figures of production (in thousand tonnes) of a sugur factory :

Year	1941	1942	1943	1944	1945
Production	80	90	92	83	94

Fit a straight line by the least squares method.

15. Fit a straight line trend to the following data on the domestic demand for motor fuel :

Year	*Average monthly demand (million barrels)*	*Year*	*Average monthly demand (million barrels)*
1978	61	1984	96
1979	66	1985	100
1980	72	1986	103
1981	76	1987	110
1982	82	1988	114
1983	90		

16. The sales figures of a company in lakhs of rupees for the years 1974-1981 are given below :

Year	1974	1975	1976	1977	1978	1979	1980	1981
Sales	550	560	555	585	540	525	545	585

Fit a linear trend equation and estimate the sales for the year 1973.

17. From the data given below, fit a curve of the type $y = a + bx$:

Year	1980	1981	1982	1983	1984
Population (in ,000's)	132	142	157	174	191

18. Calculate trend values from the following data by applying the method of least squares :

Year	1973	1974	1975	1976	1977	1978	1979
Sales (in crore rupees)	20	23	22	25	26	29	30

Estimate the likely sales for the year 1982.

19. Fit a trend line by least squares method to the following data :

Year	1997	1998	1999	2000	2001	2002	2003
Production ('000 tonnes)	70	75	90	91	95	98	100

(KU 2003)

What is the rate of growth of production ?

20. Fit a straight line trend by the least squares method for the following data :

Year	1951	1961	1971	1981	1991
y	34	50	67	75	85

Estimate the value of y of for the year 2001. *(KU 1992, 2000)*

21. Find the trend values by using least squares method. Also find the trend value for 2005.

Year	1995	1996	1997	1998	1999	2000	2001
Production (in Qtl.)	700	743	816	834	907	860	961

(KU 2002 C)

Answers

1. $y_e = 5.6 + 0.7x$, where origin = 1992 and x unit = 1 year. Trend values : 4.2, 4.9, 5.6, 6.3, 7
2. $y_e = 5.12 + 3.49\,x$ where origin = 1981, x unit = 1 year
3. $y_e = 84 + 2\,x$, with origin = 1951 and x unit = 1 year
4. $y_e = 13 + 0.75\,x$, with origin = 1975 and x unit = 1 year. Trend values are 10.75, 11.5, 12.25, 13, 13.75, 14.5, 15.25
5. $y_e = 65.75 + 7.3333\,x$, with origin = 1976.5, x unit = 1 year
6. Trend values (in lakh units) : 6.2857, 9.3714, 12.4571, 15.5428, 18.6285, 21.7142
7. $y_e = 116.0778 + 4.3017\,x$ with origin = 1964 and x unit = 1 year
8. $y_e = 135 + 3.1\,x$, where origin = 1987 and x unit = 1 year ; 153.6

9. $y_e = 71.5 + 9.69\,x$, where origin = 1966.5 and x unit = 1 year
10. $y_e = 26 + x$, where origin = 1973 and x unit = 1 year
11. 5750, 5378.57, 5007.14, 4635.71, 4264.28, 3892.85 3521.42, 3149.99
12. Rs. 95428.40
13. 61.429, 66.286, 71.143, 76, 80.857, 85.714, 90.571 ; 114.856
14. $y_e = 87.8 + 2.1\,x$, where origin = 1983 and x unit = 1 year
15. $y_e = 88.18 + 5.418\,x$, where origin = 1983 and x unit = 1 year.
16. $y_e = 555.625 + 0.4167\,x$, where origin = 1977.5 and x unit = 1 year. y_e (1973) = 553.7498
17. $y_e = 159.2 + 15\,x$, where origin = 1982 and x unit = 1 year
18. 20.071, 21.714, 23,357, 25, 26.643, 28.286, 29.929 ; estimated value for 1982 = 34.858
19. $y_e = 88.429 + 5.036\,x$, where origin = 2000 and x unit = 1 year ; 0.428
20. $y_e = 62.2 + 1.27\,x$ where origin = 1971 and x unit = 1 year, y_e (2001) = 100.3
21. 712.86 Qtl., 752.43 Qtl., 792 Qtl., 831.57 Qtl., 871.14 Qtl., 910.71 Qtl., 950.28 Qtl., Estimated production of 2005 = 1108.56 Qtl.

---

21. NON-LINEAR TREND (PARABOLIC)

There are situations where linear trend is not found suitable. Linear trend is suitable when the tendency of the actual data is to move approximately in one direction. There are number of curves representing non-linear trend. In the present section, use shall consider parabolic trends. Parabolic trends will give better trend then the straight line trends.

Let $\{(t_i, y_i) : i = 1, 2, \ldots\ldots, n\}$ be the given time series. Let x denote the deviations of the time periods $(t_1, t_2 \ldots\ldots, t_n)$ from some fixed time period, called the origin. Let y_e denote the estimated (trend) values of the variable.

Let the equation of the required parabolic trend curve be

$$y_e = a + bx + cx^2$$

where, a, b, c are constants. This trend curve will satisfy the conditions :

(*i*) $\Sigma(y - y_e) = 0$

(*ii*) $\Sigma(y - y_e)^2$ is least.

In order to meet these requirements, we will have to use those values of a, b and c in the trend curve equation which satisfies the following *normal equations* :

$$\Sigma y = an + b\Sigma x + c\Sigma x^2 \quad \ldots(1)$$

$$\Sigma xy = a\Sigma x + b\Sigma x^2 + c\Sigma x^3 \quad \ldots(2)$$

$$\Sigma x^2 y = a\Sigma x^2 + b\Sigma x^3 + c\Sigma x^4. \quad \ldots(3)$$

Here also, it is very important to mention the origin and the x unit with the trend curve equation.

There is no specific rule for choosing the origin. But if we manage to choose the origin so as to make $\Sigma x = 0$, then we shall be reducing the calculation involved in computing a, b and c. In case the time periods $t_1, t_2, \ldots\ldots t_n$ advances by equal intervals and $\Sigma x = 0$, then we will also have $\Sigma x^3 = 0$. Here, the normal equations will reduce to :

$$\Sigma y = an + b.0 + c\Sigma x^2$$

$$\Sigma xy = a.0 + b\Sigma x^2 + c.0$$

$$\Sigma x^2 y = a\Sigma x^2 + b\,.0 + c\Sigma x^4$$

or

$$\Sigma y = an + c\Sigma x^2 \quad \ldots(1')$$

$$\Sigma xy = b\Sigma x^2 \quad \ldots(2')$$

$$\Sigma x^2 y = a\Sigma x^2 + c\Sigma x^4. \quad ...(3')$$

(2′) $\Rightarrow$ $b = \Sigma xy/\Sigma x^2$. The values of a and c will be obtained by solving the equations (1′) and (3′).

Example 1. *The prices of commodities during 1978 – 1983 are given below. Fit a parabola $y = a + bx + cx^2$ to this data. Estimate the price of commodity for the year 1984.*

Year	*1978*	*1979*	*1980*	*1981*	*1982*	*1983*
Price	*100*	*107*	*128*	*140*	*181*	*192*

Also plot actual and trend values on the graph.

Sol. Here the number of periods is six. Therefore, we take $\frac{1980 + 1981}{2} = 1980.5$ as the origin. In order to avoid decimals in the deviations, we define

$$x = (\text{year} - 1980.5)2.$$

Let y denote the variable 'price'.

Parabolic Trend by Least Squares Method

S. No.	*Year*	*y*	*x*	x^2	x^3	x^4	*xy*	x^2y
1	1978	100	– 5	25	– 125	625	– 500	2500
2	1979	107	– 3	9	– 27	81	– 321	963
3	1980	128	– 1	1	– 1	1	– 128	128
4	1981	140	1	1	1	1	140	140
5	1982	181	3	9	27	81	543	1629
$n = 6$	1983	192	5	25	125	625	960	4800
Total		848	0	70	0	1414	694	10160

Let the equation of parabolic trend be

$$y_e = a + bx + cx^2.$$

The normal equations are :

$$\Sigma y = an + b\Sigma x + c\Sigma x^2 \quad ...(1)$$

$$\Sigma xy = a\Sigma x + b\Sigma x^2 + c\Sigma x^3 \quad ...(2)$$

$$\Sigma x^2 y = a\Sigma x^2 + b\Sigma x^3 + c\Sigma x^4 \quad ...(3)$$

or

$$848 = 6a + b.0 + 70c$$

$$694 = a.0 + 70b + c.0$$

$$10160 = 70a + b.0 + 1414c$$

or

$$848 = 6a + 70c \quad ...(4)$$

$$694 = 70b \quad ...(5)$$

$$10160 = 70a + 1444c \quad ...(6)$$

(5) $\Rightarrow$ $b = 694/70 = 9.914$

(4) × 35 $\Rightarrow$ $29680 = 210a + 2450c$ ...(7)

(6) × 3 $\Rightarrow$ $30480 = 210a + 4242c$ ...(8)

(7) – (8) $\Rightarrow$ $-800 = 0 - 1792c$ $\Rightarrow$ $c = 0.446.$

$\therefore$ (4) $\Rightarrow$ $848 = 6a - 70\,(0.446)$ $\Rightarrow$ $a = 136.13.$

∴ The equation of parabolic trend is

$$y_e = 136.13 + 9.914x + 0.446x^2 \text{ with origin} = 1980.5 \text{ and } x \text{ unit} = \tfrac{1}{2} \text{year.}$$

Trend values

For 1978, $x = -5$

∴ $y_e\,(1978) = 136.13 + 9.914\,(-5) + (0.446)\,(-5)^2 = 97.710$

For 1979, $x = -3.$

∴ $y_e\,(1979) = 136.13 + 9.914\,(-3) + (0.446)\,(-3)^2 = 110.402$

For 1980, $x = -1.$

∴ $y_e\,(1980) = 136.13 + 9.914\,(-1) + (0.446)\,(-1)^2 = 126.662$

For 1981, $x = 1.$

∴ $y_e\,(1981) = 136.13 + 9.914\,(1) + (0.446)\,(1)^2 = 146.490$

For 1982, $x = 3$

∴ $y_e\,(1982) = 136.13 + 9.914\,(3) + (0.446)\,(3)^2 = 169.886.$

For 1983, $x = 5.$

∴ $y_e\,(1983) = 136.13 + 9.914\,(5) + (0.446)\,(5)^2 = 196.85$

For 1984, $x = 2\,(1984 - 1980.5) = 7.$

∴ The estimated value of 'price' for 1984

$$= y_e\,(1984) = 136.13 + 9.914(7) + (0.446)\,(7)^2 = \textbf{Rs. 227.382.}$$

The graph of actual and trend values is given below :

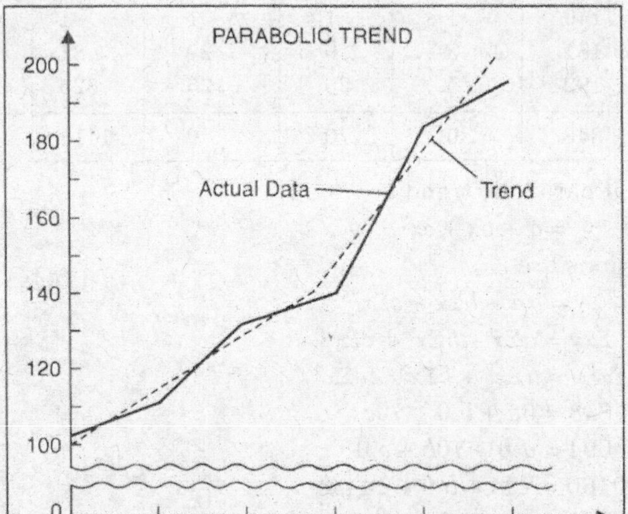

Example 2. *The following table shows our urban population as percentage of total population (1921-1961) :*

Census year	*1921*	*1931*	*1941*	*1951*	*1961*
% of total population	*11.4*	*12.1*	*13.9*	*17.3*	*18.0*

Compute the second degree trend equation for the data given above and from the equation obtained, determine the trend value for the census year 1991.

Sol. Here the number of periods is five. Therefore, we take 1941 as the origin.

Let y denote the variable "% of total population".

Second Degree Trend Equation by Least Squares Method

S. No.	Year	y	x	x^2	x^3	x^4	xy	x^2y
1	1921	11.4	– 20	400	– 8000	160000	– 228	4560
2	1931	12.1	– 10	100	– 1000	10000	– 121	1210
3	1941	13.9	0	0	0	0	0	0
4	1951	17.3	10	100	1000	10000	173	1730
$n = 5$	1961	18.0	20	400	8000	160000	360	7200
Total		72.7	0	1000	0	340000	184	14700

Let the second degree trend equation be

$$y_e = a + bx + cx^2.$$

The normal equations are :

$$\Sigma y = an + b\Sigma x + c\Sigma x^2 \quad ...(1)$$

$$\Sigma xy = a\Sigma x + b\Sigma x^2 + c\Sigma x^3 \quad ...(2)$$

$$\Sigma x^2y = a\Sigma x^2 + b\Sigma x^3 + c\Sigma x^4. \quad ...(3)$$

or

$$72.7 = 5a + b.0 + 1000c$$

$$184 = a.0 + 1000b + c.0$$

$$14700 = 1000a + b.0 + 340000c$$

or

$$72.7 = 5a + 1000c \quad ...(4)$$

$$184 = 1000b \quad ...(5)$$

$$14700 = 1000a + 340000c \quad ...(6)$$

(5) $\Rightarrow$ $b = 184/1000 = 0.184$

(4) × 200 $\Rightarrow$ $14540 = 1000a + 200000c$ ...(7)

(6) – (7) $\Rightarrow$ $160 = 0 + 140000c$ $\Rightarrow$ $c = 0.001143$

$\therefore$ (4) $\Rightarrow$ $72.7 = 5a + 1000\,(0.001143)$ $\Rightarrow$ $a = 14.3114.$

$\therefore$ The required equation of trend is

$$\mathbf{y_e = 14.3114 + 0.184x + 0.001143x^2}$$ **with origin = 1941 and x unit = 1 year.**

For 1991, $x = 1991 - 1941 = 50.$

$\therefore$ $y_e\,(1991) = 14.3114 + 0.184(50) + 0.001143(50)^2 = 26.3689.$

$\therefore$ The estimated percent of urban population for the census year 1991 = **26.3689%.**

EXERCISE 5

1. Find the equation of parabolic trend of second degree to the following data :

Year	1983	1984	1985	1986	1987
Variable	5	7	4	9	12

2. Find the equation of parabolic trend of second degree to the following data :

Year	1980	1981	1982	1983	1984	1985	1986
Outstanding loan of company 'X' (in thousand Rs.)	83	60	54	21	22	13	13

3. Estimate the value of y for the year 1979, by using the following data :

Year	1980	1981	1982	1983	1984
Variable (y)	10	12	13	10	8

For estimation, a parabolic trend is to be used. *(KU 2004)*

4. Fit a second degree parabolic trend to the data given below :

Year	1982	1983	1984	1985	1986
Variable	7	8	10	15	20

5. Fit a straight line trend and a parabolic trend to the following data :

Year	1993	1994	1995	1996	1997	1998	1999
y	12	14	12	26	42	40	50

6. The following are the production figures of an aluminium plant for the years 1990 to 2002 :

Year	*Production (in ,000 tonnes)*	*Year*	*Production (in ,000 tonnes)*
1990	12	1997	21
1991	20	1998	30
1992	10	1999	35
1993	11	2000	40
1994	12	2001	37
1995	13	2002	40
1996	10		

(*i*) Find the equation of parabolic trend.
(*ii*) Find the trend values for the years 1990—2002.
(*iii*) Plot the original data and trend values on a graph paper.
(*iv*) Estimate the production figure for the years 2003 and 2004.

Answers

1. $y_e = 5.97144 + 1.6x + 0.71428x^2$, where origin = 1985 and x unit = 1 year.
2. $y_e = 30 - 12x + 2x^2$, where origin = 1983 and x unit = 1 year.
3. 6.4003.
4. $y_e = 10.4286 + 3.3x + 0.7857x^2$, where origin = 1984 and x uint = 1 year.
5. $y_e = 25.9 + 7x + 0.524x^2$ where origin = 1996 and x unit = 1 year.

6. (*i*) $y = 17.9 + 2.69x + 0.312x^2$ where origin = 1996 and x unit = 1 year.

(*ii*) 13.28, 12.45, 12.26, 12.71, 13.80, 15.53, 17.90, 20.91, 24.56, 28.85, 33.78, 39.35, 45.56 thousand tonnes.

(*iv*) 52.41 thousand tonnes, 59.9 thousand tonnes.

22. NON-LINEAR TREND (EXPONENTIAL)

In this section, we shall study the method of finding non-linear exponential trend of a given time series.

Let $\{(t_i, y_i) : i = 1, 2, ..., n\}$ be the given time series. Let x denote the deviations of the time periods $\{t_1, t_2, ..., t_n\}$ from some fixed time period, called the origin. Let y_e denote the estimated (trend) values of the variable.

Let the equation of the required exponential trend curve be

$$y_e = ab^x \qquad ...(1)$$

where a, b are constants.

$$(1) \Rightarrow \qquad \log y_e = \log a + x \log b. \qquad ...(2)$$

The exponential trend curve will satisfy the conditions :

(*i*) $\Sigma(\log y - \log y_e) = 0$

(*ii*) $\Sigma(\log y - \log y_e)^2$ is least.

In order to meet these requirements we will have to use those values of a and b in the trend curve equation which satisfies the following *normal equations* :

$$\Sigma \log y = (\log a)n + (\log b)\Sigma x \qquad ...(3)$$

$$\Sigma x \log y = (\log a)\, \Sigma x + (\log b)\, \Sigma x^2. \qquad ...(4)$$

Here also, it is very important to mention the origin and the x unit with the trend curve equation.

If origin be chosen so that $\Sigma x = 0$, then the above normal equations reduces to

$$\Sigma \log y = (\log a)n + (\log b).0$$

and

$$\Sigma x \log y = (\log a).0 + (\log b)\, \Sigma x^2.$$

$$\therefore \qquad \log a = \frac{\Sigma \log y}{x} \quad \text{and} \quad \log b = \frac{\Sigma x \log y}{\Sigma x^2}.$$

$$\therefore \qquad \mathbf{a = AL}\left(\frac{\mathbf{\Sigma \log y}}{\mathbf{n}}\right) \quad \textbf{and} \quad \mathbf{b = AL}\left(\frac{\mathbf{\Sigma x \log y}}{\mathbf{\Sigma x^2}}\right).$$

In practical problems, we prefer to choose origin in such a way that $\Sigma x = 0$. This will facilitate the computation of constants a and b.

Example 1. *The sales of a company in lakhs of rupees for the years 1996 to 2002 are given below :*

Year	*1996*	*1997*	*1998*	*1999*	*2000*	*2001*	*2002*
Sales (in lakh ruppes)	*16*	*23*	*33*	*46*	*66*	*95*	*137*

Estimate the sales for the year 2003 using an exponential trend curve.

Sol. Here the number of periods is equal to seven, an odd number.

∴ We take 1999 (the middle most period) as the origin.

Exponential Trend by Least Squares Method

S. No.	*Year*	*Sales (in lakhs rupees) y*	*log y*	*x = year-1999*	x^2	*x log y*
1	1996	16	1.2041	− 3	9	− 3.6123
2	1997	23	1.3617	− 2	4	− 2.7234
3	1998	33	1.5185	− 1	1	− 1.5185
4	1999	46	1.6628	0	0	0
5	2000	66	1.8195	1	1	1.8195
6	2001	95	1.9777	2	4	3.9554
7	2002	137	2.1367	3	9	6.4101
$x = 7$			$\Sigma \log y = 11.6810$	$\Sigma x = 0$	$\Sigma x^2 = 28$	$\Sigma x \log y = 4.3308$

Let the equation of the exponential trend be $y_e = ab^x$.

$\therefore$ $\log y_e = \log a + x \log b$ ...(1)

The normal equations are :

$$\Sigma \log y = (\log a)n + (\log b)\Sigma x \quad ...(2)$$

and $$\Sigma x \log y = (\log a)\Sigma x + (\log b)\Sigma x^2. \quad ...(3)$$

(2) $\Rightarrow$ $11.6810 = 7 \log a + (\log b).\ 0$

$\Rightarrow$ $\log a = \dfrac{11.6810}{7} = 1.6687$

(3) $\Rightarrow$ $4.3308 = (\log a).0 + (\log b)\ .\ 28$

$\Rightarrow$ $\log b = \dfrac{4.3308}{28} = 0.1547$

$\therefore$ (1) $\Rightarrow$ $\log y_e = 1.6687 + 0.1547x.$

For the year 2003, $x = 2003 - 1999 = 4.$

$\therefore$ For 2003, $\log y_e = 1.6687 + (0.1547)4 = 2.2875$

$\therefore$ $y_e = \text{AL}\ (2.2875) = 193.8$

$\therefore$ For the year 2003, the estimated sales are **Rs. 193.8 lakh.**

Example 2. *You are given the population figures of India as follows :*

Census year	*1911*	*1921*	*1931*	*1941*	*1951*	*1961*	*1971*
Population (in crores)	*25.0*	*25.1*	*27.9*	*31.9*	*36.1*	*43.9*	*54.7*

Fit an exponential trend to the above data by the method of least squares and find the trend values. Also estimate the population for 1991 and 2001.

Sol. Here the number of periods is equal to seven, an odd number.

$\therefore$ We take 1941 (the middle most period) as the origin.

Exponential Trend by Least Squares Method

S. No.	*Census year*	*Population (in crores)*	*log y*	$x = \frac{year - 1941}{10}$	x^2	*x log y*
1	1911	25.0	1.3979	– 3	9	– 4.1937
2	1921	25.1	1.3997	– 2	4	– 2.7994
3	1931	27.9	1.4456	– 1	1	– 1.4456
4	1941	31.9	1.5038	0	0	0
5	1951	36.1	1.5575	1	1	1.5575
6	1961	43.9	1.6425	2	4	3.2850
7	1971	54.7	1.7380	3	9	5.2140
$n = 7$			$\Sigma \log y = 10.6850$	$\Sigma x = 0$	$\Sigma x^2 = 28$	$\Sigma x \log y = 1.6178$

Let the equation of the exponential trend be $y = ab^x$.

$\therefore \quad \log y = \log a + x \log b \qquad ...(1)$

The normal equations are :

$\Sigma \log y = (\log a)n + (\log b)\, \Sigma x \qquad ..(2)$

and $\quad \Sigma x \log y = (\log a)\, \Sigma x + (\log b)\, \Sigma x^2. \qquad ...(3)$

(2) $\Rightarrow \quad 10.6850 = 7 \log a + (\log b).0 \quad \Rightarrow \quad \log a = \dfrac{10.6850}{7} = 1.5264$

(3) $\Rightarrow \quad 1.6178 = (\log a).0 + (\log b).28 \quad \Rightarrow \quad \log b = \dfrac{1.6178}{28} = 0.0578.$

$\therefore$ (1) $\Rightarrow \quad \log y_e = 1.5264 + 0.0578x \qquad ...(4)$

Also $\quad \log a = 1.5264 \quad \Rightarrow \quad a = \text{AL } 1.5264 = 33.60$

and $\quad \log b = 0.0578 \quad \Rightarrow \quad b = \text{AL } 0.0578 = 1.142$

$\therefore \quad y_e = ab^x \quad \Rightarrow \quad \mathbf{y_e = 33.6 \times (1.142)x}$**, where** $\mathbf{x = \dfrac{year - 1941}{10}}$.

This represents the exponential trend equation.

Trend values

For 1911, $\quad x = -3$ and $y_e = 33.6 \times (1.142)^{-3} =$ **22.5601 crores**

For 1921, $\quad x = -2$ and $y_e = 33.6 \times (1.142)^{-2} = 33.6 \times (1.142)^{-3} \times 1.142$
$= 22.5601 \times 1.142 =$ **25.7636 crores**

For 1931, $\quad x = -1$ and $y_e = 33.6 \times (1.142)^{-1} = 33.6 \times (1.142)^{-2} \times 1.142$
$= 25.7636 \times 1.142 =$ **29.422 crores**

For 1941, $\quad x = 0$ and $y_e = 33.6 \times (1.142)^0 =$ **33.6 crores**

For 1951, $\quad x = 1$ and $y_e = 33.6 \times (1.142)^1 =$ **38.3712 crores**

For 1961, $\quad x = 2$ and $y_e = 33.6 \times (1.142)^2 = 33.6 \times 1.142 \times 1.142$
$= 38.3712 \times 1.142 =$ **43.8199 crores**

For 1971, $\quad x = 3$ and $y_e = 33.6 \times (1.142)^3 = 33.6 \times (1.142)^2 \times 1.142$
$= 43.8199 \times 1.142 =$ **50.0423 crores**

Estimated population for 1991 and 2001

For 1991, $x = \dfrac{1991 - 1941}{10} = 5.$

$\therefore \quad y_e(1991) = 33.6 \times (1.142)^5 = 33.6 \times (1.142)^3 \times (1.142)^2$

$= 50.0423 \times (1.142)^2 =$ **65.2634 crores.**

For 2001, $x = \dfrac{2001 - 1941}{10} = 6.$

$\therefore \quad y_e(2001) = 33.6 \times (1.142)^6 = 33.6 \times (1.142)^5 \times 1.142 = 65.2634 \times 1.142 =$ **74.5408 crores.**

EXERCISE 6

1. Fit an exponential trend to the following data :

Year	1998	1999	2000	2001	2002
y	1.6	4.5	13.8	40.2	135.0

2. Fit an exponential trend to the following data :

Year	1996	1997	1998	1999	2000
Profit (,000 Rs.)	65	92	132	190	275

3. Fit an exponential trend to the following data :

Year	1997	1998	1999	2000	2001
y	3.2	9.0	27.6	80.4	250.0

4. Given the following population figures of India, estimate the population for 1991 and 2001, using exponential trend :

Year	1921	1931	1941	1951	1961	1971	1981
Population (in crores)	25.1	27.9	31.9	36.1	43.9	54.8	68.5

5. Growth of Indian merchant shipping fleet from 1968 to 1977 is given below. Fit a trend function $y = AB^u$ where y represents shipping fleet measured in million gross registered tonnes and x is the year while A and B are constants :

Year	*Shipping fleet (million tonnes)*	*Year*	*Shipping fleet (million tones)*
1968	1.95	1973	2.89
1969	2.24	1974	3.49
1970	2.40	1975	3.87
1971	2.48	1976	5.09
1972	2.65	1977	5.48

Answers

1. $y = 13.79\ (2.977)^x$, where x = year – 2000
2. $y = 133\ (1.43)^x$, where x = year – 1998
3. $y = 27.54\ (2.98)^x$, where x = year – 1999.
4. $y = 38.80\ (1.19)^x$, where $x = \dfrac{\text{year} - 1951}{10}$, 77.81 crores, 92.59 crores.
5. $y = 3.07\ (1.06)^u$, where $u = 2(x - 1972.5)$.

23. CONVERSION OF TREND EQUATIONS

We have already noted that the choice of origin in computing trend equation is only a matter of convenience. We generally choose origin so as to make the sum of deviations equal to zero.

There are three characteristics of a trend equation. The first characteristic is the *origin* of time. A change in origin may alter the constants in the trend equation but the ultimate trend values will come out to be same. The second characteristic is the *unit of time*. The unit of time may be one year, one month, one week, etc. Generally the unit of time is one year. The third characteristic is the *unit of variable* of the time series. For example, the unit of time may be one year and the value of the corresponding variable may be taken as annual total or quarterly average or monthly average etc.

We shall undertake the following conversions of trend equations :

(*i*) Conversion of the origin.

(*ii*) Conversion of the trend values.

24. CONVERSION OF THE ORIGIN

Let $y_e = f(x)$ be the equation of the trend, where x denote the deviations of time periods from the origin and y is the variable of the time series. Let us suppose that the origin is to be shifted by k periods.

If the new origin is shifted *forward*, then the new trend equation is

$$\mathbf{y_e = f(x + k).}$$

If the new origin is shifted *backward*, then the new trend equation is

$$\mathbf{y_e = f(x - k).}$$

Example 1. *The parabolic trend equation of a time series is given by* $y_e = 150 + 4x - 0.3x^2$ *with origin = 1983 and x unit = 1 year. Shift the origin to (i) 1980 (ii) 1984.*

Sol. The given equation of the parabolic trend is

$$y_e = 150 + 4x - 0.3x^2.$$

The origin under reference is 1983.

(*i*) New origin is 1980.

∴ The origin is to shifted three periods in the backward direction.

∴ To obtain the required trend equation, x is to be replaced by $x - 3$ in the equation.

∴ The required equation is

$$y_e = 150 + 4\,(x - 3) - 0.3(x - 3)^2$$

or $$y_e = 150 + 4x - 12 - 0.3\,(x^2 - 6x + 9)$$

or $$\mathbf{y_e = 135.3 + 5.8x - 0.3x^2}.$$

(*ii*) New origin is 1984.

∴ The origin is to be shifted one period in the forward direction.

∴ To obtain the required trend equation, x is to be replaced by $x + 1$ in the equation.

∴ The required equation is

$$y_e = 150 + 4(x + 1) - 0.3(x + 1)^2$$

or
$$y_e = 150 + 4x + 4 - 0.3(x^2 + 2x + 1)$$

or
$$\mathbf{y_e = 153.7 + 3.4x - 0.3x^2.}$$

25. CONVERSION OF TREND VALUES

Let $y_e = a + bx$

with x unit = 1 year, y unit = annual total, be the equation of straight line trend for a time series.

If we are interested in converting this trend equation so that x unit = 1 year and y unit = monthly average, then the required equation is

$$y_e = \frac{1}{12}(a + bx) \text{ i.e. } \mathbf{y_e = \frac{a}{12} + \frac{b}{12}x.}$$

Here y will represent the monthly average during a year.

In case, we are interested in converting this trend equation so that x unit = 1 month and y unit = monthly average, then the required equation is

$$y_e = \frac{1}{12}\left(a + b\frac{x}{12}\right) \text{i.e. } \mathbf{y_e = \frac{a}{12} + \frac{b}{144}x.}$$

In case of parabolic trend, the corresponding results hold good.

Example 2. *The parabolic trend equation of a time series is given by $y_e = 15 + x - x^2$, with origin 1980 and x unit = 1 year, y = annual production. Convert the trend equation so that (i) x unit = 1 year, y = average monthly production and (ii) x unit = 1 month, y = average monthly production.*

Sol. The equation of the trend curve is

$$y_e = 15 + x - x^2$$

with origin = 1980, x unit = 1 year and y unit = annual production.

(*i*) In this case, we have only to change the y unit.

∴ The required equation is

$$y_e = \frac{1}{12}(15 + x - x^2) \text{ i.e., } \mathbf{y_e = \frac{15}{12} + \frac{1}{12}x - \frac{1}{12}x^2}$$

with origin 1980, x unit = 1 year and y unit = average monthly production.

(*ii*) In this case, we have to change the given annual trend equation to monthly trend equation.

∴ The required equation is

$$y_e = \frac{1}{12}\left(15 + \frac{x}{12} - \left(\frac{x}{12}\right)^2\right) \text{ i.e., } \mathbf{y_e = \frac{15}{12} + \frac{1}{144}x - \frac{1}{1728}x^2}$$

with origin = 1st July 1980, x unit = 1 month and y unit = average monthly production.

Example 3. *The trend equation of annual profit of a manufacturing concern is given by*

$$y_e = 157 + 15x,$$

where origin = 1st July 1985, x unit = 1 year, y unit = annual profit in thousand rupees. Step down the trend equation on monthly basis and shift the origin forward to 1st Sept. 1985.

Sol. The given trend equation is

$$y_e = 157 + 15x.$$

We shall first change the trend equation on monthly basis.

The required equation is

$$y_e = \frac{1}{12}\left(157 + \frac{x}{12}\right) \text{ i.e., } y_e = \frac{157}{12} + \frac{15}{144}x$$

with origin = 1st July 1985, x unit = 1 month and y unit = average monthly profit (in thousand rupees).

Now the origin is to shifted to 1st Sept. 1985.

∴ The new origin is 2 units in the forward direction.

∴ The required equation is obtained by replacing x by $x + 2$ in the trend equation.

∴ The required equation is

$$y_e = \frac{157}{12} + \frac{15}{144}(x + 2) \quad \text{or} \quad \mathbf{y_e = 13.2917 + 0.1042x}$$

with origin = 1st Sept. 1985, x unit = 1 month and y unit = average monthly profit.

Example 4. *Below are given the profits of a firm (in Rs. 000) for the years 1993 to 1999 :*

Years	*1993*	*1994*	*1995*	*1996*	*1997*	*1998*	*1999*
Profits	*23*	*25*	*26*	*24*	*25*	*29*	*30*

Obtain the following :

(i) Fit a straight line trend by the method of least squares and tabulate the trend values,

(ii) Convert your annual trend equation into a monthly trend equation,

(iii) Eliminate trend by assuming an additive model. What do the resulting values represent ? (KU 2002)

Sol. (*i*) Let x = year – 1996 and y denote the variable 'profit'.

Trend Line by Least Squares Method

S. No.	*Year*	*y*	*x = year – 1996*	x^2	*xy*	*Trend value* y_e *(= 26 + x)*
1	1993	23	– 3	9	– 69	26 + (– 3) = 23
2	1994	25	– 2	4	– 50	26 + (– 2) = 24
3	1995	26	– 1	1	– 26	26 + (– 1) = 25
4	1996	24	0	0	0	26 + 0 = 26
5	1997	25	1	1	25	26 + 1 = 27
6	1998	29	2	4	58	26 + 2 = 28
7	1999	30	3	9	90	26 + 3 = 29
$n = 7$		182	0	28	28	

Let the equation of trend line be $y = a + bx$.

The normal equations are :

$$\Sigma y = an + b\,\Sigma x \quad \ldots(1)$$

$$\Sigma xy = a\Sigma x + b\Sigma x^2 \quad \ldots(2)$$

(1) $\Rightarrow$ $182 = a(7) + b(0) \;\Rightarrow\; a = \dfrac{182}{7} = 26$

(2) $\Rightarrow$ $28 = a(0) + b(28) \;\Rightarrow\; b = \dfrac{28}{28} = 1$

$\therefore$ The equation of the trend line is $y_e = 26 + 1x$ *i.e.*, $\mathbf{y_e = 26 + x}$ **with origin 1996 and x unit = 1 year.**

The trend values are **23, 24, 25, 26, 27, 28, 29.**

(*ii*) The equation of the trend line on the monthly basis is

$$y_e = \frac{1}{12}\left(26 + \frac{x}{12}\right) \quad i.e., \quad \mathbf{y_e = \frac{13}{6} + \frac{x}{144}}$$

With origin = 1st July 1996, x unit = 1 month and y unit = average monthly profit.

(*iii*) The time series model is given to be *additive*.

$\therefore$ The trend eleminated values are given by $y - y_e$.

Year	y	y_e	*Trend eliminated value* $y - y_e$
1993	23	23	23 – 23 = **0**
1994	25	24	25 – 24 = **1**
1995	26	25	26 – 25 = **1**
1996	24	26	24 – 26 = **– 2**
1997	25	27	25 – 27 = **– 2**
1998	29	28	29 – 28 = **1**
1999	30	29	30 – 29 = **1**

Since the data is annual, trend eliminated values contain cyclic variations and irregular variation

26. MERITS AND DEMERITS

Merits 1. This is a mathematical method.

2. This method can also be used for forecasting.

3. This method can be used for estimating linear as well as non-linear trends.

Demerits 1. This method involves much calculation work.

2. This method of fitting trend is not flexible, because if just one more value of the variable is added to the data, the entire calculations are changed.

EXERCISE 7

1. The parabolic trend equation of a time series is given by $y_e = 1200 + 4x - 2x^2$ with origin = 1980 and x unit = 1 year. Shift the origin to (*i*) 1984 and (*ii*) 1979.

2. Convert the following trend equation in to annual trend equation :
The trend equation is $y = 5 + 0.01x$, where origin = 1st July 1984, x unit = 1 month, y unit = monthly profit (in thousand rupees).

3. Convert the following trend equation in to annual trend equation :
The trend equation is $y = 5 + 0.01x$, where origin = 15th July 1984, x unit = 1 month, y unit = monthly profit (in thousand rupees).

4. Trend equation for yearly sales (in '000 Rs.) for a commodity with 1982 as origin is $y = 507 + 60x$. Determine the trend equation to give the monthly trend values.

5. Trend equation for yearly sales (in '000 Rs.) for a commodity with 1982 as origin is $y = 507 + 60x$. Determine the trend equation to give the monthly trend values with 15 March, 1983 as origin and also calculate the trend value for August 1983.

Answers

1. (*i*) $y_e = 1184 - 12x - 2x^2$, with origin = 1984
(*ii*) $y_e = 1194 + 8x - 2x^2$ with origin = 1979.

2. $y = 12(5) + 144(.01)x = 60 + 1.44x$, where origin = 1984 and x unit = 1 year and y = annual profit (in thousand rupees).

3. $y = 12\left(5 - \frac{0.01}{2}\right) + 144(0.01)x = 59.94 + 1.44x$, where origin = 1984, x unit = 1 year and y = annual profit (in thousand rupees) (First change the origin of given equation to 1st July, 1984).

4. $y = 42.25 + 0.4167x$, where origin = 1st July, 1982, x unit = 1 month and y unit = average monthly sales (in '000 Rs.).

5. $y = \frac{507}{12} + \frac{60}{144}(x + 8.5) = 45.7919 + 0.4167x$, with origin = 15th March, 1983, x unit = 1 month and y unit = average monthly sales (in thousand rupees). Estimated value of y for August, 1983 = Rs. 47875.20.

---

27. COMPUTATION OF SEASONAL INDICES

Monthly or quarterly data relating to economics and Business show strong seasonal movements. For example, if we consider the profits figures of an ice cream factory, we find that the profits figure during the months of summer season are more than those for months of winter season. Seasonal variations are revealed only when that data is given on the monthly or quaterly basis.

A set of numbers showing relative values of a time series variable during the months (resp. quarters) of a year are called **seasonal indices.** The average of seasonal indices for the whole year must be 100 *i.e.*, the sum of the seasonal indices should be 1200 (resp. 400). For example, if the profit of a firm during I quarter II quarter, III quarter and IV quarter be 90%, 130%, 82% and 98% of the average quarterly protits for the whole year, then the numbers 90, 130, 82 and 98 gives the seasonal indices of the year. Here one can note that 90 + 130 + 82 + 98 = 400. The following are the methods of computing seasonal indices :

(*i*) Simple Average Method
(*ii*) Ratio to Trend Method
(*iii*) Ratio to Moving Average Method
(*iv*) Link Relative Method.

28. SIMPLE AVERAGE METHOD

The following are the working rules to find the seasonal indices by the simple average method :

Step I. *Find totals of different quarters (resp. months).*

Step II. *Divide the totals by the number of years. This gives quarterly (resp. monthly) average.*

Step III. *Find the average of the averages obtained in step II. This average is called the* ***grand average.***

Step IV. *Find seasonal indices by using the formula :*

$$\text{Seasonal index} = \frac{\text{Quarterly (resp. monthly) average}}{\text{Grand average}} \times 100.$$

Step V. *Check that the sum of quarterly (resp. monthly) seasonal indices is 400 (resp. 1200). If it is not so, then adjest the seasonal indices by multiplying by a suitable factor.*

Example 1. *Find the quarterly seasonal indices for the following data by using simple average method :*

Year	*Quarter*			
	I	*II*	*III*	*IV*
1996	*4*	*3*	*3*	*6*
1997	*5*	*4*	*6*	*7*
1998	*4*	*3*	*4*	*3*
1999	*5*	*4*	*5*	*5*
2000	*6*	*5*	*4*	*6*

Seasonal Indices by Simple Average Method

Year	*Quarter*			
	I	*II*	*III*	*IV*
1996	4	3	3	6
1997	5	4	6	7
1998	4	3	4	3
1999	5	4	5	5
2000	6	5	4	6
Quarterly totals	24	19	22	27
Quarterly average	$\frac{24}{5} = 4.8$	$\frac{19}{5} = 3.8$	$\frac{22}{5} = 4.4$	$\frac{27}{5} = 5.4$
Seasonal index	$\frac{4.8}{4.6} \times 100$ $= 104.35$	$\frac{3.8}{4.6} \times 100$ $= 82.61$	$\frac{4.4}{4.6} \times 100$ $= 95.65$	$\frac{5.4}{4.6} \times 100$ $= 117.39$

Grand average $= \dfrac{4.8 + 3.8 + 4.4 + 5.4}{4} = 4.6$

Sum of seasonal indices = 104.35 + 82.61 + 95.65 + 117.39 = 400.

∴ Seasonal indices are **104.35, 82.61, 95.65 and 117.39.**

Example 2. *Find the quarterly seasonal indices for the following data by using simple average method :*

Quarter	*Year*					
	1997	*1998*	*1999*	*2000*	*2001*	*2002*
I	*3.5*	*3.5*	*3.5*	*4.0*	*4.1*	*4.2*
II	*3.9*	*4.1*	*3.9*	*4.6*	*4.4*	*4.6*
III	*3.4*	*3.7*	*3.7*	*3.8*	*4.2*	*4.3*
IV	*3.6*	*4.8*	*4.0*	*4.5*	*4.5*	*4.7*

Sol. **Seasonal Indices by Simple Average Method**

Year	*Quarter*			
	I	*II*	*III*	*IV*
1997	3.5	3.9	3.4	3.6
1998	3.5	4.1	3.7	4.8
1999	3.5	3.9	3.7	4.0
2000	4.0	4.6	3.8	4.5
2001	4.1	4.4	4.2	4.5
2002	4.2	4.6	4.3	4.7
Querterly totals	22.8	25.5	23.1	26.1
Quarterly average	$\frac{22.8}{6} = 3.8$	$\frac{25.5}{6} = 4.25$	$\frac{23.1}{6} = 3.85$	$\frac{26.1}{6} = 4.35$
Seasonal index	$\frac{3.8}{4.06} \times 100$ = 93.60	$\frac{4.25}{4.06} \times 100$ = 104.68	$\frac{3.85}{4.06} \times 100$ = 94.83	$\frac{4.35}{4.06} \times 100$ = 107.14

Grand average $= \dfrac{3.8 + 4.25 + 3.85 + 4.35}{4} = 4.06$

Sum of seasonal indices = 93.60 + 104.68 + 94.83 + 107.14 = 400.25 ≠ 400.

∴ We find adjusted seasonal indices.

$$\frac{93.60}{400.25} \times 400 = 93.54 \qquad \frac{104.68}{400.25} \times 400 = 104.61$$

$$\frac{94.83}{400.25} \times 400 = 94.77 \qquad \frac{107.14}{400.25} \times 100 = 107.08.$$

∴ Adjusted seasonal indices are : **93.54, 104.61, 94.77** and **107.08.**

Example 3. *Use the method of monthly averages to determine the mon thly indices for the following data of production in lakhs of tonnes of a commodity for the years 2000, 2001 and 2002 :*

Year	*Month*											
	J	*F*	*M*	*A*	*M*	*J*	*J*	*A*	*S*	*O*	*N*	*D*
2000	*12*	*11*	*10*	*14*	*15*	*15*	*16*	*13*	*11*	*10*	*12*	*15*
2001	*15*	*14*	*13*	*16*	*16*	*15*	*17*	*12*	*13*	*12*	*13*	*14*
2002	*16*	*15*	*14*	*16*	*15*	*17*	*16*	*13*	*10*	*10*	*11*	*15*

Sol. Seasonal Indices by Simple Average Method

Year	*Month*											
	J	*F*	*M*	*A*	*M*	*J*	*J*	*A*	*S*	*O*	*N*	*D*
2000	12	11	10	14	15	15	16	13	11	10	12	15
2001	15	14	13	16	16	15	17	12	13	12	13	14
2002	16	15	14	16	15	17	16	13	10	10	11	15
Monthly Totals	43	40	37	46	46	47	49	38	34	32	36	44
Monthly average	$\frac{43}{12}=$ 3.58	$\frac{40}{12}=$ 3.33	$\frac{37}{12}=$ 3.08	$\frac{46}{12}=$ 3.83	$\frac{46}{12}=$ 3.83	$\frac{47}{12}=$ 3.92	$\frac{49}{12}=$ 4.08	$\frac{38}{12}=$ 3.17	$\frac{34}{12}=$ 2.83	$\frac{32}{12}=$ 2.67	$\frac{36}{12}=$ 3	$\frac{44}{12}=$ 3.67
Seasonal index	$\frac{3.58}{3.42}\times 100$ = 104.68	$\frac{3.33}{3.42}\times 100$ = 97.37	$\frac{3.08}{3.42}\times 100$ = 90.06	$\frac{3.83}{3.42}\times 100$ = 111.99	$\frac{3.83}{3.42}\times 100$ = 111.99	$\frac{3.92}{3.42}\times 100$ = 114.62	$\frac{4.08}{3.42}\times 100$ = 119.30	$\frac{3.17}{3.42}\times 100$ = 92.69	$\frac{2.83}{3.42}\times 100$ = 82.75	$\frac{2.67}{3.42}\times 100$ = 78.07	$\frac{3}{3.42}\times 100$ = 87.72	$\frac{3.67}{3.42}\times 100$ = 107.31

Grand average

$$= \frac{3.58 + 3.33 + 3.08 + 3.83 + 3.83 + 3.92 + 4.08 + 3.17 + 2.83 + 2.67 + 3 + 3.67}{12} = 3.42$$

Sum of seasonal indices

$$= 104.68 + 97.37 + 90.06 + 111.99 + 111.99 + 114.62 + 119.30 + 92.69 + 82.75 + 78.07 + 87.72 + 107.31$$

$= 1198.55$, which is very close to 1200.

∴ Adjustment of indices is not required.

∴ Seasonal indices are : **104.68, 97.37, 90.06, 111.99, 111.99, 114.62, 119.30, 92.69, 82.75, 78.07, 87.72,** and **107.31.**

29. MERITS AND DEMERITS

Merits 1. This method is simple to understand.

2. This is the simplest of all methods of computing seasonal indices.

Demerit. This method assumes that there is no trend component in the given time series. This is not a justified assumption.

EXERCISE 8

1. Calculate the seasonal indices for the following data by using simple average method :

Year	*I Quarter*	*II Quarter*	*III Quarter*	*IV Quarter*
1995	72	68	80	70
1996	76	70	82	74
1997	74	66	84	80
1998	76	74	84	78
1999	78	74	86	82

2. Calculate the seasonal indices for the following data by using simple average method :

Quarter	*1999*	*2000*	*2001*	*2002*
I	3.7	3.7	4.0	3.3
II	4.1	3.9	4.1	4.4
III	3.3	3.6	3.3	4.0
IV	3.5	3.6	3.1	4.0

3. The number (in hundred) of letters posted in a certain city on each day in a typical period of five weeks was as follows :

Week	*Sun.*	*Mon.*	*Tues.*	*Wed.*	*Thurs.*	*Fri.*	*Sat.*
Ist	18	161	170	164	153	181	76
IInd	18	165	179	157	168	195	85
IIIrd	21	162	169	153	139	185	82
IVth	24	171	182	170	162	179	95
Vth	27	162	186	170	170	182	120

Find the seasonal indices of the week days by using simple average method.

4. Find the seasonal indices for the following data by using simple average method :

Month	*2000*	*2001*	*2002*	*Month*	*2000*	*2001*	*2002*
Jan.	15	23	25	July	20	22	30
Feb.	16	22	25	Aug.	28	28	34
March	18	28	35	Sept.	29	32	38
April	18	27	36	Oct.	33	37	47
May	23	31	36	Nov.	33	34	41
June	23	28	30	Dec.	38	44	53

5. Find the seasonal indices for the following data by using simple average method :

Months	*1997*	*1998*	*1999*	*2000*	*2001*
Jan.	80	81	82	84	86
Feb.	84	83	80	80	85
March	76	73	75	70	75
April	70	65	53	48	52
May	65	60	55	62	64
June	60	64	70	50	56
July	55	50	45	40	45
Aug.	54	45	56	58	60
Sept.	56	60	62	55	65
Oct.	60	75	65	66	70
Nov.	75	80	70	84	85
Dec.	85	90	92	88	96

6. The following are the data relating exports of a commodity in crores of rupees. Find the seasonal indices by using simple average method :

Month	*1996*	*1997*	*1998*	*1999*	*2000*
Jan.	28	33	29	29	31
Feb.	20	25	26	25	24
March	30	25	26	30	29
April	20	18	23	24	20
May	19	20	18	19	19
June	23	20	23	23	21
July	24	22	26	21	22
Aug.	27	29	30	28	26
Sept.	26	22	26	28	23
Oct.	19	23	23	28	22
Nov.	30	26	29	28	27
Dec.	28	32	29	29	27

Answers

1. 98.43, 92.15, 108.9, 100.52
2. 98.66, 111.74, 95.3, 95.3
3. 15.75 119.71, 129.18, 118.68, 115.48, 133.43, 66.78
4. 70, 70, 90, 90, 100, 90, 80, 100, 110, 130, 120, 150
5. 121.62, 121.32, 108.66, 84.81, 90.11, 88.34, 69.20, 80.39, 87.75, 98.94, 116.02, 132.81
6. 120, 96, 112, 84, 76, 88, 92, 112, 100, 92, 112, 116.

30. RATIO TO TREND METHOD

This method is also known as *percentage trend method*.

The following are the working rules to find the seasonal indices by the ratio to trend method.

Step I.	*Given data is expressed on quarterly (resp. monthly) average basis and quarterly (resp. monthly) trend values are calculated by using least squares method.*
Step II.	*Given values are expressed as percentage of the corresponding trend values.*
Step III.	*Find seasonal indices by finding the average of quarterly (resp. monthly) percentages of the corresponding quarter (resp. month).*
Step IV.	*Check that the sum of quarterly (resp. monthly) seasonal indices is 400 (resp. 1200). If it is not so, then adjust the seasonal indices by multiplying by a suitable factor.*

Example 1. *Find the quarterly seasonal indices for the following data by using ratio to trend method :*

Year	*Quarter*			
	I	*II*	*III*	*IV*
1996	*4*	*3*	*3*	*6*
1997	*5*	*4*	*6*	*7*
1998	*4*	*3*	*4*	*3*
1999	*5*	*4*	*5*	*5*
2000	*6*	*5*	*4*	*6*

Sol. Let y be the variable 'quarterly average' of given data.

$$\therefore \quad y(1996) = \frac{4+3+3+6}{4} = 4$$

$$y(1997) = \frac{5+4+6+7}{4} = 5.5$$

$$y(1998) = \frac{4+3+4+3}{4} = 3.5$$

$$y(1999) = \frac{5+4+5+5}{4} = 4.75$$

$$y(2000) = \frac{6+5+4+6}{4} = 5.25$$

We find quarterly trend values by using least squares method.

Here the number of years is five, which is odd.

$\therefore$ We take 1998 as the origin.

Linear Trend by Least Squares Method.

S.No.	*Year*	*y*	*x = Year – 1998*	x^2	*xy*
1	1996	4	– 2	4	– 8
2	1997	5.5	– 1	1	– 5.5
3	1998	3.5	0	0	0
4	1999	4.75	1	1	4.75
5	2000	5.25	2	4	10.5
$n = 5$		23	0	10	1.75

Let the equation of the trend line by $y_e = a + bx$.

$\therefore$ The normal equations are :

$$\Sigma y = an + b\Sigma x \quad \text{...(1)}$$

and
$$\Sigma xy = c\Sigma x + b\Sigma x^2 \quad \text{...(2)}$$

(1) $\Rightarrow$ $23 = 5a + b(0)$ $\Rightarrow$ $a = \dfrac{23}{5} = 4.6$

(2) $\Rightarrow$ $1.75 = a(0) + 10b$ $\Rightarrow$ $b = \dfrac{1.75}{10} = 0.175$

$\therefore$ The equation of the trend is $y_e = 4.6 + 0.175x$, x unit = 1 year with origin = 1998.

Quarterly trend values

$b = 0.175$ $\Rightarrow$ annual increment in trend value = 0.175

$\therefore$ Quarterly increment in trend value = $\dfrac{0.175}{4} = 0.04$

Quarterly trend value for 1996 = 4.6 + (0.175)(– 2) = 4.25

(Using $x = -2$ in $y_e = 4.6 + 0.175x$)

This value correspond to the middle quarter of the year 1996 *i.e.,* half of the II quarter and half of III quarter.

$\therefore$ Trend value of II quarter of 1996 = $4.25 - \dfrac{1}{2}(0.04) = 4.23$

Trend value of I quarter of 1996 = 4.23 – 0.04 = 4.19

Trend value of III quarter of 1996 = 4.23 + 0.04 = 4.27

Trend value of IV quarter of 1996 = 4.27 + 0.04 = 4.31

Trend value of I quarter of 1997 = 4.31 + 0.04 = 4.35

Similarly, we find trend values up to IV quarter of 2000.

Quarterly Trend Values

Year	*Quarter*			
	I	*II*	*III*	*IV*
1996	4.19	4.23	4.27	4.31
1997	4.35	4.39	4.43	4.47
1998	4.51	4.55	4.59	4.63
1999	4.67	4.71	4.75	4.79
2000	4.83	4.87	4.91	4.95

Given Quarterly Values as % of Trend Values

Year	Quarter			
	I	*II*	*III*	*IV*
1996	$\frac{4}{4.19} \times 100$ = 95.47	$\frac{3}{4.23} \times 100$ = 70.92	$\frac{3}{4.27} \times 100$ = 70.28	$\frac{6}{4.31} \times 100$ = 139.21
1997	$\frac{5}{4.35} \times 100$ = 114.94	$\frac{4}{4.39} \times 100$ = 91.12	$\frac{6}{4.43} \times 100$ = 135.44	$\frac{7}{4.47} \times 100$ = 156.60
1998	$\frac{4}{4.51} \times 100$ = 88.69	$\frac{3}{4.55} \times 100$ = 65.93	$\frac{4}{4.59} \times 100$ = 87.15	$\frac{3}{4.63} \times 100$ = 64.79
1999	$\frac{5}{4.67} \times 100$ = 107.07	$\frac{4}{4.71} \times 100$ = 84.93	$\frac{5}{4.75} \times 100$ = 105.26	$\frac{5}{4.79} \times 100$ = 104.38
2000	$\frac{6}{4.83} \times 100$ = 124.22	$\frac{5}{4.87} \times 100$ = 102.67	$\frac{4}{4.91} \times 100$ = 81.47	$\frac{6}{4.95} \times 100$ = 121.21
Total	530.39	415.57	479.60	586.19
Seasonal index	$\frac{530.39}{5}$ = 106.08	$\frac{415.57}{5}$ = 83.11	$\frac{479.60}{5}$ = 95.92	$\frac{586.19}{5}$ = 117.24

Sum of seasonal indices = 106.08 + 83.11 + 95.92 + 117.24 = 402.35 ≠ 400.

∴ We find adjusted seasonal indices.

$$\frac{106.08}{402.35} \times 400 = 105.46 \qquad \frac{83.11}{402.35} \times 400 = 82.62$$

$$\frac{95.92}{402.35} \times 400 = 95.36 \qquad \frac{117.24}{402.35} \times 400 = 116.56.$$

∴ Adjusted seasonal indices are : **105.46, 82.62, 95.36 and 116.56.**

Example 2. *Find seasonal indices for the following data by using ratio to trend method :*

Querter	*Year*				
	1997	*1998*	*1999*	*2000*	*2001*
I	30	34	40	54	80
II	40	52	58	76	92
III	36	50	54	68	86
IV	34	44	48	62	82

Sol. Let y be the variable 'quarterly average' of given data.

$$\therefore \quad y(1997) = \frac{30+40+36+34}{4} = 35$$

$$y(1998) = \frac{34+52+50+44}{4} = 45$$

$$y(1999) = \frac{40+58+54+48}{4} = 50$$

$$y(2000) = \frac{54+76+68+62}{4} = 65$$

$$y(2001) = \frac{80+92+86+82}{4} = 85.$$

We find quarterly trend values by using least squares method.

Here the number of years in five, which is odd.

∴ We take 1999 as the origin.

Linear Trend by Least Squares Method

S. No.	*Year*	*y*	*x = year – 1999*	x^2	*xy*
1	1997	35	– 2	4	– 70
2	1998	45	– 1	1	– 45
3	1999	50	0	0	0
4	2000	65	1	1	65
5	2001	85	2	4	170
$x = 5$		280	0	10	120

Let the equation of the trend line be $y_e = a + bx$.

∴ The normal equations are :

$$\Sigma y = an + b\Sigma x \qquad ...(1)$$

and

$$\Sigma xy = a\Sigma x + b\Sigma x^2. \qquad ...(2)$$

$$(1) \Rightarrow \quad 280 = 5a + b(0) \Rightarrow a = \frac{280}{5} = 56$$

$$(2) \Rightarrow \quad 120 = a(0) + 10b \Rightarrow b = \frac{120}{10} = 12$$

∴ The equation of the trend line is $y_e = 56 + 12x$ with origin = 1999 and x unit = 1 year.

Quarterly trend values

$b = 12 \Rightarrow$ annual increment in trend value = 12

∴ Quarterly increment in trend value $= \frac{12}{4} = 3$

Quarterly trend value for 1997 = 56 + 12(– 2) = 32 (Using $x = -2$ in $y_e = 56 + 12x$)

This value correspond to the middle quarter of the year 1997 *i.e.*, half of the II querter and half of III quarter.

∴ Trend value of II quarter of 1997 = $32 - \frac{1}{2}(3) = 30.5$

Trend value of I quarter of 1997 = 30.5 – 3 = 27.5

Trend value of III quarter of 1997 = 30.5 + 3 = 33.5

Trend value of IV querter of 1997 = 33.5 + 3 = 36.5

Trend value of I quarter of 1998 = 36.5 + 3 = 39.5

Similarly , we find trend values up to IV quarter of 2001.

Quarterly Trend Values

Year	*Quarter*			
	I	*II*	*III*	*IV*
1997	27.5	30.5	33.5	36.5
1998	39.5	42.5	45.5	48.5
1999	51.5	54.5	57.5	60.5
2000	63.5	66.5	69.5	72.5
2001	75.5	78.5	81.5	84.5

Given Quarterly Values as % of Trend Values

year	*Quarter*			
	I	*II*	*III*	*IV*
1997	$\frac{30}{27.5} \times 100$ = 109.09	$\frac{40}{30.5} \times 100$ = 131.15	$\frac{36}{33.5} \times 100$ = 107.46	$\frac{34}{36.5} \times 100$ = 93.15
1998	$\frac{34}{39.5} \times 100$ = 86.08	$\frac{52}{42.5} \times 100$ = 122.35	$\frac{50}{45.5} \times 100$ = 109.89	$\frac{44}{48.5} \times 100$ = 90.72
1999	$\frac{40}{51.5} \times 100$ = 77.67	$\frac{58}{54.5} \times 100$ = 106.42	$\frac{54}{57.5} \times 100$ = 93.91	$\frac{48}{60.5} \times 100$ = 79.34
2000	$\frac{54}{63.5} \times 100$ = 85.04	$\frac{76}{66.5} \times 100$ = 114.29	$\frac{68}{69.5} \times 100$ = 97.84	$\frac{62}{72.5} \times 100$ = 85.52
2001	$\frac{80}{75.5} \times 100$ = 105.96	$\frac{92}{78.5} \times 100$ = 117.20	$\frac{86}{81.5} \times 100$ = 105.52	$\frac{82}{84.5} \times 100$ = 97.04
Total	463.84	591.41	514.62	445.77
Seasonal index	$\frac{463.84}{5}$ = 92.77	$\frac{591.41}{5}$ 118.28	$\frac{514.62}{5}$ = 102.92	$\frac{445.77}{5}$ = 89.15

Sum of seasonal indices = 92.77 + 118.28 + 102.92 + 89.15 = 403.12 ≠ 400.

∴ We find adjusted seasonal indices .

$$\frac{92.77}{403.12} \times 400 = 92.05 \qquad \frac{118.28}{403.12} \times 400 = 117.37$$

$$\frac{102.92}{403.12} \times 400 = 102.12 \qquad \frac{89.15}{403.12} \times 400 = 88.46$$

∴ Adjusted seasonal indices are : **92.05, 117.37, 102.12, and 88.46.**

31. MERITS AND DEMERITS

Merits 1. This method is simple to understand.

2. In this method, the seasonal indices are computed after eliminating the trend component.

Demerit. It is difficult to compute.

EXERCISE 9

1. Find the quarterly seasonal indices for the following data by using ratio to trend method :

Year	*Quarter*			
	I	*II*	*III*	*IV*
1998	36	34	38	32
1999	38	48	52	42
2000	40	55	52	53
2001	58	75	70	57
2002	82	90	88	80

2. Find the quarterly seasonal indices for the following data by using ratio to trend method :

Quarter	*Year*				
	1997	*1998*	*1999*	*2000*	*2001*
I	68	70	68	65	60
II	60	58	63	56	55
III	61	56	68	56	55
IV	63	60	67	62	58

3. Find the quarterly seasonal indices for the following data by using ratio to trend method :

Year	*Quarter*			
	I	*II*	*III*	*IV*
1	78	70	71	73
2	80	68	66	70
3	78	73	78	77
4	75	66	66	73
5	70	65	65	68

4. Find seasonal indices by the ratio to trend method for the data given below :

Year	Quarter			
	1st	*2nd*	*3rd*	*4th*
1996	60	80	72	68
1997	68	104	100	88
1998	80	116	108	96
1999	108	152	136	124
2000	160	184	172	164

Answers

1. 99.98,109.48, 104.35, 86.19
2. 106.85, 95.86, 95.35, 101.94
3. 105.82, 95.45, 97.01, 101.72
4. 92.06, 117.36, 102.12, 88.46.

32. RATIO TO MOVING AVERAGE METHOD

This method is also known as *percentage moving average method.*

The following are the working rules to find seasonal indices by the ratio to moving average method.

Step I. *If the given data is on quarterly (resp. monthly) basis, then find quarterly (resp. monthly) trend values by using 4 quarterly (resp. 12 monthly) moving averages.*

Step II. *Given values are expressed as percentages of the corresponding trend values.*

Step III. *Find seasonal indices by finding the average of quarterly (resp. monthly) percentages of the corresponding quarter (resp. month).*

Step IV. *Check that the sum of quarterly (resp. monthly) seasonal indices is 400 (resp. 1200). If it is not so, then adjust the seasonal indices by multiplying by a suitable factor.*

Example 1. *Calculate seasonal indices for the following data by using ratio to moving average method :*

Year	*Quarter*			
	I	*II*	*III*	*IV*
2000	68	61	61	63
2001	65	58	66	61
2002	68	63	63	67

Sol. We find quarterly trend values by using 4 quarterly moving average method.

Quarterly Trend Values by Moving Average Method

Year	*Quarter*	*y*	*4 Quarterly moving totals*	*4 Quarterly moving averages*	*4 Quarterly centred moving average*
2000	I	68			—
	II	61			—
			→ 253	63.25	
	III	61			→ 62.875
			→ 250	62.5	
	IV	63			→ 62.125
			→ 247	61.75	
2001	I	65			→ 62.5
			→ 253	63.25	
	II	58			→ 63
			→ 251	62.75	
	III	66			→ 63.125
			→ 254	63.5	
	IV	61			→ 64.125
			→ 259	64.75	
2002	I	68			→ 64.375
			→ 256	64	
	II	63			→ 64.75
			→ 262	65.5	
	III	63			—
	IV	67			—

Quarterly Trend Values

Year	*Quarter*			
	I	*II*	*III*	*IV*
2000	—	—	62.875	62.125
2001	62.5	63	63.125	64.125
2002	64.375	64.75	—	—

Given Quarterly Values as % of Trend Values

Year	*Quarter*			
	I	*II*	*III*	*IV*
2000	—	—	$\frac{61}{62.875} \times 100$ $= 97.02$	$\frac{63}{62.125} \times 100$ $= 101.41$
2001	$\frac{65}{62.5} \times 100$ $= 104$	$\frac{58}{63} \times 100$ $= 92.06$	$\frac{66}{63.125} \times 100$ $= 104.55$	$\frac{61}{64.125} \times 100$ $= 95.127$
2002	$\frac{68}{64.375} \times 100$ $= 105.63$	$\frac{63}{64.75} \times 100$ $= 97.30$	—	—
Total	209.63	189.36	201.57	196.54
Seasonal index	$\frac{209.63}{2}$ $= 104.82$	$\frac{189.36}{2}$ $= 94.68$	$\frac{201.57}{2}$ $= 100.85$	$\frac{196.54}{2}$ $= 98.27$

Sum of seasonal indices = 104.82 + 94.68 + 100.85 + 98.27 = 398.62 ≠ 400.

∴ We find adjusted seasonal indices.

$$\frac{104.82}{398.62} \times 400 = 105.18 \qquad \frac{94.68}{398.62} \times 100 = 95.01$$

$$\frac{100.85}{398.62} \times 400 = 101.2 \qquad \frac{98.27}{398.62} \times 100 = 98.61.$$

∴ Adjusted seasonal indices are : **105.18, 95.01, 101.2** and **98.61.**

Example 2. *Calculate seasonal indices for the following data by using ratio to moving average method :*

Year	*Quarter*			
	I	*II*	*III*	*IV*
1996	*1861*	*2203*	*2415*	*1908*
1997	*1921*	*2343*	*2514*	*1986*
1998	*1834*	*2154*	*2098*	*1799*
1999	*1837*	*2025*	*2304*	*1965*
2000	*2073*	*2414*	*2339*	*1967*

Sol. We find quarterly trend values by using 4 quarterly moving average method.

Quarterly Trend Values by Moving Average Method

Year	*Quarter*	*y*	*4 Quarterly moving total*	*4 Quarterly moving average*	*4 Quarterly Centered moving average*
1996	I	1861			—
	II	2203			—
			→ 8387	2096.75	
	III	2415			→ 2104.250
			→ 8447	2111.75	
	IV	1908			→ 2129.250
			→ 8587	2146.75	
					→ 2159.125
1997	I	1921			
			→ 8686	2171.50	
	II	2343			→ 2181.250
			→ 8764	2191.00	
	III	2514			→ 2180.125
			→ 8677	2169.25	
	IV	1986			→ 2145.625
			→ 8488	2122.00	
1998	I	1834			→ 2070.000
			→ 8072	2018.00	
	II	2154			→ 1994.625
			→ 7885	1971.25	
	III	2098			→ 1971.625
			→ 7888	1972.00	
	IV	1799			→ 1955.875
			→ 7759	1939.75	
					→ 1965.500

1999	I	1837			
			7965	1991.75	
	II	2025			2012.000
			8131	2032.75	
	III	2304			2062.250
			8367	2091.75	
	IV	1965			2140.375
			8756	2189.00	
2000	I	2073			2193.375
			8791	2197.75	
	II	2414			2198.000
			8793	2198.25	
	III	2339			—
	IV	1967			—

Quarterly Trend Values

Year	*Quarter*			
	I	*II*	*III*	*IV*
1996	—	—	2104.250	2129.250
1997	2159.125	2181.250	2180.125	2145.625
1998	2070.000	1994.625	1971.625	1955.875
1999	1965.500	2012.000	2062.250	2140.375
2000	2193.375	2198.000	—	—

Given Quarterly Values as % of Trend Values

Year	*Quarter*			
	I	*II*	*III*	*IV*
1996	—	—	$\frac{2415}{2104.250} \times 100$ = 114.77	$\frac{1908}{2129.250} \times 100$ = 89.61
1997	$\frac{1921}{2159.125} \times 100$ = 88.97	$\frac{2343}{2181.250} \times 100$ = 107.42	$\frac{2514}{2180.125} \times 100$ = 115.31	$\frac{1986}{2145.625} \times 100$ = 92.56
1998	$\frac{1834}{2070.000} \times 100$ = 88.60	$\frac{2154}{1994.625} \times 100$ = 107.99	$\frac{2098}{1971.625} \times 100$ = 106.41	$\frac{1799}{1955.875} \times 100$ = 91.98
1999	$\frac{1837}{1965.500} \times 100$ = 93.46	$\frac{2025}{2012.000} \times 100$ = 100.65	$\frac{2304}{2062.250} \times 100$ = 111.72	$\frac{1965}{2140.375} \times 100$ = 91.81

2000	$\frac{2073}{2193.375} \times 100$ = 94.51	$\frac{2414}{2198.000} \times 100$ = 109.83	—	—
Total	365.54	425.89	448.21	365.96
Seasonal index	$\frac{364.54}{4}$ = 91.14	$\frac{425.89}{4}$ = 106.47	$\frac{448.21}{4}$ = 112.05	$\frac{365.96}{4}$ = 91.49

Sum of seasonal indices

$$= 91.14 + 106.47 + 112.05 + 91.49 = 401.15 \neq 400.$$

$\therefore$ We find adjusted seasonal indices.

$$\frac{91.14}{401.15} \times 100 = 90.88 \qquad \frac{106.47}{401.15} \times 100 = 106.16$$

$$\frac{112.05}{401.15} \times 100 = 111.73 \qquad \frac{91.49}{401.15} \times 100 = 91.23.$$

$\therefore$ Adjusted seasonal indices are : **90.88, 106.16, 111.73** and **91.23.**

33. MERITS AND DEMERITS

Merits 1. This method is simple to understand.

2. In this method, the seasonal indices are computed after eliminating the trend component.

Demerits 1. It is difficult to compute.

2. In this method, quarterly trend (resp. monthly trend) values cannot be obtained for each period.

EXERCISE 10

1. Find the quarterly seasonal indices for the following data by using ratio to moving average method :

Year	*Quarter*			
	I	*II*	*III*	*IV*
1998	*30*	*81*	*62*	*119*
1999	*33*	*104*	*86*	*171*
2000	*42*	*153*	*99*	*221*
2001	*56*	*172*	*129*	*235*
2002	*67*	*201*	*136*	*302*

(MDU 2000)

2. Find the quarterly seasonal indices for the following data by using ratio to moving average method :

Year	*Quarter*			
	I	*II*	*III*	*IV*
1999	75	60	54	59
2000	86	65	63	80
2001	90	72	66	85
2002	100	78	72	93

3. Given the following quarterly sales figures in thousands of rupees for the years 1996–99, find the seasonal indices by using the method of ratio to moving average method :

Year	*Quarter*			
	I	*II*	*III*	*IV*
1996	290	280	285	310
1997	320	305	310	330
1998	340	321	320	340
1999	370	360	362	380

4. Find seasonal indices for the following data by using ratio to moving average method :

Year	*Quarter*			
	I	*II*	*III*	*IV*
1994	290	280	285	310
1995	320	305	310	330
1996	340	321	320	340
1997	370	360	362	380
1998	370	350	355	370
1999	355	336	335	350
2000	360	341	342	359

Answers

1. 39.65, 118.78, 83.26, 157.91

2. 122.37, 92.43, 84.69, 100.51

3. 104.20, 97.90, 96.50, 101.40

4. 103.12, 97.47, 97.31, 102.10.

34. LINK RELATIVE METHOD

The following are the working rules to find seasonal indices by the link relative method.

Step I. *Except for the first period, find link relative of each period by using the following formula :*

$$\text{Link relative for current period} = \frac{\text{value for current period}}{\text{value for previous period}} \times 100.$$

Step II. *Find average of quarterly (resp. monthly) link relatives of the corresponding quarter (resp. month).*

Step III. *Find chain relatives for each period as given below :*

For first period , the chain relative is taken as 100. For other periods, find chain relatives as follows :

Chain relative for current period.

$$= \frac{\text{Average of link relatives for current period} \times \text{Chain relative of previous period}}{100}$$

Step IV. *Find chain relative of the first period by using the formula :*

Chain relative for first period

$$= \frac{\text{Average of link relatives for first period} \times \text{Chain relative for last period}}{100}$$

Denote this chain relative by 100 + d and find the value of d.

Step V. *If the data is on quarter basis, subtract* $\frac{d}{4}, \frac{2d}{4}, \frac{3d}{4}$, *from the chain relatives of II, III, IV quarters respectively.*

If the data is on month basis, subtract $\frac{d}{12}, \frac{2d}{12}, \ldots, \frac{11d}{12}$ *from the chain relatives of Feb, March, ..., Dec. respectively.*

These are called corrected chain relatives.

Step VI. *The corrected chain relatives are multiplied by*

$$\frac{400}{\text{sum of corrected C.R}}\left(\text{resp. } \frac{1200}{\text{sum of corrected C.R}}\right)$$

in case quarterly (resp. monthly) figures are given. These are the required seasonal indices.

Step VII. *Check that the sum of quarterly (resp. monthly) seasonal indices in 400 (resp. 1200). If it is not so, then adjust the seasonal indices by multiplying by a suitable factor.*

Example 1. *Compute the seasonal indices by the link relative method for the following data :*

Quarter	*Prices (in rupees per kg)*			
	1999	*2000*	*2001*	*2002*
Ist (Jan. — March)	*75*	*86*	*90*	*100*
IInd (April—June)	*60*	*65*	*72*	*78*
IIIrd (July—Sept.)	*54*	*63*	*66*	*72*
IVth (Oct.—Dec.)	*59*	*80*	*85*	*93*

Sol. The given data can be arranged as follows :

Year	*Quarter*			
	I	*II*	*III*	*IV*
1999	75	60	54	59
2000	86	65	63	80
2001	90	72	66	85
2002	100	78	72	93

Seasonal Indices by Lind Relative Method

Year	*Quarter*			
	I	*II*	*III*	*IV*
1999	—	$\frac{60}{75} \times 100$ $= 80$	$\frac{54}{60} \times 100$ $= 90$	$\frac{59}{54} \times 100$ $= 109.26$
2000	$\frac{86}{59} \times 100$ $= 145.76$	$\frac{65}{86} \times 100$ $= 75.58$	$\frac{63}{65} \times 100$ $= 96.92$	$\frac{80}{63} \times 100$ $= 126.98$
2001	$\frac{90}{80} \times 100$ $= 112.5$	$\frac{72}{90} \times 100$ $= 80$	$\frac{66}{72} \times 100$ $= 91.67$	$\frac{85}{66} \times 100$ $= 128.79$
2002	$\frac{100}{85} \times 100$ $= 117.65$	$\frac{78}{100} \times 100$ $= 78$	$\frac{72}{78} \times 100$ $= 92.31$	$\frac{93}{72} \times 100$ $= 129.17$
Total of link relatives	375.91	313.58	370.9	494.2
Average of link relatives	$\frac{375.91}{3}$ $= 125.30$	$\frac{313.58}{4}$ $= 78.40$	$\frac{370.9}{4}$ $= 92.73$	$\frac{494.2}{4}$ $= 123.55$
Chain relative	100	$\frac{78.40 \times 100}{100}$ $= 78.40$	$\frac{92.73 \times 78.40}{100}$ $= 72.70$	$\frac{123.55 \times 72.70}{100}$ $= 89.82$

Corrected chain relative	100	$78.40 - \frac{12.54}{4}$ $= 75.26$	$72.70 - 2\left(\frac{12.54}{4}\right)$ $= 66.43$	$89.82 - 3\left(\frac{12.54}{4}\right)$ $= 80.41$
Seasonal index	$100 \times \frac{400}{322.1}$ $= 124.19$	$75.26 \times \frac{400}{322.1}$ $= 93.46$	$66.43 \times \frac{400}{322.1}$ $= 82.50$	$80.41 \times \frac{400}{322.1}$ $= 99.86$

New C.R. for first quarter $= \frac{125.30 \times 89.82}{100} = 112.54$

Let $112.54 = 100 + d$. $\therefore$ $d = 12.54$.

Sum of corrected chain relatives $= 100 + 75.26 + 66.43 + 80.41 = 322.1$.

Sum of seasonal indices $= 124.19 + 93.46 + 82.50 + 99.86$

$= 400.01$, which is very close to 400.

$\therefore$ Seasonal indices are : **124.19, 93.46, 82.50** and **99.86.**

Example 2. Find seasonal indices for the following data by using link relative method :

Year	*Quarter*			
	I	*II*	*III*	*IV*
1998	*60*	*62*	*61*	*63*
1999	*65*	*58*	*56*	*61*
2000	*68*	*63*	*63*	*67*
2001	*70*	*59*	*56*	*62*
2002	*60*	*55*	*51*	*58*

Seasonal Indices by Link Relative Method

Year	*Quarter*			
	I	*II*	*III*	*IV*
1998	—	$\frac{62}{60} \times 100$ $= 103.33$	$\frac{61}{62} \times 100$ $= 98.39$	$\frac{63}{61} \times 100$ $= 103.28$
1999	$\frac{65}{63} \times 100$ $= 103.17$	$\frac{58}{65} \times 100$ $= 89.23$	$\frac{56}{58} \times 100$ $= 96.55$	$\frac{61}{56} \times 100$ $= 108.93$
2000	$\frac{68}{61} \times 100$ $= 111.48$	$\frac{63}{68} \times 100$ $= 92.65$	$\frac{63}{63} \times 100$ $= 100$	$\frac{67}{63} \times 100$ $= 106.35$

2001	$\frac{70}{67}\times 100$ = 104.48	$\frac{59}{70}\times 100$ = 84.29	$\frac{56}{59}\times 100$ = 94.92	$\frac{62}{56}\times 100$ = 110.71
2002	$\frac{60}{62}\times 100$ = 96.77	$\frac{55}{60}\times 100$ = 91.67	$\frac{51}{55}\times 100$ = 92.73	$\frac{58}{51}\times 100$ = 113.73
Total of link relatives	415.9	461.17	482.59	543
Average of link relatives	$\frac{415.9}{4}$ = 103.98	$\frac{461.17}{5}$ = 92.23	$\frac{482.59}{5}$ = 96.52	$\frac{543}{5}$ = 108.60
Chain relative	100	$\frac{92.23\times 100}{100}$ = 92.23	$\frac{96.52\times 92.23}{100}$ = 89.02	$\frac{108.60\times 89.02}{100}$ = 96.68
Corrected chain relative	100	$92.23-\frac{0.53}{4}$ = 92.10	$89.02-2\left(\frac{0.53}{4}\right)$ = 88.76	$96.68-3\left(\frac{0.53}{4}\right)$ = 96.28
Seasonal index	$100\times\frac{400}{377.14}$ = 106.06	$92.10\times\frac{400}{377.14}$ = 97.68	$88.76\times\frac{400}{377.14}$ = 94.14	$96.28\times\frac{400}{377.14}$ = 102.12

New C.R. for first quarter $= \frac{103.98\times 96.68}{100} = 100.53$

Let $100.53 = 100 + d$. $\therefore$ $d = 0.53$.

Sum of corrected chain relatives = 100 + 92.10 + 88.76 + 96.28 = 377.14.

Sum of seasonal indices = 106.06 + 97.68 + 94.14 + 102.12 = 400.

$\therefore$ Seasonal indices are : **106.06, 97.68, 94.14** and **102.12.**

35. MERITS AND DEMERITS

Merits 1. This method is simple to understand.

2. In this method the seasonal indices are computed after eliminating trend component.

Demerits 1. This mehod is useful only when the data has a linear trend.

2. It is difficult to compute.

3. In the method, there is loss of one link relative.

EXERCISE 11

1. Find seasonal indices by the link relative method, for the following data :

AVERAGE QUARTERLY PRICE OF A COMMODITY

Quarter	Year				
	1996	1997	1998	1999	2000
I	30	35	31	31	34
II	26	28	29	31	36
III	22	22	28	25	26
IV	31	36	32	35	33

2. Find seasonal indices by the link relative method for the following data :

Year	Quarter			
	I	II	III	IV
1995	6.0	6.5	7.8	8.7
1996	5.4	7.9	8.4	7.3
1997	6.8	6.5	9.3	6.4
1998	7.2	5.8	7.5	8.5
1999	6.6	7.3	8.0	7.1

3. Find seasonal indices for the following data by using link ralative method :

Quarter	Quarterly figures				
	1998	1999	2000	2001	2002
I	6.0	5.4	6.8	7.2	6.6
II	6.5	7.9	6.6	5.8	7.4
III	7.8	8.4	9.8	7.5	8.0
IV	8.7	7.3	6.4	8.5	7.1

4. Find seasonal indices for the following data by using link relative method :

Year	Quarter			
	I	II	III	IV
1996	45	54	72	60
1997	48	56	63	56
1998	49	63	70	65
1999	52	65	75	72
2000	60	70	84	77

Answers

1. 108.02, 99.75, 81.23, 111.00
2. 88.18, 94.01, 113.21, 104.60
3. 97.14, 91.30, 109.96, 101.60
4. 82.67, 98.76, 115.69, 102.88.

EXERCISE 12

1. Define a time series. Explain its utility in Business and Economics.
2. Describe briefly the various characteristic movements of time series. Discuss briefly any one procedure for estimating secular trend. *(MDU 1992)*
3. What is secular trend ? Critically examine various methods of measuring trend. *(KU 1995, 97)*
4. Critically examine the different methods of measuring trend. Point out their merits ansd demerits.
5. Discuss the superiority of least square method over moving average method, in estimating secular trend of time series.
6. Write a short note on semi-average method of estimating trend of time series.
7. What is meant by a trend ? How do you fit a straight line trend by the method of least squares. *(MDU 1995)*
8. Discuss the components of time series, in detail. *(KU 1997, 99 C, 2001, 2002, 2003, 2004, 2005 C, 2006 C, 2006 ; MDU1998, 2006)*
9. Distinguish between 'Free Hand Graphic Method' and 'Simi-Average Method' of estimating trend of a time series.
10. What is the time series analysis ? What are the components of time series ? Explain the various methods of estimating the secular trend of a time series. *(KU 1996, 2000 C)*
11. What are the components of a time series ? How would you find out the trend values in a time series by the method of least squares ? Illustrate your answer with an example.
12. Discuss the method of least squares for the measurement of trend. *(MDU 1995, 2001)*
13. Explain different methods of measuring seasonal variations with their respective merits and demerits. *(KU 1999, 2006 ; MDU 2005, 2006)*
14. Distinguish between additive model and multiplicative model in the analysis of time series. *(KU 2005, 2006 C)*
15. Write a note on secular trend and seasonal variations. *(MDU 2007)*

14

Forecasting

1. INTRODUCTION

In this world, future is not certain. If the future were known with certainity, estimates for futures would have been a time wasting exercise and decisions would have been taken once for all times to come. But fortunately or unfortunately, nothing is certain in future. In economics and business, only guess work regarding future events cannot work. Even a small shopkeeper is always keen to know about his sales and profits for the times to come. Foreseeing of future events is implicit in all human action and systematic forecasting helps in proper planning and decision making. The growing competition, rapidity of change in circumstances and trend towards automation demand that decisions in business be not based purely on guesses and hunches and rather on a careful analysis of data concerning future course of events. The success of a business firm depends largely on the strategic planning based on past and present experience. The health of a business depends very heavily on the decisions regarding future. Top management is always worried about the future than to the past and the question *"What is likely to happen ?"* takes precedence over *"what has happened ?"* Foreseeing of future events is a must for all involved in economics and business activities. Even the governments are worried about their economic policies and have to foresee much regarding economic aspects.

2. MEANING OF FORECASTING

The effectiveness of future decisions in economic and business activities depends much on accuracy. The art of predicting the likelyhood of an economic or business activity for some future period under some assumptions is called **forecasting.** The point of time when the forecast is made is known as the **base point** and the future points of time which the forecast relates to is called **forecast point.** The interval between the base point and the forecast point is called the **range of forecast.** The range of forecast may be from some months to 5-10 years. Some statisticians have defined the term 'forecast' as follows :

"Forecasting refers to the using of knowledge we have at one moment of time to estimate what will happen at another moment of time. The forecasting problem is created by the interval of time between the moments.

— Frederik A. Ekeblad

"Forecasting may represent a prediction as to what might happen to one particular item of interest such as the price of gold next year or in a five years time or it may be a prediction as to the future of a much more complex entity such as the economy or a company."

— John Argenti

"Business forecasting refers to the statistical analysis of the past and current movements in a given time series, so as to obtain clues about the future pattern of the movements."

— Neter and Wasserman

"In statistics, the term (forecasting) refers to the extending or projecting time series into the future based on past behaviour of the quantitative data." **— Simpson and Kafka**

"Business forecasting is not so much the estimation of certain figures of sales, production, profits, etc. as the analysis of known data, internal and external, in a manner which will enable policy to be determined to meet probable future conditions to the best advantage."

— Wheldon

The above definitions shows that forecasting can be for a very near future or for a distant future. An important point of concern in all business activities is to assess the future business trend whether it is going to be favourable or unfavourable. This type of assessment helps the top management in taking appropriate policy decisions in advance. In order to cope with the uncertainities, it is necessary to predict the future condititions and their effect on business performance. Forecasting can provide a firm with the appropriate estimates which assume paramount importance in developing the effective short-range as well as long-range planning.

The word forecasting should not be taken as an synonym to the word 'futurology'. Futurology is based on the vision of future society and is based on exterior considerations. Topics like new sources of energy, life on planets other than earth are related to futurology. On the other hand, forecasting is a systematic attempt to make the analysis of past and current movements in a given time series in order to obtain the clues about the future pattern of movements.

3. TYPES OF FORECASTING

In forecasting, we study the expected pattern of movements of economic and business variables in future. The range of forecast may vary from some months to some years. There are two types of forecasting namely, long term forecasting and short term forecasting.

(*i*) **Long term forecasting.** If the range of forecast is about 5 to 15 years, then the forecasting is called **long term forecasting.** In long term forecasting, the main concern is to plan for the long run, sufficiently long to allow for the creation of new or reduction in the existing productive capacity. This is so because productive capacity cannot be changed in short run. The effect of population growth, habits can also be studied in long term forecasting. Long term forecasting techniques may be used in studying demand for durable goods.

(*ii*) **Short term forecasting.** If the range of forecast is about 6 months to 1 year, then the forecasting is called **short term forecasting.** In short run forecasting, we plan for the immediate future. Short run forecasting techniques may be used in studying demand for consumer goods. The risk of error increases with the increase of forecasting range. Short term forecasting also help in scheduling production. If the sales of a product are expected to go up abnormally in the very near future, it would be prudent on the part of the management to make the required adjustment in its production schedule and take necessary steps immediately so that sufficient stocks are available.

4. IMPORTANCE OF FORECASTING

One of the primary duties of top management of a business concern is of forecasting. They fix prices of their products on the basis of forecast values of raw material, wages, financial overheads etc. They also undertake production planning, recruitment of labour, purchase of raw material, raising of finance after considering the sales and market forecast. In any business organisation, the top management uses forecasting in order to take rational decisions and to a very large extent, the success or failure of business depend upon the ability to make and use forecasts successfully. The object of forecasting is not to determine a curve or a sequence of figures that will tell exactly what will happen, say, a year in advance, but it is to make analysis based on definite statistical data, which will enable an executive to take advantage of future conditions to a greater extent than he could do without them. It is rightly said that forecasting is not merely projection of trend line to find the figure for some future period. In many respects, the future tends to move like the past. This is a good thing, because without same element of continuity between past, present and future, there would be little possibility of successful forecasting. History is not likely to repeat itself and we would hardly expect economic conditions, next year or over the next ten years, to follow a clear-cut precedent. Yet, past patterns prevails sufficiently to justify using the past as a basis for forecasting the future. It is always true that proper forecasts are of paramount importance. During the last few decades, an increasingly large number of business organisations are pursuing forecasting as a formal function and using its results as the basis for future planning in almost all major areas of business activities like finance, marketing, production scheduling, adjustment of production capacity. The growing complexities and uncertainity of business life have necessitated the undertaking of effective forecasting.

5. GENERAL APPROACH TO FORECASTING

Forecasts are not expected to give exact figures. The main purpose of forecasting is to minimise the error of estimation to the minimum possible level. The error of estimation also increases with an increase in the range of forecast. Forecasting is a vary sophisticated process and it should be used only by trained professionals. The general approach to forecasting contains five steps and these steps should be observed in the given order.

Step I. ***Objective of forecasting.*** *Before commencing any data collection, the objective of forecasting should by very clear and well defined. The objective of forecasting will decide the range of forecast and the method to be used would depend upon the range of forecast.*

Step II. ***Selection of variables of forecast.*** *The forecasting of our objective may involve a number of variables. The number of variables involved in the forecasting process should be well within manageable limits. For this purpose only important variables are ascertained. For example, a multiproduct firm produces several items. It would be prudent to group these into broad categories and only important ones should be selected as the units of forecasting.*

Step III. ***Collection of data.*** *The collection of data about the variables of forecasting should be made without any personal bias. The collected data should be well scrutinised by experts.*

Step IV. *There are number of methods for long term forecasting and short term forecasting. The choice of method would depend upon the objective of forecasting, nature of available data and the range of forecasting. In general,* **trend projection method** *is used for long term forecasting and* **business indicators method** *is used for short term forecasting.*

Step V. ***Preparation of final report.*** *As the last step, the findings of the forecasting are written in a formal manner and is submitted to the top management for its execution.*

6. METHODS OF FORECASTING

For centuries, the businessmen have been trying to adjust themselves so as to make best out of the future conditions. In those days, businessmen used to decide about the future in terms of past experience and familiarity with problem at hand. With the passage of time, the business scientists succeeded in designing very efficient and reliable methods of making business forecasts. Presently, the techniques of forecasting have improved to a marked extent and are applicable to almost every sphere of business activity. The following are some of the widely used forecasting methods.

1. Trend Projection Method
2. Business Indicators Method
3. Survey Method
4. Opinion Polling Method
5. Model Building Method
6. Historical Analogy Method
7. Naive Method
8. Exponential Smoothing Method.

1. Trend Projection Method. Trend projection method is the simplest method of forecasting. This method is used for long term forecasting. This method is based on the principle that history repeats itself. For a given time series data, a trend curve (linear of parabolic or exponential) can be drawn by using the method of least squares. The trend curve describes the general tendency of movement of the variable under consideration. In the trend projective method, it is assumed that the variables influencing the time series will operate in the same direction and with same intensity in the future. In the trend projection method, the forecasting is made by projecting the trend curve to a future period.

2. Business Indicators Method. Business indicators method is a very popular method of forecasting. This method is used for short term forecasting. This method is based on time series data on important business and economic activities in the important sectors of economy. These time series are called *business indicators*. The following are some of the widely used business indicators :

1. Bonds yields
2. Consumer credit
3. Consumer prices
4. Departmental store sales
5. Disposable personal income
6. Employment
7. Export and Import volumes
8. Gross national product
9. Industrial production
10. Stock prices
11. Volume of bank deposits and currency outstanding.

The business indicators for the purpose of future forecasting must be selected very intelligently as the accuracy of the prediction depends to a large extent on the proper choice of an indicator in terms of its relevance to the type of business under consideration. A number of indicators have been selected by the National Bureau of Economic Research **(NBER)** in the U.S.A. The current series consists of 26 business indicators.

3. Survey Method. The survey method is very widely used method of forecasting. Under this method, field surveys are conducted to gather information on the intentions of the concerned people for the future. In there surveys, necessary information, both quantitative and qualitative, are obtained. Forecasts are made, by using the data of survey, about likely demand, expenditure on consumer durables etc. Such informations help a lot in planning of production. The survey method has a limitation that the information supplied may be biased. The quantum of bias may be reduced substantially by proper designing of the questionnaires, skillful conduct of interviews and by verification of results by other methods.

4. Opinion Polling Method. In the opinion polling method, opinions are invited from business experts, persons in strategic positions, sales representatives, wholesales, retailers etc. The Survey Research Centre of the University of Michigan conduct and annual poll regarding the future plans of consumers. The opinion poll of technical experts may be helpful in estimating the life of a technology. The main theme behind the opinion polling method is that the present attitudes towards business can be the real guide for evaluating the expected change in business conditions in the near future. The forecasts made by the opinion polling method are simple and least expensive. This method is best suited for short term forecasts.

5. Model Building Method. This method is considered to be the most sophisticated method of forecasting. In this method, the dependent variable is expressed in terms of the independent variables, under consideration. In the trend projection method, we use one independent variable 'time' in the trend equation. But in the model building method, we can use not only time but several other variables as well for explaining the behaviour of a dependent variable. The model building method is neither mechanistic as the trend projection method nor is very subjective as the opinion poll method. Two forecasters may choose slightly different forecasting equations to obtain defferent forecasts. The differences in their forecasts will rarely be significant.

6. Historical Analogy Method. The historical analogy method is a rough forecasting method. In this method, forecast is based on some analogous conditions prevailed elsewhere in the past. This method requires the need for search of a place and period in history, having comparable conditions. It is only a matter of chance that similar conditions are traced at some place. For example, the forecast of demand for paper in India can be based on the analogy of demand for paper in the U.S.A. in the year 1950, if it is found that the conditions now in India are very much similar to the conditions prevailing in the U.S.A. in the year 1950.

7. Naive Method. In the naive method, the forecasts are based on historical information and no attention is paid to other information. This method is highly subjective, because assumptions made about the future will vary from person to person.

Let $X_t, X_{t-1}, X_{t-2}, \ldots, X_2, X_1$ be the values of a forecasting variable for the periods $t, t-1, t-2, \ldots, 2, 1$ respectively. Let $\hat{X}_{t+1}$ represent the forecast value of the variable for the period $t+1$. If the forecaster feels that the forecasting value is to depend upon the ratios of preceding values, then he may suggest that

$$\hat{X}_{t+1} = X_t \left[\frac{1}{t-1} \sum_{i=2}^{t} \frac{X_i}{X_{i-1}} \right].$$

For example, let 28, 30, 29, 35, 39 be the values of a variable for the years 1998, 1999, 2000, 2001, 2002 respectively, then the forecast value of this variable for the year 2003 is equal to

$$39\left[\frac{1}{5-1}\left(\frac{30}{28}+\frac{29}{30}+\frac{35}{29}+\frac{39}{35}\right)\right] = \frac{39}{4}\,(1.0714 + 0.9667 + 1.2069 + 1.1143) = \mathbf{42.5032.}$$

8. Exponential Smoothing Method. In this method, forecasting figures are obtained from the given figures by using exponential smoothing. The following working rules are observed for finding forecasting figures.

Step I. *Denote the given figures by* $X_1, X_2, \ldots, X_n$.

Step II. *Find* $S_1, S_2, \ldots, S_n$ *defined as follows :*
$S_t = \alpha X_t + (1 - \alpha) S_{t-1}$ *for* $1 \le t \le n$. *The constant 'α' such that* $0 \le t \le 1$ *is called the* ***smoothing constant.*** *The initial value* S_0 *is given in the problem.* $S_1, S_2, \ldots, S_n$ *are called* ***smoothed values.***

Step III. *Find* $\Delta S_1, \Delta S_2, \ldots, \Delta S_n$ *by using* $\Delta S_t = S_t - S_{t-1}$ *for* $1 \le t \le n$.

Step IV. *Find* $T_1, T_2, \ldots, T_n$ *by using* $T_t = \alpha \Delta S_t + (1 - \alpha) T_{t-1}$ *for* $1 \le t \le n$ *and* $T_0 = 0$. *The figures* $T_1, T_2, \ldots, T_n$ *are called* ***trend values.***

Step VI. *Find* $\hat{S}_1, \hat{S}_2, \ldots, \hat{S}_n$ *by using* $\hat{S}_t = S_t + \frac{1-\alpha}{\alpha} T_t$ *for* $1 \le t \le n$. *The figures* $\hat{S}_1, \hat{S}_2, \ldots, \hat{S}_n$ *are called* ***forecasting figures.***

Step VII. *Find* $e_1, e_2, \ldots, e_n$ *by using* $e_t = \hat{S}_t - X_{t+1}$ *for* $1 \le t \le n - 1$. *These are called* ***forecasting errors.***

Example 1. *From the following values, prepare forecasts by the method of exponential smoothing taking initial estimate as 100, the value of* $\alpha = 0.4$ *and initial trend value zero.*

Year	*1997*	*1998*	*1999*	*2000*	*2001*	*2002*
Value X	*110*	*105*	*120*	*116*	*121*	*123*

Sol. **Calculation of Forecasting Figures**

Year	*Given value* X	*Smoothed value* S	ΔS	*Trend value* T	*Forecasting value* $\hat{S}$
—	—	100	—	0	—
1997	110	104	4	1.6	**106.4**
1998	105	104.4	0.4	1.12	**106.08**
1999	120	110.64	6.24	3.17	**115.39**
2000	116	112.78	2.14	2.76	**116.92**
2001	121	116.07	3.29	2.97	**120.52**
2002	123	118.84	2.77	2.89	**123.17**

Calculation of Smoothed values. We have $S_0 = 100$ and $S_t = \alpha X_t + (1 - \alpha) S_{t-1}$ for $1 \le t \le 6$.

$\therefore$
$$S_1 = (0.4)(110) + (0.6)(100) = 104$$
$$S_2 = (0.4)(105) + (0.6)(104) = 104.4$$
$$S_3 = (0.4)(120) + (0.6)(104.4) = 110.64$$
$$S_4 = (0.4)(116) + (0.6)(110.64) = 112.78$$
$$S_5 = (0.4)(121) + (0.6)(112.78) = 116.07$$
$$S_6 = (0.4)(123) + (0.6)(116.07) = 118.84.$$

Differences. We have $S_0 = 100$ and $\Delta S_t = S_t - S_{t-1}$ for $1 \le t \le 6$.

$\therefore$

$$\Delta S_1 = S_1 - S_0 = 104 - 100 = 4$$
$$\Delta S_2 = S_2 - S_1 = 104.4 - 104 = 0.4$$
$$\Delta S_3 = S_3 - S_2 = 110.64 - 104.4 = 6.24$$
$$\Delta S_4 = S_4 - S_3 = 112.78 - 110.64 = 2.14$$
$$\Delta S_5 = S_5 - S_4 = 116.07 - 112.78 = 3.29$$
$$\Delta S_6 = S_6 - S_5 = 118.84 - 116.07 = 2.77.$$

Trend values. We have $T_0 = 0$ and $T_t = \alpha \Delta S_t + (1-\alpha)T_{t-1}$ for $1 \le t \le 6$.

$\therefore$

$$T_1 = (0.4)(4) + (0.6)\,0 = 1.6$$
$$T_2 = (0.4)(0.4) + (0.6)(1.6) = 1.12$$
$$T_3 = (0.4)(6.24) + (0.6)(1.12) = 3.17$$
$$T_4 = (0.4)(2.14) + (0.6)(3.17) = 2.76$$
$$T_5 = (0.4)(3.29) + (0.6)(2.76) = 2.97$$
$$T_6 = (0.4)(2.77) + (0.6)(2.97) = 2.89.$$

Forecasting values. We have $\hat{S}_t = S_t + \dfrac{1-\alpha}{\alpha} T_t$ for $1 \le t \le 6$.

Now $\dfrac{1-\alpha}{\alpha} = \dfrac{1-0.4}{0.4} = \dfrac{0.6}{0.4} = 1.5.$

$\therefore$

$$\hat{S}_1 = 104 + (1.5)(1.6) = 106.4$$
$$\hat{S}_2 = 104.4 + (1.5)(1.12) = 106.08$$
$$\hat{S}_3 = 110.64 + (1.5)(3.17) = 115.39$$
$$\hat{S}_4 = 112.78 + (1.5)(2.76) = 116.92$$
$$\hat{S}_5 = 116.07 + (1.5)(2.97) = 120.52$$
$$\hat{S}_6 = 118.84 + (1.5)(2.89) = 123.17.$$

Example 2. *An old forecast 39 is given initially and the smoothing coefficient is 0.1. Smooth experientially the following observations :*

41, 41, 34, 39, 36, 35, 40, 36, 41, 33.

Sol. **Calculation of Forecasting Figures**

S. No.	*Given value* X	*Smoothed value* S	ΔS	*Trend value* T	*Forecasting value* $\hat{S}$
—	—	39	—	0	—
1	41	39.2	0.2	0.02	**39.38**
2	41	39.38	0.18	0.036	**39.70**
3	34	39.84	0.46	0.078	**40.54**
4	39	38.86	– 0.98	– 0.028	**38.61**
5	36	38.57	– 0.29	– 0.054	**38.08**
6	35	38.21	– 0.36	– 0.085	**37.45**
7	40	38.39	0.18	– 0.058	**37.87**
8	36	38.15	– 0.24	– 0.076	**37.47**
9	41	38.44	0.29	– 0.039	**38.09**
10	33	37.90	– 0.54	– 0.089	**37.1**

Calculation of smoothed values

We have $S_0 = 39$ and

$\therefore \quad S_t = \alpha X_t + (1 - \alpha) S_{t-1}$ for $1 \le t \le 10$.

$S_1 = (0.1)(41) + (0.9)39 = 39.2$

$S_2 = (0.1)(41) + (0.9)(39.2) = 39.38$

$S_3 = (0.1)(34) + (0.9)(39.38) = 38.84$

$S_4 = (0.1)(39) + (0.9)(38.84) = 38.86$

$S_5 = (0.1)(36) + (0.9)(38.86) = 38.57$

$S_6 = (0.1)(35) + (0.9)(38.57) = 38.21$

$S_7 = (0.1)(40) + (0.9)(38.21) = 38.39$

$S_8 = (0.1)(36) + (0.9)(38.39) = 38.15$

$S_9 = (0.1)(41) + (0.9)(38.15) = 38.44$

$S_{10} = (0.1)(33) + (0.9)(38.44) = 37.90.$

We have $S_0 = 39$ and $\Delta S_t = S_t - S_{t-1}$ for $1 \le t \le 10$.

Differences

$\therefore \quad \Delta S_1 = 39.2 - 39 = 0.2 \qquad \Delta S_2 = 39.38 - 39.2 = 0.18$

$\Delta S_3 = 39.84 - 39.38 = 0.46 \qquad \Delta S_4 = 38.86 - 39.84 = -0.98$

$\Delta S_5 = 38.57 - 38.86 = -0.29 \qquad \Delta S_6 = 38.21 - 38.57 = -0.36$

$\Delta S_7 = 38.39 - 38.21 = 0.18 \qquad \Delta S_8 = 38.15 - 38.39 = -0.24$

$\Delta S_9 = 38.44 - 38.15 = 0.29 \qquad \Delta S_{10} = 37.90 - 38.44 = -0.54.$

Trend values. We have $T_0 = 0$ and $T_t = \alpha \Delta S_t + (1 - \alpha) T_{t-1}$ for $1 \le t \le 10$.

$\therefore \quad T_1 = (0.1)(0.2) + (0.9)(0) = 0.02$

$T_2 = (0.1)(0.18) + (0.9)(0.02) = 0.036$

$T_3 = (0.1)(0.46) + (0.9)(0.036) = 0.078$

$T_4 = (0.1)(-0.98) + (0.9)(0.078) = -0.028$

$T_5 = (0.1)(-0.29) + (0.9)(-0.028) = -0.054$

$T_6 = (0.1)(-0.36) + (0.9)(-0.054) = -0.085$

$T_7 = (0.1)(-0.18) + (0.9)(-0.085) = -0.058$

$T_8 = (0.1)(-0.24) + (0.9)(-0.058) = -0.076$

$T_9 = (0.1)(-0.29) + (0.9)(-0.076) = -0.039$

$T_{10} = (0.1)(-0.54) + (0.9)(-0.039) = -0.089.$

Forecasting values. We have $\hat{S}_t = S_t + \dfrac{1-\alpha}{\alpha} T_t$ for $1 \le t \le 10$.

Now $\quad \dfrac{1-\alpha}{\alpha} = \dfrac{1-0.1}{0.1} = \dfrac{0.9}{0.1} = 9.$

$\therefore \quad \hat{S}_1 = 39.2 + 9(0.02) = 39.38$

$\hat{S}_2 = 39.38 + 9(0.036) = 39.70$

$\hat{S}_3 = 39.84 + 9(0.078) = 40.54$

$\hat{S}_4 = 38.86 + 9(-0.028) = 38.61$

$$\hat{S}_5 = 38.57 + 9(-0.0540) = 38.08$$
$$\hat{S}_6 = 38.21 + 9(-0.085) = 37.45$$
$$\hat{S}_7 = 38.39 + 9(-0.058) = 37.87$$
$$\hat{S}_8 = 38.15 + 9(-0.076) = 37.47$$
$$\hat{S}_9 = 38.44 + 9(-0.039) = 38.09$$
$$\hat{S}_{10} = 37.90 + 9(-0.089) = 37.1.$$

7. INDUSTRY VERSUS COMPANY SALES FORECASTS

The methods of forecasting discussed above are generally used to forecast the aggregate economic and business time series or industry demand or industry sales. The company sales forecasts are also made by using the same methods of forecasting. The difference of industry forecast and company forecast lies in the difference of the assumptions used in the forecasting. In making company sales forecast, the management may make the assumption that in the near future the company sales will constitute the same proportional relation with the industry sales as has been in the past. Also, the management of the company may make the assumption that may depend on the expected changes in the competitive conditions among other companies in the industry. The future market share of the company may be different from its past market share. After deciding the assumptions, the company has only to calculate its share in the total for the industry.

8. FACTORS AFFECTING COMPANY SALES

For the purpose of forecasting the sales figure for a company, its top management is expected to study the factors which may affect the sales figures. The factors affecting sales of a company are divided as *internal factors* and *external factors*. The internals factors are those factors which affect the market share of a company as a result of the changing relations among different company within the industry. Generally, these factors are under the control of the company. The internal factors include the product quality, scale of operation, price policy, advertising policy, efficiency of staff. etc. The external factors are those factors which affect the market position of the entire industry. Generally these factors are not under the control of any company. The external factors include the economic policies involving industrial import-export, fiscal, monetary, tariff of the government, population growth, changes in habits etc.

EXERCISE 1

1. Discuss the importance and scope of business forecasting.
2. Explain briefly the methods of forecasting.
3. Discuss the importance of business forecasting. Describe any one method of business forecasting.
4. Discuss the factors affecting the sales of a company.
5. Let 15, 17, 25, 31, 32, 37, be the values of the variable 'X' for the years 1997, 1998, 1999, 2000, 2001, 2002 respectively. Forecast the value of 'X' for the year 2003 by using the Naive method and the forecasting formula :

$$\hat{X}_{t+1} = X_t \left[\frac{1}{t-1}\sum_{i=2}^{t}\frac{X_i}{X_{i-1}}\right].$$

6. For the time series :

Year	1995	1996	1997	1998	1999	2000	2001	2002
Production (,000 Qtl.)	7	6	8	8	10	11	12	15

forecast the production for the year 2003 by using Naive method and the forecasting formula :

$$\hat{X}_{t+1} = X_t \left[\frac{1}{t-1} \sum_{i=2}^{t} \frac{X_i}{X_{i-1}} \right].$$

7. For the time series :

Month of the year 2002	Jan.	Feb.	March	April	May	June	July	Aug.
Sale (,000 Rs.)	85	80	90	92	98	112	130	125

forecast the sale for the month sept. 2002 by using Naive method and the forecasting formula :

$$\hat{X}_{t+1} = X_t \left[\frac{1}{t-1} \sum_{i=2}^{t} \frac{X_i}{X_{i-1}} \right].$$

8. From the following values, prepare forecasts by the method of exponential smoothing taking initial estimate as 40, the value of $\alpha = 0.2$ and initial trend value zero.

Year	1999	2000	2001	2002
Value X	42	45	57	60

9. From the following values, prepare forecasts by the method of exponential smoothing taking initial estimate as 125, the value of $\alpha = 0.4$ and initial trend value zero.

Year	1998	1999	2000	2001	2002
Value X	140	165	180	200	215

10. From the following values, prepare forecasts by the method of exponential smoothing taking initial estimale as 85, the value of $\alpha = 0.1$ and initial trend value zero.

Year	1997	1998	1999	2000	2001	2002
Value X	84	80	75	70	64	60

Answers

5. 44.64

6. 16,890 Qtl.

7. Rs. 1,32,477

8. 40.72, 42.04, 47.57, 52.54

9. 134.6, 154.92, 173.44, 193.97, 211.92

10. 84.81, 83.89, 82.16, 79.73, 76.53, 73.05.

15

Probability

1. INTRODUCTION

The words 'Probability' and 'Chance' are quite familiar to everyone. Many a times, we come across statements like, "Probably it may rain today", "Chances of his visit to the university are very few", "It is possible that he may pass the examination with good marks". In the above statements, the words probably, chance, possible etc. convey the sense of uncertainty about the occurrence of some event. Ordinarily, it may appear that there cannot be any exact measurement for these uncertainties, but in Statistics, we do have methods for calculating the degree of certainty of events in numerical value, provided certain conditions are satisfied.

2. RANDOM EXPERIMENT

When we perform experiments in science and engineering, repeatedly under very nearly identical conditions, we get almost the same result. Such experiments are called **deterministic experiments**.

There also exist experiments in which the results may not be essentially the same even if the experiment is performed under very nearly identical conditions. Such experiments are called **random experiments**. If we toss a coin, we may get 'head' or 'tail'. This is a random experiment. Throwing of a die is also a random experiment as any of the six faces of the die may come up. In this experiment, there are six possibilities (1 or 2 or 3 or 4 or 5 or 6).

Remark 1. A *die* is a small cube used in gambling. On its six faces, dots are marked as :

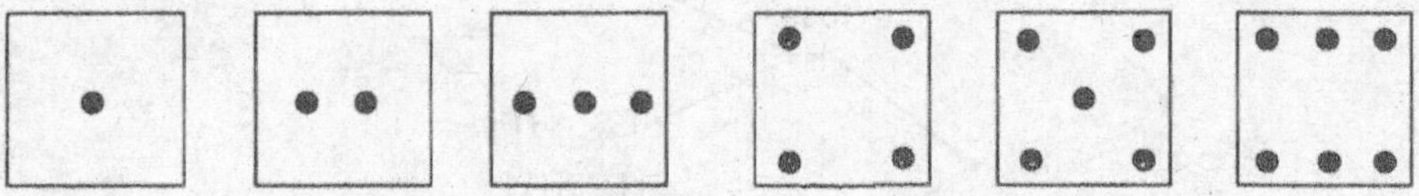

Numbers on a die

Plural of the word die is *dice*. The outcome of throwing a die is the number of dots on its upper most face.

Remark 2. A *pack of cards* consists of four suits called *Spades, Hearts, Diamonds* and *Clubs*. Each suit consists of 13 cards, of which nine cards are numbered from 2 to 10, an ace, a king, a queen and a jack (or knave). Spades and clubs are black faced cards, while hearts and diamonds are red faced cards. The kings, queens and jacks are called *face* cards.

3. SAMPLE SPACE

The **sample space** of a random experiment is defined as the set of all possible outcomes of the experiment. The possible outcomes are called **sample points.** The sample space is generally denoted by the letter S. We list the sample space of some random experiments :

Random Experiment	Sample Space
1. Throwing of a fair die	S = {1, 2, 3, 4, 5, 6}
2. Tossing of an unbiased coin	S = {H, T}
3. Tossing of two unbiased coins	S = {HH, HT, TH, TT}
4. A family of two children	S = {BB, BG, GB, GG}

4. TREE DIAGRAM

A **Tree diagram** is a device used to enumerate all the logical possibilities of a sequence of steps where each step can occur in a finite number of ways. A tree diagram is constructed from left to right and the number of branches at any point corresponds to the number of ways the next step can occur.

Illustration 1. The tree diagram of the sample space of the toss of two coins is shown in the figure.

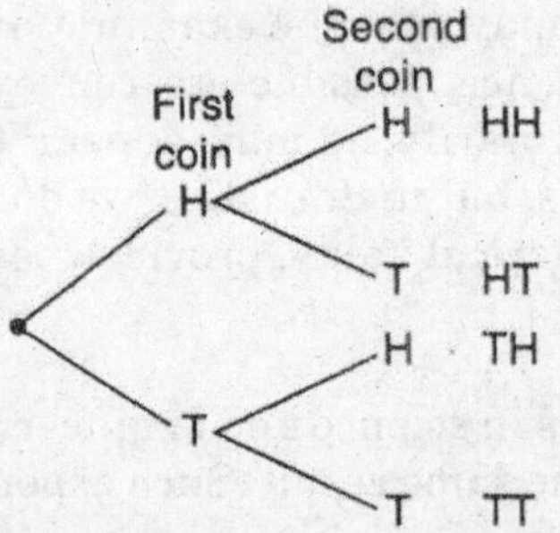

Illustration 2. The tree diagram of the sample space of the two tosses of a coin is shown in the figure.

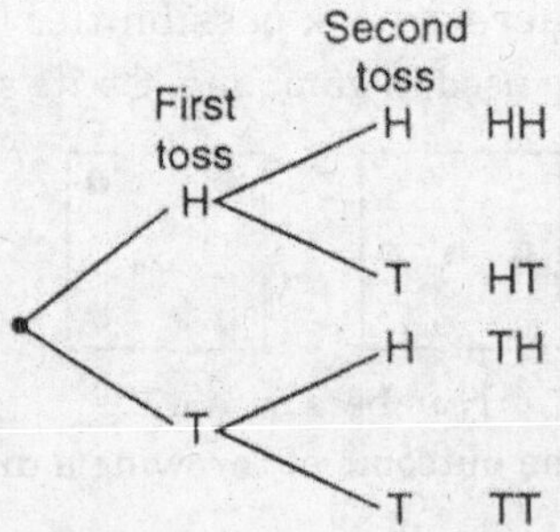

5. EVENT

An **event** is defined as a subset of the sample space. An event is called an **elementary (or simple) event** if it contains only one sample point. In the experiment of rolling a die, the event A of getting '3' is a simple event. We write A = {3}. An event is called an **impossible event** if it can never occur. In the above example, the event B = {7} of getting '7' is an impossible event. On the other hand, an event which is sure to occur is called a **certain event**. In the above example of rolling a die, the event C of getting a number less than 7 is a certain event.

In the throwing of two dice, the cases favourable to getting sum 7 are 6 *viz.* (1, 6), (2, 5), (3, 4), (4, 3), (5, 2) and (6, 1).

6. ALGEBRA OF EVENTS

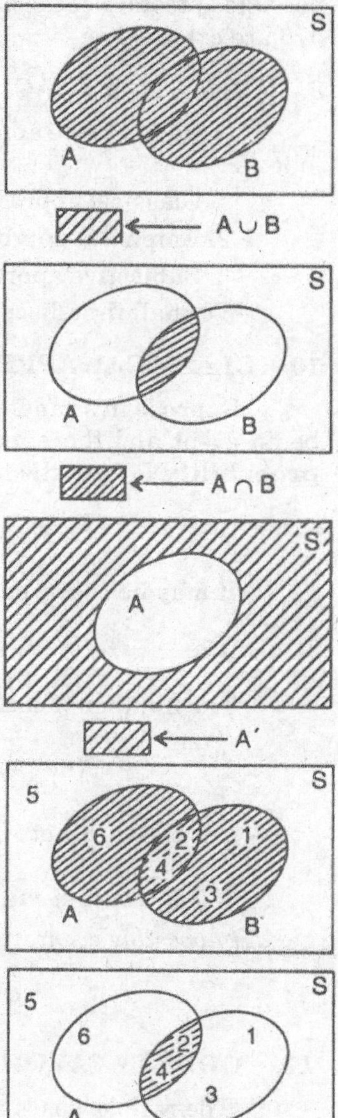

We know that the events of a random experiment are sets, being subsets of the sample space. Thus, we can use set operations to form new events.

Let A and B be any two events associated with a random experiment.

The event of occurrence of either A or B or both is written as 'A or B' and is denoted by the subset $A \cup B$ of the sample space. The event of occurrence of both A and B is written as 'A and B' and is denoted by the subset $A \cap B$ of the sample space. For simplicity, the event $A \cap B$ is also denoted by 'AB'.

The event of non-occurrence of event A is written as 'not A' and is denoted by the subset A′, which is the complement of set A. The event A′ is called the **complementary event** of the event A.

Illustration. Let a die be tossed.

$\therefore$ $S = \{1, 2, 3, 4, 5, 6\}$

Let A = event of getting an even number

and B = event of getting a number less than 5

$\therefore$ $A = \{2, 4, 6\}$ and $B = \{1, 2, 3, 4\}$

Here

$A \cup B$ = event of occurrence of either A or B or both

$= \{1, 2, 3, 4, 6\}$ *(See figure)*

$A \cap B$ = event of occurrence of both A and B

$= \{2, 4\}$ *(See figure)*

Also, A′ = event of non-occurrence of

$A = \{1, 3, 5\}$

and B′ = event of non-occurrence of

$B = \{5, 6\}$.

7. EQUALITY LIKELY OUTCOMES *(KU 2004)*

The outcomes of a random experiment are called **equally likely,** if all of these have equal preferences. In the experiment of tossing a unbiased coin, the outcomes 'Head' and 'Tail' are equally likely.

In our discussion, we shall always assume the outcomes of a random experiment to be equally likely.

8. EXHAUSTIVE OUTCOMES

The outcomes of a random experiment are called **exhaustive**, if these cover all the possible outcomes of the experiment. In the experiment of rolling a die, the outcomes 1, 2, 3, 4, 5, 6 are exhaustive.

9. THREE APPROACHES OF PROBABILITY

There are three approaches of discussing probability of events. These approaches are as follows :

1. Classical approach
2. Empirical approach
3. Subjective approach

We shall first discuss classical approach of probability.

10. CLASSICAL APPROACH OF PROBABILITY

Suppose in a random experiment, there are n exhaustive, equally likely outcomes. Let A be an event and there are m outcomes (cases) favourable to the happening of it. Then the **probability** P(A) of the happening of the event A is defined as

$$P(A) = \frac{\text{Total no. of cases favourable to the happening of A}}{\text{Total no. of exhaustive, equally likely cases}} = \frac{m}{n}.$$

It may be observed from this definition, that $0 \le m \le n$.

$$\therefore \quad 0 \le \frac{m}{n} \le 1 \text{ or } \mathbf{0 \le P(A) \le 1.}$$

The number of cases favourable to the non-happening of the event A is $n - m$.

$$\therefore \quad P(\text{not A}) = \frac{n-m}{n} = \frac{n}{n} - \frac{m}{n} = 1 - \frac{m}{n} = 1 - P(A).$$

$\therefore \quad P(A) + P(\text{not A}) = 1.$ *i.e.* $P(A) + P(\overline{A}) = 1.$

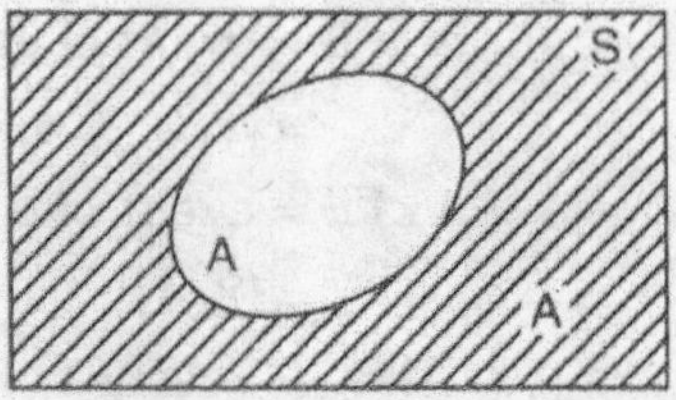

If A is a *sure event*, the $P(A) = \frac{n}{n} = 1$ and if A happen to be an *impossible event*, then

$$P(A) = \frac{0}{n} = 0.$$

11. 'ODDS IN FAVOUR' AND 'ODDS AGAINST' AN EVENT

The ratio of cases in favour of A and cases against A is called the **odds in favour** of A. Similarly, the ratio of cases against A and cases in favour of A is called the **odds against** A.

If odds in favour of A are $m : n$, then (*i*) odds against A are $n : m$ and (*ii*) probability of

$$A = \frac{m}{m+n}.$$

If odds against A are $m : n$, then (*i*) odds in favour of A are $n : m$ and (*ii*) probability of

$$A = \frac{n}{m+n}.$$

Illustration. Let $P(A) = \dfrac{3}{5}$.

Let total number of cases be 5λ.

$\therefore$ $P(A) = \dfrac{3\lambda}{5\lambda}$ and this implies that cases in favour of A are 3λ and cases against A are $5\lambda - 3\lambda = 2\lambda$.

$\therefore$ odds in favour of A are $3\lambda : 2\lambda$ or **3 : 2** and odds against A are $2\lambda : 3\lambda$ or **2 : 3**.

Example 1. *What is the probability of getting an even number in the throw of an unbiased die ?*

Sol. In this experiment, there are 6 equally likely possible outcomes 1, 2, 3, 4, 5, 6.

$$\therefore \quad S = \{1, 2, 3, 4, 5, 6\}.$$

Let A be the event of getting an even number.

$$\therefore \quad A = \{2, 4, 6\}$$

$$\therefore \quad P(A) = \frac{3}{6} = \mathbf{\frac{1}{2}}.$$

Example 2. *Find the probability of getting the sum 10 in a single throw of two dice.*

Sol. Here $S = \{(1, 1), (1, 2), (1, 3), \ldots\ldots, (6, 5), (6, 6)\}$.

$\therefore$ No. of possible outcomes $= 6 \times 6 = 36$.

Let A be the event of getting sum 10.

$$\therefore \quad A = \{(4, 6), (5, 5), (6, 4)\}$$

$$P(A) = \frac{3}{36} = \mathbf{\frac{1}{12}}.$$

Remark. In the above experiment, the sample point (a, b) means that 'a' is on the first die and 'b' is on the second die.

Example 3. *Find the probability of getting sum 10 in two throws of a die.* (KU 1997)

Sol. Here $S = \{(1, 1), (1, 2), (1, 3), \ldots, (6, 5), (6, 6)\}$

$\therefore$ No. of possible outcomes $= 6 \times 6 = 36$

Let A be the event of getting sum 10

$$\therefore \quad A = \{(4, 6), (5, 5), (6, 4)\}$$

$$P(A) = \frac{3}{36} = \mathbf{\frac{1}{12}}.$$

Remark. In the above experiment, the sample ponit (a, b) means that 'a' occurred in the first toss and 'b' occurred in the second toss.

Example 4. *If there are two children in a family, find the probability that there is at least one girl in the family.*

Sol. Let S be the sample space.

$$\therefore \quad S = \{BB, BG, GB, GG\}.$$

where B and G stand for 'Boy' and 'Girl' respectively.

Let A be the event of having at least one girl.

$$\therefore \quad A = \{BG, GB, GG\}$$

$$P(A) = \mathbf{\frac{3}{4}}.$$

Example 5. *Find the probability of getting 53 Sundays in a :*

(*a*) *non-leap year* (KU 2001)

(*b*) *leap year.*

Sol. (*a*) There are 365 days in a non-leap year.

Now $365 = 7 \times 52 + 1$

∴ A non-leap year will contain at least 52 Sundays. The possibilities for the remaining one day are :

(*i*) Sunday (*ii*) Monday
(*iii*) Tuesday (*iv*) Wednesday
(*v*) Thursday (*vi*) Friday
(*vii*) Saturday.

Let A be the events of getting 53 Sundays in a non-leap year. Therefore only (*i*) possibility is favourable to the event A.

$$\therefore \quad P(A) = \frac{1}{7}.$$

(*b*) There are 366 days in a leap year.

Now $366 = 7 \times 52 + 2$

∴ A leap year will contain at least 52 Sundays. The possible combinations for the remaining two days are :

(*i*) Sunday and Monday (*ii*) Monday and Tuesday
(*iii*) Tuesday and Wednesday (*iv*) Wednesday and Thursday
(*v*) Thursday and Friday (*vi*) Friday and Saturday
(*vii*) Saturday and Sunday.

Let A be the event of getting 53 Sundays in a leap year. Therefore, only those combinations will be favourable to the event A which contain 'Sunday'.

∴ The combinations (*i*) and (*vii*) are favourable to the happening of A.

$$\therefore \quad P(A) = \frac{2}{7}.$$

Example 6. *From a bag containing 4 red and 5 green balls, a ball is drawn at random. What is the probability that it is a red ball ?* (MDU 2002)

Sol. Total no. of balls $= 4 + 5 = 9$

No. of red balls $= 4$

$$\therefore \quad \text{Prob. of getting a red ball} = \frac{\text{Toral no. of red ball}}{\text{Total no. of balls}} = \frac{4}{9}.$$

Example 7. *Three coins are tossed. Find the probability of getting at least two heads.*

Sol. Let S be the sample space.

$$\therefore \quad S = (HHH, HHT, HTH, THH, HTT, THT, TTH, TTT)$$

Let A be the event of getting at least two heads.

$$\therefore \quad A = \{HHH, HHT, HTH, THH\}$$

∴ P(at least two heads)

$$= P(A) = \frac{\text{No. of cases favourable to A}}{\text{Total no. of exhaustive, equally likely cases}} = \frac{4}{8} = \frac{1}{2}.$$

Example 8. *A card in drawn out of a pack of cards. Find the probability that the card is (i) an ace (ii) a king (iii) a queen (iv) a card of clubs.* (MDU 1998)

Sol. Total number of cases = 52

(*i*) There are 4 aces.

$$\therefore \quad P(\text{ace}) = \frac{4}{52} = \frac{1}{13}.$$

(*ii*) There are 4 kings.

$$\therefore \quad P(\text{king}) = \frac{4}{52} = \frac{1}{13}.$$

(*iii*) There are 4 queens.

$$\therefore \quad P(\text{queen}) = \frac{4}{52} = \frac{1}{13}.$$

(*iv*) There are 13 club cards.

$$\therefore \quad P(\text{club card}) = \frac{13}{52} = \frac{1}{4}.$$

Example 9. *Find the probability of getting a 'King' or a 'Queen' in a single draw from a well-shuffled pack of playing cards.* (MDU 1995)

Sol. Let A be the event of getting a king or a queen in the draw.

$\therefore$ No. of favourable cases for the happening of the event A = 4 + 4 = 8

Total no. of cases = 52

$$\therefore \quad P(\text{King or Queen}) = P(A) = \frac{8}{52} = \frac{2}{13}.$$

Example 10. *Two unbiased dice are thrown. Find the probability that the total of the numbers on the dice is greater than 8.*

Sol. Let S be the sample space.

$$\therefore \quad S = \{(1, 1), (1, 2), (1, 3), \ldots\ldots, (6, 5), (6, 6)\}$$

There are 6 × 6 = 36 exhaustive, equally likely outcomes.

Let A be the event of getting total greater than 8.

$$\therefore \quad A = \{(3, 6), (4, 5), (5, 4), (6, 3), (4, 6), (5, 5), (6, 4), (5, 6), (6, 5), (6, 6)\}$$

$$\therefore \quad P(\text{sum} > 8) = P(A) = \frac{\text{No. of cases favourable to A}}{\text{Total No. of cases}} = \frac{10}{36} = \frac{5}{18}.$$

Example 11. *The following table gives a distribution of wages :*

Weekly wage (in Rs.)	*No. of workers*
30—35	9
35—40	108
40—45	488
45—50	230
50—55	112
55—60	30
60—65	16
65—70	7

An individual is taken at random from the above group. Find the probability (i) his wage is under Rs. 40 (ii) his wage is Rs. 55 or above (iii) his wage is either between Rs. 45—50 or Rs. 35—40. (MDU 2001)

Sol. Total number of workers = 9 + 108 + 488 + 230 + 112 + 30 + 16 + 7 = 1000.

(*i*) Number of workers having wage under 40 = 9 + 108 = 117

$$\therefore \quad \text{P(wage under Rs. 40)} = \frac{\text{No. of workers having wage under 40}}{\text{Total number of workers}} = \frac{117}{1000} = \mathbf{0.117.}$$

(*ii*) Number of workers having wage 55 or above = 30 + 16 + 7 = 53

$$\therefore \quad \text{P(wage Rs. 55 or above)} = \frac{53}{1000} = \mathbf{0.053.}$$

(*iii*) Number of workers having wage either between Rs. 45 – 50 or Rs. 35 – 40

= 230 + 108 = 338

$$\therefore \quad \text{P(wage either between Rs. 45 – 50 or Rs. 35 – 40)} = \frac{338}{1000} = \mathbf{0.338.}$$

Example 12. *Three unbiased dice are thrown simultaneously. Find the probability of getting (i) sum not greater than 5 (ii) sum at least 15 (iii) sum equal to 8.* (MDU 1999)

Sol. Let S be the sample space.

$\therefore$ S = {(1, 1, 1), (1, 1, 2), ..., (6, 6, 5), (6, 6, 6)}

There are 6 × 6 × 6 = 216 exhaustive equally likely outcomes.

(*i*) Let A = event that sum is not greater than 5.

$\therefore$ A = {(1, 1, 1), (1, 1, 2) (1, 2, 1), (2, 1, 1), (1, 1, 3),
(1, 2, 2), (1, 3, 1), (2, 1, 2), (2, 2, 1), (3, 1, 1)}

$$\therefore \quad P(A) = \frac{n(A)}{n(S)} = \frac{10}{216} = \mathbf{\frac{5}{108}}.$$

(*ii*) Let B = event that sum is at least 15

$\therefore$ B = {(3, 6, 6), (4, 5, 6), (4, 6, 5), (5, 4, 6), (5, 5, 5),
(5, 6, 4), (6, 3, 6), (6, 4, 5), (6, 5, 4), (6, 6, 3),
(4, 6, 6), (5, 5, 6), (5, 6, 5), (6, 4, 6), (6, 5, 5),
(6, 6, 4), (5, 6, 6), (6, 5, 6), (6, 6, 5), (6, 6, 6)}

$$\therefore \quad P(B) = \frac{n(B)}{n(S)} = \frac{20}{216} = \mathbf{\frac{5}{54}}.$$

(*iii*) Let C = event of getting sum 8

$\therefore$ C = {(1, 1, 6), (1, 2, 5), (1, 3, 4), (1, 4, 3), (1, 5, 2),
(1, 6, 1), (2, 1, 5), (2, 2, 4), (2, 3, 3), (2, 4, 2),
(2, 5, 1), (3, 1, 4), (3, 2, 3), (3, 3, 2), (3, 4, 1),
(4, 1, 3), (4, 2, 2), (4, 3, 1), (5, 1, 2), (5, 2, 1), (6, 1, 1)}

$$\therefore \quad P(C) = \frac{n(C)}{n(S)} = \frac{21}{216} = \mathbf{\frac{7}{72}}.$$

Example 13. *A player tosses two fair coins. He wins Rs. 5 if 2 heads appear, Rs. 2 if one head appear and Re. 1 if no head occur. Find his expected value of the amount.*

Sol. The expected value of the amount won by the player is the sum of products of various amounts with corresponding probabilities.

In the given example, let x denotes the 'number of heads'.

$\therefore$ The possible values of x are 0, 1 and 2.

Here S = {TT, TH, HT, HH}

$$\therefore \quad p_0 = P(x = 0) = P(\text{no head}) = \frac{1}{4}$$

$$p_1 = P(x = 1) = P(\text{one head}) = \frac{2}{4} = \frac{1}{2}$$

$$p_2 = P(x = 2) = P(\text{two heads}) = \frac{1}{4}$$

$\therefore$ Expected value

$$= (p_0 \times 1) + (p \times 2) + (p_2 \times 5) = \left(\frac{1}{4} \times 1\right) + \left(\frac{1}{2} \times 2\right) + \left(\frac{1}{4} \times 5\right)$$

$$= 0.25 + 1 + 1.25 = \textbf{Rs. 2.5.}$$

Example 14. *Find the probability that in a random arrangement of the letters of the world* **DAUGHTER**, *the letter* **D** *occupies the first place.*

Sol. The word **DAUGHTER** contains 8 letters and all are different.

$\therefore$ Total no. of possible arrangements

$$= 8\,! = \mathbf{40320}$$

Let A be the event of getting a word with **D** at the first place.

$\therefore$ Favourable cases to the event A

= 1 × no. of ways of arranging 7 letters (except **D**).

$$= 1 \times 7\,! = 5040$$

$\therefore$ P(**D** occupies first place)

$$P(A) = \frac{5040}{40320} = \mathbf{\frac{1}{8}}.$$

Example 15. *Find the probability that in a random arrangement of letters of the world* **INSTITUTION**, *the three* **T**'s *are together.*

Sol. The word **INSTITUTION** contains 3**I**'s 2 **N**'s, 1 **S**, 3 **T**'s, 1 **U**'s and 1 **O**.

$$\therefore \quad \text{Total no. of arrangements} = \frac{11!}{3!\,2!\,1!\,3!\,1!\,1!} = 554400$$

For finding the no. of favourable cases to the event under consideration, we shall consider 3 **T**'s as one block. So in arranging 3 **I**'s, 2 **N**'s, 1 **S**, 1 (**TTT**)'s, 1 **U** and 1 **O**, three **T** will remain together.

$$\therefore \quad \text{No. of favourable cases} = \frac{9!}{3!\,2!\,1!\,1!\,1!\,1!} = 30240$$

$$\therefore \quad P(3T\text{'s are together}) = \frac{30240}{554400} = \mathbf{0.0545}.$$

Example 16. *Find the probability that in a random arrangement of letters of the word* **MATHEMATICS**, *the consonants occur together.*

Sol. The word **MATHEMATICS**, contains 2 **M**'s, 2 **A**'s, 2 **T**'s, 1 **H**, 1 **E**, 1 **I**, 1 **C** and 1 **S**.

∴ Total no. of exhaustive cases

$$= \frac{11!}{2!2!2!} = 4989600$$

For finding the no. of favourable cases to the event under consideration, we shall consider all consonents **M, T, H, M, T, C, S** as one block. So in arranging **2 A's, 1 E's, 1 I's, 1 (MTHMTCS)**, all the consonents will occur together. The consonents **MTHMTCS** can arrange themselves in

$$\frac{7!}{2!2!} = 1260 \text{ ways}$$

$$\therefore \quad \text{No. of favourable cases} = \frac{5!}{2!1!1!1!} \times 1260 = 75600$$

$$\therefore \quad \text{P(consonants are together)} = \frac{75600}{4989600} = \mathbf{0.01515.}$$

Example 17. *A bag contains 3 white balls and 4 black balls. Two balls are drawn at random. Find the probability that both the balls are white.*

Sol. Let A be the event of getting both balls white.

$$\therefore \quad P(A) = \frac{\text{No. of selections of 2 out of 3 white balls}}{\text{No. of selections of 2 out of 7 (= 3 + 4) balls}} = \frac{^3C_2}{^7C_2} = \frac{3}{21} = \mathbf{\frac{1}{7}}.$$

Example 18. *A bag contains 10 red and 8 black balls. Two balls are drawn at random. Find the probability that :*

(i) both balls are red.

(ii) one ball is red and the other is black. (KU 2002 C)

Sol. (*i*) Total number of balls = 10 + 8 = 18

$$(ii)\ \text{P(both red balls)} = \frac{\text{No. of selections of 2 out of 10 red balls}}{\text{No. of selections of 2 out of 18 balls}}$$

$$= \frac{^{10}C_2}{^{18}C_2} = \frac{10 \times 9}{1 \times 2} \div \frac{18 \times 17}{1 \times 2} = \frac{10 \times 9}{18 \times 17} = \mathbf{\frac{5}{17}}.$$

(*ii*) P(one red ball and one black ball)

$$= \frac{\begin{pmatrix}\text{No. of selections of} \\ \text{1 out of 10 red balls}\end{pmatrix}\begin{pmatrix}\text{No. of selections of} \\ \text{1 out of 8 black balls}\end{pmatrix}}{\text{No. of selections of 2 out of 18 balls.}} = \frac{^{10}C_1 \times {}^8C_1}{^{18}C_2}$$

$$= (10 \times 8) \div \frac{18 \times 17}{2} = \frac{10 \times 8}{9 \times 17} = \mathbf{\frac{80}{153}}.$$

Example 19. *Five cards are drawn from a pack of playing cards. Find the probability that :*

(i) 4 are aces and 1 is a queen *(ii) 3 are eights and 2 are kings*

(iii) at least one queen is drawn.

Sol. (*i*) Let A be the event of drawing 4 aces and 1 queen.

$$\therefore \quad P(A) = \frac{\begin{pmatrix}\text{No. of selections of} \\ \text{4 out of 4 aces}\end{pmatrix}\begin{pmatrix}\text{No. of selections of} \\ \text{1 out of 4 queens}\end{pmatrix}}{\text{No. of selections of 5 out 52 cards}}$$

$$= \frac{{}^4C_4 \times {}^4C_1}{{}^{52}C_5} = \frac{1 \times 4}{2598960} = \frac{1}{649740} = \mathbf{0.0000015.}$$

(*ii*) Let B be the event of getting 3 eights and 2 kings.

$$\therefore \quad P(B) = \frac{\begin{pmatrix}\text{No. of selections of} \\ \text{3 out of 4 eights}\end{pmatrix}\begin{pmatrix}\text{No. of selections of} \\ \text{2 out of 4 kings}\end{pmatrix}}{\text{No. of selections of 5 out 52 cards}} = \frac{{}^4C_3 \times {}^4C_2}{{}^{52}C_5}$$

$$= \frac{4 \times 6}{2598960} = \frac{1}{108290} = \mathbf{0.0000092.}$$

(*iii*) Let C be the event of getting at least one queen

$$\therefore \quad P(C) = 1 - \text{Prob. of getting no queen}$$

$$= 1 - \frac{\text{No. of selections of 5 out of 48 non-queen cards}}{\text{No. of selections of 5 out 52 cards}}$$

$$= 1 - \frac{{}^{48}C_5}{{}^{52}C_5} = 1 - \frac{1712304}{2598960} = 1 - 0.6588 = \mathbf{0.3412.}$$

Example 20. *From a group of 8 children (5 boys and 3 girls) three children are selected at random. Calculate the probabilities that the selected group contains :*

(*i*) *no girl* (*ii*) *only one girl*

(*iii*) *only one particular girl.*

Sol. No. of girls = 3

No. of boys = 5

Let A_0, A_1, A_2 and A_3 be the events that there are no girl, one girl, two girls and three girls in the random selection of three children.

(*i*) Required probability $= P(A_0) = \dfrac{{}^5C_3}{{}^8C_3} = \mathbf{\dfrac{5}{28}}.$

(*ii*) Required probability $= P(A_1) = \dfrac{{}^3C_1 \times {}^5C_2}{{}^8C_3} = \mathbf{\dfrac{15}{28}}.$

(*iii*) The particular girl can be selected in only one way. The remaining two children in the selection must be boys.

$\therefore$ Required probability $= \dfrac{1 \times {}^5C_2}{{}^8C_3} = \mathbf{\dfrac{5}{28}}.$

EXERCISE 1

1. Find the probability of getting an odd number in a single throw of a fair die.
2. Find the probability of getting a number less than 2 in a single throw of a fair die.
3. A single letter is selected at random from the word "**PROBABILITY**". What is the probability that it is a vowel ? *(KU 1996)*
4. Find the probability of getting no head in a single toss of three coins.
5. Find the probability of getting at most two heads in a single toss of three coins.
6. A card is drawn at random from a well-shuffled pack of playing cards. Find the probability of having an ace. *(KU 2003 C)*
7. From a pack of 52 playing cards, one card is drawn at random. What is the probability that it will be a queen of club or king of diamond ?
8. Two unbiased dice are thrown. Find the probability that both dice show the same number.
9. Two unbiased dice are thrown. Find the probability that the total of the numbers on the dice is 8.
10. A ball is drawn at random from a box containing 5 white, 8 red and 10 black balls. Determine the probability that the ball drawn is not red.
11. Tickets are numbered from 1 to 100. These are well-shuffled and a ticket is drawn at random. What is the probability that the drawn ticket has a number which is greater than 75 ?
12. The following table gives a distribution of marks :

Marks	*No. of students*
0—10	7
10—20	10
20—30	15
30—40	28
40—50	23
50—60	45
60—70	12
70—80	7
80—90	2
90—100	1

An individual is taken at random from the above group. Find the probability that :

(*i*) his marks are below 50 (*ii*) his marks are below 70.

(*iii*) his marks are between 30 and 60 (*iv*) his marks are above 70.

13. Suppose an ideal die is tossed twice. What is the probability of getting a sum of 10 in the two tosses ? *(KU 1997)*
14. Find the probability that in a random arrangement of the letters of the word **VOWEL**, the letter V occupies the first place.
15. Find the probability that in a random arrangement of the letters of the word **MALENKOV**, the letter A occupies the third place.
16. Find the probability that in a random arrangement of letters the word **BHARAT**, the two A occupies the first two places.
17. Find the probability that in a random arrangement of letters of the world **INDIA**, the two I are together.
18. Find the probability that in a random arrangement of the letters of the word **STATISTICS**, the three T are in the beginning.

19. Find the probability that in a random arrangement of the letters of the word **STATISTICS**, the three T are together.

20. Two cards are drawn from a pack of 52 cards, at random. What is the probability that one is a king and the other is a queen ?

21. Four cards are drawn from a pack of playing cards. Find the probability that none is a king.

22. From a bag containing 4 red and 5 black balls, four balls are drawn at random. Find the probability of getting two red and two black balls.

23. A bag contains 6 white, 4 red and 10 black balls. Two balls are drawn at random. Find the probability that both balls are black.

24. A bag contains 7 white, 5 red and 8 black balls. Two balls are drawn at random. Calculate the probability that both balls are white.

25. A bag contains 7 white, 5 red and 8 black balls. Two balls are drawn at random. Calculate the probability that none is white.

26. A bag contains 7 white, 5 red and 8 black balls. Three balls are drawn at random. Calculate the probability that there is one ball of each colour.

Answers

1. $\frac{1}{2}$	2. $\frac{1}{6}$	3. $\frac{4}{11}$	4. $\frac{1}{8}$
5. $\frac{7}{8}$	6. $\frac{1}{13}$	7. $\frac{1}{26}$	8. $\frac{1}{6}$
9. $\frac{5}{36}$	10. $\frac{15}{23}$	11. $\frac{1}{4}$	
12. (*i*) 0.5533	(*ii*) 0.9333	(*iii*) 0.64	(*iv*) 0.0667
13. $\frac{1}{12}$	14. 0.2	15. 0.125	16. 0.0667
17. 0.4	18. 0.0083	19. 0.0667	
20. $\frac{{}^4C_1 \times {}^4C_1}{{}^{52}C_2} = \frac{8}{663}$	21. $\frac{{}^{48}C_4}{{}^{52}C_4} = 0.7187$	22. $\frac{{}^4C_2 \times {}^5C_2}{{}^9C_4} = \frac{10}{21}$	23. $\frac{{}^{10}C_2}{{}^{20}C_2} = \frac{9}{38}$
24. $\frac{{}^7C_2}{{}^{20}C_2} = \frac{21}{190}$	25. $\frac{39}{95}$	26. $\frac{14}{57}$	

12. MUTUALLY EXCLUSIVE EVENTS (*KU 2004*)

Two events associated with a random experiment are said to be **mutually exclusive** if both cannot occur together in the same trial. In the experiment of throwing a die, the events A = {1, 4} and B = {2, 5, 6} are mutually exclusive events. In the same experiment, the events A = {1, 4} and C = {2, 4, 5, 6} are not mutually exclusive because if 4 appear on the die, then it is favourable to both events A and C. The definition of mutually exclusive events can also be extended to more than two events. We say that more than two events are mutually exclusive if the happening of one of these rules out the happening of all other events. The events A = {1, 2}, B = {3} and C = {6}, are mutually exclusive in connection with the experiment of throwing a single die.

13. ADDITION THEOREM (FOR MUTUALLY EXCLUSIVE EVENTS)

If A and B are two mutually exclusive events associated with a random experiment, then

$$\mathbf{P(A \text{ or } B) = P(A) + P(B).}$$

Proof. Let n be the total number of exhaustive, equally like cases of the experiment.

Let m_1 and m_2 be the number of cases favourable to the happening of the events A and B respectively.

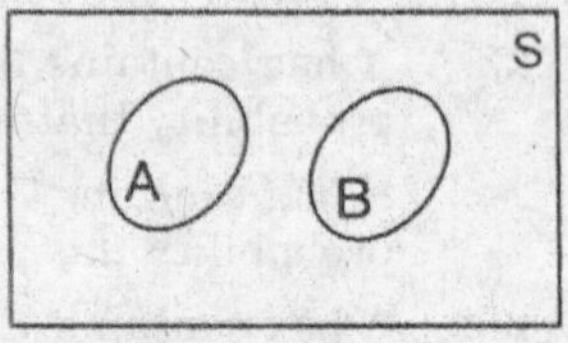

$\therefore$ $$P(A) = \frac{m_1}{n}$$

and $$P(B) = \frac{m_2}{n}.$$

Since the events are given to be mutually exclusive, therefore there cannot be any sample point common to both events A and B.

$\therefore$ The event A or B can happen in exactly $m_1 + m_2$ ways.

$\therefore$ $$P(A \text{ or } B) = \frac{m_1 + m_2}{n} = \frac{m_1}{n} + \frac{m_2}{n} = P(A) + P(B).$$

Hence, $\mathbf{P(A \text{ or } B) = P(A) + P(B).}$

This theorem can also be extended to even more than two events.

If $A_1, A_2, \ldots\ldots, A_k$ are pairwise m.e. events, then

$$\mathbf{P(A_1 \text{ or } A_2 \text{ or } \ldots\ldots \text{ or } A_k) = P(A_1) + P(A_2) + \ldots\ldots + P(A_k).}$$

Example 1. *A box contains 4 red balls, 4 green balls and 7 white balls. What is the probability that a ball drawn is either red or white ?*

Sol. Total no. of balls = 4 + 4 + 7 = 15

4 Red
4 Green
7 White

Let A = event of drawing a red ball

B = event of drawing a white ball.

The events A and B are *m.e.* because a ball cannot be both red and white.

$$P(A) = \frac{\text{No. of red balls}}{\text{Total no. of balls}} = \frac{4}{15}$$

$$P(B) = \frac{\text{No. of white balls}}{\text{Total no. of balls}} = \frac{7}{15}$$

Now A or B is the event of drawing either a red ball or a white ball. By addition theorem, the required probability

$$P(A \text{ or } B) = P(A) + P(B) = \frac{4}{15} + \frac{7}{15} = \frac{11}{15}.$$

Example 2. *The probability that a company executive will travel by plane is 2/3 and that he will travel by train is 1/5. Find the probability of his travelling by plane or train.*

Sol. Let A = event that the company executive travel by plane

$\therefore$ P(A) = 2/3.

Let B = event that the company executive travel by train

$\therefore$ P(B) = 1/5

The events A and B are mutually exclusive, because he cannot travel by plane and train at the same time.

∴ Prob. of his travelling by plane or train

$$= P(A \text{ or } B) = P(A) + P(B) = \frac{2}{3} + \frac{1}{5} = \frac{13}{15}.$$

Example 3. *In a single throw of 2 dice, determine the probability of getting total 7 or 11.* (MDU 2000)

Sol. Here $S = \{(1, 1), (1, 2), \ldots\ldots, (6, 5), (6, 6)\}$.

Let A and B be the events of getting total 7 and 11 respectively.

∴ $A = \{(1, 6), (2, 5), (3, 4), (4, 3), (5, 2), (6, 1)\}$

and $B = \{(5, 6), (6, 5)\}$

The events A and B are mutually exclusive and

$$P(A) = \frac{6}{36} = \frac{1}{6} \quad \text{and} \quad P(B) = \frac{2}{36} = \frac{1}{18}$$

∴ *By addition theorem,*

$$P(\text{total is 7 or 9}) = P(A \cup B) = P(A) + P(B)$$

$$= \frac{1}{6} + \frac{1}{18} = \frac{3+1}{18} = \frac{2}{9}.$$

Example 4. *One of the two events must happen. Given that the chance of one is two-third of the other, find the odds in favour of the other.*

Sol. Let the given events be A, B and $P(A) = \frac{2}{3} P(B)$.

Let $P(B) = x$. ∴ $P(A) = \frac{2}{3} x$.

The events A and B are exhaustive.

∴ $P(A \text{ or } B) = 1 \Rightarrow P(A) + P(B) = 1$ (∵ A and B are *m.e.*)

$$\Rightarrow \frac{2}{3} x + x = 1 \Rightarrow \frac{5x}{3} = 1 \Rightarrow x = \frac{3}{5}.$$

∴ $P(B) = \frac{3}{5}$.

$P(B) = \frac{3}{5}$ implies that the odds in favour of B are 3 : 5 – 2 *i.e.* **3 : 2**.

Example 5. *In a single throw of two dice, find the probability that neither a doublet nor a total of 9 will appear.* (KU 2007)

Sol. Here $S = \{(1, 1), (1, 2), \ldots\ldots, (6, 5), (6, 6)\}$.

∴ Number of possible outcomes $= 6 \times 6 = 36$.

Let E = event that doublet is occurred

and F = event that sum is 9.

∴ $E = \{(1, 1), (2, 2), (3, 3), (4, 4), (5, 5), (6, 6)\}$

and $F = \{(3, 6), (4, 5), (5, 4), (6, 3)\}$.

$$\therefore \quad P(E) = \frac{6}{36} = \frac{1}{6} \text{ and } P(F) = \frac{4}{36} = \frac{1}{9}.$$

P(neither a doublet nor a total of 9)

$$= P(E^c \cap F^c) = P((E \cup F)^c) = 1 - P(E \cup F) \quad ...(1)$$

The events E and F are *m.e.*

∴ By *addition theorem*,

$$P(E \cup F) = P(E) + P(F) = \frac{1}{6} + \frac{1}{9} = \frac{5}{18}$$

$$\therefore \quad (1) \Rightarrow \quad P(E^c \cap F^c) = 1 - \frac{5}{18} = \frac{13}{18}.$$

EXERCISE 2

1. A and B are mutually exclusive events for which P(A) = 0.3, P(B) = p and $P(A \cup B) = 0.5$. Find the value of p.
2. A box contains 4 white balls, 2 black balls, 3 yellow balls and 3 red balls. What is the probability that a ball drawn is either white or red ? *(MDU 2001)*
3. Find the probability that a card drawn from a pack of playing cards is either a 'queen' or a 'king'. *(MDU 1995)*
4. State with reasons, whether the following events are mutually exclusive or not : E_1 : a total of 9 ; E_2 : an odd number on each die, in a simultaneous throw of two dice.
5. A and B are two mutually exclusive events of an experiment.
   If P('not A') = 0.65, $P(A \cup B) = 0.65$ and P(B) = p, find the value of p.
6. In a class of 25 students with roll numbers 1 to 25, a student is picked up at random to answer a question. Find the probability that the roll number of the selected student is either a multiple of 5 or of 7.
7. From a set of 17 cards, numbered 1, 2, 3, ..., 16, 17, one is drawn at random. Show that the chance that its number is divisible by 3 or 7 is 7/17.
8. A, B, C are three mutually exclusive and exhaustive events associated with a random experiment. Find P(A) , given that $P(B) = \frac{3}{2} P(A)$ and $P(C) = \frac{1}{2} P(B)$.
9. Find the probability of getting the sum 9 or 11 in a single throw of two dice.
10. Find the probability of getting the sum 8 or 11 or 12 in a single throw of two dice.
11. In a single throw of three dice, find the probability of getting a total of 17 or 18.
12. Three coins are tossed simultaneously. What is the probability that there will be at least 2 heads ? *(MDU 2006)*

Answers

1. 0.2	2. $\frac{7}{12}$	3. $\frac{2}{13}$	4. yes
5. 0.3	6. $\frac{8}{25}$	8. $\frac{4}{13}$	9. $\frac{1}{6}$
10. $\frac{2}{9}$	11. $\frac{1}{54}$	12. $\frac{1}{2}$.	

---

14. ADDITION THEOREM (GENERAL)

If A and B are two events not necessarily mutually exclusive, associated with a random experiments, then

P(A or B) = P(A) + P(B) – P(AB). *(KU 1996, 97)*

Proof. Let n be the total number of exhaustive equally likely cases of the experiment.

Let m_1 and m_2 be the number of cases favourable to the happening of the events A and B respectively.

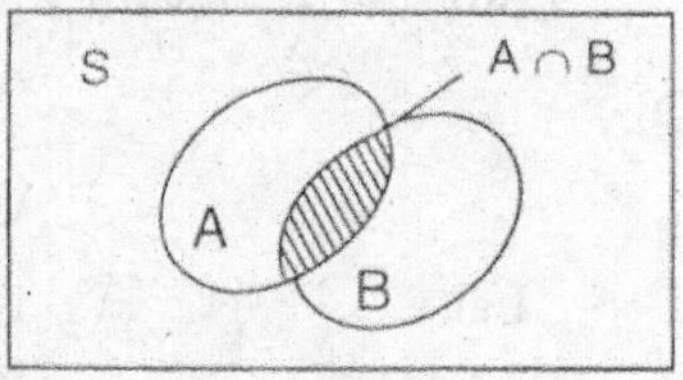

$$\therefore \quad P(A) = \frac{m_1}{n} \quad \text{and} \quad P(B) = \frac{m_2}{n}$$

Since the events are given to be not necessarily mutually exclusive, there may be some sample points common to both events A and B.

Let m_3 be number of these common sample points. m_3 will be zero in case A and B are mutually exclusive.

$$\therefore \quad P(AB) = \frac{m_3}{n}$$

The m_3 sample points which are common to both events A and B, are included in the events A and B separately.

∴ Number of sample points in the event A or B

$$= m_1 + m_2 - m_3$$

m_3 is subtracted from $m_1 + m_2$ to avoid counting of common sample points twice.

$$\therefore \quad P(A \text{ or } B) = \frac{m_1 + m_2 - m_3}{n} = \frac{m_1}{n} + \frac{m_2}{n} - \frac{m_3}{n} = P(A) + P(B) - P(AB).$$

Hence, **P(A or B) = P(A) + P(B) – P(AB).**

Corollary 1. If events A and B happen to be mutually exclusive events, then P(AB) = 0 and in this case *addition theorem* implies

$$P(A \text{ or } B) = P(A) + P(B) - P(AB) = P(A) + P(B) - 0 = P(A) + P(B)$$

$$\therefore \quad P(A \text{ or } B) = P(A) + P(B).$$

This is the same as the **addition theorem** for mutually exclusive events.

Corollary 2. If A, B, C are three events associated with a random experiment, then

P(A or B or C) = P(A) + P(B) + P(C) – P(BC) – P(CA) – P(AB) + P(ABC).

Example 1. *Find the probability that a card drawn from a pack of playing cards is either a 'queen' or a 'spade'.*

Sol. Total number of cases (cards) = 52

Let A = event of drawing a 'queen'

B = event of drawing a 'spade'

$$\therefore \quad P(A) = \frac{4}{52} \quad \text{and} \quad P(B) = \frac{13}{52}$$

Here the events are not mutually exclusive as drawing of the card 'queen of spade' is common to both events.

$$\therefore \quad P(AB) = \frac{1}{52}$$

By *addition theorem*, the probability of getting either a queen or a spade is

$$P(A \text{ or } B) = P(A) + P(B) - P(AB) = \frac{4}{52} + \frac{13}{52} - \frac{1}{52} = \frac{16}{52} = \frac{4}{13}.$$

Example 2. *A bag contains 30 balls numbered from 1 to 30. One ball is drawn at random. Find the probability that the number of the ball is a multiple of 5 or 6.*

Sol. Let A = event that the number of ball is a multiple of 5.

$$A = \{5, 10, 15, 20, 25, 30\}$$

$$\therefore \quad P(A) = \frac{6}{30}$$

Let B = event that the number of ball is a multiple of 6.

$$\therefore \quad B = \{6, 12, 18, 24, 30\}$$

$$\therefore \quad P(B) = \frac{5}{30}$$

The events A and B are not *m.e.* because the sample point 30 is common to both.

$$\therefore \quad AB = \{30\}$$

$$\therefore \quad P(AB) = \frac{1}{30}$$

By *addition theorem*, the probability of getting a multiple of 5 or 6 is

$$P(A \text{ or } B) = P(A) + P(B) - P(AB) = \frac{6}{30} + \frac{5}{30} - \frac{1}{30} = \frac{10}{30} = \frac{1}{3}.$$

Example 3. *One number is drawn from numbers 1 to 150. Find the probability that it is divisible by either 3 or 5.*

Sol. Here $S = \{1, 2, 3, ..., 149, 150\}$.

Let A = event that the number is divisible by 3

$$\therefore \quad A = \{3, 6, 9, ..., 147, 150\}$$

$$\therefore \quad P(A) = \frac{50}{150}$$

Let B = event that the number is divisible by 5.

$$\therefore \quad B = \{5, 10, 15 ......, 145, 150\}$$

$$\therefore \quad P(B) = \frac{30}{150}$$

The events A and B are not *m.e.* because the sample points 15, 30, 45, ..., 150 are common to both.

$$\therefore \quad AB = \{15, 30, 45, ..., 135, 150\}$$

$$\therefore \quad P(AB) = \frac{10}{150}$$

By *addition theorem*, the required probability of getting a multiple of either 3 or 5 is

$$P(A \text{ or } B) = P(A) + P(B) - P(AB) = \frac{50}{150} + \frac{30}{150} - \frac{10}{150} = \frac{70}{150} = \frac{7}{15}.$$

Example 4. *Find the probability of 4 turning for at least once in two tosses of a fair die.*

Sol. Here $S = \{(1, 1), (1, 2), ..., (6, 5), (6, 6)\}$.

Let A = event of getting 4 on the first die

and B = event of getting 4 on the second die.

$\therefore$ $A = \{(4, 1), (4, 2), (4, 3), (4, 4), (4, 5), (4, 6)\}$

and $B = \{(1, 4), (2, 4), (3, 4), (4, 4), (5, 4), (6, 4)\}$

$$\therefore \quad P(A) = \frac{n(A)}{n(S)} = \frac{6}{36} = \frac{1}{6} \quad \text{and} \quad P(B) = \frac{n(B)}{n(S)} = \frac{6}{36} = \frac{1}{6}.$$

The events A and B are not *m.e.* because the sample (4, 4) is common to both.

$\therefore$ $AB = \{(4, 4)\}$

$$\therefore \quad P(AB) = \frac{1}{36}$$

By *addition theorem*, the required probability of getting four at least once is

$$P(A \text{ or } B) = P(A) + P(B) - P(AB) = \frac{1}{6} + \frac{1}{6} - \frac{1}{36} = \mathbf{\frac{11}{36}}.$$

Example 5. *A student applies for a job in two firms X and Y. The probability of his being selected in firm X is is 0.7 and being rejected in the firm Y is 0.5. The probability of at least one of his application being rejected is 0.6. What is the probability that he will be selected in one of the firms ?* (KU 2002)

Sol. Let A = event of getting selected in X

B = event of getting selected in Y

$\therefore$ $P(A) = 0.7, P(B) = 1 - 0.5 = 0.5$

$P(AB) = 1 - P$ (rejecting in at least one firm) $= 1 - 0.6 = 0.4$

$\therefore$ P(selected in one of the firm)

$= P(A \cup B) = P(A) + P(B) - P(AB)$

$= 0.7 + 0.5 - 0.4 =$ **0.8.**

EXERCISE 3

1. Find the probability that a card drawn from a pack of playing cards is either a 'king' or a 'club'.
2. One card is drawn from a pack of playing cards, each of 52 cards being equally likely to be drawn. Find the probability that :
   (*i*) the card drawn is either red or a king.
   (*ii*) the card drawn is either diamond or red.
3. A drawer contains 50 bolts and 150 nuts. Half of the bolts and half of the nuts are rusted. If one item is chosen at random, what is the probability that it is rusted or is a bolt ?
4. Two dice are thrown simultaneously. Find the probability that at least one of the following two events occurs :
   E : an even total is thrown
   F : a total larger than 8 is thrown.
5. From 30 tickets marked with first 30 numerals, one is drawn at random. Find the probability that it is :
   (*i*) a multiple of 5 or 7 (*ii*) a multiple of 3 or 7.

6. Find the probability of getting an even number on the first die or a total of 8, in a single throw of two dice.
7. A construction company is bidding for two contracts A and B. The probability that the company will get contract A is 3/5, the probability that the company will get contract B is 1/3 and the probability that the company will get both the contracts is 1/8. What is the probability that the company will get contract A or B ?
8. A card is drawn at random from a well-suffled pack of playing cards. What is the probability that it is either a heart or a jack ?
9. The probability that a contractor will get a plumbing contract is 2/3 and the probability that he will not get an electric contract is 5/9. The probability of getting at least one contract is 4/5. What is the probability that he will get both contracts ?
10. A chartered accountant applied for a job in two firms x and y. He estimates that the probability of his being selected in firm x is 0.7 and being rejected in y is 0.5 and the probability of his being selected in both the firms is 0.4. What is the probability that he will be selected in at least one of the firms ?
11. Find the probability of getting at least one five, in a single throw of two dice.
12. There are 1 to 100 pages in a book. A page is opened at random. Find the probability of getting page of number which is a multiple of 6 or of 10. *(MDU 1997)*
13. There are 10 boys and 20 girls in a class ; in which half boys and half girls have blue eyes. One representative is selected at random from the class. What is the probability that he is boy or his eyes are blue ? *(MDU 2006)*

Answers

1. $\frac{4}{13}$ 2. (*i*) $\frac{7}{13}$ (*ii*) $\frac{1}{2}$ 3. $\frac{5}{8}$

4. $\frac{2}{3}$ 5. (*i*) $\frac{1}{3}$ (*ii*) $\frac{13}{30}$ 6. $\frac{5}{9}$

7. $\frac{97}{120}$ 8. $\frac{4}{13}$ 9. $\frac{14}{45}$ 10. $\frac{4}{5}$

11. $\frac{11}{36}$ 12. 0.23 13. $\frac{2}{3}$.

15. CONDITIONAL PROBABILITY *(KU 1997, 2003)*

Let us consider the random experiment of throwing a die. Let A be the event of getting an odd number on the die.

$\therefore \quad S = \{1, 2, 3, 4, 5, 6\}$ and $A = \{1, 3, 5\}$

$\therefore \quad P(A) = \frac{3}{6} = \frac{1}{2}$

Let $B = \{2, 3, 4, 5, 6\}$

If, after the die is thrown, we are given the information that the event B has occurred, then the probability of event A will no more be 1/2, because in this case, the favourable cases are three and the total number of possible outcomes will be five and not six. The probability of event A, with the condition

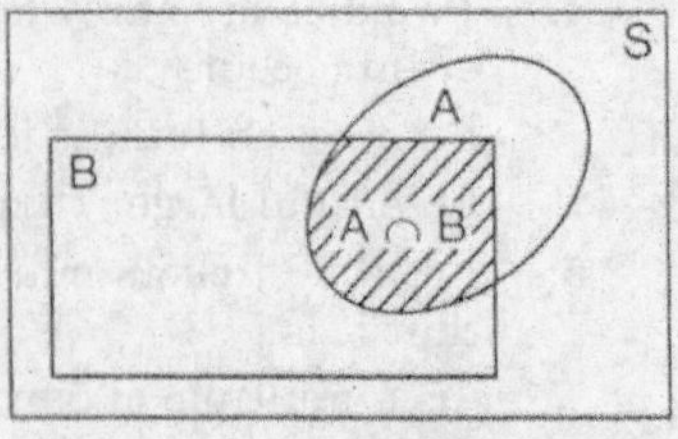

that event B has happened will be 3/5. This conditional probability is denoted as P(A/B). Let us define the concept of conditional probability in a formal manner.

Let A and B be any two events associated with a random experiment. The probability of occurrence of event A when the event B has already occurred is called the **conditional probability** of A when B is given and is denoted as P(A/B). The conditional probability P(A/B) is meaningful only when $P(B) \neq 0$, *i.e.* when *B* is not an impossible event.

By definition,

P(A/B) = probability of occurrence of event A when the event B has already occurred

$$= \frac{\text{no. of cases favourable to B which are also favourable to A}}{\text{no. of cases favourable to B}}$$

$$\therefore \quad \mathbf{P(A/B) = \frac{\text{no. of cases favourable to } A \cap B}{\text{no. of cases favourable to B}}}.$$

Also, $$P(A/B) = \frac{\dfrac{\text{no. of cases favourable to } A \cap B}{\text{no. of cases in the sample space}}}{\dfrac{\text{no. of cases favourable to B}}{\text{no. of cases in the sample space}}}$$

$$\therefore \quad \mathbf{P(A/B) = \frac{P(A \cap B)}{P(B)}}.$$

Remark 1. If $P(A) \neq 0$, the $P(B/A) = \dfrac{P(B \cap A)}{P(A)} = \dfrac{P(A \cap B)}{P(A)}$.

Remark 2. If A and B are *m.e.* events, then

$$P(A/B) = \frac{P(A \cap B)}{P(B)} = \frac{0}{P(B)} = 0 \quad \text{and} \quad P(B/A) = \frac{P(B \cap A)}{P(A)} = \frac{0}{P(A)} = 0.$$

∴ **If A and B are m.e. events, then A/B and B/A are impossible events.**

For an illustration, let us consider the random experiment of throwing two coins.

∴ S = {HH, HT, TH, TT}.

Let A = {HH, HT}, B = {HH, TH}, C = {HH, HT, TH} and D = {TT}.

$$\therefore \quad P(A) = \frac{2}{4} = \frac{1}{2}, \quad P(B) = \frac{2}{4} = \frac{1}{2}, \quad P(C) = \frac{3}{4}, \quad P(D) = \frac{1}{4}.$$

A/B is the event of getting A with the condition that B has occurred.

$$\therefore \quad P(A/B) = \frac{n(A \cap B)}{n(B)} = \frac{n\{HH\}}{n\{HH, TH\}} = \frac{1}{2}.$$

Similarly, $$P(A/C) = \frac{n\{HH, HT\}}{n\{HH, HT, TH\}} = \frac{2}{3} \quad \text{and} \quad P(B/C) = \frac{n\{HH, TH\}}{n\{HH, HT, TH\}} = \frac{2}{3}.$$

We observe that $P(A/C) \neq P(A)$, $P(B/C) \neq P(B)$.

The events A and D are *m.e.* and we have

$$P(A/D) = \frac{n(A \cap D)}{n(D)} = \frac{0}{1} = 0 \quad \text{and} \quad P(D/A) = \frac{n(D \cap A)}{n(A)} = \frac{0}{2} = 0.$$

Example 1. *If P(E) = 0.40, P(F) = 0.35 and P(E ∪ F) = 0.55, find P(E/F).*

Sol. We have $P(E) = 0.40, P(F) = 0.35, P(E \cup F) = 0.55.$

By *addition theorem,*

$$P(E \cup F) = P(E) + P(F) - P(E \cap F)$$

$$\therefore \quad 0.55 = 0.40 + 0.35 - P(E \cap F)$$

$$\therefore \quad P(E \cap F) = 0.75 - 0.55 = 0.20.$$

Required probability, $P(E/F) = \dfrac{P(E \cap F)}{P(F)} = \dfrac{0.20}{0.35} = \dfrac{4}{7}.$

Example 2. *If A and B are events associated with a random experiment such that* $P(A) = \frac{1}{3}$, $P(B) = \frac{1}{4}$, $P(A \cap B) = \frac{1}{5}$, *find :*

(i) $P(A/B)$ (ii) $P(B/A)$

(iii) $P(A \cup B)$ (iv) $P(\overline{A}/\overline{B})$

(v) $P(\overline{B}/\overline{A})$.

Sol. We have $P(A) = \dfrac{1}{3}, \quad P(B) = \dfrac{1}{4}$ and $P(A \cap B) = \dfrac{1}{5}.$

(i) We have $P(A/B) = \dfrac{P(A \cap B)}{P(B)} = \dfrac{\frac{1}{5}}{\frac{1}{4}} = \dfrac{4}{5}$

(ii) $P(B/A) = \dfrac{P(B \cap A)}{P(A)} = \dfrac{P(A \cap B)}{P(A)} = \dfrac{\frac{1}{5}}{\frac{1}{3}} = \dfrac{3}{5}$

(iii) $P(A \cup B) = P(A) + P(B) - P(A \cap B)$

$$= \frac{1}{3} + \frac{1}{4} - \frac{1}{5} = \frac{20 + 15 - 12}{60} = \frac{23}{60}$$

(iv) $P(\overline{A}/\overline{B}) = \dfrac{P(\overline{A} \cap \overline{B})}{P(\overline{B})} = \dfrac{P(\overline{A \cup B})}{P(\overline{B})} = \dfrac{1 - P(A \cup B)}{1 - P(B)}$

$$= \frac{1 - (23/60)}{1 - (1/4)} = \frac{37/60}{3/4} = \frac{37}{45}$$

(v) $P(\overline{B}/\overline{A}) = \dfrac{P(\overline{B} \cap \overline{A})}{P(\overline{A})} = \dfrac{P(\overline{B \cup A})}{P(\overline{A})} = \dfrac{1 - P(B \cup A)}{1 - P(A)}$

$$= \frac{1 - (23/60)}{1 - (1/3)} = \frac{37/60}{2/3} = \frac{37}{40}.$$

Example 3. *A coin is tossed twice and the four possible outcomes are assumed to be equally likely. If E is the event "both head and tail have occurred", and F the event : "at most one tail is observed", find P(E), P(F), P(E/F) and P(F/E).*

Sol. We have S = {HH, HT, TH, TT}

E = {HT, TH} and F = {HH, HT, TH}.

∴ $E \cap F$ = {HT, TH}.

$$\therefore \quad P(E) = \frac{n(E)}{n(S)} = \frac{2}{4} = \frac{1}{2}, \qquad P(F) = \frac{n(F)}{n(S)} = \frac{3}{4},$$

$$P(E/F) = \frac{n(E \cap F)}{n(F)} = \frac{2}{3} \quad \text{and} \quad P(F/E) = \frac{n(E \cap F)}{n(E)} = \frac{2}{2} = 1.$$

Example 4. *A die is rolled. If the outcome is an even number, what is the probability that it is a prime number ?*

Sol. Let S be the sample space of the experiment.

$\therefore$ S = {1, 2, 3, 4, 5, 6}

Let A = event of getting an even number

and B = event of getting a prime number.

$\therefore$ A = {2, 4, 6} and B = {2, 3, 5}

Also, $A \cap B = \{2\}$

Required probability = Probability of getting a prime number given that the outcome is an even number

$$= P(B/A) = \frac{P(B \cap A)}{P(A)} = \frac{P(A \cap B)}{P(A)} = \frac{1/6}{3/6} = \frac{1}{3}.$$

Alternatively,

$$P(B/A) = \frac{\text{no. of cases favourable to 'A} \cap \text{B'}}{\text{no. of cases favourable to A}} = \frac{1}{3}.$$

Example 5. *A die is thrown twice and the sum of the number appearing is observed to be 6. What is the conditional probability that the number 4 has appeared at least once ?*

Sol. Let S be the sample space of the experiment.

$\therefore$ S = {(1, 1), (1, 2), ..., (6, 5), (6, 6)}.

Let A = event of getting sum 6

and B = event of getting 4 at least once.

$\therefore$ A = {(1, 5), (2, 4), (3, 3), (4, 2), (5, 1)}

and B = {(4, 1), (4, 2), (4, 3), (4, 4), (4, 5), (4, 6), (1, 4), (2, 4), (3, 4), (5, 4), (6, 4)}.

$$\therefore \quad P(A) = \frac{5}{36} \text{ and } P(B) = \frac{11}{36}$$

Also $A \cap B = \{(4, 2), (2, 4)\} \quad \therefore \quad P(A \cap B) = \frac{2}{36}$

Now, required probability

= Probability of getting 4 on at least one die given that sum in 6

$$= P(B/A) = \frac{P(B \cap A)}{P(A)} = \frac{P(A \cap B)}{P(A)} = \frac{2/36}{5/36} = \frac{2}{5}.$$

Alternatively,

$$P(B/A) = \frac{\text{no. of cases favourable to 'A} \cap \text{B'}}{\text{no. of cases favourable to A}} = \frac{2}{5}.$$

Remark 1. In practical problems, it would be easier to use the formulae :

(*i*) $P(A/B) = \dfrac{\text{no. of favourable to 'A} \cap \text{B'}}{\text{no. of cases favourable to B}}$

(*ii*) $P(B/A) = \dfrac{\text{no. of cases favourable to 'B} \cap \text{A' } i.e. \text{ 'A} \cap \text{B'}}{\text{no. of cases favourable to A}}$.

Remark 2. The event A ∩ B is same as B ∩ A and each consists of sample points which are common to both A and B.

Example 6. *Find the probability that a single throw of a die results in a number less than 6 if (i) no other information is given (ii) it is given that the throw resulted in an add number.*

Sol. Here $S = \{1, 2, 3, 4, 5, 6\}$.

Let A = event of getting number less than 6

and B = event of getting an odd number.

∴ $A = \{1, 2, 3, 4, 5\}$ and $B = \{1, 3, 5\}$.

(*i*) P(no. is less than 6) = $P(A) = \dfrac{5}{6}$

(*ii*) P(no. is less than 6 given that the number obtained is odd)

$$= P(A/B) = \frac{P(A \cap B)}{P(B)} = \frac{3/6}{3/6} = 1. \qquad (\because \; A \cap B = \{1, 3, 5\})$$

Alternatively,

$$P(A/B) = \frac{\text{no. of cases favourable to } A \cap B}{\text{no. of cases favourable to B}} = \frac{n\,\{1,3,5,\}}{n\,\{1,3,5\}} = \frac{3}{3} = 1.$$

Example 7. *One card in drawn from a well shuffled pack of 52 cards. If E is the event "the card drawn is either a king or an ace" and F is the event "the card drawn is either an ace or a jack", then find the probability of the conditional event E/F.*

Sol. There are 4 kings and 4 aces in the pack.

∴ $$P(E) = \frac{4+4}{52} = \frac{2}{13}$$

There are 4 aces and 4 jacks in the pack.

∴ $$P(F) = \frac{4+4}{52} = \frac{2}{13}$$

The event E ∩ F contains 4 aces.

∴ $$P(E \cap F) = \frac{4}{52} = \frac{1}{13}$$

∴ Required probability $= P(E/F) = \dfrac{P(E \cap F)}{P(F)} = \dfrac{1/13}{2/13} = \dfrac{1}{2}$.

Example 8. *In a certain school, 20% of the students failed in English, 15% of the students failed in Mathematics, and 10% of the students failed both in English and Mathematics. A student is selected at random. If he failed in English, what is the probability that he also failed in Mathematics ?*

Sol. Let E and M be the events that a students is fail in English and Mathematics respectively.

$$\therefore \quad P(E) = \frac{20}{100} = \frac{1}{5}, \quad P(M) = \frac{15}{100} = \frac{3}{20} \quad \text{and} \quad P(E \cap M) = \frac{10}{100} = \frac{1}{10}.$$

Required probability $= P(M/E)$

$$= \frac{P(M \cap E)}{P(E)} = \frac{P(E \cap M)}{P(E)} = \frac{1/10}{1/5} = \frac{\mathbf{1}}{\mathbf{2}}.$$

Example 9. *Three fair coins are tossed. Find the probability that they are all tails, if :*
(*i*) *at least one of the coins show tail* (*ii*) *two coins show tail*
(*iii*) *at least two coins show head* (*iv*) *at most one coin show head.*

Sol. Here S = {HHH, HHT, HTH, THH, HTT, THT, TTH, TTT}.

Let A = event of getting all tails ∴ A = {TTT}

(*i*) Let B = event that at least one of the coins show tail

∴ B = {HHT, HTH, THH, HTT, THT, TTH, TTT}

∴ $A \cap B$ = {TTT}

$$\therefore \text{ Required probability} = P(A/B) = \frac{n(A \cap B)}{n(B)} = \frac{\mathbf{1}}{\mathbf{7}}.$$

(*ii*) Let B = event that two coins show tail

∴ B = {HTT, THT, TTH}

∴ $A \cap B = \phi$

$$\therefore \text{ Required probability} = \frac{n(A \cap B)}{n(B)} = \frac{0}{3} = \mathbf{0}.$$

(*iii*) Let B = event that at least two coins show head

∴ B = {HHH, HHT, HTH, THH}

∴ $A \cap B = \phi$

$$\therefore \text{ Required probability} = P(A/B) = \frac{n(A \cap B)}{n(B)} = \frac{0}{4} = \mathbf{0}.$$

(*iv*) Let B = event that at most one coin show head.

∴ B = {HTT, THT, TTH, TTT}

∴ $A \cap B$ = {TTT}

$$\therefore \text{ Required probability} = P(A/B) = \frac{n(A \cap B)}{n(B)} = \frac{\mathbf{1}}{\mathbf{4}}.$$

Remark. The value of P(A/B) is equal to $\frac{n(A \cap B)}{n(B)}$ which is also equal to $\frac{P(A \cap B)}{P(B)}$.

EXERCISE 4

1. If P (not A) = 0.7, P(B) = 0.7 and P(B/A) = 0.5, then find P(A/B) and $P(A \cup B)$.
2. If P(A) = 0.4, P(B) = 0.8, P(B/A) = 0.6, find P(A/B) and $P(A \cup B)$.
3. For two events A and B, P(A) = 0.5, P(B) = 0.6 and $P(A \cap B)$ = 0.3. Find the conditional probabilities P (A/B) and P(B/A).

4. (*i*) If $A \subseteq B$, show that $P(B/A) = 1$ (*ii*) If $A \cap B = \phi$, show that $P(B/A) = 0$.
(*iii*) If $A \subseteq B$, show that $P(A/C) \leq P(B/C)$.

[**Hint.** (*i*) $P(B/A) = \dfrac{P(B \cap A)}{P(A)} = \dfrac{P(A)}{P(A)} = 1.$

(*ii*) $P(B/A) = \dfrac{P(B \cap A)}{P(A)} = \dfrac{0}{P(A)} = 0.$

(*iii*) $A \subseteq B \;\Rightarrow\; A \cap C \subseteq B \cap C \;\Rightarrow\; P(A \cap C) \leq P(B \cap C)$

$\therefore \quad P(A/C) = \dfrac{P(A \cap C)}{P(C)} \leq \dfrac{P(B \cap C)}{P(C)} = P(B/C).$]

5. A die is thrown. Find the probability that the number obtained is greater than 2 if :
(*i*) no other information is given (*ii*) it is given that the number obtained is less than 5.

6. Find the probability of drawing a king, when a card is drawn from a well suffled pack of cards. It is also given that the card drawn is a face card.

7. A pair of fair dice is thrown. Find the probability that the sum is 10 or greater if 5 appears on the first die.

8. A pair of dice is thrown. If the sum is seven, find the probability that one of the dice shows 3.

9. A pair of fair dice is thrown. If the two numbers appearing are different, find the probability that the sum is 4 or less.

10. A die is thrown twice and the sum of the numbers appearing is observed to be 7. What is the conditional probability that the number 2 has appeared at least once ?

11. The probability that a person stopping at a petrol pump will ask to have his tyres checked is 0.12, the probability that he will ask to have his oil checked is 0.29 and the probability that he will ask to have both of them checked is 0.07.
(*i*) What is the probability that a person who has oil checked will also have tyre checked ?
(*ii*) What is the probability that a person stopping at the petrol pump will have either tyres or oil checked ? (*KU 2002*)

[**Hint :** Let A and B be the events of getting 'tyres checked' and 'oil checked' respectively.
$\therefore \quad P(A) = 0.12,\ P(B) = 0.29,\ P(A \cap B) = 0.07.$

(*ii*) Required probability $= P(A/B) = \dfrac{P(A \cap B)}{P(B)}$

(*iii*) Required probability $= P(A \cup B) = P(A) + P(B) - P(A \cap B)$.].

Answers

1. 0.2143, 0.85 **2.** 0.3, 0.96 **3.** 0.5, 0.6

5. (*i*) $\dfrac{2}{3}$ (*ii*) $\dfrac{1}{2}$ **6.** $\dfrac{1}{3}$ **7.** $\dfrac{1}{3}$

8. $\dfrac{1}{3}$ **9.** $\dfrac{2}{15}$ **10.** $\dfrac{1}{3}$ **11.** (*i*) $\dfrac{7}{29}$ (*ii*) $\dfrac{17}{50}$.

16. INDEPENDENT EVENTS (*KU 2004*)

Let A and B be two events associated with a random experiment. We know that

$$P(B/A) = \frac{P(B \cap A)}{P(A)} = \frac{P(A \cap B)}{P(A)}$$

$$\therefore \quad P(A \cap B) = P(A)\, P(B/A).$$

In general P(B/A) may or may not be equal to P(B). When P(B/A) and P(B) are equal, then the events A and B are of special importance.

Two events associated with a random experiment are said to be **independent events** if the occurrence or non-occurrence of one event does not affect the probability of the occurrence of the other event. For example, the events A and B are independent events when P(A/B) = P(A) and P(B/A) = F(B).

Theorem. Let A and B be events associated with a random experiment. The events A and B are independent if and only if

$$\mathbf{P(A \cap B) = P(A)\,P(B).}$$

Proof. Let A and B be independent events.

$$\therefore \qquad P(A \cap B) = \frac{P(A \cap B)}{P(B)} \times P(B) = P(A/B)\,P(B)$$

$$= P(A)\,P(B) \qquad [\because \quad P(A/B) = P(A)]$$

$$\therefore \qquad P(A \cap B) = P(A)\,P(B).$$

Conversely, let P(A ∩ B) = P(A) P(B).

$$\therefore \qquad P(A/B) = \frac{P(A \cap B)}{P(B)} = \frac{P(A)\,P(B)}{P(B)} = P(A)$$

and
$$P(B/A) = \frac{P(B \cap A)}{P(A)} = \frac{P(A \cap B)}{P(A)} = \frac{P(A)\,P(B)}{P(A)} = P(B).$$

$$\therefore \qquad P(A/B) = P(A) \text{ and } \quad P(B/A) = P(B).$$

∴ A and B are independent events.

Remark 1. P(A ∩ B) = P(A) P(B) is the necessary and sufficient condition for the events A and B to be independent.

Remark 2. Let A and B be events associated with a random experiment.

(*i*) Let A and B be *m.e.* ∴ P(A ∩ B) = 0

∴ P(A ∩ B) ≠ P(A) P(B) *i.e.* A and B are not independent events.

∴ **Mutually exclusive events cannot be independent.**

(*ii*) Let A and B be independent.

∴ P(A ∩ B) = P(A) P(B) *i.e.* P(A ∩ B) ≠ 0.

∴ A and B are not *m.e.* events.

∴ **Independent events cannot be mutually exclusive.**

Important observation. If A and B be any two events associated with a random experiment, then their physical description is not sufficient to decide if A and B are independent events or not. A and B are declared to be independent events only when we have P(A ∩ B) = P(A) P(B).

17. DEPENDENT EVENTS (*KU 2004*)

Let A and B be two events associated with a random experiment. If A and B are not independent events, then these are called **dependent events.**

∴ In case of dependent events, we have **P(A ∩ B) = P(A) P(B/A).**

Theorem. Let A and B be events associated with a random experiment. If A and B are independent, then show that the events (*i*) $\overline{A}$, B (*ii*) A, $\overline{B}$ (*iii*) $\overline{A}$, $\overline{B}$ are also independent.

Proof. The events A and B are independent.

$\therefore$ $$P(A \cap B) = P(A)\,P(B) \qquad ...(1)$$

(*i*) $(A \cap B) \cap (\bar{A} \cap B) = (A \cap \bar{A}) \cap (B \cap B) = \phi \cap B = \phi$

and $(A \cap B) \cup (\bar{A} \cap B) = (A \cup \bar{A}) \cap B = S \cap B = B.$

$\therefore$ The events $A \cap B$ and $\bar{A} \cap B$ are *m.e.* and their union in B.

$\therefore$ By *addition theorem*, we have

$$P(B) = P(A \cap B) + P(\bar{A} \cap B).$$

$$\Rightarrow \quad P(\bar{A} \cap B) = P(B) - P(A \cap B) = P(B) - P(A)\,P(B) \qquad \text{[Using (1)]}$$

$$= (1 - P(A))\,P(B) = P(\bar{A})\,P(B).$$

$\therefore$ $\mathbf{P(\bar{A} \cap B) = P(\bar{A})\,P(B)}$ *i.e.* $\bar{A}$ and B are independent.

(*ii*) $(A \cap B) \cap (A \cap \bar{B}) = (A \cap A) \cap (B \cap \bar{B}) = A \cap \phi = \phi$

and $(A \cap B) \cup (A \cap \bar{B}) = A \cap (B \cup \bar{B}) = A \cap S = A$

$\therefore$ The events $A \cap B$ and $A \cap \bar{B}$ are *m.e.* and their union is A.

$\therefore$ By *addition theorem*, we have

$$P(A) = P(A \cap B) + P(A \cap \bar{B}).$$

$$\Rightarrow \quad P(A \cap \bar{B}) = P(A) - P(A \cap B) = P(A) - P(A)\,P(B) \qquad \text{[Using (1)]}$$

$$= P(A)(1 - P(B)) = P(A)\,P(\bar{B}).$$

$\therefore$ $\mathbf{P(A \cap \bar{B}) = P(A)\,P(\bar{B})}$ *i.e.* A and $\bar{B}$ are independent.

(*iii*) $(\bar{A} \cap B) \cap (\bar{A} \cap \bar{B}) = (\bar{A} \cap \bar{A}) \cap (B \cap \bar{B}) = \bar{A} \cap \phi = \phi$

and $(\bar{A} \cap B) \cup (\bar{A} \cap \bar{B}) = \bar{A} \cap (B \cup \bar{B}) = \bar{A} \cap S = \bar{A}.$

$\therefore$ The events $\bar{A} \cap B$ and $\bar{A} \cap \bar{B}$ are *m.e.* and their union is $\bar{A}$.

$\therefore$ By *addition theorem*, we have

$$P(\bar{A}) = P(\bar{A} \cap B) + P(\bar{A} \cap \bar{B}) \qquad ...(1)$$

$$\Rightarrow \quad P(\bar{A} \cap \bar{B}) = P(\bar{A}) - P(\bar{A} \cap B) = P(\bar{A}) - P(\bar{A})\,P(B) \qquad \text{[Using part (i)]}$$

$$= P(\bar{A})\,(1 - P(B)) = P(\bar{A})\,P(\bar{B}).$$

$\therefore$ $\mathbf{P(\bar{A} \cap \bar{B}) = P(\bar{A})\,P(\bar{B})}$ *i.e.* $\bar{A}$ and $\bar{B}$ are independent.

Example 1. *If A and B are independent events such that* $P(A \cup B) = 0.6$ *and* $P(A) = 0.2$ *find* $P(B)$.

Sol. We have $P(A \cup B) = 0.6$ and $P(A) = 0.2$.

By *addition theorem*, we have

$$P(A \cup B) = P(A) + P(B) - P(A \cap B)$$

$$\therefore \quad P(A \cup B) = P(A) + P(B) - P(A)\,P(B) \qquad (\because \text{ A and B are independent})$$

$$\Rightarrow \quad 0.6 = 0.2 + P(B) - (0.2)\,P(B)$$

$$\Rightarrow \quad 0.4 = P(B)\,(1 - 0.2)$$

$$\Rightarrow \quad (0.8)\,P(B) = 0.4 \quad \Rightarrow \quad P(B) = \frac{0.4}{0.8} = \frac{1}{2} = \mathbf{0.5}.$$

Example 2. *A pair of dice is thrown. A is the event : "the sum is 8" and B is the event :"at least one odd number is obtained". Show that the events A and B are dependent.*

Sol. Let S be the sample space.

$\therefore$ S = {(1, 1), (1, 2), ..., (6, 5), (6, 6)}.

A = {(2, 6), (3, 5), (4, 4), (5, 3), (6, 2)}

B = {(1, 1), (1, 2), (1, 3), (1, 4), (1, 5), (1, 6), (3, 1), (3, 2), (3, 3), (3, 4), (3, 5), (3, 6), (5, 1), (5, 2), (5, 3), (5, 4), (5, 5), (5, 6), (2, 1), (2, 3), (2, 5), (4, 1), (4, 3), (4, 5), (6, 1), (6, 3), (6, 5)}.

$$\therefore \quad P(A) = \frac{5}{36} \quad \text{and} \quad P(B) = \frac{27}{36} = \frac{3}{4}$$

Also, $A \cap B = \{(3, 5), (5, 3)\}$. $\therefore$ $P(A \cap B) = \frac{2}{36} = \frac{1}{18}$

$$P(A)\,P(B) = \frac{5}{36} \times \frac{3}{4} = \frac{5}{48} \neq P(A \cap B).$$

The events A and B are **dependent.**

Example 3. *A coin is tossed thrice and all the eight outcomes are assumed equally likely. In which of the following cases are the events E and F independent ?*

(*i*) *E : the first throw results in head.*

F : the last throw results in tail.

(*ii*) *E : the number of heads is two.*

F : the last throw results in head.

(*iii*) *E : the number of heads is odd.*

F : the number of tails is odd.

Sol. Let S be the sample space.

$\therefore$ S = {HHH, HHT, HTH, THH, HTT, THT, TTH, TTT}.

(*i*) Here E = {HHH, HHT, HTH, HTT} and F = {HHT, HTT, THT, TTT}.

$$\therefore \quad P(E) = \frac{4}{8} = \frac{1}{2} \quad \text{and} \quad P(F) = \frac{4}{8} = \frac{1}{2}.$$

There are 2 cases favourable to the event $E \cap F$, namely HHT and HTT.

$$\therefore \quad P(E \cap F) = \frac{2}{8} = \frac{1}{4}.$$

Also, $P(E)P(F) = \frac{1}{2} \times \frac{1}{2} = \frac{1}{4} = P(E \cap F)$.

$\therefore$ The events E and F are **independent.**

(*ii*) Here E = {HHT, HTH, THH} and F = {HHH, HTH, THH, TTH}.

$$\therefore \quad P(E) = \frac{3}{8} \quad \text{and} \quad P(F) = \frac{4}{8} = \frac{1}{2}$$

There are 2 cases favourable to the event $E \cap F$, namely HTH and THH.

$$\therefore \quad P(E \cap F) = \frac{2}{8} = \frac{1}{4}.$$

Also, $P(E)\,P(F) = \frac{3}{8} \times \frac{1}{2} = \frac{3}{16} \neq P(E \cap F)$.

∴ The events E and F are **not independent.**

(*iii*) Here E = {HHH, HTT, THT, TTH} and F = {HHT, HTH, THH, TTT}.

∴ $P(E) = \frac{4}{8} = \frac{1}{2}$ and $P(F) = \frac{4}{8} = \frac{1}{2}$.

There is no case favourable to the event $E \cap F$.

∴ $P(E \cap F) = \frac{0}{8} = 0.$

Also, $P(E)P(F) = \frac{1}{2} \times \frac{1}{2} = \frac{1}{4} \neq P(E \cap F).$

∴ The events E and F are **not independent.**

EXERCISE 5

1. (*i*) Two events A and B are such that P(A) = 0.6, P(B) = 0.2 and $P(A \cap B) = 0.8$. Does this imply that A and B are independent ?

(*ii*) The events A and B are given to be independent. Find P(B) if it is given that P(A) = 0.35 and $P(A \cup B) = 0.60$.

2. For two events A and B, let P(A) = 0.4 and P(B) = p and $P(A \cup B) = 0.6$.

(*i*) Find p so that A and B are mutually exclusive.

(*ii*) Find p so that A and B are independent.

3. (*i*) If P(not B) = 0.65, $P(A \cup B) = 0.85$ and A and B are independent events, find P(A).

(*ii*) If P(not A) = 0.4, $P(A \cup B) = 0.75$ and A, B are given to be independent events, find the value of P(B).

4. A coin is tossed twice and all possible outcomes are assumed to be equally likely. E is the event : "at most one head has occurred" and F is the event : "at most one tail has occurred". Show that the events E and F are not independent.

5. A coin is tossed twice and all possible outcomes are assumed to be equally likely. A is the event : both head and tail have occurred and B is the event : at least one tail has occurred". Shcw that A and B are not independent.

6. A coin is tossed three times and all possible outcomes are assumed to be equally likely. E is the event : "both heads and tails have occurred", and F is the event : "at most one tail has occurred". Show that the events E and F are independent.

7. One card is drawn from a pack of 52 cards so that each card is equally likely to be selected. A is the event : "the card is a heart" and B is the event : "the card is a king." Show that A and B are independent.

8. One card is drawn from a pack of 52 cards so that each card is equally likely to be selected. A is the event : "the card is a spade" and B is the event : "the card is red". Show that A and B are not independent.

9. A die is thrown and the 6 possible outcomes are assumed to be equally likely. If E is the event : "the number appearing is a multiple of 3", and F is the event : "the number appearing is even". Show that the events E and F are independent.

10. One card is drawn from a pack of 52 cards so that each card is equally likely to be selected. In which of the following cases are the events E and F are independent ?

(*i*) E : the card drawn is a spade.

F : the card drawn is an ace.

(*ii*) E : the card drawn is black.
F : the card drawn is a king.

(*iii*) E : the card drawn is a king or queen.
F : the card drawn is a queen or jack.

Answers

1. (*i*) No.	(*ii*) $\frac{5}{13}$	2. (*i*) $\frac{1}{5}$	(*ii*) $\frac{1}{3}$
3. (*i*) $\frac{10}{13}$	(*ii*) $\frac{3}{8}$	10. (*i*), (*ii*).	

18. INDEPENDENT EXPERIMENTS

Two random experiments are said to be **independent experiments** if the occurrence or non-occurrence of an event in one experiment does not in any way affect the probability of occurrence of any event in the other experiment. For example, two tosses of a coin are independent experiments.

19. MULTIPLICATION THEOREM

If A and B be events associated with independent experiments E_1 and E_2 respectively, then prove that

$$\mathbf{P(AB) = P(A)P(B).}$$ (*KU 1996, 2001, 2002, 2004*)

Proof. Since the random experiments E_1 and E_2 are independent, the sample spaces of the experiments are not affected by the events.

Let n_1 and n_2 be the numbers of exhaustive, equally likely cases in the first and second experiment respectively.

Let m_1 be the number of cases favourable to the happening of the event A out of n_1 cases of the first experiment.

$$\therefore \qquad P(A) = \frac{m_1}{n_1}$$

Let m_2 be the number of cases favourable to the happening of the event B out of n_2 cases of the second experiment.

$$\therefore \qquad P(B) = \frac{m_2}{n_2}$$

By the **fundamental principle of events**, the number of cases favourable to the happening of the event AB in this specified order is $m_1 m_2$. Also the number of exhaustive, equally likely cases in the combined experiment is $n_1 n_2$.

$$\therefore \qquad P(AB) = \frac{m_1 m_2}{n_1 n_2} = \frac{m_1}{n_1} \cdot \frac{m_2}{n_2} = P(A)P(B).$$

$$\therefore \qquad \mathbf{P(AB) = P(A)\ P(B).}$$

The theorem can also be extended to even more than two events.

Let $A_1, A_2, \ldots\ldots, A_k$ be k events associated with k independent random experiments $E_1, E_2, \ldots\ldots, E_k$ with probabilities $p_1, p_2, \ldots\ldots, p_k$ respectively, then

$$P(A_1 A_2 \ldots\ldots, A_k) = P(A_1)\ P(A_1) \ldots\ldots P(A_k) = p_1\, p_2 \ldots\ldots p_k.$$

Also $\quad P(\text{not } A_1) = P(\overline{A}_1) = 1 - p_1$

$P(\text{not } A_2) = P(\overline{A}_2) = 1 - p_2$

....

....

$P(\text{not } A_k) = P(\overline{A}_k) = 1 - p_k.$

Since $A_1, A_2, ...A_k$ are associated with independents experiments, therefore, the events $\overline{A}_1, \overline{A}_2, ..., \overline{A}_k$ are also associated with independent experiments.

Now P(event of happening of at least one of $A_1, A_2, ..., A_k$)

$= 1 -$ P(event of happening of none of $A_1, A_2, ... A_k$)

$= 1 - P(\overline{A}_1 \overline{A}_2 ...... \overline{A}_k) = 1 - P(\overline{A}_1) P(\overline{A}_2) ......P(\overline{A}_k)$

(By Multiplication theorem)

$= 1 - (1 - p_1)(1 - p_2) ...... (1 - p_k).$

Remark. If A and B are events associated with experiments which are not independent, then the probability of the event 'AB' is found by using the result :

$$P(AB) = P(A)\, P(B/A).$$

This result can also be extended to more than two experiments.

Example 1. *A and B appeared for an interview for two posts. Probability of A's rejection is 2/5 and that of B's selection is 4/7. Find the probability that one of them is selected.*

Sol. The random experiments 'interview of A' and 'interview of B' are experiment.

Let $\quad$ E = event that A is selected

and $\quad$ F = event that B is selected.

$$\therefore \quad P(\overline{E}) = \frac{2}{5} \quad \text{and} \quad P(F) = \frac{4}{7}.$$

Also, $$P(E) = 1 - P(\overline{E}) = 1 - \frac{2}{5} = \frac{3}{5}$$

and $$P(\overline{F}) = 1 - P(F) = 1 - \frac{4}{7} = \frac{3}{7}.$$

Required probability = P(only one is selected)

$= P(E\overline{F} \cup \overline{E}F) = P(E\overline{F}) + P(\overline{E}F)$ **(Using addition theorem)**

$= P(E)\, P(\overline{F}) + P(\overline{E})\, P(F)$ **(Using multiplication theorem)**

$$= \frac{3}{5} \times \frac{3}{7} + \frac{2}{5} \times \frac{4}{7} = \mathbf{\frac{17}{35}}.$$

Example 2. *A husband and a wife appear in an interview for two vacancies for the same post. The probability of husband's selection is 3/5 and that of wife's selection is 1/5. Find the probability that :*

(i) both are selected $\qquad$ *(ii) exactly one is selected*

(iii) none is selected.

Sol. The random experiments 'interview of husband' and 'interview of wife' are independent.

Let H = event that 'Husband' is selected

and W = event that 'Wife' is selected.

$\therefore$ $P(H) = \frac{3}{5}$ and $P(W) = \frac{1}{5}$.

Also, $P(\overline{H}) = 1 - P(H) = 1 - \frac{3}{5} = \frac{2}{5}$ and $P(\overline{W}) = 1 - P(W) = 1 - \frac{1}{5} = \frac{4}{5}$.

(*i*) P(both are selected)

$= P(HW) = P(H)P(W)$ **(Using multiplication theorem)**

$= \frac{3}{5} \times \frac{1}{5} = \frac{3}{25}$.

(*ii*) P(exactly one is selected)

$= P(H\overline{W} \cup \overline{H}W) = P(H\overline{W}) + P(\overline{H}W)$ **(Using addition theorem)**

$= P(H)P(\overline{W}) + P(\overline{H})P(W)$ **(Using multiplication theorem)**

$= \frac{3}{5} \times \frac{4}{5} + \frac{2}{5} \times \frac{1}{5} = \frac{14}{25}$.

(*iii*) P(none is selected) $= P(\overline{H}\,\overline{W}) = P(\overline{H})\,P(\overline{W})$ **(Using multiplication theorem)**

$= \frac{2}{5} \times \frac{4}{5} = \frac{8}{25}$.

Note. In this example, it is worth while to note that $\frac{3}{25} + \frac{14}{25} + \frac{8}{25} = \frac{25}{25} = 1$.

This has happened because the events : both are selected, exactly one is selected and none is selected are *mutually exclusive* and *exhaustive.*

Example 3. *The odds in favour of one student passing a test are 3 : 7. The odds against another student passing it are 3 : 5. What is the probability that both pass the test ?*

Sol. Let A = event that first pass the test.

$\therefore$ $P(A) = \frac{3}{3+7} = \frac{3}{10}$

Let B = event the second pass the test.

$\therefore$ $P(B) = \frac{5}{3+5} = \frac{5}{8}$

The random experiments of results of students are independent.

$\therefore$ P(both pass the test) $= P(AB) = P(A)P(B) = \frac{3}{10} \times \frac{5}{8} = \frac{3}{16}$.

Example 4. *A class consists of 100 students. Out of these 25 are girls and 75 are boys. 10 of them are rich, remaining poor. Out of 100, only 20 students are fair complexioned. What is the probability of selecting a fair complexioned rich girl ?*

Sol. Let A = event that a girl student is selected

B = event that a rich student is selected

C = event that a fair complexioned student is selected.

$\therefore$ $P(A) = \frac{25}{100} = \frac{1}{4}$, $P(B) = \frac{10}{100} = \frac{1}{10}$ and $P(C) = \frac{20}{100} = \frac{1}{5}$.

Now, ABC is the event of selecting a rich, fair, complexioned girls student. The random experiments of selections are independent.

$$\therefore \quad P(ABC) = P(A)\,P(B)\,P(C) = \frac{1}{4} \times \frac{1}{10} \times \frac{1}{5} = \frac{1}{200} = \mathbf{0.005.}$$

Example 5. *A speaks truth in 60% of the cases and B in 90% of the cases. In what percentage of cases, are they likely to contradict each other in stating the same fact ?*

Sol. The random experiments of speeches of *A* and *B* are independent.

Let E = event of A speaking truth

and F = event of B speaking truth.

$$\therefore \quad P(E) = \frac{60}{100} = \frac{6}{10} \quad \text{and} \quad P(F) = \frac{90}{100} = \frac{9}{10}.$$

Probability of A and B contradicting each other = $P(E\,\overline{F} \text{ or } \overline{E}\,F)$

$$= P(E\,\overline{F}) + P(\overline{E}\,F) = P(E)\,P(\overline{F}) + P(\overline{E})\,P(F)$$

$$= P(E)(1 - P(F)) + (1 - P(E))P(F)$$

$$= \frac{6}{10}\left(1 - \frac{9}{10}\right) + \left(1 - \frac{6}{10}\right)\frac{9}{10} = \frac{6}{10} \times \frac{1}{10} + \frac{4}{10} \times \frac{9}{10} = \frac{42}{100}.$$

∴ A and B are likely to contradicts each other in **42%** cases.

Example 6. *A problem in mathematics is given to 3 students whose chances of solving it are $\frac{1}{2}, \frac{1}{3}, \frac{1}{4}$. What is the probability that the problem is solved ?*

Sol. The random experiments of trying the problem by the given students are independent.

Let A, B, C be the events of first, second, third student solving the problem.

$$\therefore \quad P(A) = \tfrac{1}{2},\ P(B) = \tfrac{1}{3} \quad \text{and} \quad P(C) = \tfrac{1}{4}.$$

∴ P(the problem is solved)

$$= P(A \text{ or } B \text{ or } C) = 1 - P(\overline{A}\,\overline{B}\,\overline{C}) = 1 - P(\overline{A})\,P(\overline{B})\,P(\overline{C})$$

$$= 1 - (1 - P(A))(1 - P(B))(1 - P(C)) = 1 - (1 - \tfrac{1}{2})(1 - \tfrac{1}{3})(1 - \tfrac{1}{4})$$

$$= 1 - (\tfrac{1}{2}).(\tfrac{2}{3}).(\tfrac{3}{4}) = 1 - \tfrac{1}{4} = \mathbf{3/4}.$$

Example 7. *A problem in statistics is given to five students A, B, C, D and E. Their chances of solving the problem are $\frac{1}{2}, \frac{1}{3}, \frac{1}{4}, \frac{1}{5}$ and $\frac{1}{6}$ respectively. What is the probability that the problem will be solved ?* *(MDU 1996)*

Sol. The random experiments of trying the problem by the given students are independent.

Let A_1 = event that A fails to solve the problem

A_2 = event that B fails to solve the problem

A_3 = event that C fails to solve the problem

A_4 = event that D fails to solve the problem

A_5 = event that E fails to solve the problem.

$\therefore$ $P(A_1) = 1 - \frac{1}{2} = \frac{1}{2}$ $P(A_2) = 1 - \frac{1}{3} = \frac{2}{3}$

$P(A_3) = 1 - \frac{1}{4} = \frac{3}{4}$ $P(A_4) = 1 - \frac{1}{5} = \frac{4}{5}$

$P(A_5) = 1 - \frac{1}{6} = \frac{5}{6}$

Now, P(event that the problem is solved by at least one student)

= 1 – P(event that the problem is not solved by any of the five students)

$= 1 - P(A_1\, A_2\, A_3\, A_4\, A_5)$

$= 1 - P(A_1)\, P(A_2)\, P(A_3)\, P(A_4)\, P(A_5)$ (By Multiplication Theorem)

$$= 1 - \left(\frac{1}{2} \times \frac{2}{3} \times \frac{3}{4} \times \frac{4}{5} \times \frac{5}{6}\right) = 1 - \frac{1}{6} = \mathbf{\frac{5}{6}}.$$

Example 8. *A bag contains 5 white and 3 black balls and another bag contains 3 white and 4 black balls. If one ball is drawn from each bag, what is the probability that one is white and the other is black ?*

Sol. The random experiments of 'drawing ball from first bag' and 'drawing ball from second bag' are independent.

Bag I	Bag II
5 White 3 Black	3 White 4 Black

Let W_i and B_i be the events of drawing white ball and black ball respectively from the ith bag, $i = 1, 2$.

Required probability = P (one is white and one is black)

$= P\,(W_1B_2 \text{ or } B_1W_2)$

$= P\,(W_1B_2) + P(B_1W_2) = P(W_1)\, P(B_2) + P(B_1)\, P(B_2)$

$$= \frac{5}{5+3} \times \frac{4}{3+4} + \frac{3}{5+3} \times \frac{3}{3+4} = \frac{20}{56} + \frac{9}{56} = \mathbf{\frac{29}{56}}.$$

Example 9. *Three bags contain 7 white 8 red, 9 white 6 red and 5 white 7 red balls respectively. One ball, at random, is drawn from each bag. Find the probability that all of them are of the same colour.*

Sol. The three random experiments of drawing balls from given bags are independent.

Bag I	Bag II	Bag III
7 White 8 Red	9 White 6 Red	5 White 7 Red

Let W_i and R_i be the events of drawing white ball and red ball respectively from the ith bag, $i = 1, 2, 3$.

Required probability = P(all balls of same colour)

$= P(W_1W_2W_3 \text{ or } R_1R_2R_3)$

$= P(W_1\ W_2\ W_3) + P(R_1R_2R_3)$

$= P(W_1)P(W_2)P(W_3) + P(R_1)P(R_2)P(R_3)$

$$= \frac{7}{7+8} \times \frac{9}{9+6} \times \frac{5}{5+7} + \frac{8}{7+8} \times \frac{6}{9+6} \times \frac{7}{5+7}$$

$$= \frac{7}{15} \times \frac{9}{15} \times \frac{5}{12} + \frac{8}{15} \times \frac{6}{15} \times \frac{7}{12} = \frac{651}{2700} = \mathbf{\frac{217}{900}}.$$

Example 10. *A can hit a target 3 times in 5 shots, B 2 times in 5 shots, C 3 times in 4 shots. Each fire a volley. What is the probability that 2 shots hit the target ?*

Sol. The three random experiments of hitting target by A, B, C are independent.

Let A, B, C be the events that A, B, C respectively hit the target.

$$\therefore \quad P(A) = \frac{3}{5}, \quad P(B) = \frac{2}{5} \quad \text{and} \quad P(C) = \frac{3}{4}.$$

$$\therefore \quad P(\overline{A}) = 1 - \frac{3}{5} = \frac{2}{5}, \quad P(\overline{B}) = 1 - \frac{2}{5} = \frac{3}{5} \quad \text{and} \quad P(\overline{C}) = 1 - \frac{3}{4} = \frac{1}{4}.$$

Required probability $= P(\text{2 shots hit the target})$

$$= P(AB\overline{C} \text{ or } A\overline{B}C \text{ or } \overline{A}BC)$$

$$= P(AB\overline{C}) + P(A\overline{B}C) + P(\overline{A}BC)$$

$$= P(A)P(B)P(\overline{C}) + P(A)P(\overline{B})P(C) + P(\overline{A})P(B)P(C)$$

$$= \frac{3}{5} \times \frac{2}{5} \times \frac{1}{4} + \frac{3}{5} \times \frac{3}{5} \times \frac{3}{4} + \frac{2}{5} \times \frac{2}{5} \times \frac{3}{4}$$

$$= \frac{6}{100} + \frac{27}{100} + \frac{12}{100} = \frac{9}{20}.$$

Example 11. *A bag has 4 red and 5 black balls, a second bag has 3 red and 7 black balls. One ball is drawn from the first and two from the second. Find the probability that out of three balls, two are black and one is red.*

Sol. The random experiments of 'drawing one ball from first bag' and 'drawing two balls from second bag' are independent.

We are to find the probability two black balls and one red ball.

Bag I	Bag II
4 Red 5 Black	3 Red 7 Black

$\therefore$ Required probability

$$= P(F_r S_{bb} \text{ or } F_b S_{rb}),$$

where F_r is the event of drawing red ball from the first bag etc.

$$= P(F_r S_{bb}) + P(F_b S_{rb}) = P(F_r)\, P(S_{bb}) + P(F_b)\, P(S_{rb})$$

$$= \frac{4}{4+5} \times \frac{{}^7C_2}{{}^{3+7}C_2} + \frac{5}{4+5} \times \frac{{}^3C_1\, {}^7C_1}{{}^{3+7}C_2}$$

$$= \frac{4}{9} \times \frac{\frac{7 \times 6}{1 \times 2}}{\frac{10 \times 9}{1 \times 2}} + \frac{5}{9} \times \frac{3 \times 7}{\frac{10 \times 9}{1 \times 2}} = \frac{4}{9} \times \frac{7}{15} + \frac{5}{9} \times \frac{7}{15} = \frac{7}{15}.$$

Example 12. *A candidate is interviewed for three posts. For the first post there are three candidates, for the second last there are four and for the third there are two. What are the chances of his getting selected for at least one post ?*

Sol. The three interviews are independent experiments.

Let A = event of getting first post

B = event of getting second post

C = event of getting third post.

$\therefore \quad P(A) = \frac{1}{3} \quad P(B) = \frac{1}{4} \quad \text{and} \quad P(C) = \frac{1}{2}.$

P(getting at least one post)

$$= 1 - P(\text{not getting any post})$$

$$= 1 - P(\bar{A}\,\bar{B}\,\bar{C}) = 1 - P(\bar{A})\,P(\bar{B})\,P(\bar{C})$$

$$= 1 - \left(1-\frac{1}{3}\right)\left(1-\frac{1}{4}\right)\left(1-\frac{1}{2}\right) = 1 - \frac{2}{3}\times\frac{3}{4}\times\frac{1}{2} = 1 - \frac{1}{4} = \frac{3}{4}.$$

Example 13. *In a hockey match, the probability of winning of Indian team against Pakistani team in 1/4. Three matches are played. Find the probability that :*

(i) India looses all the matches.

(ii) India wins at least one match.

(iii) India wins two matches. (MDU 1997)

Sol. The random experiments of matches between Indian team and Pakistani team are independent.

Let A_i to the event of winning of Indian team in the ith match, $i = 1, 2, 3$.

$\therefore \quad P(A_i) = \frac{1}{4} \quad \text{and} \quad P(\bar{A}_i) = 1 - \frac{1}{4} = \frac{3}{4}$

(*i*) P(India loosing all the matches)

$$= P(\bar{A}_1\,\bar{A}_2\,\bar{A}_3) = P(\bar{A}_1)\,P(\bar{A}_2)\,P(\bar{A}_3) = \frac{3}{4}\times\frac{3}{4}\times\frac{3}{4} = \mathbf{\frac{27}{64}}.$$

(*ii*) P(India winning at least one match)

$$= 1 - P(\text{India loosing all the matches})$$

$$= 1 - \frac{27}{64} = \mathbf{\frac{37}{64}}.$$ **[Using part (i)]**

(*iii*) P(India winning two matches)

$$= P(A_1 A_2 \bar{A}_3 \text{ or } A_1 \bar{A}_2 A_3 \text{ or } \bar{A}_1 A_2 A_3)$$

$$= P(A_1 A_2 \bar{A}_3) + P(A_1 \bar{A}_2 A_3) + P(\bar{A}_1 A_2 A_3)$$

$$= P(A_1)\,P(A_2)\,P(\bar{A}_3) + P(A_1)\,P(\bar{A}_2)\,P(A_3) + P(\bar{A}_1)\,P(A_2)\,P(A_3)$$

$$= \frac{1}{4}\times\frac{1}{4}\times\frac{3}{4} + \frac{1}{4}\times\frac{3}{4}\times\frac{1}{4} + \frac{3}{4}\times\frac{1}{4}\times\frac{1}{4} = \mathbf{\frac{9}{64}}.$$

Example 14. *First bag contains 5 red balls and 3 black balls ; second contains 4 red balls and 7 blacks balls. Find the probability that : (i) both are red ; (ii) one is red and one is black : (iii) both are black, when one ball is drawn from each bag.*

Sol. The random experiments 'drawing one ball from first bag' and 'drawing one ball from second bag' are independent.

Bag I	Bag II
5 Red 3 Black	4 Red 7 Black

Let R_i and B_i be the events of drawing red ball and black ball respectively from the ith bag, $i = 1, 2$.

(*i*) P(both are red) $= P(R_1R_2) = P(R_1)\,P(R_2)$

$$= \frac{5}{5+3}\times\frac{4}{4+7} = \frac{5}{8}\times\frac{4}{11} = \mathbf{\frac{5}{22}}$$

(*ii*) P(red and black) $= P(R_1B_2 \text{ or } B_1R_2) = P(R_1B_2) + P(B_1R_2)$

$= P(R_1)\,P(B_2) + P(B_1)\,P(R_2)$

$$= \frac{5}{5+3} \times \frac{7}{4+7} + \frac{3}{5+3} \times \frac{4}{4+7} = \frac{5}{8} \times \frac{7}{11} + \frac{3}{8} \times \frac{4}{11} = \mathbf{\frac{47}{88}}$$

(*iii*) P(both are black) $= P(B_1B_2) = P(B_1)\,P(B_2)$

$$= \frac{3}{5+3} \times \frac{7}{4+7} = \frac{3}{8} \times \frac{7}{11} = \mathbf{\frac{21}{88}}.$$

Example 15. *Three groups of children consists of respectively 3 girls and 1 boy, 2 girls and 2 boys, 1 girl and 3 boys. One child is selected at random from each group. Find the chance that three selected children comprise 1 girl and 2 boys.*

Sol. The random experiments of drawing one child from each group are independent.

Group I	Group II	Group III
3 Girls	2 Girls	1 Girl
1 Boy	2 Boys	3 Boys

Let G_i and B_i be the events of selecting a girl and a boy respectively from the *i*th group, $i = 1, 2, 3$.

∴ P(1 girl and 2 boys)

$= P(G_1B_2B_3 \text{ or } B_1G_2B_3 \text{ or } B_1B_2G_3)$

$= P(G_1B_2B_3) + P(B_1G_2B_3) + P(B_1B_2G_3)$

$= P(G_1)P(B_2)P(B_3) + P(B_1)P(G_2)P(B_3) + P(B_1)P(B_2)P(G_3)$

$$= \left(\frac{3}{4} \times \frac{2}{4} \times \frac{3}{4}\right) + \left(\frac{1}{4} \times \frac{2}{4} \times \frac{3}{4}\right) + \left(\frac{1}{4} \times \frac{2}{4} \times \frac{1}{4}\right) = \frac{18+6+2}{64} = \mathbf{\frac{13}{32}}.$$

Example 16. *A six faced die is so biased that it is twice as likely to show an even number than an odd number, when thrown. It is thrown twice. What is the probability that the sum of the two numbers thrown is even ?*

Sol. Let E and O be the events of getting an even number (2 or 4 or 6) and an odd number (1 or 3 or 5) respectively.

∴ $P(E) + P(O) = 1$ and $P(E) = 2 \times P(O)$.

∴ $P(E) = 2/3$ and $P(O) = 1/3$.

Now, the sum of two numbers is even if either both are even or both are odd.

The random experiments of throwing die twice are independent experiments.

Let E_i, O_i be the events of throwing an even number, an odd number respectively in the *i*th throw, $i = 1, 2$.

P(sum is even) $= P(E_1E_2 \text{ or } O_1O_2)$

$= P(E_1E_2) + P(O_1O_2) = P(E_1)P(E_2) + P(O_1)P(O_2)$

$$= \left(\frac{2}{3} \times \frac{2}{3}\right) + \left(\frac{1}{3} \times \frac{1}{3}\right) = \frac{4}{9} + \frac{1}{9} = \mathbf{\frac{5}{9}}.$$

Example 17. *A bag contains 6 white ball and 4 black balls. Two balls are drawn at random one by one without replacement. Find the probability that both balls are white.*

Sol. Since the first ball is not replaced before the second draw, the random experiments of drawing balls are not independent.

Let W_1 = event that first ball is white
W_2 = event that second ball is white

P(both balls are white)

$$= P(W_1W_2) = P(W_1)P(W_2/W_1)$$

$$= \frac{6}{6+4} \times \frac{6-1}{(6-1)+4} = \frac{6}{10} \times \frac{5}{9} = \frac{\mathbf{1}}{\mathbf{3}}.$$

Example 18. *Three balls are drawn successively from an urn containing 6 red balls, 4 white ball and 5 blue balls. Find the probability that these are drawn in the order red, white and blue, if each ball is not replaced.*

Sol. Since the balls are not replaced before successive draws, the three random experiments of drawing balls are not independent.

Let us define events :

A = first ball is red, B = second ball is white and C = third ball is blue.

Now ABC is the event of drawing three balls in the order red, white and blue.

By Multiplication rule,

$$P(ABC) = P(A)\, P(B/A)\, P(C/AB).$$

Now $$P(A) = \frac{\text{no. of red balls}}{\text{total no. of balls}} = \frac{6}{6+4+5} = \frac{6}{15} = \frac{2}{5}$$

$$P(B/A) = \frac{\text{no. of white balls}}{\text{total no. of balls left}} = \frac{4}{5+4+5} = \frac{4}{14} = \frac{2}{7}$$

$$P(C/AB) = \frac{\text{no. of blue balls}}{\text{total no. of balls left}} = \frac{5}{5+3+5} = \frac{5}{13}$$

$$\therefore \quad P(ABC) = \frac{2}{5} \times \frac{2}{7} \times \frac{5}{13} = \frac{\mathbf{4}}{\mathbf{91}}.$$

Example 19. *From a pack of playing cards, two cards are drawn one by one without replacement. Find the probability that :*

(*i*) *first is king and second is queen*

(*ii*) *one is king and other in queen.*

Sol. Since the first card is not replaced before the second draw, the random experiments of drawing cards are not independent.

Let K_i and Q_i be the events of drawing a king and a queen respectively in the *i*th draw, $i = 1, 2$.

(*i*) P(first is king and second is queen)

$$= P(K_1Q_2) = P(K_1)\, P(Q_2/K_1)$$

$$= \frac{4}{52} \times \frac{4}{51} = \frac{\mathbf{4}}{\mathbf{663}}.$$

(*ii*) P(one king and one queen)

$$= P(K_1Q_2 \text{ or } Q_1K_2) = P(K_1\, Q_2) + P(Q_1\, K_2)$$

$$= P(K_1)\, P(Q_2/K_1) + P(Q_1)\, P(K_2/Q_1)$$

$$= \frac{4}{52} \times \frac{4}{51} + \frac{4}{52} \times \frac{4}{51} = \frac{\mathbf{8}}{\mathbf{663}}.$$

Example 20. *A box contains 9 tickets numbered 1 to 9 inclusive. If three tickets are drawn from the box one at a time without replacements, find the probability that the numbers on the tickets are alternatively either odd, even, odd or even, odd, even.*

Sol. Since the tickets are not replaced before successive draws, the random experiments of drawing tickets are not independent.

Let O_i and E_i be the events of drawing ticket of odd number and even number respectively in the ith draw, $i = 1, 2, 3$.

Required probability

$$= P(O_1E_2O_3 \text{ or } E_1O_2E_3) = P(O_1E_2O_3) + P(E_1O_2E_3)$$

$$= P(O_1)P(E_2/O_1)P(O_3/O_1E_2) + P(E_1)P(O_2/E_1)P(E_3/E_1O_2)$$

$$= \frac{5}{9}\times\frac{4}{8}\times\frac{4}{7} + \frac{4}{9}\times\frac{5}{8}\times\frac{3}{7} = \frac{10}{63}+\frac{5}{42} = \mathbf{\frac{5}{18}}.$$

Example 21. *From a well-shuffled pack of playing cards, two cards are drawn at random one by one. Find the probability that they are both kings if the first card is : (i) replaced (ii) not replaced before the second draw.*

Sol. Let K_1 and K_2 be the events of getting kings in the first draw and second draw respectively before the second draw.

(*i*) Since the first card is replaced, the random experiments are independent.

$$\therefore \quad P(\text{both kings}) = P(K_1K_2) = P(K_1)\,P(K_2) = \frac{4}{52}\times\frac{4}{52} = \mathbf{\frac{1}{169}}$$

(*ii*) Since the first card is not replaced, the random experiments are not independent.

$$\therefore \quad P(\text{both kings}) = P(K_1K_2) = P(K_1)\,P(K_2/K_1) = \frac{4}{52}\times\frac{3}{51} = \mathbf{\frac{1}{221}}.$$

Example 22. *An urn contains 8 red, 3 white and 9 blue balls. Three balls are drawn at random one by one without replacement. Determine the probability that :*

(*i*) *all three are red* (*ii*) *all three are blue*

(*iii*) *balls are drawn in the order red, white, blue*

(*iv*) *one of each colour is drawn.*

8 Red
3 White
9 Blue

Sol. The random experiments of drawing balls without replacements are not independent.

Let R_i, W_i, B_i be the events of drawing red ball, white ball, blue ball respectively in the ith draw, $i = 1, 2, 3$.

(*i*) P(all three are red) $= P(R_1R_2R_3) = P(R_1)\,P(R_2/R_1)\,P(R_3/R_1R_2)$

$$= \frac{8}{20}\times\frac{8-1}{20-1}\times\frac{8-2}{20-2} = \frac{8}{20}\times\frac{7}{19}\times\frac{6}{18} = \mathbf{\frac{14}{285}}.$$

(*ii*) P(all three are blue) $= P(B_1B_2B_3) = P(B_1)P(B_2/B_1)P(B_3/B_1B_2)$

$$= \frac{9}{20}\times\frac{9-1}{20-1}\times\frac{9-2}{20-2} = \frac{9}{20}\times\frac{8}{19}\times\frac{7}{18} = \mathbf{\frac{7}{95}}$$

(*iii*) P(balls are drawn in the order red, white, blue)

$$= P(R_1W_2B_3) = P(R_1)P(W_2/R_1)P(B_3/R_1W_2)$$

$$= \frac{8}{20}\times\frac{3}{19}\times\frac{9}{18} = \mathbf{\frac{3}{95}}$$

(*iv*) P(one of each colour)

$= P(R_1W_2B_3 \text{ or } R_1B_2W_3 \text{ or } B_1R_2W_3 \text{ or } B_1W_2R_3 \text{ or } W_1R_2B_3 \text{ or } W_1B_2R_3).$

$= P(R_1W_2B_3) + P(R_1B_2W_3) + P(B_1R_2W_3) + P(B_1W_2R_3) + P(W_1R_2B_3) + P(W_1B_2R_3)$

$$= \left(\frac{8}{20}\times\frac{3}{19}\times\frac{9}{18}\right)+\left(\frac{8}{20}\times\frac{9}{19}\times\frac{3}{18}\right)+\left(\frac{9}{20}\times\frac{8}{19}\times\frac{3}{18}\right)+\left(\frac{9}{20}\times\frac{3}{19}\times\frac{8}{18}\right)+\left(\frac{3}{20}\times\frac{8}{19}\times\frac{9}{18}\right)+\left(\frac{3}{20}\times\frac{9}{19}\times\frac{8}{18}\right)$$

$$= 6\left(\frac{8\times3\times9}{20\times19\times18}\right) = \mathbf{\frac{18}{95}}.$$

Example 23. *A bag contains 8 red and 5 white balls. Two successive drawings of three balls are made such that (i) balls are replaced before second trial, (ii) balls are not replaced before second trial. Find the probability that 1st drawing will give 3 white and the 2nd 3 red balls.* (KU 1997, 99 S, 2000 C, 2002)

Sol. Let W_1 and R_2 be the events of getting 3 white balls in the first draw and 3 red balls in the second draw respectively.

8 Red
5 White

(*i*) Since the balls of first draw are replaced, the random experiments are independent.

$$\therefore \quad P(W_1R_2) = P(W_1)\,P(R_2) = \frac{^5C_3}{^{13}C_3}\times\frac{^8C_3}{^{13}C_3} = \frac{10}{286}\times\frac{56}{286} = \mathbf{0.0068}$$

(*ii*) Since the balls of first draw are not replaced, the random experiments are not independent.

$$\therefore \quad P(W_1R_2) = P(W_1)\,P(R_2/W_1) = \frac{^5C_3}{^{13}C_3}\times\frac{^8C_3}{^{10}C_3} = \frac{10}{286}\times\frac{56}{120} = \mathbf{0.0163.}$$

Example 24. *Let p be the probability that a man aged x years will die in a year. Find the probability that out of n men A_1, A_2 ......, A_n each aged x, A_1 will die in the year and be the first to die.* (KU 1998)

Sol. Let E_i be the event that A_i will die in a year, $i = 1, 2, ...n$.

$\therefore \quad P(E_i) = p \quad i = 1, 2, ..., n.$

P(at least one will die)

$$= P(E_1 \cup E_2 \cup ...... \cup E_n) = 1 - P(\overline{E_1 \cup E_2 \cup ...... \cup E_n})$$
$$= 1 - P(\overline{E}_1 \cap \overline{E}_2 \cap ...... \cap \overline{E}_n) = 1 - P(\overline{E}_1)\,P(\overline{E}_2) ...... P(\overline{E}_n)$$
$$= 1 - (1-p)(1-p) ...... (1-p) = 1-(1-p)^n$$

Since each of $A_1, A_2, ..., A_n$ is equally likely to be the first to die, the probability that A_1 will be first to die

$$= \frac{1}{n}\times(1-(1-p)^n) = \mathbf{\frac{1-(1-p)^n}{n}}.$$

Example 25. *In each of a set of games, it is 2 to 1 in favour of the winner of the previous game. What is the chance that the player who wins the first game shall win at least three of the next four games ?* (KU 1999)

Sol. Let W_i be the event that the winner of the first game wins the ith game, $i = 2, 3, 4, 5$.

$\therefore$ P(Winner of the first game wins at least 3 out of the next 4 games)

$$= P(W_2 W_3 W_4 \overline{W}_5 \text{ or } W_2 W_3 \overline{W}_4 W_5 \text{ or } W_2 \overline{W}_3 W_4 W_5 \text{ or } \overline{W}_2 W_3 W_4 W_5 \text{ or } W_2 W_3 W_4 W_5)$$

$$= P(W_2 W_3 W_4 \overline{W}_5) + P(W_2 W_3 \overline{W}_4 W_5) + P(W_2 \overline{W}_3 W_4 W_5) + P(\overline{W}_2 W_3 W_4 W_5) + P(W_2 W_2 W_3 W_4)$$

$$= P(W_2)\, P(W_3/W_2)\, P(W_4/W_2 W_3)\, P(\overline{W}_5/W_2 W_3 W_4)$$
$$+ P(W_2)\, P(W_3/W_2)\, P(\overline{W}_4/W_2 W_3)\, P(W_5/W_2 W_3 \overline{W}_4)$$
$$+ P(W_2)\, P(\overline{W}_3/W_2)\, P(W_4/W_2 \overline{W}_3)\, P(W_5/W_2 \overline{W}_3 W_4)$$
$$+ P(\overline{W}_2)\, P(W_3/\overline{W}_2)\, P(W_4/\overline{W}_2 W_3)\, P(W_5/\overline{W}_2 W_3 W_4)$$
$$+ P(W_2)\, P(W_3/W_2)\, P(W_4/W_2 W_3)\, P(W_5/W_2 W_3 W_4)$$

$$= \frac{2}{3}\times\frac{2}{3}\times\frac{2}{3}\times\frac{1}{3} + \frac{2}{3}\times\frac{2}{3}\times\frac{1}{3}\times\frac{1}{3} + \frac{2}{3}\times\frac{1}{3}\times\frac{1}{3}\times\frac{2}{3} + \frac{1}{3}\times\frac{1}{3}\times\frac{2}{3}\times\frac{2}{3} + \frac{2}{3}\times\frac{2}{3}\times\frac{2}{3}\times\frac{2}{3}$$

$$= \frac{8+4+4+4+16}{81} = \frac{36}{81}.$$

EXERCISE 6

1. Two cards are drawn from a pack of cards in succession (with replacement). Find the probability that the first card is spade and the second is a black king.
2. Two cards are drawn from a pack of cards in succession (with replacement). Find the probability that both cards are of the same suit.
3. A husband and a wife appear in an interview for two vacancies for the same post. The probability of husband's selection is $\frac{2}{5}$ and that of wife is $\frac{4}{5}$. What is the probability that both of them will be selected ?
4. A person is known to hit the target in 3 out of 4 shots, whereas another person is known to hit the target in 2 out of 3 shots. Find the probability of the target being hit at all, when both try.
5. A man wants to marry a girl having qualities : white complexion—the probability of getting such a girl is one in twenty, handsome dowry — the probability of getting this is one in thirty. Find the probability of his getting married to a white complexioned girl who may also bring handsome dowry.
6. The probabilities of hitting a target by three persons are $\frac{1}{3}, \frac{1}{4}$ and $\frac{1}{5}$. Find the probability that the target is hit, when they all fire simultaneously.
7. (*i*) A problem in statistics is given to three students Ram, Shyam and Radheyshyam whose chances of solving it are 0.3, 0.5 and 0.6 respectively. Find the probability that the problem will be solved. *(KU 2003)*

   (*ii*) A problem in statistics is given to three students, A, B and C whose chances of solving it are 1/2, 1/3 and 1/4 respectively. Find the probability that the problem will be solved. *(KU 2002 C)* (*iii*) A problem in statistics is given to four students A, B, C and D whose chances of solving it are $\frac{1}{2}, \frac{1}{3}, \frac{1}{4}, \frac{1}{4}$ respectively. Find the probability that the problem is solved. (*MDU 1996*)

8. A candidate is called for interview by three companies. For the first company there are 12 candidates, for the second there are 15 candidates and for the third there are 10 candidates. What is the probability of his getting selected in at least one of the companies ? (*KU 1995*)

9. The probability of A winning a race is $\frac{1}{5}$ and the probability of B winning the race is $\frac{1}{6}$. Find the probability that none will win the race.

10. The odds in favour of one student passing a test are 3 : 7. The odds against another student passing it are 3 : 5. What is the probability that both will fail ?

11. The odds in favour of 'A' solving a problem are 7 : 6, and the odds against 'B' solving the same problem are 11 : 8. What is the probability that the problem will be solved, if both try the problem ? (*MDU 1995*)

12. (*i*) 'A' speaks the truth in 75% and 'B' in 90% of the cases. In what percent cases are they likely to contradict each other in stating the same fact ? (*MDU 2003*)

(*ii*) A speaks truth in 80% cases, B in 90% cases. In what percentage of cases are they likely to contradict each other in stating the same fact ? (*KU 2005 C*)

13. The odds in favour of first speaking the truth are 3 : 2. The odds in favour of second speaking the truth are 5 : 3. In what percentage of cases are they likely to contradict each other on an identical point ?

14. There are two papers in Mathematics in a certain examination. The probability that a candidate passes in paper I is 60% and that he passes in paper II is 50%. What is the probability that the candidate passes only in one paper ?

15. What is the probability of throwing 6 with a die at least once in 3 attempts ? (*KU 1997 C*)

16. If 1 out of 10 bulbs is defective, find the probability that out of sample of 3 bulbs, with replacement :

(*i*) 2 bulbs are defective. (*ii*) no bulb is defective.

17. A can solve 75% of problems and B can solve 70%. What is the probability that at least one of them will solve the problem, selected at random. (*MDU 1996*)

18. A candidate is selected for interview for three posts. For the first post there are 3 candidates, for the second there are 4 and for the third there are 8. What are the chances of his getting at least one post ?

19. Find the probability of drawing a heart on each of the two consecutive draws of one card from a well-shuffled pack of playing cards, if the card is not replaced after the first draw.

20. An urn contains two black and three white balls. A ball is drawn at random and then a second ball is drawn at random from those left. What is the probability that both balls are white ?

21. Find the probability of drawing a king, a queen and a knave in that order from a pack of playing cards in three consecutive draws of one card. The first two cards drawn are replaced.

22. Three urns contain red and blue balls . First urn has 1 red and 2 blue, second urn has 2 red and 3 blue and third urn has 3 red and 4 blue balls. If one ball each is drawn from 3 urns, find the probability that 3 balls consist of 1 red and 2 blue balls. (*KU 2005*)

23. A bag contains 10 red and 6 black balls. 4 balls are drawn successively one by one and are not replaced. What is the probability that these are alternatively of different colours, beginning with red ?

24. A bag contains 10 red and 6 black balls, 4 balls are drawn successively one by one and are not replaced. What is the probability that these are alternatively of different colours ?

25. Two cards are drawn one by one from a well-shuffled pack of 52 cards. Find the probability that both are aces, if the first card is not replaced.

26. A bag contains 13 balls numbered from 1 to 13. Suppose an even number is considered as a success. Two balls are drawn one by one without replacement. Find the probability of getting one success.

27. Find the probability of drawing a queen, a king and a knave in that order from a pack of cards in three consecutive draws, the cards are not being replaced. *(KU 1997)*

28. A student is trying to seek admission in either of the two colleges. The probability that he is admitted in first college is 3/5 and that in second college is 1/3. Find the probability that he is admitted at least one of the colleges. *(MDU 2002)*

29. A candidate is called for interview by three companies. For the first company there are 12 candidates, for the second there are 15 candidates and for the third there are 10 candidates. What are the chances of his getting selected in at least two companies ?

30. A bag contains 2 white balls and 3 black balls. Four persons, A, B, C, D in the order named each draws one ball and does not replace it. The first to draw a white ball receive Rs. 50. Determine their expectations. *(KU 2001 C)*

[**Hint.** Let A, B, C, D themselves denote the probability of their winning.

$$\therefore \quad P(A) = \frac{2}{5} \qquad P(B) = \frac{3}{5}.\frac{2}{4} = \frac{3}{10}$$

$$P(C) = \frac{3}{5}.\frac{2}{4}.\frac{2}{3} = \frac{1}{5} \qquad P(D) = \frac{3}{5}.\frac{2}{4}.\frac{1}{3}.\frac{2}{2} = \frac{1}{10}.$$

$\therefore$ Their respective expactations are Rs. $\left(50 \times \frac{2}{5}\right)$, Rs. $\left(50 \times \frac{3}{10}\right)$,

Rs. $\left(50 \times \frac{1}{5}\right)$, Rs. $\left(50 \times \frac{1}{10}\right)$]

Answers

1. $\frac{1}{104}$ 2. $\frac{52}{52} \times \frac{13}{52} = \frac{1}{4}$ 3. $\frac{8}{25}$

4. $\frac{3}{4} + \frac{2}{3} - \frac{1}{2} = \frac{11}{12}$ or $1 - \left(1 - \frac{3}{4}\right)\left(1 - \frac{2}{3}\right) = \frac{11}{12}$ 5. $\frac{1}{600}$

6. $1 - \left(1 - \frac{1}{3}\right)\left(1 - \frac{1}{4}\right)\left(1 - \frac{1}{5}\right) = \frac{3}{5}$ 7. (*i*) 0.86 (*ii*) $\frac{3}{4}$

(*iii*) $\frac{13}{16}$ 8. 0.23 9. $\frac{4}{5} \times \frac{5}{6} = \frac{2}{3}$ 10. $\frac{7}{10} \times \frac{3}{8} = \frac{21}{80}$

11. $\frac{181}{247}$ 12. (*i*) 30% (*ii*) 26%

13. $\left[\left(\frac{3}{5} \times \frac{3}{8}\right) + \left(\frac{2}{5} \times \frac{5}{8}\right)\right]$ 100% = 47.5% 14. $\left(\frac{3}{5} \times \frac{1}{2}\right) + \left(\frac{2}{5} \times \frac{1}{2}\right) = \frac{1}{2}$

15. $1 - \left(\frac{5}{6} \times \frac{5}{6} \times \frac{5}{6}\right) = \frac{91}{216}$ 16. (*i*) $\frac{27}{1000}$ (*ii*) $\frac{729}{1000}$

17. $\frac{37}{40}$ 18. $\frac{9}{16}$ 19. $\frac{13}{52} \times \frac{12}{51} = \frac{1}{17}$ 20. $\frac{3}{5} \times \frac{2}{4} = \frac{3}{10}$

21. 0.000455 22. $\frac{46}{105}$ 23. $\frac{10}{16} \times \frac{6}{15} \times \frac{9}{14} \times \frac{5}{13} = \frac{45}{728}$

24. $\frac{45}{364}$ 25. $\frac{1}{221}$ 26. $\frac{6}{13} \times \frac{7}{12} + \frac{7}{13} \times \frac{6}{12} = \frac{7}{13}$

27. $\frac{8}{16575}$ 28. $\frac{11}{15}$ 29. $\frac{7}{360}$

30. Rs. 20, Rs. 15, Rs. 10, Rs. 5.

20. TOTAL PROBABILITY RULE

Let $E_1, E_2, \ldots\ldots, E_n$ be n mutually exclusive and exhaustive events, with non-zero probabilities, of a random experiment. If A be any arbitrary event of the sample space of the above random experiment with $P(A) > 0$, then

$$P(A) = P(E_1)P(A/E_1) + P(E_2)P(A/E_2) + \ldots\ldots + P(E_n)P(A/E_n).$$

Proof. Let S be the sample space of the random experiment.

Since $E_1, E_2, \ldots\ldots, E_n$ are exhaustive, we have

$$S = E_1 \cup E_2 \cup \ldots\ldots \cup E_n.$$

Now $A = S \cap A = (E_1 \cup E_2 \cup \ldots\ldots \cup E_n) \cap A$

$\Rightarrow$ $A = (E_1 \cap A) \cup (E_2 \cap A) \cup \ldots\ldots \cup (E_n \cap A)$ ...(1)

Since $E_1, E_2, \ldots\ldots, E_n$ are mutually exclusive, we have

$$E_i \cap E_j = \phi \text{ for } i \neq j.$$

Now $(E_i \cap A) \cap (E_j \cap A) = (E_i \cap E_j) \cap A = \phi \cap A = \phi$

$\therefore$ $E_1 \cap A, E_2 \cap A, \ldots\ldots, E_n \cap A$ are also mutually exclusive.

By **addition theorem**, (1) implies

$$P(A) = P(E_1 \cap A) + P(E_2 \cap A) + \ldots\ldots + P(E_n \cap A)$$

$\Rightarrow$ $\mathbf{P(A) = P(E_1)P(A/E_1) + P(E_2)P(A/E_2) + \ldots\ldots P(E_n)P(A/E_n).}$

Remark. In practical problems, it is found convenient to write as follows :

$$P(A) = P(E_1A \text{ or } E_2A \text{ or } \ldots\ldots \text{ or } E_nA) = P(E_1A) + P(E_2A) + \ldots\ldots + P(E_nA)$$

$\therefore$ $\mathbf{P(A) = P(E_1)P(A/E_1) + P(E_2)P(A/E_2) + \ldots\ldots + P(E_n)P(A/E_n).}$

Corollary. In particular if $n = 2$, we have

$$P(A) = P(E_1)P(A/E_1) + P(E_2)P(A/E_2).$$

Example 1. *A bag contains 4 red and 3 black balls. A second bag contains 2 red and 4 black balls. One bag is selected at random. From the selected bag, one ball is drawn. Find the probability that it is a red ball.*

Sol. Let E_1 and E_2 be the events of selecting first bag and second bag respectively.

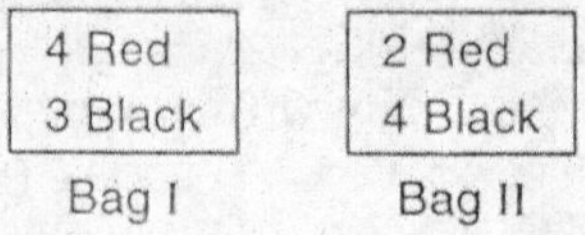

$\therefore$ $P(E_1) = \frac{1}{2}$, $P(E_2) = \frac{1}{2}$

Let R be the event of drawing a red ball.

$\therefore$ $P(R/E_1) = P(\text{Red ball is drawn from first bag}) = \frac{4}{7}$

Similarly, $P(R/E_2) = \frac{2}{6} = \frac{1}{3}$

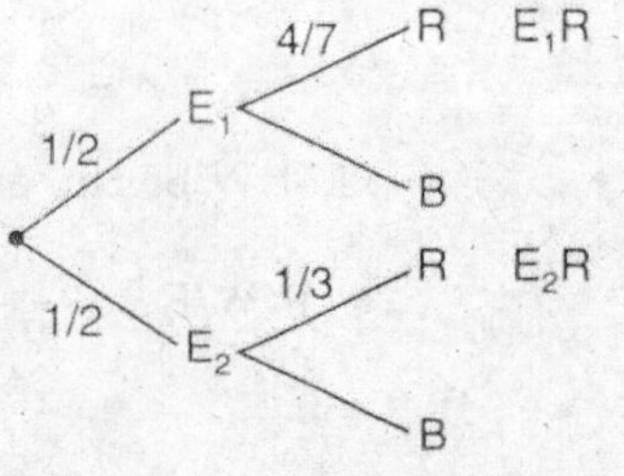

Now, P(selecting a red ball)

$$= P(R) = P(E_1R \text{ or } E_2R) = P(E_1R) + P(E_2R)$$
$$= P(E_1)P(R/E_1) + P(E_2)P(R/E_2)$$
$$= \frac{1}{2}\times\frac{4}{7} + \frac{1}{2}\times\frac{1}{3} = \frac{2}{7} + \frac{1}{6} = \mathbf{\frac{19}{42}}.$$

Example 2. *A bag contains 5 red and 3 black balls and another bag contains 4 red and 5 black balls. One of these is selected at random and two balls are drawn. What is the probability that one of them is red and the other black ?*

Sol. Let E_1 and E_2 be the events of selecting the first bag and the second bag respectively.

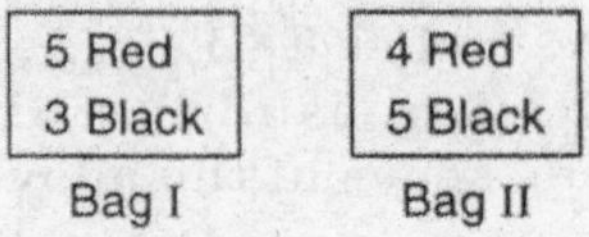

$$\therefore \quad P(E_1) = \frac{1}{2}, \; P(E_2) = \frac{1}{2}$$

Let *RB* be the event of drawing one red and one black ball.

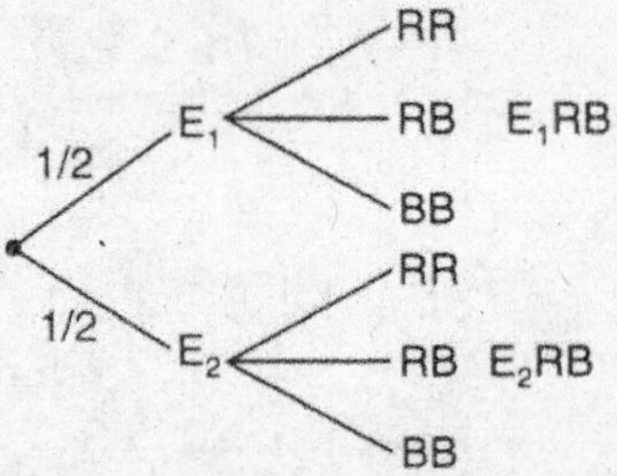

$$\therefore \quad P(RB) = P(E_1RB \text{ or } E_2RB)$$
$$= P(E_1RB) + P(E_2RB)$$
$$= P(E_1)P(RB/E_1) + P(E_2)P(RB/E_2)$$
$$= \frac{1}{2} \times \frac{{}^5C_1 \times {}^3C_1}{{}^8C_2} + \frac{1}{2} \times \frac{{}^4C_1 \times {}^5C_1}{{}^9C_2}$$
$$= \frac{1}{2} \times \frac{5\times3}{28} + \frac{1}{2} \times \frac{4\times5}{36} = \mathbf{\frac{275}{504}}.$$

Example 3. *Two urns contains 2 red, 4 white and 3 red, 7 white balls. One of the urns is chosen at random and a ball is drawn from it. Find the probability that the ball drawn is (i) red (ii) white.*

Sol. Let E_1 and E_2 be the events of choosing the first urn and the second urn respectively.

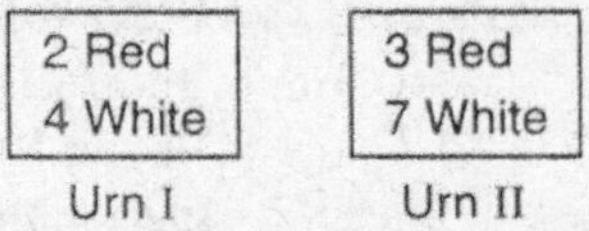

$$\therefore \quad P(E_1) = \frac{1}{2}, \; P(E_2) = \frac{1}{2}$$

(*i*) Let R be the event of drawing a red ball.

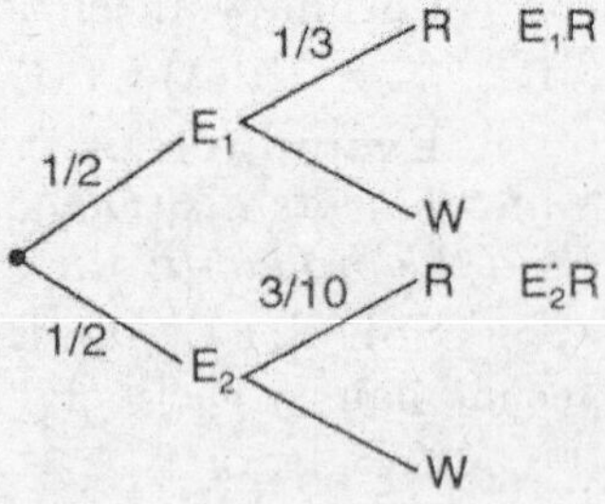

$$\therefore \quad P(R/E_1) = \frac{2}{2+4} = \frac{1}{3}$$
$$P(R/E_2) = \frac{3}{3+7} = \frac{3}{10}$$

Now P(drawing a red ball) = P(R)

$$= P(E_1R \text{ or } E_2R) = P(E_1R) + P(E_2R)$$
$$= P(E_1)P(R/E_1) + P(E_2)P(R/E_2)$$
$$= \frac{1}{2}\times\frac{1}{3} + \frac{1}{2} \times \frac{3}{10} = \mathbf{\frac{19}{60}}.$$

(*ii*) Let W be the event of drawing a white ball.

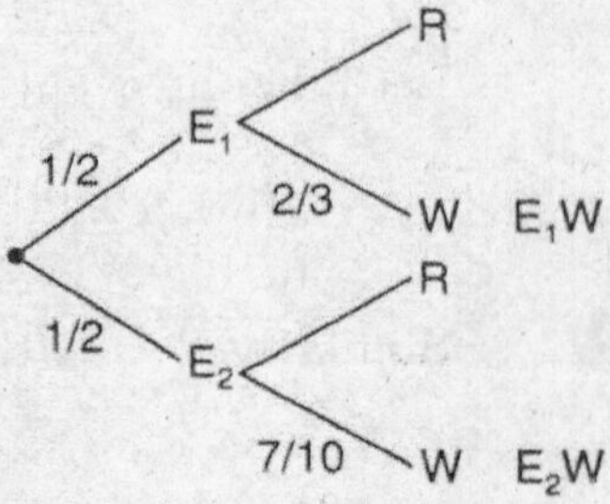

$$\therefore \quad P(W/E_1) = \frac{4}{2+4} = \frac{2}{3}$$

$$P(W/E_2) = \frac{7}{3+7} = \frac{7}{10}$$

Now P(drawing a white ball)

$$= P(W) = P(E_1W \text{ or } E_2W) = P(E_1W) + P(E_2W)$$
$$= P(E_1)P(W/E_1) + P(E_2)P(W/E_2)$$
$$= \frac{1}{2} \times \frac{2}{3} + \frac{1}{2} \times \frac{7}{10} = \mathbf{\frac{41}{60}}.$$

Example 4. *An urn contains 4 tickets numbered 1, 2, 3, 4 and another contains 6 tickets numbered 2, 4, 6, 7, 8, 9. If one of the two urns is chosen at random and a ticket is drawn at random from the urn chosen, find the probability that the ticket drawn bears the number 2 or 4.*

Sol. Let E_1 and E_2 be the events of choosing the urn I and the urn II respectively.

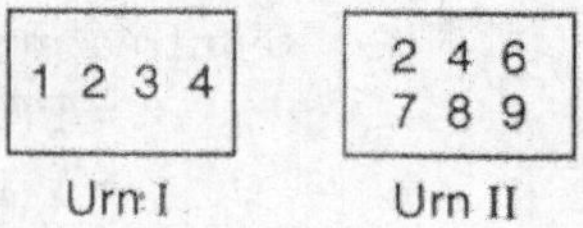

$$\therefore \quad P(E_1) = \frac{1}{2}, \quad P(E_2) = \frac{1}{2}$$

Let A be the event of drawing a ticket bearing the number 2 or 4.

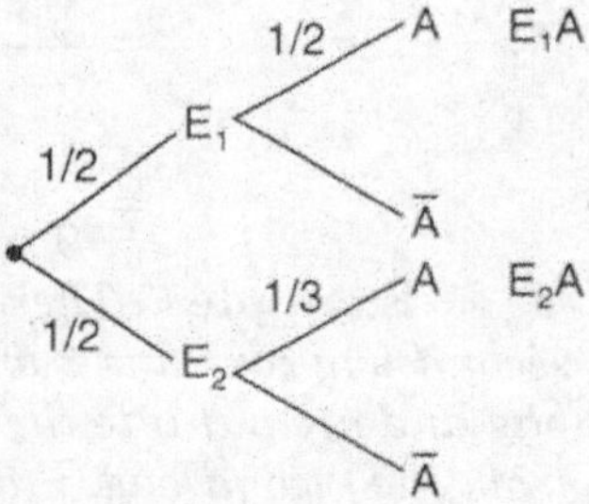

$$\therefore \quad P(A/E_1) = \frac{2}{4} = \frac{1}{2}$$

and $$P(A/E_2) = \frac{2}{6} = \frac{1}{3}$$

Required probability $= P(A)$

$$= P(E_1A \text{ or } E_2A)$$
$$= P(E_1A) + P(E_2A)$$
$$= P(E_1)P(A/E_1) + P(E_2)P(A/E_2)$$
$$= \frac{1}{2} \times \frac{1}{2} + \frac{1}{2} \times \frac{1}{3} = \frac{1}{4} + \frac{1}{6} = \mathbf{\frac{5}{12}}.$$

Example 5. *Suppose that 5 men out of 100 men and 25 women out of 1000 women are good oretor. Assuming that there are equal number of men and women, find the probability, of choosing an oretor.*

Sol. Let E_1 and E_2 be the events of choosing a man and a woman respectively

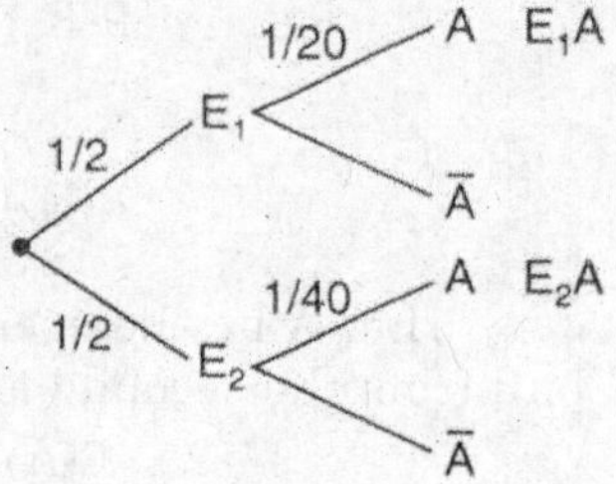

$\therefore \quad P(E_1) = \frac{1}{2}$ and $P(E_2) = \frac{1}{2}$, because there are equal number of men and women.

Let A be the event of choosing an oretor

$\therefore \quad P(A/E_1)$ = probability that a man is an oretor

$$= \frac{5}{100} = \frac{1}{20}$$

$P(A/E_2)$ = probability that a woman is an oretor

$$= \frac{25}{1000} = \frac{1}{40}$$

$\therefore \quad$ P(oretor is chosen) $= P(A) = P(E_1A \text{ or } E_2A)$

$$= P(E_1A) + P(E_2A) = P(E_1)P(A/E_1) + P(E_2)P(A/E_2)$$

$$= \frac{1}{2} \times \frac{1}{20} + \frac{1}{2} \times \frac{1}{40} = \frac{3}{80}.$$

Example 6. *One bag contains 5 white and 4 black balls. Another bag contains 7 white and 9 black balls. A ball is transferred from the first bag to the second bag and then a ball is drawn from the second. Find the probability that this ball is white.*

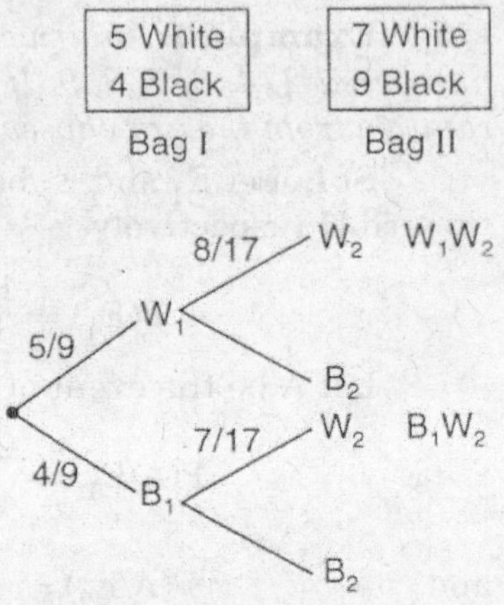

Sol. Let W_1 and B_1 be the events of transferring a white ball and a black ball from bag I to bag II respectively.

Let W_2 be the event of drawing a white ball from the bag II after the transfer of ball.

∴ Required probability

$$= P(W_2) = P(W_1W_2 \text{ or } B_1W_2)$$
$$= P(W_1W_2) + P(B_1W_2)$$
$$= P(W_1)P(W_2/W_1) + P(B_1)P(W_2/B_1)$$
$$= \frac{5}{5+4} \times \frac{7+1}{(7+1)+9} + \frac{4}{5+4} \times \frac{7}{7+(9+1)}$$
$$= \frac{5}{9} \times \frac{8}{17} + \frac{4}{9} \times \frac{7}{17} = \frac{4}{9}.$$

Example 7. *There are two bags. The first bag contains 5 white and 3 black balls and the second bag contains 3 white and 5 black balls. Two balls are drawn at random from the first bag and are put into the second bag, without noticing their colours. Then two balls are drawn from the second bag. Find the probability that these balls are white and black.*

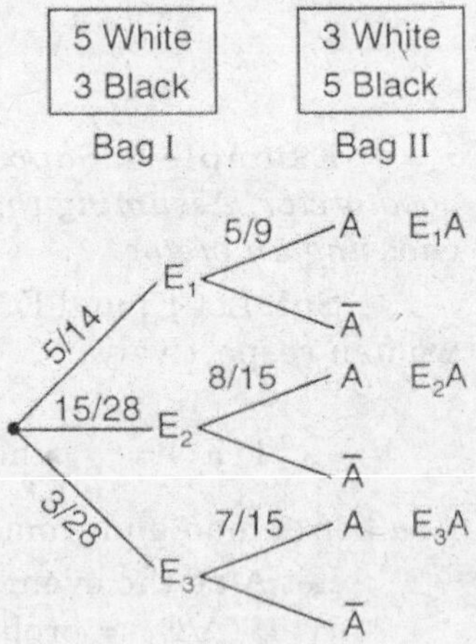

Sol. Let E_1, E_2 and E_3 be the events of transferring 2 white, 1 white and 1 black, 2 black balls respectively from the first bag to second bag.

$$P(E_1) = \frac{{}^5C_2}{{}^8C_2} = \frac{10}{28} = \frac{5}{14}$$

$$P(E_2) = \frac{{}^5C_1 \times {}^3C_1}{{}^8C_2} = \frac{5 \times 3}{28} = \frac{15}{28}$$

$$P(E_3) = \frac{{}^3C_2}{{}^8C_2} = \frac{3}{28}$$

Let A be the event of drawing one white and one black ball from the second bag.

$$\therefore \quad P(A) = P(E_1A \text{ or } E_2A \text{ or } E_3A)$$
$$= P(E_1A) + P(E_2A) + P(E_3A)$$
$$= P(E_1)P(A/E_1) + P(E_2)P(A/E_2) + P(E_3)P(A/E_3)$$
$$= \frac{5}{14} \times \frac{{}^5C_1 \times {}^5C_1}{{}^{10}C_2} + \frac{15}{28} \times \frac{{}^4C_1 \times {}^6C_1}{{}^{10}C_2} + \frac{3}{28} \times \frac{{}^3C_1 \times {}^7C_1}{{}^{10}C_2}$$
$$= \frac{5}{14} \times \frac{5}{9} + \frac{15}{28} \times \frac{8}{15} + \frac{3}{28} \times \frac{7}{15} = \frac{\mathbf{673}}{\mathbf{1260}}.$$

Example 8. *Two cards are drawn from a pack of 52 cards at random and kept out. Then one card is drawn from the remaining 50 cards. Find the probability that it is an ace.*

Sol. Let E_1, E_2 and E_3 be the events of drawing 2 aces, 1 ace and 1 non ace, 2 non aces in the first draw of 2 cards.

$$\therefore \quad P(E_1) = \frac{^4C_2}{^{52}C_2} = \frac{1}{221}, \quad P(E_2) = \frac{^4C_1 \times {^{48}C_1}}{^{52}C_2} = \frac{32}{221}$$

and
$$P(E_3) = \frac{^{48}C_2}{^{52}C_2} = \frac{188}{221}.$$

Let E be the event of drawing an ace in the second draw of one card.

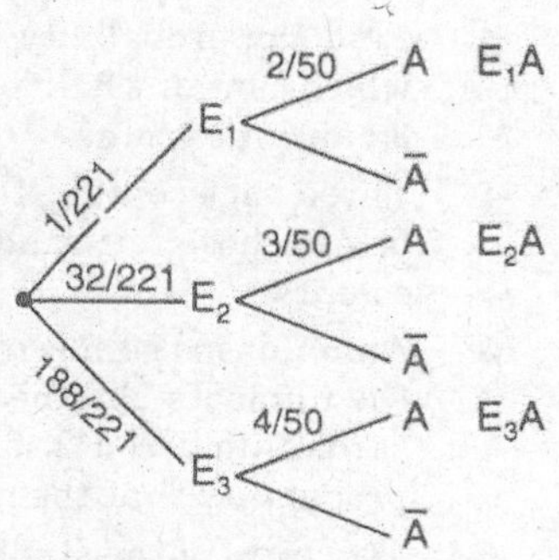

Required probability

$= P(A) = P(E_1A \text{ or } E_2A \text{ or } E_3A)$

$= P(E_1)P(A/E_1) + P(E_2)P(A/E_2) + P(E_3)P(A/E_3)$

$$= \frac{1}{221} \times \frac{4-2}{52-2} + \frac{32}{221} \times \frac{4-1}{52-2} + \frac{188}{221} \times \frac{4-0}{52-2}$$

$$= \frac{2+96+752}{221 \times 50} = \frac{850}{11050} = \frac{1}{13}.$$

Example 9. *Two machines A and B produce respectively 60% and 40% of the total numbers of a items of a factory. The percentages of defective output of these machines are respectively 2% and 5%. If an item is selected at random, what is the probability that the item is (i) defective (ii) non-defective ?*

Sol. Let E_1, E_2 be the events of drawing an item produced by machine A and machine B respectively. Let A be the event of selecting a defective item.

$\therefore$ $\bar{A}$ represent the event of selecting a non-defective item. We have

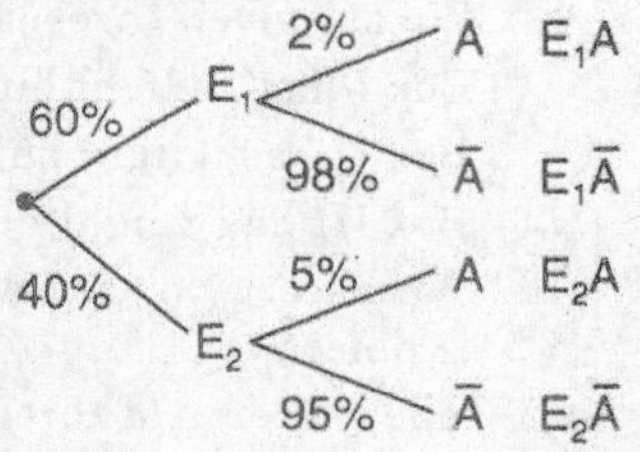

$P(E_1) = 60\%$, $P(E_2) = 40\%$.

$P(A/E_1)$ = probability that a defective item is produced by A = 2%.

$P(A/E_2)$ = probability that a defective item is produced by B = 5%.

(*i*) P(selected item is defective)

$= P(A) = P(E_1A \text{ or } E_2A) = P(E_1A) + P(E_2A)$

$= P(E_1)P(A/E_1) + P(E_2)P(A/E_2) = (60\%)(2\%) + (40\%)(5\%)$

$$= \frac{60}{100} \times \frac{2}{100} + \frac{40}{100} \times \frac{5}{100} = \frac{320}{10000} = \mathbf{0.032}.$$

(*ii*) P(selected item is non-defective)

$= P(\bar{A}) = P(E_1\bar{A} \text{ or } E_2\bar{A}) = P(E_1\bar{A}) + P(E_2\bar{A})$

$= P(E_1)P(\bar{A}/E_1) + P(E_2)P(\bar{A}/E_2) = (60\%)(98\%) + (40\%)(95\%)$

$$= \frac{60}{100} \times \frac{98}{100} + \frac{40}{100} \times \frac{95}{100} = \frac{9680}{10000} \quad \mathbf{0.968}.$$

EXERCISE 7

1. A bag contains 3 white and 2 black balls and another bag contains 2 white and 4 black balls. One bag is chosen at random. From the selected bag, one ball is drawn. Find the probability that the ball drawn is white.
2. A factory has two machines A and B. Past records show that the machine A produced 60% of the items of output and machine B produced 40% of the items. Further 2% of the items produced by machine A were defective and 1% produced by machine B were defective. If an item is drawn at random, what is the probability that it is defective ?
3. Find the probability of drawing a one-rupee coin from a purse with two compartments one of which contains 3 fifty-paise coins and 2 one-rupee coins and other contains 2 fifty-paise coins and 3 one-rupee coins.
4. Three bags coptain 1 red and 3 blue, 2 red and 1 blue and 4 red and 3 blue balls respectively. A bag is chosen at random and 2 balls are drawn. Find the probability that they are of different colours. *(KU 2006 C)*
5. An unbiased coin is tossed. If the result is a head, a pair of unbiased dice is rolled and the sum of the numbers obtained is noted. If the result is a tail, a card from a well shuffled pack of eleven cards numbered 2, 3, 4, ..., 12 is picked and the number on the card is noted. What is the probability that the noted number is either 7 or 8 ?
6. Two third of the students in a class are boys and the rest girls. It is known that the probability of a girl getting a first class is 0.25 and that of a boy getting first class is 0.28. Find the probability that a student chosen at random will get first class marks in the examination.
7. In a bolt factory, machines A, B and C manufacture 25%, 35% and 40% of the total bolts. Of their outputs 5%, 4% and 2% are respectively defective bolts. A bolt is drawn at random from the output. What is the probability that the bolt drawn is defective ?
8. Three machines A, B and C produces respectively 50%, 30% and 20% of the total number of items of a factory. The percentage of defective output of these machines are respectively 3%, 4% and 5%. If an item is selected at random, what is the probability that the item is defective ?
9. We are given three boxes as follows :

   Box I has 10 light bulbs of which 4 are defective.

   Box II has 6 light bulbs of which 1 is defective.

   Box III has 8 light bulbs of which 3 are defective.

   We select a box at random and then draw a bulb at random. What is the probability that the bulb is defective ?
10. The contents of three bags I, II and III are as follows :

    Bag I : 1 white, 2 black and 3 red balls,

    Bag II : 2 white, 1 black and 1 red balls, and

    Bag III : 4 white, 5 black and 3 red balls.

    A bag is chosen at random and two balls are drawn. What is the probability that the balls are white and red ?
11. A bag contains 5 red and 5 green balls and another bag contains 4 red and 6 green balls. A ball is taken from the first bag and without seeing its colour is put in the second bag. A ball is taken from the latter. Find the probability that the ball drawn is red. *(KU 2005 C)*
12. Bag A contains 5 red and 4 green balls. Bag B contains 4 red and 6 green balls. A ball is transferred from bag A to the bag B and then a ball is taken out of the second bag. Find the probability of this ball being red. *(KU 2006)*
13. One bag contains 5 white and 4 black balls. Another bag contains 7 white and 9 black balls. A ball is transferred from the first bag to the second bag and then a ball is drawn from the second bag. Find the probability that ball drawn is black.

14. A bag contains 3 white and 5 black balls and a second bag contains 5 white and 3 black balls. One ball is transferred from first bag to the second and then a ball is drawn from the second bag. Find the probability that the ball drawn white.

15. An urn contains 1 black and 2 white balls. Another urn B contains 2 black and 1 white balls. A ball is transferred from the urn A to the urn B. Then a ball is drawn from urn B. Find the probability that it is a white ball. *(KU 1996)*

16. An urn contains 10 white and 3 black balls, while another urn contains 3 white and 5 black balls. Two balls are drawn from the first urn and put in to the second urn and then a ball is drawn from the latter. What is the probability of drawing a white ball ?

Answers

1. $\frac{7}{15}$	2. $\frac{2}{125}$	3. $\frac{1}{2}$	4. $\frac{73}{126}$
5. $\frac{193}{792}$	6. 0.27	7. 0.0345	8. 0.037
9. $\frac{113}{360}$	10. $\frac{118}{495}$	11. $\frac{9}{22}$	12. $\frac{41}{99}$
13. $\frac{5}{9}$	14. $\frac{43}{72}$	15. $\frac{5}{12}$	16. $\frac{59}{130}$

BAYES' THEOREM

21. MOTIVATION

Let there be two or more urns, each containing some white balls and red balls. Suppose an urn is chosen at random and a ball is drawn from that chosen urn. By using *addition theorem* and *multiplication theorem*, we can find the probability of drawing a white ball (or red ball) from the urn chosen.

But in case, we are given that the ball drawn is white and we are interested in finding the probability of the event that the ball was drawn from the Ist urn or IInd urn etc., then the situation is not the same as in the previous case. Now the probability of the drawn urn will depend upon the colour of the drawn ball.

To tackle this type of problems, Bayes' theorem is used. This theorem was enunciated by British mathematician **Thomos Bayes** in 1763.

22. BAYES' THEOREM

Let E_1, E_2, ..., E_n be n pairwise mutually exclusive and exhaustive events, with non-zero probabilities, of a random experiment. If A be any arbitrary event of the sample space of the above experiment with P(A) > 0, then

$$P(E_i/A) = \frac{P(E_i)P(A/E_i)}{\sum_{j=1}^{n} P(E_j)P(A/E_j)}, \quad 1 \le i \le n.$$

(KU 1998, 98 C, 99, 99 C, 2001 C ; MDU 1998, 99)

Proof. Let S be the sample space of the random experiment.

$\therefore \quad S = E_1 \cup E_2 \cup \ldots\ldots \cup E_n \qquad (\because \; E_1, E_2, \ldots\ldots, E_n \text{ are exhaustive})$

Now $\quad A = S \cap A = (E_1 \cup E_2 \cup \ldots\ldots \cup E_n) \cap A$

$= (E_1 \cap A) \cup (E_2 \cap A) \cup \ldots\ldots \cup (E_n \cap A)$

$\therefore \quad P(A) = P(E_1 \cap A) + P(E_2 \cap A) + \ldots\ldots + P(E_n \cap A)^*$

$= P(E_1)P(A/E_1) + P(E_2)P(A/E_2) + \ldots\ldots + P(E_n)P(A/E_n)$

or
$$P(A) = \sum_{j=1}^{n} P(E_j)P(A/E_j) \qquad \ldots(1)$$

Now, $\quad P(E_i/A) = \dfrac{P(E_i \cap A)}{P(A)}, \; 1 \le i \le n$

$$\therefore \quad \mathbf{P(E_i/A) = \frac{P(E_i)P(A/E_i)}{\sum_{j=1}^{n} P(E_j)P(A/E_j)}, \; 1 \le i \le n.} \qquad \text{[Using (1)]}$$

Remark 1. If $n = 2$, then

$$P(E_1/A) = \frac{P(E_1)P(A/E_1)}{P(E_1)P(A/E_1) + P(E_2)P(A/E_2)}$$

and
$$P(E_2/A) = \frac{P(E_2)P(A/E_2)}{P(E_1)P(A/E_1) + P(E_2)P(A/E_2)}$$

Example 1. *Two urns contain 1 white, 6 red and 4 white, 3 red balls. One of the urns is selected at random and a ball is drawn from it. Find :*

(i) the probability of drawing a white ball.

(ii) the probability of drawing the ball from first urn, if the ball drawn is white.

Sol. Let E_1, E_2 be the events of drawing the first urn and the second urn respectively.

$\therefore \quad P(E_1) = \frac{1}{2}, \; P(E_2) = \frac{1}{2}.$

Urn I	Urn II
1 White	4 White
6 Red	3 Red

Let A be the event of drawing a white ball.

$\therefore \quad P(A/E_1) = \dfrac{1}{1+6} = \dfrac{1}{7}$ and $P(A/E_2) = \dfrac{4}{4+3} = \dfrac{4}{7}$

(*i*) P(getting white ball)

$= P(A) = P(E_1A \text{ or } E_2A) = P(E_1A) + P(E_2A)$

$= P(E_1)P(A/E_1) + P(E_2)P(A/E_2)$

$= \left(\dfrac{1}{2} \times \dfrac{1}{7}\right) + \left(\dfrac{1}{2} \times \dfrac{4}{7}\right) = \dfrac{5}{14}$

(*ii*) P(white ball drawn is from the first urn)

$= P(E_1/A) = \dfrac{P(E_1)P(A/E_1)}{P(E_1)P(A/E_1) + P(E_2)P(A/E_2)}$

---

* **Why this step.** Since $E_1, E_2, \ldots, E_n$ are pairwise mutually exclusive, we have $E_l \cap E_m = \phi$ for $l \ne m$.

Now $(E_l \cap A) \cap (E_m \cap A) = (E_l \cap E_m) \cap A = \phi \cap A = \phi$.

$\therefore \quad E_1 \cap A, E_2 \cap A, \ldots\ldots, E_n \cap A$ are also pairwise *m.e.* and *extended addition theorem* is applicable.

$$= \frac{\frac{1}{2} \times \frac{1}{7}}{\left(\frac{1}{2} \times \frac{1}{7}\right) + \left(\frac{1}{2} \times \frac{4}{7}\right)} = \frac{\frac{1}{14}}{\frac{5}{14}} = \frac{1}{5}.$$

Note. In finding the probability of drawing a white ball in part (*i*) we do not require the use of Bayes' theorem.

Example 2. *In 1988, there will be three candidates for the position of principal – A, B and C. The chances of their selection are in the proportion 4 : 2 : 3 respectively. The probability that A, if selected, will introduce co-education in the college is 0.3. The probability of B and C doing the same are respectively 0.5 and 0.8. What is the probability that there will be co-education in the college in 1988 ? Also find the probability that the co-education in the college was introduced by the principal B.*

Sol. Let E_1, E_2, E_3 be the events of selection of A, B, C as principal respectively. Let A be the event of introduction of co-education in the college.

$$\therefore \quad P(E_1) = \frac{4}{4+2+3} = \frac{4}{9}, \quad P(E_2) = \frac{2}{4+2+3} = \frac{2}{9}$$

and $$P(E_3) = \frac{3}{4+2+3} = \frac{3}{9}.$$

Also, $$P(A/E_1) = \frac{3}{10}, \quad P(A/E_2) = \frac{5}{10}, \quad P(A/E_3) = \frac{8}{10}.$$

Now, P(co-education is introduced in the college)

$$= P(A) = P(E_1A \text{ or } E_2A \text{ or } E_3A) = P(E_1A) + P(E_2A) + P(E_3A)$$
$$= P(E_1)P(A/E_1) + P(E_2)P(A/E_2) + P(E_3)P(A/E_3)$$
$$= \left(\frac{4}{9} \times \frac{3}{10}\right) + \left(\frac{2}{9} \times \frac{5}{10}\right) + \left(\frac{3}{9} \times \frac{8}{10}\right) = \frac{46}{90} = \frac{\mathbf{23}}{\mathbf{45}}.$$

By *Bayes' theorem*,

P(Co-education was introduced by the principal B)

$$= P(E_2/A) = \frac{P(E_2)P(A/E_2)}{P(A)} = \frac{\frac{2}{9} \times \frac{5}{10}}{\frac{23}{45}} = \frac{\mathbf{5}}{\mathbf{23}}.$$

Example 3. *Assume that a factory has two machines. Past records shows that machine I produces 30% of the items of output and machine II produces 70% of the items. Further, 5% of the items produced by machine I were defective and only 1% produced by machines II were defective. An item is drawn at random and found to be defective. What is the probability that it was produced by machine I or machine II ?*

Sol. Let E_1, E_2 be the events of drawing an item produced by machine I and II respectively. Let A be the event of drawing a defective item.

$$\therefore \quad P(E_1) = \frac{30}{100} = \frac{3}{10}, \quad P(E_2) = \frac{70}{100} = \frac{7}{10}$$

Also, $$P(A/E_1) = \frac{5}{100}, \quad P(A/E_2) = \frac{1}{100}$$

The events E_1 and E_2 are mutually exclusive and exhaustive.

By *Bayes' theorem*,

P(machine I produced the defective item) = $P(E_1/A)$

$$= \frac{P(E_1)P(A/E_1)}{P(E_1)P(A/E_1) + P(E_2)P(A/E_2)}$$

$$= \frac{\frac{3}{10} \times \frac{5}{100}}{\left(\frac{3}{10} \times \frac{5}{100}\right) + \left(\frac{7}{10} \times \frac{1}{100}\right)} = \frac{15}{15+7} = \mathbf{\frac{15}{22}}$$

Also, P(machine II produced the defective item) = $(P(E_2/A)$

$$= \frac{P(E_2)P(A/E_2)}{P(E_1)P(A/E_1) + P(E_2)P(A/E_2)}$$

$$= \frac{\frac{7}{10} \times \frac{1}{100}}{\left(\frac{3}{10} \times \frac{5}{100}\right) + \left(\frac{7}{10} \times \frac{1}{100}\right)} = \frac{7}{15+7} = \mathbf{\frac{7}{22}}.$$

Example 4. *A manufacturing firm produces steel pipes in three plants with daily production volume of 500, 1000 and 2000 units respectively. According to past experience, it is known that the fraction of defective outputs produced by the three plants are respectively 0.005, 0.008, 0.010. If a pipe is selected from a day's total production and found to be defective, find out the probability that it came from the first plant.*

Sol. Let E_1, E_2 and E_3 be the events of drawing a pipe produced by first plant, second plant and third plant respectively. Let A be the event of drawing a defective pipe.

$$\therefore \quad P(E_1) = \frac{500}{500+1000+2000} = \frac{1}{7},$$

$$P(E_2) = \frac{1000}{500+1000+2000} = \frac{2}{7} \quad \text{and} \quad P(E_3) = \frac{2000}{500+1000+2000} = \frac{4}{7}.$$

Also $\quad P(A/E_1) = 0.005, \quad P(A/E_2) = 0.008 \quad$ and $\quad P(A/E_3) = 0.010.$

The events E_1, E_2, E_3 are mutually exclusive and exhaustive.

By *Bayes' theorem*, P(Plant I produced the defective pipe) = $P(E_1/A)$

$$= \frac{P(E_1)P(A/E_1)}{P(E_1)P(A/E_1) + P(E_2)P(A/E_2) + P(E_3)P(A/E_3)}$$

$$= \frac{\frac{1}{7}(0.005)}{\frac{1}{7}(0.005) + \frac{2}{7}(0.008) + \frac{4}{7}(0.010)}$$

$$= \frac{0.005}{0.005 + 0.016 + 0.040)} = \frac{0.005}{0.061} = \mathbf{\frac{5}{61}}.$$

Example 5. *In a bolt factory, machines A, B and C manufacture 60%, 25% and 15% respectively. Of the total of their output, 1%, 2% and 1% are defective bolts. A bolt is drawn at random from the total production and found to be defective. From which machine, the defective bolt is expected to have been manufactured ?*

Sol. Let E_1, E_2, E_3 be the events of drawing a bolt produced by machine A, B and C respectively. Let A be the event of drawing a defective bolt.

$$\therefore \quad P(E_1) = \frac{60}{100}, \quad P(E_2) = \frac{25}{100}, \quad P(E_3) = \frac{15}{100}$$

$$P(A/E_1) = \frac{1}{100}, \quad P(A/E_2) = \frac{2}{100}, \quad P(A/E_3) = \frac{1}{100}.$$

The events E_1, E_2 and E_3 are mutually exclusive and exhaustive.

By *Bayes' theorem.*

P(defective bolt is produced by machine A) = $P(E_1/A)$

$$= \frac{P(E_1)P(A/E_1)}{P(E_1)P(A/E_1) + P(E_2)P(A/E_2) + P(E_3)P(A/E_3)}$$

$$= \frac{\frac{60}{100} \times \frac{1}{100}}{\left(\frac{60}{100} \times \frac{1}{100}\right) + \left(\frac{25}{100} \times \frac{2}{100}\right) + \left(\frac{15}{100} \times \frac{1}{100}\right)} = \frac{60}{60 + 50 + 15} = \frac{60}{125} = \mathbf{\frac{12}{25}}$$

P(defective bolt is produced by machine B) = $P(E_2/A)$

$$= \frac{P(E_2)P(A/E_2)}{P(E_1)P(A/E_1) + P(E_2)P(A/E_2) + P(E_3)P(A/E_3)}$$

$$= \frac{\frac{25}{100} \times \frac{2}{100}}{\left(\frac{60}{100} \times \frac{1}{100}\right) + \left(\frac{25}{100} \times \frac{2}{100}\right) + \left(\frac{15}{100} \times \frac{1}{100}\right)} = \frac{50}{60 + 50 + 15} = \frac{50}{125} = \mathbf{\frac{10}{25}}$$

P(defective bolt is produced by machine C) = $P(E_3/A)$

$$= \frac{P(E_3)P(A/E_3)}{P(E_1)P(A/E_1) + P(E_2)P(A/E_2) + P(E_3)P(A/E_3)}$$

$$= \frac{\frac{15}{100} \times \frac{1}{100}}{\left(\frac{60}{100} \times \frac{1}{100}\right) + \left(\frac{25}{100} \times \frac{2}{100}\right) + \left(\frac{15}{100} \times \frac{1}{100}\right)} = \frac{15}{60 + 50 + 15} = \frac{15}{125} = \mathbf{\frac{3}{25}}.$$

$\therefore$ Most probably, the defective bolt has been drawn from the output of machine A.

$$\left(\because \frac{12}{25} > \frac{10}{25}, \frac{3}{25}\right)$$

Example 6. *An insurance company insured 2000 scooter drivers, 4000 car drivers and 6000 truck drivers. The probability of an accident involving a scooter driver, car driver and a truck driver is 0.01, 0.03 and 0.15 respectively. One of the insured drivers meets with an accident. What is the probability that he is a car driver ?* (MDU 2000 ; KU 2001, 2002 C)

Sol. Let E_1, E_2, E_3 be the events of drawing scooter driver, car driver, truck driver respectively.

Total number of drivers = 2000 + 4000 + 6000 = 12000

$$\therefore \quad P(E_1) = \frac{2000}{12000} = \frac{1}{6}, \quad P(E_2) = \frac{4000}{12000} = \frac{1}{3} \quad \text{and} \quad P(E_3) = \frac{6000}{12000} = \frac{1}{2}$$

Let A be the event of getting an accident.

$\therefore$ $P(A/E_1) = 0.01$, $P(A/E_2) = 0.03$ and $P(A/E_3) = 0.15$

The events E_1, E_2 and E_3 are mutually exclusive and exhaustive.

$\therefore$ **By Bayes' theorem**

P(accident involved car driver) = $P(E_2/A)$

$$= \frac{P(E_2)P(A/E_2)}{P(E_1)P(A/E_1) + P(E_2)P(A/E_2) + P(E_3)P(A/E_3)}$$

$$= \frac{\frac{1}{3} \times 0.03}{\frac{1}{6} + 0.01 + \frac{1}{3} \times 0.03 + \frac{1}{2} \times 0.15} = \frac{0.01}{0.52/6} = \frac{0.06}{0.52} = \frac{3}{26}.$$

EXERCISE 8

1. A bag contains 4 black and 1 white balls and another bag contains 5 black and 4 white balls. One bag is chosen and a ball is drawn. If the ball drawn is black, find the probability that it is drawn from the first bag. *(KU 1996 C)*
2. Two urns contain 4 white, 6 blue and 4 white, 5 blue balls. One of the urns is selected at random and a ball is drawn. If the ball drawn is white, find the probability that it is drawn from the first urn.
3. Two urns contain 4 white, 6 blue and 4 white, 5 blue balls. One of the urns is selected at random and a ball is drawn. If the ball drawn is white, find the probability that it is drawn from the second urn.
4. Three urns contain 6 red, 4 black ; 4 red, 6 black and 5 red, 5 black balls respectively. One of the urns is selected at random and a ball is drawn. If ball drawn is red, find the probability that it is drawn from the first urn.
5. Assume that a factory has two machines. Past records shows that machine I produces 60% of the items of output and machine II produces 40% of the items. Further, 2% of the items produced by machine I were defective and only 1% produced by machine II were defective. If a defective item is drawn at random, what is the probability that it was produced by machine I ?
6. In a bolt factory, machines A and B manufacture equal number of bolts. Of the total of their output, 1% and 2% are defective. A bolt is drawn at random from the total production and found to be defective. From which machine, the defective bolt is expected to have been produced ?
7. In a factory, machines A, B and C produces 40%, 40% and 20% respectively. Of the total of their output 1%, 1% and 3% are defective. An item is drawn at random from the total production and found to be defective. Find the probability that this item is produced by the machine C.
8. State and prove Bayes' theorem. In a bolt factory, machines A, B and C manufacture 25%, 35% and 40% of the total of output. Of their output, 5, 4 and 2 per cent are defective. A bolt is drawn at random and is found to be defective. What is the probability that it was manufactured by the machine A, B or C ? *(KU 1999, 99 C, 2001, 2004)*
9. A manufacturing firm produces pipes in two plants with daily production volume of 5000 and 7000 units respectively. According to past experience, it is known that the fraction of defective outputs produced by the plants are 0.01 and 0.02 respectively. If a pipe is selected at random from a day's total production and found to be defective, find out the probability that it came from the second plant.
10. In a Post Office, two clerks are engaged in checking incoming mails. On an average, the first clerk (A_1) checks 60 percent mail, while the second (A_2) does the remaining. A_1 has an error rate of 0.03 and A_2 has an error rate of 0.02. A mail is selected at random from incoming mails of a day and is discovered to have an error, find the probability that it was checked by clerk A_2. *(KU 2003)*

Answers

1. 36/61	2. 9/19	3. 10/19	4. 2/5
5. 3/4	6. B	7. 3/7	8. 25/69, 28/69, 16/69
9. 14/19	10. 4/13.		

23. CRITICISM OF CLASSICAL APPROACH OF PROBABILITY

Though the classical approach of measuring probability seems to be quite simple and straight forward, but this approach is subjected to certain points of criticism.

In defining probability of an event, we assume that all the possible outcomes are equally likely. This means that all the possible outcomes of an experiment have equal chances of being occurred. In other words, the probability of occurrence of each outcome is equal. Thus, in classical approach, we define probability of an event in terms of probabilities of various outcomes of the experiment. Thus, this definition of probability is circular in nature.

The classical approach is based on abstract reasoning and is suitable under ideal conditions. For example, we say that in the experiment of throwing a die, the probability of getting 2 is 1/6. But this will be true if the die is unbiased *i.e.* it is perfect. In practice, perfection is not achieved. Thus, this approach is not realistic in nature.

24. EMPIRICAL APPROACH OF PROBABILITY

This approach is based upon repetitive experiments under uniform conditions. Suppose a coin is perfectly balanced and we toss it 100 times. In 100 tosses, we may get head 56 times. Again if we toss this coin 1000 times, we may get head 519 times. Again if we toss this coin 10,000 times, we may get head 5085 times. In these experiments, we see that the ratio 56/100, 519/1000, 5085/10000 is tending toward 1/2, which should be the probability of getting head in any toss of the coin. In empirical approach, the probability of an events is defined in terms of a ratio of the type explained above.

If an experiment is repeated n times under uniform conditions and an event E occurs 'm' times, then the probability of the event E is defined as

$$P(E) = \lim_{n \to \infty} \frac{m}{n}$$

In the definition, '$\lim_{n \to \infty}$' emphasizes the fact that n must be very large. In the real mathematical sense, we cannot measure $\lim_{n \to \infty} \frac{m}{n}$, because we cannot repeat any experiment infinitely many times. Thus, in this approach, we content ourselves by assuming that n takes large and practically possible values. If we toss a perfect coin two times, it is not expected that we shall definitely get one head and one tail. But if the same coin is tossed 5000 times, we may get about 2500 heads. Thus, the probability defined in this approach is a long run concept, because to find the probability of an event, we have to repeat out experiment a large number of times. In any experiment, we shall have $m \leq n$.

$$\therefore \quad P(E) = \lim_{n \to \infty} \frac{m}{n} \text{ implies } \quad 0 \leq P(E) \leq 1.$$

The empirical approach of probability is based on experience.

Limitations. The computation of empirical probability requires repetition of experiment, a very large number of times. This restrict the suitability of this approach. In many cases, the experiment may not be repeated large number of times. If E be the event that a particular student secures 70% marks or more in all the examinations given to him in a particular year, then this experiment cannot be repeated many number of times. This approach is also not applicable to experiments which are not expected to occur frequently in future.

25. SUBJECTIVE APPROACH OF PROBABILITY

The classical and empirical approaches of probability are *objective* in nature. In the subjective approach, the probability of an event is considered as a measure of one's confidence in the occurrence of that particular event. The probability of the event that the student 'A' will pass the examination cannot be calculated by any of the above discussed objective approaches. The events of his passing and failing are not equally likely cases. Had these cases been equally likely, we could have used classical approach and said that the probability is $\frac{1}{2}$. In this case, the experiment is such that it cannot be repeated under uniform conditions. Thus, the empirical approach also fails to comment upon the probability of this event. In such cases, the subjective approach is found useful. In subjective approach, the probability of an event represent the degree of faith which a rational person reposes in the occurrence of that certain event. The degree of faith will depend upon his judgement, personal outlook etc. In this approach, the probability of a event, differ from person to person and that is why it is called subjective approach. In this approach, the probability of an event also suffer from personal bias of its estimator.

EXERCISE 9

1. Explain the fundamental concepts of 'Probability'. *(MDU 2000)*
2. Define 'probability'. *(MDU 1998)*
3. Write the fundamental concepts of probability calculation. *(KU 2000 C)*
4. Define 'probability' and explain its importance in Statistics. *(MDU 2003)*
5. Explain the term 'Mutually Exclusive Events' by taking some examples. *(KU 2006 C)*
6. What is conditional probability ? Explain with the help of an example. *(KU 1997, 2003)*
7. Define probability and explain the Addition law of probability giving suitable examples. *(KU 2001 C, 2005 C ; MDU 2002)*
8. Explain what do you understand by the term 'probability'. State and prove the addition and multiplication theorems of probability. *(KU 1996)*
9. Explain short notes on any two :
   (*i*) Dependent and independent events *(KU 2004 ; MDU 2004)*
   (*ii*) Mutually exclusive and equally likely events
   (*iii*) Simple and compound events. *(MDU 1998)*
10. Explain the Multiplication Theorem of Probability with suitable example. *(KU 2001, 2004)*
11. Explain Bayes' theorem with the help of an example. *(MDU 1997, 98 ; KU 2001 C, 2005, 2006)*
12. Define probability in different ways. Giving their merits and demerits by examples. State which is the best. *(KU 1999)*
13. Discuss in detail the Classical and Empirical approaches to probability. *(KU 2000, 2002 C)*
14. Explain the various approaches to probability. *(KU 1995, 2000 C, 2005 ; MDU 1996)*
15. Explain the following :
    Mutually Exclusive Event, Compound Event and Dependent Event. *(KU 2007)*
16. Using illustration, explain the following :
    (*i*) Classical approach to probability (*ii*) Conditional probability. *(MDU 2007)*

16

Random Variables

1. INTRODUCTION

We have already studied a lot about frequency distributions. These distributions are based upon observations, *i.e.,* the frequencies for different values of the variable, under consideration, are based on actual observation. For example, if an unbiased coin is tossed 100 times, we may get head 57 times. Here, 57 is the observed frequency but theoretically we shall expect head 50 times. In this chapter, we shall study *probability distributions and frequecncy distributions* which are based upon theoretical considerations.

2. VARIABLES

A symbol which can assume any of a prescribed set of values is called a **variable.** A variable is generally denoted by $x, y, z,$ ......

A real valued function defined on the sample space of a random experiment is called a **random variable.** Thus, the values of a random variable are real numbers, connected with the outcomes of the experiment. In the experiment of toss of two coins, if we define the random variable (x) as the number of heads, then the values of the random variable x are 0, 1, 1, 2 corresponding to the outcomes TT, TH, HT, HH respectively. In case there are three coins, then the values of this random variable are 0, 1, 1, 1, 2, 2, 2, 3 corresponding to the outcomes TTT, TTH, THT, HTT, HHT, HTH, THH, HHH respectively.

We can define any number of rabdom variables on the same sample space.

If x denote the random variable, defined as the cube of the number of tails, in the random experiment of toss of two coins, than we have :

Sample points	HH	HT	TH	TT
x	$(0)^3 = 0$	$(1)^3 = 1$	$(1)^3 = 1$	$(2)^3 = 8$

A **discrete random variable** is a random variable which can take only finite number of values. For example, in the experiment of drawing three cards from a pack of playing cards, the random variable "no. of kings drawn" is a discrete random variable, taking 4 values 0, 1, 2, 3.

A **continuous random variable** is a random variable which can assume any value between certain limits.

3. PROBABILITY DISTRIBUTION OF DISCRETE RANDOM VARIABLE

Let x be a discrete random variable assuming values $x_1, x_2, x_3, \ldots.., x_n$ corresponding to various outcomes of a random experiment. If the probability of occurrence of $x = x_i$ is $P(x_i) = p_i$, $1 \leq i \leq n$ such that $p_1 + p_2 + p_3 + \ldots. + p_n = 1$, then the function, $P(x_i) = p_i$ is called the **probability function** of the random variable x and the set $\{P(x_1), P(x_2), P(x_3), \ldots.., P(x_n)\}$ is called the **probability distribution** of x.

Example 1. *Find the probability distribution of the discrete random variable "the number of sixes" in two tosses of a die.*

Sol. Let E be the event of getting 'six' in a throw of die.

∴ $P(E) = 1/6.$

Let x denote the discrete random variable *number of sixes.*

∴ x can take values 0, 1 and 2.

Now $P(x = 0) = P(\overline{E}_1\overline{E}_2) = P(\overline{E}_1)P(\overline{E}_2) = \frac{5}{6} \times \frac{5}{6} = \frac{25}{36}$

$P(x = 1) = P(E_1\overline{E}_2 \text{ or } \overline{E}_1 E_2) = P(E_1\overline{E}_2) + P(\overline{E}_1E_2)$

$= P(E_1)\,P(\overline{E}_2) + P(\overline{E}_1)\,P(E_2)$

$= \left(\frac{1}{6} \times \frac{5}{6}\right) + \left(\frac{5}{6} \times \frac{1}{6}\right) = \frac{10}{36} = \frac{5}{18}$

$P(x = 2) = P(E_1E_2) = P(E_1)P(E_2) = \frac{1}{6} \times \frac{1}{6} = \frac{1}{36}.$

∴ The required probability distribution is

x	0	1	2
$P(x)$	$\frac{25}{36}$	$\frac{5}{18}$	$\frac{1}{36}$

Example 2. *3 bad articles are mixed with 7 good ones. Find the probability distribution of the number of bad articles if 3 articles are drawn at random without replacement.*

Sol. Let x denote the discrete random variable *number of bad articles.*

∴ x can take values, 0, 1, 2, 3.

Now $P(x = 0) = P(\text{no bad article}) = \frac{^7C_3}{^{10}C_3} = \frac{7}{24}$

$P(x = 1) = P(\text{1 bad article}) = \frac{^3C_1 . ^7C_3}{^{10}C_3} = \frac{21}{40}$

$P(x = 2) = P(\text{2 bad articles}) = \frac{^3C_2 . ^7C_1}{^{10}C_3} = \frac{7}{40}$

$P(x = 3) = P(\text{all bad articles}) = \frac{^3C_3}{^{10}C_3} = \frac{1}{120}$

∴ The required probability distribution (P.D.) is

x	0	1	2	3
$P(x)$	$\frac{7}{24}$	$\frac{21}{40}$	$\frac{7}{40}$	$\frac{1}{120}$

Example 3. *A pair of unbiased dice is tossed. If the random variable x is the sum of two numbers obtained on two dice, find the probability distribution of x.*

Sol. Let S be the sample space of the experiment.

∴ S = {(1, 1), (1, 2), ..., (6, 5), (6, 6)}

The possible values of x are 2, 3, 4, ..., 12.

Now $P(x = 2) = P\{(1, 1)\} = 1/36$

$P(x = 3) = P\{(1, 2), (2, 1)\} = 2/36$

$P(x = 4) = P\{(1, 3), (2, 2), (3, 1)\} = 3/36$

$P(x = 5) = P\{(1, 4), (2, 3), (3, 2), (4, 1)\} = 4/36$

$P(x = 6) = P\{(1, 5), (2, 4), (3, 3), (4, 2), (5, 1)\} = 5/36$

$P(x = 7) = P\{(1, 6), (2, 5), (3, 4), (4, 3), (5, 2), (6, 1)\} = 6/36$

$P(x = 8) = P\{(2, 6), (3, 5), (4, 4), (5, 3), (6, 2)\} = 5/36$

$P(x = 9) = P\{(3, 6), (4, 5), (5, 4), (6, 3)\} = 4/36$

$P(x = 10) = P\{(4, 6), (5, 5), (6, 4)\} = 3/36$

$P(x = 11) = P\{(5, 6), (6, 5)\} = 2/36$

$P(x = 12) = P\{(6, 6)\} = 1/36.$

Also $$\sum_{i=2}^{12} P(x = x_i) = \frac{1}{36}+\frac{2}{36}+\frac{3}{36}+\frac{4}{36}+\frac{5}{36}+\frac{6}{36}+\frac{5}{36}+\frac{4}{36}+\frac{3}{36}+\frac{2}{36}+\frac{1}{36} = \frac{36}{36} = 1.$$

The required P.D. is

x	2	3	4	5	6	7	8	9	10	11	12
$P(x)$	$\frac{1}{36}$	$\frac{2}{36}$	$\frac{3}{36}$	$\frac{4}{36}$	$\frac{5}{36}$	$\frac{6}{36}$	$\frac{5}{36}$	$\frac{4}{36}$	$\frac{3}{36}$	$\frac{2}{36}$	$\frac{1}{36}$

Example 4. *Obtain the probablity distribution of the total number of heads occurring in three tosses of an unbiased coin.*

Sol. Let x denote the discrete random variable *number of heads*.

$\therefore$ The possible values of x are 0, 1, 2, 3.

Now $P(x = 0) = P(TTT) = P(T)\,P(T)\,P(T) = \frac{1}{2} \times \frac{1}{2} \times \frac{1}{2} = \frac{1}{8}$

$P(x = 1) = P(HTT \text{ or } THT \text{ or } TTH) = P(HTT) + P(THT) + P(TTH)$

$= P(H)\,P(T)\,P(T) + P(T)\,P(H)\,P(T) + P(T)\,P(T)\,P(H)$

$$= \left(\frac{1}{2}\times\frac{1}{2}\times\frac{1}{2}\right)+\left(\frac{1}{2}\times\frac{1}{2}\times\frac{1}{2}\right)+\left(\frac{1}{2}\times\frac{1}{2}\times\frac{1}{2}\right) = \frac{3}{8}$$

$P(x = 2) = P(HHT \text{ or } HTH \text{ or } THH) = P(HHT) + P(HTH) + P(THH)$

$= P(H)\,P(H)\,P(T) + P(H)\,P(T)\,P(H) + P(T)\,P(H)\,P(H)$

$= (\frac{1}{2}\times\frac{1}{2}\times\frac{1}{2})+(\frac{1}{2}\times\frac{1}{2}\times\frac{1}{2})+(\frac{1}{2}\times\frac{1}{2}\times\frac{1}{2}) = \frac{3}{8}.$

$P(x = 3) = P(HHH) = P(H)\,P(H)\,P(H) = \frac{1}{2}\times\frac{1}{2}\times\frac{1}{2} = \frac{1}{8}.$

Also $$\sum_{i=0}^{3} P(x = i) = \frac{1}{8}+\frac{3}{8}+\frac{3}{8}+\frac{1}{8} = 1.$$

$\therefore$ The required P.D. is

x	0	1	2	3
$P(x)$	1/8	3/8	3/8	1/8

Example 5. *Find the probability distribution of the number of doublets in four throws of a pair of dice.*

Sol. Let S be the sample space of the experiment.

$\therefore \quad S = \{(1, 1), (1, 2), \ldots\ldots, (6, 5), (6, 6)\}$

Let E be the event of getting a doublet in a throw of two dice

$\therefore \quad E = \{(1, 1), (2, 2), \ldots\ldots, (6, 6)\}$

$\therefore \quad P(E) = 6/36 = 1/6$

Let x denote the discrete random variable '*no. of doublets*' in four throws.

$\therefore$ The possible values of x are 0, 1, 2, 3, 4.

Now $P(x = 0) = P(\overline{E}_1 \overline{E}_2 \overline{E}_3 \overline{E}_4) = P(\overline{E}_1) P(\overline{E}_2) P(\overline{E}_3) P(\overline{E}_4)$

$$= \frac{5}{6} \times \frac{5}{6} \times \frac{5}{6} \times \frac{5}{6} = \frac{625}{1296}$$

$$P(x = 1) = P(E_1 \overline{E}_2 \overline{E}_3 \overline{E}_4 \text{ or } \overline{E}_1 E_2 \overline{E}_3 \overline{E}_4 \text{ or } \overline{E}_1 \overline{E}_2 E_3 \overline{E}_4 \text{ or } \overline{E}_1 \overline{E}_2 \overline{E}_3 E_4)$$

$$= \left(\frac{1}{6} \times \frac{5}{6} \times \frac{5}{6} \times \frac{5}{6}\right) + \left(\frac{5}{6} \times \frac{1}{6} \times \frac{5}{6} \times \frac{5}{6}\right) + \left(\frac{5}{6} \times \frac{5}{6} \times \frac{1}{6} \times \frac{5}{6}\right) + \left(\frac{5}{6} \times \frac{5}{6} \times \frac{5}{6} \times \frac{1}{6}\right)$$

$$= \frac{500}{1296}$$

$$P(x = 2) = P(E_1 E_2 \overline{E}_3 \overline{E}_4 \text{ or } \overline{E}_1 \overline{E}_2 E_3 E_4 \text{ or } \overline{E}_1 E_2 E_3 \overline{E}_4 \text{ or } E_1 \overline{E}_2 \overline{E}_3 E_4$$
$$\text{or } \overline{E}_1 E_2 \overline{E}_3 E_4 \text{ or } E_1 \overline{E}_2 E_3 \overline{E}_4)$$

$$= \left(\frac{1}{6} \times \frac{1}{6} \times \frac{5}{6} \times \frac{5}{6}\right) + \left(\frac{5}{6} \times \frac{5}{6} \times \frac{1}{6} \times \frac{1}{6}\right) + \left(\frac{5}{6} \times \frac{1}{6} \times \frac{1}{6} \times \frac{5}{6}\right)$$
$$+ \left(\frac{1}{6} \times \frac{5}{6} \times \frac{5}{6} \times \frac{1}{6}\right) + \left(\frac{5}{6} \times \frac{1}{6} \times \frac{5}{6} \times \frac{1}{6}\right) + \left(\frac{1}{6} \times \frac{5}{6} \times \frac{1}{6} \times \frac{5}{6}\right)$$

$$= \frac{150}{1296}$$

$$P(x = 3) = P(E_1 E_2 E_3 \overline{E}_4 \text{ or } E_1 E_2 \overline{E}_3 E_4 \text{ or } E_1 \overline{E}_2 E_3 E_4 \text{ or } \overline{E}_1 E_2 E_3 E_4)$$

$$= \left(\frac{1}{6} \times \frac{1}{6} \times \frac{1}{6} \times \frac{5}{6}\right) + \left(\frac{1}{6} \times \frac{1}{6} \times \frac{5}{6} \times \frac{1}{6}\right) + \left(\frac{1}{6} \times \frac{5}{6} \times \frac{1}{6} \times \frac{1}{6}\right) + \left(\frac{5}{6} \times \frac{1}{6} \times \frac{1}{6} \times \frac{1}{6}\right)$$

$$= \frac{20}{1296}$$

$$P(x = 4) = P(E_1 E_2 E_3 E_4) = P(E_1) P(E_2) P(E_3) P(E_4)$$

$$= \frac{1}{6} \times \frac{1}{6} \times \frac{1}{6} \times \frac{1}{6} = \frac{1}{1296}.$$

Also $\displaystyle\sum_{i=0}^{4} P(x = i) = \frac{625}{1296} + \frac{500}{1296} + \frac{150}{1296} + \frac{20}{1296} + \frac{1}{1296} = 1.$

$\therefore$ The required P.D. is

x	0	1	2	3	4
$P(x)$	$\frac{625}{1296}$	$\frac{500}{1296}$	$\frac{150}{1296}$	$\frac{20}{1296}$	$\frac{1}{1296}$

EXERCISE 1

1. Find the probability distribution of the number of heads in one throw of an unbiased coin.
2. Find the probability distribution of the number of heads in two throws of an unbiased coin.
3. Find the probability distribution of the number of tails in three throws of an unbiased coin.
4. Find the probability distribution of the number of sixes in a single throw of a die.
5. Find the probability distribution of the number of ones in a single throw of two dice.
6. Find the probability distribution of the number of sixes in a single throw of three dice.
7. Find the probability distribution of the number of sixes in a single throw of four dice.
8. Three cards are drawn with replacements from a pack of playing cards. Find the probability distribution of the number of spades in the cards drawn.
9. Three cards are drawn without replacements from a pack of playing cards. Find the probability distribution of the number of diamonds in the cards drawn.
10. Find the probability distribution of the number of boys in a family of three children.

Answers

1.

x (no. of heads)	0	1
$P(x)$	1/2	1/2

2.

x (no. of heads)	0	1	2
$P(x)$	1/4	1/2	1/4

3.

x (no. of tails)	0	1	2	3
$P(x)$	1/8	3/8	3/8	1/8

4.

x (no. of sixes)	0	1
$P(x)$	5/6	1/6

5.

x (no. of ones)	0	1	2
$P(x)$	$\frac{25}{36}$	$\frac{10}{36}$	$\frac{1}{36}$

6.

x (no. of sixes)	0	1	2	3
$P(x)$	$\frac{125}{216}$	$\frac{75}{216}$	$\frac{15}{216}$	$\frac{1}{216}$

7.

x (no. of sixes)	0	1	2	3	4
P(x)	$\frac{625}{1296}$	$\frac{500}{1296}$	$\frac{150}{1296}$	$\frac{20}{1296}$	$\frac{1}{1296}$

8.

x (no. of spades)	0	1	2	3
P(x)	$\frac{27}{64}$	$\frac{27}{64}$	$\frac{9}{64}$	$\frac{1}{64}$

9.

x (no. of diamonds)	0	1	2	3
P(x)	$\frac{703}{1700}$	$\frac{741}{1700}$	$\frac{234}{1700}$	$\frac{22}{1700}$

10.

x (no. of boys)	0	1	2	3
P(x)	1/8	3/8	3/8	1/8

4. MEAN AND VARIANCE OF A RANDOM VARIABLE

We know the method of finding the mean and variance of frequency distributions. In a frequency distribution, we have frequencies corresponding to different values of the variable. Similarly in a probability distribution, we have probabilities corresponding to different admissible values of the discrete random variable.

Now, we shall extend the idea of mean and variance for probability distributions.

Let x be a discrete random variable assuming values $x_1, x_2, \ldots, x_n$ with respective probabilities $p_1, p_2, \ldots, p_n$ with $p_1 + p_2 + \ldots + p_n = 1$.

We define, mean $(\mu) = \dfrac{\sum_{i=1}^{n} p_i x_i}{\sum_{i=1}^{n} p_i} = \sum_{i=1}^{n} p_i x_i$ $\qquad \left(\because \sum_{i=1}^{n} p_i = 1 \right)$

and variance $= \dfrac{\sum_{i=1}^{n} p_i (x_i - \mu)^2}{\sum_{i=1}^{n} p_i} = \sum_{i=1}^{n} p_i (x_i - \mu)^2$.

We have

$$\sum_{i=1}^{n} p_i (x_i - \mu)^2 = \sum_{i=1}^{n} p_i (x_i^2 + \mu^2 - 2\mu x_i)$$

$$= \sum_{i=1}^{n} p_i x_i^2 + \mu^2 \sum_{i=1}^{n} p_i - 2\mu \sum_{i=1}^{n} p_i x_i$$

$$= \sum_{i=1}^{n} p_i x_i^2 + \mu^2 . 1 - 2\mu.\mu = \sum_{i=1}^{n} p_i x_i^2 - \mu^2 .$$

$\therefore$ **Mean** $(\mu) = \sum_{i=1}^{n} p_i x_i$ and **variance** $(\sigma^2) = \sum_{i=1}^{n} p_i x_i^2 - \mu^2$.

In short, we write, $\mu = \Sigma px$ and variance $= \Sigma px^2 - \mu^2$.

The mean of random variable x is called the **expected value** of x and is denoted by $E(x)$. The mean and variance of a random variable are also referred to as the mean and variance of the corresponding P.D.

Remark 1. $E(x) = p_1x_1 + p_2x_2 + \ldots + p_nx_n$.

Remark 2. For the sake of simplicity, $\sum_{i=1}^{n} p_i x_i$ and $\sum_{i=1}^{n} p_i x_i^2$ are written in Σpx and Σpx^2 respectively.

Remark 3. S.D. of probability distribution $= \sqrt{\text{variance}} = \sqrt{\Sigma px^2 - \mu^2}$.

Example 1. *A die is tossed twice. A 'success' is 'getting an odd number' in a random toss. Find the expected value and variance of the number of successes.*

Sol. Let E be the event of getting a success *i.e.* of getting an odd number. On a die, odd numbers are 1, 3, 5.

$$P(E) = \frac{3}{6} = \frac{1}{2} \quad \text{and} \quad P(\overline{E}) = 1 - \frac{1}{2} = \frac{1}{2}.$$

Let x denote the random variable 'number of successes'

$\therefore$ The possible values of x are 0, 1, 2.

$$P(x = 0) = P(\overline{E}_1 \overline{E}_2) = P(\overline{E}_1)\,P(\overline{E}_2) = \frac{1}{2} \times \frac{1}{2} = \frac{1}{4}$$

$$P(x = 1) = P(E_1 \overline{E}_2 \text{ or } \overline{E}_1 E_2) = P(E_1 \overline{E}_2) + P(\overline{E}_1 E_2)$$

$$= P(E_1)\,P(\overline{E}_2) + P(\overline{E}_1)\,P(E_2) = \left(\frac{1}{2} \times \frac{1}{2}\right) + \left(\frac{1}{2} \times \frac{1}{2}\right) = \frac{1}{2}$$

$$P(x = 2) = P(E_1 E_2) = P(E_1)\,P(E_2) = \frac{1}{2} \times \frac{1}{2} = \frac{1}{4}.$$

Calculation of Mean and Variance

x	p	px	px^2
0	$\frac{1}{4}$	0	0
1	$\frac{1}{2}$	$\frac{1}{2}$	$\frac{1}{2}$
2	$\frac{1}{4}$	$\frac{1}{2}$	1
		$\Sigma px = 1$	$\Sigma px^2 = \frac{3}{2}$

$$E(x) = \text{Mean } (\mu) = \Sigma px = \mathbf{1}$$

Variance $= \Sigma px^2 - \mu^2 = \frac{3}{2} - (1)^2 = \mathbf{0.5}$.

Example 2. *Three urns contain respectively 3 green and 2 white balls, 5 green and 6 white balls and 2 green and 4 white balls. One ball is drawn from each urn. Find the expected value and variance of the probability distribution of the random variable "no. of white balls drawn".*

Sol. Let x denote the discrete random variable, '*no. of white ball drawn*'.

Urn I	Urn II	Urn III
3 Green 2 White	5 Green 6 White	2 Green 4 White

$\therefore$ The possible values of x are 0, 1, 2, 3. Let G_i, W_i be the events of drawing a green ball, white ball respectively from the urn i $(1 \le i \le 3)$.

Now $$P(x=0) = P(G_1G_2G_3) = P(G_1)P(G_2)P(G_3) = \frac{3}{5} \times \frac{5}{11} \times \frac{2}{6} = \frac{30}{330} = \frac{1}{11}.$$

$$P(x=1) = P(W_1G_2G_3 \text{ or } G_1W_2G_3 \text{ or } G_1G_2W_3)$$

$$= \left(\frac{2}{5} \times \frac{5}{11} \times \frac{2}{6}\right) + \left(\frac{3}{5} \times \frac{6}{11} \times \frac{2}{11}\right) + \left(\frac{3}{5} \times \frac{5}{11} \times \frac{4}{6}\right)$$

$$= \frac{20+36+36}{330} = \frac{116}{330} = \frac{58}{165}.$$

$$P(x=2) = P(W_1W_2G_3 \text{ or } W_1G_2W_3 \text{ or } G_1W_2W_3)$$

$$= \left(\frac{2}{5} \times \frac{6}{11} \times \frac{2}{6}\right) + \left(\frac{2}{5} \times \frac{5}{11} \times \frac{4}{6}\right) + \left(\frac{3}{5} + \frac{6}{11} + \frac{4}{6}\right)$$

$$= \frac{24+40+720}{330} = \frac{136}{330} = \frac{68}{165}.$$

$$P(x=3) = P(W_1W_2W_3) = \frac{2}{5} \times \frac{6}{11} \times \frac{4}{6} = \frac{48}{330}\ \frac{8}{55}.$$

$\therefore$ The P.D. is

x	0	1	2	3
$P(x)$	$\frac{1}{11}$	$\frac{58}{165}$	$\frac{68}{165}$	$\frac{8}{55}$

Calculation of Mean and Variance

x	$p = P(x)$	px	px^2
0	$\frac{30}{330}$	0	0
1	$\frac{116}{330}$	$\frac{116}{330}$	$\frac{116}{330}$
2	$\frac{136}{330}$	$\frac{272}{330}$	$\frac{544}{330}$
3	$\frac{48}{330}$	$\frac{144}{330}$	$\frac{432}{330}$
Total		$\frac{532}{330}$	$\frac{1092}{330}$

Now, expected value of x $= E(x) = \Sigma px = \dfrac{532}{330} = \mathbf{1.6121}$

Variance $= \Sigma px^2 - (\text{mean})^2$

$= \dfrac{1092}{330} - (1.6121)^2 = \mathbf{0.7102.}$

Example 3. *Two unbiased dice are thrown. Find the expected value and S.D. of the probability distribution of the random variable "sum of numbers on the dice".*

Sol. Let x denote the random variable '*sum of numbers on the dice*'.

We have already studied the probability distribution of the discrete random variable x.

Calculate of Mean and S.D.

x	p	px	px^2
2	$\frac{1}{36}$	$\frac{2}{36}$	$\frac{4}{36}$
3	$\frac{2}{36}$	$\frac{6}{36}$	$\frac{18}{36}$
4	$\frac{3}{36}$	$\frac{12}{36}$	$\frac{48}{36}$
5	$\frac{4}{36}$	$\frac{20}{36}$	$\frac{100}{36}$
6	$\frac{5}{36}$	$\frac{30}{36}$	$\frac{180}{36}$
7	$\frac{6}{36}$	$\frac{42}{36}$	$\frac{294}{36}$
8	$\frac{5}{36}$	$\frac{40}{36}$	$\frac{320}{36}$
9	$\frac{4}{36}$	$\frac{36}{36}$	$\frac{324}{36}$
10	$\frac{3}{36}$	$\frac{30}{36}$	$\frac{300}{36}$
11	$\frac{2}{36}$	$\frac{22}{36}$	$\frac{242}{36}$
12	$\frac{1}{36}$	$\frac{12}{36}$	$\frac{144}{36}$
Total		$\frac{252}{36}$	$\frac{1974}{36}$

Now, expected value of $x = \Sigma px = \dfrac{252}{36} = \mathbf{7}$

$$\text{S.D.} = \sqrt{\Sigma px^2 - (\text{mean})^2} = \sqrt{\frac{1974}{36} - (7)^2} = \mathbf{2.4152.}$$

Example 4. *Five defective articles are mixed with twenty good ones. Four articles are drawn simultaneously at random. Find the mean and S.D. of the defective articles drawn.*

Sol. Let x denote the discrete random variable *no. of defective articles drawn.*

∴ The possible values of x are 0, 1, 2, 3, 4.

Now

$$P(x = 0) = \frac{^{20}C_4}{^{15}C_4} = 0.3830$$

$$P(x = 1) = \frac{^{5}C_1 \times {}^{20}C_3}{^{25}C_4} = 0.4506$$

$$P(x = 2) = \frac{^{5}C_2 \times {}^{20}C_2}{^{25}C_4} = 0.1502$$

$$P(x = 3) = \frac{^{5}C_3 \times {}^{20}C_1}{^{25}C_4} = 0.0158$$

$$P(x = 4) = \frac{^{5}C_4}{^{25}C_4} = 0.0004.$$

∴ The P.D. is

x	0	1	2	3	4
$P(x)$	0.3830	0.4506	0.1502	0.0158	0.0004

Calculation of Mean and S.D.

x	p	px	px^2
0	0.3830	0	0
1	0.4506	0.4506	0.4506
2	0.1502	0.3004	0.6008
3	0.0158	0.0474	0.1422
4	0.0004	0.0016	0.0064
Total		0.8	1.2

Now, mean $= \Sigma px = \mathbf{0.8}$

$$\text{S.D.} = \sqrt{\Sigma px^2 - (\text{mean})^2}$$

$$= \sqrt{1.2 - (0.8)^2} = \mathbf{0.7483.}$$

EXERCISE 2

1. Two urns contain 5 black and 4 white balls and 4 black and 5 white balls. One ball is drawn from each urn. Find the expected value and variance of the probability distribution of the random variable "no. of white balls drawn".
2. Find the S.D. of probability distribution of the number of aces drawn, when a draw of 2 cards, one at a time, is made with replacement.
3. Find the S.D. of probability distribution of the number of aces drawn, when a draw of 2 cards, one at a time, is made without replacement.

4. **Three defective pencils are mixed with ten good ones. Two pencils are drawn simultaneously at random. Find the expected value of defective pencils drawn.**

5. **A draw of 3 balls is made from an urn containing 7 red and 6 black balls. Find the S.D. of the probability distribution of the discrete random variable "no.of black balls drawn".**

Answers

1. 1, 0.4938 **2.** 0.3768 **3.** 0.3730 **4.** 0.4616

5. 0.7882.

17

Probability Distributions

(Binomial, Poisson, Normal Distributions)

1. INTRODUCTION

We know that a real valued function defined on the sample space of a random experiment is called a *random variable*. A random variable is either discrete or continuous.

Let x be a discrete random variable assuming values $x_1, x_2, x_3, \ldots, x_n$ corresponding to the various outcomes of a random experiment. If the probability of occurrence of $x = x_i$ is $P(x_i) = p_i$, $1 \le i \le n$ such that $p_1 + p_2 + p_3 + \ldots + p_n = 1$, then the function, $P(x_i) = p_i, 1 \le i \le n$ is called the *probability function* of the random variable x and the set $\{P(x_1), P(x_2), P(x_3), \ldots, P(x_n)\}$ is called the *probability distribution* of x.

2. EMPIRICAL DISTRIBUTION

Let x be a discrete random variable assuming values $x_1, x_2, \ldots, x_n$ corresponding to various outcomes of a random experiment. Let this random experiment be repeated N times. Let the random variable x take values $x_1, x_2, \ldots, x_n$ with respective frequencies $f_1, f_2, \ldots, f_n$ where $f_1 + f_2 + \ldots, + f_n = N$.

The distribution

x	x_1	x_2	....	x_n
f	f_1	f_2	....	f_n

is called an **empirical distribution.**

Illustration. Let the random experiment be of tossing of two coins.

∴ S = {HH, HT, TH, TT}.

Let x be random variable "square of number of tails," then x takes the values $0^2 = 0$, $1^2 = 1$, $2^2 = 4$. Let this random experiment be repeated 100 times and let the observed frequencies be as follows :

HH	HT	TH	TT
↓	↓	↓	↓
24	27	23	26

∴ The empirical distribution corresponding to above experiment is

x	0 (HH)	1 (HT, TH)	4 (TT)
f	24	50 (= 27 + 23)	26

Now we shall consider three very important types of probability distributions.

BINOMIAL DISTRIBUTION

3. INTRODUCTION

The binomial distribution is a particular type of probability distribution. This was discovered by **James Bernoulli (1654—1705)** in the year 1700. This distribution mainly deals with attributes. An attribute is either present or absent with respect to elements of a population. For example, if a coin is tossed, we get either *head* or *tail*. The workers of a factory may be classified as *skilled* and *unskilled*. An item of a population of articles produced in a firm may be either defective or non-defective.

4. CONDITIONS *(KU 2000 C, MDU 2004)*

The following conditions are essential for the applicability of binomial distribution :

(*i*) **The random experiment is performed for a finite and fixed number of trials.** If in an experiment, a coin is tossed repeatedly or a ball is drawn from an urn repeatedly, then each toss or draw is called a **trial.** For example, if a coin is tossed 6 times, then this experiment has 6 trials. The number of trials is an experiment is generally denoted by 'n'.

(*ii*) **The trials are independent.** By this we mean that the result of a particular trial is not going to effect the result of any other trial. For example, if a coin is tossed or a die is thrown, the trials would be independent. If from a pack of playing cards, some draws of one card are made without replacing the cards, then the trials would not be independent. But if the card drawn is replaced before the next draw, then the trials would be independent.

(*iii*) **Each trial must result in either "success" or "failure".** In other words, in every trial, there should be only two possible outcomes *i.e., success* or *failure*. For example, if a coin is tossed, then either *head* or *tail* is observed. Similarly, if an item is examined, it is either *defective* or *non-defective.*

(*iv*) **The probability of success in each trial is same.** In other words, this condition requires that the probability of *success* should not change in different trials. For example, if a sample of two items is drawn, then the probability of exactly one being defective will be constant in different trials provided the items are replaced before the next draw.

5. BINOMIAL VARIABLE

A random variable which counts the number of successes in a random experiment with trials satisfying above four conditions is called a **binomial variable.**

For example, if a coin is tossed 5 times and the event of getting head is *success*, then the possible values of the binomial variable are 0, 1, 2, 3, 4, 5. This is so, because, the minimum number of successes is 0 and maximum number is 5.

6. BINOMIAL PROBABILITY FUNCTION

When a fair coin is tossed, we have only two possibilities : head and tail. Let us call the occurrence of head as 'success'. Therefore, the occurrence of tail would be a 'failure'. Let this coin be tossed 5 times. Suppose we are interested in finding the probability of getting 4 heads and 1 tail *i.e.*, of getting 4 successes. If S and F denote 'success' and 'failure' in a trial respectively, then there are ${}^5C_4 = 5$ ways of having 4 successes.

These are : SSSSF, SSSFS, SSFSS, SFSSS, FSSSS.

The probability of getting 4 successes in each case is $\left(\frac{1}{2}\right)^4\left(\frac{1}{2}\right)$, because the trials are independent.

∴ By using *addition theorem,* the required probability of having 4 successes is $^5C_4\left(\frac{1}{2}\right)^4\left(\frac{1}{2}\right)$, which is equal to $\frac{5}{32}$. Now we shall generalise this method of finding the probabilities for different values of *binomial variables.*

Let a random experiment satisfying the conditions of **binomial distribution** be performed. Let the number of trials in the experiment be n. Let p denote the probability of *success* in any trial.

∴ Probability of failure, $q = 1 - p$

Let x denote the binomial variable corresponding to this experiment.

∴ The possible values of x are 0, 1, 2, ..., n.

If there are r successes in n trials, then there would be $n - r$ failures. One of the ways in which r successes may occur is

$$\underbrace{SS\ldots\ldots SS}_{r \text{ times}}\ \underbrace{FF\ldots\ldots F}_{n-r \text{ times}}$$

where S and F denote success and failure in trials.

Now, P(SS ...... SFF ...... F) = P(S)P(S) ...... P(S)P(F)P(F) ...... P(F)

(∵ the trials are independent)

$$= p.p \ldots\ldots p.q.q \ldots\ldots q = p^r q^{n-r}.$$

We know that ^nC_r is the number of combinations of n things taking r at a time. Therefore, the number of ways in which r successes can occur in n trials is equal to the number of ways of choosing r trials (for successes) out of total n trials *i.e.*, it is ^nC_r Therefore, there are ^nC_r ways in which we get r successes and $n - r$ failures and the probability of occurrence of each of these ways is $p^r q^{n-r}$. Hence the probability of r successes in n trials in any order is

$$P(x = r) = p^r q^{n-r} + p^r q^{n-r} + \ldots\ldots\ ^nC_r \text{ terms} \qquad \text{(By addition theorem)}$$

or $$\mathbf{P(x = r) = {}^nC_r p^r q^{n-r},\ 0 \le r \le n.}$$

This is called the **binomial probability function.** The corresponding **binomial distribution** is

x	0	1	2	....	n
$P(x)$	$^nC_0 p^0 q^n$	$^nC_1 p^1 q^{n-1}$	$^nC_2 p^2 q^{n-2}$	....	$^nC_n p^n q^0$

The probabilities of 0 success, 1 success, 2 successes, ..., n successes are respectively the 1st, 2nd, 3rd, ..., $(n + 1)$th terms in the binomial expansion of $(q + p)^n$. This is why, it is called **binomial distribution.**

7. BINOMIAL FREQUENCY DISTRIBUTION

If a random experiment, satisfying the requirements of binomial distribution, is repeated N times, then the expected frequency of getting r $(0 \le r \le n)$ successes is given by

$$\mathbf{N.P(x = r) = N.{}^nC_r p^r q^{n-r},\ \ 0 \le r \le n.}$$

The *frequencies* of getting 0 success, 1 success, 2 successes, ..., n successes are respectively the 1st, 2nd, 3rd, ..., $(n + 1)$th terms in the expansion of $N(q + p)^n$.

Example 1. *An unbiased coin is tossed six times. Find the probability of obtaining :*

(i) no head (KU 2000 C) *(ii) all heads* (KU 2000 C)

(iii) at least one head i.e., one or more heads (KU 2000 C)

(iv) exactly 4 heads *(v) less than 3 heads*

(vi) more than 4 heads *(vii) more than 4 and less than 6 heads*

(viii) more than 6 heads.

Sol. Let p be the probability of success *i.e.,* of getting head in the toss of the coin.

$$\therefore \quad n = 6, p = \frac{1}{2} \quad \text{and} \quad q = 1 - p = 1 - \frac{1}{2} = \frac{1}{2}.$$

Let x be the binomial variable **'no. of successes'.**

By **Binomial distribution**, $P(x = r) = {}^nC_r p^r q^{n-r}, \quad 0 \le r \le n.$

$$\therefore \quad P(x = r) = {}^6C_r \left(\frac{1}{2}\right)^r \left(\frac{1}{2}\right)^{6-r} = {}^6C_r \left(\frac{1}{2}\right)^6 = {}^6C_r \frac{1}{64}, \quad 0 \le r \le n.$$

(i) $P(\text{no head}) = P(x = 0) = {}^6C_0 \frac{1}{64} = \mathbf{\frac{1}{64}}$

(ii) $P(\text{all heads}) = P(x = 6) = {}^6C_6 \frac{1}{64} = \mathbf{\frac{1}{64}}$

(iii) $P(\text{at least one head}) = 1 - P(\text{no head}) = 1 - \frac{1}{64} = \mathbf{\frac{63}{64}}$ [Using part (*i*)]

(iv) $P(\text{exactly 4 heads}) = P(x = 4) = {}^6C_4 \frac{1}{64} = \mathbf{\frac{15}{64}}$

(v) $P(\text{less than 3 heads}) = P(x < 3) = P(x = 0 \text{ or } 1 \text{ or } 2)$

$$= P(x = 0) + P(x = 1) + P(x = 2)$$

$$= {}^6C_0 \frac{1}{64} + {}^6C_1 \frac{1}{64} + {}^6C_2 \frac{1}{64}$$

$$= (1 + 6 + 15) \frac{1}{64} = \frac{22}{64} = \mathbf{\frac{11}{32}}$$

(vi) P(more than 4 heads)

$$= P(x > 4) = P(x = 5 \text{ or } 6) = P(x = 5) + P(x = 6)$$

$$= {}^6C_5 \frac{1}{64} + {}^6C_6 \frac{1}{64} = (6 + 1)\frac{1}{64} = \mathbf{\frac{7}{64}}$$

(vii) P(more than 4 heads and less than 6 heads)

$$= P(4 < x < 6) = P(x = 5) = {}^6C_5 \frac{1}{64} = \frac{6}{64} = \mathbf{\frac{3}{32}}.$$

(viii) $P(\text{more than 6 heads}) = P(x > 6) = \mathbf{0}.$ ($\because$ The event is impossible)

Example 2. *A die is thrown 4 times. Getting a number greater than 2 is a success. Find the probability of getting (i) exactly 1 success (ii) less than 3 successes (iii) more than 3 successes.*

Sol. Let p be the probability of success *i.e.*, of getting number greater than 2 in the throw of a die.

$$\therefore \quad n = 4,\ p = \frac{4}{6} = \frac{2}{3} \quad \text{and} \quad q = 1 - p = 1 - \frac{2}{3} = \frac{1}{3}.$$

Let x be the binomial variable "*no. of successes*".

By **Binomial distribution**, $P(x = r) = {}^nC_r\, p^r q^{n-r},\ 0 \le r \le n.$

$$\therefore \quad P(x = r) = {}^4C_r \left(\frac{2}{3}\right)^r \left(\frac{1}{3}\right)^{4-r},\ 0 \le r \le 4.$$

(*i*) P(exactly 1 success) = $P(x = 1)$

$$= {}^4C_1 \left(\frac{2}{3}\right)^1 \left(\frac{1}{3}\right)^{4-1} = 4 \times \frac{2}{3} \times \frac{1}{27} = \frac{8}{81}.$$

(*ii*) P(less than 3 successes) = $P(x < 3)$

$$= P(x = 0 \text{ or } x = 1 \text{ or } x = 2)$$

$$= P(x = 0) + P(x = 1) + P(x = 2) \qquad \text{(Addition theorem for m.e. events)}$$

$$= {}^4C_0 \left(\frac{2}{3}\right)^0 \left(\frac{1}{3}\right)^{4-0} + {}^4C_1 \left(\frac{2}{3}\right)^1 \left(\frac{1}{3}\right)^{4-1} + {}^4C_2 \left(\frac{2}{3}\right)^2 \left(\frac{1}{3}\right)^{4-2}$$

$$= \left(1 \times 1 \times \frac{1}{81}\right) + \left(4 \times \frac{2}{3} \times \frac{1}{27}\right) + \left(6 \times \frac{4}{9} \times \frac{1}{9}\right)$$

$$= \frac{1 + 8 + 24}{81} = \frac{33}{81}.$$

(*iii*) P(more than 3 successes) = $P(x > 3)$

$$= P(x = 4) = {}^4C_4 (\tfrac{2}{3})^4 (\tfrac{1}{3})^0 = 1 \times \frac{16}{81} \times 1 = \frac{16}{81}.$$

Example 3. *The probability of a bomb hitting a target is 1/5. It is known that the attack of 2 bombs is sufficient to destroy a bridge. If 6 bombs are targetted at the bridge, find the probability of the bridge being destroyed.* (KU 1995, 2002 C, 2005 C ; MDU 1995, 2003)

Sol. Let p be the probability of success *i.e.*, a bomb hitting the bridge.

$$\therefore \quad n = 6,\ p = \frac{1}{5} \quad \text{and} \quad q = 1 - p = 1 - \frac{1}{5} = \frac{4}{5}.$$

Let x be the binomial variable "*no. of successes*".

By **Binomial distribution**, $P(x = r) = {}^nC_r\, p^r q^{n-r},\ 0 \le r \le n.$

$$\therefore \quad P(x = r) = {}^6C_r \left(\frac{1}{5}\right)^r \left(\frac{4}{5}\right)^{6-r},\ 0 \le r \le 6.$$

Now, P(the bridge is destroyed) = $P(x \ge 2) = 1 - P(x < 2)$

$$= 1 - \{P(x = 0) + P(x = 1)\}$$

$$= 1 - \left\{ {}^6C_0 \left(\frac{1}{5}\right)^0 \left(\frac{4}{5}\right)^6 + {}^6C_1 \left(\frac{1}{5}\right)^1 \left(\frac{4}{5}\right)^5 \right\}$$

$$= 1 - \left\{ \frac{4096}{15625} + \frac{6144}{15625} \right\} = \frac{5385}{15625} = \mathbf{0.3446}.$$

Example 4. *There are 20% chances for a worker of an industry to suffer from an occupational disease. 50 workers were selected at random and examined for the occupational disease. Find the probability that (i) only one worker is found suffering from the disease ; (ii) more than 3 are suffering from the disease ; (iii) none is suffering from the disease.*

Sol. Let p be the probability of success *i.e.*, a worker is suffering from disease.

$$\therefore \qquad n = 50, p = \frac{20}{100} = \frac{1}{5} \quad \text{and} \quad q = 1 - p = 1 - \frac{1}{5} = \frac{1}{4}.$$

Let x be the binomial variable, "*no. of successes*".

By **Binomial distribution,** $P(x = r) = {}^nC_r p^r q^{n-r}, 0 \le r \le n.$

$$\therefore \qquad P(x = r) = {}^{50}C_r \left(\frac{1}{5}\right)^r \left(\frac{4}{5}\right)^{50-r}, 0 \le r \le 50.$$

(*i*) P(only one is suffering) = $P(x = 1)$

$$= {}^{50}C_1 \left(\frac{1}{5}\right)^1 \left(\frac{4}{5}\right)^{49} = 50 \times \frac{1}{5} \times \left(\frac{4}{5}\right)^{49} = \mathbf{10\left(\frac{4}{5}\right)^{49}}.$$

(*ii*) P(more than 3 are suffering) = $P(x > 3) = 1 - P(x \le 3)$

$$= 1 - P(x = 0 \text{ or } x = 1 \text{ or } x = 2 \text{ or } x = 3)$$

$$= 1 - \{P(x = 0) + P(x = 1) + P(x = 2) + P(x = 3)\}$$

$$= 1 - \left\{ {}^{50}C_0 \left(\frac{1}{5}\right)^0 \left(\frac{4}{5}\right)^{50} + {}^{50}C_1 \left(\frac{1}{5}\right)^1 \left(\frac{4}{5}\right)^{49} + {}^{50}C_2 \left(\frac{1}{5}\right)^2 \left(\frac{4}{5}\right)^{48} + {}^{50}C_3 \left(\frac{1}{5}\right)^3 \left(\frac{4}{5}\right)^{47} \right\}$$

$$= 1 - \left\{ 1 \times 1 \times \left(\frac{4}{5}\right)^{50} + 50 \times \frac{1}{5} \times \left(\frac{4}{5}\right)^{49} \right.$$

$$\left. + \left(\frac{50 \times 49}{1 \times 2}\right) \times \left(\frac{1}{5}\right)^2 \times \left(\frac{4}{5}\right)^{48} + \left(\frac{50 \times 49 \times 48}{1 \times 2 \times 3}\right) \times \left(\frac{1}{5}\right)^3 \times \left(\frac{4}{5}\right)^{47} \right\}$$

$$= 1 - \frac{4^{47}}{5^{50}} \{64 + (50 \times 16) + (1225 \times 4) + (19600 \times 1)\} = \mathbf{1 - \left(\frac{4^{47}}{5^{50}} \times 25364\right)}.$$

(*iii*) P(none is suffering) = $P(x = 0)$

$$= {}^{50}C_0 \left(\frac{1}{5}\right)^0 \left(\frac{4}{5}\right)^{50} = 1 \times 1 \times \left(\frac{4}{5}\right)^{50} = \left(\frac{4}{5}\right)^{50}.$$

Example 5. *Assuming that half the population is vegetarian so that the chance of an individual being a vegetarian is* $\frac{1}{2}$ *and assuming that 100 investigators can take samples of 10 individuals to see whether they are vegetarian, how many investigators would you expect to report that three persons or less were vegetarian.*

Sol. Let p be the probability of success *i.e.*, an individual is vegetarian.

$$\therefore \qquad n = 10, N = 100, p = \frac{1}{2} \text{ and } q = 1 - p = 1 - \frac{1}{2} = \frac{1}{2}.$$

Let x be the binomial variable, '*no. of successes*'.

By **Binomial distribution,** $P(x = r) = {}^nC_r p^r q^{n-r}$, $0 \le r \le n$.

$$\therefore \quad P(x = r) = {}^{10}C_r \left(\frac{1}{2}\right)^r \left(\frac{1}{2}\right)^{10-r} = {}^{10}C_r \left(\frac{1}{2}\right)^{10} = {}^{10}C_r \frac{1}{1024}, \ 0 \le r \le 10.$$

Now, P(3 or less vegetarian) = $P(x \le 3)$

$$= P(x = 0) + P(x = 1) + P(x = 2) + P(x = 3)$$

$$= {}^{10}C_0 \frac{1}{1024} + {}^{10}C_1 \frac{1}{1024} + {}^{10}C_2 \frac{1}{1024} + {}^{10}C_3 \frac{1}{1024}$$

$$= (1 + 10 + 45 + 120) \frac{1}{1024} = \frac{176}{1024} = 0.1719.$$

$\therefore$ No. of investigators expected to report 3 or less vegetarians in their samples $= 100\ (0.1719) = 17.19 \simeq$ **17.**

Example 6. *There are 64 beds in a garden and 3 seeds of a particular type of flower are sown in each bed. The probability of a flower being white is 1/4. Find the number of beds with 3, 2, 1 and 0 white flowers.*

Sol. Let p be the probability of success *i.e.*, the flower is white.

$$\therefore \quad n = 3, N = 64, p = \frac{1}{4}, q = 1 - p = 1 - \frac{1}{4} = \frac{3}{4}.$$

Let x be the binomial variable, '*no. of successes*'.

By **Binomial distribution,** $P(x = r) = {}^nC_r p^r q^{n-r}$, $0 \le r \le n$.

$$\therefore \quad P(x = r) = {}^3C_r \left(\frac{1}{4}\right)^r \left(\frac{3}{4}\right)^{3-r}, \ 0 \le r \le 3.$$

$$\therefore \quad \text{P(3 white flowers)} = P(x = 3) = {}^3C_3 \left(\frac{1}{4}\right)^3 \left(\frac{3}{4}\right)^0 = \frac{1}{64}$$

$$\text{P(2 white flowers)} = P(x = 2) = {}^3C_2 \left(\frac{1}{4}\right)^2 \left(\frac{3}{4}\right)^1 = \frac{9}{64}$$

$$\text{P(1 white flower)} = P(x = 1) = {}^3C_1 \left(\frac{1}{4}\right)^1 \left(\frac{3}{4}\right)^2 = \frac{27}{64}$$

$$\text{P(no white flower)} = P(x = 0) = {}^3C_0 \left(\frac{1}{4}\right)^0 \left(\frac{3}{4}\right)^3 = \frac{27}{64}.$$

$\therefore$ Number of beds with 3 white flowers

$$= 64 \times P(x = 3) = 64 \times \frac{1}{64} = \mathbf{1}$$

Number of beds with 2 white flowers

$$= 64 \times P(x = 2) = 64 \times \frac{9}{64} = \mathbf{9}$$

Number of beds with 1 white flower

$$= 64 \times P(x = 1) = 64 \times \frac{27}{64} = \mathbf{27}$$

Number of beds with no white flower

$$= 64 \times P(x = 0) = 64 \times \frac{27}{64} = \mathbf{27}.$$

Example 7. *An irregular six faced die is thrown and the probability that in 10 throws it will give five even numbers is twice the probability that it will give four even numbers. How many times in 10,000 sets of 10 throws, would you expect to give no even number.*

Sol. Let the event of getting an even number in a single throw of die be the 'success' of the experiment.

Let probability of success = p

$\therefore$ Probability of failure, $q = 1 - p$

Let x denote the number of successes in the experiment. The possible values of x are 0, 1, 2, ..., 10.

By **Binomial distribution,** $P(x = r) = {}^{10}C_r p^r q^{10-r}, 0 \le r \le 10$.

By the given condition,

$$P(x = 5) = 2.\ P(x = 4)$$

$$\therefore \quad {}^{10}C_5 p^5 q^5 = 2 \times {}^{10}C_4 p^4 q^6$$

$$\therefore \quad \frac{10.9.8.7.6}{1.2.3.4.5} p = 2 \times \frac{10.9.8.7}{1.2.3.4} q$$

$$\Rightarrow \quad p = \frac{5}{3} q \quad \Rightarrow \quad p = \frac{5}{3}(1-p)$$

$$\Rightarrow \quad p = \frac{5}{8} \quad \text{and} \quad q = 1 - \frac{5}{8} = \frac{3}{8}.$$

$\therefore$ No. of times no even number is excepted out of 10,000 sets of 10 throws

$$= 10,000 \times P(x = 0)$$

$$= 10,000\ {}^{10}C_0 \left(\frac{5}{8}\right)^0 \left(\frac{3}{8}\right)^{10} = 0.549 \simeq \mathbf{1}.$$

Example 8. *In an experiment, a fair die is thrown 6 times. The event of occurring number greater than 4 is the 'success' of the experiment. Find the Binomial distribution of the experiment. If the same experiment is repeated 3645 times, find also the Binomial frequency distribution.*

Sol. Let p be the probability of success *i.e.,* of getting number greater than 4

$$\therefore \quad n = 6, p = \frac{2}{6} = \frac{1}{3} \text{ and } q = 1 - p = 1 - \frac{1}{3} = \frac{2}{3}.$$

Let x be the binomial variable, "*no. of successes*".

By **Binomial distribution,** $P(x = r) = {}^nC_r p^r q^{n-r}, 0 \le r \le n$.

$$\therefore \quad P(x = r) = {}^6C_r \left(\frac{1}{3}\right)^r \left(\frac{2}{3}\right)^{6-r}, 0 \le r \le 6.$$

Now

$$P(x = 0) = {}^6C_0 \left(\frac{1}{3}\right)^0 \left(\frac{2}{3}\right)^6 = 1 \times 1 \times \frac{64}{729} = \frac{64}{729}$$

$$P(x = 1) = {}^6C_1 \left(\frac{1}{3}\right)^1 \left(\frac{2}{3}\right)^5 = 6 \times \frac{1}{3} \times \frac{32}{243} = \frac{192}{729}$$

$$P(x = 2) = {}^6C_2 \left(\frac{1}{3}\right)^2 \left(\frac{2}{3}\right)^4 = 15 \times \frac{1}{9} \times \frac{16}{81} = \frac{240}{729}$$

$$P(x=3) = {}^6C_3 \left(\frac{1}{3}\right)^3 \left(\frac{2}{3}\right)^3 = 20 \times \frac{1}{27} \times \frac{8}{27} = \frac{160}{729}$$

$$P(x=4) = {}^6C_4 \left(\frac{1}{3}\right)^4 \left(\frac{2}{3}\right)^2 = 15 \times \frac{1}{81} \times \frac{4}{9} = \frac{60}{729}$$

$$P(x=5) = {}^6C_5 \left(\frac{1}{3}\right)^5 \left(\frac{2}{3}\right)^1 = 6 \times \frac{1}{243} \times \frac{2}{3} = \frac{12}{729}$$

$$P(x=6) = {}^6C_6 \left(\frac{1}{3}\right)^6 \left(\frac{2}{3}\right)^0 = 1 \times \frac{1}{729} \times 1 = \frac{1}{729}.$$

∴ The required distributions are as follows :

Binomial Distribution		*Binomial Frequency Distribution*	
x	$P(x)$	x	$N.\ P(x) = 3645 \times P(x)$
0	$\frac{64}{729}$	0	$3645 \times \frac{64}{729} = 320$
1	$\frac{192}{729}$	1	$3645 \times \frac{192}{729} = 960$
2	$\frac{240}{729}$	2	$3645 \times \frac{240}{729} = 1200$
3	$\frac{160}{729}$	3	$3645 \times \frac{160}{729} = 800$
4	$\frac{60}{729}$	4	$3645 \times \frac{60}{729} = 300$
5	$\frac{12}{729}$	5	$3645 \times \frac{12}{729} = 60$
6	$\frac{1}{729}$	6	$3645 \times \frac{1}{729} = 5$

Example 9. *The probability of a man hitting a target is* $\frac{1}{4}$. *If he fires 7 times, what is the probability of his hitting the target at least twice ? How many least number of times must he fire so that the probability of his hitting at least once is greater than* $\frac{2}{3}$.

Sol. Let p be the probability of success *i.e.*, the man hitting the target.

$$\therefore \quad n = 7, p = \frac{1}{4} \quad \text{and} \quad q = 1 - p = 1 - \frac{1}{4} = \frac{3}{4}.$$

Let x be the binomial variable, "*no. of successes*".

By **Binomial distribution,** $P(x = r) = {}^nC_r p^r q^{n-r}$, $0 \le r \le n$.

$$\therefore \quad P(x = r) = {}^7C_r \left(\frac{1}{4}\right)^r \left(\frac{3}{4}\right)^{7-r}, \ 0 \le r \le 7.$$

(*i*) P(hitting at least twice) = $P(x \ge 2) = 1 - P(x < 2)$

$$= 1 - P(x = 0 \text{ or } x = 1) = 1 - \{P(x = 0) + P(x = 1)\}$$

$$= 1 - \left\{ {}^7C_0 \left(\frac{1}{4}\right)^0 \left(\frac{3}{4}\right)^7 + {}^7C_1 \left(\frac{1}{4}\right)^1 \left(\frac{3}{4}\right)^6 \right\}$$

$$= 1 - \left\{1 \times 1 \times \left(\frac{3}{4}\right)^7 + 7 \times \frac{1}{4} \times \left(\frac{3}{4}\right)^6\right\} = \mathbf{0.5551}.$$

(*ii*) Let n be the number of times, the should fire so that the probability of hitting the target at least once is greater than $\frac{2}{3}$.

In this case, $P(x = r) = {}^nC_r \left(\frac{1}{4}\right)^r \left(\frac{3}{4}\right)^{n-r}$, $0 \le r \le n$.

By the given condition,

$$P(x \ge 1) > \frac{2}{3} \quad \Rightarrow \quad 1 - P(x = 0) > \frac{2}{3}$$

$$\Rightarrow \quad 1 - {}^nC_0 \left(\frac{1}{4}\right)^0 \left(\frac{3}{4}\right)^n > \frac{2}{3} \quad \Rightarrow \quad 1 - \left(\frac{3}{4}\right)^n > \frac{2}{3} \text{ or } \left(\frac{3}{4}\right)^n < \frac{1}{3}$$

This inequility holds if $n \ge 4$.

$\therefore \qquad n = 4.$

EXERCISE 1

1. If a coin is tossed six times, what is the probability of obtaining four or more heads ? *(MDU 2004)*
2. If a die is thrown 6 times and getting either 5 or 6 is considered a success. Obtain the probability of getting 0, 1, 2, 3, 4, 5, 6 successes.
3. An unbiased coin is tossed 8 times. Find the probability of obtaining (*i*) exactly 2 heads (*ii*) more than 2 heads (*iii*) all heads.
4. An unbiased coin is tossed 32 times. Find the probability of obtaining at least 2 heads.
5. The incidence of occupational disease in a factory is such that the workers have a 25% chances of suffering from it. What is the probability that out of 6 workmen, 4 or more contact the disease ? *(KU 2003)*
6. If on an average 1 vessel in every 10 is wrecked, find the probability that out of 5 vessels expected to arrive, at least 4 will arrive safely.
7. Out of 800 families with 4 children each, what percentage would be expected to have (*a*) 2 boys and 2 girls (*b*) at least one boy (*c*) no girl (*d*) at most 2 girls ? Assume equal probabilities for boys and girls.
8. Six dice are thrown 729 times. How many times do you expect at least 3 dice to show either five or six ?
9. In a certain town, 20% of population is literate, and assume that 200 investigators takes a sample of 10 individuals to see whether they are literate. How many investigators would you expect to report that 3 persons or less are literate in their samples ?
10. Five coins are tossed 3,200 times. Find the frequencies of getting x heads $(0 \le x \le 5)$.
11. Eight coins are tossed at a time, 256 times. Find the expected frequencies of 0, 1, 2, 3 successes (getting head).
12. An insurance agent sells policies to 6 men, all of identical age. According to the acturial tables, the probability that a man of this particular age will be alive 20 years hence is 3/4. Find the probability that in 20 years (*i*) at least two men (*ii*) at most two men, will be alive.
13. During war, 1 ship out of 9 was sunk on an average in making a certain voyage. What was the probability that exactly 3 out of a convoy of 6 ships would arrive safely ?

14. A machine manufacturing screws is known to produce 5% defectives. In a random sample of 15 screws, what is the probability that there are :
(*i*) exactly 3 defectives and (*ii*) not more than 3 defectives ?

15. The probability of a man hitting a target is $\frac{1}{3}$. How many least number of times, must he fire so that the probability of hitting the target at least once is more than 90% ?

16. 10 students are chosen at random from a college in which 20% students do not reside in the college compound. Find the probability that exactly 8 of the students do not reside in the college compound.

17. An unbiased coin is tossed 10 times. Find the probability of getting exactly 5 heads ?

18. The probability that an evening student will be graduate is 0.8. Determine the probability that out of 5 students :
(*i*) none (*ii*) one (*iii*) at least one, will be graduate.

19. The probability that a student will be graduate is 0.4. Detremine the probability that out of 5 students (*i*) none (*ii*) one (*iii*) at least one (*iv*) all will be graduate. (*MDU 2002*)

20. Out of 10 watches, 4 are defective. Three watches are selected at random. Find the probability that :
(*i*) no watch is defective (*ii*) one watch is defective.

21. The sex ratio of male child is 11/20. What is the probability that in a family of 5 children all will be of the same sex ? (*MDU 2005*)

Answers

1. $\frac{11}{32}$

2. $\frac{64}{729}, \frac{192}{729}, \frac{240}{729}, \frac{160}{729}, \frac{60}{729}, \frac{12}{729}, \frac{1}{729}$

3. $\frac{7}{64}, \frac{219}{256}, \frac{1}{256}$

4. $1 - \frac{33}{2^{32}}$

5. $\frac{77}{2048}$

6. $\frac{45927}{50000}$

7. 37.5%, 93.75%, 6.25%, 68.75%

8. 233

9. 176

10. 100, 500, 1000, 1000, 500, 100

11. 1, 8, 28, 56

12. 0.9954, 0.0376

13. $^6C_3 \left(\frac{8}{9}\right)^3 \left(\frac{1}{9}\right)^3 = 0.0193$

14. (*i*) $^{15}C_3 \left(\frac{1}{20}\right)^3 \left(\frac{19}{20}\right)^{12} = 0.0307$ (*ii*) 0.9945

15. $1 - \left(\frac{2}{3}\right)^n > \frac{9}{10} \Rightarrow n = 6$

16. $^{10}C_8 \left(\frac{1}{5}\right)^8 \left(\frac{4}{5}\right)^2 = 0.000074$

17. 0.2461

18. (*i*) 0.00032 (*ii*) 0.0064 (*iii*) 0.99968

19. (*i*) 0.07776 (*ii*) 0.2592 (*iii*) 0.92224 (*iv*) 0.01024

20. (*i*) $\frac{27}{125}$ (*ii*) $\frac{54}{125}$

21. $^5C_0 (0.55)^0(0.45)^5 + {}^5C_5 (0.55)^5(0.45)^0 = 0.0688.$

PROPERTIES OF BINOMIAL DISTRIBUTION

8. THE SHAPE OF B.D.

The shape of the binomial distribution depends upon the probability of success (p) and the number of trials in the experiment. If $p = q = \frac{1}{2}$, then the distribution will be symmetrical for every value of n. If $p \neq q$, then the distribution would be asymmetrical *i.e.*, skewed. The magnitude of skewness varies as the difference between p and q. We illustrate this by taking $p = 0.1, p = 0.5, p = 0.9$ and assuming that there are 5 trials in the experiment.

Case I. p = 0.1, n = 5

We have $P(x = r) = {}^5C_r \left(\frac{1}{10}\right)^r \left(\frac{9}{10}\right)^{5-r}, 0 \le r \le 5.$

The B.D. is

x	0	1	2	3	4	5
$P(x)$	0.59049	0.32805	0.07290	0.00810	0.00045	0.00001

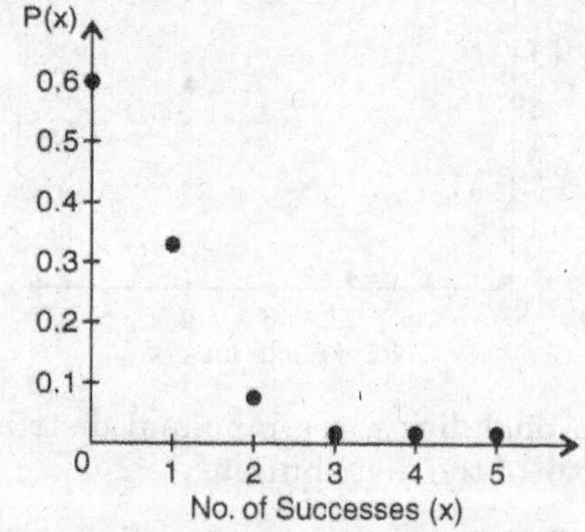

Case II. p = 0.5, n = 5

We have $P(x = r) = {}^5C_r \left(\frac{1}{2}\right)^r \left(\frac{1}{2}\right)^{5-r}, 0 \le r \le 5.$

The B.D is

x	0	1	2	3	4	5
$P(x)$	0.03125	0.15625	0.31250	0.31250	0.15625	0.03125

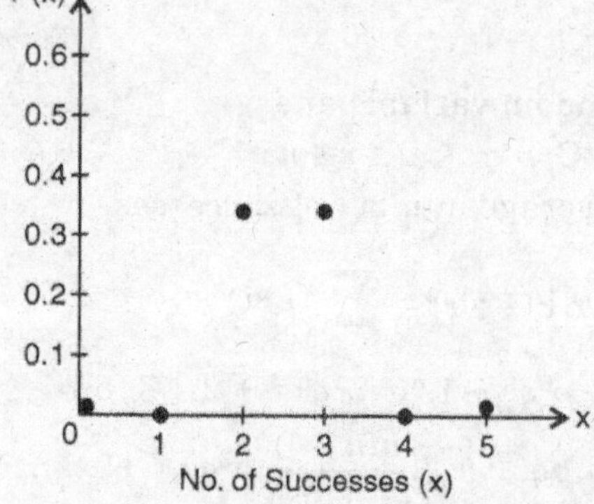

Case III. p = 0.9, n = 5

We have $P(x = r) = {}^5C_r \left(\frac{9}{10}\right)^r \left(\frac{1}{10}\right)^{5-r}, 0 \le r \le 5.$

The B.D. is

x	0	1	2	3	4	5
$P(x)$	0.00001	0.00045	0.00810	0.07290	0.32805	0.59049

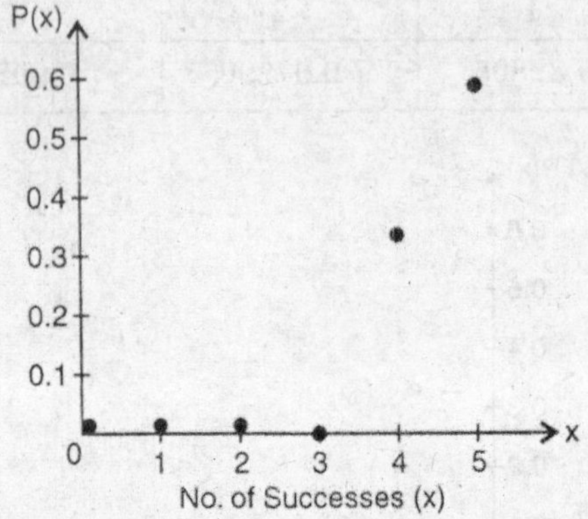

Thus, we see that the probabilities in a binomial distribution depends upon n and p. These are called the **parameter** of the distribution.

9. THE LIMITING CASE OF B.D.

(KU 2003)

As number of trials (n) in the binomial distribution increases, the number of successes also increases. If neither p nor q is very small, then as n approaches infinity, the skewness in the distribution disappears and it becomes continuous. We shall see that such a continuous, bell shaped distribution is called a *normal distribution*. Thus, the normal distribution is a limiting case of binomial distribution as n approaches infinity.

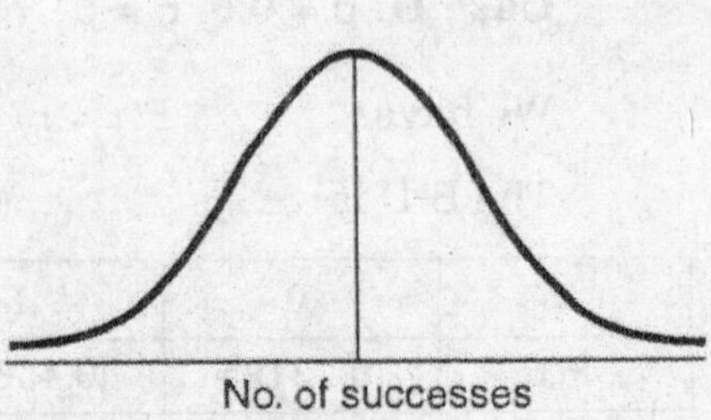

10. MEAN OF B.D.

(KU 1998 ; MDU 2006)

Let x be a binomial random variable and

$$P(x = r) = {}^nC_r p^r q^{n-r}, 0 \le r \le n.$$

The *mean* of x is the average number of successes.

$$\therefore \quad \text{Mean,} \quad \mu = \sum_{r=0}^{n} r.P(x = r) = \sum_{r=0}^{n} r.{}^nC_r p^r q^{n-r}$$

$$= 0.\,{}^nC_0 p^0 q^n + 1.{}^nC_1 p^1 q^{n-1} + 2.\,{}^nC_2 p^2 q^{n-2} + \ldots\ldots + n.\,{}^nC_n p^n.q^0$$

$$= 0 + n.pq^{n-1} + 2.\frac{n(n-1)}{1.2} p^2 q^{n-2} + \ldots\ldots. + n.1.p^n$$

$$= np\left\{q^{n-1} + \frac{n-1}{1}pq^{n-2} + ... + p^{n-1}\right\}$$

$$= np\ \{^{n-1}C_0 p^0 q^{n-1} + {}^{n-1}C_1 p^1 q^{n-2} + ... + {}^{n-1}C_{n-1} p^{n-1} q^0\}$$

$$= np\ (q+p)^{n-1} = np(1)^{n-1} = np.$$

$\therefore$ Mean of x = **np.**

11. VARIANCE AND S.D. OF B.D. *(KU 1998)*

Let x be a binomial random variable and

$$P(x = r) = {}^nC_r p^r q^{n-r},\ \ 0 \le r \le n.$$

The variance and standard deviation of x measures the dispersion of the binomial distribution and are given by

$$\text{Variance} = \sum_{r=0}^{n} r^2.P(x = r) - \mu^2$$

and $$\text{S.D} = \sqrt{\sum_{r=0}^{n} r^2.P(x = r) - \mu^2}\ .$$

Now $$\sum_{r=0}^{n} r^2.P(x = r) = \sum_{r=0}^{n} r^2.\,{}^nC_r p^r q^{n-r}$$

$$= 0.\,{}^nC_0 p^0 q^n + 1^2.\,{}^nC_1 p^1 q^{n-1} + 2^2.\,{}^nC_2 p^2 q^{n-2} + 3^2.\,{}^nC_3 p^n q^{n-3} + ... + n^2.\,{}^nC_n p^n q^0$$

$$= 0 + 1.\frac{n}{1}pq^{n-1} + 2^2.\frac{n(n-1)}{1.2}p^2q^{n-2} + \frac{3^2.\,n(n-1)(n-2)}{1.2.3}p^3q^{n-3} + ... + n^2.1.p^n.1$$

$$= np\left\{q^{n-1} + \frac{2(n-1)}{1}pq^{n-2} + \frac{3(n-1)(n-2)}{1\times 2}p^2q^{n-3} + ... + np^{n-1}\right\}$$

$$= np\left\{\left(q^{n-1} + \frac{n-1}{1}pq^{n-2} + \frac{(n-1)(n-2)}{1\times 2}p^2q^{n-3} + ... + p^{n-1}\right)\right.$$
$$\left. + \left(\frac{n-1}{1}pq^{n-2} + \frac{2(n-1)(n-2)}{1\times 2}p^2q^{n-3} + ... + (n-1)p^{n-1}\right)\right\}$$

$$= np\{(q+p)^{n-1} + (n-1)\,p(q^{n-2} + (n-2)\,pq^{n-3} + ... + p^{n-2})\}$$

$$= np\{1 + (n-1)\,p(q+p)^{n-2}\} = np\ \{1 + (n-1)\,p.1\}$$

$$= np\{1 + np - p\} = np + n^2p^2 - np^2.$$

$$\therefore\ \text{Variance} = \sum_{r=0}^{n} r^2.P(x = r) - \mu^2 = (np + n^2p^2 - np^2) - (np)^2 = np - np^2$$

$$= np(1-p) = \mathbf{npq}.$$

Also, $$\textbf{S.D.} = \sqrt{\textbf{variance}} = \sqrt{\mathbf{npq}}\ .$$

12. γ_1 AND γ_2 OF B.D.

The values of γ_1 and γ_2 for the binomial probability function

$$P(x = r) = {}^nC_r\, p^r q^{n-r},\ 0 \le r \le n$$

are given by

$$\gamma_1 = \frac{\mathbf{1 - 2p}}{\sqrt{\mathbf{npq}}} \quad \text{and} \quad \gamma_2 = \frac{\mathbf{1 - 6pq}}{\mathbf{npq}}.$$

13. RECURRENCE FORMULA FOR B.D.

Let x be a binomial random variable and

$$P(x = r) = {}^nC_r\, p^r q^{n-r}\ 0 \le r \le n.$$

For $0 \le k < n$, $P(k) = {}^nC_k\, p^k q^{n-k}$ and $P(k+1) = {}^nC_{k+1}\, p^{k+1}\, q^{n-(k+1)}$

Dividing, we get $\dfrac{P(k+1)}{P(k)} = \dfrac{{}^nC_{k+1} p^{k+1} q^{n-k-1}}{{}^nC_k p^k q^{n-k}}$

$$= \frac{n!}{(k+1)!\,(n-(k+1))!} \cdot \frac{k!\,(n-k)!}{n!} \cdot \frac{p}{q} = \frac{n-k}{k+1}\,\frac{p}{q}.$$

$$\therefore \qquad \mathbf{P(k+1) = \frac{n-k}{k+1} \cdot \frac{p}{q}\ P(k)\ \text{for}\ \ 0 \le k < n.}$$

This the required **recurrence formula.**

Example 1. *The mean and S.D. of a binomial distribution are 20 and 4 respectively. Calculate n, p and q.*

Sol. Let the binomial distribution be

$$P(x = r) = {}^nC_r\, p^r q^{n-r},\ 0 \le r \le n.$$

$$\therefore \qquad \text{Mean} = np \quad \text{and} \quad \text{S.D.} = \sqrt{npq}.$$

We are given mean = 20, S.D. = 4.

$$\therefore \qquad np = 20,\ \sqrt{npq} = 4$$

$$\Rightarrow \qquad \sqrt{20q} = 4 \quad \Rightarrow \quad 20q = 16 \quad \Rightarrow \quad q = \frac{4}{5}$$

$$\therefore \qquad p = 1 - q = 1 - \frac{4}{5} = \frac{1}{5}.$$

$np = 20$ implies $n \times \dfrac{1}{5} = 20$ *i.e.*, $n = 100$

$$\therefore \quad n = \mathbf{100},\ p = \frac{\mathbf{1}}{\mathbf{5}},\ q = \frac{\mathbf{4}}{\mathbf{5}}.$$

Example 2. *If the sum of the mean and the variance of a binomial distribution of 5 trials is 9/5, then find the binomial distribution.*

Sol. Let the binomial distribution be

$$P(x = r) = {}^nC_r\, p^r q^{n-r},\ 0 \le r \le n.$$

$$\therefore \qquad \text{Mean} = np \quad \text{and} \quad \text{variance} = npq.$$

By the given condition,

$$np + npq = \frac{9}{5} \quad \text{and} \quad n = 5.$$

$\Rightarrow \quad 5p + 5p(1-p) = \dfrac{9}{5} \quad \Rightarrow \quad 5p + 5p - 5p^2 = \dfrac{9}{5}$

$\Rightarrow \quad 25p^2 - 50p + 9 = 0 \quad \therefore \quad p = \dfrac{1}{5}$

$\therefore \quad q = 1 - p = 1 - \dfrac{1}{5} = \dfrac{4}{5}.$

$\therefore$ The binomial distribution is

$$\mathbf{P(x = r) = {}^5C_r \left(\frac{1}{5}\right)^r \left(\frac{4}{5}\right)^{5-r}, \; 0 \le r \le 5.}$$

Example 3. *Is the following statement correct ? "The mean and variance of a binomial distribution are respectively 6 and 9".*

Sol. Let the binomial distribution be

$$P(x = r) = {}^nC_r\, p^r q^{n-r}\, 0, \le r \le n.$$

Now $\quad$ mean = 6 $\quad \Rightarrow \quad np = 6$

variance = 9 $\quad \Rightarrow \quad npq = 9$

$\therefore \quad 6q = 9 \quad \Rightarrow \quad q = \dfrac{3}{2}.$

This is impossible, because probability of an event can never be greater than 1.

$\therefore$ The given statement is not correct.

EXERCISE 2

1. Determine the binomial distribution whose mean is 5 and standard deviation is $\sqrt{2.5}$.
2. Determine the probability of 3 successes in a binomial distribution whose mean and variance are respectively 2 and $\dfrac{3}{2}$.
3. For a binomial distribution, the mean is 6 and the standard deviation is $\sqrt{2}$. Find the probability of getting 7 successes.
4. Is there any inconsistency in the statement. "The mean of a Binomial Distribution is 80 and S.D. is 8." If no inconsistency is found, what shall be the values of p, q and n ?

Answers

1. $P(x = r) = {}^{10}C_r \left(\dfrac{1}{2}\right)^r \left(\dfrac{1}{2}\right)^{10-r}, \; 0 \le r \le 10$

2. 0.2076 $\qquad$ 3. 0.2341 $\qquad$ 4. $\dfrac{1}{5}, \dfrac{4}{5}$, 400.

---

14. FITTING OF A BINOMIAL DISTRIBUTION

Let x be a binomial random variable of an experiment. Let probability of x successes be given by

$$P(x = r) = {}^nC_r\, p^r q^{n-r}, \; 0 \le r \le n.$$

By fitting of a binomial distribution, we mean to find out the theoretical frequencies of the values of the binomial random variable $x = 0, 1, 2, ..., n$, when the experiment of n trials is repeated for, say, N times. The theoretical frequencies are given by

$$\mathbf{N.P(x = r) = N.\, {}^nC_r\, p^r q^{n-r},\ 0 \le r \le n.}$$

The recurrence formula can also be made use of, if desired.

Example 1. *The following data are the number of seeds germinating out of 10 on damp filter for 80 sets of seeds. Fit a binomial distribution to this data.*

x	*0*	*1*	*2*	*3*	*4*	*5*	*6*	*7*	*8*	*9*	*10*
f	*6*	*20*	*28*	*12*	*8*	*6*	*0*	*0*	*0*	*0*	*0*

Sol. **Calculation of Expected Frequencies**

x	*Observed frequency (f)*	*fx*
0	6	0
1	20	20
2	28	56
3	12	36
4	8	32
5	6	30
6	0	0
7	0	0
8	0	0
9	0	0
10	0	0
Total	80	174

Hence $n = 10, N = 80$

$$\text{Mean, } \bar{x} = \frac{\Sigma fx}{N} = \frac{174}{80} = 2.175$$

Let p denote the probability of *success* in a trial.

$\therefore$ Mean $= np \Rightarrow 10p = 2.175$

$\therefore$ $p = 0.2175$ and $q = 1 - p = 0.7825$

$\therefore$ The binomial distribution is

$$P(x = r) = {}^{10}C_r\, (0.2175)^r\, (0.7825)^{10-r},\ 0 \le r \le 10.$$

$\therefore$ For $x = 0$, expected frequency $= 80 \times P(0)$

$$= 80 \times {}^{10}C_0\, (0.2175)^0\, (0.7825)^{10} = 6.8854 \doteq \mathbf{7}$$

For $x = 1$, expected frequency $= 80 \times P(1)$

$$= 80 \times {}^{10}C_1 (0.2175)^1\, (0.7825)^9 = 19.1385 \doteq \mathbf{19}$$

For $x = 2$, expected frequency $= 80 \times P(2)$

$$= 80 \times {}^{10}C_2 (0.2175)^2\, (0.7825)^8 = 23.9382 \doteq \mathbf{24}$$

For $x = 3$, expected frequency $= 80 \times P(3)$

$$= 80 \times {}^{10}C_3(0.2175)^3 (0.7825)^7 = 17.7427 \doteq \mathbf{18}$$

For $x = 4$, expected frequency $= 80 \times P(4)$

$$= 80 \times {}^{10}C_4 (0.2175)^4 (0.7825)^6 = 8.6302 \doteq \mathbf{8*}$$

For $x = 5$, expected frequency $= 80 \times P(5)$

$$= 80 \times {}^{10}C_5 (0.2175)^5 (0.7825)^5 = 2.8768 \doteq \mathbf{3}$$

For $x = 6$, expected frequency $= 80 \times P(6)$

$$= 80 \times {}^{10}C_6 (0.2175)^6 (0.7825)^4 = 0.6636 \doteq \mathbf{1}$$

For $x = 7$, expected frequency $= 80 \times P(7)$

$$= 80 \times {}^{10}C_7 (0.2175)^7 (0.7825)^3 = 0.1046 \doteq \mathbf{0}$$

For $x = 8$, expected frequency $= 80 \times P(8)$

$$= 80 \times {}^{10}C_8 (0.2175)^8 (0.7825)^2 = 0.0108 \doteq \mathbf{0}$$

For $x = 9$, expected frequency $= 80 \times P(9)$

$$= 80 \times {}^{10}C_9(0.2175)^9 (0.7825)^1 = 0.0006 \doteq \mathbf{0}$$

For $x = 10$, expected frequency $= 80 \times P(10)$

$$= 80 \times {}^{10}C_{10}\cdot (0.2175)^{10} (0.7825)^0 = 0.000016 \doteq \mathbf{0.}$$

∴ The expected frequencies are as given in the following table :

x	0	1	2	3	4	5	6	7	8	9	10
Exp. freq.	7	19	24	18	8	3	1	0	0	0	0

Example 2. *Five dice are thrown 96 times. The number of times 4 or 5 or 6 was actually thrown in the experiment is given in the following table :*

No. of dice (Each showing 4 or 5 or 6)	*0*	*1*	*2*	*3*	*4*	*5*
Observed frequency	*1*	*10*	*24*	*35*	*18*	*8*

Fit a binomial distribution assuming :

(*i*) *the dice are perfect.*

(*ii*) *the nature of dice is not known.*

Sol. Let x be the binomial random variable** of the experiment. The possible values of x are 0, 1, 2, 3, 4, 5. Let p be the probability of getting 4 or 5 or 6 in a single throw.

Here $n = 5, \quad N = 96$

∴ The expected frequency of getting r *successes*

$$= N\,{}^nC_r p^r q^{n-r} = 96\,{}^5C_r p^r q^{5-r},\ 0 \le r \le 5.$$

(*i*) In this case, the dice are perfect.

∴ $$p = \frac{3}{6} = \frac{1}{2}$$

Also $$q = 1 - p = 1 - \tfrac{1}{2} = \tfrac{1}{2}.$$

---

*We have approximated 8.6302 to 8 in order to keep the sum of all expected frequencies equal to 80.

** The experiment of throwing 5 dice can be considered as throwing of one die 5 times.

$\therefore$ For $x = 0$, the expected frequency $= 96 \times {}^5C_0 (\frac{1}{2})^0(\frac{1}{2})^5 = \mathbf{3}$

For $x = 1$, the expected frequency $= 96 \times {}^5C_1(\frac{1}{2})^1(\frac{1}{2})^4 = \mathbf{15}$

For $x = 2$, the expected frequency $= 96 \times {}^5C_2(\frac{1}{2})^2(\frac{1}{2})^3 = \mathbf{30}$

For $x = 3$, the expected frequency $= 96 \times {}^5C_3(\frac{1}{2})^3(\frac{1}{2})^2 = \mathbf{30}$

For $x = 4$, the expected frequency $= 96 \times {}^5C_4(\frac{1}{2})^4(\frac{1}{2})^1 = \mathbf{15}$

For $x = 5$, the expected frequency $= 96 \times {}^5C_5(\frac{1}{2})^5(\frac{1}{2})^0 = \mathbf{3}.$

(*ii*) In this case, the value of p will be estimated by using the observed frequencies. We have

$$\text{Mean} = \frac{\Sigma fx}{N} = \frac{(1\times 0)+(10\times 1)+(24\times 2)+(35\times 3)+(18\times 4)+(8\times 5)}{96} = \frac{275}{96}$$

Also, mean $= np$

$$\therefore \quad 5p = \frac{275}{96} \quad \text{or} \quad p = 0.5729$$

$$\therefore \quad q = 1 - p = 1 - 0.5729 = 0.4271.$$

$\therefore$ Expected frequency for $x = r$

$$= 96\ {}^5C_r\ (0.5729)^r\ (0.4271)^{5-r},\ 0 \le r \le 5.$$

For $x = 0$, the expected frequency

$$= 96 \times {}^5C_0\ (0.5729)^0\ (0.4271)^5 = 1.3643 \doteq \mathbf{1}$$

For $x = 1$, the expected frequency

$$= 96 \times {}^5C_1\ (0.5729)^1\ (0.4271)^4 = 9.1503 \doteq \mathbf{9}$$

For $x = 2$, the expected frequency

$$= 96 \times {}^5C_2\ (0.5729)^2\ (0.4271)^3 = 24.5479 \doteq \mathbf{25}$$

For $x = 3$, the expected frequency

$$= 96 \times {}^5C_3\ (0.5729)^3\ (0.4271)^2 = 32.9281 \doteq \mathbf{33}$$

For $x = 4$, the expected frequency

$$= 96 \times {}^5C_4\ (0.5729)^4\ (0.4271)^1 = 22.0844 \doteq \mathbf{22}$$

For $x = 5$, the expected frequency

$$= 96 \times {}^5C_5\ (0.5729)^5\ (0.4271)^0 = 5.9247 \doteq \mathbf{6}.$$

EXERCISE 3

1. 8 unbiased coins were tossed 256 times. Fit a binomial distribution. (MDU 2007)
2. 7 coins are tossed and the number of the heads noted. The experiment is repeated 128 times and the following distribution is obtained :

No. of heads	0	1	2	3	4	5	6	7
Frequency	7	16	19	35	30	13	7	1

Fit a binomial distribution assuming :

(*i*) the coins are unbiased.

(*ii*) the nature of coins is not known.

3. Four dice are thrown 162 times. The number of times 5 or 6 was actually thrown in the experiment is given in the following table :

No. of dice (Each showing 5 or 6)	0	1	2	3	4
Observed frequency	22	50	50	35	5

Fit a binomial distribution assuming :

(*i*) the dice are perfect.

(*ii*) the nature of dice is not known.

4. Ten coins were tossed 1024 times and the following frequencies are observed.

No. of heads	0	1	2	3	4	5	6	7	8	9	10
Frequency	2	10	38	106	188	257	226	128	59	7	3

Compare these frequencies with the expected frequencies.

Answers

1. 1, 8, 28, 56, 70, 56, 28, 8, 1. **2.** (*i*) 1, 7, 21, 35, 35, 21, 7, 1. (*ii*) 1, 8, 23, 36, 34, 19, 6, 1.
3. (*i*) 32, 64, 48, 16, 2 (*ii*) 18, 52, 58, 29, 5.
4. 1 ($\doteq 1024\,{}^{10}C_0\,(0.5135)^0(0.4865)^{10}$), 8, 38, 107, 200, 251, 221, 133, 52, 12, 1.

POISSON DISTRIBUTION

15. INTRODUCTION

The Poisson distribution is also a discrete probability distribution. This was discovered by French mathematician **Simon Denis Poisson** (1781 – 1840) in the year 1837. This distribution deals with the evaluation of probabilities of *rare* events such as "no. of car accidents on road", "no. of earthquakes in a year", "no. of misprints in a book" etc.

16. CONDITIONS

The Poisson distribution is derived as a limiting case of binomial distribution. So, the conditions for the applicability of the Poisson distribution are same as those for the applicability of Binomial distribution. Here the additional requirement is that the probability of 'success' is quite near to zero.

17. POISSON VARIABLE

A random variable which counts the number of successes in a random experiment with trials satisfying above conditions is called a **Poisson variable.** If the probability of an article being defective is 1/500 and the event of getting a defective article is *success* and samples of 10 articles are checked for defective articles, then the possible values of the Poisson variable are 0, 1, 2, ... 10.

18. POISSON PROBABILITY FUNCTION

Let a random experiment satisfying the conditions of Poisson Distribution be performed. Let the number of trials in the experiment be n, which is very large. Let p denote the probability of *success* in any trial. We assume that p is very small, *i.e.*, we are dealing with a rare event. Let x denote the Poisson variable corresponding to this experiment.

∴ The possible values of x are 0, 1, 2, ..., n.

The Poisson distribution is obtained as a limiting case of the corresponding binomial distribution of the experiment.

It can be proved mathematically that the probability of r successes is given by

$$P(x = r) = \frac{e^{-m}\, m^r}{r!}, \qquad r = 0, 1, 2, ...$$

This is called the **Poisson probability function.** The corresponding **Poisson distribution** is

x	0	1	2	3 ......
$P(x)$	$\frac{e^{-m}m^0}{0!}$	$\frac{e^{-m}m^1}{1!}$	$\frac{e^{-m}m^2}{2!}$	$\frac{e^{-m}m^3}{3!}$ ......

The constant m is the product of n and p and is called the **parameter** of the Poisson distribution.

19. POISSON FREQUENCY DISTRIBUTION

If a random experiment, satisfying the requirements of Poisson distribution, is repeated N times, then the expected frequency of getting r successes is given by

$$N \,.\, P(x = r) = N\,\frac{e^{-m}\, m^r}{r!}, \quad r = 0, 1, 2, ...$$

Remark 1. The distribution to be used in solving a problem is generally given in the problem. If it is not given, then the student should make use of Poisson distribution only when the event in the problem is of rare nature *i.e.*, the probability of happening of event is quite near to zero.

Remark 2. The values of e^{-m} required in any particular problem is generally given with the problem itself, otherwise, the value of e^{-m} can be found out by using the table given at the end. In the examination hall, generally the table of e^{-m} is available for students. If at all the value of e^{-m} is neither given with the problem nor the table of e^{-m} is supplied in the examination hall, then the students are advised to retain their final result in terms of e^{-m}.

Example 1. *A company makes electric toys. The probability that an electric toy is defective is 0.01. What is the probability that a shipment of 300 toys will contain exactly 5 defective toys ?* (MDU 2000)

Sol. Let x be the Poisson variable, '*no. of defective toys*'

By **Poisson distribution,** $P(x = r) = \frac{e^{-m}\, m^r}{r!}$, $r = 0, 1, 2, ...$

Here $n = 300, \quad p = 0.01$

∴ $m = np = 300 \times 0.01 = 3$

∴ $$P(x = r) = \frac{e^{-3}\, 3^r}{r!}, \quad r = 0, 1, 2, ..., 300$$

$\therefore$ P(5 defective toys) $= P(x = 5)$

$$= \frac{e^{-3}(3)^5}{5!} = \frac{0.04979 \times 243}{120} = \mathbf{0.1008.}$$

Example 2. *The probability that a particular injection will have reaction to an individual is 0.002. Find the probability that out of 1000 individuals :*

(*i*) *exactly 2 individuals*

(*ii*) *at least one individual will have reaction from injection.* (KU 2000)

Sol. Let x be the Poisson variable, '*no. of individuals suffering reaction*'.

By **Poisson distribution**, $P(x = r) = \dfrac{e^{-m}\, m^r}{r!}, r = 0, 1, 2, ...$

Here $n = 1000, \quad p = 0.002$

$\therefore$ $m = np = 1000 \times 0.002 = 2$

$\therefore$ $P(x = r) = \dfrac{e^{-2}\, 2^r}{r!}, \; r = 0, 1, 2, ..., 1000.$

(*i*) P(exactly 2 suffer reaction) $= P(x = 2)$

$$= \frac{e^{-2}(2)^2}{2!} = \frac{0.13534 \times 4}{2} = \mathbf{0.27068.}$$

(*ii*) P(at least one suffer reaction)

$$= P(x \geq 1) = 1 - P(x < 1) = 1 - P(x = 0)$$

$$= 1 - \frac{e^{-2}(2)^0}{0!} = 1 - \frac{0.13534 \times 1}{1} = \mathbf{0.86466.}$$

Example 3. *10% of the tools produced in a certain factory turns out to be defective. Find the probability that in a sample of 10 tools chosen at random, (i) exactly two (ii) more than two will be defective by using Poisson approximation to binomial distribution.*

Sol. Let x be the Poisson variable, "*no. of defective tools in the sample*".

By **Poisson distribution,** $P(x = r) = \dfrac{e^{-m}\, m^r}{r!}, \; r = 0, 1, 2, ...$

Here $n = 10, p = \dfrac{10}{100} = \dfrac{1}{10}. \quad \therefore \quad m = np = 10 \times \dfrac{1}{10} = 1$

$\therefore$ $P(x = r) = \dfrac{e^{-1}(1)^r}{r!}, \; r = 0, 1, 2, ... 10.$

(*i*) P(exactly 2 defectives) $= P(x = 2)$

$$= \frac{e^{-1}}{2!} = \frac{0.36788}{2} = \mathbf{0.18394.}$$

(*ii*) P(more than 2 defectives) $= P(x > 2) = 1 - P(x \leq 2)$

$$= 1 - P(x = 0 \text{ or } x = 1 \text{ or } x = 2)$$

$$= 1 - \{P(x = 0) + P(x = 1) + P(x = 2)\}$$

$$= 1 - \left\{\frac{e^{-1}}{0!} + \frac{e^{-1}}{1!} + \frac{e^{-1}}{2!}\right\} = 1 - e^{-1}\left\{1 + 1 + \frac{1}{2}\right\}$$

$= 1 - (0.36788)(2.5) = \mathbf{0.0803}.$

Example 4. *Suppose that a manufactured product has 2 defects per unit of product inspected. Using Poisson distribution, calculate the probabilities of finding a product without any defect, 3 defects and 4 defects. (Given $e^{-2} = 0.135$).*

Sol. Let x be the Poisson variable, '*no. of defects per unit*'.

By **Poisson distribution,**

$$P(x = r) = \frac{e^{-m}\, m^r}{r!}, \; r = 0, 1, 2, \ldots\ldots$$

Here m = mean no. of defects in a unit = 2

$$\therefore \quad P(x = r) = \frac{e^{-2}\, 2^r}{r!}, \; r = 0, 1, 2, \ldots\ldots$$

$\therefore$ Probability of getting no defect in a unit

$$= P(x = 0) = \frac{e^{-2}(2)^0}{0!} = e^{-2} = \mathbf{0.135}$$

Probability of getting 3 defects in a unit

$$= P(x = 3) = \frac{e^{-2}(2)^3}{3!} = \frac{(0.135)(8)}{6} = \mathbf{0.18}$$

Probability of getting 4 defects in a unit

$$= P(x = 4) = \frac{e^{-2}(2)^4}{4!} = \frac{(0.135)16}{24} = \mathbf{0.09}.$$

Remark. For Poisson distribution, mean of $x = np$.

$\therefore$ Mean of $x = m$, because $m = np$.

Example 5. *A telephone exchange receives on an average 4 calls per minute. Find the probability on the basis of Poisson distribution ($m = 4$), of :*

(*i*) *2 or less calls per minute,* (KU 2001, 2005)

(*ii*) *upto 4 calls per minute,* (KU 2001, 2005)

(*iii*) *more than 4 calls per minute.* (Given $e^{-4} = 0.01832$) (KU 2001, 2005)

Sol. Let x be the Poisson variable "*no. of calls per minute*".

By **Poisson distribution,**

$$P(x = r) = \frac{e^{-m}\, m^r}{r!}, \; r = 0, 1, 2, \ldots\ldots$$

Here m = average number of successes *i.e.*, calls per minute = 4

$$\therefore \quad P(x = r) = \frac{e^{-4}(4)^r}{r!}, \quad r = 0, 1, 2, \ldots\ldots$$

(*i*) P(2 or less calls per minute) = $P(x \le 2)$

$= P(x = 0 \text{ or } x = 1 \text{ or } x = 2)$

$= P(x = 0) + P(x = 1) + P(x = 2)$

$$= \frac{e^{-4}(4)^0}{0!} + \frac{e^{-4}(4)^1}{1!} + \frac{e^{-4}(4)^2}{2!}$$

$$= e^{-4}\{1 + 4 + 8\} = 0.01832 \times 13 = \mathbf{0.2382}$$

(*ii*) P(upto 4 calls per minute) = $P(x \le 4)$

$$= P(x = 0 \text{ or } x = 1 \text{ or } x = 2 \text{ or } x = 3 \text{ or } x = 4)$$

$$= P(x = 0) + P(x = 1) + P(x = 2) + P(x = 3) + P(x = 4)$$

$$= \frac{e^{-4}(4)^0}{0!} + \frac{e^{-4}(4)^1}{1!} + \frac{e^{-4}(4)^2}{2!} + \frac{e^{-4}(4)^3}{3!} + \frac{e^{-4}(4)^4}{4!}$$

$$= e^{-4}\left\{1 + 4 + 8 + \frac{64}{6} + \frac{256}{24}\right\}$$

$$= 0.01832 \times 34.3333 = \mathbf{0.6289}$$

(*iii*) P(more than 4 calls per minute) = $P(x > 4)$

$$= 1 - P(x \le 4) = 1 - 0.6289 = \mathbf{0.3711}.$$ [By part (*ii*)]

Example 6. *If x follows the Poisson probability law such that :*
P(x = 1) = P(x = 2), then find the probability of 4 successes.

Sol. Let m = average no. of successes

$$\therefore \quad P(x = r) = \frac{e^{-m}\, m^r}{r!}, r = 0, 1, 2, \ldots\ldots$$

By the given condition,

$$P(x = 1) = P(x = 2)$$

$$\therefore \quad \frac{e^{-m}m^1}{1!} = \frac{e^{-m}m^2}{2!} \quad \text{or} \quad 1 = \frac{m}{2} \quad \text{or} \quad m = 2.$$

$$\therefore \quad P(4 \text{ successes}) = P(x = 4) = \frac{e^{-2}(2)^4}{4!} = \frac{0.13534 \times 16}{24} = \mathbf{0.0902}.$$

Example 7. *A manufacturer of bulbs knows that on an average 5% of his production is defective. He sells bulbs in boxes of 100 pieces and guarantees that not more than 4 bulbs will be defective in a box. What is the probability that a box will meet the guarantee ($e^{-5} = 0.0067$) ?*

(KU 1995, 2004)

Sol. Let x be the Poisson variable, '*no. of defective bulbs per box*',
By **Poisson distribution,**

$$P(x = r) = \frac{e^{-m}m^r}{r!}, \quad r = 0, 1, 2, \ldots\ldots$$

Here $\quad n = 100,\ p = \frac{5}{100}.$

$$\therefore \quad m = np = 100 \times \frac{5}{100} = 5$$

$$\therefore \quad P(x = r) = \frac{e^{-5}\, 5^r}{r!}, \quad r = 0, 1, 2, \ldots\ldots, 100.$$

P(box will meet the guarantee) = $P(x \le 4)$

$$= P(x = 0) + P(x = 1) + P(x = 2) + P(x = 3) + P(x = 4)$$

$$= \frac{e^{-5}(5)^0}{0!} + \frac{e^{-5}(5)^1}{1!} + \frac{e^{-5}(5)^2}{2!} + \frac{e^{-5}(5)^3}{3!} + \frac{e^{-5}(5)^4}{4!}$$

$$= e^{-5}\left[\frac{1}{1} + \frac{5}{1} + \frac{25}{2} + \frac{125}{6} + \frac{625}{24}\right] = 0.0067 \times 65.37499 = \mathbf{0.438.}$$

Example 8. *In a certain factory turning out razor blades, there is a small chance 1/500 for any blade to be defective. The blades are in packets of 10. Use Poisson's distribution to calculate the approximate number of packets containing :*

(i) no defective (ii) one defective and (iii) two defective blades in a consignment of 10000 packets.

Sol. Let x be the Poisson variable '*no. of defective blades in a packet*'.

∴ By **Poisson distribution,**

$$P(x = r) = \frac{e^{-m}\, m^r}{r!}, \; r = 0, 1, 2, \ldots..$$

Here $n = 10, p = \dfrac{1}{500}$.

$$\therefore \quad m = np = 10 \times \frac{1}{500} = \frac{1}{50} = 0.02$$

$$\therefore \quad P(x = r) = \frac{e^{-0.02}(0.02)^r}{r!}, \; r = 0, 1, 2, \ldots\ldots, 10.$$

(*i*) Expected no. of packets containing no defective

$$= N \times P(x = 0) = 10000 \times \frac{e^{-0.02}(0.02)^0}{0!}$$

$$= 10000 \times e^{-0.02} = 10000\,(0.9802) = \mathbf{9802}$$

(*ii*) Expected no. of packets containing one defective

$$= N \times P(x = 1) = 10000 \times \frac{e^{-0.02}(0.02)^1}{1!}$$

$$= 10000\,(0.9802)(0.02) \doteq \mathbf{196.}$$

(*iii*) Expected no. of packets containing two defectives

$$= N \times P(x = 2) = 10000 \times \frac{e^{-0.02}(0.02)^2}{2!}$$

$$= \frac{10000(0.9802)(0.02)^2}{2} \doteq \mathbf{2.}$$

Example 9. *A car-hire firm has two cars, which it hires out day by day. The number of demands for a car on each day is distributed as a Poisson distribution with mean 1.5. Calculate the proportion of days on which neither car is used and the proportion of days on which some demand is refused* ($e^{-1.5} = 0.2231$).

Sol. Let x be the Poisson variable, '*no. of demands per day*'.

∴ By **Poisson distribution,**

$$P(x = r) = \frac{e^{-m}\, m^r}{r!}, \quad r = 0, 1, 2, \ldots..$$

Here m = average number of demands per day = 1.5

$$\therefore \quad P(x = r) = \frac{e^{-1.5}(1.5)^r}{r!}, r = 0, 1, 2, ...$$

Now, proportion of days on which neither car is used

$$= P(x = 0) = \frac{e^{-1.5}(1.5)^0}{0!} = \mathbf{0.2231}$$

Also, proportion of days on which some demand is refused

$$= P(x > 2) = 1 - P(x \leq 2) = 1 - P(x = 0 \quad \text{or} \quad x = 1 \quad \text{or} \quad x = 2)$$

$$= 1 - \{(P(x = 0 + P(x = 1) + P(x = 2))\}$$

$$= 1 - \left\{\frac{e^{-1.5}(1.5)^0}{0!} + \frac{e^{-1.5}(1.5)^1}{1!} + \frac{e^{-1.5}(1.5)^2}{2!}\right\}$$

$$= 1 - e^{-1.5}\left\{1 + 1.5 + \frac{2.25}{2}\right\} = 1 - (0.2231)(3.625) = \mathbf{0.1913.}$$

Example 10. *Suppose a book of 585 pages contains 43 pages with misprints and these pages are randomly distributed through out the book. What is the probability that 10 pages, selected at random, will be free from pages with misprints ?*

Sol. Let x be the Poisson variable, "*no. of pages with misprints in the sample of 10 pages*".

By **Poisson distribution,**

$$P(x = r) = \frac{e^{-m}m^r}{r!}, r = 0, 1, 2, ...$$

Here $\quad n = 10, p = \frac{43}{585}. \quad \therefore \quad m = np = 10 \times \frac{43}{585} = 0.735$

$$\therefore \quad P(x = r) = \frac{e^{-0.735}(0.735)^r}{r!}, r = 0, 1, 2, ..., 10$$

From the table of e^{-m},

$$e^{-0.735} = e^{(-0.73 - 0.74)/2} = \sqrt{e^{-0.73} \times e^{-0.74}} = \sqrt{(0.4819)(0.4771)} = 0.4795.$$

P(sample is free from pages with misprints)

$$= P(x = 0) = \frac{e^{0.735}(0.735)^0}{0!} = \mathbf{0.4795.}$$

Example 11. *250 passengers have made reservations for a flight from Delhi to Mumbai. If the probability that a passenger, who has reservation, will not turn up is 0.016. Find the probability that at the most 3 passengers will not turn up.*

(given $e^{-4} = 0.0183$) (KU 2002)

Sol. Let x be the random variable '*no. of passengers not turning up*'.

$\therefore$ By **Poisson distribution,**

$$P(x = r) = \frac{e^{-m}m^r}{r!}, \quad r = 0, 1, 2, ...$$

Here $n = 250, p = 0.016 \quad \therefore \quad m = np = 250 \times \frac{16}{1000} = 4$

$$\therefore \quad P(x = r) = \frac{e^{-4}(4)^r}{r!}, \; r = 0, 1, 2, \ldots, 250$$

$\therefore$ Prob. that at most 3 passengers will not turn up

$$= P(x \le 3) = P(x = 0 \text{ or } x = 1 \text{ or } x = 2 \text{ or } x = 3)$$
$$= P(x = 0) + P(x = 1) + P(x = 2) + P(x = 3)$$
$$= \frac{e^{-4}(4)^0}{0!} + \frac{e^{-4}(4)^1}{1!} + \frac{e^{-4}(4)^2}{2!} + \frac{e^{-4}(4)^3}{3!}$$
$$= e^{-4}\left[1 + 4 + \frac{16}{2} + \frac{64}{6}\right] = 0.0183 \times 23.67 = \mathbf{0.433}.$$

EXERCISE 4

1. **Find the probability that at most 5 defective bolts will be found in a box of 200 bolts if it is known that 2% of such bolts are expected to be defective (you may take the distribution to be of Poisson type). ($e^{-4} = 0.0183$).**

2. **Between 2 P.M. to 4 P.M., the average number of phone calls per minute coming into a switch board of a company is 2.5. Find the probability that during one particular minute, there will be :**

(*i*) no phone call at all (*ii*) exactly three calls.

3. **A telephone exchange receives on an average 3 calls per minute. Find the probability on the basis of Poisson distribution ($m = 3$), of :**

(*i*) exactly 1 call per minute (*ii*) exactly 3 calls per minute

(*iii*) less than 3 calls per minute (*iv*) more than 1 call per minute.

4. **The experience shows that 4 industrial accidents occur in a plant on an average per month. Calculate the probability of less than 3 accidents in a certain month. Use Poisson distribution.**

5. **Assuming that the probability of a total accident in a factory during a year is 1/1200, calculate the probability that in a factory employing 300 workers, there will be at least two total accidents in a year. ($e^{-0.25} = 0.7788$).**

6. **Suppose that x has a Poisson distribution. If $P(x = 2) = (2/3)P(x = 1)$, then find the values of (*i*) $P(x = 0)$ and (*ii*) $P(x = 3)$.**

7. **The probabilities of a Poisson variate taking the values 3 and 4 are equal. Calculate the probabilities of the variate taking the values 0 and 1.**

8. **Find the probability that no defective fuse will be found in a box of 200 fuses, if experience shows that 2% such fuses are defective.**

9. **Find the probability that at most 5 defective articles will be found in a box of 200 articles, if experience shows that 2% of such articles are defective.**

10. **If the probability that an individual suffer a bad reaction from a certain injection is 0.001, find the probability that out of 2000 individuals :**

(*i*) exactly 2 (*ii*) exactly 3

(*iii*) less than 2 (*iv*) more than 2

individuals will suffer a bad reaction.

11. **Assume that the probability of an individual coal miner killed in a mine accident during a year is 1/2500. Calculate the probability that in a mine employing 2000 miners, there will be (*i*) no fatal accident and (*ii*) at least one fatal accident in a year.**

12. Supposing the probability of dialling a wrong number to be 0.02, find the probabilities of dialling (*i*) exactly 2 (*ii*) less than 2 (*iii*) more than 2 wrong numbers in 100 diallings.

13. The probability that a man aged 60 years will die within a year is 0.01125. What is the probability that out of 12 such men, at least 11 will reach their 61st birth day ?

14. An insurance company finds that 0.005% of the population die from air-crash accidents each year. What is the probability that the company must pay off to more than 3 out of 10,000 insured risks against such accidents in a given year ?

15. An office switch board receives telephone calls at the rate of 3 per minute on an average. What is the probability of receiving (*i*) no call in one minute interval and (*ii*) at the most 3 calls in one minute interval ?

16. A manufacturing concern employing a large number of workers find that, over a period of time, the average absentee rate is three workers per shift. Calculate the probability that, in a given shift :

(*i*) exactly one worker will be absent (*ii*) exactly two workers will be absent

(*iii*) at most four workers will be absent.

17. 2% bulbs, manufactured by a company are defective. Find the probability that in a sample of 200 bulbs : (*i*) less than 2 bulbs are defictive (*ii*) more than 3 bulbs are defective. (Use $e^{-4} = 0.0183$)

(*KU 2002 C*)

18. In a factory manufacturing pens, of which 0.5 percent are defective pens, each carton is packed of 100 pens. What is the percentage of such carton in which (*i*) not a single pen is defective, (*ii*) at least one pen is defective and (*iii*) two or more pens are defective ? (*KU 2001 C*)

19. In a town 10 accidents took place in a span of 50 days. Assuming that the number of accidents per day follows the Poissson distribution, find the probability that there will be three or more accidents in a day. (use $e^{-0.2} = 0.8187$) (*KU 1995 C*)

20. The probability of a defective blade produced in a factory is 1/500. If blades are supplied in packets of 10, find the expected number of packets having (*i*) no defective blade (*ii*) 1 defective blade (*iii*) 2 defective blades in a consignment of 400 packets. (Given $e^{-0.02} = 0.9802$)

(*KU 2005 C*)

Answers

1. $e^{-4}\left\{\frac{4^0}{0!}+\frac{4^1}{1!}+\frac{4^2}{2!}+\frac{4^3}{3!}+\frac{4^4}{4!}+\frac{4^5}{5!}\right\} = 0.7845$

2. (*i*) 0.0821, (*ii*) 0.2138 **3.** 0.1494, 0.2241, 0.4232, 0.8008 **4.** 0.2382

5. $1 - e^{-0.25}\left(1+\frac{0.25}{1!}\right) = 0.0265$

6. (*i*) $e^{-4/3} = e^{-1} \cdot e^{-0.33} = (0.36788)(0.7189) = 0.2645$ (*ii*) $e^{-4.3} \cdot \frac{32}{81} = 0.1045$

7. $e^{-4} = 0.01832$, $4e^{-4} = 0.07328$ **8.** 0.01832 **9.** 0.7853

10. (*i*) 0.2707 (*ii*) 0.1804 (*iii*) 0.4060 (*iv*) 0.3233

11. (*i*) 0.4493 (*ii*) 0.5507 **12.** (*i*) 0.2707 (*ii*) 0.4060 (*iii*) 0.3233.

13. P(at least 11 will survive) = P(at most one die) = $P(x \le 1) = e^{-0.135}(1 + 0.135) = 0.9916$

14. $1 - e^{-0.5}\left\{1+\frac{0.5}{1!}+\frac{(0.5)^2}{2!}+\frac{(0.5)^3}{1!}\right\} = 0.0018$ **15.** (*i*) 0.0498 (*ii*) 0.6473

16. (*i*) 0.14937	(*ii*) 0.22405	(*iii*) 0.81531	
17. (*i*) 0.092	(*ii*) 0.567	18. (*i*) 60.65%	(*ii*) 39.35%
(*iii*) 9.03%	19. 0.0012	20. (*i*) 392	(*ii*) 8 (*iii*) 0.

PROPERTIES OF POISSON DISTRIBUTION

20. THE SHAPE OF P.D.

The shape of the Poisson distribution depends upon the parameter m, the average number of successes per unit. As value of m increases, the graph of Poisson distribution would get closer to a symmetrical continuous curve.

21. SPECIAL USEFULNESS OF P.D.

The Poisson distribution is specially used when there are events which do not occur as outcomes of a definite number of trials in an experiment, rather occur randomly in nature. This distribution is used when the event under consideration is rare and casual. In finding probabilities by Poisson distribution, we require only the measure of average chance of occurrence (m) based on past experience or a small sample drawn for the purpose.

22. MEAN OF P.D. *(KU 1998 C, 99 ; MDU 2001)*

Let x be a Poisson random variable and

$$P(x = r) = \frac{e^{-m}\, m^r}{r!},\ r = 0, 1, 2, \ldots\ldots$$

The *mean of* x is the average numbers of successes.

$$\therefore \quad \text{Mean } (\mu) = \sum_{r=0} r.P(x = r) = \sum_{r=0} r.\frac{e^{-m}\, m^r}{r!}$$

$$= 0.\frac{e^{-m}\, m^0}{0!} + 1.\frac{e^{-m}\, m^1}{1!} + 2.\frac{e^{-m}\, m^2}{2!} + 3.\frac{e^{-m}\, m^3}{3!} + \ldots\ldots$$

$$= 0 + me^{-m}\left(\frac{1}{1!} + \frac{2m}{2!} + \frac{3m^2}{3!} + \ldots..\right) = me^{-m}\left(1 + \frac{m}{1!} + \frac{m^2}{2!} + \ldots..\right)$$

$$= me^{-m}.\, e^m = me^0 = m\,.\,1 = m.$$

$\therefore$ Mean of x = m.

23. VARIANCE AND S.D. OF P.D. *(KU 1998 C, 99 ; MDU 2001)*

Let x be a Poisson random variable and

$$P(x = r) = \frac{e^{-m}\, m^r}{r!}, \quad r = 0, 1, 2, \ldots\ldots$$

The variance and standard deviation of x measures the dispersion of the Poisson distribution and are given by

$$\text{variance} = \sum_{r=0} r^2.P(x = r) - \mu^2 \quad \text{and} \quad \text{S.D.} = \sqrt{\sum_{r=0} r^2.P(x = r) - \mu^2}\,.$$

Now $\sum_{r=0} r^2.P(x = r) = \sum_{r=0} r^2.\dfrac{e^{-m}m^r}{r\,!}$

$$= 0^2.\frac{e^{-m}m^0}{0\,!} + 1^2\,\frac{e^{-m}\;m^1}{1!} + 2^2\,\frac{e^{-m}\;m^2}{2\,!} + 3^2\,\frac{e^{-m}\;m^3}{3\,!}\;4^2\,\frac{e^{-m}\;m^4}{4\,!} + \ldots.$$

$$= 0 + me^{-m}\left(\frac{1}{1!} + \frac{2m}{1!} + \frac{3m^2}{2!} + \frac{4m^3}{3\,!}\ldots..\right)$$

$$= me^{-m}\left\{\left(1 + \frac{m}{1!} + \frac{m^2}{2!} + \frac{m^3}{3!} + \ldots..\right) + \left(\frac{m}{1!} + \frac{2m^2}{2!} + \frac{3m^3}{3\,!} + \ldots...\right)\right\}$$

$$= me^{-m}\left\{e^m + m\left(1 + \frac{m}{1!} + \frac{m^2}{2!} + \ldots..\right)\right\} = me^{-m}\,\{e^m + me^m\}$$

$$= me^{-m}\,e^m\,(1 + m) = me^0\,(1 + m) = m(1 + m) = m + m^2.$$

$\therefore$ Variance $= \sum_{r=0} r^2.P(x = r) - \mu^2 = (m + m^2) - m^2 = \mathbf{m}.$

Also, S.D. $= \sqrt{\text{variance}} = \sqrt{\mathbf{m}}$.

24. γ_1 AND γ_2 OF P.D.

The values of γ_1 and γ_2 for the Poisson probability function

$$P(x = r) = \frac{e^{-m}\;m^r}{r\,!},\quad r = 0, 1, 2, \ldots...$$

are given by

$$r_1 = \frac{\mathbf{1}}{\sqrt{\mathbf{m}}} \quad\text{and}\quad r_2 = \frac{\mathbf{1}}{\mathbf{m}}\,.$$

25. RECURRENCE FORMULA FOR P.D.

Let x be a Poisson variable and $P(x = r) = \dfrac{e^{-m}\;m^r}{r\,!}$, $r = 0, 1, 2, \ldots...$

For $k \geq 0$, $P(k) = \dfrac{e^{-m}m^k}{k\,!}$ and $P(k + 1) = \dfrac{e^{-m}m^{k+1}}{(k+1)!}$

Dividing, we get $\dfrac{P(k+1)}{P(k)} = \dfrac{e^{-m}m^{k+1}}{(k+1)\,!}.\dfrac{k\,!}{e^{-m}m^k} = \dfrac{m}{k+1}$.

$$\therefore\quad \mathbf{P(k + 1) = \frac{m}{k+1}\;P(k),\;\; k = 0, 1, 2, \ldots...}$$

This is the required **recurrence formula.**

Example 1. *Criticise the following statement, "The mean and standard deviation of a Poisson distribution are 5 and 2 respectively".*

Sol. Let x be a Poisson variable and

$$P(x = r) = \frac{e^{-m} m^r}{r!}, \qquad r = 0, 1, 2, \ldots\ldots$$

By the given condition,

$$\text{Mean} = 5, \text{S.D.} = 2$$

$$\therefore \quad \text{Variance} = (2)^2 = 4.$$

Now, in Poisson distribution,

$$\text{mean} = \text{variance} = m$$

$$\therefore \quad 5 = 4. \text{ This is impossible.}$$

$\therefore$ The given statement is incorrect.

Example 2. *If x is a Poisson random variable such that :*

$$P(x = 2) = 9P(x = 4) + 90P(x = 6),$$

then find mean, standard deviation and γ_1.

Sol. We have $\quad P(x = r) = \dfrac{e^{-m} m^r}{r!}, r = 0, 1, 2, \ldots\ldots$

where m is the average no. of occurrence of x.

By the given condition,

$$P(x = 2) = 9\,P(x = 4) + 90\,P(x = 6).$$

$$\therefore \quad \frac{e^{-m} m^2}{2!} = 9\frac{e^{-m} m^4}{4!} + 90\frac{e^{-m} m^6}{6!}$$

or $\quad \dfrac{m^2}{2} = \dfrac{9m^4}{24} + \dfrac{90m^6}{720} \quad$ or $\quad \dfrac{1}{2} = \dfrac{3m^2}{8} + \dfrac{m^4}{8} \qquad (\because \ m \neq 0)$

or $\quad 4 = 3m^2 + m^4 \quad$ or $\quad (m^2 + 4)(m^2 - 1) = 0$

$\Rightarrow \quad m^2 = -4, 1 \quad \Rightarrow \quad m^2 = 1 \Rightarrow m = 1 \qquad (\because \ m^2 > 0)$

$\therefore$ Mean = 1, standard deviation = $\sqrt{1} = 1$ and $\gamma_1 = 1/\sqrt{1} = 1$.

EXERCISE 5

1. The mean of a Poisson distribution is $\sqrt{8}$, find the value of its S.D.
2. Criticise the following statement : "The mean and variance of a Poisson distribution are 4 and 2.1 respectively."
3. Comment on the following statement : " The mean and variance of a Poisson distribution are equal only if the average occurrence of the Poisson variable is ≤ 4."
4. The standard deviation of a Poisson distribution is 3. Find the probability of getting 3 successes.

Answers

1. 1.6818   4. 0.0149.

26. FITTING OF A POISSON DISTRIBUTION

Let x be a Poisson random variable. Let probability of x successes be given by

$$P(x = r) = \frac{e^{-m} m^r}{r!}, \qquad r = 0, 1, 2, \ldots\ldots$$

By fitting of a Poisson distribution, we mean to find the theoretical frequencies of the values of the Poisson random variable $x = 0, 1, 2, \ldots\ldots$ when the experiment is repeated N times. The theoretical frequencies are given by

$$\mathbf{N . P(x = r) = N . \frac{e^{-m} m^r}{r!} \quad for \quad r = 0, 1, 2, \ldots\ldots}$$

The use of recurrence formula would be found very useful.

Example 1. *The distribution of typing mistakes committed by a typist is given below :*

No. of mistakes per page	*0*	*1*	*2*	*3*	*4*	*5*
No. of pages	*142*	*156*	*69*	*27*	*5*	*1*

Assuming a Poisson model, find out the expected frequencies.

Sol. **Calculation of Expected Frequencies**

No. of mistakes per page x	*No. of pages* f	fx
0	142	0
1	156	156
2	69	138
3	27	81
4	5	20
5	1	5
Total	N = 400	400

$\therefore$ m = average of no. of mistakes per page

$$= \frac{\Sigma fx}{N} = \frac{400}{400} = 1.$$

$\therefore$ The Poisson distribution is

$$P(x = r) = \frac{e^{-m} m^r}{r!} = \frac{e^{-1}(1)^r}{r!} = \frac{e^{-1}}{r!}, \qquad r = 0, 1, 2, \ldots\ldots$$

For $x = 0$, expected frequency = 400 . P(0)

$$= 400 . \frac{e^{-1}}{0!} = 400(0.36788) = 147.152 \doteq \mathbf{147}$$

For $x = 1$, expected frequency = 400 . P(1)

$$= 400 . \frac{e^{-1}}{1!} = 400(0.36788) = 147.152 \doteq \mathbf{147}$$

For $x = 2$, expected frequency = 400 . P(2)

$$= 400 \cdot \frac{e^{-1}}{2!} = 400(0.36788)/2 = 73.576 \doteq \mathbf{74}$$

For $x = 3$, expected frequency = 400 . P(3)

$$= 400 \cdot \frac{e^{-1}}{3!} = 400(0.36788)/6 = 24.525 \doteq \mathbf{25}$$

For $x = 4$, expected frequency = 400 . P(4)

$$= 400 \cdot \frac{e^{-1}}{4!} = 400(0.36788)/24 = 6.131 \doteq \mathbf{6}$$

For $x = 5$, expected frequency = 400 . P(5)

$$= 400 \cdot \frac{e^{-1}}{5!} = 400(0.36788)/120 = 1.2263 \doteq \mathbf{1.}$$

Example 2. *Letters were received in an office on each of 100 days. Assuming the following data to form a random sample from a Poisson distribution, find the expected frequencies, correct to the nearest unit, taking* $e^{-4} = 0.0183$.

No. of letters	*0*	*1*	*2*	*3*	*4*	*5*	*6*	*7*	*8*	*9*	*10*
Frequency	*1*	*4*	*15*	*22*	*21*	*20*	*8*	*6*	*2*	*0*	*1*

Sol. **Calculation of Expected Frequencies**

No. of letters x	*Frequency* f	fx
0	1	0
1	4	4
2	15	30
3	22	66
4	21	84
5	20	100
6	8	48
7	6	42
8	2	16
9	0	0
10	1	10
Total	N = 100	400

∴ m = average no. of letters per day

$$= \frac{\Sigma fx}{N} = \frac{400}{100} = 4.$$

∴ The Poisson distribution is

$$P(x = r) = \frac{e^{-m} m^r}{r!} = \frac{e^{-4} 4^r}{r!}, \; r = 0, 1, 2, \ldots\ldots$$

By recurrence formula,

$$P(k+1) = \frac{4}{k+1} P(k), \quad k = 0, 1, 2, \ldots..$$

Let $f(x)$ denote the expected frequency of x.

$$\therefore \quad f(k+1) = N \,.\, P(k+1) = 100 \,.\, \frac{4}{k+1} P(k) = \frac{4}{k+1} 100 \,.\, P(k) = \frac{4}{k+1} f(k)$$

$$\therefore \quad f(k+1) = \frac{4}{k+1} f(x), \quad k = 0, 1, 2, \ldots...$$

Now $\quad f(0) = 100\, P(0) = 100 \,.\, \dfrac{e^{-4}(4)^0}{0!} = 100(0.0183) = 1.83 \doteq \mathbf{2}$

$$f(1) = \frac{4}{1} f(0) = 4(1.83) = 7.32 \doteq \mathbf{7}$$

$$f(2) = \frac{4}{2} f(1) = 2(7.32) = 14.64 \doteq \mathbf{15}$$

$$f(3) = \frac{4}{3} f(2) = \frac{4(14.64)}{3} = 19.52 \doteq \mathbf{20}$$

$$f(4) = \frac{4}{4} f(3) = \frac{4(19.52)}{4} = 19.52 \doteq \mathbf{20}$$

$$f(5) = \frac{4}{5} f(4) = \frac{4(19.52)}{5} = 15.62 \doteq \mathbf{16}$$

$$f(6) = \frac{4}{6} f(5) = \frac{4(15.62)}{6} = 10.41 \doteq \mathbf{10}$$

$$f(7) = \frac{4}{7} f(6) = \frac{4(10.41)}{7} = 5.95 \doteq \mathbf{6}$$

$$f(8) = \frac{4}{8} f(7) = \frac{4(5.95)}{8} = 2.97 \doteq \mathbf{3}$$

$$f(9) = \frac{4}{9} f(8) = \frac{4(2.97)}{9} = 1.32 \doteq \mathbf{1}$$

$$f(10) = \frac{4}{10} f(9) = \frac{4(1.32)}{10} = 0.53 \doteq \mathbf{1.}$$

EXERCISE 6

1. A typist commits the following number of mistakes per page in typing 100 pages. Fit a Poisson distribution and calculate theoretical frequencies :

Mistakes per page	0	1	2	3	4	5
Frequency	42	33	14	6	4	1

You are given, $e^{-1} = 0.3679$. *(KU 1996, 2006 C)*

2. Below are given the number of vacancies of judges occurring in a High Court over a period of 96 years :

Fit a Poisson distribution to represent the frequencies of vacancies per year and find the expected frequencies :

No. of vacancies per year	0	1	2	3
No. of years	59	27	9	1

3. In 1,000 sets of trials for an event of small frequencies f_i, of the number of x_i successes are :

x	0	1	2	3	4	5	6	7
f	305	365	210	80	28	9	2	1

Fit a Poisson distribution to the above data and calculate the theoretical frequencies.

4. 5,000 television sets are inspected as they come off the production line and the number of defects per set is recorded below.

No. of defects	0	1	2	3	4
No. of sets	3680	720	520	70	10

Estimate the average number of defects per set and the expected frequencies of 0, 1, 2, 3 and 4 defects, assuming Poisson distribution.

Answers

1. 37, 37, 18, 6, 2, 0 **2.** 58, 29, 7, 1

3. 301, 361, 217, 87, 26, 6, 1, 0.

4. Average no. of defect per set = 0.402 ; 3351, 1341, 268, 36, 4.

NORMAL DISTRIBUTION

27. INTRODUCTION

In Binomial and Poisson distributions, we considered the probabilities of discrete random variables. Now we shall consider random variables which may take non-countably infinitely many possible values. Such a random variable is called a **continuous random variable**. The random variables corresponding to the measurement of height, weight etc. are continuous. We have already discussed probability distributions of discrete random variables. We shall also be considering the probability function of a very important continuous random variable, namely *normal variable*.

28. PROBABILITY FUNCTION OF CONTINUOUS RANDOM VARIABLE

In discrete probability distributions, the probability is defined for each and every value of the variable and the sum of all these probabilities is one. On the other hand, continuous random variables are defined over intervals of real numbers which contains non-countably infinitely many numbers. Let x be a continuous random variable. The probability of x to take any particular value is generally zero. For example, if an individual is selected at random from a large group of males, then the probability that his weight (x) is exactly 56 kg (*i.e.*,

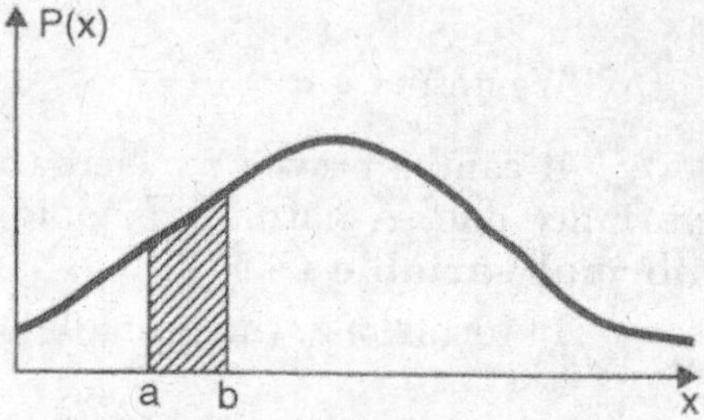

56.000 ...... kg) would be zero. On the other hand, the probability that weight (x) lying between 55.600 ...... kg and 56.200 ...... kg need not be zero. Thus, we cannot define a probability function for a continuous random variable as we did in the case of a discrete random variable. In case of a continuous random variable (x), the probability of x taking any particular value is generally zero and practically does not make any sense whereas the probability of x taking values between any two different values is meaningful.

For a continuous random variable, x, a function $P(x)$ is called a **probability function** if :

(*i*) $P(x) \geq 0$ and (*ii*) $\int_{-\infty}^{\infty} P(x)\,dx = 1$.

If $P(x)$ is a *probability function* of x, then we define :

$$P(a < x < b) = \int_a^b P(x)\,dx .$$

Thus, if $P(x)$ is a *probability function* of x, then :

(*i*) $P(x)$ is non-negative

(*ii*) area bounded by the curve and x-axis is equal to one

(*iii*) area bounded by the curve, x-axis and ordinates $x = a$, $x = b$ gives the measure of the probability that x lies between a and b.

Remark. Since the probability of x taking any particular value is generally zero, we have

$$P(a < x < b) = P(a \leq x < b) = P(a < x \leq b) = P(a \leq x \leq b).$$

29. NORMAL DISTRIBUTION

The normal distribution is a particular type of continuous probability distribution. This was discovered by **De Moivre (1667—1754)** in the year 1733. The normal distribution is obtained as a limiting case of a binomial distribution when n, the number of trials is indefinitely large and neither p nor q is very small.

30. DEFINITION

A continuous random variable x is said to have a **normal distribution** (N.D.) if its probability function is given by

$$P(x) = \frac{1}{\sigma\sqrt{2\pi}} e^{-\frac{1}{2}\left(\frac{x-\mu}{\sigma}\right)^2}, \quad -\infty < x < \infty, \qquad ...(1)$$

where μ and σ are the mean and standard deviation of the distribution respectively.

Remark. If x is a normal variable with mean μ and variance σ^2, then we write symbolically as $x \sim N(\mu, \sigma^2)$.

31. STANDARD NORMAL DISTRIBUTION

Let x be a normal variable with probability function :

$$P(x) = \frac{1}{\sigma\sqrt{2\pi}} e^{-\frac{1}{2}\left(\frac{x-\mu}{\sigma}\right)^2}, \quad -\infty < x < \infty,$$

where μ and σ are the mean and standard deviation of the distribution respectively.

We define $z = \frac{x - \mu}{\sigma}$.

It can be proved mathematically that z is also a normal variable with mean zero and variance one. A normal variable with mean zero and variance one is called a **standard normal variable (S.N.V.).**

In terms of z, the probability function of x reduces to

$$P(z) = \frac{1}{\sqrt{2\pi}} e^{-\frac{1}{2}z^2}, \quad -\infty < z < \infty.$$

Remark. Thus, if $x \sim N(\mu, \sigma^2)$ and z = S.N.V. of $x = \frac{x - \mu}{\sigma}$, then $z \sim N(0, 1)$.

32. AREA UNDER NORMAL CURVE

Let x be a *normal variable* with mean μ and standard deviation σ. Let $z = \frac{x - \mu}{\sigma}$ be the corresponding S.N.V. We know that mean and standard deviation of the variable z are 0 and 1 respectively. Therefore, the curves of standard normal variables corresponding of normal variables are identical.

This is why the curve of a standard normal variable is called the **standard normal curve**. For the standard normal curve, we have :

(*i*) area between $z = -1$ and $z = 1$ is 68.26% of total area, which is one.

$\therefore \quad P(-1 \le z \le 1) = 0.6826.$

(*ii*) area between $z = -2$ and $z = 2$ is 95.44% of total area.

$\therefore \quad P(-2 \le z \le 2) = 0.9544.$

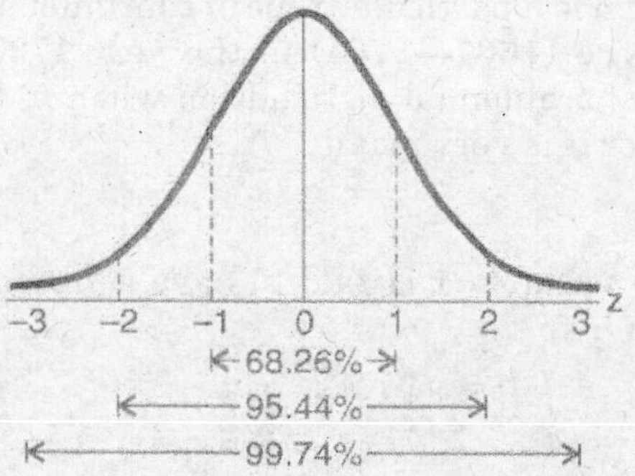

(*iii*) area between $z = -3$ and $z = 3$ is 99.74% of total area.

$\therefore \quad P(-3 \le z \le 3) = 0.9974.$

The area bounded by the curve of a S.N.V. z, z-axis and the ordinates at $z = 0$ and any positive value of z is provided by a standard table. This knowledge of measure of area in case of S.N.V. is used to find the area bounded by the corresponding normal variable x, x-axis and any two ordinates. This in turn would help us to find the probability of normal variable x lying between any two real numbers.

33. TABLE OF AREA UNDER STANDARD NORMAL CURVE

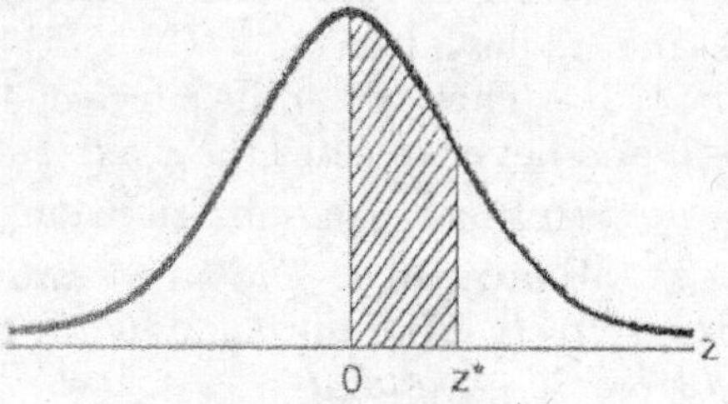

The table titled *area under standard normal curve* is given at the end. Let $z*$ be any arbitrary but fixed value of the variable z. The first column of the table provides for z values with one decimal digit and the second column gives areas bounded between z-curve and ordinates $z = 0$ and $z = z*$, which is equal to $P(0 \le z \le z*)$.

For example, from the table $P(0 \le z \le 1.4) = 0.4192$. The first row of the table provides for the second decimal digit of $z*$. For example, $P(0 \le z \le 1.43) = 0.4236$.

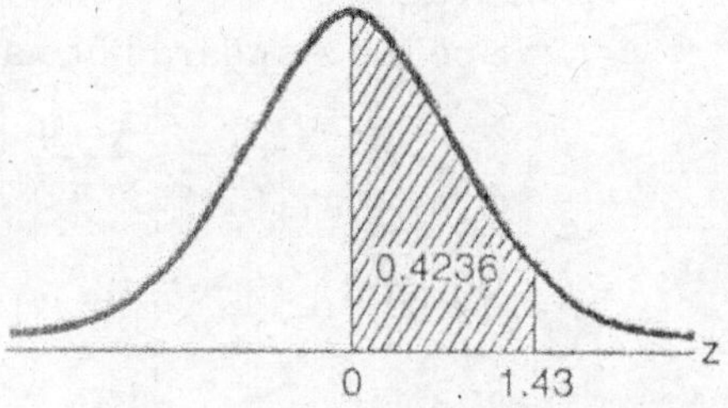

Remark. Sometimes, the table for the probabilities $P(-\infty < z \le z*)$ is given in the examination hall. In such a case, the students should find the value of $P(0 \le z \le z*)$ by using the following formula :

$$\mathbf{P(0 \le z \le z*) = P(-\infty < z \le z*) - 0.5.}$$

34. PROPERTIES OF NORMAL DISTRIBUTION

(KU 2004 ; MDU 2004)

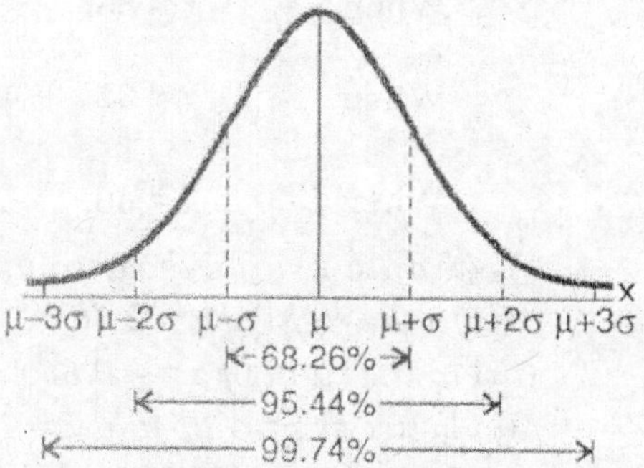

(*i*) The area bounded by the curve and the x-axis is equal to one.

(*ii*) $P(a < x < b)$, *i.e.* the probability that x lies between a and b is equal to the area bounded by the curve, x-axis and ordinates $x = a$ and $x = b$.

(*iii*) The curve is bell-shaped and symmetrical about the line $x = \mu$.

(*iv*) The mean (μ) and variance (σ^2) of a normal distribution are called its *parameters*.

(*v*) The location and shape of a normal distribution depends upon the values of its parameters.

(*vi*) If the mean and S.D. of a normal distribution are μ and σ respectively, then :

$$(a)\ P(\mu - \sigma \le x \le \mu + \sigma) = P\left(\frac{\mu - \sigma - \mu}{\sigma} \le \frac{x - \mu}{\sigma} \le \frac{\mu + \sigma - \mu}{\sigma}\right)$$
$$= P(-1 \le z \le 1) = 0.6826$$

$$(b)\ P(\mu - 2\sigma \le x \le \mu + 2\sigma) = P\left(\frac{\mu - 2\sigma - \mu}{\sigma} \le \frac{x - \mu}{\sigma} \le \frac{\mu + 2\sigma - \mu}{\sigma}\right)$$
$$= P(-2 \le z \le 2) = 0.9544$$

$$(c)\ P(\mu - 3\sigma \le x \le \mu + 3\sigma) = P\left(\frac{\mu - 3\sigma - \mu}{\sigma} \le \frac{x - \mu}{\sigma} \le \frac{\mu + 3\sigma - \mu}{\sigma}\right)$$
$$= P(-3 \le z \le 3) = 0.9974.$$

(*vii*) The mean, median and mode of a normal distribution coincide with each other.

(*viii*) For a normal distribution, $\gamma_1 = 0$ and $\gamma_2 = 0$. Therefore, normal distribution is *mesokurtic*.

(*ix*) In a normal distribution, mean deviation about mean is approximately equal to $\frac{4}{5}$ time its standard deviation.

(*x*) In a normal distribution, quartile deviation is approximately equal to $\frac{2}{3}$ times its standard deviation.

(*xi*) The tails of the curve of a normal distribution extend indefinitely on both sides of $x = \mu$ and never touches the x-axis.

(*xii*) In a normal distribution, Q_1 and Q_3 are equidistant from the median.

Example 1. *The mean and standard deviation of a normal variable x are 50 and 4 respectively. Find the values of the corresponding standard normal variable, when x is equal to 42, 84, 85, 32 and 40.*

Sol. We have $\mu = 50, \sigma = 4$.

Let z be the standard normal variable corresponding to x.

$$\therefore \quad z = \frac{x - \mu}{\sigma} = \frac{x - 50}{4}$$

$\therefore$ When $x = 42$, $z = \frac{42 - 50}{4} = -2$

When $x = 84$, $z = \frac{84 - 50}{4} = 8.5$

When $x = 85$, $z = \frac{85 - 50}{4} = 8.75$

When $x = 32$, $z = \frac{32 - 50}{4} = -4.5$

When $x = 40$, $z = \frac{40 - 50}{4} = -2.5$.

Example 2. *Find the area under the standard normal curve which lies :*

(*i*) *to the right of* $z = 2.70$ (*ii*) *to the left of* $z = 1.73$

(*iii*) *to the right of* $z = -0.66$ (*iv*) *to the left of* $z = -1.88$

(*v*) *between* $z = 1.25$ *and* $z = 1.67$

(*vi*) *between* $z = -1.85$ *and* $z = -0.90$

(*vii*) *between* $z = -1.45$ *and* $z = 1.45$

(*viii*) *between* $z = -0.9$ *and* $z = 1.58$.

Sol. The variable z is a standard normal variable (S.N.V.).

$\therefore$ Total area under the curve of z and z-axis is one.

(*i*) Area to the right of $z = 2.7$

$= 0.5 -$ area between $z = 0$ and $z = 2.7$

$= 0.5 - 0.4965$ (Using area Table)

$= \mathbf{0.0035}$.

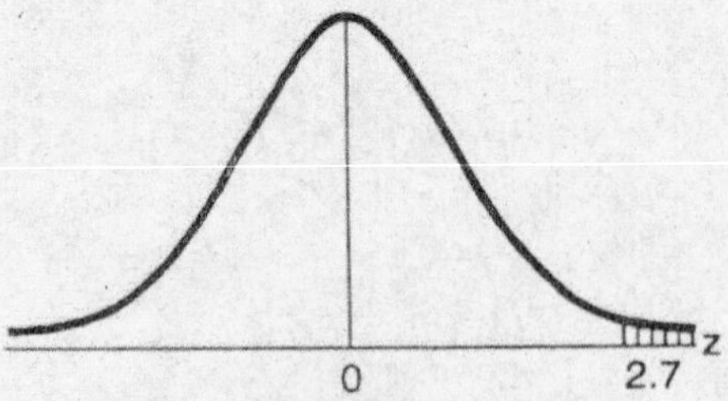

(*ii*) Area to the left of $z = 1.73$

$= 0.5 +$ area between $z = 0$ and $z = 1.73$

$= 0.5 + 0.4582 = \mathbf{0.9582}$.

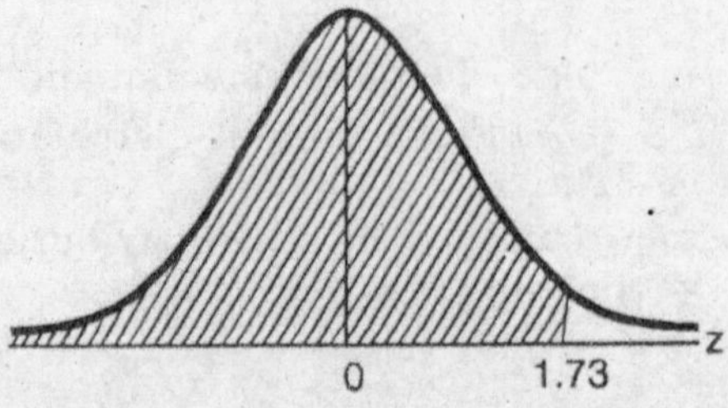

(*iii*) Area to the right of $z = -0.66$

$= (\text{area from } z = -0.66 \text{ to } z = 0) + 0.5$

$= (\text{area from } z = 0 \text{ to } z = 0.66) + 0.5$ (By symmetry of curve)

$= 0.2454 + 0.5 =$ **0.7454.** (Using Table)

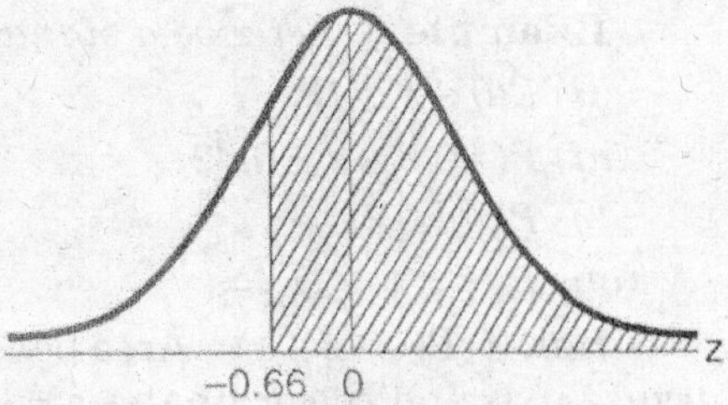

(*iv*) Area to the left of $z = -1.88$

$= 0.5 - \text{area between } z = -1.88 \text{ and } z = 0$

$= 0.5 - \text{area between } z = 0 \text{ and } z = 1.88$ (By symmetry of curve)

$= 0.5 - 0.4699 =$ **0.0301.** (Using Table)

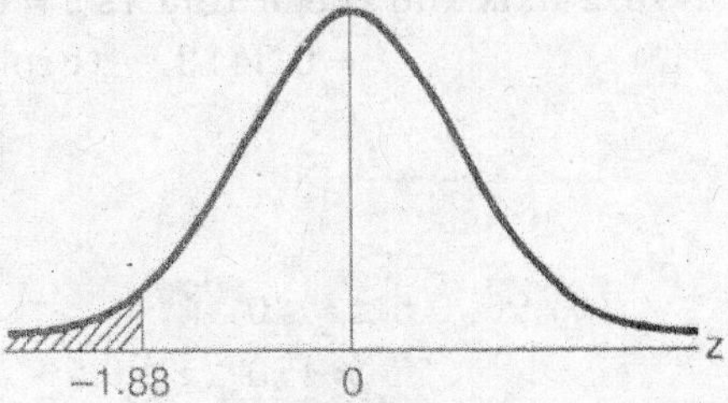

(*v*) Area between $z = 1.25$ and $z = 1.67$

$= (\text{area between } z = 0 \text{ and } z = 1.67) - (\text{area between } z = 0 \text{ and } z = 1.25)$

$= 0.4525 - 0.3944 =$ **0.0581.** (Using Table)

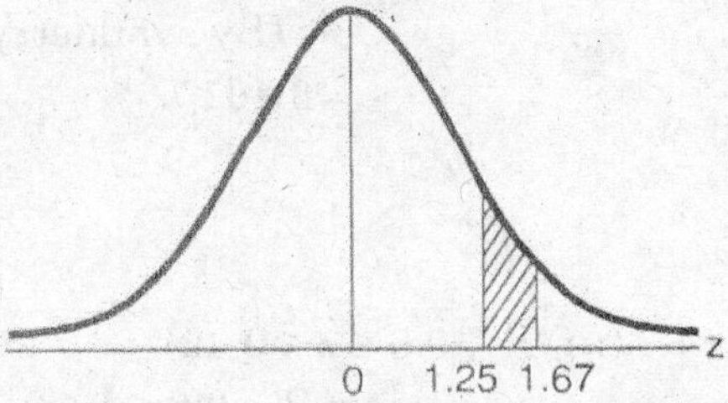

(*vi*) Area between $z = -1.85$ and $z = -0.90$

$= (\text{area between } z = -1.85 \text{ and } z = 0) - (\text{area between } z = -0.90 \text{ and } z = 0)$

$= (\text{area between } z = 0 \text{ and } z = 1.85) - (\text{area between } z = 0 \text{ and } z = 0.90)$ (By symmetry of curve)

$= 0.4678 - 0.3159 =$ **0.1519.** (Using Table)

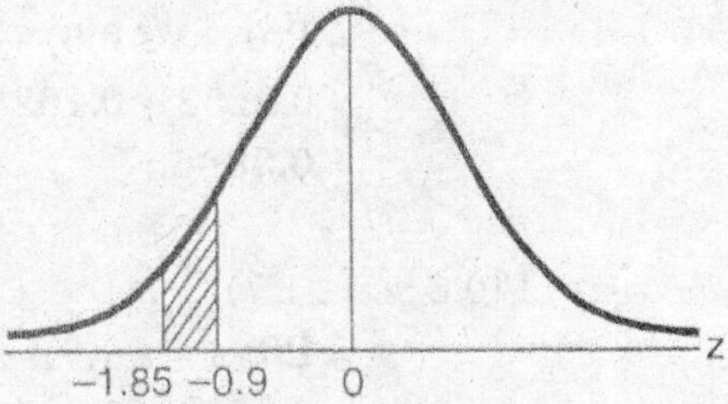

(*vii*) Area between $z = -1.45$ and $z = 1.45$

$= (\text{area between } z = -1.45 \text{ and } z = 0) + (\text{area between } z = 0 \text{ and } z = 1.45)$

$= (\text{area between } z = 0 \text{ and } z = 1.45) + (\text{area between } z = 0 \text{ and } z = 1.45)$ (By symmetry of curve)

$= 2(\text{area between } z = 0 \text{ and } z = 1.45)$

$= 2(0.4265) =$ **0.8530.** (Using Table)

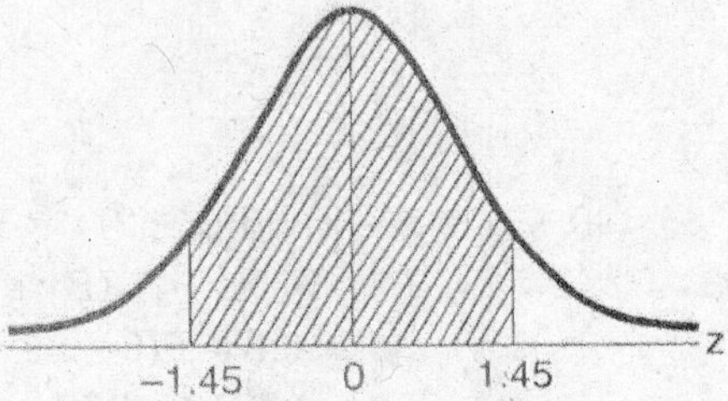

(*viii*) Area between $z = -0.9$ and $z = 1.58$

$= (\text{area between } z = -0.9 \text{ and } z = 0) + (\text{area between } z = 0 \text{ and } z = 1.58)$

$= (\text{area between } z = 0 \text{ and } z = 0.9) + (\text{area between } z = 0 \text{ and } z = 1.58)$ (By symmetry of curve)

$= 0.3159 + 0.4429 =$ **0.7588.** (Using Table)

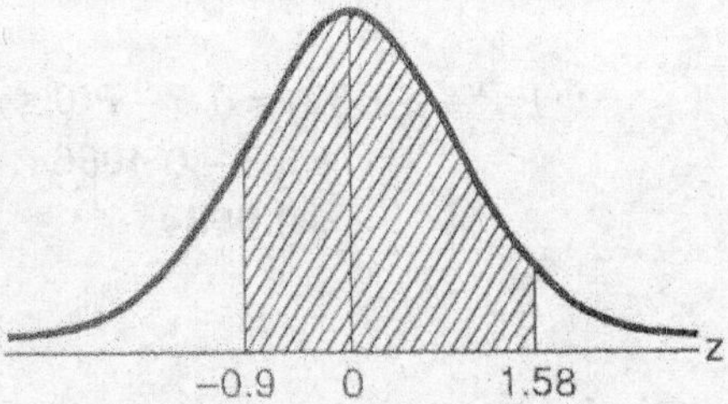

Example 3. *Let z be a standard normal variable. Find :*

(*i*) $P(0 \le z \le 1)$ (*ii*) $P(-0.5 \le z \le 0)$

(*iii*) $P(-0.6 \le z \le 0.42)$ (*iv*) $P(0.6 \le z \le 1.7)$

(*v*) $P(z \le -2)$ (*vi*) $P(z \ge 1.32)$ *and*

(*vii*) $P(|z| \ge 1)$.

Sol. (*i*) $P(0 \le z \le 1)$ = Area bounded by the z-curve, z-axis and the ordinates $z = 0$ and $z = 1$

= **0.3413.** (From the table)

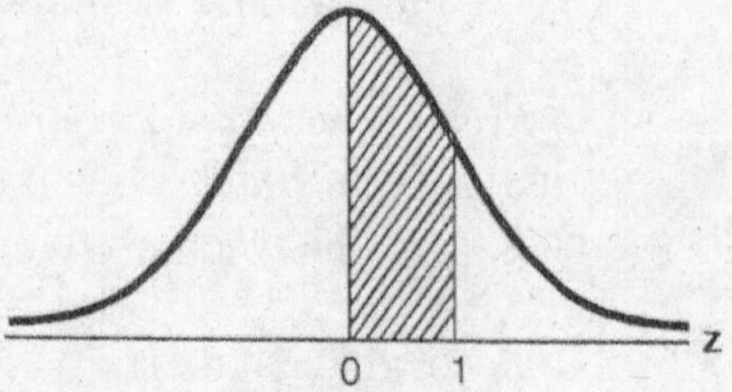

(*ii*) $P(-0.5 \le z \le 0)$

$= P(0 \le z \le 0.5)$

(By symmetry of normal curve)

= **0.1915.**

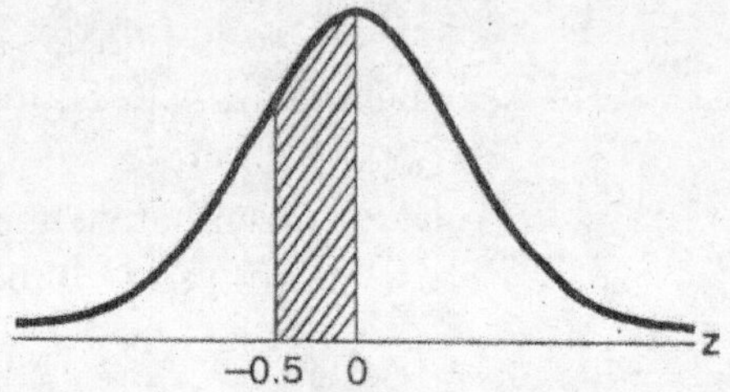

(*iii*) $P(-0.6 \le z \le 0.42)$

$= P(-0.6 \le z \le 0) + P(0 \le z \le 0.42)$

$= P(0 \le z \le 0.6) + P(0 \le z \le 0.42)$

$= 0.2258 + 0.1628$

= **0.3886.**

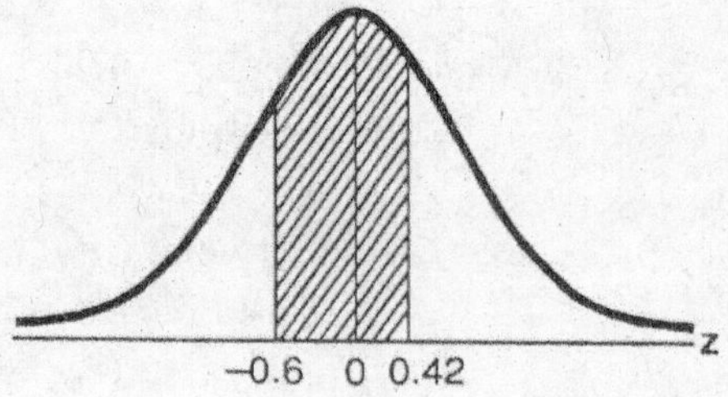

(*iv*) $P(0.6 \le z \le 1.7)$

$= P(0 \le z \le 1.7) - P(0 \le z \le 0.6)$

$= 0.4554 - 0.2258$

= **0.2296.**

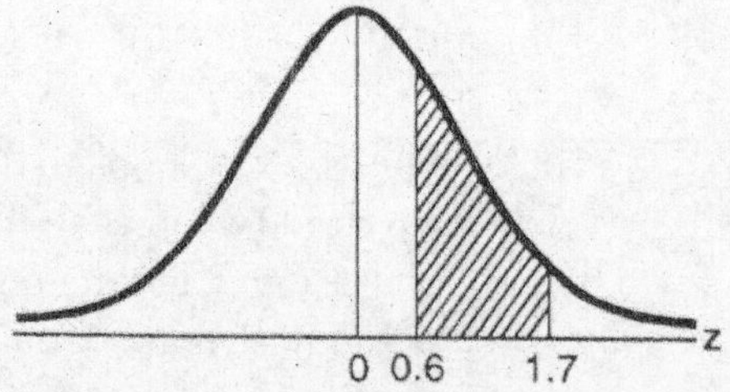

(*v*) $P(z \le -2) = P(z \ge 2)$

(By symmetry of curve)

$= 0.5 - P(0 \le z \le 2)$

$= 0.5 - 0.4772$

= **0.0228.**

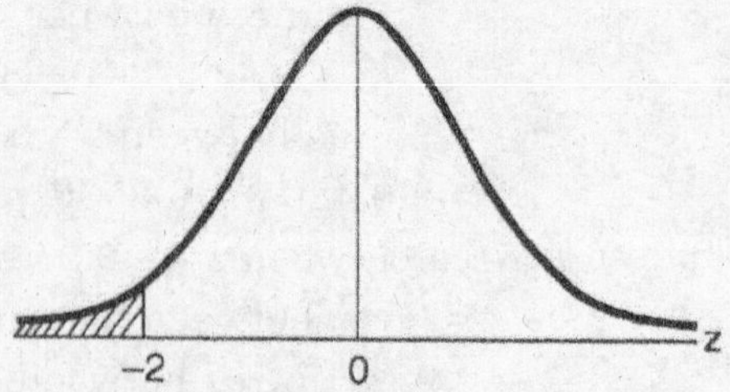

(*vi*) $P(z \ge 1.32) = 0.5 - P(0 \le z \le 1.32)$

$= 0.5 - 0.4066$

= **0.0934.**

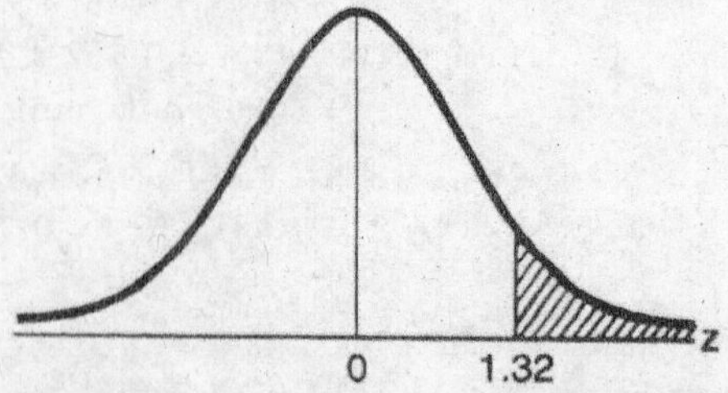

(*vii*) $P(|z| \geq 1) = P(z \leq -1) + P(z \geq 1)$
$= P(z \geq 1) + P(z \geq 1) = 2P(z \geq 1)$
$= 2\{0.5 - P(0 \leq z \leq 1)\}$
$= 2\{(0.5 - 0.3413\}$
$= \mathbf{0.3174.}$

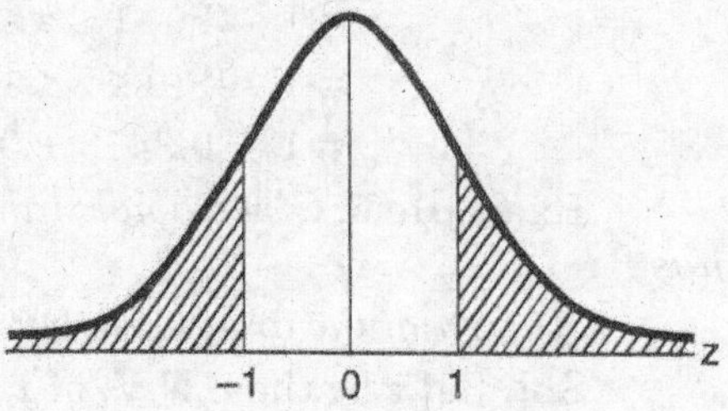

Example 4. *x is a normal variable with mean 25 and standard deviation 5. Find the probability that :*

(*i*) $x \leq 10$ (*ii*) $15 \leq x \leq 30$

(*iii*) $|x - 30| \geq 10$.

Sol. We have mean = 25, S.D. = 5.

Let z be the S.N.V. corresponding to x.

$\therefore \quad z = \dfrac{x - \mu}{\sigma} = \dfrac{x - 25}{5}$.

(*i*) When $x = 10$, $z = \dfrac{10 - 25}{5} = -3$

$\therefore$ Required probability $= P(x \leq 10)$
$= P(z \leq -3) = P(z \geq 3)$
$= 0.5 - P(0 \leq z \leq 3)$
$= 0.5 - 0.4987$
$= \mathbf{0.0013.}$

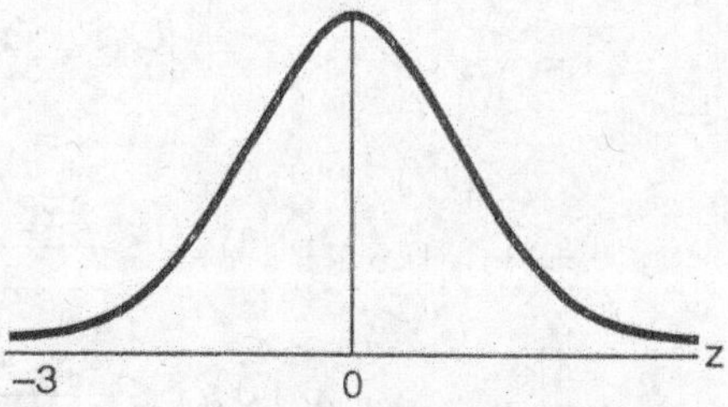

(*ii*) When $x = 15$, $z = \dfrac{15 - 25}{5} = -2$

When $x = 30$, $z = \dfrac{30 - 25}{5} = 1$

$\therefore$ Required probability
$= P(15 \leq x \leq 30)$
$= P(-2 \leq z \leq 1)$
$= P(-2 \leq z \leq 0) + P(0 \leq z \leq 1)$
$= P(0 \leq z \leq 2) + P(0 \leq z \leq 1)$
$= 0.4772 + 0.3413$
$= \mathbf{0.8185.}$

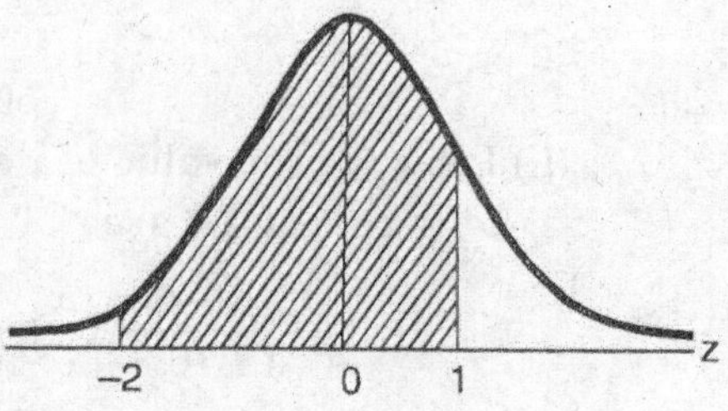

(*iii*) Required probability $= P(|x - 30| \geq 10)$
$= 1 - P(|x - 30| < 10)$
$= 1 - P(30 - 10 < x < 30 + 10)$
$= 1 - P(20 < x < 40)$
$= 1 - P\left(\dfrac{20 - 25}{5} < \dfrac{x - 25}{5} < \dfrac{40 - 25}{5}\right)$
$= 1 - P(-1 < z < 3)$

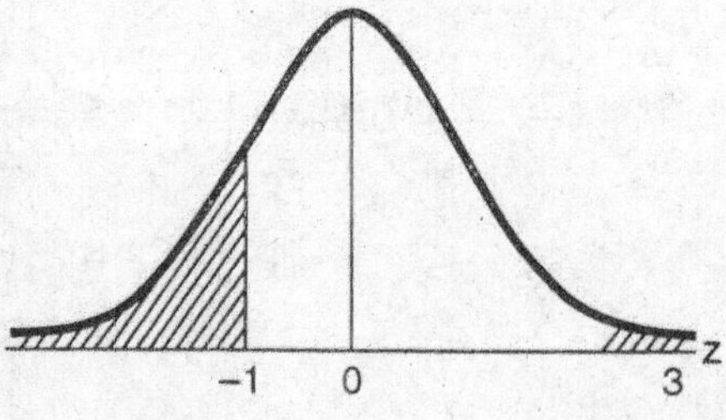

$= 1 - \{P(-1 \le z \le 0) + P(0 \le z \le 3)\}$ $\quad [\because \; P(z = -1) = P(z = 3) = 0]$

$= 1 - \{P(0 \le z \le 1) + P(0 \le z \le 3)\}$

$= 1 - \{0.3413 + 0.4987\} = \mathbf{0.16}.$

Example 5. *Given a normal distribution with x = 50 and σ = 10. Find the value of x that has :*

(i) 13% of the area to its left *(ii) 14% of the area to its right.*

Sol. Let z be the S.N.V. of x.

$$\therefore \quad z = \frac{x - 50}{10}.$$

(*i*) Let x_1 be the value of x such that $P(x \le x_1)$ = 13% of the area

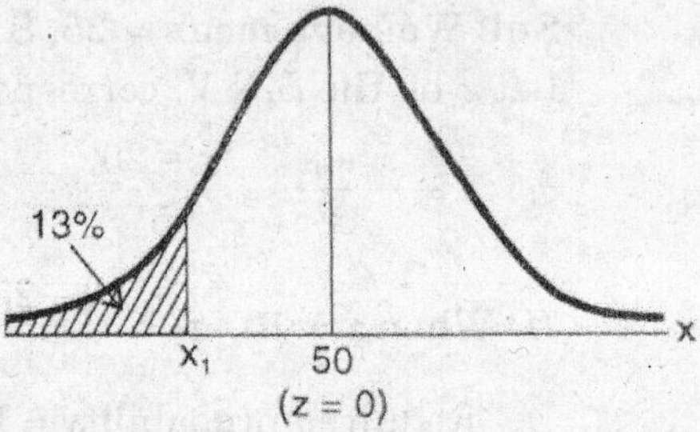

$$\therefore \quad P\left(\frac{x-50}{10} \le \frac{x_1 - 50}{10}\right) = 0.13$$

$$\Rightarrow \quad P\left(z < \frac{x_1 - 50}{10}\right) = 0.13$$

$$\Rightarrow \quad P\left(z \ge -\frac{x_1 - 50}{10}\right) = 0.13$$

(Note this step)

$$\Rightarrow \quad 0.5 - P\left(0 \le z \le -\frac{x_1 - 50}{10}\right) = 0.13$$

$$\Rightarrow \quad P\left(0 \le z \le -\frac{x_1 - 50}{10}\right) = 0.5 - 0.13 = 0.37.$$

From the area table,

$P(0 \le z \le 1.13) = 0.37$ (Approx.)

$$\therefore \quad -\frac{x_1 - 50}{10} = 1.13$$

i.e., $50 - x_1 = 11.3$ or $x_1 = 50 - 11.3 = \mathbf{38.7}.$

(*ii*) Let x_2 be the value of x such that $P(x \ge x_2)$ = 14% of the area

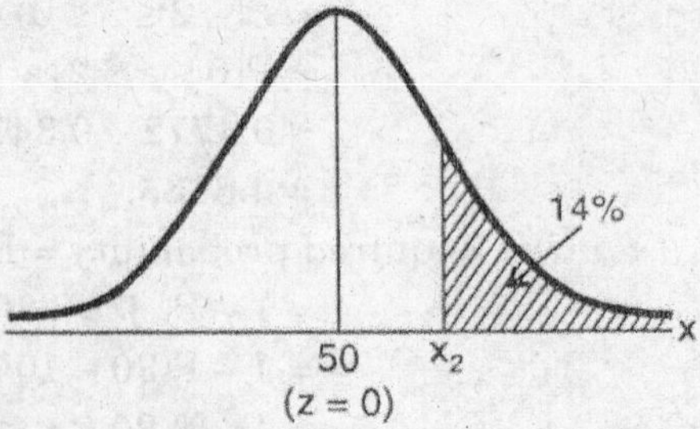

$$\therefore \quad P\left(\frac{x-50}{10} \ge \frac{x_2 - 50}{10}\right) = 0.14$$

$$\Rightarrow \quad P\left(z \ge \frac{x_2 - 50}{10}\right) = 0.14$$

$$\Rightarrow \quad 0.5 - P\left(0 \le z \le \frac{x_2 - 50}{10}\right) = 0.14$$

$$\Rightarrow \quad P\left(0 \le z \le \frac{x_2 - 50}{10}\right) = 0.5 - 0.14 = 0.36.$$

From the area table,

$P(0 \le z \le 1.08) = 0.36$ (Approx.)

$$\therefore \quad \frac{x_2 - 50}{10} = 1.08$$

i.e. $$x_2 - 50 = 10.8 \quad \text{or} \quad x_2 = 50 + 10.8 = \mathbf{60.8}.$$

Example 6. *In a normal distribution, 31% of the items are under 45 and 8% are over 64. Find the mean and standard deviation of the distribution.* (MDU 2000, 2001)

Sol. Let x be the normal variable and z be its S.N.V. Let μ and σ be the mean and standard deviation of x.

By the given conditions,

$$P(x < 45) = \frac{31}{100} = 0.31 \quad \text{and} \quad P(x > 64) = \frac{8}{100} = 0.08.$$

Since $P(x < 45) < 0.5$. $\therefore$ $x = 45$ lies on the left of $x = \mu$ and so the value of the corresponding z-variable is –ve.

When $x = 45$, let $z = \dfrac{45 - \mu}{\sigma} = -z_1 \ (z_1 > 0)$

When $x = 64$, let $z = \dfrac{64 - \mu}{\sigma} = z_2 \ (> 0)$

$\therefore$ $P(x < 45) = 0.31$

$\Rightarrow$ $P(z < -z_1) = 0.31$

$\Rightarrow$ $P(z > z_1) = 0.31$

$\Rightarrow$ $0.5 - P(0 \le z \le z_1) = 0.31$

$\Rightarrow$ $P(0 \le z \le z_1) = 0.19$

$\Rightarrow$ $z_1 = 0.5$ (From area table)

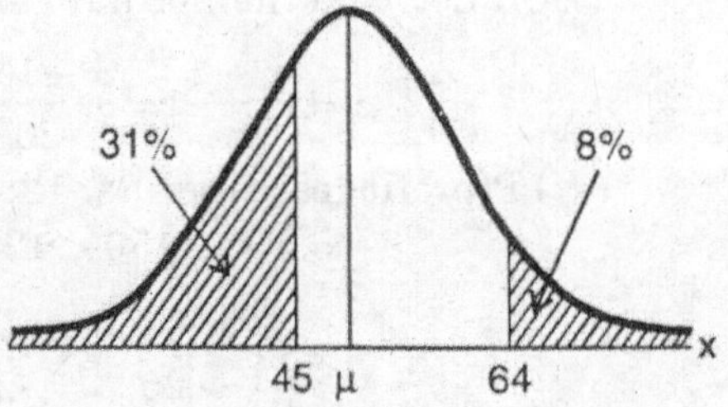

$$\therefore \quad \frac{45 - \mu}{\sigma} = -0.5 \quad \text{or} \quad 45 - \mu = -0.5\,\sigma \quad \text{...(1)}$$

Also $P(x > 64) = 0.08$

$\Rightarrow$ $P(z > z_2) = 0.08$ $\Rightarrow$ $0.5 - P(0 \le z \le z_2) = 0.08$

$\Rightarrow$ $P(0 \le z \le z_2) = 0.42$ $\Rightarrow$ $z_2 = 1.4$

(From area table)

$$\therefore \quad \frac{64 - \mu}{\sigma} = 1.4 \quad \text{or} \quad 64 - \mu = 1.4\,\sigma \quad \text{...(2)}$$

(1) – (2) $\Rightarrow$ $-19 = -1.9\sigma$ $\Rightarrow$ $\sigma = 10$

$\therefore$ (1) $\Rightarrow$ $45 - \mu = -0.5\,(10) = -5$

$\Rightarrow$ $\mu = 45 + 5 = 50$

$\therefore$ $\mu = \mathbf{50}$ and $\sigma = \mathbf{10}$.

Example 7. *Find the probability that an item drawn at random from a normal distribution with mean 5 and S.D. 3 will be between 2.75 and 4.34.* (KU 2000, 2005 ; MDU 2003)

Sol. Let x be the normal variable and z be its S.N.V.

$$\therefore \quad z = \frac{x - \mu}{\sigma} = \frac{x - 5}{3}.$$

Now, $P(2.75 < x < 4.34) = P(2.75 - 5 < x - 5 < 4.34 - 5)$

$= P(-2.25 < x - 5 < -0.66)$

$= P\left(\frac{-2.25}{3} < \frac{x-5}{3} < \frac{-0.66}{3}\right)$

$= P(-0.75 < z < -0.22)$

$= P(0.22 < z < 0.75)$

(By symmetry)

$= P(0 < z < 0.75) - P(0 < z < 0.22)$

$= 0.2734 - 0.0871 = \mathbf{0.1863}.$

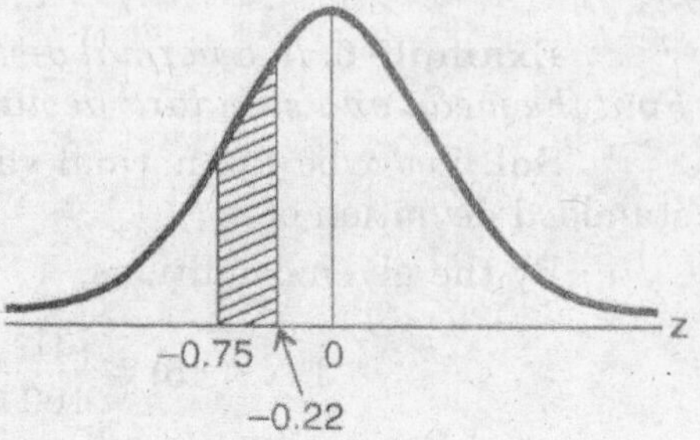

Example 8. *The profits of 400 companies are normally distributed with mean Rs. 150 lakhs and standard deviation Rs. 20 lakhs. Estimate the number of companies with :*

(*i*) *profits less than Rs. 128 lakhs*

(*ii*) *profits more then Rs. 175 lakhs*

(*iii*) *profits between Rs. 100 lakhs and Rs. 138 lakhs.* (MDU 1999)

Sol. Let x be the normal variable '*profit*'. Let z be the corresponding S.N.V.

$$\therefore \quad z = \frac{x - \mu}{\sigma} = \frac{x - 150}{20}$$

(*i*) P(profit less than Rs. 128 lakhs) $= P(x < 128)$

$= P(x - 150 < 128 - 150)$

$= P\left(\frac{x-150}{20} < \frac{-22}{20}\right)$

$= P(z < -1.1) = P(z > 1.1)$

(By symmetry)

$= 0.5 - P(0 < z \le 1.1)$

$= 0.5 - 0.3643 = 0.1357.$

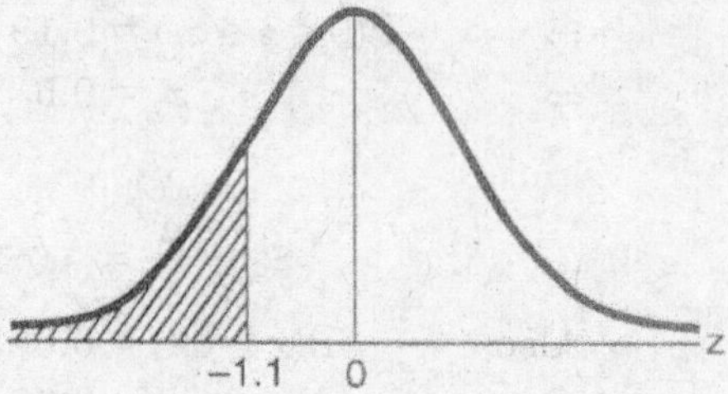

No. of companies with profit less than Rs. 128 lakhs

$= 400\ P(x < 128) = 400 \times 0.1357 \doteq \mathbf{54}.$

(*ii*) P(profit more than Rs. 175 lakhs)

$= P(x > 175) = P(x - 150 > 175 - 150)$

$= P\left(\frac{x-150}{20} > \frac{25}{20}\right) = P(z > 1.25)$

$= 0.5 - P(0 < z \le 1.25)$

$= 0.5 - 0.3944 = 0.1056.$

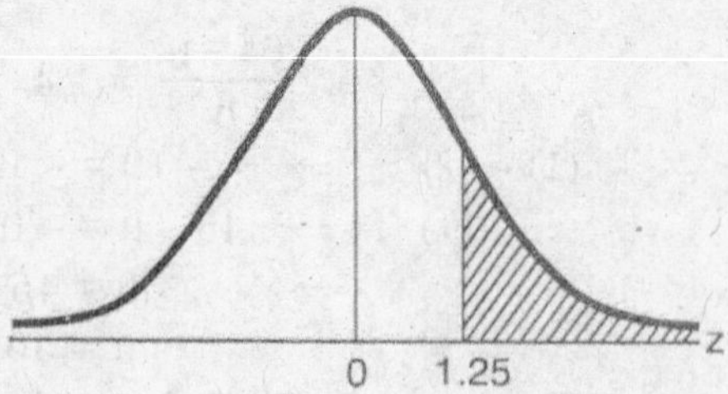

$\therefore$ No. of companies with profit more than Rs. 175 lakhs

$= 400\ P(x > 175)$

$= 400 \times 0.1056 \doteq \mathbf{42}.$

(*iii*) P(profit between Rs. 100 lakhs and Rs. 138 lakhs)

$= P(100 < x < 138)$

$= P(100 - 150 < x - 150 < 138 - 150)$

$= P\left(\frac{-50}{20} < \frac{x-150}{20} < \frac{-12}{20}\right)$

$= P(-2.5 < z < -0.6)$

$= P(0.6 < z < 2.5)$ (By symmetry)

$= P(0 < z < 2.5) - P(0 < z < 0.6)$

$= 0.4938 - 0.2257 = 0.2681.$

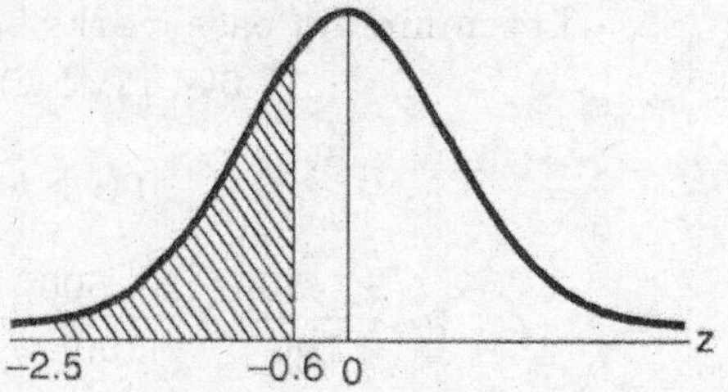

∴ No. of companies with profits between Rs. 100 lakhs and Rs. 138 lakhs

$= 400\ P(100 < x < 138)$

$= 400 \times 0.2681 = \mathbf{107}.$

Example 9. *Students of a class are given a test. Their marks were normally distributed with mean 60 and standard deviation 5. What percentage of students scored :*

(*i*) *more than 60 marks*

(*ii*) *less than 56 marks*

(*iii*) *between 45 and 65 marks both inclusive ?*

Sol. Let x denote the normal variable *marks*. Let z be the corresponding S.N.V.

∴ $z = \frac{x-60}{5}$

(*i*) P(more than 60 marks) $= P(x > 60)$

$= P\left(\frac{x-60}{5} > \frac{60-60}{5}\right) = P(z > 0) = 0.5 = \mathbf{50\%}.$

(*ii*) P(less than 56 marks)

$= P(x < 56)$

$= P\left(\frac{x-60}{5} > \frac{56-60}{5}\right) = P(z < -0.8)$

$= P(z > 0.8)$ (By symmetry of normal curve)

$= 0.5 - P(0 \le z \le 0.8) = 0.5 - 0.2881 = 0.2119 = \mathbf{21.19\%}.$

(*iii*) P(between 45 and 65 marks both inclusive)

$= P(45 \le x \le 65)$

$= P\left(\frac{45-60}{5} \le \frac{x-60}{5} \le \frac{65-60}{5}\right)$

$= P(-3 \le z \le 1) = P(-3 \le z \le 0) + P(0 \le z \le 1)$

$= P(0 \le z \le 3) + P(0 \le z \le 1) = 0.4987 + 0.3413 = 0.84 = \mathbf{84\%}.$

Example 10. *The marks obtained by students in a degree examination are normally distributed. The mean marks and S.D. of the distribution are 500 and 100 respectively. If 674 appeared in the examination and out of these, 550 are to be declared passed, what should be the minimum pass marks ?* (MDU 1995, KU 2007)

Sol. Let x denote the normal variable *marks*. Let z be the S.N.V. of x.

$$\therefore \qquad z = \frac{x - 500}{100}.$$

Let minimum pass marks be k.

$$\therefore \qquad 674\ P(x \geq k) = 550$$

$$\Rightarrow \qquad P(x \geq k) = \frac{550}{674} = 0.816$$

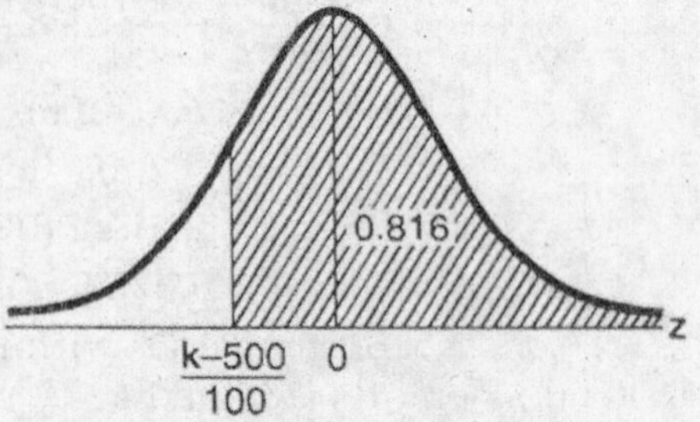

$$\text{or} \qquad P\left(\frac{x - 500}{100} \geq \frac{k - 500}{100}\right) = 0.816$$

$$\text{or} \qquad P\left(z \geq \frac{k - 500}{100}\right) = 0.816$$

$$\text{or} \qquad P\left(\frac{k - 500}{100} \leq z\right) = 0.816$$

$$\text{or} \qquad P\left(\frac{k - 500}{100} \leq z \leq 0\right) + 0.5 = 0.816$$

$$\text{or} \qquad P\left(\frac{k - 500}{100} \leq z \leq 0\right) = 0.316$$

$$\text{or} \qquad P\left(0 \leq z \leq -\frac{k - 500}{100}\right) = 0.316 \qquad \text{(By symmetry of normal curve)}$$

By area table,

$$P(0 \leq z \leq 0.9) = 0.316 \text{ (Approx.)}$$

$$\therefore \qquad -\frac{k - 500}{100} = 0.9$$

i.e., $500 - k = 90$ or $k = 500 - 90 = 410$.

$\therefore$ Minimum pass marks = **410.**

Example 11. *The incomes of a group of 10,000 persons was found to be normally distributed with mean Rs. 750 per month and standard deviation Rs. 50. Show that of this group about 15% had income exceeding Rs. 668 and only 5% had income exceeding Rs. 832. What was the lowest income among the richest 100 ?*

Sol. Let x denote the normal variable *income*. Let z be the corresponding standard normal variable. The mean and S.D. of x are Rs. 750 and Rs. 50 respectively.

$$\therefore \qquad z = \frac{x - 750}{50}.$$

(*i*) Probability of a person's income exceeding Rs. 668

$$= P(x > 668)$$

$$= P\left(\frac{x - 750}{50} > \frac{668 - 750}{50}\right)$$

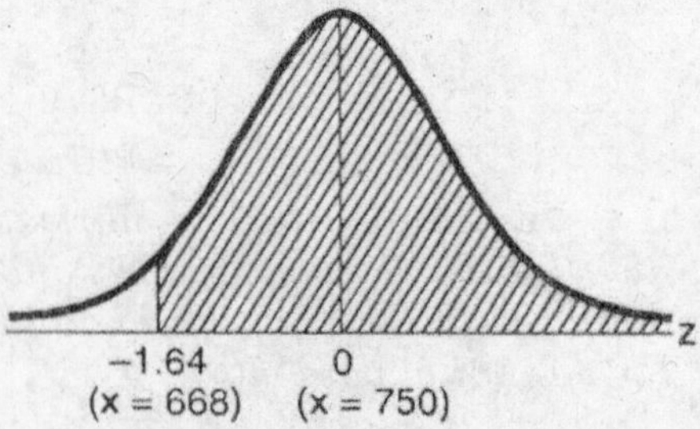

$$= P(z > -1.64) = 0.5 + P(0 \le z \le 1.64)$$

$$= 0.5 + 0.4495 = 0.9495 \doteq 0.95$$

$\therefore$ Percentage of persons getting more than Rs. 668

$$= 100\ P(x > 668)\% = 100.(0.95)\% = \mathbf{95\%}.$$

(*ii*) Probability of a person's income exceeding Rs. 832

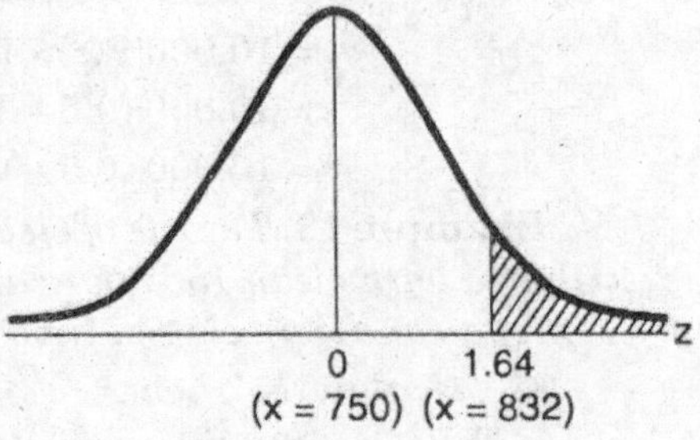

$$= P(x > 832) = P\left(\frac{x-750}{50} > \frac{832-750}{50}\right)$$

$$= P(z > 1.64) = 0.5 - P(0 \le z \le 1.64)$$

$$= 0.5 - 0.4495 = 0.0505 \doteq 0.05$$

$\therefore$ Percentage of persons getting more than Rs. 832

$$= 100\ P(x > 832)\% = 100.(0.05) = \mathbf{5\%}.$$

(*iii*) Probability of a person being among the richest 100

$$= \frac{100}{10{,}000} = 0.01$$

Let the lowest income among richest 100 = Rs. m

$\therefore$ $P(x \ge m) = 0.01$

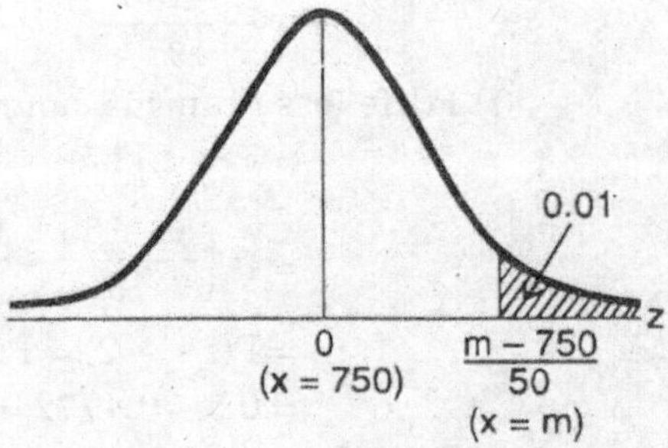

$$\therefore \quad P\left(\frac{x-750}{50} > \frac{m-750}{50}\right) = 0.01$$

or
$$P\left(z \ge \frac{m-750}{50}\right) = 0.01$$

or
$$0.5 - P\left(0 \le z \le \frac{m-750}{50}\right) = 0.01$$

$$\therefore \quad P\left(0 \le z \le \frac{m-750}{50}\right) = 0.5 - 0.01 = 0.49$$

Also from the table,

$$P(0 \le z \le 2.33) = 0.49$$

$$\therefore \quad \frac{m-750}{50} = 2.33$$

$$\Rightarrow \quad m = 50(2.33) + 750 = 866.50$$

$\therefore$ Lowest income among richest 100 = **Rs. 866.50.**

Example 12. *Assuming the mean height of soldiers to be 68.22 inches with a variance of 10.8 (inches)^2, find how many soldiers in a regiment of 10,000 would you expect to be over 6 feet tall ?* (MDU 2006)

Sol. Let x denote the variable *height*. We assume that x is normally distributed. The mean and S.D. of x are 68.22 and $\sqrt{10.8} = 3.2863$.

Let z be the corresponding S.N.V.

$$\therefore \quad z = \frac{x - 68.22}{3.2863}$$

Now, the expected number of soldiers, who are at least 6 feet (72 inches) tall

$= 10,000 \, P(x > 72)$

$= 10,000 \, P\left(\frac{x - 68.22}{3.2863} > \frac{72 - 68.22}{3.2863}\right)$

$= 10,000 \, P(z > 1.15)$

$= 10,000 \, (0.5 - P(0 \le z \le 1.15))$

$= 10,000 \, (0.5 - 0.3749) = \mathbf{1251}.$

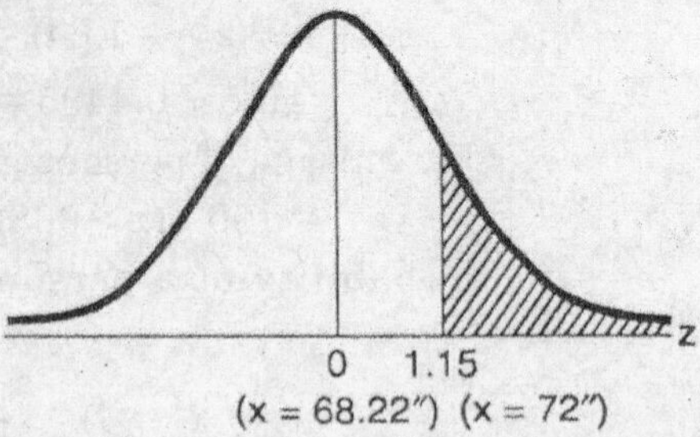

Example 13. *The life of electronic tubes of a certain type may be assumed to be normally distributed with mean 155 hours and standard deviation 19 hours. What is the probability that the life of a randomly chosen tube is :*

(*i*) *less than 117 hours*

(*ii*) *between 136 hours are 194 hours and*

(*iii*) *more than 395 hours ?*

Sol. Let x denote the normal variable *life of electronic tubes.* The mean and S.D. of x are 155 and 19 hours respectively.

Let z be the S.N.V. of x.

$\therefore \quad z = \frac{x - 155}{19}$

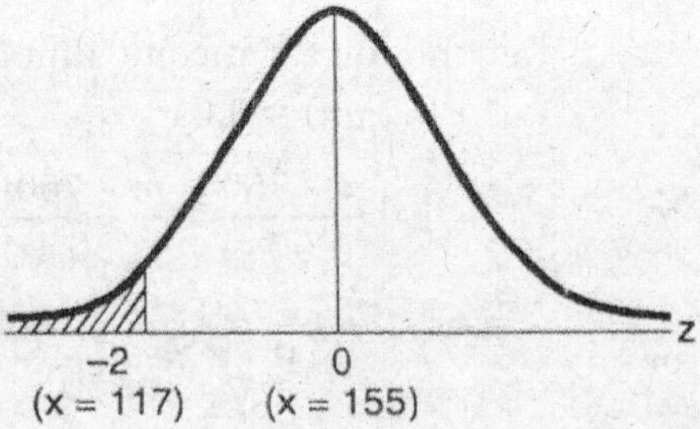

(*i*) P(life less than 117 hours)

$= P(x < 117)$

$= P\left(\frac{x - 155}{19} < \frac{117 - 155}{19}\right)$

$= P(z < -2) = P(z > 2) = 0.5 - P(0 \le z \le 2)$

$= 0.5 - 0.4772 = \mathbf{0.0228.}$

(*ii*) P(life between 136 hours and 194 hours)

$= P(136 < x < 194)$

$= P\left(\frac{136 - 155}{19} < \frac{x - 155}{19} < \frac{194 - 155}{19}\right)$

$= P(-1 < z < 2.05)$

$= P(-1 < z \le 0) + P(0 \le z < 2.05)$

$= P(0 \le z \le 1) + P(0 \le z \le 2.05)$

$= 0.3413 + 0.4798 = \mathbf{0.8211.}$

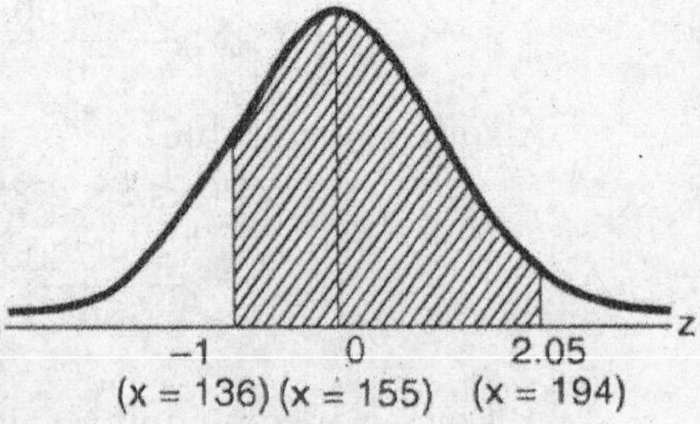

(*iii*) P(life more than 395 hours)

$= P(x > 395)$

$= P\left(\frac{x - 155}{19} > \frac{395 - 155}{19}\right)$

$= P(z > 12.63)$

$= 0.5 - P(0 \le z \le 12.63)$

$= 0.5 - 0.5 = \mathbf{0}.$

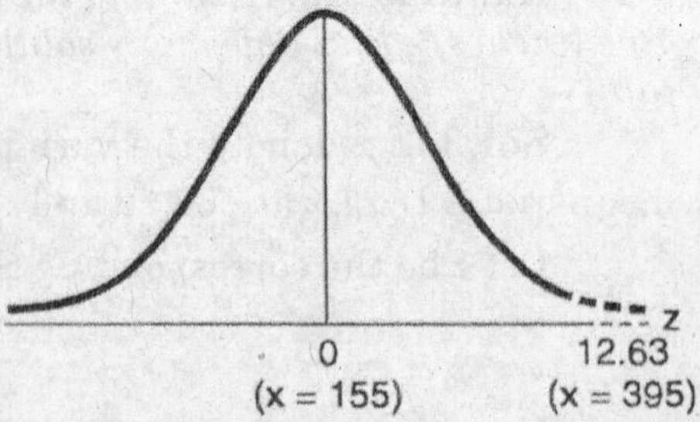

Example 14. *In a certain examination, the percentages of passes and distinctions were 45 and 9 respectively. Estimate the average marks obtained by the candidates, the minimum pass and distinction marks being 40 and 75. (Assume the distribution of marks to be normal).*

Sol. Let x denote the normal variable *marks*. Let μ and σ be the mean and standard deviation of x respectively. Let z be the S.N.V. of x.

$$\therefore \quad z = \frac{x-\mu}{\sigma}$$

Now, percentage of passes = 45% ∴ 100 P($x \ge 40$) = 45

$$\Rightarrow \quad P(x \ge 40) = 0.45 \qquad \Rightarrow \quad P\left(\frac{x-\mu}{\sigma} \ge \frac{40-\mu}{\sigma}\right) = 0.45$$

$$\Rightarrow \quad P\left(z \ge \frac{40-\mu}{\sigma}\right) = 0.45 \qquad \Rightarrow \quad 0.5 - P\left(0 \le z \le \frac{40-\mu}{\sigma}\right) = 0.45$$

$$\Rightarrow \quad P\left(0 \le z \le \frac{40-\mu}{\sigma}\right) = 0.05.$$

Also from the table, $P(0 \le z \le 0.12) \doteq 0.05$

$$\therefore \quad \frac{40-\mu}{\sigma} = 0.12 \qquad \text{...(1)}$$

Also, percentage of distinctions = 9%

$$\therefore \quad 100\, P(x \ge 75) = 9 \qquad \Rightarrow \quad P(x \ge 75) = 0.09$$

$$\Rightarrow \quad P\left(\frac{x-\mu}{\sigma} \ge \frac{75-\mu}{\sigma}\right) = 0.09 \qquad \Rightarrow \quad P\left(z \ge \frac{75-\mu}{\sigma}\right) = 0.09$$

$$\Rightarrow \quad 0.5 - P\left(0 \le z \le \frac{75-\mu}{\sigma}\right) = 0.09 \qquad \Rightarrow \quad P\left(0 \le z \le \frac{75-\mu}{\sigma}\right) = 0.41$$

Also, from the table, $P(0 \le z \le 1.34) \doteq 0.41$

$$\therefore \quad \frac{75-\mu}{\sigma} = 1.34. \qquad \text{...(2)}$$

Dividing (1) by (2), we get $\dfrac{40-\mu}{75-\mu} = \dfrac{0.12}{1.34}$

$$\Rightarrow \quad \mu = 36.5576 \doteq 37$$

∴ Average marks = 37.

EXERCISE 7

1. The mean and standard deviation of a normal variable are 35 and 5 respectively. Find the values of the corresponding S.N.V., when x = 10, 15, 22, 34, 35, 55.
2. The mean and variance of a normal distribution are 20 and 9 respectively. Find the values of x for which the values of the corresponding S.N.V. are – 2, – 1, 0.5, 3, 4.
3. If z is a standard normal variable, then find the following probabilities :
   (*i*) $P(1 \le z \le 2)$ (*ii*) $P(z \ge 3)$.
4. If z is a standard normal variable, then find the following probabilities :
   (*i*) $P(z \le -0.56)$ (*ii*) $P(-0.42 \le z \le 2)$
   (*iii*) $P(-2.3 \le z \le -1.5)$ (*iv*) $P(z \ge 0)$
   (*v*) $P(z \le 2.5)$.

5. x is a normal variable with mean 50 and standard deviation 8. Find the probabilities :
   (*i*) $x \leq 60$ (*ii*) $10 \leq x \leq 40$
   (*iii*) $x > 60$.
6. Let x be a normal variable with mean 45 and standard deviation 5. Find the probabilities :
   (*i*) $P(32 < x < 42)$ (*ii*) $P(50 < x < 60)$.
7. A normal curve has $\bar{x} = 40$ and $\sigma = 15$. Find the area between $x_1 = 25$ and $x_2 = 60$. *(MDU 2002)*
8. The mean of the distribution is 70 and S.D. = 8. Assuming that the distribution is normal: What percentage of items lie between 70 and 82 and beyond 82 ? *(MDU 2001)*
9. The income of a group of 5000 persons was found to be normally distributed with mean Rs. 700 and standard deviation Rs. 50. Find the expected number of persons getting (*i*) less than Rs. 680 (*ii*) more than Rs. 750 and (*iii*) between Rs. 680 and Rs. 750.
10. In a distribution exactly normal, 7% of the items are under 35 and 89% are under 63. What are the mean and standard deviation of the distribution ?
11. The marks obtained by a large group of students in a final examination in statistics have mean 68 and standard deviation 9. If these marks are normally distributed, what percentage of students can you expect to have secured marks between 60 and 65, both inclusive ?
12. The marks obtained by a large group of students in a final examination in statistics have mean 58 and standard deviation 8.5. If these marks are normally distributed, what percentage of students can be expected to have secured marks between 60 and 69, both inclusive ?
13. In a sample of 120 workers in a factory, the mean and standard deviation of wages were Rs. 11.35 and Rs. 3.03 respectively. Find the percentage of workers getting wages between Rs. 9 and Rs. 17 in the whole factory, assuming that the wages to be normally distributed.
14. In an intelligence test administrated to 1000 children, the average score is 42 and standard deviation 24. Find the number of children :
   (*i*) exceeding the score 60 (*ii*) with score lying between 20 and 40.
   (Assume the variable under consideration to be normal)
15. 5000 candidates appeared in a certain examination paper carrying a maximum of 100 marks. It was found that the marks were normally distributed with mean 39.5 and standard deviation 12.5. Determine the approximate number of candidates who secured a first class for which a minimum of 60 is necessary.
16. As a result of tests on 20,000 electric bulbs manufactured by a company, it was found that the life time of a bulb was normally distributed with an average life of 2040 hours and standard deviation of 60 hours. On the basis of this information, estimate the number of the bulbs that are expected to burn for
   (*i*) more than 2150 hours, and (*ii*) less than 1960 hours. *(KU 2001)*
17. In a large group of persons, it is found that 5% are under 60 inches and 40% are between 60 and 65 inches in height. Assuming the distribution to be normal, find the mean and standard deviation of the height. *(KU 2003)*
18. Assuming that height of a group of men is normal, find the mean and S.D., given that 84.13% of men have height less than 65.2 inches and 68.26% have heights between 65.2 and 62.8 inches. *(KU 2006)*
19. A sales tax officer has reported that the average sales of 500 businessmen that he has to deal with during a year amount to Rs. 36,000 with a S.D. of Rs. 10,000. Find out :
   (*i*) the number of businessmen the sales of which are over Rs. 40,000.
   (*ii*) the percentage of businessmen the sales of which are likely to range between Rs. 30,000 and Rs. 40,000 *(KU 2001)*

Answers

1. – 5, – 4, – 2.6, – 0.2, 0, 4 2. 14, 17, 21.5, 29, 32
3. (*i*) 0.1359 (*ii*) 0.0013

4. (*i*) 0.2877	(*ii*) 0.64	(*iii*) 0.0561	(*iv*) 0.5
(*v*) 0.9938	5. (*i*) 0.8944	(*ii*) 0.1056	(*iii*) 0.1056
6. (*i*) 0.2696	(*ii*) 0.1574	7. 0.7495	8. 0.4332, 0.0668
9. (*i*) 1723	(*ii*) 793	(*iii*) 2484	
10. Mean = 50.3, standard deviation = 10.33		11. 18.4%	12. 30.67%
13. 100 P(9 < *x* < 17) = 75.09%		14. (*i*) 227	(*ii*) 289
15. 252	16. (*i*) 672	(*ii*) 1836	17. 65.41, 3.28
18. 64 inches, 1.2 inches	19. (*i*) 172	(*ii*) 38.12%.	

35. FITTING OF A NORMAL DISTRIBUTION

Let x be a normal variable. Let the probability density function P(x) of x be given by

$$P(x) = \frac{1}{\sigma\sqrt{2\pi}} e^{-\frac{1}{2}\left(\frac{x-\mu}{\sigma}\right)^2}, \quad -\infty < x < \infty,$$

where μ and σ are the mean and standard deviation of the distribution respectively. For calculating the expected normal frequencies, corresponding to an observed frequency distribution, the following steps are taken :

(*i*) The values of mean (μ) and S.D. (σ) are calculated by usual methods.

(*ii*) The values of the standard normal variable $z = \frac{x-\mu}{\sigma}$ are calculated corresponding to each lower limit of classes in the given distribution.

(*iii*) Corresponding to these values of z, the areas under the normal curve to the left of these ordinates are calculated. This is done by using the table given at the end.

(*iv*) The areas for the successive classes are obtained by subtracting the corresponding areas calculated in step (*iii*).

(*v*) The areas for the successive classes are multiplied by N to get the required expected frequencies.

Example 1. *Fit a normal curve to the following data :*

Class	*0—5*	*5—10*	*10—15*	*15—20*	*20—25*	*25—30*	*30—35*	*35—40*	*40—45*
No. of items	*20*	*24*	*32*	*28*	*20*	*16*	*34*	*10*	*16*

Sol. **Calculation of Mean and S.D.**

Class	*f*	*x*	*d = x — A* *A* = 22.5	*u = d/h* *h* = 5	*fu*	*fu*^{2}
0—5	20	2.5	– 20	– 4	– 80	320
5—10	24	7.5	– 15	– 3	– 72	216
10—15	32	12.5	– 10	– 2	– 64	128
15—20	28	17.5	– 5	– 1	– 28	28
20—25	20	22.5	0	0	0	0
25—30	16	27.5	5	1	16	16
30—35	34	32.5	10	2	68	136
35—40	10	37.5	15	3	30	90
40—45	16	42.5	20	4	64	250
Total	200				– 66	1190

$$\text{Mean } (\mu) = A + \left(\frac{\Sigma fu}{N}\right)h = 22.5 + \left(\frac{-66}{200}\right) 5 = 20.85$$

$$\text{S.D. } (\sigma) = \sqrt{\frac{\Sigma fu^2}{N} - \left(\frac{\Sigma fu}{N}\right)^2} \times h = \sqrt{\frac{1190}{200} - \left(\frac{-66}{200}\right)^2} \times 5 = 12.084.$$

Calculation of Expected Frequencies

Class	*Lower class limit* x	$z = \frac{x-\mu}{\sigma} = \frac{x - 20.85}{12.084}$	*Area under normal curve to the left of ordinate at* z	*Area corresponding to class*	*Expected frequency* $= N \times$ *Area*
0—5	0	– 1.72	0.0427	0.0524	10.48 ≑ **10**
5—10	5	– 1.31	0.0951	0.0890	17.80 ≑ **18**
10—15	10	– 0.90	0.1841	0.1315	26.30 ≑ **26**
15—20	15	– 0.48	0.3156	0.1565	31.30 ≑ **31**
20—25	20	– 0.07	0.4721	0.1610	32.20 ≑ **32**
25—30	25	0.34	0.6331	0.1433	28.66 ≑ **29**
30—35	30	0.76	0.7764	0.1026	20.52 ≑ **21**
35—40	35	1.17	0.8790	0.0639	12.78 ≑ **13**
40—45	40	1.58	0.9429	0.0338	6.76 ≑ **7**
45—50	45	1.99	0.9767	—	—

EXERCISE 8

1. Fit a normal curve to the following data :

Variable	60—62	63—65	66—68	69—71	72—74
Frequency	5	18	42	27	8

2. Fit a normal curve to the following data :

Class	60—65	65—70	70—75	75—80
Frequency	3	21	150	335
	80—85	85—90	90—95	95—100
	326	135	26	4

Answers

1. **4, 21, 39, 28, 8** **2.** **3, 31, 148, 322, 319, 144, 30, 3.**

EXERCISE 9

1. What are the conditions under which Binomial probability model is appropriate ?
2. Explain the utility of Poisson distribution in practical life. *(MDU 2004)*
3. What is a normal probability distribution ? What are the salient features of a normal curve ?
4. Explain the distinctive features of Binomial and Poisson distributions.
5. What is binomial distribution ? Under what conditions will it tend to a normal distribution ? *(KU 1995)*
6. What is Poisson distribution ? Point out its role. *(MDU 1997, 2006)*
7. Explain the characteristics of Poisson distribution. *(KU 2000 ; MDU 2006)*
8. Explain the properties of a Binomial distribution. What is its relationship with Poisson distribution ? *(KU 2001 C, 2005 C, 2006)*
9. Write short note on Normal distribution.
10. Explain the properties of Normal distribution. *(KU 2001, 2002, 2003, 2004, 2007 ; MDU 2004, 2006)*
11. How does a normal distribution differ from a binomial distribution ? What are the important properties of a normal distribution ? *(KU 1996, 99 C)*
12. Discuss the conditions for the Binomial distribution. What are its important properties ? *(KU 2000 C ; MDU 2004)*
13. Define binomial distribution and explain its important features.
14. What is meant by theoretical frequency distribution ? Discuss the salient features of the Binomial and Normal distributions. *(KU 1997)*
15. Differentiate between Normal and Binomial distributions. *(KU 2000)*
16. What is meant by Theoretical Frequency Distribution ? Discuss the main features of Binomial, Poisson and Normal distributions. *(MDU 1998)*
17. What is a normal distribution ? Discuss the main characteristics of normal distributions. *(KU 2002 C, 2006 C)*
18. Explain Poisson Distribution and give any six examples where Poisson Distribution is applied. *(KU 2007)*
19. Explain the area property of normal distribution. *(MDU 2007)*

18

Methods of Sampling

1. INTRODUCTION

We know that there are two types of data, namely, primary data and secondary data. The data which is collected during the process of investigation is called *primary data.* The data which is not collected by the investigation agency during the process of investigation, but instead, it is collected from some other source, is called *secondary data.* The results of investigation would wholly depend upon the data used. If the data is not collected carefully, the results can never be expected to be valid. The investigator is supposed to be very careful in the process of collection of data. In this chapter, we shall discuss the methods of collecting data and the methods of sampling. There are two methods of collecting data :

I. Census Method II. Sample Method.

Now we shall discuss both methods in detail :

I. CENSUS METHOD

2. DEFINITION

In this method of collecting data, data is obtained about each and every individual (students, shops, factories, etc.) covered in the scope of the investigation. The totality of all individual units covered in the scope of the investigation is called a '*population*'. This is a very old method of collecting data. For example, if we intend to study the wage distribution in a textile factory then all the employees working in that factory would constitute the population. If on the other hand, our intention is to study the wage distribution in all the factories taken together, then the population would mean the totality of all the workers, working in different factories. In this case, the workers of that particular textile factory would constitute only a part of the population. In our country, data is collected about all the citizens after every 10 years by using census method. *Ya-Lun-Chou* has defined population as, "In statistics, the term population is used to mean an aggregate of Individual Items, whether composed of people or things, that are to be observed in a given problem situation". The census method of collecting data is suitable when the area to the covered is limited and great degree of accuracy is desired. This method is adopted only when the sample method is not found suitable.

Merits

(*i*) In this method, the data collected is expected to be very accurate.

(*ii*) The data collected is reliable.

(*iii*) The data collected by using this method is found quite useful as a source of secondary data.

Demerits

(*i*) This method is very expensive in respect of time,, money and labour.

(*ii*) A large number of enumerators are required in the process. They are also required to be imparted training.

(*iii*) This method is not easily used in case the area to be covered is spread over a wide range.

II. SAMPLE METHOD

3. DEFINITION

In this method of collecting data, data is not obtained about each and every individual covered in the scope of the investigation. Rather, the data is collected about only a part, covered in the scope of the investigation. The results about the entire population are drawn on the basis of the results about that 'part' of population under consideration. This is a modern method of investigation. A lot of research work has been done on this topic. The part of population which is selected to study under investigation is called a '*sample*'. In the context of sample method of conducting investigation, *Croxton* and *Cowden* have said, "It may be too expensive or too time consuming to attempt either a complete or a nearly complete coverage in a statistical study. Further more, to arrive at valid conclusion, it may not be necessary to enumerate all or nearly all of a population. We may study a sample drawn from the larger and, if that sample is adequately representative of the population, we should be able to arrive at valid conclusions". The sample used for investigation purpose is expected to be representative of the population. Suppose we want to investigate the correlation between height and weight of students of a university. This may be achieved by taking a sample of say 50 students and investigating the degree of correlation between their heights and weights. The degree of significance of this correlation for the entire population (all students of the university) would depend upon the degree of representativeness of the sample used. There are certain situations where census methods of investigation is not possible. Suppose a doctor wants to test the 'Blood Group' of a man. He would only be drawing and investigating a sample of few drops of blood from his body. The results drawn from this sample of few drops would be declared valid for the whole amount of blood flowing in the body. The sample method of investigation is suitable when the area covered in the scope of investigation is spread over a wide range. This method of investigation is also suitable when very high degree of accuracy is not necessary.

Merits

(*i*) This method is economical in respect of money, time and labour.

(*ii*) This method is easily used when the area covered in the population is spread widely.

Demerits

(*i*) This method may result in wrong conclusions if the sample investigated is not representative of the population.

(*ii*) This method cannot be used effectively if the size of the population is very small.

4. REQUISITES OF A GOOD SAMPLE

The success of sample method of collecting data depend upon the representativeness of the sample. A sample would be termed as 'good' if the results about the sample are also significant for the entire population. Now we shall discuss the requisites of a good sample.

(*i*) **Representativeness.** A good sample is expected to be representative of the entire population. The sample should bear all the characteristics of the population.

(*ii*) **Independence.** The items of the sample are expected to be selected independently. This means that all the items in the population have equal chances of being selected in the sample and the selection of any item in the sample is not linked with the selection or non-selection of any other items in the population.

(*iii*) **Adequacy.** The number of items in the sample is expected to be adequate in the sense that its items may be able to represent all the characteristics of the population. It is always recommended that the number of items in the sample should be as large as possible.

(*iv*) **Homogeneity.** By homogeneity, we mean that the items of the sample should not reveal any difference regarding the nature of data as compared with the items of the population. The results drawn from two or more samples, from the same population are expected to be almost same.

5. METHODS OF SAMPLING

We have already discussed that the degree of validity of results of samples to the entire population would greatly depend upon the degree of representativeness of the population in the samples investigated. Samples are ought to be selected very carefully and their investigation is also expected to be carried out only by expert statisticians. Mishandling of sample data would give only misleading interpretations about the populations. In the words of *Frederick F. Stephen*, "Samples are like medicines. They can be harmful when they are taken carelessly or without adequate knowledge of their effects. We may use their results with confidence if the applications are made with due restraint. It is foolish to avoid or discard them because someone else has misused them and suffered the predictable consequences of his folly. Every good sample should have a proper lebel with instructions about its use". Now we shall discuss the methods of drawing samples from the populations. This process is called **sampling**. The following methods are commonly used in practice :

(*i*) Simple Random Sampling
(*ii*) Stratified Random Sampling
(*iii*) Multistage Random Sampling
(*iv*) Systematic Random Sampling
(*v*) Judgement Sampling
(*vi*) Quota Sampling
(*vii*) Convenience Sampling.

6. SIMPLE RANDOM SAMPLING

We know that sample is a part of population. A sample is called a **simple random sample**, if every item of the population has equal chance of being included in the sample. It must be noted that 'randomness' does not mean haphazard choice of items from the population. This is infact a scientific undertaking which ensure that there had been equal chances for all the items of population, to have been included in the sample. In the words of *Lillian Cohen*, "A sample is considered a simple random one if its members are drawn in such a way that each observation of the universe has an equal chance of being included in the sample, and every possible combination of observations in the universe has the same chance of being included".

In simple random sampling, the selection of items in the sample does not depend upon the choice of the investigator. He cannot exercise his discretion and the items coming in the sample solely depend upon the chance. There are number of methods of simple random sampling. A very popular method of taking random sample is *lottery method*. In this method, all the items in the population are numbered or named on identical pieces of paper, then these papers are folded in an identical style. These folded papers regarding all the items in the population are then mixed very thoroughly in a container. After that, a sample of folded slips is drawn without exercising any prejudice. The items of population whose numbers or names appear on the slips of the sample constitutes the desired simple random sample. This selection of a simple random sample can also be made by using tables of *Random Numbers. Tippett's* random numbers table contains 10400 random numbers each of 4 digits. Fisher and Yates' *table* of random numbers contains 15000 random numbers each of 10 digits. Rand Corporation table of random numbers contain 20,000 numbers each of 5 digits. Regarding the suitability of this method *Ya-Lau-Chou* has said, "Simple random sampling is certainly an efficient procedure if the population is not large and if it is relatively easy and inexpensive to find the sampling units. It could also be a practical procedure for large populations whose elements are concentrated within a small area."

Merits

1. This method of sampling is considered as the most scientific method.
2. The sample is not at all affected by the bias of the investigator.
3. This method is based on the 'Law of Statistical Regularity' and the 'Law of Inertia of Large Numbers'.
4. This method is economical in respect of time, money and labour.
5. The theory of sampling is based on random sampling and so the measure of sampling error is possible in case of random samples.

Demerits

1. This method is not applicable when the complete list of items of population is not available to the investigator.
2. In case the items of the population are spread very widely then the items of the sample would also be expected to be widely spread and it would be difficult to cover the area to collect data about the items of the sample.
3. This method is not suitable when the items of population are heterogeneous in nature.
4. The random sample may be badly affected by the bias of the chance. In random sampling, one may get a sample which may be most non-random in appearance.

7. STRATIFIED RANDOM SAMPLING

This is a restricted random sampling method. In this method, the entire population is divided into stratas (groups) on the basis of homogeneity of items in the population. Random samples of pre-determined sizes are then drawn from each strata and the totality of these samples constitute the **stratified random sample** for the entire population. The stratified sample is called proportional if the size of random samples drawn from different stratas are proportional to the size of the respective stratas. If in a population, the most homogeneous items are grouped together in four different stratas and if the percentage of items in the stratas be 20%, 30%, 10% and 40%, then in every stratified sample of the population, 20%, 30%, 10% and 40% items would be drawn from respective groups on the basis of simple random sampling basis. On the other hand, if the size of random samples drawn from stratas are not proportional to the size of respective stratas, then the stratified sampling is termed as disproportionate. This method is found very useful when the items of the population are not homogeneous.

Merits

1. In this method, the investigator can exercise great control over the items of the samples by manipulating the number of stratas.

2. The sample drawn by using this method is more representative of the population, because it comprises of random samples drawn from every group in the population. In other words, every type of item in the population is included in the sample.

3. This method is economical in respect of time, money and labour.

4. This method is easily used when the items of the population are heterogeneous in nature.

Demerits

1. Grouping the items of population on the basis of homogeneity is a very technical job. If the stratas are not formed correctly, the stratified sample would not be true representative of the population.

8. MULTISTAGE RANDOM SAMPLING

This is also a restricted random sampling method. In this method, the process of random sampling is carried out a pre-determined number of times. At the first stage, a random sample of a pre-determined size is drawn from the population. At the second stage, a random sample of pre-determined size is drawn from the population of items of the random sample drawn at the first stage. In the third stage, again a random sample of pre-determined size is drawn from the population of items of random sample drawn at the second stage. This process is repeated a pre-determined number of times to get the final **multistage random sample** from the given population. For example, suppose a sample of 50 households is to be drawn from the entire country by using this method. At the first stage, a random sample of some states may be drawn. At the second stage, a random sample of some districts may be drawn from the population of districts of states drawn at the first stage. At the third stage, a random sample of villages/towns may be drawn from the population of villages/towns in districts drawn at the second stage. And lastly, a random sample of 50 households may be drawn from the population of households in the village/towns drawn at the third stage. This sample would be called a four-stage random sample. This method of sampling is also called **Cluster sampling.**

Merits

1. In this method, the sample is not at all affected by the bias of the investigator.

2. This method is economical in respect of money, time and labour.

3. This method is very useful in case a very wide range is to be covered in the investigation.

Demerits

1. This method is considered to be less accurate than the simple random method.

2. This method is not suitable when the area to be covered is very small.

9. SYSTEMATIC RANDOM SAMPLING

This is also a restricted random sampling method. In this method, all the items of the populations are arranged in alphabetical or geographical or numerical order. Let k be the whole number nearest to the ratio of size of population to the size of sample. The first item to the sample is drawn from the population by using the lottery method. After this, every kth item of the population is taken in the sample till the required number of items are taken in the sample. Suppose a sample of 12 students is to be drawn from a population of students numbered from 1 to 478.

Here $\frac{\text{size of population}}{\text{size of sample}} = \frac{478}{12} = 39.833$

Therefore, k = whose number nearest to 39.833 = 40.

The first student for the sample would be drawn from the population by using lottery method. Let the first student drawn be with number 192. The second student to be selected for the sample would be with number 232. The number of the third student in the sample would be 272 and so on. Thus, the numbers of students selected in the systematic random sample would be 192, 232, 272, 312, 352, 392, 432, 472, 34(472 + 40 − 478), 74, 114, 154. This method of sampling is also known as **quasi-random sampling method**.

Merits

1. This method is economical in respect of money, time and labour.
2. This method is suitable in case a very small area is to be covered in the investigation.
3. This method of sampling is very simple to operate.

Demerits

1. The sample can be badly affected by the hidden periodicities regarding some characteristics.

2. The sample drawn may be affected by the bias of the investigator. The investigator can exercise bias in alloting numbers to the items in the population.

10. JUDGEMENT SAMPLING

In this method of sampling, no particular method is used to draw sample from the population. Rather, the choice of the items for the sample is left altogether at the discretion of the investigator. The investigator is expected to draw items for the sample, which he considers as the most representative of the population. There is no element of randomness in the sample. That is why, this method is categorized as a non-random method. Suppose a sample of twenty workers is to be drawn from a population of 10,000 workers, working in different factories. Now it would be upto the investigator as to which 20 workers he considers as the most representative of the entire population. The success of this method depends upon the personality of the investigator. This method of sampling is also called **purposive sampling**.

Merits

1. This method is economical in respect of money, time and labour.
2. This method is useful in case the area to be covered in the investigation is very small.
3. This method is very useful for 'pilot-survey'.
4. This method is very much useful when there is no time for adopting other methods of sampling.

Demerits

1. This method of sampling is expected to be affected by the bias of the investigator.
2. This method is not considered to be scientific.
3. In this method of sampling, there is no measure for sampling error.

11. QUOTA SAMPLING

This is also a non-random method of sampling. In this method, the entire population is divided into groups on the basis of some pre-decided characteristics. Quota is fixed for each group for drawing items to constitute the required quota sample. The allocated number of items are drawn from each group by using the judgement method of sampling. Suppose we are to draw a sample of 20 students from a population of a 1000 students. Let the entire population of students be divided into 4 groups of students with their ages in the age groups, 15—17, 17—19, 19—21, 21 and above. Let the quota for each group be fixed as 4, 3, 6 and 7. Now these fixed number of students would be drawn from the different groups by judgement method of sampling. The totality of all these students would be a quota sample of 20 students from the population of 1000 students.

Merits

1. This method is economical in respect of money, time and labour.

2. This method is useful in case, the area to be covered in the investigation is very widely spread. In such a case, groups are formed according to areas and enumerators are deputed for different groups to collect data.

3. The data collected is reliable.

Demerits

1. The data collected is expected to be affected by the bias of the enumerators or of the investigator.

12. CONVENIENCE SAMPLING

This is also a non-random method of sampling. In this method, the investigator draws items for the sample according to his own convenience. Suppose an investigator is to draw a sample of 20 students from the population of all the students to study, "the uses of library", from students' point of view. The investigator would conveniently draw the required sample of students by visiting the nearest school or college for collecting data.

Merits

1. This is a very easy method of sampling.

2. This method is useful when the list of all the items in the population is not available to the investigator.

3. This method is economical in respect of money, time and labour.

4. This method is useful for 'pilot-survey'.

Demerits

1. The data collected may be badly affected by the bias of the investigator.

EXERCISE

1. What is 'Sampling' ? What are the essentials of a good sample ? Name the various methods of sampling and explain them in brief. *(K.U. 1996 S)*
2. Discuss the importance of the methods of random sampling in an investigation extending over a wide area.
3. Distinguish between a census survey and sample survey. What are their relative merits and demerits ?
4. "A sample may be large yet worthless, because, it is not random, or it may be random but unreliable, because it is small". Comment upon the above statement and explain the importance of sampling in our daily life.
5. What is meant by a sample method of enquiry ? When is it adopted and what are its advantages ? What are the requirements of a good sample ?
6. Describe the various methods of selecting a sample. State the merits and demerits of each, giving examples.
7. What is meant by sampling ? Explain its objects and merits over census. *(M.D.U. 1999)*

19

Curve Fitting and Method of Least Squares

1. INTRODUCTION

We know the area (A) of a circle of radius (r) is functionally related with r by the relation $A = \pi r^2$. very often in practice a functional relation may not exist between two (or more) variables. For example, the variables 'height' and 'weight' of persons are not functionally related. In the present chapter, we shall study the method of finding the equation of that curve which approximates the data relating to given variables which are not functionally related.

2. CURVE FITTING

Let x and y be two variables which are not functionally related. Let $y_1, y_2, ..., y_n$ be the values of the variable y corresponding to the values $x_1, x_2, ..., x_n$ of the variable x. We plot the points $(x_1, y_1), (x_2, y_2), ..., (x_n, y_n)$ on a rectangular coordinate system. The diagram so formed is called the *scatter diagram* of the given data.

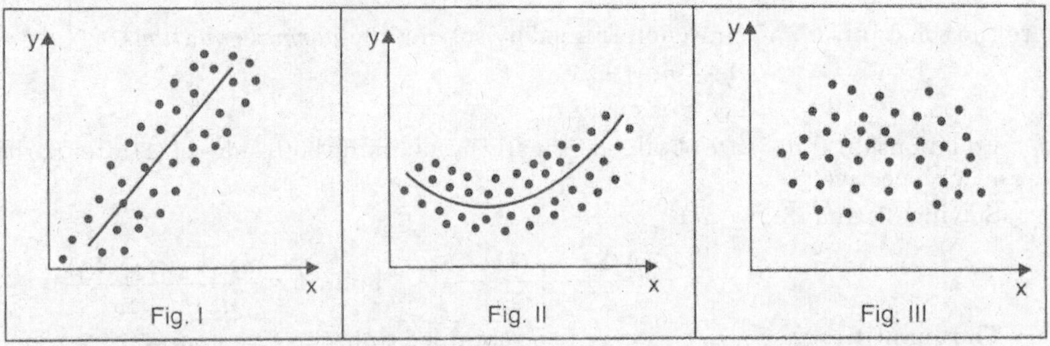

A curve which is most near to the points in the scatter diagram is called an **approximating curve**. From the above diagrams, we see that an approximating curve may be linear, non-linear or even may not exist. In the figure I, the approximating curve is a straight line, in figure II, the approximating curve is non-linear and in the figure III, there is no approximating curve.

The process of finding the equations of approximating curves is called **curve fitting.** We shall be using the *method of least squares* in curve fitting.

3. METHOD OF LEAST SQUARES

Let $y_1, y_2, ..., y_n$ be the values of a variable y corresponding to the values $x_1, x_2, ..., x_n$ of a variable x. We draw the scatter diagram of the points $(x_1, y_1), (x_2, y_2), ..., (x_n, y_n)$. Let C be an approximating curve of the given data. Let d_1 denote the difference between y_1 and the corresponding value as determined from the curve C. Here d_1 is positive. Similarly, we define $d_2, d_3, ..., d_n$ corresponding to the values $x_2, x_3, ..., x_n$ of the variable x. The differences $d_1, d_2, ..., d_n$ are called **deviations** and their values may be positive, negative or zero. If the approximating curve C is such that the sum of squares of deviations *i.e.*, $d_1^2 + d_2^2 + ... + d_n^2$ is least then the approximating curve C is called a **least-squares curve** and that approximating curve is said to have been obtained by the method of least squares.

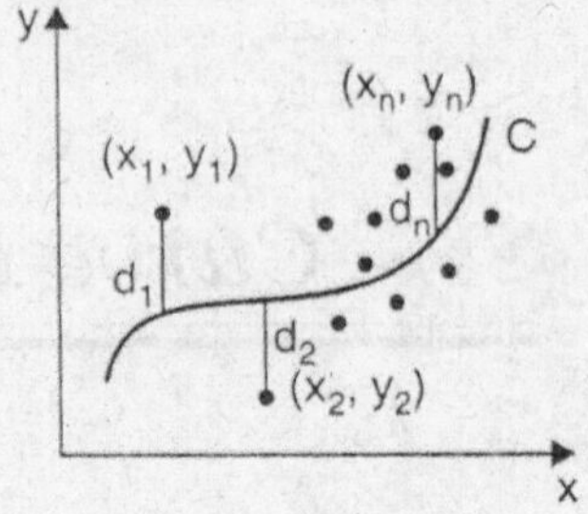

We know that an approximating curve may or may not be linear. Now we shall discuss the method of finding linear and non-linear approximating curves by the method of least squares separately.

4. LEAST-SQUARES LINE

The process of finding the least-squares line to a given data is also called the **fitting of a line.**

Let $y_1, y_2, ..., y_n$ be the values of a variable y corresponding to the values $x_1, x_2, ..., x_n$ of a variable x.

The equation of the least-squares line approximating the points $(x_1, y_1), (x_2, y_2), ..., (x_n, y_n)$ is

$$y = a + bx \qquad ...(1)$$

where the constants a and b are determined by solving the *normal equations*

$$\Sigma y = na + b\Sigma x \qquad ...(2)$$

and

$$\Sigma xy = a\Sigma x + b\Sigma x^2 \qquad ...(3)$$

Equations (2) and (3) are obtained formally by summing both sides of (1) after multiplying by 1 and x respectively.

Solving (2) and (3), we get

$$a = \frac{(\Sigma y)(\Sigma x^2) - (\Sigma x)(\Sigma xy)}{n\Sigma x^2 - (\Sigma x)^2} \quad \text{and} \quad b = \frac{n\Sigma xy - (\Sigma x)(\Sigma y)}{n\Sigma x^2 - (\Sigma x)^2}.$$

The quantities $\Sigma x, \Sigma y, \Sigma x^2, \Sigma xy$ are to be obtained from the given pairs $(x_1, y_1), (x_2, y_2), ..., (x_n, y_n)$.

Remark. For the sake of simplicity, we have written $\Sigma x, \Sigma y, \Sigma x^2, \Sigma xy$ instead of

$$\sum_{i=1}^{n} x_i, \sum_{i=1}^{n} y_i, \sum_{i=1}^{n} x_i^2, \sum_{i=1}^{n} x_i y_i \text{ respectively.}$$

Example 1. *Fit a straight line $y = a + bx$ to the following data by the method of least squares :*

x	1	2	3	4	6	8
y	2.4	3	3.6	4	5	6

Sol. The equation of the least-squares straight line is $y = a + bx$.

∴ The normal equations are :

$$\Sigma y = na + b\Sigma x \quad \text{and} \quad \Sigma xy = a\Sigma x + b\Sigma x^2.$$

S. No.	x	y	x^2	xy
1	1	2.4	1	2.4
2	2	3	4	6
3	3	3.6	9	10.8
4	4	4	16	16
5	6	5	36	30
6	8	6	64	48
$n = 6$	$\Sigma x = 24$	$\Sigma y = 24$	$\Sigma x^2 = 130$	$\Sigma xy = 113.2$

Using normal equations, we have

$$24 = 6a + 24b \quad \text{...(1)}$$

and $$113.2 = 24a + 130b \quad \text{...(2)}$$

(1) × 4 ⇒ $$96 = 24a + 96b \quad \text{...(3)}$$

(2) – (3) ⇒ $$17.2 = 34b \quad \Rightarrow \quad b = \frac{17.2}{34} = 0.506$$

(1) ⇒ $$4 = a + 4b \quad \Rightarrow \quad a = 4 - 4(0.506) = 1.976$$

∴ The least-squares straight line is $\mathbf{y = 1.976 + 0.506x}$.

Alternative method

$$a = \frac{(\Sigma y)(\Sigma x^2) - (\Sigma x)(\Sigma xy)}{n\Sigma x^2 - (\Sigma x)^2} = \frac{24(130) - 24(113.2)}{6(130) - (24)^2} = \frac{403.2}{204} = 1.976$$

and $$b = \frac{n\Sigma xy - (\Sigma x)(\Sigma y)}{n\Sigma x^2 - (\Sigma x)^2} = \frac{6(113.2) - 24(24)}{6(130) - (24)^2} = \frac{103.2}{204} = 0.506$$

∴ The least-squares straight line is $\mathbf{y = 1.976 + 0.506x}$.

Example 2. *Fit a straight line $y = a + bx$ to the following data by the method of least squares :*

x	65	63	67	64	68	62	70	66	68	67	69	71
y	68	66	68	65	69	66	68	65	71	67	68	70

Sol. The equation of the least-squares straight line is $y = a + bx$.

∴ The normal equations are

$$\Sigma y = na + b\Sigma x$$

and $$\Sigma xy = a\Sigma x + b\Sigma x^2.$$

Solving these equations, we have

$$a = \frac{(\Sigma y)(\Sigma x^2) - (\Sigma x)(\Sigma xy)}{n\Sigma x^2 - (\Sigma x)^2} \quad \text{and} \quad b = \frac{n\Sigma xy - (\Sigma x)(\Sigma y)}{n\Sigma x^2 - (\Sigma x)^2}.$$

S. No.	x	y	x^2	xy
1	65	68	4225	4420
2	63	66	3969	4158
3	67	68	4489	4556
4	64	65	4096	4160
5	68	69	4624	4692
6	62	66	3844	4092
7	70	68	4900	4760
8	66	65	4356	4290
9	68	71	4624	4828
10	67	67	4489	4489
11	69	68	4761	4692
12	71	70	5041	4970
$n = 12$	$\Sigma x = 800$	$\Sigma y = 811$	$\Sigma x^2 = 53418$	$\Sigma xy = 54107$

$$\therefore \quad a = \frac{(\Sigma y)(\Sigma x^2) - (\Sigma x)(\Sigma xy)}{n\Sigma x^2 - (\Sigma x)^2}$$

$$= \frac{811(53418) - 800(54107)}{12(53418) - (800)^2} = \frac{36398}{1016} = 35.825$$

and $$b = \frac{n\Sigma xy - (\Sigma x)(\Sigma y)}{n\Sigma x^2 - (\Sigma x)^2} = \frac{12(54107) - 800(811)}{12(53418) - (800)^2} = \frac{484}{1016} = 0.476$$

$\therefore$ The least-squares straight line is **y = 35.825 + 0.476x.**

5. CHANGE OF ORIGIN AND SCALE

Let $y_1, y_2, ..., y_n$ be the values of a variable y corresponding to the values $x_1, x_2, ..., x_n$ of a variable x.

Let $$u = \frac{x - A}{h} \quad \text{and} \quad v = \frac{y - B}{k}.$$

Let the least-squares line of v on u be $v = a + bu$.

The values of a and b are formed by solving the normal equations

$$\Sigma v = na + b\Sigma u \quad \text{and} \quad \Sigma uv = a\Sigma u + b\Sigma u^2.$$

Putting the values of u and v in the equation $v = a + bu$, we get the required least-squares line of y on x.

This method is specially used when the given values of x are equidistant because in such a case we can make $\Sigma u = 0$ and thus the normal equations reduces to $\Sigma v = na$ and $\Sigma uv = b\Sigma u^2$.

Example 3. *The weight of a calf taken at weekly intervals are given below. Fit a straight line $y = a + bx$ using the method of least squares :*

Age (x)	1	2	3	4	5	6	7	8	9	10
Weight (y)	52.5	58.7	65.0	70.2	75.4	81.1	87.2	95.5	102.2	108.4

Sol. Let $$u = \frac{x - 5.5}{1/2} = 2x - 11$$

Let the least-squares line of y on u be $y = \alpha + \beta u$.

$\therefore$ The normal equations are

$$\Sigma y = n\alpha + \beta \Sigma u \quad \text{and} \quad \Sigma uy = \alpha \Sigma u + \beta \Sigma u^2.$$

S.No.	x	y	$u = 2x - 11$	u^2	uy
1	1	52.5	− 9	81	− 472.5
2	2	58.7	− 7	49	− 410.9
3	3	65.0	− 5	25	− 325.0
4	4	70.2	− 3	9	− 210.6
5	5	75.4	−1	1	− 75.4
6	6	81.1	1	1	81.1
7	7	87.2	3	9	261.6
8	8	95.5	5	25	477.5
9	9	102.2	7	49	715.4
10	10	108.4	9	81	975.6
$x = 10$		$\Sigma y = 796.2$	$\Sigma u = 0$	$\Sigma u^2 = 330$	$\Sigma uy = 1016.8$

Using normal equations, we have

$$796.2 = 10\alpha + \beta(0)$$

$$1016.8 = \alpha(0) + \beta(330)$$

$$\therefore \quad \alpha = \frac{796.2}{10} = 79.62 \quad \text{and} \quad \beta = \frac{1016.8}{330} = 3.08$$

$\therefore$ The least-squares line of y on u is

$$y = 79.62 + 3.08u$$

$$\Rightarrow \quad y = 79.62 + 3.08(2x - 11) \quad \Rightarrow \quad \mathbf{y = 45.74 + 6.16x.}$$

This is the required least-squares line of y on x.

6. LEAST-SQUARES SECOND DEGREE PARABOLA

Let $y_1, y_2, \ldots\ldots, y_n$ be the values of a variable y corresponding to the values $x_1, x_2, \ldots\ldots, x_n$ of a variable x.

The equation of the least-squares second degree parabola approximating the points $(x_1, y_1), (x_2, y_2), \ldots\ldots, (x_n, y_n)$ is

$$y = a + bx + cx^2 \qquad \ldots(1)$$

where the constants a, b and c are determined by solving the *normal equations* :

$$\Sigma y = na + b\Sigma x + c\Sigma x^2 \qquad \ldots(2)$$

$$\Sigma xy = a\Sigma x + b\Sigma x^2 + c\Sigma x^3 \qquad \ldots(3)$$

and $$\Sigma x^2 y = a\Sigma x^2 + b\Sigma x^3 + c\Sigma x^4 \qquad \ldots(4)$$

Equations (2), (3) and (4) are obtained formally by summing both sides of (1) after multiplying by 1, x and x^2 respectively.

The quantities Σx, Σy, Σx^2, Σxy, Σx^3, Σx^2y, Σx^4 are to be obtained from the given pairs $(x_1, y_1), (x_2, y_2), \ldots\ldots, (x_n, y_n)$.

Example 4. *Fit a second degree parabola $y = a + bx + cx^2$ to the following data by the method of least squares.*

x	1.2	1.8	3.1	4.9	5.7	7.1	8.6	9.8
y	4.5	5.9	7.0	7.8	7.2	6.8	4.5	2.7

Sol. The equation of the least squares second degree parabola is $y = a + bx + cx^2$.

$\therefore$ The normal equations are :

$$\Sigma y = na + b\Sigma x + c\Sigma x^2 \quad \ldots(1)$$

$$\Sigma xy = a\Sigma x + b\Sigma x^2 + c\Sigma x^3 \quad \ldots(2)$$

$$\Sigma x^2y = a\Sigma x^2 + b\Sigma x^3 + c\Sigma x^4 \quad \ldots(3)$$

S. No.	x	y	x^2	x^3	x^4	xy	x^2y
1	1.2	4.5	1.44	1.73	2.08	5.40	6.48
2	1.8	5.9	3.24	5.83	10.49	10.62	19.12
3	3.1	7.0	9.61	29.79	92.35	21.70	67.27
4	4.9	7.8	24.01	117.65	576.48	38.22	187.28
5	5.7	7.2	32.49	185.19	1055.58	41.04	233.93
6	7.1	6.8	50.41	357.91	2541.16	48.28	342.79
7	8.6	4.5	73.96	636.06	5470.12	38.70	332.82
8	9.8	2.7	96.04	941.19	9223.66	26.46	259.31
$n = 8$	$\Sigma x =$ 42.2	$\Sigma y =$ 46.4	$\Sigma x^2 =$ 291.20	$\Sigma x^3 =$ 2275.35	$\Sigma x^4 =$ 18971.92	$\Sigma xy =$ 230.42	$\Sigma x^2y =$ 1449.00

Using normal equations, we have

$$46.4 = 8a + 42.2b + 291.20c$$

$$230.42 = 42.2a + 291.20b + 2275.35c$$

$$1449.00 = 291.20a + 2275.35b + 18971.92c$$

Solving these equations, we get

$$a = 2.588,\ b = 2.065 \text{ and } c = -0.2110.$$

$\therefore$ The least-squares second degree parabola is

$$\mathbf{y = 2.588 + 2.065x - 0.2110x^2.}$$

7. CHANGE OF ORIGIN AND SCALE

Let $y_1, y_2, \ldots\ldots, y_n$ be the values of a variable y corresponding to the values $x_1, x_2, \ldots\ldots, x_n$ of a variable x.

Let $$u = \frac{x - A}{h} \quad \text{and} \quad v = \frac{y - B}{k}.$$

Let the least-squares second degree parabola of v on u be $v = a + bu + cu^2$.

The values of a, b and c are found by solving the normal equations :

$$\Sigma v = na + b\Sigma u + c\Sigma u^2$$
$$\Sigma uv = a\Sigma u + b\Sigma u^2 + c\Sigma u^3$$

and $$\Sigma u^2 v = a\Sigma u^2 + b\Sigma u^3 + c\Sigma u^4.$$

Putting the values of u and v in the equation $v = a + bu + cu^2$, we get the required least-squares second degree parabola of y on x.

This method is specially used when the given values of x are equidistant because in such a case we can make $\Sigma u = 0$, $\Sigma u^3 = 0$ and thus the normal equations reduces to

$$\Sigma v = na + c\Sigma u^2,\ \Sigma uv = b\Sigma u^2 \quad \text{and} \quad \Sigma u^2 v = a\Sigma u^2 + c\Sigma u^4.$$

Example 5. *The profit of a certain company in the xth year of its life are given below :*

x	1	2	3	4	5
Profit (,000 Rs.) y	1250	1400	1650	1950	2300

Taking $u = x - 3$ *and* $v = \dfrac{y - 1650}{50}$, *show that the least-squares second degree parabola of* v *on* u *is* $v = -0.086 + 5.3\,u + 0.643\,u^2$. *From this deduce that the least-squares second degree parabola of* y *on* x *is* $y = 1140.05 + 72.1\,x + 32.15\,x^2$.

Sol. We have $$u = x - 3 \quad \text{and} \quad v = \frac{y - 1650}{50}.$$

Let the least-squares second degree parabola of v on u be $v = a + bu + cu^2$.

$\therefore$ The normal equations are :

$$\Sigma v = na + b\Sigma u + c\Sigma u^2$$
$$\Sigma uv = a\Sigma u + b\Sigma u^2 + c\Sigma u^3$$
$$\Sigma u^2 v = a\Sigma u^2 + b\Sigma u^3 + c\Sigma u^4.$$

S. No.	x	y	$u = x - 3$	$v = \dfrac{y-1650}{50}$	u^2	u^3	u^4	uv	u^2v
1	1	1250	− 2	− 8	4	− 8	16	16	− 32
2	2	1400	− 1	− 5	1	− 1	1	5	− 5
3	3	1650	0	0	0	0	0	0	0
4	4	1950	1	6	1	1	1	6	6
5	5	2300	2	13	4	8	16	26	52
$n = 5$			$\Sigma u = 0$	$\Sigma v = 6$	$\Sigma u^2 = 10$	$\Sigma u^3 = 0$	$\Sigma u^4 = 34$	$\Sigma uv = 53$	$\Sigma u^2 v = 21$

Using normal equations, we have

$$6 = 5a + b(0) + 10c \qquad \text{...(1)}$$
$$53 = a(0) + 10b + c(0) \qquad \text{...(2)}$$

$$21 = 10a + b(0) + 34c \qquad ...(3)$$

(2) $\Rightarrow$ $b = \frac{53}{10} = 5.3$

(1) $\Rightarrow$ $5a + 10c = 6$ ...(4)

(3) $\Rightarrow$ $10a + 34c = 21$ ...(5)

(4) × 2 $\Rightarrow$ $10a + 20c = 12$ ...(6)

(5) – (6) $\Rightarrow$ $14c = 9 \Rightarrow c = 0.643$

(1) $\Rightarrow$ $5a = 6 - 10(0.643) = -0.43$

$\Rightarrow$ $a = -\frac{0.43}{5} = -0.086$

$\therefore$ The least-squares parabola of v on u is

$$\mathbf{v = -0.086 + 5.3u + 0.643u^2.}$$

Putting the values of u and v, we get

$$\frac{y - 1650}{50} = -0.086 + 5.3(x - 3) + 0.643(x - 3)^2$$

$\Rightarrow$ $y - 1650 = 50[-0.086 + 5.3x - 15.9 + (0.643)(x^2 - 6x + 9)]$

$\Rightarrow$ $\mathbf{y = 1140.05 + 72.1x + 32.15x^2.}$

$\therefore$ The result holds.

EXERCISE 1

1. Fit a straight line $y = a + bx$ to the following data by the method of least squares :

x	0	1	2	3	4
y	1	1.8	3.3	4.5	6.3

2. Fit a straight line $y = a + bx$ to the following data by the method of least squares :

x	3	5	6	8	9	11
y	2	3	4	6	5	8

3. Fit a straight line $y = a + bx$ to the following data by the method of least squares :

x	1	3	4	6	8	9	11	14
y	1	2	4	4	5	7	8	9

4. Fit a straight line $y = a + bx$ to the following data by the method of least squares :

x	6	7	7	8	8	8	9	9	10
y	5	5	4	5	4	3	4	3	3

5. Fit a parabola $y = a + bx + cx^2$ to the following data by the method of least squares :

x	0	1	2	3	4
y	1	1.8	1.3	2.5	6.3

6. Fit a parabola $y = a + bx + cx^2$ to the following data by the method of least squares :

x	0	1	2	3	4	5	6
y	2.4	2.1	3.2	5.6	9.3	14.6	21.9

7. Fit a parabola $y = a + bx + cx^2$ to the following data by the method of least squares :

x	20	30	40	50	60	70
y	54	90	138	206	292	396

Answers

1. $y = 0.72 + 1.33x$ 2. $y = -\frac{1}{3} + \frac{5}{7}x$ 3. $y = \frac{6}{11} + \frac{7}{11}x$

4. $y = 8 - 0.5x$ 5. $y = 1.42 - 1.07x + 0.55x^2$

6. $y = 2.51 - 1.20x + 0.733x^2$

7. $y = 41.77 - 1.096x + 0.08786x^2$.

20

महत्त्वपूर्ण सैद्धान्तिक प्रश्नों के हिन्दी में उत्तर

1. सांख्यिकी का परिचय

प्रश्न 1. सांख्यिकी की परिभाषा दीजिए और इसके क्षेत्र तथा सीमाओं की विवेचना कीजिए।

उत्तर–आधुनिक युग को सांख्यिकी का युग कहा जाता है। भारत में आंकड़ों का संकलन चन्द्रगुप्त मौर्य के समय में भी था। अकबर के राज्य में उसके वित्त मन्त्री राजा टोडर मल भी जमीनों और कृषि के आँकड़े संकलित करवाया करते थे। वर्तमान समय में सांख्यिकी का प्रयोग लगभग हर विषय में होने लगा है।

सांख्यिकी शब्द को विभिन्न गणितज्ञों ने विभिन्न रूप से परिभाषित किया है। सांख्यिकी शब्द को एकवचन और बहुवचन दोनों ही रूपों में प्रयोग किया जाता है। 1935 में Dr. W.F. Wollifox ने सांख्यिकी की सौ से भी ज्यादा परिभाषाओं की सूची बनाई थी और फिर भी वह सूची पूर्ण नहीं थी।

एकवचन के रूप में सांख्यिकी शब्द का प्रयोग एक ऐसे विज्ञान के लिए किया जाता है, जो समंकों (Data) के संकलन, सम्पादन, विश्लेषण और निर्वाचन से सम्बन्धित है। यह परिभाषा Croxton और Cowden के द्वारा दी गई है।

बहुवचन के रूप में सांख्यिकी शब्द का प्रयोग समंकों (Data) के अर्थ के रूप में होता है। प्रसिद्ध सांख्यिकीय **होरेस सेक्राइस्ट** के अनुसार, ''सांख्यिकी से हमारा आशय तथ्यों के उन समूहों से है जो अनेक कारणों से पर्याप्त सीमा तक प्रभावित होते हैं, जो संख्याओं में व्यक्त किए जाते हैं, एक उचित मात्रा की शुद्धता के अनुसार संकलित या अनुमानित किए जाते हैं। और जिन्हें एक-दूसरे से सम्बन्धित रूप में प्रस्तुत किया जाता है।''

सांख्यिकी का क्षेत्र

सांख्यिकी को एक कला और एक विज्ञान, दोनों ही रूप में समझा जाता है। **टिपेट** के अनुसार सांख्यिकी विज्ञान और कला दोनों है। यह विज्ञान है क्योंकि–इसकी रीतियाँ मौलिक रूप से व्यवस्थित हैं और यह कला है क्योंकि इसकी रीतियों का प्रयोग व्यापक रूप से समस्याओं के अध्ययन के लिए किया जाता है।'' सांख्यिकीय रीतियाँ जटिलताओं को आसान करने में मदद करती हैं। सांख्यिकीय चित्र तथा बिन्दू रेखाचित्र आँकड़ों को आसान तथा सुन्दर ढंग से प्रदर्शित करने में मदद करते हैं। इसलिए सांख्यिकीय चित्रों को प्रदर्शनियों में आँकड़ों को प्रदर्शित करने के लिए प्रयोग किया जाता है।

(*i*) **सांख्यिकी और योजना**–सांख्यिकीय रीतियाँ सरकार को योजनाएँ बनाने में बहुत मदद करती हैं। आज के युग में कोई भी सरकार बगैर योजना के अपने देशवासियों का उत्थान नहीं कर सकती। दुनिया के तकरीबन सभी देशों की सरकारें भविष्य की योजनाएँ काफी पहले से ही तैयार करती हैं। आर्थिक विकास के लिए यह बहुत ही जरूरी है और इस काम के लिए सरकार सांख्यिकीय रीतियों पर बहुत निर्भर करती है। किसी भी योजना की सफलता काफी कुछ इस बात पर निर्भर करती है कि उस योजना में सांख्यिकीय रीतियों का कितना ठीक प्रयोग हुआ है।

(*ii*) **सांख्यिकी और गणित**–सांख्यिकी वास्तव में गणित की ही एक विशिष्ट शाखा है। सांख्यिकीय रीतियों का विकास गणित के ज्ञान पर ही आधारित है। गणित की सहायता से ही इस शास्त्र का विकास हुआ है। **कॉनर** के अनुसार ''सांख्यिकी व्यवहारिक गणित की ही एक शाखा है, जो समंकों में विशिष्टीकरण प्राप्त करती है।'' सांख्यिकी का विकास बगैर गणित के बिल्कुल असम्भव है। और इसका उपयोग आने वाले समय में बढ़ता ही जाएगा।

(*iii*) **सांख्यिकी और अर्थशास्त्र**–सांख्यिकी और अर्थशास्त्र में भी गहरा सम्बन्ध है। सांख्यिकी के प्रयोग से अर्थशास्त्र में प्रमाणिकता आती है। सरकार अपने कर्मचारियों को देने वाले महंगाई भत्ते का निर्धारण उपभोक्ता मूल्य निर्देशांक के आधार पर ही करती है जो कि–सांख्यिकीय रीतियों के प्रयोग से ही तैयार किए जाते हैं। सांख्यिकी का प्रयोग अर्थशास्त्र में इतना ज्यादा है कि– इसके बिना अर्थशास्त्र का विकास असम्भव सा ही है। अर्थशास्त्र की एक विशिष्ट शाखा 'Econometrics' है जिसमें सांख्यिकी का विशेष रूप से प्रयोग किया जाता है। इस शाखा को हिन्दी में अर्थनीति कहा जाता है।

सांख्यिकी की सीमाएँ

सांख्यिकी की कुछ अपनी सीमाएँ भी हैं। जिनको जानना बहुत जरूरी है। सांख्यिकी रीतियों का प्रयोग करने में इन सीमाओं का ध्यान रखना बहुत जरूरी है। इसकी कुछ सीमाएँ निम्नलिखित हैं–

(*i*) **सांख्यिकी में केवल संख्यात्मक तथ्यों का ही अध्ययन होता है**–सांख्यिकी में केवल उन्हीं समस्याओं का अध्ययन किया जा सकता है जो कि–संख्याओं के रूप में व्यक्त की जा सकें, जैसे कि–उत्पादन, आय, मूल्य, वेतन, ऊँचाई, वजन आदि। गुणात्मक रूप में प्रकट किए जाने वाले तथ्य जैसे–ईमानदारी, ख्याति, चरित्र, स्वास्थ्य आदि का सांख्यिकीय रीतियों के द्वारा अध्ययन नहीं किया जा सकता है। इन समस्याओं के अध्ययन में सांख्यिकीय रीतियाँ केवल अप्रत्यक्ष रूप में ही प्रयोग में लाई जा सकती हैं।

(*ii*) **सांख्यिकीय निष्कर्ष पूर्ण रूप से प्रमाणित नहीं होते**–सांख्यिकीय निष्कर्ष हमेशा शुद्ध नहीं होते। लेकिन इससे हम यह निष्कर्ष नहीं निकाल सकते कि–सांख्यिकीय रीतियों का कोई लाभ नहीं। किसी भी सांख्यिकीय अनुसन्धान में आम तौर पर सम्बन्धित समग्र (Population) का प्रयोग नहीं किया जाता है, बल्कि उसके स्थान पर सम्बन्धित समग्र से लिया गया कोई न्यादर्श (Sample) का ही अध्ययन किया जाता है, इसीलिए जो निष्कर्ष न्यादर्श के लिए प्रमाणित हैं, उन्हें शत-प्रतिशत सम्बन्धित समग्र के लिए प्रमाणित नहीं माना जा सकता।

(*iii*) **सांख्यिकी समूहों का अध्ययन करती हैं**–सांख्यिकी व्यक्तिगत इकाइयों का अध्ययन नहीं करती। **प्रोफेसर किंग** के अनुसार, ''सांख्यिकी अपने विषय की प्रकृति के कारण ही व्यक्तिगत इकाइयों पर न तो कभी विचार कर सकती है और न ही विचार करने की स्थिति में होगी।'' उदाहरण के लिए, यदि किसी विद्यार्थी का वजन दिया हुआ है तो सांख्यिकीय रीतियाँ इससे कोई निष्कर्ष नहीं निकाल सकेंगी और यदि हमें इसके स्थान पर विद्यालय के सभी विद्यार्थियों का वजन दिया हुआ है तो सांख्यिकीय रीतियाँ इन आँकड़ों का विश्लेषण कर सकेंगी।

(*iv*) **सांख्यिकी विशेषज्ञों के लिए ही उपयोगी हैं**–आम आदमी सांख्यिकीय रीतियों का प्रयोग नहीं कर सकता। क्योंकि हर आदमी में इतनी योग्यता सम्भव नहीं है, जितनी कि इन रीतियों को समझने के लिए आवश्यक है। कोई भी विशेषज्ञ आम जनता को यह सलाह कभी नहीं देगा कि उन्हें सड़क के बीचों-बीच चलना चाहिए, क्योंकि सड़क के बीच में चलने वालों के साथ दुर्घटनाओं की संख्या किनारे पर चलने वालों के साथ हुई दुर्घटनाओं की अपेक्षा कम होती है। **यूल और कैण्डाल** के शब्दों में, ''अयोग्य व्यक्ति के हाथों में सांख्यिकीय रीतियाँ बहुत खतरनाक हथियार हैं।''

प्रश्न 2. सांख्यिकीय अनुसंधान से आप क्या समझते हैं ? एक सांख्यिकी अनुसंधान का आयोजन करते समय आप किन बातों को ध्यान में रखेंगे ?

उत्तर–सांख्यिकी का मुख्य उद्देश्य समंकों का संकलन करके उनसे निष्कर्ष निकालना है, इस प्रक्रिया को सांख्यिकीय अनुसंधान कहते हैं। सांख्यिकीय अनुसंधान **सामान्य** और **विशिष्ट** दो प्रकार के होते हैं। विशिष्ट अनुसंधान में किसी विशेष उद्देश्य के लिए कार्यवाही की जाती है। भारत में हर दस वर्ष के बाद जनगणना की जाती है, यह एक सामान्य सांख्यिकीय अनुसंधान का उदाहरण है। किसी भी सांख्यिकीय अनुसंधान में निम्नलिखित क्रियाएँ क्रमशः की जाती हैं।

(*a*) सांख्यिकीय अनुसंधान का आयोजन

एक अच्छी योजना का होना अच्छे परिणाम के लिए बहुत जरूरी है। सांख्यिकीय अनुसंधान का कार्य बहुत ही संवेदनशील होता है और यह कार्य विशेषज्ञों द्वारा ही किया जानां चाहिए। अनुसंधान का कार्य शुरू करने से पहले ही सभी बातों पर निष्कर्ष पहले ही ले लिए जाते हैं। अनुसंधान के आयोजन में इन बातों पर ध्यान दिया जाता है।

है, अन्यथा यह समय और साधनों का दुरुपयोग ही सिद्ध होगा। **प्रोफेसर नीस्वेंगर** के शब्द में, "अनुसंधान के उद्देश्य का निश्चय करना सांख्यिकीय अनुसंधान में बहुत महत्त्व रखता है क्योंकि इसी से यह निश्चित किया जा सकता है कि कौन से समंक एकत्रित करने हैं।

(*ii*) **अनुसंधान का क्षेत्र**–अनुसंधान के उद्देश्य को निश्चित करने के पश्चात अनुसंधान के क्षेत्र को निश्चित किया जाता है इसमें यह निश्चित कर लिया जाता है कि आँकड़ें कहाँ से एकत्रित किए जाने हैं अनुसंधान का क्षेत्र, अनुसंधान की सीमाएँ भी निर्धारित करता है।

(*iii*) **सूचनाओं के स्रोत**–अनुसंधान के उद्देश्य और क्षेत्र को निर्धारित करने के बाद यह सोचा जाता है कि किस प्रकार के आँकड़े प्रयोग में लाने हैं, अगर द्वितीयक समंकों से ही काम चलने की सम्भावना हो तो अनुसंधानकर्त्ता इन्हीं को प्रयोग में लाना पसन्द करते हैं क्योंकि इससे समय, धन और श्रम की बचत होती है। अगर द्वितीयक समंक ही प्रयोग में लाने हैं तो उनकी विश्वसनीयता का पूरा ध्यान दिया जाता है क्योंकि अविश्वसनीय आँकड़े सही निष्कर्ष नहीं दे सकते।

(*iv*) **अनुसंधान की पद्धति**–सांख्यिकीय अनुसंधान की प्रक्रिया में अगला चरण यह है कि–संगणना पद्धति से आँकड़े एकत्रित करने हैं या न्यादर्श पद्धति से। जिन अनुसंधानों में संगणना पद्धति प्रयोग में लाई जाती हैं, उनमें अनुसंधान के क्षेत्र से सम्बन्धित प्रत्येक इकाई के विषय में सूचनाएँ एकत्रित की जाती हैं और न्यादर्श पद्धति में पूरे समग्र से कोई एक न्यादर्श निश्चित किया जाता है और उस न्यादर्श से सम्बन्धित प्रत्येक इकाई के सम्बन्ध में सूचनाएँ एकत्रित की जाती हैं। न्यादर्श पद्धति की अपेक्षा संगणना पद्धति को प्रयोग में लाने से अनुसंधान के निष्कर्ष काफी ज्यादा विश्वसनीय होने की उम्मीद होती है। अगर अनुसंधान का क्षेत्र काफी ज्यादा व्यापक हो तो न्यादर्श पद्धति ही प्रयोग में लाना उचित होता है।

(*v*) **अनुसंधान का समय**–अनुसंधान का समयावधि का निश्चित होना भी बहुत आवश्यक है। समय अवधि जितनी कम होगी उतना ही निष्कर्ष ज्यादा विश्वसनीय होगा। अगर समय अवधि निश्चित न की जाए तो आँकड़ों के संकलन में और उसके बाद वाली प्रक्रियाओं में अनावश्यक रूप से ज्यादा समय लग जाता है और कई बारी तो अनुसंधान के निष्कर्ष तक पहुँचने में इतना समय लग जाता है, उस वक्त ऐसा महसूस लगने लगता है कि अनुसंधान कार्य में प्रयोग किए गए आँकड़े अब ठीक नहीं हैं। किसी भी अनुसंधान की समय अवधि इतनी कम भी नहीं होनी चाहिए कि अनुसंधान कार्य को पूरा करने के लिए गणकों और विशेषज्ञों को बहुत जल्दबाजी में काम पूरा करना पड़े।

(*vi*) **सांख्यिकीय एककों** (Units) **का निर्धारण**–सांख्यिकीय आँकड़ों का संकलन शुरू करने से पहले ही यह निश्चित कर लेना चाहिए कि किन और किस प्रकार के एककों को प्रयोग में लाना है। उदाहरण के तौर पर अगर आदमियों का वजन कहीं किलोग्राम, कहीं सेर में और कहीं क्विंटल में लिखा जाएगा तो वो तथ्य तुलनात्मक दृष्टि से ज्यादा अच्छे नहीं रहेंगे। जो भी एकक प्रयोग में लाए जाएँ उनकी मात्रा निश्चित होनी चाहिए, और वो समय, स्थान और गणक के परिवर्तन से परिवर्तित नहीं होने चाहिए। उदाहरण के तौर पर जमीन नापने के एकक "मरला" में कहीं तो पच्चीस गज सम्मिलित किए जाते हैं और कहीं तीस गज। ऐसे भ्रामक एकक प्रयोग में नहीं लाने चाहिए।

(*vii*) **शुद्धता के स्तर का निर्धारण**–किसी भी सांख्यिकीय अनुसंधान में निष्कर्ष का शत-प्रतिशत शुद्ध होना सम्भव नहीं होता लेकिन फिर भी इस बात को हमेशा ध्यान में रखना चाहिए कि सांख्यिकीय अनुसंधान की प्रतिक्रियायें इस ढंग से क्रियान्वित हों कि–निष्कर्ष में शुद्धता स्तर ज्यादा से ज्यादा हो। उदाहरण के तौर पर अगर लोगों की आयु के बारे में ही समंक एकत्रित करने हैं तो कोई भी गणक उनकी वास्तविक आयु न ही लिखना पसन्द करेगा और न ही आसानी से लिखी जा सकेगी क्योंकि आयु को हम आमतौर पर वर्षों में ही लिखते हैं। समंक शास्त्री **किंग** के शब्दों में "प्रत्येक सांख्यिकीय समस्या के लिए प्रत्येक मूल्य के विषय में शुद्धता के एक निश्चित स्तर का निर्धारण पहले ही कर लिया जाना चाहिए और इस बात का पूर्ण

द्वितीयक आँकड़े कहा जाता है। किस प्रकार के आँकड़े प्रयोग में लाने हैं इस बारे में निश्चय, समय, धन, श्रम, उद्देश्य और क्षेत्र को ध्यान में रखते हुए ही किया जाता है।

(*c*) आँकड़ों का सम्पादन

आँकड़ों को एकत्रित करने के बाद सम्पादन की क्रिया की जाती है सम्पादन का कार्य किसी विशेषज्ञ द्वारा ही किया जाना चाहिए और यदि संकलित आँकड़ों में कोई चीज़ गलत हो तो उसको छोड़ दिया जाता है।

(*d*) आँकड़ों का प्रदर्शन

आँकड़ों के सम्पादन के बाद इनको तालिकाओं, चित्रों और बिन्दु रेखीय चित्रों द्वारा प्रदर्शित किया जाता है।

(*e*) आँकड़ों का विश्लेषण

सम्पादित आँकड़ों को सांख्यिकीय रीतियों के द्वारा विश्लेषित किया जाता है, इस क्रिया में गणित का बहुत प्रयोग होता है और विशेषज्ञों द्वारा ही इस क्रिया को किया जाना चाहिए।

(*f*) आँकड़ों का निर्वचन

सांख्यिकीय रीतियों के द्वारा आँकड़ों का विश्लेषण करने के बाद निष्कर्ष निकालने की प्रक्रिया की जाती है। यह काम भी किसी विशेषज्ञ द्वारा ही किया जाना चाहिए अगर निर्वचन का काम ठीक नहीं होगा तो पहले की गई सभी ठीक क्रियाएँ भी बेकार हो जाएगी।

(*g*) अंतिम रिपोर्ट को पेश करना

आँकड़ों के विश्लेषण के बाद निकाले गए निष्कर्षों को अंतिम रिपोर्ट में लिखा जाता है। अंतिम रिपोर्ट बहुत शुद्ध और स्पष्ट शब्दों में लिखी जानी चाहिए। अन्तिम रिपोर्ट में सांख्यिकीय अनुसंधान का उद्देश्य और क्षेत्र भी अंकित होना चाहिए। यह रिपोर्ट कुछ इस ढंग से लिखी जानी चाहिए कि आम आदमी भी सांख्यिकीय अनुसंधान के उद्देश्य, क्षेत्र और निष्कर्षों को समझ सकें और लाभ उठा सकें।

2. समंकों के प्रकार

प्रश्न 3. प्राथमिक एवं द्वितीयक समंकों में अन्तर स्पष्ट कीजिए तथा प्राथमिक समंक संकलित करने की विभिन्न रीतियों का वर्णन कीजिए।

उत्तर–सांख्यिकीय अनुसंधान की योजना बनाने के पश्चात समंकों का आवश्यकता अनुसार संकलन किया जाता है। समंकों के संकलन के दौरान भरपूर सावधानी का प्रयोग करना अत्यन्त आवश्यक है क्योंकि, अशुद्ध, पक्षपातपूर्ण और अपर्याप्त समंकों को प्रयोग करके कभी भी सही निष्कर्ष नहीं निकाले जा सकते। **डॉक्टर बाऊले** के शब्दों में "समंकों के संकलन में सामान्य विवेक प्रमुख आवश्यकता है और अनुभव प्रमुख शिक्षक।" समंक दो प्रकार के होते हैं।

(*a*) प्राथमिक समंक (Primary Data)

(*b*) द्वितीयक समंक (Secondary Data)

अब हम दोनों प्रकार के समंकों की विस्तार से विवेचना करेंगे।

(*a*) प्राथमिक समंक

प्राथमिक समंक वह समंक कहलाते हैं जो कि अनुसंधानकर्त्ता के द्वारा स्वयं ही एकत्रित किये जाते हैं। प्राथमिक समंक आमतौर पर विशेष प्रकार के अनुसंधान में प्रयोग किए जाते हैं। अब हम प्राथमिक समंकों को संकलित करने की विधियों के बारे में विस्तार से वर्णन करेंगे।

(*i*) **प्रत्यक्ष व्यक्तिगत अनुसंधान** (Direct Personal Investigation)–इस पद्धति में अनुसंधानकर्त्ता स्वयं ही कार्यक्षेत्र में जाकर सम्बन्धित इकाइयों के बारे में सूचनाएँ एकत्रित करता है वह स्वयं ही सूचकों से मिलता है, इस पद्धति में

अनुसंधानकर्त्ता का होशियार, ईमानदार और मेहनती होना बहुत जरूरी है। यह पद्धति तभी फायदेमन्द है जबकि–अनुसंधान का कार्यक्षेत्र बहुत सीमित हो। अगर समंकों को गुप्त रखना हो, तब भी यह पद्धति प्रयोग में लाई जाती है। इस पद्धति में क्योंकि अनुसंधानकर्त्ता खुद जाकर सूचकों से मिलता है इसलिए सूचकों का अनुसंधान के प्रति उत्साह काफी बढ़ जाता है। और अनुसंधानकर्त्ता को यह भी आसानी रहती है कि–नाजुक प्रश्नों को भी मोड़ तोड़ कर पूछकर वह सूचकों से सम्बन्धित जानकारी हासिल कर सकता है। यह पद्धति बहुत महंगी पड़ती है और समय भी काफी लगता है।

(*ii*) **अप्रत्यक्ष मौखिक अनुसंधान** (Indirect Oral Investigation)–इस पद्धति में अनुसंधानकर्त्ता सूचकों से प्रत्यक्ष रूप में तो सम्बन्ध स्थापित नहीं करता, परन्तु उन लोगों से सम्बन्ध स्थापित करके जानकारी हासिल की जाती है जोकि अनुसंधान से सम्बन्धित सूचकों के बारे में तथा अनुसंधान के उद्देश्य के बारे में सही जानकारी रखते हैं ऐसे व्यक्तियों को "साक्षी" कहा जाता है। इस पद्धति में साक्षी का ईमानदार होना बहुत जरूरी है। यह पद्धति उन अनुसंधानों में फायदेमन्द है जहाँ कि आमतौर पर अनुसंधान से सम्बन्धित सूचक जानकारी देने में झिझक महसूस कर सकते हैं। उदाहरण के तौर पर, यदि विद्यार्थियों की योग्यता के बारे में जानकारी हाासिल करनी हो तो सम्बन्धित विद्यार्थियों से बात करना लगभग बेकार सा ही सिद्ध होगा, बल्कि इसके स्थान पर उनको पढ़ाने वाले शिक्षकों द्वारा दी गई जानकारी विश्वसनीय होगी। यदि अनुसंधान का क्षेत्र काफी व्यापक है तब भी इस पद्धति का फायदा उठाया जा सकता है। इस पद्धति से धन, श्रम तथा समय की बचत होती है।

(*iii*) **स्थानीय सम्वाददाताओं के द्वारा** (Through Local Correspondents)—इस पद्धति में समंक स्वयं अनुसन्धानकर्त्ता के द्वारा एकत्रित नहीं किये जाते बल्कि अनुसंधानकर्त्ता अनुसंधान के कार्यक्षेत्र में अपने सम्वाददाता नियुक्त करता है और वो ही आवश्यक जानकारी हासिल करके समय-समय पर अनुसंधानकर्त्ता को भेजते रहते हैं। अखबार वाले भी इसी प्रणाली के द्वारा जगह-जगह से समाचार एकत्रित करवाते हैं। इस पद्धति में सम्वाददाताओं को समझदार होना बहुत जरूरी है। यह पद्धति विशेष तौर पर उन अनुसन्धानों में फायदेमन्द है जहाँ कि अनुसन्धान का कार्यक्षेत्र बड़ा हो और जहाँ सूचनाएँ लगातार प्राप्त करनी हों। इस पद्धति से धन, श्रम और समय की बहुत बचत होती है।

(*iv*) **प्रश्नावलियों को सूचकों के पास डाक द्वारा भेजकर** (Through Questionnaires Mailed to Informents)—इस पद्धति में अनुसंधानकर्त्ता अनुसंधान के उद्देश्य को ध्यान में रखते हुए सम्बन्धित प्रश्नों की एक प्रश्नावली तैयार करता है और यह प्रश्नावली सभी सूचकों को डाक द्वारा भेजी जाती है और सूचकों से प्रार्थना की जाती है कि वे इस प्रश्नावली को सही-सही भर कर अनुसंधानकर्त्ता को डाक द्वारा वापस भेज दें। आमतौर पर अनुसंधानकर्त्ता अपना पता लिखा तथा आवश्यक डाक टिकिट लगा लिफाफा प्रश्नावली के साथ ही भेज देते हैं, जिससे कि सूचकों को प्रश्नावली वापस भेजने में आसानी रहे। कई बार अनुसंधानकर्त्ता सूचकों का उत्साह बढ़ाने के लिए उन्हें उपहार भी भेज देते हैं। इस पद्धति से धन, श्रम और समय की बहुत बचत होती है और यदि कार्यक्षेत्र व्यापक हो तब भी यह बहुत उपयोगी है। यह पद्धति उन कार्यक्षेत्रों में उपयोगी सिद्ध नहीं होती जहाँ कि सूचक ज्यादातर अनपढ़ हों। आमतौर पर लोग लिखित में अपने बारे में जानकारी देना पसन्द नहीं करते इसलिए भी इस पद्धति का पूरा फायदा नहीं होता।

(*v*) **गणकों द्वारा अनुसूचियाँ भरकर** (Through Schedules Filled in by Enumerators)— इस पद्धति में अनुसन्धानकर्त्ता अनुसन्धान के उद्देश्य को ध्यान में रखकर सम्बन्धित प्रश्नों की एक अनुसूची तैयार करता है और कुछ गणकों की नियुक्ति की जाती है। वे गणंक अनुसूची की प्रतियाँ लेकर अनुसंधान से सम्बन्धित सभी सूचकों के पास पहुँचते हैं और उनसे सम्बन्धित प्रश्नों का उत्तर प्राप्त करके स्वयं ही अनुसूचियों में भरते हैं। हमारे देश में हर दस वर्ष के बाद जनगणना होती है और इसी पद्धति को प्रयोग में लाया जाता है। इस पद्धति की उपयोगिता गणकों की समझदारी पर निर्भर करती है। इस पद्धति के द्वारा प्राप्त की हुई सूचना काफी विश्वसनीय होती है। और जहाँ कि सूचक अनपढ़ हों वहाँ भी यह पद्धति बहुत उपयोगी सिद्ध होती है। इस पद्धति को प्रयोग में लाने से धन, श्रम और समय की बचत नहीं हो पाती।

(*b*) द्वितीयक समंक

यदि अनुसंधानकर्त्ता स्वयं समंक एकत्रित नहीं करता बल्कि किसी दूसरे के द्वारा एकत्रित किए गए समंकों को प्रयोग में लाता है, तो वह समंक अनुसंधानकर्त्ता के लिए **द्वितीयक समंक** कहे जाते हैं। अगर अनुसन्धान सामान्य प्रकार का हो और

द्वितीयक समंकों से काम चल सकता हो तो उन्हें ही प्रयोग में लाना चाहिए क्योंकि इससे धन, श्रम और समय की बहुत ज्यादा बचत हो जाती है। द्वितीयक समंकों को प्रयोग में लाने से पूर्व यह निश्चित करना बहुत जरूरी है कि वे समंक विश्वसनीय हैं। हमारे देश में जो जनगणना की सूचनाएँ हर दस वर्ष के बाद प्राप्त की जाती हैं उन्हें द्वितीयक समंकों के रूप में बहुत अनुसंधानों में प्रयोग किया जाता है। द्वितीयक समंक प्रकाशित स्रोतों तथा अप्रकाशित स्रोतों से प्राप्त किए जाते हैं। सरकार भी समय-समय पर विभिन्न विषयों से सम्बन्धित सूचनाएँ प्राप्त करके उन्हें प्रकाशित करवाती रहती है। विभिन्न आयोगों, समितियों तथा विश्वविद्यालयों के द्वारा भी आँकड़े प्रकाशित किए जाते हैं। इन प्रकाशित आँकड़ों को द्वितीयक समंको के रूप में प्रयोग किया जाता है।

प्रश्न 4. सांख्यिकी अनुसंधानों में प्रयुक्त संगणना रीति तथा दैव प्रतिचयन रीति के बारे में विस्तार से वर्णन कीजिए तथा न्यादर्श चुनने की विभिन्न रीतियों का वर्णन कीजिए।

उत्तर–किसी भी सांख्यिकीय अनुसंधान में उसके कार्यक्षेत्र से संबंधित सभी इकाइयों के बारे में सूचनाएँ प्राप्त करनी होती हैं। इस काम के लिए निम्नलिखित दो प्रणालियों के द्वारा समंक एकत्रित किए जा सकते हैं।

(*a*) संगणना पद्धति (Census Method)

(*b*) न्यादर्श पद्धति (Sample Method)

(*a*) **संगणना पद्धति**

इस पद्धति के अनुसार अनुसंधान से सम्बन्धित कार्यक्षेत्र की हर एक इकाई के बारे में अध्ययन किया जाता है। यह पद्धति सिर्फ उन्हीं अनुसंधानों में उचित रहती हैं जिनका कार्यक्षेत्र अधिक व्यापक ना हो। इस पद्धति के द्वारा प्राप्त किए गए समंक अधिक शुद्ध व विश्वसनीय होते हैं। क्योंकि इसमें समग्र की प्रत्येक इकाई का अध्ययन किया जाता है। हमारे देश में हर दस वर्ष के बाद जनगणना इसी पद्धति के द्वारा की जाती है। इस पद्धति को प्रयोग में लाना उन्हीं अनुसंधानों में उचित रहता है। जहाँ कि न्यादर्श पद्धति प्रयोग में न लायी जा सके और अनुसंधान का कार्यक्षेत्र ज्यादा व्यापक न हो तथा उद्देश्य संवेदनशील हो। कभी-कभी संगणना पद्धति प्रयोग में लाई ही नहीं जा सकती। उदाहरण के तौर पर जैसे कि किसी रोगी के खून की जाँच करनी हो तो उसका सारा खून नहीं निकाला जा सकता और खून के किसी न्यादर्श की ही जाँच की जाती है।

(*b*) **न्यादर्श पद्धति**

इस पद्धति के अनुसार अनुसंधान से सम्बन्धित हर एक इकाई के बारे में जाँच नहीं की जाती, बल्कि सम्बन्धित समग्र से कोई एक न्यादर्श लेकर उससे सम्बन्धित हर एक इकाई के बारे में सूचनाएँ एकत्रित की जाती हैं। यह अनुसंधान की आधुनिक रीति है। इस पद्धति के प्रयोग से अनुसंधान कार्य में काफी कम समय लगता है। और श्रम तथा समय की भी बचत होती है। अगर अनुसंधान के लिए न्यादर्श ठीक प्रकार से चुना जाए तो अनुसंधान के निष्कर्ष भी काफी ठीक निकलते हैं। किसी भी समग्र से न्यादर्श लेने के कई तरीके हैं। जिनके बारे में अब विस्तार से वर्णन किया जाएगा।

(*i*) **सामान्य दैव-निदर्शन रीति** (Simple Random Sampling)–हम जानते हैं कि न्यादर्श समग्र का ही एक हिस्सा होता है। किसी भी न्यादर्श को सामान्य दैव-न्यादर्श कहा जाता है। यदि सम्बन्धित समग्र में किसी भी इकाई का न्यादर्श के लिए चयन होना सम्भव हो। दैव-निदर्शन का मतलब यह नहीं कि जैसे मर्जी समग्र से इकाइयाँ छाँट ली जाएँ, बल्कि यह तो एक वैज्ञानिक रीति है। जिसमें यह निश्चित करना पड़ता है कि हर एक इकाई का न्यादर्श में आने की सम्भावना समान है। दैव-न्यादर्श चुनने की सबसे सरल पद्धति यह है कि समग्र की सभी इकाइयों की पर्चियाँ बना कर किसी बर्तन में डाल दी जाती हैं तथा किसी निष्पक्ष व्यक्ति के द्वारा निश्चित संख्या की पर्चियाँ उठा ली जाती हैं।

(*ii*) **स्तरित निदर्शन रीति** (Stratified Random Sampling)–इस पद्धति में सारे समग्र को कुछ स्तरों में बाँट दिया जाता है और पहले से ही निर्धारित मात्रा के न्यादर्श हर एक स्तर से ले लिए जाते हैं। इस प्रकार से जो न्यादर्श बनता है उसे पूरे समग्र का स्तरित न्यादर्श कहा जाता है। यह पद्धति सामान्य दैव-निदर्शन रीति से अधिक विश्वसनीय है और इसके प्रयोग से समय, धन व श्रम की बचत होती है।

(*iii*) **बहुस्तरीय दैव-निदर्शन रीति** (Multistage Random Sampling)–यह भी एक दैव-निदर्शन रीति है। इस रीति में समग्र से कई बार न्यादर्श लिए जाते हैं। उदाहरण के तौर पर जैसे सारे देश से 100 व्यक्तियों का न्यादर्श लेना हो तो

सारे देश के राज्यों से एक राज्य का न्यादर्श लिया जा सकता है तथा उसके बाद उस न्यादर्श से सम्बन्धित राज्यों के जिलों के समग्र से कई जिलों का न्यादर्श लिया जा सकता है और अन्त में न्यादर्श के जिलों के व्यक्तियों के समग्र से 100 व्यक्तियों का न्यादर्श लिया जा सकता है। यह पद्धति भी सामान्य दैव-निदर्शन रीति से अधिक उपयोगी है। यदि अनुसंधान का कार्यक्षेत्र बहुत अधिक व्यापक हो तो यह पद्धति विशेष तौर पर लाभकारी सिद्ध होती है।

(*iv*) **व्यवस्थित दैव-निदर्शन रीति** (Systematic Random Sampling)–यह भी दैव-निदर्शन रीति है, इस रीति के अन्तर्गत समग्र से सम्बन्धित सभी इकाइयों को किसी विशेष क्रम से लगा लिया जाता है। फिर जरूरत के अनुसार प्रत्येक दसवीं, बीसवीं या सौवीं इकाइयों को न्यादर्श में सम्मिलित कर लिया जाता है। उदाहरण के तौर पर यदि किसी समग्र में 20,000 इकाइयाँ हैं और सौ इकाइयों का व्यवस्थित दैव-निदर्शन रीति से न्यादर्श लेना हो तो समय से सम्बन्धित सभी 20,000 इकाइयों को किसी क्रम से लगा लिया जाएगा और प्रत्येक दो सौवीं इकाई को न्यादर्श में शामिल कर लिया जाएगा। इस पद्धति से भी समय, धन व श्रम की बचत होती है। यह पद्धति तभी अपनायी जानी चाहिए जबकि अनुसंधान का कार्यक्षेत्र सीमित हो।

(*v*) **अभ्यंश निदर्शन रीति** (Quota Sampling)–इस प्रणाली में न्यादर्श चुनने के लिए सारे समग्र को कुछ भागों में विभाजित कर दिया जाता है और हर भाग से लिया जाने वाला अभ्यंश निश्चित कर दिया जाता है। हर भाग से कौन-सी इकाइयाँ न्यादर्श में शामिल करनी हैं यह गणकों पर छोड़ दिया जाता है। इस प्रणाली में गणकों का योग्य होना अत्यन्त आवश्यक है। इस प्रणाली के प्रयोग से समय, धन और श्रम की काफी बचत हो जाती है। अगर गणक ईमानदारी से काम न लें तो अनुसंधान के परिणाम बहुत ठीक नहीं हो पाते।

(*vi*) **सुविधानुसार निदर्शन रीति** (Conveniance Sampling)–इस रीति में अनुसंधानकर्त्ता अपनी इच्छा के अनुसार निश्चित की गई इकाइयों का न्यादर्श समग्र में से चुन लेता है। यह रीति अवैज्ञानिक है। उदाहरण के तौर पर, अगर किसी अनुसंधानकर्त्ता ने कोई 20 विद्यार्थियों का न्यादर्श लेकर कोई निष्कर्ष निकालना हो तो वह अपनी सुविधा के अनुसार किसी नजदीक के विद्यालय या महाविद्यालय में जाकर किन्हीं 20 विद्यार्थियों से सम्पर्क स्थापित कर सकता है। इस पद्धति में अनुसंधानकर्त्ता का ईमानदार होना अत्यन्त आवश्यक है। प्रयोग में लाने की दृष्टि से यह विधि सबसे ज्यादा आसान है।

3. वर्गीकरण और प्रस्तुतिकरण

प्रश्न 5. वर्गीकरण और सारणीयन में अन्तर बताइए। वर्गीकरण के उद्देश्य, उसकी रीतियों तथा उसके महत्त्व को समझाइए।

उत्तर–किसी भी अनुसंधान में समंकों को इकट्ठा करने और संकलन करने के बाद उनको व्यवस्थित रूप से लिखा जाता है, अव्यवस्थित समंक किसी भी निष्कर्ष को निकालने में मदद नहीं कर पाते। **हिक्स** के शब्दों में, ''वर्गीकृत एवम् सुव्यवस्थित तथ्य स्वयं बोलते हैं और अव्यवस्थित समंक माँस के समान मृत होते हैं।''

एकत्रित की गई सूचनाओं के व्यवस्थीकरण में वर्गीकरण तथा सारणीयन की क्रियाएँ की जाती हैं। अब हम विस्तार से इन प्रक्रियाओं के बारे में वर्णन करेंगे।

1. वर्गीकरण

इस प्रक्रिया में संकलित समंकों को वर्गों में विभाजित कर दिया जाता है, वर्गों का विभाजन समंकों के गुणों को ध्यान में रखते हुए किया जाता है। उदाहरण के तौर पर अगर किसी शहर के वयस्कों की आय का ब्यौरा लिखना हो तो उन्हें 100 से कम, 100-200, 200-300 आदि वर्गों में विभाजित किया जा सकता है।

(*i*) **वर्गीकरण के उद्देश्य**–निम्नलिखित उद्देश्यों की पूर्ति के लिए संकलित समंकों का वर्गीकरण किया जाता है। वर्गीकरण के द्वारा समंकों को सरल रूप में प्रस्तुत किया जा सकता है, संकलित आँकड़े अपनी प्रारम्भिक अवस्था में बहुत जटिल रूप में होते हैं वर्गीकरण द्वारा संमक समझने में आसान और विश्लेषण के लिए सरल हो जाते हैं। इस प्रक्रिया द्वारा समंकों की समानताओं को उनकी असमानताओं से अलग किया जा सकता है। वर्गीकरण के द्वारा समंकों का तुलनात्मक अध्ययन भी सम्भव हो जाता है।

है।

2. सारणीयन

संकलित समंकों को वर्गीकृत करने के पश्चात् उन्हें सारणियों द्वारा प्रदर्शित किया जाता है। इसके लिए सारणियों में खाने (Columns) और पंक्तियाँ (Rows) बनाए जाते हैं। **कॉनर** के शब्दों में, ''सारणीयन किसी विचाराधीन समस्या को स्पष्ट करने के उद्देश्य से किया गया सांख्यिकीय तथ्यों का क्रमबद्ध और सुव्यवस्थित प्रस्तुतीकरण है।'' वर्गीकरण और सारणीयन एक-दूसरे से घनिष्ट रूप से सम्बन्धित प्रक्रियाएँ हैं। वर्गीकरण के पश्चात् सारणीयन किया जाता है।

सारणीयन के उद्देश्य

सारणीयन का मुख्य उद्देश्य संकलित समंकों को अनुसंधान के उद्देश्य को ध्यान में रखते हुए उन्हें सरलतम रूप में प्रस्तुत करना है। सारणीयन संकलित समंकों को प्रभावशाली तथा आकर्षक रूप में समंकों को प्रस्तुत करने में मदद करती है तथा तुलनात्मक दृष्टि से भी समंक तुलना योग्य हो जाते हैं।

वर्गीकरण तथा सारणीयन में अन्तर

वास्तव में वर्गीकरण तथा सारणीयन एक संयुक्त प्रक्रिया है जिसका प्रथम चरण वर्गीकरण है तथा दूसरा सारणीयन। संकलित समंकों को पहले वर्गीकृत किया जाता है और उसके बाद उन्हें सारणी के खानों और पंक्तियों में अंकित किया जाता है। वर्गीकरण समंकों के विश्लेषण की एक सांख्यिकीय रीति है जबकि सारणीयन वर्गीकृत समंकों को प्रस्तुत करने की रीति है। वर्गीकरण का आधार संकलित समंकों की विशेषताएँ होती हैं जबकि सारणीयन का आधार वर्गीकृत समंक होते हैं।

प्रश्न 6. सांख्यिकी में बिन्दु रेखीय प्रदर्शन की उपयोगिता पर संक्षिप्त लेख लिखिए।

उत्तर–सांख्यिकीय समंकों को आकर्षक ढंग से प्रस्तुत करने के लिए उनका चित्र और रेखाचित्र के द्वारा प्रदर्शन किया जाता है। ऐसे चित्र सांख्यिकीय समंकों की तुलना एवं प्रवृतियों को सरलता से स्पष्ट करते हैं। बिन्दु रेखीय चित्र ऐसे तथ्यों को अधिक स्पष्टता और आकर्षकता के साथ प्रस्तुत कर सकते हैं जिन्हें चित्रों द्वारा प्रदर्शित करना संभव न हो। पर्याप्त काल पूर्व ही संख्या शास्त्रियों ने अपने शोध परिणामों को बिन्दु रेखा द्वारा प्रदर्शित करने की कला को खोज निकाला था। **बॉडिक्टन** के शब्दों में, ''रेखा का घुमाव मस्तिष्क को प्रभावित करने में सारणीयकृत वितरण की अपेक्षा कहीं अधिक शक्तिशाली होता है। वह उतनी शीघ्रता से यह प्रदर्शित करने में समर्थ है कि क्या हो रहा है और क्या होने वाला है, जितनी शीघ्रता से यह कार्य हमारी आँख करने में समर्थ है।'' बिन्दु रेखाचित्रों को सिर्फ प्रदर्शन के लिए ही प्रयोग में नहीं लाया जाता बल्कि इनको विश्लेषण के यन्त्र के रूप में भी प्रयोग में लाया जाता है।

बिन्दु रेखीय प्रदर्शन के लाभ

बिन्दु रेखीय प्रदर्शन समंकों का प्रदर्शन करने की दृष्टिगत विधि है, जटिल एवं विशाल समंक समूहों को समझने में श्रम व समय की बचत करने के कारण बिन्दु रेखीय प्रदर्शन का सांख्यिकीय विधियों में महत्त्वपूर्ण स्थान है। समंकों के बिन्दु रेखीय प्रदर्शन के लाभ निम्नलिखित हैं–

(*i*) **आकर्षक एवं प्रभावशाली**–बिन्दु रेखीय चित्र समंकों को आकर्षक एवं प्रभावशाली बनाते हैं। इनको आकर्षक बनाने के लिए विभिन्न रंगों का प्रयोग भी किया जा सकता है नीरस समंक-समूहों में मनुष्य खो जाता है और पर्याप्त गूढ़ अध्ययन के पश्चात् ही वह कोई निष्कर्ष निकालने में सफल होता है। बिन्दु रेखीय प्रदर्शन पर मनोवैज्ञानिक प्रभाव पड़ता है

(*iii*) **सरलतम विधि**–सांख्यिकीय तथ्यों को प्रदर्शित करने में बिन्दु रेखा चित्र एक सरलतम पद्धति है, इसके प्रयोग में शास्त्री और अवलोकनकर्त्ता दोनों के ही समय और श्रम की बचत होती है।

(*iv*) **तुलनात्मकता**–बिन्दु रेखा चित्रों के द्वारा दो या दो से अधिक चरों को एक ही रेखाचित्र में प्रदर्शित करने से उनकी तुलना आसानी से की जा सकती है तथा उनके बीच पाये जाने वाले सहसम्बन्ध को भी समझा जा सकता है।

(*v*) **काल श्रेणियों का अध्ययन**–रेखाचित्रों की सहायता से काल श्रेणियों का अध्ययन भी आसानी से किया जा सकता है। किसी भी काल श्रेणी में मौजूद मौसमी परिवर्तनों, चक्रीय परिवर्तनों और दीर्घकालीन प्रवृत्ति को आसानी से समझा जा सकता है।

(*vi*) **आवृत्ति वितरण का प्रदर्शन**–रेखाचित्रों की सहायता से आवृत्ति वितरणों को भी आसानी से प्रदर्शित किया जा सकता है। रेखाचित्रों से किसी भी आवृत्ति वितरण से सम्बन्धित आवृत्ति चित्र (Histogram) आवृत्ति बहुभुज (Frequency Polygon) और आवृत्ति वक्र (Frequency Curve) को बनाया जा सकता है।

(*vii*) **केन्द्रीय प्रवृत्ति के अनुमान में सहायक**–किसी भी आवृत्ति वितरण से सम्बन्धित आवृत्ति चित्र बनाकर सम्बन्धित वितरण के भूयिष्ठक का मान निकाला जा सकता है। रेखाचित्र सम्बन्धित वितरण की मध्यका का मान निकालने में भी मदद करते हैं, इसके लिए सम्बन्धित आवृत्ति वितरण का संचयी आवृत्ति वक्र (Ogive) बनाया जाता है।

(*viii*) **अन्तर्गणन तथा बाह्यगणन में उपयोगिता**–रेखाचित्रों की मदद से अन्तर्गणन (Interpolation) और बाह्यगणन (Extrapolation) में भी मदद मिलती है। बाह्यगणन के लिए सम्बन्धित रेखाचित्र को आगे या पीछे बढ़ा लिया जाता है।

बिन्दु रेखीय प्रदर्शन की सीमाएँ

बिन्दु रेखीय प्रदर्शन के अत्यन्त लाभ होते हुए भी यह रीति पूर्णतया दोष रहित नहीं है। इस प्रकार के प्रदर्शन की भी अपनी कुछ सीमाएँ हैं। किसी भी बिन्दु रेखाचित्र से सम्बन्धित चर या चरों की प्रवृत्ति का तो आभास होता है लेकिन उनके मूल्यों का ज्ञान बहुत अधिक संभव नहीं हो पाता। आम लोगों के लिए बिन्दुरेखा चित्रों को बनाना तथा समझना संभव नहीं होता। **आई०आर० वैसलों** के शब्दों में ''शीघ्रता से पढ़ने में कुछ सम्बन्धों को आवश्यकता से अधिक महत्त्व देना और यहाँ तक कि अविद्यमान सम्बन्धों को देखना आसान होता है। साउद्देश्य रेखाचित्र-संरचक उन विशेषताओं को, जिन्हें वह सर्वोपरि समझता है अनुचित महत्त्व दे सकता है, तथा जिन्हें वह बेकार समझता है। उनके महत्त्व को कम करके दिखा सकता है।'' बिन्दु रेखाचित्र केवल समंकों की प्रवृत्ति तथा उनके उच्चावचनों का ही प्रदर्शन करते हैं तथा उनके वास्तविक मूल्यों का सही आभास नहीं करा पाते। रेखाचित्रों के मापदण्डों में परिवर्तन करके प्रवृत्तियों एवं उच्चावचनों के महत्त्व में परिवर्तन किया जा सकता है।

इन सब सीमाओं के होते हुए भी यह रीति सांख्यिकीय अनुसंधानों में अत्यन्त उपयोगी सिद्ध होती है।

4. केन्द्रीय प्रवृत्ति के माप

प्रश्न 7. 'सांख्यिकीय माध्य' से क्या अभिप्राय है ? एक अच्छे माध्य में कौन-कौन-सी वांछनीय विशेषताएँ होनी चाहिएँ ?

उत्तर–संख्यात्मक तथ्यों का वर्गीकरण (Classification) तथा सारणीयन (Tabulation) करने के उपरान्त भी इतने सरल, स्पष्ट तथा बोधगम्य नहीं हो पाते कि उनसे तत्काल कोई निष्कर्ष निकाला जा सके। उदाहरण के तौर पर यदि किसी कक्षा में 60 विद्यार्थी हैं और उनके कद सम्बन्धी आँकड़े दिए हों तो आँकड़ों को देखकर यह बताना अत्यन्त मुश्किल होगा कि कक्षा के विद्यार्थी लम्बे कद के हैं या ठिगने कद के।

इसी प्रकार से यदि किसी कारखाने में कार्यरत मजदूरों की आय को किसी दूसरे कारखाने में कार्यरत मजदूरों की आय से तुलना करनी हो तो यह भी सम्भव नहीं हो पायेगा कि विभिन्न मजदूरों की आय को दूसरे कारखाने के मजदूरों से तुलना की जाये। इस प्रकार की तुलना का कार्य सुगमतापूर्वक सम्पन्न किया जा सकता है, यदि हमें दोनों कारखानों में काम करने वाले मजदूरों की आय से सम्बन्धित ऐसी संख्याएँ ज्ञात हो सकें जोकि दोनों कारखानों में कार्यरत मजदूरों की आय का अलग-अलग प्रतिनिधित्व करे। इन प्रतिनिधि संख्याओं की तुलना करके हम तुरन्त यह निष्कर्ष निकाल सकेंगे कि किस कारखाने के मजदूरों को अच्छा वेतन मिल रहा है।

वर्गीकरण तथा सारणीयन की रीतियाँ आँकड़ों को संक्षिप्त रूप में प्रस्तुत करने में सहायता करती है। परन्तु ये विधियाँ आँकड़ों की सम्पूर्ण महत्त्वपूर्ण विशेषताओं पर प्रकाश डालने में असमर्थ रहती हैं। आँकड़ों को संक्षिप्त रूप से प्रकट करने के लिए सांख्यिकीय माध्यों (Statistical averages) का प्रयोग किया जाता है व किसी भी सांख्यिकीय शृंखला के माध्य को शृंखला में आये सभी आँकड़ों के प्रतिनिधि के रूप में प्रयोग किया जाता है।

क्राक्सटन एवं काऊडन (Croxton and Cowden) लिखते हैं–''माध्य आँकड़ों के विस्तार के अन्तर्गत स्थित एक ऐसा अकेला मूल्य है जिसका प्रयोग श्रेणी में समस्त मूल्यों का प्रतिनिधित्व करने के लिए किया जाता है, समंक श्रेणी के विस्तार के मध्य में होने के कारण माध्य को केन्द्रीय प्रवृत्ति का माप (Measure of central tendency) भी कहा जाता है।

सांख्यिकीय माध्य एकमात्र अंक के रूप में होता है तथा समूह के किसी विशेष गुण को मापता है। यह समूह का प्रतिरूप एवं प्रतिनिधि अंक होता है। समूह के व्यक्तिगत पद माध्य मूल्य के दोनों ओर केन्द्रित रहते हैं। इसी कारण से सांख्यिकीय माध्य को केन्द्रीय प्रवृत्ति की माप कहना उपयुक्त रहता है। **लारेन्स जे० काप्लान** (Lawrence J. Kaplan) लिखते हैं–''सांख्यिकीय विश्लेषण संक्षिप्त सूक्ष्म संख्यायें, जो विशाल संख्यात्मक तथा समूहों का विवरण दे सकें, विकसित करने की खोज करता है। इनमें से सर्वाधिक प्रयुक्त संक्षिप्त संख्याओं को 'स्थिति की मापें, (Measures of location) के नाम से जाना जाता है, जिन्हें प्राय: 'माध्य', केन्द्रीय प्रवृत्ति की मापें (Measure of central tendency) अथवा 'केन्द्रीय स्थिति' भी कहा जाता है। एक अवलोकन समूह के लिए माध्य मूल्य की गणना का उद्देश्य एक ऐसे मूल्य को ज्ञात करना है जो सभी का प्रतिनिधि हो, जिसे मस्तिष्क सरलता व शीघ्रता से समझ सके। वह एकमात्र मूल्य वह बिन्दु अथवा स्थिति है जिसके गिर्द व्यक्तिगत पद केन्द्रित रहते हैं।''

जी० पी० वाटकिन्स (G.P. Watkins) ने अत्यन्त सुन्दर तथा संक्षिप्त शब्दों में कहा है कि, ''माध्य समूह की 'प्रतिनिधि संख्या' होती है जो समूह के समंकों का अर्थ नहीं तो निचोड़ अवश्य होता है।''

ऊपर लिखित विवरण से यह स्पष्ट हो जाता है कि सांख्यिकीय माध्य संबंधित समूह का सूक्ष्म व सरल चित्र प्रस्तुत करता है तथा सम्पूर्ण समूह का प्रतिनिधित्व करता है।

अब हम विस्तार से यह अध्ययन करेंगे कि एक अच्छे माध्य में कौन-कौन-सी वांछनीय विशेषतायें होनी चाहिएँ।

1. समझने में आसान (Easy to understand)—एक अच्छे माध्य से यह अपेक्षा की जाती है कि उसकी परिभाषा आसान हो जिससे कि माध्य के विषय में समझने तथा समझाने में कोई कठिनाई न हो। उदाहरण के तौर पर गुणोत्तर माध्य (Geometric mean), भूयिष्ठक (Mode) आदि की परिभाषा सरलता से नहीं समझी जा सकती।

2. गणना में आसानी (Simple to Compute)—किसी माध्य को अधिकाधिक प्रयोग में लाने के लिए यह आवश्यक है कि उसकी गणना आसानी से की जा सके। व्यावहारिकता में वह माध्य अच्छा समझा जाता है। जिसकी गणना में विशेष परेशानी न हो। उदाहरण के तौर पर 4, 7, 10, 12, 15 की माध्यिका (Median) 10 है और यदि इन्हीं आँकड़ों का गुणोत्तर माध्य (Geometric mean), $(4 . 7 . 10 . 12 . 15)^{1/5}$ होगा, जो कि आसानी से नहीं निकाला जा सकता।

3. स्पष्ट परिभाषा (Rigidly defined)—एक अच्छे माध्य से यह अपेक्षा की जाती है कि उसकी परिभाषा बिल्कुल स्पष्ट हो तथा किसी प्रकार के संदेह की आशंका न हो। माध्य की परिभाषा में बीजगणितीय सूत्रों के प्रयोग को अच्छा माना जाता है माध्य की परिभाषा ऐसी होनी चाहिए जिससे कि किसी एक समूह के आँकड़ों के मध्य की गणना कई व्यक्ति अलग–अलग करें तो सभी के माध्य का मान एक ही आना चाहिए। माध्य की परिभाषा स्पष्ट न होने की दशा में माध्य की गणना में अवलोकन की भावना एवं योग्यता का प्रभाव पड़ेगा तथा विभिन्न व्यक्ति उसका अलग–अलग अर्थ लगायेंगे।

4. सभी संख्याओं पर आधारित (Based on all the items)—माध्य को संबंधित आँकड़ों का प्रतिनिधि माना जाता है यदि किसी माध्य की गणना में संबंधित सभी आँकड़ों का योगदान नहीं होता तो उसे वास्तविकता में सभी आँकड़ों का प्रतिनिधि नहीं माना जा सकता। उदाहरण के तौर पर 4, 5, 12, 17, 20 की माध्यिका (median) 12 है तथा 4, 5, 12, 17, 200 की माध्यिका भी 12 है, जबकि पहली श्रेणी का समानान्तर माध्य (Arithmetic mean)

$$\frac{4+5+12+17+20}{5} = 11.6 \text{ है}$$

और दूसरी श्रेणी का समानान्तर माध्य = $\frac{4+5+12+17+200}{5} = 47.6$ है।

एक अच्छे माध्य (average) से यह अपेक्षा की जाती है कि यदि किसी एक या अधिक मूल्यों में कोई परिवर्तन हो तो माध्य का मान भी प्रभावित होना चाहिए।

5. न्यूनतम तथा अधिकतम मूल्यों का कम-से-कम प्रभाव (Least effect of extreme items)—यदि किसी माध्य की गणना में सम्बन्धित सभी आँकड़ों का प्रयोग किया जाता है तो उसे एक अच्छा गुण समझा जाता है, लेकिन साथ ही यह भी अपेक्षा की जाती है कि आँकड़ों में मौजूद न्यूनतम तथा अधिकतम मूल्यों का अवांछनीय प्रभाव नहीं पड़ना चाहिये। उदाहरण के तौर पर 2, 4, 4, 5, 6 का समानान्तर माध्य = $\frac{2+4+4+5+6}{5} = 4.2$ है।

तथा 2, 4, 4, 5, 6, 1000 समानांतर माध्य = $\frac{2+4+4+5+6+1000}{6} = 170.17$ है।

पहली शृंखला में माध्य (4.2) सभी मूल्यों का प्रतिनिधित्व कर रहा है, लेकिन दूसरी शृंखला में माध्य (170.17) किसी भी मूल्य का प्रतिनिधित्व नहीं कर पा रहा है। दूसरी शृंखला में आखिरी मूल्य (1000), माध्य के मूल्य को अनावश्यक रूप से प्रभावित कर रहा है। ऊपर दी गई शृंखलाओं की माध्यिका क्रमश: 4 तथा 4.5 है जोकि अधिकतम मूल्य 1000 से अवांछनीय तौर पर प्रभावित नहीं हो रहा है।

6. बीजगणितीय विवेचन योग्य (Capable of algebraic treatment)—किसी सांख्यिकीय श्रेणी का माध्य निकालने के लिए विभिन्न तरीके हैं, इनमें से कुछ विधियाँ ऐसी हैं जिनका बीजगणितीय विवेचन किया जा सकता है। उदाहरण के तौर पर यदि किन्हीं दो या अधिक श्रेणियों का माध्य दिया हो तो हम चाहेंगे कि सभी श्रेणियों के सामूहिक मूल्यों का भी माध्य निकाला जा सके। यह गुण समानांतर माध्य (A.M.), गुणोत्तर माध्य (G.M.) तथा हरात्मक माध्य (H.M.) में विद्यमान होता है। इस गुण को किसी भी माध्य का अपेक्षित गुण माना जाता है।

7. न्यादर्शों के परिवर्तन का न्यूनतम प्रभाव (Least effected by sampling fluctuations)—मान लीजिए किसी शहर में 50,000 नागरिक हैं तथा 100 नागरिकों का न्यादर्श लेकर उनकी ऊँचाई का माध्य (average) निकाला जाता है। यदि हम 100 नागरिकों का कोई और न्यादर्श लेकर उनकी ऊँचाई का माध्य निकालें तो यह आवश्यक नहीं होगा कि जो माध्य पहले न्यादर्श का आया था वही माध्य दूसरे न्यादर्श का भी होगा। इसका कारण यह है कि न्यादर्श बदलने से ऊँचाइयों का मान भी बदलना स्वाभाविक है, लेकिन साथ ही एक अच्छे माध्य से यह अपेक्षा की जाती है कि जब अलग-अलग न्यादर्शों के माध्य निकाले जायें तो माध्य के मान में बहुत अधिक उतार-चढ़ाव नहीं आने चाहिएँ।

वास्तव में सांख्यिकीय आँकड़ों का माध्य निकालने की कोई भी ऐसी विधि नहीं है जिसमें ऊपर लिखे गये सभी गुण हों। यदि सभी अपेक्षित गुण किसी एक विधि में मिल जाते तो शायद माध्य निकालने की अधिक विधियों के अध्ययन करने की आवश्यकता ही नहीं पड़ती।

प्रश्न 8. सांख्यिकीय माध्यों की उपयोगिता के विषय में विस्तार से लिखिए।

उत्तर–किसी सांख्यिकीय श्रेणी का माध्य (average) वह संख्या होती है जोकि सभी आँकड़ों का अच्छे-से-अच्छे प्रकार से प्रतिनिधित्व कर सके। श्रेणी की संख्यायें माध्य के गिर्द केन्द्रित होती हैं। सांख्यिकीय माध्यों की निम्नलिखित उपयोगितायें हैं–

1. विशाल समंक समूहों का संक्षिप्त रूप में प्रस्तुत करना (To represent huge data briefly)—माध्य की सहायता से व्यक्तिगत मूल्यों के समूह को सरल एवं संक्षिप्त रूप से प्रस्तुत किया जा सकता है। इसकी सहायता से समूह की इकाइयों के सामान्य आकार को शीघ्रता से समझा जा सकता है। उदाहरण के तौर पर भारत के सभी नागरिकों के आय सम्बन्धी आँकड़ों को समझना एवं याद रखना अत्यन्त कठिन है लेकिन आय सम्बन्धी आँकड़ों के किसी माध्य को

आसानी से समझा और याद रखा जा सकता है। **डॉ० बाऊले** (Dr. A.L. Bowley) के शब्दों में "माध्यों के प्रयोग से जटिल समूहों तथा विशाल संख्याओं को कुछ महत्त्वपूर्ण शब्दों अथवा संख्याओं में प्रस्तुत किया जाता है।"

2. तुलनात्मक अध्ययन में सहायक (To facilitate comparative studies)—माध्यों की सहायता से विभिन्न समूहों का तुलनात्मक अध्ययन सरलता से किया जा सकता है। उदाहरण के तौर पर यदि किन्हीं दो कारखानों में कार्यरत मजदूरों की आय के विषय में यह निष्कर्ष निकालना हो कि किस कारखाने के मजदूरों को अच्छा वेतन मिल रहा है, तो इस कार्य में माध्य सहायक सिद्ध हो सकता है। यदि हम पहले कारखाने में कार्य करने वाले मजदूरों की आय की तुलना एक-एक करके दूसरे कारखाने के मजदूरों से करना चाहें तो यह व्यावहारिक रूप में सम्भव नहीं हो पायेगा। इस प्रक्रिया के स्थान पर यदि हम दोनों कारखानों में काम करने वाले मजदूरों की आय का अलग-अलग माध्य निकाल लें तो तुलना तुरन्त हो जायेगी। मान लीजिए पहले कारखाने के मजदूरों की औसत आय 950 रुपये है तथा दूसरे कारखाने के मजदूरों की औसत आय 980 रुपये है। इन माध्यों की तुलना करके हम तुरन्त निष्कर्ष निकाल सकते हैं कि दूसरे कारखाने के मजदूरों को पहले कारखाने के मजदूरों की अपेक्षा अच्छा वेतन मिल रहा है।

3. नीति निर्धारण में सहायक (Helpful in formation of policies)—नीति निर्धारण के कार्य में माध्यों का अत्यन्त महत्त्वपूर्ण योगदान रहता है। यदि देश की औसत आय पिछले वर्ष की अपेक्षा कम हो जाती है तो सरकार को अपेक्षित कदम उठाने की आवश्यकता पड़ जाती है। विभिन्न प्रकार के माध्यों की आपस में तुलना करके यह निष्कर्ष निकाला जा सकता है कि हमारा देश किस दिशा में और देशों से आगे है और किस दिशा में औरों से पीछे। अपने कर्मचारियों का उपयुक्त महंगाई भत्ता (Dearness allowance) निश्चित करने के लिए सरकार 'उपभोक्ता मूल्य सूचकांक' समय-समय पर तैयार करवाती रहती है, जिनकी रचना में माध्यों का ही मुख्य योगदान होता है।

4. सांख्यिकीय विश्लेषण का आधार (Basis of statistical analysis)—सांख्यिकीय विश्लेषण में माध्यों का अत्यन्त महत्त्वपूर्ण योगदान है। अपकिरण (Dispersion), विषमता (Skenwess), पृथुशीर्षत्व (Kurtosis) आदि के अध्ययन में माध्य आधार रूप में प्रयोग किये जाते हैं। काल श्रेणियों (Time series) के विश्लेषण में माध्यों का मुख्य योगदान है। निर्देशांकों (Index numbers) की रचना में भी माध्य प्रयोग किये जाते हैं। वास्तविकता तो यह है कि माध्यों के बिना सांख्यिकीय विश्लेषण पूर्णता असम्भव है।

प्रश्न 9. समानान्तर माध्य (Arithmetic mean) के विषय में विस्तार से लिखिए।

उत्तर—हम जानते हैं कि किसी सांख्यिकीय श्रेणी का माध्य वह मूल्य है जोकि श्रेणी में आये सभी मूल्यों का अच्छा प्रतिनिधित्व करने में सक्षम हो। किसी श्रेणी का माध्य निकालने की कई विधियाँ हैं, जिनमें समानांतर माध्य (Arithmetic mean) भी एक है। समानांतर माध्य सबसे अधिक प्रचलित माध्य है। इसी कारण से समानांतर माध्य को आम बोल-चाल की भाषा में केवल 'माध्य' ही कह दिया जाता है।

किसी सांख्यिकीय श्रेणी का **समानान्तर माध्य** निकालने के लिए श्रेणी के सभी मूल्यों को जोड़कर कुल मूल्यों की संख्या से भाग कर दिया जाता है।

मान लीजिए $\{x_1, x_2, \ldots, x_n\}$ कोई व्यक्तिगत श्रेणी (Individual series) है। इस श्रेणी का समानांतर माध्य निम्नलिखित सूत्र द्वारा निकाला जाता है :

$$\text{A.M.} = \frac{x_1 + x_2 + \ldots + x_n}{n} = \frac{\sum_{i=1}^{n} x_i}{n}$$

और संक्षिप्त में $$\text{A.M.} = \frac{\Sigma x}{n}.$$

इस विधि को समानांतर माध्य निकालने की **प्रत्यक्ष विधि** (Direct method) कहा जाता है।

प्रत्यक्ष विधि से किसी आवृत्ति आबंटन का समानांतर माध्य निकालने के लिए निम्न सूत्र प्रयोग किया जाता है–

$$\text{A.M.} = \frac{f_1x_1 + f_2x_2 + \ldots + f_nx_n}{f_1 + f_2 + \ldots + f_n} = \frac{\sum_{i=1}^{n} f_ix_i}{\sum_{i=1}^{n} f_1} = \frac{\Sigma fx}{\Sigma f} = \frac{\Sigma fx}{\text{N}}$$

इस सूत्र में मद x_i की आवृत्ति f_i $(1 \le i \le n)$ है। सभी आवृत्तियों के जोड़ Σf को आसानी के लिए N लिखा जाता है। यदि मदों का मान वर्गों के रूप में दिया हो तो विभिन्न वर्गों की आवृत्तियों का मान सम्बन्धित वर्ग के मध्य बिन्दु को माना जाता है। किसी सांख्यिकीय वर्ग का समानांतर माध्य निकालने के लिए एक और विधि का भी प्रयोग किया जाता है, जिसे **लघु-विधि** (Short-cut method) कहा जाता है।

इस विधि में मदों का किसी एक कल्पित माध्य (assumed mean), A से विचलन निकाले जाते हैं।

माना $d_1 = x_1 - \text{A}, d_2 = x_2 - \text{A}, \ldots, d_n = x_n - x_n - \text{A}$. विभिन्न विचलनों (Deviations) का मान है। समानांतर माध्य निकालने के लिए निम्न सूत्र प्रयोग किये जाते हैं–

$$\text{A.M.} = \text{A} + \frac{\Sigma d}{n}$$ (व्यक्तिगत श्रेणी के लिए)

$$\text{A.M.} = \text{A} + \frac{\Sigma fd}{N}$$ (आवृत्ति आबंटन के लिए)

यदि विभिन्न विचलनों में कोई समान गुणक (h) हो तो विचलनों से पद–विचलन (Step-deviations) निकाल लिये जाते हैं। माना

$$u_1 = \frac{d_1}{h} = \frac{x_1 - \text{A}}{h},\ u_2 = \frac{d_2}{h} = \frac{x_2 - \text{A}}{h}, \ldots\ldots, u_n = \frac{d_n}{h} = \frac{x_n - \text{A}}{h}$$

विभिन्न पद-विचलनों का मान है। समानान्तर माध्य निकालने के लिए निम्न सूत्र प्रयोग किये जाते हैं–

$$\text{A.M.} = \text{A} + \left(\frac{\Sigma u}{n}\right)h$$ (व्यक्तिगत श्रेणी के लिए)

$$\text{A.M.} = \text{A} + \left(\frac{\Sigma fu}{N}\right)h$$ (आवृत्ति आबंटन के लिए)

सामूहिक समानांतर माध्य (Combined arithmetic mean)—यदि किन्हीं दो समूहों में n_1 और n_2 मद हों और समानांतर माध्य $\bar{x}_1$ और $\bar{x}_2$ हों तो दोनों समूहों के मदों का **सामूहिक समानांतर माध्य** $(\bar{x})$ निम्न सूत्र द्वारा निकाला जाता है।

$$\bar{x} = \frac{n_1\bar{x}_1 + n_2\bar{x}_2}{n_1 + n_2}$$

इस सूत्र को दो से अधिक समूहों के लिए भी बढ़ाया जा सकता है।

भारित समानान्तर माध्य (Weighted arithmetic mean)—किसी श्रेणी का समानान्तर माध्य निकालते समय यह माना जाता है कि श्रेणी में हर एक मद को महत्ता समान है। यदि मदों की महत्ता समान नहीं हो तो एक दूसरे सूत्र का प्रयोग किया जाता है।

माना श्रेणी के मदों $x_1, x_2, \ldots, x_n$ की महत्ता (weights) क्रमशः $w_1, w_2, \ldots, w_n$ है। इस श्रेणी का **भारित समानान्तर माध्य** (Weighted arithmetic mean) निम्न सूत्र द्वारा निकाला जाता है।

$$\overline{\text{X}}_w = \frac{x_1w_1 + x_2w_2 + \ldots + x_nw_n}{w_1 + w_2 + \ldots + w_n} = \frac{\Sigma xw}{\Sigma w}$$

आर्थिक समस्याओं के अध्ययन में भारित समानान्तर माध्य का विशेष स्थान है।

समानान्तर माध्य के गुण (Merits of arithmetic mean)—

1. समानान्तर माध्य समझने में सबसे सरल प्रकार का माध्य है।
2. समानान्तर माध्य की गणना कई माध्यों से सरल है।
3. समानान्तर माध्य बीजगणितीय सूत्र द्वारा स्पष्ट रूप से परिभाषित किया जाता है।
4. समानान्तर माध्य श्रेणी में आये सभी पदों पर आधारित होता है।
5. समानान्तर माध्य बीजगणितीय विवेचन योग्य है।
6. समानान्तर माध्य पर न्यादर्श के परिवर्तन का बहुत कम प्रभाव पड़ता है।
7. समानान्तर माध्य को विशेष रूप से विभिन्न गतियों (Speeds) का औसत निकालने के लिए प्रयोग किया जाता है। यदि विभिन्न गतियों का समय समान हो तो साधारण समानांतर माध्य और यदि विभिन्न गतियों का समय समान न हो तो भारित समानान्तर माध्य औसत गति के बराबर होते हैं।

समानान्तर माध्य के दोष (Demerits of arithmetic mean)—

1. यह आवश्यक नहीं है कि किसी श्रेणी का समानांतर माध्य श्रेणी में भी हो। उदाहरण के तौर पर 4, 5, 6, 6 का समानांतर माध्य 5.25 है जोकि श्रेणी में नहीं है।

2. समानांतर माध्य की गणना गुण सम्बन्धी आँकड़ों के लिए नहीं की जा सकती।

3. समानांतर माध्य न्यूनतम तथा अधिकतम पदों से बहुत प्रभावित हो जाता है।

प्रश्न 10. गुणोत्तर माध्य (Geometric mean) के विषय में विस्तार से लिखिए।

उत्तर–किसी सांख्यिकीय श्रेणी का माध्य (average) वह मूल्य होता है जोकि सम्बन्धित श्रेणी में आये सभी मूल्यों का अच्छी प्रकार से प्रतिनिधित्व कर सकने में सक्षम हो। सांख्यिकीय श्रेणियों के माध्य निकालने की कई विधियाँ प्रचलित हैं और उनमें से एक गुणोत्तर माध्य (Geometric mean) है।

किसी सांख्यिकीय श्रेणी का **गुणोत्तर माध्य** निकालने के लिए श्रेणी के सभी मूल्यों को गुणा करके कुल मूल्यों की संख्या जितना मूल (root) ले लिया जाता है।

मान लीजिए $x_1, x_2, ..., x_n$ कोई व्यक्तिगत श्रेणी (individual series) है। इस श्रेणी का गुणोत्तर माध्य निकालने के लिए निम्नलिखित सूत्र का प्रयोग किया जाता है–

$$\text{G.M.} = (x_1, x_2, ..., x_n)^{1/n}$$

उदाहरण के तौर पर, 4, 8, 54 का गुणोत्तर माध्य $(4 \times 8 \times 54)^{1/3} = 12$ है। यदि किसी श्रेणी में 2, 3, 4, 7, 9 है तो इसका गुणोत्तर माध्य $(2.3.4.7.9)^{1/5}$ होगा, जिसकी गणना सरल नहीं है।

व्यावहारिकता में गुणोत्तर माध्य निकालने के लिए लघुगणकों (Logarithms) तथा प्रतिलघुगणकों (Antilogarithms) का प्रयोग किया जाता है। गुणोत्तर माध्य निम्न सूत्र द्वारा निकाला जाता है।

$$\text{G.M.} = \text{Antilog}\left(\frac{\log x_1 \times \log x_2 + ... + \log x_n}{n}\right) = \text{Antilog}\left(\frac{\Sigma \log x}{n}\right)$$

इस सूत्र में सभी पदों का लघुगणक निकाला जाता है और इनके जोड़ को $\Sigma \log x$ लिखा जाता है।

किसी आवृत्ति आबंटन (Frequency distribution) के गुणोत्तर माध्य निकालने के लिए निम्न सूत्र का प्रयोग किया जाता है।

$$\text{G.M.} = \text{Antilog}\left(\frac{f_1 \log x_1 + f_2 \log x_2 + ... + f_n \log x_n}{f_1 + f_2 + ... + f_n}\right)$$

$$= \text{Antilog} \frac{\sum_{i=1}^{n} f_i \log x_i}{\sum_{i=1}^{n} f_i} = \text{Antilog}\left(\frac{\Sigma f \log x}{n}\right) \quad \text{(संक्षिप्त रूप में)}$$

इस सूत्र में x_i की आवृत्ति (Frequency) f_i $(1 \le i \le n)$ है। सभी आवृत्तियों के जोड़ Σf को आसानी के लिए N लिखा जाता है। यदि मदों का मान वर्गों (Classes) के रूप में दिया हो तो विभिन्न वर्गों की आवृत्तियों का मान सम्बन्धित वर्गों के मध्य बिन्दुओं को माना जाता है।

सामूहिक गुणोत्तर माध्य (Combined geometric mean) — यदि किन्हीं दो समूहों में n_1 और n_2 मद हो और गुणोत्तर माध्य G_1 और G_2 हो तो दोनों समूहों के मदों का **सामूहिक गुणोत्तर माध्य** (G) निम्न सूत्र द्वारा निकाला जाता है–

$$G = \text{Antilog}\left(\frac{n_1 \log G_1 + n_2 \log G_2}{n_1 + n_2}\right)$$

इस सूत्र को दो से अधिक समूहों के लिए भी बढ़ाया जा सकता है।

भारित गुणोत्तर माध्य (Weighted geometric mean) — किसी श्रेणी का गुणोत्तर माध्य निकालते समय यह माना जाता है कि श्रेणी में हर एक मद की महत्ता समान है यदि मदों की महत्ता समान न हो तो एक दूसरे सूत्र का प्रयोग किया जाता है।

माना श्रेणी के मदों $x_1, x_2, ..., x_n$ की महत्ता (Weights) क्रमशः $w_1, w_2, ..., w_n$ है। इस श्रेणी का **भारित गुणोत्तर माध्य** (Weight geometric mean) निम्न सूत्र द्वारा निकाला जाता है–

$$\text{भारित गुणोत्तर माध्य} = \text{Antilog}\left(\frac{\Sigma w \log x}{\Sigma w}\right)$$

गुणोत्तर माध्य के गुण (Merits of geometric mean)—

1. गुणोत्तर माध्य बीजगणितीय सूत्र द्वारा स्पष्ट रूप से परिभाषित किया जाता है।
2. गुणोत्तर माध्य श्रेणी में आये सभी पदों पर आधारित होता है।
3. गुणोत्तर माध्य बीजगणितीय विवेचन योग्य है।
4. प्रतिशत वृद्धि, अनुपातों आदि का औसत निकालने के लिए गुणोत्तर माध्य का प्रयोग किया जाता है।
5. गुणोत्तर माध्य को विशेष तौर पर निर्देशांकों की रचना में प्रयोग किया जाता है।
6. जिन समूहों में बड़े पदों को कम भार तथा छोटे पदों को अधिक भार देना हो, उनमें गुणोत्तर माध्य अधिक उपयुक्त रहता है।
7. गुणोत्तर माध्य पर न्यादर्शों के परिवर्तन का बहुत कम प्रभाव पड़ता है।

गुणोत्तर माध्य के दोष (Demerits of geometric mean)—

1. गुणोत्तर माध्य को सरलता से नहीं समझा जा सकता है।
2. गुणोत्तर माध्य की गणना में कठिनता का सामना करना पड़ता है।
3. ऋणात्मक पदों की उपस्थिति में गुणोत्तर माध्य काल्पनिक हो जाता है।
4. यदि किसी पद का मान शून्य हो तो गुणोत्तर माध्य का मान शून्य हो जाता है, चाहे बाकी पदों का मान कुछ भी हो।

प्रश्न 11. हरात्मक माध्य (Harmonic mean) के विषय में विस्तार से लिखिए।

उत्तर–किसी सांख्यिकीय श्रेणी का माध्य (Average) वह मूल्य होता है, जो कि सम्बन्धित श्रेणी में आये सभी मूल्यों का अच्छी प्रकार से प्रतिनिधित्व कर सकने में सक्षम हो। सांख्यिकीय श्रेणियों के माध्य निकालने की कई विधियाँ प्रचलित हैं और उनमें से एक हरात्मक माध्य (Harmonic mean) है।

किसी सांख्यिकीय श्रेणी का **हरात्मक माध्य** निकालने के लिए श्रेणी के कुल मूल्यों की संख्या को सभी मूल्यों के व्युत्क्रमों (Reciprocals) के योग से भाग किया जाता है।

मान लीजिए $x_1, x_2, ..., x_n$ कोई व्यक्तिगत श्रेणी (Individual series) है। इस श्रेणी का हरात्मक माध्य निकालने के लिए निम्नलिखित सूत्र का प्रयोग किया जाता है :

$$\text{H.M.} = \frac{n}{\frac{1}{x_1} + \frac{1}{x_2} + ... + \frac{1}{x_n}} = \frac{n}{\sum \frac{1}{x}}$$

उदाहरण के लिए 4, 7, 9, 10, 15 का हरात्मक माध्य

$$\frac{5}{\frac{1}{4} + \frac{1}{7} + \frac{1}{9} + \frac{1}{10} + \frac{1}{15}} = \frac{5}{0.6706} = 7.4560 \text{ है।}$$

किसी आवृति आबंटन (Frequency distribution) के लिए निम्न सूत्र का प्रयोग किया जाता है–

$$\text{H.M.} = \frac{f_1 + f_2 + ... + f_n}{f_1\left(\frac{1}{x_1}\right) + f_2\left(\frac{1}{x_2}\right) + ... + f_n\left(\frac{1}{x_n}\right)}$$

$$= \frac{\Sigma f}{\sum f\left(\frac{1}{x}\right)} = \frac{\text{N}}{\sum \left(\frac{f}{x}\right)}. \qquad \text{(संक्षिप्त रूप में)}$$

इस सूत्र में x_i की आवृत्ति (frequency) f_i $(1 \le i \le n)$ है। सभी आवृत्ति जोड़ Σf को आसानी से लिये N लिखा जाता हैं। यदि मदों का मान वर्गों (Classes) के रूप में दिया हो तो विभिन्न वर्गों की आवृत्तियों का मान सम्बन्धित वर्गों के मध्य बिन्दुओं को माना जाता है।

सामूहिक हरात्मक माध्य (Combined harmonic mean)—यदि किन्हीं दो समूहों में n_1और n_2 मद हों और हरात्मक माध्य H_1और H_2 हो तो दोनों समूहों के मदों का **सामूहिक हरात्मक माध्य** (H) निम्न सूत्र द्वारा निकाला जाता है–

$$\text{H} = \frac{n_1 + n_2}{\frac{n_1}{\text{H}_1} + \frac{n_2}{\text{H}_2}}$$

इस सूत्र को दो से अधिक समूहों के लिये भी बढ़ाया जा सकता है।

भारित हरात्मक माध्य (Weighted harmonic mean)—किसी श्रेणी का हरात्मक माध्य निकालते समय यह माना जाता है कि श्रेणी में हर एक मद की महत्ता समान है। यदि मदों की महत्ता समान न हो तो एक दूसरे सूत्र का प्रयोग किया जाता है।

माना श्रेणी के मदों $x_1, x_2, ..., x_n$ की महत्ता (Weights) क्रमश: $w_1, w_2, ..., w_n$ है। इस श्रेणी का **भारित हरात्मक माध्य** (Weighted harmonic mean) निम्न सूत्र द्वारा निकाला जाता है–

$$\text{भारित हरात्मक माध्य} = \frac{\Sigma w}{\sum \left(\frac{w}{x}\right)}$$

हरात्मक माध्य के गुण (Merits of harmonic mean)—

1. हरात्मक माध्य बीजगणितीय सूत्र द्वारा स्पष्ट रूप से परिभाषित किया जाता है।
2. हरात्मक माध्य श्रेणी में आये सभी पदों पर आधारित होता है।
3. हरात्मक माध्य बीजगणितीय विवेचन योग्य है।
4. हरात्मक माध्य पर न्यादर्शों के परिवर्तन का बहुत कम प्रभाव पड़ता है।
5. हरात्मक माध्य को विशेष रूप से विभिन्न गतियों (speeds) का औसत निकालने के लिए प्रयोग किया जाता है। यदि विभिन्न गतियों द्वारा तय की गई दूरियाँ समान हों तो साधारण हरात्मक माध्य और यदि विभिन्न गतियों द्वारा तय की गई दूरियाँ समान न हों तो भारित हरात्मक माध्य औसत गति के बराबर होता है।

हरात्मक माध्य के दोष (Demerits of harmonic mean)

1. हरात्मक माध्य को सरलता से नहीं समझा जा सकता है।
2. हरात्मक माध्य की गणना में कठिनता का सामना करना पड़ता है।
3. हरात्मक माध्य छोटे पदों को अधिक महत्त्व देता है जो कि कुछ परिस्थितियों में अपेक्षित नहीं होता।

प्रश्न 12. माध्यिका (Median) के विषय में विस्तार से लिखिए।

उत्तर–किसी सांख्यिकीय श्रेणी का माध्य (Average) वह मूल्य होता है, जोकि सम्बन्धित श्रेणी में आये सभी मूल्यों का अच्छे प्रकार से प्रतिनिधित्व कर सकने में सक्षम हो। सांख्यिकीय श्रेणियों के माध्य निकालने की कई विधियाँ प्रचलित हैं और उनमें से एक माध्यिका (Median) है।

किसी सांख्यिकीय श्रेणी का **माध्यिका** (Median) वह मूल्य है जोकि श्रेणी को दो बराबर हिस्सों में इस प्रकार से विभाजित करता है कि एक हिस्से के मदों का मान माध्यिका से कम या बराबर होता है तथा दूसरे हिस्से के मदों का मान माध्यिका से अधिक या बराबर होता है। किसी सांख्यिकीय श्रेणी का माध्यिका ज्ञात करने के लिए श्रेणी में आये सभी मदों को आरोही (Ascending) क्रम से अनुविन्यसित कर लिया जाता है।

मान लीजिए $x_1, x_2, ..., x_n$ कोई व्यक्तिगत श्रेणी (Individual series) है और इसमें सभी मद आरोही क्रम से लगाए हुये हैं। इस श्रेणी का माध्यिका निकालने के लिए निम्नलिखित सूत्र का प्रयोग किया जाता है–

माध्यिका $= \dfrac{n+1}{2}$ स्थान वाले मद का मूल्य

इस सूत्र में यदि $\dfrac{n+1}{2}$ दशमलव में आ जायें तो बीच वाले दोनों मदों के मूल्यों को जोड़कर दो से भाग किया जाता है।

उदाहरण के तौर पर यदि श्रेणी में 9 मद हों तो माध्यिका $\dfrac{9+1}{2} = 5$ वें स्थान पर आने वाले मद का मान होगा और यदि श्रेणी में 10 स्थान हों तो $\dfrac{10+1}{2}$ का मान 5.5 होगा और माध्यिका निकालने के लिए पांचवें तथा छठे मदों के मूल्यों को जोड़ कर दो से भाग किया जायेगा–

किसी आवृत्ति आबंटन (frequency distribution) के लिए निम्न सूत्र का प्रयोग किया जाता है–

माध्यिका $= \dfrac{N+1}{2}$ स्थान वाले मद का मूल्य

इस सूत्र में श्रेणी के मदों की आवृत्तियों के योग को N से दर्शाया गया है। इस सूत्र को प्रयोग करने से पहले यह निश्चित करना आवश्यक होता है कि सभी मद आरोही क्रम में हैं। $\dfrac{N+1}{2}$ वें मद मान निकालने के लिए संचयी आवृत्ति को प्रयोग किया जाता है।

यदि आवृत्ति आबंटन में मदों को वर्गों के रूप में दर्शाया गया है तो निम्नलिखित विधि द्वारा माध्यिका का मान निकाला जाता है–

(*i*) सभी वर्गों को आरोही क्रम से लगाया जाता है।

(*ii*) विभिन्न वर्गों की संचयी आवृत्ति निकाली जाती है।

(*iii*) $\frac{N}{2}$ वें मद के वर्ग को **माध्यिका वर्ग** कहा जाता है।

माध्यिका का मान निश्चित करने के लिए निम्न सूत्र का प्रयोग किया जाता है।

$$\text{माध्यिका} = L + \left(\frac{\frac{N}{2} - C}{f}\right)h$$

इस सूत्र में,

L = माध्यिका वर्ग की निम्न सीमा

C = माध्यिका वर्ग से पहले वर्ग की संचयी आवृत्ति

f = माध्यिका वर्ग की आवृत्ति

h = माध्यिका वर्ग का वर्गान्तर

यदि वर्ग समावेशी (inclusive) हो तो माध्यिका वर्ग की वास्तविक सीमाओं का प्रयोग किया जाता है। इस सूत्र के प्रयोग में यह भी आवश्यक नहीं है कि सभी वर्गों के वर्गान्तर बराबर हों।

ग्राफ द्वारा माध्यिका का मान निकाला जा सकता है। इस कार्य के लिए ओजाइव वक्रों (Ogive Curves) का प्रयोग किया जाता है।

माध्यिका के गुण (Merits of median)

1. माध्यिका समझने में सरल प्रकार का माध्य है।
2. माध्यिका की गणना कई माध्यों की अपेक्षा सरलता से सम्पन्न हो जाती है।
3. माध्यिका को बीजगणितीय सूत्र द्वारा स्पष्ट रूप से परिभाषित किया जाता है।
4. माध्यिका पर न्यूनतम तथा अधिकतम पदों का कोई प्रभाव नहीं पड़ता।
5. खुले सिरों वाले वर्गों (Open end classes) के मामले में माध्यिका बहुत उपयुक्त माध्य होता है।
6. माध्यिका का मान ग्राफ की सहायता से भी निकाला जा सकता है।

माध्यिका के दोष (Demerits of median)

1. माध्यिका का मान श्रेणी के सभी पदों पर आधारित नहीं होता।
2. माध्यिका बीजगणितीय विवेचन योग्य नहीं है।
3. माध्यिका का मान सिर्फ तभी लगाया जा सकता है जबकि श्रेणी के सभी मद आरोही क्रम में हों।

प्रश्न 13. भूयिष्ठक (Mode) के विषय में विस्तार से लिखिये।

उत्तर–सांख्यिकीय श्रेणी का माध्य (Average) वह मूल्य होता है, जोकि सम्बन्धित श्रेणी में आये सभी मूल्यों का अच्छे प्रकार, से प्रतिनिधित्व कर सकने में सक्षम हो। सांख्यिकीय श्रेणियों के माध्य निकालने की कई विधियाँ प्रचलित हैं और उनमें से भूयिष्ठक (Mode) एक है।

किसी सांख्यिकीय श्रेणी का **भूयिष्ठक** (Mode) वह मूल्य होता है जिसके गिर्द श्रेणी के मूल्यों का जमाव सर्वाधिक हो। **क्राक्सटन** और **काउडन (Croxton and Cowden)** के अनुसार ''एक वितरण का भूयिष्ठक वह मूल्य है। जिसके

निकट श्रेणी की इकाइयाँ अधिक-से-अधिक केन्द्रित होती हैं। उसे मूल्यों की श्रेणी का सबसे अधिक प्रतिरूपी माना जा सकता है।'' किसी श्रेणी का भूयिष्ठक 'सर्वाधिक घनत्व की स्थिति (Position of greatest density) वाला मूल्य होता है। **जिजेक (Zizek)** के अनुसार ''भूयिष्ठक वह मूल्य है जो पदों की श्रेणी (अथवा समूह) में सबसे अधिक बार आता है तथा जिसके चारों और सबसे अधिक घनत्वों में पदों का वितरण रहता है।''

भूयिष्ठक का मान निकालने के लिए हमें सांख्यिकीय श्रेणी में यह देखना होगा कि किस मूल्य के गिर्द मूल्यों का जमाव अधिकतम है। इस कार्य के लिए हमें श्रेणी में आये सभी मूल्यों की आवृत्तियों का अध्ययन करना पड़ेगा। उदाहरण के लिए मान लीजिये किसी श्रेणी में मूल्य 4, 5, 6, 7, 8, 9 है तथा इनकी आवृत्तियाँ क्रमश: 27, 29, 40, 35, 16, 9 हैं। इस आवृत्ति वितरण में यह स्पष्ट रूप में देखा जा सकता है कि श्रेणी के मूल्य 6 के गिर्द मूल्यों का जमाव अधिकतम है और इसीलिए दी गई आवृत्ति वितरण का भूयिष्ठक 6 कहा जायेगा।

किसी व्यक्तिगत श्रेणी का भूयिष्ठक निकालने के लिए हमें पहले व्यक्तिगत श्रेणी को आवृत्ति वितरण में परिवर्तित करके यह देखना होगा कि श्रेणी के किस मूल्य के गिर्द जमाव (Clustering) अधिकतम है। यह भी कोई आवश्यक नहीं है कि अधिकतम जमाव वाला मूल्य श्रेणी में हो। ऐसी परिस्थिति में श्रेणी को **बहु-भूयिष्ठक** (multi-modal) कहा जाता है।

किसी आवृत्ति वितरण का भूयिष्ठक निकालने के लिए निम्नलिखित विधियों का प्रयोग किया जाता है।

1. निरीक्षण द्वारा (By inspection)—सबसे पहले चरण में यह निश्चित किया जाता है कि वितरण में आये सभी मूल्य आरोही क्रम से हैं। यदि ऐसा न हो तो मूल्यों को आरोही क्रम से कर लिया जाता है। यदि श्रेणी की आवृत्तियाँ नियमित रूप से बढ़ती रहें और अधिकतम आवृत्ति के पश्चात् नियमित रूप से घटती रहें तो सबसे अधिक आवृत्ति वाले मूल्य को श्रेणी का भूयिष्ठक कहा जाता है।

2. समूहन द्वारा (By grouping)—इस विधि में भी पहले यह निश्चित किया जाता है कि वितरण में आये सभी मूल्य आरोही क्रम से हैं। इस विधि का प्रयोग उन परिस्थितियों में किया जाता है जबकि वितरण में आवृत्तियाँ नियमित से न बढ़ रही हों तथा न ही घट रही हों। श्रेणी की आवृत्तियों का निम्नलिखित प्रकार से समूहन (Grouping) किया जाता है।

(*i*) प्रथम स्तम्भ में वितरण की आवृत्तियाँ ही रहती हैं तथा सबसे अधिक आवृत्ति को चिह्नित किया जाता है।

(*ii*) द्वितीय स्तम्भ में वितरण की दो-दो आवृत्तियों को जोड़ा जाता है तथा अधिकतम योग को चिह्नित किया जाता है।

(*iii*) तृतीय स्तम्भ में वितरण की पहली आवृति को छोड़कर दो-दो आवृत्तियों को जोड़ा जाता है तथा अधिकतम योग को चिह्नित किया जाता है।

(*iv*) चतुर्थ स्तम्भ में वितरण की तीन-तीन आवृत्तियों को जोड़ा जाता है तथा अधिकतम योग को चिह्नित किया जाता है।

(*v*) पंचम स्तम्भ में वितरण की पहली आवृत्ति को छोड़कर तीन-तीन आवृत्तियों को जोड़ा जाता है तथा अधिकतम योग को चिह्नित किया जाता है।

(*vi*) षष्ठम स्तम्भ में वितरण की पहली तथा दूसरी आवृत्तियों को छोड़कर फिर से तीन-तीन आवृत्तियों को जोड़ा जाता है तथा अधिकतम योग को चिह्नित किया जाता है।

समूहीकरण का विश्लेषण करने के लिए एक और तालिका बनाई जाती है जिसमें समूहीकरण के सारे स्तम्भों में आए अधिकतम योगों से सम्बन्धित मूल्यों को चिह्नित किया जाता हैं। वितरण के जिस मूल्य के आगे सबसे अधिक चिन्ह लगें, वही भूयिष्ठक का मान कहा जाता है। कभी-कभी ऐसा हो जाता है कि समूहन के विश्लेषण में वितरण के दो या दो से अधिक मूल्य अधिकतम बार चिह्नित हो जाते हैं। ऐसी परिस्थिति में वितरण को बहु-भूयिष्ठक कहा जाता है। ऐसा होने पर भूयिष्ठक का मान निम्नलिखित सूत्र द्वारा निश्चित किया जाता है:

$$\text{भूयिष्ठक} = 3\,\text{माध्यिका} - 2\,\text{समानांतर माध्य}$$

यदि आवृत्ति वितरण में मदों को वर्गों के रूप में दर्शाया गया है तो निम्नलिखित प्रक्रिया द्वारा भूयिष्ठक का मान निकाला जाता है–

(*i*) सभी वर्गों को आरोही क्रम से लगाया जाता है।

(*ii*) सभी वर्गों के वर्गान्तर समान न हों तो वर्गान्तरों को बराबर किया जाता है।

(*iii*) 'निरीक्षण द्वारा' या 'समूहन द्वारा' विधि से **भूयिष्ठक वर्ग** (modal class) निश्चित की जाती है।

भूयिष्ठक का मान निकालने के लिए निम्न सूत्र का प्रयोग किया जाता है–

$$\text{भूयिष्ठक} = L + \left(\frac{\Delta_1}{\Delta_1 + \Delta_2}\right)h$$

इस सूत्र में,

L = भूयिष्ठक वर्ग की निम्न सीमा

Δ_1 = भूयिष्ठक वर्ग तथा उससे पहले वाले वर्ग की आवृत्तियों का अन्तर

Δ_2 = भूयिष्ठक वर्ग तथा उससे बाद वाले वर्ग की आवृत्तियों का अन्तर

h = भूयिष्ठक वर्ग का वर्गान्तर

यदि वर्ग समावेशी (inclusive) हो तो भूयिष्ठक वर्ग की वास्तविक सीमाओं का प्रयोग किया जाता है। इस सूत्र के प्रयोग में यह आवश्यक है कि सभी वर्गों के वर्गान्तर बराबर हों।

ग्राफ द्वारा भी भूयिष्ठक का मान निकाला जा सकता है। इस कार्य के लिए आवृत्ति आयत (Histogram) का प्रयोग किया जाता है।

भूयिष्ठक के गुण (Merits of mode)

1. भूयिष्ठक की गणना कई माध्यों की अपेक्षा सरलता से सम्पन्न हो जाती है।
2. भूयिष्ठक पर न्यूनतम तथा अधिकतम पदों का कोई प्रभाव नहीं पड़ता।
3. भूयिष्ठक का मान ग्राफ की सहायता से निकाला जा सकता है।

भूयिष्ठक के दोष (Demerits of mode)

1. भूयिष्ठक को सरलता से नहीं समझा जा सकता।
2. भूयिष्ठक को स्पष्ट रूप से परिभाषित नहीं किया जा सकता। भूयिष्ठक का मान निकालने के लिए कई बीजगणितीय सूत्र प्रचलित हैं और वह आवश्यक नहीं है कि विभिन्न सूत्र भूयिष्ठक का एक ही मान देंगे।
3. भूयिष्ठक बीजगणितीय विवेचन योग्य नहीं है।

5. अपकिरण के माप

प्रश्न 14. अपकिरण के माप से क्या अभिप्राय है? एक अच्छे अपकिरण के माप में कौन-कौन-सी वांछनीय विशेषतायें होनी चाहिए ?

उत्तर–हम जानते हैं कि माध्य को सांख्यिकीय श्रेणी के प्रतिनिधि के रूप में प्रयोग किया जाता है। श्रेणी की केन्द्रीय प्रवृत्ति के प्रतिनिधि के रूप में माध्य एक महत्त्वपूर्ण एवं उपयोगी माप हैं। व्यावहारिकता में किसी सांख्यिकीय श्रेणी का विवरण प्रस्तुत करने के लिए एक ही माप का प्रयोग करने से उसमें अन्तर्निहीत अनेक महत्त्वपूर्ण तथ्य छिप जाते हैं। किसी श्रेणी को पूर्ण रूप से समझने के लिए यह आवश्यक होता है कि उनमें छिपी सभी विशेषताओं को प्रकट किया जाए। केन्द्रीय प्रवृत्ति की माप एक समंक माला के पद-मूल्यों के सामान्य स्तर को ही स्पष्ट करती है और इससे अधिक कोई विवरण देने में वह असमर्थ रहती है। किसी आवृत्ति विवरण में कई अन्य विशेषताएँ होती हैं जिन्हें जानना आवश्यक होता है केन्द्रीय प्रवृत्ति की माप यह स्पष्ट नहीं करती कि उसके सम्बन्ध में समंक माला के अन्य पदों का बिखराब किस प्रकार है। किन्हीं दो समंकमालाओं के माध्य समान हो सकते हैं, परन्तु एक समंक माला में पदों का जमाव अत्यन्त केन्द्रित हो सकता है, जबकि समंक माला में पदों का बिखराव माध्य के चारों ओर विस्तार से हो सकता है।

मान लीजिए किसी विद्यालय के सभी विद्यार्थियों की ऊँचाई का औसत 65 इंच है। औसत ऊँचाई से यह निष्कर्ष नहीं निकाला जा सकता कि सभी विद्यार्थियों की ऊँचाई 65 इंच होगी। ऐसा हो सकता है कि विद्यार्थियों की ऊँचाई 63 इंच और 68 इंच के बीच हो और सबकी ऊँचाईयों का औसत 65 इंच हो। विद्यार्थियों की ऊँचाइयाँ 59 इंच और 75 इंच के बीच भी हो सकती हैं। पहली परिस्थिति में पदों का जमाव औसत मान के गिर्द केन्द्रित रहेगा तथा दूसरी परिस्थिति में पदों का बिखराव औसत के चारों ओर विस्तार से रहेगा। विभिन्न श्रेणियों के माध्य समान हो सकते हैं परन्तु उनकी बनावट में पर्याप्त भिन्नता हो सकती है, जैसा कि निम्न तालिका से स्पष्ट होता है।

समान माध्य वाली श्रेणियाँ

क्र॰	क		ख		ग	
सं॰	मूल्य x	$\bar{x}$ से विचलन $x-\bar{x}$	मूल्य x	$\bar{x}$ से विचलन $x-\bar{x}$	मूल्य x	$\bar{x}$ से विचलन $x-\bar{x}$
1.	10	0	10	0	1	−9
2.	10	0	9	−1	2	−8
3.	10	0	8	−2	1	−9
4.	10	0	11	1	1	−9
5.	10	0	12	2	45	35
योग	50		50		50	
$\bar{x}$	$\frac{50}{5}=10$		$\frac{50}{5}=10$		$\frac{50}{5}=10$	

उपर्युक्त तीनों श्रेणियों के माध्य समान हैं, लेकिन उनकी संरचना में पर्याप्त अन्तर है। पहली श्रेणी का प्रत्येक मूल्य 10 है, अतः माध्य पूर्ण रूप से सभी मूल्यों का प्रतिनिधित्व कर रहा है। दूसरी श्रेणी का माध्य भी 10 है, परन्तु बनावट प्रथम श्रेणी से कुछ भिन्न है। इस श्रेणी के मूल्यों का माध्य से विचलन-2 और 2 के बीच में है। तीसरी श्रेणी का माध्य भी 10 है परन्तु इस श्रेणी की बनावट पहली और दूसरी श्रेणियों से अत्यन्त भिन्न है। इस श्रेणी के मूल्यों का माध्य से विचलन– 9 और 35 के बीच में है। इस श्रेणी का माध्य किसी भी मूल्य का प्रतिनिधित्व नहीं कर रहा है।

उपरोक्त विवेचन से स्पष्ट है कि किसी समंक माला के केवल माध्य मात्र से उसका सही विश्लेषण नहीं किया जा सकता। किसी समंक माला के मौलिक लक्षणों को सही रूप में जानने के लिए **'अपकिरण के माप'** (Measures of Dispersion) निकाले जाते हैं। अपकिरण के मापों में यह अध्ययन करते हैं कि श्रेणी के मूल्यों का किसी माध्य से विचलन कितना और किस दशा में है।

अपकिरण (Dispersion) की मुख्य परिभाषाएँ निम्न हैं–

1. प्रो॰ किंग (King) के शब्दों में, ''अपकिरण शब्द का प्रयोग यह स्पष्ट करने के लिए किया जाता है कि एक दिए समूह के पद-मूल्यों में भिन्नता है, दूसरे शब्दों में, उसके मूल्यों में एकरूपता का अभाव है।''

2. ब्रुक्स और डिक (Brooks and Dick) के शब्दों में, ''एक केन्द्रिय मूल्य के दोनों ओर पाए जाने वाले चरम मूल्यों के विचलन या प्रसार की सीमा ही अपकिरण है।''

3. स्पीगेल (Spiegal) के शब्दों में, ''वह सीमा जहाँ तक समंक एक माध्य मूल्य के दोनों ओर फैलने की प्रवृत्ति रखते हैं, उन समंको का विचलन या अपकिरण कहलाती है।

4. कौनर (Connor) के शब्दों में, ''व्यक्तिगत पदों में भिन्नता की मात्रा के माप को अपकिरण कहते हैं।''

5. सिम्पसन तथा काफ्का (Simpson and Kafka) के शब्दों में, ''अकेला माध्य सम्पूर्ण कहानी नहीं कहता है। शायद ही वह समूह का पूर्ण प्रतिनिधि हो, जब तक हमको यह ज्ञात न हो कि व्यक्तिगत पद-चारों ओर किस प्रकार बिखरे

हैं। समंकमाला का और आगे विवरण देना आवश्यक होता है यदि हम यह अनुमान लगाना चाहते हैं कि माध्य कितना प्रतिनिधि है।''

उपरोक्त विवरण से यह स्पष्ट हो जाता है कि अपकिरण की मापें किसी समंकमाला के मूल्यों का किसी माध्य के प्रति विचलनों का अध्ययन करते हैं।

अब हम विस्तार से यह अध्ययन करेंगे कि एक आदर्श अपकिरण की माप में कौन-कौन से गुण होने चाहिए।

1. समझने में आसान (Easy to understand)—एक अच्छे अपकिरण की माप से यह अपेक्षा की जाती है कि उसकी परिभाषा आसान हो, जिससे कि अपकिरण की माप के विषय में समझने तथा समझाने में कोई कठिनाई न हो। उदाहरण के तौर पर विस्तार (Range) की परिभाषा अत्यन्त सरल है।

2. गणना में आसान (Simple to Compute)—किसी अपकिरण की माप को अधिकाधिक प्रयोग में लाने के लिए यह एक आवश्यक है कि उसकी गणना आसानी से की जा सके। व्यावहारिकता में अपकिरण की वह माप अच्छी समझी जाती है, जिसकी गणना में विशेष परेशानी न हो। उदाहरण के तौर पर 2, 4, 5, 10, 12 का विस्तार (Range) 12 – 2 = 10 है और यदि इन्हीं आँकड़ों का समानांतर माध्य निकालना होगा, फिर सभी मूल्यों का समानांतर माध्य से विचलन लेकर, उनका वर्ग करके फिर योग करके मूल्यो की संख्या से भाग किया जाएगा। भाग करके आने वाली संख्या का वर्गमूल ही प्रमाप विचलन का मान होगा।

3. स्पष्ट परिभाषा (Rigidly difined)—एक अच्छे अपकिरण के माप से यह अपेक्षा की जाती है कि उसकी परिभाषा बिल्कुल स्पष्ट हो तथा किसी प्रकार के सन्देह की आशंका न हो। माप की परिभाषा में बीजगणितीय सूत्रों के प्रयोग को वांछनीय माना जाता है। अपकिरण के माप की परिभाषा ऐसी होनी चाहिए जिससे कि किसी एक समूह के आँकड़ों के अपकिरण के माप की गणना कई व्यक्ति अलग-अलग करें तो सभी के माप का मान एक ही आना चाहिये। माप की परिभाषा स्पष्ट न होने की दशा में माप की गणना में अवलोकन की भावना एवं योग्यता का प्रभाव पड़ेगा और विभिन्न व्यक्ति उसका अलग-अलग अर्थ निकालेंगे।

4. सभी संख्याओं पर आधारित (Based on all items)—अपकिरण के माप का उद्देश्य समंकमाला के पदों का माध्य से विचलन का अध्ययन करना होता है। यदि किसी अपकिरण के माप गणना में सम्बन्धित सभी आंकड़ों का योगदान नहीं होता तो उसे अपकिरण का उचित प्रतिनिधि नहीं माना जा सकता। उदाहरण के तौर पर 4, 5, 4.2, 4.1, 4.7, 5, 4.9, 10 का विस्तार (Range) 10 – 4 = 6 है। तथा 4, 5, 6, 9.5, 9.7, 10, 9.8, 10 का भी विस्तार 6 है। दोनों श्रेणियों के विस्तार का मान समान होते हुए भी श्रेणियों की बनावट में बहुत अन्तर है। एक अच्छे अपकिरण के माप से यह अपेक्षा की जाती है कि यदि किसी एक या अधिक मूल्यों में कोई परिवर्तन हो तो अपकिरण के माप का मान भी प्रभावित होना चाहिए।

5. न्यूनतम तथा अधिकतम मूल्यों का कम-से-कम प्रभाव (Least effect of extreme items)—यदि किसी अपकिरण के माप की गणना में सम्बन्धित सभी आँकड़ों का प्रयोग किया जाता है तो उसे एक अच्छा गुण समझा जाता है, लेकिन साथ ही यह भी अपेक्षा की जाती है कि आंकड़ों में मौजूद न्यूनतम तथा अधिकतम मूल्यों का अवांछनीय प्रभाव नहीं पड़ना चाहिए। उदाहरण के तौर पर 3, 4, 3.2, 4, 5, 4.2 का विस्तार 5 – 3 = 2 है तथा 3, 4, 3.2, 4, 5, 4.2, 18 का विस्तार 18 – 3 = 15 है। दूसरी शृंखला में आखिरी मूल्य 18 विस्तार को अनावश्यक रूप से प्रभावित कर रहा है।

6. बीजगणितीय विवेचन योग्य (Capable of algebraic treatment)—किसी सांख्यिकीय श्रेणी के लिए अपकिरण का माप निकालने की कई विधियाँ हैं, इनमें सभी ऐसी नहीं हैं जिनका बीजगणितीय विवेचन किया जा सके। उदाहरण के तौर पर यदि किन्हीं दो या अधिक श्रेणियों के अपकिरण के माप का मान दिया हो तो हम चाहेंगे कि सभी श्रेणियों के सामूहिक मूल्यों के अपकिरण का मान निकाला जा सके। यह गुण केवल प्रमाप विचलन (Standard Deviation) में विद्यमान होता है। इस गुण को किसी भी अपकिरण के माप का अपेक्षित गुण माना जाता है।

7. न्यादर्शों के परिवर्तन का न्यूनतम प्रभाव (Least effect of sampling fluctuation)—मान लीजिये किसी विद्यालय में 2000 विद्यार्थी हैं तथा 15 विद्यार्थियों का न्यादर्श लेकर उनके वजन के अपकिरण का माप (Measure

of dispersion) निकाला जाता है। यदि हम 15 विद्यार्थियों का कोई और न्यादर्श लेकर उनकी ऊँचाई के अपकिरण का माप निकालें तो यह आवश्यक नहीं होगा जो कि माप पहले न्यादर्श का था, वही माप दूसरे न्यादर्श का भी होगा। इसका कारण यह है कि न्यादर्श बदलने से वजनों का मान भी बदलना स्वाभाविक है, लेकिन साथ ही एक अच्छे अपकिरण के माप से यह अपेक्षा की जाती है कि जब भिन्न-भिन्न न्यादर्शों के अपकिरण के माप निकाले जायें तो उनके मान में बहुत अधिक उतार-चढ़ाव नहीं आने चाहिए।

वास्तव में सांख्यिकीय आँकड़ों के अपकिरण का माप निकालने की कोई विधि ऐसी नहीं है जिसमें ऊपर लिखे सभी गुण हों। यदि सभी अपेक्षित गुण किसी एक विधि में मिल जाते तो शायद अपकिरण का माप निकालने की अधिक विधियों के अध्ययन करने की आवश्यकता ही नहीं पड़ती।

प्रश्न 15. विस्तार (Range) के विषय में विस्तार से लिखिए।

उत्तर – हम जानते हैं कि किसी सांख्यिकीय श्रेणी के अपकिरण का माप वह मूल्य होता है जोकि श्रेणी में आए सभी मूल्यों का किसी माध्य के गिर्द बिखराव को दर्शाता है किसी श्रेणी के अपकिरण के माप की कई विधियाँ हैं। जिनमे विस्तार (Range) भी एक है। विस्तार अपकिरण के माप की सरलतम विधि है।

किसी सांख्यिकीय श्रेणी का **विस्तार** निकालने के लिए सबसे बड़े मूल्य में सबसे छोटे मूल्य को घटाया जाता है।

यदि श्रेणी में आये सबसे बड़े मूल्य और सबसे छोटे मूल्य क्रमश: L और S हों तो **'विस्तार'** निम्नलिखित सूत्र द्वारा निकाला जाता है–

$$\text{विस्तार} = L - S$$

यदि किसी आवृत्ति आबंटन के लिए विस्तार निकालना हो तो सबसे बड़े वर्ग की उच्च सीमा में से सबसे छोटे वर्ग की निम्न सीमा को घटाया जाता है।

दो श्रेणियो के अपकिरण के तुलनात्मक अध्ययन के लिए विस्तार का सापेक्ष माप (Relative measure) निकाला जाता है। जिसे **विस्तार गुणांक** (Coefficient of Range) कहा जाता है। किसी श्रेणी के विस्तार गुणांक का मान निम्नलिखित सूत्र द्वारा निकाला जाता है–

$$\text{विस्तार गुणांक} = \frac{L - S}{L + S}$$

उपरोक्त सूत्र में L और S क्रमश: श्रेणी के सबसे बड़े तथा सबसे छोटे मान हैं।

विस्तार के गुण (Merits of Range)

1. विस्तार समझने में सबसे सरल प्रकार का अपकिरण का माप है।
2. विस्तार की गणना अपकिरण के मापों में सबसे सुगम है।
3. विस्तार बीजगणितीय सूत्र द्वारा स्पष्ट रूप से परिभाषित किया जाता है।
4. विस्तार उन सीमाओं को स्पष्ट करता है। जिनके मध्य में ही समंकमाला के सभी मूल्य फैले रहते हैं।

विस्तार के दोष (Demerits of Range)

1. विस्तार श्रेणी में आये सभी पदों पर आधारित नहीं होता। उदाहरण के तौर पर समंक श्रेणियों 4, 5, 6, 10, 12, 18, 20 और 4, 10, 11, 11, 12, 20, दोनों का विस्तार 16 है जोकि 4 और 20 के बीच से प्रभावित नहीं हो रहा है।
2. विस्तार की गणना में न्यूनतम और अधिकतम पदों का बहुत अधिक असर पड़ता है। वास्तव में इसकी गणना में न्यूनतम और अधिकतम पदों का ही प्रयोग करना होता है।
3. विस्तार बीजगणितीय विवेचन के योग्य नहीं हैं।
4. विस्तार पर न्यादर्शो के परिवर्तन का बहुत अधिक असर पड़ता है।
5. विस्तार की गणना में केवल मूल्यों को ही दृष्टिगत रखा जाता है अत: यह आवृत्तियों से प्रभावित नहीं होता।

प्रश्न 16. चतुर्थक विचलन (Quartile Deviation) के विषय में विस्तार से लिखिए।

उत्तर–हम जानते हैं कि किसी साँख्यिकीय श्रेणी के अपकिरण का माप वह मूल्य होता है जोकि श्रेणी में आये सभी मूल्यों का किसी माध्य के गिर्द विखराव को दर्शाता है। किसी श्रेणी के अपकिरण के माप की कई विधियाँ, जिनमें चतुर्थक विचलन (Quartile Deviation) भी एक है।

विस्तार की गणना में श्रेणी के न्यूनतम और अधिकतम पदों का ही प्रयोग किया जाता है। इस कारण से विस्तार का मान ठीक प्रकार से श्रेणी के पदों के विचलन का सही माप नहीं होता। चतुर्थक विचलन की गणना में श्रेणी के बीच के 50% पदों का ही प्रयोग किया जाता है। इसका लाभ यह होता है कि श्रेणी के न्यूनतम और अधिकतम पद श्रेणी के दोनों किनारों पर ही होने के कारण अपकिरण के माप को प्रभावित नहीं कर पाते।

किसी साँख्यिकीय श्रेणी का चतुर्थक विचलन निकालने के लिये प्रथम एवं तृतीय चतुर्थकों का प्रयोग किया जाता है।

चतुर्थक विचलन (Q.D.) का मान निकालने के लिए निम्नलिखित सूत्र का प्रयोग किया जाता है–

$$\text{चतुर्थक विचलन (Q.D.)} = \frac{Q_3 - Q_1}{2}$$

इस सूत्र में प्रथम चतुर्थक और तृतीय चतुर्थक को क्रमशः Q_1 और Q_3 से दर्शाया गया है।

किसी साँख्यिकीय श्रेणी के लिए $Q_3 - Q_1$ के मान को **अन्तर चतुर्थक विस्तार** (Inter Quartile Range) कहा जाता है।

दो श्रेणियों के अपकिरण के तुलनात्मक अध्ययन के लिए चतुर्थक विचलन का सापेक्ष मान निकाला जाता है। इस सापेक्ष माप को **चतुर्थक विचलन गुणांक** (Coefficient of Quartile Deviation) कहा जाता है।

किसी श्रेणी के चतुर्थक विचलन गुणांक का मान निम्नलिखित सूत्र द्वारा निकाला जाता है–

$$\text{चतुर्थक विचलन गुणांक} = \frac{Q_3 - Q_1}{Q_3 + Q_1}$$

उपरोक्त सूत्र में Q_1 और Q_3 क्रमशः प्रथम एवं तृतीय चतुर्थकों के मान हैं।

चतुर्थक विचलन के गुण (Merits of Quartile Deviation)

1. चतुर्थक विचलन समझने में सरल प्रकार का अपकिरण का माप है।
2. चतुर्थक विचलन की गणना सुगम है।
3. चतुर्थक विचलन बीजगणितीय सूत्र द्वारा स्पष्ट रूप से परिभाषित किया जाता है।
4. किसी सांख्यिकीय श्रेणी के बीच के 50% पदों का अध्ययन करने में सहायक होता है।
5. चतुर्थक विचलन की गणना में न्यूनतम और अधिकतम पदों का प्रभाव नहीं पड़ता।
6. खुले सिरे वाली आवृत्ति आबंटन के अपकिरण का अध्ययन करने के लिये यह सबसे उपयुक्त विधि है।

चतुर्थक विचलन के दोष (Demerits of Quartile Deviation)

1. चतुर्थक विचलन श्रेणी में आये सभी पदों पर आधारित नहीं होता।
2. चतुर्थक विचलन बीजगणितीय विवेचन योग्य नहीं है।
3. चतुर्थक विचलन पर न्यादर्शों के परिवर्तन का बहुत प्रभाव पड़ता है।

प्रश्न 17. माध्य विचलन (Mean Deviation) के विषय में विस्तार से लिखिए।

उत्तर–हम जानते हैं कि किसी सांख्यिकीय श्रेणी के अपकिरण का माप वह मूल्य होता है जोकि श्रेणी में आये सभी मूल्यों का किसी माध्य के गिर्द बिखराव को दर्शाता है। किसी श्रेणी के अपकिरण के माप की कई विधियाँ हैं, जिनमें माध्य विचलन (Mean Deviation) भी एक है। माध्य विचलन की गणना में समानांतर माध्य और माध्यिका का प्रयोग किया जाता है।

किसी सांख्यिकीय श्रेणी का माध्य विचलन निकालने के लिए श्रेणी के सभी मूल्यों का माध्य (समानांतर माध्य या माध्यिका) से विचलन निकाले जाते हैं। इन विचलनों के निरपेक्ष मानों को जोड़ कर श्रेणी में आये कुल मूल्यों की संख्या से भाग कर दिया जाता है। भागफल के मान को **माध्य विचलन** कहा जाता है।

यदि माध्य विचलन की गणना में विचलन समानांतर माध्य से निकाले गये हैं तो माध्य विचलन को संकेताक्षर के रूप में M.D.$(\bar{x})$ लिखा जाता है। इसी प्रकार यदि माध्य विचलन की गणना में विचलन माध्यिका से निकाले गये हों तो सम्बन्धित माध्य विचलन का संकेताक्षर के रूप में M.D. (Median) लिखा जाता है।

मान लीजिये $x_1, x_2, ..., x_n$ कोई व्यक्तिगत श्रेणी (Individual series) है। इस श्रेणी का **माध्य विचलन** निम्नलिखित सूत्रों द्वारा निकाला जाता है–

$$\text{M.D.}(\bar{x}) = \frac{|x_1 - \bar{x}| + |x_2 - \bar{x}| + \ldots + |x_n - \bar{x}|}{n} = \frac{\sum_{i=1}^{n} |x_1 - \bar{x}|}{n}$$

$$= \frac{\Sigma |x - \bar{x}|}{n} \qquad \text{(संक्षिप्त रूप में)}$$

$$\text{M.D. (median)} = \frac{|x_1 - \text{median}| + |x_2 - \text{median}| + \ldots + |x_n - \text{meidan}|}{n}$$

$$= \frac{\sum_{i=1}^{n} |x_1 - \text{median}|}{n} = \frac{\Sigma |x - \text{median}|}{n} \qquad \text{(संक्षिप्त रूप में)}$$

किसी आवृत्ति आबंटन के लिये माध्य विचलन निम्नलिखित सूत्रों द्वारा निकाला जाता है–

$$\text{M.D.}(\bar{x}) = \frac{\Sigma f |x - \bar{x}|}{\text{N}}$$

$$\text{M.D. (median)} = \frac{\Sigma f |x - \text{median}|}{\text{N}}$$

इन सूत्रों में सभी आवृत्तियों के योग को N से दर्शाया गया है।

यदि मदों का मान वर्गों के रूप में दिया हो तो विभिन्न वर्गों की आवृत्तियों का मान सम्बन्धित वर्ग के मध्य बिन्दु को माना जाता है।

यदि सांख्यिकीय श्रेणी के समानांतर माध्य (या माध्यिका) का मान दशमलव में आने की आशंका हो तो माध्य विचलन निकालने के लिये निम्नलिखित सूत्रों का प्रयोग किया जाता है।

$$\text{M.D.}(\bar{x}) = \frac{(\Sigma fx)_A - (\Sigma fx)_B - [(\Sigma f)_A - (\Sigma f)_B]\bar{x}}{\text{N}}$$

$$\text{M.D. (median)} = \frac{(\Sigma fx)_A - (\Sigma fx)_B - [(\Sigma f)_A - (\Sigma f)_B]\text{median}}{\text{N}}$$

माध्य से अधिक एवं कम पदों से सम्बंधित योगों को क्रमशः उपसंकेत A और B से दर्शाया गया है।

दो श्रेणियों के अपकिरण के तुलनात्मक अध्ययन के लिये माध्य विचलन का सापेक्ष मान निकाला जाता है। इस सापेक्ष माप को **माध्य विचलन गुणांक** (Coefficient of Mean Deviation) कहा जाता है।

किसी श्रेणी के माध्य विचलन गुणांक का मान निम्नलिखित सूत्रों द्वारा निकाला जाता है–

$$\text{Coeff. of M.D.}(\bar{x}) = \frac{\text{M.D.}(\bar{x})}{\bar{x}}$$

$$\text{Coeff. of M.D.(median)} = \frac{\text{M.D. (median)}}{\text{median}}$$

माध्य विचलन गुणांक निकालने के लिए माध्य विचलन को सम्बन्धित माध्य से भाग किया जाता है।

माध्य विचलन के गुण (Merits of Mean Deviation)

1. माध्य विचलन समझने में सरल प्रकार का अपकिरण का माप है।
2. माध्य विचलन की गणना सुगम है।
3. माध्य विचलन बीजगणितीय सूत्र द्वारा स्पष्ट रूप से परिभाषित किया जाता है।
4. माध्य विचलन की गणना श्रेणी में आये सभी पदों पर आधारित होती है।
5. माध्य विचलन के मान पर न्यूनतम और अधिकतम पदों का विशेष प्रभाव नहीं पड़ता।
6. माध्य विचलन की गणना में किसी भी माध्य का प्रयोग किया जा सकता है, लेकिन व्यावहारिकता में केवल समानांतर माध्य एवं माध्यिका का ही प्रयोग किया जाता है।

माध्य विचलन के दोष (Demerits of Mean Deviation)

1. माध्य विचलन बीजगणितीय विवेचन योग्य नहीं है।
2. माध्य विचलन की गणना में पदों के माध्य से विचलनों के बीजगणितीय चिन्हों (+ एवं −) को छोड़ दिया जाता है।

प्रश्न 18. प्रमाप विचलन के (Standard Deviation) विषय में विस्तार से लिखिए।

उत्तर–हम जानते हैं कि किसी सांख्यिकीय श्रेणी के अपकिरण का माप वह मूल्य होता है जोकि श्रेणी में आये सभी मूल्यों का किसी माध्य के गिर्द बिखराव को दर्शाता है। किसी श्रेणी के अपकिरण के माप की कई विधियाँ है, जिनमें प्रमाप विचलन (Standard Deviation) भी एक है। प्रमाप विचलन की गणना में समानांतर माध्य का प्रयोग किया जाता है।

किसी सांख्यिकीय श्रेणी का प्रमाप विचलन ज्ञात करने के लिए श्रेणी के सभी मूल्यों के समानांतर माध्य से विचलन निकाले जाते हैं। इन विचलनों के वर्गों को जोड़ श्रेणी में आये कुल मूल्यों की संख्या से भाग करके वर्गमूल निकाला जाता है। वर्गमूल के मान को **प्रमाप विचलन** कहा जाता है।

मान लीजिये $x_1, x_2, \ldots\ldots, x_n$ कोई व्यक्तिगत श्रेणी (individual series) है। इस श्रेणी का प्रमाप विचलन निम्नलिखित सूत्र द्वारा निकाला जाता है–

$$\text{S.D.} = \sqrt{\frac{(x_1\ \bar{x})^2 + (x_2 - \bar{x})^2 + \ldots + (x_n - \bar{x})^2}{n}} = \sqrt{\frac{\sum_{i=1}^{n}(x_i - \bar{x})^2}{n}}$$

$$= \sqrt{\frac{\Sigma(x - \bar{x})^2}{n}} \qquad \text{(संक्षिप्त रूप में)}$$

इस विधि को प्रमाप विचलन ज्ञात करने की प्रत्यक्ष विधि (Direct method) कहा जाता है।

प्रत्यक्ष विधि से किसी आवृत्ति आबंटन का प्रमाप विचलन निकालने के लिए निम्न सूत्र का प्रयोग किया जाता है–

$$= \sqrt{\frac{f_1(x_1 - \bar{x})^2 + f_2(x_2 - \bar{x})^2 + \ldots + f_n(x_n - \bar{x})^2}{f_1 + f_2 + \ldots + f_n}}$$

$$= \sqrt{\frac{\sum_{i=1}^{n} f_i(x_i - \bar{x})^2}{\sum_{i=1}^{n} f_i}}$$

$$= \sqrt{\frac{\Sigma f(x-\bar{x})^2}{n}} \text{.} \qquad \text{(संक्षिप्त रूप में)}$$

इस सूत्र में मद x_i की आवृत्ति $f_i \, (1 \le i \le n)$ है। सभी आवृत्तियों के जोड़ Σf को सुगमता के लिये N लिखा जाता है। यदि मदों का मान वर्गों के रूप में दिया हो तो विभिन्न वर्गों की आवृत्तियों का मान सम्बन्धित वर्ग के मध्य बिन्दु को माना जाता है।

किसी सांख्यिकीय श्रेणी का प्रमाप विचलन निकालने के लिए एक और विधि का भी प्रयोग किया जाता है, जिसे लघु-विधि (Short-cut method) कहा जाता है।

इस विधि में मदों का किसी एक कल्पित माध्य (assumed mean) A से विचलन निकाले जाते हैं। माना $d_1 = x_1 - \text{A}$, $d_2 = x_2 - \text{A}$, ..., $d_n = x_n - \text{A}$ विभिन्न विचलनों (Deviations) के मान हैं। प्रमाप विचलन निकालने के लिए निम्न सूत्र प्रयोग किये जाते हैं–

$$\text{S.D.} = \sqrt{\frac{\Sigma d^2}{n} - \left(\frac{\Sigma d}{n}\right)^2} \qquad \text{(व्यक्तिगत श्रेणी के लिए)}$$

$$\text{S.D.} = \sqrt{\frac{\Sigma fd^2}{\text{N}} - \left(\frac{\Sigma fd}{\text{N}}\right)^2} \qquad \text{(आवृत्ति आबंटन के लिए)}$$

यदि विभिन्न विचलनों में कोई समान गुण (h) हो तो विचलनों से पद-विचलन (Step-deviation) निकाल लिए जाते हैं। माना–

$$u_1 = \frac{d_1}{h} = \frac{x_1 - \text{A}}{h}, \quad u_2 = \frac{d_2}{h} = \frac{x_2 - \text{A}}{n}, \ldots\ldots, u_n = \frac{d_n}{h} = \frac{x_n - \text{A}}{h}$$

विभिन्न पद-विचलनों के मान हैं।

प्रमाप विचलन निकालने के लिए निम्न सूत्र प्रयोग किए जाते हैं–

$$\text{S.D.} = \sqrt{\frac{\Sigma u^2}{n} - \left(\frac{\Sigma u}{n}\right)^2} \, . \, h \qquad \text{(व्यक्तिगत श्रेणी के लिए)}$$

$$\text{S.D.} = \sqrt{\frac{\Sigma fu^2}{\text{N}} - \left(\frac{\Sigma fu}{\text{N}}\right)^2} \, . \, h \qquad \text{(आवृत्ति आबंटन के लिए)}$$

व्यावहारिकता में क्रियात्मक प्रश्नों को हल करने के लिए इन्हीं सूत्रों का प्रयोग किया जाता है।

सामूहिक प्रमाप विचलन (Combined Standard Deviation)—यदि किन्हीं दो समूहों में n_1 और n_2 मद हों और समानांतर माध्य और प्रमाप विचलन क्रमशः $\bar{x}_1, \sigma_1$ और $\bar{x}_2, \sigma_2$ हो तो **सामूहिक प्रमाप विचलन** निकालने के लिए निम्न सूत्र का प्रयोग किया जाता है–

$$\sigma = \sqrt{\frac{n_1\sigma_1^2 + n_2\sigma_2^2 + n_1 d_1^2 + n_2 d_2^2}{n_1 + n_2}}$$

इस सूत्र में

σ = सामूहिक प्रमाप विचलन

$d_1 = \bar{x}_1 - \bar{x} = \bar{x}_1$ का $\bar{x}$ से विचलन

$d_2 = \bar{x}_2 - \bar{x} = \bar{x}_2$ का $\bar{x}$ से विचलन

$\bar{x} = \dfrac{n_1\bar{x}_1 + n_2\bar{x}_2}{n_1 + n_2}$ = दोनों समूहों का सामूहिक समानांतर माध्य

इस सूत्र को दो से अधिक समूहों के लिए भी बढ़ाया जा सकता है।

प्रमाप विचलन के वर्ग को **विचलन** (variance) कहा जाता है।

दो श्रेणियों के अपकिरण के तुलनात्मक अध्ययन के लिए प्रमाप विचलन का सापेक्ष मान निकाला जाता है। इस सापेक्ष माप को **प्रमाप विचलन गुणांक** (Coefficient of Standard Deviation) कहा जाता है।

किसी श्रेणी के प्रमाप विचलन गुणांक का मान निम्नलिखित सूत्र द्वारा निकाला जाता है–

$$\text{प्रमाप विचलन गुणांक} = \frac{\text{प्रमाप विचलन}}{\text{समानांतर माध्य}}, \textit{i.e.}, \text{Coeff. of S.D.} = \frac{\text{S.D.}}{\bar{x}}$$

प्रमाप विचलन गुणांक को 100 से गुणा करके आये मूल्य को **विचरण गुणांक** (Coefficient of Variation) कहा जाता है। विचरण गुणांक को संक्षिप्त रूप में C.V. लिखा जाता है।

$$\therefore \qquad \text{C.V.} = \frac{\sigma}{\bar{x}} \times 100.$$

प्रमाप विचलन के गुण (Merits of Standard Deviation)

1. प्रमाप विचलन समझने में सरल प्रकार का अपकिरण का माप है।
2. प्रमाप विचलन बीजगणितीय सूत्र द्वारा स्पष्ट रूप से परिभाषित किया जाता है।
3. प्रमाप विचलन की गणना में पदों के समानांतर माध्य से विचलनों के बीजगणितीय चिन्हों (+ एवं –) को नहीं छोड़ा जाता।
4. प्रमाप विचलन की गणना श्रेणी में आये सभी पदों पर आधारित होती है।
5. प्रमाप विचलन बीजगणितीय विवेचन योग्य है। उदाहरण के लिए यदि किन्हीं दो समूहों के समानान्तर माध्य एवं प्रमाप विचलन दिये हों तो दोनों समूहों का सामूहिक प्रमाप विचलन ज्ञात किया जा सकता है।
6. प्रमाप विचलन के मान पर न्यूनतम एवं अधिकतम पदों का विशेष प्रभाव नहीं पड़ता।
7. विभिन्न मापों की अर्थपूर्णता की जाँच (Tests of Significance) में प्रमाप विचलन अत्यन्त उपयोगी सिद्ध होता है।

प्रमाप विचलन के दोष (Demerits of Standard Deviation)

1. प्रमाप विचलन की गणना में काफी परिश्रम करना पड़ता है।
2. कुछ परिस्थितियों में प्रमाष विचलन श्रेणी में आये न्यूनतम और अधिकतम मूल्यों से अवांछनीय रूप में प्रभावित हो जाता है।

प्रश्न 19. लारेंज वक्र (Lorenz Curve) के विषय में विस्तार से लिखिए।

उत्तर–हम जानते हैं कि किसी सांख्यिकीय श्रेणी के अपकिरण का माप वह मूल्य होता है जोकि श्रेणी में आये सभी मूल्यों का किसी माध्य के गिर्द बिखराव को दर्शाता है। किसी श्रेणी के अपकिरण की कई विधियाँ हैं, जिनमें लारेंज वक्र (Lorenz Curve) भी एक है। यह अपकिरण के माप की बिन्दु रेखीय विधि है। अपकिरण की इस रीति का प्रतिपादन प्रसिद्ध अर्थ-संख्या शास्त्री **डॉ० मैक्स ओ० लारेंज** (Max O. Lorenz) ने किया था। अर्थशास्त्री विशेष तौर पर धन, आय जैसे तथ्यों के वितरण की दशा जानने का इच्छुक रहता है। व्यवसायों में लाभों के वितरण की तुलना के लिये भी इसका प्रयोग किया जाता है। **लारेंज वक्र** एक संचयी प्रतिशत वक्र (Cumulative Percentage Curve) है।

लारेंज वक्र बनाने के लिए निम्नलिखित प्रक्रिया प्रयोग में लाई जाती हैं। दिये गए मूल्यों (वर्गान्तर होने पर मध्य बिन्दुओं) के संचयी योग ज्ञात करके, अन्तिम संचयी योग को 100 मान कर प्रत्येक संचयी मूल्य को प्रतिशत में बदल दिया जाता है। इसी प्रकार, आवृत्तियों के संचयी योग ज्ञात करके, अन्तिम संचयी योग को 100 मान कर प्रत्येक संचयी आवृत्ति को प्रतिशत में बदल दिया जाता है। मूल्यों तथा आवृत्तियों के संचयी प्रतिशतों को रेखा-पत्र के भुजाक्ष (X-axis) और कोटि अक्ष (Y-axis) पर प्रदर्शित किया जाता है। भुजाक्ष और कोटिअक्ष पर पैमाना शून्य से शुरू होकर 100 तक जाता है। मूल्यों और संचयी प्रतिशतों को रेखा-पत्र पर अंकित करके, उन बिन्दुओं को मिला दिया जाता है। बिन्दुओं को मिलाने से जो वक्र प्राप्त होता है, उसे **लारेंज वक्र** कहा जाता है।

रेखा-पत्र पर (0, 0) और (100, 100) वाले बिन्दुओं को मिलाने से जो रेखा प्राप्त होती है उसे **समान वितरण की रेखा** (Line of Equal Distribution) कहा जाता है।

लारेंज वक्र, समान वितरण रेखा से जितना दूर होगा, उतना ही सम्बन्धित श्रेणी में अपकिरण अधिक होगा।

लारेंज वक्र विधि के गुण (Merits of Lorenz Curve Method)

1. लारेंज वक्र द्वारा अपकिरण का अध्ययन करना एक बिन्दु रेखीय विधि है। इस विधि द्वारा तुलनात्मक अध्ययन सरलता से हो जाता है। एक ही दृष्टि में अपकिरण का अनुमान लगाने के लिए यह अत्यन्त उपयोगी विधि है।
2. लारेंज वक्र को वे लोग भी आसानी से समझ पाते हैं, जिन्हें सांख्यिकीय रीतियों का विशेष ज्ञान नहीं होता।

लारेंज वक्र विधि के दोष (Demerits of Lorenze Curve Method)

1. इस विधि से अपकिरण की सही मात्रा का ज्ञान नहीं हो पाता।
2. लारेंज वक्र बनाने में बहुत अधिक गणना-कार्य करना पड़ता है।

6. विषमता

प्रश्न 20. विषमता (Skewness) क्या है ? अपकिरण से वह किस प्रकार भिन्न है ?

उत्तर–हम जानते हैं कि सांख्यिकीय श्रेणी का माध्य श्रेणी के पदों की केन्द्रीय प्रवृत्ति का प्रतिनिधित्व करता है। श्रेणी के पदों का माध्य से विचलन का अध्ययन अपकिरण के मापों द्वारा किया जाता है। दूसरे शब्दों में, माध्य से श्रेणी की केन्द्रीय प्रवृत्ति का ज्ञान होता है एवं अपकिरण के माप से श्रेणी की बनावट का पता चलता है। माध्य और अपकिरण के माप से श्रेणी के स्वरूप के विषय में ज्ञान नहीं हो पाता।

विषमता (Skewness) एक ऐसा सांख्यिकीय माप है जोकि श्रेणी के स्वरूप (Shape) को स्पष्ट करती है। किसी सांख्यिकीय श्रेणी के बिन्दुरेखीय चित्र में समिति (Symmetry) की कमी को विषमता कहते हैं। जब किसी श्रेणी के मूल्यों का वितरण सामान्य न हो तो उसे असमित (asymmetric) या विषम (Skewed) कहा जाता है **वेसल, विलेट** तथा **साइमोन** के शब्दो में, ''विषमता समिति का अभाव है। विषमता की कोई भी माप यह बतलाती है कि सामान्य वितरण की तुलना में एक वितरण विशेष के पदों का वितरण किस प्रकार से भिन्न है।'' —*Wessell, Willett and Simone*

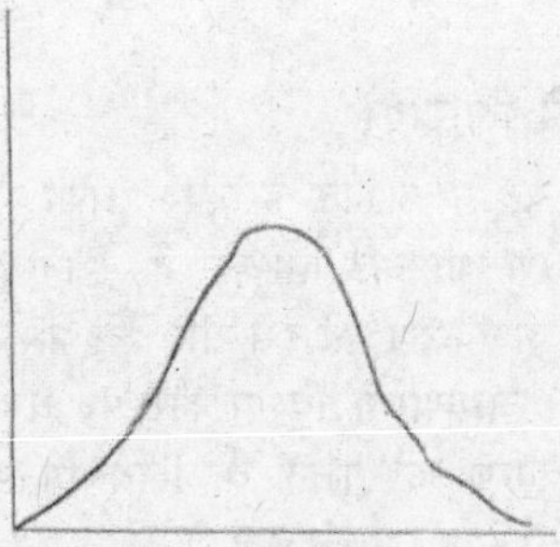

संमित वितरण

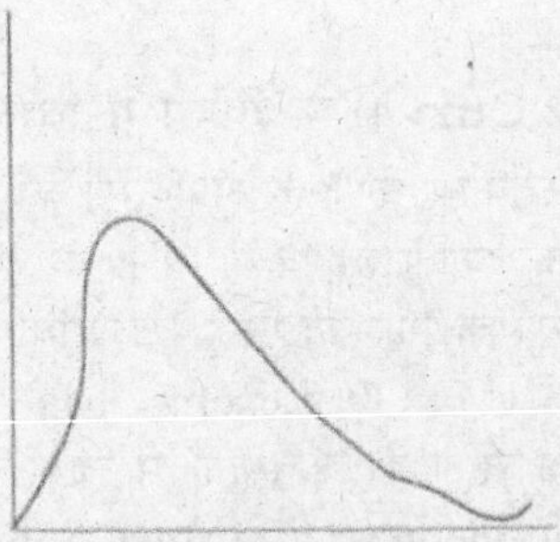

धनात्मक विषमता वितरण

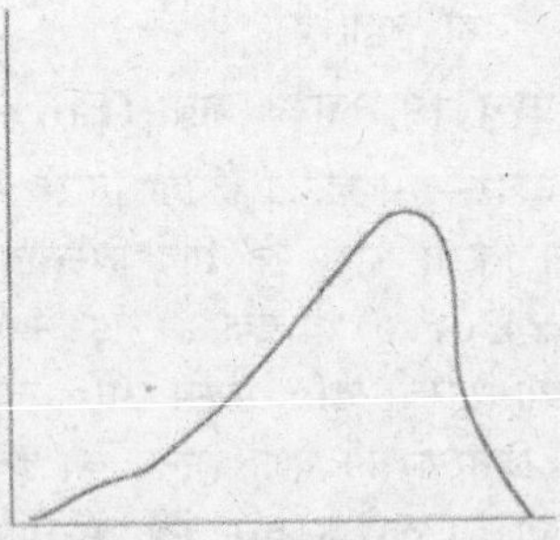

ऋणात्मक विषमता वितरण

सिम्पसन तथा **काफ्का** के शब्दों में, ''विषमता या असंमिति आवृत्ति वितरण की एक विशेषता है जो श्रेणी के एक तरफ अधिकतम आवृंत्ति के साथ दूसरी तरफ की तुलना में अधिक बढ़ जाती है। —*Simpson and Kafka*

विषमता के माप से यह ज्ञात हो जाता है कि यदि आवृति वितरण का बिन्दु रेखीय चित्र बनाया जाये तो वह संमित होगा या असंमित। किसी आवृत्ति वितरण का रेखाचित्र दो प्रकार का हो सकता है–(1) संमित या (2) असंमित। संमित वितरण में आवृत्तियाँ क्रम से बढ़ती हैं और एक बिन्दु पर पहुँच जाने के पश्चात् उसी क्रम से घटती हैं। संमित वितरण का

वक्र घंटाकार (bell-shaped) होता है तथा ऐसे वितरण में अंकगणितीय माध्य, माध्यिका और भूयिष्ठक समान होते हैं तथा वे वितरण के मध्य में स्थित होते हैं। असंमित वितरण में आवृतियों के बढ़ने व घटने के क्रम में अन्तर होता है। आवृत्ति वितरण को संमिति से विचलित होने की दशा में सांख्यिकीय माध्यों की स्थिति में परिवर्तन हो जाता है।

यदि आवृति वितरण के वक्र का झुकाव दाहिनी ओर होता है तो उसे वितरण की विषमता को **धनात्मक विषमता** (Positive Skewness) कहा जाता है। इस प्रकार के आवृत्ति वितरण में अंकगणितीय माध्य का मूल्य माध्यिका तथा भूयिष्ठक से अधिक होता है। धनात्मक विषमता वाले आवृत्ति वितरण में तृतीय चतुर्थक तथा माध्यिका का अन्तर माध्यिका तथा प्रथम चतुर्थक के अन्तर से अधिक होता है।

यदि आवृत्ति वितरण के वक्र का झुकाव बायीं ओर होता है तो उसे वितरण की विषमता को **ऋणात्मक विषमता** (Negative Skewness) कहा जाता है। इस प्रकार के आवृत्ति वितरण में अंकगणितीय माध्य का मूल्य माध्यिका तथा भूयिष्ठक से कम होता है। ऋणात्मक विषमता वाले आवृत्ति वितरण में तृतीय चतुर्थक तथा माध्यिका का अन्तर, माध्यिका तथा प्रथम चतुर्थक के अन्तर से कम होता है।

अपकिरण के माप से हमें यह पता चलता है कि श्रेणी के पदों के किसी माध्य से विचलन कितनी मात्रा में है। इस माप से हमें पदों के माध्य के गिर्द बिखराव के विषय में ज्ञान होता है। विषमता के माप से हमें यह पता चलता है कि श्रेणी का वक्र संमित है या नहीं। विषमता के अध्ययन से हमें यह पता लग जाता हैं कि पदों के माध्य से विचलन किस दिशा में अधिक और किस दिशा में कम है। अपकिरण के मापों से यह बात पता नहीं चल पाती।

प्रश्न 21. विषमता की माप की विभिन्न रीतियों का वर्णन कीजिए।

उत्तर–विषमता की माप से यह अध्ययन किया जाता है कि सांख्यिकीय श्रेणी के वक्र में संमितता (Symmetry) का कितना अभाव है। यदि सांख्यिकीय श्रेणी का वक्र संमित या कि घंटाकार हो तो यह कहा जाता है कि श्रेणी में विषमता नहीं है। ऐसी सांख्यिकीय श्रेणी को संमित श्रेणी कहा जाता है तथा ऐसी श्रेणी के लिए विषमता का मान शून्य आता है।

यदि आवृत्ति वितरण के वक्र का झुकाव दाहिनी ओर होता है तो वितरण की विषमता को धनात्मक विषमता (Positive Skewness) कहा जाता है। यदि आवृत्ति वितरण के वक्र का झुकाव बायीं ओर हो तो वितरण की विषमता को ऋणात्मक विषमता (Negative Skewness) कहा जाता है।

विषमता के माप दो प्रकार के होते–(*i*) निरपेक्ष (Absolute) और (*ii*) सापेक्ष (Relative)। विषमता के निरपेक्ष माप से यह ज्ञात होता है कि श्रेणी में विद्यमान विषमता धनात्मक (Positive) है या ऋणात्मक (Negative)। तुलनात्मक अध्ययन के लिए विषमता के सापेक्ष माप का प्रयोग किये जाते हैं। विषमता के सापेक्ष माप का मान निकालने के लिए सम्बन्धित निरपेक्ष माप का उपयुक्त आधार से भाग किया जाता है।

विषमता का माप ज्ञात करने की विधियाँ निम्नलिखित हैं–

(1) कार्ल पियर्सन विधि (Karl Pearson's Method)

(2) बाऊले विधि (Bowley's Method)

(3) कैली विधि (Kelly's Method)

अब हम विस्तार से इन विधियों का अध्ययन करेंगे।

(1) कार्ल पियर्सन विधि (Karl Pearson's Method)—विषमता की माप की इस विधि का प्रतिपादन **प्रोफेसर कार्ल पियर्सन** ने किया। यह माप सांख्यिकीय श्रेणी के अंकगणितीय माध्य, भूयिष्ठक एवं प्रमाप विचलन पर आधारित होता है। संमितिता (Symmetry) होने की दशा में अंकगणितीय माध्य तथा भूयिष्ठक का मान एक ही होता है। संमितिका के अभाव में आवृत्ति वितरण का वक्र दाहिनी ओर या बायीं ओर झुका हुआ होता है। धनात्मक विषमता होने पर अंकगणितीय माध्य का मान भूयिष्ठक के मान से अधिक होता है तथा ऋणात्मक विषमता होने पर अंकगणितीय माध्य का मान भूयिष्ठक के मान से कम होता है। कार्ल पियर्सन ने भी विषमता का मान निकालने के इन्हीं तथ्यों का प्रयोग किया है। विषमता के निरपेक्ष एवं सापेक्ष मान निकालने के लिए निम्नलिखित सूत्रों का प्रयोग किया जाता है–

विषमता का निरपेक्ष मान = अंकगणितीय माध्य – भूयिष्ठक

$$\textbf{विषमता का सापेक्ष मान} = \frac{\text{अंकगणितीय माध्य – भूयिष्ठक}}{\text{प्रमाप विचलन}}$$

संकेताक्षरों में **SK. = A.M. – Mode**

$$\textbf{Coeff. of SK.} = \frac{\textbf{A.M. – Mode}}{\textbf{S.D.}}$$

विषमता का सापेक्ष मान – 1 और 1 के बीच में रहता है। संमिति की दशा में इसका मान शून्य हो जाता है।

यदि आवृत्ति वितरण के लिए भूयिष्ठक का मान न आ रहा हो तो निम्नलिखित सूत्रों का प्रयोग किया जाता है–

$$\textbf{SK.} = \textbf{3(A.M. – Median)}$$

$$\textbf{Coeff. of SK.} = \frac{\textbf{3(A.M. – Median)}}{\textbf{S.D.}}$$

(2) बाऊले विधि (Bowley's Method)—विषमता की माप की इस विधि का प्रदिपादन **डॉ० बाऊले** (Dr. A.L. Bowley) ने किया। यह माप सांख्यिकीय श्रेणी के प्रथम चतुर्थक, माध्यिका एवं तृतीय चतुर्थक पर आधारित होता है।

संमितिका (Symmetry) होने की दशा में तृतीय चतुर्थक तथा माध्यिका का अन्तर, माध्यिका तथा प्रथम चतुर्थक के अन्तर के समान होता है। संमितिका के अभाव में आवृत्ति वितरण का वक्र दाहिनी ओर या बायीं ओर झुका होता है। धनात्मक विषमता होने पर तृतीय चतुर्थक और माध्यिका का अन्तर, माध्यिका और प्रथम चतुर्थक के अन्तर से अधिक होता है। ऋणात्मक विषमता होने पर तृतीय चतुर्थक और माध्यिका का अन्तर, माध्यिका और प्रथम चतुर्थक के अन्तर से कम होता है।

∴ धनात्मक विषमता होने की दशा में–

$$Q_3 - \text{Median} > \text{Median} - Q_1$$

$$\Rightarrow \quad Q_3 + Q_1 - 2\ \text{Median} > 0$$

ऋणात्मक विषमता होने की दशा में–

$$Q_3 - \text{Median} < \text{Median} - Q_1$$

$$\Rightarrow \quad Q_3 + Q_1 - 2\ \text{Median} < 0$$

बाऊले ने भी विषमता का मान निकालने के लिये इन्हीं तथ्यों का प्रयोग किया है। विषमता के निरपेक्ष एवं सापेक्ष मान निकालने के लिए निम्नलिखित सूत्रों का प्रयोग किया जाता है–

विषमता का निरपेक्ष मान = **तृतीय चतुर्थक + प्रथम चतुर्थक – 2 माध्यिका**

$$\textbf{विषमता का सापेक्ष मान} = \frac{\textbf{तृतीय चतुर्थक + प्रथम चतुर्थक – 2 माध्यिका}}{\textbf{तृतीय चतुर्थक – प्रथम चतुर्थक}}$$

संकेताक्षरों में–

$$\textbf{SK.} = \mathbf{Q_3 + Q_1 - 2\ Median}$$

$$\textbf{Coeff. of SK.} = \frac{\mathbf{Q_3 + Q_1 - 2\ Median}}{\mathbf{Q_3 - Q_1}}$$

विषमता का सापेक्ष मान – 1 और 1 के बीच में रहता है।

संमिति की दशा में इसका मान शून्य हो जाता है। इस विधि में गणना कार्य कार्ल पियर्सन विधि की अपेक्षा कम समय में हो जाता है।

(3) कैली विधि (Kelly's Method)—विषमता की माप की इस विधि का प्रतिपादन **प्रोफेसर कैली** ने किया। यह माप सांख्यिकीय श्रेणी के दसवें शतमक (P_{10}), माध्यिका एवं नब्बेवें शतमक (P_{90}) पर आधारित होता है।

संमितिका (Symmetry) होने की दशा में नब्बेवें शतमक तथा माध्यिका का अन्तर, माध्यिका तथा दसवें शतमक के अन्तर के समान होता है। संमितिका के अभाव में आवृत्ति वितरण का वक्र दाहिनी ओर या बायीं ओर झुका हुआ होता है। धनात्मक विषमता होने पर नब्बेवें शतमक और माध्यिका का अन्तर माध्यिका और दसवें शतमक के अन्तर से अधिक होता है। ऋणात्मक विषमता होने पर नब्बेवें शतमक और मध्यका का अन्तर, मध्यका और दसवें शतमक के अन्तर से कम होता है।

∴ धनात्मक विषमता होने की दशा में–

$$P_{90} - \text{Median} > \text{Median} - P_{10}$$

$$\Rightarrow \quad P_{90} + P_{10} - 2\,\text{Median} > 0$$

ऋणात्मक विषमता होने की दशा में–

$$P_{90} - \text{Median} < \text{Median} - P_{10}$$

$$\Rightarrow \quad P_{90} + P_{10} - 2\,\text{Median} < 0$$

कैली ने भी विषमता का मान निकालने के लिए इन्हीं तथ्यों का प्रयोग किया है। विषमता के निरपेक्ष एवं सापेक्ष मान निकालने के लिए निम्नलिखित सूत्रों का प्रयोग किया जाता है–

विषमता का निरपेक्ष मान = नब्बेवाँ शतमक + दसवाँ शतमक – 2 माध्यिका

विषमता का सापेक्ष मान = $\dfrac{\text{नब्बेवां शतमक + दसवाँ शतमक – 2 माध्यिका}}{\text{नब्बेवाँ शतमक – दसवाँ शतमक}}$

संकेताक्षरों में –

$$\textbf{SK.} = P_{90} + P_{10} - 2\,\text{Median}$$

$$\textbf{Coeff. of SK.} = \frac{P_{90} - P_{10} - 2\,\text{Median}}{P_{90} - P_{10}}$$

7. सहसम्बन्ध के माप

प्रश्न 22. सहसम्बन्ध (Correlation) के विषय में विस्तार से लिखिए।

उत्तर–व्यावहारिक जीवन में हम देखते हैं कि किसी एक चर के मान में हुए परिवर्तन के कारण और चरों के मान में भी परिवर्तन हो जाता है। उदाहरण के तौर पर जिस परिवार की आमदनी अधिक होती है उस परिवार का खर्चा भी कम आमदनी वाले परिवार के खर्चे की अपेक्षा अधिक होता है।

यदि किसी विद्यालय के विद्यार्थियों के वजन और ऊँचाई सम्बन्धी आँकड़ों को लिखा जाये तो हम पायेंगे कि जिस विद्यार्थी का वजन अधिक है उसकी ऊँचाई भी सामान्यत: अधिक ही होगी। यदि किसी चर के मान में परिवर्तन होने से किसी दूसरे चर का मान आमतौर पर बदले तो इस प्रकार के चरों (variables) को सहसम्बन्धित चर (correlated variables) कहते हैं।

सहसम्बन्ध की परिभाषा (Definition of Correlation)

सहसम्बन्ध की कुछ प्रमुख परिभाषायें निम्नलिखित हैं–

1. **प्रो॰ किंग के शब्दों में**–"दो श्रेणियों अथवा समूहों के बीच कार्य-करण सम्बन्ध को ही सहसम्बन्ध कहते हैं।"

— *W.I. King*

2. **वैसेल तथा विलेट के शब्दों में**–''जब दो भिन्न चरों से लिये गये पदों के मूल्य के समूह अंकित किए जाएं और यह पाया जाए कि मूल्यों के युग्मों में गुण-सम्बन्ध है तो यह कहा जाएगा कि दो चरों में सम्बन्ध है।''

—Wessel and Willet

3. **डेवनपोर्ट के शब्दों में**–''सहसम्बन्ध का सम्पूर्ण विषय पृथक् विशेषताओं के मध्य पाए जाने वाले उस पारस्परिक सम्बन्ध की ओर संकेत करता है जिसके अनुसार वे कुछ सीमा तक साथ-साथ परिवर्तन होने की प्रवृत्ति रखती हैं।''

—E. Davenport

4. **कोनर के शब्दों में**–''यदि दो या अधिक राशियाँ सहानुभूति में परिवर्तित हों जिससे एक में होने वाले परिवर्तनों के फलस्वरूप दूसरी राशि में भी परिवर्तन होने की प्रवृति पायी जाये, तो वे राशियाँ सहसम्बन्धित कहलाती हैं।''

—Conner

5. **ग्राहमेन के शब्दों में**–''जब दो या अधिक संख्यायें सहानुभूति में परिवर्तित होती हैं जिससे एक में परिवर्तन का परिणाम दूसरी में उसी या विपरीत दिशा में परिवर्तन हो, तो उन संख्याओं के मध्य सहसम्बन्ध होता है।''

—C.J. Grahmann

उपरोक्त परिभाषाओं से यह स्पष्ट हो जाता है कि यदि किसी एक चर के मान में परिवर्तन होने से दूसरे चरों के मानों में सहगामी अथवा विपरीतगामी परिवर्तन की प्रवृति पाये तो ऐसे चरों को सहसम्बन्धित कहा जाता है।

सहसम्बन्ध और कारण-कार्य सम्बन्ध (Correlation and Causation)

यदि कोई दो चर सहसम्बन्धित हैं तो किसी एक चर में हुए परिवर्तन के कारण दूसरे चर में परिवर्तन होने की प्रवृत्ति पाई जाती है। लेकिन इसके विपरीत यदि किसी एक चर में परिवर्तन होने से यदि दूसरे चर के मान में सहगामी अथवा विपरीतगामी परिवर्तन पाया जाए तो हमेशा यह सत्य नहीं होगा कि दोनों चर आपस में सहसम्बन्धित हैं। उदाहरण के तौर पर किन्हीं 6 विद्यार्थियों के सम्बन्ध में निम्नलिखित समंक पाये जा सकते हैं–

विद्यार्थी	A	B	C	D	E	F
पिछली परीक्षा में प्राप्त किये अंकों का प्रतिशत	42%	47%	60%	80%	55%	40%
ऊँचाई (इंचों में)	60	62	65	70	40	59

उपरोक्त समंकों का अध्ययन करने से ज्ञात होता है कि यदि किसी विद्यार्थी का प्रतिशत अधिक है तो ऊँचाई भी सामान्यत: अधिक ही है। इससे हम यह निष्कर्ष नहीं निकाल सकते कि दोनों चर आपस में सम्बन्धित हैं।

किन्हीं दो चरों में सहसम्बन्ध होने का यह भी कारण हो सकता है कि उन चरों में कारण-कार्य सम्बन्ध हो ? उदाहरण के तौर पर 'आय' तथा 'खर्च' सम्बन्धी आंकड़ों में उच्च स्तरीय सहसम्बन्ध होने का मुख्य कारण यह है कि अधिक आय ही अधिक खर्च का कारण होती है।

कुछ परिस्थितियाँ ऐसी होती हैं जबकि चरों के विषय में यह निश्चित करना सम्भव नहीं हो पाता कि कौन-सा चर दूसरे चर में हुए परिवर्तन का कारण है। उदाहरण के तौर पर किसी शहर में यदि मोटर कारों की संख्या अधिक है तो यह आशा की जा सकती है उस शहर में टेलीफोनों की संख्या भी अधिक होगी। इसका कारण यह नहीं कि यदि किसी के पास कार है तो उसके पास टेलीफोन अवश्य होना चाहिए। वास्तव में इस धनात्मक सहसम्बन्ध होने का कारण यह है कि जिसकी आय अधिक है, वह ये दोनों ही चीजें रखना पसन्द करता है।

सहसम्बन्ध के प्रकार (Types of Correlation)

1. धनात्मक और ऋणात्मक सहसम्बन्ध (Positive and Negative Correlation)–यदि दो चरों का मान औसत तौर पर एक ही दिशा में बढ़ता है, तो चरों के बीच में पाई जाने वाले सह-सम्बन्ध को **धनात्मक** (Positive) **सहसम्बन्ध** कहा जाता है। दूसरे शब्दों में, यदि एक चर का मान बढ़ता (या घटता) है तो चरों में धनात्मक सहसम्बन्ध होने पर यह आशा की जायेगी कि दूसरे चर का मान औसत तौर पर बढ़ेगा (या घटेगा)। उदाहरण के लिए, 'आय' तथा 'खर्च' सम्बन्धी आँकड़ों में धनात्मक सहसम्बन्ध पाया जाता है।

धनात्मक सहसम्बन्ध होने की दशा में यह आवश्यक नहीं होता कि एक चर का मान बढ़ने की दशा में दूसरे चर का मान भी बढ़ेगा। वस्तुत: यह आशा कि जाती है कि औसत तौर पर चर एक ही दशा में बढ़े। निम्न उदाहरण इस तथ्य को स्पष्ट करता है।

x	2	3	6	8	11
y	14	15	13	18	22

उपरोक्त आँकड़ों में जब x का मान 3 से बढ़कर 6 हो रहा है तो y का मान 15 से घटकर 13 हो रहा है। लेकिन औसत तौर पर यहीं कहा जायेगा कि x और y में धनात्मक सहसम्बन्ध है।

यदि दो चरों का मान औसत तौर पर विपरीत दिशा में बढ़ता है, तो चरों के बीच में पाई जाने वाले सहसम्बन्ध को ऋणात्मक (Negative) सहसम्बन्ध कहा जाता है।

दूसरे शब्दों में, यदि एक चर का मान बढ़ता (या घटता) है तो चरों में ऋणात्मक सहसम्बन्ध होने पर यह आशा की जायेगी कि दूसरे चर का मान औसत तौर पर घटेगा (या बढ़ेगा)। उदाहरण के लिए 'तापमान' तथा 'चाय की बिक्री' सम्बन्धी आंकड़ों में ऋणात्मक सहसम्बन्ध पाया जाता है।

ऋणात्मक सहसम्बन्ध होने की दशा में यह आवश्यक नहीं होता कि एक चर का मान बढ़ने की दशा में दूसरे चर का मान अवश्य घटेगा। वस्तुत: यह आशा की जाती है कि औसत तौर पर चर विपरीत दिशा में बढ़ेंगे। निम्न उदाहरण इस तथ्य को स्पष्ट करता है।

x	110	107	105	95	80
y	8	15	14	27	36

उपरोक्त आँकड़ों में जब x का मान 107 से घटकर 105 हो रहा है तो y का मान भी 15 से घटकर 14 हो रहा है। लेकिन औसत तौर पर यही कहा जायेगा कि x और y में ऋणात्मक सहसम्बन्ध है।

2. रेखीय और अरेखीय सहसम्बन्ध (Linear and Curvilinear Correlation)

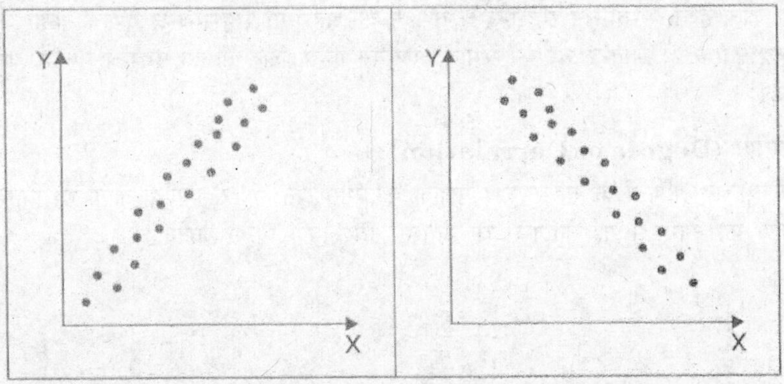

धनात्मक रेखीय सहसम्बन्ध ऋणात्मक रेखीय सहसम्बन्ध

यदि दो चरों के होने वाले परिवर्तन का अनुपात समान या लगभग समान हो तो चरों के बीच सहसम्बन्ध को **रेखीय** (Linear) कहा जाता है।

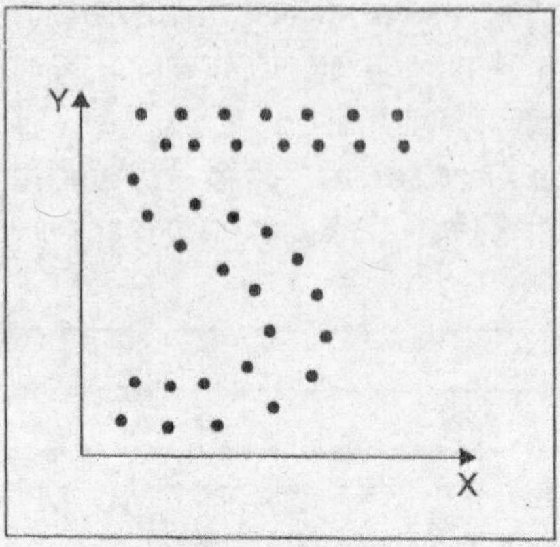

अरेखीय सहसम्बन्ध

उदाहरण के लिए, किसी विद्यालय में विद्यार्थियों की संख्या एवं उनके द्वारा दी गई मासिक फीस सम्बन्धी आँकड़ों में रेखीय सहसम्बन्ध पाया जायेगा। यदि दो चरों में रेखीय सहसम्बन्ध है तो उनके मूल्यों में परिवर्तन लगभग एक निश्चित अनुपात में होंगे।

कुछ परिस्थितियों में ऐसा भी हो जाता है कि चरों में होने वाले परिवर्तन का अनुपात समान नहीं होता, ऐसे चरों के सहसम्बन्ध को **अरेखीय** (Curvilinear) सहसम्बन्ध कहा जाता है।

उपरोक्त बिन्दु चित्र में दिखाया गया है कि x और y चरों में अरेखीय सहसम्बन्ध है। यदि किसी व्यापारिक संस्थान के विज्ञापन व्यय तथा लाभ सम्बन्धी आँकड़ों का बिन्दु चित्र बनाया जाए तो हम देखेंगे कि चित्र के बिन्दुओं की प्रवृत्ति किसी एक रेखा के गिर्द रहने की नहीं होगी। इसका कारण यह है कि यदि विज्ञापन व्यय दुगुना कर दिया जाए तो यह आवश्यक नहीं होगा कि लाभ भी दुगुना हो जाए।

3. साधारण, आंशिक और बहुगुणी सहसम्बन्ध (Simple, Partial and Multiple Correlation)–यदि केवल दो ही चरों के सहसम्बन्ध का अध्ययन करना हो तो चरों के सहसम्बन्ध को **साधारण सहसम्बन्ध** (Simple Correlation) कहा जाता है। उदाहरण के लिए, किसी संस्थान के ''बिक्री'' तथा ''लाभ'' सम्बन्धी आंकड़ों के सहसम्बन्ध को साधारण सहसम्बन्ध कहा जाएगा। यदि दो से अधिक चरों के सम्बन्धित आंकड़ों का अध्ययन करना हो तो आंशिक (Partial) तथा बहुगुणी (Multiple) सहसम्बन्ध गुणांक निकाले जाते हैं। यदि एक से अधिक चरों का प्रभाव अध्ययन आश्रित चर पर किया जाता है तो सम्बन्धित सहसम्बन्ध गुणांक को **बहुगुणी सहसम्बन्ध** गुणांक कहा जाता है। यदि एक समय में आश्रित चर पर केवल एक ही स्वतन्त्र चर का प्रभाव अध्ययन किया जाये तो सहसम्बन्ध गुणांक को **आंशिक सहसम्बन्ध गुणांक** कहा जाता है।

सहसम्बन्ध का परिमाण (Degree of Correlation)

दो चरों से सम्बन्धित श्रेणियों के सहसम्बन्ध गुणांक को सामान्यत: 'r' से दर्शाया जाता है। किन्हीं दो श्रेणियों में रेखीय सहसम्बन्ध के परिमाण का आगे दी गई तालिका के अनुसार विश्लेषण किया जाता है।

रेखीय सहसम्बन्ध का परिमाण

सहसम्बन्ध परिणाम	सहसम्बन्ध गुणांक का मान	
	धनात्मक	ऋणात्मक
पूर्ण (Perfect)	$r = 1$	$r = -1$
उच्च स्तर (High degree)	$0.75 \leq r < 1$	$-1 < r \leq -0.75$
मध्य स्तर (Moderate degree)	$0.50 \leq r < 0.75$	$-0.75 < r \leq -0.50$
निम्न स्तर (Low degree)	$0 < r < 0.50$	$-0.50 < r < 0$
सहसम्बन्ध का अभाव (No correlation)	$r = 0$	$r = 0$

प्रश्न 23. दो चरों में सह-सम्बन्ध को ज्ञात करने के लिए प्रयोग में आने वाली विधियों के बारे में संक्षिप्त में लिखिए।

उत्तर–किन्हीं दो चरों में विद्यमान सह-सम्बन्ध को ज्ञात करने के लिए निम्नलिखित विधियों को प्रयोग में लाया जाता है।

1. विक्षेप चित्र (Scatter Diagram)

दो चरों (x और y) के मूल्यों से सम्बन्धित विक्षेप चित्र बिन्दु रेखीय पत्र पर बनाया जाता है। एक चर के सम्बन्धित मूल्यों को भुजाक्ष पर मापा जाता है तथा दूसरे चर के सम्बन्धित मूल्यों को कोटि अक्ष पर मापा जाता है। प्रत्येक पदयुग्म से सम्बन्धित x और y को माप कर एक बिन्दु अंकित किया जाता है। इस प्रकार श्रेणी में जितने पद-युग्म होते हैं, उतने ही बिन्दु चित्र पर अंकित हो जाते हैं यदि दो पद-युग्मों में x और y का मान समान हो तो दो सम्बन्धित बिन्दुओं को एक के ऊपर एक न करके साथ-साथ अंकित कर दिया जाता है। इस प्रकार से जितने पद-युग्म होंगे उतने ही बिन्दु विक्षेप चित्र पर प्राप्त हो जाएँगे।

विक्षेप चित्र का विश्लेषण–यदि विक्षेप चित्र में बिन्दु बायें से दायें ऊपर की तरफ जाते हुए प्रतीत हों तो चरों में सह-सम्बन्ध धनात्मक होगा और यदि बिन्दु बायें से दायें नीचे की तरफ जाते हुए प्रतीत हों तो सह-सम्बन्ध ऋणात्मक होगा। चित्र में बिन्दु जितना चौड़ाई में बढ़े हुए होंगे, उतना ही उनके बीच सह-सम्बन्ध कम होगा। यदि चित्र में यह पता ही न लग पाए कि बिन्दु किधर बढ़ रहे हैं तथा सब तरफ फैले हुए महसूस हों तो चरों के बीच कोई सह-सम्बन्ध नहीं होगा।

2. सह-सम्बन्ध बिन्दु रेखा-चित्र (Correlation Graph)

सह-सम्बन्ध बिन्दु रेखा चित्र भी बिन्दु रेखा-पत्र (Graph Paper) पर बनाया जाता है। इस चित्र में जितने भी चरों के मान के पद-युग्म हो, उतने ही अंक भुजाक्ष पर अंकित किए जाते हैं। दोनों चरों से सम्बन्धित मान कोटि अक्ष पर ही मापे जाते हैं। दोनों चरों के न्यूनतम तथा अधिकतम मानों को देखते हुए ही कोटि अक्ष पर पैमाना (Scale) अंकित किया जाता है। इस चित्र में दोनों चरों से सम्बन्धित मानों की अलग-अलग बिन्दु रेखा डाली जाती है। इस प्रकार से इस चित्र में दो बिन्दु रेखा प्राप्त हो जाते हैं। चित्र को आकर्षक बनाने के लिए विभिन्न रंगों का प्रयोग भी किया जा सकता है।

सह-सम्बन्ध बिन्दु रेखा-चित्र का विश्लेषण–इस चित्र के द्वारा सह-सम्बन्ध का अनुमान लगाने के लिए दोनों चरों से सम्बन्धित रेखाओं के उतार-चढ़ाव का अध्ययन किया जाता है। यदि दोनों चरों के बिन्दु रेखा, पद युग्मों के हर मान के लिए औसत तौर पर एक दिशा में बढ़ें तो चरों के बीच धनात्मक सह-सम्बन्ध होता है और यदि दोनों चरों के बिन्दु रेखा, पद-युग्मों के हर मान के लिए औसत तौर पर विभिन्न दिशा में बढ़ें तो उनके बीच ऋणात्मक सह-सम्बन्ध होता है। विक्षेप चित्र तथा सह-सम्बन्ध बिन्दु रेखा-चित्र के द्वारा दोनों चरों के बीच सह-सम्बन्ध का अन्दाजा तो हो जाता है पर सह-सम्बन्ध का वास्तविक मान ज्ञात नहीं हो पाता।

3. कार्ल पियर्सन रीति (Karl Pearson's Method)

यह रीति किन्हीं दो चरों के बीच रेखीय सह-सम्बन्ध का मान ज्ञात करने की सबसे उत्तम रीति मानी जाती है। इस रीति में सह-सम्बन्ध गुणांक को 'r' से अंकित किया जाता है।

अगर $(x_1, y_1), (x_2, y_2), \ldots\ldots, (x_n, y_n)$ दो चरों x तथा y के n पद-युग्मों का मान हो तो इस सूत्र के द्वारा r का मान निकाला जाता है।

$$r = \frac{\sum_{i=1}^{n}(x_i - \bar{x})(y_i - \bar{y})}{\sqrt{\sum_{i=1}^{n}(x_i - \bar{x})^2}\sqrt{\sum_{i=1}^{n}(y_i - \bar{y})^2}}$$

यदि x और y के मानों का माध्य (A.M.) दशमलव में न हो तो इस सूत्र का प्रयोग करने में कोई कठिनाई नहीं आती, परन्तु यदि x या y या दोनों चरों का माध्य दशमलव में आ जाए तो इस रीति से r की गणना करने में बहुत समय लग जाता है। ऐसी परिस्थिति में इस सूत्र का दूसरा रूप प्रयोग में लाया जाता है। इस रीति में दोनों चरों के लिए कोई भी कल्पित माध्य A, B लिए जाते हैं। x के मूल्यों का A से विचलन $(x - A)$ निकाला जाता है और u से अंकित किया जाता है। इसी प्रकार से y के सभी मूल्यों का B से विचलन $(y - B)$ निकाला जाता है तथा v से अंकित किया जाता है। इन विचलनों को प्रयोग में लाकर निम्नलिखित सूत्र से सम्बन्धित सभी मान निकाले जाते हैं।

$$r = \frac{n\sum_{i=1}^{n} u_i v_i - \left(\sum_{i=1}^{n} u_i\right)\left(\sum_{i=1}^{n} v_i\right)}{\sqrt{n\sum_{i=1}^{n} u_i^2 - \left(\sum_{i=1}^{n} u_i\right)^2}\sqrt{n\sum_{i=1}^{n} v_i^2 - \left(\sum_{i=1}^{n} v_i\right)^2}}$$

इस सूत्र से निकाले गए r के मान को कार्ल पियर्सन सह-सम्बन्ध का गुणांक कहा जाता है। इस गुणांक का मान हमेशा -1 और 1 के बीच होता है। अगर दोनों चरों में पूर्ण धनात्मक सह-सम्बन्ध हो तो r का मान एक आता है। यदि $r = -1$ आए तो दोनों चरों में पूर्ण ऋणात्मक सह-सम्बन्ध होता है।

4. स्पियरमैन की अनुस्थिति सह-सम्बन्ध रीति (Spearman's Rank Correlation Method)

स्पियरमैन द्वारा प्रतिपादित इस रीति को विशेष तौर पर उन चरों के बीच सह-सम्बन्ध ज्ञात करने के लिए किया जाता है, जिनका संख्यात्मक माप प्रत्यक्ष रूप से सम्भव न हो। इस प्रकार के चरों को गुणात्मक चर कहा जाता है। उदाहरण के तौर पर बुद्धिमत्ता, सुन्दरता, ईमानदारी आदि गुणात्मक चर हैं। इस प्रकार के चरों में प्रत्यक्ष माप सम्भव नहीं हो पाता, परन्तु इनके मानों की अनुस्थिति जरूर निश्चित की जा सकती है। स्पियरमैन द्वारा दिए गए सूत्र को गुणात्मक तथा संख्यात्मक दोनों ही प्रकार के चरों के लिए प्रयोग किया जा सकता है। अगर कोई चर संख्यात्मक है तो उनके मूल्यों की अनुस्थिति निश्चित कर दी जाती है। दोनों चरों के मूल्यों की अनुस्थितियों को R_1 तथा R_2 से अंकित किया जाता है। इस रीति द्वारा निकाले गए सह-सम्बन्ध गुणांक को 'r_k' से अंकित किया जाता है। इसका मान निम्नलिखित सूत्र को प्रयोग करके किया जाता है।

$$r_k = 1 - \frac{6\sum D^2}{n(n^2 - 1)}$$

इस सूत्र में D का मान R_1—R_2 है तथा n पद-युग्मों की संख्या होती है। अगर किसी चर का कुछ पद-युग्मों में मान समान हो तो उसके लिए भी स्पियरमैन ने प्रावधान किया है।

5. संगामी विचलन रीति (Concurrent Deviation Method)

दो चरों में सह-सम्बन्ध का मान निकालने की यह सबसे सरल तथा व्यावहारिक रीति है। इस रीति में दोनों चरों के मानों का अपने से पहले वाले मान से विचलन की दिशा को काम में लिया जाता है। सारणी में केवल विचलनों की दिशा

ही अंकित की जाती है। अगर कोई मान अपने से पहले मान के बराबर हो तो दिशा वाले खाने में 0 अंकित किया जाता है। इसके पश्चात् दोनों श्रेणियों के विचलनों के चिन्हों को गुणा करके अगले खाने में लिखा जाता है। इस खाने में आये + चिन्हों के जोड़ को 'c' के बराबर लिखा जाता है। सह-सम्बन्ध का मान निम्नलिखित सूत्र को प्रयोग करके निकाला जाता है–

$$r_c = \pm\sqrt{\pm\left(\frac{2c - N}{N}\right)}$$

इस सूत्र में,

r_c = संगामी विचलन सह-सम्बन्ध गुणांक

N = कुल पद-युग्मों की संख्या से एक कम।

8. प्रतीपगमन विश्लेषण

प्रश्न 24. सांख्यिकीय विश्लेषण में प्रतीपगमन रेखाओं के उपयोग के विषय में लेख लिखिए।

उत्तर–सांख्यिकी में 'प्रतीपगमन' (Regression) शब्द का प्रयोग सबसे पहले **सर फ्रांसिस गॉल्टन** ने किया था। उन्होंने पिताओं तथा पुत्रों की ऊँचाइयों का अध्ययन करते हुए यह देखा कि ऊँचे पिताओं के पुत्र कम ऊँचे तथा ठिगने पिताओं के पुत्र कम ठिगने हैं। इससे उन्होंने यह निष्कर्ष निकाला कि पिताओं की ऊँचाइयों की अपेक्षा पुत्रों की ऊँचाइयाँ औसत के अधिक नजदीक हैं। इसी प्रवृत्ति को उन्होंने प्रतीपगमन की प्रवृत्ति से सम्बोधित किया।

आधुनिक सांख्यिकी में प्रतीपगमन की धारणा केवल पिता-पुत्र की ऊँचाइयों के अध्ययन तक ही सीमित नहीं रह गयी है, बल्कि अब इस धारणा का प्रयोग सामाजिक, आर्थिक, व्यापारिक सम्बन्धित चरों में भी होने लगा है। सह-सम्बन्ध के अध्ययन से तो हमें यह पता चलता है कि सम्बन्धित चर आपस में सम्बन्धित हैं या नहीं, और यदि सम्बन्धित हैं तो किस सीमा तक। अगर हमें एक चर के किसी मूल्य से सम्बन्धित दूसरे चर के मूल्य का अनुमान लगाना हो तो इस कार्य में सह-सम्बन्ध विश्लेषण हमारी सहायता नहीं कर सकता। इस प्रकार के कार्य को करने के लिए प्रतीपगमन विश्लेषण सहायक सिद्ध होता है। **डब्ल्यू॰ जेड॰ हर्ष** के शब्दों में, ''सह-सम्बन्ध विश्लेषण दो या अधिक घटनाओं में सह-परिवर्तन की घनिष्टता का परीक्षण करता है, और प्रतीपगमन विश्लेषण इस सम्बन्ध की प्रकृति व मात्रा का माप करके हमें भावी अनुमान लगाने की क्षमता प्रदान करता है।'' सांख्यिकी में प्रतीपगमन विश्लेषण का प्रयोग दिए गए चरों से सम्बन्धित समीकरण निश्चित करने के लिए किया जाता है।

प्रतीपगमन विश्लेषण की उपयोगिता

सांख्यिकी में प्रतीपगमन विश्लेषण की उपयोगिता निश्चित रूप से बहुत अधिक है। कुछ विशेष उपयोगिताएँ निम्नलिखित हैं–

1. प्रतीपगमन समीकरण ज्ञात करना–प्रतीपगमन विश्लेषण के सिद्धांतों को प्रयोग करके दो या दो से अधिक चरों से समीकरण ज्ञात किया जा सकता है। या x और y दो चर हैं तो प्रतीपगमन समीकरण x को या y को परतन्त्र चर मानकर निकाली जा सकती है। यदि x को परतन्त्र तथा y को स्वतन्त्र चर मान कर प्रतीपगमन समीकरण निकाली गई है तो उसे x का y पर प्रतीपगमन समीकरण कहा जाता है। यदि y को परतन्त्र तथा x को स्वतन्त्र चर मानकर प्रतीपगमन समीकरण निकाली गई है तो उसे y का x प्रतीपगमन समीकरण कहा जाता है।

2. सह-सम्बन्ध गुणांक का मान निकालना–प्रतीपगमन गुणांकों का प्रयोग करके सह-सम्बन्ध गुणांक का मान भी निकाला जा सकता है। वास्तव में, सह-सम्बन्ध गुणांक प्रतीपगमन गुणांकों के गुणोत्तर माध्य के बराबर होता है। जितना प्रतीपगमन रेखाओं के बीच कोण कम होगा उतना ही सम्बन्धित चरों में सह-सम्बन्ध ज्यादा होगा। अगर दोनों प्रतीपगमन रेखाएँ समकोण बनाती हैं तो चरों के बीच सहसम्बन्ध का गुणांक '0' होगा यदि प्रतीपगमन रेखाएँ बिल्कुल एक-दूसरे के ऊपर हैं, तो उनके बीच पूर्ण सह-सम्बन्ध होगा।

3. ''अर्थमिति'' विषय में प्रयोग–अर्थशास्त्र की विशेष शाखा अर्थमिति (Econometrics) सांख्यिकी के सिद्धान्तों के प्रयोग पर ही आधारित है। अर्थमिति में विशेष रूप से प्रतीपगमन रेखाओं का प्रयोग किया जाता है।

4. चरों के मूल्यों का अनुमान लगाने के लिए–प्रतीपगमन समीकरणों तथा रेखाओं का प्रयोग किसी एक चर के किसी मूल्य के लिए दूसरे चर के मूल्य का अनुमान लगाने के लिए किया जा सकता है। यदि x के किसी मूल्य के लिए y का अनुमानित मूल्य निकालना हो तो y की x पर प्रतीपगमन समीकरण का प्रयोग किया जाता है। यदि x का मान निकालना हो तो x की y पर प्रतीपगमन समीकरण का प्रयोग किया जाता है।

सह-सम्बन्ध और प्रतीपगमन में अन्तर

सह-सम्बन्ध विश्लेषण से चरों के बीच सम्बन्ध की मात्रा समझने में मदद मिलती है, जबकि प्रतीपगमन विश्लेषण के द्वारा चरों के सम्बन्ध की प्रकृति का ज्ञान होता है।

चरों के बीच सह-सम्बन्ध होने की दशा में यह हमेशा आवश्यक नहीं होता कि चरों में अवश्य ही कारण (cause) और परिणाम (effect) सम्बन्धी कोई बात होगी, जबकि प्रतीपगमन समीकरण स्पष्ट रूप से ऐसा सम्बन्ध दर्शाती है।

सह-सम्बन्ध गुणांक को किसी चर के अनुमानित मान को निकालने में सहायता नहीं कर सकता, जबकि प्रतीपगमन रेखाओं या समीकरणों को प्रयोग करके चर का कोई अनुमानित मान निकाला जा सकता है।

y on x की प्रतीपगमन समीकरण

y चर के किसी अनुमानित मान को निकालने के लिए y की x पर प्रतीपगमन समीकरण का प्रयोग किया जाता है। यदि $(x_1, y_1), (x_2, y_2), \ldots\ldots, (x_n, y_n)$ n पद-युग्मों का मान दिया गया हो तो y की x पर प्रतीपगमन समीकरण

$$y - \bar{y} = b_{yx}(x - \bar{x}) \text{ होती है।}$$

इस समीकरण में $\bar{x}, \bar{y}$ क्रमशः x श्रेणी तथा y श्रेणी के समान्तर माध्य होते हैं और इनका मान निम्नलिखित है :

$$\bar{x} = \frac{\sum x}{n}, \quad \bar{y} = \frac{\sum y}{n}$$

इस समीकरण में प्रयुक्त b_{yx} को y का x पर प्रतीपगमन गुणांक कहा जाता है। तथा इसका मान

$$b_{yx} = \frac{\sum(x-\bar{x})(y-\bar{y})}{\sum(x-\bar{x})^2} \text{ के बराबर होता है।}$$

x on y की प्रतीपगमन समीकरण

x चर के किसी अनुमानित मान को निकालने के लिए x की y पर प्रतीपगमन समीकरण का प्रयोग किया जाता है। यदि $(x_1, y_1), (x_2, y_2), \ldots\ldots, (x_n, y_n)$ n पद-युग्मों का मान दिया गया हो तो x की y पर प्रतीपगमन समीकरण

$$x - \bar{x} = b_{xy}(y - \bar{y}) \text{ होती है।}$$

इस समीकरण में $\bar{x}, \bar{y}$ क्रमशः x श्रेणी तथा y श्रेणी के समान्तर माध्य होते हैं और इनका मान निम्नलिखित है :

$$\bar{x} = \frac{\sum x}{n}, \quad \bar{y} = \frac{\sum y}{n}$$

इस समीकरण में प्रयुक्त b_{xy} को x का y पर प्रतीपगमन गुणांक कहा जाता है तथा इसका मान

$$b_{xy} = \frac{\sum(x-\bar{x})(y-\bar{y})}{\sum(y-\bar{y})^2} \text{ के बराबर होता है।}$$

9. निर्देशांक

प्रश्न 25. निर्देशांकों से आपका क्या अभिप्राय है ? निर्देशांकों का महत्त्व भी बताइए।

उत्तर–परिवर्तन प्रकृति का नियम है और यह कथन आर्थिक जगत पर भी पूरी तरह लागू होता है। आर्थिक जगत में अनेक कारणों से परिवर्तन हुआ करते हैं। ये परिवर्तन विभिन्न इकाइयों के रूप में व्यक्त होते हैं। इस प्रकार के परिवर्तनों की प्रत्यक्ष माप सम्भव नहीं हो पाती, तथा केवल अप्रत्यक्ष माप द्वारा ही अध्ययन सम्भव हो पाता है। उदाहरण के लिए प्राय: ये कथन सुनने में आये हैं कि ''हमारे देश का आयात पिछले वर्ष की अपेक्षा बढ़ गया है'', ''उपयोगी वस्तुओं का सामान्य मूल्य स्तर बढ़ रहा है'' इत्यादि। यदि सरकार यह घोषणा करती है कि आयात बढ़ रहा है, इसका अभिप्राय यह नहीं कि आयात होने वाली हर एक वस्तु का आयात बढ़ रहा है। इसी प्रकार से यदि मूल्य स्तर बढ़ रहा है तो यह कोई आवश्यक नहीं कि सभी वस्तुओं की कीमतें बढ़ रही हैं। वास्तव में, इस प्रकार के औसत मापों में सांख्यिकीय रीतियों की सहायता ली जाती है। सांख्यिकी में इस प्रकार के मापों को **निर्देशांकों** के द्वारा प्रदर्शित किया जाता है। निर्देशांकों को सूचकांक भी कहा जाता है।

निर्देशांकों की परिभाषा विभिन्न सांख्यिकी विद्वानों ने अपने-अपने ढंग से दी है। निर्देशांकों की एक सर्वमान्य परिभाषा देना कठिन है क्योंकि निर्देशांकों को बनाने की विभिन्न रीतियाँ हैं और इनको विभिन्न प्रकार से सांख्यिकीय विश्लेषण में प्रयोग किया जाता है। निर्देशांकों को औपचारिक रूप से इस प्रकार परिभाषित किया जाता है। **निर्देशांक** विशेष प्रकार के सांख्यिकीय औसत हैं, जिनके द्वारा किसी एक चल-मूल्य या आपस में सम्बन्धित चल-मूल्यों में समय या स्थान के परिवर्तन के कारण हुए परिवर्तन को प्रदर्शित किया जाता है। निर्देशांक चल-मूल्यों में हुए परिवर्तनों को सापेक्ष रूप में मापते हैं। निर्देशांक केवल एक संख्या है और इसी संख्या के द्वारा चल-मूल्यों में हुए परिवर्तनों के बारे में जानकारी हो जाती है। निर्देशांक चल-मूल्यों में हुए परिवर्तन की दिशा को औसत रूप में प्रकट करते हैं। उदाहरण के तौर पर यदि सामान्य मूल्य स्तर बढ़ रहा है तो इसका यह अर्थ नहीं कि सभी वस्तुओं के मूल्य समान दर से बढ़ रहे हैं। सम्बन्धित वस्तुओं में से किसी एक या अधिक का मूल्य घट भी सकता है।

निर्देशांकों का महत्त्व

निर्देशांक एक ऐसा सांख्यिकीय माप है जो कि सिर्फ एक ही अंक से चल-मूल्यों में हुए परिवर्तनों को प्रदर्शित कर देता है। जिस प्रकार वायुमापक यन्त्रों के द्वारा मौसम की स्थिति के बारे में जानकारी हो जाती है उसी प्रकार से निर्देशांक आर्थिक परिस्थितियों का अध्ययन करने में सहायता करते हैं। इसीलिए निर्देशांकों को आर्थिक वायुमापक यंत्र (Economic Barometers) कहा जाता है।

निर्देशांकों की सहायता से कभी-कभी ऐसे तथ्यों के परिवर्तन का माप भी सम्भव हो पाता है जिनका मापन अन्यथा सम्भव नहीं होता। बहुत-से भावात्मक तथ्य भी निर्देशांकों की सहायता से मापे जा सकते हैं।

निर्देशांकों का प्रयोग तुलनात्मक अध्ययन को भी सरल बनाते हैं, क्योंकि इनकी प्रकृति तुलनात्मक होती है।

निर्देशांको की उपयोगिता सार्वभौमिक है। वर्तमान युग में सरकार की हर नीति के आधार भी विभिन्न चरों से सम्बन्धित निर्देशांक ही होते हैं। सरकार अपने कर्मचारियों को दिए जाने वाले महँगाई भत्ते का निर्धारण भी उपभोक्ता मूल्य निर्देशांकों के आधार पर ही निश्चित करती है। सरकार का सांख्यिकीय विभाग समय-समय पर उपभोक्ता मूल्य निर्देशांकों की घोषणा करता रहता है।

अगर निर्देशांक मूल्यों में हुए परिवर्तनों को मापते हैं तो उन्हें मूल्य निर्देशांक कहा जाता है। और इसी प्रकार मात्रा निर्देशांक वस्तुओं की मात्रा में हुए परिवर्तन को मापते हैं। मात्रा निर्देशांकों का प्रयोग करके यह भी देखा जा सकता है कि हमारा देश औद्योगिक क्षेत्र में कितनी उन्नति कर रहा है।

वर्तमान युग में निर्देशांकों की उपयोगिता प्रमाणित हो चुकी है तथा लगभग सभी क्षेत्रों में इनका प्रयोग होने लगा है।

प्रश्न 26. सामान्य मूल्य निर्देशांकों की रचना करते हुए किन-किन समस्याओं का सामना करना पड़ सकता है ? उनके बारे में संक्षेप में वर्णन कीजिए।

उत्तर–सामान्य मूल्य निर्देशांकों की रचना करते हुए आमतौर पर निम्नलिखित समस्याओं का सामना करना पड़ सकता है।

1. उद्देश्य की परिभाषा (Definition of the Purpose)

निर्देशांकों की रचना में प्रथम चरण निर्देशांक के उद्देश्य को स्पष्ट रूप से जान लेना होता है। इस बारे में पहले ही निश्चय कर लिया जाता है कि क्या मापना है, किसके लिए मापना और किसलिए मापना है। विभिन्न निर्देशांकों को विभिन्न परिस्थितियों में प्रयुक्त किया जाता है। यदि सामान्य मूल्य स्तर वाले निर्देशांकों की रचना करनी है तो उसमें देश की सम्पूर्ण अर्थव्यवस्था का प्रतिनिधित्व करने वाली अधिक-से-अधिक वस्तुओं को सम्मिलित किया जायेगा।

2. वस्तुओं का चुनाव (Selection of Items)

निर्देशांक की रचना में किन-किन वस्तुओं को शामिल करना है यह निर्देशांक के उद्देश्य का ध्यान रखते हुए सोचा जाता है। उदाहरण के लिए यदि उपभोक्ता मूल्य निर्देशांक बनाना है तो सम्बन्धित हर एक वस्तु को शामिल नहीं किया जा सकता क्योंकि परिवार में प्रयोग में आने वाली वस्तुएं तो बहुत ज्यादा होती हैं। निर्देशांक की रचना में जितनी ज्यादा वस्तुएँ शामिल की जाएँगी उतना ही निर्देशांक की रचना में ज्यादा समय, श्रम तथा धन लगेगा, क्योंकि शामिल की गई वस्तुओं के सम्बन्ध में समंक भी एकत्रित करने होते हैं। निर्देशांक की रचना में वस्तुएं इतनी कम भी नहीं रखी जातीं कि निर्देशांक से सही सूचना ही प्राप्त न हो सके। चुनी हुई वस्तुएं ऐसी होनी चाहिए जो कि अपने वर्ग का उचित प्रतिनिधित्व करती हों तथा कुछ समय बाद भी आसानी से पहचानी जा सकें।

3. वस्तुओं सम्बन्धी समंकों का एकत्रित करना (Collection of Data Regarding Items)

मूल्य निर्देशांक की रचना में वस्तुओं से सम्बन्धित मूल्य तथा मात्रा सम्बन्धी समंक एकत्रित करना एक संवेदनशील कार्य है और निर्देशांक का मान इन्हीं समंकों पर आधारित होता है। यह निश्चित कर लेना चाहिए कि सम्बन्धित समंक एकत्रित करने वाले गणक ईमानदारी से काम कर रहे हैं। आमतौर पर यह भी होता है कि एक ही बाजार की दुकानों पर एक ही चीज अलग-अलग दामों पर बेची जा रही होती है। मूल्य भी हमेशा विश्वसनीय स्रोतों से ही प्राप्त करने चाहिए। साप्ताहिक निर्देशांकों के लिए सप्ताह के किसी निश्चित दिन ही मूल्य लेने चाहिए।

4. आधार समय का चुनाव (Selection of Base Period)

जिस समय से निर्देशांक में चालू समय की तुलना की जाती है, उसे आधार समय कहा जाता है। साधारण तौर पर निर्देशांकों की रचना वार्षिक आधार पर ही की जाती है। निर्देशांकों की प्रकृति साप्ताहिक, मासिक भी हो सकती है। आधार वर्ष का चुनाव करते हुए यह ध्यान में रखा जाता है कि उस वर्ष में सम्बन्धित वस्तुओं के मूल्य असाधारण रूप से बहुत ज्यादा या बहुत कम न हों। आधार वर्ष ऐसा भी नहीं होना चाहिए कि उस वर्ष कोई भूचाल, महामारी या अकाल पड़ा हो, क्योंकि ऐसे समय में वस्तुओं के मूल्यों में असाधारण परिवर्तन आने की सम्भावना रहती है। अगर कोई वर्ष सामान्य न हो तो दो या तीन साथ लगते सालों की कीमतों के औसत को ले लिया जाता है। आधार वर्ष भूतकाल में बहुत पीछे का भी नहीं होना चाहिए। निर्देशांक बनाने में यह भी निश्चित किया जाता है कि स्थिर आधार प्रयोग में लाना है या शृंखला आधार।

5. औसत का चुनाव (Selection of Average)

निर्देशांकों की रचना में सम्बन्धित वस्तुओं के मूल्यों में हुए परिवर्तनों का औसत निकालने की आवश्यकता होती है। औसत का चुनाव वस्तुओं से सम्बन्धित समंकों पर भी काफी निर्भर करता है। निर्देशांकों की रचना में साधारणतया समान्तर माध्य तथा गुणोत्तर माध्य का ही प्रयोग किया जाता है।

6. भारों का चुनाव (Selection of Weights)

व्यावहारिक जीवन में हम देखते हैं कि जो भी वस्तुएँ हम अपने प्रयोग में लाते हैं उनकी महत्ता बराबर नहीं होती। उदाहरण के लिए उपभोक्ता मूल्य निर्देशांक में जो महत्ता खाद्यानों की हो सकती है वह मनोरंजन की नहीं हो सकती। निर्देशांकों की रचना में हर वस्तु को सही भार देना बहुत आवश्यक होता है।

7. सूत्र का चुनाव (Selection of Formula)

निर्देशांकों की रचना के लिए बहुत से सूत्र उपलब्ध होते हैं। निर्देशांक की रचना किस सूत्र द्वारा की जानी है इस बारे में भी निश्चय किया जाता है। सूत्र का चुनाव समंकों की प्रकृति पर भी निर्भर करता है। सैद्धान्तिक दृष्टि से **फिशर** के सूत्र को आदर्श सूत्र माना जाता है।

10. काल श्रेणी का विश्लेषण

प्रश्न 27. '*काल श्रेणियों के विश्लेषण*' से आप क्या समझते हैं ? इसके कौन-कौन से प्रमुख संघटक होते हैं ?

उत्तर–सांख्यिकीय समंकों को किसी निश्चित आधार के अनुसार वर्गीकृत करके विश्लेषण के योग्य बनाया जाता है। समंकों को वर्गीकृत करने का आधार स्थान, आयु समय आदि कुछ भी हो सकता है। यदि किसी चर के मूल्य समय के आधार पर लिए गए हैं तो सम्बन्धित चर श्रेणी को काल श्रेणी (Time Series) कहा जाता है। यदि y चर का $t_1, t_2, \ldots\ldots, t_n$ समय के लिए मान $y_1, y_2, \ldots\ldots, y_n$ है तो सम्बन्धित काल श्रेणी को $\{(t_i, y_i) : i = 1, 2, \ldots\ldots, n\}$ की तरह लिखा जाता है। अगर हम किसी कम्पनी की पिछली बीस सालों की वार्षिक कुल बिक्री लें तो वे भी एक काल श्रेणी होगी। काल श्रेणी के लिए यह आवश्यक नहीं होता कि कम से कम 10 या 20 वर्षों के समंक लेने होंगे। यदि कोई डॉक्टर अपने मरीज का हर 15 मिनट के बाद थर्मामीटर से ताप ले रहा है तो केवल 2 दिन से सम्बन्धित समंक भी काल श्रेणी के रूप में होंगे। अगर किसी शहर की जनसंख्या हर वर्ष ली जा रही है तो वह भी काल श्रेणी बनेगी।

किसी भी काल श्रेणी से यह उम्मीद हमेशा नहीं की जा सकती कि सम्बन्धित चर के मान हर समय के लिए समान होंगे। हर काल श्रेणी में उतार-चढ़ाव स्वाभाविक है। यदि हम किसी वस्तु का औसत मूल्य लेकर काल श्रेणी बनाएँ तो उसकी बिन्दु रेखा एक सरल रेखा नहीं होगी। इस प्रकार के परिवर्तनशील तत्त्वों का अध्ययन तथा विश्लेषण करने के लिए ही काल श्रेणियों का विश्लेषण किया जाता है। काल श्रेणी के समय की इकाई घण्टे, दिन, सप्ताह, माह, वर्ष आदि कुछ भी हो सकती है। **सिसिल सी॰ मेयर्स** के शब्दों में, ''काल-श्रेणी को एक चर के समयावधिनुसार पुनर्वतित मापों के क्रम के रूप में परिभाषित किया जा सकता है।''

किसी भी काल-श्रेणी में दो चर होते हैं, एक स्वतन्त्र चर तथा दूसरा परतन्त्र चर। काल श्रेणी में स्वतन्त्र चर हमेशा समय को लिया जाता है।

काल-श्रेणी विश्लेषण का महत्त्व (Significance of Analysis of Time Series)

व्यावहारिक जीवन में हम ऐसे बहुत-से तथ्यों से सम्बन्धित होते हैं जिनके मान समय के बदलने के साथ-साथ बदलते रहते हैं। आज के युग में काल-श्रेणियों की उपयोगिता केवल अर्थशास्त्रियों तक ही सीमित नहीं रह गई है, बल्कि काल श्रेणियों के विश्लेषण का लाभ सरकार, डॉक्टर, अध्यापक, वैज्ञानिक, समाजशास्त्री, उपभोक्ता आदि कोई भी ले सकता है। किसी भी काल श्रेणी में उच्चावचनों का होना स्वाभाविक है। काल-श्रेणी के विश्लेषण की तकनीक हमें किसी काल-श्रेणी में पाए जाने वाले उच्चावचनों के उद्गम को समझने में सहायता करती है।

किसी भी काल-श्रेणी के द्वारा आगे आने वाले समय के लिए सम्बन्धित चर के मूल्य का अनुमान लगाया जा सकता है। इस तकनीक के द्वारा चालू वर्ष के चर के मान की इस वर्ष के लिए किए गए अनुमानित मान से तुलना की जा सकती है और यदि वास्तविक मान, अनुमानित मान से कम है तो इसके कारणों को खोजा जा सकता है। इस प्रकार से काल-श्रेणी का विश्लेषण इस कार्य में सहायता करता है कि हमने वर्तमान में उन्नति की या अवनति।

काल-श्रेणी के प्रयोग से तुलनात्मक अध्ययन भी सरल हो जाता है। उदाहरण के लिए किसी फर्म के लाभ से सम्बन्धित काल-श्रेणी का अध्ययन करके विभिन्न वर्षों में की गई उन्नति का आभास किया जा सकता है।

काल श्रेणियों के विश्लेषण की तकनीकों को प्रयोग करके आने वाले समय के लिये चर के अनुमानित मान को निकाला जा सकता है। सरकार भी अपनी दीर्घकालीन योजनाएँ बनाते समय काल श्रेणियों का अत्यन्त प्रयोग करती है।

काल-श्रेणियों के संघटक (Components of Times Series)

साधारणतया किसी भी काल श्रेणी में सम्बन्धित चर के मान हर एक समय के लिए समान नहीं होते। आमतौर पर काल श्रेणी का बिन्दु रेखा चित्र में एक सीधी रेखा न आकर टेढ़ी-मेढ़ी रेखा आती है। काल-श्रेणी के चर में उच्चावचन मनोवैज्ञानिक, सामाजिक तथा आर्थिक कारणों से होते हैं। किसी काल-श्रेणी में उच्चावचन पैदा करने वाले कारणों को चार प्रकार से विभाजित किया जाता है, और इनको काल-श्रेणी के **संघटक** कहा जाता है। अब हम विस्तार से काल-श्रेणी के संघटकों की चर्चा करेंगे।

***(i)* दीर्घकालीन प्रवृत्ति (Secular Trend)**–दीर्घकाल में काल-श्रेणी से सम्बन्धित चर के मान के बढ़ने या घटने की प्रवृत्ति को दीर्घकालीन प्रवृत्ति कहा जाता है। दीर्घकालीन प्रवृत्ति एक सरल रेखा के रूप में बिन्दु रेखा चित्र में दिखाई जाती है। इस संघटक में हम उन सब कारणों का समावेश करते हैं जो कि धीरे-धीरे लम्बे समय में ही काल श्रेणी को प्रभावित करते हैं। उदाहरण के तौर पर जनसंख्या, तकनीकी विकास, वैज्ञानिक खोज, लोगों की आदतें आदि कुछ ऐसे कारण हैं जोकि अपना प्रभाव तत्काल नहीं डाल सकते। अगर किसी काल-श्रेणी की दीर्घकालीन प्रवृत्ति बढ़ने की है तो इसका यह तात्पर्य नहीं की सम्बन्धित चर के वास्तविक मान भी हमेशा बढ़ते हुए ही होंगे। इसके स्थान पर यह कहना उचित होगा कि वास्तविक मान औसत तौर पर बढ़ते हुए होंगे। दीर्घकालीन प्रवृत्ति का अध्ययन करने के लिए यह जरूरी नहीं कि सम्बन्धित चर की बहुत लम्बे समय तक के मान आवश्यक रूप से लेने चाहिए। वास्तव में कितनी अवधि तक के मान लेने हैं यह इस बात पर निर्भर करता है कि कितने अन्तराल के पश्चात् चर के मान लिए जा रहे हैं।

***(ii)* मौसमी विचरण (Seasonal Variations)**–काल-श्रेणी के मौसमी विचरण संघटक में उन सब कारणों को शामिल किया जाता है। जिनका प्रभाव हर वर्ष नियमित रूप से पड़ता हो। काल-श्रेणी के मौसमी विचरण हर वर्ष के तीज-त्योहारों की वजह से भी पड़ सकते हैं। उदाहरण के तौर पर हलवाइयों को पता होता है कि उनकी बिक्री ज्यादा या तो त्योहारों के मौकों पर होगी या शादियों के दिनों में। आतिशबाजी वालों, बैण्ड-बाजे वालों का काम भी शादियों के मौकों पर अधिक होता है। मौसमी विचरण स्थान के मौसम के कारण भी पैदा होते हैं। उदाहरण के तौर पर चाय-कॉफी आदि का काम सर्दियों में अधिक चलता है। इसी प्रकार छतरी, बरसाती आदि बनाने तथा बेचने वालों का काम बरसात के मौसम में अधिक होता है। पहाड़ों पर बसे दुकानदार, होटल वाले आदि भी यह जानते हैं कि उनका काम गर्मी में सर्दी की अपेक्षा ज्यादा होता है। बैंक वालों को भी यह पता होता है कि उनका लेन-देन प्रत्येक मास के प्रथम सप्ताह में और सप्ताहों की अपेक्षा ज्यादा होता है। यदि किसी काल-श्रेणी में सम्बन्धित चर का वार्षिक तौर पर मान लिया जाए तो काल-श्रेणी में मौसमी विचरण गौण हो जाते हैं।

***(iii)* चक्रीय विचरण (Cyclical Variations)**–किसी भी काल-श्रेणी में चक्रीय विचरण के अन्तर्गत उन सब कारणों का समावेश किया जाता है जो कि सम्बन्धित चर की बिन्दु रेखा में दीर्घकालीन प्रवृत्ति के गिर्द लहरों की तरह का उतार-चढ़ाव पैदा करते हैं। इन लहरों का प्रारूप नियमित भी हो सकता है तथा अनियमित भी। आर्थिक तथा व्यापारिक काल-श्रेणियों में सामान्यतया: चक्र की अवधि एक वर्ष से ज्यादा ही होती है। किसी-किसी काल-श्रेणी में चक्र की अवधि 10 वर्ष तक की भी हो जाती है। किसी भी चक्र में निम्नलिखित चार अवस्थाएँ होती हैं :

(क) समृद्धि (Boom) (ख) प्रतिसार (Recession)

(ग) अवसाद (Depression) (घ) पुनरुत्थान (Recovery)

***(iv)* अनियमित विचरण (Irregular Variations)**–अनियमित विचरण संघटक में उन सब कारणों का समावेश किया जाता है जो कि काल-श्रेणी के चर के मान को प्रभावित कर सकते हैं और जिनके होने या न होने या कब होने के बारे में निश्चित रूप से कुछ नहीं कहा जा सकता। उदाहरण के लिए बाढ़, अकाल, युद्ध आदि कारणों से जो परिवर्तन आते हैं उन्हें इसी श्रेणी में ही रखा जाता है। इस प्रकार के परिवर्तनों का पूर्वानुमान सम्भव नहीं हो पाता।

11. पूर्वानुमान

प्रश्न 28. पूर्वानुमान के विषय में सविस्तार लिखिये।

उत्तर–परिचय (Introduction)–इस विश्व में भविष्य निश्चित नहीं है। यदि हमें भविष्य के विषय में निश्चित तौर पर सब कुछ पता लग जाये तो हमें किसी भी विषय में पूर्वानुमान लगाने की आवश्यकता नहीं रह जायेगी और एक ही बार में भविष्य के बारे में एक निर्णय लेकर निश्चित हो जाया जा सकता था। लेकिन वास्तव में यह सत्य नहीं है। मानव वर्तमान में जो कुछ करता है, वह इस आशा और सम्भावना से करता है कि भविष्य में निश्चित घटनाएँ प्रत्याशित ढंग से पूरी होंगी। भविष्य की घटनाओं के विषय में वह पिछले अनुभव और वर्तमान प्रवृत्तियों के आधार पर सर्वोत्तम अनुमान लगा सकता है। इस प्रकार प्रत्येक क्षेत्र में भविष्य के बारे में पूर्वानुमान लगाना मानव व्यवहार का एक अभिन्न अंग है। अर्थशास्त्र तथा वाणिज्य से भविष्य के बारे में केवल अंदाजों और अटकलों से निर्णय नहीं लिये जा सकते। छोटे से छोटा दुकानदार भी यह जानने के लिये उत्सुक होता है, कि भविष्य में उसकी बिक्री और लाभ की क्या सम्भावनाएँ होंगी। भविष्य के विषय में पूर्वानुमान एक अत्यन्त उपयोगी मानवीय क्रिया है और सही ढंग से किये गये पूर्वानुमान भविष्य के लिये किये जाने वाले निर्णयों के लिये अत्यन्त लाभकारी सिद्ध होते हैं। तेजी से बढ़ती हुई प्रतियोगिता और स्वचालन की दिशा में प्रवृत्ति की माँग है कि भविष्य के विषय में केवल अंदाजों और अटकलबाजियों से काम ना लिया जाये, बल्कि इसके स्थान पर वर्तमान के आँकड़ों का सांख्यिकीय रीतियों से विश्लेषण करके भविष्य के बारे में योजनाएँ बनाई जायें। किसी भी व्यावसायिक संस्थान की सफलता इसी बात में निहित है कि किस प्रकार उसका प्रबंधक मंडल भविष्य के लिये पूर्वानुमान लगाते हैं। प्रबंधक मडंल अधिक समय यही जानने के लिये उत्सुक रहता है कि भविष्य मे क्या होने वाला है और न कि पीछे क्या हुआ। भविष्य के बारे में पूर्वानुमान हर एक आर्थिक एवं व्यावसायिक क्रिया के लिये आवश्यक है। यहाँ तक कि सरकारों को भी अपनी आर्थिक नीतियों के लिये पूर्वानुमानों का सहारा लेना पड़ता है।

पूर्वानुमान-धारणा (Forecasting-Concept)–भविष्य के विषय में लिये गये आर्थिक और व्यावसायिक निर्णयों का प्रभाव लिये गये निर्णयों की यथार्थकता पर निर्भर करता है। सांख्यिकी में, संख्यात्मक तथ्यों के भूतकालीन व्यवहार के आधार पर भविष्य के लिये काल-श्रेणी को विस्तृत या विक्षेपित करने की क्रिया को **पूर्वानुमान** (Forecasting) कहते है। दूसरे शब्दों में, परिवर्तनों के भावी स्वरूप के सम्बन्ध में सूचना उपलब्ध करने के हेतु प्रस्तुत काल-श्रेणी के भूतकालीन और वर्तमान परिवर्तनों के सांख्यिकीय विश्लेषण की क्रिया को पूर्वानुमान कहते हैं। संक्षेप में, भूतकालीन व वर्तमानकालीन आर्थिक परिस्थितियों के सांख्यिकीय विश्लेषण के आधार पर सम्भावित भविष्यकालीन व्यावसायिक स्थितियों का सर्वोत्तम अनुमान लगाने की विधि को व्यावसायिक पूर्वानुमान कहते हैं। जिस समय पर पूर्वानुमान लगाया जाता है उसे **आधार बिन्दु** कहा जाता है तथा जिस समय के लिये पुर्वानुमान लगाया जाता है उसे **पूर्वानुमान बिन्दु** कहा जाता है। पूर्वानुमान बिन्दु और आधार बिन्दु के बीच के समय को **पूर्वानुमान विस्तार** कहा जाता है। पूर्वानुमान विस्तार की अवधि कुछ महीनों से लेकर 5-10 वर्षों तक की हो सकती है। सभी आर्थिक एवं व्यावसायिक संस्थानों के लिये यह जानना अति आवश्यक होता है कि भविष्य के पूर्वानुमान उनके अनुकूल होंगे या प्रतिकूल। इस प्रकार के अनुमान किसी भी प्रबंधक मंडल को निर्णय लेने में सहायक हो सकते हैं। भविष्य में आने वाली अनिश्चितताओं से बचने के लिये यह अति आवश्यक है कि भविष्य की परिस्थितियों को ध्यान में रखते हुए पूर्वानुमान लगाये जाए। किसी भी संस्था की कम विस्तार और अधिक विस्तार योजनाओं को सफल बनाने में पूर्वानुमानों का विशेष योगदान रहता है। पूर्वानुमान शब्द को भविष्य विज्ञान के पर्याय के रूप में नहीं लेना चाहिये। भविष्य विज्ञान में हम इस प्रकार के विषयों के बारे में अध्ययन करते हैं जैसे कि ऊर्जा प्राप्ति के नये साधन, पृथ्वी के अलावा किसी और ग्रह पर जीवन की सम्भावना आदि। दूसरी तरफ, पूर्वानुमान एक सांख्यिकीय प्रक्रिया है जिससे कि हम भूतकालीन तथा वर्तमानकालीन आँकड़ों का अध्ययन करके भविष्य के सम्बन्ध में अनुमान निश्चित करते हैं।

पूर्वानुमान के प्रकार (Types of Forecasting)–पूर्वानुमान में हम आर्थिक एवं व्यावसायिक चरांकों में भविष्य मे होने वाले परिवर्तनों का अध्ययन करते हैं। पूर्वानुमान का समय विस्तार कुछ महीनों से लेकर कुछ वर्षों तक भी हो सकता है। पूर्वानुमान दो प्रकार के होते हैं–

(*i*) दीर्घ अवधि पूर्वानुमान (*ii*) लघु अवधि पूर्वानुमान।

अब हम विस्तार से इन पूर्वानुमानों का वर्णन करेंगे।

(*i*) **दीर्घ अवधि पूर्वानुमान**–यदि किसी पूर्वानुमान का समय विस्तार लगभग 5 वर्षों से 15 वर्षों तक हो तो हम उस पूर्वानुमान को **दीर्घ अवधि पूर्वानुमान** कहते हैं। दीर्घ अवधि पूर्वानुमान में हमारा मुख्य उद्देश्य यह रहता है कि दीर्घ अवधि में उत्पादन क्षमता में कितना उतार-चढ़ाव किया जाये कि भविष्य में होने वाली माँग को पूरा किया जा सके। उत्पादन क्षमता को लघु अवधि में घटाया या बढ़ाया नहीं जा सकता। जनसंख्या वृद्धि, लोगों की बदलती आदतों आदि का प्रभाव केवल दीर्घ अवधि में ही महसूस किया जा सकता है। इसलिये जब भी हम दीर्घ अवधि पूर्वानुमान लगाते हैं, तो इन कारणों के प्रभाव का भी अध्ययन करते हैं।

(*ii*) **लघु अवधि पूर्वानुमान**–यदि किसी पूर्वानुमान का समय विस्तार लगभग 6 माह से 1 वर्ष हो तो हम उस पूर्वानुमान को **लघु अवधि पूर्वानुमान** कहते हैं। लघु अवधि पूर्वानुमान में हम तात्कालिक भविष्य के विषय में योजनाएँ बनाते हैं। उपभोक्ता वस्तुओं की माँग का अध्ययन करने के लिये लघु अवधि पूर्वानुमान का प्रयोग किया जा सकता है। पूर्वानुमान की समय अवधि बढ़ने के साथ ही पूर्वानुमान में गलती होने का जोखिम बढ़ता जाता है। उत्पादन की सही दर बनाये रखने के लिये भी लघु अवधि पूर्वानुमान का प्रयोग किया जा सकता है। यदि लघु अवधि पूर्वानुमान से यह निश्चित होता है कि निकट भविष्य में माँग बढ़ने वाली है, तो प्रबंधकीय मंडल तत्काल ही इस दिशा में ठोस निर्णय ले सकती है जिससे कि भविष्य में संस्था बढ़ी माँग का पूरा लाभ उठा सके।

पूर्वानुमान का महत्त्व (Importance of Forecasting)–किसी भी संस्था के प्रबंधकीय मंडल महत्त्वपूर्ण कार्यों में पूर्वानुमानों का मान निकालना होता है। व्यावसायिक पूर्वानुमान की प्रकृत्ति से यह स्पष्ट हो जाता है कि व्यवसाय में पूर्वानुमान लगाने का मूलभूत उद्देश्य स्पष्ट रूप से यह निर्धारित करना नहीं है कि निकट भविष्य में क्या होने वाला है वरन् सुनिश्चित व्यावसायिक समंकों के विश्लेषण द्वारा यह संकेत देना है कि भविष्य में क्या होने की सम्भावना है, जिससे कि व्यावसायी इन सम्भाव्य परिस्थितियों के आधार पर अपनी भावी नीतियाँ निश्चित कर सकें। अधिकतर भूतकालीन, वर्तमान और भविष्य की आर्थिक एवं व्यावसायिक घटनाओं में एक प्रकार की निरन्तरता (continuity) होती है। जिसके कारण पूर्वानुमान का कार्य सम्भव हो जाता है। प्रबंधक भी अपने उत्पाद का मूल्य निश्चित करने के लिये कच्चे माल, मजदूरी आदि के पूर्वानुमानों को प्रयोग करते है। प्रबंधक अपने उत्पादन की योजना, कच्चे माल की खरीद, मजदूरों की नियुक्ति, धन के प्रबंध आदि के लिये अपने उत्पादन की बिक्री तथा बाजार पूर्वानुमानों का उपयोग करते हैं। किसी भी व्यावसायिक संस्थान की उन्नति या पतन इस बात पर निर्भर करता है कि उस संस्थान का प्रबंधकीय मंडल किस प्रकार और कितनी मात्रा में पूर्वानुमानों का प्रयोग करता है। यह ठीक ही कहा गया है कि पूर्वानुमान से यह नहीं समझना चाहिये कि परिवर्ती रेखा को आगे बढ़ा कर किसी आने वाले वर्ष के लिये अनुमानित मान निकाल लिया जायें। पिछले कुछ दशकों से काफी मात्रा में व्यावसायिक संस्थाओं ने अपने सभी प्रकार के निर्णयों में पूर्वानुमानों का भरपूर प्रयोग शुरू कर दिया है। व्यवसायों में बढ़ती हुई अनिश्चितताओं ने पूर्वानुमानों का महत्त्व बहुत अधिक बढ़ा दिया है।

पूर्वानुमान की विधियाँ (Method of Forecasting)–हमेशा से ही व्यावसायियों का यह प्रयास रहा है कि किस प्रकार वह अपने आपको भविष्य में होने वाली घटनाओं के अनुरूप ढाल सकें। व्यावसायी की यह चाह होती है कि वह भविष्य में होने वाले परिवर्तनों का भरपूर लाभ उठा सकें। अतीत में व्यावसायी केवल भूतकालीन आंकड़ों के बल पर ही भविष्य के बारे में निर्णय लेता था। अनेक व्यवसायियों के पूर्वानुमान, अनुभवहीनता, सांख्यिकीय रीतियों के प्रति अनभिज्ञता, अपर्याप्त सूचना व त्रुटिपूर्ण तर्क के कारण कोरे अंदाज ही होते थे, जिससे उन्हें नुकसान उठाना पड़ता था। आधुनिक युग में व्यावसायिक पूर्वानुमान की अनेक वैज्ञानिक विधियों का विकास हुआ है जिनके यथोचित प्रयोग द्वारा व्यावसायी अपने व्यवसाय के जोखिम को नियन्त्रित करके भावी परिस्थितियों में अपना लाभ अधिकतम कर सकता है। व्यावसायिक पूर्वानुमान की प्रमुख वैज्ञानिक विधियाँ निम्नलिखित हैं–

(*i*) Trend Projection Method, (*ii*) Business Indicators Method, (*iii*) Survey Method, (*iv*) Opinion Polling Method, (*v*) Model Building Method, (*vi*) Historical Analogy Method, (*vii*) Naive Method, (*viii*) Exponential Smoothing Method.

12. प्रायिकता

प्रश्न 29. निम्नलिखित के बारे में संक्षिप्त में वर्णन कीजिए–

1. *प्रायिकता की परिभाषा*
2. *परस्पर अपवर्जी घटनाएँ*
3. *स्वतन्त्र घटनाएँ*
4. *परतन्त्र घटनाएँ*

उत्तर 1. प्रायिकता की परिभाषा (Definition of Probability)

हम अपने व्यावहारिक जीवन में आमतौर पर इस प्रकार के वाक्य कहते तथा सुनते हैं, जैसे कि ''आज वर्षा होने की बहुत उम्मीद है'', ''इस बार राम जरूर प्रथम श्रेणी में पास होगा'' इत्यादि। इस प्रकार के वाक्यों में किसी एक विशेष घटना (Event) के होने की सम्भावना पाई जाती है। गणित तथा सांख्यिकी में इस प्रकार के भी तरीके हैं, जिनके प्रयोग से इस प्रकार की सम्भावनाओं को माप भी किया जा सकता है, इसमें प्रयोग होने वाले सिद्धान्त को ''प्रायिकता का सिद्धान्त'' कहा जाता है।

अगर किसी दैव-प्रयोग (Random Experiment) में कुल मिलाकर (Exhaustive) n सम-सम्भावी (Equalily likely) प्रकार (Outcomes) हो, तथा इनमें से m प्रकार ऐसे हों जिनमें कि कोई एक विशेष घटना (Event) A घटित हो सकती हो तो घटना A की प्रायिकता निम्नलिखित सूत्र द्वारा निकाली जाती है–

घटना A की प्रायिकता $= P(A) = \dfrac{m}{n}$.

दूसरे शब्दों में,

$$\text{घटना } A \text{ की प्रायिकता} = \frac{\text{घटना A के अनुकूल प्रकारों की संख्या}}{\text{दैव-प्रयोग के कुल, सम-सम्भावी प्रकारों की संख्या}}$$

ऊपर लिखित परिभाषा से यह स्पष्ट है कि घटना A के प्रतिकूल प्रकारों की संख्या $n-m$ होगी। घटना A के घटित न होने की प्रायिकता को $P(\overline{A})$ से निर्देशित किया जाता है।

$$\therefore \quad P(\overline{A}) = \frac{n-m}{n} = \frac{n}{n} - \frac{m}{n}$$

$$= 1 - \frac{m}{n} = 1 - P(A)$$

$$\therefore \quad P(A) + P(\overline{A}) = 1.$$

m और n के बारे में यह भी कह सकते हैं कि m कभी भी n से बड़ा नहीं हो सकता।

$$\therefore \quad 0 \le m \le n \quad \Rightarrow \quad 0 \le \frac{m}{n} \le 1 \quad \Rightarrow \quad 0 \le P(A) \le 1.$$

यानि कि किसी भी घटना की प्रायिकता हमेशा शून्य तथा एक के बीच में ही होगी। उदाहरण के तौर पर दो पासों (Dice) को एक साथ फेंकने पर योग 10 होने की प्रायिकता 3/36 होगी, क्योंकि कुल सम-सम्भावी प्रकार 36 ; (1, 1), (1, 2), ... (6, 5) ; (6, 6) होंगे तथा योग 10 होने की घटना के अनुकूल सिर्फ 3 ; (4, 6), (5, 5), (6, 4) प्रकार होंगे।

2. परस्पर अपवर्जी घटनाएँ (Mutually Exclusive Events)

किसी भी दैव-प्रयोग से सम्बन्धित दो या दो से ज्यादा घटनाओं को परस्पर **अपवर्जी घटनाएँ** कहा जाता है। यदि किसी भी घटना के घटित होने की दशा में बाकी कोई भी घटना घटित न हो सके। उदाहरण के तौर पर एक पासे को फेंकने के प्रयोग में घटनाएँ A = {1, 2} और B = {2, 4, 5} परस्पर अपवर्जी नहीं हैं, क्योंकि अंक 2 दोनों ही घटनाओं के अनुकूल है। इसी प्रयोग में घटनाएँ C = {4}, D = {1, 2, 3} तथा E = {5, 6} परस्पर अपवर्जी हैं, क्योंकि पासा फेंकने से किसी भी एक घटना के अनुकूल अंक आता है तो वह अंक बाकी किसी भी घटना के अनुकूल नहीं होगा। इसी प्रकार से 52 पत्तों की ताश से एक पत्ता निकाला जाए तो घटनाएँ A = ''पत्ता पान का होगा'' तथा B = ''पत्ता चिड़ी का होगा'' परस्पर अपवर्जी होंगी, क्योंकि अगर पत्ता पान का होगा तो उसे चिड़ी का नहीं कह सकते तथा अगर पत्ता चिड़ी का होगा तो उसे पान का

नहीं कहा जा सकता। इसी प्रयोग में यदि घटना C = ''पत्ता गुलाम का होगा'' तो घटनाएँ A और C परस्पर अपवर्जी नहीं होंगी, क्योंकि ताश में एक पत्ता ''पान का गुलाम'' भी होता है जोकि दोनों A और C के अनुकूल होगा।

अगर किसी प्रयोग में A और B परस्पर अपवर्जी घटनाएँ हों तो उनके एक साथ घटित होने की प्रायिकता P(AB) का मान हमेशा शून्य होगा।

3. स्वतन्त्र घटनाएँ (Independent Events)

यदि किसी दैव-प्रयोग से सम्बन्धित किसी एक घटना का घटित होना या न होना अन्य किसी घटना के घटित होने या न होने की प्रायिकता पर प्रभाव न डाल सकें, तो इस प्रकार की घटनाओं को **स्वतन्त्र घटनाएँ** कहा जाता है। उदाहरण के तौर पर 52 पत्तों की ताश में से एक-एक करके दो पत्तों को निकालने के प्रयोग में यदि A = ''पहला पत्ता बादशाह का हो'' तथा B = ''दूसरा पत्ता पान का हो'' घटनाएँ हो तो इस प्रयोग में यदि दूसरा पत्ता निकालने से पहले पहला पत्ता वापिस ताश में लौटा दिया जाए तो घटनाएँ A और B स्वतन्त्र कहलाई जाएंगी, क्योंकि ऐसा करने से पहली बार में कौन-सा पत्ता आया था इसका प्रभाव B की प्रायिकता पर नहीं पड़ सकेगा और यदि दूसरा पत्ता निकालने से पहले पहला पत्ता वापिस ताश में नहीं लौटाया जायेगा तो घटनाएं A और B स्वतन्त्र नहीं कहलाई जा सकेंगी।

स्वतन्त्र घटनाओं की परिभाषा को दो से अधिक घटनाओं के लिए भी बढ़ाया जा सकता है। किसी भी प्रयोग से सम्बन्धित दो या दो से ज्यादा घटनाओं को स्वतन्त्र घटनाएँ कहा जाता है, यदि किसी भी एक घटना के घटित होने या न होने का असर अन्य किसी भी घटना के घटित होने या न होने पर ना पड़ सके।

4. परतन्त्र घटनाएँ (Dependent Events)

परतन्त्र घटनाओं को आश्रित घटनाएं भी कहा जाता है। यदि किसी दैव-प्रयोग से सम्बन्धित किसी एक घटना का घटित होना या न होना अन्य किसी घटना के घटित होने या न होने की प्रायिकता पर प्रभाव डाल सके, तो इस प्रकार की घटनाओं को **परतन्त्र घटनाएँ** कहा जाता है। उदाहरण के तौर पर 52 पत्तों की ताश में से एक-एक करके दो पत्तों को निकालने के प्रयोग में यदि A = ''पहला पत्ता बादशाह का हो'' तथा B = ''दूसरा पत्ता पान का हो'' घटनाएं हों तो इस प्रयोग में यदि दूसरा पत्ता निकालने से पहले पहला पत्ता वापिस ताश में नहीं लौटाया जाए तो घटनाएं A तथा B परतन्त्र कहलाई जाएंगी।

अगर घटनाएं A तथा B परतन्त्र घटनाएं हैं, तो P(A/B) का अर्थ होता है, घटना A की प्रायिकता यह मानते हुए कि घटना B घट चुकी है। इसी प्रकार से P(B/A) का अर्थ होगा, घटना B के घटने की प्रायिकता यह मानते हुए कि घटना A घट चुकी है।

प्रश्न 30. प्रायिकता सिद्धांत में योग प्रायिकता तथा संयुक्त प्रायिकता संबंधित प्रमेयों के बारे में लिखिए।

उत्तर–प्रायिकता सिद्धांत के योग प्रायकिता तथा संयुक्त प्रायकिता सम्बन्धित प्रमेय किसी घटना विशेष की प्रायिकता निकालने के लिए प्रयोग की जाती है।

अगर किसी दैव-प्रयोग में कुल मिलाकर n सम-सम्भावी प्रकार हो, तथा इनमें से m प्रकार ऐसे हो जिनमें कि कोई एक विशेष घटना A घटित हो सकती हो तो घटना A प्रायिकता P(A) का मान m/n होता है।

योग प्रायिकता प्रमेय (Addition Theorem Probability)

दैव-प्रयोग से सम्बन्धित घटनाओं का मान निकालने में योग प्रायिकता की प्रमेय की सहायता ली जाती है। इस प्रमेय का प्रयोग उन घटनाओं के लिए किया जाता है जोकि परस्पर अपवर्जी हैं तथा उनके लिये भी जो परस्पर अपवर्जी नहीं भी हैं। हम जानते हैं कि किसी भी प्रयोग से सम्बन्धित दो घटनाओं को परस्पर अपवर्जी कहा जाता है, यदि किसी एक के घटित होने की दशा में दूसरी घटित न हो सके। घटना A या घटना B के घटित होने की प्रायिकता को P(A or B) से अंकित किया जाता है।

अगर A और B परस्पर अपवर्जी घटनाएं हैं, तो योग प्रायिकता की प्रमेय के अनुसार A या B घटना के घटित होने की प्रायिकता A तथा B घटनाओं की अलग-अलग प्रायिकताओं के योगफल के बराबर होती है। सूत्र के रूप में हम लिख सकते हैं।

$$P(A \text{ or } B) = P(A) + P(B)$$

उदाहरण के तौर पर, 52 पत्तों के ताश में से एक पत्ता निकालने के प्रयोग में यदि

A = पत्ता पान का होगा

B = पत्ता ईंट का होगा, तो A तथा B दोनों परस्पर अपवर्जी घटनाएँ होने के कारण

P(पत्ता पान या ईंट का होगा) = P(A or B)

$$= P(A) + P(B) = \frac{13}{52} + \frac{13}{52} = \frac{1}{2}.$$

अगर A और B परस्पर अपवर्जी घटनाएं नहीं हैं, तो योग प्रायिकता की प्रमेय के अनुसार A तथा B या दोनों घटनाओं के घटित होने की प्रायिकता का मान A तथा B घटनाओं की अलग-अलग प्रायिकताओं के योगफल से A तथा B दोनों के घटित होने की प्रायिकता को घटाकर प्राप्त की जाती है। सूत्र के रूप में हम लिख सकते हैं,

$$P(A \text{ or } B) = P(A) + P(B) - P(AB)$$

ऊपरलिखित उदाहरण में यदि B = ''पत्ता इक्के का होगा'' घटना हो तो घटनाएं A तथा B आपस में परस्पर अपवर्जी नहीं होंगी, क्योंकि अगर 'पान का इक्का आ गया तो यह प्रकार दोनों A तथा B के अनुकूल होगा। इस प्रयोग के सन्दर्भ में,

P(पत्ता पान या इक्के का होगा) = P(A or B)

$$= P(A) + P(B) - P(AB)$$

$$= \frac{13}{52} + \frac{4}{52} - \frac{1}{52} = \frac{4}{13}.$$

योग प्रायिकता की प्रमेय को दो से अधिक घटनाओं के लिए भी बढ़ाया जा सकता है। अगर घटनाएं A, B तथा C परस्पर अपवर्जी हैं तो,

P(A or B or C) = P(A) + P(B) + P(C) होगी। अगर घटनाएं A, B तथा C परस्पर अपवर्जी नहीं हैं तो योग प्रायिकता की प्रमेय का रूप होगा,

$$P(A \text{ or } B \text{ or } C) = P(A) + P(B) + P(C) - P(AB) - P(BC) - P(CA) + P(ABC).$$

संयुक्त प्रायिकता की प्रमेय (Multiplication Theorem of Probability)

इस प्रमेय का प्रयोग भी दैव-प्रयोग से सम्बन्धित घटनाओं की प्रायिकताओं का मान निकालने के लिए किया जाता है। इस प्रमेय का प्रयोग स्वतन्त्र घटनाओं तथा परतन्त्र घटनाओं के सन्दर्भ में किया जाता है। हम जानते हैं कि यदि किसी एक घटना के घटित होने से या न होने से किसी दूसरी घटना के घटित होने या न होने की प्रायिकता पर प्रभाव न पड़े तो ऐसी घटनाओं को स्वतन्त्र घटनाएँ कहा जाता है। घटना A तथा B दोनों के घटित होने की प्रायिकता को P(AB) से अंकित किया जाता है। अगर A तथा B स्वतन्त्र घटनाएं हैं, तो संयुक्त प्रायिकता की प्रमेय के अनुसार A और B दोनों घटनाओं के घटित होने की प्रायिकता A तथा B घटनाओं की अलग-अलग प्रायिकताओं के गुणनफल के बराबर होती है। सूत्र के रूप में हम लिख सकते हैं–

$$P(AB) = P(A)\,P(B)$$

उदाहरण के तौर पर यदि थैली में 4 सफेद और 5 नीली गेंदें हैं और उस थैले से एक-एक करके दो गेंदें निकालने के प्रयोग में यदि A = ''पहली गेंद सफेद होगी'' और B = ''दूसरी गेंद नीली होगी'' घटनाएं हो तो A तथा B स्वतन्त्र घटनाएं तभी होंगी जबकि दूसरी गेंद निकालने से पहले पहली वाली गेंद वापिस थैले में डाल दी जाए। इस दशा में पहली गेंद सफेद होने तथा दूसरी नीली होने की प्रायिकता P(AB) होगी और इसका मान इस प्रकार से निकाला जाएगा।

$$P(AB) = P(A).\ P(B) = \frac{4}{9} \times \frac{5}{9} = \frac{20}{81}.$$

अगर A तथा B परतन्त्र घटनाएं हैं तो दोनों के घटित होने की प्रायिकता निम्नलिखित संयुक्त प्रायिकता के प्रमेय से निकाली जाती है।

$$P(AB) = P(A)\,P(B/A)$$

इस सूत्र में P(B/A) का अर्थ है घटना B के घटित होने की प्रायिकता, यह मानते हुए कि घटना A पहले घटित हो चुकी है। ऊपरलिखित उदाहरण में यदि दूसरी गेंद निकालने से पहले पहली वाली गेंद वापिस थैले में न डाली जाए तो घटनाएं परतन्त्र हो जायेंगी। ऐसे में दोनों घटनाओं के घटित होने की प्रायिकता इस प्रकार निकाली जाएगी।

$$P(AB) = P(A)\,P(B/A) = \frac{4}{9} \times \frac{5}{9-1} = \frac{4}{9} \times \frac{5}{8} = \frac{5}{18}.$$

संयुक्त प्रायिकता की प्रमेय को दो से अधिक घटनाओं के लिए भी बढ़ाया जा सकता है। अगर घटनायें A, B तथा C स्वतन्त्र हैं तो

$$P(ABC) = P(A)\,P(B)\,P(C).$$

अगर घटनाएं A, B तथा C परतन्त्र हैं तो संयुक्त प्रायिकता की प्रमेय का निम्नलिखित रूप होगा।

$$P(ABC) = P(A)\,P(B/A)\,P(C/AB).$$

13. सैद्धान्तिक वितरण

प्रश्न 31. निम्नलिखित सैद्धान्तिक आवृत्ति वितरणों की व्याख्या कीजिए तथा इनकी प्रमुख विशेषताओं पर प्रकाश डालिए–

1. *द्विपद वितरण*
2. *पायसन वितरण*
3. *प्रसामान्य वितरण*

उत्तर–आवृत्ति वितरणों की रचना **वास्तविक अवलोकनों** तथा **सैद्धान्तिक** दोनों ही आधारों पर की जा सकती है। उदाहरण के तौर पर यदि एक सिक्के को 100 बार उछाला जाए तो हो सकता है कि पट्ट 45 बार आये और चित्त 55 बार, परन्तु सैद्धान्तिक तौर पर हम उम्मीद करेंगे की 50 बार पट्ट आये तथा 50 बार ही चित्त। इस उदाहरण से सम्बन्धित आवृत्ति वितरणों को इस प्रकार लिखा जा सकता है।

वास्तविक आवृत्ति वितरण		सैद्धान्तिक आवृत्ति वितरण	
पट्टों की संख्या x	आवृत्ति f	पट्टों की संख्या x	आवृत्ति f
0	55	0	50
1	45	1	50
योग	100	योग	100

वास्तविक आवृत्ति वितरणों में आवृत्तियाँ प्रयोगों तथा निरीक्षणों के आधार पर निश्चित की जाती हैं, परन्तु सैद्धान्तिक आवृत्ति वितरणों में आवृत्तियाँ कुछ सैद्धान्तिक मान्यताओं के आधार पर निश्चित की जाती हैं। वास्तविक आवृत्तियों की सैद्धान्तिक आवृत्तियों से तुलना करके वास्तविक आवृत्तियों के उच्चावचनों के उद्गम को समझा जा सकता है। उपयोगिता की दृष्टि से निम्नलिखित सैद्धान्तिक आवृत्ति वितरण ही अधिक महत्त्वपूर्ण है–

1. द्विपद वितरण
2. पायसन वितरण
3. प्रसामान्य वितरण।

1. द्विपद वितरण (Binomial Distribution)

द्विपद वितरण का प्रतिपादन **जेम्स बर्नोली** ने वर्ष 1700 में किया। इस वितरण के लिए n बारी समान परिस्थितियों में प्रयोग किया जाता है। उदाहरण के लिए यदि एक ही सिक्के को 4 बारी उछाला जाए तो $n = 4$ लिया जाएगा। इसमें यह भी मान कर चलते हैं कि सभी n प्रयोग स्वतन्त्र हैं और एक प्रयोग का प्रभाव दूसरे किसी प्रयोग के परिणाम पर नहीं पड़ेगा। यदि एक ही सिक्के को बार-बार उछाला जाए तो यह सब प्रयोग स्वतन्त्र होंगे। द्विपद वितरण में यह भी शर्त है कि प्रत्येक प्रयोग में केवल दो ही परस्पर अपवर्जी और एक दूसरे के पूरक परिणाम होने चाहिए, ऊपरलिखित उदाहरण में ऐसा ही होगा, क्योंकि सिक्का उछालने से या तो पट्ट आएगा या नहीं आएगा और इसके अलावा कुछ नहीं होता। सम्बन्धित घटना की सफलता के प्रायिकता p द्वारा अंकित की जाती है। द्विपद वितरण के प्रयोग के लिए यह भी आवश्यक है कि हर एक प्रयोग में p का मान स्थिर रहे।

सभी n प्रयोगों में जो चर सम्बन्धित घटना की सफलताओं को दर्शाता है उसे द्विपद चर (Binomial variable) कहा जाता है तथा x से अंकित करते हैं। x के सम्भव मान 0, 1, 2, ..., n हो सकते हैं। प्रयोग में असफलता की प्रायिकता को q से प्रदर्शित करते हैं।

$$\therefore \qquad p + q = 1$$

n प्रयोगों में r सफलता की प्रायिकता निम्नलिखित सूत्र के द्वारा निकाली जाती हैं–

$$P(x = r) = {}^nC_r p^r q^{n-r} \qquad 0 \le r \le n.$$

इस सूत्र को **द्विपद प्रायिकता फलन** कहा जाता है। इन n प्रयोगों से संबंधित **द्विपद वितरण** निम्न प्रकार से लिखा जाता है।

x	0	1	2	.........n
P(x)	${}^nC_0p^0q^n$	${}^nC_1p^1q^{n-1}$	${}^nC_2p^2q^{n-2}$	.........${}^nC_np^0q^n$

यदि n प्रयोगों की शृंखला को N बार दोहराया जाता है तो r सफलताओं की सैद्धान्तिक आवृत्ति इस सूत्र से निकाली जाती है।

$$r \text{ सफलताओं की सैद्धान्तिक आवृत्ति} = N\ {}^nC_r p^r q^{n-r} \qquad (0 \le r \le n)$$

द्विपद वितरण से सम्बन्धित कुछ सांख्यिकीय माप इस प्रकार से हैं–

(*i*) समान्तर माध्य (A.M.) = np (*ii*) प्रमाप विचलन (S.D.) = $\sqrt{npq}$

(*iii*) विचरण मापांक (Variance) = npq (*iv*) $\mu_3 = npq(q - p)$

(*v*) $\mu_4 = 3n^2p^2q^2 + npq(1 - 6pq)$ (*vi*) $\gamma_1 = \dfrac{1-2p}{\sqrt{npq}}$

(*vii*) $\gamma_2 = \dfrac{1-6pq}{npq}$

2. पायसन वितरण (Poisson Distribution)

पायसन वितरण का प्रतिपादन **साइमन पायसन** ने वर्ष 1837 में किया। इस वितरण का उपयोग उन परिस्थितियों में किया जाता है जहाँ पर किसी घटना के घटने की सम्भावना (p) बहुत कम हो। उदाहरण के तौर पर किसी कारखाने के उत्पादन में खराब इकाइयाँ उत्पादित होने की सम्भावना बहुत कम होती है, किसी वर्ष भूचाल आने की सम्भावना बहुत कम होती है, किसी सड़क पर दुर्घटना होने की सम्भावना बहुत कम होती है, इत्यादि। पायसन वितरण को द्विपद वितरण के सीमांत रूप में निकाला जा सकता है, जबकि द्विपद वितरण में n का मान बहुत ज्यादा होने लगे। पायसन वितरण में भी सब शर्तें सन्तुष्ट

होनी चाहिए जो कि द्विपद वितरण के लिए आवश्यक होती हैं। इस वितरण में घटना के घटने की प्रायिकता (p) का मान भी बहुत कम होता है।

पायसन वितरण में जो चर घटना के घटित होने की संख्या बताता है, उसे **पायसन चर** कहा जाता है और उसे x से अंकित करते हैं। x के सम्भव मान 0, 1, 2, ... और ज्यादा से ज्यादा n हो सकता है।

कुल r सफलताओं की प्रायिकता निम्नलिखित सूत्र के द्वारा निकाली जाती है।

$$P(x=r)=\frac{e^{-m}\,m^r}{r!} \qquad r=0,1,2,......$$

इस सूत्र में m वितरण के समांतर माध्य के बराबर होता है। इस सूत्र को **पायसन प्रायिकता फलन** कहा जाता है। इससे सम्बन्धित **पायसन वितरण** निम्न रूप में लिखा जाता है।

x	0	1	2	3	.....
P(x)	$\frac{e^{-m}\,m^0}{0!}$	$\frac{e^{-m}\,m^1}{1!}$	$\frac{e^{-m}\,m^2}{2!}$	$\frac{e^{-m}\,m^3}{3!}$	.....

यदि n प्रयोगों की शृंखला को N बार दोहराया जाता है, तो r सफलताओं की सैद्धान्तिक आवृत्ति इस सूत्र से निकाली जाती है–

$$r \text{ सफलताओं की सैद्धान्तिक आवृत्ति } = N\frac{e^{-m}\,m^r}{r!};\ r=0,1,2\ ......$$

पायसन वितरण से सम्बन्धित कुछ सांख्यिकीय माप इस प्रकार से हैं–

(*i*) समान्तर माध्य (A.M.) $= m = np$

(*ii*) प्रमाप विचलन (S.D.) $= \sqrt{m}$

(*iii*) विचरण मापांक (Variance) $= m$

(*iv*) $\mu_3 = m$

(*v*) $\mu_4 = m + 3m^2$

(*vi*) $\gamma_1 = \frac{1}{\sqrt{m}}$

(*vii*) $\gamma_2 = \frac{1}{m}$.

3. प्रसामान्य वितरण (Normal Distribution)

प्रसामान्य वितरण का प्रतिपादन **डी॰ मायर** ने वर्ष 1733 में किया। प्रसामान्य वितरण भी द्विपद वितरण का ही एक सीमान्त रूप है, जबकि n का मान बहुत ज्यादा बढ़ जाए। परन्तु यहाँ हम यह मानते हैं कि घटना के घटने की प्रायिकता बहुत कम नहीं है, बल्कि इसके स्थान पर यह माना जाता है कि घटना के घटने की तथा न घटने की प्रायिकताएँ लगभग बराबर हैं। प्रसामान्य वितरण में घटना की सफलता की संख्या सम्बन्धी चर को अविच्छिन्न (Continuous) माना जाता है, जबकि द्विपद तथा पायसन वितरणों घटना की सफलता की सम्बन्धी चर को विच्छिन्न (Discrete) माना जाता है।

किसी भी अविच्छिन्न चर (x) को प्रसामान्य वितरण का चर कहा जाता है, यदि x से सम्बन्धित प्रायिकता फलन निम्न प्रकार के सूत्र से दिया जाए।

$$y = P(x) = \frac{1}{\sigma\sqrt{2\pi}}e^{-\frac{1}{2}\left(\frac{x-\mu}{\sigma}\right)^2} \qquad -\infty < x < \infty$$

इस सूत्र में μ और σ क्रमशः समान्तर माध्य और प्रमाप विचलन होते हैं।

प्रसामान्य वितरण को समान्य सम्भावना वक्र भी कहा जाता है। इसका आकार घंटाकार होता है।

STATISTICAL TABLE I

VALUES OF e^{-m} $(0 < m < 1)$

m	0	1	2	3	4	5	6	7	8	9
0.0	1.0000	0.9900	0.9802	0.9704	0.9608	0.9512	0.9418	0.9324	0.9231	0.9139
0.1	0.9048	0.8958	0.8869	0.8781	0.8694	0.8607	0.8521	0.8437	0.8353	0.8270
0.2	0.8187	0.8106	0.8025	0.7945	0.7866	0.7788	0.7711	0.7634	0.7558	0.7483
0.3	0.7408	0.7334	0.7261	0.7189	0.7118	0.7047	0.6977	0.6907	0.6839	0.6771
0.4	0.6703	0.6636	0.6570	0.6505	0.6440	0.6376	0.6313	0.6250	0.6188	0.6126
0.5	0.6065	0.6005	0.5945	0 .5886	0.5827	0.5770	0.5712	0.5655	0.5599	0.5543
0.6	0.5488	0.5434	0.5379	0.5326	0.5273	0.5220	0.5169	0.5117	0.5066	0.5016
0.7	0.4966	0.4916	0.4868	0.4819	0.4771	0.4724	0.4677	0.4630	0.4584	0.4538
0.8	0.4493	0.4449	0.4404	0.4360	0.4317	0.4274	0.4232	0.4190	0.4148	0.4107
0.9	0.4066	0.4025	0.3985	0.3946	0.3906	0.3867	0.3829	0.3791	0.3753	0.3716

(m = 1, 2, 3, ..., 10)

m	1	2	3	4	5	6	7	8	9	10
e^{-m}	0.36788	0.13534	0.04979	0.01832	0.006738	0.002479	0.000912	0.000335	0.000123	0.000045

Illustrations :

1. $e^{-4.37} = e^{-4} \cdot e^{-0.37} = (0.01832)(0.6907) = 0.012654$
2. $e^{-6.05} = e^{-6} \cdot e^{-0.05} = (0.002479)(0.9512) = 0.002358.$

STATISTICAL TABLE II

AREA UNDER THE STANDARD NORMAL CURVE

The entries in the table are the probabilities that a random variable having the standard normal distribution assumes a value from 0 to z, these are given by the area under the curve shaded in the figure shown on the right hand side.

Area under Normal Curve

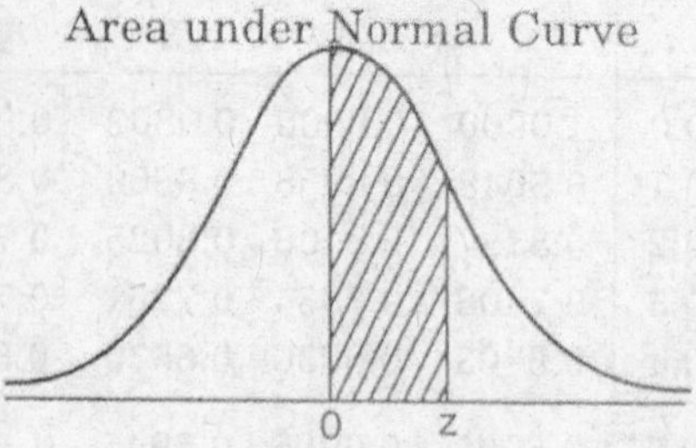

Table of Area

z	0	1	2	3	4	5	6	7	8	9
0.0	.0000	.0040	.0080	.0120	.0160	.0199	.0239	.0279	.0319	.0359
0.1	.0398	.0438	.0478	.0517	.0557	.0596	.0636	.0675	.0714	.0753
0.2	.0793	.0832	.0871	.0910	.0948	.0987	.1026	.1064	.1103	.1141
0.3	.1179	.1217	.1255	.1293	.1331	.1368	.1406	.1443	.1480	.1517
0.4	.1554	.1591	.1628	.1664	.1700	.1736	.1772	.1808	.1844	.1879
0.5	.1915	.1950	.1985	.2019	.2054	.2088	.2123	.2157	.2190	.2224
0.6	.2258	.2291	.2324	.2357	.2389	.2422	.2454	.2486	.2518	.2549
0.7	.2580	.2612	.2642	.2673	.2704	.2734	.2764	.2794	.2823	.2852
0.8	.2881	.2910	.2939	.2967	.2996	.3023	.3051	.3078	.3106	.3133
0.9	.3159	.3186	.3212	.3238	.3264	.3289	.3315	.3340	.3365	.3389
1.0	.3413	.3438	.3461	.3485	.3508	.3531	.3554	.3577	.3599	.3621
1.1	.3643	.3665	.3686	.3708	.3729	.3749	.3770	.3790	.3810	.3830
1.2	.3849	.3869	.3888	.3907	.3925	.3944	.3962	.3980	.3997	.4015
1.3	.4032	.4049	.4066	.4082	.4099	.4115	.4131	.4147	.4162	.4177
1.4	.4192	.4207	.4222	4236	.4251	.4265	.4279	.4292	.4306	.4319
1.5	.4332	.4345	.4357	.4370	.4382	.4394	.4406	.4418	.4429	.4441
1.6	.4452	.4463	.4474	.4484	.4495	.4505	.4515	.4525	.4535	.4545
1.7	.4554	.4564	.4573	.4582	.4591	.4599	.4608	.4616	.4625	.4633
1.8	.4641	.4649	.4656	.4664	.4671	.4678	.4686	.4693	.4699	.4706
1.9	.4713	.4719	.4726	.4732	.4738	.4744	.4750	.4756	.4761	.4767
2.0	.4772	.4778	.4783	.4788	.4793	.4798	.4803	.4808	.4812	.4817
2.1	.4821	.4826	.4830	.4834	.4838	.4842	.4846	.4850	.4854	.4857
2.2	.4861	.4864	.4868	.4871	.4875	.4878	.4881	.4884	.4887	.4890
2.3	.4893	.4896	.4898	.4901	4904	.4906	.4909	.4911	.4913	.4916
2.4	.4918	.4920	.4922	.4925	.4927	.4929	.4931	.4932	.4934	.4936
2.5	.4938	.4940	.4941	.4943	.4945	.4946	.4948	.4949	.4951	.4952
2.6	.4953	.4955	.4956	.4957	.4959	.4960	.4961	.4962	.4963	.4964
2.7	.4965	.4966	.4967	.4968	.4969	.4970	.4071	.4972	.4973	.4974
2.8	.4974	.4975	.4976	.4977	.4977	.4978	.4979	.4979	.4980	.4981
2.9	.4981	.4982	.4982	.4983	.4984	.4984	.4985	.4985	.4986	.4986
3.0	.4987	.4987	.4987	.4988	.4988	.4989	.4989	.4989	.4990	.4990
3.1	.4990	.4991	.4991	.4991	.4992	.4992	.4992	.4992	.4993	.4993
3.2	.4993	.4993	.4994	.4994	.4994	.4994	.4994	.4995	.4995	.4995
3.3	.4995	.4995	.4995	.4996	.4996	.4996	.4996	.4996	.4996	.4997
3.4	.4997	.4997	.4997	.4997	.4997	.4997	.4997	.4997	.4997	.4998
3.5	.4998	.4998	.4998	.4998	.4999	.4998	.4998	.4998	.4998	.4998
3.6	.4998	.4998	.4999	.4999	.4999	.4999	.4999	.4999	.4999	.4999
3.7	.4999	.4999	.4999	.4999	.4999	.4999	.4999	.4999	.4999	.4999
3.8	.4999	.4999	.4999	.4999	.4999	.4999	.4999	.4999	.4999	.4999
3.9	.5000	.5000	.5000	.5000	.5000	.5000	.5000	.5000	.5000	.5000

EXAMINATION PAPERS

M.D.U., ROHTAK

B.Com. II, Examination, April 2007

Business Statistics

(Paper IV)

Time : Three Hours] *[Maximum Marks : 90*

Before answering the question, candidate should ensure that they have been supplied the correct and complete question paper. No complaint in this regard, will be entertained after examination.

Note : Attempt any ***five*** questions. All questions carry equal marks.

1. Discuss the sources, advantages and limitations of secondary data. What precautions should be taken while using secondary data ? 18

2. Calculate the values of arithmetic mean, mode and standard deviation for the following distribution : 18

Wages (Rs.)	*No. of workers*
0—10	5
0—20	12
0—30	20
0—40	32
0—50	60
0—60	82
0—70	92
0—80	100

3. (*a*) Define kurtosis. How is it measured ? 9

(*b*) Calculate Bowley's coefficient of skewness for the following distribution : 9

x	50—100	100—150	150—200	200—250	250—300	300—350	350—400	400—450
f	8	10	16	14	10	6	4	2

4. (*a*) Does correlation always show cause and effect relationship between two variables ? 5

(*b*) Why are there two lines of regression ? 6

(*c*) Define regression coefficients and describe their utility. How are they related with Karl Pearson's coefficient of correlation ? 7

5. The following series shows the heights of fathers and sons in inches :

Height of Fathers	*Height of Sons*
65	67
66	68
68	64
69	72
71	70
73	69
67	70
68	68
70	68
72	73
69	65

Estimate :

(*i*) the height of son if the height of the father is 64 inches and

(*ii*) the height of father if the height of the son is 71 inches.

Also calculate the value of Spearman's coefficient of correlation between them. 6, 6, 6

6. (*a*) Why are index numbers called economic barometers ? 5

(*b*) Using illustration, explain how are chain base index numbers computed ? 5

(*c*) Write a note on secular trend and seasonal variations. 8

7. From the following data, calculate quantity index numbers using :

(*i*) Laspeyre's

(*ii*) Paasche's and

(*iii*) Fisher's methods.

Commodity	*1980*		*1985*	
	Price	*Value*	*Price*	*Value*
A	50	350	60	540
B	20	80	30	150
C	24	240	20	300
D	100	600	150	600

Which of the above methods satisfy factor reversal test ? Show. 3, 3, 3, 9

8. Calculate the trend values by least square method for the following time series :

Year	1980	1981	1982	1983	1984	1985	1986	1987	1988
Sales (000'Rs.)	53	79	76	66	69	87	79	95	104

Also calculate the trend values by taking 4-years moving average period. 18

9. Using illustrations, explain the following : 6, 6, 6

(*i*) Classical approach to probability

(*ii*) Conditional probability

(*iii*) Area property of normal distribution.

10. (*a*) A bag contains 9 red balls, 7 white balls and 4 green balls. Three balls are drawn randomly, without replacement. Find the probability of getting : 9

(*i*) one ball of each colour

(*ii*) only two red balls

(*iii*) no white ball.

(*b*) If 8 coins are tossed 256 times, find the expected frequencies of getting various number of heads. 9

K.U., KURUKSHETRA

B.Com. II, Examination, April 2007

Business Statistics

(Paper IV)

Time : Three Hours] *[Maximum Marks : 90*

Note : Attempt ***five*** questions in all, selecting at least ***one*** question but not more than ***two*** questions from each unit. Log tables and Graph paper are to be supplied on demand.

UNIT I

1. Define Statistics. Discuss its importance. Why people distrust in statistics ? 6 + 8 + 4

2. (*a*) Calculate Mean, Median, Q_1, Q_3, P_{67} and D_4 from the following data :

Marks Less Than	80	70	60	50	40	30	20	10
No. of Students	100	90	80	60	32	20	13	5

(*b*) A man travelled by a car for 3 days. He covered 480 kms. each day. On the first day he drove for 10 hours at 48 kms. an hour, on the second day he drove for 12 hours at 40 kms. an hour and on the last day he drove for 15 hours at 32 kms. an hour. What was his average speed ? 12 + 6

3. (*a*) Explain Skewness.

(*b*) Calculate Karl Pearson's coefficient of skewness from the following data :

Marks above	0	10	20	30	40	50	60	70	80
No. of students	150	140	100	80	80	70	30	14	0

4 + 14

4. (*a*) Calculate Coefficient of Rank Correlation from the following data :

X	15	10	20	28	12	10	16	18
Y	16	14	10	12	11	15	18	12

(*b*) The following regression equations are given :

$$3x + 4y = 44$$
$$5x + 8y = 80$$

Variance of $x(\sigma_x^2) = 30$.

Calculate the following : $\bar{x}$, $\bar{y}$, r_{xy} and σ_y. 6 + 12

UNIT II

5. Explain any **three** from the following :
   (*a*) Cyclical Oscillations
   (*b*) Consumer Price Index
   (*c*) Deflating of Index Numbers
   (*d*) Utility of Time Series. 6 + 6 + 6
6. Calculate 'FISHER'S IDEAL INDEX NUMBER' from the following data and show that it satisfies Time Reversal Test and Factor Reversal Test :

Commodities	*2004*		*2003*	
	Price	*Value*	*Price*	*Value*
A	10	120	8	80
B	12	96	10	120
C	5	50	5	40
D	3	60	4	56
E	25	150	20	100

12 + 6

7. Fit a straight line trend by the method of Least Square to the following data. Show the Trend on Graph Paper and also estimate the value for the year 2004.

Year	1995	1996	1997	1998	1999	2000	2001	2002
Profit (in Rs. Crores)	80	90	92	83	94	99	97	104

12 + 4 + 2

UNIT III

8. Explain any **Two** from following :
   (*a*) Mutually Exclusive Event, Compound Event and Dependent Events.
   (*b*) Explain Poisson Distribution and give any six examples where Poisson Distribution is applied.
   (*c*) Explain Properties of Normal Distribution. 9 + 9
9. (*a*) If a pair of dice is thrown, find the probability that :
   (*i*) the sum is neither 7 nor 11.
   (*ii*) neither a doublet nor a total of 9 will appear.
   (*b*) A number was drawn at random from the tickets numbered 1 to 50 from a box. What is the probability that the drawn number will be a multiple of 2 or 3 ? 12 + 6
10. (*a*) The mean and standard deviation of a graduation examination following normal distribution are 500 and 100 respectively. If 550 students are to be passed, out of 674 students, what would be the minimum marks for passing the examination ?
    (*b*) Suppose that a manufacturing product has 4 defects per unit of product inspected. Using Poisson distribution calculate the probability of finding a product with 2 defects. (Given $e^{-4} = .01832$) 12 + 6

LOGARITHMS

	0	1	2	3	4	5	6	7	8	9	1	2	3	4	5	6	7	8	9
10	0000	0043	0086	0128	0170						5	9	13	17	21	26	30	34	38
						0212	0253	0294	0334	0374	4	8	12	16	20	24	28	32	36
11	0414	0453	0492	0531	0569						4	8	12	16	20	23	27	31	35
						0607	0645	0682	0719	0755	4	7	11	15	18	22	26	29	33
12	0792	0828	0864	0899	0934						3	7	11	14	18	21	25	28	32
						0969	1004	1038	1072	1106	3	7	10	14	17	20	24	27	31
13	1139	1173	1206	1239	1271						3	6	10	13	16	19	23	26	29
						1303	1335	1367	1399	1430	3	7	10	13	16	19	22	25	29
14	1461	1492	1523	1553	1584						3	6	9	12	15	19	22	25	28
						1614	1644	1673	1703	1732	3	6	9	12	14	17	20	23	26
15	1761	1790	1818	1847	1875						3	6	9	11	14	17	20	23	26
						1903	1931	1959	1987	2014	3	6	8	11	14	17	19	22	25
16	2041	2068	2095	2122	2148						3	6	8	11	14	16	19	22	24
						2175	2201	2227	2253	2279	3	5	8	10	13	16	18	21	23
17	2304	2330	2355	2380	2405						3	5	8	10	13	15	18	20	23
						2430	2455	2480	2504	2529	3	5	8	10	12	15	17	20	22
18	2553	2577	2601	2625	2648						2	5	7	9	12	14	17	19	21
						2672	2695	2718	2742	2765	2	4	7	9	11	14	16	18	21
19	2788	2810	2833	2856	2878						2	4	7	9	11	13	16	18	20
						2900	2923	2945	2967	2989	2	4	6	8	11	13	15	17	19
20	3010	3032	3054	3075	3096	3118	3139	3160	3181	3201	2	4	6	8	11	13	15	17	19
21	3222	3243	3263	3284	3304	3324	3345	3365	3385	3404	2	4	6	8	10	12	14	16	18
22	3424	3444	3464	3483	3502	3522	3541	3560	3579	3598	2	4	6	8	10	12	14	15	17
23	3617	3636	3655	3674	3692	3711	3729	3747	3766	3784	2	4	6	7	9	11	13	15	17
24	3802	3820	3838	3856	3874	3892	3909	3927	3945	3962	2	4	5	7	9	11	12	14	16
25	3979	3997	4014	4031	4048	4065	4082	4099	4116	4133	2	3	5	7	9	10	12	14	15
26	4150	4166	4183	4200	4216	4232	4249	4265	4281	4298	2	3	5	7	8	10	11	13	15
27	4314	4330	4346	4362	4378	4393	4409	4425	4440	4456	2	3	5	6	8	9	11	13	14
28	4472	4487	4502	4518	4533	4548	4564	4579	4594	4609	2	3	5	6	8	9	11	12	14
29	4624	4639	4654	4669	4683	4698	4713	4728	4742	4757	1	3	4	6	7	9	10	12	13
30	4771	4786	4800	4814	4829	4843	4857	4871	4886	4900	1	3	4	6	7	9	10	11	13
31	4914	4928	4942	4955	4969	4983	4997	5011	5024	5038	1	3	4	6	7	8	10	11	12
32	5052	5065	5079	5092	5105	5119	5132	5145	5159	5172	1	3	4	5	7	8	9	11	12
33	5185	5198	5211	5224	5237	5250	5263	5276	5289	5302	1	3	4	5	6	8	9	10	12
34	5315	5328	5340	5353	5366	5378	5391	5403	5416	5428	1	3	4	5	6	8	9	10	11
35	5441	5453	5465	5478	5490	5502	5515	5527	5539	5551	1	2	4	5	6	7	9	10	11
36	5563	5575	5587	5599	5611	5623	5635	5647	5658	5670	1	2	4	5	6	7	8	10	11
37	5682	5694	5705	5717	5729	5740	5752	5763	5775	5786	1	2	3	5	6	7	8	9	10
38	5798	5809	5821	5832	5843	5855	5866	5877	5888	5899	1	2	3	5	6	7	8	9	10
39	5911	5922	5933	5944	5955	5966	5977	5988	5999	6010	1	2	3	4	5	7	8	9	10
40	6021	6031	6042	6053	6064	6075	6085	6096	6107	6117	1	2	3	4	5	6	8	9	10
41	6128	6138	6149	6160	6170	6180	6191	6201	6212	6222	1	2	3	4	5	6	7	8	9
42	6232	6243	6253	6263	6274	6284	6294	6304	6314	6325	1	2	3	4	5	6	7	8	9
43	6335	6345	6355	6365	6375	6385	6395	6405	6415	6425	1	2	3	4	5	6	7	8	9
44	6435	6444	6454	6464	6474	6484	6493	6503	6513	6522	1	2	3	4	5	6	7	8	9
45	6532	6542	6551	6561	6571	6580	6590	6599	6609	6618	1	2	3	4	5	6	7	8	9
46	6628	6637	6646	6656	6665	6675	6684	6693	6702	6712	1	2	3	4	5	6	7	7	8
47	6721	6730	6739	6749	6758	6767	6776	6785	6794	6803	1	2	3	4	5	5	6	7	8
48	6812	6821	6830	6839	6848	6857	6866	6875	6884	6893	1	2	3	4	4	5	6	7	8
49	6902	6911	6920	6928	6937	6946	6955	6964	6972	6981	1	2	3	4	4	5	6	7	8

LOGARITHMS

	0	1	2	3	4	5	6	7	8	9	1	2	3	4	5	6	7	8	9
50	6990	6998	7007	7016	7024	7033	7042	7050	7059	7067	1	2	3	3	4	5	6	7	8
51	7076	7084	7093	7101	7110	7118	7126	7135	7143	7152	1	2	3	3	4	5	6	7	8
52	7160	7168	7177	7185	7193	7202	7210	7218	7226	7235	1	2	2	3	4	5	6	7	7
53	7243	7251	7259	7267	7275	7284	7292	7300	7308	7316	1	2	2	3	4	5	6	6	7
54	7324	7332	7340	7348	7356	7364	7372	7380	7388	7396	1	2	2	3	4	5	6	6	7
55	7404	7412	7419	7427	7435	7443	7451	7459	7466	7474	1	2	2	3	4	5	5	6	7
56	7482	7490	7497	7505	7513	7520	7528	7536	7543	7551	1	2	2	3	4	5	5	6	7
57	7559	7566	7574	7582	7589	7597	7604	7612	7619	7627	1	2	2	3	4	5	5	6	7
58	7634	7642	7649	7657	7664	7672	7679	7686	7694	7701	1	1	2	3	4	4	5	6	7
59	7709	7716	7723	7731	7738	7745	7752	7760	7767	7774	1	1	2	3	4	4	5	6	7
60	7782	7789	7796	7803	7810	7818	7825	7832	7839	7846	1	1	2	3	4	4	5	6	6
61	7853	7860	7868	7875	7882	7889	7896	7903	7910	7917	1	1	2	3	4	4	5	6	6
62	7924	7931	7938	7945	7952	7959	7966	7973	7980	7987	1	1	2	3	3	4	5	6	6
63	7993	8000	8007	8014	8021	8028	8035	8041	8048	8055	1	1	2	3	3	4	5	5	6
64	8062	8069	8075	8082	8089	8096	8102	8109	8116	8122	1	1	2	3	3	4	5	5	6
65	8129	8136	8142	8149	8156	8162	8169	8176	8182	8189	1	1	2	3	3	4	5	5	6
66	8195	8202	8209	8215	8222	8228	8235	8241	8248	8254	1	1	2	3	3	4	5	5	6
67	8261	8267	8274	8280	8287	8293	8299	8306	8312	8319	1	1	2	3	3	4	5	5	6
68	8325	8331	8338	8344	8351	8357	8363	8370	8376	8382	1	1	2	3	3	4	4	5	6
69	8388	8395	8401	8407	8414	8420	8426	8432	8439	8445	1	1	2	2	3	4	4	5	6
70	8451	8457	8463	8470	8476	8482	8488	8494	8500	8506	1	1	2	2	3	4	4	5	6
71	8513	8519	8525	8531	8537	8543	8549	8555	8561	8567	1	1	2	2	3	4	4	5	5
72	8573	8579	8585	8591	8597	8603	8609	8615	8621	8627	1	1	2	2	3	4	4	5	5
73	8633	8639	8645	8651	8657	8663	8669	8675	8681	8686	1	1	2	2	3	4	4	5	5
74	8692	8698	8704	8710	8716	8722	8727	8733	8739	8745	1	1	2	2	3	4	4	5	5
75	8751	8756	8762	8768	8774	8779	8785	8791	8797	8802	1	1	2	2	3	3	4	5	5
76	8808	8814	8820	8825	8831	8837	8842	8848	8854	8859	1	1	2	2	3	3	4	5	5
77	8865	8871	8876	8882	8887	8893	8899	8904	8910	8915	1	1	2	2	3	3	4	4	5
78	8921	8927	8932	8938	8943	8949	8954	8960	8965	8971	1	1	2	2	3	3	4	4	5
79	8976	8982	8987	8993	8998	9004	9009	9015	9020	9025	1	1	2	2	3	3	4	4	5
80	9031	9036	9042	9047	9053	9058	9063	9069	9074	9079	1	1	2	2	3	3	4	4	5
81	9085	9090	9096	9101	9106	9112	9117	9122	9128	9133	1	1	2	2	3	3	4	4	5
82	9138	9143	9149	9154	9159	9165	9170	9175	9180	9186	1	1	2	2	3	3	4	4	5
83	9191	9196	9201	9206	9212	9217	9222	9227	9232	9238	1	1	2	2	3	3	4	4	5
84	9243	9248	9253	9258	9263	9269	9274	9279	9284	9289	1	1	2	2	3	3	4	4	5
85	9294	9299	9304	9309	9315	9320	9325	9330	9335	9340	1	1	2	2	3	3	4	4	5
86	9345	9350	9355	9360	9365	9370	9375	9380	9385	9390	1	1	2	2	3	3	4	4	5
87	9395	9400	9405	9410	9415	9420	9425	9430	9435	9440	0	1	1	2	2	3	3	4	4
88	9445	9450	9455	9460	9465	9469	9474	9479	9484	9489	0	1	1	2	2	3	3	4	4
89	9494	9499	9504	9509	9513	9518	9523	9528	9533	9538	0	1	1	2	2	3	3	4	4
90	9542	9547	9552	9557	9562	9566	9571	9576	9581	9586	0	1	1	2	2	3	3	4	4
91	9590	9595	9600	9605	9609	9614	9619	9624	9628	9633	0	1	1	2	2	3	3	4	4
92	9638	9643	9647	9652	9657	9661	9666	9671	9675	9680	0	1	1	2	2	3	3	4	4
93	9685	9689	9694	9699	9703	9708	9713	9717	9722	9727	0	1	1	2	2	3	3	4	4
94	9731	9736	9741	9745	9750	9754	9759	9763	9768	9773	0	1	1	2	2	3	3	4	4
95	9777	9782	9786	9791	9795	9800	9805	9809	9814	9818	0	1	1	2	2	3	3	4	4
96	9823	9827	9832	9836	9841	9845	9850	9854	9859	9863	0	1	1	2	2	3	3	4	4
97	9868	9872	9877	9881	9886	9890	9894	9899	9903	9908	0	1	1	2	2	3	3	4	4
98	9912	9917	9921	9926	9930	9934	9939	9943	9948	9952	0	1	1	2	2	3	3	4	4
99	9956	9961	9965	9969	9974	9978	9983	9987	9991	9996	0	1	1	2	2	3	3	3	4

ANTILOGARITHMS

	0	1	2	3	4	5	6	7	8	9	1	2	3	4	5	6	7	8	9
.00	1000	1002	1005	1007	1009	1012	1014	1016	1019	1021	0	0	1	1	1	1	2	2	2
.01	1023	1026	1028	1030	1033	1035	1038	1040	1042	1045	0	0	1	1	1	1	2	2	2
.02	1047	1050	1052	1054	1057	1059	1062	1064	1067	1069	0	0	1	1	1	1	2	2	2
.03	1072	1074	1076	1079	1081	1084	1086	1089	1091	1094	0	0	1	1	1	1	2	2	2
.04	1096	1099	1102	1104	1107	1109	1112	1114	1117	1119	0	1	1	1	1	2	2	2	2
.05	1122	1125	1127	1130	1132	1135	1138	1140	1143	1146	0	1	1	1	1	2	2	2	2
.06	1148	1151	1153	1156	1159	1161	1164	1167	1169	1172	0	1	1	1	1	2	2	2	2
.07	1175	1178	1180	1183	1186	1189	1191	1194	1197	1199	0	1	1	1	1	2	2	2	2
.08	1202	1205	1208	1211	1213	1216	1219	1222	1225	1227	0	1	1	1	1	2	2	2	3
.09	1230	1233	1236	1239	1242	1245	1247	1250	1253	1256	0	1	1	1	1	2	2	2	3
.10	1259	1262	1265	1268	1271	1274	1276	1279	1282	1285	0	1	1	1	1	2	2	2	3
.11	1288	1291	1294	1297	1300	1303	1306	1309	1312	1315	0	1	1	1	2	2	2	2	3
.12	1318	1321	1324	1327	1330	1334	1337	1340	1343	1346	0	1	1	1	2	2	2	2	3
.13	1349	1352	1355	1358	1361	1365	1368	1371	1374	1377	0	1	1	1	2	2	2	3	3
.14	1380	1384	1387	1390	1393	1396	1400	1403	1406	1409	0	1	1	1	2	2	2	3	3
.15	1413	1416	1419	1422	1426	1429	1432	1435	1439	1442	0	1	1	1	2	2	2	3	3
.16	1445	1449	1452	1455	1459	1462	1466	1469	1472	1476	0	1	1	1	2	2	2	3	3
.17	1479	1483	1486	1489	1493	1496	1500	1503	1507	1510	0	1	1	1	2	2	2	3	3
.18	1514	1517	1521	1524	1528	1531	1535	1538	1542	1545	0	1	1	1	2	2	2	3	3
.19	1549	1552	1556	1560	1563	1567	1570	1574	1578	1581	0	1	1	1	2	2	3	3	3
.20	1585	1589	1592	1596	1600	1603	1607	1611	1614	1618	0	1	1	1	2	2	3	3	3
.21	1622	1626	1629	1633	1637	1641	1644	1648	1652	1656	0	1	1	2	2	2	3	3	3
.22	1660	1663	1667	1671	1675	1679	1683	1687	1690	1694	0	1	1	2	2	2	3	3	3
.23	1698	1702	1706	1710	1714	1718	1722	1726	1730	1734	0	1	1	2	2	2	3	3	4
.24	1738	1742	1746	1750	1754	1758	1762	1766	1770	1774	0	1	1	2	2	2	3	3	4
.25	1778	1782	1786	1791	1795	1799	1803	1807	1811	1816	0	1	1	2	2	2	3	3	4
.26	1820	1824	1828	1832	1837	1841	1845	1849	1854	1858	0	1	1	2	2	3	3	3	4
.27	1862	1866	1871	1875	1879	1884	1888	1892	1897	1901	0	1	1	2	2	3	3	3	4
.28	1905	1910	1914	1919	1923	1928	1932	1936	1941	1945	0	1	1	2	2	3	3	4	4
.29	1950	1954	1959	1963	1968	1972	1977	1982	1986	1991	0	1	1	2	2	3	3	4	4
.30	1995	2000	2004	2009	2014	2018	2023	2028	2032	2037	0	1	1	2	2	3	3	4	4
.31	2042	2046	2051	2056	2061	2065	2070	2075	2080	2084	0	1	1	2	2	3	3	4	4
.32	2089	2094	2099	2104	2109	2113	2118	2123	2128	2133	0	1	1	2	2	3	3	4	4
.33	2138	2143	2148	2153	2158	2163	2168	2173	2178	2183	0	1	1	2	2	3	3	4	4
.34	2188	2193	2198	2203	2208	2213	2218	2223	2228	2234	1	1	2	2	3	3	4	4	5
.35	2239	2244	2249	2254	2259	2265	2270	2275	2280	2286	1	1	2	2	3	3	4	4	5
.36	2291	2296	2301	2307	2312	2317	2323	2328	2333	2339	1	1	2	2	3	3	4	4	5
.37	2344	2350	2355	2360	2366	2371	2377	2382	2388	2393	1	1	2	2	3	3	4	4	5
.38	2399	2404	2410	2415	2421	2427	2432	2438	2443	2449	1	1	2	2	3	3	4	4	5
.39	2455	2460	2466	2472	2477	2483	2489	2495	2500	2506	1	1	2	2	3	3	4	5	5
.40	2512	2518	2523	2529	2535	2541	2547	2553	2559	2564	1	1	2	2	3	4	4	5	5
.41	2570	2576	2582	2588	2594	2600	2606	2612	2618	2624	1	1	2	2	3	4	4	5	5
.42	2630	2636	2642	2649	2655	2661	2667	2873	2679	2685	1	1	2	2	3	4	4	5	6
.43	2692	2698	2704	2710	2716	2723	2729	2735	2742	2748	1	1	2	3	3	4	4	5	6
.44	2754	2761	2767	2773	2780	2786	2793	2799	2805	2812	1	1	2	3	3	4	4	5	6
.45	2818	2825	2831	2838	2844	2851	2858	2864	2871	2877	1	1	2	3	3	4	5	5	6
.46	2884	2891	2897	2904	2911	2917	2924	2931	2938	2944	1	1	2	3	3	4	5	5	6
.47	2951	2958	2965	2972	2979	2985	2992	2999	3006	3013	1	1	2	3	3	4	5	5	6
.48	3020	3027	3034	3041	3048	3055	3062	3069	3076	3083	1	1	2	3	4	4	5	6	6
.49	3090	3097	3105	3112	3119	3126	3133	3141	3148	3155	1	1	2	3	4	4	5	6	6

ANTILOGARITHMS

	0	1	2	3	4	5	6	7	8	9	1	2	3	4	5	6	7	8	9
.50	3162	3170	3177	3184	3192	3199	3206	3214	3221	3228	1	1	2	3	4	4	5	6	7
.51	3236	3243	3251	3258	3266	3273	3281	3289	3296	3304	1	2	2	3	4	5	5	6	7
.52	3311	3319	3327	3334	3342	3350	3357	3365	3373	3381	1	2	2	3	4	5	5	6	7
.53	3388	3396	3404	3412	3420	3428	3436	3443	3451	3459	1	2	2	3	4	5	6	6	7
.54	3467	3475	3483	3491	3499	3508	3516	3524	3532	3540	1	2	2	3	4	5	6	6	7
.55	3548	3556	3565	3573	3581	3589	3597	3606	3614	3622	1	2	2	3	4	5	6	7	7
.56	3631	3639	3648	3656	3664	3673	3681	3690	3698	3707	1	2	3	3	4	5	6	7	8
.57	3715	3724	3733	3741	3750	3758	3767	3776	3784	3793	1	2	3	3	4	5	6	7	8
.58	3802	3811	3819	3828	3837	3846	3855	3864	3873	3882	1	2	3	4	4	5	6	7	8
.59	3890	3899	3908	3917	3926	3936	3945	3954	3963	3972	1	2	3	4	5	5	6	7	8
.60	3981	3990	3999	4009	4018	4027	4036	4046	4055	4064	1	2	3	4	5	6	6	7	8
.61	4074	4083	4093	4102	4111	4121	4130	4140	4150	4159	1	2	3	4	5	6	7	8	9
.62	4169	4178	4188	4198	4207	4217	4227	4236	4246	4256	1	2	3	4	5	6	7	8	9
.63	4266	4276	4285	4295	4305	4315	4325	4335	4345	4355	1	2	3	4	5	6	7	8	9
.64	4365	4375	4385	4395	4406	4416	4426	4436	4446	4457	1	2	3	4	5	6	7	8	9
.65	4467	4477	4487	4498	4508	4519	4529	4539	4550	4560	1	2	3	4	5	6	7	8	9
.66	4571	4581	4592	4603	4613	4624	4634	4645	4656	4667	1	2	3	4	5	6	7	9	10
.67	4677	4688	4699	4710	4721	4732	4742	4753	4764	4775	1	2	3	4	5	7	8	9	10
.68	4786	4797	4808	4819	4831	4842	4853	4864	4875	4887	1	2	3	4	6	7	8	9	10
.69	4898	4909	4920	4932	4943	4955	4966	4977	4989	5000	1	2	3	5	6	7	8	9	10
.70	5012	5023	5035	5047	5058	5070	5082	5093	5105	5117	1	2	4	5	6	7	8	9	11
.71	5129	5140	5152	5164	5176	5188	5200	5212	5224	5236	1	2	4	5	6	7	8	10	11
.72	5248	5260	5272	5284	5297	5309	5321	5333	5346	5358	1	2	4	5	6	7	9	10	11
.73	5370	5383	5395	5408	5420	5433	5445	5458	5470	5483	1	3	4	5	6	8	9	10	11
.74	5495	5508	5521	5534	5546	5559	5572	5585	5598	5610	1	3	4	5	6	8	9	10	12
.75	5623	5636	5649	5662	5675	5689	5702	5715	5728	5741	1	3	4	5	7	8	9	10	12
.76	5754	5768	5781	5794	5808	5821	5834	5848	5861	5875	1	3	4	5	7	8	9	11	12
.77	5888	5902	5916	5929	5943	5957	5970	5984	5998	6012	1	3	4	5	7	8	10	11	12
.78	6026	6039	6053	6067	6081	6095	6109	6124	6138	6152	1	3	4	6	7	8	10	11	13
.79	6166	6180	6194	6209	6223	6237	6252	6266	6281	6295	1	3	4	6	7	9	10	11	13
.80	6310	6324	6339	6353	6368	6383	6397	6412	6427	6442	1	3	4	6	7	9	10	12	13
.81	6457	6471	6486	6501	6516	6531	6546	6561	6577	6592	2	3	5	6	8	9	11	12	14
.82	6607	6622	6637	6653	6668	6683	6699	6714	6730	6745	2	3	5	6	8	9	11	12	14
.83	6761	6776	6792	6808	6823	6839	6855	6871	6887	6902	2	3	5	6	8	9	11	13	14
84	6918	6934	6950	6966	6982	6998	7015	7031	7047	7063	2	3	5	6	8	10	11	13	15
.85	7079	7096	7112	7129	7145	7161	7178	7194	7211	7228	2	3	5	7	8	10	12	13	15
.86	7244	7261	7278	7295	7311	7328	7345	7362	7379	7396	2	3	5	7	8	10	12	13	15
.87	7413	7430	7447	7464	7482	7499	7516	7534	7551	7568	2	3	5	7	9	10	12	14	16
.88	7586	7603	7621	7638	7656	7674	7691	7709	7727	7745	2	4	5	7	9	11	12	14	16
.89	7762	7780	7798	7816	7834	7852	7870	7889	7907	7925	2	4	5	7	9	11	13	14	16
.90	7943	7962	7980	7998	8017	8035	8054	8072	8091	8110	2	4	6	7	9	11	13	15	17
.91	8128	8147	8166	8185	8204	8222	8241	8260	8279	8299	2	4	6	8	9	11	13	15	17
.92	8318	8337	8356	8375	8395	8414	8433	8453	8472	8492	2	4	6	8	10	12	14	15	17
.93	8511	8531	8551	8570	8590	8610	8630	8650	8670	8690	2	4	6	8	10	12	14	16	18
.94	8710	8730	8750	8770	8790	8810	8831	8851	8872	8892	2	4	6	8	10	12	14	16	18
.95	8913	8933	8954	8974	8995	9016	9036	9057	9078	9099	2	4	6	8	10	12	15	17	19
.96	9120	9141	9162	9183	9204	9226	9247	9268	9290	9311	2	4	6	8	11	13	15	17	19
.97	9333	9354	9376	9397	9419	9441	9462	9484	9506	9528	2	4	7	9	11	13	15	17	20
.98	9550	9572	9594	9616	9638	9661	9683	9705	9727	9750	2	4	7	9	11	13	16	18	20
.99	9772	9795	9817	9840	9863	9886	9908	9931	9954	9977	2	5	7	9	11	14	16	18	20